The Book of
Latin American Cooking

The Book of Latin American Cooking

Elisabeth Lambert Ortiz

An Imprint of HarperCollinsPublishers

Some of the recipes in this book first appeared in *House & Garden* magazine,
copyright © 1969 by The Condé Nast Publications, Inc., and in *Gourmet*
magazine in July, September, and October 1969, September 1971, December 1973,
January and December 1974, October 1975, and December 1977.

Library of Congress Cataloging-in-Publication Data

Ortiz, Elisabeth Lambert.
    The book of Latin American cooking/Elisabeth Lambert Ortiz.
        p. cm.
    Originally published: New York : Knopf, 1979.
    Includes index.
    ISBN 0-88001-382-6
    1. Cookery, Latin American.   I. Title.
TX716.A1077   1994
641.598—dc20   94-12452

06 FOLIO/HADDON 10 9 8 7

For my husband and colleague, César Ortiz-Tinoco,
whose knowledge and enthusiasm were of
inestimable help in writing this book,
and for Judith Jones, most perceptive and helpful of editors

Contents

Acknowledgments

It is hard to know where to begin with thanks. Surely no one has had friends more generous with their time, their knowledge, and their kitchens than I have had. I would like to thank Mr. and Mrs. José Fernández de Córdoba, Mr. and Mrs. Belisario Fernández de Córdoba, Mr. and Mrs. Arturo Montesinos, Mr. and Mrs. Galo Plaza, Col. and Mrs. Edmundo García Vivanco, Mr. and Mrs. Vincente Umaña Méndez, Margarita Pacini, Cecilia Blanco de Mendoza, Mr. and Mrs. Guillermo Power, Jorge Manchego, Mr. and Mrs. Genaro Carnero Checa, Noreen Maxwell, Dr. and Mrs. Alberto Gormaz, Alejandro Flores Zorilla, Mr. and Mrs. Salvador Ferret, Dr. Raúl Nass, Mr. and Mrs. Carlos August León, Simón Reyes Marcano, Raymond Joseph Fowkes, Lolita de Lleras Codazzi, Phyllis Bird, Emma Vásquez, Mirtha Stengel, Mr. and Mrs. Gilberto Rizzo, Mr. and Mrs. Raúl Trejos, María J. Troconis, Jeanne Lesem, José Wilson, Copeland Marks, Lua de Burt, Josefina Velilla de Aquino, María Teresa Casanueva, Mr. and Mrs. Abél Quezada, Mr. and Mrs. Humberto Ortiz Reyes, Humberto Ortiz Azoños, Mr. and Mrs. Héctor Fernández, Mr. and Mrs. Efraín Huerta, Dr. and Mrs. Antonio Delgado, Raquel Braune, Victor Simón Bovier, Alwyne Wheeler, James A. Beard, Mr. and Mrs. Victorino A. Althaparro, Dr. Raúl

Noriega, Dr. and Mrs. Andrés Iduarte, Elizabeth Borton de Treviño, Mr. and Mrs. Julio César Anzueto, Lucy de Arenales, Mr. and Mrs. Jason Vourvoulias, Mr. and Mrs. Mario Montero, Ruth Kariv, Mr. and Mrs. Antonio Carbajal, Mr. and Mrs. Eugenio Soler Alonso, Ambassador and Mrs. Mario Alvírez, and Alan Eaton Davidson CMG.

I am deeply indebted to Dr. David R. Harris of London University and Dr. Wolfgang Haberland of Munich for their scientific findings on the origins of agriculture in Latin America and for their advice and encouragement, and to Walter Sullivan, who first brought this new work to my attention. My thanks to my friend and colleague the late Dr. Alex D. Hawkes for helping me with botanical problems relating to tropical plants and herbs. I am immensely grateful to Alan Davidson, that great authority on fish and shellfish and writer of cookbooks on the subject, and to Alwynne Wheeler of the British Museum of Natural History, who both helped me on the identification of the chilean fish *congrio*.

I would have been lost without the work done by Dr. Jorge Hardoy, of Argentina, and Dr. Leopoldo Castedo, of Brazil, who make brilliantly clear the urban nature of the great civilizations of pre-Columbian Latin America. I owe them a great debt.

My thanks also to Sally Berkeley at Knopf for the marvelous job she did in helping to find illustrative material for this book and to Karolina Harris, the designer, for her imaginative selection and placement of the illustrations.

Elisabeth Lambert Ortiz,
New York

Introduction

I first became interested in Latin American food when I was at school for some time in Jamaica. It was the flavor of hot peppers that beguiled me, especially one that Jamaicans call a Scotch bonnet — small, lantern-shaped, fiery, and flavorful. I also had Cuban and Brazilian friends who gave me a tantalizing glimpse into this enormous cuisine that stretches from the Rio Bravo (Rio Grande) to the Antarctic. It wasn't until shortly after I was married, twenty odd years ago, and my husband was transferred from headquarters in New York to another United Nations assignment in Mexico, that I was able to pursue my research into flavors I have never been able to forget. So it was chance that I started with Mexico, perhaps the most complex and unique cooking of the whole region. Even now, when I have traveled to all the world's continents, Mexican food is still the most exotic of all.

Mexican cooking still rests firmly on its Aztec, and to a lesser extent Mayan, origins, interwoven with the cooking of Spain. But Spain itself was for almost eight hundred years dominated by the Arab empire, so its food has a strong Middle Eastern influence. All through my investigation of Mexican cooking I kept stumbling into the Middle East. Later on I went to the Middle East, Spain, and Portugal to sort out the influences. So many strands are woven into this complicated tapestry that I still find it hard to unravel them completely.

But no matter the sources, the reward is in the eating. From the start I was enchanted by the dishes of the corn kitchen, the most purely Mexican aspect of the food. My palate was utterly bewitched by simple snacks like *quesadillas de flor de calabaza* where an unbaked tortilla is stuffed with a savory mixture of cooked squash blossoms, folded over, and fried, or more rarely, baked. I had mouth-watering deep-green peppers stuffed with mashed beans, batter-coated, and fried; or even more exotic, stuffed with meat and masked with a fresh cheese and walnut sauce and garnished with pomegranate seeds. I had *huachinango a la Veracruzana*, beautiful red snapper with mildly hot *jalapeño* peppers in a tomato sauce very lightly perfumed with cloves and cinnamon. And *Mole Poblano de Guajolote*, that extraordinary mixture of different types of dried peppers, nuts, herbs, spices, and a little bitter chocolate made into a sauce for turkey and origi- nally a favorite dish at Moctezuma's court. It was wholly unfamiliar, wholly delicious.

I found wonderful descriptions of the markets of pre-Conquest Mexico in the monumental work of a Spanish priest, Fray Bernardino de Sahagún, who was there before the Conquest was consolidated. A lively writer, he brought the markets to life, even describing how the local prostitutes lounged about, clicking their chewing gum. I hadn't realized that *chicle* (chewing gum) from the *zapote* tree was also a Mexican gift to the world, and that this same tree bears the pleasant *chico zapote* (sapodilla) fruit. Father Sahagún characterized and identified all the various kinds of tortil- las on sale, and clearly he was not averse to sampling some of the cooked foods since he described a shrimp stew and other dishes with such relish one can almost taste them. I needed no more urging — I went off to the markets, realizing they were still the best places in which to learn.

Because peppers, along with corn and beans, play such a vital role in the Mexican cuisine, and because my palate was still haunted by the flavor of the hot Jamaican peppers of my school days, I began to research this fascinating fruit. Botanically it is *Capsicum annuum* or *Capsicum frutes- cens* of the *Solanaceae* family, to which potatoes, tomatoes, and eggplant also belong. There has never been an accurate count of peppers, which were first cultivated as far back as 7000 B.C. The reason is that they are wind-pollinated and cross-fertilize easily, and since they have been doing this for thousands of years, there are now a great many different kinds. Some botanists put the number as low as sixty, while others can name over a hundred. Long before Columbus they had spread all over the Caribbean, as well as Central and South America. And since Columbus they have sprung up all over the world and have become so thoroughly naturalized that their national origin has been forgotten. They are sweet, pungent, or hot. They are first green, then change to yellow or red as they ripen — and some of them have all three colors in their cycle. They range from ¼ to 7 inches in length. They are used fresh or dried. Some are wrinkled; some are smooth; and quite apart from sweetness, pungency, or heat, they have flavor.

My first visit was to the large San Juan market. It was a blaze of color. There were enormous piles of ripe crimson tomatoes; and heaps of yellow squash blossoms, soft green zucchini, ripe red bell peppers and pimientos, bright green bell peppers and darker green *poblanos*; stalls selling the dried, wrinkled red peppers — *ancho, mulato,* and *pasilla* — brick red *chipotle* and *morita*, smooth red *guajillos*, and the little peppers, *cascabel* and *pequin*. There were more kinds than I could possibly take in at a single visit.

The sellers were mostly women with their dark hair in plaits, dressed in full cotton skirts and snowy white blouses with the traditional *rebozo* (stole) around their shoulders. Some, sitting on the ground, had before them only tiny piles of herbs or spices, or a pyramid of purple-skinned avocados. Others, often with husbands and children, had proper stalls laden with oranges; grapefruit; the paddles of the *nopal* (prickly pear) cactus, *nopalitos*; or its fruit, *tuna* — globes of green or purplish red. They called to me as I passed: *"Qué va a llevar, marchanta?"* ("What are you going to buy, customer?") and when I explained that I wanted to learn about Mexican food, they were generous with their help. I found the pepper I had remembered from my school days. It came from Yucatán and was called, paradoxically, *habanero* (pepper from Havana), a migrant returned. Later I found it all over the Caribbean, in Bahia in Brazil, and in Guatemala where it is called *caballero*, gentleman pepper — one clearly to be reckoned with.

I bought peppers of all kinds, took them home, photographed them, learned their names, and cooked them. I have listed them in the ingredients section — not all, of course, only the ones I think are useful to North American cooks.

That first day I asked one of the market women how to make *quesadillas de flor de calabaza* (squash blossom turnovers), and she was delighted. She shouted to a tortilla seller to come over, and gradually gathered all the ingredients needed, then showed me how to put them together, folding the squash-blossom mixture in a tortilla and then frying it. She was careful to explain that she was using an already baked tortilla for convenience. Whereupon she sent me off to a stall to buy a fresh lump of tortilla dough, which is made from the special cooked and ground corn that is sold dried as *masa harina* (literally "dough flour," in markets such as this one, it is already mixed with water). That was a lovely day and I became a regular visitor to markets whether in La Merced, San Juan; or Medellín in Mexico City; in Guadalajara, Querétaro; in Mérida, Yucatán; or in Cuernavaca. Wherever I went I found wonderfully knowledgeable teachers, good friends who introduced me with great generosity and enthusiasm to all manner of new foods.

Tortillas are an essential accompaniment to Mexican food. I learned easily to make them from packaged *masa harina,* using a tortilla press, which is a very splendid colonial invention. Mexican cooks can pat a tortilla with their hands into a thin pancake, then slap it on to a *comal* (griddle) to bake. But I found I could make only rather thick, clumsy ones this way, so I tried using a cast-iron tortilla press (the original presses were made of wood). It works very well and can be bought, as can *masa harina,* from specialty stores selling Mexican foods.

Beans are also an integral part of Mexican food, whether served in bowls as a separate course — not dry, rather soupy — or mashed and fried in lard to make *Frijoles Refritos,* a rich-tasting bean paste, used in all sorts of delectable ways.

A key ingredient is the tomato, and I can't imagine Mexican cooking without it, whether it is the familiar red or yellow tomato of everyday use, or the little Mexican green tomato (*Physalis ixocarpa*) — a small pale-green or yellow tomato covered with a papery husk, whose flavor develops only as it is cooked, and which is usually available to us only canned, except in parts of the Southwest. Both types of tomato are used in cooked and fresh sauces, and in *Guacamole,* the avocado salad cum sauce that is another essential on the Mexican table.

Mexico, and indeed all of Latin America, adopted rice enthusiastically and it goes excellently with the *mollis* (Mexican stews) and most other dishes. Cooks all over the continent pride themselves on their rice. No matter what method they use to cook it, each grain is tender and separate.

During the years I lived in Mexico I traveled all over the country, from the northern cattle ranges where my husband's family comes from to Mayan Yucatán, from the Caribbean to the Pacific, in enthusiastic pursuit of recipes from family, friends, strangers, markets, and restaurants, captivated as I was by the exuberance of this wonderfully varied food. I worked happily in my kitchen to faithfully reproduce the dishes I found so seductive, and back in New York I put my discoveries into a cookbook. Then chance again, or should I say good fortune, took me to Central America, beginning with Guatemala — once the heart of the Mayan empire — and I realized there was a whole continent of intriguing new cookery, linked with Mexican food, still to discover.

My interest was stimulated by recent discoveries of food origins that showed that agriculture had been born simultaneously in the Middle East and in the Valley of Mexico about 7000 B.C. In the Middle East animals such as sheep, goats, pigs, and cattle were domesticated, and barley, wheat, peas, and lentils cultivated. Gradually this produce spread all over Europe and Asia. Rice was introduced from Asia about 3500 B.C. Peanuts, Guinea yams, and millet came from Africa some centuries later. At the same time in Mexico, that other cradle of agriculture, peppers, squash, and avocados were the first cultivated food plants. A couple of thousand years later corn and the common bean followed, then lima beans, and later still, in 700 A.D., the tomato. These foods gradually spread all over the Americas. Potatoes and sweet potatoes, cultivated in the Andean highlands by the predecessors of the Incas about 2500 B.C., spread through the continent, and so did manioc (cassava) and peanuts from Brazil. Peanuts, as a matter of fact, have a dual origin, as they were independently cultivated both in Brazil and West Africa by 1500 B.C. All this cultivation was, of course, an ongoing process, with more and more fruits, vegetables, and crops being developed, so that by the time Columbus arrived, he found not only a whole new world, but a whole new world of food. These discoveries gave me an insight into the nature of the cuisine, for very soon after the Conquest there was a blending of cooking strains that evolved into the rich and varied cookery of Latin America today.

I knew it would take me a long time to travel the huge continent, to visit markets, to talk to cooks, to collect recipes, to learn about the food, and to cook it back home in my own kitchen. I also knew I would have a magnificent time doing so and I set off with enthusiasm, this book beginning to take tentative shape in my mind.

I found visiting the archaeological sites of the old Mayan empire a good way to trace the boundaries of the ancient cuisine. The Mayan empire began in Guatemala, spread to nearby Honduras, and into the states of Yucatán, Chiapas, and Campeche and the territory of Quintana Roo in Mexico. In this area today the cooking is Mayan, not Aztec Mexican. Since the civilization was already in decline at the time of the Conquest, not a great deal has survived. I wish more had, as it is subtle and delicate, except when it comes to fresh hot pepper sauce, which is really fiery. I love to cook with ground annatto seeds, which have a flowery fragrance when used whole, quite unlike the flavor of the colored oil or lard made from just the reddish-orange pulp surrounding the seeds. The cooking of the rest of Central America — Belize, El Salvador, Nicaragua, Costa Rica, and Panama, which together with Guatemala and Honduras make a land bridge between North and South America — is a mixture of Mayan, Aztec Mexican, Colombian, and Spanish cuisines, with cosmopolitan influences from recent times. There is also a Caribbean influence, mostly from island people coming to work in the banana plantations.

The Caribbean seemed my next logical step, and I went off island-hopping and again found generous-hearted cooks who welcomed me with my notebook into their kitchens and shared their cooking secrets with me. Of that great arc of islands that stretches from Florida in the north to the coast of Venezuela in the south, and which Columbus discovered in 1492, only Cuba, the Dominican Republic, and Puerto Rico are part of Latin America. When Columbus arrived, first at Hispaniola (now the Dominican Republic and Haiti), the islands were inhabited by warlike Caribs and gentle Arawaks, both from South America. The Arawaks were good farmers and soon cultivated corn and peppers from Mexico, and sweet potatoes, yams, and manioc (cassava) which they must have brought with them. Their influence on the food of the islands persists in the wide use of root vegetables, hot peppers, allspice, and corn. African settlers brought okra and their own yams, but fundamentally the cooking of the Spanish-speaking islands is that of Spain — using a mixture of indigenous and intro-duced foods. It is a surprisingly rich and varied kitchen, particularly in the Dominican Republic where a *cocido* (stew) of chicken, beef, ham, and sausages, cooked with an assemblage of vegetables, is a veritable feast.

I could now see the pattern that the common heritage of Spain and Portugal and an early shared agriculture wove into the tapestry that makes Latin American food into a richly diverse unity. And so I set off on a series of journeys to South America, lucky to have friends all over the continent to help me. I began with the Andean countries — Venezuela, Colombia, Ecuador, Peru, Bolivia, and Chile — visiting them one by one.

The 4,000-mile mountain chain of the Andes, which runs along the Pacific coast of South America from Venezuela to the tip of Chile, domi-nates the continent. The foothills begin at the coast, which is lushly sub-tropical in the north and desert from Peru on south. The mountains rise range upon range interspersed with high plateaus and cut by wild mountain rivers, until they descend into the valley of the Amazon. It is awe-inspiring country, and traveling in it I felt as if I were in a sea of mountains. Before air travel became commonplace, journeys were difficult so that cuisines developed independently of each other. It was just as hard for people and goods to get from the coast to the highlands as from country to country, so there is a tropical and a temperate cuisine as well. Modern roads and transportation have changed this, blurring the distinctions.

Venezuela's cuisine is small, as there was no great indigenous Indian civilization. The country was discovered in 1498 by Columbus when he found the mouths of the Orinoco River. Spanish settlement began in 1520.

The basis of the cookery is colonial more than anything else with borrowings and adaptations from other Latin American countries. Black beans are a great favorite and Venezuelans call their mashed black beans *caviar criollo*, native caviar, surely the ultimate culinary compliment. The national dish is as eclectic as the rest of the cooking. It is based on a sixteenth-century Spanish recipe, *Ropa Vieja* (Old Clothes), made from shredded flank steak in a rich tomato sauce — very good, despite its name — and is served with fried eggs, black beans, rice, and fried plantains. There is also a good avocado sauce, *Guasacaca*, derived from Mexico's *Guacamole*, and a fine fish dish, *Corbullón Mantuano* (Striped Bass in Sweet Pepper Sauce), that echoes Mexico's famous *Pescado a la Veracruzana* (Fish, Veracruz Style). The local corn bread is the *arepa*, made in a similar way to Mexico's tortillas but with a different type of corn. *Arepas* are much thicker, more like buns than pancakes, and the corn flavor is much less pronounced than in tortillas. German settlers of the last century are responsible for the very good cheeses of Venzuela and the excellent beer, for that matter. There is a delicious runny fresh cream cheese that turns an *arepa* into a feast when the corn bread is served hot, then pulled apart and stuffed with the cheese.

Colombia has a very grand geography with two seacoasts — one on the Pacific, one on the Caribbean — which gives the country a large choice of fish and shellfish. Three great mountain ranges, from six thousand to nineteen thousand feet, rise from the coast like the steps of a giant staircase, forming a series of plateaus at different heights so that the country has every type of climate and produces every kind of food. Wandering around the markets in the capital, Bogotá, I found piles of coconuts, bananas, plantains, pineapples, cherimoyas, papayas, sugarcane, avocados, guavas, and tropical root vegetables like yams, taros, sweet potatoes, cassava roots, and *arracacha* sharing space with peaches, pears, apricots, apples, grapes, and plums.

The conquering Spanish intermarried with the dominant Indians, the Chibchas, great gold workers who had a highly advanced civilization. The modern cuisine is very varied, sophisticated, and original. The coastal kitchen makes imaginative use of coconut milk — with rice, fish, meats, and poultry. I particularly like *Arroz con Coco y Pasas* (Rice with Coconut and Raisins) and its twin dish *Arroz con Coco Frito y Pasas* (Rice with Fried Coconut and Raisins): the rice is dry and quite firm, *bien graneado*, which is the equivalent of *al dente* in pasta. I also like the subtle flavor of *Sábalo Guisado con Coco* (Shad Fillets in Coconut Milk), easy to make at home in the spring when shad is plentiful. The highlands produce wonderful stews, perhaps the most famous of which is *Ajiaco de Pollo Bogotano* (Bogotá Chicken Stew). There is the even grander *Sancocho Especial* (Special Boiled Dinner) with a great selection of meats and vegetables, some from the tropics. It is a splendid dish for a family gathering or a party. As in all of Latin America, fresh coriander is used a great deal and there is always a fresh hot pepper sauce on the table to be taken at one's discretion.

My next trip was to Ecuador. The highland region was part of the Incan empire. The tropical lowlands were not conquered until the arrival of the Spanish. Quito, the capital, at nearly ten thousand feet lies within an extinct volcano, Pichincha, which rises to fifteen thousand feet. Eight volcanoes — among them the fabled Chimborazo, over twenty thousand feet, and Cotopaxi, over nineteen thousand feet — can be seen on clear days from Quito. The equator is only fifteen miles away, giving the highlands a gentle climate. There is a great contrast between tropical sea level cuisine and highland cookery, especially as one was Incan, the other not.

On the wall of the cathedral in the main plaza of Quito is a plaque that says that the glory of Ecuador is that it discovered the Amazon River down which Francisco de Orellana floated in a homemade boat, arriving at the source in 1541. I think it could also be claimed that the glory of the Ecuadorian kitchen is its *seviches* (fish "cooked" in lime or lemon juice). They are quite different from other countries' *seviches* mostly because of the use of Seville (bitter) orange juice in a sauce of onion, garlic, and oil. I tasted *seviches* made from bass, shrimp, lobster, and an interesting black conch. They are best accompanied by chilled beer. In Latin America there is never any problem finding beer of excellent quality with a nice bite to it, sharp on the tongue, refreshingly dry.

Potatoes play a large role in Ecuadorian highland cooking. A favorite dish is *Locro*, a thick potato and cheese soup that is sometimes served with avocado slices. I find it makes a splendid light lunch or supper if followed by a dessert or fruit. With Ecuadorian friends at midday dinner, still the main meal in most of Latin America, I had it as a course that followed a corn soufflé and preceded the meat. It was made with a little sweet paprika, but the coastal version uses annatto (achiote), which has a more pronounced flavor. Another favorite potato dish is *Llapingachos*, fried potato and cheese patties that are served with various accompaniments either as a first or as a main course according to what goes with them. They make an admirable addition to broiled or grilled meat, fish, or poultry. On the coast they are usually fried in annatto lard or oil. Coastal rice is also usually cooked with annatto, which yellows it.

Vegetables are highly esteemed in Ecuador and are served in that gentle climate at room temperature, several at a time. Since water at ten thousand feet boils at a much lower temperature than at sea level, vegetables are always crisply tender without the cook making a great effort. I think of this as a cuisine that builds bridges between the exotic and the known, using mustard in imaginative ways and contrasting texture and flavor. I was once served hot roast pork, cut into cubes and arranged in a circle on a serving dish, the center filled with slightly chilled, chopped ripe tomatoes. Delicious. There is, as everywhere, a hot sauce, *Salsa de Aji*, to be taken or not as one pleases, this one made from fresh hot red or green peppers simply ground with salt and mixed with a little chopped onion.

Of all the Andean countries the cuisine of Peru is the most exciting, though in creating it the brilliant agriculturists of the region had a most formidable geography to contend with. The narrow coastal plain is desert except where rivers create a brief oasis. The mountains rise abruptly, completely barren, but they create fertile valleys with great rivers running through them, and wide plateaus with temperate farm- and pastureland, though already as high as eleven thousand feet. Higher still, at fourteen thousand feet, are only barren, windswept uplands.

It was in the temperate highlands, the steep mountainsides terraced to provide more land for crops, that the ancient people of the region developed the sweet potato and over a hundred varieties of the potato some time around 2500 B.C. They freeze-dried potatoes, using the cold of the Andean highlands to freeze the vegetables overnight, thawing them in the morning sun and squeezing out the moisture. The resulting rock-hard potatoes were called *chuño* and kept indefinitely. The only large domestic animals were the cameloids — the llama and the alpaca — used by the Incas for their wool, as pack animals, and for meat, and they made a fresh cheese from their milk.

The Incan empire had an extensive highway system to which only the Roman is comparable, linking its more than thirty towns and cities. Farmers in this highly organized, highly urban society sent their produce to market in the town or city nearest them. A sophisticated cuisine developed with a characteristic use of hot peppers, *aji*. Peruvians like their food *picante* and are lavish in their use of peppers, of which they have a considerable variety, just about all of them hot. They are a wonderful sight in the markets, enormous piles of *rocotos* and *mirasols*, great heaps of sun yellow, flaming orange, or red as well as green peppers in various sizes, but it is the yellow ones that catch the eye. I like to speculate about this use of yellow in the food of countries that were sun worshipers before the Conquest brought Christianity. I don't think it can be an accident that Peru uses the herb *palillo*, ground to a sunshine-yellow powder, to color and flavor food. And there are the yellow potatoes — true potatoes, not sweet potatoes — which have yellow flesh, as well as yellow sweet potatoes, and plantains, yellow when ripe. The yellows continue in the squash family from the pale yellow of the huge *zapallo* to the deep yellow of other types, and in fresh corn. There are potato dishes that are a symphony of yellow and white, perhaps honoring the sun god and the moon goddess. In any case, they are lovely food in a cuisine full of marvelous dishes.

Little is known of the cooking of the Bolivian highlands, though this region was once the site of impressive civilizations. From the cook's point of view the altitude is rather daunting, for Bolivia tends to be high, higher, and highest. Lake Titicaca, which Bolivia shares with Peru, lies at 12,500 feet. Legend has it that an island in the lake is the legendary home of the Incas. Quite nearby are the ruins of Tiahuanaco, a pre-Incan city. After the Conquest Bolivia became part of Peru and was known as *El Alto Peru*, highland Peru. With independence the name was changed to Bolivia to honor the liberator, Simón Bolívar. Like the Peruvians, the Bolivians like their food hot and are lavish in their use of hot peppers. Their most popular dishes are stews and hearty soups. However, my favorite is a very good chicken pie with a corn topping, *Pastel de Choclo con Relleno de Pollo*, which I recommend with enthusiasm.

The geography of Chile poses very different problems. The northern third of this stringbean of a country, twenty-six hundred miles long and sandwiched between the Pacific Ocean and the Andes, is unrelieved desert, the most total desert on earth. Flying over it, the shadows are so intensely dark they look like pools of water, a tantalizing illusion. It is strangely, movingly beautiful. The southern third is mountainous and storm-swept, with more rain than it needs, but the middle third is lovely, temperate, and fertile, with green valleys full of vineyards that produce very fine wines, splendid vegetables and fruits, among them notable strawberries. The southern part of this felicitous third is heavily forested with a series of lakes, a landscape of rare loveliness. And, of course, the snowcapped Andes make a permanently dramatic backdrop.

The cold Humboldt Current gives Chile the most unusual seafood in the world. I can only think of the giant sea urchins, *erizos*; giant abalone, *locos*, tender as chicken when properly beaten; of *picoroccos*, strange, beaked shellfish that taste like crabs; giant crabs; mussels; clams; shrimp; langostines; oysters; and *congrio*, a splendid fish unique to these waters. Only in Chile can one enjoy these gifts of the cold current. All the same I found many interesting dishes that are not dependent on special ingredients — dishes like *Congrio en Fuente de Barro* (Fish with Tomatoes and Onions), *Pollo Escabechado* (Pickled Chicken), and *Porotos Granados* (Cranberry Beans with Corn and Squash).

There was no great Indian civilization in what is now Argentina and Uruguay. Though they are today separate countries, before independence from Spain they were both part of the viceroyalty of the River Plate. Spanish cooking methods using indigenous and introduced ingredients produced the local cuisine, which has been somewhat modified by newer arrivals — Italian influence being predominant. Like Chile, Argentina produces good wine, and its beef ranks with the best in the world. *Matambre*, which translates literally into kill hunger, and into kitchen parlance as stuffed rolled flank steak, is an example of what Argentine cooks can do with a comparatively humble cut of beef. And the *Empanadas,* the pastry turnovers, variously stuffed, are the best I've ever had. There are some unusual and good meat stews with fruit, such as *Carbonada Criolla* (Beef Stew, Argentine Style) with peaches and *Carbonada en Zapallo* (Veal Stew in Baked Pumpkin), which includes pears and peaches and finishes cooking in a large, hollowed-out squash. It is a delicious combination.

Paraguay is a small landlocked country where Guaraní, the language of the Indians of the region, is co-equal with Spanish as an official language. The cooking is Spanish and Guaraní, with some international food, mostly French and Italian. My favorite Paraguayan dish is the magnificently named *So'O-Yosopy* (the last syllable is pronounced with an explosive PEH), that translates into Spanish as *sopa de carne* (beef soup). I know of nothing more restorative when one is worn-out. I'm almost as fond of *Sopa Paraguaya,* which is not a soup at all but a rich cheese and cornmeal bread that is traditionally served with steak; but as far as I am concerned, it is good by itself and goes with almost everything. Paraguay is also the home of *Mate* tea, a very ancient Indian drink that is pleasantly stimulating, since it has a good deal of caffeine.

Of all the cuisines in South America, the Brazilian is the most exuberant and varied. The country, taking up nearly half the continent of South America, is enormous, stretching from the tropics in the north to the temperate south, with great highlands and a long coastline. It bulges generously out into the South Atlantic toward Africa with which it is once believed to have been joined — perhaps accounting for the dual origin of the peanut. The ethnic mix is as varied as the climate, which ranges from torrid to temperate. There are the original Indians, the Portuguese, Africans, Italians, Germans, and so on. And there are all the foods of the world plus many cooking techniques, making a rich amalgam. The sheer size of the country has made for authentic regional cooking.

There was no great Indian civilization in Brazil. Today's cuisine has developed since the arrival of the Portuguese who in 1539 founded Salvador in the state of Bahia on the northeast coast, planted sugarcane, and brought in African slaves to work in the cane fields. From a combination of the foods and cooking methods of local Indians, Africans, and Portuguese,

Brazil's most exciting cooking, the *cozinha baiana*, Bahian cookery, developed. The primary ingredients are *dendè* (palm) oil from Africa, which has a nutty flavor and colors food an attractive orangey-yellow, coconut, fresh coriander, fresh and dried shrimp, and nuts — almonds, cashews, peanuts — and of course, hot peppers. A hot sauce made with tiny *malaqueta* peppers steeped in *dendè* oil and *farofa* made from manioc (cassava) meal, often colored yellow with *dendè* oil, is always on the table. Brazilians in all parts of the country sprinkle meat, poultry, and other dishes with *farofa*, as others might use grated Parmesan cheese.

The cooking of Rio de Janeiro which supplanted Salvador as the capital in 1763 seems almost subdued by comparison. It is closer to Portuguese, using local ingredients, except for *Feijoada Completa*, a regional recipe from Rio which is now recognized as the national dish. It is a very splendid, colorful meal of meats and black beans cooked together so that the many flavors are blended, and it is served, lavishly garnished, with sliced oranges, rice, cooked kale or collard greens, *farofa*, and a hot pepper and lime juice sauce. I cannot think of a better dish for a party.

São Paulo and Minas Gerais to the south share a regional cuisine. It was the Paulistas who, in the seventeenth century, set out looking for gold and found it, together with diamonds and other mineral wealth in the mountainous country to the northeast. This is now the state of Minas Gerais, which means general mines, a succinct description of what the Paulistas found. It is hearty food, well suited to the cooler climate. One of its best dishes is *Cozido à Brasileira* (Stew, Brazilian Style), a splendidly robust pot-au-feu. The most famous dish is *Cuscuz Paulista*, an adaptation of the couscous that originated in Arabia and spread to North Africa. It is made with cornmeal instead of wheat, looks marvelously decorative, and is surprisingly easy to make.

Desserts all over Brazil are rich and very much in the Portuguese egg-yolk-and-sugar tradition with its strong Moorish overtones.

Throughout Latin America there are examples of the oldest form of cooking, the neolithic earth oven, now superseded for centuries by stoves of one kind or another from charcoal to electric or gas. It has persisted as holiday cooking. Country people in Mexico cook a whole lamb in an earth oven for a *barbacoa*, and less rural people have *barbacoa* parties on Sundays and holidays at special restaurants devoted to this form of cooking. In Yucatán the earth oven is called a *pib*; in the Andes it is called *pachamanca* from the Quechua words for earth and pot. In southern Chile they have a *curanto*, best described as a clambake like those in New England. It is often lavish and includes a suckling pig as well as Chile's magnificent shellfish.

Argentina, Uruguay, and Brazil all have barbecues like the kind popular in the United States. In Argentina there are splendid restaurants where meats are cooked on wall-size grills, and in Brazil there are *Churrascarias* where all manner of grilled meats are served. I think the best proof I ever had of the popularity of this form of cooking was on a main street in Montevideo, Uruguay, when I watched some road repairmen settle down to lunch. They made a fire, put a piece of wire netting on top of it, grilled a steak, opened a bottle of red wine, and with the addition of some good bread had an excellent meal.

Looking back to the day when I determined to collect Latin American recipes — true gems of cookery — into a book gives me a feeling of great pleasure. I have done what I so deeply wanted to do, to bring these delectable dishes into American kitchens. I have spent a long time on my research; I have made many exciting journeys and eaten a great deal of very good food. It has been infinitely worthwhile. I sought out the historical hows and whys of this intriguing cuisine and found academic answers which I recorded in my endless notebooks in a special kind of cook's shorthand. A fascinating analysis to be sure, of ancient peoples and cities, of the birth of agriculture, of the coming together, in the kitchen, of very different cultures. That was only part of what I sought. I found the rest quite simply in wonderful food, the focal point of family and social life. So the best part of my quest has been coming back to my own kitchen and bringing to life those scribbled words, turning them into dishes with the authentic flavors of Latin American cooking.

It isn't food that is difficult to cook or bristles with complicated techniques. For the most part it is straightforward and easy, though there are some cooking methods that may seem odd at first, like frying a paste of peppers and other ingredients in lard or oil as a preliminary to making a Mexican *mole*. And I did have to learn about unfamiliar fruits and vegetables and seek them out in my own markets back home, where I found them without much trouble. I remembered flavors, and altered recipes until the taste was right, and had loving friends and family in to share splendid meals with me. It was a joyous experience and I have never been happier than when I received the accolade bestowed on good cooks in Latin America, *"tiene buena mano,"* "She has a good hand." It is my hope that readers will want to share my experience, and will cook, enjoy, and adopt these recipes as family favorites.

The Book of
Latin American Cooking

Ingredients

Aceite o Manteca de Achiote (Annatto Oil or Lard) is made by briefly steeping annatto seeds in hot oil or lard, then straining and cooling the fat, colored a deep orange-gold by the seeds, see page 324. It is used for both color and flavor in Latin America as well as in some non-Spanish-speaking parts of the Caribbean.

Aliño Criollo (Creole Style Seasoning Powder), a Venezuelan seasoning mixture made of herbs and spices, used with meat and poultry, in stews, and so on. Available in shaker-top glass jars from the spice section of supermarkets. Easy to make at home, see recipe, page 325.

Allspice or **pimiento** (*Pimenta officinalis*), the *pimiento de Jamaica* or *pimienta gorda* of the Spanish-speaking countries is the small, dark brown berry of an evergreen tree of the myrtle family found by the Spaniards growing wild in Jamaica. Most exports still come from the island. The dried berries, which closely resemble peppercorns, combine the flavor of cinnamon, nutmeg, and cloves. Available whole or ground wherever spices are sold.

Annatto is the English name given to the seeds of a small flowering tree of tropical America. Known as *achiote* in Spanish from the Nahuatl (Aztec) *achiotl*, the seeds are sometimes called *bija* or *bijol* in the Spanish-speaking islands of the Caribbean. The Caribs and Arawaks called the seeds *roucou*, a name by which they are still known in parts of the region. The hard orange-red pulp surrounding the seeds is used to make *Aceite o Manteca de Achiote* (Annatto Oil or Lard) and serves as a coloring and flavoring for meat, poultry, and fish dishes in the Caribbean, Colombia, Ecuador, and Venezuela. In Yucatán the whole seed is ground with various spices (such as cumin and oregano) into a paste, giving a more pronounced flavor. The taste is hard to define, fragrant, light, and flowery. Available in stores specializing in foods from Latin America or India.

Antojitos, literally little whims or fancies, the name given by the Spanish to the finger foods made with a base of tortillas that they found in Aztec Mexico. These foods fit perfectly into today's meal patterns as hors d'oeuvres or first courses. A large version, the *antojos*, whims or fancies, are ideal for light lunches or suppers.

Apio — see **Arracacha.**

Arepas, the corn bread of Venezuela, made from special flour of pre-cooked Venezuelan corn, available, packaged, from Latin American groceries. See **Tortillas** for additional information.

Arracacha (*Arracacia xanthorrhiza*) is a leggy root vegetable found in markets in Colombia. It is a member of the celery family indigenous to the northern part of South America and a favorite pre-Columbian vegetable. Venezuela has a cylindrically shaped root vegetable called *apio*, also said to be *Arracacia xanthorrhiza.* They do taste the same, faintly reminiscent of celery with a hint of sweetness, a potatolike texture, and very pale yellow flesh. The only difference I've found is that *apio* is easier to peel. As *apio* is often available in tropical markets and *arracacha* only occasionally, they can be used interchangeably. Confusion arises from the fact that *apio* is the Spanish for celery. Venezuelans solve the problem by calling celery *apio de España* or *apio de Castilla* (Spanish celery). It can be a delicious substitute for potatoes, and makes a lovely dessert when cooked with pineapple.

Arrowroot, the edible starchy powder made from the underground rhizomes of *Maranta arundinacea*, is a delicate thickening agent for soups, stews, and sauces. It is widely available.

Avocado (*Persea americana*), of the laurel family, was cultivated in Mexico as far back as 7000 B.C. and was known as *ahuacatl* in Nahuatl, the language of the ancient Mexicans. Today it is called *aguacate*. It spread to South America before Columbus arrived and was cultivated in the Inca empire, where it was called *palta*. Today it is known in Quechua by that name though in many parts of South America it keeps its Mexican name. In Brazil it is called *abacate*. The fruit may be rough or smooth-skinned, green or black. It is hard when unripe but ripens in a few days if put into a brown paper bag and left at room temperature. An avocado is ripe when it yields to a gentle pressure at the stem end. Once an avocado is cut, it discolors quickly. Sprinkling lime or lemon juice on it helps, and if you are going to try to keep an unused portion of an avocado, leave the skin on, let the pit rest in the cavity, rub the cut sides with lemon or lime, wrap tightly in plastic wrap, and refrigerate.

An easy way to mash avocados is to cut them in half, remove the pits, and mash them in their shells with a fork, holding the shell in the palm of the left hand. Scoop out the flesh with a spoon and mash any bits that may have escaped the fork. This method is much easier than having them slither round a bowl and gives a texture with character. Avocado leaves are sometimes used in Mexican cooking in the same way as bay leaves and there is also the charming bonus of being able to grow the pits into very beautiful house plants. To toast avocado leaves, place them on an ungreased *comal* (griddle) or a heavy iron skillet and cook on both sides over moderate heat for about 1 minute.

Bacalao, Spanish for dried salted codfish, called *bacalhau* in Brazil, is extremely popular in all of Latin America. It is available in Latin American markets and in many supermarkets and fish stores, especially in the Northeast.

Bananas and banana leaves. Both green and ripe bananas are used in Latin American cooking, the green bananas as a vegetable. When a recipe calls for plantains (page 15), bananas make a good substitute. Banana leaves, sometimes available in specialty food stores, are used as a wrapping in which to cook foods. Kitchen parchment or aluminum foil make good substitutes.

Beans, black (turtle), red kidney, pink, mottled pinto, white Navy, or pea beans, all belong to the large grouping called *Phaseolus vulgaris* of the legume family, which originated in Mexico about 5000 B.C. They are an essential part of the Latin American kitchen and turn up in many guises. I follow the Mexican rules for cooking beans — namely, that they should not be soaked but should be put on to cook in cold water with their seasonings and that hot water is added as necessary during the cooking time. Salt should not be added until the beans are tender. It is impossible to give an exact time for cooking beans as it can vary from 1½ to 2½ hours according to the age of the beans. It is wise to buy beans from shops with a quick turnover, as stale beans may take a very long time to cook and even when cooked may have a dry texture. If there is reason to suspect that beans are stale, a desperate remedy may be in order. Soak them overnight in cold water with a little bicarbonate of soda (baking soda), ¼ teaspoon to 2 cups of beans, then rinse the beans very thoroughly before putting them on to cook in fresh water. It works wonders.

The Spanish and Portuguese brought chickpeas, sometimes called garbanzos or ceci (*Cicer arietinum*), also of the legume family, to the New World with them. These hard, round, yellow peas, native to the Middle East, do need soaking overnight in cold water before cooking. Another popular bean from the Middle East is the broad bean, also called fava or habas (*Vicia faba*). Other popular local beans are limas from Peru and cranberry or shell beans and, to a lesser extent, black-eyed peas, which originated in Africa. Whenever beans need soaking before cooking, instructions are given in individual recipes.

Calabaza, also called *ahuyama*, *zapallo*, *abóbora*, and, in English, West Indian or green pumpkin, is a winter squash available in Latin American and Caribbean markets. Not to be confused with American pumpkin, it comes in a variety of shapes and sizes but is usually large and either round or oval. Hubbard, or other winter squash, is a good substitute.

Carne sêca is the sun-dried salt beef, known in the United States as jerked beef, that is used in the Brazilian national dish *Feijoada Completa* (Black Beans with Mixed Meats). It is available in Latin American markets and in some specialty butcher shops. The salt beef used in *Sancocho Especial* (Special Boiled Dinner, see page 163) from Colombia could be used instead, as the technique of salting and drying is similar.

Cassava (*Manihot utilissima*), also called manioc, mandioca, aipím, or yucca, is a handsome tropical plant whose tuberous roots, at least 2 inches in diameter and about 8 to 10 inches long, are best known as the commercial source of tapioca. Cassava originated in 1500 B.C. in Brazil and is widely used in the kitchens of Latin America. The roots are covered with a brown, barklike, rather hairy skin. Cassava should be peeled under running water and immediately dropped into water, as its white flesh tends to discolor on contact with the air. It may be boiled and used as a potato substitute in stews, or to accompany meat and poultry dishes, or it may be fried and served like potato chips.

In Brazil manioc meal is used to make *farofa*: the meal is toasted and mixed with butter and other ingredients such as onion, eggs, or prunes and served with *Feijoada* or with poultry, steaks, or roasted meats. *Farofa*, which looks like coarsely grated Parmesan cheese, is as common on Brazilian tables as salt and pepper.

Cassava is also used for making bread or cakes, mostly sold commercially in South America. To make them, you need cassava that is finely ground like cornstarch, not easily obtainable in the United States — and, anyway, the results are not particularly delicious.

Chayote (*Sechium edule*), of the squash family, is also known a: christophene, cho-cho, and chuchu. The vegetable originated in Mexico, and the name comes from the Mexican *chayotl.* It is now widely grown in semitropical regions throughout the world. About 6 to 8 inches long, and roughly pear-shaped, chayote is usually a light, pretty green (though there are white varieties), with a slightly prickly skin and a single edible seed. The texture is crisp with a delicate flavor a little like zucchini but more subtle. It is best when young and firm. Avoid soft or wrinkled ones.

Chicha, a beerlike drink made from dried corn. Usually only slightly alcoholic. Popular throughout South America.

Chicharrones are fried pork rinds available packaged in Latin American markets and in supermarkets.

Coconuts and **coconut milk.** Choose coconuts that are full of liquid. Shake them to check. Nuts with little liquid are stale. Avoid those with moldy or wet "eyes." With an ice pick, screwdriver, or similar sharp implement, pierce two out of the three eyes of the nut using a hammer to bang it through if necessary. Drain out and reserve the liquid. Strain it before use as there may be bits of coconut fiber in it. A medium-sized coconut yields about ½ cup liquid. Bake the coconut in a preheated hot (400° F.) oven for 15 minutes. Then put the coconut on a hard surface and hit it all over with a hammer. The hard shell will fall away. Lever out any bits that are left with a knife or screwdriver. If making coconut milk it is not necessary to peel off the brown inner skin, but if grated coconut is to be used in a recipe, peel this off with a small, sharp knife. Chop the coconut pieces coarsely, then put into a blender or food processor fitted with a steel blade and grate as fine as possible. The grated coconut is now ready for use. If the coconut water is not to be used separately in a recipe, add it to the blender or food processor with the coconut pieces as this helps in the grating. This makes about 4 cups per coconut.

To make thick (rich) coconut milk squeeze the grated coconut through a damp cloth, squeezing and twisting the cloth to remove as much liquid as possible. Set this aside. To make ordinary coconut milk put the squeezed-out coconut into a bowl and pour 1 cup boiling water over it. Let it stand 30 minutes. Squeeze out the liquid through a damp cloth, add the coconut water, and set aside. Repeat the entire process. Discard the coconut.

Unless a recipe calls for thick coconut milk to be used separately, mix the thick and ordinary coconut milk together and use. When thick coconut milk is left to stand, the cream rises to the top. This is delicious instead of cream with desserts. If the coconut water drained out of the nut at the beginning is not needed for any culinary purpose, it makes a wonderful mix with gin or vodka.

If coconuts are not available, canned moist coconut is a good substitute for grated fresh coconut. Creamed coconut available from tropical markets and specialty stores is a good substitute for coconut milk. Simply dilute to the desired consistency with warm water or milk.

Freshly grated coconut keeps well frozen.

Coriander (*Coriandrum sativum*), of the carrot family, indigenous to the Mediterranean and the Caucasus, is a very old herb, mentioned in Sanskrit and ancient Egyptian writings. Its antiquity is proved by the fact that the Romans introduced it to Britain before the end of the first century A.D. It has spread throughout the world and is very important in Indian and Thai cooking, indeed in most of Asia including China. It is often sold as Chinese parsley and though the leaves are a lighter green, it does resemble flat-leafed parsley, also of the carrot family and a close relative.

Many Mexicans think of coriander as indigenous. Certainly it is hard to imagine the Mexican green tomato dishes or *Guacamole* (Avocado Sauce) without it. If there could be said to be a favorite herb in the Mexican kitchen it would be coriander, though oregano, cumin, and to a lesser extent the indigenous herb *epazote* are all popular. I have never been able to find out when coriander first arrived in Mexico, but I think it was introduced after the Conquest and was adopted with enthusiasm. Certainly it is popular in all of Latin America. But there is a puzzle here. Coriander is not used in Spanish cooking today, although it is a favorite Middle Eastern herb and Spain was occupied for nearly eight centuries by the Arabs. In fact, Columbus had discovered America before Spain had reconquered all its occupied provinces, so the Spanish of that time, eating Arab foods, may have brought coriander with them to the New World. Or it may have arrived via the Philippines, where it is popular; there was a great deal of trade between Mexico and the Philippines, then a Spanish possession, in early colonial times. Some kitchen mysteries may never be solved, though it is great fun trying. There is no mystery, however, about its arrival in Brazil, as it is a favorite Portuguese herb.

The fresh herb is increasingly available. Latin American, Chinese, and

Korean markets, as well as some specialty stores, carry it. In Latin American markets it is called cilantro, less usually *culantro* or *culantrillo*. In Chinese and Korean markets it is called Chinese parsley, or, in Chinese, *yuen-sai*. It is sold with its roots on and it does not keep well. The roots should not be removed for storage and the coriander should not be washed but simply wrapped in paper towels, roots and all, and stored in a plastic bag in the refrigerator. This is the simplest method and the one I use. Some recommend washing the coriander with its roots on, drying thoroughly, and refrigerating in a jar with just enough water to cover the roots. Others simply refrigerate roots and all in a glass jar with a screw top.

To have coriander available for flavoring soups and stews, I remove the roots, wash the coriander well, and purée it, including the stems, without the addition of any water in a food processor, then freeze the purée in an ice cube tray. When frozen, I store the cubes in a plastic bag. One cube is the equivalent of about 1 tablespoon of the freshly chopped leaves. This works well where flavor — not appearance — is what matters. Sometimes the coriander roots are quite sizeable. In Thailand, the country, incidentally, in which I became a coriander addict, they are scraped and used in curries. They add a very intense flavor. I always keep an eye out for these fat roots, a happy bonus.

The tiny brown seedlike fruits of coriander are also used in cooking, especially in curries, and to flavor gin. They are available in jars in the spice section of supermarkets and I have grown coriander from them.

Crème fraîche. Venezuela has a lovely runny fresh cream cheese that is wonderful with hot *arepas* (corn bread). It is very like French *crème fraîche*. A good imitation of *crème fraîche* can be made by mixing 1 tablespoon of buttermilk with 1 cup heavy cream and heating the mixture to lukewarm in a small saucepan. Pour it into a jar and let it stand until it has thickened, about 8 hours in a warm room. It will then keep for several days refrigerated.

Dendê oil (palm oil), originally from Africa and very much used in Bahian cooking in Brazil. It is a deep, beautiful orange-gold and has a pleasant nutty flavor. Available in Latin American stores and specialty markets. It lends color and some flavor to dishes but one can manage without it.

Epazote (*Chenopodium ambrosioides*), one of the Anserinas, from the Nahuatl *epazotl*, known under a variety of names in English — Mexican tea, wormseed, lamb's quarters, goosefoot, and Jerusalem oak. It is ubiquitous, growing wild all over the Americas and in many parts of Europe. It dries excellently and is often available dried in Latin American markets.

To dry it yourself, pick the epazote or lamb's quarters on a dry morning (early if possible, as the sun draws out the volatile oil) and spread on paper towels in a dark, warm cupboard until dry, turning occasionally. This may take a week. Or put on a tray in the oven with the pilot light on. Turn from time to time. This will take only a matter of hours. Strip the leaves from the stalks when dry, put into a screw-top glass jar, and store away from light. It is used quite a lot in Mexican cooking, especially in the center and south, in black bean and tortilla dishes. There is no substitute. Fortunately the herb is not vital to the success of the dishes.

Garlic. Peruvian garlic, purple-skinned, and Mexican garlic, sometimes purple-skinned, sometimes white, are both often available in specialty food stores and supermarkets. They have quite enormous cloves, which comes in handy when one has to peel a number of them. The size of garlic cloves varies so widely, as does a taste for garlic, that I have adopted in most instances the system of simply giving the number of cloves needed so that those who are particularly fond of garlic may seek out the big ones with a clear conscience.

Guascas or **huascas** (*Galinsoga parviflora Lineo*) is a Colombian herb that grows in the Andes. It is sold in jars, dried and ground into a green powder, in Colombian food shops. Though it has no relationship whatsoever to Jerusalem artichokes, its smell is reminiscent of that vegetable. It adds a delicious flavor to soups and stews, particularly those made with chicken. Since specialty food stores constantly increase the range of their imports, I have included it here in case it should become available, but it is not essential to the success of any of the recipes in this book.

Hearts of palm, in Spanish and Portuguese *palmito*, are the tender heart buds of any one of several species of palm trees. Their delicate flavor is exquisite in salads and soups. Though they are eaten fresh in the countries of origin, they are always canned for export and are available in supermarkets.

Huacatay, an herb of the marigold family, is used in Peru in sauces and dishes such as *Picante de Yuca* (Cassava Root with Cheese Sauce). It is not available here and there is no substitute. The flavor is unusual and is certainly an acquired taste, rather rank at first try. I find I don't miss it.

Jerusalem artichokes, despite their name, are the edible tubers of a plant native to Canada and the northern United States. Their botanical name is *Helianthus tuberosus*, and they are a species of sunflower belonging to the daisy family. Jerusalem is apparently a corruption of *girasole*, the Italian word for sunflower. They are called *topinambur* in South America and are sometimes called sunchokes in U.S. markets. They have a lovely crisp texture reminiscent of water chestnuts. They make a delightful soup, an excellent salad, and are a lovely change of pace from the more usual potatoes as a starchy root vegetable. They are a little tricky to peel since the small tubers are knobby in shape. I always pick out the largest and least knobby ones available, but I have also found recently that newer varieties are easier to peel. When I scrape them I'm not all that fussy about a bit of skin left on, as it is not at all unpleasant, and I just shave off the little knobs. It is very important not to overcook them since they lose their crisp texture and turn mushy.

Jícama, pronounced HEE-kama (*Exogonium bracteatum*), of the morning glory family, is a tuberous turnip-shaped root vegetable with a light brown skin, originally from Mexico, where it is usually eaten raw, sliced, with a little salt and a sprinkling of hot chili powder (cayenne), or in salads. It has crispy, juicy white flesh. Water chestnuts or tart green cooking apples are the best substitutes. It is available in markets in the Southwest and in markets specializing in tropical fruits and vegetables.

Malanga — see **Taro**.

Mate, a tea made from the dried leaves of the South American evergreen *Ilex paraguayensis*. Especially popular in Paraguay, Uruguay, Argentina, and Brazil. Available in specialty and health food stores. Make according to package directions, or see page 337.

Mole, pronounced MO-lay, from the Nahuatl (Mexican) word *molli*, meaning a sauce made from any of the peppers, sweet, pungent, or hot, usually a combination, together with other ingredients. The most famous of the *moles* is the *Mole Poblano de Guajalote*, the turkey dish from Puebla using bitter chocolate, but there are a host of others playing variations on a theme.

Nopal is the prickly pear cactus. It is available canned in stores selling Mexican foods and fresh in some markets in the Southwest. Used mainly in salads, it has an attractive fruit, *tuna*, which may be green or pinkish red.

Oranges, bitter, sour, Seville, or Bigarade, to give this fruit all the names by which it is commonly known, are not raised commercially in the U.S., but can sometimes be found in specialty food stores or markets. The large, rough-skinned, reddish-orange fruit has a delicate and quite distinctive flavor, but the pulp is too sour to be eaten raw. The juice, which is used a great deal in Latin American cooking, freezes successfully, and the peel need not be wasted but can be used to make marmalade. A mixture of one-third lime or lemon juice to two-thirds sweet orange juice can be used as a substitute.

Palillo is a Peruvian herb used dried and ground to give a yellow color to food. Since so many Peruvian foods are yellow or white, I'm sure it is a reflection of pre-Conquest Inca sun (and moon) worship. *Palillo* is not available here but I have found that using half the amount of turmeric gives much the same result.

Pepitas, Mexican pumpkin seeds, available in jars in supermarkets and health food stores.

PEPPERS

Peppers, sweet, pungent, and hot, all belong to the genus *Capsicum annuum* or *Capsicum frutescens* of the *Solanaceae* family, to which potato, tomato, and eggplant also belong. They were first cultivated in the Valley of Mexico about 9,000 years ago and their original name in Nahuatl was *chilli*. Varieties are legion and have not yet been fully classified botanically. They have spread all over the world and become naturalized so quickly that their national origin has been forgotten. Peppers are widely used in Latin American cooking, especially in Mexico and Peru. The number of varieties used is, fortunately, limited. They are widely available in markets specializing in Latin American and tropical foods and often in supermarkets and neighborhood stores. They fall into two main categories, the dried and the fresh.

The Dried Peppers

Ancho. This is the most widely used of all the peppers in the Mexican kitchen. It is quite large, with a wrinkled skin, about 4 inches long by about 3 inches wide. It has a deep, lovely color and a rich, full, mild flavor. It is the base of many cooked sauces.

Chipotle and **morita.** These are dried wrinkled peppers, brick red in color. Both are smaller than *ancho* peppers, with the *morita* smaller than the *chipotle*. Though they are available dried and sometimes ground, they are more usually canned. They have the most distinctive flavor of all the

Mexican peppers and are very, very hot. If used sparingly, the exciting flavor comes through without excessive heat.

Guajillo. This is a long (4-inch), slender, tapering, smooth-skinned bright red pepper, which, like its fresh counterpart, the pale green *chile largo*, is mostly used whole to flavor pot-au-feu dishes.

Mulato. Much the same size and shape as the *ancho* but darker in color, closer to brown than red, and longer and more tapering. Its flavor is more pungent than the mild *ancho*. It is wrinkled.

Pasilla. This is a long, slender pepper, 6 to 7 inches in length and about an inch or so wide, and very much darker in color than the *ancho*. Like ancho and mulato peppers, it is wrinkled and some varieties are so dark they are called *chile negro* (black peppers). It is very hot but at the same time richly flavored. In Mexico these three peppers are often used in combination.

SMALL HOT DRIED PEPPERS
There are a number of small hot dried red peppers under various names, *cascabel, pequín, tepín*, which can be used interchangeably whenever dried hot red peppers are called for. One variety, a Japanese migrant, is called *hontaka* and should be treated with respect as it is very hot indeed. Hot paprika or cayenne pepper can be used instead: ⅛ teaspoon is about the equivalent of a whole *pequín*.

Mirasol. This is a medium-sized tapering, wrinkled, dried hot pepper from Peru, which may be either red or yellow. It is not available here, but dried hot red peppers are an excellent substitute. The larger ones like the Japanese *hontaka* are the most suitable.

How to Use Dried Red Peppers
The method used in Mexican cooking is the same for *ancho, pasilla, mulato, chipotle*, and *morita* chilies. Rinse in cold water, tear off the stem end, and shake out the seeds. Tear the chilies roughly into pieces and soak in warm water, about 6 to 1 cup, for half an hour. If they are very dry, soak them a little longer. Purée them with the water in which they have soaked in a blender or food processor fitted with a steel blade. The resulting almost pastelike purée is then ready to be cooked in hot lard or oil with the other ingredients specified in the recipe to make the sauce.

Canned *chipotle* and *morita* chilies are puréed right out of the can without soaking, or used as the recipe specifies. The small hot dried red chilies are usually just crumbled with the fingers.

Always wash the hands in warm soapy water after handling chilies. Hot chili accidentally rubbed in the eyes can be temporarily very painful.

Dried chilies are best stored in plastic bags in the refrigerator or another cool place. They dry out if exposed to the air.

The Fresh Peppers

HOT FRESH PEPPERS

A number of small and medium-sized hot green peppers are sold fresh in supermarkets and greengrocers all year round. They are not usually identified beyond being called hot peppers. In Mexico the most commonly used small fresh peppers are the *serrano*, about 1½ inches long, tapering, smooth-skinned, medium green, and the *jalapeño*, which is slightly darker in color and larger, about 2½ inches long. Both are quite hot. *Jalapeño is* sold interchangeably with *cuaresmeño*, a pepper so like it that some botanists classify them as the same. The shape is slightly different and I think the *cuaresmeño* is hotter. As most of the heat in these peppers is in the seeds and veins, remove them, unless fiery heat is wanted. These peppers are also sold canned in Mexican food stores and are very useful since they can be used when fresh peppers are not available.

There is a tiny hot pepper that in Brazil is called *malagueta*. It is fiery. A larger one, sometimes called cayenne chili, is widely available year round in greengrocers and can also be found in Chinese and Japanese markets. These two are sometimes sold ripe, when they have turned red. They are then slightly less hot, and have a somewhat richer flavor.

In the West Indies there is a lantern-shaped pepper that the Jamaicans call Scotch Bonnet, usually quite small, about 1½ inches long, with a most exquisite flavor. It is the *habanero* of Yucatán and is also popular in tropical Brazil. This pepper is sold green, yellow, and red in its three stages of ripening. It is fiery hot but has a flavor that makes it worth seeking. I have found it fresh in Caribbean markets and also bottled, usually imported from Trinidad. The bottled version keeps indefinitely in the refrigerator.

Any of these peppers can be used when fresh hot red or green peppers are called for.

Peppers vary a great deal in strength. There is only one way to find out how hot they are and that is by tasting. Nibble a tiny bit of hot pepper, and if it seems very fiery, use it sparingly. But tastes vary as much as peppers do, so the only true guide is to please yourself. As with dried peppers, always wash your hands in warm, soapy water after handling.

Visiting markets in Peru, I came upon great heaps of yellow peppers, *ají amarillo* (fresh hot yellow peppers), an astonishment to the eye. Surely nothing short of gold is as yellow as these peppers. Yellow peppers are almost never available here. Fresh hot red or green peppers are just as good from the point of view of flavor.

SWEET FRESH PEPPERS

Perhaps the most widely used of all peppers is the green bell pepper, available year round everywhere. There is a splendid Mexican pepper, the *poblano*, dark green and tapering and about the same size as the bell pepper, which is not available in Eastern markets. It is used especially for stuffed peppers and the bell pepper makes a good substitute. There is another sweet green pepper, pale green and tapering, called California or Italian pepper. It is similar to the Mexican *chile güero* and can be used whenever chopped bell peppers are called for. These tapering peppers are not usually large enough to be stuffed.

The green bell pepper turns red when ripe. A similar pepper, though a different variety, is the pimiento, tapering in shape where the bell pepper is squat. It is always sold canned or in jars, often labeled *pimientos morrones*. It is tomato red whereas the ripe bell pepper is a true crimson. When red bell peppers are unavailable, use the canned pimientos. Already peeled and cooked, they can be used straight from the jar and make a very attractive garnish.

How to Peel Red or Green Bell Peppers

Stick a cooking fork into the stem end of the peppers and toast them over a gas flame or electric burner, turning frequently, until the skin blisters and blackens. Wrap the peppers in a cloth wrung out in hot water and leave for 30 minutes. The burned part of the thin papery skin will rinse off easily under cold running water and most of the rest can be pulled away. If a few bits of skin remain, it does not matter. Toasting the peppers in this way also brings out their flavor.

Piloncillo, Mexican brown sugar packaged in pyramid-shaped pieces. Similar molded brown sugar is called by a variety of names. Use dark brown sugar instead.

Plantains, *plátanos* in Spanish, are members of the same family as bananas — bird-of-paradise (*Strelitzia*). They are much larger and are not edible until cooked even when they are quite ripe and their skins are black. They are fried or boiled green, half-ripe, and ripe, and are usually served as a starchy vegetable to accompany meat, poultry, or fish. They also make a good cocktail nibble when green (*verde*), thinly sliced, and deep fried.

How to Peel a Plantain or Green Banana
Neither plantains, except very ripe ones, nor green bananas peel readily by hand. The simplest method is to make shallow lengthwise cuts along the natural ridges of the fruit and pull the skin off in sections.

Potatoes. The people we call the Incas for convenience, though it was quite likely a much earlier civilization, now lost in time, first cultivated potatoes in the high Andes. They developed a bewildering variety, some of which survive today. Among the survivors are large, yellow-fleshed potatoes that look beautiful used in the Peruvian potato dishes. However, this is more a matter of aesthetics than flavor as any good-quality potato that takes to boiling can be used instead. Colombia has a small version of the Peruvian potato. They are also yellow-fleshed, are called *papas criollas*, and are the size of new potatoes. As they stay firm when cooked, Colombians use them in stews with other, softer potatoes, which disintegrate to thicken the gravy, leaving the *papas criollas* intact. Any good small new potato, especially a waxy one, does very well as a substitute.

Sausages. There are no problems in finding the right sausages for Latin American cooking. Chorizos, Spanish-style hot, spicy pork sausages, are widely available in the United States. Blood sausages are very little different from *morcilla*, and Polish *kielbasa,* available in supermarkets, is a splendid substitute for Spanish *longaniza* or Brazilian *linguiça.*

Shrimp (dried) are used a great deal in Bahian cooking in Brazil. They are tiny and are ground before being used in dishes like *vatapá*. A food processor fitted with a steel blade takes the hard work out of this chore. A blender can also be used. If the shrimp are very dry, a brief soaking in warm water helps. Available in Chinese and Japanese markets and in Latin American markets.

Sierra (Spanish mackerel) is a large fish that can reach 10 to 15 pounds. It is very attractive, with yellow the predominating color on its back scales instead of the steely blue of Atlantic mackerel. Found off Florida and the Gulf coast, it is a popular fish in South America and is used in *Sopa de Almejas* (Clam Soup) from Colombia. Red snapper, or similar fish, is a better substitute than Atlantic mackerel, which is too strongly flavored.

Smoked ham. When South American recipes call for smoked ham, the one most usually used is Spanish *jamón serrano*, which has been aged in spices. Italian prosciutto, German Westphalian, French Ardennes, or Bayonne hams are perfect substitutes.

Squash blossoms or **pumpkin flowers**, whatever they are called, are the pretty golden yellow blooms of one or other of the cucurbits of the squash family. They are not the female blossoms, which would turn into little squash, but are the male flowers, which if not gathered and cooked would die upon the vine. Female blossoms have recognizably squashlike swellings behind them; male blossoms do not. The latter make a marvelous soup among other things.

Sweet potato (*Ipomoea batatas*) is an edible tuber originally from tropical America, though its precise birthplace is not known. Only slightly sweet, it is in no way related to the potato family. The most popular variety grown in the United States is the Louisiana yam, with moist, orange-colored flesh and brown skin. Its name is also confusing as it is not related to the yams, which are an entirely different botanical group, the Dioscoreas. The white sweet potato with drier white flesh and pink or white skin is known as *boniato* (pronounced bon-ee-AH-toe) and is the variety most popular in Latin America. It is widely available in tropical markets and increasingly in ordinary greengrocers. It makes a delicious substitute for potatoes.

Taro and **malanga** are tropical plants that bear edible tubers and are members of the very large *Arum* family. There are a great many of them and they have been cultivated for more than 2,000 years. I think of all the root vegetables they are, apart from potatoes, the most subtly flavored, the most delicious. The type of taro most widely cultivated in the United States is called *dasheen* and can be found in tropical markets, though in some markets specializing in Caribbean foods it may be called *coco* or *eddo*. They can also be found in Japanese markets as *sato-imo*, or Japanese potatoes. A closely related group, the malangas, which belong to the genus *Xanthosoma*, are known by a wide variety of names, malanga, tannia, and *yautía* being the ones most likely to be encountered in tropical markets in the U.S. The skins are usually brown, the flesh white to yellow, and they can be cooked like potatoes. When I first went looking for them in markets, I wrote down all the names and asked for them in a sort of litany. I found people very understanding and helpful, and they sorted things out for me in a charmingly good-humored way.

Tomatoes, green or husk (*Physalis ixocarpa*), which have a loose, brown papery outer covering, should not be confused with ordinary green (unripe) tomatoes. Though members of the same family, they are a different species. The Aztecs called the fruit *miltomatl*, but today in Mexico it is usually called *tomatillo* (little tomato), as it is never very large, usually only about an inch across. It has other names, *tomate verde*, *tomatitto*, and *fresadilla*. In English it is sometimes called Spanish tomato. When the tomatoes, which cannot be skinned as nothing would be left of them, are marketed as peeled, it means that the papery brown husk has been removed. The green tomato is very important in Mexican, and to a lesser extent Guatemalan, cooking, giving a distinctive flavor to the "green" dishes and sauces. The flavor is delicate and slightly acid, and the fruit must be cooked for 2 or 3 minutes for its special flavor to develop. It is available fresh in markets in the Southwest and canned from stores specializing in Mexican foods. The canned version needs no further cooking and is ready to use. The flesh is rather delicate and the can may be full of broken fruit. When this happens, use the liquid from the can in a sauce, reducing the amount of stock or other liquid, and save the whole fruit for sauces where no liquid is required. Green tomatoes are grown easily from seed.

Tortillas and **arepas.** The tortilla of Mexico, and the *arepa* of Venezuela, and to a lesser extent Colombia, are unique in the world of bread since they are made from cooked flour. Dried corn kernels are boiled with lime (to loosen the skin), then the kernels are drained and ground, and, if not for immediate use, are dried and packaged as flour. Though the method of cooking the corn is the same for both tortillas and *arepas*, the end result is very different because of the difference in the type of corn used. The corn for *arepas* has very large kernels, giving a rather starchy flour. The packaged flours identify themselves very clearly as *masa harina* (literally dough flour) for tortillas, or flour for *arepas*. It is not possible to confuse them. Shops specializing in Latin American foods carry them.

Yams are members of a vast assemblage of edible tubers of the Dioscorea family, which has about 250 different species, most of them originating in the tropical regions of the world. They can be as small as a new potato or weigh up to 100 pounds, though most of them weigh about a pound and are the size of a large potato. The skins are usually brown and may be rough, smooth, or hairy, and the shape is usually cylindrical. The flesh is white or yellow, the texture mealy, and the flavor pleasantly nutlike. They are available in tropical markets and increasingly in supermarkets and greengrocers. They may be encountered in markets as *ñame* (pronounced ny-AH-may), yampi, cush-cush, mapuey, or a number of other names. A good plan on seeing an unfamiliar tuber in a market is to ask if it is a kind of yam, always remembering that these yams should not be confused with the Louisiana yam, which is a sweet potato. They may be cooked in the same way as potatoes. The smaller varieties are usually the best ones to buy for texture and flavor, and they are well worth getting to know.

Hors d'Oeuvres and Appetizers

Entremeses

Hors d'oeuvres and appetizers in our modern sense were not a large part of the traditional cooking of Latin America. But there are innumerable small foods that were once used as accompaniments to main dishes or were served only to gentlemen in bars or eaten from stalls in the market, which have been adapted for comparatively new styles of eating: finger foods to go with drinks, or light first courses at lunch or dinner, often taking the place of soup.

From country to country they rejoice in a variety of names, which are as different and varied as the hors d'oeuvres themselves. They are known as *botanas*, meaning literally the stoppers on leather wine bottles; *bacaditos*, little mouthfuls; *antojitos*, little whims or fancies; *boquillas*, things to stop the mouth; *fritangas*, fried things and fritters; *tapados*, nibbles; *picadas*, things on a toothpick; *entremeses*, side dishes; *entradas*, dishes to be served at table; *salgadinhos frios*, small, cold, salty things; and *salgadinhos quentes*, small, hot, salty things.

These are the hors d'oeuvres I find exciting, not the almost universal modern canapes, which are mostly borrowed or adapted from our own cocktail foods and have become popular throughout Latin America in recent years as industrialization has changed social patterns from feudal to modern. One comes upon canapes of caviar, ham, shrimp, anchovies; even *crudités* turn up. There are clam or onion-soup dips, cheese cubes alternating with pineapple on toothpicks, tiny frankfurters, salmon caviar with sour cream, and grilled bacon-wrapped prunes. They appear in recipe books under the heading *Cocina Internacional*, International Cookery, and have a certain glamour in Latin America because they are foreign and unfamiliar, which is very understandable.

But fortunately they have not elbowed out the traditional appetizers with exciting flavors that are new to us. These traditional foods range from the simplest of nibbles — toasted corn, fried chickpeas, tiny fried potatoes, French fried plantain slices, yucca and banana chips — to the heartier *Empanadas* (Turnovers) and the *seviches* (fish cooked in lime or lemon juice), which make particularly splendid first courses for summer dining. And the *antojitos* (little whims or fancies) and *tacos, chalupas, sopes, quesadillas*, which all derive from some form of tortillas imaginatively stuffed and seasoned, can compose a whole cocktail buffet or informal luncheon.

All of these appetizers are easy to make and most of them are served at room temperature. They can be prepared ahead of time, and some, like the *empanadas*, can be made well in advance and frozen. They make ideal hors d'oeuvres for a cocktail party. I have enjoyed them in restaurants and in the homes of friends throughout Latin America. They fit perfectly into the pattern of today's living, where meals tend to have fewer courses and be less elaborate than in the past, and where the habit of having drinks before lunch or dinner is increasingly accepted.

It is surprising that the hors d'oeuvres of the region owe so little to their Spanish heritage. Though one might have expected the *tapas* of Spain to appear on New World tables changed, but recognizable, this has not happened. It always surprises me in the world of culinary borrowings, what gets taken, what gets left — and this is especially true of appetizers. After nearly eight centuries of Moorish domination, Spain gained its independence and united its provinces into a nation, turning its back at the same time on the *mezze*, the hors d'oeuvres of the Middle East, which are one of the most attractive features of the food of that region. Latin America, with a few exceptions such as *empanadas*, has behaved in much the same way, so that it is the ancient dishes of the pre-Columbian kitchens and the dishes of the creole cuisine that have been adapted as today's appetizers.

The old tradition of foods eaten in the market has survived in Latin America in a very charming way. Snack foods, cakes, and drinks of all kinds are served in *confeitarías* in Brazil, in *sandwicherías* in Uruguay, and *whiskerías* in Argentina, while each station on the subway in Buenos

Aires has a stall selling coffee, a variety of drinks, and snack foods. In Chile *empanadas*, cakes, and snack foods of all kinds are sold in *salas de onces*. *Onces* (*once* is the number eleven), named for the English custom of having tea or coffee and cookies at eleven in the morning, have become, by some extraordinary transmutation, afternoon tea, so that a *sala de onces* is a tea shop. Ecuador has restaurants devoted to its famous *seviches* while Mexico has its *taquerías*, with an astonishing variety of fillings for the simple *tortilla*.

Anticuchos PERU
Skewered Beef Heart

These are without doubt the most famous of all the Peruvian *entradas*, or appetizers — dishes traditionally served sometimes before, sometimes after the soup, but before the roast in the days when appetites were more robust than they are now. Many of the *entradas* make excellent lunches or suppers; some, like these spiced pieces of beef heart that are skewered and grilled, make a good first course but are also fine as a snack or an accompaniment to drinks. When served as lunch or supper they may be accompanied by corn on the cob, boiled sweet potatoes, and boiled yucca (cassava), bland foods that go very well with the spicy beef hearts. Peruvians like their *picante* foods to be really hot and *anticuchos* are no exception. The dried chili used is *mirasol*, not available here. I have found the *hontaka*, dried hot red chili peppers sold packaged in Japanese markets, to be an admirable substitute.

The amount of peppers given in the recipe, 1 cup, will make a very fiery sauce just the way Peruvians like it but too hot for most of us. A good idea is to begin with ⅛ cup peppers. If the sauce seems too bland, add more peppers. Peppers themselves vary a great deal in hotness, and I have found when dealing with them it is wise to experiment.

Anticuchos are a very old, pre-Columbian dish; I suspect they used to be made with llama hearts since there were no cattle until after the Conquest. The name translates from the Quechua into "a dish from the Andes cooked on sticks."

My favorite place to buy *anticuchos* is from stalls outside Lima's *plaza de toros*, built in 1768 and said to be the second oldest bullring in the world. Eaten right there, accompanied by beer and rounded out with a dessert of *picarones*, deep-fried sweet potato and pumpkin fritters, they make a wonderful impromptu meal.

Serves 8 to 10 as an hors d'oeuvre, or 6 as a main course

1 beef heart, weighing about 4
    pounds
1 head garlic (about 16 cloves),
    peeled and crushed
1 tablespoon fresh hot red or green
    peppers, seeded, coarsely
    chopped, and puréed in a
    blender or food processor

1 tablespoon ground cumin
Salt, freshly ground pepper
1 cup red wine vinegar

FOR THE SAUCE

1 cup dried hot red peppers
1 tablespoon ground annatto
    (achiote) seeds

1 tablespoon vegetable oil
Salt

Remove the nerves and fat from the beef heart, and cut it into 1-inch cubes. Place in a large bowl. Combine the garlic, fresh hot peppers, cumin, salt, pepper, and vinegar, stir to mix, and pour over the beef heart, adding more vinegar, if necessary, to cover. Refrigerate, covered, for 24 hours. Remove the beef heart from the marinade and set them both aside.

Shake the seeds out of the dried peppers and soak in hot water to cover for 30 minutes. Drain the peppers and put them into a blender or food processor with the annatto, oil, and about ¾ cup of the reserved marinade. Season to taste with a little more salt if necessary and blend until smooth. The sauce should be quite thick. Thread the beef-heart cubes on skewers. Brush them with the sauce, and broil, turning to cook all sides, either over charcoal or under a gas or electric broiler, about 3 inches from the heat, for about 4 minutes. Serve with the remaining sauce on the side. Accompany with boiled corn, sweet potato, and yucca.

Acarajé   BRAZIL
Black-Eyed Pea Fritters

Black-eyed peas are originally African, brought to the New World by slaves. The fritters turn up all over the Caribbean as well as in South America. The most elegant version, *acarajé*, comes from Bahia in Brazil and makes an unusual cocktail nibble. I have occasionally come across packaged black-eyed pea flour, *harina para bollitos*, which I have found very good indeed and useful when one is in a hurry. It is worth looking out for in Latin markets. As the flour is a ready mix and needs only the addition of water, it saves one all the bother of cooking the peas, rubbing off the skins, and grinding them. To make the fritters from the pea flour, simply follow package instructions. The *dendê* (palm) oil, used a great deal in Bahian cooking, is also an African contribution. A rich reddish-orange in color, it turns the fritters a beautiful deep gold. They have a crispy texture and a nutty flavor with an attractive hint of shrimp from the sauce.

Makes 24

1 pound (2 cups) black-eyed peas	*Salt*
½ cup dried shrimp	*Dendê (palm) oil*
1 medium onion, chopped	

Soak the black-eyed peas overnight in cold water to cover. Drain. Rub off and discard the skins. Soak the shrimp in cold water to cover for 30 minutes. Put the peas, shrimp, and onion through the fine blade of a food grinder, or purée them in a blender or food processor. Season to taste with salt if necessary. The shrimp may be quite salty. Pour enough *dendê* oil into a deep fryer or saucepan to fill it to a depth of 2 to 3 inches. When the oil is hot (365° F. on a frying thermometer), fry the mixture by the tablespoon, turning the fritters once, until they are golden. Drain on paper towels and serve at room temperature with *Môlho de Acarajé*.

Môlho de Acarajé

Black-Eyed Pea Fritter Sauce

Makes about 1¼ cups

½ cup dried shrimp	*½ teaspoon chopped fresh ginger*
1 medium onion, chopped	*root*
1 tablespoon crushed dried hot red	*3 tablespoons dendê (palm) oil*
peppers	

Soak the shrimp in cold water to cover for 30 minutes. Drain the shrimp and pulverize them in a blender or food processor with the onion, peppers, and ginger root. Heat the oil in a skillet and sauté the shrimp mixture for about 3 minutes. Transfer to a bowl and serve with the *acarajé*.

Variation: For *Abará* (Steamed Black-Eyed Peas), make 1 recipe *Acarajé* (Black-Eyed Pea Fritters), but do not fry them. Beat the mixture thoroughly until it is fluffy with 3 tablespoons *dendê* oil and fresh hot red peppers, seeded, coarsely chopped, and puréed in a blender or food processor, to taste. Place tablespoons of the mixture in the center of 6-inch squares of kitchen parchment or aluminum foil, push a whole dried shrimp into the center of the pea mixture, then fold up into a neat package. If using parchment, tie securely with kitchen string. Steam the packages for 1 hour and serve directly from the packages at room temperature. Traditionally, banana leaves, which are sometimes available from specialty shops, are used for *Abará*. Makes about 24.

Variation: There is a simpler, but very attractive, version, *Buñuelitos de Frijol* (Bean Fritters) from coastal Colombia. The black-eyed peas are soaked overnight in cold water and the skins rubbed off and discarded. The peas are ground fine and seasoned with salt, then beaten with a wooden spoon until they are light and fluffy. They are deep fried by the tablespoon in vegetable oil or lard until golden brown.

Garbanzos Compuestos MEXICO
Toasted Chickpeas

Chickpeas were brought to the New World by the Spanish and even though the common bean (red kidney, etc.) was first cultivated in the Valley of Mexico as early as 5000 B.C. and had long spread to other parts of the continent by the time of the Conquest, chickpeas were given a warm welcome and have been widely used in the kitchen ever since. I think, however, that toasted chickpeas as a cocktail nibble are a piece of culinary borrowing from South America, where a special type of large-kernel white corn was developed by the Incas, presumably sometime after corn reached them from Mexico, its birthplace. Called *cancha* in Peru, the corn is soaked, fried in lard, seasoned with salt, and served alone, or with *seviche*, *anticuchos*, and so on. In Ecuador the same dish is called *Maíz Tostado* and is always served with the *seviches*.

Makes about 4 cups

Two 1-pound cans of chickpeas, or ½ cup olive oil
    1 pound dried chickpeas, 1 clove garlic
    soaked overnight Ground hot red pepper
1 teaspoon salt

Drain the chickpeas, cover with fresh water, and simmer for 30 minutes. Add the salt and continue cooking until the chickpeas are tender. Drain and cool. Heat the olive oil in a skillet and sauté the chickpeas with the garlic until they are golden brown. Drain on paper towels and sprinkle with the hot pepper.

    If using cooked canned chickpeas, rinse, drain, and then fry them.

Patacones

Green Plantain Chips

Fried plantain slices are popular in many parts of Latin America under different names and cooked by slightly different methods. Sprinkled lightly with salt, they are served with drinks, or as an accompaniment to meat, fish, or poultry. My favorite is this one from the northern coast of Colombia.

Vegetable oil for deep frying
1 large green plantain, peeled and
    cut into 1½-inch slices
Salt

Pour enough oil into a deep fryer or saucepan to fill it to a depth of 2 to 3 inches. Heat to moderate, 325° F. on a frying thermometer. Drop in the plantain slices and fry until tender, about 5 minutes. Lift out and drain on paper towels. Cover with wax paper and press until each is about ¾ inch thick. I find a clenched fist does as well as anything. In fact in Costa Rica, where the usual name is *tostones*, they are sometimes called *plátanos a puñetazos*, "plantains hit with the fist."

Raise the temperature of the oil to hot, 375° F. on a frying thermometer, and fry the slices until they are brown and crispy on the outside, tender inside, a minute or two. Traditional cooks dip the slices in cold, salted water before this second frying to make them crustier. I don't find this extra fussiness makes much difference. Sprinkle lightly with salt before serving.

Variation: In Venezuela the chips are called *tostones de plátano*, and cut into 1-inch slices. Some cooks put them in overlapping pairs after the first frying and before flattening them. This gives a very thick, soft center with crispy edges. In lieu of the clenched fist, the heel of the hand, or a rolling pin, I've seen cooks on this coast use large stones from the beach to do the flattening for them.

Variation: *Tostones* in Puerto Rico, cut diagonally into ½-inch slices, are soaked for 30 minutes in cold, salted water before they are either sautéed, or deep fried in oil or lard. They are dipped again in salted water before the second frying.

Variation: Also in Puerto Rico green plantains are very thinly sliced, soaked in ice water for 30 minutes, drained, patted dry, deep fried until crisp in hot oil or lard, and sprinkled with salt before serving. Called *platanutri*, they are *tostoncitos* in the Dominican Republic and *chicharritas de plátano verde* in Costa Rica. Green bananas are often used in the same way. They make a pleasant change from potato chips.

Yuca Frita   COLOMBIA
Cassava Chips

In Colombia hors d'oeuvres are called *picadas* and any fried *picada* is called a *fritanga*. Cassava chips, deliciously light and crisp and no trouble at all to make, are among the *fritangas* I enjoy most. This root vegetable is such an astonishment. First cultivated in northern Brazil in 1500 B.C. it has now spread all over the world. I once saw it growing outside a country pub in Wiltshire, England, where its tall spike of white flowers towered flamboyantly over roses and wallflowers. We know it best as tapioca, but Latin America uses it much more widely, added to stews, boiled and mashed. Its squeezed-out juice is the basis of *cassareep*, used in the Guyanese national meat and poultry stew. And of course there is always a bowl of *farofa* (cassava meal) on the table in Brazilian restaurants and homes (see page 6). I like cassava in all its forms whether it is called yucca, manioc, mandioca, aipím, cassava, or botanically, *Manihot utilissima*.

1 pound cassava (yucca) root,	*Salt*
about	*Vegetable oil or lard*

Peel the vegetable under cold running water as it discolors quickly. Cut into 1-inch slices and boil in salted water to cover until tender, about 30 minutes. The pieces often break up during cooking but this does not matter. Drain, pat dry with paper towels. In a skillet heat about ½ inch oil or lard and fry the pieces until they are crisp and golden all over. Serve at room temperature with drinks. The chips are also a pleasant accompaniment to meats or poultry.

For crisper chips, freeze the boiled vegetable for an hour or so before frying it and fry it frozen. The chips can be deep fried if preferred.

Variation: In the Colombian highlands *Papas Criollas Fritas* (Fried Creole Potatoes) are a popular appetizer. These are small local potatoes with yellow flesh; the smallest bite-sized ones are chosen and deep fried, skin and all, sprinkled with salt and eaten while still hot as an accompaniment to drinks. They are sometimes available in tropical markets; if not, use very small new potatoes.

Variation: Puerto Ricans use breadfruit to make *Hojuelas de Panapén* (Breadfruit Chips). Peel and core a breadfruit and quarter it. Cut it into thin crosswise slices and drop into boiling salted water. Boil for 2 to 3 minutes, drain, and pat dry. Fry in deep oil or lard until the chips are golden and crisp. Sprinkle with salt and serve at room temperature. Canned breadfruit can be used, in which case simply pat it dry, slice, and fry it.

SEVICHE

Seviche or *ceviche* — the spelling varies — is raw fish marinated in lime or lemon juice. The fish loses its translucent look as the juice "cooks" it and needs no further cooking. It doesn't taste raw. The idea almost certainly originated in Polynesia and like all migrant dishes has evolved in its new home; I have found versions of it all over Latin America. The best *seviches* in Mexico are from the state of Guerrero, especially from Acapulco on the Pacific coast. The fish principally used are sierra, or Spanish, mackerel, pompano, and porgy. I am always rather surprised at how well the mackerel *seviche* comes out, with the full-flavored and oily fish tempered by the lime or lemon juice. *Seviche* in Peru, served with sweet potatoes, lettuce, ears of corn, and toasted corn (*cancha*), is almost a meal in itself. The most popular fish there is bass, which makes a very delicate *seviche*, though octopus, conch, and scallops are also used. I've enjoyed *seviche* in restaurants overlooking Acapulco Bay, with its indestructible charm, and at a beach club in the strangely beautiful desert landscape of the Peruvian coast, but I think the best *seviches* I've ever had were in Ecuador. They are quite different from the Mexican variety though not wholly unlike those from Peru since bitter (Seville) oranges are used in both countries. Made from shrimp, lobster, bass, and an interesting local black conch, they have a reputation for being a splendid pick-me-up, and one is encouraged to try them at noon with a glass of cold beer. Marinated fish or shellfish should be eaten 5 to 6 hours after the marinating was begun.

Aguacate Relleno con Seviche de Camarones
Avocado Stuffed with Marinated Shrimp

MEXICO

This unusual variation on the standard *seviche* is from Acapulco and makes a rather grand and rich beginning to a special lunch or dinner. It would make an admirable light lunch served with soup as a first course and a dessert to finish.

Serves 2

½ pound small shrimp, shelled
   and deveined
½ cup or more fresh lime or lemon
   juice
1 medium tomato, peeled and
   chopped
1 canned jalapeño chili, rinsed,
   seeded, and cut in strips
1 pimiento, chopped
1 tablespoon fresh coriander
   (cilantro), chopped, or use
   parsley

½ small white onion, finely
   chopped
6 small pitted green olives, halved
4 tablespoons vegetable oil
Salt, freshly ground pepper
1 large avocado, halved and pitted
Lettuce leaves

If small shrimp are not available, cut larger ones into ½-inch pieces. Put into a bowl with enough lime or lemon juice to cover, about ½ cup. Refrigerate for about 3 hours, or until the shrimp are opaque. Add the tomato, chili, pimiento, coriander, onion, olives, oil, and salt and pepper to taste. Toss lightly to mix.

Spoon the shrimp mixture into the avocado halves and serve on plates garnished with lettuce leaves.

Seviche de Sierra
Mackerel Marinated in Lime Juice

MEXICO

Serves 6

1 pound skinned fillets of
   mackerel, or use pompano or
   porgy, cut into ½-inch
   squares

1½ cups lime or lemon juice,
   about
2 medium tomatoes, peeled and
   chopped

4 canned serrano chilies, rinsed
    and chopped
¼ cup vegetable oil
1 teaspoon oregano

Salt, freshly ground pepper
1 medium onion, finely sliced
1 large avocado, peeled, pitted,
    and sliced

Put the fish into a glass or china bowl and pour the lime or lemon juice over it. There should be enough to cover the fish. Add a little more, if necessary. Refrigerate the fish for 3 hours, turning it from time to time. Add the tomatoes, chilies, oil, oregano, and salt and pepper to taste. Toss lightly to mix and divide among 6 bowls. Garnish with the onion slices and the avocado.

Seviche de Corvina
Bass Marinated in Lime Juice

PERU

Serves 8

1½ pounds fillets of striped bass,
    or similar fish, cut into 1-inch
    pieces
Salt, freshly ground pepper
2 fresh hot red peppers, seeded and
    thinly sliced
1 teaspoon paprika

1 large onion, thinly sliced
1 cup lemon or lime juice
1 cup bitter (Seville) orange juice*
1 pound sweet potato, preferably
    the white type
2 ears corn, each cut into 4 slices
Lettuce leaves

Put the fish into a large glass or china bowl and season to taste with salt and pepper. Add 1 of the peppers, the paprika, and the onion, reserving a few rings for the garnish. Add the lemon or lime and bitter orange juice, mix lightly, cover, and refrigerate for about 3 hours, or until the fish is opaque, "cooked" by the juices.

Peel the sweet potatoes, cut into 8 slices, drop into salted water, bring to a boil, and cook until tender, about 20 minutes. Drop the slices of corn into boiling salted water and boil for 5 minutes. Drain and reserve the vegetables.

Line a serving platter with lettuce leaves. Arrange the fish on the platter, garnish with the reserved onion rings and the hot pepper strips. Arrange the corn and sweet potato slices around the edge of the dish. Serve with *cancha* (toasted corn).

---

*If bitter (Seville) orange juice is not available, use 1½ cups lemon juice and ½ cup orange juice.

Seviche de Corvina
ECUADOR

Bass Marinated in Lime Juice

Serves 6 to 8

1 ½ pounds fillets of striped bass,
    or similar fish, cut into
    ½-inch pieces
1 cup lime or lemon juice
1 cup bitter (Seville) orange juice*
1 fresh hot red or green pepper,
    seeded and finely chopped

1 medium onion, thinly sliced
1 clove garlic, chopped
Salt, freshly ground pepper
1 cup vegetable oil

Put the fish into a large glass or china bowl and add the lime or lemon juice to cover, adding a little more if necessary. Refrigerate for about 3 hours, or until the fish is opaque, "cooked" by the lime or lemon juice. Drain. Transfer to a serving bowl and mix with the bitter orange juice, pepper, onion, garlic, salt and pepper to taste, and the oil. Serve with *Maíz Tostada* (Toasted Corn) on the side.

Seviche de Camarones
ECUADOR

Marinated Shrimp

Serves 6

2 pounds medium shrimp, shelled
    and deveined
Salt
2 cups bitter (Seville) orange
    juice†
1 medium onion, finely chopped

1 fresh hot red or green pepper,
    seeded and finely chopped
1 large tomato, peeled, seeded,
    and chopped
Freshly ground pepper

Drop the shrimp into a large saucepan of boiling salted water and boil for 2 or 3 minutes, or until the shrimp are cooked. Drain and mix with the orange juice, onion, hot pepper, tomato, and salt and pepper to taste. Let stand an hour before serving. Serve with *Maíz Tostada* (Toasted Corn) on the side.

*If bitter (Seville) orange juice is not available, use ½ cup lime or lemon juice and ½ cup orange juice.

†If bitter (Seville) orange juice is not available, use 1½ cups orange juice and ½ cup lemon juice.

Seviche de Ostras GUATEMALA
Oysters Marinated in Lime Juice

I came across this unusual *seviche* in Guatemala, where there are still echoes of Mayan cooking, which must have been an exciting one.

Serves 8

4 dozen oysters, shucked
1 cup lime or lemon juice
3 large tomatoes, peeled and
   chopped
1 large onion, finely chopped
1 fresh hot red pepper, seeded and
   chopped

2 tablespoons mint leaves,
   chopped
Salt, freshly ground pepper
Lettuce leaves

Put the oysters into a large glass or china bowl with the lime or lemon juice, cover, and refrigerate overnight. Strain the oysters, reserving the juice. In the bowl combine the oysters with the tomatoes, onion, hot pepper, mint leaves, and ¼ cup of the reserved juice. Season to taste with salt and pepper. Line a serving bowl with lettuce leaves and pour in the oyster mixture.

Siri Recheado BRAZIL
Stuffed Crabs

A similar dish, *crabes farcies*, is popular in the French Caribbean islands. I think it is very probable that the original inspiration came from West Africa. Whether in the West Indies or in Brazil, I have never had exactly the same version of stuffed crabs, which makes eating them a perpetual adventure. Cooks let imagination, not rule books, guide them.

    If live crabs are not available, use ¾ pound (12 ounces) fresh, frozen, or

canned crab meat, picked over to remove any shell or cartilage, and stuff
scallop shells.

Serves 3 to 6

6 small, *live hard-shelled crabs*
Olive oil
2 tablespoons lime or lemon juice
2 cloves garlic, crushed
Salt, freshly ground pepper
1 medium onion, grated
2 scallions, chopped, using white
    and green parts
2 medium tomatoes, peeled,
    seeded, and chopped

2 tablespoons fresh coriander
    (cilantro), chopped
1 or 2 fresh hot red peppers, seeded
    and chopped
1 cup fresh breadcrumbs
1 egg, beaten
Fine bulgar wheat
Lettuce leaves
Small black and green olives

Plunge the crabs into boiling water and boil for 10 minutes. Lift out and
cool. Carefully remove the meat from the shells and claws, and chop.
Discard the spongy fiber. Scrub the empty shells, dry them, and brush the
insides with a little olive oil. Season the crab meat with the lime or lemon
juice, garlic, salt and pepper to taste, and set aside.

Heat 2 tablespoons olive oil in a skillet and sauté the onion, scallions,
and tomatoes until the mixture is soft and well blended. Cool to room
temperature and combine it with the crab mixture. Add the coriander
leaves, the hot peppers, and the breadcrumbs, and mix well. Stuff the crab
shells with the mixture, brush with beaten egg, and sprinkle with a little
bulgar wheat. Bake in a preheated moderate (350° F.) oven for 30 minutes,
or until lightly browned. Garnish serving plates with the lettuce leaves and
olives. Serve as a first course.

Variation: Parsley is sometimes used instead of coriander leaves and mandioca (cassava, or manioc, meal) is used instead of bulgar wheat. In Bahia
dendê (palm) oil often replaces olive oil.

EMPANADAS
Turnovers

One could write a small book on *empanadas, empanaditas, pasteles,
pastelitos, empadhinas,* and *pastèizinhos* — those delicious turnovers, patties, and pies, stuffed with meat, poultry, fish, shellfish, and other mix-

tures, and baked or fried, which are so popular throughout Latin America. Each country has its own favorite pastries, its own favorite filling, and the *empanadas* of Argentina and Chile are as different as one turnover can be from another. They come in small sizes for cocktails, larger ones for first courses, snacks, light luncheons, or picnics. They are very versatile, and I often use a pastry from one country, a filling from another, according to my fancy. I am not attempting to give a representative selection of these delights, only those I have especially enjoyed making and eating.

I remember at Viña del Mar, on the Chilean coast, sitting on the terrace of a friend's house overlooking the sea in the cold winter sunshine and eating *empanadas de locos* bought from a small shop in nearby Quintero and washing them down with the local, very acceptable champagne. *Locos* are the enormous abalone of this coast, where the cold Humboldt Current makes for a fabulous harvest of fish and shellfish. There were also turnovers with other fillings, but it is the juicy onion-enriched abalone ones I remember best, and for which I have worked out an approximation. Use the recipe for the 6-inch Argentine *Empanadas* (Turnovers) pastry, page 38, with 2 tablespoons filling. Have ready equal amounts of coarsely chopped, canned abalone and finely chopped onion. Sauté the onion in *Color Chilena* (Paprika Oil), page 324. Add the abalone, salt, pepper, and a little chopped parsley. Place the filling across the center of the pastry, top with 2 small black olives, pitted, and a slice of hardboiled egg.

As for the *empanadas* of Argentina, some of which I ate decorously in a *whiskería* (a felicitously evolved tea shop) in Buenos Aires, the crust was so light and flaky I felt the *empanada* might fly from the plate. The filling combined beef with pears and peaches — utterly delicious. I remember too taking some with me for an al fresco lunch on the banks of the River Plate, the Rio de la Plata, which looked like a vast sea of silver, not like a river at all. And on the other side of the river, later in Montevideo, in Uruguay, eating *empanadas* in a *sandwichería*, which again belied its name by selling all manner of marvelous small foods as well as drinks.

Empanadas of course have strong echoes of Spain, Portugal, and the Middle East. They probably originated in the Middle East, which would be natural enough considering that wheat was cultivated there as early as 7000 B.C. But they are of mixed ancestry. The *pasteles* of the Middle East, for example, are believed to have been taken to Turkey from Spain or Portugal by Sephardic Jews a long while ago. They are very like the *empadhinas* of Brazil, which are cousins of the *empanadas*. However, many of the turnovers incorporate foods of the New World — potatoes, tomatoes, peppers, even using corn for the pastry, thus linking them with the indigenous Indian kitchens.

EMPADHINAS and PASTÈIZINHOS
Little Pies and Turnovers

One of my pleasantest memories of Brazil is of eating *empadhinas* and *pastèizinhos*, little savory pies and turnovers in a *confeitaria*, a pastry shop in downtown Rio which seemed to me to be full at all hours with people eating pies and cakes and drinking tiny cups of exquisitely strong coffee. The generic term for these pies and turnovers is *salgadinhos*, little salt things, and they form an enchanting part of the Brazilian cuisine, allowing the inventive cook endless freedom to experiment. If you make them in larger sizes, they are called *empadas* and *pastéis*, and they are fine for lunches.

Massa Para Empadhinas   BRAZIL
Pastry for Little Pies

Makes about 30

2½ cups all-purpose flour
½ teaspoon salt
4 tablespoons (¼ cup) lard
4 tablespoons (¼ cup) butter

2 egg yolks
Water
1 egg

Sift the flour with the salt into a large bowl. Cut the lard and butter into little bits and rub into the flour with the fingertips to make a coarse meal. Make a well in the center of the flour and stir in the egg yolks with enough cold water (4 to 5 tablespoons) to make a soft but not sticky dough or mix quickly in a food processor. Cover with wax paper and refrigerate for 1 hour. Roll out on a lightly floured surface to ¹/₁₆th-inch thickness and cut into circles 1½ inches larger than the circumference of the cupcake, muffin, or tart tin you are using. Cut an equal number of circles the same size as the tins. Press the larger circles into the tins. Add enough filling to come about three-quarters of the way up the tin, and if the recipe calls for it a small piece of sliced hardboiled egg and a slice of pitted olive. Moisten the edges of the pastry with a little egg beaten with ½ teaspoon water, cover with the smaller circle of pastry, and seal firmly with the fingers. Brush the tops with egg and bake in a preheated moderate (350° F.) oven for 30 minutes or until golden brown. Makes about 30 in muffin tins measuring 2½ inches across.

The pastry may be used to make 1 large double-crust pie, in which case use a 9-inch pie tin and bake the pastry for about 10 minutes longer.

Picadinho de Carne
Meat Filling

Chopped beef fillings are popular all over Latin America. In this one the meat is steamed, making it moist and giving it a softer texture and more delicate flavor than its namesake, Mexican *picadillo*.

Makes about 2 cups

1 tablespoon olive oil	2 tomatoes, peeled and chopped
¾ pound lean ground beef	1 fresh hot red pepper, chopped
Salt, freshly ground pepper	(optional)
2 cloves garlic, crushed	2 hardboiled eggs, sliced
1 medium onion, grated	Sliced pitted black or green olives

In a skillet heat the oil and add the beef, salt, pepper, and garlic, mixing well. Sauté for a minute or two, then add the onion, tomatoes, and the hot pepper, if liked. Stir to mix, cover, and cook over low heat until the meat is tender, about 20 minutes. Allow to cool. Then fill the pies three-quarters full and put a piece of sliced egg and a slice of olive on top of each before covering with the top crust.

Recheio de Sardinhas
Sardine Filling

Makes about 2 cups

1 tablespoon olive oil	2 cans (4-ounce) sardines, drained
1 medium onion, finely chopped	2 teaspoons lime or lemon juice
2 medium tomatoes, peeled,	2 tablespoons chopped fresh green
seeded, and chopped	coriander (cilantro)
½ fresh hot red pepper, seeded and	2 hardboiled eggs, chopped
chopped	4 pitted black or green olives,
Salt, freshly ground pepper	sliced

In a skillet heat the oil and sauté the onion until it is softened. Add the tomatoes and the pepper, season to taste with salt and pepper, and simmer, stirring from time to time, until the mixture is thick and well blended, about 10 minutes. Cool. Mash the sardines with the lime or lemon juice and coriander, and fold into the tomato mixture with the eggs and olives.

Recheio de Queijo
Cheese Filling

Makes about 2 cups

¾ pound (1 ½ cups) ricotta cheese
Salt, freshly ground white pepper
½ teaspoon sweet paprika

4 scallions, trimmed and chopped,
    using white and green parts
3 egg yolks, lightly beaten

Mix all the ingredients together. Chill slightly before using.

Recheio de Camarão Baiano
Shrimp Stuffing, Bahian Style

Makes about 2 cups

¼ cup dendê (palm) oil
1 medium onion, finely chopped
1 medium green bell pepper,
    seeded and chopped
1 fresh hot red or green pepper,
    seeded and chopped
1 pound fresh shrimp, peeled and
    chopped

Salt
½ cup palm hearts, chopped
2 egg yolks
½ cup thick coconut milk (page 7)
1 tablespoon fresh green coriander
    (cilantro), chopped

In a skillet heat the palm oil and sauté the onion and the peppers until they are softened. Add the shrimp, salt to taste, and palm hearts, and cook for a minute or two. Beat the egg yolks with the coconut milk and stir into the shrimp mixture. Add the coriander and cook, stirring over low heat until the mixture has thickened. It should have the consistency of a medium white sauce. If necessary thicken with ½ teaspoon arrowroot or cornstarch dissolved in 1 teaspoon water and cook for a minute or two longer. Cool.

Recheio de Galinha
Chicken Filling

Makes about 2 cups

2 tablespoons butter
½ cup mushrooms, finely chopped
4 scallions, trimmed and chopped,
　using white and green parts
1 cup finely diced cooked chicken
　breast

1 cup thick Béchamel sauce (page
　325)
1 tablespoon grated Parmesan
　cheese (optional)

In a skillet melt the butter and sauté the mushrooms over fairly brisk heat until they have given up all their liquid and are very lightly browned, about 4 minutes. Stir the mushrooms, scallions, and chicken meat into the Béchamel sauce, which should be highly seasoned. Add the grated cheese, if liked. Cool before using.

I sometimes like to follow the example of Brazilian cooks who vary the sauce by using equal amounts of chicken stock and milk, making the sauce lighter with a beautiful chickeny flavor.

Massa Para Pastéis Fritos　　　　BRAZIL
Pastry for Fried Turnovers

Makes 50 to 60 turnovers

2 cups all-purpose flour
½ teaspoon salt
2 tablespoons butter

2 eggs, lightly beaten
Vegetable oil for deep frying

Sift the flour with the salt into a large bowl. Cut the butter into little bits and rub into the flour with the fingertips to make a coarse meal. Make a well in the center of the flour and pour in the eggs. Stir with a fork to mix and add enough water (about 1 tablespoon) to make a soft but not sticky dough. Knead until the pastry is elastic. A food processor may be used to mix and knead the dough; spin until the dough forms a ball. Cover and allow to stand for 1 hour. Roll out on a floured surface to a thickness of ¹/₁₆ inch, cut into 3-inch rounds with a cookie cutter, or a glass, and stuff with 2 teaspoons of any of the fillings on pages 2 – 3. Moisten the edges with water or milk, fold over, and press together. Seal with the tines of a fork. I sometimes put a small piece of sliced hardboiled egg and a slice of black or green olive on top of the filling, a very popular touch in Brazil.

To fry: Pour enough oil into a fryer or saucepan to reach a depth of 2 to 3 inches. Heat to moderate, 350° to 360° F. on a frying thermometer. An easy way to check the temperature is to stir the oil with wooden chopsticks, then wait to see if tiny bubbles form on the sticks. If they do, the temperature is right. Fry the turnovers, a few at a time, until golden brown, turning once, cooking a total of 4 to 5 minutes. Drain on paper towels and keep warm.

Empanadas
Turnovers

ARGENTINA

Makes 16 first-course or luncheon-size turnovers

FOR THE PASTRY

4 cups all-purpose flour
2 teaspoons baking powder
1 teaspoon salt

1½ cups lard, or ¾ cup each lard
  and butter

Sift the flour, baking powder, and salt into a large bowl. Cut the fat into small pieces and rub into the flour with the fingertips to form a coarse meal. Mix to a fairly stiff dough with cold water, gather into a ball or mix in a food processor, and refrigerate, covered with wax paper, for 1 hour. Roll out on a floured surface to about ⅛ inch thick. Cut into 6-inch circles using a small plate or bowl as a guide.

FOR THE FILLING

2 medium onions, finely chopped
2 cups finely diced raw potatoes
1 pound finely chopped lean round
  steak

Salt, freshly ground black pepper
3 tablespoons beef stock
1 egg, beaten with ½ teaspoon
  water

Mix all the ingredients, except the egg, together. Spoon 2 tablespoons of the mixture across the center of each circle of pastry, leaving ¼ inch at the edges. Moisten the edges of the pastry with the egg and fold the pastry over to make a turnover, pressing the edges firmly together. Curve the turnover slightly to form a crescent shape, then turn about ¼ inch of the pastry back over itself, pinching it between the thumb and forefinger to form a ropelike pattern round the edge. Prick the tops of the turnovers 2 or 3 times with the tines of a fork and brush with the egg mixture. The *empanadas* are now ready to bake and may be frozen until ready to use. Let them thaw for 3 hours at room temperature before cooking.

To bake: Bake the turnovers on an ungreased cookie sheet for 10 minutes in a preheated hot (400° F.) oven. Reduce the heat to 350° F. and bake for 30 minutes longer, or until golden brown.

ANOTHER FILLING

2 tablespoons butter
1 medium onion, finely chopped
1 green bell pepper, seeded and
*   chopped*
1 pound lean ground beef
1 large tomato, peeled and
*   chopped*

1 large pear, peeled, cored, and
*   chopped*
2 large peaches, peeled, pitted,
*   and chopped*
Salt, freshly ground pepper
¼ cup dry white wine

Heat the butter in a skillet and sauté the onion and pepper over moderate heat until softened. Add the meat, breaking it up with a fork, and sauté for a few minutes longer. Add all the remaining ingredients and cook for 5 minutes over low heat. Cool and stuff the turnovers with the mixture in the same way as for the other filling. If using both fillings, double the amount of pastry.

Variation: In Cuba a similar pastry is enlivened by the addition of ½ cup dry sherry, 2 eggs and 2 egg yolks, and a tablespoon of sugar. The lard and butter are reduced to 2 tablespoons each. This is a very old recipe from colonial times and an attractive one. The fillings used are any cooked meat or poultry, chopped and mixed with chopped onion, sautéed in butter, peeled and chopped tomatoes, raisins, olives, capers, and chopped hardboiled eggs, combined and seasoned with salt and pepper. Wonderful for using leftovers.

Empanaditas
Little Turnovers

Makes 75 cocktail turnovers

FOR THE PASTRY

3 cups all-purpose flour
½ teaspoon salt

6 ounces (¾ cup) butter
1 egg and 1 yolk, lightly beaten

Sift the flour with the salt into a large bowl. Cut the butter into small pieces and rub into the flour with the fingertips to form a coarse meal. Or use a food processor. Make a well in the center of the flour and add the egg and yolk, stir to mix, and add water (about ⅓ cup), tablespoon by tablespoon, mixing with a fork, to make a soft but not sticky dough. Form the dough into a ball and refrigerate it, covered, for 1 hour. Roll out the dough on a floured surface to ¹/₁₆th inch thick and cut into 2½-inch squares. Put a teaspoon of filling into the center of each square, fold over, and seal the edges. The turnovers may be frozen at this point until ready to use. Let them thaw for 3 hours at room temperature before cooking. If preferred, they may be completely covered and simply reheated in the oven just before serving.

To fry: Fry as for the Colombian *Pastelitos Rellenos de Cerdo* (Pork-Filled Turnovers), page 41.

FOR THE FILLING

1 pound lean boneless pork, chopped
2 tablespoons vegetable oil
1 medium onion, finely chopped
1 green bell pepper, seeded and finely chopped
2 medium tomatoes, peeled and chopped

1 tablespoon small pimiento-stuffed green olives, chopped
1 tablespoon capers, chopped
1 tablespoon seedless raisins
Salt, freshly ground pepper
Aliños criollos en polvo, to taste*
½ cup dry sherry
1 hardboiled egg, chopped

Put the pork into a saucepan with water barely to cover and simmer, covered, until tender, about 30 minutes. Drain, reserving the pork stock. In a skillet heat the oil and sauté the onion and pepper until they are softened.

Aliños criollos en polvo is a Venezuelan seasoning sold ready made. It is a mixture of sweet paprika, cumin, black pepper, ground annatto, garlic powder, oregano, and salt. Add a little of all or any of the ingredients to the filling according to taste. *Aliño*, sold as *Aliño Preparado* by McCormick in a glass shaker bottle, may sometimes be available in Latin markets. It makes a characteristic and remarkably pleasant addition to soups, stews, etc., and also adds a little color. It is easy to make at home (see page 325).

Add the pork and sauté for a minute or two longer. Add the tomatoes, olives, capers, raisins, salt, pepper, *aliño criollo* to taste, and the sherry. If the mixture seems a little dry, add some of the reserved pork stock. Simmer, uncovered, until the liquid has almost evaporated. Allow to cool. Add the egg, mixing well.

Variation: Chile has a turnover very similar to the Venezuelan one. It may be fried or baked. Make the pastry in the same way. Use chopped sirloin steak or top round instead of pork, omit the green bell pepper, the capers, and the *aliño,* and add 1 tablespoon sweet paprika, ½ tablespoon hot paprika, and ½ teaspoon ground cumin (or to taste). Cut the pastry into 5-inch rounds using a small bowl or plate as a guide, stuff with about 1½ tablespoons of the mixture, paint the edges with a little egg mixed with ½ teaspoon water, fold over, and seal firmly, pressing the edges with a fork. Cut 2 or 3 slits in the top, brush with the egg mixture. To bake, place the turnovers on an ungreased cookie sheet in a preheated hot 400° F. oven for 10 minutes, then reduce the heat to 350° F. and cook for about 20 minutes longer, or until golden brown. The turnovers may be fried in the same way as the Venezuelan and Colombian ones.

A great many different fillings are used for turnovers in Chile; a piece of cheese, such as Münster or Monterey Jack, very thick béchamel sauce, highly flavored and mixed with grated Parmesan cheese, or with chopped cooked green vegetables such as green beans, spinach, Swiss chard, or with shrimp, fish, or any of the marvelous shellfish that the coast of Chile is blessed with. The seafood is often mixed with a thick béchamel seasoned with tomato.

Some turnovers are even simpler. Just a little chopped onion, salt and pepper, the shellfish, and its natural juices, baked in a pastry shell. There is no end to the inventiveness of Chilean cooks when it comes to *empanadas.*

Pastelitos Rellenos de Cerdo COLOMBIA
Pork-Filled Turnovers

Makes about 100

FOR THE PASTRY

2 cups all-purpose flour
½ teaspoon salt
¼ pound (½ cup) butter

½ teaspoon lemon juice
½ cup lukewarm water
Vegetable oil for deep frying

Sift the flour and salt into a large bowl. Cut the butter into small pieces and rub into the flour with the fingertips to form a coarse meal. Mix the lemon juice with the water. Using a fork, stir in the water quickly to make a soft dough. Gather into a ball and refrigerate, covered with wax paper, for 30 minutes. Roll out the pastry on a floured surface to a thickness of 1/16 inch and cut into 2½-inch circles with a cookie cutter or glass. Put ½ tablespoon of filling in the center of each pastry circle, fold the pastry in half to make a turnover, and seal the edges by pressing with the tines of a fork. The turnovers may be frozen at this point until ready to use. Let them thaw for 3 hours at room temperature before cooking.

To fry: Pour enough vegetable oil in a fryer or saucepan to reach a depth of 2 to 3 inches. Heat to moderate, 350° F. on a frying thermometer. An easy way to check the temperature is to stir the oil with wooden chopsticks, then wait to see if tiny bubbles form on the sticks. If they do, the temperature is right. Fry the turnovers, a few at a time, until golden brown, turning once, about 5 minutes. Drain on paper towels and keep warm.

If preferred the *pastelitos* may be baked. Brush with egg yolk beaten with a little water in a preheated hot (400° F.) oven for 5 minutes. Reduce the heat to 350° F. and bake for 15 minutes longer, or until golden brown. Serve as an accompaniment to drinks.

They may also be cooked and later reheated in the oven just before serving.

FOR THE FILLING

½ pound ground pork
1 large onion, grated
4 tablespoons capers
1 hardboiled egg, finely chopped

½ cup deviled ham, or ¼ pound
  finely chopped boiled ham
Salt, freshly ground pepper to taste

Thoroughly mix all the ingredients together. Instead of pork, ground beef, chicken breast, or drained, canned tuna fish may be used. If using tuna, omit the ham and use 2 hardboiled eggs instead of 1.

ABOUT TORTILLAS

If one were to compile all the recipes that are in existence for tortilla-based appetizers, one would end up with an encyclopedia that would dizzy the reader. So I am giving here only my favorites, though I confess the choice has not been easy.

The Spaniards named them *antojitos*, little whims or fancies, and to me they are perhaps the most exciting aspect of pre-Columbian Mexican cooking. We have some very good descriptions of the markets of old Tenochtitlán, now modern Mexico City, before the Conquest was completed, when the city was virtually untouched by the invaders. In his *Historia General de las Cosas de Nueva España* Fray Bernardino de Sahagún, a Spanish priest, tells, among other things, of the types of tortilla on sale in the market; it is enough to make one's head spin — with envy. That marvelous early war correspondent, Bernal Díaz del Castillo, a captain who was with Cortés before and during the campaign, gives in his memoirs, *Historia de la Conquista de Nueva España*, a remarkable picture of dining in Mexico, so we do know that there was a great deal more, now alas lost, of this cuisine. However, loss was soon balanced by gain, as post-Conquest Mexicans made good use of the foods the Spanish brought from Europe and Asia, and their *antojitos* were enhanced by beef, pork, chicken, olives, almonds, raisins, and so on.

With the exception of *arepas*, the corn bread of Venezuela, tortillas are unique among breads in being made from a cooked, not a raw, flour. Dried corn is boiled with lime until the skins are loosened and the cooked, skinned kernels are then dried and ground to make the *masa harina*, dough flour, that is used for tortillas. Happily for anyone wanting to make them, it is sold packaged by the Quaker Company. The flour is mixed with water to a fairly soft dough, pressed on a tortilla press or patted into a flat pancake by hand, and baked on a *comal*, an ungreased griddle, for a minute or so. It is not possible to speak of a raw tortilla, only of an unbaked one. Tortillas for those who don't want to make them are available frozen.

Arepas are also made from a cooked flour, and since it was in the Valley of Mexico in 5000 B.C. that corn was first cultivated, not arriving in South America until about 1500 B.C., it is a safe bet that the technique of cooking the corn before making it into flour was established in Mexico long before Venezuela invented *arepas*. In any event they are quite different.

Tortillas for *antojitos* are made in a variety of shapes and sizes and with a variety of fillings. Sternly traditional cooks parcel the fillings out among the shapes with some rigidity. However, when we make such things in the States, we should have the freedom to follow our own whims and fancies.

A selection of *antojitos* makes a fine buffet lunch when accompanied by a dessert.

Tortillas

Mexican cooks pat out tortillas by hand. They take a small ball of tortilla dough and with quick, deft movements pat the dough from one hand to the other, transforming it in no time at all into a thin pancake, which is then baked. I have managed to produce a recognizable tortilla by this method, though most of my hand-patted ones were a little on the thick side. I am pretty sure that if I had spent two or three years at it I could have mastered the art of making tortillas by hand! However, since colonial Spain had faced the problem and come up with the solution in the form of a tortilla press, I gave up trying and bought myself a press. The old colonial ones were made of wood. Mine is cast iron. It works extremely well and many Mexican cooks who can hand-pat a tortilla use it for convenience. I use a plastic liner on the press — a plastic bag cut in half is ideal. However, some people prefer to use wax paper.

Makes about eighteen 4-inch tortillas

2 *cups* masa harina   1⅓ *cups lukewarm water*

Put the *masa harina* into a bowl, pour in 1 cup of the water, and stir to mix to a soft dough. Add the remaining water if necessary, as it probably will be. It is impossible to be absolutely precise about the amount of water needed. If the *masa harina* is very fresh it will need less water, and I have even found that an extremely humid day has its effect. The corn flour picks up moisture from the air. The dough should be flexible and hold together nicely. If it is too wet, it will stick to the tortilla press, in which case simply scrape it off the plastic sheet or wax paper, and add it to the dough with a little more flour. The dough is not hurt by being handled. If the dough is too dry, floury bits will show up on the cooked tortilla. Sprinkle the dough with a little more lukewarm water. Traditionally salt is not added to tortillas. However, a teaspoon of salt may be added to the flour by those who find the unsalted tortilla insipid.

Divide the dough into balls the size of small eggs and flatten on the tortilla press between 2 sheets of plastic or wax paper to thin pancakes about 4 inches across. Peel off the top piece of plastic or paper. Put the tortilla, paper side up, in the palm of the left hand, peel off the paper, then flip the tortilla onto a moderately heated, ungreased *comal* or griddle. It's a knack, but very easily learned. Cook until the edges begin to curl, about 1 minute, then, using a spatula or the fingers, turn the tortilla over and cook for about a minute longer. It should be very lightly flecked with brown. The side that is cooked first is the top. Pressing the first side with a spatula while the second side is cooking will turn it into an *inflado* — meaning something swollen with air; it subsides on being taken off the *comal* — which is said to be good luck. It certainly makes the stuffing of *panuchos* easier.

As they are done, stack the tortillas in a cloth napkin. When a dozen are stacked up, wrap them, napkin and all, in foil and put them into a preheated barely warm (150° F.) oven, where they will stay warm for hours. If it is necessary to reheat cold tortillas, dampen the hands and pat the tortillas between them. Place the tortillas over direct heat, fairly low heat, turning constantly for about 30 seconds.

For appetizers use a piece of dough about the size of a walnut and flatten it out to about 2 inches. Even smaller tortillas may be made if desired, using a piece of dough about the size of a large grape.

Variations

Tacos. Make 4-inch tortillas, stuff them with any filling, roll them into a cylinder, and eat by hand, or secure them with a toothpick and fry them in shallow oil or lard until crisp. Usually called soft and fried tacos.

Sopes. Pinch off a piece of tortilla dough about the size of a walnut, roughly 2 teaspoons, and pat or press it into a pancake about 2 inches in diameter. Bake it on an ungreased griddle, iron skillet, or *comal* until it is lightly flecked with brown on both sides, about 1 minute a side. Pinch up a ¼-inch border all round the *sope*, then fry in vegetable oil or lard on the flat side. Stuff with any filling, the most usual of which is *Frijoles Refritos* (Refried Beans), page 242, topped with a little grated cheese, a little chopped white onion, and a hot chili sauce with a radish slice for a garnish. The basic tortilla dough for *sopes* is often mixed with another ingredient. Half a cup of cottage cheese may be added to the dough, or 2 or 3 *ancho* chilies, soaked and ground, or 2 or 3 *serrano* chilies, seeded and ground in a blender or food processor.

Chalupas (little canoes). These are oval tortillas with a pinched-up rim. Pinch off a piece of tortilla dough, about 2 tablespoons, and roll it into a cylinder about 4 inches long. Flatten it into an oval on a tortilla press or pat it into shape by hand. Bake on a *comal* or griddle in the usual way, then pinch up a ¼-inch rim all the way round. Fry in vegetable oil or lard on the flat side. Some cooks spoon a little hot fat into the *chalupa* when frying it. Use any filling, but the most usual is shredded chicken or pork, crumbled or grated cheese, and a red or green chili sauce.

Totopos. Ordinary tortillas cut into 4 or 6 wedges, fried until crisp in lard or vegetable oil, and used for dips or with *Frijoles Refritos* (Refried Beans) are usually called *tostaditas*. However, in Mexico's Federal District they are often called *totopos*. This leads to some confusion as there is an

entirely different *antojito* also called a *totopo*. To make *totopos* remove
the seeds from 3 *ancho* or *pasilla* chilies, soak them in hot water, and purée
them in a blender. Mix the chilies with the *masa harina* and ½ cup cooked,
mashed red kidney beans. Season with salt and make into rather thicker
than usual tortillas using about 2 teaspoons of dough for each *totopo*. Fry
the *totopos* in hot lard or vegetable oil on both sides. Drain on paper towels
and spread with *guacamole* topped with grated Parmesan cheese, or use
any topping.

　　Tostadas. These are 6- or 4-inch tortillas fried until crisp in hot lard or
vegetable oil and topped with various combinations of poultry, meat, fish,
or shellfish and various garnishes, lettuce, chili sauce, and so on. Use
2-inch tortillas for appetizers.

FILLINGS

The most popular fillings are shredded chicken, shredded pork, or *Picadillo*
(Chopped Beef), combined with various sauces such as *Salsa Cruda* (Uncooked Tomato Sauce), *Salsa de Tomate Verde* (Green Tomato Sauce), and
Salsa de Jitomate (Cooked Tomato Sauce); chilies such as *serrano* or
jalapeño, available canned; shredded lettuce, romaine or iceberg; grated
cheese such as Parmesan or Münster; and *Frijoles Refritos* (Refried Beans).
Guacamole can be added to almost any *antojito* to advantage. Radishes,
sliced or cut into radish roses, and olives are a popular garnish.

　　Chorizo. Skin chorizos (hot Spanish sausage) and chop coarsely. Sauté
in vegetable oil with a little chopped onion, and tomato if liked. Drain any
excess fat. Mix with a little grated Parmesan or Romano cheese (in Mexico
queso de Chihuahua or *queso añejo* would be used). If not using tomato,
add a little tomato sauce, red or green. Garnish with shredded lettuce.

　　Sardine. Sauté a medium onion, chopped, in 1 tablespoon vegetable
oil, add 2 medium tomatoes, peeled, seeded, and chopped, and chopped
serrano or *jalapeño* chilies to taste. Cook until thick and well blended.
Mash in 1 cup *Frijoles Refritos* (Refried Beans), page 242, mixing well. Fold
in 1 can sardines packed in olive oil, drained, boned, and chopped. Sprinkle
with Parmesan cheese.

　　Cream cheese. Mash 3 ounces cream cheese with 3 tablespoons heavy
cream and combine with 1 cup shredded pork or chicken. Top with a
tomato sauce or a bottled chili sauce and garnish with shredded lettuce.

Panuchos   MEXICO
Fried Stuffed Tortillas

Panuchos are one of the most popular appetizers in the Mayan cuisine of the Yucatán peninsula. The garnish may vary slightly, but black beans are always used. They make a fine snack or light meal, and I have found that if I make my tortillas a little thicker than usual, they are easier to stuff. Pressing down lightly on the tortilla with a wooden spoon, or a spatula, when it is baking makes it puff up and this puffed-up layer is easy to lift up to insert the stuffing.

Serves 4 to 6

1 cup black beans
1 teaspoon epazote *(see page 9),*
*   if available*
Salt
1 medium onion, thinly sliced
½ cup mild white vinegar
Twelve 4-inch tortillas
½ cup lard or vegetable oil

Shredded lettuce, romaine or
*   iceberg*
1 whole cooked chicken breast,
*   boned and shredded*
12 slices tomato

Wash the beans and pick them over. Put into a saucepan with cold water to cover by about ½ inch, add the *epazote*, crumbled, and simmer, covered, until tender, adding a little hot water from time to time if necessary. Add salt when the beans are tender and continue cooking, uncovered, until almost all the liquid has evaporated. Mash to a thick paste. Keep warm.

Chop the onion and soak it in salted water for 5 minutes. Drain. Transfer the onion to a small saucepan, pour in the vinegar, bring to a boil, remove from the heat and cool. Strain, discard the vinegar, and set the onion aside.

Using the point of a small sharp knife, lift up the top skin of the tortilla, leaving the skin still attached to the tortilla on one side. Carefully spread a layer of beans inside each little pocket. Replace the tortilla layer. Heat the lard or oil in a skillet and fry the tortillas, bottom side down, until lightly browned. Drain on paper towels. Place a layer of lettuce, chicken, and onion on each tortilla, and top with a slice of tomato.

Variation: If liked, a slice of hardboiled egg may be put on top of the beans. Use 2 eggs for 12 tortillas. Cooked shredded pork may be used instead of chicken breast.

Sambutes

Stuffed Miniature Tortillas

Sambutes, sometimes spelled *salbutos*, are another Yucatán specialty — they taste just as good no matter how they are spelled.

Makes about 18

FOR THE FILLING

2 tablespoons vegetable oil
½ pound lean ground pork
1 medium onion, chopped

2 medium tomatoes, peeled and
    chopped
Salt, freshly ground pepper

Heat the oil in a skillet and sauté the pork until it is lightly browned. Purée the onion and tomatoes in a blender or food processor and add to the pork. Season to taste with salt and pepper and simmer, uncovered, until the mixture is thick and fairly dry. Set aside.

FOR THE TORTILLAS

2 cups masa harina
1 teaspoon salt

4 tablespoons all-purpose flour
Vegetable oil for deep frying

Mix the *masa harina*, salt, and flour together. Add enough water (about a teaspoon) to make a fairly stiff dough. Pinch off pieces of the dough about the size of walnuts and roll into balls. Flatten on the tortilla press into miniature tortillas not more than 2 inches across. Do not bake. Holding one tortilla in the palm of the hand, place a tablespoon of the filling on it. Cover with another tortilla and pinch the edges together. Continue until all the tortillas and the fillings are used up.

Into a fryer or saucepan pour enough oil to reach a depth of 2 to 3 inches. Heat to about 375° F. on a frying thermometer. Fry the stuffed tortillas, a few at a time, turning once, until they are golden brown, about 3 minutes. Drain on paper towels and eat hot.

If liked, these can be made even smaller, an inch across, pinching off a piece of dough not much bigger than a good-sized grape. Fill with 1 teaspoon of the stuffing.

Sambutes are often served as an appetizer accompanied by the same pickled onion as in *Panuchos* (page 47) and with a tomato sauce made by peeling and chopping ½ pound tomatoes and reducing them to a purée in a blender or food processor with 1 fresh hot seeded pepper, or 1 canned *serrano* chili. The sauce is not cooked and is spooned on top of the stuffed tortilla, which is then topped with a little onion. They make a marvelous accompaniment to drinks.

Soups

Sopas

Soup is extremely popular in Latin America, and most people there would regard a main meal without soup as a poor thing indeed. Soups were not part of the indigenous cooking but were introduced in the colonial period and range from the bowl of richly flavored amber chicken consommé, so highly esteemed at the beginning of Sunday or holiday midday dinner in Mexico, to the hearty soup-stews, the pot-au-feu dishes that Colombia, particularly, excels in, and that are a meal in themselves.

From a very large array of soups, I have made a small selection of those I have particularly enjoyed. The varied soup repertoire evolved from local ingredients, chayote, zucchini, squash blossoms, sweet red peppers, corn, coconut, winter squash, yams, yucca, hearts of palm, and from the marvelous fish and shellfish of the region's coasts. They are not run-of-the-mill soups, of which Latin America has its full share — the soups one could call universal — vegetable, onion, cream of tomato, celery, watercress, green pea. No matter how good these may be, their Latin American cousins have not changed enough from the versions with which we are all familiar to make it worthwhile including them. My choice has been soups that will introduce new combinations of flavors, refreshing to any palate that is pleased with change.

Nowadays, with excellent canned beef or chicken stock available, one need not go to the trouble of making one's own stock. But Latin American cooking methods do have a pleasant bonus. Many dishes are cooked on top of the stove because, in the past, cooking was done mostly over charcoal, and ovens were not greatly used. As a result, when poaching a flank steak for a Venezuelan *Pabellón Caraqueño*, or a chicken for a Mexican *mole*, I get stock as an extra. I seldom freeze it, just refrigerate it, though I make a point of boiling it up and simmering it for 3 or 4 minutes if it hasn't been used in 2 or 3 days, which doesn't happen often as one always seems to need stock in the kitchen. And a nice thing is that stock does not sneer at leftovers or bits of this and that but welcomes them. When I boil up a refrigerated stock, I take the opportunity of adding any extras I may have around. The good rich stock comes in very handy for soup making.

Sopa de Aguacate   MEXICO
Avocado Soup

Avocado soup is popular in Latin America from Mexico all the way south to Chile. I don't think I've ever had an avocado soup I didn't enjoy. The beautiful pale green color and the buttery richness of the flavor are seductive, yet one of my favorite avocado soups is also one of the simplest. It comes from Mexico and is good hot, marvelous chilled. It is vitally important when making the soup not to let the avocado cook, as cooked avocados tend to develop a bitter taste. I like the soup garnished with chopped fresh coriander leaves as this adds a very special flavor.

Serves 6

2 large, ripe avocados
4 cups rich chicken stock
1 cup heavy cream
Salt, freshly ground white pepper
1 tablespoon fresh green coriander
    (cilantro), finely chopped
    (optional)

6 tortillas, quartered and fried
    crisp in lard or oil

Peel and mash the avocados and put them through a sieve. Place them in a heated soup tureen. Heat the chicken stock with the cream. Pour the stock into the avocados, stirring to mix, or beat lightly with a wire whisk. Season to taste with salt and pepper. Sprinkle with the coriander, if desired. Serve immediately with the crisp tortillas.

For summer dining the soup is splendid chilled. In which case do not heat the tureen and make sure that the chicken stock has been skimmed of all fat. Combine the avocados, stock, cream, salt, and pepper in a blender or food processor and blend until it is smooth. Chill quickly and serve as soon as possible, as the soup tends to darken on top if left for long. If it darkens, simply stir it before serving. The flavor is not affected and the small amount of darkening won't show. Keeping air from the soup helps to minimize darkening, so it is useful to cover it with plastic wrap while it is chilling.

Variation: This *Sopa de Paltas* (Avocado Soup) from Chile is an interesting example of a culinary combination from the opposite ends of the earth. The avocado and the Béchamel go very well together, producing a soup that is subtly flavored. In a fairly large saucepan heat 4 tablespoons butter and sauté 1 medium onion, finely chopped, until it is soft. Add 4 tablespoons flour, and cook, stirring, for about 2 minutes over low heat without letting the flour take on any color. Gradually add 2 cups milk, stirring constantly until the mixture is smooth and thick. Stir in 2 cups chicken stock and continue to cook over low heat, stirring from time to time, for about 5 minutes. Cut 2 large, ripe avocados in half and remove the pits. Mash them in their shells, turn them into a warmed soup tureen, season with a little lemon juice, and continue to mash until they are quite smooth. Pour the hot béchamel mixture over the avocados, stirring to mix, or beat with a wire whisk. Season to taste with salt and pepper. Serves 4 to 6.

Variation: For *Sopa de Aguacate y Papas* (Avocado Vichyssoise) from Colombia, peel and dice 1 pound potatoes and put into a large saucepan with the white part of 2 leeks, washed and sliced, and 1 medium onion, sliced. Pour in 4 cups chicken stock, cover, and simmer until tender. Put the vegetables and broth through a sieve, return the mixture to the saucepan, stir in a cup of heavy cream, and heat just to a boil. Peel and mash 2 large avocados and put them into a heated soup tureen. Add the hot soup and stir to mix thoroughly. Season to taste with salt and white pepper. The soup is also very good served chilled. Serves 6.

Variation: For *Sopa de Aguacate* (Avocado Soup) from Venezuela, scoop out the flesh of 2 large avocados and put into a blender with 1½ cups clam juice, 1½ cups chicken stock, 1 cup light cream, and salt and white pepper to taste. Blend until smooth, chill, and serve garnished with a little chopped parsley and a little sweet paprika. If preferred, omit the cream and use 2 cups each chicken stock and clam juice. Serves 6.

Sopa de Creme de Palmito   BRAZIL
Creamed Hearts of Palm Soup

Hearts of palm are a commonplace in Brazil, where their delicate flavor and texture is taken for granted. I will always think of them as a luxury, even though most supermarkets have them canned. I particularly like to serve this soup when I am having a beef dish as a main course and want something elegantly light in contrast to the robust flavor of the meat. The soup can be prepared ahead of time and finished at the last minute. It is simplicity itself with a lovely, unusual, delicate flavor.

Serves 6

2 tablespoons rice flour
1 cup milk
A 14-ounce can hearts of palm

5 cups chicken stock
Salt, white pepper
2 egg yolks

In a small bowl mix the rice flour with the milk. Drain and chop the hearts of palm and purée in a blender or food processor with 1 cup of the chicken stock. Pour the mixture into a saucepan and stir in the rice flour mixture and the rest of the chicken stock. Season to taste with salt and pepper and cook, stirring, over low heat until the soup is smooth and thickened slightly. In a bowl beat the egg yolks. Beat in a little of the hot soup, then pour the egg yolk mixture into the soup, and cook, stirring, for about 1 minute. Do not let the soup boil as it will curdle.

Antonia's Sopa de Chayote   MEXICO
Chayote Soup

This soup from Cuernavaca in the state of Morelos has a lovely light texture and delicate flavor. The main ingredient, chayote, the pale green pear-shaped vegetable, is worth looking out for in tropical markets.

Serves 6

2 large chayotes, peeled and sliced
Salt
1 medium onion, finely chopped
1 clove garlic, chopped

2 tablespoons butter
1 tablespoon flour
4 cups chicken stock
White pepper

Put the chayotes in a saucepan with salted water to cover and simmer, covered, until they are tender, about 20 minutes. Transfer the chayotes to a blender or food processor with 2 cups of the cooking liquid and blend until smooth. Discard any remaining cooking liquid.

In a saucepan sauté the onion and garlic in the butter until the onion is soft. Stir in the flour and cook, stirring, for a minute without letting it brown. Add the chicken stock and cook, stirring, until the mixture is smooth. Combine the stock with the chayote mixture, season to taste with salt and white pepper, and simmer, covered, for 5 minutes longer, stirring from time to time. If liked, the soup may be put through a sieve for a finer texture.

Variation: I found an interesting variation of this soup in Nicaragua. It is made in exactly the same way except that just before serving, 1 cup (about ½ pound) cooked, shredded chicken breast is added and heated through, and the soup when served is garnished with croutons.

Sopa de Jitomate   MEXICO
Tomato Soup

This is a very fresh, simple tomato soup from Mexico, where the tomato originated and where it is sold large and ripe and sweet. I wait until the tomato season reaches its peak before cooking this, or better still until some home-grown tomatoes are ripe on the vine. I sometimes add a tablespoon of dry sherry to each serving, but mostly I prefer the unadorned flavor of tomato.

Serves 6

2 tablespoons butter or vegetable oil
1 large onion, finely chopped
1 clove garlic, chopped
6 large ripe tomatoes, peeled and coarsely chopped

4 cups chicken or beef stock
Salt, freshly ground pepper
6 tablespoons dry sherry (optional)

Heat the butter in a fairly large saucepan and sauté the onion and garlic until the onion is soft. Add the tomatoes and cook, stirring, for 2 or 3 minutes. Pour in the stock and simmer the mixture for 10 minutes. Cool slightly and purée in two or three batches in a blender or food processor. Reheat, add salt and pepper to taste, and serve in bouillon cups with the sherry, if liked.

Sopa de Pimientos Morrones   MEXICO
Sweet Red Pepper Soup

When I was first married and my husband was transferred to Mexico for
some years, my mother-in-law found me a cook who had long associations
with the family. Her name was Francisca and she was a Zapotecan Indian
from Oaxaca, a tiny woman with a beautiful tranquil high-cheekboned
face, framed by long plaits, quite gray. This soup was one she made for me,
using bell peppers for their rather more robust flavor. It is important that
they be smooth and shiny, as even slightly wrinkled peppers will have less
flavor and the texture of the finished soup will not be so smooth. This is a
beautiful soup to look at with its deep, rich color and I love its pleasantly
unusual flavor. The addition of hot peppers to the pot is a matter of
taste — I prefer it without.

Serves 6

2 tablespoons vegetable oil
1 medium onion, finely chopped
3 large ripe red bell peppers
4 cups chicken or beef stock
1 cup tomato juice

1 fresh hot red or green pepper,
*   whole and with stem left on*
*   (optional)*
Salt, freshly ground pepper

Heat the oil in a small skillet and sauté the onion until it is soft. Set aside.
Peel the peppers according to the instructions on page 15. Seed and chop
coarsely. Purée the peppers with the onion and a little stock in a blender or
food processor. Transfer the purée to a saucepan, add the rest of the stock,
the tomato juice, and if liked the hot pepper. Season to taste with salt and
pepper. Simmer, covered, for 15 minutes. Remove and discard the pepper.

Sopa de Flor de Calabaza   MEXICO
Squash Blossom Soup

Squash, one of the oldest vegetables in the world, originated in Mexico.
The flowers used in this recipe are usually from zucchini, although blossoms from any type of squash or pumpkin can be used. A popular Italian
dish consists of the flowers dipped in batter and fried, so that Italian as well
as Latin American markets are good places to go looking for squash blossoms. These are the male flowers, which produce no fruit. It is the female

flower that gives us the zucchini, so one may eat the blossoms with a clear conscience. The male blossoms are attached to short, thin stems; the female flowers are attached to miniature squashes. *Epazote*, which adds a slight but distinctive flavor to the soup, is not often available in local markets, but the soup, with its subtle flavor, is still very good without it.

Serves 6

1 pound squash blossoms	*5 cups chicken stock*
4 tablespoons butter	*Salt, freshly ground pepper*
1 medium onion, finely chopped	*1 sprig* epazote, *page 9 (optional)*

Remove and discard the stems from the squash blossoms and chop the flowers coarsely. Heat the butter in a saucepan and sauté the onion until it is soft. Add the flowers and sauté for 3 or 4 minutes longer. Pour in the stock, season to taste with salt and pepper, cover, and simmer until the blossoms are tender, about 5 minutes. Purée in a blender or food processor, in more than one batch if necessary. Return to the saucepan and reheat with the sprig of *epazote* if it is available. Discard the *epazote* before serving.

Variation: For *Sopa de Flor de Calabaza con Crema* (Cream of Squash Blossom Soup), a rather richer soup, whisk 2 egg yolks with 1 cup of heavy cream, then whisk 1 cup of the hot soup into the egg mixture, beat this into the soup, and cook, without letting it boil, until the soup is lightly thickened. Mexican cooks always use only egg yolks. I find whole eggs do a much better job, and I use them even though this is a departure from tradition.

Variation: For *Sopa de Flor de Calabaza con Jitomate* (Squash Blossom and Tomato Soup), add 2 medium tomatoes, peeled, seeded, and chopped, to the onion with the squash blossoms. This makes a very pleasantly different soup with an interesting blend of flavors.

Caldo de Zapallo Tierno   PARAGUAY
Zucchini Soup

This lovely simple recipe was given me by a friend, Josefina Velilla de Aquino, when I visited her in Asunción, Paraguay. She is a gifted cook and teacher of cooking, with a great feeling for traditional cuisine. Another version of it, from a family cook in Cuernavaca, is even more simple, and I often make that one when I am alone, or in a hurry, and the more elaborate one when I have guests. I often leave the rice out of the Paraguayan recipe for a more purely vegetable flavor.

Serves 6

2 tablespoons vegetable oil
1 medium onion, finely chopped
1 clove garlic, chopped
5 cups chicken stock
3 tablespoons raw rice
1 pound zucchini, grated

Salt, freshly ground pepper
1 egg
3 tablespoons freshly grated
    Parmesan cheese
1 tablespoon finely chopped
    parsley

Heat the oil in a fairly large saucepan and sauté the onion and garlic until the onion is soft. Add the chicken stock and the rice and simmer, covered, for 10 minutes. Add the zucchini. Season to taste with salt and pepper and simmer until the zucchini is very tender, about 15 minutes. In a soup tureen beat the egg with the cheese and parsley, then whisk in the soup, mixing well.

Variation: Antonia Delgado's *Sopa de Calabacita* (Zucchini Soup) from Cuernavaca, Mexico. In a saucepan sauté 1 medium onion, finely chopped, and 1 large scallion, using the white and green parts, coarsely chopped, in 2 tablespoons butter until the onion is soft. Add 1 pound zucchini, coarsely chopped, and stir for a minute. Pour in 5 cups chicken stock and simmer, covered, until the zucchini is tender, about 15 minutes. Purée in two or three batches in a blender or food processor. Pour the soup back into the saucepan, season to taste with salt and pepper, and reheat. Remove from the heat and stir in ½ cup heavy cream. Serve immediately. Serves 6.

Sopa de Crema de Coco   COLOMBIA
Cream of Coconut Soup

This is a subtle and unusual soup from Cartagena in coastal Colombia, where coconut plays a large role in the kitchen. I like it especially as the beginning to a summer lunch or dinner.

Serves 6

1 coconut
5 cups chicken stock
2 tablespoons butter

1 medium onion, grated
2 tablespoons flour
Salt, freshly ground white pepper

Follow the instructions for extracting the thick milk from a coconut (page 7), and set it aside. There will be ¾ to 1 cup. Heat 1 cup of the chicken stock and pour it over the grated coconut, from which the thick milk has been squeezed, and let it stand about 30 minutes. Squeeze out the liquid through a double layer of dampened cheesecloth. Repeat the process two or three times to extract as much flavor from the coconut as possible. Set aside. Do not mix the two lots of milk. Discard the grated coconut.

Heat the butter in a saucepan and sauté the onion until it is very soft. Stir in the flour and cook, stirring, over low heat for 2 minutes. Gradually whisk in the thin coconut milk made with the stock, and the rest of the stock. Add a little more stock if there is only ¾ cup of the thick coconut milk, to make 6 cups in all. Season to taste with salt and pepper, cover, and simmer for 15 minutes. Stir in the thick coconut milk and heat the soup through but do not let it boil. Serve in bouillon cups.

Sopa de Repollo
Cabbage Soup

CHILE

Chile's temperate, sunny climate produces lovely fruits and vegetables and the cabbages are no exception, firm and heavy in the hand. Green cabbage is the best kind for this delicious, fresh-tasting soup.

Serves 6

*1 small green cabbage, weighing
    about 1 pound*
1 large or 2 medium potatoes
1 large leek
3 tablespoons butter
4 cups beef or chicken stock

Salt, freshly ground pepper
*1 cup coarsely grated Münster or
    similar cheese*

Wash and finely shred the cabbage. Peel the potato, slice thinly, then cut each slice into 3 or 4 fingers. Trim the leek and split it lengthwise. Wash thoroughly, then slice finely. Heat the butter in a saucepan large enough to hold all the ingredients. Add the cabbage, potatoes, and leek and cook, stirring with a wooden spoon, until the vegetables have absorbed the butter and the cabbage and leek are wilted, about 3 or 4 minutes. Pour in the stock, season to taste with salt and pepper, and simmer, covered, over moderate heat for 30 minutes, until the cabbage is tender. Stir in the cheese, and serve in soup bowls.

Sopa de Lima   MEXICO
Lime Soup

This soup is one of Mexico's great regional dishes. It comes from Yucatán, where the Mayan kitchen predominates, and it owes its unique flavor to a local species of lime that is seldom available, even in Mexico, outside the Yucatán peninsula. I have sometimes found these limes in the great Mexico City markets, but even then not regularly or often. Fortunately I've found that the soup loses very little of its authentic — and marvelous — flavor when made with our limes. In Mérida, Yucatán's capital, I had an interesting and very pleasant variation of the soup. Instead of the chicken gizzards and livers, a whole chicken breast, boned, poached, and shredded, was added. The chicken breast was cut in half, then simmered very gently in the stock for 10 minutes, allowed to cool, then skinned, boned, and shredded with the fingers. It was added to the soup just long enough to heat through before serving.

Serves 6

Lard *or vegetable oil*
1 medium onion, finely chopped
1 medium tomato, peeled and
    chopped
½ green bell pepper, seeded and
    chopped
2 or 3 canned serrano *chilies,*
    chopped
6 cups chicken stock
Juice *of ½ lime and the shell*

3 chicken gizzards
6 raw chicken livers, chopped
Salt, freshly ground pepper
6 tortillas, cut into thin strips
1 lime, thinly sliced

Heat 2 tablespoons of lard or vegetable oil in a saucepan and sauté the onion until it is softened. Add the tomato and sweet pepper and sauté for 2 or 3 minutes longer. Add the chilies, the chicken stock, the lime juice, and lime shell. Simmer for 2 minutes. Remove and discard the lime shell.

Put the chicken gizzards into a small saucepan with water to cover. Bring to a boil, reduce the heat, cover, and simmer gently until the gizzards are tender, about 30 minutes. Drain, remove the gristle, chop, and set aside. Add the gizzards to the soup with the chicken livers. Simmer until the livers are done, about 5 minutes. Season to taste with salt and pepper. Have ready the tortillas, fried until crisp in lard or vegetable oil and drained on paper towels. Serve the soup garnished with the tortilla strips and thin slices of lime.

Quibebe
Winter Squash Soup

This is a Bahian specialty but it is a safe bet to say that winter squash soup in one form or another is popular throughout Latin America, reflecting the New World origin of the vegetable. The *calabaza* (West Indian pumpkin) available in many tropical markets is closer in flavor to the varieties used in Latin America but I have had successful results using Hubbard, butternut, and crookneck squashes. Our American pumpkin won't do. It is both too strongly flavored and too sweet.

Serves 6

4 tablespoons (¼ cup) butter
1 medium onion, chopped
1 medium tomato, peeled, seeded,
    and chopped
1 clove garlic, minced
1 or 2 fresh hot red peppers, seeded
    and chopped
2 pounds winter squash,
    preferably calabaza (West
    Indian pumpkin), peeled and
    cut into ½ inch cubes

4 cups beef stock
Salt
¼ teaspoon sugar
Parmesan cheese (optional)

Melt the butter in a large saucepan; add the onion, tomato, garlic, and hot peppers; and cook until the onion is softened and the mixture thick and well blended. Add the squash and the stock to the saucepan, season to taste with salt, stir in the sugar, and simmer, covered, for 20 minutes or until the squash has disintegrated and thickened the soup, which should retain some texture and not be completely smooth. If liked, the soup may be sprinkled with 1 tablespoon Parmesan cheese for each serving.

Variation: In Chile the squash is cooked in stock or water, mashed until smooth, and combined with a sautéed onion and an amount of milk equal to the stock, 3 cups of each to 1 pound of squash. At the last minute a well-beaten egg is stirred into the soup.

Variation: In Colombia 2 pounds of squash are cooked in beef stock until the squash is tender. The soup, which should be thick, is put through a sieve or reduced to a purée in a blender or food processor. A little butter is added just before serving.

Variation: In Argentina, as in Chile, the soup is a thinner one, using 1½ pounds of squash to 3 cups each beef stock and milk. It is served with croutons. At the last minute 2 egg yolks beaten with a tablespoon or so of Parmesan cheese are stirred into the soup.

Variation: In Paraguay ¼ cup raw rice is cooked with the squash. At the last minute a whole egg is beaten with a tablespoon or so of grated Münster or Parmesan cheese together with a tablespoon of chopped parsley and stirred into the soup.

Variation: In Ecuador the squash is put on to cook with 1 sliced onion, 1 medium sliced tomato, peeled, 1 clove garlic, chopped, and water barely to cover, about 3 cups. When the squash is tender, purée it in a blender with all the liquid and return the soup to the saucepan. Add 2 cups milk and season to taste with salt and pepper. Mix 2 tablespoons butter with 2 tablespoons flour, and add, bit by bit, to the soup. Simmer gently, stirring, over low heat until the soup is thickened. Serve with grated Münster cheese.

Locro   ECUADOR
Potato Soup

This is a highlands dish. There is a coastal version in which 1 teaspoon ground annatto is used instead of the paprika.

Serves 6 to 8

4 tablespoons (¼ cup) butter
1 teaspoon sweet paprika
1 medium onion, finely chopped
4 pounds potatoes, peeled and
    sliced

1 cup each milk and light cream
½ pound Münster cheese, grated
Salt

In a large, heavy saucepan heat the butter and stir in the paprika. Add the onion and sauté over moderate heat until the onion is softened. Pour in 4 cups water, bring to a boil, add the potatoes, and simmer over low heat, uncovered, stirring occasionally. When the potatoes are almost done, add the milk and cream and continue to cook, stirring from time to time, until the potatoes begin to disintegrate. Stir the cheese into the potatoes, season to taste with salt, and serve immediately. Avocado slices are sometimes served with the *Locro*, on separate plates but to be eaten at the same time.

Variation: In coastal Ecuador shrimp fritters are sometimes added to the potato soup. Peel 2 dozen medium shrimp and set them aside. In a skillet heat 1 tablespoon butter and sauté the shrimp shells until they turn pink. Put the shells into a small saucepan with 1 cup water, cover, and simmer for 5 minutes. Strain, discard the shells, and stir the stock into the *Locro*. Chop the shrimp. Grate a medium ear of corn — there should be ½ cup. In 1 tablespoon butter sauté 1 medium onion, very finely chopped, with 1 medium tomato, peeled, seeded, and chopped, until the onion is tender and the mixture very thick and well blended. Allow the mixture to cool. Season to taste with salt and pepper, add the shrimp, the corn, and 1 egg, lightly beaten. Fry by the tablespoon in hot lard or vegetable oil until lightly browned on both sides. Add to the soup when serving.

Sopa de Elote
Corn Soup

CUBA

Serves 6

4 cups corn kernels, preferably
    fresh; if frozen, thoroughly
    defrosted
2 cups chicken stock

1 cup light cream
Salt, freshly ground white pepper
2 eggs, lightly beaten
2 tablespoons chopped parsley

Put the corn into a blender or food processor with the chicken stock and blend to a purée. Do this in two batches. Pour the purée into a saucepan, stir in the cream, and simmer over very low heat, stirring from time to time, for 5 minutes. Work the purée through a sieve, return it to the saucepan, and season it to taste with salt and pepper. If it is very thick, thin it with a little more chicken stock, and bring to a simmer. Stir ½ cup of the soup into the eggs, then stir the egg mixture into the soup and cook, stirring, for 1 or 2 minutes. Serve garnished with a little chopped parsley.

Sopa de Maní
Peanut Soup

ECUADOR

Peanut soup turns up all over Latin America, each version a little different from the others, though not very much so. My favorite is this creamy, delicate soup from Ecuador.

Serves 6

2 tablespoons butter
1 medium onion, finely chopped
1 cup toasted peanuts, finely
    ground
1 pound fresh potatoes, cooked
    and chopped

4 cups chicken or beef stock
1 cup light cream
Salt, freshly ground pepper
2 tablespoons chopped chives

Heat the butter in a skillet and sauté the onion until it is soft. In a blender or food processor combine the onion and any butter in the skillet, the peanuts, potatoes, and a little of the stock. Blend to a smooth purée, pour into a saucepan, stir in the rest of the stock, and simmer gently, covered, for 15 minutes. Stir in the cream, season to taste with salt and pepper, and simmer just long enough to heat through. Pour into soup bowls and garnish with the chopped chives.

Sopa de Topinambur   CHILE
Jerusalem Artichoke Soup

Chile was the only country in South America where I encountered this soup. Though differently made, it reminded me of my mother's artichoke soup, a family favorite. Autumn is the season for Jerusalem artichokes and I have found the soup comforting on a blustery evening, though it is richly delicate rather than hearty.

Serves 4

¾ pound Jerusalem artichokes
1 large onion, finely chopped
3 ½ cups chicken stock
Salt, freshly ground white pepper
1 cup heavy cream
2 tablespoons fresh coriander
    (cilantro) or parsley, chopped

Wash and scrape the artichokes and slice thinly. Put into a saucepan with the onion and the chicken stock, bring to a boil and simmer, covered, until the artichokes are soft, about 20 minutes. Reduce to a purée in a blender or food processor and pour back into the saucepan. Season to taste with salt and pepper, stir in the cream, and heat through. Pour the soup into bowls and garnish with the chopped coriander or parsley.

Sopa de Plátano Verde
Green Plantain Soup

Traditionally the plantains for this soup, which I first had in Puerto Rico, are grated on a grater but I find a blender or food processor does the job admirably. Recipes vary from country to country though not in essentials.

Serves 6

1 green plantain (see page 15)
6 cups chicken or beef stock
Salt, freshly ground pepper

Grate the plantain on the second finest side of a grater, or chop it and purée it in a blender or food processor with a little stock if necessary. Pour the cold stock into a saucepan, add the plantain, and cook over moderate heat, stirring with a wooden spoon, until the soup is thick. Season to taste with salt and pepper and simmer, covered, for 10 minutes.

Sopa de Batata Doce   BRAZIL
Sweet Potato Soup

This is one of the most delicious soups I have ever had, whether as *sopa de camote* in Spanish-speaking Latin America or as *sopa de batata doce* in Brazil. It is a beautiful golden-yellow color with a lovely tart hint of tomato flavor balancing the slight sweetness of the potato. The type of sweet potato used is the delightful *boniato*, which has a pink or brownish skin and white flesh and is available in Caribbean markets — it is well worth looking for.

Serves 6

1 pound boniatos (white sweet
    potatoes)
Salt
4 tablespoons butter
1 medium onion, finely chopped
4 medium tomatoes, peeled and
    chopped
4 cups beef stock

Freshly ground pepper
2 tablespoons chopped parsley or
    fresh coriander (cilantro),
    optional

Peel the sweet potatoes, slice thickly, and put into a saucepan with cold salted water to cover. Bring to a boil, reduce the heat, and simmer, covered, until tender, about 20 minutes. Drain thoroughly and chop coarsely.

Heat the butter in a skillet and sauté the onion until it is soft. Add the tomatoes and cook for about 5 minutes longer. Put the mixture into a blender or food processor with the sweet potatoes and 1 cup of the stock and reduce to a smooth purée. Pour into a saucepan with the rest of the stock. Season to taste with salt and pepper and reheat. I have sometimes had the soup garnished with chopped parsley or coriander, and though it looks pretty I feel this really adds very little to the incomparable flavor of the soup.

So'O-Yosopy
Beef Soup

PARAGUAY

This is a wonderfully comforting soup and needs little more than dessert to make a light supper. Its name in Guaraní, an official language in Paraguay, translates in Spanish into *sopa de carne*. It is easy to make if the simple rules are followed.

Serves 6

2 pounds ground lean sirloin or
    round steak
2 tablespoons vegetable oil
2 medium onions, finely chopped
1 green bell pepper, seeded and
    finely chopped, or 1 or 2 fresh
    hot peppers, seeded and
    chopped

4 medium tomatoes, peeled and
    chopped
½ cup rice or vermicelli
Salt
Grated Parmesan cheese

Have the butcher grind the meat twice, then mash it in a mortar to make sure it is completely pulverized, or use a food processor. Set the meat aside together with any juices.

Heat the oil in a skillet and sauté the onions and pepper until the onions are softened. Add the tomatoes and cook until the mixture is thick and well blended, about 5 minutes longer. Cool the mixture slightly. Put the beef and its juices into a saucepan. Stir in the sautéed onions, pepper, and tomatoes, known as the *sofrito*, and 8 cups cold water, mixing well. Bring to a boil over moderate heat, stirring with a wooden spoon. Add the rice or noodles and simmer, still stirring, until tender, about 15 minutes. At this point, season to taste with salt. If salt is added earlier, the meat and liquid, which should be completely blended, may separate. Some cooks believe that constant stirring is the most important step, others that the point at which the salt is added is the vital factor. Superstition has it that if anyone who does not enjoy cooking is present in the kitchen they may cause the *So'O-Yosopy* to separate and spoil the dish.

Serve with a baked sweet potato or a thick slice of boiled yucca (cassava), or both, and *Sopa Paraguaya*, Paraguayan Corn Bread despite its misleading name. Sprinkle, if liked, with grated cheese. Water biscuits may also be served with the soup.

Variation: Omit the rice or noodles and add 2 thinly sliced carrots to the onion and tomato mixture with a teaspoon of oregano and freshly ground pepper.

Variation: *Chupi* (Meat Soup) from Argentina is a very simple but traditional soup, easy to make and grand in winter weather. It is obviously related to Paraguay's exotically named *So'O-Yosopy*. Heat ¼ cup vegetable oil in a saucepan and sauté 1 large onion, finely chopped, and 1 red bell pepper, seeded and chopped (or use 2 canned pimientos, chopped), until onion and pepper are both tender. Add 1 pound lean beef, round or sirloin, coarsely chopped in a food processor, or by hand, and sauté, stirring to break up the beef for a few minutes. Add 3 medium potatoes, peeled and cubed, 1 tablespoon chopped parsley, ⅛ teaspoon of cayenne (optional), 6 cups beef stock or water, and salt and pepper to taste. Bring to a simmer and cook, covered, for 30 minutes, stirring once or twice during the cooking time. Serves 6.

Sopa de Garbanzo MEXICO
Chickpea Soup

Though this is a regional Mexican dish from Oaxaca, its overtones are very Middle Eastern with its union of chickpeas and mint. It is clearly an old colonial dish. The fried egg is an interesting addition.

Serves 6

4 tablespoons vegetable oil
1 medium onion, finely chopped
1 clove garlic, minced
1 tablespoon fresh mint leaves,
    chopped, or ½ tablespoon
    dried
3 cups beef or chicken stock

2 cups cooked chickpeas
    (1¼-pound can), or ½ pound
    dried chickpeas, soaked
    overnight in cold water
Salt, freshly ground pepper
6 eggs

Heat 2 tablespoons of the oil in a skillet and sauté the onion and garlic until the onion is soft. Transfer the contents of the skillet to a blender or food processor, add the mint leaves, and ½ cup of the stock, and reduce the mixture to a purée. Pour the mixture into a medium-sized saucepan.

Put the cooked chickpeas in the blender or food processor with the liquid from the can. If using dried chickpeas, cook these in water to cover until tender, about 1 hour. Purée the chickpeas in a blender with 1 cup of the water in which they have cooked. Add the chickpea purée to the onion mixture and stir in the remaining stock. Season to taste with salt and pepper, bring to a simmer, and cook, stirring from time to time, until the flavors are blended, about 5 minutes.

Heat the remaining 2 tablespoons of oil in a skillet and fry the eggs. Pour the soup into bowls. Slide a fried egg into each bowl.

FISH SOUPS

The fruits of the sea, with which Latin America is so lavishly endowed, are used in some very fine soups, robust enough to be the main course of lunch or dinner. They may be enriched with corn, tomatoes, sweet peppers, or beans, with root vegetables like yams, yucca (cassava) root, or potatoes, with okra, zucchini, or other green vegetables, with coconut milk as well as stock, sometimes enlivened with a touch of hot pepper, and always with well-orchestrated seasonings, a symphony of flavors.

Sopa de Almejas   COLOMBIA
Clam Soup

This clam soup is a coastal favorite in Colombia, which is richly blessed in having both the Caribbean and the Pacific wash its shores. I had it with Colombian friends at a family gathering when there were twelve of us to lunch. The day was hot, the sun brilliant, and the soup hearty, but this did not stop even more substantial dishes following. At home I like it as a winter soup and make it the central dish of a family lunch or dinner, serving larger helpings; this recipe would serve 3 or 4 as a main dish, 6 as a soup.

In Colombia the large Spanish mackerel sierra (see page 16) is used. The stronger flavored Atlantic mackerel won't do for this dish, so substitute red snapper if Spanish mackerel is not available.

Serves 6

¼ cup olive oil
1 medium onion, finely chopped
1 clove garlic, chopped
1 red and 1 green bell pepper, or
    use 2 red or 2 green peppers,
    seeded and chopped
3 medium tomatoes, peeled,
    seeded, and chopped
1 pound (about 3 medium)
    potatoes, peeled and sliced
Salt, freshly ground pepper
1 bay leaf

Pinch ground cloves
⅛ teaspoon cumin
½ teaspoon sugar (optional)
3 dozen clams, well washed
2 pounds fillets of Spanish
    mackerel, red snapper, or
    similar fish, cut into 12 pieces
2 cups clam juice
2 cups water
2 tablespoons finely chopped
    parsley

Heat the oil in a fireproof casserole and sauté the onion, garlic, and peppers until the onion is soft. Add the tomatoes and sauté for a minute or two longer. Add the potatoes. Season to taste with salt and pepper. Add the bay leaf, cloves, cumin, and sugar (if desired). Cover and simmer until the potatoes are almost tender, about 15 minutes. Add the clams, pieces of fish, clam juice, and water. Cover and simmer for 5 minutes longer, or until the clams have opened and the fish has lost its translucent look. Sprinkle with parsley and serve in soup bowls.

Chupe de Camarones
Shrimp Stew

PERU

More like a bouillabaisse, this soup is really a meal in itself. The word "chupe" actually means a savory stew containing potatoes, cheese, eggs, etc. Peru, Ecuador, and Chile all have magnificent *chupes.*

Serves 6

¼ cup vegetable oil
2 medium onions, finely chopped
2 cloves garlic, chopped
2 medium tomatoes, peeled and
  chopped
1 or 2 fresh hot red or green
  peppers, seeded and chopped
½ teaspoon oregano
Salt, freshly ground pepper
3½ quarts fish stock, or half clam
  juice, half water
2 medium potatoes, peeled and
  cut into 1-inch cubes
2 pounds jumbo shrimp

½ cup rice
3 large potatoes, peeled and
  halved
1½ pounds peas, shelled, or use
  one (10-ounce) package frozen
  peas, thawed
2 ears corn, each cut into 3 slices
3 eggs
1 cup light cream
2 tablespoons finely chopped fresh
  green coriander (cilantro), or
  use parsley, preferably flat
  Italian

Heat the oil in a large saucepan and sauté the onions and garlic until the onions are softened. Add the tomatoes, hot peppers, oregano, salt and pepper to taste, and cook for a few minutes, stirring to mix well. Add the fish stock and the diced potatoes. Peel the shrimp and add the shells to the saucepan. Set the shrimp aside. Bring to a boil, reduce the heat, and simmer gently, covered, for about 30 minutes. Strain through a sieve, pressing down on the solids to extract all the juices. Rinse out the saucepan and return the broth to it.

Add the rice, halved potatoes, and peas, cover, and simmer until the potatoes are tender, about 20 minutes. Add the corn and the shrimp and cook for 5 minutes longer. Break the eggs into the soup, one at a time, stirring, so that the eggs coagulate in strips. Pour in the cream and cook just long enough to heat through. Pour into a warmed soup tureen and sprinkle with the coriander or parsley. Ideally this is served in large, deep, old-fashioned rimmed soup plates. Serve in large bowls holding about 2 cups.

Variation: Use only 1 pound of shrimp. Add six 1-inch slices of fillet of bass, fried in oil at the last minute. Leave out the stirred-in eggs and top each soup plate with a poached egg and, if liked, a strip of lightly sautéed sweet red or green pepper. Serves 6.

Variation: In Chile, that paradise of fish and shellfish, there is a simple, very pleasant version of these hearty fish soup-stews, *Chupe de Pescado* (Fish Stew). It is light enough to serve as a soup, not as a meal in itself. Peel, quarter, and boil in salted water 6 fairly small potatoes. Set aside. In a saucepan sauté 2 finely chopped onions in 3 tablespoons vegetable oil and 1 tablespoon sweet paprika until the onions are soft. Add 2 cups freshly made breadcrumbs, 1 finely grated carrot (optional), 3 cups milk, 1½ cups fish stock or clam juice or water, salt and pepper to taste, ½ teaspoon oregano, and 1 pound mackerel fillets or hake or cod, cut into 1-inch pieces. Add the potatoes. Cover and simmer gently until the fish is done, about 5 to 8 minutes. The *chupe* should be about as thick as a medium Béchamel sauce. If it seems too thick, add a little more milk. Serve sprinkled with finely chopped hardboiled egg, using 2. Serves 6.

Sopa de Candia con Mojarras   COLOMBIA
Okra and Pompano Soup

The foods of the Andean countries, Venezuela, Colombia, Ecuador, and Peru, have more distinctive regional characteristics because the countries, until recently, were so cut off from one another. Though now with modern transportation they enjoy one another's foods, the old regional kitchens have, happily, retained their identity. This is a typical coastal dish from Cartagena, which has a very lively cuisine. I first enjoyed it high up in Bogotá.

Serves 6

2 quarts fish stock
2 medium onions, finely chopped
2 cloves garlic, chopped
1 large tomato, peeled, seeded, and chopped
2 fresh hot peppers, seeded and chopped
¼ teaspoon each ground cumin and allspice
Salt
4 tablespoons lemon juice

½ pound small, fresh okra, quartered
1 pound small yams, peeled and cut into 1-inch pieces
2 ripe plantains, peeled and sliced
2 tablespoons butter
6 fillets pompano
2 tablespoons tomato paste
1 tablespoon Worcestershire sauce
Salt, freshly ground pepper

In a kettle combine the fish stock, onions, garlic, tomato, hot peppers, and cumin and allspice. Bring the mixture to a boil and simmer it, covered, for 15 minutes over low heat. To a saucepan of boiling salted water add the lemon juice and okra. Bring back to a boil, remove from the heat, drain the okra, and rinse it in cold water. Add the okra to the kettle with the yams and plantains and cook, covered, over very low heat for 1 hour.

In a skillet heat the butter and sauté the fish until the fillets are golden. Cut the fish into 1-inch pieces and add to the soup with the tomato paste, Worcestershire sauce, and salt and pepper to taste. Simmer for 30 minutes longer.

Variation: Coconuts are used a great deal in coastal cooking. Instead of the fish stock, use 3 cups thin coconut milk (see page 7), increase the cumin to ½ teaspoon, and omit the allspice. Add 1 pound yucca (cassava) root, peeled and cut into 1-inch pieces, when adding the okra. Omit the tomato paste and Worcestershire sauce. When the soup is ready, pour in 1 cup thick coconut milk and simmer for a few minutes longer.

Chupe de Corvina y Camarones   ECUADOR
Striped Bass and Shrimp Stew

This is Ecuador's version of the Peruvian *Chupe de Camarones* (Shrimp Stew), but a distinctively different dish.

Serves 6

1 ½ pounds striped bass fillets, cut into 1 ½-inch slices
Flour
Salt, freshly ground pepper
¼ cup vegetable oil
1 pound small or medium shrimp
4 tablespoons butter
1 teaspoon sweet paprika

1 large onion, finely chopped
2 pounds potatoes, peeled and sliced
2 cups milk or half milk, half light cream
½ pound Münster cheese, grated
3 hardboiled eggs, sliced

Rinse the fish and pat dry with paper towels. Season the flour with salt and pepper. Dredge the fish in the flour. Heat the oil in a skillet and sauté the fish slices until lightly browned on both sides. Set aside.

Shell the shrimp, reserving the shells. Cut the shrimp into ½-inch pieces and set aside. Melt a tablespoon of the butter in a saucepan, add the shrimp shells, and cook, stirring, until the shells turn pink. Add 3 cups water, bring to a boil, cover, and simmer for 5 minutes. Strain, discard the shells, and measure the stock. Bring it up to 3 cups with a little water if necessary. Set the stock aside.

Heat the rest of the butter in a large saucepan. Add the paprika and the onion and sauté until the onion is softened. Add the potatoes and the shrimp stock, cover, and simmer until the potatoes are tender, about 20 minutes. Add the milk, or milk and cream, to the saucepan and continue to cook the potatoes, stirring from time to time, until they are partly disintegrated. Add the cheese and stir to mix thoroughly. Season to taste with salt and pepper, then fold in the fish and the shrimp. Cook over low heat for about 3 minutes, or until the shrimp are cooked. Serve in bowls topped with slices of hardboiled egg. This should be thick, but still recognizable as a soup. Thin with a little milk if necessary.

Variation: This is also Ecuadorian, a simpler version, *Chupe de Corvina* (Striped Bass Stew). Heat 4 tablespoons butter in a large saucepan. Add 1 tablespoon sweet paprika; 1 large onion, finely chopped; 2 cloves garlic, chopped, and sauté until the onion is soft. Add 2 pounds potatoes, peeled and sliced, and 3 cups water. Cover and simmer until the potatoes disintegrate. Season to taste with salt and pepper, stir in 1 cup light cream and ½ pound grated Münster cheese or, if available, Spanish *queso blanco*, crumbled. Cut 1 pound striped bass fillets into 1-inch slices. Dust with flour and fry in vegetable oil until golden brown on both sides. Drain and fold into the potato soup. Serve garnished with slices of hardboiled egg, using 2 eggs. Serves 4 to 6.

Caldillo de Congrio  CHILE
Fish Soup

Congrio is a magnificent firm-fleshed fish found in Chilean waters. I have found cod to be the most acceptable substitute.

Serves 4

2 pounds cod, cut into 4 steaks
Salt
¼ cup lemon juice
2 carrots, scraped and thinly
   sliced
2 pounds small potatoes, peeled
   and thinly sliced
2 medium onions, halved and
   thinly sliced

2 cloves garlic, chopped (optional)
Freshly ground pepper
½ teaspoon oregano
1 cup dry white wine
4 cups fish stock
4 tablespoons olive oil

Put the fish steaks into a casserole, preferably earthenware, large enough to hold them in a single layer. Season with salt and the lemon juice. Cover with a layer of carrots, then a layer of half the potatoes, then the onions and garlic, and the rest of the potatoes. Season with salt, pepper, and oregano. Pour in the wine, fish stock, and olive oil. Bring to a boil, reduce the heat, and simmer until the potatoes and carrots are tender, about 30 minutes. Serve in soup bowls accompanied by crusty bread and butter. With the addition of dessert, or cheese, this makes a splendid lunch or dinner.

Fanesca

ECUADOR

Spring Soup

A traditional dish for Lent, when spring vegetables — peas, green beans, and so on — are first available, this soup is a meal in itself.

Serves 8 to 10

1 pound salt cod
4 tablespoons (¼ cup) butter
2 medium onions, finely chopped
1 clove garlic, minced
¼ teaspoon oregano
¼ teaspoon ground cumin
1 bay leaf
Freshly ground pepper
1 cup long-grain rice cooked in 1
    cup milk and 1 cup water
1 cup cooked corn kernels
2½ cups cooked shredded
    cabbage
2 cups cooked, mashed winter
    squash

2 cups cooked, chopped zucchini
1 cup cooked baby lima beans or
    broad (fava) beans
1 cup cooked green peas
1 cup cooked green beans, cut into
    ½-inch pieces
½ cup peanuts, ground
4 cups milk
1 cup light cream
1 cup Spanish fresh cheese (queso
    fresco or queso blanco) or
    Münster, chopped
Salt
3 hardboiled eggs, sliced
Grated Parmesan cheese

Soak the cod in cold water to cover for 12 hours or more, changing the water frequently. Drain the fish and put it into a saucepan with fresh water to cover. Bring to a boil, lower the heat, and simmer until the fish is tender, about 15 minutes. Drain, and reserve the fish stock. Remove any skin and bones from the fish and cut it into ½-inch pieces. Set aside.

Heat the butter in a large saucepan and sauté the onions and garlic until the onions are soft. Add the oregano, cumin, bay leaf, and several grinds of black pepper and sauté for a minute or two longer. Add 1 cup water, bring to a boil, and add the cooked rice, corn, cabbage, squash, zucchini, lima or fava beans, peas, green beans, ground peanuts, the fish and fish stock, the milk, and the cream. Stir to mix and simmer very gently for about 5 minutes to blend the flavors. Add the chopped cheese and salt to taste. The soup should be about as thick as a minestrone. If it seems too thick, thin it with a little more milk and simmer for a few minutes longer.

Pour the soup into a tureen and serve in soup plates. Garnish the servings with sliced hardboiled egg. Have the grated Parmesan cheese in a bowl on the table to be used as liked.

Sopa de Frijol Negro con Camarones MEXICO
Black Bean Soup with Shrimp

This is a recipe from Oaxaca, where avocado leaves are often used in cooking. Since I find it hard to prune my potted avocado trees, lost as I am in affectionate admiration for their beautiful glossy foliage, I am grateful to recipes like this, which urge me to pluck a couple of leaves. The flavor they add is less pronounced than bay leaf, which is also often used. The leaves may be toasted lightly before they are added to the pot. Some cooks insist this is a vital step, but from experience I do not think it matters a great deal, if at all. The soup is absolutely delicious with a most exciting flavor, the richness of the black beans contrasting unexpectedly with the fresh flavor of the shrimp.

Serves 4

¾ cup black beans, washed and
    picked over
⅛ teaspoon ground cumin
¼ teaspoon oregano
1 bay leaf, or 2 avocado leaves
2 tablespoons olive oil
1 medium onion, finely chopped
1 clove garlic, chopped
1 medium tomato, peeled and
    chopped

Salt, freshly ground pepper
2 cups chicken stock
½ pound peeled raw shrimp, cut
    into ½-inch pieces
4 tablespoons dry sherry

In a medium saucepan combine the beans, cumin, oregano, bay leaf or avocado leaves, with 3 cups water. Bring to a boil over moderate heat, reduce the heat to low, cover, and simmer until the beans are very tender, about 2½ hours. Cool a little, remove, discard the bay leaf or avocado leaves, and pour the beans and liquid into a blender or food processor.

Heat the oil in a skillet and sauté the onion and garlic until the onion is soft. Add the tomato and simmer until the mixture is well blended, 2 or 3 minutes. Season to taste with salt and pepper and add to the blender or food processor. If necessary do this in two batches. Reduce the mixture to a smooth purée and pour it into the saucepan. Stir in the chicken stock and bring to a simmer over moderate heat. Add the shrimp and cook for 2 minutes longer. Serve immediately, as overcooking toughens shrimp. Stir 1 tablespoon of sherry into each serving.

Fish and Shellfish

Pescados y Mariscos

As I have noted, fish and shellfish in Latin America are superb, with the cold Humboldt Current that runs up the coasts of Chile and Peru being responsible for some of the most magnificent seafood in the world. *Erizos*, the sea urchins of Chile, which often measure as much as 4 and 5 inches across, provide an unrivaled gastronomic experience. I remember having *erizos al matico*, raw sea urchins served with a sauce of chopped onion, parsley, oil, and lemon juice, a soup spoon, and a pile of thin, hot buttered toast, at the Hotel Crillon's dining room in Santiago, and marveling not only at their exquisite flavor but at their astonishing size.*

It is the same with *locos* (abalone), which also reaches wildly generous proportions yet loses nothing in delicacy and flavor. At a beach club near Lima, Peru, I had huge scallops with their coral served on the half shell and accompanied only by the small tropical lemon-lime that I am sure is indigenous to tropical America, its flavor more lemon than lime, but muted, delicate. Shrimp, crabs, oysters, lobsters, clams, and scallops are found in abundance, and there are also strange shellfish like the *picoroccos*, beaked

---

*Erizos (sea urchins) are sometimes available canned from specialty stores. Serve them with *Salsa de Perejil* (Parsley Sauce).

creatures that live in colonies of rocklike tubes and taste like crabs when cooked. Among the fish, *congrio* with its large head and tapering body is unique, and *corvina*, sea bass, is very fine. Mexico's waters produce excellent shrimp, conch, red snapper, and other fish and shellfish, and the same is true of the waters off Ecuador, Colombia, Argentina, and Brazil.

Perhaps because of this abundance of good seafood, recipes are not as numerous, or as varied, as for meat and poultry dishes, since the best way to cook splendid fish and shellfish is often the simplest. But there are a number of very good, original recipes, especially those from Brazil, suitable for fish usually available in any fish store. And there are the *seviches*, fish and shellfish "cooked" in a marinade of lime or lemon juice, and the *escabeches*, lightly pickled fish.

Salt cod is as popular in South America as it is in Spain and Portugal, with cooks combining indigenous and introduced foods to create exciting new dishes. Mexico cooks salt cod with a sauce of the mild but richly flavored *ancho* pepper and almonds. The north of Brazil marries coconut milk with tomatoes and sweet peppers for its salt cod Bahia style, in great contrast to the cod of Minas Gerais to the south, where tomatoes, sweet peppers, and cabbage are included.

Pescado a la Veracruzana MEXICO
Fish, Veracruz Style

Pescado a la Veracruzana (Fish in the Style of Veracruz) is Mexico's best-known fish dish and rightly so for it is admirable. There are a great many versions of it, each one differing in minor details. This is the one I prefer and I never tire of it. When I first visited Venezuela, I realized I was meeting its culinary, and almost certainly younger, cousin, *Corbullón Mantuano*, made with striped bass, and in Buenos Aires the *Corvina a la Porteña*, also with bass, seemed to be the Argentine cousin. Subtle variations make all three worth trying; they come to table surprisingly different.

Serves 4

2 pounds red snapper fillets
Salt, freshly ground pepper
Juice of a small lemon or lime
⅓ cup olive oil
2 medium onions, finely chopped
2 cloves garlic, chopped
6 medium tomatoes, peeled and
    chopped
3 tablespoons capers

20 small pimiento-stuffed green
    olives
2 or 3 canned jalapeño chilies,
    seeded and cut into strips
12 small new potatoes, freshly
    cooked, or 6 medium
    potatoes, halved
3 slices firm white bread
Butter for frying

Season the fish with salt and pepper and the lemon or lime juice. Set aside.
Heat the oil in a skillet and sauté the onions and garlic until the onions are
soft. Reduce the tomatoes to a purée in a blender or food processor and add
to the skillet with the capers, olives, *jalapeño* chilies, and the fish. Season
with a little more salt and pepper and cook over very low heat until the fish
is tender and the sauce slightly thickened, about 10 to 15 minutes. Transfer to a warmed platter and garnish with the potatoes. Cut the bread into 6
triangles, sauté in butter until golden, and arrange as a border round the
edge of the platter.

Variation: *Corbullón Mantuano* (Striped Bass in Sweet Pepper Sauce) from
Venezuela. Remove the head and tail from a 2½-pound striped bass and cut
it into 1½-inch slices. Season with salt and freshly ground pepper. Heat 4
tablespoons butter and 1 tablespoon olive oil in a large skillet and sauté the
fish until it is lightly browned on both sides. Transfer the fish to a platter
and keep it warm. In the fat remaining in the pan sauté 2 medium onions,
thinly sliced, and 1 green and 1 red bell pepper, seeded and thinly sliced,
until the onions are soft. Add 6 medium tomatoes, peeled and chopped, ½
small fresh hot red pepper, or ¼ teaspoon ground hot red pepper (cayenne),
2 tablespoons capers, and 20 small pimiento-stuffed green olives, and
simmer for 2 or 3 minutes. Add 1 cup dry red wine and ¼ cup olive oil and
simmer until the sauce is well blended, about 10 minutes. Add the fish and
cook just long enough to heat it through. Arrange on a warmed platter. Peel
and slice 1½ pounds potatoes and boil, covered, in salted water until tender, about 15 to 20 minutes. Drain and arrange around the edge of the
platter with the fish. Serves 4.

Variation: *Corvina a la Porteña* (Striped Bass, Buenos Aires Style) is an
Argentine cousin of both dishes. Cut a 2½- to 3-pound striped bass with
head and tail removed into 1½-inch slices and dredge them in flour. Pour
½ cup olive oil in a baking dish and arrange the fish slices in it. In a skillet
heat another cup of olive oil and sauté 2 medium onions, chopped, until

softened. Add 2 tomatoes, peeled and chopped, 2 sliced green bell peppers, a bay leaf, ½ teaspoon oregano, and salt and freshly ground pepper to taste. Simmer the mixture until it is thick and well blended. Pour the sauce over the fish and bake in a preheated moderate (350° F.) oven for 20 minutes, or until the fish is done. Discard the bay leaf. Transfer to a warmed platter and sprinkle with a tablespoon of chopped parsley. Serves 4.

Corvina a la Chorrillana   PERU
Striped Bass with Vegetables

This is bass in the style of Chorrillos, a resort 10 miles out of Lima. The annatto oil gives a distinctive flavor to this robust and satisfying dish. Chorrillos means literally "the little streams," which flow down from the Andes creating a green patch on this desert coast so that the town can exist — and hence the dish.

Serves 6

1 tablespoon annatto oil (see page 324)
2 large onions, finely sliced
2 cloves garlic, chopped
2 large tomatoes, peeled and sliced
2 large or 4 small fresh hot red or green peppers, seeded and sliced
½ teaspoon oregano
Salt, freshly ground pepper

3 pounds striped bass, cut into 6 steaks
2 tablespoons peanut oil
Juice of 1 lemon

Pour the annatto oil into a heavy casserole so that it covers the bottom evenly. Make a layer of half the onions, garlic, tomatoes, and peppers. Sprinkle with half the oregano and season to taste with salt and pepper. Arrange the fish on top of the vegetables and cover with the remaining vegetables. Season with the rest of the oregano, salt and pepper, the peanut oil, and the lemon juice. Cover the casserole and cook over low heat for 20 to 30 minutes, or until the vegetables are tender. Serve with *Arroz Graneado* (Peruvian Style Rice).

Variation: Omit the oregano and use 2 tablespoons finely chopped fresh green coriander (cilantro) instead.

Corvina Rellena   ARGENTINA
Stuffed Striped Bass

Serves 4

A 3- to 3½-pound striped bass,
   cleaned and boned, with head
   and tail left on
Salt, freshly ground pepper
1 medium onion, finely chopped
2 cloves garlic, finely chopped or
   crushed

½ cup finely chopped parsley
1 cup fresh breadcrumbs
Milk
1 tablespoon butter
1 tablespoon olive oil
1 cup dry white wine

Rinse the fish and pat dry with paper towels. Season the inside of the fish with salt and pepper. In a bowl combine the onion, garlic, parsley, breadcrumbs, and salt and pepper to taste. Moisten the mixture with a little milk and stuff the fish with the mixture. Fasten with toothpicks. Butter a shallow, heatproof casserole that will hold the fish comfortably, and arrange the fish in it. Dot the fish with the butter and pour the olive oil over it, then pour the white wine over it. Bake in a preheated hot (400° F.) oven for 40 minutes, or until the fish feels firm when pressed with a finger. The wine will have reduced, combining with the butter and oil to form a sauce. Serve directly from the casserole. Accompany with rice or potatoes and a green vegetable or salad.

Mero en Mac-Cum   MEXICO
Striped Bass in Sauce

This dish with achiote (annatto), cumin, and Seville orange juice is typical of the Mayan kitchen of Yucatán.

Serves 4

2 pounds striped bass, or any
   firm-fleshed, non-oily white
   fish, cut into 4 steaks
4 large cloves garlic, crushed
Black pepper
¼ teaspoon ground cumin
½ teaspoon oregano

1 teaspoon achiote (annatto),
   ground
Salt
½ cup Seville (bitter) orange juice,
   about, or a mixture of
   two-thirds orange juice to
   one-third lime juice

½ cup olive oil
1 large onion, thinly sliced
2 cloves garlic, minced
2 tomatoes, sliced
2 medium red bell peppers, seeded
    and sliced, or 2 canned
    pimientos, cut into strips

1 fresh hot pepper, seeded and
    chopped (optional)
2 tablespoons chopped parsley

Put the fish steaks on a platter in a single layer. Make a dressing of the garlic, 6 or more grinds black pepper, cumin, oregano, achiote (annatto), salt to taste, and enough orange juice to make a thin paste. Coat the steaks on both sides with the mixture and let stand for 30 minutes. Pour a little of the olive oil into a shallow baking dish large enough to hold the fish steaks. Use only enough oil to coat the bottom of the dish. Arrange the fish steaks, with any remaining marinade, in the dish. Top the steaks with the onion, minced garlic, tomatoes, and peppers. Pour the rest of the oil over the fish, cover, and cook over low heat until the fish loses its translucent look, about 15 minutes. Sprinkle with the parsley and serve with rice. Fresh hot tortillas may also be served.

Peixe em Môlho de Tangerina   NORTHERN BRAZIL
Fish in Tangerine Sauce

Serves 4

A 3-pound red snapper or bass,
    cleaned, with head and tail
    left on
2 tablespoons lemon juice
Salt, freshly ground pepper
Butter
1 tablespoon olive oil

1 tablespoon melted butter
¼ pound mushrooms, sliced
1 tablespoon chopped parsley
1 scallion, chopped, using green
    and white parts
1 cup dry white wine
½ cup tangerine juice

Season the fish with lemon juice, salt, and pepper. Put the fish in a buttered baking dish just large enough to hold it and pour over it the olive oil and melted butter. Sprinkle the fish with the mushrooms, parsley, and scallion. Pour the wine and tangerine juice over it and bake in a preheated hot (400° F.) oven for 25 to 30 minutes, or until it flakes easily when tested with a fork.

Pescado con Cilantro   MEXICO
Fish with Coriander

Fresh coriander leaves give this dish a delectable flavor, especially for addicts of the herb, of which I am one. It is a colonial dish, and very easy to make, which is unusual as many of the older recipes are rather long-winded. Plain White Rice (*Arroz Blanco*), cooked in the Mexican style, is the perfect accompaniment.

Serves 6

3 pounds fillets of red snapper,
    striped bass, flounder, or any
    firm white-fleshed fish
Salt, freshly ground pepper
¼ cup lemon juice
5 tablespoons vegetable oil

1 medium onion, finely chopped
½ cup chopped fresh coriander
    (cilantro)
3 canned jalapeño chilies, rinsed,
    seeded, and chopped

Season the fish with salt and pepper and sprinkle with the lemon juice. Heat 4 tablespoons of the oil in a skillet and sauté the onion until it is soft. Lightly film with oil the surface of a shallow ovenproof casserole large enough to hold the fish comfortably, in more than one layer if necessary. Arrange the fish fillets, with any liquid they may have yielded, in the casserole, cover with the onion and the oil, and sprinkle with the coriander and chilies. Drizzle with the remaining tablespoon of oil. Bake in a preheated moderate (350° F.) oven for 20 minutes, or until the fish has lost its translucent look.

Pescado Frito
con Salsa de Vino Tinto
Fried Fish with Red Wine Sauce   COLOMBIA

The red wine and tomatoes combine here to make a full-flavored sauce with the subtle pinch of allspice that I find very attractive and out of the ordinary.

Serves 4

2 pounds fish steaks, cut into 4
    pieces, using any firm-fleshed
    white fish such as red
    snapper, striped bass, tile fish,
    etc.
Salt, freshly ground pepper
Flour
4 tablespoons vegetable oil

2 medium onions, finely chopped
2 cloves garlic, minced
4 medium tomatoes, peeled and
    chopped
1 bay leaf
Pinch each cayenne pepper and
    ground allspice
1 cup dry red wine

Season the fish steaks with salt and pepper and coat lightly with flour, shaking to remove the excess. Heat the oil in a skillet and sauté the fish until lightly browned on both sides. Transfer to a platter and keep warm. In the oil remaining in the pan (add a little more if necessary), sauté the onions and garlic until the onions are soft. Add the tomatoes, bay leaf, cayenne pepper and allspice, and salt and pepper to taste, and sauté, stirring from time to time, until the mixture is thick and well blended, about 5 minutes. Stir in the wine and bring to a simmer. Add the fish and simmer for 2 or 3 minutes. Transfer the fish to a warmed serving dish and pour the sauce over it. Serve with rice, potatoes, or any starchy accompaniment.

Pargo al Horno   VENEZUELA
Baked Red Snapper

Serves 4

A 3- to 3½-pound red snapper,
    cleaned and boned, with head
    and tail left on, or striped or
    black bass
Salt, freshly ground pepper

4 tablespoons butter
¼ cup lime or lemon juice
1 cup fish stock or clam juice
½ cup heavy cream
1 teaspoon Worcestershire sauce

Rinse the fish and pat dry with paper towels. Season the fish inside and outside with salt and pepper. Using 1 tablespoon of the butter, grease a shallow, heatproof casserole that will hold the fish comfortably and arrange the fish in it. Combine the lime or lemon juice and fish stock and pour over the fish. Dot the fish with 1 tablespoon of the butter and bake in a preheated hot (400° F.) oven for 30 minutes, or until the fish feels firm when pressed with a finger. Using 2 spatulas, lift the fish out onto a serving platter and keep warm. Pour the liquid from the casserole into a small saucepan. Stir in the heavy cream and bring it to a simmer over moderate heat. Cut the remaining 2 tablespoons of butter into small pieces and stir in. Taste for seasoning and add more salt and pepper if necessary. Spoon a little of the sauce over the fish and serve the rest separately in a sauceboat. Accompany with potatoes or rice and a green vegetable.

Congrio en Fuente de Barro   CHILE
Fish with Tomatoes and Onions

Congrio, that very splendid large fish found in Chilean waters, is considered by Chileans to be the finest of all their food fishes. There are three kinds, *congrio colorado, congrio negro,* and *congrio dorado,* red, black, and gold fish. They made a fine sight when I saw them hanging up in a Santiago fish market, looking rather like eels with their big heads and tapering bodies — which explains their equivocal common name, for *congrio* is the Spanish word for eel. Eels these are not. They are *Genypterus chilensis,* living in the waters off Chile's long Pacific coast and existing as far north as Peruvian waters. Their only known relatives are a New Zealand fish known as ling, but not to be confused with the European ling to which it is not related.

The fish is firm-fleshed and when cooked breaks into large flakes. In my experience cod is the best substitute, though any firm-fleshed non-oily fish can be used successfully. The term *"fuente de barro"* simply means cooked in earthenware. Though any casserole may be used, the dish is better when cooked in earthenware. A lovely, satisfying, full-flavored dish.

Serves 4

2 pounds fillets of scrod or cod, cut
    into 4 pieces
Salt, freshly ground pepper
2 tablespoons lemon juice
3 tablespoons butter
1 teaspoon sweet paprika
1 large onion, finely chopped
4 medium tomatoes, peeled and
    chopped

4 slices firm white bread, fried in
    butter, or 1 pound potatoes,
    boiled and sliced
2 hardboiled eggs, sliced
1 sweet red pepper, seeded and
    cut into strips
½ cup milk (optional)
1 tablespoon chopped parsley

Season the fish with salt, pepper, and lemon juice, and set aside. Heat the butter in a skillet, stir in the paprika, add the onion, and sauté over moderate heat until it is soft. Add the tomatoes and sauté for a few minutes longer. Butter an earthenware casserole and put a layer of the tomato mixture, then the fish, more tomato, the fried bread or potatoes, and more tomato. Repeat until all these ingredients are used up. Or you may have a casserole large enough to hold the fish in a single layer. Top with the sliced hardboiled eggs and pepper strips. Cover and bake in a preheated moderate (350° F.) oven for 30 minutes. If the dish seems to be drying out during cooking, add up to ½ cup milk. This should not be necessary if the tomatoes are fully ripe and juicy. Sprinkle with parsley and serve.

Variation: I was quite astonished one day in Asunción, capital of land-locked Paraguay, to be given a dish remarkably like *Congrio en Fuente de Barro* from Chile, which is more seacoast than anything else and has a most remarkable harvest of fish and shellfish. The fish in this *Guiso de Dorado* was from the Paraguay River, a great, noble waterway. It seemed to me in flavor and texture very like the Spanish *dorado*, dolphin fish, and so it turned out to be, though not, of course, to be confused with the mammalian dolphin. *Dorado* is a famous fish of Paraguayan rivers and wholly delectable. Any firm-fleshed white fish would make a suitable substitute.

For *Guiso de Dorado* (Fish Stew), put 2 pounds fish, cut into 4 steaks, into a flat dish and season them with salt and pepper. Pour ¼ cup lemon juice over the steaks and let them stand 1 hour, turning once or twice. Lift out, pat dry with paper towels, and dust with flour. Heat ½ cup olive or vegetable oil in a casserole and sauté the fish steaks until golden on both sides. Arrange half the fish steaks in the casserole. Have ready 2 medium onions, thinly sliced, 2 cloves garlic, minced, 2 tomatoes, peeled and sliced, 2 red or green bell peppers, seeded and sliced, and 2 medium potatoes, peeled and thinly sliced. Arrange half of the onions, garlic, to-matoes, peppers, and potatoes over the fish. Top with a bay leaf, a sprig of thyme, and 2 or 3 sprigs of parsley. Season to taste with salt and pepper and top with the rest of the fish and the remaining vegetables. Season again with salt and pepper. Pour ½ cup each dry white wine and fish stock, or clam juice, or water, over the fish, cover tightly, bring to a simmer, and cook for 20 to 30 minutes, or until the potatoes and fish are both tender. Check to see if the fish is drying out during the cooking time and add a little more stock or wine if necessary. Serves 4.

Pescado en Escabeche   PERU
Fish in Oil and Vinegar Sauce

Pescado en Escabeche is very popular throughout Latin America. The cooking technique is of Spanish origin, but cooks have changed recipes adding an herb or vegetable, altering things a little, so that there is a whole group of New World *escabeche* dishes that make splendid appetizers or main courses.

Serves 6

3 pounds of any firm-fleshed white
    fish such as red snapper or
    striped bass, cut into 6 fillets
    or 6 steaks
Salt, freshly ground pepper
Flour
3 tablespoons butter or lard

1 cup olive oil or vegetable oil
3 medium onions, thickly sliced
1 or 2 fresh hot red or green
    peppers, seeded and cut into
    strips
¼ teaspoon oregano
4 tablespoons white vinegar

Season the fish with salt and pepper and dredge in flour, shaking to remove the excess. Heat the butter or lard in a skillet and sauté the fish until lightly browned on both sides. Transfer the cooked fish to a shallow serving dish and keep warm. Heat the oil in a medium-sized saucepan, add the onions and pepper strips, and cook over low heat until the onions are soft and very lightly browned. Stir in the oregano and cook for a minute longer. Pour in the vinegar, stir, and pour over the fish. Serve immediately.

For a more robust dish, garnish with 3 ears of freshly cooked corn, each cut into 4 slices, 3 hardboiled eggs, halved, lettuce leaves, and olives.

Variation: This Argentine version, *Merluza a la Vinagreta* (Hake in Vinaigrette Sauce), is quite different from the Peruvian one. Wash and pat dry 3 pounds of hake fillets, cut into 12 pieces, or use cod or any firm-fleshed white fish. Sprinkle the fish with salt, preferably coarse salt, and let stand for 1 hour. Rinse and dry. Dredge in flour, shaking to remove the excess, and sauté in 3 tablespoons olive oil until the fish has lost its translucent look. A good rule is to measure the thickness of the fish and give it 10 minutes to the inch, 5 minutes on each side. Arrange the cooked fish in a shallow dish and pour on a sauce made by mixing 1 clove garlic, peeled and finely chopped, 4 cornichons, chopped, 2 hardboiled eggs, chopped, 2 tablespoons capers, 2 tablespoons finely chopped parsley, salt, freshly ground pepper, 1 cup wine vinegar, and 1 cup olive oil. Let the fish stand for at least an hour before serving. Serve, garnished with lettuce leaves, at room temperature. Serves 12 as a first course.

Variation: *Pescado en Escabeche* from Mexico can be made with a variety of fish including pompano, mackerel, red snapper, or snook. Cut 2 pounds of fish fillets into 8 pieces and sprinkle them with 3 tablespoons lemon juice. Let the fish stand for 15 minutes, turning the pieces once. Rinse gently in cold water and pat dry. In a skillet heat 4 tablespoons of olive oil and sauté the fish until it has lost its translucent look and is lightly browned on both sides. Lift the fish out of the skillet and place in a dish.

In a saucepan combine 2 whole cloves, a 1-inch piece of stick cinnamon, 6 peppercorns, 2 cloves garlic, ⅛ teaspoon ground cumin, ¼ teaspoon thyme, ½ teaspoon oregano, 2 bay leaves, 2 whole fresh hot green peppers, preferably *serrano*, with stems left on, 6 sliced scallions, using white and green parts, salt to taste, and 1 cup white vinegar. Bring to a boil, lower the heat, and simmer, uncovered, for 2 or 3 minutes, or until the scallions are soft. Set aside. In another small saucepan or skillet heat 1 cup olive oil with 2 cloves garlic and fry the garlic over low heat until browned. Lift out and discard the garlic. Pour the oil into the saucepan with the vinegar mixture, heat to a simmer, and pour the mixture over the fish. Allow to cool, cover, and refrigerate for 24 hours. To serve, lift out the fish onto a shallow serving platter and sprinkle with a little oregano crumbled between the fingers, if liked. Garnish the platter with shredded lettuce tossed in vinaigrette sauce (page 326), 2 tablespoons capers, 2 canned *jalapeño* chilies, cut into strips, 1 bunch radishes, cut into flowers, and about 24 small pimiento-stuffed green olives. Serve with tortillas as an appetizer for 8. This makes a pleasant light lunch for 4.

Variation: For *Pescado en Escabeche* from Cuba, sauté 2 pounds fillets of red snapper or similar fish, cut into 8 pieces, in 1 cup olive oil until the fish has lost its translucent look and is lightly browned on both sides. Lift out the fish and arrange it in a shallow casserole or serving dish. Sauté 3 medium onions, thinly sliced, and 2 cloves garlic, chopped, in the oil remaining in the skillet until the onion slices are soft. Pour the onions, garlic, and oil over the fish. In a small saucepan heat ½ cup wine vinegar with 1 bay leaf, 6 peppercorns, ¼ teaspoon each thyme and marjoram, and 1 teaspoon paprika. Pour the mixture over the fish, allow to cool, and refrigerate for 24 hours. Serve as a first course garnished with lettuce leaves, small pitted green olives, and cornichons. Serves 8.

Variation: For *Escabeche de Atún* (Fresh Tuna in Oil and Vinegar Sauce), put a 1-pound slice of tuna in a skillet with ¼ cup olive oil, 4 tablespoons lemon juice, and a bay leaf and simmer, turning once, until the fish is done, 10 minutes for each inch of thickness. Lift out, remove any bones and skin, and cut into 4 pieces. Rinse out and dry the skillet. Heat ¼ cup olive oil in the skillet and sauté 2 medium onions, thinly sliced, and 2 red bell peppers, seeded and sliced, until the onions are tender. Add ½ pound cooked, sliced carrots, ½ pound cooked green beans cut into 1-inch pieces, and ½ pound cooked potatoes, peeled and sliced. Sauté for 2 or 3 minutes. Add the tuna, 2 tablespoons vinegar, and salt and pepper to taste. Remove from the heat, cool, and serve on a bed of lettuce. Mustard pickles are sometimes served with this. Serves 4 as an appetizer, 2 as a main course.

Sábalo Guisado con Coco   COLOMBIA
Shad Fillets in Coconut Milk

Coconut milk is used a great deal in the cooking of coastal Colombia, giving dishes an interestingly different flavor, rich yet delicate.

Serves 6

3 pounds boned shad fillets, cut
  into 6 pieces
3 medium tomatoes, peeled,
  seeded, and chopped
1 medium onion, finely chopped
1 or 2 fresh hot red or green
  peppers, left whole with
  stem on

Salt, freshly ground pepper
4 cups thin coconut milk, about
  (see page 7)
1 cup thick coconut milk (see
  page 7)

Arrange the fish fillets in a shallow flameproof casserole and cover with the tomatoes and onion. Lay the hot peppers on top. Season to taste with salt and pepper. Pour in the thin coconut milk, and simmer for about 10 minutes or until the fish is no longer translucent. A simple rule is to measure the thickness of the fish and cook it 10 minutes to the inch. Carefully lift out the fish onto a serving platter and keep warm. Discard the hot peppers. Reduce the liquid in the casserole to about 1 cup over brisk heat. Add the thick coconut milk and simmer just long enough to heat the sauce through. Strain the sauce but do not push the solids through the sieve. Pour the sauce over the fish. Serve with rice.

The fish may be cooked in a preheated moderate (350° F.) oven. In this case bring the liquid just to a simmer on top of the stove, transfer the casserole to the oven, and cook for 10 minutes to the inch, which will be about 10 minutes for fillets. Make the sauce in the same way. Any firm-fleshed white fish can be used for this dish when shad is not in season, making it *Pescado Guisado con Coco* (Fish Cooked in Coconut Milk).

If the peppers are very hot (nibble a tiny bit to check), the sauce may be too *picante* for some tastes. A simple solution is to take the peppers out of the sauce after 2 or 3 minutes instead of leaving them there for the full cooking time.

MOQUECAS

The mixture of indigenous Indian, African, and Portuguese cooking that makes up Bahian cuisine is particularly apparent in the *moquecas*, which I translate as stews for want of a better word. According to that great authority on the Bahian kitchen Darwin Brandão, *moquecas* were originally Indian *pokekas* — dishes wrapped in banana leaves and cooked over charcoal. Africans brought over as slaves and working as cooks for the Portuguese in the great houses of the sugar plantations around Bahia modified the indigenous dishes, and today *moquecas*, whether of shrimp, fish, crab, or whatever, are cooked in a saucepan on top of the stove. Coconut milk, *dendê* oil, and hot peppers are typical ingredients in these flavorful dishes.

Moqueca de Peixe   BRAZIL
Fish Stew

Serves 6

*3 pounds fillets of sole or any
    white fish
2 medium onions, chopped
1 or 2 fresh hot peppers, seeded
    and chopped
3 medium tomatoes, peeled and
    chopped*

*1 clove garlic, chopped
2 tablespoons fresh coriander
    (cilantro)
Salt
4 tablespoons lime or lemon juice
¼ cup dendê (palm) oil*

Cut the fish into 2-inch pieces and place in a large bowl. In a blender or food processor combine the onions, hot peppers, tomatoes, garlic, coriander, salt to taste, and the lime or lemon juice, and reduce to a purée. Pour the purée over the fish, mixing lightly, and allow to stand for 1 hour. Transfer the fish and the marinade to a saucepan. Add ½ cup cold water and ⅛ cup of the *dendê* oil. Cover and simmer until the fish is done, about 8 minutes. Pour in the remaining ⅛ cup *dendê* oil and cook just long enough to heat the oil through. Transfer the stew to a heated serving platter and surround with a border of plain white rice.

Variation: *Moqueca de Camarão* (Shrimp Stew). This is a very interesting *moqueca*. Substitute 2 pounds raw shrimp, shelled and deveined, for the fish. Shorten the cooking time to about 3 minutes, or just long enough for the shrimp to turn pink and lose their translucent look. Stir in 1 cup thick coconut milk with the shrimp. Omit the water. Serves 6.

Moqueca de Camarão
Bahian Shrimp Stew

BRAZIL

Serves 6

¼ cup olive oil
1 large onion, finely chopped
2 small carrots, scraped and thinly
    sliced
1 green bell pepper, seeded and
    chopped
1 red bell pepper, seeded and
    chopped

4 medium tomatoes, peeled,
    seeded, and chopped
Salt, freshly ground pepper
2 pounds large shrimp, shelled
    and deveined
2 tablespoons dendê (palm) oil

Heat the olive oil in a large, heavy skillet and sauté the onion, carrots, and green and red peppers until the onion is soft. Add the tomatoes and salt and pepper to taste, and cook for a few minutes longer over moderate heat. Stir in the shrimp and the *dendê* oil and cook, turning the shrimp once or twice, until the shrimp are pink and have lost their translucent look, about 3 minutes. Serve on a warmed platter surrounded by white rice. Serve separately with *Môlho de Pimenta e Azeite de Dendê* (Hot Peppers in Palm Oil), page 313, or *Môlho de Pimenta e Limão* (Hot Pepper and Lime Sauce), page 313.

SHRIMP DISHES

Shrimp in Latin America are magnificent in quality and abundant in quantity and in my experience almost always beautifully cooked, juicy, and well flavored. It takes discipline in Bahia to eat anything *but* shrimp, they are so delicious. Tomatoes and peppers, both sweet and hot, are used a great deal with shrimp, but because each country uses different seasoning, or different ways of preparing them, the finished dishes are quite varied in flavor. Perhaps the most unusual is the *Vatapá de Camarão e Peixe* (Shrimp and Fish in Coconut, Nut, and Shrimp Sauce), which illustrates the exuberance of this extraordinarily imaginative kitchen, where improbable combinations, such as dried and fresh shrimp, almonds and cashew nuts, *dendê* oil and coconut milk, marry in an exciting way — a lovely dish for a party (and fortunately a food processor simplifies the work).

Vatapá de Camarão e Peixe   BRAZIL
Shrimp and Fish in Coconut, Nut, and Shrimp Sauce

Serves 6 to 8

1 cup dried shrimp
¼ cup dendê *(palm) oil or olive oil*
2 medium onions, grated
2 cloves garlic, crushed
1 cup cashew nuts, ground
1 cup blanched almonds, ground
1 cup fresh breadcrumbs
4 cups thin coconut milk (see
   page 7)

2 or more tablespoons dendê
   (palm) oil
2 tablespoons olive oil
2 pounds see bass fillets, or other
   white fish
1 pound shrimp, shelled and
   deveined

Soak the dried shrimp in warm water to cover for 15 minutes. Drain the shrimp, then purée in a blender or food processor, or put through a food mill, using the fine blade. Set aside.

Heat ¼ cup *dendê* or olive oil in a heavy skillet and sauté the onions, garlic, cashew nuts, almonds, and the puréed shrimp for 5 minutes. Stir in the breadcrumbs and the coconut milk, and simmer, stirring occasionally, until the mixture has the consistency of a thick béchamel sauce. Add more breadcrumbs if necessary. Remove from the heat and stir in 2 or more tablespoons of *dendê* oil to taste.

Heat 2 tablespoons olive oil in a skillet and sauté the fish lightly. Add the fresh shrimp, and sauté for about 2 minutes, or until the shrimp turn pink. Fold the shrimp and fish mixture into the coconut milk sauce. Serve with *Angú de Arroz* (Molded Rice) and a hot pepper sauce (see page 311), if liked.

Camarones Acapulqueños
Shrimp, Acapulco Style

MEXICO

Serves 4

1 pound medium to large shrimp	3 tablespoons tomato paste
4 tablespoons butter	Salt, freshly ground pepper
2 cloves garlic, minced	1/3 cup brandy
1/4 cup parsley, finely chopped	
3 medium tomatoes, peeled and chopped	

Peel and devein the shrimp and set aside. Put the shrimp shells into a small saucepan with 2 cups water, bring to a boil, reduce the heat, and simmer, uncovered, for 20 minutes. Strain and discard the shells. Measure the liquid. There should be 1 cup. If necessary, reduce it over brisk heat or make up the quantity with water. Reserve.

Heat the butter in a casserole and add the garlic and parsley, and sauté for 2 minutes, taking care not to let the garlic burn. Add the tomatoes and simmer until the mixture is thick, about 10 minutes. Add the reserved shrimp stock and the tomato paste, stir to mix, season with salt and pepper, and add the brandy. Bring to a simmer, add the shrimp, cover, and cook for 2 to 3 minutes, according to the size of the shrimp, until they are pink, taking care not to overcook. Serve on a bed of rice.

Camarão com Leite de Côco   BRAZIL
Shrimp in Coconut Milk

A Bahamian dish that I find enticing.

Serves 6

1 ½ pounds large shrimp
3 cloves garlic, crushed
6 tablespoons lime or lemon juice
Salt, freshly ground pepper
¼ cup vegetable oil
1 large onion, grated

3 scallions, chopped, using white
  and green parts
3 medium tomatoes, peeled,
  seeded, and chopped
1 ½ cups thick coconut milk (see
  page 7)

Peel and devein the shrimp, saving the shells. Put the shrimp in a bowl with the garlic, lime or lemon juice, and salt and pepper to taste. Set aside.

Place the reserved shrimp shells in a saucepan with 3 cups water and simmer briskly, uncovered, for 30 minutes, or until the liquid is reduced to ¾ cup. Strain, discard the shells, and set the stock aside.

Heat the oil in a skillet and sauté the onion and scallions for 3 minutes, or until the onion is softened. Add the tomatoes and the shrimp stock to the skillet and simmer until the mixture is well blended and quite thick, about 5 minutes. Stir in the thick coconut milk and the shrimp with their liquid, and cook, uncovered, until the shrimp are pink and have lost their translucent look, about 3 minutes. Turn the shrimp over once or twice during the cooking. Be careful not to overcook the shrimp as they toughen very quickly. Taste for salt and pepper and add a little more if necessary. Serve on a bed of plain white rice.

Cuajado de Camarones   COLOMBIA
Shrimp and Potato Omelet

Cuajado means a dish made in a skillet with meat, fish, or fruit, and eggs to hold it together. "Omelet" seems the best word to describe it but the eggs do not play as large a role as they would in a French omelet, pushed off center stage by the onions, tomatoes, potatoes, and shrimp. Though not a heavy dish, this is robust and satisfying and served with a green salad makes an excellent lunch or dinner.

Serves 4

3 tablespoons butter
1 teaspoon sweet paprika
2 medium onions, finely chopped
3 large tomatoes, peeled, seeded,
    and chopped
Salt, freshly ground pepper
2 medium-sized new potatoes,
    cooked and cubed

4 large eggs, separated
1 pound small or medium-sized
    raw shrimp, peeled and cut
    into ½-inch pieces

Heat the butter in a large (10-inch) skillet, stir in the paprika and the onions and sauté over moderate heat until the onions are soft. Add the tomatoes and salt and pepper to taste and cook until the mixture is thick and well blended, about 5 minutes. Add the potatoes and cook for a few minutes longer. Beat the egg yolks until they are thick and lemony. In a separate bowl beat the egg whites until they stand in firm peaks. Fold the whites and yolks together with a spatula. Return the skillet to the heat, fold the shrimp into the sauce, cook 2 minutes for small shrimp, 3 for medium-sized ones. Then fold in the eggs, mixing thoroughly. Cook until the eggs are lightly set.

Arroz con Mariscos   PERU
Rice with Shellfish

This is a really festive dish with its shrimp-flavored rice and rich mixture of shellfish. The secret is in cooking the shellfish just until they are done and not a second longer as they toughen very quickly with overcooking.

Serves 4 to 6

4 tablespoons olive oil, about
1 large onion, finely chopped
2 cloves garlic, minced
2 fresh hot peppers,* preferably
    red, seeded and cut into strips
2 cups long-grain rice
4 cups shrimp stock
1 or 2 tablespoons fresh coriander
    (cilantro), chopped

½ pound medium-sized shrimp,
    about 18
½ pound scallops — if small, left
    whole; if large, halved
12 cherrystone or littleneck clams
12 oysters

---

*Peruvians for the most part like their food hot and are lavish in their use of *ajíes*, hot peppers, which in fact lend flavor as well as heat. A wicked Peruvian friend of mine says that his compatriots like *picante* food as it gives them an excuse to quench the fire with *pisco* sours, a lovely local drink, or with anything else alcoholic. However, use just as much, or as little, of the hot pepper as suits your personal taste.

Heat the oil in a skillet and sauté the onion, garlic, and pepper strips until the onion is soft. Using a slotted spoon, transfer the onion mixture to a casserole. There should be about 2 tablespoons oil left in the skillet. Add a little more if necessary. Add the rice and sauté until the rice has absorbed the oil, taking care not to let it brown. Transfer the rice to a casserole. Add the shrimp stock, bring to a boil over high heat, reduce the heat to low, and cook, covered, until the rice is tender and all the liquid absorbed, about 20 minutes. Add the coriander and the shrimp, scallops, and clams, folding them well into the rice. Cook, covered, over low heat for about 3 to 5 minutes, or until the shrimp have turned pink and lost their translucent look. Add the oysters, folding them into the rice and cook just long enough to plump them, about 1 minute. Serve immediately.

To make shrimp stock: In a small saucepan heat 1 tablespoon olive oil and toss the shrimp shells in this until they turn pink. Add 1 sprig parsley, 1 slice onion, or a sliced scallion, using white and green parts, 1 sprig thyme or ⅛ teaspoon dried, 3 or 4 peppercorns, and 4 cups water. Bring to a boil, reduce the heat, and simmer, covered, for 30 minutes. Strain and measure. There should be about 3 cups. Measure the liquid from the oysters and clams. If there is more than 1 cup, reduce the shrimp stock, uncovered, over brisk heat so that there will be 4 cups stock. Cool the stock and stir in the oyster and clam liquid. Season to taste with salt.

Moqueca de Siri Mole

BRAZIL

Softshell Crabs in Coconut Milk

Serves 2

6 softshell crabs, cleaned and
    ready for cooking
2 tablespoons dendê (palm) oil or
    olive oil
1 small onion, finely chopped
2 medium tomatoes, peeled and
    chopped
1 tablespoon fresh coriander
    (cilantro), chopped

1 or 2 fresh hot red peppers, seeded
    and chopped
1 tablespoon lime or lemon juice
¾ cup thin coconut milk (see
    page 7)
Salt, freshly ground pepper

Rinse the crabs, pat them dry with paper towels, and set aside. In a skillet heat the oil and add the onion, tomatoes, coriander, hot peppers, and lime or lemon juice. Cook, stirring from time to time, over moderate heat for 5 minutes. Add the coconut milk and the crabs and cook for about 8 minutes, turning the crabs once or twice. Serve with plain rice or *Pirão de Arroz* (Rice Flour Pudding).

Variation: Omit the coconut milk and use 4 tomatoes.

SALT COD DISHES

Many fish stores, some supermarkets, and most Latin American markets and specialty stores sell salt cod, so that it will be easy to duplicate these typical Latin American dishes. It is sold packaged by the pound, sometimes in a box, sometimes as a piece cut from a whole fish, often very large. There is no important difference between the two except that the packaged fish is usually boneless while pieces from the whole fish may be quite bony, involving a little extra work.

Bacalao en Salsa de Chile Ancho y Almendra   MEXICO
Salt Cod in Mild Red Chili and Almond Sauce

Serves 4 to 6

2 pounds salt cod
1 medium onion, chopped
1 whole clove garlic

1 recipe Salsa de Chile Ancho y Almendra *(Mild Red Chili and Almond Sauce), page 315*
1 teaspoon red wine vinegar

Soak the cod in cold water to cover for 12 hours or more, changing the water 5 or 6 times. Drain the fish and put into a saucepan with the onion and garlic and cold water to cover. Bring to a boil, reduce the heat, and simmer, covered, for 15 minutes, or until the fish is tender. Drain the fish. Strain and reserve the stock. Remove any skin and bones from the fish and cut into 2- to 3-inch pieces.

Make the sauce and thin it with 2 cups of the reserved fish stock, stir to mix, and simmer for a minute or two. Add the fish and the vinegar and simmer for 5 minutes. Serve with rice.

Bacalhau a Baíana   BRAZIL
Salt Cod, Bahia Style

This Brazilian dish of salt cod cooked in a tomato mixture is the most original of these popular dishes, but other versions are good, too.

Serves 4

1 pound salt cod
3 tablespoons vegetable oil
1 medium onion, grated
1 clove garlic, crushed
2 sweet peppers, 1 red, 1 green,
*   seeded and chopped*
3 tomatoes, peeled and puréed

1 cup hot water
Salt, freshly ground pepper
1 tablespoon dendê (palm) oil
1 cup thick coconut milk (see
*   page 7)*
1 cup scallions, chopped, using
*   white and green parts*

Soak the cod in cold water to cover for 12 hours or more, changing the water frequently. Drain the fish and remove any skin and bones. Pat the fish dry with paper towels and cut it into 2-inch pieces. Heat the oil in a saucepan and sauté the onion, garlic, and peppers until the onion and peppers are soft, about 5 minutes. Add the tomatoes, fish, and hot water. Cover and simmer for 15 minutes, or until the fish flakes easily when tested with a fork. Season to taste with salt, if necessary, pepper, and *dendê* oil. Stir in the coconut milk and the scallions and heat through without letting the mixture boil.

Variation: *Bacalao a la Criolla* (Salt Cod, Creole Style), from Venezuela. Prepare the cod as for *Bacalhau a Baíana*. Heat 4 tablespoons of olive or vegetable oil in a casserole and sauté 1 large onion, finely chopped, with 3 cloves garlic, minced, until the onion is tender. Add 3 large tomatoes, peeled and chopped, ½ teaspoon cumin, ½ teaspoon oregano, pepper to taste, and a bay leaf, and simmer for 5 minutes. Add the fish, 1 cup dry white wine, 2 tablespoons lemon juice, and salt if necessary. Simmer until the fish is tender, about 15 minutes. Accompany with rice. Serves 4.

Bacalhau a Mineira

BRAZIL

Salt Cod and Cabbage, Minas Gerais Style

Serves 4

1 pound salt cod
3 tablespoons olive oil
1 onion, finely chopped
1 clove garlic, crushed
1 sweet red pepper, seeded and
    chopped, or 1 green pepper
3 medium tomatoes, peeled and
    chopped

¼ cup chopped parsley
½ cup dry white wine
Freshly ground pepper
1 pound (5 cups) shredded
    cabbage
Salt

Soak the cod in cold water to cover for 12 hours or more, changing the water frequently. Drain the fish and remove any skin and bones. Pat the fish dry with paper towels and cut it into 2-inch pieces. Heat the oil in a large skillet and sauté the onion, garlic, pepper, tomatoes, and parsley for 5 minutes, stirring occasionally. Add the fish, wine, pepper to taste, and cabbage. Stir to mix and simmer, partially covered, until the cabbage is tender and the fish flakes easily when tested with a fork, about 15 minutes. Season with salt, if necessary.

Pudim de Bacalhau com Ovos   BRAZIL
Salt Cod with Eggs

This is an unusual and delicious first-course or breakfast dish. The salt cod in the tomato-flavored white sauce makes a rich topping for the egg.

Serves 6 as a first course, 3 as a breakfast

½ pound salt cod fillets
2 tablespoons cornstarch
2 cups milk
4 tablespoons (¼ cup) butter plus
   1 tablespoon
1 medium onion, grated
2 medium tomatoes, peeled,
   seeded, and chopped

2 tablespoons drained capers
Salt, freshly ground pepper
Butter for ramekins
6 eggs
3 tablespoons grated Parmesan
   cheese

Soak the cod in cold water to cover, changing the water several times, for 24 hours. Drain and rinse the fish. Put it into a saucepan with water to cover and poach it for 15 to 20 minutes, or until it flakes easily when tested with a fork. The water should just simmer. Drain and flake the fish and set it aside.

Mix the cornstarch with a little of the milk, add the rest of the milk, and pour the mixture into a small saucepan. Add 1 tablespoon of butter and cook, stirring, over moderate heat until the mixture is smooth and lightly thickened. Set aside.

In another saucepan heat the 4 tablespoons of butter, add the onion, and cook, stirring, for a few minutes. Add the tomatoes and cook until the mixture is thick and well blended. Stir in the Béchamel sauce and the capers. Fold in the codfish and add a little salt if necessary. Season generously with pepper. Cool slightly.

Butter six ⅔-cup-size ramekins and break an egg into each. Pour the codfish mixture over the eggs and sprinkle each ramekin with ½ tablespoon grated Parmesan cheese. This may also be cooked in a single shallow Pyrex dish. Bake in a preheated hot (400° F.) oven for 8 minutes.

Meats
Carnes

Nowhere in Latin American cooking is there such a coming together of introduced and indigenous foods and cooking methods as there is in the meat and poultry dishes. All of South and Central America, as well as Mexico, was poorly supplied with animals for meat. There were no sheep, goats, or cattle, all of which had been domesticated thousands of years before in the Middle East, and no domestic pigs or chickens, which had been supplying meat for a long while in Asia.

But the Aztecs did cultivate turkeys, ducks, quails, and doves among other birds, and they hunted a type of wild boar. Yucatán was known as the land of *Faisán y Venado* (the curassow pheasant and deer). From Mexico on south there were many rabbitlike animals from the small *agouti* to the *ñeque* or *paca*, the *viscacha*, and the huge *capybara*, weighing up to 150 pounds; this may explain why modern Latin America has so many splendid rabbit recipes. The *cuy* (pronounced kwee), a type of guinea pig, is still popular in Peru and tastes like young rabbit. The Incas bred the llama, vicuna, and alpaca from *guanacos*, small camel-like animals that still roam wild in herds in the Andean highlands. They supplied milk, meat, and soft, fleecy wool, while the llama did extra duty carrying loads as well.

The Spanish introduced sheep, goats, cattle, pigs, and chickens quite soon after the Conquest, and these were welcomed with varying degrees of enthusiasm into the Aztec, Inca, and Chibcha kitchens, among others. Pork and chicken were the favorites, reflected in the cooking of today. The new meats were incorporated into existing local dishes and, as the colonial kitchens evolved, new dishes were created, some with echoes from Spain's own colonial past, when the country had been dominated for nearly eight centuries by the Arabs. The Middle Eastern influence can still be seen in meat dishes cooked with almonds, raisins, cinnamon, and cloves, or with fruits, either dried or fresh. In Brazilian meat dishes, once again you find the contributions of the rich Portuguese cuisine, the indigenous foods of Africa like yams, nuts, and palm oil, blending with the local produce of the Indians. Dried shrimp and nuts may be ground together and mixed with coconut milk and rice flour to form a sauce colored gold with *dendê* oil — as luscious to the palate as to the eye.

The meeting of conqueror and conquered produced astoundingly rich and varied results, new food and old combined in a harmony of contrasting flavors, exuberant often, but never bland or dull. Chili peppers join chocolate to make an exotic sauce for Mexico's national dish, *Mole Poblano de Guajalote* (Turkey in Chili and Chocolate Sauce). Peppers and tomatoes used with nuts, and the herbs of both Old and New Worlds make aromatic sauces. In Peru, Brazil, and Ecuador shellfish, especially shrimp, make fascinating combinations with both meats and poultry. Fruits, fresh as well as dried, enhance beef or veal stews in Argentina and may be cooked in a large, hollowed-out squash, the vegetable itself becoming the cookpot. Tropical root vegetables, yams, taros, and sweet potatoes, transform everyday dishes into something unctuous, attractive, and different, and beans make all sorts of unusual combinations in dishes ranging from grand affairs like Brazil's *Feijoada Completa* (Black Beans with Mixed Meats) to simple ones like their *Tutú a Mineira* (Black Beans, Minas Gerais Style), where the vegetable dominates. Annatto and allspice, very much New World spices, enliven meat dishes.

Many traditional meat dishes in Latin America are types of stew, cooked on top of the stove, largely because reliable ovens are a comparatively new feature in kitchens where until recently tiled charcoal stoves were commonplace. Also much of the continent is mountainous and altitude is an important feature in cooking. It was discovered early that long, slow cooking gives very flavorful results, making meat tender and juicy. An advantage is that dishes can be prepared ahead of time and need little watching.

Argentina, which is famous for its beef, and Brazil, whose south is great cattle country, both have wonderful outdoor feasts, the *asado criollo* and the *churrasco.*

On this diverse continent there is a whole new world of flavors to be explored.

MEAT STEWS
WITH VEGETABLES AND WITH FRUIT

There is a seemingly inexhaustible range of meat stews — made from beef, veal, pork, lamb, kid — with vegetables and with fruits in the Latin American kitchen. Taste, texture, and aroma are balanced in excitingly different combinations, gentle, pungent, fiery, earthy, or elegant. Unusual ingredients are put together in subtle partnerships to produce a wonderful array of dishes, splendid for everyday eating, grand for guests as all the work can be done ahead of time. And despite a rich complexity of ingredients, cooking is straightforward. Long, slow simmering makes even the cheaper cuts of meat juicy and tender. Orange juice, wine, or vinegar is used to flavor and tenderize, nuts are used for flavor and to thicken the already richly flavored cooking liquid, and fruits, fresh and dried, lend a hint of acid blended with sweetness to the robustness of meat.

Seco de Carne   PERU
Beef Stew

This stew is very curiously named, since *seco* means dry. Once upon a time stews were very much more soupy than they are now and the *seco* here is simply to indicate that this is not a soupy stew like a pot-au-feu.

The ingredients are not exotic but the flavor of the finished stew is far from ordinary, as the garlic, hot pepper, fresh coriander, and lemon juice combine to give the sauce a fine flavor.

A similar stew made with kid, *Seco de Cabrito*, is a great favorite. Kid is more strongly flavored than beef and Peruvian cooks take advantage of this, adding extra coriander and white wine or *chicha*, a sort of corn beer, as well as stock to the dish, with very savory results. *Seco de Carnero* (Lamb Stew) and *Seco de Chancho* (Pork Stew) belong to the same family.

In Peru the potatoes used would be ones with yellow flesh, not to be confused with sweet potatoes. Though they are delicious as well as pretty, they taste the same as ordinary white potatoes.

Serves 6

4 tablespoons lard or vegetable oil
4 cloves garlic, finely chopped
1 medium onion, finely chopped
1 teaspoon ground hot pepper or
*   cayenne*
3 pounds beef chuck, cut into
*   1-inch cubes*

2 cups beef stock
Salt, freshly ground pepper
2 tablespoons fresh coriander
*   (cilantro), chopped*
Juice of 1 lemon
2 pounds potatoes, boiled and
*   halved*

Heat the lard or oil in a casserole and sauté the garlic, onion, hot pepper, and beef cubes until the beef is lightly browned. Add the beef stock, salt and pepper to taste, and the coriander. Cook, partially covered, over low heat until the beef is tender, 1½ to 2 hours. The liquid should be reduced so that the sauce is quite thick and not very abundant. Just before serving stir in the lemon juice and cook a minute or two longer. Heap the stew onto a warmed serving platter and surround with the freshly cooked, hot potato halves.

Variation: *Seco de Cabrito.* Make the stew as for the beef stew above, using 3 pounds boneless kid cut into 1-inch pieces instead of the beef. Use 1 fresh hot red or green pepper, seeded and finely chopped, instead of cayenne pepper, and increase the amount of fresh coriander to 1 cup. Use equal amounts of dry white wine and stock for the cooking liquid but use only enough barely to cover the meat. An authentic Peruvian touch would be to use 1 cup of *chicha* (corn beer). When the stew has been simmering, partially covered, for 2 hours, or when the kid is almost tender, add 6 medium-sized potatoes, peeled and halved, and cook for 20 minutes longer, or until both kid and potatoes are tender. Omit the lemon juice and add 1 cup cooked green peas just before serving. The stew is cooked partially covered to reduce the liquid as the gravy should not be abundant. Serves 6.

Carne en Jocón   GUATEMALA
Beef in Tomato and Pepper Sauce

This is called *Carne en Adobo* in some parts of Guatemala.

Serves 6

¼ cup peanut oil
1 medium onion, finely chopped
2 cloves garlic, chopped
2 red or green bell peppers, seeded
  and chopped
1 fresh hot red or green pepper,
  seeded and chopped
3 pounds lean, boneless beef
  chuck, cut into 1-inch cubes
A 10-ounce can Mexican green
  tomatoes and liquid from the
  can

4 medium tomatoes, peeled and
  coarsely chopped
1 bay leaf
2 cloves
½ teaspoon oregano
Salt, freshly ground pepper
½ cup beef stock, more or less
2 stale tortillas, or 2 tablespoons
  masa harina, or 2 tablespoons
  cornmeal

Heat the oil in a heavy saucepan or casserole and sauté the onion, garlic, and peppers until the onion is soft. Add the meat and all the other ingredients except the tortillas. The liquid should barely cover the meat. Add a little more stock, if necessary. Cover, and simmer gently until the beef is tender, about 2 hours. If using tortillas soak them in cold water, squeeze them out, and crumble like breadcrumbs. Add to the casserole and simmer, uncovered, until the sauce is thickened. If using *masa harina* or cornmeal, mix it with a little cold water and stir into the stew, cooking just until the sauce is thickened (cornmeal will take a few minutes longer to thicken). Serve the stew on a bed of *Arroz Guatemalteco* (Rice, Guatemalan Style).

Tomaticán   CHILE
Beef and Tomato Stew

Serves 4

4 tablespoons paprika oil (*Color
  Chilena*), see page 324
1½ pounds lean, boneless beef,
  cut into 1½-inch cubes

1 large onion, chopped
1 clove garlic, chopped
½ teaspoon oregano

1 tablespoon parsley, finely
    chopped
Salt, freshly ground pepper
8 medium tomatoes, peeled and
    chopped

4 medium potatoes, peeled and
    quartered
1 cup corn kernels

Heat the paprika oil in a heavy casserole and add the beef, onion, garlic, oregano, parsley, and salt and pepper to taste, and sauté, stirring frequently, for about 5 minutes. Add the tomatoes, cover, and cook over very low heat until the meat is almost tender, about 1½ hours. Add the potatoes and cook until both meat and potatoes are tender, about 30 minutes longer. Stir in the corn and cook for 5 minutes longer. If liked, the dish may be garnished with slices of hardboiled egg. Some cooks fry the potatoes in oil before adding to the casserole.

Ternera en Pipián Verde   MEXICO
Veal in Pumpkin Seed Sauce

Pipián is a stew of meat or poultry where the liquid is thickened with ground nuts or seeds — pumpkin, sesame, peanuts, almonds — whatever the cook chooses. It may be red or green according to the type of peppers and tomatoes used. This one has a delicious flavor and is a lovely color. It looks truly elegant accompanied by rice, and green beans for their contrastingly darker green.

Serves 6

3 pounds boneless veal, shoulder
    or shank, cut into 2-inch
    pieces
2 cups chicken or veal stock,
    about
¾ cup pepitas (pumpkin seeds)
1 medium onion, chopped
1 clove garlic, chopped
3 fresh hot green peppers, seeded
    and chopped (serrano or
    jalapeño peppers, if available)

½ cup chopped fresh coriander
    (cilantro) leaves
A 10- or 12-ounce can of Mexican
    green tomatoes, drained
6 romaine lettuce leaves,
    preferably the darker green
    outside leaves, chopped
2 tablespoons lard or vegetable oil
Salt, freshly ground pepper

Put the veal into a heavy casserole and pour in the stock, adding a little more if necessary barely to cover. Simmer over low heat, covered, until the meat is tender, about 1½ hours. In an ungreased skillet toast the pumpkin seeds for a few minutes. Cool slightly and pulverize in a blender or food processor fitted with a steel blade. Add to the blender or food processor the onion, garlic, hot peppers, coriander, green tomatoes, and romaine, and reduce to a pastelike purée. If necessary add a little of the stock.

In a skillet heat the lard or vegetable oil and cook the pumpkin seed mixture, stirring, for about 3 minutes. Thin the pumpkin seed mixture with about 2 cups of the stock, or until it is the consistency of heavy cream. Season to taste with salt and pepper. Drain the veal and set the meat aside. Return the veal to the casserole, pour on the sauce, and cook just long enough to heat through.

Ternera con Zanahorias   PERU
Veal with Carrots

I have often admired the great heaps of small, deep orange carrots in markets throughout Latin America, exquisitely clean and glowing with color. They make a great contribution to this veal stew.

Serves 6

3 pounds shank or shoulder of
    veal, cut into 2-inch pieces
Salt, freshly ground pepper
⅛ teaspoon grated nutmeg
2 large cloves garlic, crushed
1 cup dry white wine

4 tablespoons butter
1 medium onion, finely chopped
1 pound small young carrots,
    scraped and thinly sliced
1 cup beef stock, about

Season the veal pieces with salt, pepper, nutmeg, and garlic and put into a large bowl. Pour the wine over them. Cover and marinate in the refrigerator for about 4 hours, turning once or twice.

Heat the butter in a heavy casserole and sauté the onion and carrots until the onion is very soft, about 10 minutes. Add the veal and the marinade and enough beef stock barely to cover. Simmer, covered, over very low heat until the veal is tender, about 1½ hours. The carrots should be very soft, almost disintegrating in the sauce. Serve with a green vegetable.

Chancho Adobado

Spicy Pork

Serves 6

1 whole head garlic
2 tablespoons ground annatto
(achiote)
2 teaspoons ground cumin
Salt, freshly ground pepper
1 cup white vinegar

3 pounds shoulder of pork, cut
into 2-inch cubes
2 tablespoons lard or vegetable oil
Juice of 1 Seville (bitter) orange, or
¼ cup orange juice
1 ½ pounds sweet potatoes

Peel the garlic cloves and reduce them to a purée in an electric blender with the annatto, cumin, salt and pepper to taste, and vinegar. Put the pork pieces into a large bowl and pour the garlic marinade over them, mixing well. Marinate overnight in the refrigerator, covered. Strain, reserving the marinade. Pat the pork cubes dry with paper towels. Heat the lard or oil in a large skillet and sauté the pork pieces until golden brown all over, transferring them to a casserole as they are done. Pour the reserved marinade over the pork, add the orange juice, cover, and cook over very low heat until the meat is tender, 1½ to 2 hours. If the meat seems to be drying out, add a little water; 3 or 4 tablespoons will probably be enough. There should be very little gravy when the dish is finished.

Peel the sweet potatoes and cut them into slices about ¾ inch thick. Cook in boiling salted water until tender, 15 to 20 minutes. Drain.

To serve, heap the pork in the center of a large warmed platter and surround with the sweet potato slices moistened with a little of the meat gravy. White rice is another traditional accompaniment to this dish.

Seco de Chancho
ECUADOR
Pork Stew

Serves 6 to 8

2 tablespoons annatto oil or lard
  (see page 324)
3 pounds lean pork shoulder, cut
  into 2-inch cubes
1 large onion, finely chopped
2 large cloves garlic, minced
1 large tomato, peeled, seeded,
  and chopped
1 red bell pepper, seeded and
  coarsely chopped, or 2 canned
  pimientos, chopped

1 fresh hot red or green pepper,
  seeded and finely chopped
1 tablespoon fresh coriander
  (cilantro), chopped coarsely
½ teaspoon ground cumin
½ teaspoon oregano
Salt, freshly ground pepper
Pinch sugar (optional)
2 cups beer

Heat the oil or lard in a heavy skillet and lightly sauté the pork cubes. With a slotted spoon remove the pork pieces to a heavy flameproof casserole. Remove all but 2 tablespoons of fat from the skillet, add the onion and garlic, and sauté the mixture until the onion is soft. Add the tomato, the sweet and hot peppers, coriander, cumin, and oregano, and simmer until the mixture is well blended, about 10 minutes. Season to taste with salt and pepper and, if liked, the pinch of sugar. Pour over the pork, add the beer, cover, and cook over very low heat until the pork is tender, about 2 hours. The sauce should be quite thick. If it seems at all watery, partially uncover the casserole during the second hour of cooking. Serve with rice.

Jamón del País
PERU
Peruvian Fresh Ham

Though this is called ham (*jamón*), it is really fresh pork spiced and cooked in a most unusual way — marinated, simmered until tender, then browned in hot fat. Very different and marvelous for a buffet either hot or transformed when cold into a delicious dividend, *Butifarras*, special Peruvian sandwich rolls. It can be made with a boned leg of pork but I find the shoulder a more manageable size. Incidentally, though the meat is strictly speaking stewed, the finished dish is more like a baked meat.

Peruvian and Mexican garlic have quite enormous cloves, which comes in handy when one has to peel a number of them. I have specified large cloves of garlic but if these are not available, a whole head of garlic should be used. It will not overpower the other flavors.

Serves 12 or more

12 large cloves garlic, peeled, or 1 whole head
2 tablespoons annatto (achiote) seeds, ground
1 teaspoon cumin, ground
Salt, freshly ground pepper
About 6 pounds pork shoulder (cali), boned and rolled
4 tablespoons lard

Crush the garlic cloves and mix to a paste with the annatto, cumin, and salt and pepper to taste. Spread this on the pork, put the pork into a baking dish, cover loosely with foil, and refrigerate overnight. Put the pork, and any liquid in the pan, into a very large saucepan or kettle and pour in enough water to cover it. Cover, bring to a boil, reduce the heat to low, and simmer gently until the meat is tender, 2½ to 3 hours. When it is cool enough to handle, remove it from the cooking liquid and pat it dry with paper towels. Heat the lard in a very large skillet or baking dish and sauté the pork until it is browned all over. Transfer the pork to a serving platter and serve hot, sliced with rice or potatoes, a green vegetable or a salad, or allow to cool and use to make *Butifarras* (Peruvian Ham Sandwiches).

Variation: For *Butifarras*, put thinly sliced onions into a bowl with an equal amount of thinly sliced radishes; fresh hot peppers, seeded and sliced; and salt and pepper to taste. Pour in enough white vinegar to cover the vegetables and let them stand at room temperature for 2 hours before using. The amount of hot peppers will depend on taste. Strain and discard the vinegar. Have ready crusty rolls, cut three-quarters of the way through. Butter the rolls if desired and place a lettuce leaf, a slice of ham, and a layer of the pickled vegetables in each roll. Serve as a snack.

Cordero Criollo   PERU
Lamb, Creole Style

Lamb and kid are used interchangeably in Latin America, though kid requires a little longer cooking time. There are not a great many recipes calling for these meats, but the few that exist are very good indeed. Annatto (achiote) lends a marvelous fragrance to this Peruvian roast leg of lamb. The herbs and spices in the dressing are the same as those in *aliño criollo* (Venezuelan creole style seasoning powder), and I find the prepared version exactly right for this dish, though I add a large clove of crushed garlic to the mixture. Shoulder of lamb or kid can also be used successfully.

Serves 6

A 4-pound leg or shoulder of lamb
    or kid
2 tablespoons aliño criollo (see
    page 325)
¼ cup red wine vinegar
1 large clove garlic, crushed

½ cup olive oil
3 large potatoes, peeled and
    halved lengthwise
Lettuce leaves, preferably romaine
1 canned pimiento, cut into strips

Trim the lamb of all but a thin layer of fat. Mix the seasoning powder with the vinegar, add the garlic, then beat in the oil with a fork. Rub this marinade into the lamb and let it stand for at least 2 hours, turning the meat from time to time and spooning the marinade over it. When ready to cook scrape off and reserve the marinade. Put the lamb into a baking pan brushed over with oil and surround with the potatoes. Bake in a preheated moderate (325° F.) oven for 1 hour (15 minutes to the pound), for rare lamb, 130° to 135° F. on a meat thermometer. Cook for 15 minutes longer if medium rare lamb is preferred. Baste every 20 minutes with the reserved marinade and any pan juices. Turn the potatoes halfway through the cooking time.

Remove the lamb to a carving board and let it stand 15 minutes before carving. Arrange the potatoes round the edge of a serving platter and keep warm in the turned-off oven. Slice the lamb and arrange it on the platter. Garnish the edge of the dish with lettuce leaves and strips of pimiento. Spoon the fat off the pan juices and put into a gravy boat with the juices from the meat as it is carved. Either spoon over the meat or serve as gravy. There will not be a great deal.

Variation: A most delicious variation, which has overtones of the Middle East in its use of mint, is *Carnero o Cabrito al Horno* (Roast Lamb or Kid). Make a dressing of 3 tablespoons butter creamed with 8 large cloves crushed garlic, salt, freshly ground pepper, and 4 tablespoons finely chopped fresh mint. Spread over the lamb or kid and roast as above. Baste with 1 cup dry white wine instead of the marinade.

Cazuela de Cordero
Lamb Casserole

CHILE

This lamb stew is a Chilean standby, a family favorite, both rich and simple at the same time. The winter squash slightly thickens the sauce, and the final whisking in of beaten eggs finishes it.

Serves 6

2 pounds boneless lamb for stew,
    cut into 2-inch pieces
1 onion, coarsely chopped
1 leek, sliced
1 carrot, scraped and sliced
Small stalk of celery with leaves
½ teaspoon oregano
Pinch of ground cumin
1 sprig parsley
1 bay leaf
6 small potatoes, peeled, or 3 large
    potatoes, peeled and halved
½ pound winter squash, peeled
    and cut into 1-inch cubes

Salt, freshly ground pepper
3 small zucchini, cut into 1-inch
    slices
½ pound green beans, cut into
    1-inch pieces
2 cups fresh corn kernels
2 eggs, lightly beaten

Put the lamb, onion, leek, carrot, celery, oregano, cumin, parsley, and bay leaf into a large saucepan or casserole. Pour in enough water to cover, about 6 cups, bring to a boil, skim off any froth that rises to the surface, lower the heat, cover, and simmer until the meat is almost tender, about 1½ hours. Lift out the pieces of lamb onto a plate and set aside. Strain the stock, pressing down to extract all the juices. Discard the solids. Rinse out and dry the casserole.

Return the lamb pieces to the casserole and add the potatoes and winter squash. Pour in the strained stock, adding a little water if necessary to cover the lamb and vegetables. Season to taste with salt and pepper and simmer 15 minutes. Add the zucchini, beans, and corn, and simmer until the beans are tender, about 10 minutes.

Whisk a cup of the hot stock gradually into the eggs, then pour the mixture into the saucepan, stirring to mix. Do not let the liquid boil, as the eggs will curdle. Cook over very low heat until the eggs have thickened the sauce. The winter squash will have disintegrated, also thickening the sauce slightly. Serve in soup plates, making sure that each serving has a little of everything.

Arvejado de Cordero   CHILE
Lamb Stew with Green Peas

This Chilean lamb stew is characterized by the interesting use of paprika oil (*Color Chilena*).

Serves 6

3 tablespoons paprika oil (Color
   Chilena), *see page 324*
2 pounds boneless lamb for stew,
   cut into 1-inch pieces
1 large onion, finely chopped

1 tablespoon flour
Salt, freshly ground pepper
2 cups fresh green peas
2 eggs, lightly beaten
¼ cup chopped parsley

Heat the paprika oil in a casserole or large saucepan. Add the lamb pieces and the onion, and sauté until the onion is soft. Add the flour and cook for a minute or two longer, stirring with a wooden spoon to mix thoroughly. Add 2 cups water, season to taste with salt and pepper, cover, and simmer until the lamb is almost done, about 1½ hours. Add the peas, bring back to a simmer, and cook for 15 minutes longer, or until the peas are tender. Transfer the meat and peas to a serving dish and keep warm. Stir the eggs and parsley into the liquid in the casserole and cook over very low heat, stirring constantly with a wooden spoon, until the sauce has thickened lightly. Do not let it boil, as it will curdle. Pour the sauce over the lamb and serve with boiled potatoes or any puréed root vegetable or plain rice.

Carnero en Adobo   MEXICO
Lamb in Chili and Vinegar Sauce

Lamb and kid are very popular in the north of Mexico, much of it mountain country well suited to these animals. Julia, the cook of my husband's uncle, General Procopio Ortiz Reyes, who lives in Torreón, Coahuila, cooked this for me and gave me her recipe. It is easy yet exotic. *Ancho* chili is mild and full flavored, *mulato* chili a little *picante*. Using both gives a sauce full of character.

Serves 6

3 pounds boneless lamb (shoulder
   or leg), cut into 1½-inch
   pieces

2 medium onions, chopped
2 cloves garlic, chopped
3 or 4 sprigs fresh coriander

Salt   *2 tablespoons red wine vinegar*
3 ancho *and* 3 mulato *chilies*   *3 tablespoons lard or vegetable oil*
⅛ *teaspoon ground cumin*
½ *teaspoon oregano*

Put the lamb into a heavy saucepan or casserole with 1 onion, 1 clove garlic, the coriander sprigs, salt, and water barely to cover. Bring to a boil, lower the heat, and simmer, covered, over moderate heat until the meat is tender, about 1½ hours. Drain the lamb, strain the stock, and set aside. Rinse out and dry the casserole and return the lamb to it.

Prepare the chilies (page 13) and put them with the soaking water into a blender or food processor fitted with a steel blade. Add the remaining onion and garlic, the cumin, oregano, vinegar, and salt, and blend until fairly smooth. The mixture should be more of a paste than a purée. Heat the lard or oil in a skillet and cook the mixture, stirring constantly with a wooden spoon, for about 5 minutes, over moderate heat. Thin with 1½ cups of the reserved lamb stock. The mixture should be the consistency of a medium white sauce. Add more stock if necessary. Pour the sauce over the lamb and simmer over very low heat for 20 minutes. Serve with rice, beans, and a green vegetable. Tortillas are good with this.

Variation: Mexican friends who like their food hot and very highly flavored suggest adding a canned *chipotle* or *morita* chili to the blender when making the sauce. It makes a delicious change.

Variation: For *Carnero en Salsa de Chile Ancho* (Lamb in Mild Red Chili Sauce) from Mexico, sauté the lamb in 2 tablespoons olive oil in a skillet and transfer to a casserole. Prepare 6 *ancho* chilies (page 13) and put them with the soaking water into a blender or food processor fitted with a steel blade. Add 1 chopped onion, 1 clove garlic, and 4 medium tomatoes, peeled and chopped, and reduce to a purée. If necessary, add enough oil to the skillet to make the quantity of fat up to 2 tablespoons. Add the chili mixture and cook, stirring constantly, for about 5 minutes over moderate heat. It has a tendency to splutter. Pour over the lamb, season to taste with salt and freshly ground pepper, a pinch of cinnamon, and ⅛ teaspoon of cloves. Cover and simmer over low heat until the lamb is tender, about 1½ hours. Soak ¼ cup small, pimiento-stuffed olives, about 12, in cold water for 15 minutes to get rid of the brine, drain and halve them. Put the lamb in a serving dish and garnish with the olives and ¼ cup slivered, toasted almonds. Serve with rice and a green vegetable. Depending on the juiciness of the tomatoes, it may be necessary to add a little more liquid to the lamb, though the sauce should not be abundant. Add tomato juice, stock, or water. Serves 6.

Seco de Carnero
Lamb Stew

PERU

Don't be afraid of the amount of garlic used here. The flavor will not be at all aggressive, indeed it will be quite gentle as the pungent oils cook out. The coriander, garlic, fruit juices, and hot peppers combine into a most delicious sauce.

Serves 6 to 8

1 cup fresh coriander (cilantro), chopped
2 or 3 fresh hot red or green peppers, seeded and chopped
1 whole head garlic, peeled and chopped
½ cup olive oil
2 medium onions, finely chopped
4 pounds lean, boneless lamb (shoulder or leg), cut into 1-inch cubes
Salt, freshly ground pepper
½ cup bitter (Seville) orange juice, or use two-thirds fresh orange juice and one-third lime or lemon juice

2 pounds potatoes, peeled and sliced
1 pound green peas, or 2 packages frozen peas

In a blender or food processor combine the coriander leaves, hot peppers, and garlic, and reduce to a purée. Set aside. Heat the oil in a casserole and sauté the onions until they are soft. Stir in the coriander mixture and cook for a minute or two longer. Add the lamb pieces and cook for about 5 minutes, turning the pieces to coat them with the sauce. Season to taste with salt and a generous amount of pepper. Add the bitter (Seville) orange juice or the orange and lime (or lemon) juice mixture and enough water to cover, about 1½ cups. Cover and simmer until the lamb is tender, about 1½ hours. The stew may be cooked to this point a day ahead and refrigerated so that any fat may be removed. Let the casserole stand until it reaches room temperature before reheating.

Boil the potatoes in salted water until they are tender. Drain and add to the casserole. Boil the peas in salted water until they are tender, drain, and add to the casserole. Bring the casserole to a simmer and cook just long enough to heat it through.

Posta en Frutas Secas   COLOMBIA
Beef and Dried Fruit Stew

This is one of the Latin American meat and fruit stews that have links, via Spain when it was a Moorish colony, to ancient Persia, where these delectable dishes were first concocted. Interestingly there are also links with the cooking of present-day Morocco, where dishes very similar to those of ancient Persia survive. Most Colombians take advantage of modern marketing and use an 11-ounce package of dried mixed fruit, but you can make the mixture yourself.

Serves 6

An 11-ounce package mixed dried
    fruit (prunes, dried apricots,
    peaches, and pears)
3 tablespoons olive or vegetable
    oil
3 pounds lean beef, preferably top
    round, cut into 1-inch cubes
1 medium onion, finely chopped
1 clove garlic, minced
1 medium carrot, scraped and
    chopped
Salt, freshly ground pepper

1 cup dry red wine
1 tablespoon soft butter (optional)
1 tablespoon flour (optional)

Put the mixed dried fruit into a bowl with 1½ cups warm water and leave to soak for 1 hour, turning the fruit from time to time. Drain, reserve the soaking water, and set the fruit aside.

Heat the oil in a heavy casserole or saucepan and sauté the beef, onion, garlic, and carrot for about 5 minutes. Season with salt and pepper. Pour in the wine and the reserved soaking water from the fruit. Bring to a boil, reduce the heat to low, and simmer, covered, for 2 hours, or until the beef is almost tender. Add the fruit. The prunes and apricots should be left whole, the pears and peaches halved or quartered. Cover and simmer 30 minutes longer. If the sauce is too thick, add a little more wine. If you want a slightly thicker sauce, mix the butter and flour together and drop a few smooth pieces into the casserole, blending well. Serve with rice.

Carne con Salsa de Frutas   ECUADOR
Beef in Fruit Sauce

A particularly delicious beef stew, with the flavors of the fruits and the tomatoes subtly blended and enriched by the cream, though still nicely tart.

Serves 6

6 tablespoons vegetable oil
1 large onion, finely chopped
3 pounds boneless beef chuck, cut
    into 1-inch cubes
1 cup dry white wine
1 cup beef stock
Salt, freshly ground pepper
2 quinces, peeled, cored, and
    chopped, or 2 peaches, peeled,
    pitted, and chopped

2 apples, peeled, cored, and
    chopped
2 pears, peeled, cored, and
    chopped
2 large tomatoes, peeled and
    chopped
Sugar to taste
1 cup heavy cream

Heat 4 tablespoons of the oil in a skillet and sauté the onion until it is soft. Using a slotted spoon transfer the onion to a casserole. In the oil remaining in the skillet sauté the beef until it is browned on all sides. Add it to the casserole with the wine, stock, and salt and pepper to taste. Cover and simmer until the meat is tender, about 2 hours. Arrange the meat on a serving platter and keep warm. Reserve the stock.

Heat the remaining 2 tablespoons of oil in a saucepan and add the fruit, including the tomatoes. Cook for a few minutes, stirring. Add a little sugar, if liked. The sauce should be quite tart. Add enough of the reserved stock barely to cover, and simmer, stirring from time to time, until the mixture is thick and well blended. In the old days cooks had to work the mixture through a sieve, a tedious procedure; today a blender or food processor does the job. Return the purée to the saucepan and taste for seasoning, adding a little salt if necessary. Stir in the cream and cook just long enough to heat through. Pour the sauce over the meat. Serve with rice.

Variation: Guava shells or nectarines may be used instead of quinces or peaches. Boneless pork loin may be used instead of beef. The sauce is also pleasant served with grilled lamb chops. If preferred, serve with *Llapin-gachos* (Potato Cakes) instead of rice.

Chuletas de Cerdo con Frutas
DOMINICAN REPUBLIC

Pork Chops with Dried Fruit

The use of dried fruits, especially apricots, in meat dishes is very much a Middle Eastern thing. In Iran lamb and dried apricots are used together in a most delectable dish. A lot of old dishes have survived in the Dominican Republic and this one was obviously brought over by the Spanish, using pork instead of lamb. It works beautifully.

Serves 4

¼ pound, about 1 cup, pitted prunes
¼ pound, about 1 cup, dried apricots
¼ pound, about 1 cup, dried pears
4 pork loin chops, weighing 2 pounds

Salt, freshly ground pepper
2 tablespoons vegetable oil
1 medium onion, finely chopped
1 clove garlic, chopped
1 cup chicken stock, about
1 cup dry white wine, about

Put the prunes in a bowl with the apricots, halved, and the pears, quartered. Pour in enough cold water barely to cover and let soak for 30 minutes.

Season the chops with salt and pepper. Heat the oil in a skillet and sauté the chops until golden on both sides. Transfer the chops to a casserole. In the fat remaining in the pan sauté the onion and garlic until the onion is softened. Add to the casserole. Arrange the fruit over and around the pork chops. Pour in the chicken stock and wine, adding a little more of each if necessary to cover. Cover the casserole with aluminum foil, then the lid, and bake in a preheated moderate (350° F.) oven for about 1½ hours or until the pork is tender.

Chirmole de Puerco   MEXICO
Pork Stew with Peppers and Greengage Plums

Serves 6

3 pounds lean, boneless pork, cut
    into 2-inch cubes
6 ancho *chilies*
3 *fresh or canned hot green* serrano
    peppers, seeded
2 cloves garlic, chopped
1 large onion, chopped
¼ teaspoon ground cinnamon
Salt, freshly ground pepper
1 pound greengage plums

4 medium tomatoes, sliced
½ teaspoon crumbled, dried
    epazote *(optional)*
¼ cup masa harina
¼ cup Seville (bitter) orange juice,
    or use two-thirds orange juice
    and one-third lime juice
2 tablespoons lard or vegetable oil
    (optional)

Put the pork into a large, heavy saucepan or casserole, add water barely to cover, and simmer, covered, until almost tender, about 1½ hours.

Pull off the stems and shake out the seeds from the peppers and tear them into pieces. Rinse and put into a bowl with ½ cup hot water. Let the peppers soak for 1 hour, turning them frequently. Combine the *ancho* chilies, the water in which they were soaked, the *serrano* peppers, garlic, onion, and cinnamon in an electric blender or food processor and reduce to a coarse purée. Drain the pork, reserving the stock, and return the meat to the saucepan. Add enough of the stock to the purée to make a thin sauce. Season to taste with salt and pepper and pour over the pork, mixing well. Pit the greengages and cut each plum into 4 pieces. Add them to the pork. Add the tomato slices, and if it is available the *epazote*. Simmer, covered, until the pork is tender. Mix a little of the remaining stock with the *masa harina*. Stir the orange juice into this mixture and add to the pork stew. The lard or vegetable oil may be added at this time, if liked. Simmer, stirring gently, for a minute or two longer.

Ternera en Salsa de Ciruelas Pasas   MEXICO
Veal in Prune Sauce

This is an old colonial dish that I particularly like to serve when friends are coming to dinner. The prunes give the dark sauce a rich, subtle flavor.

1 ½ cups large, pitted prunes,
　chopped
1 cup dry red wine
4 tablespoons lard or vegetable oil
2 ½ to 3 ½ pounds boneless veal
　roast, preferably top round

2 medium onions, finely chopped
2 cloves garlic, chopped
3 medium tomatoes, peeled,
　seeded, and chopped
2 cups beef or veal stock, about
Salt, freshly ground pepper

Put the prunes to soak in the wine for at least 2 hours.

Heat the lard or oil in a heavy casserole and sauté the veal until it is golden brown all over. Lift out of the casserole and set aside. In the oil remaining in the casserole sauté the onions and garlic until the onions are soft. Add the tomatoes and cook until the mixture is well blended. Add the prunes and wine. Add the veal and pour in just enough stock to cover. Simmer, covered, over low heat until the veal is tender, about 2 hours. Lift out the veal to a serving platter, slice, and keep warm. Season the sauce to taste with salt and pepper. During cooking the prunes should have disintegrated, thickening the sauce. If necessary, cook the sauce over fairly brisk heat, stirring, for a few minutes to amalgamate the solids and reduce the sauce a little. It should be thick but not completely smooth. Spoon a little sauce over the veal slices and serve the rest in a sauceboat. Serve with rice or any starchy root vegetable.

Ternera con Aceitunas   MEXICO
Veal with Olives

The stuffed green olives add a distinctive flavor to this dish.

4 tablespoons olive or vegetable
　oil
2 pounds shank or shoulder of
　veal, cut into 1-inch cubes
2 ounces boiled ham, coarsely
　chopped
1 medium onion, finely chopped
1 clove garlic, chopped

½ cup chopped parsley
36 small pimiento-stuffed green
　olives
1 cup dry white wine
1 cup beef stock
Salt, freshly ground pepper
2 eggs

Heat the oil in a skillet and sauté the veal with the ham. Lift out into a casserole. In the oil remaining in the skillet sauté the onion and garlic until the onion is soft. Add to the casserole with the parsley. Soak the olives in cold water for 10 minutes, drain, and add to the casserole. Pour in the wine and stock, season to taste with salt and pepper, cover, and simmer until the veal is tender, about 1½ hours. Lightly beat the eggs, then whisk ½ cup of the hot liquid into them. Pour the mixture back into the casserole and cook, stirring, until the sauce is lightly thickened. Do not let the sauce boil, as it will curdle. Serve with rice or a starchy root vegetable and a green vegetable or salad.

FLANK STEAK DISHES

South Americans hold flank steak in high esteem for its fine flavor and adaptability. It may be braised, stewed, and broiled, stuffed, baked, or shredded. And it may be served hot or cold. It is used for the national dish of Venezuela with the traditional accompaniments of rice, black beans, and fried plantains. It is stuffed with spinach, or even more exotically with an omelet, asparagus tips, and strips of pimiento to make a party dish that is not only satisfyingly hearty but elegant in appearance. It has the added merit of being a lean and tender cut that is also economical.

Pabellón Caraqueño   VENEZUELA
Steak with Rice, Black Beans, and Plantains

This national dish of Venezuela is said to look like a flag (*pabellón*) because of the different colors of meat, rice, beans, and plantains. It is a robust and satisfying dish.

Serves 6

1 ½ pounds flank steak or skirt
    steak
1 ½ cups beef stock, about
1 medium onion, finely chopped
1 clove garlic, minced
2 medium tomatoes, peeled,
    seeded, and chopped
Salt
2 tablespoons olive oil

1 recipe Arroz Blanco (White
    Rice), page 248
6 eggs, fried in olive oil
1 recipe Caraotas Negras (Black
    Beans), page 243
1 ripe plantain, or 2 underripe
    bananas
2 tablespoons vegetable oil

Cut the steak into 2 or 3 pieces to fit conveniently into a saucepan, and add the stock to cover. If necessary add a little more. Bring to a simmer and cook, covered, over very low heat until the meat is tender, 1½ to 2 hours. Allow to cool in the stock, drain, reserve the stock for another use, and shred the meat with the fingers. Combine the meat with the onion, garlic, and tomatoes. Season to taste with salt. Heat the oil in a skillet and sauté the meat mixture until the onion is cooked and the mixture is quite dry. Put the rice in the center of a large, warmed platter and heap the meat on top of it. Arrange the fried eggs on top of the meat. Surround the rice with the black beans and decorate the edge of the platter with the fried plantains or bananas.

To fry the plantains or bananas: Peel the plantains and cut them in half lengthwise, then crosswise into thirds. If using bananas, peel and cut into thirds. Heat the oil in a skillet and fry the plantains or bananas until golden brown on both sides, about 2 or 3 minutes.

Matambre   ARGENTINA
Stuffed Rolled Flank Steak

This translates literally as "kill hunger" and it is indeed a very satisfying dish whether eaten hot as a main course, or cold with salads, ideal for a picnic. In more modest amounts, it makes an unusual first course.

Serves 4

1 teaspoon oregano
2 cloves crushed garlic
1½ pounds flank steak
Salt, freshly ground pepper
1 cup spinach leaves, about

1 small carrot, thinly sliced
1 hardboiled egg, thinly sliced
Cayenne pepper (optional)
8 cups beef stock, about

Mix the oregano and garlic and spread over the steak. Season the steak with salt and pepper to taste, then cover with the spinach leaves, leaving about a ½-inch margin. Top the spinach with the carrot and egg and sprinkle with a little cayenne pepper, if liked. Roll up with the grain and tie with kitchen string at about 1-inch intervals. Place in a casserole into which it fits comfortably but quite snugly. Pour in the beef stock. There should be enough to cover the steak. Bring to a boil, skim off any froth that rises, reduce the heat, and simmer gently for 1½ to 2 hours, or until the beef is tender. Lift out, remove the strings, slice, and serve hot, moistening the steak with a little of the stock. Serve with potatoes or rice. Or allow the steak to cool in the stock and serve cold, sliced, with salad. Reserve the leftover stock for another use. Serve with *Salsa Criolla* (Creole Sauce), page 320.

Variation: For *Matambre al Horno* (Baked Flank Steak), put the stuffed steak into the casserole with 3 cups stock. Bring the stock to a boil on top of the stove, cover the casserole, and transfer to a preheated moderate (350° F.) oven for about 1 hour, or until the steak is done.

Variation: In Uruguay, where this dish is also popular, the steak is sometimes just seasoned and stuffed with spinach.

Variation: *Matambre a la Cacerola* (Casseroled Flank Steak). Heat 2 tablespoons butter in a skillet, add 1 small onion, finely chopped, ½ cup finely chopped celery, and 1 small carrot, scraped and finely chopped. Sauté until the onion is soft, about 5 minutes. Remove from the heat and stir in 2 tablespoons finely chopped parsley and 2 cups cubed bread. Season with salt and pepper. Stir in 2 tablespoons beef stock, mix well, and spread over the steak, leaving a ½-inch margin. Roll up with the grain and tie at 1-inch intervals with kitchen string. Heat 2 tablespoons vegetable oil in a casserole large enough to hold the steak, and brown the steak all over. Pour in enough stock, about 8 cups, to cover, and simmer for 1½ to 2 hours. Or cook in a preheated moderate (350° F.) oven for 1 hour or so, in which case add only enough stock to come about one-third of the way up the steak, about 3 cups. If liked, thicken about 2 cups of the stock with a beurre manié (see page 328). Serve with carrots and potatoes and a green vegetable.

Variation: *Malaya Arrollada* (Rolled Flank Steak) is a Chilean version of *Matambre*, and why this particular cut of steak is called a *malaya* in Chile is entirely beyond me. Admittedly, women in Malaya wear sarongs and sarongs are wrapped around ladies, while the *malaya* is wrapped around a filling, but this is surely stretching a linguistic point too far. Season the steak with salt, pepper, and 1 teaspoon oregano. Cover it with 1 onion, finely chopped, 1 stalk celery, finely chopped, 1 carrot, scraped and finely sliced, and 1 hardboiled egg, thinly sliced. Roll up with the grain, tie with string, and place in a flameproof casserole that holds it snugly. Pour in enough stock to cover and simmer until it is tender, 1½ to 2 hours. Let it cool in the stock. Lift out, remove the string and slice. Serve as a first course with any salad. Serves 8.

Sobrebarriga
Flank Steak

Serves 4 to 6

A 2-pound flank steak, with layer
  of fat left on
1 medium onion, chopped
2 cloves garlic, chopped
2 medium tomatoes, chopped
1 carrot, scraped and chopped
1 bay leaf
2 or 3 sprigs parsley

½ teaspoon thyme
½ teaspoon oregano
Salt, freshly ground pepper
Beef stock or water
1 or 2 tablespoons butter, softened
  at room temperature
1 cup fresh breadcrumbs

Put the steak into a large saucepan with the onion, garlic, tomatoes, carrot, bay leaf, parsley sprigs, thyme, oregano, and salt and pepper to taste. Add enough stock or water to cover the meat and cook it, covered, over low heat for about 2 hours, or until it is tender. Remove the meat from the liquid, pat it dry with paper towels, and place it in a broiling pan, fat side up. Spread the butter over the meat and cover with breadcrumbs. Broil until the crumbs are golden brown. Slice the steak and arrange it on a heated platter. Strain the hot seasoned liquid into a sauceboat. Serve with *Papas Chorreadas* (Potatoes with Cheese, Tomato, and Onion Sauce) and *Ensalada de Aguacate* (Avocado Salad).

Sobrebarriga Bogotana
Flank Steak, Bogotá Style

Serves 4 to 6

1 medium onion, finely chopped
2 cloves garlic, chopped
2 medium tomatoes, peeled and
  chopped
1 tablespoon parsley, chopped
½ teaspoon thyme
1 bay leaf, crumbled
1 teaspoon prepared mustard
1 teaspoon Worcestershire sauce

Salt, freshly ground pepper
A 2-pound flank steak, trimmed of
  all fat
2 cups beef stock or water, about
2 cups dark beer, about
2 tablespoons butter, softened at
  room temperature
1 cup fresh breadcrumbs

Mix together the onion, garlic, tomatoes, parsley, thyme, bay leaf, mustard, Worcestershire sauce, and salt and pepper to taste. Spread the mixture on the steak. Roll the steak up with the grain and tie securely with string. Place in a flameproof casserole, cover, and refrigerate until the following day. Cover with equal quantities of beef stock or water, and dark beer. Bring to a boil, reduce the heat to a bare simmer, and cook, partially covered, until the steak is tender and the liquid reduced, about 2 hours. Remove the steak from the casserole, brush it with the butter, and roll it in the breadcrumbs. Arrange the steak in a baking tin and bake in a preheated hot (400° F.) oven until the crumbs are lightly browned, about 15 minutes. Heat the sauce remaining in the casserole and serve in a sauceboat. Slice the steak and arrange on a warmed platter. Serve with *Papas Chorreadas* (Potatoes with Cheese, Tomato, and Onion Sauce) and *Ensalada de Aguacate* (Avocado Salad).

Roupa Velha   BRAZIL
Old Clothes

This is the Brazilian version of the Spanish dish *Ropa Vieja* (Old Clothes). Ideally flank steak is used since the cooked meat should be shredded, as old clothes can be said to shred into rags and tatters. The dish is infinitely more appetizing than its name, and occurs very widely in Spanish- and Portuguese-speaking countries, varying from place to place. The Brazilian version, though it is not as rich as, for example, the Cuban version, is very good. Traditionally leftover beef from a *cozido* (pot-au-feu), or similar dish, is used, and if you have some, by all means use it.

Serves 4 to 6

A 2-pound flank steak, or 2 pounds cooked boiled beef	1 sprig parsley
	1 bay leaf
1 medium onion, stuck with a clove	1 clove garlic
	6 peppercorns
1 carrot, scraped and halved	1 tablespoon salt
1 stalk celery	

Put the steak into a flameproof casserole with the onion, carrot, celery, parsley, bay leaf, garlic, peppercorns, and salt and enough cold water to cover. Bring to a boil, simmer for 5 minutes, and skim the froth that rises to the surface. Cover, lower the heat, and simmer for 1½ hours, or until the steak is tender. Leave the steak in the stock until it is cool enough to handle. Lift it out of the stock onto a chopping board. Strain the stock into a jar and refrigerate for another use. Cut the steak in half crosswise, then shred it along the grain into strips. Set aside.

FOR THE SAUCE

¼ cup olive oil
2 medium onions, thinly sliced
2 medium tomatoes, peeled and
*   sliced*
½ cup finely chopped parsley

Salt, freshly ground pepper
Pinch of sugar
2 tablespoons vinegar
Tabasco sauce (optional)

Heat the oil in a skillet and sauté the onions until they are lightly browned. Add the tomatoes, parsley, salt and pepper to taste, and the sugar. Cook the mixture for 5 minutes longer, stirring occasionally. Add the steak, vinegar, and a little Tabasco sauce, if liked, and cook, stirring, until the steak is heated through. Transfer to the center of a heated platter and surround it with plain white rice.

PORK LOIN DISHES

Pork is one of the best-liked meats in Latin America, and pork loin one of the favorite cuts. In my view pork shoulder is just as attractive and much more economical though it will need a little longer cooking time. Recipes are quite varied, ranging from an Ecuadorian dish where the meat is larded with raw shrimp and braised, reminding one of the flavors of Chinese food, to an Argentine dish where the meat is baked in milk and emerges deliciously tender with a creamy sauce, to pork simmered in orange juice, tender and delicate, to pork loin, Chilean style, served with a fiery pepper sauce to be taken with discretion.

Lomo con Camarones   ECUADOR
Pork Loin with Shrimp

The combination of pork and shrimp braised in wine is unusual and exciting — the flavor exquisite. This is one of my party favorites.

Serves 6

A 3-pound boned loin of pork
½ pound raw shrimp, peeled and
*   coarsely chopped*
1 hardboiled egg, chopped
Salt, freshly ground pepper
2 cloves garlic, crushed
4 tablespoons butter
2 cups dry white wine
1 tablespoon flour
White wine or chicken stock

With a steel, or with a sharp, narrow knife, make holes about the thickness of one's thumb all over the loin, almost to the center of the meat. Season the shrimp and egg with salt and pepper. With your fingers, stuff half the holes with the shrimp, the other half with chopped egg, or mix the shrimp and egg together and use as a stuffing. Season the loin with salt, pepper, and the crushed garlic. Heat 3 tablespoons of the butter in a flameproof casserole large enough to hold the loin comfortably (an oval casserole is best) and sauté the meat until it is golden all over. Pour in the wine and bring to a simmer. Remove from the heat. Cover with aluminum foil and the casserole lid and bake in a preheated moderate (325° F.) oven for 2 hours, or until the pork is tender. Lift the pork onto a warmed serving platter and remove the string. Slice the pork and keep warm. Mix the flour with the remaining tablespoon of butter and stir it, over moderate heat, into the casserole, stirring until the sauce is lightly thickened. If the liquid has reduced a great deal during cooking and the sauce is too thick, add a little wine or chicken stock to thin it to medium consistency. Taste, and season with more salt and pepper, if necessary. Spoon a little of the sauce over the pork slices, and pour the rest into a sauceboat. Serve with shoestring potatoes, sliced tomatoes, and *Ensalada de Habas* (Fresh Broad Bean Salad).

Lomo de Cerdo a la Caucana　　ARGENTINA
Pork Loin Baked in Milk

This is an unusual version of a meat cooked in milk. The lemon juice clabbers the milk slightly and also tenderizes the pork. At the end of the cooking time there are about 3 cups of slightly thickened milk in the baking dish. This makes a very light and attractive sauce when reduced. Boned shoulder of pork, a more economical cut, can also be used, in which case increase the cooking time by about half an hour.

Serves 6

2 pounds boneless pork loin or
　　boned shoulder
4 cups milk
¼ cup lemon juice
Salt, freshly ground pepper
2 tablespoons butter

Put the pork into an oblong Pyrex or other flameproof baking dish that will just hold it comfortably. Mix the milk with the lemon juice and pour it over the pork. Cover the dish lightly and leave overnight in a cool place. When ready to cook, lift the pork out of the milk mixture and pat it dry. Season with salt and pepper. Heat the butter in a skillet and brown the pork lightly all over. Put the pork back into the dish with the milk together with the pan drippings, and bake it, uncovered, in a preheated moderate (350° F.) oven for 1½ to 2 hours, or until the pork is tender. Lift the pork out onto a warmed serving platter and remove the string tying it up. Skim the fat from the sauce and pour the sauce into a saucepan. Reduce it over brisk heat to 1½ cups. Pour it into a sauceboat and serve separately. Slice the meat and serve hot with rice or potatoes and a green vegetable.

　　This is also good served cold with *Guasacaca* (Avocado Sauce) from Venezuela (page 317) or *Guacamole* (Avocado Sauce) from Mexico (page 316) and salad.

Lomo en Jugo de Naranja

Pork Loin in Orange Juice

ECUADOR

Serves 6

3 tablespoons butter
1 large onion, finely chopped
1 clove garlic, minced
A 3-pound loin of pork, boned
Salt, freshly ground pepper
1 tablespoon grated orange rind
1 fresh hot red or green pepper,
    seeded and ground, or 1
    teaspoon hot pepper sauce
    such as Tabasco
2 cups orange juice
Chicken stock
2 teaspoons cornstarch

Heat the butter in a skillet and sauté the onion and garlic until the onion is soft. With a slotted spoon transfer the onion and garlic to a flameproof casserole large enough to hold the pork loin. Season the pork with salt and pepper and brown all over in the fat remaining in the skillet. Add the pork to the casserole with the grated orange rind, the hot pepper or hot pepper sauce, orange juice, and enough stock barely to cover. Bring to a bare simmer and cook, covered, over very low heat for about 2 hours, or until the meat is tender. Put the meat on a serving platter, slice it, and keep it warm. Measure the liquid in the casserole and reduce it over brisk heat to 2 cups. Mix the cornstarch with a little water and stir it into the sauce. Cook, stirring, over moderate heat until the sauce is lightly thickened. Spoon a little of the sauce over the pork and serve the rest separately in a sauceboat. Accompany the pork with a salad made of cooked sliced beets, carrots, and potatoes in a vinaigrette sauce made with a teaspoon of Dijon mustard. If liked, toss the vegetables separately in the vinaigrette sauce and arrange them in heaps on a bed of lettuce leaves on a platter. Or serve with plain rice and a green vegetable.

Chancho a la Chilena
CHILE

Pork Loin, Chilean Style

Serves 6 to 8

¼ cup vegetable oil
4 pounds boneless pork loin
2 medium onions, sliced
2 cloves garlic, chopped
1 carrot, scraped and sliced
1 stalk celery, cut into 1-inch
    pieces

1 bay leaf
½ teaspoon oregano
½ teaspoon thyme
¼ teaspoon ground cumin
Salt, freshly ground pepper
½ cup red wine vinegar

Heat the oil in a large flameproof casserole and brown the meat lightly all over. Add all the other ingredients to the casserole with enough water to cover. Bring to a boil, cover, reduce the heat, and simmer gently until the meat is tender, about 3 hours. Allow the meat to cool completely in the stock, then remove to a serving platter. Reserve the stock for another use.

    Serve the pork sliced with *Salsa de Ají Colorado* (Red Pepper Sauce), page 311, separately. In Chile the pork slices would be covered with the sauce. But since it can be quite incendiary if the peppers used are very hot, it is wiser to test one's palate with a little at a time.

GROUND MEAT DISHES

Albóndigas
URUGUAY

Meatballs

Albóndigas enjoy great popularity in Latin America and are obviously inspired by the Middle East, where the range and variety of delicious meatballs seem inexhaustible. The countries of Latin America, adding their own very special touches, make their meatballs with beef, veal, or pork or a combination. They are usually lightly sautéed first, then cooked in a broth or sauce, seasoned quite differently from the meatballs themselves, thus creating a counterpoint of flavors that is very intriguing. Often there is the added richness that wine gives to the sauce. In Mexico the full-flavored yet mild *ancho* chili or the peppery, exotic *chipotle* adds unusual flavor to the sauces. With such variety in seasonings it would be hard to tire of them.

Makes about 18 meatballs, serves 4 to 6

5 tablespoons vegetable oil
1 medium onion, finely chopped
1 medium tomato, peeled and
    chopped
1 fresh hot red pepper, seeded and
    chopped
1 teaspoon sugar
Salt, freshly ground pepper
1 pound veal, finely ground

1 cup fresh breadcrumbs
4 tablespoons grated Parmesan
    cheese
¼ cup seedless raisins
¼ teaspoon grated nutmeg
2 eggs
Milk, if necessary
Flour

FOR THE BROTH

1 tablespoon vegetable oil
1 medium onion, finely chopped
1 ½ cups beef stock
1 ½ cups dry red wine
¼ teaspoon thyme

¼ teaspoon oregano
1 bay leaf
Salt, freshly ground pepper
Additional stock and wine, if
    necessary

In a skillet heat 2 tablespoons of the oil and sauté the onion until it is soft. Add the tomato, hot pepper, sugar, and salt and pepper to taste. Cook, stirring from time to time, until the mixture is thick and quite dry. Let the mixture cool. In a bowl mix together the veal, breadcrumbs, Parmesan cheese, raisins, nutmeg, and the tomato mixture. Add the eggs, mixing thoroughly. If the mixture is too dry to hold together, add a very little milk. Form into balls, about 2 inches in diameter, and flour them lightly. Heat the remaining 3 tablespoons of oil in the skillet and sauté the meatballs until lightly browned. As they are done, lift them out and set aside.

To make the broth: Heat the tablespoon of oil in a saucepan and sauté the onion until it is very soft. Add the stock, wine, thyme, oregano, and bay leaf, and simmer for a few minutes to blend the flavors. Season to taste with salt and pepper. Add the meatballs, cover, and cook over low heat until they are done, about 30 minutes. If necessary to cover the meatballs, add more stock and wine in equal amounts.

Serve the meatballs with rice or any starchy vegetable, using the broth as gravy. The broth may be a little thin, or too abundant, in which case lift out the meatballs to a serving dish and keep them warm. Reduce the broth over brisk heat until it is slightly thickened. If any is left over, I find it comes in handy for use in other sauces. *Ensalada de Habas* (Fresh Broad Bean Salad) from Ecuador makes a very pleasant accompaniment.

Variation: For *Albóndigas* from Chile, use ground beef instead of veal and mix the beef with 1 finely chopped onion, 1 cup fresh breadcrumbs, salt, pepper, and 2 eggs, adding a little milk if the mixture is too dry. Form into balls, and poach in beef stock until tender, about 30 minutes. While the meatballs are poaching, make a sauce: In a saucepan heat 2 tablespoons butter and sauté 1 onion, finely chopped, until it is soft. Add 1½ cups each beef stock and dry red wine, 1 very finely grated carrot, ¼ teaspoon ground cumin, 1 bay leaf, and salt and pepper to taste. Bring to a boil and simmer, covered, for 30 minutes, then strain. Return the sauce to the pan and thicken with a beurre manié. Mix 2 teaspoons flour with 2 teaspoons butter and stir it into the hot sauce bit by bit. Reserving the poaching stock for another use, remove the meatballs to a serving dish and pour the sauce over them. Serve with rice. Serves 4 to 6.

Variation: For *Albóndigas en Caldo* (Meatballs in Stock) from Paraguay, thoroughly mix together 1 pound ground beef, 1 cup cornmeal or fresh breadcrumbs, 1 onion, finely chopped, 1 clove garlic, minced, 2 tablespoons finely chopped parsley, 1 fresh hot red pepper, minced, ¼ teaspoon oregano, salt and pepper to taste, and 2 eggs. Add a little stock if the mixture seems too dry. Form into balls, about 2 inches in diameter, putting a piece of hardboiled egg in the center of each ball. Set aside. Heat 1 tablespoon vegetable oil in a saucepan and sauté 1 onion, finely chopped, 2 medium tomatoes, peeled and chopped, 1 fresh hot red pepper, seeded and chopped, and salt and pepper, until the onion is soft. Add 3 cups beef stock and bring to a boil. Add the meatballs and simmer until they are done, about 30 minutes. Serve with rice. Serves 4 to 6.

If liked the meatballs may be made small, 1 inch in diameter, and the amount of stock increased to 8 cups. Cook the meatballs with 3 tablespoons well-washed rice for 20 minutes and serve in soup plates, with the stock, as a soup. The cornmeal will give this version a slightly drier texture, the breadcrumbs a very soft one. Both are good. Serves 4 to 6.

Variation: For *Albóndigas Picantes* (Peppery Meatballs) from Paraguay, put 1½ pounds lean beef, ground twice, in a bowl with 2 cloves garlic, minced, 1 cup fresh breadcrumbs, ½ teaspoon each ground oregano and cumin, salt and pepper to taste, and a beaten egg. Mix very thoroughly, adding a little milk or stock if the meat mixture seems too dry. Make into balls 1½ inches in diameter and roll lightly in flour. Sauté the balls in vegetable oil until lightly browned all over and set aside.

Next make a sauce: Heat 3 tablespoons vegetable oil in a saucepan and sauté 2 medium onions, finely chopped, 1 bell pepper, seeded and chopped, preferably red (if red peppers are not available, use 2 canned pimientos, chopped). Add 2 fresh hot red or green peppers, seeded and chopped, or use 1 teaspoon cayenne pepper or 1 teaspoon hot pepper sauce such as Tabasco. (If using cayenne or Tabasco, add these later with the tomato purée.) When the onion is soft, add 1 bay leaf, 1 teaspoon sugar, and salt and pepper to taste. Stir in 2 cups beef stock and 6 cups tomato purée and simmer, covered, for 15 minutes. Remove and discard the bay leaf and purée the liquid in a blender or food processor. Return to the saucepan and bring to a simmer, add the meatballs and simmer, uncovered, for 15 minutes longer, or until the meatballs are done. Serve with white rice. There should be a generous amount of sauce to go over the rice. It may be reduced over brisk heat or thickened with a little flour if it is too abundant. Serves 4 to 6.

Variation: Perhaps of all the meatballs in Latin America, the Mexican ones are the most exotic. There is one version with a choice of sauces — either a gentle *ancho* chili sauce or a hot *chipotle* or *morita* chili sauce, so that all tastes are accommodated happily.

For *Albóndigas Mexicanas*, in a bowl thoroughly mix together ½ pound each twice-ground beef, pork, and veal. Add ½ cup fresh bread-crumbs, 1 medium onion, finely chopped, ½ teaspoon oregano or ground cumin, according to preference, salt, freshly ground pepper, and 1 egg, lightly beaten. Mix thoroughly, adding a little milk if necessary. Form into 1½-inch balls, roll lightly in flour, and set aside. If liked, a little cooked rice, a little hardboiled egg, or a slice of green olive, or a combination of all three, may be put in the center of each meatball. Makes 24 meatballs.

For the Ancho Chili Sauce: Pull the stems off 3 dried *ancho* chilies, shake out the seeds, and tear the peppers into pieces. Rinse and put to soak in a bowl with ½ cup warm water. Leave to soak for about 1 hour, turning from time to time. Put into a blender or food processor with the liquid and reduce to a purée. Set aside. In a skillet heat 3 tablespoons vegetable oil and sauté 1 medium onion, finely chopped, with 1 clove garlic, minced, until the onion is soft. Add the puréed *ancho* chili and 2 cups peeled, seeded, and finely chopped tomato, and sauté, stirring frequently, for 5 minutes over moderate heat. Pour the mixture into a fairly large saucepan, add 1 cup or more of beef stock to thin the mixture to a souplike consistency. Season to taste with salt, pepper, and ¼ teaspoon sugar. Bring to a simmer, add the meatballs, and simmer, uncovered, until the meatballs are tender, about 20 minutes. Serve with rice. Serves 4 to 6.

For the Chipotle or Morita Chili Sauce: Follow the instructions for the preceding sauce, but omit the *ancho* chili. Put the 2 cups peeled, seeded, and chopped tomato in a blender or food processor with 1 *chipotle* or 2 *morita* chilies, coarsely chopped, and blend to a purée. Sauté with the onion and thin with the beef stock, adding more stock if necessary. The sauce will be quite hot, and very much thinner than the mild but full-flavored *ancho* sauce.

Variation: For *Albóndigas* from Venezuela, in a bowl combine 1 pound finely ground lean beef, ¼ pound boiled ham, ground, 1 finely chopped onion, ½ cup fresh breadcrumbs, 2 lightly beaten eggs, and salt and freshly ground pepper to taste. Mix thoroughly and form into balls about 1 inch in diameter. Heat 4 tablespoons vegetable oil in a skillet and sauté the meatballs, in batches, until they are browned all over. Transfer to a flameproof casserole or saucepan. In a blender or food processor combine 1 onion, chopped, 1 tablespoon chopped parsley, 4 medium tomatoes, peeled and chopped, salt and freshly ground pepper to taste, and 1 cup dry white wine. Blend until the mixture is smooth. Pour over the meatballs, adding a little beef stock if necessary to barely cover. Simmer, covered, over low heat until the meatballs are cooked, about 20 minutes. Serve with rice or potatoes, and a green vegetable or salad as a main course. Serves 6.

The meatballs may be made half size, speared with toothpicks and served as an accompaniment to drinks. Drain them thoroughly and reserve the sauce for another use.

Picadillo MEXICO
Seasoned Chopped Beef

Picadillo is a great favorite throughout Latin America and every country has its own version. In Mexico it is much appreciated as a filling for tacos, *empanadas*, tamales, and green peppers. In the north of the country it is popular on its own and is eaten as a main dish, accompanied by rice, beans, *guacamole*, and tortillas.

Serves 6

3 tablespoons olive or vegetable oil
2 pounds lean ground beef
1 large onion, finely chopped
1 clove garlic, finely chopped
3 medium tomatoes, peeled and chopped
2 tart cooking apples, peeled, cored, and chopped
1 or more fresh hot green peppers, seeded and chopped, or 2 or 3 canned jalapeño chilies, seeded and chopped

½ cup raisins, soaked 10 minutes in warm water
½ cup pimiento-stuffed olives, halved crosswise
½ teaspoon oregano
½ teaspoon thyme
Salt, freshly ground pepper
1 tablespoon butter
½ cup slivered almonds

Heat the oil in a large, heavy skillet. Add the beef and sauté until it is lightly browned, stirring to break up any lumps. Add the onion and garlic and sauté for 5 minutes longer. Add all the remaining ingredients except the butter and the almonds. Mix well and simmer, uncovered, over moderate heat, stirring from time to time, for 20 minutes. In a small skillet heat the butter and sauté the almonds until they are golden brown. Mound the beef onto a serving platter and sprinkle with the almonds. Surround it with a border of *Arroz Blanco* (White Rice).

Variation: Instead of oregano and thyme, use a pinch or two of cinnamon and ⅛ teaspoon ground cloves. This makes an interesting difference in flavor, giving the dish an almost Middle Eastern taste.

Variation: In Chihuahua, the apple is left out and 4 medium potatoes, cooked and cubed, and 2 cups cooked green peas are added to the beef at the end of the cooking time for just long enough to heat them through. This makes a nice one-dish meal.

Variation: *Picadillo de la Costa* from the state of Guerrero, best known for the beach resort of Acapulco, uses the tropical fruits in which the region abounds, and instead of beef uses an equal mixture of ground pork and veal. The method is the same but the meats, with the onion, garlic, tomatoes, hot peppers, salt, and pepper, are cooked, uncovered, for 15 minutes. Then 1½ cups pineapple chunks, 2 pears, peeled, cored, and cut in chunks, and 2 bananas, peeled and sliced, are added and the mixture simmered for 15 minutes longer over low heat. Sprinkle with almonds just before serving. This is a delicious summer dish, good with plain rice.

Picadinho de Porco   BRAZIL
Pork Hash

Serves 6

1 tablespoon butter
1 medium onion, grated
2 large tomatoes, peeled, seeded,
  and chopped
2 pounds ground pork
½ pound chorizo or other spiced,
  smoked pork sausage,
  skinned and chopped

4 tablespoons lemon juice
Salt, freshly ground pepper
¼ cup chopped parsley
2 hardboiled eggs
3 large bananas, peeled
Butter

Heat the butter in a skillet and sauté the onion for 2 minutes. Add the tomatoes and cook, stirring occasionally, until the mixture is thick and well blended. Add the pork and the sausage and continue cooking for 20 minutes until the pork is cooked through, breaking up the meat with a fork. Add the lemon juice and salt and pepper to taste and cook for a few minutes longer. Transfer the hash to a warmed serving dish and sprinkle with the parsley, the egg whites, finely chopped, and the egg yolks, sieved. Keep warm.

Halve the bananas crosswise, then lengthwise, and sauté in butter until lightly browned. Surround the hash with the bananas.

If preferred, omit the bananas and serve with *Angú de Farinha de Milho* (Molded Cornmeal), or include with both accompaniments.

RABBIT DISHES

Rabbit, with its lean, flavorful meat, is very adaptable, taking happily to a wide variety of seasonings. In Latin America, where it is a favorite, having superseded its indigenous relatives like the *agouti* or *paca* in modern markets, it may be cooked with white wine in the simplest of ways, or exotically with sweet peppers and thick coconut milk, with annatto, with orange juice, or even more exotically with ground peanuts. A friend of mine uses peanut butter, but I prefer the texture of the sauce when home-ground nuts are used. Excellent quality frozen rabbit cut up in ready-to-cook pieces is available in supermarkets. However, a whole rabbit is very easy to cut up.

Usually the head has already been removed. If not, cut it off using a sharp, heavy knife. Split it in two and use it to enrich the dish. There is a small amount of meat on it and the brains can be eaten separately. Cut off the forelegs — easy, as they are not jointed. Cut across the rabbit just under the rib cage, then cut the rib cage in half. Cut across the section with the hind legs, then split it in two, separating the legs. Cut the part remaining, the saddle, into two pieces crosswise. One piece will contain the kidneys. There will be eight pieces in all but the two rib pieces have very little meat.

Guiso de Conejo

PERU

Rabbit Stew

Serves 4

6 cloves garlic
1 teaspoon each cumin, oregano,
    and rosemary
Salt, freshly ground pepper
½ cup vegetable oil
¼ cup white wine vinegar

A 2½-pound rabbit, or 2½ pounds
    of kid, cut into serving pieces
3 slices bacon, chopped
2 cups dry white wine
12 small white onions, peeled

Grind the garlic, cumin, oregano, and rosemary together with a mortar and pestle or in a small blender jar. Add salt to taste and a generous amount of pepper. Mix with ¼ cup of the oil and all the vinegar. Put the rabbit pieces in a bowl and pour the mixture over them. Cover with plastic wrap and marinate overnight in the refrigerator, turning once or twice. Lift out the rabbit pieces, pat dry. Reserve the marinade.

In a skillet heat the remaining ¼ cup of oil and sauté the bacon until it is crisp. Push it to one side of the skillet and sauté the rabbit pieces in the fat until they are golden. Transfer the rabbit and the contents of the skillet to a flameproof casserole or heavy saucepan. Add the marinade, the wine, and the onions. Cover and simmer until the rabbit is tender, about 1½ hours. Arrange the rabbit and the onions in a serving dish and keep warm. Reduce the sauce over brisk heat until it is slightly thickened. Pour over the rabbit. Garnish if liked with black olives and parsley sprigs and serve with boiled potatoes.

Conejo con Leche de Coco

COLOMBIA

Rabbit in Coconut Milk

In Colombia this is made with *ñeque* or *paca*, an animal like a hare, but rabbits are enough like hares for the substitution to succeed. It is a coastal dish and uses both annatto and coconut milk, typical of the cooking of this region. *Conejo Guisado con Coco* (Rabbit Stew with Coconut Milk), also from the coast, uses coconut milk too, but the flavors of the two dishes are very different and demonstrate the versatility of this attractive cuisine.

6 large cloves garlic
1 teaspoon salt
¼ teaspoon cayenne pepper
½ teaspoon ground cumin
12 grinds black pepper, about
3 tablespoons white vinegar
A 2½-pound rabbit, cut into
    8 serving pieces

1 tablespoon annatto oil or lard
    (see page 324)
1 medium onion, chopped
1 large tomato, peeled, seeded,
    and chopped
1 tablespoon tomato paste
½ cup thick coconut milk (see
    page 7)

In a mortar crush the garlic with the salt, cayenne pepper, cumin, and black pepper. Stir in the vinegar. Spread this mixture over the pieces of rabbit in the casserole in which they are to be cooked and marinate at room temperature for about 4 hours, turning the pieces once or twice.

Heat the annatto oil or lard in a skillet and sauté the onion until it is softened. Add it to the rabbit with the tomato and tomato paste and enough water barely to cover. Bring to a boil, cover, and cook over low heat until the rabbit is tender, about 1½ hours. Lift the rabbit pieces onto a serving dish and keep warm. Over brisk heat reduce the liquid in the casserole to about 1 cup, stirring frequently. Stir in the coconut milk and heat it through. Do not let it boil. Pour the sauce over the rabbit. Serve with rice.

Conejo Guisado con Coco   COLOMBIA
Rabbit Stew with Coconut Milk

3 tablespoons butter
A 2½-pound rabbit, cut into
    8 serving pieces
1 large onion, finely chopped
2 cloves garlic, chopped
1 green bell pepper, seeded and
    chopped
1 fresh hot red or green pepper,
    seeded and chopped

1 large tomato, peeled and
    chopped
1 pimiento, chopped
Salt, freshly ground pepper
2 cups beef or chicken stock
½ cup thick coconut milk (see
    page 7)

Heat the butter in a skillet and sauté the rabbit pieces until they are lightly browned. Transfer the rabbit to a flameproof casserole. In the fat remaining in the skillet sauté the onion, garlic, and the sweet and hot peppers. Add to the casserole with the tomato, pimiento, salt and pepper to taste, and the stock. Bring to a boil, cover, and cook over very low heat until the rabbit is tender, about 1½ hours. Remove the rabbit pieces to a serving dish and keep warm. Over brisk heat reduce the liquid in the casserole to about half. Lower the heat and stir in the coconut milk. Cook, stirring, for a few minutes, then pour the sauce over the rabbit. The sauce should be quite thick. Serve with rice.

Variation: Omit the coconut milk, and reduce the amount of stock to 1 cup and add 1 cup red wine instead. Reduce the liquid in the casserole in the same way, as the sauce should not be abundant.

Conejo con Maní
Rabbit in Peanut Sauce

CHILE

Serves 4

¼ cup vegetable oil
1 tablespoon sweet paprika
A 2½-pound rabbit, cut into
    serving pieces
2 large onions, finely chopped
1 clove garlic
1 cup roasted peanuts, finely
    ground

Salt, freshly ground pepper to taste
½ teaspoon ground cumin
1 tablespoon white wine vinegar
1½ cups chicken stock
1½ cups dry white wine

Heat the oil in a heavy casserole and stir in the paprika, taking care not to let it burn. Add the rabbit pieces and sauté lightly. Lift out and set aside. Add the onions and garlic to the casserole and sauté until the onions are softened. Return the rabbit pieces to the casserole. Add all the other ingredients, mix well, cover, and simmer until the rabbit is tender, about 1½ hours. Serve with rice and a salad.

Variation: Peru has a *Conejo con Maní* using the very hot yellow peppers that are a feature of this kitchen. It can however be made with fresh hot red or green peppers instead. Sauté the rabbit pieces in a mixture of 2 tablespoons vegetable oil and 2 tablespoons butter. Transfer the rabbit to a casserole. In the fat remaining in the skillet sauté 3 medium onions, cut into thick slices, and add to the casserole with 1 or 2 hot peppers ground in a blender with 2 cloves garlic and 1 teaspoon salt. Cover with chicken stock or water, 2 to 3 cups, and simmer for 1 hour. Add 1 cup roasted ground peanuts and simmer until the rabbit is tender, about 30 minutes longer. Just before serving, add 8 small whole cooked potatoes. The peanuts will thicken as well as flavor the stew.

Conejo en Salsa de Naranja CHILE
Rabbit in Orange Sauce

Serves 4

2 tablespoons vegetable oil
A 2½-pound rabbit, cut into
    serving pieces
2 medium onions, finely chopped
1 clove garlic, chopped
1½ cups dry white wine
1½ cups orange juice

Salt, freshly ground pepper
1 tablespoon flour
1 tablespoon butter
2 eggs, lightly beaten
1 hardboiled egg, finely chopped
1 tablespoon chopped parsley

Heat the oil in a skillet and sauté the rabbit pieces until they are lightly browned. Transfer to a flameproof casserole. In the oil remaining in the pan, adding a little more if necessary, sauté the onions and garlic until the onions are softened. Add to the casserole. Pour the wine into the skillet and scrape up all the brown bits. Pour into the casserole. Add the orange juice to the casserole and season to taste with salt and pepper. Cover and simmer until the rabbit is tender, about 1½ hours. Transfer the rabbit pieces to a serving dish and keep them warm.

Work the flour and butter into a paste. Add it to the liquid in the casserole and cook over low heat, stirring, until it is lightly thickened. Beat ½ cup of the sauce into the eggs, then pour the eggs into the casserole, stirring constantly. Do not let the sauce come to a boil, as it will curdle. Pour the sauce over the rabbit and sprinkle with the egg and parsley. Serve with rice, potatoes or noodles, and a green vegetable.

INNARDS, OR VARIETY MEATS

✳ Tripe Dishes

Of all the *interiores* (innards) none is so popular in Latin America as tripe, understandably so since few dishes are as appetizing when well prepared from an imaginative recipe. Tripe, which generally means the first and second stomach of beef, comes to the market from the packing house, ready prepared and partially cooked. The best kind is honeycomb, but plain tripe is also good. Pig and sheep tripe are also sometimes sold. Tripe is quite tough and needs to be simmered 2 or more hours to tenderize it, but a word of warning must be sounded — much depends on how long the tripe has been precooked before being sold. It is wise to test from time to time during the cooking process so as not to overcook it. It should be tender but with a good, firm texture, a nice bitey resistance. Overcooked tripe has no character.

I have chosen a group of recipes that come from Mexico and all over South America — all deliciously appetizing, easy to cook, earthy dishes to be enjoyed at any time of the year. They need little in the way of accompaniment, potatoes if they are not already included in the recipe, or perhaps rice, a green vegetable, or a salad. And your excellent dish of tripe has the added merit of being inexpensive.

Mondongo Serrano   MEXICO
Tripe, Mountain Style

This is quite a fancy dish from northern Mexico, with a wonderful blending of flavors and a fine aroma. I like to serve it to close friends or family.

Serves 6 to 8

3 pounds honeycomb tripe, cut
    into 1-inch squares
¼ cup lemon juice
3 cups beef stock, about
½ cup vegetable oil
1 large onion, finely chopped
4 chorizos (hot Spanish sausages),
    coarsely chopped
A ½-pound piece boiled ham, cut
    into ½-inch dice
A 1-pound can cooked garbanzos
    (chickpeas), or ½ pound dry
    chickpeas, soaked overnight
    and boiled until tender (about
    2 hours)
⅓ cup seedless raisins

⅓ cup blanched almonds, ground
⅔ cup orange juice
2 fresh hot green peppers, seeded
    and chopped, or canned
    Mexican serrano or jalapeño
    chilies
½ cup small pitted green olives,
    halved
Pinch each ground cloves and
    cinnamon
¼ teaspoon thyme
¼ teaspoon oregano
1 bay leaf
Salt, freshly ground pepper
Freshly grated Parmesan cheese

Wash the tripe in water mixed with the lemon juice, rinse, and put into a heavy saucepan or casserole with the beef stock, adding a little more if necessary to cover. Cover and simmer over low heat until the tripe is barely tender, about 1 to 2 hours. Test often for doneness, as the cooking time for tripe varies greatly. Lift the tripe out of the stock with a slotted spoon and pat dry with paper towels. Reserve the stock.

Heat the oil in a skillet and sauté the onion and chorizos until the onion is soft. Lift out with a slotted spoon and put into the casserole. In the fat remaining in the pan sauté the tripe and add to the casserole with all the remaining ingredients except the cheese. Pour in the reserved stock, cover, and simmer over very low heat for 30 minutes, or until the tripe is tender. Add a little more stock if necessary as the sauce should be quite abundant. Serve in rimmed soup plates with the cheese served separately. Accompany with crusty bread and a green salad.

Tripa de Vaca a Brasileira BRAZIL
Tripe with Vegetables, Brazilian Style

This is another rather fancy dish made special by the fresh coriander and the dry Madeira, which lend a lovely flavor.

Serves 6

3 pounds honeycomb tripe
4 tablespoons lime or lemon juice
3 cups beef broth
3 tablespoons olive oil
1 large onion, finely chopped
1 large clove garlic, chopped
1 sweet red pepper, seeded and
   chopped

3 medium tomatoes, peeled and
   chopped
1 bay leaf
3 tablespoons fresh coriander
   (cilantro), chopped
¼ cup dry Madeira
18 small pitted black olives
½ cup grated Parmesan cheese

Wash the tripe in cold running water and cut it into strips about ¾ inch by 2 inches. Put the tripe into a flameproof casserole and add the lime or lemon juice, stir to mix, and leave for 5 minutes. Add the beef broth to the casserole. Heat the oil in the casserole and sauté the onion, garlic, and Drain the tripe and set it aside. Reserve the broth. Rinse out and dry the casserole. Heat the oil in the casserole and sauté the onion, garlic, and sweet pepper until the onion is soft. Add to the casserole the tomatoes, bay leaf, fresh coriander, Madeira, tripe, and 2 cups of the reserved stock. Simmer, partially covered, until the tripe is tender and the sauce slightly thickened, about 1 hour. Stir from time to time with a wooden spoon to prevent the tripe from sticking. Add the olives and cook for a minute or two longer. Stir in the cheese. Serve with *Angú de Farinha de Milho* (Molded Cornmeal).

Chupe de Guatitas   CHILE
Tripe Stew

A very flavorful stew with a modestly fiery accent from the hot pepper combined with the richly subtle flavor of sweet red peppers. Chileans often use breadcrumbs, as is done here, to thicken sauces.

Serves 4 to 6

2 pounds honeycomb tripe	½ teaspoon oregano
½ cup paprika oil (Color Chilena), page 324, made with olive or vegetable oil	1 fresh hot red pepper, seeded and chopped, or ½ teaspoon cayenne
1 medium onion, finely chopped	Salt, freshly ground pepper
1 red bell pepper, seeded and chopped, or 2 canned pimientos, chopped	1 cup fresh breadcrumbs
	1 cup milk
¼ cup parsley, chopped	½ cup grated Parmesan cheese
	1 hardboiled egg, sliced

Put the tripe into a large saucepan or flameproof casserole with cold, unsalted water to cover, bring to a boil, lower the heat, and simmer, covered, until the tripe is barely tender, about 1 to 2 hours. Test during the cooking period as tripe varies greatly. Drain, cut the tripe into strips about ½ inch by 2 inches, and set aside. Reserve the stock.

Heat the paprika oil in the saucepan and add the onion and bell pepper. If using pimientos, add later with the parsley. Sauté until the onion and pepper are soft. Add the parsley, oregano, hot pepper or cayenne, salt and freshly ground pepper to taste, and the pimientos, if using. Stir to mix, and simmer, uncovered, for about 5 minutes, or until well blended.

Put the breadcrumbs and milk into a small saucepan and cook, stirring from time to time, for about 5 minutes. Purée in a blender or food processor. This step is not absolutely necessary but it does give a finer textured sauce. Add the breadcrumb sauce to the casserole, stirring to mix. Add the tripe. If the sauce is very thick, thin with ½ cup or more of the reserved tripe stock. Simmer, uncovered, over very low heat, stirring from time to time, for 20 minutes to blend the flavors. Pour into a heated serving dish. Sprinkle with the grated cheese and garnish with the hardboiled egg slices. Serve with crusty bread and a green salad.

Variation: For *Guatitas con Tomates* (Tripe with Tomatoes), cook the tripe in the same way but omit the bell pepper in the first sauce, and omit the breadcrumb sauce altogether. Sauté the onion and garlic, then add 6 medium tomatoes, peeled and chopped, and 2 carrots, scraped and grated. When the tomato sauce is well blended, add 6 medium potatoes, peeled and quartered, the tripe, and enough of the reserved tripe stock to cover. Simmer, covered, over low heat until the potatoes are tender. Thicken the sauce with 1 tablespoon flour mixed with a little stock to a paste, stirred into the casserole, and simmered until the sauce is lightly thickened. Omit the hardboiled egg garnish, and sprinkle the dish with grated Parmesan cheese.

Variation: A simple dish, great as a meal in itself, *Mondongo a la Criolla* (Tripe, Creole Style) is popular throughout Latin America. This is an Argentine recipe. Soak ½ pound dried lima beans overnight, drain, and put into a saucepan with salted water to cover. Simmer until the beans are tender, 1 to 1½ hours. Drain and set aside. In a flameproof casserole heat ½ cup olive oil and sauté 1 large onion, finely chopped, 1 large stalk celery, chopped, and 1 red bell pepper, seeded and chopped, until the onion is soft. Add 2 large tomatoes, peeled and chopped, and simmer for a few minutes to blend the flavors. Add 2 pounds honeycomb tripe cut into 1½- by ½-inch strips, 1 bay leaf, ¼ teaspoon each thyme and oregano, 2 cups beef stock, 1 tablespoon tomato paste, and salt and pepper to taste. Simmer, covered, over low heat for 1 to 2 hours, or until the tripe is barely tender. Test often, as the cooking time for tripe varies greatly. Add 1 cup well-washed long-grain rice and simmer until the rice is tender, about 20 minutes. If necessary add a little more stock as there should be plenty of sauce. Add the beans and heat through. Serve in rimmed soup plates with plenty of freshly grated Parmesan cheese, crusty bread, and a green salad.

Two 1-pound cans of *cannellini* (white kidney beans), rinsed and drained, and 2 canned pimientos, chopped, can be used instead of lima beans and bell pepper. Add just before serving and heat through.

Variation: The ground peanuts used in this Ecuadorian recipe for *Guatita* (Tripe) may seem a little startling at first. They add a delightful nutty taste, not at all overwhelming, and thicken the sauce at the same time. The annatto adds a subtle grace note of flavor, light and fragrant, while giving the dish an attractive yellow color. This is a most imaginative recipe yet the flavor of the finished dish is in no way bizarre.

Cook the tripe in the same way as for *Chupe de Guatitas* (Tripe Stew, see page 140). In a skillet heat 4 tablespoons annatto oil or lard (see page 324) and sauté 1 large onion, finely chopped, 2 cloves garlic, minced, 1 green bell pepper, seeded and chopped, until the onion is soft. Add 1 large tomato, peeled, seeded, and chopped, season with salt, and cook until the mixture is well blended. Stir in 1 cup ground peanuts and enough of the reserved tripe stock to thin to a medium thick sauce. Add the tripe and 1 pound potatoes, cooked and cubed, and simmer until heated through. Serve sprinkled with chopped coriander or parsley. Accompany with a green vegetable or a salad. Serves 4.

Variation: For *Caucau a la Limeña* (Tripe, Lima Style), Peruvian cooks would use hot yellow peppers, but I find fresh hot red or green peppers a perfect substitute, and where Peruvians would use 1 tablespoon of ground *palillo*, a yellow herb, I use 1½ teaspoons of turmeric, with fine results. Cook the tripe in the same way as for *Chupe de Guatitas* (Tripe Stew, see page 140). In a large, heavy skillet that has a lid, heat 1 cup vegetable oil and add 1 or more, according to taste, fresh hot red or green peppers, seeded and pounded in a mortar or puréed in a blender, 4 medium onions, finely chopped, and 6 cloves garlic, chopped. Sauté over moderate heat until the onions are soft and beginning to brown. Add the tripe and 2 pounds potatoes, peeled and cut into ½-inch cubes. Sauté for 2 or 3 minutes, then add 1½ teaspoons ground turmeric mixed with ½ cup tripe stock, a sprig of mint or parsley, and salt and freshly ground pepper to taste. Cover and simmer over low heat until the potatoes are almost done. Cook, uncovered, until the dish is quite dry. If necessary add a little more tripe stock during cooking, but only enough to cook the potatoes. Before serving pour a tablespoon of oil over the tripe, folding it into the mixture. Serves 4.

※ Tongue

Lengua en Salsa Picante   CHILE
Tongue in Hot Pepper Sauce

Fresh beef tongue is popular as a main dish in all of Latin America. This dish from Chile is not very peppery. There is just enough hot chili in the sauce to justify the name, but only enough to give a pleasant piquancy.

Serves 6 to 8

A fresh beef tongue, weighing about 3 pounds	*1 small stalk celery*
1 onion, sliced	*1 bay leaf*
1 sprig each parsley and coriander (cilantro)	*2 teaspoons salt*

Wash the tongue and put into a large saucepan or flameproof casserole with all the remaining ingredients and enough cold water to cover. Bring to a boil, skim as necessary, reduce the heat, cover, and simmer until the tongue is tender, about 3 hours. Uncover and leave in the stock until it is cool enough to handle. Lift out onto a platter, remove skin and any bones or fat, and cut into ½-inch slices. Strain the stock into a jug. Rinse out and dry the casserole and return the tongue to it.

FOR THE SAUCE

2 shallots, finely chopped	2 cups tongue stock
½ cup red or white wine vinegar	1 or more fresh hot peppers,
2 tablespoons butter or vegetable	preferably red, seeded and
oil	finely chopped
2 tablespoons flour	2 tablespoons chopped parsley

Put the shallots into a small saucepan with the vinegar and simmer until the shallots are tender, about 3 minutes. Set aside. Heat the butter or oil in a saucepan and add the flour. Cook, stirring constantly with a wooden spoon, for 2 minutes over low heat without letting the flour brown. Stir in the stock and simmer over low heat for 10 minutes. Stir in the vinegar and shallot mixture, the hot pepper, and parsley, and pour over the tongue. Simmer just long enough to heat the tongue through. Arrange on a platter and serve surrounded by halved cooked potatoes, or with rice served separately.

Variation: Ecuador has a similar recipe. Also called *Lengua en Salsa Picante*, the tongue is cooked in the same way but the sauce differs, and I find it makes an interesting change from the Chilean version. In 2 tablespoons vegetable oil or butter, sauté 1 medium onion, finely chopped, with 1 clove garlic, chopped, until the onion is soft. Stir in 1 tablespoon dry mustard, mixing well. Add 1½ cups stock from the cooked tongue and simmer for 5 minutes. Add 1 tablespoon capers, 2 tablespoons chopped parsley, 1 pimiento, coarsely chopped, 1 tablespoon lemon juice, and salt and pepper to taste. Pour the sauce over the sliced tongue and simmer just long enough to heat through.

Variation: The very first Mexican dish I learned to cook was *Lengua en Salsa de Tomate Verde* (Tongue in Green Tomato Sauce), using the little green husk tomatoes that have such a special, and delicious, flavor. The tongue is cooked in the same way as in the previous recipes. In a blender or food processor combine 1 medium onion, coarsely chopped, 2 cloves garlic, chopped, ½ cup coriander (cilantro) sprigs, chopped, 1½ cups canned Mexican green tomatoes, drained, and 3 or 4 canned *serrano* chilies, or 1 or 2 fresh hot green peppers, seeded and chopped, and reduce to a coarse purée. Heat 3 tablespoons lard or vegetable oil in a skillet, pour in the purée, and cook, stirring, for about 4 minutes. Add 1 cup stock from the cooked tongue, season to taste with salt, and pour over the tongue. Simmer just long enough to heat through. Serve with small new potatoes.

If fresh Mexican green tomatoes are available, peel off the brown outer husk and chop coarsely before adding to the blender or food processor.

Variation: Another favorite Mexican recipe is *Lengua en Salsa de Chile Ancho y Almendra* (Tongue in Mild Red Chili and Almond Sauce). Simply heat the tongue through in 2 cups of the sauce (see page 143).

Variation: There is usually quite a lot of stock left over from cooking a tongue, and Latin American cooks frequently use it to make soup, saving the trimmings of the tongue for garnish. Recipes are not very formal. Vegetables such as carrots, turnips, potatoes, Swiss chard, or cabbage are cubed or chopped and may be cooked in a little butter for a few minutes before being added to the stock, or just added and simmered until tender, about 25 minutes. A little sherry is sometimes added to the finished soup, and sometimes it is sprinkled with grated cheese. Rice, vermicelli, or cornmeal is also sometimes added, in short whatever is on hand. The result is a very pleasant unpretentious soup augmented by a feeling of virtue for having avoided waste.

✳ Pig's Feet

Patitas de Cerdo   ARGENTINA
Pig's Feet

Pig's feet, with their bland flavor and delicious gelatinous quality, are a favorite wherever pork is eaten. Latin America has some excitingly different recipes for this splendidly economical dish. I sometimes like to serve the pig's feet whole, instead of boned and cut up. I have borrowed a trick from James Beard, a dear friend always generous with help. I wrap the feet in cheesecloth and tie them with string before cooking them. It gives them a neat and tidy look, prevents broken skin, and makes for a much more attractive presentation.

Serves 4

8 pig's feet
1 ripe red bell pepper, seeded and
    chopped

2 cloves garlic

FOR THE DRESSING

1 teaspoon Spanish (hot) paprika
   or cayenne
1 cup red wine vinegar
Salt

1 cup vegetable oil
1 ripe red bell pepper, peeled (page
   15) and seeded
Lettuce leaves

Wrap each of the pig's feet tightly in cheesecloth and tie with string. Put into a large saucepan with the pepper and garlic and enough water to cover. Bring to a boil, reduce the heat, and simmer, covered, for 3 to 4 hours, or until tender. Let the pig's feet stand in the pan until cool enough to handle. Lift out and remove cheesecloth wrapping. Put into a shallow dish and pour on the dressing. Let stand at room temperature, turning once or twice, for at least an hour before serving.

    To make the dressing mix the ground hot paprika or cayenne with the vinegar and salt to taste. Beat in the oil. Cut the pepper into strips and add. Serve the pig's feet on plates garnished with lettuce leaves, 2 per person, as a main course, or serve 1 per person as an appetizer. Accompany with crusty bread and butter.

Patitas de Cerdo con Chile Poblano   MEXICO
Pig's Feet in Poblano Pepper Sauce

In Mexico the flavorful dark green *chile poblano* would be used for this recipe. Green bell pepper is a good substitute.

Serves 4

8 pig's feet
1 medium onion, coarsely
   chopped
⅛ teaspoon thyme

⅛ teaspoon oregano
1 bay leaf
1 sprig parsley or coriander
   (cilantro)

FOR THE SAUCE

1 medium onion, chopped
2 cloves garlic, chopped
6 medium tomatoes, peeled and
   chopped
4 tablespoons vegetable oil

3 green bell peppers, peeled (page
   15), seeded, and cut into
   strips
Pinch of sugar
Salt, freshly ground pepper

Wrap each of the pig's feet tightly in cheesecloth and tie with string. Put into a large saucepan with the onion, thyme, oregano, bay leaf, and parsley or coriander, and enough water to cover. Bring to a boil, reduce the heat, and simmer, covered, for 3 to 4 hours, or until tender. Let the pig's feet stand in the pan until cool enough to handle. Lift out and remove the cheesecloth wrapping. Return to the saucepan.

To make the sauce put the onion, garlic, and tomatoes into a blender or food processor fitted with a steel blade and reduce to a purée. Heat the oil in a skillet and add the tomato mixture and the pepper strips. Add the sugar and season to taste with salt and pepper. Simmer, uncovered, stirring from time to time, until the mixture is thick and well blended. Pour over the pig's feet and simmer until they are heated through. Serve with tortillas.

Variation: Leftover sauce from dishes like *Ternera en Pipián Verde* (Veal in Pumpkin Seed Sauce), *Pollo Verde Almendrado* (Chicken in Green Almond Sauce), *Pollo en Pipián de Almendra* (Chicken Stew with Almonds), *Mole Coloradito de Oaxaca* (Chicken in Red Sauce, Oaxaca Style), or *Salsa de Chile Ancho y Almendra* (Mild Red Chili and Almond Sauce), page 315, can be used with pig's feet.

Patitas de Chancho a la Criolla   PERU
Pig's Feet, Creole Style

Served at room temperature, this is more a salad for a luncheon main course or an hors d'oeuvre.

Serves 4 as luncheon dish,
8 as first course

2 pig's feet, about 2 pounds
Salt
2 medium onions, very thinly
  sliced
2 medium tomatoes, peeled and
  sliced
1 fresh hot red or green pepper,
  seeded and sliced lengthwise

2 cooked medium-sized potatoes,
  halved and sliced
6 tablespoons vegetable oil
2 tablespoons white vinegar or
  lemon juice, or a mixture
Salt, freshly ground pepper
Lettuce leaves for garnish

Wash the pig's feet and put them into a saucepan with salted water to cover, bring to a boil, reduce the heat, and simmer, covered, for 3 hours, or until tender. Cool in the stock, lift out, bone, and cut into 1-inch pieces, about. Discard the stock.

In a large bowl combine the pig's feet, onions, tomatoes, hot pepper strips, potatoes, oil, vinegar or lemon juice, salt and pepper to taste, and mix lightly. Allow to stand for about 15 minutes, then place in a serving dish garnished with lettuce leaves and serve at room temperature.

Picante de Pata Arequipeña

PERU

Spicy Pig's Feet, Arequipa Style

Serves 4

3 pig's feet
3 sprigs fresh mint
1 or more fresh hot red or green
    peppers, seeded and ground
2 tablespoons lard or vegetable oil
2 medium onions, finely chopped
3 cloves garlic, minced

½ teaspoon oregano
½ cup roasted peanuts, finely
    ground
Salt, freshly ground pepper
3 medium potatoes, about 1
    pound, cooked and cut into
    1-inch cubes

Wash the pig's feet and put them into a saucepan large enough to hold them comfortably, preferably in a single layer. Add the mint and enough water to cover by about 1 inch. Cover and simmer until the pig's feet are tender, about 3 hours. Let them cool in the stock, then lift out, remove the bones, and cut into 1-inch pieces. Set aside. Strain and reserve the stock.

Grind the peppers with a mortar and pestle or in a small blender jar.

Heat the lard or oil in a flameproof casserole and sauté the onions, garlic, oregano, and hot peppers until the onions are soft. Stir in the peanuts and sauté for 1 or 2 minutes longer. Season to taste with salt and pepper. Stir in 1 cup of the reserved stock and simmer for a few minutes to blend the flavors. Add the pig's feet and the potatoes and simmer just long enough to heat them through. The sauce should be thick and highly spiced but one's own taste should determine the number of hot peppers used. If the sauce is too thick, add a little more of the reserved stock. In Peru this would be served with rice. I prefer it with a green vegetable or a salad.

Coração Recheado

BRAZIL

Stuffed Beef Heart

Stuffed beef heart has been a favorite dish of mine since childhood, so I was delighted when a Brazilian friend gave me her recipe, which is quite grand. I was also pleased to be given a Chilean version of this old favorite in a new guise, a simpler recipe than the Brazilian one. I like both. Calf's heart is also good. It usually weighs about 1 pound so use about one-quarter of the stuffing and reduce the cooking time to 1½ hours. It would serve 2 or 3.

Serves 8

1 beef heart, weighing about 4
    pounds
4 tablespoons butter
1 medium onion, finely chopped
1 cup corn kernels
½ cup freshly made breadcrumbs
2 hardboiled eggs, chopped
½ sweet red pepper, peeled (see
    page 15), seeded and chopped
8 pimiento-stuffed olives, halved

1 small fresh hot red or green
    pepper, seeded and chopped
2 tablespoons chopped parsley
Salt, freshly ground pepper
1½ cups dry red wine
1½ cups beef stock
1 clove garlic, chopped
2 teaspoons cornstarch or
    arrowroot

Thoroughly wash the heart and remove the membrane inside that divides the two chambers if the butcher has not already done this. Trim away any fat. In a skillet heat 2 tablespoons of the butter and sauté the onion until it is soft. Purée the corn in a food processor or blender and stir into the onion off the heat. Add the breadcrumbs, the eggs, sweet pepper, olives, hot pepper, parsley, and salt and pepper to taste, mixing well. Stuff the heart with the dressing. Sew it up or skewer it and lace with string. In a flame-proof casserole large enough to hold the heart comfortably, heat the remaining 2 tablespoons of butter and brown the heart all over. Pour in the wine and stock, add the garlic, and bring the liquid to a boil. Cover the casserole with foil, then with the lid, and cook in a preheated moderate (350° F.) oven for about 3½ hours, or until tender. Lift the heart out onto a serving platter and remove the sewing thread or the skewers and string. Cut the heart into crosswise slices and keep warm. Reduce the cooking liquid over brisk heat to 2 cups. Mix the cornstarch or arrowroot with a little cold water, stir into the sauce, and cook, stirring, for a few minutes until the sauce is thickened. Pour a little sauce over the sliced heart and serve the rest in a sauceboat. Serve with mashed potatoes and string beans or peas.

Variation: For *Corazon Relleno* (Stuffed Heart) from Chile, prepare the heart in the same way. For the stuffing soak 4 slices firm white bread in milk, then squeeze out and mix with 1 medium onion, finely chopped, 2 tablespoons parsley, finely chopped, 4 slices of bacon, chopped, salt and pepper to taste, and 1 egg, lightly beaten. Stuff the heart with the mixture and sew or skewer it closed. Heat 2 tablespoons vegetable oil in a flame-proof casserole and brown the heart all over. Add to the casserole 1 onion, coarsely chopped, 1 carrot, scraped and sliced, ½ teaspoon thyme, 1 sprig parsley, 1 bay leaf, and 1½ cups each beef stock and dry red wine. Cook as for *Coração Recheado*.

✳ Brains

Brains are popular in Latin America, particularly French Calf's Brains in Black Butter, which sounds very splendid in Spanish as *Sesos con Salsa de Mantequilla Quemada*. But there are several interesting recipes common to a number of countries that provide us with some new ways to cook this delicacy. A preliminary soaking and peeling are always necessary, followed by a simmering in seasoned liquid, except when the brains are to be stewed as in the first of these recipes.

Sesos Guisados COLOMBIA
Stewed Brains

This recipe is as appetizing as it is simple.

Serves 6

1½ pounds brains
1 medium onion, finely chopped
1 clove garlic, chopped
3 medium tomatoes, peeled and
    chopped

1 tablespoon butter
Salt, freshly ground pepper

Soak the brains in several changes of water for about 2 hours. Carefully pull off the thin membrane that covers the brains. This is not difficult but requires patience. Rinse the brains in fresh cold water. Then simmer in enough water to barely cover, with the onion, garlic, tomatoes, butter, and salt and pepper to taste for 30 minutes. Lift out the brains and cut each one into 4 to 6 slices. Arrange in a warmed serving dish. Reduce the liquid in the saucepan over brisk heat until it is slightly thickened, then pour over the brains. Serve with rice or potatoes or any other starchy vegetable.

Variation: For *Sesos Rebozados* (Sautéed Brains), soak 1½ pounds brains and remove the membranes in the usual way. Then simmer, in enough water to cover, with 1 small chopped onion, 1 clove garlic, and ½ teaspoon salt for 30 minutes. Cool in the cooking liquid, lift out, and pat dry with paper towels. Cut each brain into 4 to 6 slices. Beat 2 egg whites until they stand in peaks. Fold the whites into 2 egg yolks beaten with ½ teaspoon salt. Dip the brain slices in flour, then in the beaten egg, and sauté in 4 tablespoons butter until golden brown on both sides. Serve with rice or potatoes and a fresh Hot Pepper Sauce (page 311), or lemon wedges.

Variation: For *Sesos en Vino* (Brains in Wine Sauce), soak and simmer 1½ pounds brains as for *Sesos Rebozados*. Cut into cubes and put into a buttered casserole. Heat 2 tablespoons butter in a skillet and sauté 1 medium onion, finely chopped, and 1 clove chopped garlic until the onion is soft. Add to the casserole. Season to taste with salt and pepper. Fold 3 cups diced cooked potatoes into the brains and pour 1½ cups dry white wine over the mixture. Simmer very gently for 15 minutes to blend the flavors, sprinkle with 2 tablespoons chopped parsley, and serve surrounded by 12 triangles of white bread fried in butter.

Variation: For *Sesos con Jamón* (Brains with Ham), soak and simmer 1½ pounds brains as for *Sesos Rebozados*. Halve the brains, dip in flour seasoned with salt and pepper, and fry in butter, about 4 tablespoons, until golden on both sides. Sauté 6 thin slices of ham in butter and arrange on a warmed platter. Put the halved brains on top of the ham and mask with 1½ cups *Môlho ao Tomate* (page 318).

✳ Liver

Hígado en Salsa de Hongos CHILE
Calf's Liver in Mushroom Sauce

Chile's excellent wine turns an ordinary dish into a fine one in this simple recipe. Either a dry white or red wine, which I prefer, may be used.

Serves 4

6 tablespoons butter
2 tablespoons oil
1 medium onion, finely chopped
¼ teaspoon oregano
½ pound mushrooms, sliced
1½ cups dry red wine
Salt, freshly ground pepper
1 pound calf's liver, cut into
 ¼-inch slices

Heat 3 tablespoons of the butter and 1 tablespoon of the oil in a skillet and sauté the onion and oregano until the onion is soft. Add the mushrooms and cook over fairly high heat, stirring from time to time with a wooden spoon, until the mushrooms are lightly browned, about 5 minutes. Pour in the wine and cook, stirring, until the wine is reduced to half and the sauce is slightly thickened.

In another skillet heat the remaining 3 tablespoons butter and 1 tablespoon oil and sauté the liver over moderate heat for 2 minutes. Turn the pieces and sauté for 1 minute longer. Add the liver and the juices in the pan to the skillet with the mushrooms, stir to mix, and simmer for about 1 minute. Be careful not to overcook the liver—it should be pink inside. Transfer to a warmed serving dish and serve with potatoes or rice and a green vegetable.

Hígado con Vino
COLOMBIA

Calf's Liver in Red Wine Sauce

The red wine marinade gives this calf's liver a special delicate flavor.

Serves 2

½ pound calf's liver, cut into
　½-inch slices
Salt, freshly ground pepper

1 large clove garlic, crushed
¾ cup dry red wine
3 tablespoons butter

Arrange the liver slices in a large shallow dish, season with salt and pepper and the garlic. Pour the wine over them. Leave at room temperature for 2 hours, turning the slices from time to time. When ready to cook, lift out the liver slices and pat them dry with paper towels. Reserve the marinade. In a large skillet heat the butter and sauté the liver slices over moderate heat for about 2 minutes on the first side and 1 minute on the second side. The liver should remain pink inside. Pour the marinade into a small sauce-pan and reduce to half its volume. Arrange the liver on a warmed platter. Pour any liquid from the skillet into the wine sauce, stir to mix, and pour over the liver.

✳ Kidneys

Riñones con Vino
CHILE

Kidneys in Wine Sauce

I love to make this simple, quick Chilean kidney dish just for myself with two lamb kidneys or one pork. It is a fine dish for a hurried supper.

Serves 3 to 4

1 beef kidney
Salt, freshly ground pepper
4 tablespoons butter
1 medium onion, finely chopped

4 tablespoons parsley, chopped
1 cup dry white wine
4 medium potatoes, freshly
　cooked and cubed

Trim the surplus fat from the kidney, and cut the kidney into thin slices. Season with salt and pepper. Heat the butter in a skillet and sauté the kidney slices for about 5 minutes, turning frequently. Lift out and set aside in a covered dish. In the butter remaining in the pan sauté the onion until it is soft. Add the parsley and sauté for a minute longer. Add the wine and the potatoes. Add the kidney slices and cook just long enough to heat them through without further cooking, which would toughen them. Serve immediately.

If cooking this for one and using lamb or pork kidneys, remove the thin skin and any fat from the kidneys and slice them thinly. Use one-quarter of the remaining ingredients, and cook as above.

Variation: In Argentina cooks use a similar recipe for *Riñones a la Porteña* (Kidneys, Buenos Aires Style) except that veal kidney, chopped instead of sliced, is used and is sautéed in oil instead of butter.

Variation: For the Brazilian *Rim de Vitela* (Veal Kidney) or *Rims de Carneiro* (Lamb Kidneys), the kidneys are cleaned and sliced, and sautéed in 2 tablespoons olive oil. They are then heated through in the following sauce: Sauté 1 chopped onion and ½ green bell pepper, seeded and chopped, in 2 tablespoons olive oil until the onion is soft. Add 1 chopped tomato, ¼ cup chopped parsley, and salt and pepper. Simmer until well blended. Stir in ⅛ cup dry sherry and the kidneys. Reheat the kidneys without letting the sauce boil. For those who like a fiery touch, 1 small fresh hot pepper may be added with the bell pepper, or a dash of Tabasco with the sherry.

BARBECUES

The great cattle countries of Argentina and Brazil have marvelous outdoor feasts, elaborate and sophisticated barbecues that are superb for informal, warm weather entertaining, and easy to copy in the United States.

The *asado criollo*, the Argentine spit-roasted barbecue, originated with the gauchos — the cowboys of the *pampas*, those wide, rolling plains that stretch like a sea of grass for thousands of miles. The cowboys tended cattle, and later sheep, and when they were hungry killed an animal, spit-roasted it, and had dinner. In comparison, today's barbecue is a very grand affair. In addition to barbecued meats there are salads, sauces, bread, and wine, as well as the cowboy's favorite beverage, *mate*, the green herb tea popular in many parts of South America for its refreshing, slightly bitter flavor. But the essentials are the same — meat, salt, and a fire.

The word "barbecue" comes from the Spanish *barbacoa*, derived from a Haitian word in the Taino Indian language. It meant a rude framework either for sleeping or for drying meat over a fire, and reached the United States with that meaning by 1697. By 1809 its American meaning had changed to an outdoor social entertainment at which animals were roasted whole. Because of the growing popularity of outdoor cooking, grills of various kinds can easily be bought, and it is not difficult to build a do-it-yourself grill in the Argentine or Brazilian style provided there is yard space.

To make a *parrilla* (grill) for an Argentine *asado* (roast), dig a pit about 1 foot deep and about 3 feet long by 2 feet wide. Make sure the fire bed is level and cover it with a layer of sand. Surround it with bricks at ground level or, for a more luxurious grill, extend them to waist level, and cover with an iron grate. Also needed are a long three-pronged fork, a small work table to cut up the cooked meat, canvas work gloves, an asbestos oven mitt for hot jobs, tongs for turning meats and lifting them from the grill, a bowl for the *salmuera* (brine) to baste the meats, a brush or bunch of twigs for basting, and a bottle with a sprinkler top, filled with water, to discipline unruly flames.

It takes about an hour for a fire of wood and charcoal to burn down to embers that are ready to be used, and whoever looks after the grill has to put the meats on in sequence so that they are served hot and crispy brown on the outside, red and juicy inside. It is a considerable art and one that can be mastered only by experience, common sense, and a watchful eye. Meats are not basted with a barbecue sauce. Brine is used, usually a simple solution of salt and water. When the meat is seared on one side it is basted with brine and turned, and the other side seared and basted. After that the meat is turned and basted frequently until done.

Argentine hosts are generous in their estimate of how much meat is enough. They work it out roughly as a pound a person. The *asado* always begins with grilled sausages, either a halved chorizo, or 2 or 3 slices of grilled *longaniza*, nothing else, served with a glass of dry red wine. The sausages are just to hold off starvation, not to destroy appetite, while guests wait for the meats on the grill to cook. For ten people the traditional meats for the *parrillada* (barbecue) would be 2 pounds short ribs, 2 pounds rump or chuck steak, 1½ pounds flank steak, 1 pound blood sausage, 1 or 2 beef kidneys or a whole calf's liver, 1½ pounds sweetbreads, and 1½ pounds tripe, cut into strips about 1 inch wide. Traditionally intestines, udders, and prairie oysters are part of the roast. Intestines are grilled, then sliced. Udders are grilled, then cut into ½-inch slices. And prairie oysters are peeled, halved, grilled, and sliced.

After the sausages, the "innards" are served, and then the meats. Guests go to the grill to be served, then eat informally at simple wooden tables set with baskets of French bread and bottles or carafes of red wine. There are bowls of salad — lettuce, tomatoes, and sliced onions or scallions in a garlic-flavored oil and vinegar dressing, or a more robust one of potatoes, beets, hardboiled eggs, chopped celery, and radishes, also in a vinaigrette dressing. *Crudités* are sometimes served, raw carrot sticks, celery, and radishes. And there is always a bowl of hot pickled peppers as well as the traditional bowls of sauces — *Salsa Criolla* (Creole Sauce), a really fiery one to be taken with discretion, or sauce *Chimichurri*, an untranslatable name, hardly any milder. There is another less lethal sauce, *Salsa para Asados* (Barbecue Sauce) from nearby Uruguay, where barbecues are also popular.

The barbecue pit with a grate over it is really a sophisticated refinement. Whole animals, a lamb, kid, suckling pig, or a side of beef, can be spit-roasted in the true gaucho manner. The animals are split and impaled on iron rods that have a crosspiece to keep them flat. The rods are thrust firmly into the ground at an angle of about 20 degrees, toward a wood fire and about a foot away. They too are basted with brine and with their own fat and turned as they brown so that both sides cook evenly.

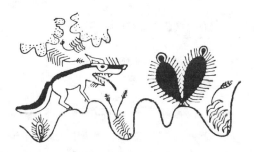

It is difficult to give more than approximate times for barbecuing as the heat of the fire and the thickness of the meats vary, as well as the degree of doneness preferred. Sausages will take about 10 minutes a side. A 2½- to 3-pound chicken, split down the back, will take about 1 hour. A medium-sized suckling pig will take 3 to 3½ hours, and baby lamb and kid about the same time. A 3-pound piece of short ribs should be cooked 10 to 15 minutes, rib side down, then turned, salted, and cooked for about 30 minutes longer. Rump or sirloin takes 20 to 30 minutes according to size. Flank steak, over high heat, starting fat side down, takes about 7 minutes a side.

The Brazilian barbecue, *Churrasco a Gaucha* from the cattle state of Rio Grande do Sul, has its own refinements and sophisticated extras. Originally the meat was spitted on long iron skewers and stuck in the ground at an angle to the fire much as the gauchos of Argentina did. It is still done for a traditional *churrasco*, but more and more people find a barbecue pit with a grate on top much more convenient for backyard barbecues. Short ribs and rump are the preferred meats. Though traditionally beef is the only meat used, many people temporarily tired of beef, like to have a *galeto*, a chicken, instead. This is split down the back and grilled whole. A whole parsley plant is used as a baster to apply the brine, seasoned sometimes with chopped onion and parsley, or crushed garlic cloves.

Slices of grilled *linguiça* (Portuguese sausage) may be served with a *Caipirinha* or a *batida* (Brazilian cocktails), page 333, as a first course. The meats are accompanied by *Farofa de Ouro* (Cassava Meal with Hardboiled Eggs) or *Farofa de Manteiga* (Cassava Meal with Butter). A nice variation is to add 4 bananas, cut into ½-inch slices and fried in 2 tablespoons of butter, to the cassava meal and mixed together. There is always a lettuce and tomato salad in an oil and vinegar dressing, and *Môlho de Tomates* (Tomato Sauce). Brazil's excellent beer is the popular drink to serve.

✳ Sauces for the Barbecues

Salsa Criolla   ARGENTINA
Barbecue Sauce, Creole Style

Makes about 5 cups

1 tablespoon hot paprika or
    cayenne pepper
½ tablespoon dry mustard
½ cup red wine vinegar
½ cup olive oil

Salt, freshly ground pepper
2 green bell peppers, seeded and
    finely chopped
1 medium onion, finely chopped
3 medium tomatoes, chopped

Mix the paprika or cayenne and mustard to a paste with a little of the vinegar, then stir in the rest of the vinegar. Beat in the oil. Season to taste with salt and a generous amount of freshly ground pepper. Add the remaining ingredients and stir to mix. The sauce has a lot of liquid. The solids should float in the bowl, so add a little more oil and vinegar if necessary. This is very hot.

Variation: Brazilian *Môlho ao Tomate* (Tomato Sauce). In a bowl combine 4 medium tomatoes, coarsely chopped, 2 medium onions, chopped, 2 cloves garlic, chopped, ½ cup each chopped parsley and coriander, salt, pepper, 1 cup olive oil, and ½ cup red wine vinegar. Mix lightly and serve at room temperature. Makes 4 to 5 cups.

Chimichurri
Vinegar Sauce

This is a popular sauce with barbecued meats or with any broiled or roasted meat or poultry.

Makes about 1 ½ cups

4 tablespoons olive oil
1 cup red wine vinegar
4 tablespoons hot paprika or
   cayenne pepper
4 cloves garlic, crushed

1 teaspoon black peppercorns
1 teaspoon oregano
1 bay leaf, crumbled
½ teaspoon salt

Combine all the ingredients in a bottle, shake well to mix, and put in a cool place, or refrigerate, for 4 or 5 days for the flavor to develop. Shake a few drops on meat or poultry.

Brine

½ cups coarse salt

2 cups water

Mix the salt and water thoroughly and use to baste meats.

Salsa Para Asados
Barbecue Sauce

Makes about 3 cups

1 cup olive oil
½ cup red wine vinegar
8 cloves garlic, chopped
1 cup finely chopped parsley
1 teaspoon oregano

1 teaspoon thyme
2 teaspoons hot paprika or
   cayenne pepper
Salt, freshly ground pepper

Combine all the ingredients and mix thoroughly. Allow to stand for 2 or 3 hours before serving. Serve with barbecued meats. This sauce may also be used as a marinade.

POT-AU-FEUS

The pot-au-feu (literally, pot on the fire) is one of the earliest cooking methods and probably goes back to the Bronze Age. Bronze cauldrons from 3500 B.C. are not very much different from the casseroles and kettles in use today, and there is hardly a country on earth that does not have a pot-au-feu in its repertoire. In Latin America this type of stew may be called a *sancocho* (literally parboiled, a dish where foods are added to the pot after some have already been partially cooked), a *pozole* (from an Aztec word meaning beans boiled with other things), a *puchero* (a glazed earthenware pot for cooking meat and vegetables together), a *carbonada* (a meat stew from the New World), a *cocido* (a cooked meat dish), and an *ajiaco* (a dish made of boiled meat and vegetables from South America). Essentially, as elsewhere, it is a whole meal cooked in a single pot on top of the stove.

In Latin America over the years versions of the pot-au-feu have served as plantation meals, useful for feeding large numbers of people. There is often an enormously long list of ingredients including the marvelous root vegetables, the yams, taros, and cassava, that flourish in this region, where many of them originated; they vary in texture and flavor and lend variety to any stew they grace. Plantains are another widely used ingredient, as are the winter squashes and, of course, that greatest of all Inca achievements, the potato. Meats introduced by Spain and Portugal — beef, kid, lamb, chicken, and pork — are all used. So are beans, both the indigenous beans (*Phaseolus vulgaris*, kidney, Navy, pea, lima, turtle, etc.) and such exotics as chickpeas (*garbanzos, hummus*), brought by Spain from the Middle East. In addition there are all the green vegetables, and onions, scallions, and garlic — a grand assemblage, needing only a degree of selection, and a knowledge of when to add them to the pot.

These dishes are still very popular in Latin America for parties and family gatherings, since it is not really possible to cook them for small numbers like two or four. They are usually presented in a grand manner with various meats on one platter, vegetables on another, the soup in a large tureen, sauces on the side, and the table set with generous-sized rimmed soup plates. With a little planning, they are easy and you don't have to spend time at the last minute in the kitchen, since the ingredients can all be prepared ahead of time, the work being mostly the peeling and cutting up of vegetables. What is essential is a large enough pot; I have often solved this problem by using two fairly big casseroles and dividing the ingredients equally between them. Since such a dish comprises the entire meal, the whole stove is available for its cooking. Permutations and combinations of ingredients have resulted in a group of wonderfully diverse dishes.

Carbonada en Zapallo ARGENTINA
Veal Stew in Baked Pumpkin

West Indian pumpkin (*calabaza*) is available in many Caribbean and Latin American markets and is ideal for this colorful and quite spectacular dish, as it is usually possible to get just the size needed. However, any large winter squash can be used, the Hubbard shape probably being the best. U.S. pumpkins won't do; they are too watery. The stew is served from the squash itself, which plays a dual role as both container and ingredient. The squash will be very soft and mashes into the sauce, thickening it. It has a lovely flavor, which mingles with the stew.

Serves 6 to 8

A 10- to 12-pound West Indian pumpkin (calabaza) or other large winter squash, such as Hubbard
¼ cup vegetable oil
2 pounds boneless veal, cut into 1-inch cubes
1 large onion, finely chopped
1 green bell pepper, seeded and chopped
1 or 2 fresh hot peppers, seeded and chopped (optional)
1 large tomato, peeled and chopped
1½ cups chicken stock
1½ cups dry white wine

1 pound potatoes, peeled and cut into 1-inch cubes
1 pound sweet potatoes, preferably boniatos (white sweet potatoes), peeled and cut into 1-inch cubes
2 ears corn, cut into 1-inch slices
2 large pears, peeled and sliced
3 large peaches, peeled, pitted, and sliced
1 tablespoon chopped chives
1 tablespoon sugar
Salt, freshly ground pepper
½ cup long-grain rice, soaked for 1 hour and drained

Scrub the pumpkin. Cut a slice off the top to make a lid, then scrape out the seeds and stringy fibers from the pumpkin and lid. Bake the pumpkin on a baking sheet in a preheated moderate (350° F.) oven for 45 minutes.

Meanwhile, heat the oil in a heavy skillet and sauté the veal pieces until they are golden all over. Lift them out into a flameproof casserole with a slotted spoon. In the fat remaining in the pan sauté the onion, pepper, and hot peppers, if using, until the onion is soft. Add the tomato and cook until the mixture is well blended, about 5 minutes. Add to the casserole with the chicken stock and wine. Bring to a boil, reduce the heat, and simmer, covered, for 40 minutes. Add the potatoes and sweet potatoes and cook 15 minutes. Add the corn and cook 5 minutes longer. Remove from the heat and add the pears, peaches, chives, and sugar. Season to taste with salt and pepper. Add the rice. Transfer the contents of the casserole to the pumpkin. Replace the lid and bake in a preheated moderate (350° F.) oven for 30 minutes or until the rice is cooked. Transfer the pumpkin to a large serving platter and serve directly from it, taking care when scooping out the cooked pumpkin not to break the shell.

Variation: If liked, 2 quinces, peeled and sliced, may be added when the potatoes and sweet potatoes are put into the casserole.

Variation: Lean beef chuck may be used instead of veal.

Variation: Six dried apricots, soaked for 20 minutes in cold water, drained, and quartered, may be used instead of the peaches.

Carbonada Criolla

ARGENTINA

Beef Stew, Argentine Style

This is a simpler, less spectacular version of *Carbonada en Zapallo* (Veal Stew in Baked Pumpkin). Once more it demonstrates the Argentine flair for combining meat and fruit.

Serves 6

¼ cup olive oil
2 pounds lean beef, cut into 1-inch
    cubes
1 large onion, finely chopped
1 clove garlic, chopped
3 medium tomatoes, peeled and
    chopped
½ teaspoon oregano
1 bay leaf
1 teaspoon sugar
1 tablespoon tomato paste
Salt, freshly ground pepper
1 cup beef stock, about
1 cup dry red wine, about
1 pound sweet potatoes,
    preferably boniatos (white
    sweet potatoes), peeled and
    sliced
1 pound potatoes, peeled and
    sliced

1 pound West Indian pumpkin
    (calabaza) or any winter
    squash, peeled and sliced
6 small peaches, peeled
4 ears corn, each cut into 3 slices

Heat the oil in a large, heavy casserole and sauté the beef until it is lightly browned all over. Push it to the side and add the onion and garlic. Sauté the onion until it is soft. Add the tomatoes and cook for 5 minutes longer. Add the oregano, bay leaf, sugar, tomato paste, salt and pepper to taste, the stock, and the wine. Cover and simmer for 1½ hours, or until the meat is almost tender. Add the sweet potatoes and potatoes and a little more stock and wine if necessary to cover. Simmer for 10 minutes, then add the pumpkin or squash and peaches, and simmer for a further 10 minutes. Add the corn and cook 5 minutes longer, or until all the ingredients are tender. Some cooks add ½ cup rice or vermicelli during the last 20 minutes of cooking.

Cozido à Brasileira   BRAZIL
Stew, Brazilian Style

This is a dish from São Paulo that was taken by Paulistas to Minas Gerais. I have met it both in the new capital, Belo Horizonte, and the old one, Ouro Prêto. This recipe was given me by the mother of a good friend, Gilberto Rizzo, a Paulista.

Serves 12

2 pounds top round of beef, cut into 1-inch cubes
6 pork chops, boned
4 medium onions, grated
4 cloves garlic, crushed
4 scallions, including the green tops
2 or 3 sprigs each parsley and fresh coriander (cilantro)
Beef broth
A 3-pound chicken, cut into 6 pieces
A 2-pound linguiça *sausage, or use a similar sausage such as Spanish* longaniza *or Polish* kielbasa
6 small whole carrots, scraped
1 small bunch celery, with stalks cut into 3- to 4-inch pieces

1 small whole cabbage
6 small whole potatoes, peeled or scraped
3 small sweet potatoes, peeled and halved
1 ½ pounds cassava root (manioc, yucca), peeled and cut into 2-inch slices
2 pounds West Indian pumpkin (calabaza) or any winter squash, peeled and cut into 2-inch cubes
2 ears corn, each cut into 3 slices
Salt, freshly ground pepper
3 medium slightly underripe bananas, or 2 half-ripe plantains
1 cup cassava meal (manioc, mandioca)

In a kettle or saucepan large enough to hold all the ingredients put the beef, pork chops, onions, garlic, scallions, parsley and coriander sprigs, and enough beef broth to cover. Simmer, covered, over low heat for 1 hour. At the end of that time add the chicken, sausage, and more beef broth as necessary to cover, and cook for 30 minutes longer. Add to the kettle the carrots, celery, cabbage, potatoes, sweet potatoes, cassava root, pumpkin or winter squash, corn, salt and pepper to taste, and more beef broth to cover.

In a separate saucepan put the bananas or plantains, cover with cold water, and simmer, covered, for 20 minutes. If using plantains, cook them for 30 minutes. When cool enough to handle, lift out and peel. Halve the bananas, or cut the plantains into thirds, and add to the ingredients in the kettle just long enough to heat through. Have ready two large, deep, warmed platters. Arrange the meats on one of the platters. Place the cabbage in the center of the second platter and cut it into wedges. Arrange the other vegetables on the platter in decorative groups.

Remove and discard the parsley and coriander sprigs from the broth in the kettle. Moisten the meats and vegetables with some of the broth. Measure 4 cups of the broth and pour it into a saucepan. Stir in the cassava meal, then simmer, stirring constantly, over moderate heat until the cassava has thickened the liquid to a porridgelike consistency. Pour this *pirão* into a bowl and serve it as a sauce with the *cozido*.

Sancocho Especial COLOMBIA
Special Boiled Dinner

The Spanish verb *sancochar* means to parboil and has come to be applied to a number of South American dishes of the pot-au-feu family in the sense of adding new ingredients to already parboiled ones in the pot. The more ingredients there are in a *sancocho*, the more of a party dish it becomes. This one is very festive. It has to be done ahead of time, as it takes about a week. Simplified by the omission of some of the vegetables and meats, it will still be very good indeed. The salted beef gives a distinctive, though not pronounced, flavor to this special *sancocho*.

Serves 6 to 8

1 pound beef chuck, cut into
    1½-inch cubes
1 pound lean pork, cut into
    1½-inch cubes
1 pound salted beef, well washed
    and cut into 1½-inch cubes
    (see below)
2 large onions, sliced
3 cloves garlic, chopped
2 large tomatoes, peeled, seeded,
    and chopped
1 pound yucca root (cassava),
    peeled and sliced
1½ quarts beef stock
1½ quarts chicken stock
A 3½-pound chicken, cut into
    serving pieces
1 pound sweet potatoes, peeled
    and sliced

1 pound yams, peeled and sliced
1 pound winter squash, peeled
    and cubed
1 pound potatoes, peeled and
    sliced
2 green plantains, peeled and cut
    into 2-inch slices
2 ripe plantains, peeled and cut
    into 2-inch slices
3 ears corn, each cut into 3 slices
Salt, freshly ground pepper
3 or 4 limes, quartered

Put the beef, pork, salted beef, onions, garlic, tomatoes, yucca, and the beef and chicken stock into a soup kettle or pot large enough to hold all the ingredients. Bring to a boil over moderate heat, skim off the froth, and reduce the heat so that the liquid barely moves. Cook, covered, for 1¼ hours. Add the chicken pieces, sweet potatoes, yams, winter squash, potatoes, and green and ripe plantains and simmer until the chicken is tender, about 45 minutes longer. Add the corn, season to taste with salt and pepper, and cook for 5 minutes longer.

Arrange the meats on a warm platter, the vegetables on another warm platter, and pour the broth into a soup tureen. Serve in large soup plates with side dishes of quartered limes, and *Salsa de Ají* (Hot Pepper Sauce).

Salted beef, Colombia style. The salted beef, which is a special feature of this dish, is easy to do, and once done keeps indefinitely in the refrigerator. It is well worth the effort.

Cut a 3- to 4-pound piece of bottom round of beef into horizontal slices about ½ inch thick, stopping short of the far side of the meat so that it opens like a book. Pour 1 pound salt over the beef, between the slices, and on the top and bottom. Place on a large platter and cover lightly with cheesecloth. Leave it to stand in a cool place overnight and in the morning pour off the liquid that has accumulated. There will be a lot of it the first day. Check that the meat is still heavily coated with salt, adding more if necessary. Repeat the process, leaving the beef to stand for another 24 hours and again pouring off the liquid. If necessary add more salt. Place on a piece of heavy aluminum foil, or on a platter, cover with cheesecloth, and put in the sun to dry, turning the meat over daily. It will take about a week. Shake out the excess salt, wrap the beef in foil, and store in the refrigerator. Wash well before using. I have found that Brazilian *carne sêca* (sun-dried salt beef, or jerked beef) works very well. If plantains are not available, use unripe (green) bananas for green plantains and barely ripe bananas for the ripe plantains. Reduce the cooking time to about 20 minutes for green bananas, 5 minutes for the barely ripe ones.

Pozole Tapatío   MEXICO
Pozole, Guadalajara Style

Tapatío is an affectionate term for the people of Guadalajara, the capital of Jalisco, and is also used for special dishes from the city. It comes from a colonial dance from Guadalajara, the *Jarabe Tapatío* (The Hat Dance), those who danced it being *tapatíos*. In Mexico the hominy used here would not always be bought canned but is very often prepared at home. Whole, large white corn kernels are soaked overnight, then boiled with lime. The skins are then rubbed off and the *"cabecita,"* little head, at the base removed. The corn is then ready to be cooked. It is a long and time-consuming process and I have found canned whole hominy an excellent substitute.

Serves 8 to 10

6 ancho *chilies*
3 *pig's feet*
1 *head garlic, peeled*
3 *quarts chicken stock*
1 *pound boneless pork loin, cut*
  into 1-inch cubes

A 3½- *to 4-pound chicken, cut*
  into serving pieces
Salt
2 *cups canned whole hominy*

FOR THE GARNISH

1 *large onion, finely chopped*
½ *head iceberg lettuce, shredded*
1 *bunch radishes*
½ *pound Spanish fresh cheese*
  (*queso fresco or queso blanco*),
  optional
Oregano

Ground hot pepper, or hot pepper
  sauce such as Tabasco
Fresh hot tortillas, or tortillas cut
  into triangles and fried in hot
  lard or vegetable oil
3 *limes or lemons, cut into wedges*

Break off the stems and shake the seeds out of the chilies. Rinse the chilies and tear them into pieces. Put them into a bowl with 1 cup hot water and leave to soak for 1 hour, turning them from time to time. Put them into a blender or food processor and reduce to a purée. Set aside.

Put the pig's feet into a large saucepan or kettle with the garlic and chicken stock. Bring to a boil, reduce the heat, cover, and simmer for 3 hours. Add the pork loin and simmer for 1 hour, then add the chicken pieces and the puréed chilies. Add a little salt if necessary. Simmer for 40 minutes, add the hominy, and cook for 5 minutes longer. By this time all the ingredients should be tender. Simmer for a little longer if necessary.

To serve put the meats and broth into a large soup tureen and set the table with large-rimmed soup plates. Put the onion, lettuce, radishes, and crumbled cheese into bowls, and the oregano and ground hot pepper or hot pepper sauce into small bowls. Serve the tortillas, in a straw basket, wrapped in a napkin. To eat, add the garnishes to each serving of meat and broth, with squeezes of lime or lemon juice.

Cocido a la Dominicana
DOMINICAN REPUBLIC

Spanish Stew, Dominican Style

Serves 6 to 8

½ pound dried chickpeas, or a
    1-pound can
4 tablespoons vegetable oil
A 4-pound chicken, cut into
    serving pieces
½ pound beef, cut into 1-inch
    cubes
A ½ pound slice of smoked ham,
    such as prosciutto or Spanish
    Jamon Serrano, cut into
    1-inch cubes
½ pound chorizo (hot Spanish)
    sausages, sliced, or use hot
    Italian sausages
1 medium onion, chopped
4 cloves garlic, chopped
2 pounds potatoes, peeled and
    sliced

1 large carrot, scraped and sliced
1 small cabbage, cut into 8
    wedges
½ pound West Indian pumpkin
    (calabaza) or winter squash,
    peeled and cubed
1 fresh hot red or green pepper, left
    whole with stem on
1 bay leaf
1 tablespoon white vinegar
8 cups beef stock
Salt
6 small pitted green olives, sliced
1 tablespoon finely chopped
    parsley

If using dried chickpeas, soak them overnight in cold water to cover. Drain, cover with fresh water, and simmer, covered, for 1 hour. Drain, measure the liquid, and use it to replace some of the beef stock. Set aside. If using canned chickpeas, drain, rinse in cold water, and set aside.

Heat the oil in a skillet and sauté the chicken pieces until golden on both sides. Transfer to a large saucepan or soup kettle. In the oil remaining in the skillet sauté the beef cubes, ham, and sausages, and add them to the saucepan. In the remaining oil, adding a little more if necessary, though the sausages will give off quite a lot of fat, sauté the onion and garlic until the onion is soft. Add the mixture to the kettle with the potatoes, carrot, cabbage, pumpkin or winter squash, whole hot pepper, bay leaf, vinegar, the chickpeas and liquid or the canned, drained, chickpeas, the stock, and salt to taste. Cover and simmer until all the ingredients are tender, about 1 hour. The pumpkin or squash will have disintegrated, slightly thickening the broth. Remove and discard the bay leaf and hot pepper. Transfer the stew to a warmed tureen or serving dish, add the olives, and sprinkle with the parsley.

Variation: There is an interesting variation, *Sancocho de Longaniza y To-cino* (Sausage and Bacon Stew), also from the Dominican Republic. Soak 1½ pounds bacon, in a single piece, for 15 minutes in cold water, rinse, drain, and cut into 1-inch cubes. Slice 2 pounds *longaniza* (Spanish garlic) sausages, or *linguiça* or *kielbasa*, into 1-inch slices. Heat 4 tablespoons vegetable oil in a skillet and sauté the bacon cubes and sausage slices until lightly browned. Transfer to a flameproof casserole. In the fat remaining in the skillet sauté 1 large onion, finely chopped, 3 cloves garlic, chopped, and 1 green bell pepper, seeded and chopped, and add to the casserole with 1 tablespoon red wine vinegar and 2 tablespoons Seville (bitter) orange juice, or two-thirds orange juice and one-third lime or lemon juice. Add 3 quarts beef stock, and simmer, covered, for 1½ hours, then add 1 pound cassava

(yucca) root, peeled and sliced, 1 pound taro (*yautía*), peeled and sliced, 1 pound yam (*ñame*), not orange sweet potatoes, and 1 pound West Indian pumpkin (*calabaza*) or winter squash, peeled and cubed. Season to taste with salt, freshly ground pepper, 1 teaspoon oregano, and hot pepper sauce (such as Tabasco) to taste. Simmer, covered, until all the ingredients are tender. In a separate saucepan, in water to cover, boil 2 green plantains in their skins for 30 minutes, cool, peel, slice, and add to the casserole just long enough to heat them through. The plantains may be omitted, if pre-ferred, or green (underripe) bananas may be used instead, in which case boil them for 20 minutes. Put the meats and vegetables on a heated serving platter, pour the broth into a tureen, and serve in soup plates. Serves 6 to 8.

Puchero Estilo Mexicano   MEXICO
Mexican Pot-au-Feu

If you want to present everything in this pot-au-feu at the same time, serve
the soup in bowls, the meats and vegetables on plates. The green vegetables may be varied to suit the cook. Cabbage and turnips may be added,
chayotes may be used instead of zucchini.

Serves 8 to 10

½ pound dried chickpeas, or a
    1-pound can
1 pound lean boneless beef chuck,
    cut into 1-inch cubes
1 pound boneless lamb, cut into
    1-inch cubes
½ pound raw ham, cubed
½ pound chorizo (hot Spanish
    sausages), sliced
1 large onion, chopped
2 cloves garlic, chopped
⅛ teaspoon peppercorns
1½ quarts chicken stock
1½ quarts beef stock
Salt
A 3½- to 4-pound chicken, cut
    into serving pieces
4 carrots, scraped and sliced
4 zucchini, sliced
1 pound green beans, cut into
    ½-inch pieces

1 pound sweet potatoes, peeled
    and sliced
3 ears corn, cut into 1-inch slices
4 tablespoons lard or vegetable oil
1 pound potatoes, peeled and
    sliced
2 green plantains, or 2 large green
    (underripe) bananas, peeled
    and cut into 1-inch slices
3 large peaches, peeled, pitted,
    and quartered
3 large pears, peeled, cored, and
    quartered
1 tablespoon chopped fresh
    coriander (cilantro)
Fresh hot tortillas
Guacamole (Avocado Sauce), page
    316
2 limes or lemons, cut into wedges
Hot pepper sauce (Tabasco or any of
    the sauces on pages 311 – 13)

Soak the chickpeas overnight, drain, and rinse. Put them into a large soup
kettle. If using canned chickpeas, drain, rinse, and set aside until later. Add
to the kettle the beef, lamb, ham, chorizo, onion, garlic, peppercorns,
chicken and beef stock, and salt to taste, if necessary. Bring to a boil, skim
any froth that comes to the surface, reduce the heat, cover, and simmer
gently for 45 minutes. Add the chicken pieces and simmer for 30 minutes
longer. Add the carrots, zucchini, green beans, sweet potatoes, and canned
chickpeas, if using, and cook for 15 minutes longer. Add the corn and cook
for 5 minutes.

    Heat the lard or vegetable oil in a skillet and sauté the potatoes and
plantains or green bananas until tender. Lift out onto a platter and keep
warm. Take a cupful of stock from the kettle and gently poach the peaches

and pears, between 10 and 15 minutes. Add to the kettle with the stock.

Check that all the ingredients are tender. Arrange the meats in the center of a large platter and surround with the vegetables and fruits. Moisten with a little stock and keep warm. If liked, the chickpeas may be left in the soup, or put on the platter. Pour the soup into a tureen and sprinkle with the chopped coriander. Serve the soup in bowls. Serve the meats, fruits, vegetables, and the fried potatoes and plantains as a second course accompanied by hot tortillas, *Guacamole*, lime or lemon wedges, and hot pepper sauce.

Sancocho de Gallina
VENEZUELA
Chicken Pot-au-Feu

Tropical markets carry an astonishing variety of root vegetables so if *apio* (*arracacha*) is not available, use taro (*yautía, dasheen*), or white sweet potato (*boniato*), or more than one type of yam. None of the vegetables has a dominating flavor, and all cook in about the same time so it is easy — and perfectly acceptable — to make substitutions. It is also a good way to get to know more about these delicious vegetables.

Serves 8 to 10

Two 3½-pound chickens, cut into serving pieces
3 quarts chicken stock
1 leek, well washed and halved lengthwise
1 large onion, chopped
1 head garlic, peeled
3 white turnips, peeled and quartered

3 carrots, scraped and cut into 4 slices
1 large tomato, peeled, seeded, and chopped
2 or 3 sprigs fresh coriander (cilantro)
Salt, freshly ground pepper

THE VEGETABLES

1 pound cassava root (yucca), peeled and cut into ½-inch slices
1 pound West Indian pumpkin (calabaza) or any winter squash, peeled and cut into ½-inch slices
1 pound yam (ñame, not orange sweet potatoes), peeled and cut into ½-inch slices

1 pound apio (arracacha), peeled and cut into ½-inch slices
1 pound potatoes, peeled and cut into ½-inch slices
1 small cabbage, blanched and cut into 8 wedges
3 ears corn, each cut into 4 slices
2 green plantains (optional), or 3 large green bananas

Put all the ingredients except those listed under vegetables into a large saucepan or soup kettle. Bring to a boil, reduce the heat to a bare simmer, and cook, covered, for 30 minutes. Add all the vegetables except the corn and plantains, and continue cooking until the chicken and vegetables are tender, 20 to 30 minutes. Add the corn in the last 5 minutes of cooking. In a separate saucepan boil the unpeeled green plantains in water to cover for 30 minutes. When they are cool enough to handle, lift out, peel, and cut into 1-inch slices. Add to the chicken and vegetables just long enough to heat through. If using green bananas, cook for 15 minutes, peel, slice, and add to the kettle. Arrange the chicken pieces on a large, heated serving platter and surround with the vegetables. Strain the soup into a soup tureen. Serve in soup plates with *Guasacaca* (Avocado Sauce) or *Salsa de Ají* (Hot Pepper Sauce), separately.

Traditionally a large stewing hen (*gallina*) is used for this dish, but stewing hens are no longer readily available and require long, slow cooking. I find 3½-pound chickens very satisfactory. The dish can also be made with beef, using 4 pounds lean, boneless beef such as chuck, cut into 1-inch cubes. It is then called *Hervido*.

Ajiaco   CUBA
Meat and Vegetable Stew

Serves 8 to 10

3 pounds lean, boneless pork, cut into 2-inch cubes
1 pound corned beef, cut into 2-inch cubes
2 quarts beef stock
2 quarts water
1 pound cassava root (yucca), cut into ½-inch slices
1 pound taro (yautía), peeled and cut into ½-inch slices
1 pound yam (ñame, not orange sweet potatoes), peeled and cut into ½-inch slices
1 pound sweet potatoes, preferably white (boniatos), peeled and cut into ½-inch slices

1 pound West Indian pumpkin (calabaza) or winter squash, peeled and cubed
2 ears corn, cut into 1-inch slices
2 chayotes, peeled and sliced, or use zucchini
2 ripe plantains, peeled and cut into 1-inch slices
4 tablespoons olive oil
2 medium onions, finely chopped
2 cloves garlic, minced
1 green bell pepper, seeded and coarsely chopped
2 or more fresh hot red or green peppers, seeded and finely chopped

3 medium tomatoes, peeled and
   coarsely chopped
Salt, freshly ground pepper

2 green plantains (optional)
Juice of 2 limes

Put the pork and corned beef into a large saucepan or soup kettle with the stock and water. Bring to a boil, boil for a minute or two, and skim the froth that rises to the surface. Reduce the heat to a bare simmer, and cook, covered, for 1 hour. Add the cassava root, taro, and yam, and cook 15 minutes longer. Add the sweet potatoes, pumpkin or winter squash, corn, chayotes, and ripe plantains, and continue to simmer gently. If using zucchini do not add until later.

Heat the oil in a skillet and sauté the onions, garlic, and sweet and hot peppers until the onions are soft. Add the tomatoes, season to taste with pepper and salt, if necessary (the corned beef may have added enough saltiness), and cook until well blended, about 5 minutes longer. Add to the kettle with the zucchini, if using, and continue cooking at a gentle simmer until everything is done, which should be about 2 hours from starting. The pumpkin or winter squash will disintegrate, slightly thickening the broth.

Boil the green plantains in a separate saucepan in water to cover for 30 minutes. Cool, peel, and cut into 1-inch slices. Add to the kettle just long enough to heat through. Add the lime juice, stir, and serve. Arrange the meat and vegetables on a large heated serving platter, or if preferred, on two separate, smaller platters. Pour the broth into a soup tureen. Serve in soup plates with a hot pepper sauce on the side. This is wonderful with crusty rolls and butter.

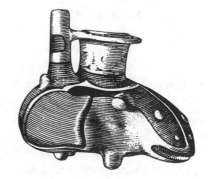

Poultry
Aves

CHICKEN

There is no doubt that chicken — inexpensive and extremely versatile — is the favorite bird in the kitchens of Latin America. It is impossible to tire of chicken with so many delectable ways to cook it.

Most Latin American recipes are variations on a poaching theme. Chicken is gently simmered with herbs and spices and vegetable flavorings like onion and garlic, and deliciously sauced in a great variety of ways. Also, corn plays a special role in dishes like *Cuscuz de Galinha* (Garnished Steamed Chicken and Cornmeal) and *Pastel de Choclo con Relleno de Pollo* (Chicken Pie with Corn Topping) — see Substantial Dishes.

Out of a vast array of recipes I have chosen dishes that I have enjoyed, not just once, but time and again.

Pollo con Naranja

Chicken in Orange Sauce

Serves 4

A 3- to 3½-pound chicken,
    quartered
Salt, freshly ground pepper
3 tablespoons butter
1 cup chicken stock

1 cup orange juice
Grated rind of 1 orange
1 tablespoon flour
2 eggs
1 tablespoon heavy cream

Season the chicken pieces with salt and pepper. Heat the butter in a heavy casserole and sauté the chicken pieces, one or two at a time, until golden on both sides. Set aside as they are done. Pour off the fat from the casserole into a small bowl and reserve. Return the chicken pieces to the casserole, putting the legs in first with the breasts on top, as the breasts cook more quickly. Add the chicken stock, orange juice, and grated orange rind. Cover and simmer for 30 to 45 minutes, or until the chicken is done. Lift out the chicken onto a serving dish and keep warm. Mix the flour with a tablespoon of the reserved fat and stir it into the liquid in the casserole. Bring to a boil and cook, stirring, for a minute or two. Reduce the heat to low. Beat the eggs with the cream. Stir 1 cup of the thickened liquid from the casserole, 1 tablespoon at a time, into the egg mixture, then pour the mixture into the casserole and cook, stirring with a wire whisk, until the sauce is lightly thickened, a minute or two. Do not let the sauce boil, as it will curdle. Pour some of the sauce over the chicken and serve the rest in a sauceboat. Serve with rice or mashed or French fried potatoes.

Frango com Bananas

Chicken with Bananas

This chicken dish from Brazil's Mato Grosso is simmered with white wine and tomatoes, then topped with lightly fried bananas; a most attractive and unusual combination of flavors, slightly sweet, slightly sour.

Serves 4

A 3-pound chicken, quartered
¼ cup lemon juice
2 teaspoons salt
3 tablespoons butter
1 medium onion, grated
2 tomatoes, peeled, seeded, and
    chopped

⅛ teaspoon sugar
1 cup dry white wine
¼ cup vegetable oil
6 ripe bananas, peeled and halved
    lengthwise
1 cup grated Parmesan cheese
1 tablespoon butter

Season the chicken with the lemon juice and salt. Heat the butter in a flameproof casserole and stir in the onion, tomatoes, and sugar. Add the chicken pieces and any of their liquid. Simmer for 5 minutes, uncovered, turning the chicken pieces once. Add the wine, cover the casserole, and simmer until the chicken is tender, about 45 minutes.

Heat the oil in a skillet and sauté the bananas until they are lightly browned on both sides. Arrange the bananas, cut side down, on top of the chicken pieces and sprinkle them with the grated cheese. Dot with the butter, cut into little bits. Place the casserole in a preheated hot (400° F.) oven and bake until the cheese is lightly browned, about 10 minutes. Serve with white rice.

Pollo en Piña   GUATEMALA
Chicken in Pineapple

Serves 4 to 6

A 3½- to 4-pound chicken, cut
    into serving pieces
1 ripe pineapple, weighing about
    1½ pounds, peeled, cored,
    and coarsely chopped, or a
    1-pound can unsweetened
    pineapple, in its own juice
2 medium onions, finely chopped
2 cloves garlic, chopped
2 whole cloves

A 1-inch piece of stick cinnamon
2 bay leaves
½ cup olive oil
½ cup white vinegar
½ cup dry sherry
2 medium tomatoes, peeled and
    coarsely chopped
Salt, freshly ground pepper
Chicken stock, if necessary

Put the chicken pieces into a heavy saucepan or casserole. If using fresh pineapple, be careful to save and use all the juice. If using canned pineapple, use the juice. Add all the rest of the ingredients, including salt and pepper to taste. If using fresh pineapple, it may be necessary to add a little chicken stock to cover the chicken pieces, as the fresh fruit will not have as much juice as the canned. Cover and simmer over low heat until the chicken is tender, about 45 minutes. If the sauce is very abundant, cook partially covered for the last 15 minutes. Serve with rice.

Ají de Gallina
Chicken in Pepper Sauce

PERU

Serves 6

A 3½- to 4-pound chicken, quartered
3 cups chicken stock, about
¼ cup vegetable oil
2 medium onions, finely chopped
2 cloves garlic, minced
2 cups fresh breadcrumbs
2 cups milk

8 fresh hot red or green peppers, seeded
2 medium tomatoes, peeled and seeded
4 ounces walnuts, ground
Salt, freshly ground pepper
½ cup grated Parmesan cheese

Put the chicken pieces into a large saucepan or flameproof casserole with the stock, adding a little more if necessary to cover, and poach until the chicken is tender, about 45 minutes. Let the chicken cool in the stock. Remove the skin and bones and shred the meat into pieces about 1½ inches long and ¼ inch wide. Set the shredded chicken aside and reserve the stock.

Heat the oil in a flameproof casserole and sauté the onions and garlic until the onions are golden. Soak the breadcrumbs in the milk and mash to a paste. Add the breadcrumb mixture to the casserole. In a blender or food processor reduce the peppers and tomatoes to a purée and stir into the casserole. Add the ground walnuts. Season to taste with salt and pepper, and cook, stirring, over moderate heat for about 5 minutes. Add the chicken, 1 cup of the stock, and the cheese, and cook just until heated through. The sauce should be thick. Serve the chicken and sauce on a heated platter surrounded by halved, boiled potatoes, hardboiled eggs, sliced lengthwise, and black olives.

Cecilia Blanco de Mendoza's Ajiaco

COLOMBIA

Chicken Stew

This is a very special *ajiaco* (chicken stew) with subtle seasonings that include *guascas* or *huascas*, a Colombian herb whose botanical name is *Galinsoga parviflora Lineo*. It is sold, dried and ground, in jars in Colombian markets and has a mild flavor vaguely reminiscent, to my palate, of Jerusalem artichokes, to which, I am assured by a Colombian botanist, it bears no relationship whatsoever. It might one day appear in a specialty food shop and will enhance any soup or stew, as the flavor is delicate and unobtrusive. However, though *guascas* is an attractive extra, it is not essential to the deliciousness of this dish, which depends on a combination of flavors including scallions and coriander.

Also in the stew are three types of potatoes: Idahos or any similar potato, small red potatoes, and *papas criollas.* These last are delicious small Colombian potatoes that are sometimes available in Latin American markets. They have yellow flesh and stay whole through prolonged cooking. Small white new potatoes make a very good substitute, perhaps not as pretty to look at, but equal otherwise.

Serves 6

A 3½- to 4-pound chicken, left
    whole
4 whole scallions
6 sprigs fresh coriander (cilantro)
1 teaspoon ground **guascas**
3 cups chicken stock or water
Salt, freshly ground pepper
4 small ears corn, cut into 1-inch
    slices
2 pounds Idaho or similar
    potatoes, peeled and cut into
    ¼-inch slices

2 pounds small red potatoes,
    peeled and cut into ¼-inch
    slices
1 pound **papas criollas** or small
    white new potatoes, unpeeled
2 cups milk
1 small can Vienna sausages,
    sliced
½ cup cooked baby peas
1 or 2 tablespoons capers
2 hardboiled eggs, sliced
6 tablespoons heavy cream

In a soup kettle or large saucepan combine the chicken, scallions, coriander, *guascas* (if available), chicken stock or water, and salt and pepper to taste. Bring to a boil and skim off any froth that rises to the surface, reduce the heat, cover, and simmer gently until the chicken is tender, about 45 minutes. Let the chicken cool in the broth, lift it out, cut it into 6 serving pieces, and set it aside, covered. Strain the broth and add the corn to it.

Bring the broth to a simmer over moderate heat and add all the potatoes. Simmer until the broth thickens. The Idaho potatoes will disintegrate and thicken the broth, the red potatoes will retain some texture, and the *papas criollas* or new potatoes will remain whole. Add the milk and the chicken pieces and cook just long enough to heat them through. To serve, have ready six large, deep soup plates. Put a piece of chicken in each, 2 or 3 slices of Vienna sausage, 1 tablespoon peas, a few capers, a slice of egg, and the broth, making sure each gets a *papa criolla* or new potato. Pour a tablespoon of heavy cream over each serving. Serve with knife, fork, and soup spoon.

Ajiaco de Pollo Bogotano COLOMBIA
Bogotá Chicken Stew

Serves 6

4 tablespoons (¼ cup) butter
A 3½-pound chicken, cut into
   serving pieces
2 large onions, finely chopped
8 small potatoes, peeled and thinly
   sliced
8 cups chicken stock

12 whole, peeled papas criollas, if
   available (otherwise 6 new
   potatoes halved)
Salt, fresh ground pepper
2 ears corn, each cut into 3 slices
3 tablespoons capers
1 cup heavy cream

Heat the butter in a heavy casserole and sauté the chicken pieces with the onions until the chicken is golden on both sides. Add the thinly sliced potatoes and the stock, cover, and cook over very low heat until the chicken is about half done and the potatoes are beginning to disintegrate, about 25 minutes. Add the 6 halved new potatoes and continue cooking until both chicken and potatoes are tender. With a slotted spoon, remove the chicken pieces and potatoes from the casserole and keep warm. Work the stock through a sieve. It will have been thickened by the sliced potatoes. Return the stock to the casserole, season to taste with salt and pepper, add the chicken and potatoes, the corn and capers, and simmer for 5 minutes longer. Add the cream and continue cooking just long enough to heat it through. Serve in deep soup plates with *Ají de Huevo* (Avocado Sauce) on the side.

Carapulcra

Chicken, Pork, and Potatoes in Peanut Sauce

When I decided to test *carapulcra* in New York, having enjoyed it in Peru, I was told I could regard one of its ingredients, *chuño* or *papaseca* (freeze-dried potato) as optional, to be replaced with fresh potatoes, since I couldn't buy the commercially packaged article here. I decided that what the Inca women could do I could do. When the Inca, who were the first people to cultivate the potato back in 2500 B.C., faced crop storage problems, they invented freeze-drying, and there is every reason to believe that they were the first people to do so. Raw, unpeeled potatoes were put outside their houses at night in the icy cold of the Andean highlands, where they froze solid. In the morning they thawed in the sun and the water was trampled out of them by Inca women, and the process repeated until they were thoroughly dry.

The sixteenth floor of a New York high-rise is not to be compared with the Andes, whose soaring peaks topple the imagination, so I put my potatoes, 3 large Idahos, in the freezer overnight. In the morning, since I have a small terrace with a southern exposure, I put them in the sun to thaw. One cannot trample the water out of 3 potatoes — it takes a whole crop to make that possible — so I squeezed the water out of my potatoes by hand. At the end of three days they were like stone, strange skinny objects. The flesh had turned quite dark, almost black. I kept one for two years before I used it, just to see, and it was as good as ever. The others I used in this *carapulcra*. I had a lot of fun making *chuño*, but I can honestly say my Peruvian friends were right when they said it was all right to substitute fresh potatoes for it.

Serves 6

2 freeze-dried Idaho potatoes, or 2 fresh potatoes
A 2½-pound chicken, cut into serving pieces
1 pound boneless loin of pork, cut into ¾-inch cubes
2 cups chicken stock, about
4 tablespoons lard or vegetable oil
1 large onion, finely chopped
4 cloves garlic, minced
½ teaspoon Spanish (hot) paprika or cayenne

⅛ teaspoon ground cumin
Salt, freshly ground pepper
½ cup roasted peanuts, finely ground
6 small potatoes, freshly cooked
3 hardboiled eggs, sliced
20 medium-sized pitted black or green olives

Put the dried potatoes on to soak in warm water to cover for about 2 hours. If using the fresh potatoes instead of the dried ones, add them to the stew, peeled and diced at the same time the dried potatoes would be added. When the dried potatoes have been soaked, drain them, and chop coarsely. Set aside.

Put the chicken and pork pieces into a saucepan and add enough chicken stock to cover. Cover and simmer until tender. Drain and set the stock aside. Bone the chicken and cut the meat into cubes about the same size as the pork. Set aside with a little stock to moisten the meats.

Rinse out and dry the saucepan or use a flameproof casserole, and heat the lard or oil in it. Add the onion, garlic, hot paprika or cayenne, and cumin, and sauté until the onion is soft. Add the potato and about a cup of the reserved stock, cover, and simmer gently until the potato has disintegrated, thickening the mixture, about 1 hour. Season to taste with salt and pepper and stir in the ground peanuts. Cook for a minute or two, then add the chicken and pork pieces. The sauce should be thick, but add a little more stock if necessary. Simmer just long enough to heat through and blend the flavors.

Arrange the chicken and pork mixture on a heated serving platter and garnish it with the fresh, hot potatoes, the hardboiled egg slices, and olives.

Pollo Borracho ARGENTINA
Drunken Chicken

This is a typical *criollo* dish and with slight variations occurs all over Latin America.

Serves 4

1 tablespoon butter
½ pound boiled ham, cut into strips about 2 inches by ¼ inch
A 3½-pound chicken, cut into 4 serving pieces
Salt, freshly ground pepper
¼ teaspoon ground cumin
¼ teaspoon ground coriander

¼ cup white wine vinegar
2 cups dry white wine
1 cup chicken stock, about
3 cloves garlic, minced
12 medium pimiento-stuffed olives
3 tablespoons capers

Melt the butter in a flameproof casserole. Make a layer of one-third of the ham. Season the chicken pieces with the salt, pepper, cumin, and coriander, and add the chicken legs to the casserole with another third of the ham on top. Arrange the chicken breasts over the ham and sprinkle with the remaining ham strips. Pour in the vinegar, wine, and enough chicken stock to cover. Add the garlic, cover, and simmer over low heat for 45 minutes, or until the chicken is tender. Rinse the olives and soak them for 15 minutes in cold water. Drain. Rinse and drain the capers. Place the chicken pieces and ham strips in a serving dish and keep warm. Measure the liquid in the casserole and reduce it, over brisk heat, to 2 cups. Moisten the chicken with a little of the liquid and serve the rest in a gravy boat. Garnish the chicken with the olives and capers.

If liked, the sauce may be lightly thickened. Mix 1 tablespoon flour with 1 tablespoon butter, stir into the liquid, and simmer over low heat, stirring constantly, until the sauce is thickened. Serve with plain boiled potatoes or white rice and a green vegetable or salad.

Pollo en Pepián Dulce   GUATEMALA
Mayan Chicken Fricassee

Because Guatemala was the heart of the Mayan empire, with its capital city of Tikal, the kitchen of post-Columbian Guatemala is close to that of Yucatán in Mexico. This dish unites a medley of flavors, which the chicken absorbs during cooking. They blend harmoniously in the sauce, which is as thick as heavy cream and delicious with plain rice.

Serves 6

A 3½- to 4-pound chicken, cut
    into serving pieces
2 cups chicken stock, about
1 tablespoon sesame seeds
½ cup pepitas (Mexican pumpkin
    seeds)
3 red bell peppers, seeded and
    coarsely chopped, or 5 canned
    pimientos, chopped
3 medium tomatoes, peeled and
    coarsely chopped

1 medium onion, chopped
2 cloves garlic, chopped
2 tablespoons lard or vegetable oil
¼ cup Seville (bitter) orange juice,
    or use two-thirds orange juice
    and one-third lime juice
½ teaspoon ground allspice
Salt, freshly ground pepper
¼ cup seedless raisins
Butter
¼ cup chopped almonds

Put the chicken pieces into a heavy casserole, pour in the stock, adding a little more to cover, if necessary. Cover and simmer until almost tender, about 30 minutes. In a blender or food processor grind the sesame and pumpkin seeds as fine as possible and shake through a sieve. Set aside. Put the peppers, tomatoes, onion, and garlic into a blender or food processor and reduce to a coarse purée. Mix the purée with the ground sesame and pumpkin seeds. Heat the lard or vegetable oil in a skillet, add the purée, and cook, over moderate heat, stirring constantly with a wooden spoon, for 5 minutes. Drain the chicken, reserve the stock, and return the chicken to the casserole. Add to the purée 1 cup of the stock, the Seville (bitter) orange juice, allspice, and salt and pepper to taste. Stir to mix, and pour over the chicken. Cover and simmer gently until the chicken is tender, about 15 minutes. Add a little more stock if necessary. The sauce should be thick. Soak the raisins in cold water to cover for 15 minutes. Drain thoroughly. Heat a little butter in a skillet and sauté the almonds until they are golden. Drain. Transfer the chicken and sauce to a warmed serving dish and sprinkle with the raisins and almonds. Serve with rice.

Pollo Verde Almendrado MEXICO
Chicken in Green Almond Sauce

I find all the Mexican green chicken dishes delicious; this one is enchanting, not only for its very subtle flavor but because the green sauce is downright pretty to look at.

Serves 6

A 3½-pound chicken, cut into
    serving pieces
2 cups chicken stock
1 medium onion, chopped
1 clove garlic, chopped
1 cup parsley sprigs, coarsely
    chopped
1 cup coriander (cilantro) sprigs,
    coarsely chopped
1 heart of romaine lettuce,
    coarsely chopped

1 or 2 fresh hot green peppers,
    seeded and chopped, or 2
    canned jalapeño or 3 canned
    serrano chilies, seeded and
    chopped
4 ounces ground almonds, about
    ¾ cup
3 tablespoons vegetable oil or lard
Salt

Put the chicken pieces into a heavy casserole with the stock, bring to a boil, reduce the heat, and simmer gently, covered, for 45 minutes, or until tender. Lift the chicken out onto a platter and set aside. Pour the stock into a jug. Rinse out and dry the casserole.

In a blender or food processor combine the onion, garlic, parsley, coriander, lettuce, hot peppers, and almonds, and reduce to a coarse purée. Do not overblend as the finished sauce should have some texture, not be entirely smooth. Heat the oil or lard in a large, heavy skillet and pour in the purée, which will be almost pastelike because of the almonds. Cook the mixture, stirring constantly with a wooden spoon, for 3 to 4 minutes over moderate heat. Transfer it to a casserole. Stir in 2 cups of the stock, season to taste with salt. Add the chicken pieces, cover, and simmer just long enough to heat the chicken through.

Arroz Blanco (White Rice) is good with this. For a completely Mexican meal, serve the chicken with the rice and with tortillas, *Frijoles* (Beans), and *Guacamole* (Avocado Sauce).

Pollo en Pipián de Almendra   MEXICO
Chicken Stew with Almonds

Pipián is one of the best dishes in the Mexican kitchen and one of the hardest to define. The dictionary of the Spanish Royal Academy says it is an American stew made of meat, chicken, turkey, or other fowl with salt pork and ground almonds. Other dictionaries describe it as a kind of Indian fricassee. The *Nuevo Cocinero Méjicano*, a dictionary published in Paris in 1888, gives a more complete description. It says that *pipián* is a Mexican stew made with red or green peppers, pumpkin seeds, almonds, or oily seeds such as sesame or peanuts. The stew may be made with turkey, chicken, duck, or indeed any bird, as well as with meats or fish and shellfish. There are even vegetarian versions using fruits and vegetables. It should not be salted until the moment of serving, as salt is said to make the sauce separate.

Serves 4

A 3-pound chicken, cut into
    serving pieces
2 or 3 scallions
2 or 3 large sprigs fresh coriander
    (cilantro)
1 carrot, scraped and halved
2 cups chicken stock, about
6 ancho *chilies*

½ cup (4 ounces) almonds,
    blanched
2 tablespoons lard or vegetable oil
⅛ teaspoon ground cloves
¼ teaspoon ground cinnamon
¼ teaspoon oregano
Salt

Put the chicken pieces into a large, heavy casserole or saucepan with the scallions, coriander, and carrot. Pour in the chicken stock, adding a little more if necessary to cover. Bring to a boil, reduce the heat, and simmer, covered, for 45 minutes, or until the chicken is tender. Lift the chicken pieces out of the stock. Strain and reserve the stock, discarding the solids. Rinse out the casserole and put the chicken pieces back in it. Shake the seeds out of the chilies and rinse them. Tear them in pieces and put them to soak for 1 hour in about ½ cup hot water, turning them from time to time. If they absorb all the water, add a little more. Reduce the chilies to a paste in a blender or food processor, using a little of the soaking water. Put them into a bowl. Toast the almonds in a skillet and pulverize them in a nut grinder, blender, or food processor, shake them through a sieve, and add to the chilies, mixing thoroughly. Heat the lard or oil in a skillet, add the chili and almond mixture, and sauté, stirring constantly with a wooden spoon, for 4 or 5 minutes over moderate heat. Thin with about 2 cups of the reserved chicken stock to make a medium-thick sauce. Stir in the cloves, cinnamon, and oregano, and pour over the chicken pieces in the casserole. Cook at a bare simmer over very low heat for 15 minutes, or until the chicken is heated through and the flavors have blended. Season to taste with salt. Serve with rice, beans, tortillas, *guacamole* or other salad, and a green vegetable, if liked.

Despite the solemn warnings in ancient cookbooks and from experienced Mexican cooks, I must confess I have never found that salting the sauce earlier makes it separate, so I leave this question open.

Some cooks reserve the seeds of the *ancho* chilies, toast them, and grind them with the almonds. I have not found this a good idea. The seeds seem to coarsen the sauce and blur the delicate flavor of the almonds. Also more stock has to be added, making too much sauce.

Pollo en Salsa de Almendra   MEXICO
Chicken in Almond Sauce

Serves 4

4 tablespoons (¼ cup) butter
A 3- to 3½-pound chicken, cut
    into serving pieces
3 cups chicken stock, about
1 medium onion, finely chopped
1 fresh hot red or green pepper,
    seeded and finely chopped, or
    1 canned serrano or jalapeño
    chili, rinsed

½ cup toasted almonds, finely
    ground
2 hardboiled eggs, chopped
1 cup freshly made breadcrumbs
Salt, freshly ground pepper

Heat the butter in a large skillet and sauté the chicken pieces until lightly golden all over. Transfer the chicken to a heatproof casserole, add enough chicken stock to cover, bring to a boil, lower the heat, cover, and simmer gently until the chicken is tender, about 45 minutes. Lift out the chicken pieces and keep warm. Pour the stock into a container and set it aside. Rinse out and dry the casserole.

In the fat remaining in the skillet sauté the onion with the hot pepper until the onion is soft. Add the almonds, eggs, breadcrumbs, and salt and pepper to taste, and sauté for a minute or two longer. Stir in 2 cups of the reserved chicken stock, pour the mixture into a blender or food processor, and reduce it to a purée. Do not overblend. The sauce should have some texture. Return the chicken pieces to the casserole and pour the sauce over them. Simmer just long enough to heat the chicken through. Serve with rice.

Pollo Pibil
Chicken, Yucatán Style   MEXICO

This is an old dish from the distant past. It would have been wrapped in banana leaves and cooked in a *pib*, an earth oven, one of the earliest methods of cooking. A modern oven does well but not as well as the *pib*. Sometimes one still gets a chance to have *pollo pibil* cooked in the traditional way and it is a grand experience.

Serves 4

12 peppercorns
½ teaspoon oregano
¼ teaspoon cumin seeds
2 teaspoons achiote (annatto)
* seeds*
1 teaspoon salt
4 large cloves garlic

1 cup Seville (bitter) orange juice,
* or use two-thirds orange juice*
* and one-third lime juice*
A 3½- to 4-pound chicken,
* quartered*
Banana leaves (or kitchen
* parchment or aluminum foil)*

Using mortar and pestle, a blender, or a food processor, grind together the peppercorns, oregano, cumin, achiote seeds, salt, and garlic. Transfer the mixture to a large bowl and mix thoroughly with the orange juice. Add the chicken pieces, mixing well to coat them with the marinade. Cover and refrigerate for 24 hours, turning two or three times.

Wrap each piece of chicken in a square of banana leaf, kitchen parchment, or aluminum foil, about 12 inches by 12 inches, dividing the marinade equally among the pieces. Arrange the packages in a casserole, cover, and bake in a preheated moderate (325° F.) oven for about 2 hours, or until the chicken is very tender. Serve with hot tortillas.

Pollo Ticuleño   MEXICO
Chicken, Ticul Style

This is a favorite Mayan dish from Yucatán. The delicate chicken breast makes a fine contrast to the robust flavor of black beans and tortilla, all enhanced by the very pure flavor of the tomato sauce. Put the beans on to cook about 3 hours ahead of time, so they will be ready when needed. The dish really needs no accompaniment other than the garnishes and, for lovers of the *picante, Ixni-Pec,* the hot pepper sauce from Yucatán (page 312).

Serves 4

FOR THE TOMATO SAUCE
3 *medium tomatoes*   *Salt, freshly ground pepper*
1 *small onion*

FOR THE CHICKEN
8 *tablespoons (½ cup) butter*   4 *tortillas, fried crisp in vegetable*
2 *whole chicken breasts, boned*   *oil*
   and halved   1 *cup black beans cooked as for*
Flour   *Panuchos (see page 47)*
1 *egg, lightly beaten*   4 *tablespoons freshly grated*
2 *cups breadcrumbs, about*   *Parmesan cheese, about*

FOR THE GARNISH
1 *onion prepared as for* **Panuchos**   8 *to 12 radish flowers*
   (see page 47), but thinly sliced   1 *or 2 medium tomatoes, sliced*
   instead of chopped   *(optional)*
1 *cup cooked green peas*
2 *ripe plantains, halved crosswise,*
   then lengthwise, and fried
   until golden brown in
   vegetable oil

To make the tomato sauce, peel and chop 3 medium tomatoes and add to a blender or food processor with 1 small onion, chopped. Reduce to a purée. Pour the mixture into a small saucepan and simmer, uncovered, over very low heat for 15 minutes, or until thick and well blended. Season with salt and freshly ground pepper to taste.

Chop the butter coarsely and put it into a small, heavy saucepan. Melt the butter over very low heat. Skim off the foam that rises to the top and carefully pour the butter into a heavy skillet, discarding the milky sediment. Roll the chicken breasts in flour, dip in the egg, then in breadcrumbs. Heat the clarified butter and sauté the breasts for about 4 minutes on each side, taking care not to overcook them. Spread the tortillas with the beans, place the chicken breasts on top of the tortillas, pour a little tomato sauce over them, and sprinkle with the grated cheese. Place 1 tortilla on each of four warmed serving plates and garnish with the onion, peas, plantains, radishes, and, if liked, sliced tomatoes.

Xinxim de Galinha   BRAZIL
Chicken with Shrimp and Peanut Sauce

This is a Bahian dish, as the use of *dendê* (palm) oil indicates. The mixture of flavors is unusual and exciting, but not difficult for the unaccustomed palate to accept.

Serves 6

*A 3-pound chicken, cut into
    serving pieces*
4 tablespoons lime or lemon juice
2 cloves garlic, crushed
Salt
2 tablespoons olive oil
1 medium onion, grated

1 cup dried shrimp, finely ground
*½ cup dry roasted peanuts,
    ground*
*1 fresh hot red pepper, seeded and
    chopped (optional)*
½ cup chicken stock, about
¼ cup dendê (palm) oil

Season the chicken with the lime or lemon juice, the garlic, and salt to taste. Set aside.

In a heavy saucepan heat the oil and sauté the onion, dried shrimp, peanuts, and hot pepper for 5 minutes, stirring from time to time. Add the chicken pieces and their liquid, and cook for a few minutes, turning the pieces once. Add the chicken stock, cover, and simmer gently until the chicken is tender, about 30 minutes, turning once during the cooking and adding a little more stock if necessary. When the chicken is tender, taste for seasoning, pour in the *dendê* (palm) oil, and cook for a minute or two longer. The sauce should be thick and not very abundant. Serve with white rice and *Farofa de Azeite de Dendê* (Cassava Meal with Palm Oil).

Vatapá de Galinha

Chicken in Shrimp and Almond Sauce

Vatapá is one of the great dishes of the Bahian kitchen of Brazil, but it does take quite a lot of work. It is an exciting dish for guests and I find their pleasure in this truly exotic food makes it well worth the effort. The coconut milk can be made ahead of time and tedious jobs like grinding the dried shrimp are made easy with the help of a food processor. I so well remember the first time I had *vatapá* in Salvador, Bahia. It was a revelation, with so many unfamiliar and delicious flavors to beguile the palate.

Serves 6 to 8

3 tablespoons olive oil
2 medium onions, finely chopped
4 scallions, chopped, using white
　and green parts
2 large cloves garlic, chopped
4 medium tomatoes, peeled,
　seeded, and chopped
1 or 2 fresh hot peppers, seeded
　and chopped
Salt, freshly ground pepper
3 tablespoons lime or lemon juice
4 tablespoons fresh coriander
　(cilantro), or use flat-leafed
　Italian parsley

Two 2½-pound chickens,
　quartered
Chicken stock, if necessary
1¾ cups finely ground almonds
2 cups dried shrimp, finely ground
3 cups thin coconut milk (see
　page 7)
1 cup thick coconut milk (see
　page 7)
1 tablespoon rice flour
4 tablespoons dendê (palm) oil

In a large skillet heat the oil and sauté the onions, scallions, garlic, tomatoes, and hot peppers for 5 minutes. Season the mixture to taste with salt and pepper and stir in the lime or lemon juice and the coriander or parsley. Add the quartered chickens, cover, and cook until the chickens are tender, 30 to 35 minutes. Add a little chicken stock to the skillet if the mixture seems too dry. With a slotted spoon, transfer the chickens to a dish and let them cool. Skin and bone the chickens and chop the meat coarsely. Put the vegetable mixture through a sieve, pressing down hard on the vegetables to extract all the liquid. Discard the solids and reserve the liquid.

　　In a saucepan combine the almonds, ground shrimp, the thin coconut milk, and the reserved liquid from cooking the chicken. Bring to a boil and simmer for 15 minutes. Add the thick coconut milk and the rice flour mixed with a little water, and cook, uncovered, stirring frequently, until the mixture has the consistency of a thick béchamel. Add the chicken pieces and the *dendê* (palm) oil. Cook just long enough to heat through, about 5 minutes. Serve with *Pirão de Arroz* (Rice Flour Pudding).

Variation: To make *Vatapá de Camarão* (Shrimp and Fish in a Shrimp and Almond Sauce), in place of the chicken, substitute 1 pound raw shrimp, shelled and deveined, and 3 pounds fillets of any firm white fish, cut into 2-inch pieces. Add 1 tablespoon of finely chopped fresh ginger to the onion and tomato mixture, and cook the fish for 10 minutes, the shrimp only until they turn pink and lose their translucent look, about 3 minutes.

Pollo en Salsa de Huevos   ECUADOR
Chicken in Egg Sauce

Ecuador was once part of the great Inca empire, which had its center in Cuzco, Peru, and dominated the whole Andean region, stretching as far as northern Chile. Even today the dominant language of the Inca empire, Quechua, is still spoken in both countries. Coastal Ecuador was not gathered into the Inca fold, and with its vastly different climate and vegetation has a distinct regional kitchen, whose notable feature is the use of plantains, especially the *verde* (green, or unripe) plantain. The secret of the cooking lies in combining foods not usually put together, pork stuffed with shrimps, for example, or Seville (bitter) orange used for the *seviches* (marinated fish). Dry mustard is used interestingly in the chicken dishes — sautéed with chopped onion first so that it adds an elusive flavor to the finished dish. Elsewhere ground walnuts make a wonderfully rich sauce for chicken, with that hint of bitterness and sweetness peculiar to walnuts. Wine, vinegar, both orange and lemon juice, eggs, sweet red peppers, and nuts are all used one way or another with chicken, making for a very versatile yet simple cuisine, requiring no elaborate techniques.

Serves 4 to 6

*4 tablespoons (¼ cup) butter or
    vegetable oil
A 3½- to 4-pound chicken, cut
    into serving pieces
1 large onion, finely chopped*

*1 clove garlic, minced
1 tablespoon dry mustard
Salt, freshly ground pepper
2 cups chicken stock, about
6 hardboiled eggs, finely chopped*

Heat the butter in a skillet and sauté the chicken pieces until golden on both sides. Transfer them to a casserole. In the butter remaining in the skillet sauté the onion and garlic with the mustard, stirring to mix. When the onion is soft, transfer the contents of the skillet to a flameproof casserole. Season with salt and pepper to taste and pour in the stock, adding a little more barely to cover the chicken, if necessary. Cover and simmer until the chicken is tender, about 45 minutes. Transfer the chicken to a warmed serving platter and keep warm. Over brisk heat reduce the sauce until it is of medium thickness. Taste the sauce for seasoning and add a little salt and pepper if necessary. Stir in the eggs and cook just long enough to heat through. Pour the sauce over the chicken and serve, or serve the sauce separately in a sauceboat. Accompany with rice or potatoes, mixed vegetable salad, or a green vegetable.

Variation: For *Pollo en Salsa de Nuez* (Chicken in Nut Sauce), omit the hardboiled eggs and add 1½ cups ground walnuts to the sauce.

Variation: For *Pollo con Aceitunas* (Chicken with Olives), use 1 cup red wine in place of 1 cup of the stock, and omit the mustard. Instead of the hardboiled eggs, add 1½ cups sliced, green, pimiento-stuffed olives to the sauce. Rinse the olives in warm water before slicing.

Variation: For *Pollo a la Criolla* (Chicken, Creole Style), omit the mustard and the hardboiled eggs, adding with the stock, ½ cup oil, 2 tablespoons vinegar, and 1 bay leaf. Serve with fried potatoes.

Variation: For *Pollo con Pimientos* (Chicken with Sweet Red Peppers), omit the hardboiled eggs. Use 1 cup stock and 1 cup dry red wine. Increase the dry mustard to 2 tablespoons and add to the sauce one 8-ounce can of pimientos, drained and puréed in a blender. Simmer the sauce for a few minutes longer, and if necessary add enough fresh breadcrumbs to make it of medium consistency. It should not be thin.

Variation: For *Pollo al Limón* (Chicken with Lemon), omit the hardboiled eggs. Reduce the chicken stock to 1½ cups and add ½ cup fresh lemon juice. Traditionally the sauce is thickened by adding 1 cup fresh breadcrumbs and stirring over moderate heat until the sauce is smooth and thick. I prefer to reduce the sauce over brisk heat, or to thicken it with 1 tablespoon flour mixed with 1 tablespoon of butter. The flavor is not changed, it is simply a matter of texture.

Variation: For *Pollo en Salsa de Almendras* (Chicken in Almond Sauce), omit the mustard and reduce the hardboiled eggs to 3. When the chicken is cooked, transfer it to a platter and keep it warm. Reduce the stock to 1½ cups over brisk heat. Pulverize ¾ cup blanched almonds in a blender, add the eggs and stock, and reduce to a smooth purée. Heat the sauce, spoon a little over the chicken, and serve the rest separately. A deceptively simple dish. The eggs and almonds give the sauce a very subtle flavor.

Variation: For *Pollo en Jugo de Naranja* (Chicken in Orange Juice), omit the hardboiled eggs. Omit the mustard and use 1 tablespoon sweet paprika instead. In place of 2 cups chicken stock, use 1 cup stock and 1 cup orange juice. Add 6 ounces coarsely chopped boiled ham to the chicken in the casserole. Before serving, reduce the sauce over brisk heat to medium thick.

Variation: For *Pollo al Jerez* (Chicken with Sherry), omit the hardboiled eggs. Reduce the amount of dry mustard to 1 teaspoon, and instead of 2 cups chicken stock, use 1 cup stock, 1 cup dry sherry. Thicken the sauce with 1 cup of breadcrumbs, or reduce it over brisk heat.

Variation: For *Pollo con Queso* (Chicken with Cheese), omit the hardboiled eggs. When adding the stock to the casserole, add 1 bay leaf and ½ teaspoon each thyme and oregano. When the chicken is done, lift it out onto an ovenproof serving dish and sprinkle it generously with grated Parmesan cheese, about ½ cup, and dot with 2 tablespoons butter. Put it into a preheated moderate (350° F.) oven until the cheese is golden brown. Strain the sauce and reduce it to half over brisk heat. Serve in a gravy boat.

In Ecuador a fresh, or bottled, hot pepper sauce would be on the table to be taken with any of these dishes according to individual taste.

Pollo con Arroz   PARAGUAY
Chicken with Rice

It would be impossible to have a book of Latin American food without including recipes for *Arroz con Pollo*, a perennial favorite, almost always translated as Chicken with Rice though literally it is Rice with Chicken. This simplest of dishes is also somewhat of a paradox. Its ingredients are not, for the most part, native to Spain, and the dish there is sometimes called *Arroz a la Valenciana* (Rice, Valencia Style). It is also often thought of as a cousin of *paella*, Spain's famous rice, chicken, and shellfish dish. The dish is quintessentially international, for the chickens originally came from India, the saffron arrived with Phoenician traders, the Arabs brought the rice from Asia, and the tomatoes and peppers are the gift of Mexico. It is tremendously popular in the Spanish-speaking Caribbean and in Mexico, as well as in South America, and differs a little from country to country not only in ingredients and technique but in the name as well. One of my favorites, in which the name is reversed to *Pollo con Arroz* (Chicken with Rice), is perhaps the simplest of all the versions I've encountered.

Serves 4 to 6

2 tablespoons oil, preferably olive
   oil
A 3- to 3½-pound chicken, cut
   into serving pieces
1 medium onion, finely chopped
1 green or red bell pepper, seeded
   and chopped

3 tomatoes, peeled and chopped
Salt, freshly ground pepper
4 cups chicken stock or water
⅛ teaspoon saffron
2 cups long-grain rice

Heat the oil in a heavy skillet and sauté the chicken pieces until they are golden on both sides. Transfer the chicken to an earthenware or enameled iron casserole. In the oil remaining in the skillet sauté the onion and pepper until they are soft. Add to the casserole with the tomatoes, salt and pepper to taste, 2 cups of the chicken stock or water, and the saffron, crumbled. Simmer, covered, over low heat for 30 minutes.

Lift out the chicken pieces onto a dish or plate and set aside. Pour the liquid through a sieve, reserving the solids. Measure the liquid and make the quantity up to 4 cups with the rest of the chicken stock. Pour it into the casserole, add the rice and the reserved solids, stir to mix, and bring to a boil over fairly brisk heat. Arrange the chicken pieces on top of the rice, cover, and cook over very low heat until the rice is tender and all the liquid absorbed, about 20 minutes. Serve directly from the casserole. If liked, artichoke hearts, about 12, may be scattered through the chicken.

Variation: Venezuela has an interesting version of this dish. It is a little more elaborate and has raisins, olives, and capers mixed with the rice. In a blender purée 4 medium tomatoes, skinned and chopped, 2 medium onions, chopped, 1 green and 1 red bell pepper, seeded and chopped, 2 leeks, well washed and chopped, and 1 clove garlic. Season the mixture with salt and freshly ground pepper and pour it over a 3- to 3½-pound chicken, cut into serving pieces, in a flameproof casserole. Add ½ cup dry white wine and a little chicken stock to cover, if necessary, and simmer, covered, for 30 minutes. Lift out the chicken pieces onto a plate or dish, and measure the liquid. Make up the quantity to 4 cups, if more liquid is needed, with chicken stock. Rinse out and dry the casserole. Heat 4 tablespoons (¼ cup) butter in the casserole and stir in the rice. Stir constantly with a wooden spoon over moderate heat, taking care not to let the rice burn. Pour the chicken stock mixture over the rice. Add ½ cup seedless raisins, 12 pimiento-stuffed green olives, halved, and 2 tablespoons capers, and stir to mix. Bring to a simmer. Arrange the chicken pieces on top of the rice, cover, and cook over low heat until the rice is tender and the liquid absorbed, about 20 minutes. Serves 4 to 6.

Variation: Coastal Colombia uses annatto (achiote) in its version of *Arroz con Pollo*; interesting, since this was a favorite seasoning of the Maya, the Caribs, and the Arawaks as well as the Colombian coastal people of pre-Conquest times. It is still popular in Yucatán, coastal Colombia, and the Caribbean today. Put 2 tablespoons of *aceite de achiote* (annatto oil), see page 324, in a heavy casserole, and add a 3- to 3½-pound chicken, cut into serving pieces, 4 medium tomatoes, peeled and chopped, 2 medium onions, finely chopped, 1 large carrot, scraped and chopped, 2 stalks celery, chopped, 3 or 4 scallions, trimmed, 1 fresh hot pepper, seeded and chopped (optional), 1 bay leaf, ⅛ teaspoon ground cumin, 2 cloves, 1 tablespoon vinegar, and salt and pepper to taste. Cover and simmer over low heat for about 30 minutes, or until the chicken is barely tender. If more liquid is needed, add a little chicken stock. Lift out the chicken pieces onto a plate or dish. Remove and discard the scallions, bay leaf, and cloves. Strain the liquid and reserve the solids. Make up the quantity of liquid to 4 cups. Pour the liquid into the casserole, add 2 cups long-grain rice and the reserved vegetables, stir to mix, and bring to a boil. Arrange the chicken pieces on top of the rice, cover, and cook over low heat until the rice is tender and all the liquid absorbed, about 20 minutes. Serves 4 to 6.

Variation: The Dominican Republic has its own, very attractive *Arroz con Pollo*. In this version the chicken is marinated in a mixture containing hot pepper, and the marinade later mixed with the rice. Put a 2- to 2½-pound chicken, cut into serving pieces, into a bowl with 2 cloves garlic, crushed, 1 medium onion, finely chopped, 1 tablespoon parsley, chopped, 1 bay leaf, crumbled, 1 fresh hot red or green pepper, seeded and finely chopped, salt and freshly ground pepper to taste, and 2 tablespoons vinegar, and let it stand for about an hour. Some cooks like to add 2 ounces cubed boiled ham to the chicken. Lift the chicken pieces out of the marinade and pat them dry with paper towels. Reserve the marinade. Heat 4 tablespoons vegetable oil or lard in a heavy casserole and fry the chicken pieces until they are golden on both sides. Add the reserved marinade and cook for a minute or two. Add 2 cups rice and stir into the oil and vegetable mixture. Cook for 2 or 3 minutes. Pour in 4 cups chicken stock or water mixed with 2 tablespoons tomato purée and bring to a boil over fairly high heat. Cover and cook over low heat until the chicken and rice are both tender and all the liquid absorbed, about 30 minutes. Add ½ cup pimiento-stuffed green olives, sliced, 1 tablespoon capers, ½ cup cooked green peas or cut green beans, and 1 or 2 pimientos, cut into strips. Cook just long enough to heat through and serve from the casserole. Serves 4.

Variation: From Mexico I have a family recipe for *Arroz con Pollo* given me by my husband's maternal grandmother, Doña Carmen Sarabia de Tinoco.

She was a fabulous cook and when she made *tamales del norte* (tamales, northern style) for a party, all the world scrambled for an invitation. I think it is a dreadful pity that grandmothers are usually so much older than their granddaughters-in-law. I could have learned so much more from a very wonderful teacher. Her recipe is interesting for having both saffron and hot peppers.

For Mexican chicken with rice, season a 3- to 3½-pound chicken, cut into serving pieces, with salt and pepper. Heat 3 tablespoons olive oil in a skillet and sauté the chicken pieces until they are golden on both sides. Put the chicken pieces into an earthenware casserole heavy enough to go on direct heat, or any heavy casserole. In the oil remaining in the skillet sauté 1 medium onion, finely chopped, and 2 cloves garlic, chopped, until the onion is soft. Add to the chicken. Add 4 medium tomatoes, peeled and chopped, 1 or 2 canned *jalapeño* chilies, seeded and chopped, ¼ teaspoon ground cumin, and ⅛ teaspoon saffron, crumbled. Pour in 3 cups chicken stock or water, or enough to cover the chicken. Bring to a boil, reduce the heat to low, cover, and simmer gently for 30 minutes. Lift out and set aside the chicken pieces and measure the stock. Make up the quantity to 4 cups. In the oil remaining in the skillet sauté 2 cups rice until the rice grains are well coated. Do not let the rice brown. Add the rice to the casserole, pour in the stock, and stir to mix. Bring to a boil, add the chicken pieces, reduce the heat, cover, and cook over very low heat until the rice is tender and all the liquid absorbed. Garnish with 2 pimientos, cut into strips. Serve directly from the casserole.

Two ounces of dry sherry may, with advantage, be poured over the chicken and rice at the end of the cooking and the dish cooked for a minute or two longer. The *jalapeño* chilies may be left out, if preferred. Serves 4 to 6.

Pollo Escabechado
Pickled Chicken

CHILE

In this recipe the chicken literally stews in the oil, which is poured or spooned off the sauce at the end of the cooking time. It makes for a very delicate, moist, and tender bird. Though the name of the dish translates as pickled chicken, the small amount of vinegar used leaves just a pleasant echo on the palate. Since the chicken is served cold, it is done ahead of time, which makes it perfect for a family meal in summer. It is an attractive dish in its pale, translucent jelly, lovely for a cold buffet accompanied by salads such as *Ensalada de Aguacate* (Avocado Salad), *Ensalada de Habas* (Fresh Broad Bean Salad), or *Ensalada de Verduras* (Vegetable Salad).

Serves 6 to 8

A 4-pound roasting chicken, cut
    into serving pieces
1 cup vegetable oil
½ cup white wine vinegar
1 teaspoon salt

6 peppercorns
1 bay leaf
2 medium onions, thinly sliced
2 carrots, scraped and thinly
    sliced

Place all the ingredients in a large kettle or heavy casserole, cover, and cook over very low heat until the chicken is tender, about 1½ hours. Allow to cool. Place the chicken pieces on a serving platter with the vegetables arranged around them. Remove and discard the peppercorns and bay leaf. Pour the liquid in the casserole into a bowl, then spoon off all the oil (it is easier to do it this way). Save the oil, incidentally, for sautéing other meats and poultry. Pour the stock over the chicken pieces and refrigerate. The liquid will set into an aspic. If a firmer jelly is preferred, add to the stock ½ tablespoon unflavored gelatin softened in water and stir to dissolve, over low heat, before pouring it over the chicken. In very hot weather I find this is sometimes necessary. If any oil escapes being spooned off, it will separate out when the jelly sets. Just tip the dish and pour it off, or remove it with a piece of blotting paper or paper towel.

To serve, decorate a platter with lettuce leaves, sliced tomatoes, cooked green peas and beans, and sliced pimiento or other suitable vegetables such as artichoke hearts.

Variation: *Pollo a la Paisana* (Country Chicken), also from Chile, can, I suppose, be considered a variation of *Pollo Escabechado* (Pickled Chicken) though it is served hot not cold and is a much simpler dish. It is in fact simplicity itself and is most useful when one is both busy and hungry for delectable food. The chicken emerges from the pot wonderfully moist and tender and with a subtle flavor that the cook can vary by the use of different vinegars. Tarragon vinegar and Japanese rice vinegar both spring to mind and I have used them with great success, though I doubt whether Japanese rice vinegar is a commonplace in Chile. I claim cook's privileges for this departure from strict tradition.

For *Pollo a la Paisana* (Country Chicken), cut a 3½- to 4-pound chicken into serving pieces and put it into a heavy earthenware or enameled cast iron casserole with 4 scallions, cut into 1-inch pieces and using both white and green parts, 4 cloves garlic, left whole, salt and freshly ground black pepper to taste, 1 or 2 sprigs parsley, 6 tablespoons olive oil, and 2 tablespoons vinegar. Cover and cook over very low heat until the chicken is tender, 45 minutes to 1 hour. Serve with either shoestring potatoes or French fries and a lettuce or watercress salad or a green vegetable. Serves 4 to 6.

TURKEY

Pavo Relleno
Stuffed Turkey

MEXICO

Until recently when industrialization brought gas and electric stoves into the kitchens of Mexico to replace the charcoal stoves of the past, there was very little oven cooking done, except for the baking of breads and cakes. This roast turkey with its hearty meat stuffing is an exception. I was a little taken aback the first time I encountered it; it seemed such a double richness, meat and bird. But I very soon adopted it with enthusiasm, for it is delicious. In Mexico the bird would be served with a garnish of chopped lettuce, sliced tomatoes, and avocado, in oil and vinegar dressing, and olives and radish roses, but I prefer these garnishes served separately as a salad.

Serves 6 to 8

1 recipe Picadillo *(Seasoned*
   Chopped Beef), page 131
A 6- to 8-pound turkey, ready to
   cook

Butter
1 cup dry white wine
3 tablespoons flour
Salt, freshly ground pepper

Make the *Picadillo* stuffing and allow it to cool. Fill the cavities of the bird with the stuffing and close them with skewers. Truss the bird and place it breast side up on a rack in a roasting pan. Have ready a double thickness of cheesecloth large enough to cover the bird. Soak it in melted butter and drape it over the bird. Roast in a preheated moderately slow (325° F.) oven for 2 to 2½ hours, or until the bird is done, basting through the cheesecloth several times with pan drippings or melted butter. While the bird is roasting, make a stock by covering the neck, giblets, and liver with water and 1 cup white wine and simmer 45 minutes to 1 hour. Remove the cheesecloth 30 minutes before the bird is done so that it will brown, basting twice during this period. Lift the bird onto a platter and remove the trussing strings and skewers. Let it rest 15 minutes before carving. Skim all but 3 tablespoons of fat from the roasting pan and stir in the flour, blending thoroughly over moderate heat. Stir in 1 cup of the stock and blend well, adding a little more if the gravy is too thick. Season to taste with salt and pepper and serve separately in a sauceboat.

Variation: For another popular stuffing, substitute 2 pounds ground pork for the beef. Omit the oregano and thyme and add ⅛ teaspoon of cloves and half that amount of ground cinnamon. Ground cumin (⅛ teaspoon) may be added to either stuffing. This spice is very popular in Mexican cooking and I find it makes a pleasant change.

Pavita Rellena a la Criolla   ARGENTINA
Hen Turkey with Creole Stuffing

Quinces, when they are available, may be used instead of peaches in this delicious turkey stuffing.

Serves 10 to 12

8 slices firm white bread	*3 tablespoons pitted green olives,*
Milk	* chopped*
2 tablespoons butter	*2 cups pitted, peeled, and chopped*
1 medium onion, finely chopped	* peaches*
2 pounds sausage meat	*Salt, freshly ground pepper*
1 bay leaf, crumbled	*3 eggs, lightly beaten*
1 teaspoon oregano	*A 10- to 12-pound turkey,*
1 tablespoon parsley, finely	* preferably a hen turkey*
* chopped*	*Olive oil*
2 hardboiled eggs, finely chopped	*Butter for basting*

Soak the bread in milk, squeeze out, and fluff. In a saucepan heat the butter and sauté the onion until it is golden. Add the sausage meat and cook until it has lost all its color, mashing with a fork to break it up. Remove the saucepan from the heat. Add the bread, herbs, hardboiled eggs, olives, and peaches. Season to taste with salt and a generous amount of pepper. Stir in the lightly beaten eggs. Stuff the bird with the mixture and truss it in the usual way. Rub the bird all over with olive oil and bake in a preheated moderate (325° F.) oven for 3 to 3½ hours, or until it is done. Baste every 30 minutes with ½ cup melted butter and when this is used up, the drippings in the pan. If necessary, use a little more butter. If any dressing is left over, bake it separately in a foil-covered container. If liked, make a gravy by simmering the giblets and neck in water to make 3 cups of stock, stir 4 tablespoons flour into 4 tablespoons fat from the roasting pan, add the stock, and cook, stirring, until the gravy is thickened.

Pavo Guisado   DOMINICAN REPUBLIC
Turkey Stew, Dominican Style

Perhaps because it remained out of the mainstream, the cooking of the Dominican Republic has preserved some of the best dishes of the Spanish colonial period, when indigenous and introduced foods combined very happily in the stewpot.

Serves 8 to 10

An 8- to 8½-pound turkey, cut into serving pieces
4 cloves garlic, crushed
Salt, freshly ground pepper
2 tablespoons red wine vinegar
½ cup vegetable oil
1 cup tomato purée
1 green bell pepper, seeded and chopped

24 small pitted green olives
4 tablespoons capers
3 pounds potatoes, peeled and sliced
1 pound fresh peas, shelled, or a 10-ounce package frozen peas, thawed

Season the turkey pieces with the garlic, salt and pepper to taste, and the vinegar. Leave for 1 hour at room temperature. Heat the oil in a heavy casserole or Dutch oven large enough to hold the turkey pieces comfortably. Pat the turkey dry with paper towels, and reserve any marinade that remains. Sauté the turkey pieces, two or three at a time, until lightly browned on both sides. Arrange the turkey in the casserole and add the marinade. Add the tomato purée, the bell pepper, and enough water to cover. Cover and simmer over moderate heat for 1 hour. Add the olives, capers, and potatoes, and cook for 20 minutes longer. Add the peas, and cook for about 10 minutes longer, or until both the turkey and vegetables are tender. If using frozen peas, add only for the last 5 minutes of cooking. To serve arrange the turkey pieces on a warmed serving platter and surround with the potatoes. If the liquid is very abundant, reduce it over brisk heat and pour over the turkey.

MOLE DISHES
Turkey or Chicken

Mole Poblano de Guajalote   MEXICO
Turkey in Chili and Chocolate Sauce

This is Mexico's most famous dish and though it is native to the state of Puebla, it is served all over the republic on truly festive occasions. It can be absolutely sensational for a party when served with tortillas, Mexican rice and beans, and *Guacamole* (Avocado Sauce). I always put a small bowl of canned *serrano* or *jalapeño* chilies on the table for the bold souls who claim no dish is hot enough for them. Actually *Mole Poblano* is not hot though I have come across versions of it where a *chipotle* chili or two had been added, introducing both heat and this chili's very exotic flavor. For a more everyday dish, chicken or pork may be used instead of turkey.

There is a charming but apocryphal legend, that a group of nuns at the convent of Santa Rosa in Puebla invented the dish in early colonial times to honor a visiting viceroy and archbishop. But, in fact, it had long been a royal dish of the Aztec court; since it contained chocolate, it was forbidden to women, and among men it was reserved for royalty, the military nobility, and the higher ranks of the priesthood. It is on record that the Spanish conquistador Hernán Cortés was served a version of the dish at the court of Aztec Emperor Moctezuma. All the same I do think we owe the sisters a debt. They recorded the recipe, which might otherwise have been lost, and they substituted familiar ingredients for some of the more exotic herbs and spices used in the emperor's day. I'd be prepared to swear that in the past allspice (a native spice) was used instead of cloves and cinnamon brought by Spain from the East, but since the flavor is much the same, why fuss?

Since *mole*, which comes from the Nahuatl word *molli*, means a sauce made from any of the chilies, hot, pungent, or sweet, there are more *moles* in Mexico than one can count. Out of the innumerable array, I have chosen this one and some of the *moles* from the state of Oaxaca, where I am always aware of the mysteries of the past and where the cooking of today brings the past very much to life.

Serves 10

An 8-pound turkey, cut into   2 cloves garlic, chopped
   serving pieces   Salt
1 medium onion, chopped   6 tablespoons lard

FOR THE SAUCE

6 ancho *chilies*	4 *tablespoons sesame seeds*
6 mulato *chilies*	½ *teaspoon ground coriander seed*
4 pasilla *chilies*	½ *teaspoon ground anise*
2 *medium onions, chopped*	2 *whole cloves*
3 *cloves garlic, chopped*	A ½-*inch piece of stick cinnamon*
3 *medium tomatoes, peeled,*	½ *cup lard, about*
seeded, and chopped	1 ½ *squares (1 ½ ounces)*
2 *tortillas, or 2 slices toast, cut up*	*unsweetened chocolate*
1 *cup blanched almonds*	*Salt, freshly ground pepper*
½ *cup peanuts*	1 *tablespoon sugar (optional)*
½ *cup raisins*	

Put the turkey pieces into a large heavy saucepan or casserole with the onion, garlic, and water to cover. Season with salt, bring to a boil, lower the heat, and simmer, covered, for 1 hour, or until the turkey is barely tender. Drain off and reserve the turkey stock. Lift out the turkey pieces and pat them dry with paper towels. Heat the lard in a large skillet and sauté the turkey pieces until they are lightly browned on both sides. Set them aside.

To make the sauce, remove the stems and seeds from the *ancho, mulato,* and *pasilla* chilies. Tear them into pieces, put them in a bowl, and pour hot water over them barely to cover, about 2 cups. Let them stand for 30 minutes, turning the pieces from time to time. In a blender or food processor combine the chilies and the water in which they have soaked with the onions, garlic, tomatoes, and tortillas or toast, and blend the mixture until it forms a paste. Do this in two lots if necessary. Transfer the paste to a bowl. Rinse out and dry the container of the blender or food processor and add the almonds, peanuts, raisins, 2 tablespoons of the sesame seeds, the coriander seed, the anise, the cloves, and the cinnamon stick, broken up, and blend the mixture well. Mix thoroughly with the chili paste. Measure the lard left in the skillet from sautéing the turkey and add enough to bring the quantity up to 4 tablespoons. Add the chili paste and sauté over moderate heat, stirring, for 5 minutes. Transfer the mixture to the saucepan or casserole in which the turkey was cooked. Stir in 2 cups of the reserved turkey stock and the chocolate, cut into pieces. Season to taste with salt and pepper. Cook the mixture over low heat, stirring until the chocolate is melted and adding more turkey stock if necessary to make the sauce the consistency of heavy cream. Stir in the sugar, if liked. Add the turkey and simmer it, covered, for 30 minutes. Arrange the turkey and sauce in a serving dish. In a small skillet toast the remaining sesame seeds and sprinkle them over the turkey. Serve with Tortillas, *Arroz Blanco, Frijoles,* and *Guacamole.*

For an authentic Mexican fiesta meal, start with *Seviche de Sierra* (Mackerel Marinated in Lime Juice) and finish with *Chongos Zamoranos* (Custard Squares in Syrup).

Mole Negro Oaxaqueño   MEXICO
Chicken in Chili Sauce, Oaxaca Style

Though *Mole Poblano de Guajalote* (Turkey in Chili and Chocolate Sauce) is probably the most famous of all Mexican dishes, *mole* Oaxaca style is not far behind. Traditionally made with a hen turkey (*pípila*) weighing about 8 pounds, it is equally good with chicken, which I have used here. These are both very old dishes, served at pre-Conquest courts to emperors and kings. They are essentially royal dishes because of the chocolate, and they have obviously been modified since colonial times, using some ingredients not available before the Conquest — peppercorns, cinnamon, cloves, and almonds, for example. The chilies used in the Oaxacan *mole* include *chilhuacle*, a rather bitter pepper that gives the dish a very dark color. This is not available here and I have found *guajillo* chili, which is available, a very good substitute from the point of view of flavor, though the color is lighter. This is a very good party dish especially as the sauce is improved by being made a day ahead.

Serves 8

Two 3½-pound chickens, cut into
    serving pieces
Chicken stock
12 guajillo *chilies (about 2 ounces)*
4 ancho *chilies*
4 pasilla *chilies*
1 medium onion, chopped
2 cloves garlic, chopped
2 medium tomatoes, peeled and
    chopped
¼ cup dried apricots, soaked and
    chopped
¼ cup almonds, ground
¼ cup peanuts, ground
2 tablespoons sesame seeds
2 slices French bread or firm white
    bread, fried in lard or
    vegetable oil

⅛ teaspoon ground cloves, or 2
    whole cloves
4 peppercorns
1 teaspoon thyme
1 teaspoon oregano
⅛ teaspoon ground cinnamon, or
    a small piece of stick
    cinnamon
8 tablespoons lard or vegetable oil
2 squares (2 ounces) unsweetened
    chocolate
1 or 2 avocado leaves (optional)
Salt

Put the chicken pieces in a large flameproof casserole or saucepan and pour in enough chicken stock to cover. Bring the stock to a simmer, cover, and cook over low heat for 30 minutes. Set aside.

Shake the seeds out of the chilies, rinse them, and tear them into pieces. Put them in a bowl with 1 cup warm water, using a little more water if necessary. Let them soak for 1 hour, turning them from time to time. Combine the chilies, onion, garlic, tomatoes, apricots, almonds, peanuts, 1 tablespoon of the sesame seeds, the bread, broken into pieces, the cloves, peppercorns, thyme, oregano, and cinnamon, and reduce to a purée, bit by bit, in a blender or food processor. Heat the lard or oil in a large skillet and add the purée, which should be quite thick. Fry the mixture, stirring constantly with a wooden spoon as it tends to splatter, for 5 minutes.

Lift the chicken pieces out of the casserole or saucepan and set them aside in a dish. Pour out and measure the stock. Rinse out the saucepan or casserole and pour in the chili mixture. Stir in 3 cups of the chicken stock and the chocolate. Drop the avocado leaves briefly into boiling water and add to the saucepan. Season to taste with salt. Stir over low heat until the chocolate has melted. The sauce should be rather thicker than heavy cream; if it is too thick, add a little more chicken stock. Add the chicken pieces, cover, and simmer over very low heat for 30 minutes, or until the chicken is tender. Remove the avocado leaves. Put the chicken pieces and the sauce in a large serving dish. Toast the remaining sesame seeds in a skillet over moderate heat until they begin to pop, a minute or two, and sprinkle them over the *mole*. Serve with *Arroz Blanco* (White Rice), *Frijoles* (Beans), *Guacamole*, and Tortillas.

Variation: If using a turkey, cut an 8-pound bird into serving pieces and put into a large saucepan or kettle with water to cover. Season with salt, bring to a boil, reduce the heat, and simmer gently, covered, for 1 hour. Drain and pat dry with paper towels. Use the turkey broth to thin the chili mixture. Heat 4 tablespoons lard or vegetable oil in a skillet and sauté the turkey pieces until they are browned on both sides. Add them to the chili sauce and simmer over very low heat, covered, until the turkey is tender, about 30 minutes.

Variation: Cut 3 pounds lean, boneless pork into 2-inch pieces and put into a saucepan with water barely to cover. Season with salt and simmer gently, covered, for 1 hour. Drain. Use the pork broth to thin the chili mixture. Add the pork to the sauce and simmer gently, covered, until the pork is tender, about 30 minutes.

Mole Amarillo

MEXICO

Chicken in Yellow Sauce

Serves 6

A 3½- to 4-pound chicken, cut
    into serving pieces
4 cloves garlic
4 canned largo chilies, or use any
    fresh hot light green pepper,
    seeded
2 tablespoons lard or vegetable oil
1 medium onion, chopped
4 medium tomatoes, peeled and
    chopped

½ teaspoon oregano
⅛ teaspoon ground cumin
Salt, freshly ground pepper
1 pound zucchini, sliced
½ pound green beans, cut into
    1-inch pieces
Masa harina

Put the chicken into a saucepan with 2 of the cloves of garlic, crushed, and water barely to cover. Bring to a boil, lower the heat, cover, and simmer until the pork is tender, about 2 hours. Put the chilies into a blender or food processor and reduce them to a purée. If necessary add a tablespoon of the chicken stock. Heat the lard or oil in a skillet and sauté the chili purée, stirring constantly with a wooden spoon, for 3 or 4 minutes. Put the remaining 2 cloves garlic, the onion, and tomatoes in a blender or food processor and reduce them to a purée. Pour the mixture into the skillet with the chili and cook, stirring from time to time, until the mixture is thick and well blended, 3 or 4 minutes. Drain the pork but leave the meat in the saucepan. Pour 2 cups of the stock into the skillet, stir to mix, season with the oregano, cumin, salt and pepper, and pour the mixture over the pork. Cook the zucchini (about 8 minutes) and the beans (about 10 to 15 minutes) separately in boiling salted water, drain them, and add to the saucepan. Simmer over very low heat for 10 to 15 minutes to blend the flavors. I like to thicken the sauce with a little *masa harina* (tortilla flour) if it seems too thin; mix a tablespoon of the flour with a little of the stock and stir it into the saucepan and cook for a minute or so longer. Serve with rice.

Variation: Instead of the *largo* chilies use 6 *guajillo* chilies. Shake out the seeds and soak the chilies in ½ cup warm water for 30 minutes, then purée in the blender or food processor in the soaking water. Sauté the chili purée in the lard or oil. Instead of the tomatoes, use two 10-ounce cans Mexican green tomatoes, drained and puréed in a blender with 2 medium romaine lettuce leaves. The red tomatoes and green peppers give a yellow sauce, and here the green tomatoes and red peppers give the same color result though with a subtly different flavor. If liked, chayotes may be used instead of zucchini.

Variation: 3 pounds boneless pork, loin or shoulder, cut into 1-inch pieces may be used instead of chicken.

Variation: Traditionally *chochoyotes* are added to the stew in the last few minutes of cooking. These are small balls made by mixing 1½ cups *masa harina* (tortilla flour) with a little salt and 4 tablespoons lard with just enough water to hold them together. A little dent is made in each of the balls, which are about 1 inch in diameter. But I do not think these can be made successfully with the dried, packaged flour. The fresh, moist dough sold in local markets is what is needed. Oaxaca in Mexico is known as the land of the seven *moles*. The dishes are distinguished by color. There is *mole negro* (black sauce), perhaps the most famous, as well as yellow, red, light red, green, and two others, *mancha manteles* (tablecloth stainer) and *chichilo*, made with the distinctive local chili, *chilhuacle*, which is also used in the *mole negro*. Versions of *mancha manteles* turn up all over the republic, but the others are exclusively Oaxacan. Not all of them can be reproduced faithfully outside Oaxaca, but some can and I have included them here: *negro*, *verde*, *amarillo*, and *coloradito*.

Mole Verde de Oaxaca
Chicken in Green Sauce, Oaxaca Style

MEXICO

Serves 6

1 cup Great Northern, Navy, pea
  beans, or lima beans
Salt
1 medium onion, finely chopped
3 cloves garlic, chopped
A 10-ounce can Mexican green
  tomatoes, drained
1 canned jalapeño chili, or 2
  canned serrano chilies, rinsed
  and chopped
3 tablespoons lard or vegetable oil

1 pound boneless pork loin, cut
  into 1-inch cubes
2 cups chicken stock or water,
  about
A 3- to 3½-pound chicken, cut
  into serving pieces
1 cup parsley sprigs, fairly tightly
  packed
1 cup fresh coriander leaves, fairly
  tightly packed
2 tablespoons masa harina

Pick over and rinse the beans. Put them into a saucepan with cold water to cover, put the lid on, and bring to a boil over moderate heat. Let stand 35 to 40 minutes off the heat, covered. Drain, rinse, and put on to cook with cold water to cover. Simmer the beans, covered, until they are tender, about 1 hour. Season with salt to taste in the last 30 minutes of cooking. Drain, reserve the cooking liquid, and set the beans aside.

In a blender or food processor combine the onion, garlic, Mexican green tomatoes, and chilies, and reduce to a purée. In a skillet heat the lard or vegetable oil and sauté the tomato mixture for 3 or 4 minutes. Pour the mixture into a saucepan and add the reserved cooking liquid from the beans. Add the pork loin and a little chicken stock or water, if necessary, to cover. Cover and simmer for 1 hour. At the end of this time, add the chicken, and a little more stock, if necessary. Continue cooking until both chicken and pork are tender, about 1 hour. Add the cooked beans and simmer just long enough to heat them through.

Put the parsley and coriander into a blender or food processor with a little stock if necessary and reduce to a purée. Stir into the saucepan and cook without letting the mixture return to a boil for a minute or so. If the mixture boils, the sauce will lose its fresh green color. If the sauce is too thin, thicken with the *masa harina* mixed with a little stock. Serve with rice and *guacamole*.

Variation: Sometimes when Mexican green tomatoes are hard to find I have used a 7-ounce can of *Salsa Verde Mexicana* (Green Mexican Sauce) put up by Herdez. In this case, I omit the onion, garlic, green tomatoes, and chilies. The sauce does contain coriander (cilantro) but I do not find I need to alter the amount of fresh coriander. If liked, ½ pound cooked green beans and/or cooked, sliced zucchini may be added to the finished *mole*. I have a trick I sometimes use to make sure of the bright green color of the green dishes. Purée 2 or 3 leaves of romaine lettuce with the parsley and coriander if the color seems at all pallid. The lettuce also slightly thickens the sauce but does not alter the flavor to any perceptible extent.

Mole Coloradito de Oaxaca
MEXICO

Chicken in Red Sauce, Oaxaca Style

Serves 4 to 6

A 3½- to 4-pound chicken, cut
    into serving pieces
3 cups chicken stock, about
6 ancho *chilies*
1 medium onion, chopped
1 clove garlic, chopped
4 medium tomatoes, peeled and
    chopped

⅛ teaspoon cinnamon
¼ teaspoon oregano
2 tablespoons sesame seeds,
    toasted and ground
2 tablespoons lard or vegetable oil
Salt, freshly ground pepper

Put the chicken pieces into a large saucepan or heatproof casserole and pour in enough chicken stock to cover. Bring to a boil, lower the heat, cover, and simmer gently until the chicken is tender, about 45 minutes. Lift out the chicken pieces and set aside. Pour the stock into a container and set aside. Rinse out and dry the saucepan or casserole.

Pull off the stems and shake out the seeds of the *ancho* chilies. Tear the chilies into pieces, put them into a bowl with ½ cup warm water, and soak, turning them from time to time, for about 1 hour. Transfer the soaked chilies and any liquid to a blender or food processor. Add the onion, garlic, tomatoes, cinnamon, oregano, and sesame seeds and reduce to a coarse purée. Heat the lard or oil in a skillet and add the purée. Sauté, stirring constantly with a wooden spoon, until the mixture is thick and heavy, about 5 minutes. Turn the chili mixture into the casserole and stir in 2 cups of the reserved stock. Season to taste with salt and pepper. Add the chicken pieces and simmer, uncovered, until the chicken is heated through and the sauce slightly thickened. Serve with rice, tortillas, *guacamole*, and beans.

Variation: Pork may also be used for this *mole*. Instead of the chicken, use 3 pounds boneless pork loin, cut into 1-inch cubes, and cook, with 2 or 3 large cloves garlic, in water barely to cover until tender, about 2 hours. Strain the stock before using it for the sauce.

Many cooks in Oaxaca like to add an avocado leaf or two to the sauce in its final simmering. The leaves may be toasted lightly before they are added. They are discarded, like a bouquet garni, before the dish is served.

Variation: There is a pleasant vegetarian version of this *mole*. Instead of chicken or pork, add to the sauce ½ pound each cooked, cut-up potatoes, green beans, and peas. Any other vegetables such as zucchini, chayote, or cauliflower may be added. I particularly like cooked green bananas with this *mole* instead of rice. Choose very green (unripe) bananas and cut through the skin lengthwise in 2 or 3 places to peel off the skin. Boil the bananas in salted water for 10 to 15 minutes, or until tender, drain and add them to the vegetarian *mole*, or serve as a side dish.

DUCK

Arroz con Pato   PERU
Duckling with Rice

It is not surprising that this is Peru's favorite duckling dish. The coriander and cumin unite in a most subtle way with the dark beer in which the rice is cooked, and the rich flavor of the duckling permeates the whole.

Serves 6

A 4½- to 5-pound duckling, cut
   into 6 serving pieces
Vegetable oil
1 large onion, finely chopped
3 fresh hot red or green peppers,
   seeded, coarsely chopped, and
   puréed in a blender or food
   processor
6 large cloves garlic, crushed

2 tablespoons fresh coriander
   (cilantro), chopped
1 teaspoon ground cumin
Salt, freshly ground pepper
4 cups chicken stock, about
2 cups long-grain rice
2 cups dark beer
½ cup cooked green peas

GARNISH
Sliced tomatoes and fresh hot
   peppers, seeded and cut into
   flower shapes

Prick the skin of the duckling all over with the tines of a fork. Film the bottom of a heavy skillet with a small amount of oil and sauté the duckling pieces — about 10 to 15 minutes — until they are lightly browned all over in their own fat, which will run out during the cooking. Transfer the duckling pieces to a heavy casserole. Pour off all but 3 tablespoons of fat from the skillet in which the duckling was browned, and in the remaining fat sauté the onion, peppers, and garlic until the onion is golden. Add the vegetables to the casserole with the coriander, cumin, salt and pepper to taste, and the chicken stock, which should just cover the duckling pieces. Add a little more if necessary. Cover and simmer over low heat until the duckling is almost done, about 45 minutes. Drain off the stock and measure it. Add the rice to the casserole with 2 cups of the stock and the dark beer. Cover, bring to a boil, reduce the heat to low, and cook until the rice is tender and quite dry. Fold in the peas. Serve hot on a large platter garnished with tomato slices and fresh hot peppers.

Pato al Vino
Duckling in Wine

COLOMBIA

Spices from the New and Old Worlds — allspice, cinnamon, and cloves — combine to give this duckling a full, rich flavor. It may be cooked on top of the stove, but I find it much more satisfactory to use the oven as do many modern Latin Americans.

Serves 3 to 4

A 4½- to 5-pound duckling
Salt, freshly ground pepper
2 tablespoons butter
2 large onions, finely chopped
1 bay leaf
2 whole cloves
A 1-inch piece of stick cinnamon

4 allspice berries
1 whole fresh hot red or green
    pepper
1 cup dry red wine
1 cup duck stock, made by
    simmering giblets, neck, and
    liver for 1 hour

Pull the loose fat from inside the duckling and prick the bird all over with a fork to help release the excess fat. Season inside and out with salt and pepper. Heat the butter in a heavy casserole and sauté the duckling until it is golden brown all over. Lift out and set aside. Spoon off all but 4 tablespoons fat from the casserole. Add the onions and sauté until soft. Return the duckling to the casserole. Tie the bay leaf, cloves, cinnamon, allspice berries, and hot pepper in a square of cheesecloth and add to the casserole with the red wine and duck stock. Season to taste with more salt and pepper if necessary and bring to a boil on top of the stove. Cover with aluminum foil, then with the casserole lid, and cook in a preheated moderate (350° F.) oven for 1½ hours, or until the duckling is tender. Lift out onto a serving platter and keep warm. Remove and discard the cheesecloth bag. Spoon excess fat from the sauce, and if it is very abundant, reduce it over brisk heat for a few minutes. Spoon a little sauce over the duckling and serve the rest separately. Serve with *Arroz con Coco y Pasas* (Rice with Coconut and Raisins) and a green salad.

Variation: *Pato Borracho* (Drunken Duckling) is a popular duck dish all over Latin America. Cook as for *Pato al Vino* but use white wine instead of red. Omit the cloves, cinnamon, allspice, and hot pepper, and use instead a bouquet garni of parsley and thyme tied in a cheesecloth square with the bay leaf. Add 3 cloves of chopped garlic to the onions, and when they are soft, add 4 tomatoes, peeled, seeded, and chopped.

Variation: *Pato com Ameixas* (Duckling with Prunes), from Brazil, is a full-flavored, robust dish. Cook as for *Pato al Vino* but omit the cloves, cinnamon, allspice berries, and hot pepper. When sautéing the onions, add 2 cloves garlic, chopped. When the onions are soft, add 3 large tomatoes, peeled, seeded, and chopped, and ½ teaspoon thyme. Instead of 1 cup dry red wine, add 2 cups dry white wine and the cup of duck stock, and 1½ cups pitted prunes, quartered. Just before serving stir in ¼ cup dry Madeira.

Pato en Jugo de Naranja   MEXICO
Duck in Orange Juice

This is a very old colonial dish that has remained popular, with slight variations, throughout Latin America, though it seems to have originated in Mexico. I have chosen a modern version where the duck is braised in the oven, instead of on top of the stove.

Serves 4

1 duckling weighing about 4 pounds	¼ teaspoon thyme
2 tablespoons butter	¼ teaspoon marjoram
1 medium onion, finely chopped	1 bay leaf
2 cloves garlic, chopped	¼ cup raisins
3 medium tomatoes, peeled, seeded, and chopped, about 1 cup pulp	1 tablespoon white wine vinegar
	1 cup orange juice
	¼ cup toasted, slivered almonds

Pull out the loose fat from inside the duckling and prick the bird all over with a fork to help release the excess fat. Heat the butter in a large skillet and brown the duckling lightly all over. Transfer the duckling to a flame-proof casserole large enough to hold it comfortably. Spoon off all but 2 tablespoons of fat from the skillet and sauté the onion and garlic until the onion is soft. Add to the casserole with all the remaining ingredients except the almonds. Add the duck giblets to enrich the sauce. Bring the liquid in the casserole to a boil on top of the stove. Cover the casserole with foil, then with the lid, and cook in a preheated moderate (325° F.) oven for 1 ½ hours, or until the duckling is tender. Lift the bird out and carve it. Put it onto a serving platter and keep warm. Spoon off the fat from the sauce, take out and discard the giblets and bay leaf. If the sauce is very abundant, reduce it over brisk heat for a few minutes. Spoon a little of the sauce over the duckling and sprinkle with the almonds. Pour the rest of the sauce into a sauceboat and serve separately with rice and green peas or green beans.

SQUAB

Latin America has a marvelous way with pigeons (or what we call squab), which everyone loves. They range from the beautifully simple Mexican favorite *Pichones al Vino* (Squab with Wine) to the exotic *Pichones con Salsa de Camarones* (Squab in Shrimp Sauce) of Peru. They make an ideal dinner party dish, with each guest served a plumply elegant, full-flavored bird. You may also substitute fresh Rock Cornish game hens.

Pichones con Salsa de Camarones PERU
Squab in Shrimp Sauce

The shrimp sauce turns this into an excitingly different dish, the apparently contradictory flavors deliciously complementing each other.

Serves 6

4 tablespoons clarified butter
   (page 328)
6 squab, each weighing about 8
   ounces
1 medium onion, finely chopped
1 clove garlic, chopped
2 tablespoons flour
1 ½ cups dry white wine

1 ½ cups chicken stock
Pinch of nutmeg
Salt, freshly ground pepper
½ pound raw shrimp, peeled and
   coarsely chopped
2 eggs, lightly beaten
2 tablespoons finely chopped fresh
   coriander

Heat the butter in a skillet and sauté the squab until they are golden on both sides. Transfer to a heavy casserole. In the butter remaining in the skillet sauté the onion and garlic until the onion is soft. Add the flour and cook, stirring, for a minute or two. Add the wine, stir, add the stock and the nutmeg, and simmer, stirring, until the mixture is smooth. Season to taste with salt and pepper and pour over the squab. Cover the casserole with foil, then with the lid, and simmer over moderate heat until the squab are tender, about 1½ hours. Lift out the squab and arrange on a serving dish. Keep warm. Add the shrimp to the liquid in the casserole and cook for about 2 minutes. Then stir in the eggs and the coriander and cook, stirring, over low heat until the sauce is lightly thickened. Do not let the sauce boil once the eggs are added, as it will curdle. Spoon a little of the sauce over the squab and serve the rest separately in a sauceboat. Serve with white rice or boiled potatoes and a green vegetable or a salad.

Pichones al Vino MEXICO
Squab with Wine

Dry sherry is sometimes used in this recipe and though it is pleasant I prefer the equally traditional dry red wine. Baked *boniato* (white sweet potato) is a splendid accompaniment.

Serves 4

4 squab, each weighing about 8 ounces
2 cloves garlic, chopped
16 scallions, trimmed and cut into 1¼-inch pieces, using both green and white parts
4 medium-sized carrots, scraped and thinly sliced
½ teaspoon thyme
½ teaspoon marjoram
⅛ teaspoon freshly ground black pepper
⅛ teaspoon ground allspice
1 whole clove
Salt
1 small fresh hot pepper, seeded and chopped
¼ cup olive oil
2 tablespoons red wine vinegar
1 cup dry red wine or dry sherry
½ cup chicken stock, about

Arrange the squab in a flameproof casserole just large enough to hold them comfortably. Add all the ingredients except the chicken stock and mix well. Marinate in the refrigerator overnight, turning once or twice. When ready to cook, add the stock, using a little more if necessary barely to cover. Bring to a simmer on top of the stove, then cook, covered, in a preheated moderate (350° F.) oven until tender, about 1½ hours. Arrange the squab on a warmed serving dish, spoon a little of the sauce over them. Serve the rest of the sauce separately.

Pichones Saltados

Squab Stew

This is a deceptively simple dish, very easy to cook yet with a fine, rich flavor.

Serves 4

*4 squab, each weighing about 8
    ounces*
Salt, freshly ground pepper
½ cup olive oil
1 large onion, finely chopped
*1 fresh hot red or green pepper,
    seeded and chopped*

2 tablespoons flour
2 teaspoons sweet paprika
1 cup dry white wine
1 cup chicken stock

Season the squab inside and out with salt and pepper. Heat the oil in a flameproof casserole and sauté the squab over moderate heat until they are golden brown all over, about 15 minutes. Lift out and set aside. Add the onion and the hot pepper to the oil remaining in the casserole and sauté until the onion is soft. Stir in the flour and the paprika and cook, stirring, for a minute longer. Add the wine, stir to mix, then stir in the stock. Return the squab to the sauce, cover the casserole with a piece of foil, then with the lid, and simmer over low heat until the squab are tender, about 1½ hours. Lift out the squab onto a serving dish. Taste the sauce and add more salt and pepper if necessary. Pour a little sauce over the squab and serve the rest in a sauceboat. Serve with rice, mashed potatoes, or a purée of any starchy root vegetable such as sweet potato or yams, or with a purée of winter squash, and a green vegetable.

Pichones en Jugo de Naranja   COLOMBIA
Squab in Orange Juice

Orange juice and white wine combine to make a delicate sauce for the richness of the squab, a balancing of flavors that is typical of Colombian cooking.

Serves 6

4 tablespoons butter
6 squab, each weighing about 8
    ounces
1 medium onion, finely chopped
1 cup dry white wine

1 cup orange juice
Salt, freshly ground pepper
Pinch of cinnamon
2 teaspoons cornstarch

Heat the butter in a skillet and sauté the squab until golden brown all over. Transfer them to a heavy casserole. In the butter remaining in the skillet sauté the onion until it is soft. Pour in the wine and the orange juice, bring to a boil, and stir, scraping up all the brown bits. Season to taste with salt and pepper and add the cinnamon. Pour the mixture over the squab, cover, and simmer over low heat until the squab are tender, about 1½ hours. Transfer the squab to a serving dish and keep warm. Mix the cornstarch with a little cold water and stir into the casserole. Simmer, stirring, until the sauce is lightly thickened. If the sauce seems very abundant, reduce briskly over fairly high heat for a few minutes before adding the cornstarch. Serve with any root vegetable or rice and a green vegetable.

Substantial Dishes

Platillos Fuertes

Including Beans and Rice

There are a number of hearty dishes in the Latin American cuisine that combine fish, meat, or poultry with beans, rice, corn, potatoes, or other root vegetables. These once served as a course in a meal as soup or appetizers do now. To our modern appetites they are main dishes, so I have put them into a category of their own. I have included the festive dish *Feijoada Completa* (Black Beans with Mixed Meats) here because beans are such an important part of it. This is not a very sharply defined category but I think it is a useful one.

Feijoada Completa   BRAZIL
Black Beans with Mixed Meats

This exuberant mixture of black beans, meats, vegetables, and garnishes is Brazil's national dish. It was created in Rio de Janeiro but has now spread all over the country. It is magnificent for parties and well worth the work involved. And it is versatile as one can eliminate or substitute many of the meats if some are not available. Polish or Spanish sausage (*kielbasa* or *longaniza*) can substitute for *linguiça*, fresh pork hocks can be used instead of pig's feet, ears, and tail. Kale can be used for collard greens, and any fresh hot peppers can be used in the hot pepper sauce. To serve the *Feijoada*, the meats are sliced and arranged on one or more platters, the beans, which should be quite soupy with an almost saucelike consistency, are served in a tureen or large serving bowl with a soup ladle or generously sized serving spoon, and accompanied by *Arroz Brazileiro* (Brazilian Rice), *Couve a Mineira* (Kale or Collard Greens, Minas Gerais Style), *Farofa de Manteiga* (Cassava Meal with Butter) or *Farofa de Ouro* (Cassava Meal with Hardboiled Eggs), as well as 6 peeled and sliced oranges arranged in a serving dish, *Môlho de Pimenta e Limão* (Hot Pepper and Lime Sauce) and *Salada de Palmito* (Hearts of Palm Salad).

The table looks very splendid with this array of food. Guests put a serving of everything onto a single plate, then sprinkle *farofa* over the lot. The flavors blend delightfully, an orchestra of taste and texture. *Cachaça*, Brazilian rum, is traditionally served with *Feijoada* but to the uninitiated this can be traumatic. Ideally either *batidas* or *Caipirinhas*, two *cachaça* drinks made with lime or lemon juice, are served before the meal, and chilled beer with it.

Brazilian friends say *Feijoada* should be eaten for Saturday lunch so that one may sleep it off. I've done that but I find I prefer *Feijoada* for dinner, or for a festive Sunday luncheon party. It is a truly international dish since the beans and hot peppers come originally from Mexico, the cassava (manioc) meal from pre-Portuguese Brazil, the meats and sausages from Europe by way of Portugal, and the cooking genius that put it all together from Africa.

An admirable dessert to accompany this feast is *Quindins de Yáyá* (Coconut Cupcake Dessert), which is deliciously rich and sweet.

4 pig's ears
1 pig's tail
Salt
3 pig's feet, split
A 1-pound piece carne sêca
    (sun-dried salted beef or
    jerked beef), see page 6
A 3-pound smoked beef tongue
A ½-pound piece of lean bacon
4 cups black (turtle) beans
A 1-pound piece of lean beef
    chuck or bottom round
1 pound linguiça sausage (see page
    16), or use longaniza or
    kielbasa sausage

1 pound fresh pork sausages
2 tablespoons lard or vegetable oil
2 onions, finely chopped
2 cloves garlic, minced
2 tomatoes, peeled, seeded, and
    chopped
1 fresh hot pepper, seeded and
    minced, or ⅛ teaspoon
    Tabasco (optional)
Salt, freshly ground pepper

Two days ahead of time put the pig's ears and tail into a mixing bowl and sprinkle thoroughly with salt. Cover and refrigerate for 2 days. Lift out of the bowl, discard the liquid, and rinse the meats thoroughly in cold water. Put into a large saucepan with water to cover, bring to a boil, lower the heat, and simmer for 10 minutes. Drain. Set aside until ready to cook.

The night before put the pig's feet on to cook in cold water to cover and simmer, covered, for 1½ hours. Cool and refrigerate in a covered container in the cooking liquid until ready to use.

Also on the night before cut the jerked beef in half lengthwise. Put the jerked beef, the beef tongue, and the bacon to soak overnight in cold water to cover. Start soaking early in the evening and change the water 2 or 3 times if possible. Thoroughly wash and pick over the beans and put them to soak in cold water to cover.

When ready to cook, allowing 4 hours for the actual cooking time, put the beans and their soaking liquid into a kettle or casserole large enough to hold all the ingredients. Drain and add the pig's feet. Reserve the jellied liquid from the pig's feet for some other time to make stock. Add enough cold water to cover by 2 inches. Bring to a boil, then simmer over low heat, covered, for 1½ hours.

While the beans are cooking, put the tongue, jerked beef, and bacon into a large saucepan with fresh cold water to cover, bring to a boil over moderate heat, then simmer, covered, over low heat for 1 hour. When the beans have cooked for 1½ hours, add the bacon and jerked beef to the bean pot but continue to simmer the tongue separately. At the same time add the fresh beef, pig's ears and tail to the beans. Add hot water as necessary to cover and simmer, covered, for 2 hours longer. By this time the tongue will be tender. Remove from the heat and allow to cool. As soon as it is cool enough to handle, peel it and remove any gristle and bones. Add the tongue to the beans with hot water if necessary to keep the beans covered. Stir the pot with a wooden spoon from time to time to prevent the beans from sticking.

Fill the pot in which the tongue was cooked with fresh water, bring to a boil, and add the *linguiça* (or its substitute) and the fresh pork sausages. Bring back to a boil and simmer for 1 minute. Drain and add the sausages to the beans, which by now will have been cooking for 3½ hours.*

Heat the lard or oil in a skillet and sauté the onions and garlic until the onions are soft. Add the tomatoes and the hot pepper or Tabasco, if liked, and simmer until the mixture is well blended. Season to taste with salt and pepper. Remove 1 cup of the cooked beans and add, smashing them into the sauce. Stir the mixture back into the beans and simmer for 15 minutes longer, or until the beans have been cooking for 4 hours. The beans should be very soft, almost falling apart. Lift out the meats and continue to simmer the beans, uncovered, over low heat. Remove any bones from the meats. Slice the pig's ears and tail into 4 or 5 pieces. Slice all the meats and arrange on a platter with the tongue in the center, its traditional position. Use two platters if necessary. Moisten the meats with a little bean liquid and keep warm. Pour the beans into a tureen or large serving bowl.

*The *Feijoada* can be cooked ahead to this point and kept overnight in a cool place, or refrigerated, until half an hour before it is to be served. Bring it to room temperature before adding the onion, tomato, and mashed bean mixture.

Tutú a Mineira
Black Beans, Minas Gerais Style

This is a sort of junior *Feijoada*, much simpler than that grand feast but nonetheless a hearty dish. It is really a dish of mashed beans and cassava (manioc) meal generously garnished with meat and eggs. It is a very old dish going back to the days of slavery and was a great favorite with small children. Somehow the infants, lisping the word purée, converted the sound into *tutú* and that is what it has been called ever since.

Serves 6

1 recipe Feijão Preto *(Black Beans), page 243*
4 large eggs
A ¾-pound linguiça, *or similar sausage such as* longaniza *or* kielbasa

1 tablespoon lard
8 slices bacon, chopped
2 medium onions, finely sliced
⅓ cup cassava (manioc) meal (farinha de mandioca)

Have ready the black beans, freshly cooked. Put the eggs into a large saucepan and boil them for 8 minutes. Shell under cold running water. Halve the eggs and set them aside. Put the sausage in a saucepan with cold water to cover and simmer for 30 minutes. Drain and cut into ½-inch slices. Heat the lard in a skillet and sauté the sausage slices and bacon until the bacon is crisp. Transfer the sausage and bacon to a dish lined with paper towels and keep them warm. In the fat remaining in the skillet sauté the onions and keep them warm.

Put the beans into a large saucepan and mash over low heat. Stir in the cassava meal and cook, stirring, until the mixture has the consistency of rather heavy mashed potatoes, adding a little more cassava meal if necessary. Transfer the mashed beans to a deep, hot serving dish and pat them down lightly to an even layer. Pour the onion and bacon fat mixture over the beans. Arrange the sausage and bacon at opposite ends of the dish and put the hardboiled eggs in a row down the middle. Serve with *Couve a Mineira* (Kale, Minas Gerais Style) and, if liked, a hot pepper sauce.

Variation: Some cooks serve the *Tutú* with eggs fried in butter instead of hardboiled eggs. Roast pork, cut into small slices, may be substituted for the chopped bacon or the *Tutú* may be served with *Roupa Velha* (Old Clothes), a traditional Brazilian shredded beef dish.

Ocopa Arequipeña   PERU
Potatoes with Cheese, Walnut, and Hot Pepper Sauce

Having "invented" the potato, the Incas developed splendid recipes using this most versatile of all root vegetables. I am sure dishes like the *ocopas* and the *causas* are pre-Columbian, slightly changed, I think for the better, by food introduced by the Conquest — walnuts, for example. In colonial times (and still today for a really traditional Peruvian meal), these were considered dishes to have before the main course. As far as I am concerned, they make a complete meal with the addition of a light dessert. They are very useful when one wants a vegetarian meal or something a little different made with fish or shrimp. In Peru *mirasol* pepper would be used. Hot dried red peppers are an excellent substitute.

Serves 6

6 hot red dried peppers, about 1 ½
    to 2 inches long
½ cup peanut oil
1 medium onion, thickly sliced
2 cloves garlic, finely chopped
1 cup walnut meats, ground
¼ pound Spanish fresh cheese
    (queso blanco or queso fresco),
    crumbled, or use grated
    Münster cheese

1 cup milk
1 teaspoon salt, or to taste
Lettuce leaves
6 warm, freshly cooked medium
    potatoes, peeled and halved
    lengthwise
6 hardboiled eggs, halved
    lengthwise
12 black olives
Strips of pimiento for garnish

Shake the seeds out of the peppers and put them to soak in ¼ cup hot water for 30 minutes. Drain and set aside. Heat the oil in a small skillet and sauté the onion and garlic over very low heat until the onion is golden. Put the oil, onion, garlic, hot peppers, walnut meats, and fresh cheese in a blender or food processor. Add the milk and salt and blend to a smooth sauce, about the consistency of a heavy mayonnaise. Add milk and oil in equal quantities to thin the sauce if necessary.

Arrange a bed of lettuce leaves on a large, warmed platter. Arrange the potatoes, cut side down, on top of the lettuce. Mask the potatoes with the sauce, then garnish the dish with the eggs, cut side up, the black olives, and the strips of pimiento.

Variation: For *Ocopa de Camarones* (Shrimp and Potatoes with Cheese, Walnut, and Hot Pepper Sauce), reduce the walnut meats to ½ cup and add to the blender or food processor ½ pound cooked, chopped shrimp. In addition garnish the platter with ¼ pound cooked, peeled shrimp, preferably medium-sized.

Papas a la Huancaina   PERU
Potatoes with Cheese and Hot Pepper Sauce

This is from Huancayo, in the Peruvian highlands at 11,000 feet. It is a typical highlands dish, very Indian, especially in the use of the local herb *palillo*, which colors food a bright yellow. Turmeric, used sparingly, is an admirable substitute.

*Serves 8 as a first course,
4 as a light luncheon dish*

¼ cup lemon juice
⅛ teaspoon cayenne pepper
Salt, freshly ground pepper
1 medium onion, thinly sliced
8 medium potatoes
*3 cups coarsely chopped Spanish
    fresh cheese (queso blanco or
    queso fresco), or use Münster
    cheese*
*1 or more fresh hot yellow
    peppers, seeded and chopped,
    or use red or green peppers*

1 teaspoon palillo, *or ½ teaspoon
    turmeric*
1½ cups heavy cream
⅔ cup olive oil
Lettuce leaves
4 hardboiled eggs, halved
*2 or 3 ears of corn, cooked and cut
    into 8 slices*
8 black olives

In a bowl combine the lemon juice, cayenne pepper, and salt and pepper to taste. Add the onion, separated into rings, and set it aside to pickle at room temperature.

Boil the potatoes in their skins until tender. Drain, peel, and keep warm. In a blender or food processor combine the cheese, hot peppers, *palillo* or turmeric, and the cream. Blend until smooth. Heat the oil in a skillet, pour in the cheese mixture, reduce the heat to low, and cook, stirring constantly with a wooden spoon, until the sauce is smooth and creamy.

Garnish a platter with the lettuce leaves. Arrange the potatoes on the platter and pour the sauce over them. Arrange the eggs, corn slices, and olives around and in between the potatoes. Drain the onion rings and arrange them over the potatoes.

Causa a la Chiclayana

PERU

Potatoes with Fish and Vegetables

This is a very decorative dish and looks lovely on a buffet with lettuce leaves framing the serving platter and the mound of mashed potatoes garnished with strips of hot red pepper, onion rings, wedges of cheese, and black olives, in the center surrounded by the fried fish, sliced green bananas, corn, and slices of tropical root vegetables. The potatoes are transformed into something quite exciting with the vinaigrette dressing. It makes a hearty and satisfying one-dish meal.

Serves 6

¼ cup finely chopped onion
½ cup lemon juice
⅛ teaspoon cayenne pepper
Salt, freshly ground pepper
3 pounds boiling potatoes, peeled
   and halved
1 ½ cups olive oil plus 4
   tablespoons
1 pound sweet potatoes, peeled
   and cut into 6 slices
1 pound cassava (yucca) root,
   peeled and cut into 6 slices
3 green plantains or green bananas
2 ears corn
Flour
2 pounds striped bass fillets, cut
   into 2-inch pieces, or any firm
   white fish

3 fresh hot red peppers, about 4
   inches long, or use hot green
   peppers
3 medium onions, cut into ⅛-inch
   slices
½ cup white vinegar
Lettuce leaves
½ pound Spanish fresh cheese
   (queso blanco or queso fresco)
   or Münster cheese, cut into 6
   wedges
Lettuce leaves
Black olives

In a small bowl combine the finely chopped onion, lemon juice, cayenne pepper, and salt and pepper to taste. Set aside. Cook the potatoes in salted water until they are tender, but not mushy. Drain well and mash. Add 1 cup of the olive oil to the onion and lemon juice. Pour this dressing over the potatoes, mixing thoroughly. Make a mound of the potatoes in the center of a large round platter and keep warm, not hot.

Boil the sweet potatoes and cassava in salted water for 20 minutes, or until they are tender. Drain and keep warm. It does not matter if the cassava slices have broken up. In a separate saucepan boil the plantains, unpeeled but cut in half if necessary to fit the pan, until tender, about 30 minutes. Green bananas will take less time, about 15 minutes. Peel and cut into 12 slices. Keep warm with the sweet potatoes and cassava. Drop the corn into a large saucepan of boiling salted water and boil for 5 minutes. Cut each ear into 3 slices and put with the other vegetables.

Season the flour with salt and pepper. Dredge the fish pieces in the seasoned flour, shaking to remove the excess. In a skillet heat the 4 tablespoons of olive oil and fry the pieces of fish until they are golden brown on both sides, about 3 or 4 minutes. Drain on paper towels and keep warm.

Cut the peppers into ⅛-inch strips and put, with the sliced onions, into a saucepan of boiling water. Blanch for a few minutes then drain well. Add the remaining ½ cup olive oil, the vinegar, and salt and pepper to taste. Bring to a boil over low heat and cook, covered, for 2 or 3 minutes.

To serve, garnish the platter round the edge with lettuce leaves. Arrange the fish fillets, corn, sweet potato, cassava, and plantains or bananas on the lettuce leaves. Pour the onion and pepper mixture over the potatoes and garnish the mound with the wedges of cheese and black olives.

Variation: For *Causa a la Limeña* (Potatoes with Shrimp and Vegetables), add a seeded and finely chopped fresh hot red or green pepper to the chopped onion pickle. Omit the plantains and fish. Instead drop 6 jumbo shrimp (or more if using smaller shrimp) into boiling salted water and cook until just tender, 3 to 5 minutes. Hardboil 3 eggs and cut them in halves lengthwise. To serve arrange lettuce leaves round the edge of the mound of potatoes and arrange the cassava and sweet potato slices on the lettuce leaves. Make a circle on the edge of the mound of potatoes with the corn, then another circle on the potatoes with the cheese and shrimp alternately, and finally place the eggs and black olives on top of the potatoes. Serves 6.

Ocopa de Pichones   PERU
Potatoes and Eggs in Pigeon and Walnut Sauce

This is a most exotic and delectable dish, ideal for a summer lunch or dinner when hot food is unappetizing and the palate longs for something light yet substantial. The flavor of the pigeon is subtly enhanced by the walnuts, cheese, and oil-stewed onion, to make a most sumptuous sauce for the potato and hardboiled egg. Start with a corn or sweet red pepper soup and follow the *Ocopa* with *Mazamorra Morada* (Peruvian Fruit Compote) for dessert. A dry white wine or a rosé makes extremely pleasant drinking.

Serves 6

4 pigeons, each weighing about 8
   ounces
Salt, freshly ground pepper
6 medium onions
4 medium tomatoes
1 large hot dried red pepper, or 2
   small
4 tablespoons olive oil
1 cup walnut meats, about 8
   ounces

FOR THE GARNISH
Lettuce leaves
Black and green olives
4 fresh hot red peppers (optional)

8 ounces fresh cheese, or Spanish
   queso fresco *or* queso blanco,
   or use Münster *or a similar*
   cheese
Milk
6 eggs
6 medium potatoes

Split the pigeons in half and season on both sides with salt and pepper. Thinly slice 4 of the onions and put them in the bottom of a heavy casserole. Arrange the pigeons on top of the onions. Peel the tomatoes and cut them into thin slices, about ⅛ inch. Make a layer of the tomatoes over the pigeons. Cover the casserole with foil and then with the casserole lid. Cook over very low heat, using an asbestos mat if necessary to keep the contents from burning. Cook until the pigeons are tender, about 3 hours, shaking the casserole from time to time. Let the pigeons cool thoroughly in the casserole. Lift the birds out and bone them. Chop the meat coarsely and set aside. Reserve the pan juices. Rinse out and dry the casserole. Shake the seeds out of the hot dried pepper and put it to soak in warm water.

    Cut the remaining 2 onions into thick slices, about ¾ inch. Heat the oil in the casserole and add the onion slices. Cook over low heat, turning once, until they are golden brown on both sides. Allow to cool slightly, then put into a blender or food processor fitted with a steel blade, with the oil, the pigeon meat, and the pan juices. Drain the pepper, chop, and add. Add the walnuts and cheese and reduce to a purée, adding milk as necessary to make the sauce the consistency of a thick mayonnaise. Purée in batches if necessary.

    Hardboil the eggs, shell them, and halve them lengthwise. Boil the potatoes and drain them. Arrange the eggs, yolk side up, and the potatoes while still warm on a large warmed serving platter. Pour the sauce over them. Decorate the edge of the platter with lettuce leaves and arrange the olives on top of the potatoes and eggs. Slice the peppers from the tip to the stem and into 4 or 5 sections, which will then curl back, forming flowers.

Place them round the edge of the dish. This is optional but I like to do it, as there is always someone who really enjoys nibbling on hot peppers.

If serving this as an appetizer, halve the potatoes lengthwise and serve half a potato and half a hardboiled egg per person. Serves 12.

Cuscuz de Galinha   BRAZIL
Garnished Steamed Chicken and Cornmeal

This *Cuscuz* from São Paulo is made of cornmeal. The original *couscous* — the national dish of the Maghreb, the North African countries of Morocco, Tunisia, and Algeria — is made of wheat. There are other differences, which help to illustrate the Brazilian cook's ability to absorb foreign influences and to transform what is borrowed. This is a delicious dish, easy to make and wonderfully festive looking.

Serves 6 to 8

*A 3½-pound chicken, cut into
    serving pieces*
2 tablespoons lemon juice
4 tablespoons (¼ cup) butter
*4 scallions, chopped, using white
    and green parts*
*2 medium tomatoes, peeled,
    seeded, and chopped*
Salt, freshly ground pepper

1 cup dry white wine
½ cup chicken stock
1 tablespoon olive oil
*½ pound chorizo or other spiced
    smoked pork sausage, cut into
    ¼ inch slices*
¼ cup chopped parsley
*1 or 2 fresh hot red peppers, seeded
    and chopped*

Put the chicken pieces in a bowl with the lemon juice. Mix well and let stand 15 minutes. Lift out the chicken pieces, pat dry, and reserve the liquid. Heat the butter in a flameproof casserole and sauté the chicken pieces lightly. Add the scallions and tomatoes and season to taste with salt and pepper. Pour in the wine and chicken stock. Bring to a simmer, cover, and cook over low heat until the chicken pieces are tender. Let them stand, off the heat, until they are cool enough to handle. Lift them out of the stock, skin and bone them, and shred the meat into pieces about 1 inch by ¼ inch. Strain the stock and discard the solids. There should be 1½ cups. Make up the quantity if necessary with chicken stock. Return the chicken to the stock.

Heat the olive oil in a skillet and sauté the sausage until browned on both sides. Drain on paper towels and add to the chicken with the parsley and hot peppers. Set aside.

FOR THE CORNMEAL MIXTURE

4 cups white cornmeal
½ pound (1 cup) butter
2 medium tomatoes, thinly sliced
A 10-ounce can hearts of palm,
*   drained and thinly sliced*
3 hardboiled eggs, sliced

12 pitted black olives, halved
1 cup cooked fresh green peas or
*   cooked frozen peas*
2 oranges, preferably Seville
*   (bitter) oranges, peeled and*
*   thinly sliced*

Toast the cornmeal in a heavy skillet over moderate heat, stirring constantly with a wooden spoon, until it is golden, about 5 minutes. Sprinkle 1 cup boiling water over the cornmeal and stir to mix. Cook, stirring, for 2 minutes. Melt the butter in a small saucepan and pour it over the cornmeal, mixing well. Stir the cornmeal, little by little, into the reserved chicken, sausage, and stock mixture, combining it gently but thoroughly. Test the mixture to see if it holds its shape when pressed into a ball. If it is too crumbly, add a little warmed chicken stock and mix, testing again to see that the mixture keeps its shape.

If using a *cuscuzeiro* (*couscoussière*) butter the upper part. Otherwise, butter the inside of a fine-holed colander. Place a tomato slice in the center of the colander or *couscoussière*. Divide the remaining tomato, the hearts of palm, eggs, and olives into 3 equal parts. Divide the peas into 2 parts. Arrange one-third of the tomatoes, palm hearts, eggs, and olives in a decorative pattern around the bottom and sides of the colander. They will stay in place because of the butter. Put one-third of the cornmeal mixture into the colander and pat it down lightly. Sprinkle with half of the peas and another third of the garnish. Cover with another third of the cornmeal. Add the remaining ½ cup of peas and the remaining garnish and top with the remaining cornmeal. Cover with a cloth napkin, then cover the colander tightly with foil, tucking the foil firmly under the rim. Pour boiling water into a deep pot large enough to hold the colander comfortably (or into the bottom half of the *couscoussière*), taking care that the water is not deep enough to reach the bottom of the colander. Cover and steam over low heat for 1 hour, adding a little boiling water during the cooking period if necessary. Turn off the heat and let the colander stand for a few minutes. Remove the napkin and unmold the *Cuscuz* onto a serving dish. It will look like a steamed pudding decorated with the tomato, hearts of palm, and so on. Garnish the dish with the sliced oranges.

Pastel de Choclo
con Relleno de Pollo

BOLIVIA

Chicken Pie with Corn Topping

This is simply delicious, with a combination of flavors that is new to our palates though none of the ingredients is hard to find. As it can be prepared ahead of time, it makes an ideal party dish.

Serves 6

A 3½-pound chicken, cut into
   serving pieces
2 cups chicken stock, about
¼ cup seedless raisins
3 tablespoons olive or vegetable
   oil
2 medium onions, finely chopped
3 medium tomatoes, peeled and
   chopped

Salt
1 or 2 pinches ground cinnamon
2 hardboiled eggs, coarsely
   chopped
12 small pimiento-stuffed olives,
   rinsed and halved

FOR THE TOPPING

½ cup butter or lard, or a mixture
   of both
4 cups corn kernels
1 tablespoon sugar, or less to taste
2 teaspoons salt, or to taste
4 eggs
Sweet paprika

Put the chicken pieces into a large saucepan or casserole, pour in the stock, adding a little more if necessary to barely cover. Bring to a boil, cover, and simmer over low heat until the chicken is tender, about 45 minutes. Let it cool in the stock. When it is cool enough to handle, lift it out of the stock, remove the skin and bones, and cut the meat into 1-inch pieces. Set aside. Reserve the stock for another use. Put the raisins to soak in cold water to cover for 10 minutes. In a skillet heat the oil and sauté the onions until they are soft. Add the tomatoes and cook for about 5 minutes longer, or until the mixture is well blended. Season with salt, drain, and add the raisins, cinnamon, chopped eggs, olives, and chicken. Set aside.

    To make the topping, melt the butter or lard in a small saucepan. Put the corn kernels in a blender or food processor and reduce to a purée. Pour into a saucepan and stir in the melted butter or lard. Stir in the sugar and salt. Cook over very low heat, beating the eggs in one by one. Cook, stirring with a wooden spoon, until the mixture has thickened. Allow to cool slightly.

Butter a 2-quart soufflé dish and spoon in about one-third of the corn mixture, patting it up to cover the sides of the dish. Carefully spoon in the chicken mixture, then cover with the rest of the corn. Sprinkle with sweet paprika. Bake in a preheated moderate (350° F.) oven for 1 hour, or until the topping is set and lightly browned. Serve hot.

The pie may be prepared ahead and refrigerated until ready to bake, in which case let it come to room temperature before baking.

Variation: There is a slightly simpler Chilean version of this dish in which cooked, boned chicken, either in small or large pieces, is put into a buttered earthenware casserole or soufflé dish and topped with slices of hardboiled egg, a few raisins, and pitted green olives. The corn topping is then spooned over the chicken. The topping is sprinkled with 1 tablespoon sweet paprika and 1 tablespoon of either superfine or confectioners' sugar, and the pie is baked as for *Pastel de Choclo con Relleno de Pollo.*

Variation: Another, and very popular, filling is *Pino de Carne* (Beef Hash), reminiscent of Mexican *Picadillo.* Sauté 1 pound lean beef, chopped by hand, with 4 finely chopped medium onions in 2 tablespoons oil until the beef and onions are both tender — 2 or 3 minutes. Season with salt, pepper, 1 tablespoon sweet paprika, ⅛ teaspoon cayenne, ½ teaspoon ground cumin, and ⅛ cup seedless raisins, soaked 15 minutes in warm water. Sauté for a few minutes, then put in an earthenware casserole or soufflé dish and top with 2 sliced hardboiled eggs. Cover with the corn topping and bake as for the *Pastel de Choclo con Relleno de Pollo.* If the meat mixture seems a little dry, it may be moistened with beef stock before adding it to the casserole.

Variation: Latin America is not only corn country, it is very much potato country, and the *Pino de Carne* turns up in a potato pie, *Pastel de Papas.* For this make the *Pino* as described above and set it aside. Peel and slice 3 pounds of potatoes and boil them in salted water until soft. Mash them with enough light cream, about 1 cup, to make a purée, then, over low heat, beat in 1 well-beaten egg. In a buttered earthenware casserole or soufflé dish make alternate layers of potato and beef hash, beginning and ending with potato. Bake in a preheated moderate (350° F.) oven until the potato pie is heated through and the top lightly browned. Serves 6. If liked, the amount of *Pino de Carne* may be doubled.

Pudín de Choclo   ECUADOR
Corn Soufflé

This is less like a French soufflé than like an American corn pudding. It is a
rich-tasting dish, but not heavy, nice for a light meal, or as the first course
of a grand one.

Serves 6

2 cups kernels of young corn, or 2   *Salt, white pepper*
   cups frozen corn, thawed   *5 eggs, well beaten*
½ pound Münster cheese, cubed   *Butter*
4 tablespoons (¼ cup) butter, cut
   into small pieces

Combine the corn, cheese, and butter in a blender or food processor. Season
to taste with salt and pepper and pour in the eggs. Blend on high speed until
the mixture is smooth. Pour into a buttered 1½-quart soufflé dish and set
the dish in a pan of hot water in a preheated moderate (350° F.) oven. Bake
for 1 hour, or until a knife inserted in the soufflé comes out clean.

Chouriço, Brócolos,
y Creme de Milho   BRAZIL
Sausage and Broccoli with Puréed Corn

This dish from the state of Minas Gerais is a fine one-dish family meal.
The corn purée makes a lovely sauce for the broccoli.

Serves 4

A 1½-pound bunch of broccoli   *Oil*
4 tablespoons (¼ cup) butter plus   *¾ pound chorizo or other spiced*
   1 tablespoon   *smoked pork sausage*
Salt, freshly ground pepper   *4 cups raw corn kernels*

Rinse the broccoli in cold water and cut off and discard the tough stems.
Chop the broccoli. In a saucepan heat the 4 tablespoons butter, add the
broccoli, stir, and cook for 2 minutes. Add 1 tablespoon water, cover, and
cook until the vegetable is tender, about 8 minutes. Season with salt and
pepper. Put in a serving dish and keep warm.

Film the bottom of a skillet with oil and sauté the chorizos until browned all over, about 5 minutes. They will cook in their own fat. Drain on paper towels and slice, or halve crosswise. Arrange the sausage around the broccoli and keep warm.

Purée the corn in a blender or food processor. In a saucepan melt the tablespoon of butter, add the corn, and cook stirring constantly with a wooden spoon for about 5 minutes over low heat. Season with salt and pepper. Pour the corn purée over the broccoli.

Chilaquiles de Estudiante   MEXICO
Student's Tortilla Casserole

My husband says this dish reminds him of his days at the university in Mexico, when he was perpetually hungry but often lacked the time to get home for the main meal at midday and found no one very interested in feeding him at night, when only *merienda*, a light supper, was served. *Chilaquiles* is essentially a leftover dish using anything the kitchen has to offer, usually leftover chicken, or turkey *mole*, or any pork. This one is very special indeed, quite approaching elegance. I suspect that only a very warm-hearted family cook, who understood that acquiring knowledge provokes appetite, would have gone to the trouble of preparing it for the evening meal of a hungry student and three of his friends, equally hungry, since it serves 4. I also suspect the cook must have overbought the pork for the midday meal to have had a pound left over. Made on purpose with no students around, it makes a fine lunch or supper dish.

Serves 4

FOR THE TORTILLAS
1 recipe tortillas (page 44)
4 tablespoons vegetable oil or
    lard, about

Make the tortillas the previous day, if possible, as they should have time to dry out a little. Simply wrap them in a cloth and leave them in the kitchen. If they are freshly made, dry them in the oven with the pilot light on for an hour or two. When ready to use, cut the tortillas with kitchen shears into strips about ½ inch wide. Heat the oil or lard in a skillet and fry the tortilla strips in batches, but do not let them brown. Drain on paper towels and set aside. Reserve the oil in the skillet.

FOR THE FILLING

1 pound of any leftover cooked
    pork, cut into 1-inch pieces
2 medium tomatoes, peeled and
    chopped
1 medium onion, chopped
2 cloves garlic, chopped

3 tablespoons seedless raisins
16 small pimiento-stuffed olives,
    halved
1 tablespoon red wine vinegar
½ teaspoon sugar
Salt and pepper to taste

Put the pork into a heavy saucepan with water just to cover and simmer, covered, over low heat until the pork is tender, about 1½ hours. Allow the pork to cool in the stock. Lift out and shred the meat. Reserve the stock. Put the tomatoes, onion, and garlic in a blender or food processor and reduce to a purée. Measure the oil remaining in the skillet and if necessary make up the quantity to 2 tablespoons. Add the tomato mixture and cook, stirring, for 2 or 3 minutes. Add the pork, raisins, olives, vinegar, sugar, and salt and pepper to taste, and simmer over low heat until the mixture is quite thick, about 5 minutes. Make a layer of half the tortilla strips in a greased ovenproof casserole, preferably earthenware, and spread the pork mixture on top. Cover with the remaining tortilla strips. Set aside.

FOR THE SAUCE

4 ancho *chilies*
1 medium onion
1 clove garlic
⅛ teaspoon cinnamon
Pinch of ground cloves
1 teaspoon sugar
Salt, freshly ground pepper

3 tablespoons vegetable oil or lard
2 medium tomatoes, peeled and
    chopped

Pull the stems from the *ancho* chilies, shake out the seeds, rinse in cold water, and tear into pieces. Put into a bowl with ½ cup warm water and soak, turning from time to time, for about 1 hour. Put the chilies and any soaking water into a blender or food processor with the onion and garlic and reduce to a purée. It should be quite thick and heavy. Do not over-blend, as it should have some texture. Add the cinnamon, cloves, sugar, salt, and pepper. Heat the oil or lard in a skillet and add the *ancho* mixture. Cook, stirring, for about 5 minutes. Purée the tomatoes in the blender and add to the skillet and simmer for 2 or 3 minutes longer. Add 2 cups of the reserved pork stock. If there is not enough stock, add a little chicken stock or water. Stir to mix, heat through, and pour over the contents of the casserole. Bake the casserole in a preheated moderate (350° F.) oven until heated through, about 30 minutes. Serve directly from the casserole. Accompany with a green salad.

Mucbi-Pollo
Chicken and Pork Tamal Pie

MEXICO

This is a very old, traditional Mayan dish from Yucatán, a sort of corn pie wrapped in banana or plantain leaves and baked in a *pib* or earth oven, though nowadays it is usually cooked in an ordinary gas or electric oven. As banana or plantain leaves are fairly difficult to come by, kitchen parchment or aluminum foil may be used as substitutes. If the herb *epazote* is not available, its absence from the dish is no great matter since it is the achiote (annatto) that gives the *tamal* pie its characteristic flavor and appearance. Traditionally a whole chicken, cut into serving pieces, is used but there seems to be no logical reason why the chicken should not be boned for ease in assembling and serving the dish. I have had it both ways and there is no difference in flavor, which is what matters.

Serves 4 to 6

FOR THE FILLING

1 large onion, chopped
3 medium tomatoes, peeled and
    chopped
2 cloves garlic, chopped
½ teaspoon oregano
¼ teaspoon cumin
2 tablespoons ground achiote
    (annatto)
Salt
A 2½-pound chicken, quartered
1 pound lean, boneless pork, cut
    into 1-inch cubes

1½ cups chicken stock, about
¾ cup masa harina

Put the onion, tomatoes, garlic, oregano, cumin, achiote, and salt to taste in a blender or food processor and reduce them to a purée. Put the chicken and pork into a saucepan or casserole and pour the purée over them. Add enough chicken stock to cover, about 1½ cups. Cover and simmer until the chicken is tender, about 45 minutes. Lift out the chicken pieces and set aside. Continue to cook the pork until it is tender, about 30 minutes longer. Bone the chicken and cut it into large pieces. Set it aside with the pork. Strain the stock. Put the *masa harina* in a small saucepan and add enough of the stock to make a very thick sauce, stirring over low heat for a minute or two. Pour the sauce over the chicken and pork.

FOR THE DOUGH

3 cups masa harina
1 cup (½ pound) annatto oil or
    lard, page 324
1 ½ tablespoons achiote (annatto)
    seeds
Chicken stock
Salt

Put the *masa harina* in a bowl, stir in the annatto oil or lard and the achiote seeds, and when thoroughly mixed add just enough hot chicken stock and a pinch of salt to make a thick, smooth dough. Cut a 12- by 24-inch strip of kitchen parchment or aluminum foil, or use a banana leaf, if available. Spread half of the *masa harina* dough on the parchment or foil, leaving room at the sides. Arrange the chicken, pork, and sauce on top of the dough. Cover with the rest of the dough. Fold up the parchment into a parcel and put it into a greased baking pan, fold side down. Bake in a preheated hot (400° F.) oven for 30 minutes. Unwrap to serve. The outside will be crisp, the inside, with the chicken and pork filling, moist. Serve with *Ixni-Pec* (Hot Pepper Sauce), page 311.

Queso Relleno   MEXICO
Stuffed Cheese

This dish, though popular for a long time in its birthplace, the Caribbean island of Curaçao (where it is called *Keshy Yena* in the patois of the island), was introduced to Yucatán by Dutch and German coffee men sometime in the last century. Its foreign origins are obvious in that a Dutch Edam cheese is the main ingredient, hollowed out and stuffed with a rich pork mixture. For some reason Yucatecans almost invariably use saffron rather than achiote, which is more characteristic of their kitchen, and they usually steam rather than bake the cheese; the sauce, too, is a further Mayan enhancement. The dish looks quite spectacular when brought to the table as the cheese expands during the cooking and, when cut into wedges and served, the soft cheese shell combines deliciously with the pork filling. All that is needed as an accompaniment is a salad.

Serves 6 to 8

A 4-pound Edam cheese
6 eggs
2 pounds lean pork, ground
Salt
4 tablespoons lard or vegetable oil
1 medium onion, finely chopped
1 red bell pepper, seeded and
    chopped, or use 2 canned
    pimientos
2 cloves garlic, chopped

2 tomatoes, peeled, seeded, and
    chopped
½ teaspoon oregano
¼ teaspoon ground cloves
Freshly ground pepper
¼ cup small, pitted green olives
¼ cup seedless raisins
¼ cup capers
¼ cup dry sherry

FOR THE SAUCE

3 tablespoons butter
3 tablespoons all-purpose flour
The reserved pork stock
⅛ teaspoon powdered saffron, or
    thread saffron ground in a
    mortar with a pestle

1 red bell pepper, seeded and
    chopped, or use 2 canned
    pimientos, chopped
Salt, freshly ground pepper
¼ cup small, pitted green olives,
    halved

Peel the red wax covering off the cheese. Cut an inch-thick slice from the top and hollow it out slightly. Scoop out the cheese, leaving a shell ½ to ¾ inch thick. Reserve the scooped-out cheese for another use. Put the shell and lid in a large bowl of cold water to cover, and soak for 1 hour. Hardboil the eggs and drop them into cold water. When they are cool enough to handle, shell them. Carefully remove the whites, leaving the yolks whole. The best way to do this is with the fingers. Finely chop the whites and set both whites and yolks aside.

Put the pork into a saucepan with enough water to cover and salt to taste. Cover and simmer until the meat is tender, about 30 minutes. Heat the lard or vegetable oil in a skillet and sauté the onion, bell pepper, and garlic until the onion is soft. If using the pimientos, add with the tomatoes. Add the tomatoes and cook until the mixture is quite thick, about 5 minutes. Drain the pork and reserve the stock. Add the onion and tomato mixture to the pork with the oregano, cloves, salt and pepper to taste, the chopped egg whites, olives, raisins, capers, and sherry, mixing well. Remove the cheese shell and lid from the water, drain, and pat dry. Divide the meat mixture into three parts. Put one-third of it into the cheese, patting it down firmly. Halve the egg yolks. Make a layer of 6 halved yolks on top of the meat. Spoon in another third of the meat mixture and pat down lightly. Make a layer of the remaining 6 halved egg yolks, and top with the rest of the meat mixture. Place the lid on the cheese and rub the cheese all over with lard or oil. Wrap it in a double layer of cheesecloth, then place on a rack in a steamer, and steam over boiling water for 40 minutes.

Meanwhile prepare the sauce: Heat the butter in a saucepan. Add the flour and cook, stirring constantly with a wooden spoon, for a minute. Do not let the flour brown. Add the reserved pork stock, making up the quantity with water to 2 cups, if necessary. Add the saffron, the bell pepper or pimientos, salt and pepper to taste, and the olives. Cook, stirring frequently, for 15 minutes. Pour over the cheese just before serving.

Lift the cheese out of the steamer and remove the cheesecloth. Place the cheese on a warmed serving platter and pour the sauce over it. To serve, cut the cheese in wedges.

Arroz com Porco
Rice with Pork

BRAZIL

This dish is typical of São Paulo and the regions the Paulistas developed.

Serves 6

FOR THE MARINADE

½ cup dry white wine
½ cup white vinegar
1 large clove garlic, crushed
1 medium onion, grated
Salt, freshly ground pepper
1 tablespoon chopped fresh
  coriander (cilantro)

1 fresh hot red pepper, chopped, or
  ½ teaspoon hot pepper sauce
  (such as Tabasco or Môlho de
  Pimenta e Limão, page 313)
2 pounds lean boneless pork, loin
  or shoulder, cut into 1-inch
  cubes

FOR THE STEW

2 tablespoons vegetable oil
1 medium onion, chopped
1 green bell pepper, seeded and
  chopped
1 clove garlic, chopped
1 tablespoon chopped fresh
  coriander (cilantro)

2 cups long-grain rice
Salt, freshly ground pepper
¼ pound boiled ham, diced
¼ cup freshly grated Parmesan
  cheese plus 2 tablespoons
1 tablespoon butter

In a large bowl combine the wine, vinegar, garlic, grated onion, salt and pepper to taste, coriander, and hot pepper or hot pepper sauce. Add the pork and mix lightly. Cover the bowl and refrigerate for about 8 hours, stirring once or twice. Lift out the pork pieces and pat them dry with paper towels. Strain and reserve the marinade. Discard the solids.

Now begin the stew: Heat the oil in a casserole and sauté the pork pieces until they are lightly browned. Add the onion, green pepper, garlic, and fresh coriander, and sauté for 3 or 4 minutes longer. Add the strained marinade, cover, and simmer until the pork is tender, about 1 hour.

About 20 minutes before the pork is done, wash the rice, drain, and put it into a heavy saucepan with 4 cups cold water. Bring to a boil over high heat, stir in ½ teaspoon salt, cover, and cook over low heat until the rice is tender and all the liquid absorbed, about 20 minutes.

Taste the pork for seasoning, adding a little more salt and pepper if needed. Add the ham and stir in the ¼ cup of cheese.

Arrange half the rice on an ovenproof serving platter. Spread the pork mixture over the rice, which should be quite dry. Arrange the rest of the rice over the pork. Sprinkle the rice with the 2 tablespoons of Parmesan cheese and the butter, cut into small bits. Put the platter into a preheated moderately hot (375° F.) oven until the top is lightly browned, about 10 minutes. Serve with a freshly made tomato sauce (*Môlho ao Tomate*, see page 318).

Arroz con Chancho   PERU
Pork and Rice

This Peruvian pork and rice dish is much simpler than the Brazilian version, but the annatto used in the cooking liquid for both pork and rice gives the finished dish a pleasantly distinctive flavor and an attractive yellow color.

Serves 6

2 tablespoons lard or vegetable oil	1 fresh hot red pepper, seeded and
2 pounds boneless pork loin or	chopped, or ½ teaspoon
shoulder, cut into 1-inch	cayenne
cubes	Salt
2 teaspoons finely chopped garlic	2 cups long-grain rice
½ teaspoon ground annatto	1½ cups fresh green peas, shelled
1 tablespoon sweet paprika	

Heat the lard or oil in a flameproof casserole and sauté the pork pieces until they are lightly browned all over. Add the garlic, annatto, paprika, fresh hot pepper or cayenne, and salt to the casserole and sauté for a minute or two longer. Add enough water barely to cover and simmer, covered, over low heat until the pork is tender, about 1½ hours. Drain the liquid from the casserole and measure it. Add enough water to make the quantity up to 4 cups. Return the liquid to the casserole, stir in the rice and the peas, cover, and bring to a boil. Reduce the heat as low as possible and cook until the rice and peas are tender and all the liquid absorbed. Serve with a green vegetable or a salad.

Carne Rellena
Stuffed Steak

VENEZUELA

This is an unusual dish and looks quite spectacular, as the egg and vegetables show attractively in each slice. The flavor matches the looks. The stuffed omelet makes a rich accompaniment to the tender, juicy steak.

Serves 6

A 3-pound flank steak, or two
　　1½-pound steaks
4 large cloves garlic, crushed
Salt
¼ cup olive oil
4 eggs

Vegetable oil
A 10-ounce can green asparagus
　tips
2 whole pimientos, cut into strips
2 tablespoons butter
1¼ cups dry red wine

Trim the steak of any fat and place in a baking dish or any shallow dish large enough to hold it comfortably. Mix the garlic with 2 teaspoons salt and the olive oil and rub the mixture into both sides of the steak. Let it stand at room temperature for about 2 hours.

Break the eggs into a bowl and beat them lightly with 1 teaspoon salt and 2 tablespoons water. Heat a 7-inch omelet pan and pour in just enough vegetable oil to film the surface. The pan should be about the same width as the steak. A rectangular Japanese omelet pan is ideal for this; if using a round pan, trim the omelet later to fit the steak. Pour the eggs into the pan and make an omelet in the usual way, stirring vigorously with the flat of a fork over moderate heat until the eggs begin to set, then cook until the eggs have set. Slide the omelet out of the pan and place it on top of the steak. If using 2 smaller steaks, make 2 omelets. Trim the omelet to fit. On top of the omelet lay alternate horizontal rows of asparagus tips and pimiento strips, starting and ending about ½ inch from the edge. Roll up the steak and tie it securely with string. Put the steak into a baking tin and dot it with the butter. Bake in a preheated moderate (350° F.) oven for 45 minutes for rare steak, basting it several times with the wine. Cook for 15 minutes longer if a well-done steak is preferred.

Lift the steak out onto a warmed serving platter and remove the string.

Reduce the wine and pan juices quickly over brisk heat and pour into a sauceboat. Cut the steak into 1-inch slices, and serve with plain white rice, *Caraotas Negras* (Black Beans), and fried plantains or bananas.

Molondrones con Camarones   DOMINICAN REPUBLIC
Okra with Shrimp

This is a lovely dish from the Dominican Republic with okra, bananas, shrimp, and coriander making an unusual combination of flavors.

Serves 3 to 4

½ cup vegetable oil
1 medium onion, finely chopped
4 cups small, fresh okra pods, cut
  into ¼-inch slices
3 underripe bananas, peeled and
  cut into ½-inch slices
2 medium tomatoes, peeled and
  chopped

¼ cup lemon juice
1 small fresh hot red or green
  pepper, seeded and chopped
1 tablespoon fresh green coriander
  (cilantro), chopped
Salt, freshly ground pepper
1 pound medium-sized shrimp,
  shelled and deveined

Heat the oil in a skillet and sauté the onion until it is soft. Add the okra and sauté for 2 to 3 minutes longer. Add the bananas, tomatoes, lemon juice, hot pepper, coriander, and salt and pepper to taste. Simmer the mixture for about 5 minutes, or until the okra is tender. Add the shrimp and cook for about 3 minutes longer, or until the shrimp turn pink. Serve with rice.

Repollo Relleno   BOLIVIA
Stuffed Whole Cabbage

A whole stuffed cabbage with a highly seasoned meat stuffing makes a most delectable luncheon or family supper dish. I've come across it with variations in the filling in the Andean countries of Bolivia, Peru, Venezuela, and Colombia. Its obvious ancestor is *sou-fassum*, the stuffed cabbage of Provence. When I cook it, I borrow a trick from Richard Olney, who wraps his *sou-fassum* in cheesecloth, making it a lot easier to handle than when it is merely tied round with a piece of string. I save the leftover stock for making soup.

Serves 6 to 8

1 large Savoy cabbage, weighing about 3 pounds
1 recipe Picadillo (Seasoned Chopped Beef), page 131, using pork instead of beef and omitting the apples and almonds

Beef or chicken stock
1 recipe Salsa de Jitomate (Tomato Sauce), page 319

Trim the cabbage, removing any wilted outer leaves. Drop the cabbage into a large saucepan full of briskly boiling water and let it simmer for 10 minutes. Lift out the cabbage into a colander and let it drain thoroughly. When it is cool enough to handle, place it on a large square of double cheesecloth and carefully open the outer leaves, spreading as flat as possible without breaking them off. Cut out the heart of the cabbage, discard the core, chop fine, and add it to the seasoned chopped pork, mixing thoroughly. Cut away as much of the core as possible while leaving the cabbage intact. Form the meat into a ball and pack it into the center of the cabbage. Press the outer leaves back into shape, re-forming the cabbage. Gather up the cheesecloth and tie it up with string. Put the cabbage into a large saucepan into which it fits comfortably and pour in enough stock to cover. Bring to a boil, reduce the heat, and simmer the cabbage for 3 to 3½ hours. Lift out into a round serving dish or soup tureen, untie, and slide out the cheesecloth, lifting the cabbage with a spatula to do so. Spoon a little tomato sauce over the cabbage and serve the rest in a sauceboat. To serve cut the cabbage into wedges. Accompany with rice.

Variation: Reduce the amount of pork to 1 pound and add 1 pound potatoes, peeled and cut into ¼-inch cubes. Serve with crusty bread instead of rice.

Variation: In Venezuela, cooks add 1 teaspoon *Aliño Criollo* (Creole Style Seasoning Powder), page 325, to the meat mixture, which gives it a very interesting flavor.

Variation: In Brazil, where stuffed cabbage is also popular, a mixture of pork and beef, seasoned with ½ teaspoon nutmeg, is used. Two slices of chopped bacon may be added as well as ¼ cup well-washed raw rice.

Flan de Legumbres   ECUADOR
Vegetable Soufflé

Vegetables are handled imaginatively by Ecuadorian cooks. This mixture of eggs and vegetables makes a satisfying meal when served with soup and dessert.

Serves 4 to 6

6 slices bacon, cut into julienne
1 cup fresh breadcrumbs
½ cup milk
3 tablespoons tomato sauce
1 cup chicken stock
2 tablespoons melted butter
1 tablespoon chopped parsley

Salt, freshly ground pepper
2 cups cooked mixed vegetables
    such as corn, peas, carrots,
    cauliflower, green beans, and
    green pepper, all chopped
3 eggs, well beaten
½ tablespoon butter

Cook the bacon in a skillet over moderate heat until crisp, and drain on paper towels. Combine the bacon with the breadcrumbs, milk, tomato sauce, chicken stock, melted butter, parsley, and salt and pepper to taste. Fold in the mixed vegetables. Fold in the eggs and pour the mixture into a buttered 1½-quart soufflé dish. Stand the dish in a baking tin, half-filled with hot water, in a preheated moderate (350° F.) oven, and cook for 1 hour, or until a knife inserted into the soufflé comes out clean.

Torta de Plátano   MEXICO
Savory Green Banana Cake

There is a hint of sweetness in this very original old colonial dish from
Oaxaca in Mexico: the bananas g well with the robust flavor of the beans,
a combination that is both unusual and good with meat and poultry when
served instead of rice or potatoes.

Serves 6 to 8

2 cups cooked kidney beans	6 green (unripe) bananas, or 4
1 medium onion, finely chopped	green plantains
1 bay leaf	½ cup grated Parmesan cheese
4 tablespoons lard or vegetable oil	4 tablespoons butter
Salt, freshly ground pepper	2 eggs, lightly beaten

If dried beans are used, simmer 1 cup well-washed and picked-over kidney
beans in water to cover with ½ medium onion, chopped, and a bay leaf,
until the beans are tender, about 2 hours. If the beans dry out during the
cooking, add a little hot water. Drain, reserve ½ cup of the cooking liquid,
remove and discard the bay leaf, and purée the beans with the reserved
liquid in a blender. Black beans may also be used.

Put the beans with about ½ cup of the cooking liquid in a blender or
food processor and reduce them to a purée. Heat the lard or oil in a heavy
skillet and sauté the onion until it is very soft. Add the beans and cook,
stirring with a wooden spoon, until they form a soft paste. They should not
be dry. Season to taste with salt and pepper. Set aside.

Cut through the skins of the bananas lengthwise and peel them. Put
them into a saucepan with salted water to cover, bring to a boil over
moderate heat, reduce the heat, and simmer, uncovered, until they are
tender, 10 to 15 minutes. Plantains will take about 30 minutes. Drain and
mash with a fork while they are still warm. Mash in the grated cheese and
3 tablespoons of the butter. Stir in the eggs, mixing well. Butter a soufflé
dish and make a layer of half the banana mixture, cover with the bean
mixture, and top with the remaining banana mixture. Dot with the remaining tablespoon of butter, and bake in a preheated moderate (375° F.)
oven for 30 minutes. Serve directly from the dish.

Variation: Some cooks add 4 tablespoons of flour to the banana mixture
with the cheese but I find this makes the topping very dense and heavy.
However, for another Mexican version of the dish, *Frijoles con Plátanos*

(Beans with Bananas), which is made with ripe bananas, flour is necessary (1 tablespoon flour for each banana), as the ripe fruit has more sugar and less starch. For this the banana mixture is fried in oil, 1 tablespoon at a time as a fritter, until browned on both sides, about 5 minutes. To serve put 1 teaspoon hot mashed black beans in the center and fold the fritter over. These can be eaten with cream cheese as a dessert but are delicious with plainly cooked meats or poultry as a side dish.

Variation: In Oaxaca the *torta* is sometimes made into *Empanadas* (Turnovers). Pat the cooked green banana mixture plus 4 tablespoons flour into flat cakes 2 to 3 inches in diameter, stuff with a little of the bean mixture, fold over, pressing the edges together to seal in the filling, and fry in lard or vegetable oil until golden on both sides.

Variation: I came across a similar dish in Guatemala, *Empanadas de Plátano* (Banana Turnovers), also called, more picturesquely, *Niños Envueltos* (Babies in a Blanket). Green plantains were preferred to green bananas though both were used, and flour was added, but the beans used were black beans, never any other kind. Sometimes the turnovers were stuffed with fresh cream cheese instead of, or as well as, the mashed beans, and the turnovers were deep fried. I once had them sprinkled with sugar and served with cream as a dessert. They were remarkably pleasant.

BEANS

Beans are important in Latin America not only because so many of the world's varieties of this useful vegetable originated there but because they supplied valuable protein in a region where there were none of the sources of high protein that Europe had, such as cattle, sheep, goats, pigs, and so on. Fortunately beans were not pushed out of the kitchen by the Conquest. They are just as popular today as they ever were. They are an essential part of Mexico's main meal, served after the main course and before dessert, in small bowls. They are quite soupy and are eaten with a spoon, accompanied by tortillas, which can also be used to scoop up the beans. I like to serve them, as do many modern Mexicans, with the meal. So essential are beans to the Latin American kitchen that there is a saying when unexpected guests arrive: *"Pónle más agua a los frijoles,"* meaning "Add more water to the beans." They are immensely popular as *frijoles refritos*, refried beans. It took me some time to understand why they are called "refried" when clearly they are fried only once. It is partly a matter of euphony since *frijoles fritos* sounds awful whereas *frijoles refritos* makes a pretty sound.

It is also a nice economy of language as the beans are first boiled then fried, with the "re" standing for twice and pointing out the double cooking.

Venezuelans make a charming joke about their black beans, *Caraotas Negras*. They call them *"caviar criollo,"* creole caviar, and serve them mashed, usually with *Arepas* (Corn Bread) as an hors d'oeuvre. They are also an essential part of the national dish, *Pabellón Caraqueño.* They are the heart of Brazil's national dish, *Feijoada Completa* (Black Beans with Mixed Meats).

Because they were so important, cooks evolved their own special ways of seasoning the slowly simmered beans. I cook my beans according to the rules laid down by my husband's grandmother. I think of her recipe as Seven Precious Beans because seven ingredients are added to the beans, which she, along with lots of other cooks in Mexico, insist must never be presoaked. There are exceptions, notably black beans for *Feijoada.* Soaking instructions are given for the exceptions in the recipes in which they occur. Added are onion, garlic, hot pepper, oil or lard, salt, *epazote* or bay leaf, and tomato. Beans themselves have a good, full flavor and when well seasoned and slowly cooked over the most gentle heat are quite irresistible.

Lentils, which like beans are members of the legume family and also a very ancient food, are very popular all over Latin America though not to the point of rivaling beans.

Frijoles
Beans

MEXICO

Serves 6 to 8

2 cups red kidney, black, pinto, or
    pink beans
2 medium onions, finely chopped
2 cloves garlic, chopped
2 canned serrano chilies, or 1
    jalapeño chili, chopped, or 1
    teaspoon dried hot red
    peppers, crumbled

1 sprig epazote (see page 9), or 1
    bay leaf
2 tablespoons lard or vegetable oil
Salt
1 medium tomato, peeled and
    chopped

Wash and pick over the beans but do not soak. Put the beans into a large saucepan with cold water to cover by about 1 inch. Add half the chopped onions and garlic, the chilies, and the *epazote* or bay leaf. Cover, bring to a boil, and simmer gently, adding hot water as needed. When the beans begin to wrinkle, after about 15 to 20 minutes of cooking, add 1 tablespoon of the lard or vegetable oil. When the beans are tender (cooking may take 1½ to 3 hours), add salt to taste and continue to simmer for 30 minutes longer but without adding any more water. There should not be a great deal of liquid when the beans are done.

In a skillet heat the remaining tablespoon of lard and sauté the remaining onions and garlic until soft. Add the tomato and sauté for 2 or 3 minutes longer. Take about ½ cup of beans and any liquid from the saucepan and add them, by the tablespoon, to the skillet, mashing the beans into the tomato mixture over moderate heat to form a fairly heavy paste. Stir this back into the beans in the saucepan, and simmer over low heat for a few minutes to thicken the remaining liquid.

Variation: For *Frijoles Refritos* (Refried Beans), cook the beans as above but use a large skillet to sauté the onions, garlic, and tomato. Over moderate heat, gradually mash in all the beans, tablespoon by tablespoon, together with any liquid. Add a tablespoon of lard from time to time until the beans form a heavy, creamy paste. The amount of lard or vegetable oil used is a matter of taste.

For *antojitos* the beans are used as a spread. If the beans are served as a side dish, they are formed into a roll, sprinkled with grated cheese, and stuck with *tostaditas*, triangles of crisply fried tortilla.

Frijoles Estilo Mexicano   MEXICO
Beans, Mexican Style

This does not mean beans as cooked all over the republic of Mexico. It means as cooked in the state of Mexico and the federal district, where the capital, Mexico City, is located.

Serves 8

2 cups pinto, pink, or red kidney
    beans
1 onion, chopped
1 sprig epazote (optional; see page
    9), or 1 bay leaf

3 tablespoons lard or vegetable oil
Salt

Wash and pick over the beans and put them into a heavy saucepan with the onion and *epazote*, if available, or the bay leaf. Add enough water to cover the beans by 1 inch. Simmer the beans, covered, until they begin to wrinkle, after about 15 to 20 minutes of cooking. Add 1 tablespoon of the lard or oil and continue to cook the beans, covered, adding hot water as necessary until they are tender (1½ to 3 hours). Add salt to taste. Discard the *epazote* or bay leaf. Remove the beans with a slotted spoon to a bowl. Measure ¼ cup beans and mash them until smooth. Stir the mashed beans into the liquid in the saucepan. In a skillet heat the remaining 2 tablespoons of lard or oil and sauté the remaining beans until they are dry, about 5 minutes. Add them to the liquid in the saucepan and simmer the mixture, stirring frequently, until the liquid is thickened.

Caraotas Negras
Black Beans

VENEZUELA

Serves 6

2 cups black (turtle) beans
3 tablespoons olive oil
1 medium onion, finely chopped
1 red bell pepper, seeded and
    chopped, or 2 pimientos,
    chopped
4 cloves garlic
1 teaspoon ground cumin
1 tablespoon sugar
Salt

Wash and pick over the beans. Put the beans to soak for 2 to 4 hours in a saucepan in enough cold water to cover by 2 inches. Add enough water to cover the beans by 1 inch as they will have absorbed much of the soaking water, bring to a boil, cover, and cook until the beans are tender, about 2 hours. In a skillet heat the oil and sauté the onion and bell pepper until both are soft. Add the garlic, cumin, sugar, and the pimientos, if using instead of bell pepper. Sauté for a minute or two, then stir into the beans. Season with salt to taste, and cook, partially covered, over low heat for ½ hour longer. The beans will be quite dry. Serve as a side dish or with *Pabellón Caraqueño* (Steak with Rice, Black Beans, and Plantains).

Feijão Preto
Black Beans

Serves 6 to 8

2 cups black (turtle) beans
2 tablespoons bacon fat
1 medium onion, grated

1 clove garlic, crushed
Salt, freshly ground pepper

Thoroughly wash the beans and put them into a heavy saucepan. Cover with cold water and soak them for about 4 hours. Add enough water to cover the beans by about 1 inch, bring to a boil, lower the heat, and simmer the beans, covered, until they are tender, about 2 hours. Heat the bacon fat in a skillet and add the onion and garlic. Sauté until the onion is soft, then scoop out a cupful of the beans with their cooking liquid and add to the skillet. Continue cooking, at the same time mashing the beans over low heat until the mixture is smooth and thick. Stir the mixture into the pot with the beans, season to taste with salt and pepper, and cook, uncovered, over very low heat for 30 minutes longer.

Porotos Granados
Cranberry Beans with Corn and Squash

This very popular Chilean dish is also very Indian since its main ingredients are all indigenous foods — beans, tomatoes, corn, and squash. In Chile fresh *porotos* (cranberry beans, sometimes called shell beans) are available almost all year round. If they are not available, dried cranberry or Navy beans can be used. *Calabaza*, the West Indian pumpkin, is best to use if available — otherwise use any winter squash.

Serves 4 to 6

2 cups fresh cranberry beans, or 1
    cup dried cranberry or Navy
    beans
3 tablespoons olive oil
2 tablespoons sweet paprika
1 large onion, finely chopped
4 medium tomatoes, peeled and
    chopped

½ teaspoon oregano
Salt, freshly ground pepper
1 pound (about 2 cups) winter
    squash, peeled and cut into
    1-inch cubes
½ cup corn kernels

Wash the fresh beans and put them into a saucepan with cold water to cover, bring to a boil, lower the heat, and simmer, covered, until the beans are tender, about 45 minutes. If using dried beans, rinse them and put them to soak in cold water for 3 or 4 hours. Simmer the beans in unsalted water to cover until they are barely tender, 1½ to 2 hours. Drain the fresh or dried beans and set aside. Reserve the cooking liquid.

Meanwhile heat the oil in a skillet and stir in the paprika over moderate heat with a wooden spoon, taking care not to let it burn. As soon as the paprika and oil are thoroughly mixed, stir in the onion and sauté until the onion is tender. Add the tomatoes, oregano, salt, and freshly ground pepper, and simmer the mixture, stirring from time to time, until it is thick and well blended. Add this mixture and the squash to the saucepan with the beans, stir to mix, and add enough of the reserved cooking liquid barely to cover. Cover and simmer gently for 15 minutes. The squash will disintegrate and thicken the sauce. Stir in the corn and simmer for 5 minutes longer. Serve in soup plates with a little *Pebre* (Chilean Hot Pepper Sauce), if liked.

Frijoles con Puerco Estilo Yucateco   MEXICO
Beans with Pork, Yucatán Style

Serves 6

2 cups black (turtle) beans
2 pounds lean, boneless pork, cut
    into 1½-inch cubes
2 large onions, finely chopped
1 whole fresh hot pepper, or 1
    canned hot pepper

½ teaspoon chopped epazote, *if
    available*
2 or 3 sprigs fresh coriander
    (cilantro)
Salt, freshly ground pepper

FOR THE GARNISH

1 large onion, finely chopped
½ cup fresh coriander (cilantro),
    chopped

12 small radishes, chopped
6 lemon wedges

FOR THE TOMATO SAUCE

4 medium tomatoes
2 fresh or canned hot green
    peppers
Salt

Thoroughly wash and pick over the beans. Put the beans into a large saucepan or flameproof casserole with water to cover by about 2 inches. Bring the beans to a boil, cover, reduce the heat, and simmer for 1 hour. Strain the beans, measure the liquid, and make it up to 8 cups. Return the beans and liquid to the saucepan. Add the pork, onions, hot pepper, *epazote*, if available, coriander sprigs, and salt and pepper to taste. Simmer, covered, until the meat and beans are both tender, about 1½ hours. Discard the hot pepper and coriander sprigs. Lift out the pork pieces with a slotted spoon and place them in the center of a warmed platter. Strain the beans and arrange them round the pork. Pour the bean liquid into a soup tureen. Serve the soup in bowls and the beans and pork on plates at the same time. Serve the garnishes in bowls at the table to be eaten with both the soup and the beans.

To make the tomato sauce: Peel and chop 4 medium tomatoes and simmer them for 15 minutes with 2 fresh or canned hot green peppers and salt to taste. Pour the mixture into a blender or food processor and reduce to a purée. Pour back into the saucepan and heat through. Pour into a bowl and serve over the meat.

Lentejas
Lentils

COLOMBIA

Serves 6

½ pound lentils
2 tablespoons olive oil
2 medium onions, finely chopped
2 cloves garlic, chopped
2 large tomatoes, peeled, seeded,
    and chopped
Salt, freshly ground pepper

Pinch of sugar
1 teaspoon chopped fresh
    coriander (cilantro)

Put the lentils in a large saucepan with water to cover by about 1 inch and cook until they are almost tender, about 1 hour. The quick-cooking variety (noted on package) will be done in about 25 minutes. Drain and set aside.

In a skillet heat the oil and sauté the onions and garlic until the onions are softened. Add the tomatoes, salt, pepper, sugar, and coriander, and simmer gently until the mixture is thick, about 10 minutes. Stir the sauce into the lentils and cook over very low heat for 10 minutes longer to blend the flavors. Serve instead of potatoes or rice.

Angú de Farinha de Milho   BRAZIL
Molded Cornmeal

Brazilians are fond of this simple corn pudding. Traditionally it is served with *Picadinho de Porco* (Pork Hash), and *Couve à Mineira* (Kale or Collard Greens, Minas Gerais Style), accompanied by *linguiça* sausages. It may also accompany any meat or poultry dish, or fish and shellfish.

Serves 6

3 cups water	3 tablespoons butter plus butter
1 teaspoon salt	for the mold
1 cup cornmeal	

In a heavy saucepan bring the water and salt to a boil and pour in the cornmeal in a thin, steady stream, stirring constantly with a wooden spoon. Cook over moderate heat until the mixture is smooth and thick. Stir in the 3 tablespoons of butter. Butter a 1½-quart mold and turn the cornmeal mixture into it. Pat it down, then unmold onto a serving dish.

Bacon fat may be used instead of butter.

RICE

Rice is enormously popular in Latin America and cooks pride themselves on their ability to cook rice to perfection, as this is often considered the measure of their skill in the kitchen. There are many ways to cook plain white rice and all of them produce rice that emerges tender, and with every grain separate. In Peru, Colombia, and Ecuador, cooked rice is drier than ours and is called *Arroz Graneado. Graneado* has a dual meaning in Peruvian Spanish—choice or select, and grainy. It is an attractive texture. There are also more elaborate rice dishes like *Arroz a la Mexicana* (Rice, Mexican Style), which is served as a separate course, *sopa seca*, or dry soup, at *comida*, the big midday meal. It comes after soup and before the main course. I serve it with the main course as our meals are not as elaborate as they are traditionally in Mexico. In coastal Colombia rice is cooked in coconut milk and garnished with raisins, giving it a tantalizing hint of sweetness. In addition to plain white rice and more elaborate rice dishes, Brazil makes rice into molded puddings that are served with the traditional dishes of Bahia. It is important always to use a heavy saucepan with a tightly fitting lid. If the rice is not to be used immediately, cover the saucepan with a folded dish towel, then the lid to prevent condensed moisture from making the rice mushy. The rice will stay hot for about 15 minutes.

Arroz Blanco   MEXICO
White Rice

Serves 6

1 ½ cups long-grain rice
¼ cup vegetable oil
1 small onion, finely chopped
2 cloves garlic, finely chopped

3 cups cold water
Salt
1 fresh hot green pepper (optional)

Wash the rice thoroughly in several changes of water, drain, and put into a saucepan with hot water to cover. Let stand 15 minutes. Drain in a sieve, letting it stand for about 10 minutes. Heat the oil in a saucepan, add the rice, onion, and garlic, and sauté over low heat, stirring constantly with a wooden spoon, until the rice begins to take on a pale gold color and the oil is absorbed, 3 or 4 minutes. Add the water and salt to taste. Bring to a boil over high heat, reduce the heat to as low as possible, and cook, covered, until the rice is tender and all the liquid absorbed, about 20 minutes. I sometimes like to add a whole fresh hot green pepper when adding the water. It is discarded when the rice is cooked. This gives just a hint of peppery flavor.

Variation: For *Arroz Graneado* (Peruvian Style Rice), pour 2 tablespoons vegetable oil into a saucepan and add 1 clove crushed garlic. Sauté over low heat for 1 or 2 minutes, being careful not to let the garlic burn. Add 4 cups water, 1 teaspoon lemon juice, and salt to taste, and bring to a boil. Stir in 2 cups long-grain rice, washed and drained, bring back to a boil, cover, and cook on the lowest possible heat until the rice is tender and all the liquid absorbed, about 25 minutes. Serves 4 to 6.

Variation: *Arroz Blanco* (White Rice) from Venezuela is traditionally served with *Pabellón Caraqueño* (Steak with Rice, Black Beans, and Plantains) but may accompany any fish, meat, or poultry dish. Thoroughly wash and drain 1½ cups long-grain rice. Heat 3 tablespoons butter in a saucepan and stir in the rice, 1 medium onion, finely chopped, ½ red or green bell pepper, seeded and chopped, and 1 clove garlic, chopped. Sauté, stirring, over low heat for 3 or 4 minutes, or until the butter is absorbed. Do not let the rice brown. Add 3 cups water and salt to taste, bring to a boil, and cook, covered, over very low heat for about 20 minutes, or until all the liquid is absorbed and the rice tender. Serves 6.

Variation: *Arroz de Amendoim* (Peanut-Colored Rice) is not only the color of roasted peanuts, but has a fine, nutty flavor. Thoroughly wash the rice and let it drain in a sieve for 30 minutes. Pour 2 tablespoons peanut oil into a saucepan, add the rice, and sauté, stirring constantly with a wooden spoon, over low heat until the rice is the color of roasted peanuts, a light brown, about 10 minutes. Be careful not to let the rice get too dark in color as it will have a bitter taste. Add 2 tablespoons lemon juice, 1 teaspoon salt, and 3 cups water. Bring to a boil over high heat, then simmer, covered, over very low heat, 15 to 20 minutes, or until the rice is tender and all the liquid absorbed. Serves 6.

Variation: For *Arroz Brasileiro* (Brazilian Style Rice), thoroughly wash and drain 2 cups long-grain rice. Heat 3 tablespoons vegetable oil or lard in a saucepan and sauté 1 onion, finely chopped, and 1 clove garlic, chopped, until the onion is soft. Add the rice and cook, stirring, until the fat has been absorbed. Add 3½ cups water and salt to taste, bring to a boil, cover, and simmer over very low heat until the rice is tender and all the liquid absorbed, about 20 minutes. An attractive variation is to add 1 peeled, seeded, and chopped tomato to the rice just before adding the water, or add ⅓ cup tomato purée. Serves 6, but should be enough for 8 to 10 when served with a *Feijoada Completa* (Black Beans with Mixed Meats).

Arroz a la Mexicana

MEXICO

Rice, Mexican Style

Serves 6 to 8

2 cups long-grain rice
2 tomatoes, peeled, seeded, and
    chopped
1 medium onion, chopped
1 clove garlic, chopped
3 tablespoons lard or vegetable oil
3½ cups chicken stock
2 carrots, scraped and thinly
    sliced
1 cup fresh raw peas or frozen
    peas, thawed

1 green pepper, seeded and
    chopped, or 2 serrano (hot,
    green) chilies, seeded and
    chopped
1 tablespoon chopped fresh
    coriander (cilantro) or
    parsley, preferably flat Italian
    parsley

Thoroughly wash the rice in several changes of water and let it soak for 15 minutes. Drain thoroughly in a sieve. Put the tomatoes, onion, and garlic in a blender or food processor and reduce to a purée. Heat the lard or vegetable oil in a flameproof casserole and sauté the rice, stirring constantly, until it is golden. Be careful not to let it brown. Add the tomato mixture and cook it, stirring occasionally, until all the moisture has evaporated. Stir in the chicken stock, carrots, peas, and green pepper. Bring the mixture to a boil, cover it, and simmer over very low heat until the rice is tender and all the liquid absorbed, about 20 minutes. Serve the rice garnished with the chopped coriander or parsley.

Variation: Slice 2 chorizo sausages, fry in a little oil, drain, and garnish the rice with the sausages, 1 large avocado, sliced, and 2 hardboiled eggs, sliced.

Variation: *Arroz Guatemalteco* (Rice, Guatemalan Style) is traditionally served with *Carne en Jocón* (Beef in Tomato and Pepper Sauce), but it may also be served with any dish that would be accompanied by plain rice, such as a meat or poultry stew. Heat 2 tablespoons peanut oil or butter in a heavy saucepan, add 2 cups long-grain rice, and sauté lightly, stirring with a wooden spoon, until the rice has absorbed all the fat, being careful not to let it color. Add 1 cup mixed vegetables (carrots, celery, sweet red peppers, chopped finely, and green peas), salt and pepper, and 4 cups chicken or beef stock. Bring to a boil, cover, and reduce the heat to low. Cook until the rice is tender and all the liquid absorbed, about 20 minutes. Serves 6 to 8.

Arroz con Coco y Pasas COLOMBIA
Rice with Coconut and Raisins

There are two versions of this dish, *Arroz con Coco y Pasas* (Rice with Coconut and Raisins) and *Arroz con Coco Frito y Pasas* (Rice with Fried Coconut and Raisins). Either makes an excellent and unusual accompaniment to meat dishes. They are typical of the cooking of coastal Colombia, where coconut is very much used.

Serves 6

½ *pound raisins*
5 *cups coconut milk (see page 7)*
2 *cups long-grain rice*

2 *teaspoons sugar*
1 *tablespoon butter*
Salt

Put the raisins into a heavy saucepan with a tightly fitting lid, pour in the coconut milk, and let the raisins soak for 30 minutes. Add the rice, sugar, butter, and salt to taste. Cover, bring to a boil, stir once, reduce the heat to very low, and cook the rice, covered, until it is tender and dry (20 to 25 minutes).

Variation: For *Arroz con Coco Frito y Pasas* (Rice with Fried Coconut and Raisins), heat the thick milk made from 1 coconut, about 1 cup or less, in a saucepan over moderate heat, stirring from time to time until the oil separates from the grainy golden residue. In Colombia this is called *titoté*. Add 1 tablespoon brown sugar and cook, stirring, for a few minutes longer. Add 4 cups thin coconut milk and ½ pound raisins and simmer over low heat for 10 minutes. Add 2 cups long-grain rice and salt to taste and cook, stirring frequently, for 10 minutes longer. Stir in 4 tablespoons (¼ cup) butter, or omit this step if preferred. Cover the rice and cook over very low heat until all the liquid is absorbed and the rice is dry and grainy, 20 to 25 minutes.

Angú de Arroz   BRAZIL
Molded Rice

Brazilians like to make molded puddings of rice or rice flour, which are served at room temperature as an accompaniment to dishes like *Vatapá* or with Bahian fish, shellfish, or meat dishes. They make a pleasant change from plain white rice and look very attractive when unmolded.

Serves 6 to 8

2 cups short-grain rice
1 teaspoon salt
1 cup thin coconut milk (see
    page 7)
Butter

Thoroughly rinse the rice until the water runs clear. Put the rice into a saucepan with 4 cups water and leave it to soak overnight. Stir in the salt, cover, bring to a boil, and cook over low heat for 20 minutes, or until the liquid has been absorbed and the rice is mushy. Stir in the coconut milk and cook, mashing the rice with a wooden spoon, for 2 minutes. Turn the rice into a buttered 1½-quart mold and allow to cool. Unmold the rice by covering with a platter and turning over quickly. If it doesn't unmold readily, hit the bottom of the mold with the flat of your hand. Serve at room temperature.

Variation: For *Pirão de Arroz* (Rice Flour Pudding), which goes with the same dishes as does *Angú de Arroz*, combine 1 cup rice flour, 1 teaspoon salt, and 2½ cups coconut milk made by combining both thick and thin coconut milk (see page 7) in a saucepan. Cook over low heat, stirring constantly with a wooden spoon, until the mixture is smooth and thick, about 5 minutes. Pour the mixture into a buttered bowl and let it stand for a few minutes. Turn out onto a serving dish and serve at room temperature. Serves 6 to 8.

Arroz de Haussá

BRAZIL

Haussá Rice

This is an Afro-Brazilian specialty named for the Haussa tribe of Nigeria, who are great rice eaters. The jerked beef used is Brazilian sun-dried salt beef, *carne seĉa*, often available in specialty stores. It makes a fine main course for rice lovers.

Serves 4

1 pound carne sêca *(jerked beef)*,
    see page 6
4 tablespoons butter
2 medium onions, thinly sliced
1 recipe **Arroz Brasileiro** *(Brazilian*
    Style Rice), page 249
1 recipe **Môlho de Acarajé**
    (Black-Eyed Pea Fritter
    Sauce), page 23

Soak the beef overnight in cold water to cover. Drain, put into a saucepan with fresh cold water to cover, bring to a boil over moderate heat, and drain. When the beef is cool enough to handle, chop it coarsely, or shred it with the fingers. Heat the butter in a skillet and sauté the onions until they are lightly browned. Add the beef and cook, stirring, until it is lightly browned and heated through. Arrange the rice in the center of a serving dish and surround it with the beef and onion mixture. Serve with *Môlho de Acarajé* (Black-Eyed Pea Fritter Sauce), a hot sauce.

Vegetables and Salads

Verduras y Ensaladas

One of the great excitements of Latin American markets is the vegetable stalls with great heaps of orange carrots, little tender green zucchini, bright red tomatoes, bursting with ripeness, green beans, crisply tender, corn, young onions looking like giant scallions, great, green pumpkins cut to show the vivid yellow flesh inside, bright green okra pods, new potatoes so clean and unblemished they look as though they had sprung from some celestial soil, avocados, black- and green-skinned, green globes of cabbage, peas ready shelled for the buyer, deep red beets, and peppers — vivid green, red, yellow, and orange, in more shapes and sizes than seems possible — spinach, Swiss chard, and a bewildering array of root vegetables — the sweet potatoes, the yams, the taros and malangas, dark brown and light brown, enormous or tiny, smooth-skinned and rough-skinned, knobbly or nicely symmetrical in shape — and the dried beans, black, red, creamy yellow, pink, and speckled, in lavish heaps.

It is no wonder that vegetables play such an important role in the Latin American kitchen — so much so that they are often served as a separate course. What I have learned from South America has changed my own cooking habits considerably. Now I love to serve whole platters of cooked vegetables, lightly dressed with oil and vinegar, at room temperature, either as an accompaniment or as a first course, and I have picked up so many new uses for our more familiar produce that vegetables are never uninspired.

AVOCADOS

Aguacates Rellenos   ECUADOR
Stuffed Avocados

Avocados are much more widely used in soups and sauces than in the States but they're most popular as a first course, stuffed. For a grand occasion, especially a meal in the Latin American tradition, this is fine. I also find that, accompanied by a glass or two of dry white wine and a dessert of cheese, stuffed avocados make a delicious lunch or light supper.

Serves 6

3 large avocados
1 cup chopped, cooked ham
3 hardboiled eggs, chopped
Salt, freshly ground pepper

1 cup mayonnaise, about
Romaine or iceberg lettuce,
*   shredded*

Carefully peel the avocados, cut into halves lengthwise, and remove and discard the pits. In a bowl combine the ham and hardboiled eggs, season to taste with salt and pepper, and fold in enough mayonnaise to bind the mixture, about 1 cup. Fill the hollows of the avocados with the mixture. Make a bed of lettuce on six salad plates and put half an avocado on each. Serve as a first course or light luncheon dish. A vinaigrette sauce may be used instead of mayonnaise.

   Avocados discolor quickly, so if it is necessary to prepare this ahead of time, dip the avocados in lemon juice, or leave them unpeeled, though they will look less elegant. Chopped cold roast pork or chicken may be used instead of the ham mixed with 1 cup cooked mixed vegetables instead of the hardboiled eggs. This is a dish that welcomes the improviser. Ecuadorian cooks sometimes substitute tomato sauce or béchamel for mayonnaise, though I find this less attractive.

Variation: For *Paltas Rellenas con Mariscos* (Avocados Stuffed with Shrimp) from Chile, peel and halve 3 avocados and arrange them on a bed of lettuce on six salad plates. Make 1 recipe *Salsa Golf* (Tomato- and

Cognac-Flavored Mayonnaise), page 327, and mix half of it with 1 pound cooked shrimp, quartered if large, left whole if small. Pile the shrimp mixture into the avocados and serve the rest of the mayonnaise in a sauceboat.

Variation: Venezuela varies the Chilean shrimp-stuffed avocado slightly and calls it *Aguacates Rellenos con Camarones*. The avocados are not peeled, just halved, with the pits removed. The flesh is mashed lightly with a fork and a little vinaigrette dressing is mixed in. They are then stuffed with shrimp in vinaigrette. If small avocados are used, this does make a very nice first course.

Variation: For *Paltas Rellenas* (Stuffed Avocados) from Peru, halve and remove the pits from 3 avocados. Mash a fourth avocado with 1 fresh hot pepper, seeded and chopped, and about ¾ cup vinaigrette dressing made with mustard. Toss the dressing with ½ cup each cooked diced green beans and carrots, ½ cup cooked green peas, ½ cup finely chopped celery, 6 small pimiento-stuffed olives, chopped, and 2 hardboiled eggs, finely chopped. Fill the avocados with the mixture and mask them with mayonnaise. Garnish with slices of hardboiled egg and a little finely chopped parsley. If liked, garnish also with a fresh hot red pepper, cut into a flower shape by slicing it into thin strips almost its full length, stopping short of the stem end. Put the peppers into ice water for several hours, or until the cut ends curl back.

Variation: A simpler version of the Peruvian dish, which is very rich, comes from Cuba. For *Aguacates Rellenos* (Stuffed Avocados), peel the avocados and dip them in lemon juice to prevent discoloring. Cut them in half lengthwise and discard the pits. Arrange each half on a bed of lettuce and fill with a mixture of diced cooked vegetables, using any of the following: potatoes, carrots, beets, green peas, green beans, asparagus tips, finely chopped green or red bell peppers, or chopped cucumbers. Toss the vegetables in a vinaigrette dressing before putting into the avocados, and mask with mayonnaise.

Variation: For *Paltas Rellenas con Salsa Cruda* (Avocados with Uncooked Tomato Sauce) from Bolivia, peel and halve the avocados lengthwise, or simply halve them and remove and discard the pits. Fill them with a sauce made by combining 2 medium tomatoes, peeled and chopped, 1 medium onion, finely chopped, ½ green bell pepper, seeded and chopped, salt and freshly ground pepper to taste, 1 teaspoon vinegar, and 1 tablespoon vegetable oil. This should be made at the last minute if possible, as the sauce loses its fresh flavor if it stands for long.

Variation: For *Paltas Rellenas con Pollo* (Avocados Stuffed with Chicken) from Chile, peel 3 large avocados, dip them in lemon juice, halve them lengthwise, and remove and discard the pits, or simply halve them without peeling. Peel and mash a fourth large avocado and mix it with 1 whole cooked chicken breast, finely chopped. Season to taste with salt, pepper, and lemon juice and fill the avocados with the mixture.

Variation: In Chile leftover cooked rice is also used as a filling. The avocados are prepared as above. Season the mashed avocado with salt, pepper, and ½ cup vinaigrette dressing made with lemon juice. Mix with the rice, about 1 cup, and 12 pimiento-stuffed green olives, sliced. Fill the avocados with the mixture.

ZUCCHINI

Calabacitas Picadas   MEXICO
Chopped Zucchini

Zucchini are surely Mexico's favorite green vegetable, perhaps because they have so long a history in the country, going back to 7000 B.C. They are available all year round and are picked when they are only 3 to 4 inches long, young and tender. Though vegetables in Mexico are traditionally served as a separate course before the main dish, I find they go admirably with meat, poultry, or fish, and in today's Mexico more and more people are serving them in this way.

Serves 4 to 6

3 tablespoons vegetable oil
1 medium onion, finely chopped
1 clove garlic, chopped
3 medium tomatoes, peeled, seeded, and chopped
1 sprig coriander (cilantro) or epazote
2 small fresh hot green peppers, seeded and chopped, or canned *serrano or* jalapeño *chilies*

Salt, freshly ground pepper
1 pound small, young zucchini, cut into ½-inch cubes
1 cup corn kernels (optional)

Heat the oil in a saucepan and sauté the onion and garlic until the onion is soft. Add the tomatoes, coriander or *epazote*, the hot peppers, salt and pepper to taste, the zucchini, and the corn, if using. Cover and simmer over very low heat until the zucchini is tender, 30 to 40 minutes, which may seem excessively long. It is because the acid in the tomatoes slows up the cooking of the zucchini.

The corn makes the dish more robust. I add it when the main dish is a light one and leave it out when I want a more purely green vegetable dish to go with a hearty meat.

Calabacitas Poblanas   MEXICO
Zucchini, Puebla Style

The state of Puebla in Mexico, home of the country's most famous dish, the *mole poblano*, is noted for its cooking and for the wonderfully rich flavor of the *poblano* chili, a large, deep green pepper that can be mild or quite hot. Since I cannot get *poblanos*, I use green bell peppers, with very good results, for this unusual vegetable dish.

Serves 4 to 6

3 green bell peppers, toasted,
    peeled (see page 15), and
    seeded
1 medium onion, chopped
1 clove garlic, chopped

3 tablespoons vegetable oil
1 pound small, young zucchini,
    cut into ½-inch cubes
Salt, freshly ground pepper
⅓ cup heavy cream

Chop the peppers coarsely and purée them in a blender or food processor with the onion and garlic. Heat the oil in a saucepan and sauté the purée, stirring constantly with a wooden spoon, for 3 or 4 minutes. Add the zucchini, and season to taste with salt and pepper. Add a little water, about ½ cup is all that should be needed, cover, and simmer until the zucchini is tender, about 30 minutes. Check to see if more water is needed — there should be only just enough liquid to cook the zucchini. Stir in the heavy cream and simmer, uncovered, just long enough to heat it through. Serve as a green vegetable with any plainly cooked meat, poultry, or fish.

Variation: Topped with slices of fresh cheese (Spanish *queso blanco* or *queso fresco*, or if not available Münster), about 2 ounces per person, this makes an attractive vegetarian luncheon dish. Serves 2 as a main course.

SPINACH

Espinacas con Anchoas　　　　VENEZUELA
Spinach with Anchovies

Here anchovies add a flavorful salty accent to the blandness of the spinach.
I borrow a Japanese trick of squeezing the excess moisture out of the
spinach by rolling the drained spinach in a *sudare* (a matchstick bamboo
mat like a place mat), and squeezing gently. Swiss chard can be used in any
of the spinach recipes.

Serves 6

2 pounds spinach or Swiss chard
3 tablespoons olive or vegetable
　oil

Freshly ground pepper
A small can anchovy fillets,
　drained and mashed

Wash and drain the spinach or Swiss chard and trim any coarse stems.
Drop the spinach into a large saucepan of briskly boiling water. Bring back
to a boil over high heat and boil for 5 minutes. Drain the spinach, rinse
quickly under cold water, and drain again. Squeeze out the excess moisture
by hand or by rolling the spinach in a bamboo mat and squeezing gently.
Chop the spinach coarsely. Heat the oil in a large skillet, add the spinach,
and sauté, stirring frequently, for about 3 minutes. Season generously with
freshly ground pepper. Add the mashed anchovies, tossing to mix well.
Serve as a vegetable with any plainly cooked meat or poultry, or topped
with fried or poached eggs as a dish by itself.

Espinacas Saltadas　　　　PERU
Spinach with Tomatoes

Serves 6

2 pounds spinach or Swiss chard
3 tablespoons vegetable oil
1 medium onion, finely chopped
2 cloves garlic, chopped
4 medium tomatoes, peeled and
　chopped

1 fresh hot red or green pepper,
　seeded and chopped
Salt, freshly ground pepper
Grated rind of ½ lemon

Cook the spinach or Swiss chard as for *Espinacas con Anchoas* (Spinach with Anchovies) and set aside. Heat the oil in a skillet and sauté the onion and garlic until the onion is soft. Add the tomatoes and hot pepper, season with salt and pepper, and cook until the mixture is well blended, about 5 minutes. Add the grated lemon rind. Stir the spinach into the tomato mixture and cook just long enough to heat through. Serve as a vegetable with any plainly cooked meat, poultry, or fish. For a more robust dish add 6 medium potatoes, boiled and tossed in butter.

Variation: For this version from the Dominican Republic, cook the spinach as above and set aside. Heat 2 tablespoons butter in a skillet and sauté 1 medium onion, finely chopped, until it is soft. Add 2 cups tomatoes, peeled and chopped, salt, pepper, a pinch of sugar, a pinch of ground cloves, and a bay leaf, and simmer until the mixture is thick and well blended. Add the spinach and cook until heated through.

Variation: For *Espinacas con Crema* (Spinach with Cream) from Mexico, cook the spinach as above and set aside. Peel, seed, and chop 2 green bell peppers (page 15) and purée in a blender or food processor with 1 medium onion, chopped. Heat 3 tablespoons oil in a skillet, add the purée, and sauté for 3 or 4 minutes, stirring with a wooden spoon. Add the spinach and season with salt and pepper. Stir in ⅔ cup heavy cream and simmer just long enough to heat through. Serve as a vegetable dish or as a dish by itself garnished with 6 halved hardboiled eggs.

Acelgas en Crema ARGENTINA
Swiss Chard in Cream Sauce

Both the white and green parts of the chard are used here. When only the green part is called for, I use the white part the next day, cut into 1-inch pieces, boiled in salted water until tender (about 10 minutes), and served either with a plain béchamel sauce or with a cup of grated cheddar stirred into the sauce. Not Latin American, but it avoids wasting this attractive vegetable.

Serves 6

3 tablespoons butter
1 medium onion, finely chopped
1 medium carrot, cut into julienne
    strips
1 medium-sized potato, cut into
    ½-inch cubes

1 ½ pounds Swiss chard
Salt, freshly ground pepper
3 tablespoons heavy cream

Heat the butter in a saucepan and sauté the onion, carrot, and potato until the vegetables are tender. Wash and drain the Swiss chard and cut both white and green parts into thin strips crosswise. Add to the saucepan, stir to mix, and season to taste with salt and pepper. Cover and simmer over very low heat until the chard is tender, about 10 minutes. Stir in the heavy cream and simmer, uncovered, for a few minutes longer.

KALE OR COLLARD GREENS

Couve a Mineira BRAZIL
Kale or Collard Greens, Minas Gerais Style

Collard greens, or simply collards, are a variant of kale. Both vegetables are members of the enormous crucifer family and can best be described as a sort of nonheaded cabbage. They can be used interchangeably in this recipe.

Serves 6

2 pounds kale or collard greens
Salt

¼ cup bacon fat
1 clove garlic (optional)

Wash the kale or collard greens under cold running water. Trim the leaves from the stems and shred the leaves finely. Put the leaves in a large bowl and pour boiling salted water over them. Allow to stand for 5 minutes, then drain thoroughly. Heat the bacon fat in a large skillet with the clove of garlic, if liked. Add the kale and sauté for a minute or two. Season to taste with salt, cover the skillet, and cook until the kale is tender, about 15 minutes. Discard the garlic and serve.

Variation: For a slightly different, but equally traditional, dish cut enough salt pork into ¼-inch cubes to make 1 cup and sauté them in a skillet until they have given up all their fat and are crispy and brown. Lift them out and reserve. Cook the kale as above in the fat and just before serving fold in the pork fat cubes.

CABBAGE

Guiso de Repollo   BOLIVIA
Cabbage in Sauce

Cabbage, that universal vegetable, is found all over Latin America often cooked in borrowed ways. Green, white, and red varieties are all available. Cole slaw turns up everywhere, usually as *ensalada de repollo crudo* (raw cabbage salad) and I have found *choucroute* (sauerkraut), another popular borrowed dish, as *chuckrut*. But there are also attractive and original recipes for cabbage that are worth our borrowing. The Bolivian *Guiso de Repollo* (Cabbage in Sauce) is a hearty dish that needs only a broiled lamb chop, a small steak, or a piece of fried chicken to make a complete main course since it combines cabbage with potatoes in a pleasantly spicy tomato sauce.

Serves 4

1 small white or green cabbage, weighing about 1 pound
Salt
3 tablespoons vegetable oil
1 medium onion, finely chopped
3 medium tomatoes, peeled and chopped
1 fresh hot red or green pepper, seeded and chopped

Salt, freshly ground pepper
1 tablespoon tomato purée
2 tablespoons fresh coriander (cilantro) or parsley, chopped
4 medium potatoes, freshly cooked and halved

Wash the cabbage and shred it finely. Drop it into a large saucepan of boiling salted water, bring back to a boil, and simmer for 5 minutes. Drain thoroughly and set aside. In a skillet heat the oil and sauté the onion until it is soft. Add the tomatoes and hot pepper and cook until the mixture is well blended, about 5 minutes. Season with salt and pepper. Stir in the tomato purée and the coriander or parsley. Fold in the cabbage, add the potatoes, and cook until the mixture is heated through.

Variation: For the Brazilian version of the dish, *Repôlho com Vinho* (Cabbage with Wine), omit the potatoes. Sauté 1 green bell pepper, seeded and chopped, with the onion in olive oil. When adding the tomato purée, stir in ½ cup chopped parsley, and when adding the cabbage, stir in ½ cup dry white wine.

CAULIFLOWER

Cauliflower is a popular vegetable in all of Latin America and most ways of cooking it are common to a number of countries, but here are some new twists.

Coliflor en Salsa de Almendra CHILE
Cauliflower in Almond Sauce

This is an exquisitely delicate dish that makes cauliflower into something special.

Serves 6

1 medium-sized cauliflower, about 8 inches across	1 recipe Béchamel (White Sauce), page 325
Salt	½ cup finely ground almonds

Trim the cauliflower and cut a cross in the bottom of the stem end. This speeds up the cooking of the stalk so that it is tender at the same time as the flowerets. Drop, stem end down, into a large saucepan of boiling salted water, cover, and simmer for 15 to 20 minutes, or until just tender. Lift out and place in a serving dish, preferably round, to show off the cauliflower.

Meantime make the Béchamel. Stir in the ground almonds, and cook, stirring, over low heat for about 2 minutes to blend the flavors. Mask the cauliflower with the sauce and serve as an accompaniment to any plainly cooked meat, poultry, fish, or shellfish.

Variation: Use ground walnuts instead of the almonds — less delicate but very rich tasting.

Variation: Mask the cauliflower with 1 recipe *Salsa de Choclos* (Sweetcorn Sauce), page 323, for a marvelous combination of flavors, the delicate taste of the cauliflower enhanced by the rich taste of the corn.

Variation: Heat 4 tablespoons olive or vegetable oil in a skillet and add 2 large cloves garlic, crushed in a garlic press, and ¼ cup finely chopped parsley. Sauté for a minute or two, then stir in 1 tablespoon red wine vinegar, salt, and freshly ground pepper, and pour, hot, over the cooked cauliflower. This pleasant, simple dish is from Bolivia.

Variation: Put the freshly cooked cauliflower into a flameproof serving dish and mask with 1 recipe *Môlho ao Tomate* (Tomato Sauce), page 318. Sprinkle with ¼ cup freshly grated Parmesan cheese and run under a broiler just long enough to brown the cheese. I have found it makes a pleasant change to leave out the cheese and instead sprinkle the cauliflower with 2 tablespoons finely chopped fresh coriander or parsley.

Variation: This dish from the Dominican Republic is robust enough to serve 4 as a main course at lunch. Heat 4 tablespoons butter in a large skillet and sauté 1 finely chopped onion until it is soft. Stir in 1 clove garlic, crushed in a garlic press. Add 4 medium tomatoes, peeled and chopped, 1 tablespoon tomato purée, 1 tablespoon lemon juice, a pinch of sugar, salt and pepper to taste, and 1 bay leaf. Simmer for about 10 minutes to blend the flavors. Remove and discard the bay leaf and fold in 1 large freshly cooked potato, cubed, 1 medium-sized cauliflower, cooked and separated into flowerets, and 1 cup cooked cut green beans. Cook the mixture just long enough to heat through. Serve with freshly grated Parmesan cheese separately.

CHAYOTE

Chayotes Rellenos COSTA RICA
Stuffed Chayotes

Chayotes, with their crisp texture and delicate flavor, are a favorite vegetable from the Caribbean to Brazil. Often they are just peeled, sliced, and simmered until tender in salted water, drained, and served with butter and perhaps a few grinds of black pepper. This is a more elaborate recipe and is served as a separate course before the main dish. It makes a good lunch or light supper dish if the servings are doubled. In Brazil almost identical ingredients are made into a pudding, *Pudim de Chuchu*.

Serves 3 to 6

3 chayotes, peeled and halved
Salt
3½ cups freshly made
*   breadcrumbs*
2 cups grated Münster or mild
*   cheddar cheese*
Freshly ground pepper
2 eggs, lightly beaten

3 tablespoons grated Parmesan
*   cheese*
Butter

Parboil the chayotes in salted water for 10 minutes. Drain thoroughly, then scoop out the flesh, leaving a ½-inch shell and taking care not to break the vegetables. Chop the flesh coarsely and mix with 3 cups of the breadcrumbs, the grated Münster or cheddar cheese, salt and pepper, and the eggs. Pile the mixture back into the shells. Mix the remaining ½ cup breadcrumbs with the Parmesan cheese and sprinkle over the chayotes. Dot with butter and bake in a preheated hot (450° F.) oven for 15 to 20 minutes, or until the dish is heated through and the top nicely browned.

Variation: *Pudim de Chuchu* is an interesting example of how very similar ingredients can result in a very different dish. This is closer to a soufflé than anything else. Peel and halve 2 large chayotes, each weighing about ¾ pound. Simmer in salted water to cover until tender, about 15 minutes. Drain and allow to cool. Remove the edible seed. Chop the vegetable coarsely and set aside. In a bowl mix together 1 cup freshly made breadcrumbs, 1 cup grated cheese such as Münster, Gruyère, or cheddar, salt and freshly ground pepper, 2 tablespoons melted and cooled butter, and 3 lightly beaten egg yolks. Beat 3 egg whites until they stand in stiff peaks. Fold into the chayote mixture. Pour into a buttered 1-quart mold and bake in a preheated moderate (375° F.) oven for about 30 minutes, or until a knife inserted in the pudding comes out clean. Serve with *Môlho ao Tomate* (Tomato Sauce), page 318, as a light lunch or supper dish, or as a separate course, or to accompany any plainly cooked meat, poultry, or fish. Serves 3 to 4.

Tayotes Revueltos con Huevos
Chayotes Scrambled with Eggs

DOMINICAN REPUBLIC

Chayotes are called tayotes in the Dominican Republic, where the cuisine is remarkably rich and varied. This dish is most versatile since it could serve for a late breakfast, light lunch, or supper, or accompany plainly cooked meat, poultry, or fish. The cooked seed of the chayote is delicious. I always claim it as cook's perks.

Serves 2

1 large chayote, weighing about ¾
    pound
Salt
3 tablespoons vegetable oil
1 medium onion, finely chopped
1 clove garlic, finely chopped
2 medium tomatoes, peeled and
    chopped

1 small fresh hot red or green
    pepper, seeded and chopped
Freshly ground pepper
1 tablespoon tomato purée
4 eggs, lightly beaten

Peel and halve the chayote and cook in salted water to cover until tender, about 15 minutes. Remove the seed and eat it. Drain thoroughly and cut into ½-inch cubes. Set aside. Heat the oil in an 8-inch skillet and sauté the onion over medium heat until it is soft. Add the garlic, tomatoes, and the hot pepper and simmer until the mixture is well blended and most of the liquid evaporated. Season with salt and pepper and stir in the tomato purée. Add the chayote and cook until heated through. Add the eggs and cook, stirring with the flat of a fork to reach all the surfaces of the pan until the eggs are set. Serve immediately.

Variation: For a more robust dish, add 4 ounces chopped ham to the skillet with the cubed chayotes.

EGGPLANT

Eggplant is a much-loved vegetable throughout Latin America. It may be simply sliced and fried in oil, or dipped in beaten egg and breadcrumbs, or in batter, before frying. It is served stuffed with a cheese and ham mixture, or with a *picadillo* (hash) made of pork or beef, or cooked with shrimp. Recipes do not differ a great deal from country to country. Stuffed eggplant may be served as a separate course or as a main dish for lunch or supper. A perennial favorite is *Caviar de Berengena* (Eggplant Caviar), sometimes called *berengena Rusa* (Russian eggplant), served as a cold hors d'oeuvre or salad. It is amusing to note that this dish, an international favorite, is known in both the Caucasus and the Middle East as poor man's caviar. The type of eggplant found in Latin America is the beautiful shiny deep purple kind.

Berenjena Rellena con Picadillo CHILE
Eggplant Stuffed with Hash

Serves 2

1 medium eggplant, weighing about 1 pound	1 tablespoon tomato purée
Salt	1 tablespoon red wine vinegar
4 tablespoons vegetable oil	2 tablespoons parsley or fresh coriander, chopped
½ pound chopped pork or beef	Salt, freshly ground pepper
1 medium onion, finely chopped	2 tablespoons grated Parmesan cheese
1 clove garlic, chopped	
3 medium tomatoes, peeled, seeded, and chopped	

Cut the eggplant in half lengthwise and score with a small sharp knife in both directions at ½-inch intervals. Sprinkle with salt and leave for 30 minutes. Squeeze the eggplant gently to remove the bitter juice, rinse quickly in cold water, squeeze again, and pat dry. With a grapefruit knife cut round the eggplant, leaving a ½-inch shell. Pull out the flesh and cut away any bits left in the shells. Chop the eggplant coarsely and set aside. Heat the oil in a skillet and sauté the pork or beef with the onion and garlic until the onion is soft and the meat lightly browned. Add the eggplant and sauté, stirring, for 2 or 3 minutes longer. Add the tomatoes, the tomato purée, vinegar, parsley or coriander, and salt and pepper. Stir to mix and simmer for 5 minutes longer. Spoon the mixture into the eggplant shells, sprinkle with the cheese, and arrange on a baking sheet or in a baking pan. Bake in a preheated moderate (350° F.) oven for 30 minutes.

Variation: For *Berenjena Rellena con Queso* (Eggplant Stuffed with Cheese), sauté 1 medium onion, finely chopped, in 3 tablespoons butter. Add the chopped eggplant and sauté for a few minutes longer. Stir in 1 cup freshly made breadcrumbs, 1 cup grated Münster or cheddar cheese, 2 ounces ham, coarsely chopped, salt, pepper, ⅛ teaspoon cayenne, and 1 egg, lightly beaten. Pile the mixture into the eggplant shells, sprinkle with 2 tablespoons Parmesan cheese, dot with butter, and bake in a preheated moderate (375° F.) oven for 30 minutes. Serve with *Môlho ao Tomate* (Tomato Sauce), page 318.

Variation: For *Berinjela com Camarão* (Eggplant with Shrimp) from Brazil, sauté 1 medium onion, finely chopped, 1 clove garlic, chopped, 1 small fresh red or green pepper, seeded and finely chopped, and the eggplant in 3 tablespoons olive or vegetable oil until the onion is soft. Stir in ½ pound raw, coarsely chopped shrimp and sauté for 1 minute longer. Add 1 cup freshly made breadcrumbs, ½ cup chopped parsley or fresh coriander, 1 cup tomatoes, peeled, seeded, and chopped, 1 tablespoon tomato purée, and salt and pepper. Mix thoroughly, then pile into the eggplant shells. Sprinkle with 2 tablespoons grated Parmesan cheese, dot with butter, and bake in a preheated moderate (350° F.) oven for 30 minutes.

Berenjenas con Vainitas
VENEZUELA

Eggplant with Green Beans

A very pretty dish, it is also the sort of combination of vegetables that is popular in Latin America. Excellent with broiled meats, poultry, or fish, it also makes a fine salad, tossed with vinaigrette instead of butter, and served slightly chilled or at room temperature.

Serves 6

2 pounds eggplant
Salt
6 tablespoons vegetable oil
1 medium onion, finely chopped
4 medium tomatoes, peeled and
    chopped
Pinch of sugar
Freshly ground pepper
20 small pimiento-stuffed olives,
    about 2 ounces

1 pound green beans, cut into
    1-inch pieces
2 tablespoons butter, or 4
    tablespoons Vinaigrette
    (page 326)
2 tablespoons finely chopped
    parsley

Cut the eggplant into ½-inch slices, then cut each slice into fingers crosswise. Put into a colander, sprinkle with salt, and leave for about ½ hour to drain the bitter juice. Rinse in cold water, squeeze lightly, and pat dry with paper towels. Heat the oil in a skillet, add the onion and eggplant. Sauté, turning the eggplant pieces once or twice, until the onion and eggplant are both soft. Add the tomatoes, salt to taste, sugar, and pepper. Stir in the olives and cook for about 5 minutes longer, or until the mixture is fairly dry. Cook the beans in boiling salted water until they are tender, 10 to 15 minutes. Drain thoroughly, return to the saucepan with the butter, and toss over moderate heat until the butter is melted. Arrange the eggplant mixture in the center of a serving dish, surround it with the beans, and sprinkle with the parsley.

Caviar de Berenjena
Eggplant Caviar

*1 large eggplant, weighing about 2
    pounds, or two 1-pound
    eggplants*
1 medium onion, finely chopped
*1 sweet red pepper, peeled (page
    15), seeded, and chopped*
2 medium tomatoes, chopped
*2 tablespoons fresh coriander,
    chopped*

Salt, freshly ground pepper
4 tablespoons olive oil
*1 tablespoon red wine vinegar or
    lime or lemon juice*
Lettuce leaves and black olives

Bake the eggplant on the middle rack of a preheated moderate (375° F.) oven for about 45 minutes, or until tender. Cool, peel, and chop coarsely. Add the onion, sweet pepper, tomatoes, coriander, salt and pepper, and mix well. Beat the oil and vinegar together and stir into the eggplant mixture. Serve garnished with lettuce leaves and black olives as an hors d'oeuvre with crackers, or as a salad.

STUFFED PEPPERS
Chiles Rellenos

Stuffed peppers are eaten all over Latin America but it is in Mexico, where they use the lovely dark green *poblano* pepper, that they are most famous (I substitute bell peppers instead with fine results). The best known of all the stuffed peppers is *Chiles en Nogada* (Peppers in Walnut Sauce) from Puebla. They are traditionally served on St. Augustine's Day, August 28, and also on September 15, Mexican Independence Day, the colors of the dish — red, white, and green — being the colors of the Mexican flag. Fresh walnuts, which are in season in late August and early September, are used in the sauce, but packaged walnut meats will do.

Chiles en Nogada
Peppers in Walnut Sauce

Serves 6

6 poblano *or large green bell
    peppers, peeled (page 15)*
1 *recipe* Picadillo *(Seasoned
    Chopped Beef), made with
    pork and 1 of the apples
    replaced by a peach (page 131)*
2 *eggs, separated*
½ *teaspoon salt*
Flour
Vegetable oil for frying

FOR THE SAUCE

1 *cup walnuts, finely ground*
An 8-ounce package cream cheese
1 *cup light cream, about*
1 *tablespoon sugar (optional)*
*Pinch of ground cinnamon
    (optional)*
Salt

FOR THE GARNISH

Seeds from 1 pomegranate

Slit the peppers down one side and remove the seeds, taking care not to break the peppers. Stuff with the *Picadillo*. Beat the egg whites until they stand in firm peaks. Beat the egg yolks lightly with the salt and fold into the whites. Pat the peppers dry with paper towels and dip them in the flour, then in the egg. Heat enough oil in a heavy skillet to come to a depth of at least ½ inch. Fry the peppers, in more than one batch so as not to crowd the pan, until they are lightly golden all over. The egg will seal in the filling. Drain on paper towels. Arrange them on a shallow platter.

In a blender or food processor fitted with a steel blade, combine the walnuts, cream cheese, cut into bits, and half the cream. Traditionally sugar and cinnamon are added but this is not to everyone's taste so it may be left out. (I personally prefer the sauce without.) Add a little salt and blend the mixture until it is smooth with the consistency of heavy mayonnaise, adding as much of the cream as necessary. Mask the peppers with the sauce, and garnish with the pomegranate seeds.

Variation: Of all the stuffed peppers, the one simply known as *Chiles Rellenos* (Stuffed Peppers) is most often served. Taste and texture combine to make this a splendid dish. Prepare the peppers and stuff them with *Picadillo* (Seasoned Chopped Beef), page 131, or *Picadillo de la Costa* (Seasoned Meat, Coastal Style), page 132. Coat with the egg mixture and fry in oil until golden brown. Drain on paper towels. Make 1 recipe *Salsa de Jitomate* (Tomato Sauce), page 319, and thin it to the consistency of a heavy broth with chicken stock, about 1 cup, and pour it into a large saucepan. Add the stuffed peppers. The broth will come about halfway up them. Simmer just long enough to heat through and serve with the broth. The peppers can be prepared ahead of time and added to the tomato broth to heat through just before serving.

Variation: For *Chiles Rellenos con Frijoles* (Peppers Stuffed with Beans), prepare the peppers and stuff them with about 3 cups of *Frijoles Refritos* (Refried Beans), page 242. Coat in the egg mixture in the usual way and fry in oil. Drain on paper towels. Arrange in an ovenproof dish, pour ½ cup heavy cream over them, and sprinkle with 4 ounces shredded Münster, Monterey Jack, or mild cheddar cheese. Heat the dish in a preheated moderate (350° F.) oven for 30 minutes, or until it is heated through and the top lightly browned.

Variation: Make the peppers in the usual way but stuff with slices of Münster or mild cheddar cheese, and serve with *Salsa de Jitomate* (Tomato Sauce), page 319.

Variation: The Chileans have a good way of using up leftover cooked beef or pork. Prepare the peppers for stuffing in the usual way. To make the filling sauté 1 finely chopped medium onion in 2 tablespoons butter, add 2 cups cooked meat, chopped or shredded, 2 cups cooked corn kernels, 1 cup freshly made breadcrumbs, ½ cup chopped parsley, 1 fresh hot red or green pepper, seeded and finely chopped, ½ teaspoon oregano, and salt and pepper to taste. Stir to mix and sauté for a minute or two. Stuff the peppers and fry in the egg batter in the usual way. Serve with *Pebre* (Chilean Hot Pepper Sauce), or with *Salsa Chilena* (Chilean Sauce), or with *Salsa de Jitomate* (Tomato Sauce).

POTATOES

Papas Chorreadas   COLOMBIA
Potatoes with Cheese, Tomato, and Onion Sauce

This is a marvelously rich, beautifully flavored potato dish.

Serves 6

6 large potatoes, scrubbed
1 tablespoon lard and 1
    tablespoon butter, or 2
    tablespoons butter
1 medium onion, finely chopped

2 large tomatoes, peeled and
    chopped
Salt, freshly ground pepper
½ cup heavy cream
1 cup grated Münster cheese

In a large saucepan boil the potatoes until they are tender. Drain the potatoes, peel, and keep them warm. In a skillet heat the lard and butter, or the butter, and sauté the onion until it is softened. Add the tomatoes and salt and pepper to taste, and cook, stirring, for about 5 minutes. Stir in the cream and cheese and cook, stirring, until the cheese is partially melted. Pour the sauce over the potatoes.

Llapingachos   ECUADOR
Potato Cakes

This is a typical *sierra* (mountain) dish with a number of variations. It may be served as a first course, 2 cakes to a serving, accompanied by lettuce, avocado slices, and tomato. The potato cakes may be topped with fried eggs, and on the coast it is usual to add slices of fried, ripe plantains and *Salsa de Maní* (Peanut Sauce). Often served with slices of fried bass as a main course, the *Llapingachos* are then accompanied by hot white rice and tomato, lettuce, avocado, cauliflower, green beans, and green peas, all at room temperature, as a salad.

Serves 6

2 pounds potatoes, peeled and
    sliced
Salt
4 tablespoons (¼ cup) butter

2 medium onions, finely chopped
2 cups Münster cheese, shredded
Lard, butter, or oil, or annatto lard
    or oil (page 324) for frying

Boil the potatoes in salted water until soft. Drain and mash. Heat the butter in a skillet and sauté the onions until they are very soft. Add the onions to the mashed potatoes, mixing well. Shape the potatoes into 12 balls. Divide the cheese into 12 parts and stuff each of the potato balls with the cheese, flattening them as you do so into cakes or patties about 1 inch thick. Chill in the refrigerator for about 15 minutes. In enough lard, butter, or oil (with or without annatto as you please) to cover the bottom of a skillet, sauté the potato cakes until they are golden brown on both sides. The onions may be omitted, or the potato may be mixed with the cheese instead of the cheese being used as a stuffing.

TROPICAL ROOT VEGETABLES

Tropical root vegetables like the taros, malangas, cassava (yucca), yams, sweet potatoes (including the white sweet potato better known as *boniato*), *arracacha*, *apio*, and Jerusalem artichokes add a new dimension to any meal whether it is a Latin American one or not. Generally speaking they can be cooked as potatoes are, peeled and boiled, then dressed with butter, salt, and freshly ground pepper, or mashed to a purée with butter and a little milk or cream, or baked in the oven, unpeeled like potatoes in their jackets. It is not possible to give exact cooking times for all the root vegetables as they vary so much in size, shape, and texture. However, as a guide, a *boniato* weighing 1 pound takes about 1½ hours in a preheated moderate (350° F.) oven. There is one yam called a *mapuey* that has a marvelously dry texture and positively thirsts for butter. I like to bake or boil it and serve the butter with a lavish hand. Other root vegetables have a moist texture and are nice just with sauce or gravy from the main course. West Indian pumpkin, also called *calabaza*, and other winter squash, though they're not root vegetables, are also marvelous baked or boiled and mashed with butter, or with sauce or gravy. Many of the tropical root vegetables discolor quickly when exposed to the air, so it is wise to peel them under running water and drop them into cold water as soon as they are peeled.

The best way to get to know these enchanting vegetables is to buy and cook them. Markets specializing in tropical foods carry them and the men and women in the markets are usually a mine of information. The various types are discussed in the ingredients section.

✳ Jerusalem Artichokes

Jerusalem artichokes, despite their name, are a root vegetable native to North America. There are not many recipes for them in Latin America.

Topinambur al Horno
Baked Jerusalem Artichokes

CHILE

I found these in Chile. They make a nice change as an accompaniment to steaks or chops.

Serves 6

2 pounds Jerusalem artichokes
Salt
Butter

1 recipe Béchamel (White Sauce),
    page 325
½ cup grated Parmesan cheese

Wash and scrape the artichokes and cook in salted water until tender, about 10 to 15 minutes. Drain and slice. Butter a shallow Pyrex or similar dish and arrange the sliced vegetables in it. Pour the Béchamel over the artichokes, sprinkle with the cheese, dot with butter, and bake in a pre-heated moderate (375° F.) oven for 20 minutes, or until the dish is heated through and lightly browned on top. Serve with steak, chops, or any plainly cooked meat or poultry.

Variation: There is an interesting interplay of textures in this recipe, which is also from Chile. Instead of all Jerusalem artichokes, use 1 pound Jerusalem artichokes and 1 pound potatoes, arrange roughly in layers in the baking dish, and cook as above.

✳ Cassava

Cassava root, whether eaten as a root vegetable or made into cassava meal as the Brazilians do, is much appreciated throughout Latin America.

Farofa de Azeite de Dendê   BRAZIL
Cassava Meal with Palm Oil

A Brazilian meal would not be complete without some form of *farinha de mandioca* (cassava, or manioc, meal). It may be toasted in a skillet on top of the stove or in a shallow pan in the oven until it is a very light brown. It is then put into a *farinheira*, a sort of shaker, and sprinkled on meat, poultry, and vegetables at the table. As I don't have the traditional shaker, I serve it from a small bowl, and spoon it over foods. It has a light, nutty flavor, quite subtle. The *farofas* are more elaborate and are served with any main course.

Serves 6 to 8

2 cups cassava (manioc) meal
4 tablespoons dendê *(palm) oil*

In a skillet, over low heat, toast the cassava meal until it begins to turn a very pale brown. Stir frequently so that it does not burn. Stir in the *dendê* (palm) oil and cook until it is well blended and the mixture is bright yellow. Transfer to a serving bowl. Serve with *Xinxim de Galinha* (Chicken with Shrimp and Peanut Sauce), or with any meat or poultry.

Variation: For *Farofa de Manteiga* (Cassava Meal with Butter), use butter instead of *dendê* (palm) oil. If liked 1 small onion, finely chopped, may be sautéed in the butter, then scrambled with 1 egg, lightly beaten. The cassava meal is then added, seasoned with salt, and garnished, when ready to serve, with a little finely chopped parsley.

Farofa de Ouro
BRAZIL
Cassava Meal with Hardboiled Eggs

2 cups cassava (manioc) meal
¼ pound (½ cup) butter
Salt
3 hardboiled eggs, peeled and
    chopped

In a heavy skillet, preferably iron, toast the cassava meal until it turns a pale beige, stirring constantly with a wooden spoon so that it colors evenly. Put the butter into a small saucepan and melt it over low heat. Pour the butter over the cassava meal, stirring to mix evenly. Season to taste with salt and stir in the eggs. Serve in a bowl as an accompaniment to meats or poultry, or with *Feijoada Completa* (Black Beans with Mixed Meats).

Variation: Garnish the *Farofa* with 1 cup small pitted black or green olives. If liked, chop 6 slices bacon and fry until crisp. Drain and discard the fat. Fold the bacon bits into the cassava meal after the butter has been added.

Picante de Yuca
PERU
Cassava Root with Cheese Sauce

One of the most original cassava dishes is this Peruvian one where the vegetable is masked by a lively cheese sauce made hot with fresh peppers. The peppers used should be quite large ones, 3 or 4 inches in length, not the tiny very hot ones, as they lend flavor as well as heat. The number of peppers can, of course, be reduced according to individual taste but Peruvians like their food hot and this is how they would have it. They would also use an herb called *huacatay,* of the marigold family, in the sauce, but it is not available here and there is no substitute. The flavor is unusual, a little rank, and it is certainly an acquired taste. I find the sauce good without it. The dish makes an attractive accompaniment to plainly cooked meats or poultry and is also good by itself. The recipe makes about 2½ cups of sauce, which is lovely with corn on the cob or over green vegetables such as green beans or cauliflower to make a vegetarian luncheon dish.

Serves 6

½ *pound Spanish fresh cheese*
  (queso fresco or queso blanco),
  crumbled, or use grated
  Münster cheese
10 *fresh hot red or green peppers,*
  seeded and chopped
1 *cup olive or vegetable oil*

Salt, freshly ground pepper
2 *pounds cassava (yucca) root,*
  peeled and sliced
2 *hardboiled eggs, sliced*
Black olives
Lettuce leaves

Put the cheese into a blender or food processor with the peppers and the oil
and reduce it to a heavy cream. Season to taste with salt and pepper and set
aside. Boil the cassava (yucca) root in salted water until it is tender, about
30 minutes. Drain and arrange the slices on a serving platter and pour the
sauce over them while they are still hot. Garnish the platter with the eggs,
olives, and lettuce leaves.

Budín de Yuca   GUATEMALA
Cassava Root Soufflé

Guatemala has an interesting way of making cassava root into a soufflé,
which can be served instead of rice or other starchy vegetables with meat
and poultry dishes, or with *Môlho ao Tomate* (Tomato Sauce), page 318, or
Salsa de Jitomate (Tomato Sauce), page 319, and grated Parmesan cheese as
a first course or light luncheon dish.

Serves 4

1 *pound cassava (yucca) root*
Salt, freshly ground pepper
6 *tablespoons butter*

1 *cup milk, about*
4 *egg yolks*
5 *egg whites*

Peel the cassava (yucca) root under cold running water, as it discolors
quickly. Slice it and drop it into a saucepan of salted water. Bring to a boil,
lower the heat, cover, and simmer until tender, about 30 minutes. Drain
the cassava, mash, season to taste with salt and pepper, and beat in the
butter. Heat the milk and stir it gradually into the mashed vegetable until
it has the consistency of mashed potatoes. Use a little more hot milk if
necessary. Beat in the egg yolks one by one. Beat the egg whites with a
pinch of salt until they stand in firm peaks. Fold them into the vegetable
mixture lightly but thoroughly and pour into a 2-quart soufflé dish. Bake in
a preheated moderate (350° F.) oven for 35 minutes or until well puffed and
lightly browned.

SALADS

Ensalada Mixta   ECUADOR
Mixed Salad

Of all the countries in Latin America, Ecuador has the most imaginative and original approach to vegetables. Cooks there never cease to astonish me with the variety of their salads, many of which I find pleasant for a simple lunch if served in double portions. Because it is only 15 miles from the equator, Quito, Ecuador's capital, has equal day and night so that all year round 12 hours of sunshine encourage fruits and vegetables to grow. This part of the country also has a fantastically deep subsoil and good rainfall so that the raw materials for making salads are of superb quality. At 9,500 feet above sea level, water boils at a lower temperature and vegetables do not get overcooked, and since at this altitude it is always cool in the shade, salads are served at room temperature rather than chilled. I find this enhances flavor, though at sea level in hot summer an unchilled salad will be a wilted and drooping one.

Serves 4

2 cups chopped lettuce
2 hardboiled eggs, chopped
2 cups cooked, cubed potatoes
2 cups cooked green beans, cut
    into ½-inch pieces

½ cup Vinaigrette dressing (page
    326)

Combine all the ingredients in a salad bowl and toss lightly to mix.

Variation: For *Ensalada de Hongos* (Mushroom Salad), combine equal amounts of cooked corn kernels, cooked chopped carrots, cooked green beans, cut into ½-inch pieces, cooked green peas, and sliced mushrooms, and toss in vinaigrette dressing.

Variation: For *Ensalada de Garbanzos* (Chickpea Salad), combine cooked chickpeas with half the amount of cooked, coarsely chopped Brussels sprouts and toss in Vinaigrette dressing made with mustard (page 326). Chopped lettuce and cubed boiled potatoes may be added and the Brussels sprouts omitted.

Variation: For *Ensalada de Alcachofas* (Artichoke Heart Salad), mix together equal amounts of cooked, sliced artichoke hearts and sliced apples with Mayonnaise (page 326) to taste.

Variation: For *Ensalada de Papas* (Potato Salad), omit the lettuce, add 2 cups chopped celery and 1 medium tomato, peeled and chopped.

Variation: For *Ensalada de Tomate* (Tomato Salad), combine 4 medium tomatoes, peeled and chopped, with 4 hardboiled eggs, chopped, and 1 cup chopped lettuce. Toss with vinaigrette dressing made with lemon juice.

Variation: For *Ensalada de Pepinos* (Cucumber Salad), peel 2 cucumbers if they are waxed, if not leave them unpeeled and slice very thinly. Put them in a bowl with 1 teaspoon salt, mixing well, and let stand for 30 minutes. Rinse and drain thoroughly. Peel and chop 2 medium tomatoes and combine with the cucumbers. Toss with a vinaigrette dressing.

Variation: For *Ensalada de Papas y Pimientos* (Potato and Sweet Red Pepper Salad), combine 2 cups cooked sliced potatoes, 2 sweet red bell peppers, peeled and sliced, 2 medium-sized mild onions, sliced, or 1 large, halved and sliced, and 2 cucumbers, peeled, seeded, and sliced with ¾ cup Vinaigrette dressing (page 326), made with lemon juice and seasoned with 2 pinches nutmeg. Let the salad stand for 1 hour before serving. Mix lightly just before serving.

Ensalada de Habas
ECUADOR

Fresh Broad Bean Salad

Fresh young broad beans are often hard to get. If the beans are older, shell them, drop them into boiling water, let them stand a few minutes, then peel off the tough outer skin. I find English canned broad beans or Italian canned broad beans labeled fava beans a good substitute. These need no cooking and should just be rinsed and drained. I sometimes use baby lima beans. The 12-ounce package of frozen baby limas serves 4.

Serves 4

2 cups young broad beans, shelled
2 tablespoons butter
Salt, freshly ground pepper

1 tablespoon white vinegar or
  lemon juice

Cook the beans in water to cover until they are tender, about 15 minutes. Drain and cool. Melt the butter in a saucepan, add the beans, season to taste with salt and pepper, and cook for about 1 minute, turning the beans with a rubber spatula so that all are coated with the butter. Remove from the heat and pour the vinegar or lemon juice over them, stirring to mix. Serve at room temperature as an accompaniment to meats or poultry.

Salada de Palmito

Hearts of Palm Salad

Serves 6 to 8

Two 1-pound cans hearts of palm

FOR THE *MÔLHO PARA PALMITO* (Hearts of Palm Dressing)

1 tablespoon lime or lemon juice   *Salt, freshly ground pepper*
1 tablespoon Dijon mustard   *4 tablespoons vegetable oil*

Thoroughly drain the hearts of palm and cut them into ½-inch slices. Set aside.

In a bowl beat together the lime or lemon juice with the mustard and salt and pepper to taste. Gradually beat in the oil. Pour the dressing over the palm heart slices and toss lightly.

Ensalada de Aguacate

Avocado Salad

This salad is simplicity itself as well as being surprisingly good. The true flavor of the avocado comes through in all its buttery richness.

Serves 6 to 8

6 tablespoons olive oil   *Salt, freshly ground pepper*
2 tablespoons white wine vinegar   *2 large, ripe avocados*

In a salad bowl beat together the oil and vinegar. Season to taste with salt and pepper. Peel the avocados and remove the pits. Cut the flesh into cubes and toss lightly with the dressing. If liked, serve in a bowl lined with lettuce leaves.

Chojín
Radish and Fried Pork Rind Salad

Serves 6 to 8

24 small red radishes, ½ pound
    about, finely chopped
12 fresh mint leaves, finely
    chopped
3 cups chicharrones (fried pork
    rinds), finely chopped

Salt to taste
¼ cup Seville (bitter) orange juice,
    or use two-thirds orange juice
    to one-third lemon juice

Combine all the ingredients in a bowl and serve as a salad first course. If possible, use a Latin American type of *chicharrón*, as it is more flavorful.

Variation: For *Picado de Rábano* (Radish Salad), omit the *chicharrones* (fried pork rinds) and serve as a salad.

Ensalada de Coliflor
Cauliflower Salad

This cauliflower salad looks quite grand on a buffet, the white of the vegetable just visible beneath the pale green of the masking avocado sauce, very summery and pretty especially when garnished with radish roses.

Serves 4 to 6

1 medium-sized cauliflower,
    cooked and placed in a
    serving dish (page 263)

½ recipe for Guacamole (Avocado
    Sauce), page 316, or Guacamole
    del Norte (Avocado Sauce,
    Northern Style), page 317

Allow the cooked cauliflower to cool, then mask it with the avocado sauce. Serve immediately as avocado tends to darken. Garnish with radish roses.

Variation: Dominican Republic cooks have their own way of doing this. Mash 1 large avocado with salt, pepper, 1 tablespoon white wine vinegar, 3 tablespoons vegetable oil, and ¼ cup finely ground almonds. Mask the cauliflower with the mixture. The oil and vinegar used in this recipe help to keep the avocado sauce from darkening. Garnish with radish roses.

Ensalada de Topinambur
Jerusalem Artichoke Salad

A good change from potato salad. Choose the largest artichokes available to give the finished salad a more attractive look, and be careful not to overcook them as they should be crisp not mushy.

Serves 6

2 pounds Jerusalem artichokes
Salt

1 recipe Vinaigrette (Oil and
Vinegar Dressing), page 326

Wash and scrape the artichokes and cook in salted water until tender, about 10 to 15 minutes. Drain and slice. Allow to cool, then toss with the Vinaigrette.

For a richer salad, mix the artichokes with 1 cup Mayonnaise (page 326), or *Salsa Golf* (Tomato- and Cognac-Flavored Mayonnaise), page 327.

Ensalada de Verduras   ECUADOR
Vegetable Salad

This is a favorite way of serving vegetables in Ecuador and is often presented as a separate course, before the main course. The vegetables are arranged in rows on a large platter and are served freshly cooked at room temperature. I have had them without any dressing, simply seasoned with salt during the cooking, with a dressing only of oil, salt, and pepper, and with a vinaigrette made with 3 parts oil to 1 part vinegar or lemon juice, and seasoned with salt and pepper. The platter may be decorated with shredded lettuce or garnished with slices of hardboiled egg, or with olives, green or black. The vegetables should be cooked and tossed with the dressing separately. The dressing should not be abundant. The vegetables may be arranged as the cook sees fit: in rows, in heaps, or in circles. The vegetables listed below are the ones most frequently used. I like to serve the platter of mixed vegetables to accompany a main course, especially an Ecuadorian one.

Green peas
Diced beets
Cauliflower, separated in
    flowerets
Green beans, cut into ½-inch
    slices
Corn kernels
Diced carrots
Diced potatoes

Diced celery
Asparagus, cut into 1-inch pieces
Artichoke hearts, halved or
    quartered
Tiny sliced raw zucchini, or larger
    zucchini, cooked and diced
Sliced raw tomatoes
Sliced avocados

Ensalada de Nopalitos
Cactus Salad

MEXICO

This is Mexico's most traditional salad. It is lovely for summer as the juicy yet crisp young cactus pieces are very refreshing.

Serves 6

Two 10-ounce cans nopalitos
    (cactus pieces)
3 medium tomatoes, peeled,
    seeded, and chopped
½ medium white onion, finely
    chopped

2 tablespoons fresh coriander,
    chopped
½ cup Vinaigrette dressing (page
    326)

Rinse the cactus pieces gently in cold water and drain them thoroughly. Combine all the ingredients in a salad bowl and mix lightly. Chill before serving.

Variation: For a more elaborate salad, line the bowl with lettuce leaves, add the salad, and garnish it with canned *jalapeño* chili rinsed, patted dry, and cut into strips, about ¼ pound crumbled fresh cheese (*queso fresco* or *queso blanco* or cottage cheese), or 3 tablespoons grated Parmesan cheese, with ¼ teaspoon oregano sprinkled on top of the salad.

Pico de Gallo

MEXICO

Rooster's Beak

The root vegetable used in this salad, *jícama*, comes originally from Mexico but is now grown in the States and can be found in tropical markets. This is the traditional recipe from Jalisco, where the salad is most often served as an hors d'oeuvre with drinks. I like it served as a salad in lieu of dessert.

Serves 6

2 *small* jícamas, *weighing about 1
    pound, peeled and coarsely
    chopped*
4 *navel oranges, peeled, sectioned,
    and coarsely chopped*

Salt
Cayenne pepper

Combine the *jícama*, oranges, and salt to taste in a bowl. Sprinkle with cayenne and chill thoroughly before serving.

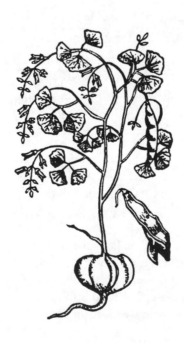

Breads
and Desserts
Panes y Postres

The people of pre-Columbian America had no breads as we know them but they had their own special flat breads made from corn, *Arepas* and *Tortillas* (already discussed as appetizers). In the colonial period other breads like *Sopa Paraguaya* were invented. Modern Latin American bakeries produce commercial breads like our own as well as *pan dulce,* the sweet breakfast breads of Spain. They are truly international. I have chosen breads that are either indigenous or colonial, like a delicious banana bread from Guatemala, *Pan de Banano*; Mexico's bread rolls, *Bolillos*; Venezuela's corn pancakes, *Cachapas de Jojoto*; and Paraguay's rich and splendid corn bread, *Sopa Paraguaya.* They are not hard to make and add an authentic and different touch to a Latin American meal.

There were few indigenous desserts; people mostly finished a meal with fresh fruits. Some, like pineapple, papaya, the *zapotes* and *anonas,* and *tuna* (fruit of the *nopal* cactus), were unknown to Europe at the time. The Aztecs stuffed tamales with strawberries, that universal fruit; honey was used as a sweetening by both Mayas and Aztecs; and the Incas made desserts from squash and sweet potatoes, but they lacked wheat flour, butter, cream, and sugar to make the pies, puddings, and rich desserts of

Europe. It was not until the colonial period and the introduction of sugar cane that desserts began to flourish. Spanish nuns in Peru and Mexico, especially in Puebla, made colonial desserts famous. In Brazil, primarily in Bahia, cooks in the great houses of the sugar plantations created a whole new world of cakes and sweet things for desserts. They drew on the Portuguese tradition of using lots of egg yolks and sugar. Out of this huge array I have chosen a small selection of favorites which I think are suited to the modern palate.

BREADS

Sopa Paraguaya   PARAGUAY
Paraguayan Corn Bread

This is a wonderfully hearty well-flavored corn bread with two kinds of cheese to enrich it and onions sautéed in butter to add to the flavor. It is traditionally served with *So'O-Yosopy* (Beef Soup) and with grilled steaks, but is fine with any meat or poultry dish, or by itself.

8 tablespoons (½ cup) butter
2 medium onions, finely chopped
½ pound farmer or cottage cheese
½ pound Münster cheese, grated
2 cups cornmeal
2 cups grated corn kernels, or a
*   1-pound can cream-style*
*   sweet corn*

1 teaspoon salt, preferably coarse
1 cup milk
6 eggs, separated

Grease a baking tin, about 10 by 13 inches, and sprinkle with 1 tablespoon flour. Shake to remove the excess.

In a skillet heat 4 tablespoons of the butter and sauté the onions until they are softened. Set aside. Cream the remaining 4 tablespoons of butter and add to the farmer or cottage cheese, blending thoroughly. Add the Münster cheese and the onions. In another bowl combine the cornmeal, corn, salt, and milk, and mix thoroughly. Combine the corn mixture with the cheese mixture, blending thoroughly.

Beat the egg whites until they form soft peaks and beat the yolks separately. Combine the two and stir them into the cornmeal and cheese mixture. Pour the batter into the baking tin. Bake in a preheated hot (400° F.) oven for 45 minutes, or until a cake tester comes out clean.

A pinch of ground aniseed may be added to the mixture, if liked. Another pleasant variation is to cut enough of the Münster into tiny cubes to measure ½ cup and stir this into the batter at the last moment, if liked. This gives a slightly different texture to the finished bread.

Pan de Banano   GUATEMALA
Banana Bread

This easy-to-make banana bread is lovely for a snack. Spread with honey or topped with fresh fruit, it can be dressed up with cream or ice cream to make an attractive dessert.

Makes one 9-inch loaf

¼ *pound (½ cup) butter*
½ *cup sugar*
1 *pound ripe bananas (2 or 3 large)*
½ *teaspoon salt*
1 *teaspoon ground cinnamon*

1 *tablespoon lemon juice*
1 *egg, well beaten*
1½ *cups all-purpose flour*
2 *teaspoons baking powder*

Soften the butter at room temperature and cream it with the sugar in a mixing bowl until light and fluffy. Mash the bananas and add to the butter and sugar mixture. Add the salt, cinnamon, lemon juice, and egg. Sift the flour with the baking powder and fold it into the liquid mixture. Pour the batter into a greased (9- by 5-inch) loaf pan. Bake in a preheated moderate (350° F.) oven for 1 hour, or until a cake tester comes out clean. Serve with honey as a cake bread, or as a pudding with cream or ice cream.

Tortillas   MEXICO
Makes about eighteen 4-inch tortillas

To make tortillas, see page 44.

Tortillas that are served instead of bread with Mexican meals may be made slightly larger, 5 or 6 inches across, though the 4-inch ones are perfectly acceptable. When they are eaten in this way, or made into soft tacos (stuffed, rolled tortillas), they should be brought to the table wrapped in a napkin, then placed in a small woven reed or straw basket. The napkin is always folded back over the tortillas when one is taken so as to keep them warm and soft. In Mexico no one ever takes the top tortilla of the stack, always the second or third to be sure of getting a good hot one. Leftover tortillas are never wasted, as they are the prime ingredient of *chilaquiles*, fried strips of day-old tortilla baked in a chili sauce. They are also used as a garnish in certain soups.

Arepas
Corn Bread

VENEZUELA AND COLOMBIA

The *Arepas* of Venezuela and Colombia are made from corn processed into flour in the same way as the flour for Mexican corn tortillas, but the *arepa* is not a flexible pancake like the tortilla. It looks rather like a pure white round bread roll. The outside is crisp, the inside doughy. In Caracas I have had *Arepas* served with cream cheese as an unusual first course. The doughy inside is pulled out of the *arepa* and it is then filled with the delicious local runny cream cheese. French *crème fraîche* (page 9) is a good substitute, as it is very like the Caracas cream cheese. I've found that cream cheese softened at room temperature and mashed with a little heavy cream also serves nicely as a substitute for the Venezuelan original. Easy to make and taking little time, *Arepas* make a pleasant change from everyday bread and are especially good with Venezuelan dishes. When eaten as bread, the doughy inside is split open, pulled out with the fingers, and the remaining shell is buttered, or the *Arepas* are simply split and buttered. I often top the butter with a little cream cheese as I find the combination irresistible.

Makes 8 to 10

2 cups corn flour for Arepas (see
    page 4)

1 teaspoon salt
2 cups water, about

In a bowl mix the *arepa* flour with the salt. Stir in the water to make a stiffish dough. Add a little more if necessary. Let the dough stand for 5 minutes, then form into balls flattened slightly to 3 inches across and about ½ inch thick. Cook on a heavy, lightly greased griddle over moderate heat for 5 minutes a side, then bake in a preheated moderate (350° F.) oven for 20 to 30 minutes, turning them two or three times during cooking.

They are done when they sound hollow when tapped. Serve hot. Traditionally they are wrapped in a napkin and served in a straw basket.

Variation: For *Arepas de Queso* (Corn Bread with Cheese), add 1 cup finely chopped or crumbled *queso fresco* or *queso blanco* (Spanish fresh cheese), or grated Münster cheese.

Variation: For *Arepas de Chicharrones* (Corn Bread with Pork Rinds), add 1 cup *chicharrones* (fried pork rinds), crumbled.

Variation: For *Arepas Santanderinas* (Corn Bread, Santander Style), mix 2 tablespoons lard into the flour before adding the water, working it in thoroughly with your fingers, then make as usual.

Variation: For *Arepas Fritas* (Fried Corn Bread), mix 1 cup grated cheese with the flour. Beat an egg yolk with the water and salt, and mix it with the flour and cheese, kneading the dough thoroughly (about 5 minutes). Roll out into thin circles about 4 inches in diameter and fry in lard or oil until lightly browned on both sides. These may be made smaller, about 1½ inches in diameter, and served as an accompaniment to drinks.

Variation: For *Arepas Fritas Infladas* (Puffed Fried Corn Bread), add to the dough 1 cup grated cheese, ½ cup all-purpose flour, ¼ teaspoon ground anise, and 1 tablespoon sugar, preferably brown. Knead the dough until it is very smooth, about 5 minutes. Form it into small balls and roll them out on a lightly floured board to make thin 3-inch pancakes. Deep fry in hot oil. They should puff up. Serve immediately. I find it easier to lift them with a slotted spoon as they are very soft.

Cachapas de Jojoto   VENEZUELA
Corn Pancakes

These are pleasant eaten instead of bread with a meal. Miniaturized (about 1½ inches across) and wrapped round a piece of Spanish fresh cheese, (*queso fresco* or *queso blanco*), or Münster, they make an attractive cocktail nibble.

Makes about 12

1½ cups corn kernels, if frozen
    thoroughly defrosted
½ cup heavy cream
1 egg
3 tablespoons all-purpose flour

¼ teaspoon sugar
½ teaspoon salt
2 teaspoons butter, melted
Butter for frying

Put all the ingredients into a blender or food processor and mix until smooth. Grease a skillet or omelet pan by rubbing a piece of crumbled wax paper over a stick of butter, then rubbing the pan with the paper. Repeat this process for each pancake. Drop the mixture, 2 tablespoons at a time, into the skillet and fry until lightly browned on both sides, turning once. Serve hot.

Variation: For *Cachapas de Hojas* (Corn Mixture Steamed in Leaves), put 2 tablespoons of the corn mixture into the center of a dry corn husk and fold it up into a package. Arrange the corn husks in a steamer, and steam, covered, over boiling water until firm, about 30 minutes. *Cachapas de Budare* (Corn Mixture in Banana Leaves) are made by stuffing a piece of banana leaf with the corn mixture, folding the leaf into a package, and cooking it over moderate heat on a griddle, turning it twice, then standing it at the side of the griddle to finish cooking. Ideally the *Cachapas* should be baked on a *budare*, a special Venezuelan griddle, and finished at the back of a wood-burning stove. It is possible to improvise using aluminum foil and a heavy griddle, setting both over very low heat on top of two asbestos mats. Faced with the difficulty of getting fresh banana leaves, I have contented myself with *Cachapas de Jojoto*, which are extremely good and present no difficulties at all.

Bolillos   MEXICO
Mexican Bread Rolls

These are the marvelous *petits pains* of Mexico, acquired during the short, unhappy reign of Maximilian and Carlota, wished on the Mexicans by Napoleon III and vigorously resisted by the infant republic. Mexico preferred to remain independent but was in no way reluctant to accept the world's best bread — French bread. To this day I find that *Bolillos*, the spindle-shaped rolls that are sold fresh twice a day in the bakeries of Mexico, are equaled only by bread in France. I find I can make a good approximation of them with little trouble if I get a good, hard wheat flour.

Makes 18

1 package (¼ ounce) active dry   5 cups sifted bread flour*
    yeast, or ½ ounce fresh yeast   Butter for the bowl
1 ½ teaspoons salt

*Bread flour is one with a higher mixture of hard wheat. All-purpose flour may be substituted.

Put the yeast into a large bowl and soften it in ¼ cup lukewarm water. When it has liquefied completely, stir in 1¾ cups lukewarm water and the salt, and stir to mix. Gradually mix in the flour to make a dough that comes away from the sides of the bowl with a little stickiness. Knead the dough on a lightly floured board for 10 minutes, or until it is smooth and elastic and has lost all its stickiness. Put the dough in a buttered bowl, cover it with a clean cloth, and leave it to rise in a warm place until it has doubled in bulk, about 2 hours.

The oven with just the pilot light lit is a good place to put the dough to rise in cold weather. This is a slow-rising dough and it is important to allow it enough time.

At the end of this time punch the dough down, cover it, and let it rise a second time until again doubled in bulk, about 1 hour. Turn it out onto a lightly floured board and knead it for about 5 minutes. Divide the dough in half. Roll each piece out into an oblong, about 18 inches by 6 inches. Roll each piece up like a jelly roll. Cut each roll into 9 slices, making 18 in all. Pinch the ends of each slice to form a spindle shape and arrange on a buttered baking sheet. Cover and let the rolls rise until they have doubled in bulk, about 1 hour. Brush them lightly with water and bake in a preheated hot (400° F.) oven for about 30 minutes, or until they are golden brown.

DESSERTS

Creme de Abacate   BRAZIL
Avocado Cream

Apart from avocado ice cream, which I confess I do not care for, this is the only dessert using avocados that I have come across. It was part of our kitchen repertoire during the years we lived in Jamaica, and later on I was puzzled by this as it was so clearly not a Jamaican dish. The mystery was solved by my mother, who told me it had been given her by the Brazilian lady who was the previous tenant of the house we rented — a sort of parting gift.

Serves 6

3 large, ripe avocados, chilled
4 tablespoons fresh lime juice
6 tablespoons superfine sugar

Halve the avocados, remove the pits, and mash them in their shells with a fork. Turn them out into a bowl and mash until smooth with the lime juice and sugar. Pile the mixture into glass serving dishes and garnish, if liked, with a little grated lime peel or a slice of lime.

Mazamorra Morada   PERU
Peruvian Fruit Compote

Mazamorra is a dish made with cornstarch and sugar or honey. This *Mazamorra* is made with *maíz morado*, the purple corn of Peru that gives off a most beautiful deep purple color when it is simmered in water. It has a delicate, flowery, lemony taste. Purple corn is not readily available outside Peru but fortunately the Hopi Indians grow it in Arizona and it can be ordered by mail. However, I have found I can get the same lovely color by using blackberries, and, by orchestrating the flavors a little differently, the same flavor may be obtained as well. This is a luscious and refreshing dessert, lovely for a summer buffet.

Serves 8 to 10

½ pound purple corn kernels
6 cups water
2 cups sugar
6 cloves
A 3-inch piece of stick cinnamon
½ small pineapple, peeled, cored, and cubed
2 quinces, peeled and sliced
2 pears, peeled and sliced

2 peaches, pitted, peeled, and sliced
1 pound cherries, pitted
½ pound dried apricots, halved
½ pound dried peaches, quartered
4 tablespoons cornstarch
Juice of 2 lemons, about 6 tablespoons
Ground cinnamon (optional)

Put the purple corn kernels into a saucepan with the water, bring to a boil, and simmer until the corn is cooked, about 30 minutes, and the water is a deep purple. Strain and discard the corn. Measure the liquid and add more water to make 6 cups, if necessary. Return the purple water to the saucepan and add the sugar, cloves, cinnamon stick, pineapple, quinces, pears, peaches, cherries, dried apricots, and dried peaches. Bring the liquid to a simmer, cover the saucepan, and cook gently over low heat until the fruit is tender, about 15 minutes. Remove and discard the cloves and cinnamon. Dissolve the cornstarch in ¼ cup water and stir it into the fruit mixture. Cook until the liquid is thickened, then stir in the lemon juice. Chill the compote and serve it sprinkled with a little cinnamon, if liked.

Variation: Cook the fruit in plain water. Add 2 apples, peeled and sliced, and ½ pound blackberries to the other fruit, otherwise make the dish in the same way.

Flan de Piña   COLOMBIA
Pineapple Custard

This is a very old family recipe given to me by my friend Cecilia Blanco de Mendoza, an authority on traditional Colombian cooking.

Serves 6

¼ cup sugar	1 cup sugar
1 cup unsweetened pineapple juice	4 eggs

In the top of a double boiler (6½-cup size) over boiling water melt the ¼ cup sugar over moderate heat, stirring constantly, until it has melted and is a rich caramel color. Dip the bottom of the container into cold water for a second or two, then turn the mold so that the caramel coats sides as well as bottom. Set aside.

In a saucepan combine the pineapple juice and 1 cup sugar and cook, stirring, until the liquid is reduced to half and is quite thick. Cool the syrup. Beat the eggs until they are thick and lemon-colored. Pour the syrup into the eggs in a thin, slow stream, beating all the time. Pour the mixture into the prepared caramelized container. On the top of the stove cook the custard, covered, over barely simmering water for about 2 hours, or until it is set. Cool and refrigerate until ready to serve. Before serving unmold by running a knife between the custard and the container, then place a serving dish over the mold and invert quickly.

Dulce de Piña con Arracacha   COLOMBIA
Arracacha and Pineapple Dessert

This is an unusual use of a root vegetable. The leggy vegetable (page 4) can be found in tropical markets and is well worth looking for. It has a taste reminiscent of celery, which marries well with the pineapple juice it is simmered with. The sweet has a fresh, invigorating flavor.

Serves 4 to 6

1 ½ pounds apio
4 cups unsweetened pineapple
 juice

1 cup sugar, or more to taste

Peel and slice the *apio* and put it on to cook in a saucepan with cold water
to cover. Simmer, covered, until it is tender, about 30 minutes. Drain and
mash. Add the pineapple juice and the sugar and cook the mixture, uncovered, over low heat, stirring frequently, until it forms a thick paste and the
bottom of the saucepan can be seen when the spoon is drawn across it.
Transfer to a dessert dish and chill. Serve by itself, or with whipped cream
or ice cream.

Mousse de Castanhas de Caju e Chocolate

BRAZIL

Cashew Nut and Chocolate Mousse

Serves 6 to 8

2 ounces (2 squares) unsweetened
 chocolate
½ cup sugar
5 egg yolks
1 cup roasted cashew nuts, finely
 ground
1 cup heavy cream
5 egg whites

Break the chocolate into small pieces and put with 2 to 3 tablespoons of
water into the top of a double boiler over boiling water. Add the sugar and
stir until the chocolate is melted and the sugar dissolved. Remove the pan
from the heat and beat in the egg yolks, one at a time, beating well after
each addition. Stir in the ground cashew nuts. Beat the cream until it
stands in firm peaks and fold it into the chocolate mixture. Beat the egg
whites until they stand in firm peaks and fold into the chocolate mixture,
lightly but thoroughly. Pour into a 1-quart soufflé dish and refrigerate
overnight or for several hours. Serve, if liked, with sweetened whipped
cream.

Capirotada   MEXICO
Bread Pudding

This is a very special bread pudding, a great favorite in Mexico during Lent
and a marvelous dessert at any time, especially for a holiday buffet. I make
my *Capirotada* from a recipe given me by my husband's grandmother, and
I use brown sugar flavored with cinnamon and cloves for the syrup in
which it is drenched before baking. A good friend, the writer Elizabeth
Borton de Treviño, sent me a grandly extravagant recipe for the syrup,
which she was given by a friend, Señora Estela Santos Coy de Cobo, who
had it from her grandmother. It is a blend of disparate flavors — orange rind,
tomato, onion, cloves, green or red pepper — which one would never expect
to work, yet work it does, lusciously.

Serves 6 to 8

FOR THE SYRUP

*2 cups piloncillo or brown sugar,
    firmly packed*
A 2-inch piece of stick cinnamon
1 small onion, stuck with 3 cloves
*1 medium red or green bell pepper,
    seeded and halved*
*Peel from 1 medium orange,
    shredded*

*½ cup fresh coriander (cilantro),
    chopped*
*1 small tomato, peeled, seeded,
    and chopped*
4 cups water

Combine all the ingredients in a saucepan, bring to a boil, reduce the heat,
and simmer, partially covered, for 30 minutes. Allow to cool a little. Strain,
discard the solids, and set the syrup aside.

FOR THE PUDDING

Butter
*6 cups of ½-inch cubes toasted
    French or firm white bread*
*3 apples, peeled, cored, and thinly
    sliced*

1 cup raisins
1 cup chopped blanched almonds
*½ pound Münster, Monterey Jack,
    cheddar, or similar cheese,
    coarsely chopped*

Butter a 2-quart ovenproof casserole or soufflé dish and make a layer of
cubes of toast. Add a layer of apple slices, raisins, almonds, and cheese.
Repeat until all the ingredients are used up. Pour the syrup over the dish.
Bake in a preheated moderate (350° F.) oven for 45 minutes, or until heated
through. Serve hot.

Variation: For a slightly richer dish sauté the bread cubes in ½ cup vegetable oil or butter.

Variation: For a simpler syrup simmer 2 cups brown sugar with a 2-inch piece of stick cinnamon, 2 cloves, and 4 cups water to make a light syrup. Remove the cinnamon and cloves before using.

Dulce de Queso
Cheese Sweet

COLOMBIA

Serves 4 to 6

1 pound mozzarella cheese, about
2 cups dark brown sugar

1 cup water
A 2-inch piece of stick cinnamon

Let the cheese come to room temperature. Using a very sharp knife, cut the cheese horizontally into ¼-inch slices and arrange them in a shallow Pyrex dish. In a small saucepan combine the sugar, water, and cinnamon, and bring to a boil, stirring to dissolve the sugar. Boil for 5 minutes without stirring. Pour the syrup over the cheese and serve immediately. For a softer cheese, put the prepared dish in a preheated 350° F. oven for 5 minutes.

✳ Coconut Desserts

Coconut is used a great deal in Latin American desserts. Since fresh coconuts are available in tropical markets and supermarkets all year, I prefer to use them rather than packaged coconut. Brazilian cooks have worked out an excellent method of getting the coconut out of the shell, and a food processor makes the rest of the work easy (see page 7).

Cocada
Coconut Custard

MEXICO

Serves 6

1½ cups sugar
A 2-inch piece of stick cinnamon
Liquid from a medium-sized
     coconut, ½ cup, about
2 cups grated coconut (page 7)

3 cups milk
4 whole eggs, lightly beaten
2 tablespoons butter, or ½ cup
     toasted slivered almonds

In a saucepan combine the sugar, cinnamon stick, and coconut water. Stir the mixture over low heat until the sugar is dissolved. Add the coconut and continue to cook the mixture, stirring, until the coconut is transparent, about 5 minutes. Remove and discard the cinnamon stick. Stir in the milk, mixing thoroughly. Simmer, over moderate heat, stirring from time to time, until the mixture has thickened and a spoon drawn across the bottom leaves a clean path. Pour ½ cup of the mixture into the eggs, beating constantly with a whisk. Pour the egg mixture back into the saucepan and cook, stirring constantly, over low heat until it has thickened. Do not let it boil. Remove from the heat and pour into a flameproof serving dish (a 1-quart soufflé dish is fine), cool, then refrigerate for several hours. Just before serving, dot the pudding with the butter, and put it under the broiler until the top is lightly browned; or garnish with the slivered almonds.

Variation: For *Dulce de Coco* (Coconut Sweet) from Colombia, soak ¾ cup raisins in hot water for 15 minutes, drain, and put into a heavy saucepan with 4 cups grated coconut, the coconut water made up to 1 cup with water, 4 tablespoons lemon juice, 1½ cups sugar, and a 3-inch piece of stick cinnamon. Bring to a boil, reduce the heat, and simmer until the syrup forms a thread when tested in cold water. Remove and discard the cinnamon stick. Beat 3 egg yolks in a bowl until they are thick and lemon-colored. Beat in 3 tablespoons of the coconut syrup, a tablespoon at a time. Gradually pour the yolk mixture into the coconut mixture and cook over low heat, stirring constantly, for 5 minutes without letting it boil. Cool and refrigerate several hours before serving. Serves 6.

Variation: *Doce de Leite Baiana* (Bahian Style Coconut and Milk Pudding) is a simpler, but still delicious, version of coconut custard. Combine 4 cups finely grated fresh coconut with 4 cups milk and 2¼ cups firmly packed light brown sugar in a heavy saucepan and cook over moderate heat until the mixture is thick and has the consistency of custard. Stir the mixture from time to time with a wooden spoon until it begins to thicken, then stir constantly. Transfer the pudding to a serving dish and serve at room temperature. Serves 6 to 8.

Variation: Writer and friend Elizabeth Borton de Treviño gave me this recipe, given her by the Acapulco cook of the Limantour family at their *quinta* Los Bichitos. It needs less watching than top-of-the-stove versions and has a rather denser texture. For this *Cocada*, simmer 3 cups milk with 1½ cups sugar in an uncovered saucepan for 20 minutes, or until the mixture is slightly thickened. Let it cool. Lightly beat 6 eggs, then beat them into the milk mixture. Stir in ½ teaspoon almond extract and 3 cups freshly grated coconut. Pour into a buttered Pyrex dish. Set in a pan of water so that the water comes 2 inches up the side and bake in a preheated moderate (350° F.) oven for 1½ hours, or until a cake tester comes out clean. Cool and chill before serving. Serves 6 to 8.

Variation: *Pudim de Côco* (Coconut Pudding) from Brazil is a rather richer version of coconut custard. Combine 1 cup sugar with ⅓ cup water in a small saucepan and simmer until it spins a thread (234° F. on a candy thermometer). Remove from the heat and stir in 4 tablespoons (¼ cup) butter. Cool. Stir in 2 cups grated coconut. Thoroughly beat 5 egg yolks until they are very light, and fold into the coconut mixture. Pour into a buttered 3-cup baking dish or soufflé dish, set in a pan of water so that the water extends 2 inches up the side, and bake in a preheated moderate (350° F.) oven for 1 to 1½ hours, or until a cake tester comes out clean. Serve at room temperature. Traditionally the pudding is served with cheese. Use Spanish fresh cheese (*queso fresco* or *queso blanco*), Münster, or similar cheese. Serves 6.

Manjar de Coco com Môlho de Ameixas

BRAZIL

Coconut Blancmange with Prune Sauce

Serves 6

FOR THE BLANCMANGE

4 cups finely grated fresh coconut
4 cups milk

Sugar to taste
4 tablespoons cornstarch

In a saucepan combine the coconut and milk and bring to a simmer. Remove from the heat and steep for 30 minutes. Strain the liquid through a cheesecloth-lined sieve into a bowl, squeezing the cloth to extract all the liquid. There should be 4 cups. If necessary add a little milk to make up the quantity. Season with sugar to taste. Rinse out and dry the saucepan. Mix a little of the coconut milk with the cornstarch and stir it into the rest of the milk. Pour the mixture into the saucepan and cook, stirring constantly with a wooden spoon, over moderate heat until it is smooth and thick, about 5 minutes. Pour it into a 1-quart mold rinsed out with cold water and refrigerate until set. Unmold onto a serving plate and surround with the prune sauce.

FOR THE SAUCE

½ pound, about 24, pitted prunes *1 ½ cups sugar*
¾ cup tawny port *½ cup water*

Put the prunes into a bowl with the port and let them macerate for 30 minutes. In a medium saucepan combine the sugar and water. Simmer for 5 minutes to make a fairly heavy syrup. Add the prunes and port and simmer for 5 minutes longer. Cool, chill, and use to garnish the *Manjar de Coco.*

Quindins de Yáyá
Coconut Cupcake Dessert

BRAZIL

Makes 24

2 cups freshly grated coconut
2 tablespoons softened butter
1 ½ cups light brown sugar
8 large egg yolks
1 egg white, well beaten
Butter
1 cup sifted all-purpose flour
    (optional)

In a large bowl mix together the coconut, butter, and sugar, beating to mix thoroughly. One by one beat in the egg yolks, beating thoroughly after each addition. Fold in the egg white beaten until stiff peaks form. Some cooks add a little flour, in which case beat in the flour after all the other ingredients have been combined. The addition of flour gives a lighter, more cakelike texture. Butter 24 muffin tins. Pour the mixture into the tins and stand them in a baking pan with hot water to reach about halfway up the sides of the tins. Bake in a preheated moderate (350° F.) oven for about 45 minutes, or until a toothpick inserted into the cakes comes out clean.

Some modern cooks use a 9- or 10-inch pie plate instead of individual muffin tins. The cooking time should be increased to 1½ or 2 hours, or until a toothpick inserted into the cake comes out clean.

✳ Pumpkin and Squash Desserts

Torta de Zapallo
Pumpkin Cake

ECUADOR

Calabaza (West Indian pumpkin), which is used so much all over Latin America as a vegetable and in soups and stews, is also used in some delectable puddings, cakes, and fritters.

Serves 8

1 ½ pounds peeled and cubed
    West Indian pumpkin
    (calabaza) or any winter
    squash, or use two 12-ounce
    packages cooked, frozen
    squash
½ teaspoon cinnamon

1 cup sugar
½ cup heavy cream
2 tablespoons butter
2 ounces dark rum
1 cup seedless raisins
1 cup grated Münster cheese
3 large eggs, well beaten

Cook the squash in water to cover until tender, about 15 minutes. Drain thoroughly. If using frozen squash, simply thaw it. Put the squash in a saucepan and stir in the cinnamon, sugar, heavy cream, and 1 tablespoon of the butter. Mash the squash and cook it over low heat until the sugar has dissolved and the mixture is fairly firm, not watery. Remove from the heat and allow to cool. Add all the remaining ingredients, except the reserved butter. Using the butter, grease a 2-quart soufflé dish and pour in the squash mixture. Bake in a preheated moderate (350° F.) oven until the cake is firm to the touch, about 1 hour. An ounce of rum may be poured over the cake while it is still hot, if liked. Serve as a pudding from the soufflé dish plain, or with whipped or sour cream.

Pudim de Abóbora
Pumpkin Pudding

BRAZIL

Serves 6

4 large eggs
½ teaspoon salt
½ cup light brown sugar
½ teaspoon ground ginger

¼ teaspoon ground cinnamon
¼ teaspoon ground cloves
¼ teaspoon ground nutmeg

1 ½ cups cooked mashed winter
    squash or, preferably, West
    Indian pumpkin (calabaza)

1 cup evaporated milk or light
    cream
Butter for the mold

Break the eggs into a large bowl and beat them lightly. Beat in the salt, brown sugar, ginger, cinnamon, cloves, nutmeg, squash, and evaporated milk or cream. Butter a 1-quart mold or pudding basin and pour in the custard. Set it in a pan of hot water so that the water extends 2 inches up the side and bake in a preheated moderate (350° F.) oven until a toothpick inserted into the custard comes out clean, about 1½ hours.

Picarones
Sweet Fritters

PERU

Serves 8 to 12

½ pound West Indian pumpkin
    (calabaza) or any winter
    squash, peeled and sliced
½ pound sweet potato, preferably
    white sweet potato (boniato),
    peeled and sliced
1 teaspoon salt

¼ teaspoon ground aniseed
4 cups all-purpose flour, sifted
1 envelope (¼ ounce) yeast
Vegetable oil for deep frying

Cook the pumpkin or squash and sweet potato in water to cover until they are tender. Drain the vegetables, mash them, and force them through a sieve. Mix in the salt, aniseed, and flour. Soften the yeast in ¼ cup of lukewarm water and mix it into the flour to make a fairly firm dough, adding a little more water if necessary, though the pumpkin and sweet potato will probably supply enough moisture. Knead the dough until it is smooth and satiny, about 5 minutes. Place it in a bowl, cover with a cloth, and allow to stand in a warm, draft-free place for 2 or 3 hours, or until it has doubled in bulk. Pull off pieces of dough by tablespoons and shape them into rings. Deep fry them in hot oil (370° F.) until they are browned on both sides. Drain on paper towels and serve with *Miel de Chancaca* (Sugar Syrup).

MIEL DE CHANCACA (Sugar Syrup)

2 cups dark brown sugar
1 cup sugar
2 cups water

1 piece lemon peel
1 piece orange peel

Combine all the ingredients in a saucepan and simmer until the syrup is quite thick. Remove and discard the orange and lemon peel. Serve as a dipping sauce with the *Picarones.*

Pristiños

Pumpkin Fritters

Serves 6

2 cups all-purpose flour
1 teaspoon baking powder
1 teaspoon salt
2 tablespoons grated Parmesan
    cheese

¼ pound (½ cup) butter, softened
    at room temperature
1 cup cooked, mashed West
    Indian pumpkin (calabaza)
Oil or lard for deep frying

Sift the flour, baking powder, and salt into a bowl. Add the cheese. Work the butter into the mixture with your fingers, then the pumpkin with a fork. The pumpkin should supply enough moisture to make a soft but not sticky dough. Turn the dough onto a floured board and roll out to a ½-inch thickness. Cut it into strips 1 inch wide and 6 inches long. Form each strip into a ring, pinching the ends lightly together. Deep fry in hot oil or lard (350° F. to 365° F.) until golden brown on all sides. Drain on paper towels and serve with cinnamon syrup.

CINNAMON SYRUP

2 cups dark brown sugar, firmly
    packed

A 1-inch piece of stick cinnamon

In a saucepan combine the sugar with 1 cup water and the cinnamon stick. Stir the mixture to dissolve the sugar and simmer over moderate heat for 5 minutes. Discard the cinnamon stick.

✳ Milk Pudding

There is a dessert made from milk simmered with sugar until it is thick that is popular throughout Latin America. It has a variety of names — *Manjar Blanco, Natillas Piuranas, Arequipe, Dulce de Leche, Cajeta de Celaya* — and the cooking technique varies slightly from country to country. I think milk pudding is about the most practical translation. Making this can be time-consuming, about 1½ hours, if one stands at the stove and conscientiously stirs the mixture with a wooden spoon, but I have found that if the heat is kept low one can make the pudding, stirring from time to time, while doing other things in the kitchen. Once the mixture begins to thicken, however, it does need constant stirring or the texture suffers and is grainy instead of smooth. But this is only in the last 5 minutes or so. Everyone in Latin America knows the *truco*, or trick, of boiling an un-opened can of sweetened condensed milk until it caramelizes, but most cooks prefer the results of the longer method. However, there is a very quick Colombian version using sweetened condensed milk and evaporated milk that is delicious, and a nice compromise. It is amazing how great a difference in taste and texture is produced by small differences in pro-portions and cooking methods for this most delicate of desserts.

Natillas Piuranas
Brown Sugar Pudding

PERU

Ideally this should be made with goat's milk but I have found that using a mixture of milk and cream or evaporated milk gives a very good result.

Serves 4 to 6

2 cups dark brown sugar
¼ cup water
3 cups milk
1 cup light cream or evaporated
    milk

½ teaspoon baking soda
½ cup finely ground walnuts

In a large, heavy saucepan combine the brown sugar and the water and cook over low heat, stirring constantly with a wooden spoon, until the sugar is dissolved. In another saucepan combine the milk, light cream or evaporated milk, and the baking soda. Stir to mix and bring almost to a boil over fairly high heat. Pour into the dissolved sugar, stirring to mix thoroughly, and cook, stirring frequently, until the mixture is thick and caramel-colored and the bottom of the pan can be seen when the spoon is drawn across it. Stir in the walnuts, mixing well. It will take about 1 hour. Serve either chilled or at room temperature.

Manjar Blanco
Milk Pudding

CHILE

Serves 6

8 cups milk
2 ½ cups sugar

A 2-inch piece of vanilla bean

In a heavy saucepan combine all the ingredients and bring to a simmer. Cook, stirring from time to time, over low heat until the mixture begins to thicken. Remove the piece of vanilla bean. Simmer, stirring constantly with a wooden spoon, until the mixture is thick enough so the bottom of the pan can be seen when the spoon is drawn across it. It will take about an hour. Do not overcook or the pudding will turn into candy. Turn into a serving bowl and serve either slightly chilled or at room temperature.

Variation: For *Dulce de Leche* (Milk Sweet or Dessert) from Paraguay, combine 10 cups milk, 1 teaspoon vanilla essence, ½ teaspoon baking soda, and 2 cups sugar in a saucepan and stir from time to time, off the heat, until the sugar is dissolved. Bring to a simmer and cook over very low heat, to prevent the milk from boiling over, stirring occasionally with a wooden spoon until the mixture is thick and caramel-colored. When the mixture begins to thicken, stir constantly. The pudding is ready when the bottom of the saucepan can be seen when the spoon is drawn across it, or when a spoonful on a plate no longer runs but retains its shape. The pudding may be varied by increasing the amount of sugar to 3 cups or by increasing the amount of milk to 12 cups. Serves 6 to 8.

Variation: For *Arequipe* (Milk Pudding) from Colombia, there is a recipe almost identical to the one above from Paraguay but using 12 cups milk to 4 cups sugar.

Variation: There is another *Arequipe* that is very successful and a splendid shortcut. Put 2 cups evaporated milk and 2 cups sweetened condensed milk into a heavy saucepan, stir to mix thoroughly, bring to a simmer, and cook, stirring constantly, until the mixture is thick and golden and the bottom of the pan can be seen when the spoon is drawn across it. Serve with wedges of cheese, preferably Spanish fresh cheese (*queso fresco* or *queso blanco*), or with Münster, Edam, or Gouda.

Variation: For *Dulce de Leche Con Huevos* (Milk Sweet with Eggs), simmer 8 cups of milk with 2 cups sugar, a vanilla bean, and a 2-inch piece of stick cinnamon until the mixture begins to thicken. Remove the vanilla bean and cinnamon stick. When the pudding is thick, remove from the heat and stir in 4 well-beaten egg yolks. Return the pudding to the heat and cook, stirring, for 2 minutes. Remove from the heat. Beat 4 egg whites until they stand in peaks and add to the pudding, off the heat. Return the pudding to the heat and cook, stirring constantly, until it is again thick. Off the heat beat the pudding until it is cool. Turn into a dessert dish and chill until ready to serve. Serves 6 to 8.

Variation: The best milk puddings of Mexico come from the rich mining and farming state of Guanajuato. The most famous of them is *Cajeta de Celaya*, which means literally box from the town of Celaya and refers to the small wooden boxes in which the sweet is packaged. Put 3 cups each cow's and goat's milk, mixed with ½ teaspoon baking soda and 2 teaspoons cornstarch, in a heavy saucepan with 2 cups sugar and a fig leaf, if available, and simmer the mixture in the usual way until thick. Discard the fig leaf and pour the pudding into a serving bowl. Serve chilled or at room temperature. Goat's milk is sometimes available in health or specialty stores.

For *Cajeta Envinada* (Milk Pudding with Wine), stir ½ cup sherry, muscatel, or Madeira into the finished sweet. For *Cajeta de Leche Quemada* (Pudding of Burned Milk), the sugar is caramelized before the milk is added. To do this the sugar is put into a heavy saucepan over low heat and stirred constantly with a wooden spoon until it melts and turns coffee color. The milk should be added little by little, off the heat, and stirred well to mix. The pudding is then cooked in the usual way. It is a deep, rich amber color. There is a little *truco* here that some cooks use — they substitute light brown sugar for white sugar. For *Cajeta de Almendra Envinada* (Milk Pudding with Almonds and Wine), add ¼ cup ground almonds and ½ cup sherry, muscatel, or Madeira. Serve the pudding by itself, or with ice cream or slices of pound cake or cookies. Serves 6.

Chongos Zamoranos   MEXICO
Custard Squares in Syrup

This is a different kind of milk pudding, and as great a favorite in Mexican households today as it was in colonial times. There are many versions. This one from Zamora in Michoacán is the one I like best. *Chongo* means a tuft of hair tied on top of the head — a very fanciful way to describe this dessert.

Serves 8

2 quarts (8 cups) milk
4 egg yolks, lightly beaten
4 rennet tablets

1 ½ cups sugar
A 2-inch piece of stick cinnamon

Heat the milk to lukewarm. Off the heat, beat in the egg yolks. Pour the mixture into a deep, straight-sided flameproof dish about 8 inches by 10 inches. Dissolve the rennet tablets in ¼ cup cold water and add to the milk mixture. Let the mixture stand in a warm place until it is set, about 1 hour. Using a sharp knife cut it into 2-inch squares disturbing it as little as possible. Sprinkle with the sugar. Break up the cinnamon stick and sprinkle the bits over the junket. Place over the lowest possible heat, using an asbestos mat if necessary to keep the liquid below simmering point, for about 2 hours. The sugar and the whey from the junket will form a thick syrup. Chills before serving.

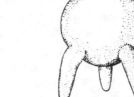

Quimbolitos
Steamed Puddings

ECUADOR

Serves 6

4 tablespoons (¼ cup) butter
6 tablespoons sugar
2 eggs, well beaten
¼ cup milk
½ cup all-purpose flour

½ cup cornstarch
2 teaspoons baking powder
½ cup grated Parmesan cheese
⅓ cup seedless raisins
2 tablespoons cognac or light rum

Soften the butter at room temperature. In a bowl cream together the butter and sugar until the mixture is light and fluffy. Add the eggs mixed with the milk. Sift together the flour, cornstarch, and baking powder, and stir into the batter mixture. Stir in the cheese, raisins, and cognac or rum.

Cut either kitchen parchment or aluminum foil into six 8- by 12-inch rectangles. Drop a scant 3 tablespoons of the mixture into the center of each, and fold up into an envelope. Arrange in a steamer and cook over boiling water for 45 minutes. Serve hot, with or without cream.

In Ecuador the *Quimbolitos* are cooked in *achira* leaves, the leaf of the taro plant, perhaps better known as *dasheen* or *yautía*. Nothing seems to be lost by cooking them in parchment or foil, however.

✳ Cakes

Torta del Cielo   MEXICO
Heavenly Cake

This cake is served on all kinds of special occasions in Yucatán: engagement parties, weddings, baptisms, first communions, birthdays, and so on. There are many versions, some using no flour at all, just ground almonds. This is the version I prefer and I find it aptly named.

Serves 12

8 ounces blanched almonds   *1 teaspoon vanilla extract*
½ cup cake flour   *Pinch of salt*
1 teaspoon baking powder
10 eggs, separated
1 ¼ cups sugar

Cut a piece of wax paper to fit a 10-inch springform pan and oil it lightly. Fit it into the bottom of the pan. Do not oil the sides.

Grind the nuts, ½ cup at a time, in a blender, food processor, or nut grinder, and shake them through a sieve. Sift the flour with the baking powder into a bowl and mix thoroughly with the nuts. In another bowl beat the egg yolks, adding the sugar gradually until they are light, thick, and lemon-colored and form a ribbon when lifted from the bowl. Stir in the vanilla. Beat the egg whites with the pinch of salt until they stand in firm peaks. Sprinkle the flour and nut mixture onto the egg yolks, add the whites, and, using a rubber spatula, lightly fold them all together. Do not overmix, fold only until the last patches of white disappear. Pour the mixture into the prepared pan and bake in a preheated moderate (375° F.) oven for 50 minutes, or until a cake tester comes out clean. Invert on a wire rack and allow to cool thoroughly for 1 to 2 hours. Remove from the pan and peel off the wax paper. Turn right side up and dust with confectioners' sugar. The cake may be served with whipped cream, ice cream, fruit salad, or by itself. It may be frosted with a butter cream frosting, if liked.

Variation: Use 1 pound ground almonds and omit the flour and baking powder. Beat the egg whites until they stand in firm peaks, then beat in the yolks, two at a time, adding 2 extra yolks. Then beat in the almonds, ¼ cup at a time, and 1 pound confectioners' sugar, ¼ cup at a time. Stir in the vanilla.

Torta de Castanhas-Do-Pará   BRAZIL
Brazil Nut Cake

This rich yet light cake from Brazil makes a splendid dessert. I like it as a change from *Quindins de Yáyá* (Coconut Cupcake Dessert) to follow *Feijoada Completa* (Black Beans with Mixed Meats). Brazil nuts take the place of flour in the cake itself, an airy thing of egg whites. The egg yolks make a luscious filling, while the chocolate frosting adds the final luxurious touch.

Serves 12 to 14

FOR THE CAKE

12 egg whites   8 ounces Brazil nuts, finely ground
1 cup sugar   Butter

Beat the egg whites until they stand in firm, unwavering peaks. Gradually beat in the sugar. Fold in the nuts, gently but thoroughly. Have ready two 8-inch cake tins lined with buttered wax paper or kitchen parchment. Pour in the cake batter and bake in a preheated moderate (350° F.) oven for 40 minutes. The cakes will puff up but will fall as they cool. When they are cool, spread generously with the filling and sandwich the cakes together. Cover with chocolate frosting.

FOR THE FILLING

1 cup sugar   6 egg yolks
½ cup water

Combine the sugar and water in a small saucepan and cook over moderate heat until the syrup reaches the soft ball stage, when a little of the syrup dropped on a saucer holds its shape but flattens out, 234° F. on a candy thermometer. Beat the egg yolks until they are thick and lemon-colored, then beat in the cooled syrup. Pour into the top of a double boiler and cook, stirring constantly with a wooden spoon, over low heat until the mixture is thick. Cool before using to fill the cake.

FOR THE FROSTING

2 ounces semisweet chocolate,   ¼ cup coffee or water
   broken into bits   ½ egg white, beaten until stiff
¼ cup sugar

In the top of a double boiler over moderate heat, combine the chocolate, sugar, and coffee or water, and cook, stirring, until the sugar is dissolved and the mixture smooth. Cool. Beat in the egg white. Spread over the cake. Refrigerate the cake until the frosting is firm.

For a simpler frosting melt 2 ounces semisweet chocolate in 2 tablespoons coffee or water in the top of a double boiler over moderate heat. Off the heat, beat 4 tablespoons unsalted butter, cut into bits, into the chocolate mixture. Continue to beat the mixture until it is cool. Spread over the cake.

Sauces
Salsas

Because the sauce is incorporated into so many Latin American dishes, there is not a large body of separate sauces. At the same time it could be said with justification that Mexican cuisine is one of sauces with infinite variations played on a theme. The same is true of Peruvian cooking. No one has ever codified these sauces and it might, if it could be done, complicate rather than simplify matters. Every country has some form of hot pepper sauce, always present on family tables, so that the amount of fire in one's food is discretionary, though Peruvian dishes tend to be pretty hot in their own right. French sauces, sometimes with names that startle a little, have migrated to Latin America, and so has the technique of the *sofrito*, that useful mixture of sautéed onion and garlic, which began in Spain and Portugal and was expanded during the colonial period from its simple original form to include peppers and tomatoes, gifts of the New World. The avocado-based sauces are well represented, as are sauces with tomato.

Pebre
Chilean Hot Pepper Sauce

The number of hot peppers used in this sauce is purely discretionary. Some people like it very hot, and it is then just called *Salsa Picante* (Hot Sauce). As many as 8 hot peppers might be used. Others prefer it mild. Hot red peppers may be used instead of green.

Makes about 1 cup

1 medium onion, finely chopped
1 clove garlic, minced
2 tablespoons finely chopped fresh
   coriander (cilantro)
1 tablespoon finely chopped
   parsley

1 or more fresh hot green peppers,
   seeded and finely chopped
3 tablespoons olive oil
1 tablespoon lemon juice
Salt to taste

Combine all the ingredients in a bowl and let stand for about 1 hour before serving for the flavor to develop. Serve with any meat and with *Porotos Granados* (Cranberry Beans with Corn and Squash).

Salsa de Ají
Hot Pepper Sauce

Makes about 1 cup

½ pound fresh hot red or green
   peppers

1 teaspoon salt, or to taste
1 medium onion, finely chopped

Remove the seeds from the peppers and chop them coarsely. In a blender or food processor grind them to a pulp with the salt. Add the chopped onion and mix well.

Salsa de Ají Picante
Hot Pepper Sauce

There are many versions of hot pepper sauce. This one is from the coast.

Fresh hot red or green peppers *Lemon juice*
Red onion *Salt*

Seed the peppers and cut them into small strips. Combine the peppers with an equal amount of finely chopped red onion in a wide-mouthed glass jar. Cover the vegetables with lemon juice, add salt to taste, and let the sauce stand for 3 to 4 hours before using. The lemon juice may be diluted by adding a little hot water.

Ixni-Pec   MEXICO
Hot Pepper Sauce

Pronounced roughly schnee-peck, this is the fresh, hot pepper sauce that always appears on Yucatecan dining tables in a small bowl or sauceboat. It should be taken with discretion for, though it has a lovely flavor, it is very hot. The pepper used is the yellow *habanero.* I have found that pickled hot peppers from the Caribbean, usually from Trinidad or Jamaica, have an almost identical flavor and make a splendid substitute.

Makes about 1 cup

¼ cup each finely chopped onion, *Seville (bitter) orange juice, or use*
tomato, and hot chili pepper, *two-thirds orange juice to*
rinsed if pickled *one-third lime juice*
  Salt

In a bowl combine the onion, tomato, and hot pepper and add enough orange juice to make it soupy, about ¼ cup. Season to taste with salt. Serve with Yucatecan dishes or whenever a hot pepper sauce is called for. The sauce should be eaten the same day or the next.

Variation: Though *Ixni-Pec* is very hot indeed, I have encountered an even hotter sauce called simply *Salsa Picante* (Hot Sauce). It consisted of green *habaneros* peeled by toasting over a flame, seeded and chopped and diluted with a little Seville (bitter) orange juice.

Môlho de Pimenta e Limão   BRAZIL
Hot Pepper and Lime Sauce

The peppers used in Brazil are the small, very, very hot *malagueta* peppers not usually available here. Any very hot pepper can be substituted but I have found pickled Caribbean peppers, usually from Jamaica or Trinidad, a good substitute.

Makes about ¾ cup

3 or 4 hot red or green peppers,
   seeded
1 onion, chopped

1 clove garlic, chopped
Salt
½ cup lime or lemon juice

Crush the peppers, onion, and garlic with salt to taste in a mortar with a pestle, adding the lime or lemon juice little by little, or purée in a blender or food processor. Serve in a bowl to accompany meat, poultry, or fish dishes and with *Feijoada Completa* (Black Beans with Mixed Meats).

Môlho de Pimenta
e Azeite de Dendê   BRAZIL
Hot Peppers in Dendê (Palm) Oil

This is a common sauce on Bahian tables. The pepper used is the tiny, ferociously hot *malagueta* pepper.

Makes about ½ cup

6 or more small fresh hot red or
   green peppers

Dendê (palm) oil, to cover

Put the peppers in a small bowl and pour in enough oil to cover them. Let them stand for several hours before using. The oil will be quite hot and flavored by the peppers, while the heat of the peppers themselves will be slightly reduced.

Variation: For *Môlho de Pimenta e Azeite de Oliva* (Hot Peppers in Olive Oil), use olive oil instead of palm oil. This is a more usual hot sauce in other parts of Brazil, where palm oil is not used.

Salsa de Ají Colorado
Red Pepper Sauce

CHILE

Makes about 2½ cups

24 fresh hot red peppers, seeded
    and cut into strips
1 cup wine vinegar

1 clove garlic, chopped
1 teaspoon salt
¾ cup vegetable oil

Put the pepper strips into a bowl and add the vinegar. Leave overnight, stirring with a wooden spoon once or twice. Drain, reserving the vinegar. Put the peppers into a blender or food processor with the garlic, the salt, and enough of the vinegar to reduce them to a purée. Beat in the oil, adding about ¼ cup of the vinegar to give the sauce the consistency of mayonnaise. For a milder sauce discard the vinegar in which the peppers were soaked and use fresh vinegar. A lot of the heat of the peppers will have soaked out into the vinegar.

Serve with *Chancho a la Chilena* (Pork Loin, Chilean Style) or with any plainly cooked meat, poultry, or fish, or with cold meats.

Ajíes en Leche
Hot Peppers in Milk

VENEZUELA

The hot peppers used in Venezuela are medium-sized round or lantern-shaped ones, extremely hot and very well flavored. Any hot peppers may, of course, be used.

Makes about 1¼ cups

1 cup milk
½ teaspoon salt
6 fresh hot red or green peppers,
    stemmed and halved
    lengthwise

1 slice onion
1 clove garlic
3 or 4 fresh mint leaves (optional)

Pour the milk into a saucepan, add the salt, bring to a boil and immediately remove from the heat. Allow to cool. Put the hot peppers, onion, garlic, and mint leaves in a glass jar and pour the milk over them. Let stand overnight. To serve, pour into a bowl and eat the peppers as a sauce with any meat, poultry, or fish dish.

Salsa de Chile Ancho y Almendra   MEXICO
Mild Red Chili and Almond Sauce

The Mexican kitchen is extraordinarily rich in sauces, *mollis* in Nahuatl, the language of the Aztec empire, modified to *moles* in Spanish. This mild and gentle sauce was probably made originally with peanuts, which were indigenous, having found their way north from Brazil, instead of almonds. Certainly almonds make a subtler sauce than do peanuts, though both are good.

The sauce is used with salt cod, another import, in *Bacalao en Salsa de Chile Ancho y Almendra* (Salt Cod in Mild Red Chili and Almond Sauce). It is also excellent with poultry, pork, or veal (chicken stock is fine for all three). The meat is poached in stock or water until it is almost tender. The sauce is then thinned with a little of the stock and the meat is simmered in the sauce until it is tender and the flavors are blended, about 5 minutes.

Makes about 5 cups

6 ancho *chilies*
1 *medium onion, chopped*
¼ *pound (¾ cup, about) toasted almonds, ground*
⅛ *teaspoon ground cinnamon*
⅛ *teaspoon ground cloves*

¼ *teaspoon oregano*
¼ *teaspoon sugar*
Salt
4 *tablespoons vegetable oil*
2 *cups chicken, beef, or fish stock*

Pull the stems off the chilies, shake out and discard the seeds, rinse in cold water, tear into pieces, and put into a bowl with 1 cup hot water. Let soak for about 1 hour, longer if the chilies are very dry, turning them from time to time. Put the chilies, any soaking water, and the onion into a blender or food processor and reduce to a purée. Add the almonds to the chili mixture with the cinnamon, cloves, oregano, sugar, and salt to taste. The mixture will be quite heavy, almost a paste. Heat the oil in a heavy skillet and sauté the chili mixture, stirring constantly with a wooden spoon, for 5 minutes over moderate heat. Add 2 cups of the appropriate stock, stir to mix, and simmer for a few minutes longer. Clam juice may be used instead of fish stock.

The sauce, which should be of medium consistency, is now ready to use with salt cod, poultry, pork, or veal. It may also be used with fresh fish, preferably fillets, in which case the uncooked fish may be simmered in the sauce until done, or put into a greased, shallow flameproof casserole with the sauce poured over it and baked in a preheated moderate (350° F.) oven until tender, about 20 minutes.

Guacamole
Avocado Sauce

In Mexico *Guacamole* is eaten with everything — meat, poultry, fish, shellfish, beans, cheese, and by itself with *tostaditas,* triangles of fried tortilla. *Antojitos* are unthinkable without it. Very old recipes give *guacamole* simply as avocado with chili and I have had it simply mashed with a little salt, very elegant. However, recipes from the seventeenth century on give it as a mixture of tomatoes, fresh green coriander (cilantro), onion, and chopped *serrano* chilies, the small hot green mountain peppers very much used in the Mexican kitchen. I find the canned *serranos* are a better choice than fresh hot peppers of another variety, since it is their flavor as well as their heat that is needed. Fresh *serranos* are sometimes available in Latin American markets.

There is a lot of superstition about preventing *Guacamole* from darkening when exposed to air. One is that putting the avocado pit in the center of the finished sauce will do this. Long and careful research has convinced me of the falseness of this claim but I must confess I like the look of the brown pit sitting in the bowl of creamy green sauce. Next to making the sauce at the last minute the best solution is to cover the bowl tightly with plastic wrap and refrigerate it.

There are two basic versions of *Guacamole,* one with tomatoes, the other *Guacamole del Norte* (Avocado Sauce, Northern Style) made with Mexican green husk tomatoes, which does not discolor quite so quickly, perhaps because the green tomato is more acid than ordinary tomatoes. Certainly sprinkling lime or lemon juice on a cut avocado does help prevent darkening. Also a very ripe avocado will darken more quickly than one that is just at its moment of ripe perfection but not a minute over it.

I find that the best way to mash an avocado is to cut it in half, unpeeled, remove the pit, and holding the pear in the left hand mash the flesh with a fork, scoop it out with a spoon and mash any solid bits that have escaped. This gives the finished purée a good texture.

Makes about 4 cups

2 large ripe avocados, pitted and
   mashed
2 medium tomatoes, peeled,
   seeded, and chopped
1 tablespoon onion, finely
   chopped

3 canned serrano chilies, or 1
   teaspoon seeded and finely
   chopped fresh hot green
   pepper
1 tablespoon fresh green coriander
   (cilantro), chopped

Salt to taste

Mix all the ingredients thoroughly and place in a serving dish with the pit of one of the avocados in the center, if liked. Serve as a dip with triangles of fried tortilla, or as a sauce.

Variation: For *Guacamole del Norte* (Avocado Sauce, Northern Style), substitute half of a 10-ounce can of Mexican green tomatoes (about 6), drained and mashed, for the tomatoes. If fresh green husk tomatoes are available, peel off the papery husk and drop them into boiling salt. Cook for 2 minutes, drain, and allow to cool. Chop finely. Then proceed as for *Guacamole*.

Guasacaca   VENEZUELA
Avocado Sauce

There was a great deal of trade between Mexico and South America in pre-Conquest times and it is entirely possible that this is a migrant version of an original *guacamole* somewhat modified in later colonial days.

Serves 4

4 tablespoons olive oil	1 large avocado, peeled and diced
1 tablespoon red wine vinegar	1 medium tomato, peeled and
Salt to taste	chopped
½ teaspoon finely chopped,	1 medium ripe red bell pepper, or
seeded, fresh hot red pepper, or	use a green pepper, finely
½ teaspoon ground hot red	chopped
pepper	1 small onion, finely chopped

In a bowl combine the oil, vinegar, salt, and hot pepper, and beat with a fork to mix thoroughly. Add the rest of the ingredients, tossing to mix. Serve with grilled meats.

Variation: Add 1 tablespoon of finely chopped fresh green coriander (cilantro) or parsley.

Variation: Add 1 hardboiled egg, finely chopped.

Ají de Huevo   COLOMBIA
Avocado Sauce

This is another migrant recipe that evolved when the Chibcha of Colombia used to export their exquisite gold work to Mexico. I suspect the reverse trade included more than recipes. It is interesting to see how this one differs from the original Mexican recipe and from the next-door Venezuelan one. The name of the sauce really defies translation. *Ají* is the South American word for hot pepper. *Huevo* is egg. Literally one gets "hot pepper of egg." Avocado is a better way of describing it.

Makes about 1 ½ cups

1 large avocado, pitted and
    mashed
1 hardboiled egg yolk, mashed
1 tablespoon finely chopped fresh
    green coriander (cilantro)
1 fresh hot green pepper, seeded
    and chopped

1 finely chopped scallion, using
    white and green parts
1 hardboiled egg white, finely
    chopped
1 tablespoon white wine vinegar
Salt, freshly ground pepper

Mix the avocado and egg yolk thoroughly. Add all the rest of the ingredients and mix well. Serve as a sauce with *Sobrebarriga Bogotana* (Flank Steak, Bogotá Style) or *Ajiaco de Pollo Bogotano* (Bogotá Chicken Stew).

Môlho ao Tomate   BRAZIL
Tomato Sauce

Makes about 2 cups

3 tablespoons olive oil
6 large, ripe tomatoes, coarsely
    chopped
1 clove garlic, minced

3 or 4 fresh basil leaves, chopped,
    or 1 teaspoon dried basil
Salt, freshly ground pepper

Heat the oil in a saucepan and add the tomatoes, garlic, and basil. Simmer over low heat for 3 or 4 minutes, stirring occasionally. Season to taste with salt and pepper and stir in ½ cup warm water. Simmer over low heat, stirring from time to time, until the mixture is quite thick. Work the mixture through a sieve.

Salsa de Maní   ECUADOR
Peanut Sauce

Serve this with *Llapingachos* (Potato Cakes).

Makes about 1½ cups

2 tablespoons annatto (achiote)
    oil or lard (see page 324)
1 onion, finely chopped
1 clove garlic, chopped
1 medium tomato, peeled, seeded,
    and chopped

½ cup finely ground peanuts, or 2
    tablespoons peanut butter
Salt, freshly ground pepper

Heat the annatto oil or lard in a skillet and stir in the onion, garlic, and tomato. Cook over moderate heat until the onion is tender and the mixture well blended. Stir in the peanuts, season to taste with salt and pepper, and cook for a few minutes longer. The sauce should be thin enough to pour. If necessary, add a little tomato juice or water and cook just long enough to blend.

Salsa de Choclos   CHILE
Sweetcorn Sauce

This is a colonial sauce developed at a time when corn was a make-do vegetable, not yet esteemed in its own right, as it was later on. The sauce is light and delicious, the flavor of the fresh sweetcorn coming through beautifully. It can be used as a sauce with meats or poultry, but I prefer it over green vegetables and especially with cauliflower.

Makes about 3 cups

2 cups sweetcorn kernels; if using
    frozen corn, thaw thoroughly
1 cup milk
1 teaspoon sweet paprika

Salt, freshly ground white pepper
1 or 2 eggs, lightly beaten
    (optional)

In a blender or food processor combine the corn, milk, sweet paprika, salt, and pepper and reduce to a smooth purée. Pour into a saucepan and cook, stirring constantly, over low heat for 5 minutes, or until the mixture is well blended. If necessary, thicken the sauce by stirring in 1 or 2 eggs, lightly beaten, and cooking over low heat, stirring, until the sauce is thickened. I find corn varies considerably, so I use my judgment about thickening the sauce, using no eggs, or 1 or 2 as required.

Color Chilena   CHILE
Paprika Oil

This oil is used a great deal in Chilean cooking, and since it keeps indefinitely can be made in quantity. However, if you want to make less, paprika can simply be added to oil in the ratio of 1 teaspoon paprika to every 2 tablespoons oil, with garlic used proportionately.

Makes 2 cups

2 cups vegetable oil or lard   *5 tablespoons sweet paprika*
3 cloves garlic

Heat the oil or lard in a saucepan and add the garlic cloves. Sauté the garlic until it is brown, then lift out and discard. Off the heat, stir in the paprika until it is well mixed with the oil. Cool and bottle.

Aceite o Manteca de Achiote   COLOMBIA
Annatto Oil or Lard

This is used a good deal as both a coloring and a flavoring in the Caribbean, Colombia, Ecuador, and Venezuela (see page 4).

Makes ½ cup

4 tablespoons annatto seeds   *4 tablespoons vegetable oil or lard*
   (achiote)

Combine the annatto seeds and oil in a small, heavy saucepan and place over moderate heat until the seeds begin to give up their color, a deep orangey-red. If the seeds are fresh, the color will be abundant and deep and will be given off very quickly, within about 1 minute. Watch for the moment when the color starts to change to golden and remove immediately from the heat. Strain and bottle. The oil or lard will keep indefinitely.

Aliño Criollo
Seasoning Powder, Creole Style

This mixture of ground herbs and spices, which varies slightly from cook to cook, is used as a seasoning in many Venezuelan dishes, and I have found it a pleasant addition to stews and casseroles even outside the Venezuelan or Latin American kitchen. It can be bought ready-made from spice shelves in Venezuelan supermarkets as *Aliño Preparado* (Prepared Seasoning). I make it without garlic so that it keeps, but I add a large clove of crushed garlic to 2 tablespoons of the powder when I use it in cooking.

Makes about ½ cup

1 tablespoon garlic salt
1½ teaspoons ground cumin
1 tablespoon ground annatto
   (achiote) seeds

¼ teaspoon ground black pepper
1 tablespoon oregano
3 tablespoons sweet paprika

Thoroughly mix all the ingredients and put into a small glass jar. Store in a cool, dark place. Keeps indefinitely.

BASIC SAUCES

Béchamel
White Sauce

Makes about 2 cups

2 tablespoons butter
2 tablespoons flour
2 cups milk

Salt, white pepper
Pinch of nutmeg

In a small, heavy saucepan melt the butter. Stir in the flour with a wooden spoon and cook, stirring, over low heat for 2 minutes. Gradually pour in the milk, stirring constantly to mix, and bring to a boil. Simmer, stirring frequently, for 5 minutes. Season to taste with salt, white pepper, and nutmeg.

For a thick béchamel, use only 1 cup of milk. For a medium sauce, use 1½ cups, and for the more usual, creamy sauce, use 2 cups.

If the sauce should be lumpy, which is unlikely if it is properly made, simply whirl it in a blender or food processor.

Vinaigrette

Oil and Vinegar, or French, Dressing

Makes about ½ cup

2 tablespoons wine vinegar or
    other mild vinegar
Salt, freshly ground pepper

1 teaspoon Dijon mustard
8 tablespoons peanut, corn, or
    olive oil

Put the vinegar in a bowl with the salt and pepper to taste and the mustard and beat with a fork to mix well. Then beat in the oil, little by little, until the sauce is well blended. Taste for seasoning, adding more vinegar, or salt and pepper.

    Lemon juice may be used instead of vinegar. For a mustard-flavored vinaigrette, increase the amount of Dijon mustard to 2 tablespoons.

Mayonnaise

This is my preferred recipe for mayonnaise. Any standard recipe may be used, and blender mayonnaise is perfectly acceptable. However, I find this is richer with a better texture, and since it takes only minutes to make I will give it in detail.

Makes about 1 ½ cups

2 large egg yolks
½ teaspoon Dijon mustard
Salt, freshly ground pepper
1 cup corn, peanut, or olive oil,
    about

4 teaspoons vinegar or lemon
    juice, or 2 teaspoons each
    vinegar and lemon juice

Put the egg yolks into a rimmed soup plate. I find this makes beating easier than using a bowl, though a bowl, of course, will do. Beat the egg yolks lightly with a fork, and beat in the mustard, and salt and pepper to taste. Drop by drop beat in the oil until the yolks thicken. When about half the oil is beaten in and the mixture is very thick, beat in the vinegar or lemon juice, or a mixture of the two. Beat in the remaining oil, pouring it in a thin, steady stream. Taste the mayonnaise and add more vinegar or lemon, or salt and pepper, if liked. If the mayonnaise is too thick for personal taste, thin with a teaspoon or so of hot water.

If the mayonnaise fails to thicken, or separates, place an egg yolk in a bowl and beat in the failed mayonnaise, tablespoon by tablespoon, to restore the sauce.

The type of vinegar used is a matter of choice, but it should never be a coarse vinegar. Wine vinegar is the most commonly used, but I do find that a Japanese rice vinegar gives a delicious result, as of course do the herb-flavored tarragon or basil vinegars.

Salsa Golf
Tomato- and Cognac-Flavored Mayonnaise

CHILE

This is a delicious mayonnaise. I have come across it served in Colombia as a dressing for avocado and described as an international recipe; it may also be used with any cold fish or shellfish. It is generally credited to Chile, where perversely it is sometimes called *Salsa Americana*. I can find no explanation whatever for its being called *Salsa Golf* and my imagination fails me.

Makes about 1 ½ cups

2 egg yolks
1 teaspoon Dijon mustard
Pinch of cayenne pepper, or dash
    of Tabasco
Salt to taste
2 teaspoons lemon juice
1 tablespoon white wine vinegar
1 cup vegetable oil
¼ cup olive oil
2 tablespoons tomato ketchup or
    thick tomato purée
1 tablespoon cognac

Put the egg yolks, mustard, cayenne or Tabasco, salt, lemon juice, and vinegar in a bowl, and beat until thick and well blended. Beat in the vegetable and olive oil, drop by drop, until the mayonnaise begins to thicken, then beat in the remaining oil in a thin, steady stream. Add the tomato ketchup or purée and the cognac. The finished mayonnaise will be a delicate pink.

For *Palta Rellena* (Stuffed Avocado), peel and halve an avocado and remove the pit. Fill the center of each half with *Salsa Golf*. Serves 2 as an appetizer, 1 as a luncheon.

BASIC PROCEDURES

Beurre Manié to Thicken a Sauce

Thoroughly mix 1 tablespoon butter, softened at room temperature, with 1 tablespoon flour. The most convenient way to do this is to put the flour and butter in a cup and mix with a fork. Stir bit by bit into the liquid to be thickened, over moderate heat. This is enough to lightly thicken the average stew. Quantities can be adjusted as required.

To Clarify Butter

Cut the butter into chunks and put into a heavy saucepan over moderate heat. Skim the foam off the surface as it rises. When the butter has melted and looks quite clear let it stand for a few minutes for all the solids to sink to the bottom. Strain the butter through a sieve lined with damp cheesecloth. The residue need not be thrown away but can be poured over green vegetables or stirred into a stew.

To Peel and Seed Tomatoes

Ripe tomatoes picked off the vine in one's own garden can often be peeled simply by pulling off the skin with the fingers. I've often peeled market-bought tomatoes in Latin America this way and hothouse tomatoes are sometimes peelable in this manner. Otherwise, choose ripe, red tomatoes and drop them into boiling water, one at a time, for 10 seconds. Lift out, rinse quickly under cold water, and peel with a paring knife from the stem end. To remove the seeds, cut the tomato in half crosswise and squeeze out the seeds gently.

Drinks

Bebidas

Latin America does very well with drinks from tea, coffee, wine, and beer, which were introduced there, to native chocolate, *mate*, tequila, *pisco*, rum, and the beerlike drinks, *pulque*, *chicha*, and *tepache*. There is lots of Scotch whisky, gin, and vodka as well as the soft drinks of both the antique and colonial past, and modern soft drinks.

Thanks to Germans, who missed the beer of their homeland, all of Latin America has very good beer indeed. And thanks to French, Spanish, Portuguese, Italians, Germans, and Swiss, who missed their native wines, Chile and Argentina, and to a lesser extent Brazil, Uruguay, Paraguay, and Mexico, have either good or acceptable wines.

Brazil's coffee is notable and one drinks it as *cafezinho*, very strong demitasse with a lot of sugar, often as not with *bôlos* (cakes), while in Colombia, whose coffee is also notable, what one takes in a demitasse is called a *tinto*. Other fine coffees are produced in smaller quantities in Guatemala, El Salvador, Costa Rica, and Mexico. For breakfast Brazil takes its coffee as *café com leite*, the same strong coffee of the demitasse diluted with hot milk, the *café con leche* of the rest of the continent. Mexico adds brown sugar, cinnamon stick, and cloves to make its *Café de Olla* (Pot Coffee).

Tea is not as popular as coffee, though it is esteemed for afternoon tea. Also popular are the herbal teas, the *tisanas* like mint and chamomile, and, of course, *mate*. Chocolate is a popular drink especially in Mexico, where it is packaged already sweetened, flavored with cinnamon and cloves, and mixed with ground almonds. It can be bought in specialty food shops here.

Many of the local soft drinks or beerlike drinks are either not available here, or are impractical to make at home, but I have sometimes come across a concentrated bottled form of *guaraná* in shops selling Brazilian foods. This is made from a Brazilian shrub and is delicious as a soft drink as well as being a good mix for gin, vodka, or rum.

Many of the mixed drinks of Latin America are as international as Scotch and soda, or gin and tonic. I have chosen local drinks I have enjoyed in their home countries and which I have been able to make in the States.

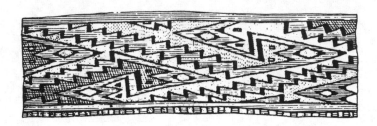

Pisco Sour   PERU
Peruvian Brandy Sour

Pisco, Peruvian brandy, is used in this sour, which is also popular in Chile, where they use the very similar Chilean *pisco*. *Pisco* is also popular in Bolivia. The small tropical lemon-limes used in the drink have a very subtle flavor. They are sometimes available in California. Our limes and lemons are rather more strongly flavored, and a little more sugar may be needed.

Serves 1

1 teaspoon egg white   2 ounces pisco (Peruvian brandy)
1 teaspoon superfine sugar   2 or 3 ice cubes
2 teaspoons lime or lemon juice   Angostura bitters

Combine all the ingredients except the Angostura bitters in a cocktail shaker and shake vigorously. Strain into a sour glass and shake a few drops of Angostura bitters on top.

Biblia con Pisco

Peruvian Brandy Eggnog

Serves 1

1 whole egg
1 tablespoon superfine sugar
1 ½ ounces pisco (Peruvian
brandy)

⅛ teaspoon ground cinnamon or
nutmeg

Beat the egg with the sugar, either by hand or with an electric beater, until the sugar is dissolved. Beat in the *pisco.* Pour into a 6-ounce goblet or punch cup, chill thoroughly, sprinkle with cinnamon or nutmeg, and serve. If preferred, 1 or 2 ice cubes may be added to the drink instead of chilling it.

Yungueño

Peruvian Brandy with Orange Juice

Serves 1

1 ½ ounces pisco (Peruvian
brandy)
1 ½ ounces orange juice

¼ teaspoon superfine sugar
½ cup cracked ice

Combine all the ingredients in a cocktail shaker and shake vigorously. Pour, unstrained, into an 8-ounce wine glass or a tumbler.

Gin Fizz

It was said to me once that the greatest glory of Uruguay was the gin fizz (pronounced jeen feez) made in the capital city of Montevideo. This may well be true, and I think the secret lies in the delicate flavor of the tropical lemon-limes of the region. I find using a little more sugar with our lemons balances the flavor and gives almost the same result.

Serves 1

2 teaspoons superfine sugar

2 tablespoons lemon juice

2 ounces gin

½ cup crushed ice

Combine the sugar and lemon juice in a cocktail shaker and stir until the sugar is dissolved. Add the gin and crushed ice and shake very thoroughly. Strain into a narrow straight-sided glass about 4 inches high, or into a small tumbler.

Coco Fizz

MEXICO

Serves 4

2 cups coconut water

3 tablespoons superfine sugar

1 cup gin

1 cup crushed ice

⅓ cup lime juice

Club soda

In a cocktail shaker combine the coconut water and the sugar and stir until the sugar is dissolved. Add all the remaining ingredients, except the club soda, and shake vigorously. Pour into four 9-ounce glasses and add a splash of soda to each.

Coconut water is the liquid in the green coconut, sometimes available in tropical markets. There is some coconut water in mature coconuts, about 1 cup usually, enough for 2 drinks.

Cola de Lagarto

MEXICO

Lizard's Tail

Serves 1

¾ cup dry white wine

⅓ cup vodka or gin

1 tablespoon lime juice

1 teaspoon superfine sugar

1 teaspoon crème de menthe

3 or 4 ice cubes

Combine all the ingredients in a cocktail shaker and shake vigorously. Strain into a chilled tumbler.

Caipirinha

Rum Sour

The name of this drink means literally "country bumpkin," perhaps because the lime is coarsely chopped and the drink served unstrained, unlike the *Batida de Limão* (Lime Batida), where only juice is used and the drink is strained, refined. Or perhaps because it is a splendid drink for that country feast, *Churrasco à Gaucha*, the Brazilian barbecue.

Serves 1

½ lime
1 teaspoon superfine sugar

2 ounces Cachaça *(Brazilian
    rum) or white rum*

½ cup crushed ice

Coarsely chop the lime and transfer it to the mixing glass of a cocktail shaker with the sugar, adding more if liked. Muddle thoroughly to extract all the juice and oil from the lime peel. Add the rum and ice. Shake vigorously and pour, unstrained, into a cocktail glass.

Batida de Limão

Lime Batida

Serves 1

2 tablespoons lime or lemon juice
1 teaspoon sugar

2 ounces Cachaça *(Brazilian rum)
    or white rum*

½ cup crushed ice

Combine all the ingredients in a cocktail shaker and shake vigorously. Strain into a cocktail glass.

Variation: For *Batida de Coco* (Coconut Milk Batida), substitute 2 tablespoons thick coconut milk (see page 7) for the lime juice.

Variation: For *Batida de Maracujá* (*Granadilla* or Passion Fruit Batida), substitute 2 tablespoons of *granadilla* or passion fruit juice for the lime juice and increase the sugar to 1½ teaspoons. *Granadilla* or passion fruit juice is often available in specialty food shops.

Variation: For *Batida de Abacaxi* (Pineapple Batida), substitute 2 ounces pineapple juice for the lime juice.

Margarita

Serves 1

½ shell of lime or lemon
Salt
1 ½ ounces white tequila

½ ounce Triple Sec or Curaçao
1 ounce lime or lemon juice
2 or 3 ice cubes

Rub the rim of a cocktail glass with the rind of the lime or lemon. Pour salt into a saucer and spin the rim of the glass in it. Combine the remaining ingredients in a bar glass and stir until thoroughly chilled. Strain into the prepared cocktail glass.

Tequila Sunrise

This and its variation, Tequila Cocktail, are very popular tequila drinks.

Serves 1

½ lime
2 ounces white tequila
½ teaspoon crème de cassis
1 teaspoon grenadine syrup
Club soda
Ice cubes

Squeeze the lime, pour the juice into an 8-ounce highball glass together with the shell of the lime. Add the tequila, *crème de cassis*, and grenadine syrup. Add enough club soda to fill the glass three-quarters full, stir to mix, then drop in 2 or 3 ice cubes.

Variation: For Tequila Cocktail, combine 1½ ounces tequila with the juice of 1 lime, about 3 tablespoons, and ½ ounce grenadine syrup or to taste. Stir to mix and pour over crushed ice in a cocktail or saucer champagne glass. Serve with two short straws. Serves 1.

Vampiros   MEXICO
Tequila Bloody Marys

Serves 4

1 ¼ cups tomato juice
½ cup orange juice
2 tablespoons lime juice
2 tablespoons chopped onion

½ teaspoon Worcestershire sauce
Salt, cayenne pepper to taste
6 ounces white tequila

Combine all the ingredients, except the tequila, in a blender and blend until smooth. Pour into a jug and chill for at least 4 hours. To serve pour 1½ ounces white tequila into each of four Old-Fashioned glasses and pour in ½ cup of the tomato mixture. Stir to mix. If liked, the drink may be served over ice cubes.

Aperitivo Chapala   MEXICO

There is a lot of controversy over this drink, a chaser for tequila, created by the widow Sanchez at her restaurant at Lake Chapala. Her original was made without tomato juice and had Seville (bitter) orange juice and grenadine syrup. I find ordinary orange juice just as good. The hot pepper gives it a nice lift. I was served it as *Aperitivo Chapala* when I stayed at the lake so I have kept that name here.

Makes about 6 servings

1 cup orange juice
3 tablespoons grenadine syrup
½ teaspoon salt

½ teaspoon cayenne pepper or any
   ground hot red pepper

Mix all the ingredients thoroughly and chill. Serve in small, straight-sided 1½- to 2-ounce tequila glasses with another glass of tequila served separately. Drink alternately sip by sip. Traditionally the drink is accompanied by small, dried, fried fish, available packaged in many specialty food shops.

Sangrita   MEXICO

Sangrita made with tomato juice is also a splendid accompaniment to tequila. I like the modern way of serving it, combining the Sangrita and the tequila over ice cubes in an Old-Fashioned glass.

Makes 18 to 24 servings

3 cups tomato juice
1 cup orange juice
½ cup lime juice
½ small white onion, chopped
1 teaspoon sugar
1 teaspoon salt, or to taste

2 teaspoons seeded and chopped
    fresh hot green or red pepper,
    or 1 teaspoon cayenne pepper
White tequila
Halved limes
Salt

Combine the tomato juice, orange juice, lime juice, onion, sugar, salt, and hot pepper or cayenne in a blender or food processor and blend until smooth. Strain into a jug and chill thoroughly. Serve in small, straight-sided 1½- to 2-ounce tequila glasses with another glass of tequila served separately. Squeeze a little lime juice into either the Sangrita or the tequila and drink sip by sip, or put a little salt on the lime and take a little suck of it as liked.

Sangría   MEXICO

This is the Spanish wine drink that Mexico has both adopted and adapted to its own use. It is light and pleasant, especially in hot weather.

Makes about 10 servings

1 cup orange juice
½ cup lime or lemon juice
¼ cup superfine sugar, or to taste

1 bottle dry red wine, preferably
    Spanish
Ice cubes

In a jug combine the orange juice, lime or lemon juice, and the sugar and stir until the sugar is dissolved. Taste and add a little more sugar if liked. Pour in the wine, stir to mix, and chill thoroughly in the refrigerator. To serve, put 2 or 3 ice cubes in a 6-ounce goblet or tumbler and fill with Sangría.

Agua de Jamaica
MEXICO

Sorrel or Rosella Drink

This is a popular soft drink and is made from the sepals of a tropical flower known in Mexico as *flor de Jamaica* and in Jamaica as sorrel, elsewhere as rosella or roselle. It can be bought dried in tropical markets usually as rosella or sorrel.

Makes about 10 servings

2 cups rosella sepals   Sugar to taste
2 quarts water

Rinse the rosella sepals and put them into a large saucepan with the water. Bring to a boil over moderate heat, remove from the heat, and allow to cool. Strain into a jug. Sweeten to taste and chill thoroughly. Serve in tumblers with ice cubes.

Mate
PARAGUAY

Mate, from the Quechua word, is a mildly stimulating, nonalcoholic drink made from the powdered dried leaves of the South American evergreen *Ilex paraguayensis*. It can be bought in many health or specialty food shops and made according to package directions. It is not necessary to have the special silver-trimmed gourd and the *bombilla*, a special silver straw, to sip it through. A teapot and a cup do just as well, and it may be drunk either hot or cold. The *mate*, the name for the gourd in which the tea is made, is called a *chimarrao* in southern Brazil, where the drink is as popular as it is in Paraguay, Uruguay, and Argentina. In South America, especially in Argentina, the rules for making *mate* can be quite complicated, and many lovers of the tea insist that the water must be just under a boil.

To make the tea, heat a teapot by rinsing it out in boiling water, add 1 tablespoon *mate* per cup, pour in boiling water, let the tea steep for 5 minutes, strain, and serve either plain, or with sugar and/or milk, if liked. To drink cold, make the *mate* double strength and pour it over ice cubes. Serve plain or with sugar and lemon.

Café de Olla

MEXICO

Pot Coffee

In Mexico, which is coffee country, this is served in small pottery mugs each holding 4 ounces (½ cup) as an after-dinner coffee. In Mexico *pilon-cillo*, the local brown sugar, would be used. Our dark brown sugar is about the same. Coffee for breakfast, *Café con Leche* (Coffee with Milk), is very strong, served in large cups, and diluted half and half with hot milk.

Serves 6

3 cups water
⅓ cup dark brown sugar
2-inch piece of stick cinnamon

3 whole cloves
3 cups coffee

Combine the water, sugar, cinnamon, and cloves in an earthenware or any heatproof coffee pot and bring the water to a boil over moderate heat. Add the coffee, bring again to a boil, simmer for 1 minute, stir, cover, and leave in a warm place for a few minutes for the grounds to settle. Pour through a strainer into earthenware mugs, or use any demitasse cups.

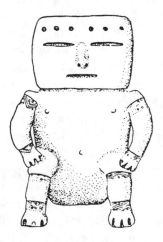

Sources of Latin American Foods

New York
Casa Moneo
210 West 14th Street
New York, N.Y. 10011
Casa Moneo carries a very wide range of Mexican and South American specialties. Mail order.

La Marqueta is an enclosed market that extends from 112th to 116th streets on Park Avenue.

Mara's West Indies Market
718 Nostrand Avenue
Brooklyn, New York 11216

H. Roth & Son
1577 First Avenue
New York, New York 10028
Roth's has a lot of Brazilian foods including *carne sêca* and cassava (manioc) meal.

Trinacria Importing Company
415 Third Avenue
New York, New York 10016

Perello, Inc.
2585 Broadway
New York, New York 10025
I've been able to get Seville (bitter) oranges here.

Ninth Avenue from about 38th Street to the fifties is a marvelous source for root vegetables, seafood, special cuts of pork, and so on.

Washington, D.C.
La Sevillana, Inc.
2469 18th Street, N.W.
Washington, D.C.

Safeway International
1110 F Street, N.W.
Washington, D.C. 20004

Casa Peña
1638 17th Street
Washington, D.C. 20009

Chicago
La Preferida, Inc.
117-181 W. South Water Market
Chicago, Illinois 60608

La Casa del Pueblo
1810 Blue Island
Chicago, Illinois 60608

Casa Esteiro
2719 West Division
Chicago, Illinois 60622

Los Angeles
El Mercado
First Avenue and Lorena
East Los Angeles, California 90063

San Francisco
Mi Rancho Market
3365 20th Street
San Francisco, California 94110

Casa Lucas Market
2934 24th Street
San Francisco, California 94110

La Palma
2884 24th Street
San Francisco, California 94110

San Antonio, Texas
Frank Pizzini
202 Produce Row
San Antonio, Texas 78207

Dallas
J. A. Mako Horticultural Enterprises
P.O. Box 34082
Dallas, Texas 75234
J. A. Mako has authentic Mexican
chili pepper seeds, for those who
want to grow their own. Mail order.

Boston
Garcia Superette
367 Center Avenue
Jamaica Plain
Boston, Massachusetts 02130

Cambridge
Star Market
625 Mt. Auburn Street
Cambridge, Massachusetts 02238

Cardullo's Gourmet Shop
6 Brattle Street
Cambridge, Massachusetts 02138

Miami
The Delicatessen Burdine's
Dadeland Shopping Center
Miami, Florida 33156

Albuquerque
Hopi Indians
Bucks General Store
P.O. Box 13561
Albuquerque, New Mexico 87112

Blue corn can be ordered from the
Hopi.

Index

THE SPIRIT LENS

PRELUDE

Philosophers claimed the Blood Wars had irredeemably corrupted magic. Historians insisted that Sabria's growing sophistication in physics, astronomy, and alchemistry—the almost daily discoveries that exposed another spell as nonsensical and another magical practitioner as a charlatan—was but a grand human evolution, on the order of our discovery of fire, the wheel, or sail. Whoever had the right of the discussion, a sensible man could not but admit that the practice of magic had lost its glamour—and I was an unendingly sensible man.

Of course it was not good sense, but rather my own incapacity that had caused me to relinquish my aspiration to life as a mage of the Camarilla Magica. Sixteen years' residence at the sole remaining school of magic in Sabria and I could not charm a flea to a dog's back.

With encouragement from my mentor, I had faced disappointment squarely, weathered the storm that followed, and accepted what solace was offered me. Yet somewhere, nurtured by the lost dreams of youth and exposed in the ruthless self-examination required to recover from despair, lay a small, intractable conviction. A seed that would not let me spit it out. A stone that would not be shaken from my shoe. I ought to be more than I was. Even if I lacked the blood-born talents of a mage, somewhere, in some

capacity, my service would make a difference in this world. Perhaps that's why the summons intrigued me so, though it made no good sense at all.

The odd missive had arrived in the late afternoon. Spring sunlight streamed through the casements of the collegia library, stretching all the way across the scuffed floor to the book cupboard labeled FORMULARY: POTIONS AND HERBALS. Only incidentally did the beams illuminate the fold of fine paper in my hand.

I peered again at the outside of the page. No insignia had manifested itself in the broken wax seal in the past few moments. The handwriting that spelled out my name remained unrecognizable.

> *Portier de Duplais, Curator of Archives*
> *Collegia Magica de Seravain*

Bold and angular—a man's hand, I judged. Seven years of intensive study in this library and nine more as its keeper, with little companionship but five thousand mouldering manuscripts and a transitory stream of increasingly vapid students, had left me unskilled in the discipline most important to me, but knowledgeable in many arcane branches of learning.

I flipped back to the enigmatic message.

> *Portier de Savin-Duplais:*
>
> *Present yourself at Villa Margeroux on the Ventinna Road no later than 17 Trine on a matter of urgent family business. A mount awaits you at the hostelry in Tigano. We require utmost discretion.*
>
> *Your kinsman*

No PERSONAL SIGNATURE. No POLITENESSES. I had no acquaintance with Villa Margeroux or with any person who lived in the vicinity of Ventinna.

The note could be a prank, perpetrated by some student I had reprimanded for marking in books or dripping lamp oil onto irreplaceable pages. Mage Rutan's much-praised validator, the small pewter charm I had wheedled out of the old sturgeon only with extraordinary groveling, wavered maddeningly between dullness and brilliance, refusing to designate the message as truth or falsehood.

Yet the request was stated with a certain directness uncharacteristic of students. Uncharacteristic, too, was the distance involved; Ventinna lay a good four days' ride westward. And a particular detail tickled my imagination, one that might escape a reader unburdened by the excessive expectations of names and bloodlines—or the private convictions of some greater destiny too embarrassing to mention, even to his longtime mentor. The outer address used my common appellation, *Duplais* being my father's unprepossessing demesne. But the inner included *Savin*, the family name I had long discarded, which could not but lead my thoughts to one particular kinsman and couch the imperious tone of the message in an entirely different light. *Present yourself . . . We require . . .*

A prickle of excitement minimized all sober considerations, such as how to request leave from my duties while maintaining *utmost discretion*, and how ridiculous it was to imagine that my fifteenth cousin, the King of Sabria, had summoned me to a clandestine meeting. I had never even met the man.

My finger traced the Savin family device scribed on the back of my left hand at birth, then moved inevitably to the ragged, nine-year-old scar that bisected it, scoring my wrist and vanishing up my sleeve. *If not now, Portier, when?*

In an instant's resolve, I stuffed the missive inside my threadbare doublet, snatched up my compass, journal, and pen case, and locked my desk without so much as returning my books to the shelves. A hastily scribbled note directed students to see Adept Nidallo for access to the archives or the vault. At the modest age of two-and-thirty, I'd spent precisely half my life inside these walls. My bones had near fossilized. Did my royal cousin bid me suckle his children, I'd do it.

"COUSIN PORTIER. WE'VE NOT MET before, I believe." The tall, broad-shouldered man in maroon and silver stood by a grand window that opened onto the sprawling country estate called Margeroux. His clear voice resonated with confidence. His extended hand bore a ruby signet, crested with Sabria's golden tree.

"Indeed, sire, I've not had that privilege." I dropped to one knee and kissed his proffered ring. "How may I serve you?"

I felt immensely relieved and a bit foolish. Four long days in the saddle give a man occasion to recall every synonym for *idiot*. Philippe de Savin-Journia was a sovereign in his prime. His wealth and open-mindedness had artists, explorers, scholars, and academicians of every science flocking to his court. What possible need had he of a librarian, schooled in a fading art? I had decided that, at best, the kinsman awaiting me would turn out to be some moronic relation as bereft of fortune and prospects as I. Worse cases abounded.

But the King of Sabria enveloped my left hand with his own—a broad, hard, warm hand, scribed with the myriad honorable scars of a warrior's life, as well as the same Savin family device that marked mine—and hauled me to my feet. Eyes the deep blue of Sabria's skies took my measure.

"I've a mystery needs solving, cousin. The matter is delicate, and certain aspects require me to seek counsel beyond my usual circles. Where better than with a member of my own family?"

"I'm honored you would think of me, sire." Mystified, to be precise. Curious.

His well-proportioned face relaxed into a welcoming smile. "Good. I've heard decent reports of you over the years and was sure you were the man I needed. I've delayed this unconscionably, hoping— Ah, you'll hear all the sordid complications soon enough. Come along."

He led me on a brisk walk through a series of pleasant, sunny rooms to a deserted kitchen in the back of the house. Pausing only to light a lamp from the banked kitchen fire, which seemed odd in the bright midafternoon, he headed outdoors.

"Tell me, Portier," he said, striding across a shady courtyard. "The methods of sorcerous practice have not changed in these years of my estrangement with the Camarilla, have they? No revelation of opticum or mechanica, no new-writ treatise on anatomy or mathematics or the composition of minerals has altered the teaching of spellwork?"

"Not at all, sire. Indeed some progressive mages believe that instruments such as the opticum will support our understanding of the physical melding of the five divine elements." Not many. Most magical practitioners stubbornly maintained their posture that the *mundane sciences* offered nothing to sorcerers.

"And your brethren yet renounce superstition and demonology?"

"Mages of the Camarilla work entirely within the bounds of earth. They practice as methodically as do the scientists and natural philosophers you embrace."

Had I ever imagined having the opportunity to seed the king's mind with some good feeling for the art of sorcery, I would have prepared more refined arguments. Philippe was known as a man of lively intellect and devouring curiosity.

"Sire, it seems a sad waste that political disagreements with the Camarilla have so undermined your confidence in an art that has so much to offer your kingdom."

He choked down a laugh. "I will not argue science and magic with you, Portier. My bodyguard reports that you yourself carry a compass rather than some 'directional charm' that might fail inexplicably at the dark of the moon and lead you off a cliff."

We left the path and crossed a dark corner of the yard to a narrow downward stair. Wading through a litter of dead leaves, twigs, and walnut husks, we descended the stone steps to an iron grate that blocked the lower end.

Philippe twisted the latch and tugged a rusty handle, the grate rising more smoothly than its appearance and location would suggest. The low-ceilinged passage beyond, much older than the house, smelled of stagnant water and old leaves. The king adjusted his lamp to shine more brightly. Once the grate slid closed behind us, a fierce sobriety wiped away my cousin's affable demeanor.

"Last year, on the twenty-fifth day of Cinq, an arrow penetrated my mount's saddle, not three millimetres from the great vein in my thigh. By the grace of the Pantokrator's angels, the villain archer's hand wavered, and he lies dead instead of me. Gross evidence implicates my wife."

"Sainted ancestors! I never heard—" Well, perhaps a traveling mage had brought gleeful rumors of a foiled assassination plot, but I'd thought nothing of it. Few mages held excessive love for Philippe, who had set out to dismantle the Camarilla Magica's pervasive influence in Sabrian society, scholarship, and business, and done exceeding well at it. But the queen . . . *the shadow queen*, rumor named her, or *the lady of sorrows*, who had lost one husband already, her parents in a fire, her firstborn to an infant fever, and three others miscarried . . .

We proceeded deliberately through a warren of dank passages. "Few know the complete story, in particular that the nature of the archer, and certain other aspects of the event, evidenced the collaboration of one from your magical fraternity. Somewhere a sorcerer has, for whatever reason, decided that his king ought to be dead. Though her two pet mages have no use for me, I utterly reject the idea that my wife could be involved."

"Sorcery."

"That's why I chose you, cousin. I need a sorcerer to serve as my confidential agent in this matter."

The snaky uneasiness in my belly quickly tangled itself into a familiar knot of disappointment. Though I held no grievance against Philippe, man or king, or his predecessor, King Soren, I forever cursed their presence in my family tree. As early as age ten, I had realized that our royal connection and its excess of expectations had ruined my father, leaving him with no true friends, no money, no useful purpose to his life, and a marital contract sufficient to produce me, but naught else.

At fourteen, I learned that no girl with a wit larger than an acorn would touch a male who wore the interlaced *S* and *V* on the back of his hand. The Camarilla mandated severe penalties for promiscuity, and when one of the parties hailed from the most notable, if not the most vigorous, of Sabria's seventeen remaining magical bloodlines, inquisitorial scrutiny was assured.

In the very year I turned sixteen and began my studies at Seravain, the coolness between the young King Philippe and the Camarilla broke into an open struggle for dominance. Determined to make my way in the society of mages, I had quickly dropped the *Savin* from my name. Seven years later, my ambition had died its humiliating death, my Savin bloodline too weak to carry me farther in a life of sorcery.

"My lord . . ."

At the end of a branched passage, Philippe touched a most ordinary-seeming door of thick oak. The door swung open all of itself. Cool air rushed out, bristling with enchantment. For one moment I allowed the mystical wave to engulf me, a sensory pleasure as deeply human as the smell of damp earth in spring. But nine years of practiced honesty required I speak nature's inescapable verdict.

"My lord, I must confess: I am no sorcerer, nor will I ever be."

He swung around to face me.

"I am failed, sire," I said, lest he had not heard enough. "Incapable of spellwork."

"I see. Yet you excelled in your studies. Reports say you are as intimately familiar with the history and practice of magic as anyone in Sabria—including those who wear the collar of a Camarilla mage. Is that true? Answer squarely, cousin. False modesty has no place here."

The truth was not so simple. Yes, I had read widely. But who would ever separate *knowledge* of sorcery from its practice? "I suppose one could say that, but—"

"Skills can be bought. Knowledge takes much longer to acquire, and the ability to question, analyze, interpret, and deduce longer still. The capacity for loyalty is born in a man, reinforced, I believe, with family connection. I believe you the fit person to pursue a confidential, objective inquiry into a matter of sorcery. The burden of judgment is my duty and my prerogative. But if you take on this task, I shall give you freedom and resources to pursue matters as you think best. If you deem yourself unfit, turn right around and be on your way. My time is exceeding short."

Royal assassination. Magic bent to murder. The queen suspected. Were my eyes wholly dazzled with royal flattery that I would consider

treading such dangerous ground? Did unseemly curiosity cloud my judgment? Or was I clinging to the improbable certainty that my life had meaning beyond breathing and dying?

Perhaps reasons didn't matter. My mentor, Kajetan, had instilled in me a determination to honesty, and I allowed that to be my guide. "Beyond the practice of sorcery itself, sire," I said, "I do believe myself fit for such a task."

"Good. Because now I must unnerve you a bit more." Philippe moved through the open door, his boots rapping sharply on the uneven paving of yet another passage. "The last man I set to this investigation, a skilled warrior and experienced diplomat, vanished nine months ago and is not found. For private reasons, I've allowed the public inquiry to lapse. Yet conscience nags that we speak not only of my personal safety, but of the security of Sabria herself."

We halted beside an iron door. Philippe hung his lamp from a bracket and unlocked the door with a plain bronze key, but he did not open it right away. The lamplight ringed his pale eyes with shadow and carved false hollows in his firm-fleshed cheeks.

"I don't believe in magic, Portier. For most of my eight-and-thirty years, I have judged its practice entirely illusion, trickery, or coincidence. Alchemists demonstrate every day that matter is not limited to sorcery's five divine elements. An opticum lens reveals that *wood* is not homogeneous, but is itself made up of water, air, and fibers. *Water* contains unseeable creatures and can be fractured into gaseous matter. *Spark* is but an explosive instance of heat and light and tinder. Similarly with *air* and *base metal*. Natural science brings logic and reason to a chaotic universe. We have discovered more of truth in the past twenty years than in the past twenty centuries, stimulating our minds, benefiting Sabria and her citizens in innumerable ways. However, in this room, it pains me to confess, we find something else again."

He dragged open the door and gestured me in, and though I held ready arguments against his inaccurate understanding of the divine elements, an eager excitement drew me into the small, bare chamber. Swept and brushed, the close room smelled of naught but damp stone and lamp

oil. On a stone table at its center lay an arrow, its point, splintered shaft, and ragged fletching stained deep rusty red; a brass spyglass, as a military commander or shipboard officer might use; and an untarnished silver coin. Simple evidence, an observer might say, unless he could sense the enchantment that belched from them in a volcanic spew.

"Sight through the glass, Portier. Then I'll tell you my story of magic and murder."

Magic, as I had told the king, was entirely of the human world and subject to its laws. So it was bad enough that I peered through the enchanted glass and saw a man staggering through a tangle of leafless thorn trees toward a barred iron gate—a view nothing related to the place where I stood. Far worse was my eerie certainty of the land he traveled. To glimpse the Souleater's ice-bound caverns or spy on the surpassing mystery of the Creator's Heaven could be no more fearsome, for every passing soul must first endure the Perilous Demesne of Trial and Journey—Ixtador of the Ten Gates, the desolation that lies just beyond the Veil separating this life from the next. Most unsettling of all was the reason for my certainty. The wailing, exhausted traveler was my father, a man nine years dead.

ONE SHORT HOUR LATER, DREAD, like Discord's Worm, had taken up permanent residence in my bowels. I would have yielded my two legs to return to my dull library.

Less than two hundred years had passed since Sabria had retreated from near dissolution. A century of savagery, fueled by rivalries between the great magical families and between those blood families and the civil authorities, had left our cities in ruins, half of our villages empty or burnt, and more than two-thirds of Sabria's nobles, scholars, and sorcerers dead. Entire magical bloodlines had been wiped out. Even a whisper of those times yet caused cold sweats and shudders in every Sabrian.

Now someone had dredged up the foulest magic of those days to create an assassin and had dispatched him to murder Sabria's golden king. Philippe was convinced that his mysterious enemy, who might or might

not be his wife, would make a second attempt on the anniversary of the first, some two months hence. The king's death by unholy sorcery must surely relight the smoldering embers of the Blood Wars, and the mysterious spyglass hinted that this time the conflagration might drive us into realms uncharted. I, Portier de Savin-Duplais, librarian and failed student of magic, was charged to stop it.

"As the secrecy of your investigation must preclude our public relationship, I've engaged you a partner *agente confide*." Philippe led me, still speechless, back into the sunny, peaceful house. I felt out of time, as if I'd just returned from the Souleater's frozen demesne. "Cousin Portier, meet Chevalier Ilario de Sylvae."

A tall, fair, long-nosed young man, garbed in an eye-searing ensemble of red silk sleeves, green satin waistcoat, gold link belt and bracelets, and lace—god's finger, ruffled lace everywhere—swept off a feathered hat and dropped to one knee as we entered the reception room. "Gracious lord. Such a delight to attend you on this glorious spring day—though 'tis a bit warmish for the season—and I am so forever humbled and ennobled to serve you, though my spirit trembles at the requirement for discretion. . . ."

Another hour and I was truly flummoxed. After charging me to halt the revival of the Blood Wars in the span of two short months, the king had paired me with an imbecile.

But I had sworn him my service. Indeed, the implications of the spyglass could not be ignored, and left my first move clear. I needed a sorcerer.

CHAPTER ONE

33 TRINE
64 DAYS UNTIL THE ANNIVERSARY

"Tell me again, good Portier," called my lanky companion over his shoulder, the plumes of his velvet toque bouncing despite the oppressive woodland damp. "Right or left at the chestnut tree? By my sacred mater's nose, headings and inclinations slip through my ears like sand through a sieve. I could lose my way in a bath!"

"Bear right, Lord Ilario," I said, biting back the oh-so-sweet temptation to send the pretty-faced moron the wrong way. "The plowman was most specific. Are you certain you'd not prefer to wait back in Bardeu? There's no need to discomfort—"

"La, brave comrade! How could I, a Knight of Sabria, leave you alone to beard this fearsome mage in his woody den—our first foray into the world as partner *agentes*?" My companion reversed the course of his palfrey with effortless grace, his idiot grin blazing like unwelcome sunrise in a drunkard's eye. "Surely I must collapse in shame, never again able to face our noble king or my fellow knights. Though, naturally, I could not discuss our business with my fellow knights until released from my vow of silence. I don't know that I've taken a vow of silence before. . . ."

With a sigh I checked my compass heading against the map I'd sketched in my journal that morning. All seemed correct. I waved the mewling

popinjay onward, hoping to still his prattle with movement if I could neither send him away nor throttle him. Knight of Sabria, indeed. Ilario de
Sylvae had been fostered since babyhood with his half sister, Queen Eugenie. If he had ever drawn his fine sword outside Merona's fencing halls,
I'd eat my boots.

Philippe had claimed that Ilario's rank could gain me access to information none other could manage and that the young lord's determination
to prove his half sister's innocence would provide me a trustworthy ally.
Fifteen days together had eliminated my concerns that the fop's motives
might be more complicated. Philippe's were yet in question. Even the
humiliating need to hire a better sorcerer was easier to bear than the implication that, in my sovereign's eyes, my service ranked on par with an
idiot's.

As the spreading canopy of oak and chestnut dimmed the feeble daylight, I spurred my mount past Ilario's. *Turn right from the Carvalho road at
the point where it leaves the village,* so the Bardeu plowman had directed me.
*Proceed through a beynt of wheat fields and cow pasture (closing the hedge-gate
behind you, if you please, sonjeur) and across the weedy bog. Then keep right of the
great chestnut and pray the Pantokrator's angels the sorcerer's not bound a confusion
spell to lose you in the groves. A well-trod path,* he'd said, his great shoulders
shuddering.

Both the obscurity and the local popularity . . . and the shudder . . .
had encouraged my decision to seek out this man. Only a skilled mage
would be able to explain the spyglass and untangle the workings of complex and illicit sorcery. And every other mage I knew of lived under the
inquisitive eye of the Camarilla Magica, scarce an objective position, considering the eighteen years' hostility between the king and Camarilla.

"Halloo! Most fearsome mage, are you to home?" Lord Ilario's cheerful trumpeting caromed off the crowding trees, only to die a quick death
in the breathless stillness.

"Chevalier, I must ask again that you adhere to our plan," I said
through clenched teeth. "We agreed to be oblique in our approach until
we're sure of him. And please, sir, curb your . . . good humor. Rumor
names this mage easily offended and unaccustomed to courtly manners."

"Nonsense. Any man of the blood will have had a proper upbringing, whether in the bosom of his family or at Collegia Seravain."

"This mage is unusual, Chevalier. His hand bears no blood family's mark. Nor did he study at Seravain."

That a man not kin to one of the noble families who carried the trait of magical talent, and not formally schooled in the accumulated knowledge of sorcery, much of which was secret, could earn a mage's collar was as likely as a rabbit writing a treatise on the movement of the planets. But so this fellow had done.

Three years previous, he had arrived at Seravain and demanded to sit for examination, naming himself *Exsanguin—Bloodless*. After five rigorous days, he had won through to the rank of master, leaving the collegia faculty in an uproar. Not only had he earned the right to practice sorcery without supervision, and to oversee and instruct other mages, but he was eligible to be named to the Camarilla Prefecture—those who ruled on the accuracy of teachings and charted the course of sorcery in the world. But to the amazement of all, in the same hour his silver collar was sealed about his neck, he had walked away, vanishing into the obscurity from which he'd come.

I had never met Exsanguin, but as Seravain's archivist, I had duly recorded his collaring and the demesne he'd claimed as residence. Twelve days traveling on the back roads of Louvel and much cajoling of reticent villagers had brought Ilario and me to Bardeu. The villagers did not know the sorcerer's true name, either.

"Saints Awaiting!" mumbled Ilario. "Rogue mages are the Souleater's servants. At the least, I've some protection." He pulled a lump of black string, seashells, scarlet beads, and silver bangles from his pocket and dangled it from silk-gloved fingers. "Adept Fedrigo made this for me before I traveled to the sea last summer, as I had expressed my mortal fear of crocodiles. I think it must be a most efficacious charm. For certain, I suffered neither scratch, bite, nor sighting of the wicked creatures. Indeed, I could not even complain about a poor bed upon my travels. Do you think it will suffice in this dismal wood?"

I closed my eyes and inhaled deeply. "Certainly, Chevalier. I'd wager we'll encounter not a single crocodile today."

Hilarity bubbled out of him until he near choked on it. At least he took no offense when my annoyance burst its bounds so injudiciously— damnable idiot.

Our mounts' hooves thudded solidly on the well-beat track through a tunnel of oaks and chestnuts. Stray gleams of sunlight glinted on bits of polished tin hung here and there on the lower branches. No matter the Camarilla's strictures against illicit practice, the ignorant would ever pay hedge witches and marketplace conjurers for such useless trinkets, thinking to ward their travels on perilous paths.

As we rounded a curve, the path opened into a trampled clearing. The unhandsome stone house with sagging thatch might have been a particularly large acorn dropped from one of the thick-boled oaks. I signaled a halt.

"At last!" Ilario flung a long leg over his beast and dropped lightly to the turf. With a flourish, the lanky young lord removed his traveling cloak and tossed it across his saddle, exposing a sky blue satin waistcoat and uselessly thin and tight leather breeches of the fashionable sort deemed suitable for "rustic" excursions. He swept his arm in my direction. "Lead me, good Portier."

I disembarked from my lead-footed mare and smoothed my sober gray tunic. No one would ever call me a "fashionable young twit" or "a preening peacock with a mind less weighty than his feathers." Sighing, I scuffed a clot of dung from my boots. Quite a duet we made—Ilario the Fop, the laughingstock of Merona, and Portier de Duplais, librarian, bound together like a peacock and a tortoise, ready to face the assaults of the unholy.

"Divine grace shine upon thee and thy ancestors, master mage!" I called.

No one answered. Ilario kissed his luck charm, and though his expression maintained a proper sobriety, he winked at me in the intimate manner that I had not yet deciphered, but which felt most unseemly.

I called again, a little louder this time. "Master mage, a word with you, if we might."

No leaf stirred in the thicket of saplings, buckthorn, and laurel that

obscured much of the ugly house. No smoke rose from the peak of the roof.

"Bother, if the fellow is away." Ilario pursed his lips, blew a disappointed note, and propped his arms on his saddle, gazing mournfully at me across his beast. Even his plume seemed to droop.

Dried mud, gouged with footprints, bore witness to a great number of visitors—both men and women, many in thick, nailed boots and others on horseback. Some had come in sodden winter; others within the past tennight, as approaching summer tempered the rains. Horses had been tethered here for hours at a time.

"Ill-tempered," the locals had told us. "Wouldn't cross him . . . not for a purse full of kivrae." Yet yeomen, merchants, tradesmen, and even the poorest of husbandmen and laborers sought him out, and he served them willing. "'E fixes them as is cursed in the mind," was the clearest report we'd scavenged. That could mean anything from providing sleeping draughts to excising bits of brain tissue like the storied Mad Healer of Dock Street.

So why the shabby surroundings? Even in these times, when magical practitioners' prestige had ebbed to the level of jongleurs or card cheats, a master mage could live as well as a duc. Privacy could be bought in fairer packages than an ugly hut in a chestnut grove.

I rapped on the door but jerked my hand away. The awareness of living enchantment slithered up my arm like a fiery snake. I'd never felt the like. I grasped a small, smooth stone inside my coin pocket. The courret, a rare wardstone borrowed from Seravain, chilled my fingers, declaring that the lingering enchantment posed no danger. I'd no other way to tell. Disentanglation, discerning the particular nature of the enchantments or magical residues my trained senses perceived, required spellwork, and thus lay beyond my abilities.

Footsteps crunched in the brush.

"Who's there?" The resonant voice was a presence in itself, deep, substantial, brittle, cold as the north wind off the barrens of Delourre.

I whipped my head around.

A lean, wiry man halted at the edge of the trees. His gaunt face was

unshaven. The dark hair that dangled wild and loose at front and sides had escaped from a shaggy tail. Despite the imperious greeting, the pick and three iron lever bars dangling from his belt, and the heavy boots, russet tunic, and work-stained canvas slops named him a common countryman. And though he measured scant centimetres taller than my own modest height, I was uncomfortably certain he could snap my scrawny limbs like twigs. He balanced a sizable stone on his shoulder with only one hand. He appeared entirely unlike any mage I had ever met, and yet . . .

"We've come to see the mage on important business, goodman. Is he nearby?" Ilario dabbed his long nose with a kerchief and craned his neck, peering deeper into the trees.

If I could but glimpse the man's neck . . . Mages were forbidden to hide or remove their silver collars, the Camarilla's concession to the fears of the powerless.

"Identify yourselves." The fellow emerged from the gloom and halted in the center of the clearing. Indeed, a seamless band of silver encircled his sinewed neck, wholly incongruous with his rough attire. And the collar's fine lay of gold designated the wearer a master mage. Yet it was the voice that marked him as worthy of note . . . and the eyes set deep under heavy brows. The fiery green of new oak leaves, those eyes could slice paper edge-on. For certain, no common laborer had such.

The fop snapped his hands to his sides and inclined his head. "Ilario de Sylvae, Chevalier ys Sabria, sir mage. And my good companion, Portier de Duplais."

"Divine grace, Master," I said, bowing with my left hand laid on my right shoulder, the mark of my blood family clearly exposed. "We would appreciate a word with you on a matter of interest."

"I share no interests with aristos."

"I am the archivist at Collegia Seravain," I said. "When examining our records—"

"Go away. I dislike company." The sorcerer hefted his burden a little higher and vanished into the oak and blackthorn scrub crowding the left side of the house.

Ilario bolted after him like a startled doe. "Hold on, sir mage!"

"Please, Master! Chevalier!" My call might have been floating dust for all it slowed them.

I had no choice but to follow. I needed a talented outsider to pursue this investigation. If this mage had skills to match his arrogance, the level of knowledge his collar bespoke, and some quantity of honor that could be claimed or bought, we might have found our man.

Thorny branches snagged my clothes, and my boots sank into the soft earth.

However, the gangly fop darted through the tangle unhindered. "Hear me out, sir mage," he called brightly. "We've brought you an invitation . . . an opportunity, one might say. If we could but sit for a moment, share a glass of wine, perhaps. My mistress will be most distressed if her offer is unheard. Most distressed . . ."

Mistress? Enthroned god! I'd told the fool to let me handle this.

Wrenching my sleeve from the barbed grip of the brush, I stumbled into a small, sunny garden: a few orderly hills and rows of vegetables, and a raised bed of close-planted herbs, swarming with bees. Garlic shoots and thick, low masses of dusty greenery bordered the plot.

Astonishing. From the mage's wild appearance, and the smoldering fury that tainted his words, one might better have expected devilish machinery or smoking pits.

"I've tasks enough to occupy my time. Take your opportunity elsewhere." The earth quivered when he dropped his loaf-shaped stone to the barren ground on the far side of the garden. At least fifty similarly shaped stones lay about the area, some stacked, some scattered randomly, some carefully trimmed and fitted into three walls set square to one another. Chips and flakes of stone littered the dirt.

Ilario blotted his cheeks with his lace kerchief. "Please, good sir mage—"

The mage whirled, his fiery gaze raking Ilario's turnout from purple plume to sleek boots. He flared his nostrils. "If my oven was built, I could bake bread and serve a noble guest and his companion properly. Even a coarse meal would better suit your taste than converse with the likes of me. But my bakefire cannot be lit as yet, so you must leave my home un-

satisfied." He removed the pick and the iron bar from his belt and tossed them to the dirt. "*Leave*. Do fine gentlemen like you understand a plain-spoke word?"

Shivers cooled my overheated skin. No welcome here; the villagers had not erred in that.

Squatting with his back to us, the mage shoved the new stone close to the others. His wide, long-fingered left hand palmed the height and width of the block as if to measure it against its fellows. The back of that hand, thick with black hair, was clean of any family mark, as the tale of Exsanguin bespoke. Odd how the right hand stayed so firmly inside his tunic. Was he armed?

Despairing, I ventured into the dismissive silence. "If you would but allow me to explain, Master. My position as archivist led me to your name—"

"We are *sent*, sir mage!" Ilario bellowed at the man's back, while bulging his eyes and waggling his brows at me incomprehensibly. "My mistress believes that current mania for scientific advancement has unfairly turned popular opinion against the mystic arts. She has assembled a consilium of mages, graciously lending her particular prestige to their works." He began to march up and down, bobbing his feathered cap like a cock in a hen roost. "Certainly your next question will be *what works might these be?* Unfortunately, I am incapable of telling you. Though I represent a woman whose intellect scales great heights, my own wit plods along the solid earth. My comrade Portier, here, himself a learned practitioner of your fantastical arts, could explain our aims better, but, of course, he is a modest man of modest rank and shy of intruding in conversation between his betters. Besides, my lady has particularly charged *me* to offer *you* her patronage. . . ."

Blessed saints, the mage would believe we were both flea-wits. The fool Ilario had gotten it wholly muddled. We had agreed that I would assess the mage by luring him into a test of his capability and honor. Only when I was satisfied would we broach the matter of the queen's mages and what we needed him to do. The queen knew—and could know—nothing about this mission.

Yet, indeed, the mage twisted around and stared at Ilario with an intensely curious expression.

"My lady relishes nurturing new talent. I can assure you . . ." Ilario's prattle skidded to a stop under the weight of the mage's scrutiny.

The disconcerting gaze shifted to me. My skin itched. Unease swelled in my belly, reaching full growth, then relaxed again like a flower that buds, blooms, and fades all in the space of ten heartbeats. My soul felt abraded—exposed. Likely it was my conscience. Surely this man recognized the lies.

"What game is this you play?" said the mage softly, returning his attention to Ilario. His dark brows knit a line. "Speak as yourself this time, lord."

Ilario's lips parted, but no sound issued from between them. I, too, felt rendered mute.

"Does truth pain a Sabrian chevalier so much?" The mage extracted a stylus from a jumble of tools in a wooden chest and scored the new block across several of its faces, rolling and marking it entirely with his left hand. "So, one or the other of you can tell me truthfully why you're here. Or I can draw it out of your asses with a billhook. Or you can go away and leave me to my *common labor*."

A sighing breeze shifted the overhanging branches. The sultry gloom deepened. I rubbed my arms through the worn velvet of my doublet.

I was no gullible stable hand who believed charmed cats could cure his pox or pond scum make his wife fertile. Though all agreed that Sabria's greater magic had faded, I had studied the testimony of those who had seen mages soothe whirlwinds and stem the advance of poisoned tides. I myself had felt the balance of the five divine elements and the flow of power through my veins and deepest self—no matter that the result was naught but a sputter in the scheme of the world. But the vibrant and richly textured power swirling about this sunny garden was no more kin to the magic I had experienced than a sunset is cousin to a candle flame. Pressing the back of my hand to my mouth, I fought a compulsion to spew King Philippe's secrets, though the mage had not even raised his uncommon voice.

Ilario's golden skin took on the hue of sour milk. He swallowed, blinked, and dabbed at his quivering lower lip, then straightened his long neck as if for the headsman. "My apologies, sir mage. Allow me to clarify. That my kinswoman defies popular beliefs with support of sorcery is true. What I failed to mention is that she is interested in certain areas of magical pursuit that many people might consider . . . unsavory. And I must confess that my mistress has not yet heard of you. I took this inquiry upon myself after hearing Portier's report—"

"My lord!" Father Creator, he was ready to tell all. "Discretion, sir!"

"We must tell him the truth, Portier! For my lady's sake. Sir mage, some days ago, my friend Portier told me of your unusual collaring at Collegia Seravain. I bade him locate you in hopes you might take an interest in my mistress's needs. In fact, I've been thinking of hiring my own mage. I've no staff at all save my valet, which is highly improper for a person of rank, depending on others to see to my requirements. . . ." Ilario, lost in his prattling deception, flashed me a desperate look. My head threatened to split.

The mage tossed his stylus aside and settled onto the dirt, resting his folded arms on his drawn-up knees, as if prepared to lecture us. "What part of my history leads you or *you*"—he glared ferociously at me—"to believe that I might be willing to be kept in some aristo's menagerie alongside the horses, hounds, and birds? I work as I please and study what I please, and no one demands my time be spent making love philtres or skin glamours or servicing whatever 'unsavory' desires your mistress wishes to indulge. I've countless better things to do."

As I tried not to stare at the mage's now-exposed right hand—a red-scarred, twisted claw living ugly and useless at the end of a well-muscled arm—my mind raced to knit Ilario's unraveled stupidity into a useful story. The fop had skewed the truth just enough to leave me an opening for the very test of skill and character I wished this visit to encompass. If only I knew how to entice the mage into revelations. Obviously, he cared naught for comforts or renown. What induced him to accommodate those who came here seeking his help?

"Because the opportunities we offer are unique," I blurted, insight like

a blade between my ears. "Your history and this place"—I waved my hand to encompass his odd home—"and gossip of a forbidding mage who untangles the mysteries of broken minds led me—us—to believe we might find in you a certain . . . nontraditional . . . approach to your work. A talented man interested in puzzles."

"Go on."

Scarce daring to believe I'd guessed right, I laid down another thread. "We could offer virtually unlimited resources to advance whatever studies you wish—books, funds, connections to information and materials from every corner of the known world, the most prominent mages in Sabria as your colleagues. You would have the opportunity to collaborate in magic of a grander scale than you could—"

Mirthless laughter halted me midargument. "So you *are* more fools than villains," said the mage. "Unfortunately for you, it has been many years since I concluded that large-scale magical works are entirely sham and chicanery, and that the 'most prominent mages' in Sabria have not the least concept of true sorcery. In short, your benevolent mistress is misguided at best, some duc's whore perpetuating a fraud at worst, and she could not offer me gold enough to participate in such a mockery."

"Speak no slander, sir!" Ilario's words dropped in the mage's lap like a challenge glove. "We serve the Queen of Sabria."

"Lord Ilario!" I snapped, horrified. The fop had almost got me believing he had a wit.

"The queen?" The mage guffawed. "So the 'prominent' colleagues you offer are the shadow queen's trained Camarilla pups? I'd sooner bed a leper than ally myself with clowns and fools."

No reasoning man could wholly discount the charges laid against sorcerers—that some of us paraded grand illusion in the guise of true sorcery. But this brutish arrogance was insupportable.

"Civilized men do not belittle those they do not know," I snapped, summoning what dignity I could muster ankle deep in a vegetable patch. "You may be gifted, sir, but the mages of the Camarilla have proved their talents over centuries."

He only grew quieter and more contemptuous. "Show me the great

work of a Camarilla mage, *student*, and I will show you with what tools a minimally talented hod carrier can duplicate it. Show me one of your own great works. Or perhaps . . . even a small one?"

And so was Ilario's challenge glove returned to my own lap, along with the mage's choice of weapons. I had not thought my failed status so obvious.

Annoyed at my slip of control, I gathered my temper. I had not come here to demonstrate my own magical worth. If we were to fail at this, all the better this man believe me Ilario's intellectual peer.

"No," I said, crushing doubt and pride alike with the hammer of necessity. "*You* show *us*. Elsewise, we shall assume you're naught but a trickster with a crude mouth, afraid to speak your own name, and with no better concept of magical truth than those you disdain. I can provide interesting, magically challenging employment for a skilled mage who values truth, scorns danger, and bears no loyalty to the Camarilla or any other magical practitioner."

One corner of his mouth twisted in what might pass for amusement. Far more satisfying was the spark of curiosity that flared in his green eyes. "What employment might that be? You do not sacrifice your pride before a forbidding and unpleasant man for a charm to calm your horse."

Swallowing my discomfiture at his insight, I laid down my challenge. "If you are interested, clean yourself, dress as befits a master mage, and join us at Villa Margeroux, off the Tallemant Road, within three days. A hired mount will await your use in Bardeu. Be prepared to dazzle us with your demonstration of magical truth. If we are satisfied with your application, Master Exsanguin, we will explain our dangerous proposition."

I bowed to the fop and motioned him back through the underbrush to the horses. Lord Ilario nodded in return and marched away, patting my shoulder as if he had given birth to me.

The green gaze scorched my back as I followed Ilario out of the garden. "Dante," said the uncommon voice behind us. "My name is Dante."

CHAPTER TWO

I had believed the mage intrigued. Something had induced him to yield his name. Dante. *Exsanguin*. Bloodless. By the holy Veil, even the memory of his stare set me glancing over my shoulder. But the third day had almost waned before the Contessa de Margeroux's housekeeper announced a visitor.

"He will not step inside, Conte Olivier." The comfortable gray woman of middling years huffed as if the report scalded her mouth. "He says he's come to see—forgive me, lord, but he's charged me to repeat his words exactly—the student and the dancepole and no . . . inbred aristos. Is it certain he's the person expected? Such a dirty, crude ruffian?"

I doubted the housekeeper's protective loyalty to the elderly Conte de Margeroux and his much younger Lady Susanna was much tested. Though valued friends of the king, the couple lived quietly in this remote demesne. The conte directed an inquiring scowl at Ilario.

"Your report but confirms his identity, good Hanea," said Ilario, shuddering. "And you'd best obey. Cross him and he'll likely change you into an ox. He is entirely yours, Portier. I've no wish to lay eyes on the creature." He waggled his glittering, ringed fingers, his beloved lace cuffs dangling unchecked into his brandy—a measure of his disturbance.

He had determinedly not spoken of Dante since we'd left the chestnut wood.

As I set out to meet our visitor, Conte Olivier retired. I wasn't sure how much the elderly lord and his wife knew of Philippe's personal troubles, but the king clearly trusted their discretion. Not only did they house the assassin's implements, but for fifteen days they had treated Ilario and me as familiar guests, never inquiring of our business.

A bit of wilderness had been allowed to flourish amid the pristine cultivation of Lord Olivier's sprawling demesne. Old joint-pines, creeping laurel, and budding strawberry trees created a fragrant and secluded haven. The footman reported that the visitor had made his way there straightaway.

"Have you an aversion to sunlight, Master Dante?" I said when he spun in his tracks at my approach.

His silver collar shone dully above the same shabby tunic he'd worn three days before, topped by a buff jerkin. Three days' growth had left his chin bristling with black spikelets akin to fen sedge. His dreadful hand was tucked inside his garments. The other hand gripped a white walking stick.

"I've a need to stretch out the knots of beast riding," he said, resuming his brisk pace as soon as I joined him. "Wasn't born to it."

Of all things, I'd never expected to smile in this man's presence. No wonder it had taken him so long to get here.

"I've scorched thighs myself," I said. "Tending a library gives one few opportunities to ride out, even did Seravain have mounts to lend. The chevalier must have a steel ass underneath his silk stockings."

The mage glanced sidewise at me, flaring his nostrils as if an ill odor accompanied us. "How well do you know the pretty peacock?"

I saw no reason to dissemble. "Lord Ilario is harmless and good natured, saints bless his empty-headed ancestors. I did not choose him to partner in this task."

"Perhaps." He slowed to a walk. "So you expected to do the choosing . . . and *you* chose to approach me. Why?"

"As I said, your history speaks of exceptional talents—which you have

yet to demonstrate—and a certain independence of thought—which you most clearly possess. And even after our short meeting, I cannot imagine a danger that would deter you, did you find your work intriguing." Until that moment I had not articulated, even to myself, this certainty that he was the partner we needed. "I cannot and will not say more until I have your assurances—"

"I am no courtier who barters trust like paper words that can be burnt, or ink-drowned, or swept aside by any wind," he snapped. "I speak plain and expect the same respect. You'll get no assurances until I understand the whole of what you want. I don't know why I've wasted my time with you."

I hoped my satisfaction did not show. He did not understand his own hunger. "Clearly a man hiring a mage for a secret and dangerous task cannot reveal everything at once," I said. "So let us proceed step by step. But I'll promise you this: If I decide you are the right person, you will know everything I know before we begin."

He considered that as we strolled deeper into the woodland. "If I agree to the work," he said at last, "I deal with you and not the lordling. I'll not abide deceivers."

"Agreed." My spine relaxed at such easy negotiation. "Now before we proceed, I must inquire about your parentage."

No porcupine could bristle so vividly. "That is *not* your business."

"Bloodlines often hint at areas of expertise. I have been tasked to solve a mystery, and your expertise is your qualification."

"Bloodlines are irrelevant. I've queried witnesses who vouch this body burst from my common mother's womb thanks to my common father's seed. The two of them bequeathed me naught but this." He yanked out his ruined hand. "Speak not to me of blessed ancestors or blood-born magic. I've neither worth the telling."

"But your talents . . ."

"Everything I possess of spellmaking is learnt or discovered." He thrust his maimed hand back into hiding, planted the walking stick, and moved on, visibly quenching his flared temper. "Does that intrigue you, Portier de Duplais, failed student?"

He sped his steps, and I could not read his back. What kind of *agente confide* could I be if a new acquaintance could deduce my own history so easily?

"Show me, Master," I said, more forcefully than I intended. "You boast and scoff, and I hear naught but a marketplace shill, luring me into a diviner's tent where I'll be told the name of my true love for a mere two kivrae. Teach me your *discovered* truth of magic. I may be only a student who has discerned his natural limits, but I am a very *good* student."

He halted, waiting for me, his folded arms resting on his chest, the staff tight in the crook of his arm. His mouth twisted oddly, narrowed eyes gleaming fierce in the failing light. Assessing me. I did my best not to squirm.

"All right, then. I presume you have memorized the formulas for many spells. You've learnt to balance the five divine elements—water, wood, air, spark, and base metal—by choosing appropriate particles to embody each formula and adjusting those particles according to the spell's particular requirements: selecting a smaller shard of limestone to make a gate ward less rigid, or choosing three spoons of dust to increase the proportion of air and wood, allowing a sleeping fog to be easily dispersed, or adding a lock of hair from the person to be healed or warded or glamoured so that your enchantment will be tight bound to its focus. But tell me, are the particles themselves—or any other natural object—ever altered by your spellworking?"

"Certainly not." Certainly not in my case—but not in anyone else's case, either. "A particle can be glamoured—disguised with light to fool the eye—but the other senses would reveal its unchanged state. Or the particle, as any other object, can be used as a receptacle, linked to the spell so the enchantment can be transported. But magic itself is ephemera. Dust is naught but dust. Stone is stone. A thistle is a thistle. The Pantokrator has rendered nature immutable."

We rounded a corner and came to an open glade. At one end of the clearing, stones had been stacked and fitted and a flow of water channeled to imitate a rocky waterfall. A stone bench sat to one side of the burbling font.

"Yet we melt silver and shape it," said Dante, motioning me not to the bench, but to the ground in front of the font. "We alloy zinc and copper to make brass. We steep leaves in water to make tea."

Irritated at his condescending tone, I cleared away a litter of thorny branches and last year's leaves and sat cross-legged on the cool ground like a child in village school. A rabbit scuttered through the underbrush to find a new hiding place. "I am not an idiot, mage. Such are blendings or reshaping, not fundamental alterations. Brass is but a variant formulation of the divine elements. The metalsmith has added spark, and the new metal's properties—weight, mass, hardness, malleability—remain appropriate to the combined elements. It is not magic."

"Just what I'd expect a squawking parrot to report. Sit knees together, close your eyes, and quiet your thoughts."

Curiosity—and a determination to see through whatever conjury he planned—goaded me to obey. From beyond my eyelids came a shifting and scraping and a grunt of effort. Whatever I expected, it had naught to do with an anvil being set in my lap. *No, not an anvil, but one of the stones from the font.* The cool solidity weighed heavy on my knees.

"Your masters at Collegia Seravain would have you believe they can recreate a memorized formula and bind a potion to smooth the skin of an old woman or generate a finger of holy fire to ensure a royal counselor's honesty. They preen when they succeed and provide a litany of excuses when the crone dies wrinkled and the counselor is caught embezzling from the treasury. They fail to inform their patrons that a common laborer could hold the lenses they've used to focus beams of light or that any decent herbalist can provide a salve of apricots and olive oil to improve the skin as long as the woman is not *too* old and eats well and stays out of the sun."

The mage's warm fingers arranged my hands side by side on the cool flattish stone in my lap. His hardened palm remained atop my hands. "True sorcery begins with small things," he said, his ever-present scorn yielding to something more kin to reverence. "Every natural object in this world— tree, stone, person, honeybee—carries with it a pattern of sound and light that our eyes and ears cannot perceive. Some call it the object's *cast.* . . . "

I released my held breath. What a hypocrite! *Cast* was naught but old-

wife twaddle—the trickster's love philtres, ghekets, and fairy rings this man purported to disdain. Yet before I could protest, the space behind my eyes—the center of my thinking self—began to heat like a glowing ember.

". . . but it is more accurately called *keirna*, for this patterning lies beyond our natural senses. A properly disciplined mind can perceive these patterns, just as refined lenses can perceive stars invisible to our eyes. Consider this particular object you hold. . . ."

Against the dark background inside my eyelids appeared lines of shimmering gray light, some lighter, some darker, stacked one atop the other like some arcane glyph, the line at the bottom thicker than the one at the top. I'd never experienced the like.

"The pattern reflects the solidity and strength that is the stone's nature. . . ."

As the mage spoke, another line appeared at the top of the stack curving gracefully around to connect at the bottom, touching every other line in the array.

". . . as are its continuity, enclosure, boundedness. Now consider the specifics of *this* rock, the minerals it contains, the shape and weight and source and history that make it like no other."

And woven in and out of the gray lines appeared slender threads of bright red, dull gold, and other colors I could not name. Permeating all was a low thrum, a sound so precise it was almost visible, a pulse that gave the pattern life.

"Were I to strike the rock with a chisel, I would alter this pattern—its keirna—but only in small ways. Because I study the language of keirna, the pattern would yet speak to me of stone, cut from yonder crags, formed in fire in the recesses of history and shaped apurpose to build this font."

Ridiculous. Stone was stone—an amalgam of the divine elements of wood, water, and base metal. Stone was softer or harder—more or less of the wood that made it firm and the base metal that made it impermeable. It was black or red or white, grainy or smooth. Such properties helped us judge the concentration of the elements in a particle and create the proper balance to bind spells. No magical *essence* hung about it.

"Human thoughts have patterns, as well." The mage's rich and resonant voice seemed strained, as if he balanced fifty such stones high above his head, demonstrating their shapes and sizes to the world. "Those of true talent—and though there are more of them in this world than you might suspect, few wear mage's collars or reside in palaces—are capable of extending their patterns of thought and will to touch keirna, to link and bind and manipulate the keirna of various objects . . . creating . . . magic."

Into my vision intruded a finger of light, a pinpoint of dark blue brilliance with a tail of silver and crimson. The finger shredded the thick lower line and picked out some of the thinner weavings. In that same moment, as the surety of enchantment settled over me like a garment, I would have wagered my life that someone lifted the stone from my knees, though my hands told me it had not moved and had not changed in length or breadth or thickness. And when I opened my eyes, unable to contain myself longer, indeed *nothing* had changed but the weight of the massive stone. A burden little heavier than a pebble rested on my lap.

No, no, you cannot alter the fundamental properties of a particle—an object of the Pantokrator's creation. I lifted my hands, shoving his away, and shifted my knees, expecting to disrupt his illusion. Nothing changed. I inserted my fingers between the stone and my thighs and hefted it. Turned it over. Shook it. Held it in one hand and raised it higher than my head, before resting it in my lap again and staring at it. A child could have tossed the thing into the air or skipped it on a pond. Illusions deposited a faint magical residue the texture of dry meal. Dante's left the air crackling like summer lightning.

The green eyes bored into mine, watching, waiting, judging me. I stared into their fiery depths and felt the foundations of my world crack.

The mage did not smile, but nodded as if a conversation had been concluded. "That, student, is the truth of sorcery."

His clawed hand gripped his walking stick, and he rested his head on it. A sighed word and the stone's full weight pressed down on my knees again.

I could not ask him how he'd learned it. To do so would have been to admit that I had failed not only in my aspiration, but in my striving. That

I had wasted sixteen years. That my chosen masters, the priests of my mind's temple, the most honored mages of history— By the Ten Gates to Heaven, I had *read* their teachings hunting answers to my failure, and none gave a moment's credence to *cast*—the idea that magic lived not solely in the blood and will of a practitioner, but in all of nature, waiting to be drawn out. How could they all be wrong about the fundamental truths of the world?

I wanted to scream at Dante that he was the Souleater's servant, a trickster demon. Yet I knew better. Illusions deceived the external senses, but this strange patterning of light and sound had appeared inside my mind where only I could render judgment. Unless I was myself a madman, he had shown me truth.

Perhaps he understood the lump the size of his rock that had lodged itself in my throat, for he spoke quietly and without rancor or hubris. "The mages at Seravain proclaim that only those they choose, only those born of proven bloodlines, only those who memorize their lists and follow their formulas, can work magic. Sorcery acknowledges no such limits. Most of the truly gifted work their small magics by rote, imitating what their grannies told them, or by instinct, because they have not separated themselves from nature by dividing all things into five divine boxes. Some of these people actually sense keirna and are able to manipulate a pattern as I did."

"Why don't we hear of this?" I said, grasping at arguments that evaporated with my touch. Fools and tricksters everywhere swore by their charms, philtres, wards, by their mother's healing power or their uncle's virility potion. What few claims ever proved true had been traced to a blood family's bastard or some true practitioner's deception.

"All those I've met work blind," said Dante, scritching the end of his staff in the dirt. "None claim to see the actual structure of keirna or attempt to display it for another as I did with you. Yet even if they did, who would believe? The Camarilla would name them cheats and deceivers and fine them into starvation, or torture them until they recant and brand them on the forehead, all to prove that collared mages alone hold the mighty reins of power. Cursed be their blackguard souls—"

He bit off a snarl, and his good hand tugged at his silver collar, as if it chafed; as if the masters at Seravain, jealous of his talent and despising his rude manner, had left a burr inside its enchanted circle or unbalanced its elements so that it would not accommodate the play of his muscles. No wonder they had been happy to forget him. His results and the lack of a blood mark on his hand must have confounded them. And he was correct; if the Camarilla had any idea of the magical heresies he propounded, they would bury him so far below Sabria's deepest dungeon, he would never see light again.

The mage had leaned his back against the fountain and closed his eyes as if to sleep. Not a peaceful sleep, but that of a wary traveler on an unknown road. "So, do I pass your test?"

I could not accept an entire reversal of my beliefs. Somewhere between his truth and mine must lie a connection I was too simple to recognize. But I could not deny him. Sainted ancestors, if all this were true, my mind could not encompass the possibilities of his talent.

I raised my head and sucked in the heaviness that weighed upon my spirit far more than the stone I had rolled off my knees. "If you agree to the terms of our partnership, I'll show you what we face and what I propose for you to do about it."

OF COURSE, DANTE ACCEPTED MY terms: absolute secrecy, loyalty to Sabria's interests, and acknowledgment of my direction. These were not difficult oaths for him, I thought, a man who had secrets of his own. He clearly cared naught for the gold or political gain that could come from betrayal. More significant to my mind, this unpleasant and forbidding man had opened a small window into himself and shown me the one thing in the world he cared about—magic. What greater offering of trust exists than that? I liked him.

As night fell on Lady Susanna's wild garden, I led Master Dante down the courtyard stair to the Conte Olivier's iron-bound cell. "Fifteen days ago, I was brought down here, sworn to the same oath I asked of you, and told a strange story. One afternoon nigh on a year ago, the King of Sabria

rode out to exercise with his household guard—the Guard Royale—as he does every tennight. He jousted, sparred with his favored partners, shot close targets with a pistol, and practiced with his longbow. His captain of the guard, a man who had stood at his back since he was crowned, challenged him to a wrestling match—a sport he much enjoyed in his youth. Though the king was soundly thumped, both he and the captain were laughing at the end of it."

I unlocked the door with the key my royal cousin had entrusted to me. The arrow, the spyglass, and the coin lay on the stone table, exactly as the king and I had left them.

"As His Majesty rode from the field, this arrow struck his saddle, scarce missing the great vein in his thigh, to the peril of his life"—I locked the door behind us and hung the lamp from a wire loop above the table— "for, naturally, he had not donned his armor after the wrestling. The horse fell, but the king managed to leap free, unharmed.

"His guardsmen scoured the field, in a fury that so bold an attempt was made in their very midst. Two of them noted a man wearing their own livery drop his bow behind a tree. They attempted to question him, but discovered the man incapable of speech. Before they could alert their comrades, he hamstrung one of his captors and strangled the other. As he ran away, he dropped this spyglass. When he retrieved it, the hamstrung guardsman threw his ax, and fortunately or unfortunately as you may see it, felled the assailant before he himself died. The villain would have gone free if he'd kept running."

Dante's brow creased. He leaned his walking stick in the corner and squatted low to get a closer look. He did not touch the artifacts. "Go on."

"The guard captain stripped the corpus in search of his identity, and instantly forbade any other to come near. The man's arms and legs were scored and scabbed, bruising, scars, and cupping marks every centimetre. . . ."

"Transference," said Dante softly, his two fingers tracing the line of the half-split arrow shaft without actually touching it. "The archer was a source—a mule. And the sorcerer who leeched the archer's blood to grow

his own power persuaded . . . induced . . . forced him to wield the nasty bit of weaponry. Did the arrow deliver poison?"

"The king assumes so, as the horse convulsed and died. Philippe immediately commanded his most loyal friend, Michel de Vernase, Conte Ruggiere, to investigate the assault. The conte ordered the horse and saddle burned in place as a precaution against a contaminating poison or a lingering spell-trap. With a mage implicated, Vernase-Ruggiere chose not to call in a practitioner to examine the arrow."

"But you've looked at it."

"I detect no extant enchantment, only a strong magical residue. But I've no skill to analyze it."

He took no note of my admission. "I'd guess the aristo lackwit had the assassin-mule's corpse burnt, as well."

"They could not allow word to get out." A hint that an unknown mage was practicing blood transference would send blood families running to their fortresses, unraveling two centuries of concord between factions. "The conte immediately arrested the guard captain, for on any other exercise day, the king would not have shed his armor before leaving the practice field. And there the problem becomes infinitely more complex."

The mage glanced up at me, sharp-eyed. "Could it be the *queen* set the captain to propose the grapple?"

No longer amazed at his quickness, I nodded. "There is a history of strain between our liege and his wife—their marriage when she was widowed so young, her failure to birth a living heir since their first boy died, disagreements over the role of sorcery in their aligned households, and more, I think, that he did not tell me. His own counselors have long pressured him to set her aside. Yet he holds determined faith in her innocence and would not . . . and will not . . . have her questioned."

"So what is the coin?"

"Likely nothing," I said, "though you'll see it is a double strike. Some people consider a two-faced coin lucky. The conte found it in the mule's jerkin, the sole item he carried. I sensed no enchantment on it, yet—" I could not explain the sensation that had come over me when I'd first held

the coin. It was as if I'd been thrown into a plummeting waterfall and emerged to the nauseating certainty that my body had been turned wrong side out or hung up by my feet, and all the blood rushed to my head. "There is a strangeness about it."

"The noble investigator has no theories?"

And so to the next element of the mystery. "A month after the attempt, Michel de Vernase wrote a letter to the king stating he'd found new evidence and hoped to have a solid case before too many more days passed. He said he planned 'a second visit to Collegia Seravain.' No one has seen or heard from him since."

"Mayhap he found the villain he was hunting." Dante's attention shifted to the spyglass. "And this?"

I swallowed hard and glared at the instrument, its tarnished surface gleaming dully in the light. It seemed wrong that such a fine invention, a marvel not so many years ago, could so strike my heart with dread.

"Naught is known of its origin or purpose. But when you sight through it, you'll understand why our dilemma is so much more than marital disaffection, more even than the revival of such evil practice as blood transference. And you'll see why we need a talented mage to help unravel this mystery." The memory of my own looking made me wish to creep into a cave and hide.

Dante drew his fingers along the artifact's tarnished case and around each of its knurled grips. He brushed dust and damp from the lenses, and while bracing it awkwardly with his scarred right fingers, he examined its construction, expanding and collapsing its length and twisting the grips.

"This was not expertly made," he said. "Its mechanisms are unbalanced, its material impure." He glanced up. "This takes no magic to learn, if you're wondering, but only the teaching of a skilled instrument maker. But the making shapes its keirna, and it's nae possible to comprehend keirna without understanding function and composition."

Stepping back from the light, he balanced the brass instrument in the claw of his ruined hand and peered through the eyepiece. The color drained from his cheeks as it surely had from mine. He set the instrument gingerly upon the stone table and snatched his hands away, breath rapid,

lips compressed, his eyes squeezed tight as if a dagger had pierced his skull.

Dante did not tell me what he'd seen. But as we locked the cell door, I guessed that he, too, had glimpsed a scene beyond this life—a scene not even the most sophisticated enchantments should be able to show us.

"The Veil teachings have never made sense to me," he said. "Why would a god who bothers to create living persons suddenly decide to ship them off someplace worse than this life when they're dead, all in hopes of some heaven that no one can describe? If I have to depend on my kin or some benevolent stranger to get me through ten gates to a paradise that might or might not be better than this, I might as well give up right now. Dead is dead, or so I've claimed. . . ."

I disliked such bluntness. In my youth I had accepted what I'd been taught at the temple: that the Blood Wars had brought humankind to such a state of depravity that the Pantokrator had altered his creation, setting the bleak and treacherous Ixtador between the Veil and Heaven. Those souls who journeyed the trackless desolation and passed Ixtador's Ten Gates would be well purified, worthy of the Pantokrator's glory. Those who failed would be left for the Souleater to devour on the last day of the world.

Unfortunately the dead could do little to further their own cause. The honor and virtuous deeds of the family left behind must provide the strength and endurance for a soul's journey. As I came to see that my weak family connections were unlikely to provide much support for Ixtador's trials, and that my prospects for improving the situation were exceedingly poor, I had shoved such concerns to the back of my mind, unwilling to relinquish either hope or belief. The spyglass insisted I confront the issue.

The mage rubbed the back of his neck tiredly and tugged at his silver collar again. "But then we must ask what is this devilish glass? Gods, if you think I can answer that for you, you've less wit than that rock in the garden. It would take a deal of study. Experimentation. So that's the job, is it? To find out the use of these things. Or, I suppose, it's truly to tell your employer, who is the *king*, I'm guessing, and not his treacherous

wife"—he paused and waited; I nodded and shoved open the outer cell block door—"what sorcerer in this blighted kingdom could create such enchantments and why an assassin—a voiceless mule—would carry them." He ground the heel of his staff into the stone. "Did anyone see the mule *use* the glass?"

"Not that we know."

"His Dimwit Majesty ought to question his queen. I could do *that* for him."

I had no doubt he could. His rumbling undertone shook me like the earth tremors I'd felt when I was a boy, on the day a godshaking had razed the city of Catram eight hundred kilometres away.

"Yes, the king wants to know who's responsible for transference and attempted murder," I said. "He wants his queen exonerated. He wants to know how this instrument can show him a sixteen-year-old battlefield disgorging its dead men, many of whom he knows, into a wilderness that perfectly fits every description of Ixtador Beyond the Veil. And he very much desires to know what's become of Michel de Vernase. Though he's received no demand for ransom or favor in exchange for Michel's life, he refuses to accept that his friend is dead."

We started up the dungeon stair.

"Beyond all that lies his duty to Sabria. The king believes magic is dying, and he bids it good riddance. He sees it as a chain that binds us to superstition and causes us to descend into myth-fed savagery such as the Blood Wars. This event tells him that someone is attempting exactly that, seeking power of such magnitude as to touch the demesne of the dead. But for what purpose? As Sabria's protector, he must understand what's being done and by whom and why. He doesn't trust the Camarilla . . . the prefects . . . any mage . . . knowing how they resent him."

"But for some reason he trusts you, who lives and works among them. You're his spy."

"I prefer the title *agente confide*." It bore a certain gentility; less reso-nances of ugly execution. "As it happens, I am His Majesty's distant kinsman—fortunately for you, *very* distant, so I'll not take exception to your loose-tongued name calling. Though we'd never met until a half

month ago, my cousin subscribes to the old virtues in the matter of family, thus has charged me to protect his life and search out the answers he needs. He believed I was—"

Again came the uncomfortable confession. Nine years previous, Master Kajetan had first forced me to admit failure aloud. As my mentor, he had insisted I speak the verdict to my parents, else I would be tempted to live forever with a delusion. My father, who had ever lived in his own delusions, had taken umbrage. I still wore the scars—within and without. The ugly episode had left me shy of discussing my paucity of talent.

Dante waited. I inhaled deeply. "As you judge correctly, Master, I cannot even begin to unravel such magic. Though I have informed the king of my lacks, he insists he trusts me to solve his mystery. As for the spying— well, for that we must include the chevalier in our conversation. Are you willing to go on, Master Dante? It is time for yea or nay, in or out."

The lamplight scarce touched the bottomless well of the descending stair, and the sinewy, black-haired mage with the unsettling gaze might have been Dimios himself, returning to the world of light for his annual visit, the blighted hand the manifest evidence of his corruption. He halted just below me.

"I doubted you could present me a mystery that I would take on—a librarian with self-loathing so exposed as to make him bold. But I don't like events that contradict my view of the world. So, go on, tell me the rest."

I took that as a *yea*.

CHAPTER THREE

Ilario's lanky frame sprawled like a creeping vine over an armchair at Lady Susanna's card table. He was spinning his crocodile charm above his head like a pinwheel, occasionally rattling a crystal-globed lamp or clinking his wineglass. The lady herself, a serene, intelligent beauty with the most luxuriant black hair I had ever seen, laid down her fan of cards when I tapped on the open door. She was a gracious hostess indeed to tolerate Ilario for more than a tennight without the least ripple of aggravation.

"Pardon, my lady," I said, bowing. "I'm sorry to steal your company. Chevalier, you wished to speak to our visitor. . . ."

"No matter," said Susanna, shifting a richly colored shawl to her shoulders as she rose. Her smile illumined her large eyes and the deep cinnamon glow of her complexion. "I am a hopeless night bird. My husband is long to bed, and I have teased poor Ilario into one game too many in search of evening's amusement. Though he carries the most perfect tenor, he will sing only when we play at cards. Alas, he seems to have run out of cheerful ditties."

Indolence abandoned, Ilario contracted his spread limbs and slithered to the edge of his chair, peering curiously through the empty doorway behind me. "Your exceptional loveliness demands excellence, dear lady, a

responsibility that weighs heavy on my bardic soul. My supply of drivel is endless; my supply of poetry not so, especially when awaiting a visit from a fiend. My companion Portier, as you see, is of a depressive cast of mind, but this fellow who's come to visit us makes Portier appear but a frippery. Where is the devilish visitor, good curator?"

"He awaits us in the wild garden," I said.

"You must persuade him to come inside," said the lady. "The night closes very dark. If he prefers more privacy, Hanea will open the guesthouse."

Ilario got out an answer more quickly than I. "Lovely Susanna, I fear indelible bruises on your innocent soul must result were his company forced upon you."

Lady Susanna laughed, a throaty ripple that issued from a deep center, and then kissed the fop on his flaxen head. "Sweet Ilario, innocent? Me? You must quit all indulgence in wine. I'll leave you to your fiendish visitor, but rest assured, naught can bruise my soul. I am well hardened."

She had scarce vanished, when she poked her head back around the doorjamb, her eyes glimmering with pleasure. "One matter of interest, Sonjeur de Duplais. Our son, Edmond, returns home tomorrow on leave from his posting in the south. You needn't fear; he is reliable and discreet. Yet I would not have him . . . compromised . . . by awkward situations. You understand."

She didn't wait for confirmation, but glided out of sight in a whisper of silk. Ilario gazed after her, as if admiring the afterglow such a luminary must leave behind. "Is any woman so much a vision of Heaven's angels? How fortune leads us. . . ." Then he lifted his head abruptly. "I could have had her, you know. She wasn't highborn. Even an offside pedigree such as mine would have raised her up. Yes, she's a few years older, but egad . . . this fossil she's got instead! Eugenie says Conte Olivier was His Majesty's first commander. Taught him everything about leading troops and bedding down in muck and staying on his feet in a battle. He was Soren's first commander, too, but I doubt he taught the shitheel much. Soren believed he knew everything already."

Eugenie de Sylvae—Ilario's half sister—had been but a child when wed to King Soren, Philippe's predecessor and an even more distant cousin

of mine. When Soren fell in a miscalculated raid on the witchlords of Kadr, he had not yet bedded the girl, much less begat an heir. Through a happenstance of Sabrian custom, my fifteenth cousin, a wild young duc entirely unprepared for the throne, had inherited the demesne of Sabria. To preclude any dispute of his position, Philippe had immediately wed Soren's child widow, inheriting her virginity, the support of her powerful relatives, and her bastard half brother, Ilario. My overly sentimental mother had insisted that political necessity had grown into a true love match between Philippe and Eugenie—despite the burden of the ridiculous half brother. But who could say what love meant, especially in such rarified circles? I doubted my mother knew.

"Thanks be, young Edmond got his mother's wit as well as her looks," mused Ilario. "Old Olivier has the cleverness of a turnip in anything but war making and wife picking."

Feeling the press of time, I dropped my voice. "I've judged that Mage Dante's talents will . . . suffice. And he agrees that the level of magic the glass signifies is extraordinary."

Ilario bobbed his fair head and clapped his hands. "Excellent, Portier. I knew he would work out." As if he'd thought of it. "Go to it."

"If we are to be partner *agentes*, the three of us must agree on our next steps."

He flared his straight nose and stretched his long saffron-colored legs in front of him. "Heaven's messengers, I near piss myself when he glares at me, and these are my favorite hose."

My royal cousin had insisted that Ilario was trustworthy and that his close bond with his half sister could help us discover the truth. I could accept that, but playing nursemaid to the fop would test a saint's patience. "You must attend, Chevalier. It is your duty as a Knight of Sabria, your sister's champion, one might say."

"Oh. Quite right." He jumped to his feet and inhaled until his bony ribs threatened to pop the buttons on his gold waistcoat. "You understand, Portier, Eugenie could not have done this thing—conspired. It is not in her nature."

I had never seen him so somber when he wasn't frighted out of his wits

or reeling drunk. Thus I found myself believing him—which was entirely foolish so early on. I had vowed to withhold judgment in *all* these matters until evidence led me to the truth.

"I understand, Chevalier. We do this for her safety as well as His Majesty's . . . and Sabria's." I didn't think a reminder of our larger purposes would go amiss. Uncounted thousands of Sabria's people had died in the Blood Wars, the flower of her nobility, the most powerful of her magical families. A second orgy of death and ruin would destroy us all.

THE EVENING HAD COOLED. SCENTS of thyme, lavender, and waking earth rose in the spring damp, and the soft rasping twitter of tree crickets engulfed the trees. Ilario steeled his courage by clutching his spalls—the shards of onyx and jade he carried to remind him of the ancestors he held sacred: surely including the father he shared with Queen Eugenie, and her mother, who had so generously taken her husband's bastard infant into her home and raised him as her own.

We found the stone bench empty when we reached the glade. I whirled in a full circle, relieved when the lamplight caught a band of silver near the font. "Master! I feared you'd left us."

The dark figure hunched on the ground raised his eyes. Ilario promptly dropped his pouch, scattering his spalls across the rocks.

Dante's lip curled. "I was relishing the *quiet*."

His collection retrieved, the lord sank to the end of the stone bench farthest from the mage. I took the other end of the bench, which set me between them, a position I feared might become familiar. As I set down the lamp and pulled out my journal, I searched for the right words to launch our odd collaboration.

"So we are to be spies," I said. "No matter how distasteful the word, I suppose we must accustom ourselves to it. Michel de Vernase made a public show of his investigation. The king refuses to believe his disappearance coincidence, which is why *we* must work in secret."

"In secret?" said Dante, scornfully. "With one of us the guilty queen's pet?"

"A fair question," I said, laying a hand on Ilario's arm to prevent him drawing his sword. "We are investigating treason, with all its heavy consequences. But His Majesty believes entirely in Lord Ilario's sincere determination to keep our secrets unshared. I choose to accept the king's word."

Though the pooled lamplight showed Dante's face impassive, his restless energies roiled the deepening night. I hastened onward, opening my journal to the notes I had made thus far, my eyes automatically deciphering my encoded script.

"So to our case and our plan. As far as the king knows, Michel learned very little. The assault on King Philippe occurred at Castelle Escalon. The assailant, who was never identified, wore royal livery. The evidence of his scars and bruises named him a mule used to feed a mage's power. Thus, we know he was of the blood. He wore no mage collar, and unfortunately, de Vernase reported his handmark obscured by scars. So we are hunting a mage with talent and knowledge enough to work transference and the . . . complex . . . spyglass spells."

Dante stirred from his contemplative posture. "Hired by the shadow queen?"

"The queen's suggestion to the guard captain that he persuade the king to wrestle and thus divest himself of armor might only be a wife's concern for her husband's amusement. We shall not be privy to the personal disagreements between their majesties that feed the king's disturbance. However, the queen does support two household mages, and it only makes sense to investigate them first." I deferred to Ilario, tapping his knee when he failed to take my cue. "Chevalier?"

"Orviene is pleasant enough," he said, avoiding the mage's heated gaze, "though a bit oily to my taste, always smarming after ladies above his station. But Gaetana is frightful. Women so large are surely an aberration of Father Creator, and she glares at me quite as much as you do."

"Orviene has an indifferent reputation at Seravain," I said, trying to add more pertinent information, "competent, reasonable, pleasant enough. He has never achieved a master's rank. Gaetana has. She is reputed to be quite brilliant, but left teaching years ago, as she is more interested in research than students. Neither ever instructed me. They've resided in the

queen's household since the mortal illness of the infant Prince Desmond seven years ago. Gaetana returns frequently to Seravain for study and research. She is polite but never familiar, and, alas, it has never been my habit to pry into what mages study in my library."

"These two have apprentices, I presume," said Dante.

"Several, who seem to change quite often . . ."

"Only Adept Fedrigo and Adept Jacard have been at court more than a year," said Ilario. "Fedrigo is quite gentleman-like and ever helpful. I don't know Jacard, as he is presently loaned out to some friend of my foster mother's. The rest scurry about like ants, fetching and sweeping, or they disappear into the mages' laboratorium for days at a time, only to reappear unkempt and entirely too exhausted to do a man a favor."

I dipped my head in acknowledgement and continued. "Neither the king nor Lord Ilario knows of any other mage with access to the queen's household, and both have expressed a feeling that Orviene and Gaetana have . . . insinuated . . . themselves between the queen and her family. Unfortunately, the lady made it known to her husband, and thus to Michel de Vernase, that no one in her household would be available for questioning. Without more specific evidence linking her to the assault, the king is unwilling to contradict her in the matter."

Dante shrugged and drew his walking stick across his lap. "Dancing about tender feelings will never get you answers. Did these mages inquire about the spyglass? Hunt for it?"

"Not that we know—which means very little. Evidently, Michel de Vernase never made any secret of his disdain for sorcery or his belief that a sorcerer planned the attack on the king. He tried to interrogate the Camarilla prefects without prior negotiation—a violation of the Concord de Praesta—and when refused, took his inquiries to Seravain. With such—"

"The conte quite insulted poor Fedrigo," blurted Ilario. "Called him a 'trickster taking advantage of his station' just because he makes these excellent charms for Eugenie's friends."

"With such a bullheaded approach," I concluded, "I doubt the conte could have learned the door warden's name at Seravain. No one directed him to my library, I can tell you."

"But if no one saw the mule use the spyglass, why was it there at all?" said Dante.

A good question that pricked not a hint of an answer in *my* mind. "The larger problem," I said, "is that even if the queen allows her mages to be questioned, they're not going to tell me—or any interrogator—the kind of information we seek. They'll deny knowing the assassin. They'll deny building instruments that show us the demesnes of the dead. They will most certainly deny any knowledge of transference or other prohibited practices. Thus we need someone to join their little consilium and learn what they're about. Only a person of their own rank might have a chance to observe their practices and judge if they are capable of the sorcery we've seen."

I paused, awaiting the explosion. It came quietly, but with intensity that near knocked me off the stone bench.

"You want *me* to pose as a court mage?" said Dante, blowing a derisive breath. "I thought you had a semblance of mind, Portier. My reputation is fairly earned. I've no manners. I know naught of bowing or titles or mouthing pleasantries to fools. You see my finest garments." He spread his arms, his grotesque hand purple in the lamplight. "Hardly what's expected of a queen's puppet."

"A certain distance might work to your advantage, Master." I dropped my eyes that he might not think me staring at his ropelike scars. "And with your permission, of course, we can teach you whatever you need to know of court life, can we not, Chevalier?"

Ilario hunched his shoulders without even a sidewise glance at Dante. "I'll loan my tailor and my barber, but . . . some tasks are impossible."

Dante hoisted himself up with his stick and strode back toward the path and the house. Before I could decide whether to chase him down, he halted, spun in place, and jabbed a finger toward Ilario. "Dress me like this strutting cock, and I still could not get near them. Do I walk up to the gate and apply for the position of queen's assassin?"

"I made you an offer three days ago," said Ilario, dabbing at his nose with a lace kerchief. "You scoffed."

"And in which layer of lies was this offer couched?"

"Please, Master. Please, Chevalier!" How was I to harness these two most irritating men, both of whom outranked me? "We are charged with our kingdom's safety. Philippe has reason to believe another attempt at murder will be made on the twenty-fifth day of Cinq—the anniversary of last year's attempt, which happens also to be the seventh anniversary of his infant son's death—which happens to be one-and-sixty days from this. Each of you has a unique gift to bring to the task."

"Give me the demonish glass, and I'll divine its use," said Dante, "perhaps even something of its maker. Give me the coin and the arrow. Such mysteries intrigue me. But do not expect me to pretend I care for an aristo's domestic troubles. I'm as like to spit on him and be done with the matter. And it's sure I'll end up prisoned myself anyway, when the Camarilla gets wind of my heretical opinions. Find another plan."

I reached for patience. "Lord Ilario . . . graces . . . society throughout Castelle Escalon and the royal city. As he mentioned at our first meeting, his half sister has set herself the charge to support magical scholarship in rivalry to the king's support of the new sciences. It would be only natural for the chevalier to bring her a new talent he has encountered. He can secure you a position—"

"Pursuing magics that 'many people might consider unsavory'? Those were your words, were they not, Chevalier?" snapped the mage. "So tell me, what are these unsavory wishes your mistress might ask me to indulge? Transference, perhaps? Enough to set me up as scapegoat for this crime?"

"Certainly not," I said. "Lord, you must explain."

No matter his pique, no matter his care for the queen's reputation, Ilario could not hide this last piece of our puzzle. Neither could he pass it off with his usual foolery. "My lady has suffered an overburden of griefs in her life: our beloved parents lost to fire not a year after her too-early marriage; an adored husband, the late king, fallen in battle; her own child dead before his first birthday, a daughter stillborn, and two more miscarried. She seeks . . . solace."

"Surely these two jackleg mages can concoct a sleeping draught. Or is it illusions she wants?"

Dante's brutal frankness drove Ilario to his feet and into the night beyond the pool of lamplight. "Portier, this is most unseemly. I'll not discuss a gracious lady with a damnable rogue."

"Mage Dante is our partner in this endeavor, lord chevalier, and has sworn to keep private all he hears. If you don't tell him all, then I must, else we'll never lift this cloud of suspicion from your royal sister. Better this come from one who can tell us her true mind . . . gently."

Evidently, Michel de Vernase had disdained Ilario, never bothering to interview him. And until Philippe himself had spoken to the chevalier, he did not comprehend the nature and intensity of his wife's unhealthy yearnings.

"They've tried illusions with varying success," said Ilario, his breath shaking. "But more than anything in the world, my sister desires her mother's comforting hands and our father's shoulder on which to weep. She yearns to hear that her dead children are not frightened as they assay the trials of Ixtador."

The mage stiffened. "Necromancy?" he said in hushed fury. "She's mad. You're all mad. Even if it's possible—and naught's certain of that— lest you've forgotten, mucking with the dead is frowned upon. If the Temple were to get wind of this . . . gods . . . the tetrarchs might slap a queen's wrists, but they'll hang the sorry practitioner in the temple square by his thumbs as fodder for rats and ravens."

"We're aware of that," I said, intestines clenching at thoughts of both the crime and the punishment.

The Camarilla discouraged deadraising; many said because they no longer knew how to do it. But the Temple claimed that to breach the Veil between life and death was to violate creation itself. Ixtador was our penalty for the depredations of the Blood Wars, including transference and necromancy. Did we transgress again, the tetrarchs and prophets implied we would be barred from Heaven everlastingly. No matter how pallid one's private convictions, the sway of public sentiment kept deadraising a dangerous activity.

"I'd not want you to mistake the possible complications, Master. But we're not asking you to practice necromancy, only to hint that you could.

That you might. To demonstrate skills that suggest you are capable. The queen's mages claim they are unable to satisfy her wishes for these very reasons you name. But we must wonder if a spyglass that seems to focus in Ixtador, and a mule whose very existence speaks of unholy practice, indicate that they are, in fact, attempting such wickedness. This is the way for you to get close to the queen and her mages and find out what we need to know."

Eyes closed, Dante crossed his arms over his bent head as if to smother the curiosity that—I hoped—would drive him to find answers. Ilario kept mercifully quiet. An owl flapped away from a nearby oak, the rushing spread of wings near stopping my heart.

At last the mage clasped his walking stick and tapped its heel on the packed dirt. "So, peacock," he said, "have you ever seen your little sister playing with this naughty glass?"

"This is insupportable." Ilario waved his arms weakly, his protest lackluster beside Dante's resonant conviction. I kept silent, giving him no permission to back away.

The chevalier heaved a suffering sigh. "Her Majesty does not include me in her mages' rituals. It is a *great kindness*, for she knows they frighten me. I've never seen her or anyone else using that foul implement. I suppose I could ask her. . . ."

My chest constricted. "No, no, best avoid any appearance of interest in such activities. Forget about the spyglass altogether when in her presence. Your caution is the best help you can give . . . along with your gift of a new mage, who will help dismiss these foul suspicions. Agreed?"

I waited until Ilario flicked his hand to acknowledge my warning before turning to our new partner. "Master, unless you suggest something better, I propose that Lord Ilario present you to the queen seven days hence. You will say what is necessary to secure employment in her household. Once you are assigned chambers in the palace, I will arrange for the spyglass, the arrow, and the coin to be delivered to you there." I tapped a forefinger on my journal. "Time is critical. Tomorrow is the first day of Qat. We've sixty-one days."

"What of you, student?" said Dante. "If a brutish sorcerer is to be

made into a courtier, and a peacock into an informant, where is *your* place in Castelle Escalon? No one will say anything useful in the hearing of a king's kinsman."

I smoothed the pages of my journal and closed it, happy no one had ever deciphered its encoding. My future likely held a potful of frustrations to express outside the public eye. "Once Lord Ilario has secured your position at court, I shall follow you to Castelle Escalon, where I intend to have a flaming public row with my royal cousin and take on a dismal, unhappy palace job of my own just to flout him. Everyone will pity me and believe I am dreadfully abused, and, I hope, divulge all manner of useful things."

"What job?" For the first, and likely last, time, Ilario and Dante spoke in unison.

"Lord Ilario's private secretary. It was the worst thing I could think of."

For the first, and likely last, time, the three of us together burst out laughing.

ON THE NEXT MORNING, I stood in the cool, sheltered carriageway with Lady Susanna and her son, Edmond, who had arrived sometime in the night. The tall, sleepy-headed young officer indeed reflected his handsome and intelligent mother.

After worrying at the problem for a fruitless hour, I had solicited my hostess's assistance in preparing Dante for his introduction at court. "He and Ilario get along like a wildcat and a magpie," I said. "The chevalier insists *I* see to it, but I've business that can't wait."

"I'll gladly do what I can," said the lady.

"Let me take it on," said Edmond. "I've been tasked with the very same duty for young officers promoted in the field. And, begging your pardon, my most refined and gracious mother"—he beamed at Lady Susanna—"some men don't appreciate a lady's introducing them to forks and serviettes and chamberpots. As it happens I've supply dispatches need delivering in Merona. The mage and I could stay on in our town house. I'll not embarrass the fellow . . . nor you nor Papa, either."

Shadows dimmed Lady Susanna's smile, and her dark eyes darted from her son to me. "I don't think . . . Perhaps this is too private a matter. You've duties here, Edmond."

But to me it sounded ideal. Edmond de Roble exuded his mother's serenity in a stalwart, soldierly package. "If you're willing, Greville, it could save several lives at once. I'll introduce——"

A bellow exploded from the inner courtyard. The three of us raced through the vine-covered gate to find Ilario flattened to the brick wall like a lizard caught between the blooming bougainvillea and honeysuckle. The tip of Dante's white staff was pressed to the chevalier's throat, in vivid illustration of our dilemma.

"Touch this again, peacock," said Dante in the quiet manner that shivered my toes, "and it will burn a hole straight through this dainty flesh." The mage tightened his grip on the carved stick, eliciting a squirm from Ilario. "Do you comprehend?"

Ilario emitted some unintelligible squeak. As the glowering mage jerked his stick away and stepped back, the bedraggled chevalier stumbled across mounds of alyssum and wallflowers, not stopping until he stood at my shoulder, glaring back at his attacker. "Madman," he croaked between coughing spasms. "I . . . was just . . . interesting carving . . . just looking . . ." He sucked greedily at an opaline flask he'd pulled from his cloak.

"You agreed I'd deal with you alone, Portier," snapped the mage. "Not with a sniveling, creeping aristo who thinks he has rights to anything he chooses."

"Divine grace, sonjeur." Edmond inhaled sharply as sun glints sparked from the silver band circling Dante's neck, but the young man did not hesitate to incline his back. "Excuse me . . . Mage. I am Edmond de Roble, Greville in the Guard Royale. I understand you're to be presented at Castelle Escalon. May I offer my services as escort to Merona and your host as you get your bearings in the city?"

In moments, all was calm and ordered at Villa Margeroux. If only Philippe had assigned this young man to our partnership instead of the dithering Ilario, I might have better hopes of success.

CHAPTER FOUR

The shutters of the palace waiting room had not yet been opened to the mild spring air, and scented candle smoke, the cloying aroma of blooming orchids, and the stifling heat had my stomach in full rebellion. Or perhaps it was only anxiety. My court debut awaited me in the Royal Presence Chamber.

"Dame Renche, present yourself." An aide in red and gold livery awaited my companion in misery—a wilting dowager come to petition the king for her son's reassignment to a regiment quartered in Tallemant. The young man was currently billeted on the *Destinne*, the vessel chosen to sail beyond the Mouth of Hedron in search of the legendary Isles of Koshavir. The woman claimed she needed her son to manage her vineyard, but her effortless domination of her serving man and the succession of footmen, secretaries, and aides a petitioner encountered en route to this room led me to conclude she did not want for managerial skills. As she repeatedly referred to voyages of exploration as "frivolous and ungodly," and the *Destinne*, in particular, as an ill-omened ship, I assumed she just didn't want to risk her boy.

The lady swept from the room. I waited and churned.

From my persistent difficulties in obtaining this audience, I assumed

Ilario had outlined my scheme to His Majesty. And from the lack of any alternative information since their arrival in Merona, I presumed that young Edmond de Roble-Margeroux had survived his sevenday with Dante, and that Ilario had successfully introduced Dante to his royal sister. Barring disaster, I had forbidden them from communicating with me.

Another rivulet of sweat dampened my threadbare velvet doublet.

"Sonjeur de Duplais, present yourself."

I adjusted my attire and trailed after the stiff-backed aide through a series of more elaborate waiting rooms and across a puddled courtyard, steamy with the previous night's rain. Halfway down a majestic promenade, footmen swung open a pair of bronze doors to reveal an expansive chamber and an eye-filling swarm of ruffed collars, plumed hats, curled beards, jeweled necks, and billowing skirts. My escort motioned me inside.

Truly this meeting place of king and subject had been designed to impress. My royal cousin sat beneath a gold-mosaic dome, where chips of lapis, tourmaline, and malachite depicted a Sabrian monarch accepting the gifts of earth, sea, and sky from the enthroned Pantokrator. On the barreled ceiling vaults hovered painted angels so lifelike, one could believe the damp, flower-scented breeze that wafted through the chamber's open arches a product of their wings. Or perhaps the shifting air emanated from the exquisite planetary suspended in the vault behind the king—the gleaming brass model of Heaven's fiery orb, circled unendingly by its five children planets in the mathematical precision calculated by Philippe's astronomers.

A half circle of ten to fifteen courtiers stood in favored attendance on Philippe. Across the dais to his right, a separate group of eight or ten clustered about a velvet-cushioned chair—empty on this day.

"I had hoped to present my petition to both king and queen," I whispered to the stiff-backed aide at my side.

"The queen no longer attends His Majesty's public audiences," he said, his eyes fixed forward. "Be ready."

So rumor was correct in that respect, at least.

Ilario's height and flaxen hair left him easy to spot at the back of the queen's party. But it was two wearing silver collars who drew my interest.

The statuesque master mage, Gaetana, held the position of favor at the immediate right of the queen's chair. The First Counselor's iron gray hair was twisted tight at the back of her head. Her pale gaze reflected chilly disinterest. The tidy, elegantly gray-haired mage standing in her formidable shadow would be Orviene. Dante was not present.

" . . . thus it is our best judgment that Augustin de Renche receive no exception to his sworn obedience." Whether by virtue of wizardry or architecture, my cousin's natural voice rang clear even at this remotest end of the chamber. "Indeed, sonjeura"—Philippe leaned down from his gilt chair and spoke with perfectly audible intimacy—"I surmise that your son's share of the *Destinne*'s discoveries shall enable you to hire three bailiffs and an entire crew of vineyard overseers next season. *Judis ainsi.*"

Philippe's formal assertion of conclusion brought a liveried aide to whisk the dowager Renche away.

"Portier de Savin-Duplais, present yourself." Was it only imagination that the herald's announcement of my name quieted the bustle of skirts and gossip? Certainly a fervid mumbling swelled as the aide escorted me up the long central aisle and pointed to a tiled circle at the foot of the dais. Head bowed, I sank to one knee and waited.

Curse the arrogant devil, where was Dante? It would be nice to know the mage was safely in play before enduring this unpleasantness.

"*Savin*-Duplais? Do we know you?"

A twitch of the aide's gloved hand brought me to my feet. Philippe's expression—clear eyes, the light brows that matched his neatly trimmed mustache and beard—held steady, cool, and disinterested.

All right then. The game was on. Time to destroy, at least for the present, what hopes I held of sober reputation in the wider circles of the world.

"Heaven's grace be with you, Majesty. My late father, Onfroi de Savin-Duplais, scholar and gentleman, was fourteenth-degree Savin out of Renferre de Savin-Gorsiet. But alas, you and I have never met, gracious sire, a seeping wound which is the matter of my petition this day. The intermediaries who rightly defend your presence from the common hordes have taken it upon themselves to refuse your kinsman private audience."

The fair brows lifted. I plunged onward, trying to ignore the titters that broke here and there.

"Insulted and demeaned by these servants, your devoted cousin has been forced to resort to this public airing of his necessities . . ." I allowed the pause to extend just past comfort. "Unless your most gracious majesty would overrule them and consent to retire behind yon doors that I might speak in private."

"Our householders reflect our mind and our instructions, *cousin*. What could you have to say that would require abandoning these other honored petitioners?" The king's wave encompassed the crowd of gaping, sniggering courtiers. I doubted many were public petitioners. "Speak, kinsman. What necessity has brought you?"

"My desire to serve you, lord. For fifteen years, my family has petitioned a place in your household appropriate for one who bears the Savin name." I tossed a bundle of letters onto the mosaic dragon whose scarlet tail encircled my feet. "Refused. Every one. Nine years ago, my honored father passed beyond the Veil. I have strived to aid his journey through the Ten Gates by prayer, virtuous living, and honorable study and employment at Collegia Seravain. But temple readers assess his tessila"—to the inhaled breath of the onlookers and a modicum of guilt on my own part, I produced the palm-sized carving of red jasper sanctified by my father's spirit—"and tell me he does not progress. He waits for his only son to supply deeds of proper quality to advance him toward his heavenly life. It is my conviction that those deeds must fall under the aegis of family. And so, gracious sire, I have dedicated myself to seek worthy service at your side."

Philippe collapsed laughing into the depths of his great chair. "Collegia Seravain!" he bellowed in great humor. "By the Ten Gates, have we a kinsman mage?"

"Nay, Majesty." I rubbed my bare neck as if to show him. "An acolyte only, but I—"

"So you have mastered reading and writing arcana, but demonstrate no skills of the blood—even by the assessment of those who *believe* in skills of the blood?"

The presence of the queen's mages only heightened the humiliation of the wretched confession. "True, sire, but—"

"Fortunately for you, Portier de Savin-Duplais, we take but small offense at this odor of failure attached to our family name. Clearly you have been cloistered with your supernatural fraternity too long and are sorely misinformed. We employ no mages in our household. No adepts. And indeed, not even acolytes. The Camarilla Magica exists by our royal sufferance, but without credence in our counsels. Thus you must seek employment elsewhere. We would advise you look to mathematics, physics, and astronomy"—he opened his hand in the direction of the gleaming planetary—"to find the true magic the Pantokrator has granted human-kind. *Judis ainsi.*"

Cheeks ablaze, I sank to my knee and winced at the risks of violating protocol by opening my mouth again. But, truly, a night in the public stocks could heap no worse disgrace upon my name than what I had just done, and a little stalwart whining should entrench my character in the public perception. Thus, when the aide tapped my shoulder to vacate my position, I rose to a posture of offended dignity. "I *shall* find a way to serve in your house, Majesty. For my honored father's soul, I shall."

"Impertinent cousin!" Philippe roared, flicking a finger at the aide. "Ill manners reap one night's service at least—in our household jail. Alas for you, Lady Justice requires a balanced hand, even for those who bear the Savin name. *Judis ainsi!*"

The aide scooped up my hastily manufactured letters and stuffed them into my arms. The soldiers of the Guard Royale gripped my shirt collar, propelled me down the long aisle, and shoved me through the door.

PHILIPPE'S PRIVATE JAIL HOUSED A prisoner in comfort when compared to a public dungeon or the Spindle, the bleak tower perched on a barren rock in the deepest channel of the river Ley. Plastered walls surrounded a real bed with sheets and blanket, approximately clean. A tin washing bowl and covered night jar sat in one corner. A small window at eye level, albeit barred, opened to a moldy brick courtyard cluttered with dustbins. Yet

the sturdy lock on the thick door and the lack of any illumination source to supplant the failing sunlight could not but reinforce a vague nausea at my first experience of prisoning.

Sitting on the bed, propped against the outer wall, I consoled myself that it was one night only, and necessary to make my humiliation real. I flicked a finger at two spiders that crept down the peeling wall and kicked a large beetle out of the sheets.

Truly, the "row" had gone well. If I was to be the king's pawn, it was reassuring that he was an intelligent manipulator. Yet, even though I knew his opinions, Philippe's bald declaration of scorn for sorcery had shocked me. He had, in essence, called his wife's mages cheats as the two of them stood not fifteen metres from him. I wished I had dared look up to gauge their expressions. Surely *marital discord* must be too sweet a term to describe the friction between the two royal households. What an ugly mess.

A fractured laugh escaped my throat at my naive hopes that Philippe's summons would somehow lead to my imagined "destiny." I'd not even two months to unravel a mystery whose chief suspects I was forbidden to question. And what if we were wrong about Orviene and Gaetana and had to look in some entirely different direction?

The lock scraped and rattled, reminding my stomach that hunger might be causing my gut's upheaval. A full day had passed since I'd supped.

But the short, robust young woman who entered my cell bore a lamp, not dinner. The ring of keys dangling from her leather belt evidenced responsibilities, yet her jeweled earrings, smoothly coiled hair, and full-sleeved gown of indigo silk hardly bespoke a jailer.

"I'll knock when I'm ready to leave," she announced to the hesitant guard. "I doubt Sonjeur de Duplais poses any risk to health or virtue."

Of a sudden acutely aware of my unseemly posture, I kicked off the sheets and jumped to my feet. My spall pouch dropped to the floor. I bent to retrieve it, noting the regrettably threadbare state of my stockings. My cheeks flamed. Alas, the guards had taken my shoes and belt, and I had to settle for buttoning my gaping doublet with the spall pouch inside and

running fingers through my straggling hair. *Dithering fool.* But then, far more time had passed since a woman had graced my bedchamber than since I had dined.

"Divine grace, damoselle," I said, bowing, left hand properly exposed on my shoulder.

"Maura ney Billard," she said, baring her own left hand.

Though many might judge the lady plain, the earthen hues of her hair, eyes, and round cheeks glowed warmly in the lamplight. Her voice, on the other hand, was decidedly cool and precise.

After a brisk survey of my chamber, eyeing the rumpled bed where the beetle and several of its friends had taken up residence again, she seated herself on the three-legged stool in the corner. Its proximity to the bare floor did no more to diminish her self-assurance than did her diminutive height or her brief nose. "I serve as administrator of the queen's household, including the *Consilium Reginae*—Her Majesty's advisors in matters of sorcery. Please sit down."

I perched on the edge of the bed, near swallowing my tongue. Were we found out? Ilario . . . Dante . . . Ixtador's Gates, what had they done?

The lady cocked her head and leaned forward, examining me as if she were a kennelmaster considering a new pup. "I witnessed your petition to the king, sonjeur. This afternoon, as someone recounted the tale to Her Majesty, Mage Gaetana mentioned that you had served as archivist and librarian at Collegia Seravain. Is that true?"

"Yes, my lady."

"Her Majesty has just taken on a new advisor," said the lady, setting her lamp on the floor, "a master mage unfamiliar with court life. The mage deems an assistant necessary, in particular an acolyte or adept who might acquire and maintain the books he needs for his duties. Never having retained his own assistant, he has no name in mind and has left the hiring to me. I am here to offer you the position."

Caught between relief and confusion, my mind snarled like a sprung clockwork. *Ilario*, not Dante, was supposed to put about that he was in desperate need of a personal secretary.

"But I—" What to say? This was all wrong. If I refused her offer . . .

insulted this lady or somehow made myself undesirable . . . how could I then apply to work for Ilario?

"Your determination to serve the royal family would be well satisfied by this position, sonjeur. And your qualification of good family and sincere piety, as well as your experience, seems a fortuitous match. Naturally, we would require references, but I've no doubts they'll be satisfactory and see no reason to delay."

"References . . ." Blood pounded my temples. This was absurd. I couldn't work for Dante. I needed to go places he'd have no reason to go; inquire about things he had no reason to know. Dante had agreed with my plan.

Think, Portier. I breathed deeply twice, a remedy I'd often used to force time and thought to slow. Dante was not stupid. He must have some compelling reason to contravene our plan. And this whole matter . . . the woman's haste . . . seemed odd.

Billard. A major blood family. She would have numerous contacts at Seravain and elsewhere—adepts and acolytes who would relish court service. And her use of *ney* Billard, instead of *de* Billard, indicated that her mother's family outranked her father's, which often meant even *more* relatives eager for advancement. Why would she choose an unknown? She embodied a quiet authority, yet her plump fingers had twined themselves into a knot in her lap.

"I would need to write letters," I said, slowly—testing. "Explain my need for references. It could take a tennight or two, perhaps a month. But I could certainly consider your kind offer."

Disappointment melted her cool mask, and rue tweaked a friendly smile. "I abhor dissembling, Sonjeur de Duplais, and thus I must inform you that this offer promises no comfortable employment. I pounced upon your qualifications both because of your desire to be at court and also because the longer this new mage resides at Castelle Escalon, the more difficult it will be to fill the position. Master Dante is a most . . . *intense* . . . man."

"How so, lady? You intrigue me." I buried my mouth in my hands, lest the smile grown on my own face give me away. She had caught Dante perfectly.

She frowned and stared at the ceiling for a moment, as if determining how to couch her description. To her credit, when she spoke, she looked me square on. "His words, his opinions, and his scrutiny carry weight beyond the usual. I can't describe it better than that. His manners demonstrate little grace. His frankness is more akin to flaying than speech, and he has no patience with frivolity or hesitation. Yet he comes highly qualified, recommended by persons Her Majesty trusts. Her Majesty was entirely satisfied after their private interview."

All right. Perhaps she didn't want to subject any personal friends to the strange mage's whims. That made sense. She was here because Dante had demanded an assistant in such terms that I was the glaringly obvious choice. He knew my plan and the reasoning behind it. I had to trust him.

I rose to my stockinged feet and bowed. "Damoselle ney Billard, your honesty becomes you and honors your mistress. I hear naught to make a determined spirit quake. Indeed, this prospect, while daunting, saves me the difficulties of exploring other opportunities in the royal household that would likely result in situations far less suited to my experience. In short, I am humbly grateful and accept the position."

She popped up from the stool, as if the weight of the sky had lifted from her shoulders. "Consider me in your debt, Sonjeur de Duplais. If the situation becomes too burdensome, I insist you come to me and I shall seek remedy from Her Majesty. The mage has been brought in to do my lady service, and I've no doubt that any who aid him will also reap her deepest gratitude."

My skin crept at recalling the *service* Eugenie de Sylvae desired of Dante. Royal gratitude could certainly be useful, but the mage had better have a damned good reason for this.

DAMOSELLE MAURA WAS NOTHING IF not efficient. Morning brought a plate of cold lamb and olives with her compliments. Still groggy from a night of empty dreams, I'd scarce dug in when the lady herself arrived.

"Did you sleep well in this unfortunate place, sonjeur?" she asked,

wrinkling her nose. The door remained open behind her, and the draft from the courtyard outside the barred window strengthened the miasma of mold and urine.

"As well as could be expected, damoselle," I said, scrambling off the bed while dabbing at my greasy mouth with the back of my hand. Few activities are less graceful than eating, especially when one lacks knife, spoon, or serviette. "I feel thoroughly chastised. My court protocol shall certainly *not* slip again."

She did not quite laugh, as if the bounds of her business kept such demonstrations inside her. Yet the heightened glow of her richly colored skin and the evidence of a slight dimple in one cheek made the prospects of the day immensely brighter.

"The guard holds your release papers and personal belongings. As Master Dante insists you attend him right away, I've come to show you the way to his chambers myself."

"My deepest gratitude, damoselle. I cannot tell you—" But she was already out the door, leaving my tongue hanging out like a thirsty pup's.

I blotted my mouth again, wiped my hands quickly on the bed sheets, and followed, reciting to myself the unfortunate realities of family connection that had kept my life celibate. The lady, daughter of a blood family, would know the rules. The door guard returned boots, belt, journal, compass, and the silver phial my mentor had given me with his best potion for my recurrent headaches. The courret remained tucked away in my spall pouch.

Once out of the cell, I felt as if I'd shed an excessively tight suit of clothes. But I could not forget I had a role to play, even if Dante had changed the playscript out from under me.

"Damoselle, if you please," I said, catching up to her. "Why would the mage need me so soon? I mean, I'm happy to go, but after a night confined, I feel unkempt. If this mage is very exacting . . . Are you certain he will accept me?"

"Her Majesty is providing the assistant her servant has requested. He'll not dare refuse." A pleasant animation softened the blunt assertion. A bold young woman indeed.

The open galleries and gardens of Castelle Escalon were built in the sprawling Fassid style. As Damoselle Maura briskly navigated the confusing route from my cell, housed in the cellar of an old barracks, I did my best to memorize landmarks. A long gray underground passage. A round crossing-room banded by lozenge-shaped window openings. A fragrance garden. An arcade where a Fassid love poem had been scribed in the tiled floor and its erotic images painted on panels in the vaulted ceiling.

"You're very kind to show me the way," I said. "It would be easy to get lost here."

"Her Majesty's household comprises the entire east wing," she said, pointing beyond three wide steps of whorled rose marble flanked by sculpted oak trees. "Her ladies, her brother Lord Ilario, and her counselors, including her mages, all live here."

At the top of the steps a broad gallery swept a long curve, its open arches overlooking the slate rooftops of Merona and the wide band of the river Ley, shimmering in the morning light. Just before the gallery ended in a wide, upward stair, a passage branched off to the right.

"These are Mage Gaetana's apartments," said the lady, pointing to the first doors along the soft-lit passage. "These Mage Orviene's, and these"— we arrived at the single door closest to the far end of the passage—"Mage Dante's."

The administrator's brisk knock elicited a curt, "Enter."

The lady gasped as we stepped through the door. Gray smoke wafted from the hearth, stinging our eyes and offending our nostrils with a sulfurous stench. Despite the discomfort, I had to smother amusement, even while breathing a prayer the mage would not get himself booted out of the palace too quickly. Luxurious draperies of heavy, blood-colored satin had been tied up in ugly knots, spilling sunlight from the broad windows across a scene of destruction. Armchairs, cushions, ebony tables, and delicate statuary had been piled haphazardly on damask couches shoved against the walls. At least three crumpled rugs had been thrown atop the pile.

A deep, narrow groove had been gouged into the rare mahogany floor, forming a circle some four metres in diameter. Clad in his old russet tunic,

rather than one of the embroidered jackets Edmond de Roble had provided him before leaving Villa Margeroux, the mage knelt inside the circle, tracing the deep channel with the still smoking end of a charred stick.

"Master Dante, what have you—?" The woman visibly choked back a reprimand. "I've brought your new assistant, Portier de Savin-Duplais."

"Good. He can finish this while I get on with the underlayment." He glanced up and caught Damoselle Maura's displeasure. "What? Do these other mages not *work* at Her Majesty's business? Perhaps that's why they achieve no results. To prepare a new circumoccule for every trial is inefficient and error-prone. Accuracy. Precision. Repeatability. Without them, you've naught but accidents and happenstance."

He popped to his feet, thrust the smoldering stick into my hand, and crouched beside the hearth. The offending stench and smoke rose from a crucible set upon a tripod over an unnaturally intense fire. "I need worktables," he said as he dropped yellow clots from a paper packet into the crucible, causing rills of blue flame to flare across his stinking mixture. "Three of them, each exactly three metres long. One with a polished stone surface, the others planed oak. And cupboards with lockable doors. Two at the least. Four would be better."

"You didn't inform the steward of these needs, when we spoke to him yesterday?"

"How was I to expect that folk hiring a mage had no idea what a mage needs to do his work?" He poked at the belching contents of the crucible with a stirring rod, then glared at me over his shoulder. "Well, get on then, apprentice. The sooner you've done, the sooner we clear this damnable stink."

"Sonjeur de Duplais is King Philippe's cousin, Master Dante," stated the lady firmly, "engaged to acquire and catalog books. If you need manual labor, we can fetch a workman."

"He might be the Pantokrator's maiden aunt for all I care. He does what I tell him in the manner I prescribe or he's no good to me and might as well dive headfirst out the window right now. Is that understood?"

Arrogant. Unyielding. Ungraceful. Even the cool Damoselle ney Billard fumed.

"I serve at the queen's pleasure, Master," I said quickly. "To that end, I shall be honored to take on whatever tasks you assign and to learn whatever you might teach." Especially why a man who disdained common sorcerous practice needed a circumoccule, a ring used to enclose particles arranged for traditional spellworking. And to learn why he had dragged me into a position that would make our investigation impossible. And to learn why this chamber thrummed as if a hundred musicians played at once, all of them different tunes.

Raising my brows and venturing a grin to soothe the lady's concerns, I shrugged out of my wrinkled doublet and bent to the work, first reheating the smoldering end of the stick—once a chair rung, I guessed—then shoving it through the gouge. Soot and char brought a minimal useful balance of spark, air, and wood to spells that focused heavily on the elements of base metal and water. A standard practitioner would embed other preferred particles into a permanent ring—fragments of colored glass, perhaps, or a few well-chosen herbs, and always nuggets or links of silver—the most perfect substance, encompassing all five of the divine elements. But who knew what Dante's plan was? The sulfur bespoke unsavory complexities.

"Get it hotter and move faster," snapped Dante. "The wood must be well seared as I lay down the lead."

"Very well then," said the administrator, equanimity recovered, though the toe of her elegantly small foot tapped rapidly on the ruined floor. "Have Sonjeur de Duplais bring a list of your additional requirements to my office this afternoon. Shall I have these excess furnishings removed?"

"Aye," said Dante, carefully ladling the first dipper of molten lead into a charred segment of the groove. "And the window rags as well. They're useless and ugly. I'll keep yon bed and the eating table and such." He jerked his head toward an open doorway in the end wall. "And you can leash your simpering maidservants and prancing footmen. None sets foot in my chambers unless I give them leave. The assistant will clean what needs cleaning. Now out with you, and let us to our work."

"Certainly, Master. Divine grace, and to you also, Sonjeur de Duplais.

As I mentioned earlier, I am at your service." The lady gazed at me intently, communicating a sincere concern and intent to help, which pleased me considerably. I acknowledged her kindness as well as I could from my ungraceful posture on the floor.

My task completed, I sat back on my heels. I expected Dante would stop once Maura had gone, but in fact his focus narrowed, his capable left hand dribbling an almost perfect thread of molten lead in the grooved circle. It was easy to overlook his doing almost everything one-handed. His ruined appendage had remained out of sight the entire time the lady was in the room. A touch of vanity, perhaps.

When he had closed the circle of lead, he returned his ladle to the empty crucible and used his staff to disperse the pile of white-hot coals across the floor of the hearth. If I hadn't been watching so carefully, I might have missed the moment when he pressed his narrow lips together as if muting a word they were intending to shape. The coals dulled instantly and fell to ash. For that one moment, I would have sworn I'd gone naked and feathers stroked my skin.

Dante rose, hurried to the windows, and threw open the casements, clinging to the iron frames as he heaved great breaths of the morning air. "Discord's realm . . . This place is going to drive me mad." Then he spun in place, his gaunt face hungry, his green eyes snapping and sparking like the fires of midsummer. "But it will be a fine madness, student. We've so much nastiness afoot in Castelle Escalon, it will take us a year to sort it out. They've found another corpse—another mule."

CHAPTER FIVE

It was an unfortunate fact that the actual blood of someone like me could so dramatically enhance another sorcerer's spellmaking, when it could not provide me enough power to work magic of my own. Transference, the direct infusion of magical blood into a sorcerer's veins, had been practiced since the awakening of magic. A few practitioners bled themselves, distilled the product, and reinfused their own strengthened ichor. But as this led determinedly to self-destruction, most incidents of transference involved an unwilling victim, leeched to provide magical sustenance for the unscrupulous. Some blood family's bastard, feeble-minded brother, or demented aunt might "wander off" or "take a sudden fever," perhaps to reappear bruised, pale, and scarred, perhaps never to be seen again.

Until the practice had exploded into a plague of abduction, torture, and murder in service of the grand power rivalries that came to be called the Blood Wars, no one had acknowledged its use among otherwise respectable members of the Camarilla Magica. And only then did ordinary Sabrians learn of mules—victims repeatedly bled until their veins collapsed and their minds disintegrated. The Temple tetrarchs declared that the mules' souls bled away as well, an irretrievable corruption.

The Concord de Praesta, the accord that ended the Blood Wars, required every mage to wear the permanent silver collar that supposedly kept his or her workings well scrutinized. And all children born to the blood were permanently marked on the back of the left hand and required to display that mark at every encounter, warning others that we might be purveyors of illicit magic. Abductions were punishable by death, and promiscuity among blood families by public penance and heavy fines, lest unrecorded bastards provide temptation for evildoers—or provide more evildoers. Despite all such precautions, it appeared that someone was bleeding poor sods into mindless idiots right under the nose of the Camarilla, the Temple, the king, and the educated citizenry of Merona. Two mules discovered within a tenmonth would strike fear in any heart. It could not be coincidence.

"A mule, are you sure?"

"Yestermorn the queen's chief panderer summoned me to his chambers." Dante perched on the broad window seat, the sunlight at his back. His white staff lay across his lap. "This Orviene, as sweet a talker as any marketplace barker, was wheedling at me to tell where I'd trained, and dancing about talk of necromancy. He even offered to lend books and materials, though revealing naught of his own skills or current work, to be sure. Yon crucible and such came from his stock, so I decided to make good use of them while I waited for you to arrive. Never thought to hear you'd got yourself thrown in jail. You were to be the *hidden* partner."

"Exactly so," I said. "So Orviene told you of the mule?"

"No. The woman Gaetana's chambers are right across the passage from Orviene's. While I was with Orviene, one of her adepts brought her a message that 'the verger would not release the dead mule.'"

"Are you sure you heard the report accurately from such a distance?" Across a passage?

"I've a spell . . . my staff . . . it's not important."

"Not *important*?" Sorcery could trick the senses; it could not alter their quality, any more than it could enable a man to eat poison without consequence.

"Gaetana was furious. Agitated. She felt"—he closed his eyes and

waved his hands about his head as if grasping for the right word—
"betrayed. This . . . this mule's death . . . this risk of their exposure . . .
isn't supposed to be happening, which means we must take advantage
before they seal whatever wall of secrets has been breached."

"Without thinking hard, I can devise fifty possibilities that would
bring an agitating message to Gaetana. The last thing we need is to fly off
on imaginings."

"I *must* see that corpse," he said. "You are the planner, the leader, so
make it happen before they burn the creature."

Impossible that he could have surmised so much from a message muffled by two walls and a passageway. Yet his belief was as undeniable as a
hurricane.

"All right. I'll do what I can. Find the deadhouse. Get you in there
today." And then find a way to renege on my agreement with Damoselle
Maura without jeopardizing my chances for Ilario's position. "Surely you
could have come up with a simpler scheme to see the body than to engage
me as your assistant. Something to do with Orviene's questions, the
deadraising . . ."

"But they've no idea I know about the mule. Don't you see? If they
suspect I can hear beyond walls, they'll never trust me near them."

Unreasonably reasonable. "All right. But I cannot work with you beyond this. I *must* have the freedom of opportunity Lord Ilario's employ
can give me."

"Do what you must, but get me in to see this new corpse. What use is
a plan if it hides the very truth we need to examine?"

That was inarguable.

I hadn't even poked my arms into my discarded doublet when the
mage dragged a crate of jumbled metal strips, spools, and packets into the
center of his circumoccule. "Hold on. We've work to do while you consider your course. Lay the strips of tin to either side of the lead. The
bronze links should lie at the sixteen compass points. You *are* capable of
determining true compass headings, are you not?"

My bewildered fumbling for my compass must have impressed him as
a *no*, for he snatched up his staff, rubbed his thumb on some particular bit

of carving, and used the soot stick to place sixteen marks on the scarred mahogany rim of his circle.

"Braid the linen, cotton, and silk thread together and lay it around the outer edge. Then fill in all the gaps and holes with wood shavings; there's a rasp in the box, and I don't care which wood you use. Spread a thin layer of sand over all. When you've done, I'll seal the ring with fire."

Exasperated, I shook my head. "Master, I'm not going to—"

"I might as well have use of you while you're in my service. Meanwhile I'll write the list of materials I need from that housekeeper or whatever she is. She pities you, so you should be able to get whatever I want. I doubt she'll be so generous when I'm on my own again." He vanished into the other room.

Mumbling unseemly responses at his vanished back, I snatched up the spall pouch I had laid aside with my doublet. I had no intention of continuing his humiliating little game of master and servant now Maura had gone. But as my thumb traced the outline of the red jasper tessila inside the heavy little bag, the glimmering of a plan took shape. A Damoselle Maura who pitied me could surely tell me where to find the palace deadhouse, and Dante's list would give me a perfect excuse to seek her out right away. Grumbling, I threw my doublet aside, knelt inside the circummoccule, and bent to the mage's work.

As I crawled about the sooty floor placing the metal and braided threads and converting the rest of a broken chair into splinters and shavings enough to fill the trough, I considered what else we needed to know about the dead mule. But the odd construction of Dante's circumoccule soon distracted me. Sand created a dispersed weight of base metal and wood. Braided threads effected proximity of silk's component water and linen's wood. But why cotton? The juxtaposition of particles fit no formula I knew. I argued with myself that Dante's chosen materials were not based on the balance of the five elements, but rather on this keirna he believed in, and then wondered for the fiftieth time if his magic relied upon particles at all. By the time I'd poured a thin layer of sand from the hearth box atop the filled ring, I was wholly filthy and wholly confused.

"I've finished, Master," I said, poking my head through the doorway in the end wall, "and I—"

Dante sat at a small writing desk next to an open window. The desktop was littered with paper, pens, and an ink bottle, and he'd wedged a small knife blade into the wood at one side, which puzzled me until the scattered shavings explained that this was how a man with one useful hand sharpened his quills. But the mage was not writing and did not acknowledge my presence. His elbow rested on the desk, and his forehead rested on his curled left fist as if he were in the deepest contemplation. His staff, wedged in the claw of his damaged hand, quivered almost imperceptibly.

"Master, are you ill?" I whispered, not truly believing it so. His posture was too deliberate, the vibrant energies of the small room as vivid as midsummer sunlight along Aubine's seacoast.

Indeed he did not move or answer, and I lowered myself to the tidy bed lined up against the adjoining wall. This was a much smaller chamber than the other, intended as a wardrobe or manservant's quarters, scarce room to walk between the bed, the desk, the night cupboard, and a small table. At the foot of the bed, atop an unopened traveling case, sat a worn leather satchel, stuffed to bursting with books and papers. Nowhere did I spy altar stone, tessila, spall pouch, or the smallest ikon of the Pantokrator. Not only was he heathen, but he didn't care who knew it, a more honest display than some of us dared.

The open satchel tempted me to discover what books he valued, but a distant bell striking the quarter hour stayed my hand. Just as well, for only moments later, Dante stirred and propped his staff against the wall. Grimacing, he massaged his temple, then ran his fingers down the scribbled papers on the desk as if to remind himself of what he'd written. "Are you finished yet, student?" he bellowed, without lifting his attention from the page. "Time passes."

"A while ago, Master," I said, childishly pleased that he near knocked over his chair as he jerked around to find me so near. "You're not ill." A statement, not a question.

"No." Curt and stone-faced, he gathered a stack of sheets and passed

them over. "Here's what I need to begin work—both on the mystery and the deadraising—and enough things I *don't* need to confuse anyone who reads the list. The last page tallies books. Most I've only heard about; don't know if they really exist. Perhaps you'll know better ones."

Resigned that he would reveal nothing until he was ready, I glanced through the lists. "A boar's tooth, three pearls, camphor oil, black alder bark, an Arothian dagger, myrrh . . . all right. But nightshade? Smut rye? Shepherd's purse? You think they're going to supply a stranger with poisons, especially these last two that cause women to *miscarry*?"

He shrugged and grabbed his staff. "If it gives them pause, so be it. I did warn the queen that if I am to tease Death itself, I must work with things that Death enjoys. She agreed. When can I get the spyglass and the other things?"

"I'll send for them today. Three or four days and we should have them. These books"—I glanced over the odd amalgam of standard texts, guessed titles, and terse descriptions—"can you read any of the ancient languages?"

"I've a skill with languages. I'm likely better with Aljyssian than Orcasi."

Orcasi. Only people native to remote Coverge named our common tongue *Orcasi* instead of *Sabrian.* The ill-educated population of Sabria's northernmost demesne scarce admitted six hundred years of Sabrian hegemony and spoke an ugly, guttural dialect of their own. That a man grown up in harsh, mountainous Coverge could read was astonishment enough, no matter that he could work the sorcery of a master mage. It explained a great deal about Dante's rough manners.

"If you ever need to leave anything for me, stuff it in that satchel," he said. "It will always be out, but won't necessarily be in the same place. No one can take aught from it. . . ."

Naturally, my fingers were drawn to test his declaration.

"Ouch!" Invisible steel teeth near ripped my fingernails out by their roots. I fell back on the bed, clutching my hand and groaning.

"Not even you. The sensation gets worse, the longer one keeps contact with it. Eventually it would—well, you'll know to be quick and not stuff my satchel with rubbish."

Wriggling my stinging fingers and cursing the day I lured Dante from his forest hovel, I followed him into the great chamber, where he was circling the ring, inspecting my work.

"I've never seen a circumoccule quite like it," I said.

"Good. I intend it to keep them guessing." He leaned heavily on his staff.

"Them? The other mages?"

"Whoever it was sneaked in here in the late watches. I weened it might take a bit longer for them to grow so bold, but then I've no experience of palace custom in the matter of sneaking. I suppose the Camarilla's been dithered about me these three years past, yes?" Grimacing, he tugged at the band about his neck. "Every day of my life I suspect they put some devilish poison in this collar to drive me mad and bring me back to Seravain."

Understanding seeped through my thick skull. Naturally the two mages would be mad to know what Dante was up to. One of them—or some trusted adept or acolyte—would certainly try to examine his work. If they probed his circumoccule, they'd be flummoxed by its odd composition. "Yes. They're most certainly curious. They'll judge this worthless "

"And then, someday perhaps, I'll raise a dead man in the center of it." Eyes fixed on the center of the circle, he could not have seen me stop breathing.

"Your purpose is not to *practice* necromancy, Master."

He shrugged, refusing to meet my gaze. "Likely any true sorcery would confuse them."

"If all goes well, I'll fetch you to the deadhouse tonight after sunset. Then we'll decide how to dissolve this unfortunate connection so I can begin asking some questions."

He nodded and folded his arms. Silently, dark brow drawn up in a knot, he watched me dab at the sorry grime of my shirt collar and gather his lists.

"Divine grace, Master," I said when I felt ready.

He did not return the farewell, but as I laid a hand on the door latch,

words spilled out of him as boiling water breaks over the rim of a pot. "Tell your king to be wary. Some violence is brewing, but I can't say what as yet."

"How——?" But he had already retreated into the little bedchamber and slammed the door behind him.

DAMOSELLE MAURA HELD COURT IN a writing room three corridors and two courtyards away from the mage's apartments. A footman waved me to a velvet-cushioned bench beside the passage wall, where I waited alongside several other supplicants and stewed over Dante's mysterious warning.

"Present, Adept Fedrigo de Leuve."

I glanced up at a dark-bearded, bull-necked giant wearing an adept's gray gown and a red sash. His nose looked to have been broken a number of times. So this was the perpetrator of Ilario's crocodile charm and other "excellent magics" for Queen Eugenie's household. Evidently his business was not as simple as the other supplicants'. Even the thick door could not mask the sound of agitated voices. He emerged, red-faced, after a lengthy consultation and stormed away.

"Present, Sonjeur de Duplais," said the footman, pointing at the door.

The administrator welcomed me warmly. "So soon? Is all well with you?"

"Perhaps better than with you," I said, inclining my head toward the door.

"We must all deal with thorns in our shoes," she said, wrinkling her nose. "Some are more difficult to be rid of than others. Ah, you've brought your thorn's lists."

An hour we spent puzzling out Dante's requirements. The lady accepted the more sinister materials with better grace than I had, and did not balk at oddities such as a *barrel of battleground soil* or a *used rat trap*.

"Everyone in my family practices the art, sonjeur. I myself attended Collegia Seravain. But I found the constant study and repetition tedious,

and when I heard that Her Majesty was searching for ladies of rank who were comfortable with magic, I leapt at the chance to move on." A rosy flush deepened the rich brown of her complexion.

Likely she had found little more success at Seravain than I. Though she had surely attended during my tenure as archivist, I'd neither met nor heard reports of her. Not so unusual. Seravain's tutorial schedules were tight and demanding, and some students found little use from the library.

"Unfortunate for the collegia, you didn't find your proper calling there," I said. "They need administrators so accommodating and efficient . . . and kind." I'd met few people so easy to talk to. Women over age seventeen generally left me in mumbling incoherence.

She radiated pleasure. "Here I serve only three mages, nine adepts, and seventy householders, not Seravain's three hundred fifty. And I much prefer a royal budget to an academic one. Which reminds me, we must see to your accommodations. . . ." She jumped up.

Ignoring two waiting supplicants, the lady herself escorted me first to the palace steward to obtain the keys to an apartment in the male householders' wing, and then to his accommodating third secretary to arrange for someone to fetch my belongings and for delivery of letters and parcels. With entrancing wit, the lady dispensed bits of history to accompany each landmark along our route. By the time we returned to her writing room, I was wholly and entirely smitten.

"From the traffic in this room, you must surely administer more than the queen's consilium," I said, struggling to revert to my more sinister business.

She settled back in the chair behind the writing desk. "I accommodate Her Majesty's family and a few other courtiers, as well—juggling apartments or personal servants, ordering books, hiring musicians for special occasions, making use of the contacts I've developed in my regular work. I know everyone in the palace and most tradesmen in Merona." She tilted her head and peered at me closely. "Tell me, sonjeur, is something troubling you?"

I steepled my fingers and pressed them to my mouth, attempting a

show of contemplation before forging ahead. Perhaps not entirely a show. The subjects of death, faith, and Veil passages always left me discomforted. "No. No. I don't think . . . You've done more than I can thank you for already."

"There, you see, something preys on your mind. Come, tell me. Mage Dante is despicably rude, setting you to such low tasks. I could speak a word to Her Majesty . . . release you. . . ."

"Please no, damoselle. I am determined to stay on in the royal household. A few insults are bearable." First things first. "I'm wondering—perhaps you could make a recommendation. After my presentation to His Majesty yesterday, I'm sore in need of a temple reader. Surely my father's spirit flags after my injudicious references to his journey. And I must have his tessila resanctified after profaning it so selfishly. This fire in me has been so strong, I fear I failed in judgment."

She leaned across her writing table in great concern and laid a kind hand on mine. "Your devotion must surely speed your father on to Heaven. We have a temple minor here and so, three readers. But, of course, the only reader who can also sanctify tessilae is a deadhouse verger. . . ."

And being precise and efficient as she was, Damoselle Maura drew me a small map to find the deadhouse, set between the temple minor and the swan garden. And she dispatched a note to Verger Rinaldo de Soinfe, saying that Portier de Duplais would be visiting him in the late evening for a reading and sanctification.

I took Damoselle Maura's small, warm hand and bowed over it. "You have been most kind, lady."

"There are more than just you who seek meaningful service in the world, sonjeur. If I can aid your search, I'm glad of it."

Lies I had expected in the role of *agente confide*; crass manipulation of sincere good feeling, I had not. I left the administrator's office feeling soiled in more than my garments.

I NEEDED TO DO SOMETHING about my crumpled, sooty attire before visiting the verger, so I sped off to locate my new apartment. No sooner had I

opened the door than a trim young fellow carrying a pillow and towel darted in, skidded to a stop, and gave a jerky bow.

"Divine grace, sonjeur." He dashed a lock of yellow hair from his eyes. "I'm Heurot, manservant for your honored self and four other gentlemen as lives on this passage. I'll empty slops, lug your wash water, and such. Leave your boots outside the door each night and I'll see to 'em before morning. And what clothes need cleaning, lay out atop yon chest in the morning. Ye'll take meals in the gentlemen's refectory at the end of the passage. Have ye nowt I should put away, sonjeur?" He peered around the bare little room as if clothing and boots might pop out of the woodwork.

"A small case should be arriving soon. More in a few days. But I don't need much looking after. I value my privacy."

No more than sixteen, he displayed a ready grin. "I'm pleased to leave ye to yerself. Four gentlemen's already a race to handle."

It was impossible not to return his breathless cheer. "Two small requests before you go. Are paper and ink available? And a clothes brush, if you would."

"Paper in the desk cupboard, sir; brush in the chest." He yanked at a sticky door latch on the cupboard mounted above the writing table. Behind the door were two shelves and a shallow drawer, containing a sheaf and an ink bottle. "If it's not enough, I can fetch more."

"These will do nicely."

He wielded the clothes brush with a deft hand and youthful vigor, ridding my doublet and breeches of prison dirt and Dante's soot and sawdust. "Thank you, Heurot. Divine grace go with you. Oh—"

My abortive call halted him in the doorway. "Sonjeur?"

"You wouldn't know . . . I've an appointment at the deadhouse this night, and I've heard a man was found dead within the palace precincts some few days ago. Are there funeral rites tonight? I'd not like to intrude."

"I've heard nowt of any such. There's only Contessa Bianci dead as I know of, Lady Antonia's waiting lady what popped off in her sleep this morning, and high time, too, the old pecking crow—angels forgive me

for speaking ill of the dead. I doubt her rites'd be so soon. But a friend of mine, Grinnel, is a guardsman and's posted evening watch at the temple gate this tennight. He'll know."

"Fine. Good. Well done. I'll seek him out."

The youth vanished in a breath of soap and boot polish.

I made grateful use of the lukewarm water and towel that waited atop the washing table. Then I unstoppered the ink and set to work.

As the palace bells rang sixth hour of the evening watch, I threaded my way through the palace maze. Letters to my mother, her steward, and the family's man of business, giving notice of my changed residence, went into the steward's post bag, along with a brief commission to a tailor in the village of Margeroux. In only a few days I should receive a package containing a new skirted doublet suitable for court wear, along with a silver coin, a bloody arrow, and a most unusual spyglass. Satisfied, I headed off to question a temple guardsman, fetch the mage, and visit the dead.

CHAPTER SIX

11 QAT
50 DAYS UNTIL THE ANNIVERSARY

The deadhouse gates swung open at my touch. The garden beyond lay quiet in the night, its thick plantings like a second wall, a moat of scent and thorn completely enclosing the blocklike stone building. Lantana and prickly juniper clogged the air with sickly, pungent aromas, and ghastly white blooms masked the sharp spines of blackthorn trees. Sabrians did not encourage the dead to linger. We wanted them to find their way through Ixtador to Heaven, lest the Souleater devour them on the last day of the world.

The echo of the gate bell faded. But from the vast palace precincts behind me rose a mournful cry that chilled my soul, sounding far more like a despairing human than dog or feral cat. The business that awaited could not but make a man skittish and heartsick. The dead mule we'd come to see was a girl, so Heurot's guardsman friend had told me.

A balding, moon-faced man awaited me in the flickering yellow torchlight of the entry. "Sonjeur de Duplais?" he said, exposing his left hand on his shoulder. "I am Verger Rinaldo."

"Divine grace," I said, swiping thumb to forehead in respect before exposing my own hand. "I appreciate your seeing me so late of an evening."

"I'm happy to serve your need, sonjeur." He held the door open.

I resisted the temptation to glance over my shoulder. Dante should be hidden in the shadowed peripheries of this garden. As I crossed the threshold, I dragged my hand across the mechanism of the lock, scraping it with the brass ring he had given me. No sooner had I whispered the key *inclavio*, than I snatched my hand away and stuffed it under the opposite elbow. My fingers stung as if I'd dipped them in a wasp nest. The mage had warned me his spell was crudely made and lacked shielding for the user.

Much of a student's first year at Seravain was spent training the senses to detect the existence of bound enchantments, the active energies of their release, and the residue that remained after some or all of those energies were used. Unlike the subtle sensations I had learned to associate with spellwork, Dante's magic nipped at my senses like a wolverine's bite— sharp, vital, as ferocious as everything else he did. I bled envy.

The mage's precaution to ensure his passage served well, as the verger shot the bolt once we were inside. Easy to see why. A thousand lamps hung from the age-mottled ceiling—lamps small and large, wrought of silver and gold, ancient lamps of the simplest design, others intricately wrought, etched, filigreed, or set with gems and jewel-hued glass. The Revelation of the Veil taught us that families could speed an ancestor's progress through Ixtador's Ten Gates only by honor and righteous living, not with material offerings. That was a difficult teaching for those who believed gold and jewels could buy anything.

Only a few of the lamps were lit, just enough to illumine our way across the foyer and through the circles of stone benches that surrounded a display of sand, miniature gates, and glazed water bowls. From the Chamber of Contemplation wide marble steps descended into a maze of polished walls etched with the names of the dead who had passed through this house.

Rather than continuing down a second stair to visit the Chamber of the Dead, where those brought to the deadhouse were washed and wrapped to lie in peace until their funeral rites, or to the tessilactory, where craftsmen shaped the stone artifacts to be sanctified at those rites,

the verger led me down a side passage to a reading room. Built to exact dimensions, two and a half metres in height, width, and length, the close little chamber reeked of incense and scented soap from the verger's purification.

Already my head throbbed unmercifully. Incense forever induced the headaches that had plagued me since the explosive ending of my magical studies—the day I confronted my father with the truth of my failure and reaped the whirlwind.

Rinaldo scribed my father's full name on his slate and lit three-and-fifty candles, one for each year of my father's life. We sat cross-legged on either side of the loaf-sized altar stone, and I laid out the smoothed shape of red jasper and its matching spall—the little wedge chipped from the tessila on my father's funeral day.

"Now why do you believe you have profaned your father's memory?" asked the verger kindly.

"In passion and duty resulting from a recent temple reading . . ." I recounted my braid of lies yet again, feeling vaguely guilty and vaguely heretical—and decidedly foolish for such emotions. My beliefs about Ixtador and its perilous gates had been uncertain for many years. Yes, I kept my altar and carried a spall pouch and judged my every deed as to its efficacy for my honored dead. But extensive reading had brought me to view the Revelation as merely a historically necessary call to reformation after the Blood Wars. Now the spyglass vision had wholly confused my beliefs.

A gentle man, Rinaldo did not condemn me for my "dutiful zeal," but counseled me to leave the tessila in its proper place on my home altar next time I needed to grovel before the king and to carry only the unsanctified spall as a reminder of my family duty. "Let us step through the resanctification first. Then I'll attempt to assess your father's progress."

"Many thanks, Verger."

He raised his hands in supplication. "Holy angels, messengers of Heaven, bear my petition for hearing and grace to sanctify this memorial of Onfroi Guillame de Savin-Duplais. . . ."

As the verger recited the lengthy prayers and blessings required to

purge the tessila of profanation, he poured and drank a thimble-cup of thick red liquid and lit the dish of herbs that sat on the altar beside the tessila and spall. I tried not to fidget as I imagined Dante slipping through the enspelled door lock and seeking out the mule's corpse. I tried not to breathe as the vapors roiled my stomach, and sharp-edged visions of curved swords and smoking battlefields etched themselves into my pounding head.

Just after the palace bells clanged the quarter hour, Rinaldo lapsed into the trancelike state of a reader probing the mysteries of Ixtador. I shook off my own drowsy half dreams, retrieved a pinch of sleeping herbs from my spall pouch, and dropped it into the smoldering dish. Rinaldo's trance state would be a bit deeper than usual and last for at least half an hour. I rose quietly and sped down the passage and the lower stair into the Chamber of the Dead.

Ranks of blocklike catafalques stood like some morbid army, silhouetted against the deeper blackness of the frigid chamber. Few were occupied. The soft white gleam from Dante's staff directed me to our quarry, a plain bier in a corner roped off for the unsanctified—suicides, felons, blasphemers, and mules.

As my mind encompassed the obscenity laid out on the stone slab, sin and grief took on new meanings for which my sheltered existence could not have prepared me. The bruised, lacerated body that lay amid the tousled grave wraps belonged to a once-fair girl of no more than sixteen summers. Scars defiled every portion of her pale skin, their number and varied age witnessing to years, not months, of torment. Even did the sorcerer extract but a thimbleful at each bleeding, a body could not replenish so much in any shorter span. Worse yet, life and mystery knotted so tightly that each wound screamed from my own flesh. For I knew her. *Ophelie . . .*

"The leech is expert," said Dante, his finger tapping the ranks of pale scars along the girl's arm and those on her neck, exposed when someone had hacked her dulled hair to a knucklebone's length. "Clean. Precise. Methodical. But I believe the mule began by bleeding herself. These oldest cuts on her thighs are ragged and tentative. And this"—he exposed the

ugly red ruin of her left hand, where her family mark would be—"the mutilation of her identity was done quite recently." He dropped the flaccid limb onto the stone slab. "The body's keirna reveals—"

"She is not just a body, not just a mule," I blurted harshly, throttling a rising anger.

I could not but glimpse the flash of golden hair in the lamplight of the Seravain library, hear her spritely laughter in the company of her friends. I disliked children and resented when the younger students invaded my library. But the age of fourteen saw some become tolerable, especially the brightest minds as they began to comprehend the true dimensions of the world, the wonders that lay in life, in books, in magic. . . .

"Her name was Ophelie de Marangel," I said, "a diligent student, intelligent and insightful. Three or four years ago, she stood on the verge of dismissal, incapable of spellwork. Then, as happens from time to time, she all at once broke through that . . . barrier." The barrier that separates those who reach for power and find magic in their grasp from those who reach, but find their palms empty.

I could still hear Ophelie's desperation when she had come to me in confidence, begging me for some volume that might open the gates of magical understanding. I'd had to tell her no such work had ever been written. I had rejoiced to learn of her awakening. But evidently her palms had gripped a lancet and no true power at all. Self transference—reinfusing her own blood to fuel her magic. Only a child's perverse reasoning would judge slow death a sensible exchange for magic. And then, what? What villain, what filth, what maggot-souled fiend had discovered Ophelie's secret sin and taken up the task?

Dante glanced up from his examination of a small wound beneath her breastbone. "You discovered so much from a guardsman?"

I shook my head, unable to remove my eyes from the translucent skin stretched over her fine bones like gossamer sails on a master-wrought ship. She could have no flesh beneath that skin. With purpose and without mercy, a sorcerer had bled her dry.

A fury woke in me, hardening into certainty of purpose. "I knew her at Seravain. Last year, not long after passing her second adept's testing, we

heard she fell ill and was sent back to her family in Challyat. She never returned to school." I inhaled the blended reeks of lamp oil, incense, and dead flesh, scribing the sight and stink upon my memory with the indelible medium of outrage. "The temple guardsman knew only that a knight found a dead girl at the base of the orchard wall with a dagger in her gut. The Guard Royale assumed she had climbed the outer wall in an attempt to breach the palace precincts and attack the king, but lost her grip and fell on her own weapon."

"Unlikely." Dante uncurled her hand, and I quickly averted my eyes. The girl's fingers were little more than ragged, blood-crusted stubs. "She'd never have topped any wall with hands like these. More likely she was trying to get *out* of the palace precincts."

"Why would anyone do that to her?" I said, swallowing hard. "Was stealing her blood not cruel enough?" What could be more dreadful than watching your own blood stolen drop by drop, knowing that your soul must eventually drain away with it?

"Identification," said the mage, crouching beside the bier, touching each torn stub in turn, using a small blade to scrape dried blood into a glass vial. I could not bear to watch. "We leave a trace of ourselves on every spell we work."

"And the Bardeu test on her fingers might reveal it," I murmured. The old formula purported to link a sorcerer and a worked spell, though I had never seen it work successfully.

"There are surer ways, but yes. Not only did our knaves leech her blood to empower magic, but I'd also guess they induced her to work some spell they wanted, just as they forced the assassin to shoot the arrow at the king. But they didn't want her work identified, which tells me that they expected someone to be analyzing her spells." He glanced up, his eyes dark pits in the gloom. "Remember the coming violence I spoke of? Odds on, she was to be a part of it."

"We should take these despicable mages down," I snapped. "Have them arrested right now."

"Without knowing what spells she's worked? Without knowing if a trap is already in place?" Dante slipped around the end of the catafalque,

cut off a snippet of the girl's hair, and moved on to examine her right hand. "The actual removal of her fingers occurred a tennight or more past, which suggests her work was complete. This fresh damage comes from her attempt to climb the wall. If we cannot establish a connection between the queen's mages and either one of the mules, the Camarilla could as easily blame this on me."

Certainly the miscreants must be terrified at the girl's exposure. The discovery of a second mule would warn the king of a coming attempt. And if someone recognized the girl, the lie about her "illness" could be traced to an accomplice at Seravain. I'd have wagered my life that Ophelie's family believed her still at the collegia, too busy with her studies to write.

"I'll find the connection," I said, skin and soul ablaze. Fifty days yet remained until the anniversary of Prince Desmond's death. "Now, will you stop touching her? It's unseemly."

Ignoring my protest, the frowning mage again palpated the knife wound beneath her breast. Though she had not been washed, little blood and only a small bruise marked the hole.

"This guardsman's story makes no sense," he said, looking up at me. "How could she have a knife? She'd no strength to disable a jailer. She'd have been desperate to escape and would never have taken time to hunt a weapon she could not wield. As she could not climb, she could not have fallen on it by accident. Even the placement of the wound is odd. So precise. How likely is it to 'fall on a knife' in the exact spot and at the exact angle to instantly stop the heart?"

"But her captors didn't kill her. You said Gaetana was upset at her exposure. They'd never have abandoned her corpse where she could be found."

Dante tapped the deadly puncture. "Find me the weapon that did this. Its keirna will tell us—"

From beyond the silent stairs and chambers behind us a clanging bell broke the silence, and a resounding thud signaled the opening of the great bronze door. "Verger Rinaldo?" bellowed a man's voice. "Would a bit of light be too much to ask in a house of the dead? Bring that torch, Jacard.

The rest of you, wait here." Heavy footsteps echoed through the upper chambers.

"Sainted bones," I whispered. "I've got to get back."

Abandoning Dante to tuck the coarse grave cloth about Ophelie, I pelted through the aisles and crept up the lower stair. The last of the hanging lamps were sputtering, as I threaded the maze of Chamber of Remembrance and dodged down the side passage into the reading room.

The verger had not moved. I dropped to the kneeling cushion opposite him just as heavy boots crossed the vestibule.

"We require Verger Rinaldo," snapped the elderly gentleman who filled the reading room doorway. The egg-sized emerald that fastened his black velvet cloak, the high starched ruff, and a heavy pectoral chain, carrying an amulet of woven silver and amber, testified to his exalted station.

"Pardon, lord," I whispered. "We are engaged in a reading."

"I don't care about your reading!" he bellowed. "My wife lies profaned!"

Wife!

Rinaldo's shoulders jerked. The verger pressed his fingers to his eyes before staring across at me and then up to the newcomer. Dazed, he wobbled to his feet. "Conte Bianci . . ."

The name quickly erased my shock. My valet had spoken of a newly deceased waiting woman.

"Verger, is it true that a corrupt corpus lies in your deadhouse alongside my wife?"

"Indeed not," said the verger, his back stiff and his eyes clearing. "That is, a corrupted body lies in the house, but we provide separate accommodation for the unsanctified. No harm shall come to your lamented lady."

"I'll not have it. Corrupt dead are to the Souleater's minions as honey to flies. Rid this house of the unsanctified, or I shall carry my wife to the Temple Major in my arms. The tetrarchs will strip you of your office. You'll be washing bodies and scrubbing floors."

"Come, come, good lord . . ."

Dante had been right to press for a quick viewing. Saints grant, this

uproar might cover his departure. There was no outside exit from the Chamber of the Dead.

Those hopes died quickly. The verger swept his arms toward the doorway. "Let us set your mind at rest. You'll see that every care has been taken. Grief must not spur haste."

As the conte stepped out, mumbling sentiments to the effect that proximity less than the moon's distance would be too close, Rinaldo laid a hand on my shoulder. "Pardon this unfortunate interruption, Sonjeur de Duplais," he whispered. "Were it anyone but a man who's lost his wife of nine-and-forty years, I'd send him packing. In any case, your father's reading seemed dreadfully confused. Come back another time, and we'll try again."

A slender, sharp-featured young man in adept's robes lit the passage with a jeweled lamp. My blessing words trailed after the verger, as he, the conte, and the adept swept out. I scooped up my tessila and spall and hurried after, willing Dante to be up the stairs and out of the deadhouse before the conte reached the lower chamber. We must not have our interest—or our confederacy—exposed.

"Adept Jacard, would you please tend the stairway lamps?" asked Verger Rinaldo, gesturing the conte to wait before descending into the dark. As I held quiet at the end of the passage, the nimble young man used the verger's long-handled brass taper to light a good third of the hanging lamps over the downward stair. *Blast!* No one would pass beneath them unseen.

Cursing Dante for leaving the entry door unlatched, I climbed the upward stair. I was nearing the main level when a clamor broke out both from above and below me. Conte Bianci shouted unintelligibly from below, while from the direction of the foyer, a ferocious baritone intoned, "Portier de Duplais, show yourself, you talentless maggot!"

I raced upward, unable to mistake Dante's resonant tones. A handful of gentlemen cowered in front of the entry doors.

The mage stood in the center of the foyer, his staff belching flames and a thundering noise that rattled the hanging lamps and set them swaying, chains and pendants jangling as in a whirlwind. "Where is my *servant*?" he bellowed.

As my mouth opened and closed soundlessly, the mumbling conte boiled up the stair behind me. "Burn that cursed mule tonight, Verger!"

As if propelled forward by the nobleman's wrath, I stumbled into the foyer, straight into Dante's glare. "There you are, insect!"

The conte's party halted at my back. "What in the infernal depths—?"

"Did I give you permission to pursue your own activities, apprentice?" Dante's visage pulsed the purpled black of a stormy sunset. "Floors unswept. Materials scattered. Accounts incomplete. Never . . . *never* . . . do you take it upon yourself to decide when to come or go. Return to my chambers and finish your work or I'll encase your feet in lead before the next sunrise."

He reversed direction and waved his flaming staff at the oaken entry doors. One of them flew open, crashing against the wall as if a battering ram had struck it. At least ten nearby lamps smashed into the tiled floor, sending the cringing gentlemen attendants scurrying to Conte Bianci's side. The sharp features of Bianci's adept glazed with awe. Mine likely did, as well.

As the mage swept into the thorny garden, one scheme, then another, careened through my head. For better or worse, I was left with the span of a moment to set my course. I had best trust my original plan.

I folded my arms around myself and set my shoulders shivering. "Witness, great lord, holy verger, good gentlemen," I said with appropriately trembling voice, "that I resign my commission as Master Dante's apprentice as of this hour. Should I fail to survive the night, I beg you invoke the Camarilla to avenge this affront."

As the white flames vanished beyond the hedges, I tucked my chin into my chest and fled, leaving the gentlemen attendants jabbering like magpies and young Adept Jacard laughing.

CHAPTER SEVEN

12 QAT
49 DAYS UNTIL THE ANNIVERSARY

On the next morning, Lord Ilario perched atop a waist-high wall in a private courtyard, feet dangling in the yellow wallflowers. His mouth gaped with a horror grown throughout my recounting of the deadhouse venture.

"Honestly, lord chevalier, the venture itself could not have worked out better," I said, attempting to ease his concern before he toppled backward into the fishpond. "Damoselle Maura placated Dante by assuring him that she would have me fetch his books from Seravain until she could assign him a new assistant. Then she offered me the position as your secretary, as we've planned all along."

My appreciation for the lady had increased yet again after I had burst in upon her the previous night, begging her to release me from Dante's service. I had not needed to feign awe at his magics, and my outrage at Ophelie's fate had sufficed for trembling.

"But, Portier, encased in lead!" He stretched his long legs straight out and gawked at his elegant boots. "You would be crippled forever! Well, I suppose you might drag your feet one by one, unless"—a sharp inhale signaled a new imagining—"he might encase them both in one block. You would have to be hauled about in a barrow!"

"He never would have done it, lord," I said, halfway between exasperation and amusement. "Dante wanted to make Conte Bianci's men forget that he had not entered through the outer door. The story of his outburst has spread throughout the palace and everyone is terrified and in awe of his magic. Just as we wish."

Certainly my spirit yet stung with the memory of Dante's enchantment. The thrill of power had raged through the deadhouse foyer like untamed lightning, filling the emptiness that gaped inside me as the ocean fills a sea cave.

"Truly, he did well. I've been freed to serve you, yet I've a perfect excuse to come and go in his chambers."

"Bless the Saints Awaiting, I did not see the poor girl." Ilario shuddered dramatically. "I would surely dream of it over and again."

After a sleepless night hearkening to Ophelie's pleas for vengeance, I could not argue. "Dante needs the weapon that killed her. But I've no idea what might have been done with it and no excuse to inquire. You do understand the questions surrounding the girl's death, Chevalier?"

"Certainly I understand," he said, springing from the wall as gracefully as a dancer. "I have a mind, after all, Portier."

"I didn't mean to imply—"

"Indeed you did. I'm not wholly unaware of what's said. No one credits that a gentleman who understands fashion and proper manners and refuses to dwell on upsetting matters in the presence of ladies can also be quite serious and scholarly." He dabbed at his hands and dusted the grit from his white hose with a lace kerchief, before tucking it into his sleeve. "The orchard, you say? I suggest that if we wish to know about the weapon, we speak to Audric de Neville. Would the present moment suit, or must you hurry off to attend to my trivial concerns or your own more sober ones?"

He strutted across the flower-filled yard toward an open gate without waiting for my answer, waving one hand as if he were an orator in the public forum. "I believe I shall enjoy having a private secretary. I have decided to host an exposition. How I love that word! *Exposition*. It sounds delightfully modern and studious. I daresay such a display shall reverse

this canard that has been spread about my sobriety. You shall make all the arrangements. . . ."

"But we've more pressing—?" As he vanished into the larger garden beyond the gate, my thoughts gummed like feathers in pine sap. I hurried after him.

Only after we had traversed the flower garden, innumerable court-yards and corridors, three kitchens and a vast kitchen garden, and de-scended a short slope toward a forested bend of the great palace wall did Ilario's long legs slow enough to allow me to ask who was Audric de Nev-ille. Yet by then the pungent scents of lemon and almond blossoms rising from ordered ranks of trees left the question unnecessary. A house knight had found Ophelie dead in an orchard.

The red-liveried chevalier was sleeping, back against the sun-drenched wall, jaw dropped in the way of the very old. His perfectly shined black boots stuck out in front of him as if he'd folded in the middle and sat straight down from standing guard. A pink almond blossom petal had settled on his white hair.

"He's the only knight in Castelle Escalon posted in an orchard," Ilario confided. "A noble spirit and proper chevalier. Philippe assigned him to guard this corner of the wall for as long as he chooses to serve. Lamenta-bly, his attention doesn't last so long as it once did."

Ilario waved me forward and propped his knee on an empty crate left among the unbloomed pomegranate trees.

"Divine grace, Chevalier Audric," I said as I crossed the grassy strip paralleling the wall.

The old knight jerked and snorted and struggled to his feet, watery yellow eyes blinking rapidly. "Who comes?"

I exposed my hand and bowed. "Portier de Duplais. I've come about the dead girl found here. The mule."

"Demon hand! Souleater's servant!" His rapier was in hand with a speed entirely unlikely for a man his age, and his face wore the wrath of the Pantokrator casting out Dimios at the founding of the world. "I'll see you dead—I'll—Ah!"

Breathing hard as if he'd run the length and breadth of his orchard

post, the old man choked back the sentiments that sudden waking had startled out of him.

"I am the girl's friend," I said, "her mourner, rather. My employer, a kindly man horrified by this tale, has ordered me to identify the girl and contact her family."

"Don't know aught. How could I? Found her dead." His hands trembled so violently, his blade hummed. As the emotion trying to escape him so belied this mumbled answer, I did not believe him in the least.

"We must tell her family how she died, what weapon finished her, so they might speed her way through Ixtador's gates." My bare hand stilled his blade. "'Twill be a mercy to all. Tell us, Chevalier."

As quickly as he'd drawn his weapon, the old man sagged to his knees. Sword dropped to the emerald grass, he crossed his arms and gripped his shoulders as if to keep his heart from flying out of his breast. "She begged me. Soon as she found the wall too steep to climb. Wild, she was. Could scarce speak and most of it babbling nonsense. But she shed no tears. Not a one. I'm damned forever to have done it, though she promised to carry word to the saints to defend me."

"Damned? But *you* didn't—" I shook off a grotesque image of the old man leeching her. It wasn't leeching he spoke of. "You found her *alive*. What did she tell you?"

"Claimed a devil woman bled her. Claimed the two forced her to terrible sin. To treason and murder. To the betrayal of a good man. Yet she'd no strength to save herself. She pawed at me. Tore at me. Begged on her knees and pressed the tip to her breast. Mad, as if the Souleater himself had gnawed her reason. I couldna refuse her. Do ye see that? I had to save her."

Dread truth stared me in the face yet again, as Audric uncrossed his arms and lifted his rapier on open palms.

Suicide. The old chevalier's rapier might have pierced her breast, but the Pantokrator, the all-seeing Judge, would know she had driven him to it. What sin could frighten her more than traversing the Veil corrupt—a mule who had sought her own death? Ixtador's gates would be barred to her.

I swallowed bile and accusation. "A name, Chevalier. In all this, did she speak a name?"

"Only near the end. She held my hand and spake it over and over in the midst of her weeping, so's I didn't know what to make of it. *Michel . . . captured . . . betrayed . . . Altevierre . . . save me . . .* Over and over. *Michel . . . captured . . . betrayed . . . . Altevierre . . . save me . . . Michel . . .*"

Michel de Vernase . . . Our first word of Philippe's lost investigator. My blood raced.

Half-crazed with shame and guilt too long suppressed, the old knight poured out his story. It illumined little. He could provide no clue to assassination plots; no hint as to Michel de Vernase's fate; no identification of Ophelie's captors beyond the *devil woman* and the vague *two*; no idea what the word *Altevierre* referred to, and yes, it might have been something other, but his hearing was so cursed feeble. . . .

The Guard Royale had not questioned the bloodied poniard Audric had left with the girl as if she'd fallen on it. Audric had told no one that he'd found Ophelie living. The deception had likely saved his life.

We plied the old knight with valerian tea from the opaline flask Ilario carried for his digestion. Now that the boil of his shame had been lanced, Audric vowed to perpetuate his silence. To soothe his conscience, I suggested he sanctify a tessila for the mysterious girl. "If she sought to avoid forced sin, then perhaps her soul was not entirely expended in unholy magic. Though you're not blood kin, your deed, for good or ill, has surely bound you to her fate."

Audric, eased by that consideration or the valerian or both, insisted on remaining at his post.

I was near dancing with urgency. We were closing on information of importance. Michel de Vernase had vanished nigh a year ago and nothing had been heard of him, so Philippe had told me. No sightings. No demands. Everything had pointed to his death. And Ophelie had come to Audric from *inside* the castle walls, as Dante had surmised.

"Where could these mages hold secret prisoners?" I demanded, once a swath of trees separated Ilario and me from the knight. "If Ophelie and Michel were held prisoner together, it must be somewhere close." *Perhaps*

he is still there, I dared not say aloud. *Perhaps he is in the same state as Ophelie.*

Ilario blotted his forehead, then wagged the knotted kerchief northward. An ancient blocklike keep squatted atop a low mound near the northern wall like a wart upon Castelle Escolan's warm yellow face. "Eugenie and I used to play in the old dungeons. Yet watchmen wander in from time to time, so you couldn't keep a secret prisoner." He swiveled westward toward the river. "Then there's the Spindle. . . ."

"Spindle Prison is outside the walls, and Ophelie didn't row a boat to get away. She was held here at the palace. A place the mages could come and go unremarked, with thick walls or well out of the common way. They'd not want anyone to hear what was going on." *Cries for help. Pleading, as a child's blood was drained away. Father Creator, forgive.*

Ilario pivoted full circle, mumbling the merits and demerits of various possibilities as his gaze traversed kitchen buildings, courtyard walls, guard towers; nurseries, toolsheds, and stables; deadhouse, swan garden, and the marble-columned temple minor. His brow lifted and smoothed. "There," he declared with the certainty of a man choosing white bread over brown.

I summoned patience. "The temple? But there's no—"

"The royal crypt lies underneath," he said, setting off at a brisk pace. "The King's Gate is kept locked until a sovereign dies, is crowned, or takes a notion to alter the name of his heir. But Eugenie found another way down." He shuddered dramatically. "She wanted to explore the secret chambers. She forced me to go. Called me a ninny, but I kept imagining those fifty kings, sitting in their niches in the dark, rotting."

As we crossed the sweltering gardens, his pace slowed and he lowered his voice. "Michel could not be used as a mule, you know. He's as common as a barnyard—most certainly not of the blood. And he despises sorcery. Cursed preachy about it, too. Stubborn as the pox."

"A perfect hostage, however," I said, matching his quiet voice. "The king's closest friend."

"True enough." Ilario shrugged and aimed his unfocused eyes in the direction of the sun-washed temple roof. "They served together for years.

Drank one another's wine and covered one another's sins. Long before anyone knew Philippe was Soren's heir, Michel took a sword strike for Philippe that near cost his arm. Philippe stood goodfather to Michel's children, and Michel did the same for Prince Desmond, angels guide the poor dead mite."

A white stone chip appeared in Ilario's hand. He touched the spall to his heart, forehead, and lips, before returning it to the silk pouch at his waist, scarce interrupting his commentary.

"Philippe's first act when crowned was to name Michel his First Counselor, displacing old Baldwin whose family had held the office since the Founding. Then he granted Michel the Ruggiere demesne that's never been held by less than royal kin, and without so much as consulting its overlord. Neither move was at all fitting. Geni's always felt the two of them were closer—" Ilario swallowed the sentiment, jerked the string closure on his spall pouch, and angled across the temple lawn.

It struck me as no surprise that a friendship founded on youth and war might bloom more intimate than a marriage founded on political necessity. But the tenor of Ilario's words gave me pause, serious as they were, and threaded with such profound dislike. I observed him closely.

Eyeing me sidewise, he wrinkled his mouth like a dried currant. "Well, all right. You've caught me out. Michel de Vernase and I get along like cats and fish. He is a brute and a bully and has not the least sense of fashion or manners or respect. He usurps places that are not his. But I'd not wish that"—he jerked his head in the direction whence we'd just come—"on anyone."

Nor would I. Nonetheless, I had been proceeding on the assumption that Michel de Vernase's disappearance had resulted solely from his position as investigator, that the king's regard for his friend had somehow made Michel's own character unimportant. *A lesson, Portier: Judge each player objectively, individually, and entirely.*

"Who is the overlord of the Ruggiere demesne?"

Ilario snapped his head around. "Dumont, of course. The Duc de Aubine." He narrowed his eyes. "No, no, Portier, quiet your nefarious imaginings. Dumont is not at all your man. He cares for naught but his

birds. Now, back when Philippe granted Ruggiere to Michel, the demesne was held by Dumont's grandfather, who was as friendly as a rabid dog. He called the grant *theft*. If not for my foster mother, the old devil would have hauled Michel out of Ruggiere naked and bound in thorn ropes."

Comprehension required some wrestling with bloodlines and inheritance. King Soren had married Eugenie de Sylvae when she was but a child, and his mother, Lady Antonia, had fostered Eugenie and her half brother, Ilario, after their parents died in a fire. "So Lady Antonia persuaded her father, the *old* duc of Aubine, not to fight Philippe's grant to Michel?"

"Antonia is very persuasive. And she believes a king can grant what he wills. It helped that the slavering old hound doted on her until the day he died choking on an olive." Ilario waved his hand dismissively. "As for the present duc—Dumont—I promise you he doesn't care who holds his demesnes unless they've beaks and feathers. Michel de Vernase earned plenty of enemies elsewhere."

A serving man was sweeping the wide, shallow steps of the temple portico as we approached. A few ladies stood in the breezy shade of the pediment, as triumphant angels, painted scarlet, emerald, and gold, bent down from the facade as if to eavesdrop on their gossip.

Ilario bowed gracefully to the women as he tripped lightly up the steps and crossed the portico. As I entered the dim vestibule, he was disappearing, not into the light-filled vastness of the temple nave, but through a lesser doorway on the left. "It's far too long since I venerated my father's tomb," he was declaiming loudly. "I've been thinking it requires a new offering urn. You must arrange for it, secretary."

Two veiled women trudged past us. We hurried down the broad passage between a wall of carved memorial stones and a rank of increasingly elaborate sarcophagi. Midway down the aisle, Ilario's closed fingers touched his lips, then brushed a vault of rosy marble capped with the sculpted figure of a Knight of Sabria.

We halted in a memorial bay at the farthest end of the aisle. With a glance back down the aisle—now deserted—Ilario ducked under the bay's

gilded rail and dodged behind a massive carving of some saintly king. I followed.

The dark alcove stank of musty wine and ancient incense. "Make us a light," Ilario said, from somewhere ahead of me. "Twiddle your fingers or whatever you sorcerers do."

"Twiddle . . ." My cheeks heated. Any more and they'd provide flames enough to see by.

I retreated past the effigy and the rail, returning moments later with a votive lamp from some marquesa's tomb hidden under my cloak. "This will have to do."

In the first moment I uncovered the lamp, I caught Ilario frowning at me. "Well, I assumed you could do *something* magical."

He dropped to his knees and probed the latch with a dainty knife more suited to picking teeth than breaking locks. Twice he fumbled and dropped the implement with a clatter. "Blast!" he said. "This used to be easier."

"Let me try," I said, trading him the lamp for the knife.

"This is the Tetrarch's Gate," Ilario whispered over my shoulder. "On coronation day, the new sovereign has to go down to the crypt to scribe the name of his heir. He uses the King's Gate—behind the font in the temple nave. A tetrarch is supposed to greet the new king down below in the name of all the dead kings, but it appears rude if he bullies past to descend first. So, instead, he slips aside and goes down this way."

In a moment's whimsy, I attempted a simple spell I'd used with some success when a child—a marvel that had sparked my magical ambitions. I broke off a thread dangling from the hem of my doublet. Twisting the thread about the knife blade and touching the latch with the knife, I blew upon their intersection—adding air to the balance of wood and metal—and infused the simple spell with my will. Not the least trickle of power cooled my veins. *Idiot.*

I twisted the handle and yanked on the door in frustration. To my astonishment, it flew open.

"Well done!" said Ilario, beaming.

"It was already unlocked," I snapped, angered at my inability to let go of what was ended.

"Impossible. No one ever goes down here. And this gate is always latched from the inside."

Impossible. Always. Dangerous words for an investigator. "Perhaps Ophelie escaped this way," I said.

Ilario blanched, blew a shaky breath, and motioned me through the opening. We closed the door softly and tiptoed down a spiraled stair. At the end of a downsloping passage lay a cavernous vault, hewn from the great rock underlying Castelle Escalon.

Massive columns incised with Fassid symbols, centuries older than the temple they supported, crowded the vast chamber. Censers of tarnished silver and brass dangled from the damp-stained ceiling like old moss, glittering and fading in our lamplight as we threaded a path between them. Every breath reeked of old incense, old stone, and old earth.

Not a step, not a breath, disturbed the stillness. What prisoner might have been held down here was no longer.

A single red lamp beamed brightly through the forest of columns, marking a great black stone bowl set atop a stepped pyramid some eight or ten metres across. Disproportionately elongated figures of men and women, hacked roughly from the gray stone, supported the bowl.

"The Coronation Font," said Ilario quietly. "Step up and take a look. It's a marvel."

The rounded lip felt cold to my hands as I peered into the font. Five half-height pillars protruded a few centimetres above the dark, still surface of the water, providing stepping stones to the center, where the watch lamp's ruby glow illumined a marble pedestal. A stone tablet lay on the pedestal. "Is that the Heir's Tablet?"

"The thing itself."

It behooved a sovereign to be specific when he scribed the name of the one who would succeed him, should he die without issue. Soren had written the *Duc de Journia,* who at the time was Armand de Savin, the white-haired Chancellor of Sabria. By the time Soren died, the Duc de Journia was the late chancellor's twenty-one-year-old son, Philippe, whom Soren detested.

"I thought it would be locked away," I said, astonished, "so no one could tamper with it."

"No need," said Ilario, from below me. "Stretch your hand out over the water."

When I did so, the water began to churn. Swirling, burbling, the dark flood quickly swelled upward toward the lip of the font, swamping the half columns.

I snatched my hand away, and the heaving water calmed. The residue of massive enchantment settled on my skin like spiderwebs, smelling of musty leaves and mildew.

"Happens it requires a few drops of an anointed king's blood to prevent all that folderol," said my companion. "And if a person gets swept off the stepping stones into the water, a hellacious clamor breaks out in the temple, and people come running and pull you out half drowned, and you think some pompous temple aide is going to slap you into one of these cells for the rest of your life, though you just wanted to get a look. . . ."

Ilario's rueful expression—and the image of a lanky young boy's dripping humiliation—elicited an unexpected laugh. But I was quickly sobered by a serious question that should have been the first out of my mouth when my royal cousin handed me this mess.

"Lord Ilario, whose name is scribed on that tablet? Since the boy died . . ."

Prince Desmond had died seven long years previous, and three more babes had failed since. Even as the distraught queen grew more reclusive, the suspicion grew that the sad lady was cursed and Philippe should be rid of her. No matter how devotedly my cousin believed his wife would yet produce a living heir, I could not imagine Philippe abandoning his beloved Sabria to the closest male of the Savin line, the near-illiterate Conte Parnasse.

"No one can pry it out of him," said Ilario. "After Catalin was stillborn, he came down here and scribed a new name, but he told no one *whose* name. Not even Eugenie. He said only that she didn't need to fret; that if the worst befell, his heir would be a person of strong and noble heart, who would care for her as his own sister . . ."

He tapped one elegant toe. Then he huffed, sighed deeply, and climbed

the black stone steps to stand at my side. I waited, grasping that his thought was not quite ended.

"And then, a month later, on the anniversary of Desmond's death—that would be not quite two years ago now—Philippe's horse went mad and threw him. Broke his leg and three ribs. Damned bad luck. I offered to fetch him a charm from Fedrigo, but, as always, he scoffed."

I gaped at Ilario, who in turn stared at the tablet, its secret barricaded with enchantments I doubted any mage of our day could duplicate. And I wondered about luck and coincidence and if, perhaps, my royal cousin's certainty that his son's deathday would bring him mortal danger was based on more than a single incident. "Have there been other unfortunate occurrences on Prince Desmond's deathday?"

"The year prior to the mad horse, their daughter, Catalin Jolie, was stillborn."

Holy saints! When Philippe named a new heir, had the queen been relieved that the burden of Sabria's future did not rest in her womb, or had she been angry that her husband's throne would pass to someone she did not know, as if he had lost faith in her? Or perhaps . . . Rumor said Queen Eugenie had first brought mages to Castelle Escalon when the little prince lay dying.

"Lord Ilario, does your sister blame the *king* for Prince Desmond's death?"

"Certainly not. The boy was sickly from birth." Ilario spun in place and tripped down the stepped dais. "We'd best move on. We came looking for evidence of Michel."

The royal tombs of Sabria's kings nestled in cold, dark bays between the heavy piers. Thick iron doors broke the occasional spaces of flat wall.

"Preparation rooms, chapels, storehouses, who knows what they were?" said Ilario, as we peered into the airless chamber behind one such door. Anyone of adult stature would have to duck to enter. Despite the cramped doorway, the ceiling stood at a reasonable height. "The verger says the lintels were built low so dead souls could not escape." He shuddered.

We opened and closed every door. Some revealed bare cells. Some

revealed heaps of what might be rotted carpeting, or worse. We found splintered shelves, broken chisels, and a rusty vise.

The crypt must have held fifty royal tombs—some sarcophagi little more than stone boxes, carved with symbols, some marked with elaborately adorned altars and graven memorial stones, some adorned with carvings of horses, wine casks, and other symbols of wealth and prosperity. More than once I jumped when our lamp revealed a pale face with solid black eyes—a nouré, a statue erected to honor the dead, its naked form swathed in real garments and jewelry, lacking only lifelike eyes so as not to be mistaken for the departed one.

Time had ravaged most of the tombs. Once-bright paint had faded on walls and furnishings. The fine garments that draped the nouri hung threadbare, ravaged by insects, vermin, and damp. Gemstones sat in tarnished settings or had been dug out and replaced with less precious stones.

The weight of so many tombs and altars, pillars, and cells oppressed my soul. The black, accusing stare of the nouri from their dark recesses dredged up my own long-buried darkness. And when I caught a whiff of cedar, the old wounds hidden underneath my doublet flared with pain, igniting searing memory. . . .

The hammering fire so unexpected . . . and then another piercing blow comes fast. The world explodes in pain and blood. Shoulder. Back. Searing agony, accompanied by a flailing blade and madman's cries: "Failure! Fool! Incapable."

"Father . . . don't!"

Lancing fire splits my left arm elbow to wrist. Life escapes in warm floods. Knees buckle. Side skewered with flame . . .

"Master, help me! Dufreyne . . . Garol . . . Mother!"

Get up, get up. On your feet or die this moment. Sweet angels defend! He's strong as a rabid dog. Grab his wrist. Ignore the pummeling; that hand holds no blade.

The earth wavers . . . light shimmers . . . fades into gray . . . Let go of his knife hand and you die. Hold on and you'll collapse . . . and die. So, let go, then. Aim for his throat. One chance . . .

"Soren's tomb is the farthest in. I hope he's kept his clothes on at the least. Viewing your sovereign in the raw is different when you actually *knew* the fellow."

Ilario's prattle dispersed my vision as the wind scatters feathers. But the pain lingered, and I could still smell the reek of blood and mortal panic. The scent of dry cedar never failed to rouse these persistent fragments of horror—memories of the day my father had tried to kill me, and I killed him instead.

"Portier, are you quite well?"

"Yes, yes, I'm fine," I said, near breathless from a burgeoning headache. Half-sick, hands trembling and hot as if yet drenched in nine-year-old blood, I fought to lock away the cursed past like a stray book in its proper cupboard.

When I opened my eyes, Ilario wore an expression of drawn worry so at odds with his raked cap and dangling feathers, I had to smile. "All right, I am not fine," I said. "As with you, Chevalier, crypts and deadhouses give me the frights. Now, what were you saying about Soren?"

Soren's tomb was the newest memorial, erected only eighteen years past, so it was only to be expected that it would show less deterioration than the others. Rosemary and lavender had been sprinkled liberally about the alcove to deter insects, and the rich colors of its frescos had been laid on deeply. But not only did the nouré's robes of silk and ermine appear to have been taken from the royal wardrobe that very morning, but at least three hundred candles burned in wrought-iron sconces. Fresh-cut iris and purple flax bloomed in pewter urns.

"The crypt must not be so unvisited as you thought," I said.

Ilario stared at the tomb bathed in candlelight, one arm folded across his sleek doublet, elbow resting in his hand, allowing him to chew a thumb thoughtfully. "Whatever are you doing, *caeri*?"

My skittish nerves prompted a rude answer. But I bit it off. The softly voiced question was not for me, but rather for the dear *one* he believed had supplied these adornments.

After a few moments, he snapped his head around. "It's surely Antonia

who maintains all this. Soren was her only true son, nigh a god to her. Though, certainly, she has been all kindness to Geni and me. She had no need to adopt us . . . me, especially."

He returned his gaze to the altar, and the half-again-larger-than-truth nouré of his foster brother looming. I didn't think he believed his assertion. Queen Eugenie, wed to another man—another king—had been lavishing her dead husband's tomb with love. How much more evidence against her would Philippe need?

"Onward," said Ilario, with far less enthusiasm than he'd shown up to now.

When Ilario pulled open the iron door tenth from Soren's tomb, the chamber sighed a tainted breath: sweat, ordure, and the acrid stink of pain, torment, and despair that seeped from walls and ceiling. Our lamplight pooled on a stained stone floor, and a litter of long, pale shards of freshly splintered wood.

A single sturdy chair stood bolted to the floor in the center of the room. An accusation. A monument to evil. Even as my soul recoiled, the *agente confide* inside me noted that I would need to bring Dante to examine its stained arms. Perhaps some residual enchantment might identify the devils who had tormented a young girl in this pit. The metallic flavor of blood drowned my tongue, as if the stolen ichor hung in the air like mist.

"*Sancte angeli*," whispered Ilario, touching the chain dangling from the ancient wall—steel links not rusted, but new and sleek and merciless. The manacle at its end gaped open, warped and twisted, a jagged break splitting the thick metal. "However did the girl manage this?"

He held out the torn metal. The cursed thing pricked my fingers like stinging nettle.

"Magic," I croaked, cramming my fingers under my arm and fighting not to drop the lamp. "Someone's magic broke it. Perhaps her own . . . but a mule so near the end . . . unlikely."

Swallowing bile, I held the lamp high and circled the chamber, examining every centimetre of the damp walls. Ophelie had learned Michel's name. But the conte had no power for magic. There should be one more

chain, at the least, two if the sorcerer who had freed Ophelie had been a prisoner as well.

On the wall opposite the dangling chain, another bolt had been fixed to the wall. Close examination revealed more. "Chevalier, come. . . ."

I shone the lamp on markings scratched in the wall near the floor, scarce distinguishable from the dirt and mold that crusted the stone. A series of minute tick marks—eleven in a ragged row, with the first nine crossed over in the manner of one counting off a tenday. More interesting were what appeared to be an *R*, encircled by a twisted rope or vine, and a word scratched in tiny letters—*Altevierre*.

Ilario, crouched beside me, touched the first mark. "The Ruggiere device," he said, confirming my guess. "Michel was here." But wherever the conte had gone, his chains and manacles had gone with him. If the tick marks indicated the length of Michel's imprisonment in this cell, then he had been held here only a short time.

Neither of us knew what *Altevierre* might signify, only that Ophelie had repeated it in her dying mania. As I sketched the wall markings in my journal, Ilario hunted more, but without success.

"We need to take the manacle," I said. "Dante might be able to identify the spellworker."

Without speaking the need aloud, we moved with accelerating urgency. Those who had used this room knew verger's schedules and little-used stairways better than we did. Even Ilario would have difficulty explaining our presence.

With a rusty gripping tool left in the crypt by some ancient bronze-worker, I worried a small piece of the torn manacle free and dropped it in my spall pouch. The shard had to be enough. Our lamp was fading. Then, as if our anxieties had made themselves manifest, a distant grind of metal heralded light footsteps on the grand stair and women's voices murmuring.

I pressed the chevalier's arm. Shielding the lamp with our cloaks, we glided through the maze of columns, past the glistening black font. Thready enchantments brushed spirit and flesh like a storm of spiderwebs.

Halfway from the font to the tetrarch's stair, our lamp died. *Saints and angels!* Blinded, I stretched out my arms.

"You feel it, lady? Someone's here." The woman's voice came from the direction of the King's Gate. "Who's there? Step out!" Yellow beams danced through the forest of pillars.

Edging one foot forward, I cursed my stubborn pride for refusing to commission charms. A guidespell would have been useful. But as I slid around the next pillar, a fan of pale blue light stretched out in front of me, just bright enough to enable me to avoid inconveniences like dangling lamps waiting to collide with my head. Astonishingly, the light emanated from Ilario's hand.

"Stop right where you are!"

We dodged through the remaining pillars, ducked into the passage, and raced up the Tetrarch's Stair. Guided by better light than Ilario's blue fan, the footsteps pounded the lower stair at the same time I poked my head through the door.

"All clear," I whispered. The side aisle was deserted, but we had no hope of getting away before our pursuers emerged behind us. Venturing into the temple nave would be even more foolish, as the domed vastness offered no better cover than a few benches and potted flowers.

"Duck behind Albriard," said Ilario, as we shut the door quietly and huddled in the memorial alcove. "He'll not mind. Stay put until they've gone."

It took me a moment to realize *Albriard* was the kingly statue looming over my head. As I weighed the wisdom of remaining three steps from the doorway, Ilario darted down the aisle. He dropped to his knees before the tomb he'd venerated on our arrival and touched forehead to stone.

The door burst open, sending me deep into the shadow of King Albriard's effigy. A tall, gray-haired woman paused a handsbreadth from me and glared down the aisle. I did not breathe. Of formidable stature, sturdy limb, and smooth, well-defined features, she might have stepped off a temple fresco—the very image of the warrior angel who cast the Souleater into the abyss. Once one had met Mage Gaetana, one would not forget her.

Another woman passed the Tetrarch's Door. Clothed in emerald silk, she, too, stood above an average woman's height, though unlike that of her robust companion, this woman's presence scarce moved the air.

Slender-boned, frail, her luminous skin pale as moonlight framed in heavy loops of ebon hair, she seemed almost transparent. "Who is it?" she said, in breathless quiet.

"Your bastard brother is the only visitor I see," said the sorceress, her muted contralto as chilly as the stones and tinged with hostility. "What would he be doing down below?"

A laugh rippled like starlight on water. Gentle humor, in no wise mocking. "Ilario? Ah, dear Gaetana, my brother would not visit the crypt were his tailor to set up shop there. Dark places frighten him terribly—my fault, I fear. It's only some temple aide or a wayward child has visited the kings today. Go back. I'll rejoin you soon."

The Queen of Sabria glided down the memorial aisle, laid a hand on Ilario's shoulder, and knelt beside him, making the same ritual gesture—a kiss of her fingers to lay on the stone. After a few moments, sister and brother stood and embraced.

"I was missing him today, Geni," said Ilario, as they strolled down the aisle arm in arm, the dark head and the fair almost touching. "You'll not tell anyone, will you? Of all things in the world, I'll *not* be seen as a Moping Mariah who lurks about tombs. My reputation!"

Gaetana stepped back through the Tetrarch's Door and closed it softly behind her. Expelling my long-held breath, I sagged against King Albriard's monument.

Eugenie laid her head on Ilario's shoulder. "Ah, sweet brother, I miss him, too. So very much. Someday . . ." They moved out of hearing before she completed her thought.

Was it possible Philippe and Ilario were so wrong about this lovely woman? Could one who appeared so fragile wreak the Souleater's own torments on a girl of sixteen? Heaven bless that I was but the investigator of this mystery and not the judge.

Only as the two walked away did I notice the implement dangling from Ilario's left hand. Absurdity filled the dark voids left by our delving and my own brief odyssey into past despair, and I slid to the floor with a disbelieving chuckle. Our guiding light had come from Ilario's crocodile charm.

CHAPTER EIGHT

"I'll say this investigating is not half so entertaining as I thought it would be. Murders. Mules. Crawling around in dreadful places." Goblet of wine in hand, Ilario leaned on his wrought-iron balcony rail that overlooked the swan garden.

Though sunlight, clear skies, and potent refreshment made the royal crypt seem a world distant, only a day had passed since our venture into the wretched dark. A day of frustration. Twice I had tried to take Dante the shard of Ophelie's broken manacle. Twice I'd found his apartments locked and strongly warded. What was he up to?

"I've written to Ophelie's family," I said, setting aside my own cup. "I hope to find out if anyone from Collegia Seravain contacted them about her 'illness.' *Someone* spread the lies about her leaving school. I need to go to the collegia soon, as well. Perhaps I can discover what Michel was looking for or what he might have uncovered that led to his disappearance. Why would someone risk taking such a prominent hostage, then not tell anyone what they want for him?"

Ilario wagged a long finger at my nose, his gold ring and its ruby-eyed phoenix flashing sunbeams in my eyes. "We must also begin arrangements for my exposition. I require it to be spectacular, splendors

of science and magic displayed side by side for the entire court to witness."

I leaned my elbows on the iron rail, pressing fingers to temples to stave off another headache before the world went gray. I had been ready to dismiss Ilario's folly of an "exposition." Yet preparations for such an event could give me reason to speak to a variety of people, and Dante needed to observe and analyze some large-scale work of the queen's mages. If they did not accept him into their circle, such a ruse might be the only way.

Ilario rattled on. "Perhaps I could design a cloud and lightning display. Mage Orviene would certainly work the caelomancy for me, especially if Eugenie encouraged him. She has him tend the weather over her family's vineyards—not to any beneficial effect that I've ever seen. But he's a good sort of fellow. Congenial. Well mannered."

"Lord Ilario, consider—" I clamped my lips before I lashed out at his thoughtlessness. Had he forgotten so soon that Mage Orviene might have bled a child to self-murder to fuel his weather-working?

Despite the day's warmth, I shivered and rubbed the back of my left hand. Consideration of the Blood Wars chilled anyone of the blood. The very mark that identified us as potential sorcerers also identified us as potential mules.

"Very well," I said. "But as I take care of these other matters, you must do all you can to watch for clues. Anything to do with the queen's mages or their assistants. Anything sudden or surprising, because Ophelie's escape must surely alter the villains' plans. Even the smallest matters—those they speak to, those they dine with, what small magics they work, how they prepare for your exposition—might be important. That is the role you agreed to."

I could not but hope that the sister Ilario so clearly adored was not stained with the foulness we had glimpsed. But neither could I forget her words: *I miss him, too. So very much. Someday . . .* She longed to speak to her dead parents. She had hired Dante to bring them back. The spyglass seemed to reach beyond death, linking assassination, unholy magic, and the queen's unhealthy desires.

"I'll do what's needed," said Ilario, who had drained his wine cup and

moved indoors to flop on a couch. "Though I don't like deception. If I'd not spoken out and asked Eugenie why she'd come to the temple, I'd never have remembered it was Soren's deathday."

The queen's answer might explain the flowers and extra candles, but had addressed neither Gaetana's presence nor the nouri's wealth of jewels and silks, nor the wax built up so thickly on candlesticks and altar stone that one must conclude the attentive vigil had lasted years, not days. Did Philippe know?

Gratefully, I followed Ilario out of the sultry heat. "One more thing, Chevalier. We must pass this new information to His Majesty. Dante's warning of violence, Ophelie and the possibility that Michel is alive and captive. Can you manage that without anyone's remarking it?" I could not afford an audience with Philippe. I was too visible as yet, so soon after my introduction at court and Dante's well-reported tirade.

"Oh, there's a way." Ilario's face soured like that of a boy commanded to kiss an ill-favored aunt. "The king enjoys trouncing me at stratagems. Does anyone but mention the tedious game, he insists on a match, no matter that he knows how I detest it. Who dares refuse a king's whim? But I oft insist on a private venue to deprive him of an audience for his triumph. None will remark it."

"Excellent," I said, unable to imagine flighty Ilario shifting knights, warriors, tetrarchs, and queens through the complex landscape of a stratagems board. "We'll not take advantage too often."

As if pricked by a hay fork, Ilario leapt from his couch, snatched up a feathered hat, and tucked his pale locks behind one ear to reveal a dangling earring of rainbow-colored stones. "Come along, Portier," he said, charging across the carpet toward the door. "Enough of maudlin business. If it is Third-day, as I suspect, and midafternoon, as I notice, then it is time for my foster mother's salon. I dare not shirk my duty, as I am charged to amuse the ladies especially. Today, I shall display my sober side. All shall marvel that I have myself a private secretary."

He halted abruptly, pressing his back to the outer door, and examined me head to toe. "Do you have that journal you're forever messing about with?"

"Always."

"Get it out. It makes you look properly serious and secretarial. We'll say your luggage has been lost and you've had to borrow clothes from your valet. La, we must get you to my tailor and my barber soon, else the entire court will guess you're a spy. None will believe I've hired a shaggy-headed slip of a fellow who wears velvet in spring."

I sighed and followed him. I would much rather have sought out Philippe's disgraced guard captain or researched the meaning of *Altevierre*—the word scratched on the crypt wall and flown from Ophelie's lips as she begged for death. But Antonia de Foucal had stood at the center of Castelle Escalon as queen, queen mother, and now as Eugenie and Ilario's adoptive mother. She must know everyone and everything. What better resource for an investigator?

ILARIO SWEPT INTO LADY ANTONIA'S grand drawing room like a benevolent west wind, touching, ruffling, and tweaking every sleeve, cheek, and temper within view. A head taller than everyone else, and adorned in blazing scarlet, he could not vanish into any crowd. He wept over a deceased cat with a thready dowager and commiserated with a fellow dandy over the poor quality of Hematian brocades. He promptly threatened a duel with a local tetrarch when a weak-chinned marquesa reported that the clergyman had complained of Ilario juggling eggs on the temple lawn. Without noting scornful smirks or guests rolling their eyes, he declared his longing that one of the sainted Reborn could choose ridding the world of crocodiles as his heroic task.

I heeled like a well-trained hound. From time to time, Ilario would pause his conversation, spin around, and point at me, declaring, "Make a note that I must speak to Teb about the exposition," or, "Pen a letter to my old swordmaster, Portier. I shall require practice before this duel."

I would acknowledge with a half bow and scratch notes in my journal, all the while learning names, listening, observing.

Ilario's sole temperate moment occurred when he encountered a man wearing the phoenix badge of the Cult of the Reborn. Cultists believed

the saints to be souls who had willingly relinquished their hope of Heaven in order to serve the needs of humankind in this life, reborn time and again at the Pantokrator's whim. I thought it nonsense.

"You must be the new secretary. Duplais, is it? *Savin*-Duplais?" Based on her unimposing height, unexceptional figure, and unguessable age, the mature woman who stood at my shoulder could have been any court lady. Yet she had shunned the heavy, smooth-woven coils of current fashion and organized her gray-streaked black hair into masses of small, stiff curls about her face—a style one saw only on thousand-year-old Fassid carvings. And just like those ancient figures, she had completely plucked out her eyebrows, giving herself a permanent look of ingenuous surprise. Such flagrant defiance of fashion demanded concentrated attention. No common courtier would be so bold.

"Indeed, my lady," I said, making all proper deference. "I am Portier de Savin-Duplais, though it might serve me ill to emphasize the *Savin* at present."

Her laugh rippled, pleasant and knowing. "Royal relations tread a more strenuous road than any outside our odd circle might suspect. You must join me for tea some afternoon. We shall exchange strategies for maintaining our equilibrium."

"I would forever prize such an event." I appreciated the absence of scorn in her good humor. Swallowing my usual inhibitions, I did not stop with politeness. "May I speak to your secretary to set a day?"

Her painted eyes widened. "What a bold young snippet! Not so craven as I was told."

She patted me on the cheek with three jeweled fingers and swept onward without answering, instantly the center of each group she encountered. She could be none but the Lady Antonia.

When Ilario spied her, he spun in a whirl of silken cloak and dangling jewelry and dropped to one knee, spreading his arms as if awaiting a message from Heaven. "Divine grace, lady mother."

Lady Antonia acknowledged this overeager obeisance with a touch to his shoulder and a pained expression. She moved on before he could rise or open his mouth again.

Sighing hugely, Ilario scrambled to his feet and took up the tale of his recent sojourn on the Aubine seacoast for two young ladies whose pasted smiles begged for escape. Perhaps they, as well as Lady Antonia, had heard the tales of crocodile charms and therapeutic mud bathing too often already.

My spirits rose when I spied Damoselle Maura poised in the doorway. Yet before I captured her notice, she set course for two wind-scoured gentlemen. Sober blue jackets, trimmed in gold, and broad-brimmed hats pinned up on one side suggested naval connections. Maura smoothed their path around the refreshment and card tables to an elaborately draped corner where Lady Antonia now bantered with a cluster of admiring ladies and gentlemen.

Though Maura lacked the dainty perfection of Ilario's bejeweled ladies or the languid elegance of the ingenue who enthralled five gallants in the garden doorway, I found the softer curves of her body and the spare authority of her movements quite pleasing. When she glanced up and caught me watching her, I'd have sworn a smile crinkled the corners of her eyes, though she continued to participate fully in her conversation with Sabria's dowager queen.

Not wishing to be rude, I shifted my attention to the refreshment table, browsing the quails' eggs and pickled leeks, the sweetmeats and lemon tarts, while observing the comings and goings. My interest focused sharply when a tidy, wide-browed mage entered from a side chamber. His gray-threaded locks were sleekly dressed, his doublet as elegantly skirted as Ilario's. His mage's collar gleamed amid his starched shirt ruffles. On the occasion of my ignominious debut in court society, he had stood behind Gaetana. Orviene, certainly.

Was it possible that this newcomer who floated from one group to the next, extending a quiet greeting or a smile, touching a young woman's hand, laughing, and offering referrals to magical practitioners who could help with every condition from limp hair to lingering curses, had hacked off Ophelie's fingers and prisoned her in a crypt next to fifty dead men? It struck me as a fearful thing that such depravity might be couched in so ordinary a figure. Surely a monster should wear a horned cap and blood-

soaked black, reeking of brimstone, and not peacock blue brocade and hair pomade.

"The demonish mage has not wreaked vengeance on you, has he?"

My head snapped around, and I near bit my tongue. Maura had somehow got across the room without my noticing it. Her round cheeks glowed with her smile, as terror constricted my throat. Had I somehow voiced my thoughts?

"I've promised to find him a new assistant." Dante. She referred to Dante.

"No vengeance," I said. "But then I've not yet encountered the devil again. Will he be here?"

The administrator clasped her hands modestly at her waist and knotted her brow in mock sobriety. "I doubt anyone has thought to invite him. I'm not sure even Mage Orviene's generosity would extend so far."

Generosity? Only a considered breath kept me from choking. "I'm not sure I'm ready to meet Mage Orviene, either," I said. "I would like to establish some solid reputation at court before greeting its most formidable figures."

Maura's eyes livened with amusement. Some might call her stiff, but she seemed to me a well-contained person, her feelings clear to anyone who took the time to observe her closely. Even before her descent into permanent genteel hysteria, my mother had lived in a constant state of fractured emotions, liberally shared with anyone within reach, and the female students at Seravain seemed forever thrashing about between the overexcited activity of squirrels and the argumentative despondency of hibernating bears.

"Mage Orviene is anything but formidable," she said. "He ever has a kind word for those who seek his help. You should speak to him. That's the purpose of a lady's salon."

"My mother hosted such events when I was a boy. Awful, awkward afternoons. I am wholly out of practice. Lord Ilario insisted I accompany him today, else I'd have spent a happy hour on his latest whim. He intends to sponsor a scientific exhibition in the coming months."

"Indeed." She ducked her head, and her finger pressed a smile from her lips. "I've heard rumor of this . . . uh . . . fancy. If you need advice . . ."

I bowed. "An accomplished administrator who knows everyone at court and most of the tradesmen in Merona could save my life. Again."

Her laughter bubbled just beneath the surface, a pleasing animation of mouth and eyes that was at once unembarrassed and quite private. Warmth flooded through my limbs and . . . everywhere. Gracious angels, it had been so long.

Of a sudden Maura's brows lifted and she tilted her head as if to see better beyond my shoulder. Then she leaned forward slightly and spoke directly into my chest, "On your guard, good sir. Thy nemesis doth approach."

I shifted around slowly, as if adrift in the sea of conversation. Framed in the doorway to the outer passage stood Dante. Clean shaven, dressed in black knee breeches and hose with an elegant short cloak swept over his right arm, he cut a fine, if sober, figure. A plain, silver earring adorned one ear. I offered fervid thanks to young Edmond de Roble and his tailor, and, foolishly, felt quite proud. Relieved, too; Dante did not carry his staff.

Across the room, Mage Orviene laughed with another admirer. Lady Antonia embraced two bejeweled ladies at once. Ilario's prattling floated atop the general buzz of voices like a gemsflute against a room full of hurdy-gurdies.

Dante's gaze swept the room like a sea storm, rousing a first tremor of uncertainty. Voices faded. Heads turned. His attention seemed to settle on a destination, and as he moved forward, the guests parted to let him through. His broad left hand cupped a glittering heap of glass or jewelry. He halted in front of Ilario.

Ilario aborted his monologue in midsentence.

"A serving man graced me these'n yestertide, along with your requirements for 'an enchanted musical gaud, suitable for a gift to an aged baroness.'" None in the large chamber could fail to hear the measured menace in Dante's quiet statement, issued in the rough patois of Coverge. "I spoil for to clarify a few mots as to your request." With a twist of his hand, he tossed the heap into the air.

Ilario's young ladies gasped, and the chevalier himself leapt backward. Yet the glittering pieces did not strike any guest, nor did they plummet. Rather they hovered a handsbreadth from Ilario's long nose—a jumble of colored glass shards, small mirrors, strings of pearls, lapis, jade, and slips of metal.

The guests withdrew into a gaping circle. As every eye widened in wonder—mine not least—the shimmering mass rose toward the coffered ceiling, organizing and collecting itself into a revolving fountain of light and music. Rings of glass prisms focused light into crossed beams; rings of mirrors reflected the light in a hundred dazzling directions. The colored beads twisted and draped like a canopy of ribbons; dangling bits of bronze and silver rang clear and joyous as the structure spun.

The guests pointed and gasped, shocked murmurs growing into laughter and expressions of awe and admiration. Yet how many of them could truly comprehend the magnificence of what they saw? This was no illusion, no scant veil of sensory deception draped over a decorated wire frame. Naught supported these glittering elements or interlaced their light beams but purest magic.

"Is this what you had to mind, great lord?"

Ilario moved underneath the sparkling font of light, bobbing his head, whirling on his heeled boots. "Oh, yes! Magnificent! Marvelous!"

Only those who heeded the mage's tight voice, only those who tore their eyes from the creation to the creator, would have seen Dante brush his silver earring, then point a steady finger at the spinning enchantment.

The glancing light soured to a thunderous purple; the melodic jingle rose to a mind-jarring cacophony.

"Lord, beware!" I darted forward and yanked Ilario from underneath the quivering folly just as it shattered, raining splintered glass and fractured beads.

Ladies screamed. Gentlemen shouted and pressed the circle of onlookers backward. Ilario tripped on my feet and stumbled to his knees.

Dante stood over Ilario, pinning him to the floor with his scorn. "I do *not* make gauds. I do *not* take orders from trivial men. Sorcery is *not* an amusement."

Before a speechless Ilario could rise, Dante had gone.

Whispers rushed through the shocked crowd like a swarm of insects. *Illusion . . . Madman . . . Who is he? Insufferable . . . dangerous . . . Who?*

Lady Antonia pushed through the frantic crowd and gazed down at the mess, Orviene at her side. The mage dropped to a knee. Closing his eyes, he swept widespread fingers over the debris in a dramatic, but entirely unnecessary, gesture. An experienced examiner sensed magical residue on his skin, on his tongue, in his bones.

As he bounced to his feet, Orviene palmed a few slips of silver and colored beads from the floor and slid them into his doublet. *Yes, test them. Feel them. I'll wager you've never felt the like.* The residue of Dante's enchantment sparkled and shimmered through my skin and spirit as no fragments of glass or metal could ever do. *Well done*, I thought. *Very well done.* Orviene could not but be impressed with his new colleague's talents.

The dapper mage waved dismissively. "No enchantment remains. You are all quite safe."

A twitch of Lady Antonia's fingers brought liveried servants with brushes and dustpans to collect the not-at-all illusory debris. The crowd sighed as one and the anxious murmurs grew into a strident babbling.

I gave Ilario a hand up and a raised brow of inquiry. He shook his head ever so slightly. He had not prompted the event. No sooner was he on his feet than he was besieged by ladies and gentlemen alike. "Dante," he said, "his name is Dante. A master mage. I brought him here to amuse Eugenie, but I never imagined . . . I am wholly flummoxed."

Dante and his display were the primary topics of conversation for the next hour. Ilario repeated his story of finding Dante by way of his search for a new crocodile-slaying spell at least a hundred times, elaborating as he went along. I retired to the wine steward.

I'd scarce downed a sip when Maura joined me, dragging Mage Orviene alongside her. "Portier, meet Her Majesty's Second Counselor, Orviene de Cie. Orviene, this is Portier de Savin-Duplais, Lord Ilario's new secretary."

"Divine grace, Mage," I said, trying not to stare.

"And with you, sonjeur, an acolyte yourself, I hear." The mage's pale

eyes moved from my exposed hand to my face in polite interest. "Fresh from Seravain."

"My studies ended many years ago, sir. I've served as the collegia librarian for almost a decade." The courret tucked into my waist pocket remained chilly. Surely it should react in the presence of evil, as it would for poisons or unsheathed weapons.

With another not quite a smile that near melted my bones, Maura excused herself.

Orviene smiled broadly. "A scholarly gentleman with an appreciation of the mystical arts will always be welcome in the household. *Common* breeding will ever display itself, eh?" Though he leaned close, as if to share a confidence, any guest within ten metres could have heard. "If your duties allow, you must stop by my chambers and I'll introduce you to my assistants. Though I'd gladly show you our current work, I doubt you'd quite grasp the intricacies."

The mage did not so much as take a breath, much less register my embarrassment. "I'd be interested to hear news of Seravain. . . ."

For half an hour, he plied me with questions about the collegia, allowing no more than a bell's strike for me to answer. Each query would launch a humorous anecdote or a reminiscence of his own student days. Eventually he ceased bothering to ask anything, but provided avuncular advice as to court dress—modesty served best for those of us in service, even when family connection supported more opulent attire—court ladies—Sabria's most luminous treasures—perfumes—best kept muted so as not to compete with the ladies—and wine—I should seek out Giorgio, the third wine steward, for the best recommendations if I planned to entertain.

By the time the mage apologized that he really must move on and attend to a few more acquaintances, my head swam with trivia. Either Orviene was the most skilled deceiver in Sabria or he was a genial, self-important, silver-tongued gadfly, who truly believed that his most critical decisions each day were which coat and scent to wear as he monitored the queen's wards and charms. I was entirely confused.

"Many thanks for the introduction, damoselle," I said when, to my

delight, I encountered Maura at the refreshment table. "Not so fearsome after all."

She smiled sagely. "I told you—"

"Excuse me, damoselle." Ilario, appearing from nowhere, snatched my arm, and dragged me away. "Come, come, Portier. No time for self-indulgence. Important business awaits."

Quivering like a captive bird, he urged me insistently toward the doorway, snatching the cup from my hand and shoving it at the first person we passed, a startled Mage Orviene. "Ah, sir mage! I do hope you and your colleagues will grace us with your participation in my Grand Exposition. My private secretary here will be handling the arrangements. But excuse us; we've urgent business waiting."

"Tell me, Chevalier, have you seen Adept Fedrigo today?" Orviene called after us. "Three days he's missed an important tutorial. I know you often preempt his time for small projects. . . ."

"Not for aeons," said Ilario, whisking me into the passage and around the corner before Orviene's question had faded.

"It's the *Destinne*," he burst out the moment his ornately carved door slammed behind us. His earrings and jeweled bracelets jangled as he hurried across the thick carpet to shut the paned garden doors. "She is scheduled to sail on the morning tide, day after tomorrow. Her captain just informed Antonia. His first officer, the other fellow who was there, is some grandnephew's cousin's eldest boy or something like."

"The exploration voyage?" I struggled to switch my thinking away from spinning gauds and unexpected mages.

"Don't you see? You told me to listen for sudden changes. The sailing date's been moved up by more than a month." Ilario threw his hands in the air as if expecting me to congratulate him.

"I'm sure there's good reason for the change. The tides . . ."

"But, Portier, it *had* been scheduled for the twenty-fifth day of Cinq."

My heart stuttered. "Prince Desmond's deathday. The anniversary." Our deadline.

Ilario lapped the room with his long strides, his brow drawn up in a

knot. "Philippe chose that date apurpose, as he's dedicated the voyage to Desmond, you see, to honor the child and see him through Ixtador. Now something's changed and the *Destinne* sails early."

"The king will insist on being at the docks to send her off," I said. "Out in the open where there will be a thousand places to lurk and a thousand times a thousand places for spell-traps to be hidden. A perfect place for a public murder."

"So I was right that this was important?"

"Saints and angels, yes. You must play that game of stratagems with Philippe tonight. Put him on his guard. And whatever you need do to arrange it, Dante and I must be near the king that day."

Scarce more than a day. Too little time to send sorcerers to detect spell-traps. Too few courrets remaining in the world for them to use. This was too soon. We didn't know enough.

CHAPTER NINE

On my way to apprise Dante of the new threat, I devised an excuse to stop in at the palace steward's office. The steward's third secretary, Henri de Sain, had been a friendly sort and had invited me to return if I needed anything. I needed information.

I found the harassed secretary jotting notes in his ledger book about a large, ill-smelling crate at his feet. "It's the dung," he said, when I slapped a kerchief to my nose. "Rare mushrooms growing in a crate full of dung. As if we didn't have enough trouble with this business of the *Destinne* . . ."

In fact, the steward's office was in an uproar, taxed with hasty arrangements for honor guards, musicians, a viewing stand, a celebratory feast with an invocation from the High Tetrarch, a smooth-tongued diplomat to coax the prefects of the Camarilla to attend in a show of unity, and little more than a day to do it all. But nothing in the reports of the changed sailing enlightened me.

"By the way," said Henri, as I rose to leave, "you may not need my tailor's service after all. Not an hour ago, we received a box from a tailor in Margeroux and sent it on to your apartment."

From Margeroux . . . The arrow and spyglass! I hadn't thought I could feel *more* urgency. Without so much as a thank-you, I bolted.

"How can a captain change the sailing day on his own?" With his skilled left hand, Dante unraveled the last knot binding the canvas-wrapped box from Margeroux. He'd set himself and the bundle on the floor at the center of his circumoccule immediately on my arrival.

"The captain holds full authority on his ship," I said. "Not even the king can gainsay him. The steward's secretary says the crew was near mutiny at sailing on a prince's deathday."

My cousin had sapped his own authority in the first year of his reign, issuing a declaration that disenfranchised the Camarilla in maritime matters. Until Philippe's pronouncement, the Camarilla had required every vessel to carry a mage, who could overrule a captain's decision at a whim. To mollify the prefects, enraged at their loss of influence, Philippe had decreed that neither temple nor civil officials could overrule a ship captain, either.

I helped myself to wine from the pitcher on a low bench. Dante's apartments had been transformed in the past two days. The heavy draperies and excess furnishings had been removed. Two chairs, one long couch, and one small table remained in front of the tall east windows, while his required cupboards and worktables had been installed about the rest of the room. A variety of implements had been tossed on the worktables alongside a clutter of boxes and bins.

"Your king's a fool if he goes to the docks," said the mage. "Let the ship sail and make his prayers at home if he must."

Dante had heeded my news of the Destinne's new launch with only half his attention, clearly more interested in the artifacts of the first assassination attempt than in anything we might do to prevent a second. He had responded to my congratulations on his "salon debut" with a shrug. "I assumed you'd control Lord Fool's reaction."

Even my report of Ophelie's death and her prisoning in the crypt had elicited few questions. My eager offering of her broken manacle had prompted a promise to "look into it" when he'd more time. Indeed, I had not pushed. Our first priority must be to protect Philippe.

"Kings are not so easily dissuaded," I said. "Especially warrior kings turned natural philosophers, who have staked their kingdom's prosperity on voyages such as this. Surely, if we can locate the threat, you can do something to protect him."

He didn't bother to answer, but yanked the thin rope loose from the dusty canvas. I needed to engage him. "I've a courret."

That caused him to look up even as the wrapping fell away to expose a flat leather case near as long as my arm. "Indeed? And how would a librarian come by such a rarity? Not a mage living knows how to make a wardstone."

I squirmed under his stare, green as jade and hot as a smith's furnace. "It's borrowed."

"Demonfire, you've stolen it!" Pure astonishment erased the wariness and suspicion he wore like a temple dancer's mask. "*You*—that I thought might be the first honest man I've ever met."

"I did *not* steal it," I said, exasperated that we'd wandered so easily from the needs of the hour, confounded again that I could be so easily read. "I found it in a crate of texts we brought from a ruin in Xarles two years ago. The courret was likely the only decent thing to come out of that house. The Mondragoni were—"

No. Better not to speak of them, though they had been on my mind since the inception of this enterprise.

But Dante's hand had fallen still. "*What* were they?"

Ixtador's Gates, the man's ears must be keener than a hawk's to hear what lingered unspoken on a man's tongue. "Necromancers," I said. "Leeches. Demonists. Torturers. A blood family that was everything foul and unholy. Some say their overreaching fired the Blood Wars. The few of them not wiped out in the wars were beheaded after, and none have ever disputed the rightness of it."

"Ah." He twisted the brass key I'd given him to unlock the leather case. The latch clicked. "I'd give a deal to see those texts—if I'm to make a show of deadraising. Orviene and Gaetana may not have the talent they think, but they'll not be easily deceived."

I pulled out my journal, my hand itching for my pen. I'd only plum-

met to hand, but I could ink the reminder later: *Bring Dante the Mondragoni texts.*

Puzzled, I stared at the open page and the words already taking shape. I had no intention of fetching the Mondragoni books.

I glanced up. Dante's eyes had fixed on the case, but his hand had stilled.

"Stop this immediately, Master." I slammed my journal onto the worktable before fury—or fear—crumpled it.

Dante hungered for knowledge as the poor hunger for evidence of the god. And because providing access to the filthiest underside of our art was the last thing I would do for anyone, friend or foe, I knew for certain this time that the compulsion I felt was entirely unnatural. No one should be able to influence a man so . . . directly.

"I don't know what spell you've worked on me, Master Dante, but you will stop it now. Tell me what you want. Tell me why. And when I make my own choice, yes or no, argue with me if you will, but with honest words, not sorcery. If you persist in this, our partnership is ended."

"I've told you what I want and why. So will you bring me these Mondragoni texts or will we argue it?" Stubborn. Prideful. Contemptuous. The manners of a badger, as Ilario had said.

Streaming sunlight transformed the circumoccule's glassy surface into a ring of amber encircling the mage. With a pair of locking forceps, he lifted the bloodstained arrow from its nest of Lady Susanna's worn silks and laid it on the floor beside his staff. The spyglass remained snugged in its wrappings. He closed the case and set it outside the circle.

I gripped my convictions tightly. "Fortunately, in this matter, I've no choice. The Mondragoni scripts are locked in the Seravain vault. And do not *will* me to break the locks. The texts are encrypted and entirely unreadable. I kept them . . ." I could not say why I'd kept them, save that destroying works of such antiquity did not come easy to me. Kajetan, my mentor, the chancellor of the collegia, and a prefect of the Camarilla, had supported my judgment.

I wasn't sure Dante heard me. Hunched over where he could see it

closely, he nudged the arrow with the forceps once, then again and again, examining its length with each rotation.

The hour ticked away in silence. I waited as long as I could bear before curiosity trumped anger. "Dante, tell me what you're—"

"Deeping fires!" Dante slammed his implement to the floor. "When did you transform into a babbling idiot like the peacock? Have you no discipline? No patience? No wonder you're incapable of spellwork."

I did not rise to the insult. "What do you see, Master?"

"What does your *borrowed* courret tell you?"

I'd not even thought of it. Which meant . . . The silver pebble I pulled from my waist pocket was as cold as the first day of Estar on Journia's highest peak. A poisoned arrow less than two metres distant should have it scorching. "It's telling me nothing."

"Step inside the circumoccule." He pulled a flask from his pocket and dribbled its contents in a small oval close around the arrow. "And bring a willow wand with you, one with a forked end. There's a basket of them over there." He gestured vaguely in the direction of the worktables.

By the time I found the basket and rummaged through the fifty or so slender branches to find what he wanted, the painted oval had dried to brown.

"Well come along. If you want to *know.*"

I stepped across the amber ring of the circumoccule and promptly dropped the courret. The wardstone clattered to the floor and rolled toward Dante. It had near burnt a hole in my palm. "Gates of Heaven!"

"One needs a secure enclosure to work on dangerous matters," he said, nudging the silver pebble in my direction. "This circumoccule suffices. The painted boundary merely isolates the object of our study from other objects, enchanted or otherwise. As we've no idea of its dangers, you'd best use the branch to touch the arrow. Willow, simple and known, will disturb its keirna far less than a finger attached to a human person, especially one who disciplines his spirit no better than a bumpkin child."

Leaving the courret where it lay, I knelt facing Dante, the arrow and its enclosing strip of paint between us, the forked end of the willow wand

wedged snugly about the arrow shaft. The mage touched the joined arrow and wand with his staff and closed his eyes, visibly retreating into that state of profound stillness I had witnessed in his bedchamber two days before. I didn't need him to tell me to close my eyes as well.

"Quiet your spirit," he said after a moment. "Naught can reflect on a turbulent sea. Calm it."

I tried. Fear—or excitement—at the revelations to come hollowed my belly. The day's urgencies could not be dismissed by merely willing it so. I shifted position. Stretched my neck and shoulders. Breathed deep. Yet I saw naught but blackness.

Determined not to miss what he would teach me, I accepted Dante's command as literal instruction. I imagined my internal landscape as the roiling ocean beyond the shores of Tallemant, and my will as the finger of the Creator at the dawn of the world. I calmed each wave, smoothed each ripple, stilled its unsettled surface until my mind's slate gleamed black as obsidian.

Against the shining blackness, a font of deep, healthy green surged upward . . . quickly overlaid with wedges of brilliant yellow and blue, angled sharp as the arrow point itself, and a series of brown marks like the crosshatching motifs on old pottery, save for an unpleasing irregularity. From the base of the rune, as I thought of the display, pooled an inky black splotch that stretched into a long, straight line twined with bruised purple. A faint waved line appeared below it.

"The keirna—this pattern you see writ in shapes and colors—tells us that this is an implement of death, precisely made from living wood, steel, and poison." Dante spoke softly, as if sharper words might jar our tenuous connection. "Splintered now—see the irregularity of the hatching—but made to fly . . . straight . . . to penetrate . . . "

A very long while passed and I thought perhaps to see no more. But then, outside my head, the mage expelled a great sigh of effort, while inside, a sparkling net of white scored the darkness and enclosed the colored marks, binding, containing, masking its entirety.

". . . everything."

After a moment of quiet, I felt the shift of limbs clothed in fabric and

leather and a release as Dante dissolved the bond between us. The pattern vanished. Wood scraped softly on wood.

When I opened my eyes, Dante sat cross-legged on the floor, the carved staff across his lap. He was staring puzzled at the arrow, which had changed neither its position nor its rusty tale of a dead horse and a lucky king and the twisting yank of whoever had withdrawn it from its victim.

I waited, confident the mage would tell me what bothered him so, for I had a sudden inspiration that sharing this marvel had not been his original intent, but an apology for his brutish attempt to manipulate me, offered in the only coin he knew. He would always prefer to investigate magic's mysteries alone.

"They were overeager, our assassins," he said at last. "That's all I can calculate. So determined to cast blame on Her Gullible Majesty that they concocted this foolery of guard captains and wrestling matches. Or perhaps that whole complication was naught but coincidence, and your guard captain the unluckiest of men."

Penetrate everything. "You're saying the arrow would have penetrated the king's armor no matter what, so there was no point in getting him out of it."

In one startling motion, he picked up the arrow and slammed it to the mahogany plank beside him. The impact left the stained head buried in the wood and a magical residue stinging my eyes like blown sand.

"This arrow would penetrate a marble slab," he said. "An iron cliff."

Stunned, I could not budge my gaze from the quivering shaft protruding from the floor. Yet my mind raced. I did not believe in coincidence. "Perhaps casting blame on the queen was never the end, but a means—a confusion to embroil an investigator in domestic argument, masking the true perpetrators."

"Or perhaps the murderous wife did not trust her mages to do what they promised," said Dante, dry as the deserts of Aroth. "The wrestling ploy marked the game as amateur."

"No amateur worked transference or enspelled an arrow to penetrate iron." What was this protective instinct already so plain in Philippe and

Ilario where Eugenie de Sylvae was concerned? I'd need to do better. Philippe was relying on me to be thorough and objective.

The mage, distracted, acknowledged my point with head and hand. He closed his eyes and knotted his brow, not quiet this time, but tapping his fingers on his staff. After only a few moments, he launched the staff across the room, growling in frustration.

"There's something more here," he said, as staff and a stack of boxes clattered on the floor. "Keirna tells a story, and the story of this arrow seems clear. Only the human conspiracy surrounding it tangles our minds. Yet I've this notion . . . Some piece of the pattern is missing. If I'd studied a hundred poisoned arrows launched at kings, I might know better what to look for."

"I'll find out what more I can about that day," I said, retrieving my courret and stepping quickly outside the circumoccule before the silver pebble set my pocket afire. "But the day after tomorrow looms much larger just now. You *will* come to the docks."

"If I must." Dante dragged his horrid right hand out of his tunic and crossed his arms atop his knees, glaring at the arrow as if it had thwarted him apurpose. "I'll need those texts, you know. With some work, I can likely break the ciphers. If I'm to tease death and wickedness . . ."

He must work with them. My mind completed his assertion, as he knew it would. I pretended not to hear. I chose to go in search of Calvino de Santo, former captain of His Majesty's personal guard, condemned to serve his former underlings for his failure in judgment. Perhaps *he* would answer my questions.

My FIRST STOP IN MY search for the disgraced soldier was a cluttered temple guardpost. Its sole occupant, a craggy-faced veteran with red hair and huge feet, was quite willing to recommend where a newcomer to Merona could get the best view of the king and the launch of the *Destinne*. Bored and alone in his watch, the soldier was easily coaxed into a lengthy discussion of the difficulties of protecting a monarch who insisted on mingling with his subjects.

"Of course, I've heard the closest to death the king's come in years occurred last year among his own guards," I said, as if I didn't know what Guardsman Veryl's red livery signified. I perched on a stool, watching him light the lamps in the sooty corners of the guardroom. The place smelled of cleaning oil, musty boots, and the spreading lawn of the temple minor beyond the open door. "Heard a guardsman near killed him."

The soldier's back stiffened, and his overlarge lower lip pooched out even farther from his red beard. "'Tweren't no fault of the guards. Nor even the cap'n's, though he's paid the price and will do till he passes the Veil."

"He's still alive? After betraying the king? I'd have wagered a year's pay the hangman had dropped him into the Souleater's maw long since." I was becoming well practiced at disingenuous surprise.

Veryl pulled a cloth-wrapped bundle from a leather pocket and extracted a slab of coarse bread spread thickly with nettle cheese and olive paste. "Nawp, you'll see the cap'n round all the posts here, wiping floors or hauling coal." He nodded to the filled scuttle beside the brazier. "He's forbid to speak to us, though we oft hear him crying out in the night. Pity. He was a decent officer got led down the path by—" He bit off a large chunk of the pasty bread and stuffed the rest back into its wrapping. "I'd best be off now. I've rounds to make."

"Sorry to delay you." I jumped up, wishing I dared push harder. But I couldn't afford to be remarked. "It's just . . . I thought I'd feel safer inside Castelle Escalon's walls than out in the countryside. But rumors of scarred assassins with no blood left in them get a man's mind working, especially when his blood skills fall short."

Veryl's gaze darted to my marked hand. As he hitched the leather pocket over his shoulder, he jutted his thick jaw toward the open door, as if it represented all of the wide world. "I was on the practice field that day, but never saw aught for myself. Just hunted the bowman and heard the rumors like everyone else. The fellow what took that shot was carried off and burnt so fast, naught but a few ever saw his body, and they wouldn't talk about it. But if I wore such a mark on my hand as you do, I'd keep

close to my lord, no matter he's a fool, and not wander the palace nor city nor dockside at night. Just my thought on it."

That's the way life had been during the Blood Wars. Hired rogues lurking in the dark places, ready to snatch those fool enough to walk out alone. Anyone remotely kin to a blood family stalked and whisked away at the first misstep, never to be seen again. And now we were marked.

I laid fist to breast and inclined my back in respect. "Divine grace, guardsman, and angels companion all who protect Sabria and my lords and such poor accounts as me."

Veryl shouldered a halberd and grunted his own farewell blessing. As he marched into the night, I pulled out my journal and reviewed my sketches of Castelle Escalon's geography. I would visit the guardposts one by one until I found Calvino de Santo.

Left skitterish by the guardsman's warning, I hurried through the darkening alleyways with an extra urgency in my steps.

THE SEVENTH POST I VISITED, a brightly lit room off the wall walk near the postern, resounded with boisterous invocation of those saints and demons who chart the fall of dice. The middle-night watch bells had just rung. Uncertain at confronting more guardsmen with the same false story, wishing I'd brought my own lantern, and feeling an increasing burden of futility, I held back in the dark courtyard below, uncomfortable in a night that seemed to twine itself about my limbs like a sneaking cat.

"Saint Calvino!" shouted a thick-tongued figure who appeared in the lit doorway. "This butt's gone dry! Do we shrivel of thirst, our wives'll take rakes to your traitorous hide."

I near cracked my head on the brick wall, startled when a dark figure darted from behind a pile of emptied crates and casks piled in a corner of the yard and vanished into the base of the tower. The man soon reappeared rolling an ale cask. As the heavy butt rumbled up the ramp to the wall walk and the tower room, all I could note was that he was a big, bearded man of dark complexion.

The arrival of a full cask was greeted with cheers, whoops, and no few

references to its handler's "holiness" and "exemplary leadership." The man soon reappeared, rolling an empty cask down the ramp. Each time the butt insisted upon wedging itself in the crooks of the wall, he jarred it loose with a violent kick. Though spared the traitor's doom of headsman or hangman, a proud soldier and once-trusted captain could find such base servitude naught but torment. What kept such a man from slamming his head into a wall?

He shoved the emptied cask into the corner, threatening to topple the entire stack, then retreated into the shadows whence he'd come. As I crossed the yard, I made sure he could see me in what light fell from the tower room. "Calvino de Santo?"

"I'm bound by law to warn thee: Royal judgment forbids me speak to any man of arms, any squire, any woman, child, or servant, or any who's weak-minded or foolish." Bitterness as thick as old honey flowed from the shadows.

"I am none of those. Nor am I here to shame you, nor to condemn or defend your past actions. Rather, I am a servant of Sabria tasked to find answers to certain questions about the very incident that resulted in this heavy judgment. To fulfill my charge, I call upon what core of honor caused you to devote your life's service to the Guard Royale, and what desire you might harbor to expose the deeper truth of that terrible event."

A harsh laugh accompanied the big man to the edge of the shadow. What tale his filthy slops, unwashed skin, ragged hair, and bleak eyes began, his half-cropped ears must complete. The hideous scars named him a convicted dupe to an unconvicted treacher, condemned to unending humiliation in the only employment that would ever be open to him.

"What gives you to think honor or truth mean aught to me, servant of Sabria?"

To avoid a glib answer required careful consideration. "You are alive. That fact speaks of inner strength. It speaks of a history and character that convinced your king your failings were in judgment, not loyalty, at a time when no other witness would speak for you."

His glare weighed on my shoulders like an iron yoke. When he re-treated into shadow again, I followed, but assumed I'd lost my gamble that honesty might outweigh contrivance. I was wrong.

"I told Vernase-Ruggiere everything I knew," he said, in earnest pain. "Fifty times, I told him. I answered everything he asked me, and never did I waver from my story, not when he showed me the headsman's ax and told me it was too good for me, not when he let me hear him order gal-lows built. Not during that ruination of a trial, nor after, when he brought in the butcher . . . Shite!"

"But you were terrified and angry, disbelieving and confused—as any man would be. Now, months have passed, and you've had time to think. You've gone over it all a thousand times. Surely something has revealed itself to you—a word . . . a look . . . a detail."

When he did not deny it right away, I knew I'd lanced the proper vein.

My eyes could pick out his shape now. He had slumped to the ground, his back to the wall. I crouched low and dropped my voice. "The events set in motion that day have not yet been graven in history, despite what hard experience tells you. I cannot—*will* not—drive you with unsubstan-tial hopes, but surely truth cannot hurt you more than this."

"You know naught of hard experience. Why do you roust a dogsbody when those as might tell all remain unquestioned? I'm forbid to speak, forbid to say who it was suggested I wrestle the king that day. But I hear enough to know who sits on silk cushions and eats fresh figs and who hides protected behind her skirts. Not my wife, who's disowned me and gone back to her parents. Not my children, who will ne'er again in this world hear my name nor speak it. Not the poor stupid wretch whose blood got stolen by devils, nor any of those *he* cared for."

His fury might be justifiable indignation or the sour dregs of failed con-spiracy, but his meaning lay clear. "You *knew* him! The mule who lofted that cursed arrow. By the Ten Gates, man, who was he? I'll swear—" What could I offer for such a prize? My cousin had granted me no power of pardon and no purse full enough to salve the wounds of this man's dis-grace. But perhaps I could ease his fears.

"I am partnered with a very powerful man, Captain. He bears no loyalty to those you blame and is joined with me to see this truth uncovered. We can do naught for the dead man, save name him with pity in our prayers. But I promise you, the two of us shall stand between those you would protect and those whose wrath you fear."

I left it there and waited while he sounded my words as I had sounded his.

"You trust this other?"

If I hoped to gain de Santo's trust, I must not delay an answer. Thus I spilled the first words that flitted into mind. "He has trusted me with what he values most, and he knows my own shame, yet treats me as an honest man. Our safety and our pride are bound up with each other's secrets."

"Naught of evil will come down on the mule's family or mine?"

"No sorcerer of the Camarilla, no adept, no acolyte, no blood-marked man or woman will learn that you spoke this name unless you give me leave. With every resource I can muster, I will see to his family's sustenance and your family's as well. I give you my hand on it."

"His name was Gruchin." Though he ignored my proffered hand, he sounded relieved to share what he knew. "At first I didn't recognize him; he was so changed. When I saw the assassin was a mule, I kept everyone away, so none could be harmed by whatever spells or corruption might linger on him. Thus no one else saw him to recognize." De Santo leaned forward, knees drawn up, hands covering his mutilated ears. "I've quarters in the barracks, but I've no peace when I'm with other men. I'd rather stay out here. But the nights get long, and I don't sleep well . . . and I see him every night."

"In your dreams."

He near choked on a barbed laugh. "Dreaming, I see him. Waking, I see him. I see him in alleys, in courtyards, on the walls, in the trees, inside my eyelids. That bloodless, battered wreck of a face was the last I saw that wasn't calling me traitor, and now he'll not leave me be. Gruchin was an expert bowman, but a sniveling sort of fellow. Always complaining. Always insisting I promote him. It was well after I took him on that I discovered he was of the blood—some laggard of a family mostly died out.

One night he was in his cups and starts whining about his ill luck and how he had tried to be a mage, but got booted out of Seravain. Claimed he'd played adept to the queen's mage, but only—"

"To Orviene?"

"Nay, the woman mage. But she'd dismissed him. Accused him of leeching. *Him*." Another despairing laugh. "Not a day after Gruchin told me this, he started with the shakes. Soon he couldn't hit a cliff from ten paces. Within a month I had dismissed him, too, and never gave him another thought. It's only fit we spend our nights together now."

"And his family?"

"He'd a wife in Riverside and a girl child same age as mine. I think of her . . . the little one . . . and wonder . . . Great Kingfather of us all, what if the devil took her, too?"

His voice broke, and I rose to go, thankful for the night and shadows that gave him a measure of privacy, if not comfort. Yet I needed an answer to one more question. "You told Michel de Vernase that the mule—Gruchin—ran away, then came back to retrieve a dropped spyglass, and one of your men killed him as he ran off again. Did Gruchin do anything else with the glass? Work magic . . . ?"

"He never ran. Hrogar said Gruchin *walked* away to pick up the glass, then came back and stood there. Hrogar flung his ax and hit the vein in his thigh. As if— Souleater's fire, he wasn't two metres away and just stood there. Hrogar, poor sod, mostly dead himself, couldn't have hit anyone running."

Such a difference to hear the exact story, knowing of Ophelie. Had Gruchin, too, preferred death to infamy? But then . . . he'd already lofted the spelled arrow. What further infamy awaited? Was it more bleeding he feared? Or the glass? "Where did you find the spyglass?"

"Had to pry it from Gruchin's hand."

So Gruchin hadn't intended to hide it or dispose of it or even to use it. That made no sense. "Tell me, did you look through it?"

"Aye," he said harshly. "A man does, doesn't he? As if it might tell him something."

"But you didn't see anything . . . unusual?"

"Naught but Gruchin laying there dead, and he's naught but bones and skin, looking back at me with eyes sunk into his skull. In the two years since I'd sacked him, I'd never asked what became of him. My own soldier. I'd never asked if his family was eating. The king sent Michel de Vernase to clean up the mess, and I gave him the glass along with everything else and told him all I learned from them as saw anything. Then the whoreson *arrested* me."

"And no one's ever come asking you about it since then?"

"None. By every saint and demon, I'd see them all strung up and bled like pigs." He buried his head in his arms, muffling a roar of anguish.

"Divine grace, Calvino," I said softly, leaving him to his misery. "I'll do what I can for you."

Mind reeling with thoughts of desperate mules and unfathomable motives, I retraced my route, too far from any familiar venue to risk a shortcut. My boots rang on the cobbled paths and bounced off the courtyard walls, far too loud. The deserted storehouses and bakehouses looked different from this direction. Bigger. Darker. And the air in the cramped alleys felt dank and chill as if Desen's month yet lingered there from wintertide.

I did not believe in ghost hauntings. No spirit, no incorporeal being swathed in mist, wandered the demesne of the living after the heart ceased its beating. I believed the Veil a barrier of iron, not silk. Whatever happened after a person's final breath was beyond our knowing, unless the spyglass could penetrate that barrier to show us truth. . . .

From the night-filled alleys and courtyards behind me rose a wild, despairing, terrified howl that echoed from the storehouses, barracks, and corner towers. I broke into a run and squeezed my eyes to a slit. I didn't want to see what made Calvino de Santo wail.

CHAPTER TEN

The moment I arrived at his apartments the next morning, Ilario whisked me off on a round of calls: the chambers of the chancellor, the king's appointment secretary, the current captain of the Guard Royale, and ten other untitled dignitaries. "I've a plan for tomorrow," he said. "You'll see. You told me we should do something unexpected."

After an hour, my nerves felt shredded. While my lord nattered about racehorses, shared tea, inquired about relatives, slandered an errant boot-maker, and wheedled some concession about "placement" and "accompaniment" and "appropriate honors," I sat on cushioned benches and fidgeted. I needed to tell Dante of my encounter with de Santo. Some crumb or tidbit in my talk with the ruined guard captain taunted me with overlooked importance, and I could not grasp it. Dante's acid reason might.

As we returned from our morning's excursions, I slipped over to the mages' passage. Dante was not in his chambers, so I tore a transcript of Calvino de Santo's testimony from my journal and stuffed it in his warded satchel. I hoped he could pick up the thread that escaped me.

"Philippe agreed to be on his guard tomorrow," Ilario said when I rejoined him in his apartments. He fluffed the lace of his third change of

attire since breakfast. "But he offered no assistance with our placement for the launch. Honestly, the man has no patience with me even at a game table where he is sure to win. You'd think we stood at Carabangor itself, he takes the cursed play so seriously."

"And the girl . . . the news of Michel . . . of the crypt? What did he say when you told him?"

"First he wiped out my entire line of warriors, both tetrarchs, and my queen. I do hate it when he takes both tetrarchs, as I think they are the most exquisite pieces. . . ."

"Lord, what did he *say*?"

"He said those responsible would pay dearly, and that we—the three of us—should continue. Truly, Portier, I thought he would snatch me up and toss me into the box with the game pieces!"

Ilario's reference to Carabangor described no trivial testiness on Philippe's part. The costly victory at the desert city, ending eighteen years of barbaric incursions from Kadr, stood as Philippe's first great achievement as sovereign. It was friends and good soldiers fallen at Carabangor that the spyglass had shown him wandering in an arid wasteland—lost, terrified, and despairing.

"But after our game"—Ilario leaned close, as if spies might have embedded themselves among the brocade doublets, satin cloaks, and silk shirts stuffing his wardrobe room—"he wanted to view the cell in the crypt. Portier, it was clean! No chains. No filth. No chair."

"You're sure it was the same?" Of course, he would be sure. Yet another twist tightened my knotted gut. "And Soren's tomb?"

Had the light in the wardrobe room been better, I might have been surer of the flush that colored Ilario's cheeks. "The display was . . . reduced. He did not note it. Come, Portier, don't look so grim. You'll ruin your complexion. Even Philippe said it was only to be expected that they'd clear out that wretched hole."

Yes, but the timing was so close. The queen and her sorceress knew someone had been poking about in the crypt. The king had commanded me to withhold judgment, but that was becoming more and more difficult.

"Now, dust yourself off. I've more calls to make."

I could glean no more specific report of their talk, nor could I break away to consult Dante, for Ilario fussed and threatened tantrums until I accompanied him. "If you insist on my accomplishing these tedious tasks, Portier, then the least you can do is provide me this smidge of assistance. My dislike of all serious business is well-known. I simply refuse to suffer frown lines and hair falling out all over. Besides, my gifts lie so completely in the area of gentle amusements and refined sport, it would be seen as simply greedy were I to strive for the same accomplishment in business or arms. But I'm finding that if I travel with a private secretary, I am instantly accorded a certain respect that allows serious conversation. So you see, it is your own fault. . . ."

Ilario's life flowed like a river flooded out of its banks—senseless, directionless, yet hugely impossible to divert. The afternoon visits took us to a hunchbacked dowager, whose town house smelled like soured apple parings, but boasted a sweeping view of the Ley and the bristling masts clustered at its wharves; then on to a black-bearded marqués, and the pink marble halls of the collegia botanica. As the sun slipped into the western sea, Ilario exchanged whispers and drank tiny cups of spiced tea with a Fassid silk merchant whose silk-draped display pavilion could have held my entire family estate.

I could not recall a single word of sense spoken in those hours. Yet at the end of the day, the fop set off to play another game of stratagems and inform the king of his arrangements. A party of important personages, representing all elements of the city's society, would accompany the king and queen to the launch of the *Destinne*. Rather than mounting a viewing platform on shore or anywhere Philippe and Eugenie might be expected, they would observe the launch from the private, well-secured pleasure barge of the Fassid silk merchant. It was a good scheme—perhaps enough to confound an assassin. Perhaps.

SCARLET AND GOLD PENNANTS WAFTED lazily against the sheeted silver of the dawn sky. The merry strains of shawm and sackbut danced across the

water. As the broad river Ley rippled and slurped against piers and barges and muddy banks, cockboats ferried the last supplies to the caravel *Destinne,* lying so grand at her anchorage in the center of the channel.

As I clung to the rail of the *Swan,* Massimo Haile's elegantly outfitted pleasure barge, the sight of the *Destinne* struck hard upon my imagining. In less than an hour, it would set sail for the lands of diamond-crusted streets, trees taller than temples, cities ruled by naked women, or whatever truly lay across the seas beyond the Mouth of Hedron. Or perhaps her brave crew would sail the *Destinne* off the edge of the world and plummet into the Souleater's abyss, as some few yet believed. To embark on such a voyage on such a morning must surely drive mind and spirit to the highest reaches. Gracious saints, what I would give for such purpose and adventure. The king's ever-more-sordid mystery had stripped the warmth and color from my already-sober world, leaving it danker and grayer yet.

Despite the early hour and the damp from overnight rain, the dockside lanes and merchants' wharves teemed with people. Bread and tea sellers cried their morning wares. Dockhands and carters, beset by swooping, screeching gulls, bawled at women and romping boys to clear a path. Viewing stands had been hastily constructed on the mud flats and draped in soggy buntings. A platform near the shore had been reserved for a crowd of scholars, displaying their distinctive regalia—brick red gowns and berets for the collegiae astronomica, sky blue for the collegiae mathematica, green gowns and black velvet tams for the collegiae botanica.

A circle of the Guard Royale kept the crowd well away from our mooring, and the slowly brightening morning revealed liveried archers atop the warehouses and pikemen posted at every door and alleyway. Massimo Haile's sturdy hirelings controlled access to the pleasure barge. They claimed to have manned their posts all through the night.

Even so, I had clutched my courret and traversed every centimetre of the gilded barge: the promenade along the elaborately carved, newly painted bulwarks; the open-air viewing galleries fore and aft; the lounging pavilion tucked behind billowing draperies in the center of the barge, and each of its cushioned couches, inlaid tables, and hanging lamps. I had even visited the cramped wine and food store beneath the exotic arch of

the *Swan*'s tail, and the forward rowing banks where sixteen bare-chested Fassid of impressive physique stared insolently while stretching backs and arms or downing mugs of ale. My talisman had indicated no untoward risks anywhere aboard, yet I felt no easier. The attempt would come today, not six-and-forty days from now.

Cheers rolled through the crowd as trumpet blasts and the royal ensign heralded the king's arrival. As Philippe traversed the wharfside, he tossed memorials—buttons, coins, or somewhat—into the crowd, leaving a wake of scrabbling backsides. He dismounted at the cordoned-off foot of Haile's gangway, exchanging greetings with two dignitaries in starched ruffs and wide-brimmed hats. Haile's dockhands unloaded a number of tight-rolled bundles, wider than my armspan, from a waiting dray, then carried the linen rolls and the king's furled ensign up the ramp. Our rail-thin host and two fellow merchant princes wrapped in fur-lined mantles waited under a silken canopy on deck.

The cheering faded into scattered shouts and rolling murmurs, as a blue painted coach passed the guarded perimeter. First out, aided by a footman in the queen's livery, was Damoselle Maura. Rising from her curtsy, she spoke an earnest message to Philippe. Unease nibbled at my gut. Though too far away to hear her, I had no difficulty in reading the king's displeasure at her news. My cousin strode angrily up the gangway. Maura trailed after him alone, as the coach rolled away. Queen Eugenie had not come.

What I would not give for Dante's spell to hear across distances! What could possibly keep the queen from the launch of an expedition honoring her son's memory? What wicked magic had the villains planned for Ophelie to work this day, and who would work it in her stead? What role was planned for a captive Michel de Vernase?

Sainted ancestors! I massaged my aching jaw. My teeth had near ground themselves flat these past two days. No matter which way I turned, my back felt vulnerable. I returned to the small, forward gallery, tucked between the lounging pavilion and open hull where the rowers sat. The venue allowed me to observe ship, shore, and a sky now hazed with scudding clouds.

Two rows of elaborately carved posts, more than twice a man's height and topped with gold-and-red painted birds, formed a great rectangle at the center of the barge. From slender crossbeams hung garlands of flowers, the silken draperies that shielded Massimo Haile's lounging pavilion from the public eye, and the stretched canopies that protected his guests on the aft gallery from excess sun. The silk merchant's dockside crew stretched new spans of line even higher on the posts between the carved birds. To each taut span the dockhands lashed one of the linen rolls—celebration banners, I guessed.

A steward hoisted the king's black and silver stag above the *Swan*'s high curved tail. The ensign snapped sharply, near ripped from its mooring by a stray gust.

Ilario arrived with the guests of the queen's party—the black-bearded marqués, the hunchbacked dowager, and, to my astonishment, all three mages. Mage Orviene paused for a laughing conversation with a Fassid aide before mounting the gangway. Gaetana swept aboard with the other guests. Dante, his long hair plaited, his black brows and gaunt cheeks made more severe by a black tunic and deep blue gown, ascended the ramp alone. Both guests and crew kept their distance, which likely suited him very well.

Though immeasurably relieved to see Dante, I was not sure whether to be fearful or reassured at the presence of our two principal suspects. Yet I doubted their own hands would be soiled with this day's work. Once more I scanned every person on the barge, the ring of guards, the people lining the wharves, the dinghies and shallops that dotted the broad reaches of the river. Where would the attack commence? It *would* come; I was sure of it.

Deckhands hauled in the gangway. I forced myself to breathe.

The bargemaster barked orders from a small railed platform facing the oarsmen. *"Seiche mar!"* Rowers settled into position and grasped the oars. *"Disema!"* Deck boys dressed in red tunics and gold arm rings cast off the mooring lines. *"Kise fa!"* Sixteen oars raised as one. *"Kise diche!"* As one the sweeps dipped into the murky water. Smooth as its namesake, the *Swan* glided away from its berth above Merona's port and eased into the

channel upriver, between the *Destinne* and the grim stone finger of Spindle Prison.

The rising wind shifted the furled banners and billowed the barge's filmy draperies and silken canopies. The king's ensign set up a steady whapping. I grabbed my narrow-brimmed hat to prevent it from making its own journey beyond the Mouth of Hedron.

"Slack water!" We'd not yet dropped anchor when the cry echoed through every bobbing boat, shallop, and skiff on the river. Another wave of raucous cheers and merry music swelled on shore. On board the caravel, copper-skinned seamen scrambled into the rigging, and more gathered at the *Destinne*'s bow and stern.

Philippe, Haile, Ilario, the marqués and marquesa, gathered at the *Swan*'s stern rail, to watch a *Destinne* seaman hoist Sabria's scarlet and gold. Guests crowded behind them on the grand gallery. A few, including two Fassid merchants and Maura, strung out along the starboard rail. I abandoned the chanting rowers and strolled toward Maura, thinking to find out why her mistress was not here.

"Sonjeur de Duplais." I swiveled. Gaetana had come up behind me, serenely sober, as if bleeding young girls for power had never occurred to her. Dante, sour faced, stood a few steps behind.

"Divine grace, Master Gaetana, Master Dante," I said, inclining my head. "Indeed a bright day." Yet the hazy sky was shading anything but fine at present. We'd see storms by afternoon.

"Dante, have you met Lord Ilario's secretary, Portier de Savin-Duplais?" asked the woman mage, extending a hand toward each of us. "Portier was our quite-competent librarian at the collegia. Knowledgeable as far as a layman can be." The barbed compliment reflected the sentiments of most at Seravain.

Dante's stare could have frosted flame. "I've doubts as to competence. But until yon female overseer finds me a proper servant, this knock-kneed craven's to fetch my books—assuming he can manage a task for a body with a *mind* attached." Ilario's current boisterous recitation of "The Lay of Hedron's Mouth" in the stern gallery would do naught to dispel Dante's scorn.

"Chevalier de Sylvae is a loyal supporter of our art," said Gaetana. "Her Majesty favors him."

A trumpet fanfare from Philippe's heralds made further conversation impossible. The stern anchor raised, the *Destinne*'s crew now hauled on their bow cable as if to draw the great ship all the way upstream to the Spindle by strength of their arms. But a shouted command loosed the spritsail, and the caravel began to come about. When the bow anchor lurched free, another scrap of sail high in the rigging was unfurled, and to the roar of Merona's delighted citizenry, the *Destinne* harnessed the quartering wind and rounded slowly into the Ley's current and the outgoing tide.

Gaetana beckoned Dante to resume their movement aft, toward the king's party. But as Dante passed between me and the furled banners, he swiveled suddenly and grabbed my neck. His iron hand shut off my breath. Green eyes blazing, he pressed me to the rail and snarled. "Do you think me deaf? I'll have no murmured resentments as I pass. Keep out of my sight until you are summoned, librarian. The stink of failure offends me."

A brutal twist and a powerful shove and I crashed to the deck, sliding headfirst toward the chanting rowers. Chest burning, cheek scraping the polished planks, I was only vaguely aware of blaring trumpets.

From a corner of my watering eye, I glimpsed Haile's man haul on the lines. A cascade of painted linen unfurled from the bird-topped posts, first the king's own black and silver standard, then the gold-on-scarlet tree of Sabria, and lastly a new ensign—a sky blue field with a white ship, a golden sun, and the words Honor and Remember and a third word that might have been Destinne, only the banners' unfolding tails crackled and spat, and the world an arm's length above my head erupted into a blinding spray of white flame.

Chaos erupted in every quarter. Gluttonous flames swallowed the *Destinne*'s banners as if they had never been and raced along greased ropes and varnished crossbeams, quickly engulfing the next banner and the next, and licking at the billowing canopies.

Rolling, scrambling away from the fire, I tumbled over the edge of the

gallery decking into the open hull, very nearly into a shocked oarsman's lap. My right hand sirened pain, as if sparks of molten iron had penetrated flesh and bone.

Bellowing oarsmen shot up from their benches, brushing frantically at skin and hair. A writhing, screaming few jumped into the river, while still others tried to slosh water over the bulwarks to douse the burgeoning fires. The bargemaster, whose platform had placed him directly in front of the forward-facing banner, lay draped over his handrail, unmoving, pitted skin smoking like a field of geysers. Heavenly angels . . . Philippe!

Eyes streaming, I strained to see the rear of the barge where I'd last seen my cousin, but billowing smoke and flame obscured the way. The whoresons who'd done this could not have found better tinder than the inked linen banners, the silken furnishings, and the *Swan*'s newly painted wood.

The oarsman nearest me twisted and danced in macabre torment, screaming and clawing at his face. I lurched upward and reached out to steady him, but the current and the changing tide caught the barge and swung it around drunkenly. We both staggered. His partner in the lead bank, a brawny fellow with a gold strap across his chest, shoved us aside and yelled, *"Seicha mar! Seicha mar!"*

A few men grabbed flapping oars and sat, though flames had burst out here and there like demonic seeds scattered from a plowman's hand. I needed to move. But the back of my right hand had become a paralyzing agony, the raw wounds smoking . . . great Heaven . . . as if I burned from the inside out.

As the lead oarsman yelled and the few at the sweeps took up a ragged rhythm, I ripped the cloth band from my hat, dipped it in the water, and wrapped it tightly about my hand. I wasn't going to be able to do anything if I started screaming, too. I needed to get aft . . . to the king . . . to Maura . . . Ilario . . . Dante.

Cradling my hand, I scrambled onto the gallery deck. Blistering heat, dense white smoke, and licking flame barred the promenades on either side of the lounging pavilion. The only way to make it aft was to forge

straight through the pavilion itself. Greedy flames licked at the sagging roof canopy and gnawed at the support poles. I took a deep breath and charged in.

Impossible. The smoke was blinding; the walls ablaze. I tripped over a couch and crashed to the decking. A drifting ribbon of flaming silk settled on my sleeve.

Rolling to the side, I slapped at the fire and scrabbled forward, straining to recall the room's arrangement from my morning inspection. *Around the low tables, over a divan, shove the chair aside.*

New flames exploded before and behind. Searing, thundering, they drowned out the screams and wails that had guided me. Everyone on the barge could be dead for all I knew. *Father Creator, no air here.* My throat scorched; my eyes streamed and blurred. *Which way?*

Instinct clamored that my friends lay beyond the thickest battlements of white-hot flame. Near blind . . . panicked . . . I drove through the roaring wall. My feet stumbled on the aft steps. I scrabbled upward, and burst into the air, gasping and swatting at my smoldering hair.

The marqués and two deckboys were passing buckets of water to Haile and his steward, battling the encroaching flames on the port side. The dowager, half her body seared like roasted meat, wailed piteously. Ilario, pale hair and fine garments blackened, had stretched his long body over her to shield her from fiery debris as the flames crept ever closer. His head jerked up and his eyes widened as a post and crossbeam crashed beside me. The blazing fountain catapulted me forward. I curled in a knot, my seared lungs fighting for air.

Calls for help from the starboard promenade spurred me to my feet again. I doused a cushion in the river and beat at a towering wall of flame, ever more frantic as the cries became screams of mortal pain and terror. I might as well have been trying to snuff the stars in a middle-night sky.

The barge lurched and wallowed. The horizon spun. My boots slipped and I crashed to the deck. Coughing, breathless, I clutched my wrapped hand to my breast and pressed my head to the planks. The flames flared higher, engulfing the entire center structure beam to

beam. I was no hero who could defeat an inferno. The agonized cries became mindless bleats until the thunder of flames silenced them. *Please, saints and angels, let Maura . . . Philippe . . . Ilario . . . Dante . . . not be in there.*

Portier, get up! The stern voice of conscience lifted my head from the blistering deck, just as a wind gust cleared a hole in the heavy smoke. Philippe sat wedged against a bulwark, his head bleeding, a charred beam crushing his middle. An unknown man in tattered garments was attempting to shift it. I scrambled across the steaming deck. "Sire, are you well?"

"See to the others," mumbled Philippe, adding what strength he could muster as we hefted the beam and shoved it overboard. Wrapping his arms about his ribs, the king curled his head to his knees, coughing.

Another gust stirred the gray smoke. On the far side of the stern gallery, Orviene and Gaetana had laid out scraps of charred silk, a great deal of shattered glass, a palm-sized golden flask, a silver drinking cup, and a brass fitting from the ship. Using a rope, they had created a ritual enclosure about the particles and themselves. Gaetana knelt at one vertex of a triangle, the rope looped round her waist. Orviene stood at a second vertex, the rope wound about his arm. They had enlisted Maura, hair straggling, one shoulder bare and blistered, to support the third vertex of the enclosing triangle. I did not need to see Gaetana's grip on a string of rubies twined around her fingers or Orviene's focused concentration on the array to guess they had already infused a spell—something huge to require so elaborate a rite. The air crackled with more than fire.

Helpless rage consumed me. To charge into the middle of an ongoing ritual risked worse disaster. But Dante . . .

The mage, apparently unsinged, leaned against the stern rail between me and the other two, arms folded around his staff—doing nothing. Was he deaf? Blind?

"Dante!" I yelled. "The oarsmen are trapped. People are dying. The king is in *peril*."

I could not tell if he heard me over the thunderous fire. His dark brows shadowed his eyes at such a distance. But he did not move.

Another explosion ripped through the holocaust, and I threw myself atop Philippe, expecting a scourge of fire and splinters. But the droplets that spattered my head and back did not burn. Cold, wet, soothing; the spattering quickly became a gentle drumming, as enchantment riddled my innermost being, and the sky brought forth a deluge.

CHAPTER ELEVEN

15 QAT

46 DAYS UNTIL THE ANNIVERSARY

Eight people died in the fire on the *Swan*: the two heralds, a botanist, one of the Fassid merchants, the bargemaster, and three oarsmen—one burned, two drowned. One rower was blinded by the explosion. The disfigured dowager was likely to die as well, sooner or later. Almost everyone suffered burns, many far worse than mine. The rain had saved our lives.

After the pleasure barge limped into port, King Philippe, the blood cleansed from his face, had proclaimed to the awestruck crowd that the Pantokrator himself had surely sent his blessed rain to douse the fires begun by a "faulty brazier" on Massimo Haile's vessel. The king reminded his subjects that the glory of the event must not be sullied by an accident that could happen on any common day. The *Destinne* and her noble crew were safely launched on their noble voyage, giving honor to Sabria and bearing the dead infant prince on his journey to Heaven.

Beloved and honored as Philippe had been since his defeat of Kadr—unlike the Blood Wars, the kind of wholesome conflict that creates heroes—he soon had his people cheering. He walked all the way up to Castelle Escalon, as if to show himself uninjured and unafraid. I suspected he had cracked ribs and could not bear the jostle of riding. Along the way he

distributed another barrelful of memorial coins imprinted with his dead son's likeness on one side, and the words HONOR, REMEMBER, and DESTINNE scribed around a ship's emblem on the obverse.

It took no time at all for the rumors to begin—that the fire had been no accident, that the celebration banners had been enspelled with the white waxy substance known as *devil's firework*, that the queen's mages had worked terrible spells *before* the fire, and that the queen's absence meant— Some dared not complete their conclusion, but many others did, inside and outside the palace.

On the morning after the fire, a new chapbook showed up in Merona's markets—and in many a courtier's gloved hands. The story told of a Syan concubine who decided to burn her land's emperor to bring back the spirits of her former lovers. That afternoon, the queen's coach, transporting two of her ladies to the lace market, was battered by a barrage of rock-centered mudballs. Despite the crowded street, no witnesses to the incident could be found. If rumor and innuendo shadowed truth, the king would be able to stave off the hounds baying at his wife for very little longer.

Ilario summoned me to his apartment that evening. His barber had trimmed his scorched hair short, save for one fair lock that dangled over his right temple, hiding a raw red streak. Twirling an ivory-headed walking stick, he paced and fidgeted, entirely unlike himself, as we exchanged platitudes about the dreadful event.

"It is a grace the queen was not aboard the *Swan*," I said. Head muddled and stomach churning from the incessant pain of my hand, I offered this sentiment entirely without innuendo.

Ilario slammed his stick onto a table so hard, the maple cane broke away and flew across the room, shattering a mirror. "She fell ill!" he shouted, and launched the ivory elephant that remained in his hand clear through the open door and off his balcony. "For her to sail would have been torture."

"Certainly, Chevalier. Certainly." His vehemence shocked me out of my sleepless stupor.

"And everyone in Merona knows it is customary for the queen to sup-

ply celebration banners." Ilario's ferocious kick buckled the leg of a delicate chair that likely cost ten times my year's pay; then he snatched up a tasseled pillow and began ripping out its threads. "*Anyone* could have enspelled them. She herself stitched only the *Destinne* ensign. Others sewed and finished them."

Great Heaven! Grim certainty infused my heart, alongside sympathy and sorrow for both husband and brother.

"Perhaps . . ." Ilario's slender hands paused in their destructive agitation, and he made another circuit of his room. "Now Philippe has seen evidence of true sorcery, perhaps he will broaden his mind. Compromise. He and Michel forever scoffed at her requests for caelomancers or healers. That's why Geni took it on herself to find help when Desmond fell so ill. If some mages are corrupt and wicked, it is no fault of the magic . . . or of my sister."

"My lord, if you could persuade Her Majesty to allow us to question—"

"Don't ask it!" He swung his long body around. "By the sainted Reborn, she'll not do it for her husband; she's certainly not going to do it for me. Her household is her only pride, her only demesne. Deeds of honor that can further her family's progress through Ixtador must be her own. Not lent. Not granted by a husband. She will not yield control. And she will *not* be treated like a common thief."

Of all the prattle that had fallen from Ilario de Sylvae's lips in these past days, the sincerest and most sober were those that embraced his half sister. No matter his flighty ways, he cared deeply for her. And he was terribly afraid. Rightly so. No queen's crown or wedding vow was proof against a charge of treason. I did not point out how unlikely it was for Philippe to compromise with Eugenie about anything after this disaster. Had her husband been any but Philippe de Savin-Journia, she would already have been in custody. So might Ilario, as well. He had arranged our presence on the barge.

"Lord Ilario, look at me." I used the most commanding voice I could manage without splitting my skull.

He halted, startled, as if he'd already forgotten I was in the room.

"Tell me, lord chevalier, who prompted you to choose Massimo Haile's barge for the king's launch party?"

You'd have thought I'd just asked him why the Pantokrator created the world. "*You* did, Portier, or near enough. You said to do whatever I needed to keep the assassins off balance and ensure that you and the confounded Dante were near Philippe. No King of Sabria has ever graced a Fassid's barge, and no mage and no minor secretary have ever accompanied the king to any such event. You don't think Massimo—?"

The full import of my question struck him as a boot to the gut. He blanched and collapsed onto a silken divan that directly faced my own stool. "Merciful hosts . . . you think that *I* . . ."

"Certainly not. It's only I must have answers for the king." More ill by the moment, I could not answer further.

He peered closely at my face that felt as clammy as sweating cheese, then popped up from his seat. In moments he returned with restored composure, a small towel, and a vase stripped of its flowers.

"When I saw you burst from that hellish fire alive, I thought you must be one of the Saints Reborn, come to save us. Now you look as if we should cart you to the deadhouse." He dipped the towel in the vase and slopped the cool, wet thing over my head. "Go to bed, Portier. And think. If I want Philippe dead, and Geni and me hanged at Merona's gates, all I have to do is propose a game of stratagems and walk into his private study wearing a poison ring. His guards don't even search me anymore."

He tossed the emptied vase onto his silk divan, hauled me to my feet, and shoved me toward the door. "Philippe will never believe such scurrilous charges," he said, "especially now Orviene and Gaetana have been redeemed—and such a justification of Eugenie's wisdom *that* is. No, these events have been perpetrated by some rogue from Seravain. You must shift your inquiries there."

And so was *I* stymied, as well. For, indeed, our structure of ill-informed suppositions had collapsed the moment Orviene and Gaetana followed the cursed banners onto the *Swan* and raised a rainstorm. The queen might still be the enemy Philippe feared, but our only *magical* suspects had saved the king, not slain him.

ILARIO RETIRED TO HIS COUNTRY house for a few days to recover his spirits and grow out his hair, so he said, but insisted I stay behind and work on his scientific exposition. "I want it held on the Anniversary—to honor Prince Desmond as the launch was meant to do. Mayhap it will blot out the taint of this wickedness. Eugenie will be pleased. Philippe, too."

The Anniversary. Six-and-forty days away. Little more than a month to arrange a scientific and magical display "unequaled in this age." I could not even begin.

My attempts to address our more important business were equally futile. Plagued with persistent pain and nausea, a lingering cough from the smoke, and an internal storm of guilt and failure, I could neither follow the confusing trail of evidence nor devise any stratagem to further our investigation—assuming Philippe wished me to continue. Every hour I expected a summons and a dismissal.

The echoed screams of those dying on the *Swan* ruined what sleep my sickness allowed, and a pernicious dread grew in me every hour. On the third night from the fire, I huddled on the floor in the corner of my bedchamber, my head buried in my arms. A familiar, seductive inner voice insisted there was no use forcing myself to impossible tasks, no use striving to be something I was not, no use eating or drinking or sleeping or breathing. . . .

Nine years it had been since failure had so unraveled me, since the day I had killed my father in defense of my own life. On that occasion, illness, guilt, and despair had come near finishing what my father's knife had begun. Past, present, and future had faded to gray. My dreams of destiny had withered, replaced by blinding headaches and unfocused anxieties. A month it had been until I could speak my own name; two until I could engage in conversation; six until I could complete a simple task on my own; a year until I had relieved my mentor of his burden and resumed responsibility for my own life.

Not this time, I mumbled, as the sky lightened yet again. *You've sworn loyalty and perseverance to souls other than your own. If you cannot move forward, go back and start again.*

To begin, I drafted a letter to my solicitor, expressing a desire to locate the family of a disgraced guard captain and direct the paltry thread of my family allowance to its sustenance. It would be enough to stave off starvation. I sought out Verger Rinaldo and told him of a muddled "vision" of a family in danger, mentioning naught but Riverside and a girl child and a guardsman/father gone missing. He promised to investigate. If Gruchin's family were to be found, he would do it.

Then I returned to the more difficult task. The keys to Ophelie's torment and Michel de Vernase's fate must surely lie at Seravain. To travel there unremarked, I needed Dante's cooperation. Yet conscience demanded I tell him what I thought of a gifted man who could hear fellow humans suffer and die without so much as raising his hand. Such frankness would risk our partnership. But I could not stay silent.

Once resolved to the necessity, I shouldered my journal like a flimsy shield and pressed through the busy byways of the east wing. I had scarce lifted my hand to knock on the mage's door when it flew open. Dante yanked me inside by my belt.

"Gods, where have you been?" he said, before I could speak even one of my carefully rehearsed words. "I near fright the serving men out of their trousers every time they bring me a dinner tray. We need—" He grabbed the wrist of my bandaged hand. "Damn the vile creatures, are you burnt?"

With a grip kin to a mad dog's jaws, he dragged me to the sunny end of his apartment, shoved me roughly onto the couch, and kicked a stool into place so he could sit close. Fortunately, he took better care as he laid my hand on his lap and unwrapped the bandages.

"Stop," I said, pain scrambling my arguments. "There's no need—"

"*Never* bind a burn so tight. And *never* slather a burn with ointments like this. Burns need air. Joints need movement. Can you uncurl your fingers?"

"Somewhat. It's only— Aagh!" He had laid the back of my hand open to view, forcing my fingers out straight. The whole was swollen and seeping. Though smaller than warts, the fifteen or twenty angry wounds yet stung as if burning spikes had been driven through flesh and bone. My

stomach heaved as had become its unfortunate habit. It was all I could do to hold back until he supplied a rag to catch the remnants of my breakfast.

Dante disposed of the foul mess, poured a slick, bitter potion down my throat, and took up exactly where he'd left off, wriggling each of my fingers in turn. "It's well that it hurts. You understand that much?" My sweat-beaded face must not have reassured him. "If the burn is too deep, it destroys the underlying nature of flesh—the very senses that give you pain or pleasure. The physicians washed your wounds with natron, as I told them?"

My left hand massaged my head, which prickled as if tiny brooms were sweeping away the cobwebs of fever and sleeplessness. "Natron . . . yes. *You* told them?"

"People assume that every mage knows healing." He jumped up and scrabbled through the paraphernalia on his worktable, returning with an amber flask and a wad of clean linen. "Unfortunately, the study of healing requires a patience I've only recently developed. At the time I had the chance to learn, I desired grander magic."

He dampened a square of linen and dabbed at the raw wounds. I strove for mental discipline, hoping to prevent further humiliation. One would think the particles had burned straight through my gut to the roots of my toenails.

"I can scarce distinguish bone from muscle or liver from heart," he said, "nor can I soothe so much as an itch out of mind, whether by conjury or practical wisdom." He patted all dry, then bound a length of fresh bandage loosely about each finger before rewrapping my whole hand in the same fashion. "Burns, though"—he snugged the trailing end of the bandage, then grimaced at his own scarred appendage—"burns I know. Now tell me, did we not judge these villains rightly? So very clever they are. I'd never have understood what they were up to had you not laid the very revelation in my lap. Well done." He jumped up and kicked the stool away in sheer exuberance.

Thrown completely out of mind, hand throbbing, stomach curdled at imagining a burn that could have caused so terrible a ruin as Dante's hand,

I could not comprehend in the least what he was talking about. We had been entirely *wrong* about the mages.

Dante seemed to need no response from me. He circled the room, the fever of discovery propelling steps and speech.

"I'd never have thought you subtle enough to extract such secrets, but then I've no understanding of *talk*, as you've seen. Only the magic. An arrow that could penetrate iron, placed in the hands of an expert marksman. Caelomancy prepared in advance to douse a sudden conflagration."

Halfway through his second circuit of the room, he snatched up the flask, linens, and bandages and returned them to his worktable.

"So now, student, bend your mind to the villains' purpose. It's not just to lay suspicion on the lady queen—though her absence from the *Swan* fits that purpose like the popinjay fits his hose. That requires no such elaborate plotting. Nor can I think they were just looking to raise the reputation of sorcery, though Gaetana looked sour enough to gnaw her own arm when she heard the king speak of the 'Pantokrator's blessed gift of rain.' If His Majesty refuses to admit what saved him, then next time they might decide to actually kill the royal fool!"

My reviving faculties began to knit these rambling threads together. "You're saying they planned—they weren't trying to kill Philippe at all!"

And then, of course, the revelation—the elusive mystery of Calvino de Santo's testimony—dropped into my own lap like an enchanted stone. Gruchin, the first mule, had been *an expert marksman*. He had aspired to be a sorcerer, but Gaetana had dismissed him from her service, accusing him of using transference. Yet she had not reported this offense. The threat of exposure and certain execution would ensure his silence about anything he'd seen or done . . . until the fool got drunk enough to babble about it to his captain. Only then did his accuracy with a bow begin to fail. And when de Santo dismissed him for his shaky hands, he had vanished with no one to notice save a wife and child. Gaetana . . . someone . . . had bled Gruchin for two years.

What if Gruchin's marksmanship had not truly failed, but had been

only temporarily blocked? What if the mages had promised him redemption and healing if he placed the arrow exactly where they told him?

"Gruchin's arrow was *supposed* to miss," I said. "Supposed to penetrate the saddle and kill the horse and come ever so close to killing the king, making everyone believe that someone wanted the king dead—most likely his queen. Supposed to leave everyone afraid and suspicious. And then Orviene and Gaetana caused the fire on the *Swan*, but you believed— you knew—they intended all the while to bring on the rain to save Philippe."

Dante scooped up a flat box and several other items from the worktable and headed back toward me. "Gaetana is a calculating witch. She would hardly have come sailing with us without a way to undo whatever mischief they intended. Orviene is thick enough to go sailing in his own piss. It just took me damnably long to figure out the banners were the danger. I wasn't close enough to them until we stood talking to you, and I smelled the wax. If I'd discovered the truth sooner, I'd have found some less drastic way to warn you."

"You saved my life," I said, stupidly. And my eyes, a gift of no less value. Yet with eight dead souls screaming in my head, how could I thank him?

He tossed an open book aside and set the flat box, a ball of string, and a knife beside me on the couch. He didn't meet my gaze. "It has occurred to me I might need you to get me out of here someday. To vouch for my good purposes and all that."

"Too bad we couldn't have warned a few others, even if they were less useful to you."

Dante's face, body, and spirit froze. "Speak this accusation completely, Portier." His voice reverted to the soft, cool precision so much more menacing than heated fury. "And while you're about it, lay out the terms of our agreement. If you wish me to salvage every sorry dullwit who strays into the path of wicked sorcery, then state that right now. Or if you wish me to curry these mages' favor and allow myself to be drawn into their trusted circle, state *that*. But understand that I am not so talented as to do both."

"People were burning . . . dying. You did nothing."

"Great works of magic that thwart murderous nature—works that might shield a man from fire or pain or drowning—cannot be devised in a heartbeat like a mother's trick to divert a naughty child. And I claim no subtlety to tease men out of danger or in half a moment create an impregnable excuse to heave sixteen oarsmen overboard. You told me at the beginning that this was a dangerous undertaking. I thought you understood what that meant."

This naive misunderstanding was certainly the truth. I had aspired to service, to useful purpose, hoped to prove that an accident of birth need not condemn a man to a hollow life. Never had I imagined Philippe's charge would cause me to see a man's eyes seared to blindness or to hear a human mind disintegrate as fire consumed its living body. Perhaps I had allowed Dante's undeniable talents to impress me overmuch with confidence in his skills, and his enthusiasm for the hunt to induce me to forget that he despised his fellow men. Yet never could I have believed that the right course of my service must be to approve the choice Dante had made. What of simple mercy?

Furious with Dante, with myself, with circumstance that forced such choices, I could see naught but to go on. Allowing such crimes as had been done to Ophelie and Gruchin to continue was unthinkable, as well.

"Fair enough," I said, gritting my teeth. "Clearly I held unreasonable expectations. Have the mages made overtures? Welcomed you into their secrets?"

"It has begun," he said, all his eager ferocity locked away. "Gaetana informed me that certain members of the queen's household were invited to the launch of the *Destinne* in company with the king. I assumed the arrangement was your work and agreed to come." As I had demanded of him.

He strode to the window and threw open the casements. "They have also asked if I would teach them how I worked the little frippery at the lady's party. I refused. They'll ask again."

"And is it both of them? You said Orviene is thick. I see him as trivial."

"She leads. He follows. Whether he knows where he goes or how, I cannot say."

The silence stretched. Questions, strategies, misunderstandings swirled in my head, and I could not leave without addressing them.

The box he'd set beside me contained thirty or forty small cloth bags filled with fragrant herbs. "What are these?"

"I need them tied shut. It's a thing I can't do." Brittle words; frigid. His maimed hand twitched, but he didn't turn around.

I took up the task, more to give myself time to think than to assist him. I had to gather the mouth of each bag and grip it with my left hand, using my injured right to do the tying—an awkward process that I could not accomplish without flexing my painful fingers. With every twinge, I cursed him.

Yet, as the hour ticked away, whatever potion he had used to bathe my wounds seemed to ease them. And I had released my festering anger, no matter how unsatisfactory the resolution. As a result, I was able to think more clearly than at any time since the fire.

"This doesn't make sense," I said after a while. "Why would Orviene and Gaetana work this weather marvel to rescue the king, a wonder that could revive people's appreciation of sorcery, and then risk its association with the worst blights of magical history—mules and transference?"

Dante snorted. "Gods, student, you are blind. Do you truly believe that collection of refuse they spread out on the deck drew the rain from the sky? The pattern was flimsy and absurd. No, the real caelomancy had already been worked and linked to a receptacle—some object they brought aboard. Not something picked up by chance to balance the magical elements. This enchantment was so huge and so complex, it required the strength of both mages to quicken it. I've never . . ." He tugged at his collar, a fretful move I'd come to think signaled uncertainty. "I am not skilled enough to dissect such spells as yet." His clipped words dripped scorn— for himself, not me.

I recalled Dante's still, focused posture in the stern of the *Swan*, as the fire raged. I had desired him to work some miracle to save the dying, be- cause I had already tried and failed. Helpless, frightened, I had wanted

him to pounce on the two mages and withhold a coming doom. He had not, because he believed their spellwork benign—as it had proved. He had been feeling, sensing, examining, using whatever was this talent that enabled him to see the very structure of spellwork, doing what I had engaged him to do.

"But no matter my incompetence." He turned slowly and settled himself on the window frame, staring at something far beyond his chamber, arms folded. "I'll swear on anything you care for that their gold flask drew forth the rain. The surge of power"—he closed his eyes as if to envision it again—"was as like the Camarilla's usual magic as a hurricane is to a baby's breath, as arsenic to mother's milk."

"Power fueled by Ophelie's blood infused into the spellworker's veins."

"Whoever has done this—their contempt is monumental." Dante ran his fingers through his untamed hair. "I believe the mule—the girl—was meant to be discovered. Not as she was—before the event and able to speak. But after, so she could be linked to the murderous 'magic' of the banners, which those few who understand the properties of the mineral phosphorus will understand to be no magic at all; a wax seal prevents its untimely combustion. Everyone would believe she ensorcelled the banners, and without her fingers, it could not be proved otherwise. Some well-laid trail would link the banners to the queen, whereupon we would be forbidden to search further. Another mystery unsatisfactorily 'solved.' And the lady of sorrows blamed."

He aimed his storm-hued gaze at me. "Now *you* tell *me*, great sympathizer with sorry humankind: Why did the girl believe she had to die before this happened? Whatever her captors would do with her blood had already been settled. She could not stop it. She spoke of betraying a 'good man,' not a 'good *queen*.' What would an aristo student of magic call *sin* or *betrayal*?"

I had assumed Ophelie's "betrayal" meant royal assassination—murder. But if they'd never planned to murder Philippe, then what?

"I've not a guess," I said after a fruitless few minutes. "The conspirators are taunting Philippe, forcing him to look the other way because

elsewise he must blame his wife. A queen who champions sorcery accused of treason by a king already considered an enemy of the Camarilla—it would destroy the Concord; throw the kingdom into chaos. But they're taunting *us*, as well. They might not know who we are, but they suspect that *someone* is examining what they've done . . ."

"Perhaps."

". . . which means they're up to something that a persistent investigator *will* see if they don't distract him. Something that requires the kind of power they cannot draw from their innate talents. Ophelie was bled for near a year; Gruchin for almost two. Who knows how many other mules they've used. What else have they done?"

As if taking the cue from my conviction, Dante strode into his bedchamber and returned with two wads of fabric. Shoving the box of half-tied herb bags onto the floor, he sat beside me and unwrapped the smaller one—a kerchief containing the twisted shard of metal from the crypt—Ophelie's manacle.

"This piece teases," he said. "I've no doubt it bound the girl. The blood"—he showed me the dark residue in the jagged tear that had freed Ophelie—"matched the keirna of the samples I took from her body. But *she* didn't break it. I found no commonalities between her blood, or anything you've told me of her, and the magic that tore the metal. Nor did I discover any commonalities with the magic worked on the *Swan*. True, that was a very different spell, and a joint working, but I would judge . . ."

". . . that the magic that freed her was worked by someone else entirely." So easy to complete his logic—forcing an astonishing conclusion. "We've yet *another* sorcerer involved."

Dante rewrapped the shard and gave it to me. "The magic was not only tremendously explosive, but entirely undisciplined. Not even a spell as we think of it. It felt as random as a lightning strike, its pattern utterly simple, but as raw and dangerous as the torn edge of the metal."

As I fingered the wrapped manacle and marveled at the story it told, he unwrapped the larger bundle. The spyglass lay innocent in the folds of a cambric shirt. A bit of metal dropped to the floor and rolled to my feet. I picked up the silver coin.

"That's an oddment," said Dante. "Its keirna is very different from that of other coins, but then coins pass through so many hands for so many different purposes, they have quite a complex pattern to begin with. The oddities might come from its being a double strike or from being in a mule's pocket at the moment of his death. But whatever its history, it is now magically inert. It carries no spells. Stranger yet, none I've tried seem to affect it in any way."

The silver disk induced no odd sensations as I had experienced the first times I'd held it. "And the glass?"

He lifted the spyglass and shoved its wrappings aside. "I've taken it apart. Studied it a bit with no ill effects. I've no doubt you'll inform me if I take on an even more fiendish bent."

"I'll certainly speak out if I sniff brimstone in here again," I said, but no wry spark illumined his shuttered face.

"Is your royal cousin a devout man?"

I rolled the double-faced coin between my fingers as I considered the odd question. "I'd say not, though that's pure supposition. What other Savins I know keep private altars, but they live . . . heedless."

I glanced up to see if he understood. He inclined his head.

"You said the king saw dead men he knew, wandering in desolation, when he looked through the glass," he said. "What did *you* see? If I'm to explain this particular mystery, I need evidence."

His request made sense. But no sooner had I sketched out my vision than he began to pick at its threads, gathering intensity like a lowering storm. *What kind of gate?* Iron. *Was it embedded in a wall?* No, it stood alone. But the way—*no,* I didn't see an actual path—led through it. I just knew. *Was your father's attire familiar?* Yes. His favorite hunting coat. *Was the land-scape known to you?* A dry hillside could be a thousand different places in Sabria, but the gate . . . *Did your father ever attempt sorcery?* Not that I ever saw or heard. He was weak in all ways. *Was there physical violence between your father and you when you were a boy?* No. *As a man?* Once. Only once. *Do you pray for your father?*

"That's quite enough," I said, jumping to my feet, trembling as the old scar on my left arm throbbed in time with my burns. I could not afford

headaches or memories of daydreams that bled truth, or any of the turbulence these topics forever roused. "What does this have to do with the spyglass?"

He didn't answer. Didn't look up. Didn't speak at all for a while, as he carefully unscrewed the outer brass ring from the wide end of the spyglass and lifted out a second, this one with the glass lens fitted in it. With a small prying implement he removed five tiny brass fasteners from the rim, then pointed to a pattern scratched on the lens ring. "I think this might be the mark of the lens maker," he said. "Can you see it?"

Still flustered, I motioned him to turn the ring into the sunlight. A squint revealed the scribed image of an eye with three rays spreading out from it. "I'll find out whose mark it is," I said. "But what does my private business have to do with this? What have you learned about the glass?"

"Nothing certain, though I doubt it provides a window into some divine hunting ground. The spellwork pattern is erratic, like a quilt jointly made by a royal seamstress and a blacksmith. Some aspects are quite subtle, using properties of light and aether I've never conceived of; some are little more than acolyte's fumbling. The power that infused the spell is weak. And, as I told you at the beginning, the instrument's physical construction is uneven, as well. Like this . . ." He removed the brass rim and exposed the hidden edge of the lens. Bubblelike voids and tiny cracks marred the wavy edge of the glass. "Filled with flaws. Again, I believe, we have a different practitioner. Less skilled even than Orviene. Far less raw talent than the one who burst the manacle."

"If it doesn't penetrate the Veil, then what, in Heaven's name, does it do?"

He didn't seem to hear my question. "This guard captain, de Santo, he is not of the blood?"

I thought back to the way de Santo had spoken of Gruchin's blood ties, and my glimpses of his grimy hands . . . bare of family marks . . . covering his head. "I don't believe so."

"And you don't think he could be working for Orviene or Gaetana?"

"Definitely not. He believes the king has betrayed him—that Philippe

sacrificed him and his family in order to shield the queen and the mages who work for her."

"I want to see the captain. Tonight."

I bristled at his demand. "Why? Was my interview flawed? My report incomplete? De Santo saw nothing of Gruchin's attack."

Dante, closed and cold, carefully reassembled the spyglass. Only when he had tightened the outer ring did he answer. "He may have seen more than he thinks."

Further questioning did naught but close him tighter. Eventually I yielded. "Tonight, then. Meet me at the temple minor at ninth hour. Meanwhile, I need you to make a fuss about your books. It's time to go to Serav—"

A rapping at the door sent both of us to our feet. Dante hurriedly rewrapped the spyglass and tossed it onto his jumbled worktable. "Enter."

As I crammed Gruchin's coin into my pocket, the door opened to Gaetana.

CHAPTER TWELVE

Gaetana's chilly gaze slid from me to Dante and back again.

Dante snatched up the book that yet lay open on the floor and thrust it into my arms. "Does no one in this wretched place heed a man's word? Keep this nursery tale, librarian, and bring me the books I asked for. I don't care if you must copy them yourself or crawl all the way to Seravain to find them."

I hunched my shoulders and gave a curt bow. "I just thought—"

"That's the problem, isn't it?" he said, taking up his staff. "I didn't ask you to think. Another delay and perhaps I'll prevent your thinking altogether. Now. Get. Out."

His staff blurted fire and I scurried out the door, not stopping until I reached the window gallery. Gaetana's derisive laughter followed me, scalding my ears as if I, too, could hear through walls.

I slid my journal into my doublet and smoothed the crumpled pages of the book Dante had shoved at me. Annoying to note my hands yet trembled, near an hour since his questioning. By all saints, why did any mention of my father throw me over? He couldn't spring a knife on me again. Onfroi Guillame de Savin-Duplais was nine years over and done with, no matter what the cursed spyglass showed.

When I noted the title of Dante's book, I almost laughed at the irony. Translated from the ritual language of the Kadr witchlords, its title *Rolfkhedri Muerge* meant *Manifestations of the Dead*.

As it happened, I had read the text before. It recounted a history of hauntings and phantasms, enumerating the distinctions between ghosts and spectres, spirits and souls. The writer had been the first to propose the idea that those we Sabrians called saints, the holy dead designated by the Pantokrator as his hand in the living world, actually walk among us reborn into bodily form—a manifestation he called a *biengasi*. The Cult of the Reborn had grown up around this theory.

Had Dante given me the tattered volume merely to support our diversion, or to keep the book from the woman's observation, or as material for study? Some day I would force the damnable mage to answer a question or two. I hiked the overlong distance to my apartments, stowed the book behind my armoire, and set out for the administrator's office to arrange my journey to Collegia Seravain.

THE SUPPLICANT BENCH SAT UNOCCUPIED when I reached Damoselle Maura's office. The lady herself sat at her writing table, her eyes focused somewhere distant, her tightly folded hands pressed to her mouth. A pen lay idle on her writing table beside an unstoppered ink bottle and a ledger book.

"Divine grace, damoselle," I said, tapping on her door, "are you well?"

The smudged eyes searched my face and promptly filled with tears.

I shut the door behind me. "Lady, may I be of some service? Fetch you wine . . . or some friend . . . a physician or apothecary, or"—it occurred to me that she might be of a religious bent—"perhaps a temple reader?"

"You still hear them, don't you, sonjeur? They break your sleep, as well?"

No need to ask whom she meant. "Aye, damoselle. I try to believe . . . There was naught we could have done differently to save them."

"I try that, too. Though I'm so afraid—" She quickly pressed finger-

tips to her lips, and a tremor racked her shoulders. Then she forced her features into something not quite a smile and picked up her pen. "What business brings you here this morning?"

That moment's break between grief and resignation revealed emotion more disquieting than our shared memory of horror. "Lady, what frightens you so?"

"As you said, some matters we cannot alter. Some promises we cannot undo." She tapped her pen on the table. "And now, please, sonjeur, your business . . ."

Without encouragement, I had no choice but to move on, yet I resolved to return to the question. "Two matters, damoselle. First, Mage Dante has become . . . um . . . insistent . . . about his books. I must travel to Collegia Seravain. My familiarity with the collegia's policies suggests that some official representation of his position in Her Majesty's household will facilitate his book borrowing. As to the second matter, you likely recall how Lord Ilario has tasked me to set up a scientific festival. . . ."

We spent the entire morning together laying out Ilario's exposition, making lists and sketching venues, laughing at the infinite possibilities of magical and scientific exhibits that could astound Merona's worldly citizens. The easy grace of her company, her bright mind and incisive wit, her consideration for the needs of guests and household only strengthened my growing admiration.

By midafternoon, she had obliged me with an official letter of request to the collegia for whatever materials I would specify, sealed with her authority as the queen's representative. She also provided me a letter of credit and an instruction for the steward's office to provide me a mount and expense money for my journey. And naturally, she offered referrals to a number of Merona's tradesmen who might craft the scientific displays. Among them were several lens makers who might also provide a pair of spectacles at a reasonable price to a private secretary who had not yet received an advance on his pay.

I blotted the page where my unburnt left hand had awkwardly scribed the list of tradesmen, closed my journal, and stood to go, Maura's letters

in my grasp. "Damoselle, this day has been . . . exceptional. And now, please, will you not allow . . . Might I assist *you* in some more personal fashion? Or perhaps you have some other friend to confide in?"

I felt like a stammering fool. But throughout my worst days, the ready ear of my mentor, Kajetan, had coaxed me out of my skin's armor, allowing me to release grief and fear and burdens held close since childhood.

She walked me to the door. "Ah, kind sonjeur, you have not lived long at Castelle Escalon. Friends are rare enough for one who holds the queen's keys. Trustworthy confidants extremely so." At least I had prompted a smile, however forlorn. "For the present, I must attend my lady and report on the day's business."

"I'll be off, then. But good lady"—my hand rested on the door lever, still refusing to press it—"when I return from Seravain, would you consider—? I would deem it a great honor, and a great favor, if you would forego business and walk out with me some afternoon. I vow by my royal cousin's head to provide you a trustworthy ear. Or you could regale me wholly with nonsense, if you prefer, as my appreciation of that art has grown deeper with recent experience."

As the warmth from a morning fire sweeps quietly through a chamber to devour the night's chill, so did the lady's pleasure smooth her brow, soften her smile, and flush her cheeks to an even deeper hue. She dipped a knee and tilted her head most charmingly, causing my body to respond in ways it had near forgotten. "It would be my delight to engage in such a venture. Far too long has passed since I've spent an afternoon walk exchanging nonsense."

"Well. All right, then." I pulled open the door.

"Divine grace smooth thy journey, Portier," she said as I stepped out, her voice enriching my name as clotted cream improves whatever sorry fruit it sits on.

It required the long, steep hike down to the lower city to replace unseemly distraction with my afternoon's purpose. But mind triumphed over flesh, and I spent the rest of the afternoon exploring Merona's craftsmen's district. After a start on exposition business, I turned to the lens makers.

With six scattered shops on the list, it would have been simpler merely to ask if someone knew which shop used the radiant eye as its crafter's mark. But Michel de Vernase might have pursued these same lines of inquiry, and I deemed it wise not to walk too obviously in his footsteps. Unfortunately, I completed my last interview at the last shop on the list without encountering any such mark on signboard, doorway, or lintel.

"Your spectacles will be ready tomorrow morning, sonjeur," said a lanky young man named Watt at a tidy workshop called the Glass House.

I had not truly intended to buy spectacles, not being of an age to require such aids. Yet I had been astonished at the clarity of fine-printed text when reading through some of Watt's sample lenses. When he proffered a guess that I might suffer blurred vision and watery eyes after prolonged reading, especially in poor light—which was exactly true—I asked how he knew. On a slate he used to tally up costs, he sketched a diagram of the human eye, as presented in a lecture at the collegia medica, he told me. With deft strokes he showed how rays of light enter the eye's own lens at various angles from close and far objects, forcing the marvelous structure to alter its very shape.

I marveled at this knowledge and could have discussed the subject for another hour. The artistry of such a creation would surely convert a nonbeliever to the Pantokrator's service. But as Watt totted up what I owed him, his sketch prompted me to one last inquiry.

I tapped a finger beside the drawing. "I've seen this pattern before," I said. "An eye with rays of light streaming in or out. Simpler perhaps, but very like. I can't think where. Has someone erected a copper plaque to memorialize this insightful scholar? I seem to recall it etched in metal."

Watt laughed and from a shelf on his wall pulled out a common magnifying lens, its scuffed ring of tarnished brass fastened to a yellowed ivory handle. He pointed to a scratch on the brass ring. "Was this the mark?"

My soul exulted at the chance so nearly missed. "That's it exactly. Is it your own?"

"Nay. 'Tis the mark of Reven Skye, a fellow artisan known more as a lampwright, who crafts both instruments and lenses to order. He's a de-

cent sort who works cheap. Only two streets over. In confidence"—he leaned forward—"he's only a bargain if you don't care about finish or precision. I can refer you to three instrument makers will do you better for a lord's exhibition—and my lenses come second to no one's. You'll hear it said all over."

I asked no further details, insisting my master would not tolerate poor work. But I explored the area "two streets over" from the Glass House and found Reven Skye's grimy little shop down an alley. No one in such a place was going to believe I'd come to consult about a royal exhibit, so I presented the equally grimy Reven Skye a different story.

"A fellow from Castelle Escalon recommended you as one who could make *uncommon* instruments," I said, exposing my hand quickly, so he could not identify the family mark. His own left hand was bare. "Perhaps incorporating a particular lens I've made myself."

"Aye," he said, and licked his yellow-brown front teeth. "I've done specialty work for your like. What kind of instrument? And who's your friend?"

"He'd rather me not say, as he's employed high, you know," I said. "And the matter's confidential. I've a need to peep in a gent's window. See if my wife's visiting. He said you do a fine spyglass."

"Gruchin!" He leapt from his stool, sending tools and metal bits crashing to the floor. I was wholly unprepared when he barreled into me, his soft, heavy body crushing me against the table, fetid breath bathing my face and a rasp pointed at my eye. "Where is the whoreson villain? Near three years and he's never paid me for the instrument. Sneaking bellycrawler, with his precious lenses and grand schemes. Claimed his luck had turned. Said the thing'd make us a fortune."

"He's dead . . . honestly, Goodman Skye . . . I've no money. . . ." My babbling attempts to divert his wrath soon convinced him I wasn't worth a charge of murder.

"I don't believe Gruchin's dead," he grumbled, grinding his rasp on a lump of bronze. "Some said it when his house burnt. But they only found his wife and youngling in it, and maybe his *luck* is what had him away from home when it happened. For sure as I'm born, not a year ago, he

stole that cursed spyglass right out of here. Thieving weasel. I spotted him running away with it."

A half hour and all the coins in my pocket save Gruchin's double strike silver—the dead man's luck charm, so I learned—and Reven Skye was back at work, mumbling of vengeance, thievery, and cheats. Climbing the hill to Castelle Escalon, I pieced together the story. After Gruchin was dismissed from the mages' service, he had fashioned lenses with spells he'd learned from them. Skye said the guardsman had decided to make himself a sensation by selling glimpses through his magic spyglass, "Though I never saw the use of a *miracle glass* that showed naught but a blur."

Verger Rinaldo would find no girl child to rescue. According to the lens maker, Gruchin's house had burned shortly after his dismissal from the Guard Royale, well before the fateful arrow shot. I added the child and her mother to the tally of murders. Perhaps Gruchin had learned what they'd done to his family and planned his revenge all the months they'd bled him. But, for certain, early on the very day Gruchin donned the armor of a royal guardsman and joined the Guard Royale's exercises, likely the only moment of freedom he'd had in almost two years, he had stolen the "useless" spyglass from Reven Skye's workshop. Once he had taken his not-quite-murderous aim at the king, the mule had grasped his unholy glass and stood where the fallen guardsman could not possibly fail to kill him. Though his captors had muted him, he had found a way to expose something of their work.

Nothing suggested the mages had come looking for the spyglass, either before or after Gruchin's death. An eager ferocity rushed through me. It seemed to me that unless a captive Michel de Vernase had told them, they didn't know it existed.

CALVINO DE SANTO UNHARNESSED HIMSELF from the coal cart in the pale glow of a watchlamp.

"Speak to him or leave him be," I murmured to Dante as we crouched in the alley watching. "Does it give you pleasure to spy on a good soldier's shame?"

The tarry night of the stale, filthy alley behind the Guard Royale barracks obscured my companion's face, though I doubted I could read any more answer there than usual. Dante had devoured my tale of Gruchin's spyglass like a starving dog cleans a bone, then insisted on searching out the disgraced guard captain immediately, while revealing naught in return. We had expended an hour of the unseasonably warm evening hunting de Santo, and three more following him about his night's drudgery. Every time I made a move to approach the man, Dante's iron hand had held me back.

"Will you just—keep—silent?" he snapped through gritted teeth. "I've worked a theory."

De Santo's yoke and straps clattered as he threw them into the cart. He left it standing beside the black hill of coal that fed the guardpost braziers throughout the palace, then disappeared into the barracks doorway.

Annoyed at the wasted evening and Dante's surly company, I stood, stretched out my aching legs and back, and cradled my throbbing hand. It was almost middle-night. "I'd like some sleep. I'm off to Seravain tomorrow early. We can test your theory when I get back."

Dante's cold grip encircled my ankle. De Santo had reappeared in a stream of yellow light spilling from the doorway, a blanket thrown over his shoulder and a pail in one hand. As the closing door shut off all but the pale watchlight, he turned away from us and trudged farther into the alley, where an iron fence barred the end, and the shadows were deep.

Metal clanked dully on stone. Water sloshed. The man coughed and spat. Silence fell, but Dante did not release his grip. Moments later, de Santo began to speak. "Holy angels, messengers of Father Creator"—the familiar prayer rose from the distant dark—"heed my petition for hearing and grace to ease the journey of Galtero de Santo, honored father, and Nicia, beloved mother, of Barela and Guilia, sisters fallen in their childhood, and Roland, son of my body. Let neither my dishonor nor my corruption taint their memorials or slow their steps. . . ."

His prayers were lengthier than those I dashed off each evening, and heartfelt as only a man who asked naught for himself could make them. I growled at Dante and dragged at his shoulder to come away. We had no

right to hear this. But the mage would not budge. He gripped his staff and stared into the dark and whispered, "Discipline."

I closed my eyes and crushed my rising temper, and in that fathomless darkness behind my eyes appeared a snarled tangle of scarlet threads and purple barbs, and disjointed blots of shaded gray crossed with livid stripes. How could a pattern of color writ on the inside of my eyelids turn my knees to jelly?

"And for one other lost traveler, unmourned"—de Santo's voice quavered—"hear me, most gracious angels and holy saints. . . . No, no, no!"

Shifting air stirred the warm stink of piss and rot in the windless alleyway. The chill, dry intrusion spoke of earth and dusty leaves and cedar.

"By Heaven's grace, leave me be!"

When de Santo's panic wrenched my eyes open, I thought Dante's magical seeing had seared through my head. Faint silver flashes and purple flickering outlined the captain's kneeling form. Not lightning. Only the great bulk of the palace armory stood beyond the iron fence at de Santo's back. My stomach rolled.

"What do you want of me?" de Santo cried. "I pray for you. I can do no more than that."

The light crawled about de Santo, shooting out tendrils of livid green and purple, charging the air to bursting. De Santo's pleas disintegrated into a despairing moan.

I pressed my back to the brick and sank down beside Dante. "By the Creator's hand, what . . . ?"

The question died on my lips. The mage had pulled out the spyglass, propping the brass body in his clawed right hand while holding the eyepiece with his functioning fingers. When he tried to adjust the eyepiece, the wider end slipped out of his dead fingers. Swearing softly, he tried again, with the same result.

I slipped my shoulder underneath as a prop and steadied the glass with my unbandaged hand. Better to be the support than the one peering through that cursed lens.

Dante's breath caught; then he exhaled, long and slow. After a moment, he eased his grip on the glass and pressed it urgently into my hands. No mistaking his intent.

A sickly, wavering light now cocooned the wailing Calvino de Santo. Dread shriveled my skin like old grapes. But I raised the glass.

Sainted bones! I could not but recall Watt's sketched light, the straight rays bending as they passed through curved glass and again as they penetrated the textured eye. But the artisan's rendering had shown the object of vision clarified, unblurred, not wholly altered, not reshaped from green and purple lightning into a man's starved likeness. Protruding teeth. Receding jaw, bony and stubbled. Scars and mouthlike wounds gaping everywhere on knobbed gray limbs. Small, close eyes, blacker than a nouré's obsidian gaze, accusing and terrible.

You don't believe in ghosts, Portier. Dead is dead. I snatched the glass from my eye. My throat near clogged when I picked out Dante's dark shape creeping along the alley wall toward de Santo and the flickering light. Cursed idiot . . . as manic a fool as Ilario . . . to seek out horror . . .

Responsibility dragged me along the wall behind the mage. Someone who cared for the weeping soldier ought to be alongside. Yet, with every step forward, mind and body escalated their war. My skull ached as if crushed in an iron clamp. Despite the night's warmth, I could not stop shivering.

De Santo remained oblivious to our presence. Poised a few paces behind him, Dante stretched his arms wide, as if to embrace the poisonous vision. Indeed, for a few moments the writhing fire flared brighter as if the mage were new kindling to feed on.

Like a virulent outwash of the encounter, bitter anger settled in my bones. Purulent hatred clung to my spirit like sap from broken cedars. Prayers of unseemly gratitude bubbled from my soul as I huddled to the clammy brick. Gracious angels be thanked, this horror was not mine.

When, after a fathomless time, the last purple wisps faded, Calvino de Santo slumped into a silent, shapeless blackness, and Dante withdrew. The mage nudged me down the passage and around a corner before sinking to the filthy cobbles, uncurling his broad back against the brick wall, and

clutching his staff between drawn-up knees. His breath came in hard gasps, as if he'd run a footrace.

"Some might call blood-born power a curse when it refuses the summons of will, as yours has done," he said after a moment. "But I think it serves you." He removed the forgotten spyglass from my paralyzed grasp and weighed it in his own wide palm. With a grimace, he stuffed the instrument into his shirt.

"My blood serves me? How? Blessed saints, what did we just see?"

"I believe that when you first looked into this glass, it played on a particular guilt and horror you carry with you about your father's end. The same for your king, who saw friends and good servants he has led to their deaths. The factor you hold in common is your Savin blood, however ineffectual that may be in magical circles. When de Santo first looked through the glass, he glimpsed the mule at the moment he crossed the plane of death, and guilt left him vulnerable to the glass's spell, as it did for you. But the captain is not of the blood, and for him the enchantment did not resolve fully, as if his own spirit became caught in a trap of wire and broken glass and cannot get free of the unresolved vision of the mule. Whenever the captain opens his spirit, when he prays, for example, as a devout man does every night, he brings the mule's spectre to life again."

"The spyglass *bound* Gruchin's spirit to de Santo? His soul cannot pass beyond the Veil?"

Tales in every age spoke of sorrowful spirits who lingered after death, chained by vengeance, grief, or urgency to the earthly plane. Ghosts, shades, visible spirits . . . The implications of magic that could force a soul to such incomplete existence were beyond imagining.

"What we saw was *not* Gruchin's ghost, not anything you'd name a soul. Believe me, there was no intelligence, no person there." Dante shook himself as if to be rid of the encounter. "A spectre is only a splash of energies . . . a phantasm or seeming . . . a vivid memory. A nasty, vicious one in this case, no argument there. The mule died committing a purposeful act of vengeance, filled with malice and rage, and this spectre encompasses and inflicts that pain every moment of its manifestation."

"There must be more to it," I said. "Why guilt? De Santo didn't even realize who Gruchin was until later."

Dante shrugged. "Guilt knows little of truth. As far as the guard captain knew, the mule was an assassin who'd come a hairsbreadth from slaying the king he'd sworn his life to protect. And the king was shed of his armor by de Santo's act. Perhaps excitement or fear would do the same."

"But *I* never glimpsed the man, living or dead, and I know as well as I know anything in this life that the face I just saw was Gruchin."

"Aye. The consolidation of the spectre, the accuracy of the likeness, that's a considerable wonder. But perhaps not so much as when one with a bent for magic spies through the glass. De Santo experiences a fragment. You and your king see something wholly real. We just don't know what."

"Reven Skye saw naught but a blur."

"Perhaps the key to the spell had not been spoken. Perhaps the lens maker was never affected by anyone's death. I don't know. But the lenses seem to focus these overpowering emotions and metaphysical realities connected to death, fix the resulting energies to physical memory, and so create a phantasm. A considerable accomplishment. Yet—think about this—not at all what the *queen* has in mind."

Of course. It was so easy to get caught up in the moment's wonders and forget the driving force behind Dante's investigation. The queen did not desire phantasms.

My grateful fingers clung to the rough edges of the solid, mundane brick behind my back. "Then the spyglass enchantment was a failed experiment," I said.

Dante sighed and hauled himself up with his staff. "That's my belief. As the fop told us—as the lady herself expressed to me at my interview—the queen wishes to speak to her mother and have the dead lady answer back. She desires neither spectres nor ghosts, but *engasi*—embodied spirits, returned from the dead to walk the earth. An entirely different matter."

"True necromancy."

"I've never seen it done," he said, almost speaking to himself. "Of all my teachers— I don't know if it's even possible. That's why I need the books. *All* of them I asked for."

Teachers—it was Dante's first mention of his schooling, and curiosity near overwhelmed my sense. But it came to me that I might be more likely to get an answer if I *didn't* pounce this time. Odd and testy as Dante was, I liked him. And I respected him beyond my wonder at his considerable gifts, and I believed he must have good reason for the bitterness that drove him, as my own peculiar history drove me. That's why I'd been so angry at what I'd seen as his failure in compassion. I'd been angry at myself for failure in judgment. Someday I would learn.

I sighed and rubbed my tired eyes. "I still don't see what necromancy has to do with Philippe. He has long turned a blind eye to the queen's illicit desires. The Temple is too weak to contradict his judgment. The Camarilla won't; they've never condemned necromancy, only its abuse, bending to the Temple's rule in the matter only to ensure their own survival after the Blood Wars. Philippe's subjects love him well enough that *they'll* not be prompted to rebellion by rumors of his unlucky wife's grieving. So these distractions of feigned assassinations, mules, and transference are hiding . . . what?"

"I don't know."

He offered me a hand, dragging me to my feet as if I were but a stripling. We set out through the warm night, neither of us able to answer this most critical question. A dog barked in the distance. A flurry of invisible wings greeted us as we passed through a deserted garden. A fountain rippled and gurgled. Peaceable sounds to contrast with what we'd seen.

"Michel de Vernase must have trod close to the answer," said Dante after a while. "The king has received no ransom demands? No encouragement to change . . . anything . . . in exchange for the conte's life?"

"No. I hope to pick up Michel's trail at Seravain."

Dante paused between the two arched gates that led into the more traveled pathways of the palace. He was little more than an angular shape in the dark. "This morning Gaetana asked if I could translate a treatise on the divine elements, written in her family's private cipher. They seem to have lost the spellkey to the code. I accepted the task."

Heat rushed through my limbs and fluttered my belly. After a day that seemed to have wrung every possible emotion out of me, it took me a

moment to recognize sheer excitement. My eyes met Dante's. Their feral brightness near blinded me.

"Good," I said, matching his ferocity. "Excellent."

He nodded. "I should make my own way from here. You're off tomorrow, you said?"

"Yes. I'll be gone three days. Four at most. If you need something right away, Ilario returns to Merona in the morning."

He turned to go, but hesitated halfway round. "You oughtn't trust the peacock. His untruth is seated so deep, it is scarce detectable. Your king trusts him at his peril."

"Lies about what?"

"If I knew, I'd hardly keep it secret, now would I?"

"I've questioned Ilario," I said. "I've had my own reservations about him, especially after the *Swan*. But I see naught but a good-hearted, ridiculous man, who loves his half sister inordinately. He's made a place for himself in this world—not one you or I would want, but one that seems to suit him. Give me evidence of something else, and I'll take it to the king."

Dante shrugged. "I've no source you'd credit."

"Tell me when you do. And by the bye"—I raised my bandaged hand, ignoring the barbed spikes that shot up my arm with every movement—"thank you for this. It feels better already."

He snorted rudely. "Lies do not become you, student. Tend the hand. Use it. You'll be glad."

He started for the gate, a strange, lonely figure, his white staff marking his passage. Where, in the Father's creation, had he come from? "Master," I called after him. "Does *your* blood shield you from the spectres of the spyglass?"

His answer drifted backward as his shape merged into the dark of the garden arch. "I don't pray."

CHAPTER THIRTEEN

The sultry breeze ruffled the pages of five years' worth of logbooks heaped on the library table. Nidallo, the soft-bodied adept temporarily assigned to my position as Collegia Seravain's curator of archives, hovered at my shoulder, disapproving. "You must allow me to close the casement, Acolyte Duplais. Constant temperature and gentle handling are critical to preservation. And I don't understand why you need so many logbooks out at once."

The sun-sweetened airs of Seravain's rocky vale had cleansed the musty odors of deadhouses, royal crypts, and haunted alleyways from my head. I wasn't about to shut them out. How had I borne fifteen years in these stifling precincts—nine of them closeted in this dusty labyrinth of book cupboards, lamp-grimed walls, and age-darkened study tables?

"Note the dryness of the parchments in the older journals," I said. "Experience informs us that more water would improve the balance of elements in the preservation spells. The moisture in the air will suffice. Surely you don't suggest immersing the books in water, Nidallo?" My recent practice at fabricating lies served many circumstances on this journey.

"Certainly not!" He shook his head sharply, as if trying to extract sense from my logic.

"Then keep the windows open. And if you could give me a better idea who might have borrowed *A Treatise on Heaven and Earth*, I would not need so many volumes. Visiting scholars borrow books every week. You must keep a running tally, compiled monthly at the very least. I've a notion it was Ydraga de Farnese who last requested this work, but have no idea when the good woman last visited. If you had to deal with this new mage at Castelle Escalon, you would understand my determination! He is the most unreasonable, crude, demanding . . ."

Angels protect me, I babbled like Ilario. The torrent of words poured from my mouth, each whorl and eddy leading poor Nidallo farther from espying my purpose—or so I hoped.

The adept retreated to his search for the missing treatise. He had not seen me slip the exquisite little volume into my pocket within a half hour of my arrival at my old haunts.

I stretched out my newly unbandaged fingers and settled back to work in the quiet niche. Nidallo's irritated mumbling at the disappearance of a valuable text kept me apprised of his location.

Switching logbooks frequently enough to prevent anyone from noting which most interested me, I jotted more entries in my journal. The gate warden's log confirmed that Michel de Vernase had indeed visited Seravain twice the previous year, the first time shortly after the assassination attempt, the second a tenday after his letter to the king hinting at new information and an extended journey. He had met with six senior mages on the first occasion, and only two on the second. Both times he had spoken with Kajetan, as well. That was only to be expected. Seravain's chancellor received every high-ranking visitor.

As I recorded Michel de Vernase's visits and appointments, I encoded them with shifted notation, even within my usual cipher. I shifted times, dates, and other names in a similar fashion. The need to mask my inquiries wrenched my soul. Collegia Seravain had been my haven from family upsets and an unwelcoming world, a serene community of the mind where I could explore and contemplate the wonders of a mystical universe. Yet its genteelly crumbling walls enfolded ugly secrets, tainting my memories as if mold had crept out of its corners. A sorcerer associated with the col-

legia had vilely abused Ophelie de Marangel right under our noses for *months*. How could those of us entrusted with children's minds—myself included—have been so inexcusably blind?

I recorded and encoded every reference to Ophelie, as well. In the early days of her residency, the girl had made occasional day visits to Seravain village, usually in company with the same few students—names duly noted. She had spent short holidays with the families of these same girls, only returning to her home in Challyat for the month-long harvest recess.

Library records scribed in my own hand indicated that three years ago, against all earlier indications, Ophelie had advanced to the rank of adept. That is, she had demonstrated sufficient talent and skill to study serious magic. The timing jibed with Dante's estimate of when she had begun bleeding herself. Only lunatics and desperate children could find logic in bleeding away one's soul to unblock the wellsprings of magic. Ironically, only an innately talented child could derive benefit from the attempt.

Sometime in the next year—long before she had been moved to the crypt at Castelle Escalon—a more experienced hand had begun taking her blood. Certainly in the months after her advancement, Ophelie's habits had changed dramatically. She left the school only rarely, at first alone, later in company with a different girl, a younger student named Lianelle ney Cazar.

Everyone knew the Cazar girl. Tutors considered her talented but erratic, and were forever chastising her lack of discipline. I recalled her as unremittingly annoying. She would demand to read every work in the library, even the most advanced texts, on obscure topics such as animal summoning or bone reading, rather than choosing a broader selection of materials suited to her age and level. And she had plagued me with endless questions about impossibilities, such as invisibility or altering time. I had never realized she and Ophelie were friends.

I jotted another date . . . then jerked my pen from the page. "But that's the same—" The words slipped out before I knew it.

"Is something wrong, Portier?" Nidallo imposed his beaky face into

my light again as I flapped a page of my journal back and forth and back again to verify what I had just noticed.

"No, no. I just thought I had found Ydraga's name in Mage Gadevron's appointment list for the thirty-first of last Ocet, but my eyes played tricks on me. I'm not yet accustomed to these spectacles."

But the surprise had nothing to do with Ydraga, and there was no mistake. As I had encoded the last instance of Ophelie and Lianelle visiting the village, it struck me that I had encoded the same date on a previous page. It was the exact day of Michel de Vernase's first visit to Collegia Seravain.

I quickly scanned the gate log for additional references to Lianelle ney Cazar. The younger girl had gone out on her own early that same morning of Michel's visit, noting her intended destination as *the fields*, and her purpose as *to collect fresh herbs for a formulary project*. She had returned an hour later.

Flipping through the wide pages, I skipped to the occasion of Michel's second visit. A scrawled notation glared up at me. Lianelle had left the school on *that* morning, as well, with destination *Tigano* and purpose *to return a stray dog*. She had returned to the collegia less than an hour before Michel de Vernase's arrival. I gave no credence to coincidence.

Not daring to feel excitement, I spent the next hour retrieving all the information I could glean about the Cazar girl from the archives. She returned to the Cazar demesne for school recesses, but otherwise left the collegia only on class outings. She took no more of the "village market" excursions she had taken with Ophelie. She had appeared before disciplinary boards at least twelve times in three years, and had been placed on probation twice.

It would be awkward to find the girl. Classes were already completed for the day. Only specialized tutorials went on in the hour before supper. For students not involved, it would be free time. . . .

I pushed away from the desk enough to spy around a corner to Nidallo's desk. The handwritten paper posted on a nail beside it provided a possibility.

"Adept Nidallo!" I called. "I need assistance retrieving some additional materials for Master Dante. Have you this month's restriction list?"

Lianelle ney Cazar had spent half her time on the restriction list since she had arrived at Seravain.

I smothered a smile as I perused the notice. Indeed the girl's name appeared along with those of six other students available for extra work during their free hours due to disciplinary infractions. Nidallo roused a student from a corner table to fetch the two malefactors I selected.

As I waited, I occupied my twitching fingers by reshelving logbooks. On a whim, I flipped the student log to Maura's records, thinking to discover some common bent that might lead to conversation outside palace business. I'd spent much of the two-day journey to Seravain reliving our pleasant hours working on the Exposition and planning what I might say when we next met. Unpracticed at casual conversation and with so much of my present life secret and my past dull or melancholy, I felt as nervous as an acolyte.

The record provided only one interesting tidbit. I had assumed Maura abandoned her studies for the same reasons I had, but indeed she had passed the intermediate examinations for adept's rank with high recommendations in all disciplines. Her claim that sheer boredom had sent her to court must be the truth. The reason was certainly not lack of talent.

Shuffling footsteps rounded the corner into my niche. I shoved the logbook back into its place.

"Divine grace, Benat, Lianelle," I said, exposing my hand to a fidgeting, spotty youth of about fifteen and a wiry, sun-browned girl a little younger.

"And w-with you, Ac-c-colyte . . ." The stammering boy exposed the back of his hand.

"Sonjeur de Duplais," said the girl, scarce dabbing her small hand on her shoulder. Her gray eyes raked me from head to boot. "Are you come back to Seravain, then, Curator? Everyone says you gave up and left because you couldn't read your way past the examinations."

Lianelle was exactly as I remembered her. Dark green student's gown stained and wrinkled. Hair escaped from two braids and frizzed about a smudged face. Speech neither belittling nor sarcastic, but merely uncomfortably frank for a girl of thirteen.

"I am now attached to Queen Eugenie's household," I said. "And I require assistance obtaining materials for Her Majesty's mages. As you may remember, I like to ensure that students on restriction make good use of their time." To be sure, I had called on the quiet Benat, continually disciplined for his inability to speak clearly, more often than the brittle-edged Lianelle.

I whipped out my transcriptions of Dante's odd requests, items ranging from crystals of blue-white antimonium to several types of exotic feathers to shards of Fassid pottery and Syan porcelain, many of which were difficult to obtain outside a sorcerer's supply room. The requirements were so numerous and so varied, requiring trips to the aviary, the metallurgical store, and several individual mages in addition to the general supply cupboards, it should take the students several hours to fetch them all—longer, in truth, as I had split the list most unfairly, leaving all the most difficult acquisitions to poor Benat.

Once the two were dispatched on their errands, I began packing a stack of borrowed volumes into crates destined for Dante. Inevitably my mind turned to the Mondragoni texts. Since the day I had refused his demands to acquire them, our mystery had spiraled deeper into a darkness where innocents died in fire and a conjured spectre drove a decent man to despair. Illicit power for sorcery and transgressing the boundaries of death were exactly the specialties of the Mondragoni, who had named their family the Brotherhood of Malevolent Spirits. How could I deny Dante any resource that might lead to understanding our quarries' aims?

Acquiring the texts would not be easy. Assuming I could find an excuse to visit the vault and abscond with forbidden materials, in no way could I take them all. The collection comprised more than fifty bound manuscripts and scrolls—far too many to escape notice were anyone to come looking and find them missing.

"Adept," I called, "could someone have shelved our missing treatise in the vault by mistake?" The short downward stair to the library vault began in an alcove just past the curator's desk. Impossible to pass without Nidallo's noticing.

"No," he snapped, slamming a large herbal on my book stack. "Every visit to the vault is supervised. Just because you no longer serve as curator does not mean the library has fallen to ruin."

"No, no. Certainly not. But you see, I myself might have put the book there a few months ago. I seem to recall hearing that the Challyat copy had been destroyed in a fire. I was concerned that our original would be the only remaining version. Perhaps we could take a look." As I had done frequently during the day, I tapped my fingers idly on Maura's document authorizing my access to all Seravain's resources.

Huffing in profound offense, Nidallo retrieved the keys from his desk. The vault door swung open with a dull clang. The adept hung a lamp from the drop chain in the center of the small stone room, then planted his back against the door frame and waved a hand at the two small cupboards and three chests—one of wood, one of leather, and one of iron. "Quickly, if you please."

The cool, windowless chamber housed what few magical texts had survived the Blood Wars. I touched the brittle volumes reverently, noting a threadbare cloth cover that had split, and a gilded title that had tarnished to unreadability. Few people ever looked at the fragile, fading texts. Many, like the Mondragoni collection, were encrypted. A few appeared entirely blank, their information beyond our current skills to retrieve, though age, wear, and the presence of encrypting enchantments bespoke certain significance. Some texts had been composed in obscure dialects or comprised little more than extensive references to even older works we did not possess. The essential knowledge from the readable texts had long been distilled into the *Encyclopaediae of Workable Formulae*, ten volumes filled with detailed instructions that students were required to memorize and practice. What spells responded to a particular student's talents might take a lifetime to master. It left little time for browsing.

A librarian, on the other hand, had plenty of time for study. Nine years had I scoured these source works for explanation of my failure. Though providing no answers, the effort had taught me a great deal about the deterioration of our art. Page after page referred to magic unknown to our experience—control of earth movements, protective wards reliable

enough to prevent the spread of diseases, techniques to address afflictions of the mind. . . .

What had the Bardeu villagers said of Dante? *'E fixes them as is cursed in the mind.* I had assumed the mage worked such standard remedies as sleeping potions or sedating enchantments. But back then I'd not yet experienced the strength of his will, the compulsions he could induce, the explosive energies of his magic. Could he truly address aberrant reason? What a blessing such an ability would be, and what terrible risk, too, if such power belonged to one without scruple or moderation. We knew so little about him.

But then again . . . I flexed my fingers, pocked with healing burns. Perhaps my experience of the man spoke more of his true nature than his own words did. For better or worse, I trusted him.

My survey of the cupboards complete, I rummaged through a heap of leather scroll cases in the wooden chest. "No books at all in here," I said, as if unfamiliar with the contents.

Nidallo rolled his eyes and fondled his keys.

Whispering the spellkey to release the locks and wards, I thumbed the slight indentation on the side of the iron chest. As I opened the lid, a stench of black mold rolled out. I pressed the back of my hand to my nose, aghast.

Four or five mold-ravaged texts, each marked with the scorpion device of the Mondragoni family, all that remained of thirty-three bound volumes, lay half submerged in a sea of green-black slime. Only three of nineteen leather scroll cases had survived, soggy parchment protruding from long cracks in their sides.

My thumb brushed one of the sodden pages. For one seemingly endless moment, the bones of my hand screamed with a cracking pressure. Then scroll and case slumped into a formless mass as would a lead slug thrown into a smithy furnace.

Was I meant to believe that ordinary mold and rot had so completely devoured these manuscripts in the two years since I'd brought them to the vault? Did someone think my senses too dull to recognize such powerful, corrosive spellwork?

Scrambling for explanations, I shut the lid and sensed nature's sigh as the magical wards settled back into place. The chest's magical protections remained intact—unforced. Even if Kajetan had changed his mind and chosen to destroy the documents, he'd never have destroyed them in place. The Gautieri, a powerful blood family, had encrypted all Mondragoni works as unfit for common readership, and then themselves been wiped out in the Blood Wars. Perhaps they had sealed the pages with destructive spells, as well, and we had triggered them by moving the documents here. I could not recall the last time I had inspected the chest.

"Mold's got in here," I said, tapping the iron box. "Best purge the entire chest, lest the blight spread to other books."

"When I have time," said Nidallo with a yawn. "I've more important things to do than play charwoman." Either he knew very well what had happened to the collection or he had no idea of its significance.

"You'd best make time to clean it up," I snapped. "These were incredibly rare. Master Kajetan will pillory you for this—and likely me, as well! Is your logbook complete?"

He frowned, blinking rapidly, thinking. "No one's come in here without signing the book. I'm sure of it."

The vault log lay open on its lectern. The open page covered two years. In the month since my departure, only two people had visited—Mage Samiel, a healer who frequently found an ancient herbal to be of use, and Mage Eliana, who studied family bloodlines. But Gaetana's tight signature glared from earlier on the page.

I had opened the vault for Gaetana many times. She had never demonstrated any interest in the Mondragoni chest, but then her frequent visits would have left her familiar with the drawer where I kept the vault keys. Perhaps she had removed some of the works—or most of them—before destroying the rest. As ever, I cursed my inability to identify magical imprints.

"No luck," I said, frustration finding an outlet as I slammed the last chest shut. "Is the *Heaven and Earth* treatise lost to mold, as well?"

"Honestly, Portier, I've taken good care of everything. I'm working here only until the chancellor appoints a proper curator." Nidallo had

sloughed off his self-important hurry and seemed genuinely concerned. "You'll not report me?"

I slapped him on the shoulder. "No. Maybe you'd best leave the mess locked up after all. If there's a scandal, I'll do what I can."

Nidallo huffed as we climbed the short stair. Awaiting us at the top was Lianelle ney Cazar. The girl hefted a basket half her height, heaped with packets, vials, and boxes. "I've got these things you wanted. May I go now?"

Nidallo returned to his desk, and the girl and I returned to my niche. "Empty the basket."

I surveyed her acquisitions. "Not at all correct or complete," I said, flipping through the contents of three leather packets. "Someday, Acolyte Cazar, you will learn to examine your work with a careful eye. Come along, let us try again."

"What are you talking about? I did everything just as—"

Grabbing the girl's arm, I hauled her past Nidallo and down the library stair. Clanging bells summoned students to supper. Thus, rather than exiting the main doors into the crush of people in the collegia's central yard, I drew her downward to the library cellar.

"Where are we going?" she croaked. "I fetched you everything on that ridiculous list."

"We need to discuss that," I said, moving even faster as she started wriggling.

A winding trip through deserted binding and copying rooms led us to the back exit and into a weedy enclosure. Around and above us, throughout the sprawl of collegia buildings, lights winked on one after another, like stars in the darkening sky.

"You're hurting me." Her voice rose, and her free hand flailed at my face. "What's wrong with you? Let me go."

She jerked away with strength enough that I needed both hands to keep her. I halted and gave her a firm shake. "Keep silent or I'll see you on restriction for the next seven years."

That at least gave her pause. I propelled her across the uneven bricks and through a gate into the long-neglected outer gardens. Honeysuckle

vines tangled in the arched trellises of an old pergola would shield us nicely from view.

"My regrets for the rough handling, Lianelle," I said. "I needed privacy to speak with you on a matter of grave importance. Will you listen?"

"I've nothing to tell you or anyone," she said.

Her belligerent stance only confirmed my suspicions. This was as stubborn a child as any at Seravain. "Your friend Ophelie de Marangel is dead."

Her small body stilled instantly.

"Cruelly dead from sorcery so wicked and terrible, I'll not speak of it unless you force me."

"Ophelie was *not* wicked." A child of thirteen ought to be more surprised at such news. She certainly knew what had killed Ophelie. Elsewise, nothing in the world would have prevented Lianelle ney Cazar from insisting I tell her.

"No, she was not," I said. "She was immensely brave and determined to expose the villains who hurt her so dreadfully. Unfortunately, I found her too late to help her."

"How—where did you find her?" Her voice quavered only slightly.

"At Castelle Escalon. She broke free of her captors. Just too late to survive."

"*Captors?* But they were supposed—but she went home!" Lianelle was not fast enough to cover her slip. She expected Ophelie to be somewhere else. Not home, but safe. "She was sick."

"Here's what I believe. Ophelie was bleeding herself to empower her magic. Someone here discovered it and began taking her blood for themselves. Lianelle, who was bleeding her? Did she see their faces?"

"I don't know what you're talking about. Ophelie never told me anything." No wavering this time. She was stubborn and angry, as only a child on the verge of adulthood could be. "She helped me with schoolwork, that's all. You've no cause to question me."

She tried again to wriggle away. I needed another tack.

"I've every right and reason to question you. Murder—this kind of

murder—is more serious than friendship or promises. No one who believes in justice can let it pass." Retaining a hold on her arm, I sat on a peeling bench and drew her close. "Let's start again. A simple exchange. Facts won't hurt anyone or betray confidences. I can discover facts in many ways, but asking you is easiest, because you were Ophelie's friend. When did you last see her? Last year, I know. Sometime after midsummer."

If I was right, the girls' meeting with Michel had occurred on 13 Siece. Michel's last letter to Philippe had been dated 17 Siece, and the conte had visited Seravain for the second time on the thirty-fourth day of that month.

"Sometime in Siece," she said after a long stare, as if to plumb the depths of my nefarious questioning. "Or maybe it was later in Nieba. Ophelie helped me with schoolwork. I'm terrible at memorizing. She had been sick all spring. She got worse and worse, but the adepts in the infirmary couldn't make her well. So she ran away home." The answer marched out of her as perfect and unnatural as a tutorial recitation.

"But just today I've checked the infirmary log and it shows no entries for Ophelie in the month of Siece or Nieba or at any time last year."

"Oh!" That surprised her, or at least set her thinking. "Why ask, if you already know?"

"In Siece of last year, a nobleman came here to question the mages about a crime in Merona—about someone who suffered the same injury as Ophelie. I'm thinking you might have heard about the man and his inquiries. Maybe you sneaked out early one morning to meet him, before taking Ophelie to see him. He returned here some days later. Was Ophelie still at the collegia when he came that second time? It can't hurt her to tell me that, and I can surely search the archives and find out. Give me the truth, and I'll tell you something important about that man."

Something in my patchwork of facts and guesses had struck home. She'd gone rigid as a post. Her pulse pounded like that of a frighted deer, choosing whether to run or stand her ground.

"Help me, Lianelle. The truth can't hurt her. Not anymore."

"She was still here." She near swallowed the words.

"All right. Good. Now I'll give *you* something. You may or may not know that the man's name was Michel de Vernase, Conte Ruggiere. He is a great friend of King Philippe. I need to know what you and Ophelie told him. I believe he's held captive by these same villains."

She jerked free of my grasp. I cursed the deepening dark that obscured her face, for I would have sworn she swallowed a cry. In any case, this answer came promptly. "We didn't meet any gentleman. No one took her." Quiet. Solid. Certain. Stubborn. "I can't tell you anything. I won't. I don't know you."

She was right to be cautious, no matter that we had seen each other on hundreds of occasions in the three years of her residency at Seravain. And yet—I rubbed my aching temple—her very assertion that she didn't know me was a deviation from her steadfast testimony . . . as if she might be able to tell me something if she *did* know me. If she trusted me.

That led me to examine the facts again . . . and they fell into perfect alignment. "Michel *took* her! He came back here that second time to fetch Ophelie. And you . . . you promised to keep it secret and helped confuse the days so no one would realize he'd taken her. *You* spread the rumor that she'd been sick and wanted to go home. That she'd run away. No one denied it. Those who had hurt Ophelie certainly wouldn't, and the collegia staff would be embarrassed that an ailing student had left without their knowing. But the villains guessed what Michel had done, caught up with them, and took them both. And if so . . . Child, you are in terrible danger. If anyone suspects you know what happened to her, who was hurting her . . ."

"Ophelie ran away. She just wanted to go home. Everyone heard us talking about it. Why would I stay here if I knew anything dangerous? I'm not stupid." The faintest tinge of panic colored her bravado.

"Listen to me, Lianelle. Go home to your family." The Cazars were a very old blood family, descendants of ferocious marauders who had holed up in the mountains of Nivanne before even the Fassid had invaded southwestern Sabria. They could protect her. "Feign your own sickness. Fail your classes. Just get away from Seravain. You've no reason to trust me, else I'd take you myself. But you *must* go."

"Fail my classes?" Even afraid and angry, the girl trumpeted scorn. "Do you think I'm a loony? I've talent leaking out my ears, could the old cods here bear to admit it. I should already be studying for an adept's level. There's nowhere else I can earn my collar or stay in the Camarilla's grace. No one can make me give up my place here. *No one.*"

Souleater, spare me; how could I, of all men, argue that? What right had I to steal her future? She had survived for almost a year. And yet . . .

"Do you understand what these leeches do, child? Every day they pierce your veins and attach their cups and tubes and pumps. *Only a few millilitres today,* they say. *Only a thimbleful.* But over the months, as the blood drains away, your flesh withers until you cannot tolerate food or drink. Your soul withers until you're incapable of reason. They leave you nothing."

"I don't know what you're talking about." Her face but a pale blotch, she backed away to the end of the pergola. "I don't need you. Stay away from me."

Indeed, this very conversation dragged her deeper into danger. Why hadn't Michel de Vernase taken both girls? Had this one convinced him so easily, or was he simply careless of her safety? Blessed angels, the girls had trusted him. Yet I'd seen naught to evidence him as sympathetic to the wreckage he'd left in the wake of his investigation. First Calvino de Santo, then Ophelie . . . Perhaps Ilario's opinion of Michel was not so far off the mark.

"Lianelle, just tell me one more thing: Why did he wait? The conte? Why didn't he take Ophelie that first day, when he saw what they were doing to her? It was cruel . . . despicable . . . to leave her in such circumstances."

"He was *not* cruel!" she cried, her armored silence cracked.

As ruthless as any villain, I plunged my fist into that crack. "The conte *killed* Ophelie, Lianelle. Waiting . . . leaving her here those extra days . . . killed her."

"No! Ophelie agreed to go back. He *had* to know where to find what he was looking for; the place where everything started. As soon as she learned the name, I wrote him a letter, and he came for her. Only, I

guess"—a sob escaped her—"I guess it was too late." Her presence fluttered like that of a bird poised to take flight.

"What was the name, child? I swear on everything good and worthy in this world, I mean no harm to you or the conte. What did your brave, beautiful friend tell him? *What* was the place he was looking for?"

She bolted as she spoke, leaving the answer hanging in the thick air: "Altevierre."

CHAPTER FOURTEEN

*A*ltevierre. The word scratched on the crypt wall. The word Ophelie de Marangel had spoken with her last breath. The mystery Michel de Vernase had pursued to his doom. The *place* where everything started. I held the name close as I scurried back to the library and stomped up the stair, grumbling loudly about recalcitrant students. Was it a town, a village, a crossroads, a house?

Nidallo sat at his high desk near the library entrance, reading a volume of the *Encyclopaediae of Workable Formulae*. He broke off pieces of a steamed bun as he read, dabbing his fingers on a kerchief before turning each page. The *Catalog Geographia,* a bloated volume that purported to list all place names in the kingdom, sat enticingly nearby on a book stand. But its size made it impossible to disguise amid my lists and books, and my purported mission provided me no cause to consult it. Nidallo's presence put me back to work, sorting and packing the materials Lianelle and Benat had gathered.

As ninth hour of the evening watch boomed from the clock tower, I stuffed the last packet into Dante's crates. The last student had scurried off to his bed. Nidallo was dozing.

I had no sooner opened the *Catalog,* excited at the prospect of enlight-

enment, than a rangy, silver-haired man burst through the library door, his blue robes flying, his long arms spread in welcome. "Portier! Bless my heart, it is good to see you. I squeeze in a long-delayed sabbatical to visit my family—a short few months only—and what happens? My prized curator takes a whim to abandon his outpost of sanity and take up residence at Castelle Escalon! Do tell me you've come to reclaim your seat."

"Master Kajetan!" The room felt excessively hot of a sudden, as guilt robbed a long-delayed reunion of its pleasure.

"No pouting, Nidallo!" The mage waved an eloquent hand at the groggy adept, stumbling to his feet. "You know Portier has ever been my goodson. Absent yourself for half an hour."

I crossed to my worktable before the chancellor's exuberant survey of my turnout could take in the open *Catalog*. "It's fine to see you, sir. No one told me you were expected back any time soon." In fact I had rejoiced that my long-time mentor remained on leave. Far easier to tell him lies in prose than while facing his iron gray gaze.

"I'm not actually returned." Kajetan paused as a sullen Nidallo gathered bun and book and left us. "To speak truth, I was visiting my sister in Tigano," he said, silver collar flashing in the lamplight, "debating whether to extend my leave a while longer. But Charica sends me a daily report on collegia business, and there at the top is your name. So I needs must come and demand explanation." He spun and surveyed the open crates, stacked books, and my journal, ink, and scattered lists. "Are you truly reduced to groveling for your cousin's favor? I believed I had instilled in you some sense of your own worth."

"It's very complicated, Master. I . . . needed to move on. Or rather, to come to some resolution about my father. I'd like to get the past out of my head once and for all. You know the conflicts it has caused me. . . ." I embellished those points of motivation and uncertainty that jibed with what he knew of me—likely more than anyone in the world, including my mother.

Philippe could not know what hardship he had imposed when compelling me to deceive this man. As a new student at Seravain, I had lived in awe of Kajetan's magic, skills that allowed me to explore cities while

sitting in a forest or to stroke a purring cat in my lap when only a block of wood lay there. But as I grew more sophisticated in analyzing spellwork, I came to see that his illusions resembled pretty paintings on silk more than fully fleshed sculptures. His greater gifts were incisive intellect and devotion to a world enriched and strengthened by our glorious art. Inspired by his eloquence and demand for excellence, every student at Seravain held strong against the winds of popular scorn.

The chancellor had personally assumed my tutorial when a broken leg forced me to spend my first harvest holiday at Seravain. Unlike most of the collegia's mages, he had never chastised me as I repeatedly failed at the magical tasks he set, nor had he offered maudlin sympathy when I recognized my defeat. Rather, with unyielding candor, he forced me to confront the truth of my failed magic and confess it aloud, so that I might hear the verdict in both ear and heart, and then he guided me through the storm that followed. He had saved my life both in metaphor and in literal truth. For on that terrible night when I confessed my failure to my father and became a father-slayer, Kajetan had stanched the bleeding. Once I had recovered, he gave me a refuge among these books, a position ordinarily forbidden to incapable sorcerers. I could never repay such debts.

"I don't understand this need to humiliate yourself to enhance Onfroi's afterlife," he said, resting his backside on my worktable. "You despised your father—and rightly so. Weak and willfully blind, he allowed an insignificant detail of birth to consume his life. He turned his back as his only son came near destroying himself to prove himself a man of substance, and then laid his own hand to complete that destruction. Onfroi deserves to languish in Ixtador and endure whatever unpleasantness that entails. Let the Souleater take him on the Last Day."

"Master, please don't. . . ."

He clapped me on the shoulder. "But then, you've always had a tender heart. No matter that I've tried to stiffen it a bit."

He had hammered honesty into me, and honesty stripped away any argument that might rebut his disrespectful logic. So I let the matter drop. When he picked up the spectacles I'd set aside and waved them in the air,

I yielded to his good humor and returned his teasing grin. "You forced me to study too much, Master. My eyes are old before their time."

But I near choked as he set the spectacles aside and fluttered the pages of my journal. And I relaxed only slightly when he picked up Dante's scrawled list of materials. I truly did *not* want to explain my day's work. Kajetan was intimately familiar with my record keeping and knew how unlikely I was to forget the very details I'd used to confuse Nidallo.

As much as Kajetan was my friend and mentor, he was a prefect of the Camarilla. The mages I pursued lived under the aegis of the Camarilla, as well. In no way could I imagine Kajetan a partner in horrors, but, as I had oft told Ilario, personal feelings could not chart our course. Our success and safety as *agentes confide* mandated absolute secrecy.

"So this mage who can dispatch you on errands like a mindless lackey is our mysterious *Exsanguin*?" he said.

"It seems he is."

I deliberately released my fingers that were clenched in nail-digging knots. Dante had earned his rank legitimately. He served at the queen's pleasure, under her protection, and had done nothing to draw Camarilla censure. It was only natural Kajetan would be curious.

"My current employer, the queen's foster brother who is addicted to charms and luck spells, ran across this Dante practicing in some village in southern Louvel, the very demesne *Exsanguin* claimed as residence. His collar is properly sealed with the Seravain mark; yet the woman who administers the consilium told me he submitted no references and refused to claim even a birthplace as a surname. Master Dante told her the Camarilla wouldn't know him, save by 'the annoyance of his collaring.'"

"I don't like it," said Kajetan, his lean face skewed to a frown. "Naturally, the Camarilla requires regular communications from Orviene and Gaetana, but their work has so little commonality with what we do here, their reports are quite arid and dismissive. I think those two are something jealous of their privileges." His brows lifted and his full lips stretched wide in good humor. "So tell me about our extraordinary mage. Have you witnessed his work?"

"Some." Knowing with what severity the Camarilla viewed uncan-

onical teaching, I was inclined to minimize the truly startling aspects of Dante's practice. Yet our plans required that Dante tread the boundaries of legality close enough to avoid Camarilla indictment, while demonstrating power of the kind valuable to rogues. Kajetan communicated with everyone in the Camarilla and his rumor could only further our aims. Thus, I set about filtering the truth. Omitting all mention of spyglasses and strange patterns written inside my eyelids, I reported my experience of Dante. "He is ill-mannered and has an unwholesome affinity for violent behavior, but I'll say I've rarely sensed such power as he wields. . . ."

The chancellor did not interrupt as I told of the strangely composed circumoccule, the fiery display in the deadhouse, the shattered gaud, the rumors of mind healing, and the extraordinary, lingering virility of Dante's public magic.

When I'd done, Kajetan's fingers combed his close-trimmed silver beard. "Hearing of such strength in an unknown of such erratic temper. We've heard rumor of transference revived—"

"No, no, Master!" My explosive dismay sharpened Kajetan's attention, leaving me fumbling to recover. "I mean, I can't believe *any* mage would be mad enough to start that up again. Even Dante, disagreeable as he is."

But how could I defend him? A mage so driven to discovery and so little grounded by family, society, or moral persuasion as Dante was certainly *capable*.

Kajetan fingered the scattered pages on my table. "Portier, would you feel it unseemly to leave me a copy of these lists? We live in a delicate balance. Should our art be dragged into evil yet again, I cannot imagine we would survive it."

Our art. *We.* The Camarilla. My kind mentor had never overdrawn the line that excluded me from his fraternity. Yet Kajetan's quiet request, spoken with such sincere concern, exposed that boundary for an uncomfortable fracture. My mentor and I did not, and would never, share a position in life, or experience the "delicate balance" of sorcerous power and political governance in the same way. But I dared not challenge him on it, lest it suggest some personal investment in Dante's concerns.

"I understand, sir. I see no harm in leaving you Dante's lists. He never claimed them private. I'll leave copies with Nidallo."

Kajetan smiled and clasped my hand, his smooth thumb tracing the Savin mark on the back of my hand and the knife scar that scored my wrist and vanished under my sleeve. "I could not persuade you to come back here, my son? Nidallo, for all his gifts, has not your good mind or your love for the art, both of which have been left stronger, I believe, by your deficiency in practice. I feel better trusting all this"—he waved his hand to encompass library and archives—"to one who has actually *read* our history."

I drew my hand away, and my gaze dropped to the region of his hem lest he observe my guilt. "Someday, Master, perhaps. The world remains an uncomfortable place."

"Indeed so. Have you found acquaintances in Merona? Here, alas, you seemed caught between students and staff. I hoped your new situation might provide you companionship at least."

"Not many at court deem a fool's private secretary worth cultivating, though I've met a few friendly sorts—the steward's third secretary, a guardsman or two."

"Your blush betrays you, lad. Could you have found a woman undaunted by your awkward connections?" Though his own wife chose to reside with her wealthy family in Tallemant, Kajetan had ever urged me to ensure my future beyond the Veil by contracting marriage—through a marriage agent, if naught else. "Tell me, who is she?"

"I've met someone amiable. Likely no more will come of it than usual." No matter my disclaimer, thoughts of Maura induced a most pleasurable anticipation. She was so different from anyone I'd met—so sensible, so lacking in artifice.

He laughed heartily and jumped up. "Forget the past, Portier, and forge ahead. I'll be awaiting happy news. Now, I must be off. If I wish to continue my sabbatical, I must be away again before Charica hears I've come."

"Good night, Master."

He paused in the doorway, sobriety erasing good humor. "I must in-

sist, Portier: Anything you learn of this Dante, send it to me. Particles that fit no known formulas, mind healing, extraordinary power—his practice feels most disturbing."

Had my old friend made this request a month before, I would have acceded instantly. I'd have agreed that a prefect of the Camarilla could not but draw on every resource to ensure magic's purity. But no matter urgency or righteousness, my newfound understanding of spying made his demand distasteful. Unlike Philippe, whose position gave him authority to demand such uncomfortable service, and with whom I had no personal bond but common ancestry, Kajetan compelled my obedience with ties of respect, affection, and gratitude. Transference—the worst perversion of sorcery—had occurred here, under his own watch. Did he suspect? How could he have missed it?

I could speak none of these arguments, nor question him. Sure as I stood there, he would prod and poke for explanation. I rubbed my arm, where the ragged scar yet pricked from his touch, an indelicate reminder of debts unpaid.

"Certainly, Master. As you wish." It was the only answer possible. "Though I fully intend to avoid the man, now I've satisfied his requirements. As ever, I am an abject coward at confrontation."

"Nay, lad. Speak not so slighting of my best work." His elegant hand touched my cheek, and with his usual wink and flourish, he hurried away.

Unsettled with these conflicts, propelled with a heightened urgency to complete my mission before Nidallo returned, I sped to the lectern and leafed quickly to the alphabetical listing of the *Catalog Geographia*. No entry corresponded with the name Ophelie had bled to discover.

The royal geographers who assembled the *Catalog* were known for their prejudices. They listed locales in Louvel, Aubine, Nivanne, and Tallemant in detail. But they frequently left out much from the less-prosperous demesnes-major, or places that lay in the demesne-minor of a personal or family rival. To find the most accurate information, of which the *Catalog* was but an organized extract, one had to look to the unwieldy volumes of the Survey, the census taken at the outset of each Sabrian king's reign.

Hastening into the Survey Room, I pulled out the index volume of the *Survey Philippi*. Even more than before, the painful sense that I must not expose my purposes consumed me.

Altevierre did not appear in the Survey's summary list of great houses, nor anywhere in its sparse index. I removed my spectacles and pressed the heels of my hands into my gritty eyes, forcing myself to concentrate. I had no time to read the entire Survey. The spelling of *Altevierre* rooted the word in central Louvel, whose lexicon had become standard as printed books spread throughout the kingdom. But Ophelie might have misspelled an overheard name. Perhaps the word drew from an older tradition. . . .

Altevierre could be interpreted as *highest view*. I pulled out the Survey volume devoted to Grenville, the rugged demesne to the north, where local dialects had evolved from the same invaders who had populated Dante's Coverge. I scoured every entry—every farmstead, house, village, and crossroads—and found nothing.

Growling in frustration, I tore through the slim collection of pages devoted to mountainous Coverge, but Sabria's poorest demesne-major had no great houses, farms, or towns, only scattered mining settlements, none of which came anything close. I ran my fingers over the remaining volumes. As a fish hooked and drawn, my finger halted on the slender volume entitled *Demesnes-major: Arabasca*. I snatched the book from the stack.

A door slammed. Measured footsteps echoed on the library stair. I dared not stop. Who knew when I might get another chance?

My finger sped through the pages, pausing at any name remotely similar. And there it was.

Eltevire: Seven-and-thirty residents. Nine men of arms-bearing age. A hundred eleven goats. Eight stone houses. A temple ruin and watchtower, ca 450 SE, both scavenged for building stones. Watering hole. Dry well. Thirteen knives. Two axes. Access by goat track and stone bridge, three kilometres due north of the shrine at Canfreg Spring.

A goat track to access a watchtower—a highest view. I shoved the Arabascan volume into the stack and slammed the book cupboard shut.

Then I snatched up the lamp and turned to go. Nidallo loomed in the archway opposite.

"Your lists made no mention of Survey volumes," he said, glaring at my hands, as if expecting evidence of theft. "They do not leave the library."

Emboldened by discovery and fueled by an unfocused anger, I had no trouble with this play. "I've taken no Survey volumes. Count them, if you wish. You are not privy to every matter my mentor and I discuss. Now, I've closed Mage Dante's crates with tamper seals. If you could provide rope . . ."

I oversaw the delivery of Dante's crates to a local drayman and left Collegia Seravain without another word to anyone.

Altevierre. Eltevire. I should have known to look to Arabasca first. Some two years before, I had retrieved a cache of books unearthed from the ruins of a once-fortified Arabascan town called Xarles. Before and during the Blood Wars, Xarles and that entire corner of Sabria's eastern borderlands—crags and stony tablelands pocked with wildcat dens, hermits' caves, and robbers' lairs—had been the demesne of the Mondragoni necromancers.

HAD IT NOT BEEN MIDDLE-NIGHT at the dark of the moon, I would have set out for Arabasca immediately; yet simple wisdom insisted that investigating Eltevire on my own would be a fool's gambit. Despite my youthful dreams that had repeatedly anointed me the boldest of knights, I lacked the weapons to dispatch even a single despicable mage. Trained awareness of enchantments, paper knowledge, and a borrowed courret could scarce stand against magic bolstered by transference. And the manly art of righteous combat was as alien to me as the practices of sculpture or painting. The only "gentleman's swordmaster" my father could afford had been a drunken tavern brawler. I needed Dante.

A dreadful night in the local hostelry affirmed the sensible course. In the dark wakings between my own nightmares of glaring spectres and fleshless mules, and the mumbling, snoring, wind-ridden sleep of my

companions in the bachelor's loft, I resolved to save Lianelle ney Cazar. I would not force myself on the girl, but neither would I follow Michel's example and abandon her. Ilario would know her family. Somehow, in his odd way, he could devise a scheme to remove the girl from Seravain. Once that was settled, I'd devise some ruse to roust Dante and ride for Eltevire.

Even such resolution did not ease me into sleep. I spent the last hours of darkness huddled over a corner table in the inn's common room. Meg, the yawning, drop-shouldered woman who kept the shabby establishment, brought me ale and cold steamed buns left from the previous day.

"Yer back to Merona with first light, then," she said as she spitted a slab of bacon over her newly stoked fire.

"Aye. The great wicked city, all fish and sour wine, with evils round every corner." My mirthless humor echoed the common local opinions.

Meg bobbed her head, knowingly. "There was a lad from out near Oncet what went to Merona and near got hisself starved. . . ."

Citizens of Tigano prided themselves on exchanging lurid tales. Living in the shadow of the collegia magica seemed to expand everyone's imagination into the realms of the fantastic. This common room witnessed many a night of competitive tale-spinning. Yet made-up stories paled beside a plotted web that linked royal assassination and transference, Merona and Collegia Seravain, the living and the dead.

Of a sudden, my sluggish curiosity woke. What had people seen roundabout Seravain and Tigano? One sure way to prompt more stories . . .

"Your Oncet boy fared lucky even so," I said, issuing my challenge as soon as the woman's story wound to a bittersweet end. "Fellow in my lodging house at Merona was found murdered not long since. Ears, nose, and fingers cut off. Corpus dropped in an alley near the docks, emptied entire of his blood. The whore who lives upstairs says the man's ghost lingers in the lane. Scared three customers away. Dreadful things like *that* don't happen in Tigano."

Meg, dusted with flour and smelling of smoke, scooped up my emptied mug and refilled it from the tap. "Nah, boy. 'Tis not only in the city ghosts are walking. Every morn Bets the Seamer spies her gammy what

was hanged a'dangling beside her washing line, and Dame Fanny herself says her dead sons creep about their old rooms in the manse. None dares go to our deadhouse save in best daylight. But it's true, we've seen no grueish murders such as you're telling of."

"Be thankful," I said.

When she issued no new attack in our lurid joust, I drained my cup and gathered my traveling case to go. Too much to hope that evidence lay about the countryside awaiting my eye. I'd had a moment's thought that if Gaetana or someone else was practicing transference at the collegia, some evidence of a mule might have turned up here. They'd not dare use a second student.

"But then . . ." The woman's hand slowly turned her bacon. "I've not seen a man so staggered as Adept Coperno when Constable called him down from Seravain and he declared Grafer Wheelwright three times dead. Emptied half my tun afore he spake a word."

Meg blotted her sweaty brow with her sleeve, and she did not look up to make sure her tale had created the proper state of horrified amazement on my face. This tale frightened *her*, as well.

I lowered myself to the stool. For a constable to call in aid from Seravain was not uncommon. For an adept to be frightened by a corpse was something else again. And for that adept to be a cocky former classmate who had left Seravain abruptly a few years previous mandated a hearing. "Three times dead? I never heard such."

Though her complexion took on the color of soured milk, she could not resist the telling. "Grafer got drunk and beat his wife. As was his common way, he run 'ta the wood to sleep it out. But a trimonth passed and he never come home."

She filled herself a mug and dragged a stool up to my table. "Then it happ'd one night a crate was left in my own yard to be shipped off to Merona. No one spake me, but only left the proper coin with it. Come daylight, the drayman and his helper, loading their wain, dropped the crate"—she leaned close until I smelled the ale and garlic on her breath—"and 'twas Grafer curled up inside—dead. Constable called the coroner. But the coroner couldn't say what killed Grafer, as the lad had marks of

strangling on his neck, and yet had green scum lodged in his throat as though he were breathing and fell into Breek's Ditch."

She drank deep of her ale. "Adept Coperno come down from Seravain and worked his magic to seek which way Grafer died, so they could name the murderer. Three . . . four . . . five times over he worked it, till he puked all over the deadhouse floor, for he'd no magic left in his blood to fire his spellmaking. Once he drunk up my ale, all Coperno said was, 'Three times dead. Strangled and died. Stabbed and died. Drowned at the last. And maybe more besides, but my seeing failed me.' And then he stumbled out and's ne'er again come down the hill."

A story to make anyone blanch. A story that teased and nagged and roused a certainty that this was no exaggeration, but very much a part of the exact same story I lived. "That's a cruel, wicked tale, mistress. This happened when? Six . . . seven . . . years ago?"

"'Twas exactly three years past, come midsummer, as it happened when my daughter was confined with her youngest, and we had a charm-singer in to ward her house from—" The innkeeper flushed and jumped up, as if she'd just recalled that I, too, was a follower of the Camarilla, who lashed or fined such unsanctioned practitioners as charm-singers. "Best get to my baking. Everyone will be up soon."

She stuck out her hand for payment. I rummaged in my belt purse, and the first coin I pulled out was the double-strike silver—Gruchin's luck charm. I'd never returned it to Dante. No reason not to spend it; silver was silver. But I slid the coin into my boot, then pulled out twenty copper kivrae and tossed them on the table.

"One more thing, Mistress Meg," I said, snagging her apron as she scooped up the coins. "Did the constable send after the one who was to receive the crate? Surely that person would have knowledge of the crime. I'd like to think such mystery simply explained—and well punished."

She downed her ale and shook color back into her sagging cheeks. "Constable thought same as you, but my lads had already broke up the crate and thrown it in their morning fire, and none recalled what was writ. Some say Grafer haunts Breek's Ditch. I've not seen him, but I don't go down there no more. 'Tis a wicked age we live in. Temples deserted.

Disbelievers growing bold. Folk forget their ancestors and make demon-ish devices that steal the stars from the heavens, and prison time itself in jewel cases. My mam said the dead rise to give us warning of evil times, and so I believe." She jerked her apron from my hand.

I rousted the stable lad, preferring to lead my mount until the light grew than to remain in Tigano one more moment. As I trudged along the rutted road, I could not shake the notion that Adept Coperno had met a fate no fairer than Grafer Wheelwright. Had the frightened adept gone back to Seravain and asked one question too many? For I would swear on my hope of Heaven that he had left the collegia exactly three years ago at midsummer without a word to anyone.

The rare physician could retrieve a life whose spark had dimmed past common detection. But only a sorcerer of uncommon power—only three I'd read of—had ever reclaimed a dying person from the very folds of the Veil. Only a sorcerer exploring the unholy might see use in repeatedly driving a man to that brink and snatching him back again.

The light grew, tinting the scant clouds with vermillion and rose. Old Meg's story had raised such dread in me that I felt near drowning in it. I retrieved a flask from a saddlebag and drew down a long pull of ale, then pressed my face against my horse's flank. And in that moment of warm, living darkness, memory raised an image of freshly splintered wood . . . not Grafer Wheelwright's crate, broken and thrown in a fire, but long strips scattered in Ophelie's cell in the royal crypt. Great Heaven, had someone transported *her* to Castelle Escalon in a crate? And Michel—

My heart near stopped its beating. I had *seen* such a crate as could hold a tightly bound man, not two days after Ophelie de Marangel had escaped her prison. A crate exuding the stink of "mushrooms growing in dirt and dung" had sat in Castelle Escalon's steward's office. Had it held a dead man or . . . the god save us all . . . a living one?

I threw myself on my horse and pushed the poor beast unmercifully all the way to Merona.

CHAPTER FIFTEEN

The morning air hung heavy and damp in the bustling passages and courtyards of Castelle Escalon. I ducked my head as I forged through the ever-moving river of courtiers and servants. The sense would not leave me that anyone I *noticed* would turn up dead.

I had arrived the previous evening after two long days on the road, only to find the tally of the fallen grown to yet more dire proportions. Waiting in my apartments was a message from a devastated Ilario. Mage Orviene's adept Fedrigo, Ilario's favored maker of crocodile charms and stomach elixirs, was reported knifed in a tavern brawl near the docks and thrown dead into the river. And beside Ilario's scented paper lay a letter scribed in my own hand, still sealed, returned along with a message informing me that the Marqués and Marquesa de Marangel and their two young sons had met an unfortunate fate. An *explosion of devil's firework* had devoured Ophelie's home and family not a tenday past. Someone felt us on the trail of discovery. Every hour since learning this news had been filled with a creeping dread, the first tremors of an earthshaking that set birds and beasts to flight.

My morning's first task was to settle the matter that had gnawed at my vitals all the way from Seravain. Henri de Sain, third secretary to the palace steward, was my quarry of the moment. Assuming *he* lived.

Henri was sweeping his private office, which was not at all private and very unlike an office, being little more than a closet off the stone-floored, north-wing undercroft. Casks, trunks, and teetering stacks of crates shared the vast undercroft with a legion of undersecretaries, paymasters, footmen, draymen, and ladies' maids.

"Divine grace, Henri," I said, as if our two brief encounters had made us personal friends, "I just wanted to thank you again for the recommendation of your tailor. As soon as I've pay in hand, I'm determined to give him fair custom."

"Oh, very good," he said, looking a bit surprised as I occupied his stool, drawing up my knees and wrapping my arms round as if set to stay awhile. He set his broom in the corner and brushed off his sleeves. "Is there something I can do for you, Sonjeur de"—his eyes darted to my exposed left hand—"Savin-Duplais, is it? Portier?"

I bobbed my head. "Honestly, you're the only person in the palace who's been civil, so I didn't think you'd mind another inquiry. I've just returned from Collegia Seravain whence I shipped three book crates back here for this wolfhound of a mage, Dante." I screwed up my face in disgust. "The taverner told me a dreadful story about a crate that had been dropped in her yard, only to find a *dead man* in it. A *corpus* . . . to be shipped *here* to Castelle Escalon, she said! And not respectfully in a decent coffin as a family might do, with a verger's blessings and proper pall over all, but curled up tight in a nailed-up box as one would never suspect. Have you ever heard of such wickedness?"

"Nay." His nostrils flared in distaste. "Such a violation would be—"

"Exactly so. But you see"—I dropped my voice, drawing him nearer with every word—"I recalled that stinking crate you had in here not a tenday ago, just before the fire on the *Swan*, and it gives me the frights to think it might have been a corpse, as well. And I'm wondering— This Dante has already laid threats on me, you see. I'm bound by my duties to deal with him, but if he's the one shipping corpses about the kingdom or having them sent, I'm thinking to resign my post and hie me back to academe."

Henri's knotted brow softened. "You needn't fear, good Portier. He's

neither sent nor received any parcel whatsoever. That particular nasty crate—living mushrooms as I recall, destined for an apothecary in Mattefriese—originated with the least likely person to be engaged in abominations of any kind, Damoselle ney Billard herself."

The sunlight pouring into the dusty hall dimmed to gray. I heard myself laughing and prating about foolish anxieties and country superstitions. But all the time Maura's own words crowded my memory. "Some matters we cannot alter. Some promises we cannot undo." Eugenie herself had stitched only the new Destinne ensign on the celebration banners. Who but Maura would have seen to the ordering of linen and hiring of seamstresses and the delivery of the finished rolls? Maura, the queen's trusted household administrator, who had been unstrung since the fire on the *Swan*. And Mattefriese lay on the Louvel-Arabascan border, the last town of any size between Merona and Eltevire. Blessed angels . . .

My spirit recoiled. Rebelled. Yet, as if I had split into two persons at once, Portier, *agente confide*, nattered with Henri about his busy life in the palace, and all the crates and bundles that came through the palace, exclaiming how easy it must be to get them confused.

"As do you, I keep a journal," he said. "Everyone says I can recall names and dates and sizes as some recall their children's birth stars and lineage." Flushed, he waved off my feigned amazement. "I'll send notice when your boxes arrive. Then you'll be finished with this fearsome Dante. A footman I know saw the mage set fire to his food with his eyes. He was at table with the queen's ladies and claimed the meat was off. And the maid who washes his linen swears he can see through walls, as he forever opens the door before she knocks! Could that be true?"

"I'd put no outlandish talent past him," I said, truthfully. "But I'd best hush. What if he finds out I've spoken ill of him?"

Henri blanched.

"One more small thing," I said. "You've surely heard about this event Lord Ilario plans for Prince Desmond's deathday? I'll need banners to be made. . . ."

Numb already, I was scarce surprised to hear that the palace seamstress

who had sewn the banners for the *Swan* had slit her wrists, horrified that her faithful work had been used to endanger her king.

The third secretary would make a fine, credible witness, said I, the king's chosen *agente*, a lunatic who had dared imagine that out of this snarl of ghosts and murders something new and good might take root in his own sorry life. I made it as far as the wide steps of whorled marble that led into the queen's wing of the palace before I dived into a small fragrance garden to be sick.

The heaving seemed to purge my head as well as my stomach. Maura could *not* be involved in these crimes. I did not question my growing certainty that Henri's crate had held a living prisoner, but any of two hundred people could have attached Maura's name to it. She did favors for everyone in the queen's household. And surely fifty other people had been involved with the delivery of the banners to the *Swan*. Unlike her mistress, Maura had boarded the ship.

Questioned outright, she could surely provide an explanation for everything . . . only I could not ask. Secrecy must be maintained. Exoneration was not my prerogative. My charge was to gather evidence, make linkages, investigate, deduce.

I wiped my mouth on my sleeve and plucked mint leaves from a spreading plant. Chewing the pungent leaves, I headed for the east wing and Ilario's apartments, speeding through the curved window gallery that displayed the ruddy rooftops of Merona. I would task Ilario with saving Lianelle ney Cazar, and then persuade Dante to come with me to Eltevire. Unmask the true conspiracy, find the murderers, and all would be clear.

"Duplais!"

I near jumped out of my skin. A firm hand on my sleeve drew me out of the stream of footmen and maidservants to the window wall. "I've been hoping to speak with you, and here you manifest in my own haunts."

"Mage Orviene!" Every distraction receded as I bestowed my entire attention on the neat little man with pomaded hair, silver collar, and pleasant smile. I inclined my back. "Divine grace, sir. How may I serve you?"

His wide, soft features drew into a focused concern. "Excuse my ab-

ruptness, Sonjeur de Duplais, but I hoped you might be able to enlighten a grievous darkness."

"Whatever I can." Curiosity scorched my mouth dry.

"My assistant, Fedrigo, has gone missing for more than a tenday. A reliable report says he's been stabbed in a brawl and drowned, but I"—a nervous finger rubbed his rounded chin—"I cannot accept it. Drigo was an abstemious man, not at all inclined to gaming or rowdiness. I'm extremely worried about him."

Had I charms or amulets or enchanted swords to defend myself, every one would have been raised. Why would Orviene come to *me* with this?

"A grievous matter indeed," I said carefully, "but I scarce see how I can help you. Though my employer ever sings Adept Fedrigo's praises, I've met the fellow only once."

Orviene propped himself on the window seat and examined me with a sharp, wry glance. He cleared his throat. "Well, this *is* about your employer. Lord Ilario frequently hires Fedrigo for private spellworking, so I thought perhaps he might know why the lad might have gone down to Riverside or whom he might have met there. But your chevalier forever behaves as if I am a goblin lurking in his closet and refuses to speak with me beyond formalities. If *you* could enlighten me, I'd need not bother your master. And truly . . ." Of a sudden, the mage's whole posture shifted, as if a mask had dropped away. "My apprentices are as sons to me, Acolyte Portier. Drigo has no family save his mother in Delourre. How can I write her of his death, offering no more explanation than drunken foolery? She cannot even claim his remains."

The world stilled. "His body's not been found, then," I said.

The mage motioned me to bend my head closer. "You'll have heard whispers of the resurgent evil abroad in Merona, and that the practice might even be linked to the events on the *Swan*. I wish I could declare such rumor false. Any with a marked hand is at risk. I've urged my aides to stay wary, and so you should, as well. I fear greatly for Drigo's fate."

No trace of the bantering courtier remained, but only a sincerely troubled man afraid his missing apprentice might face a death more terrible than a tavern rowdy's blade in his craw. Dared I believe him?

"I can try to find out, sir mage," I said, slowly. "Naturally, I could not betray Lord Ilario's confidence."

"I'd never presume that."

"But if he knows aught of your assistant, I'll let you know."

"I would be most grateful." He offered his hand, palm up, requesting a trust bond—an old-fashioned custom among magical practitioners. Though I had no magic to forego, I laid my palm on his without qualm. Warm and steady, his hand conveyed no ill.

"Mage," I said, seizing an opportunity unexpected, "if you've evidence . . . or suspicion . . . that the fire on the *Swan* was linked to illicit practice, should not the Camarilla be warned? So many died."

One small hand flew to his mouth; the other jittered in a vigorous denial. "Merciful saints," he whispered, eyeing the passing maidservants and courtiers. "Forget the ravings of a loose tongue. Of all men, you should understand my position. Do I speak my suspicions, all will name it jealousy and ambition, an attempt to divert attention from my own . . . limitations. Even so, if the murderous fire *itself* gave me pause, I would speak out. But, it was not in the crime but in the remedy I felt the stirring of strength . . . extraordinary."

"In the caelomancy, then," I said. "You believe transference enhanced the magic wielded to bring the rain?" That jibed with Dante's experience.

He winced at the word spoken aloud. "We all reached for strength beyond our own that day. That was likely what I felt. If you hear aught of Fedrigo . . ."

"I'll inform you right away, of course."

Orviene could certainly be accused of jealousy and ambition. Gaetana was a master mage and the queen's First Counselor, privy to the queen's secrets, always first to be consulted, always at her right hand. No matter Orviene's popularity with courtiers and servants, it must appear impossible to gain ground on her. Was this only a play for sympathy or did he suspect my role? I could get no firm sense of the man.

I watched the mage hurry up the queen's stair, then turned into the passage where the three mages had their apartments. Morning light re-

vealed naught but dancing dust motes. When I rapped on Dante's door, enchantment grazed my knuckles like broken glass.

"He'll not answer."

I lurched around and slammed my back to the door. Truly, the morning had my nerves shredded.

A dark young man in adept's gray lugged a desk toward me, a stool upended on its top. His sharp features and trim beard looked vaguely familiar, which could likely be said of every young male adept in Sabria. Every one of them had passed through Seravain's library at some time or other. And every one of them grew a manly beard once he escaped the collegia's strictures.

"Is the mage away, then?" I asked, lending him a hand with the heavy table.

"Not that I know. He's only given up answering the door." He bobbed his head toward the stretch of wall beside Dante's door. "Just there, if you would."

We placed the desk as he wished, and he unstacked the stool, setting himself on it to catch his breath. "If the door is locked and warded, even I can't get in, which is why I've commandeered this desk. I'm hopeful that if I demonstrate a resolute spirit, my new master will decide he can use me after all."

"You're Master Dante's new assistant." Curse my distracted mind, where had I seen him?

He entwined his long fingers and rested them on the desk. "I confess it. Assigned three days ago. I've hopes of learning a great deal once he allows me into his chamber. You're the librarian from Seravain, the royal cousin. I'm greatly reassured that you survived your fiery resignation."

The deadhouse! This was Conte Bianci's adept. Recalling my craven posturing on that night set my complexion ablaze. "Aye, that's me," I said. "My temperament is ill suited to violence."

"Mine, as well," he said, grinning, "but the magic is incomparable." He flicked coal-dark eyes to Dante's door. "I'd sell my gammy to learn how he does it."

"I just know my gullet clamps shut whenever he points that staff at

me," I said, resisting the temptation to compare experiences of Dante's wonders. The poorer the common assessment of my capabilities, the better. "Paper knowledge feeds the soul and intellect, but provides little defense against fire spouts that char your clothes." I exposed my hand and bowed. "Portier de Duplais."

He returned the courtesy. "Jacard de Viole. I never thought to see you outside your archives, Curator. You were as imposing as the library facade. I believed you must have lived there unaging all the centuries since it was built and had accumulated all the knowledge to be found there. Your direction helped me through many an examination."

But not the final examination as yet. He wore no collar.

Many adepts left the collegia to apprentice with master mages, hoping to make the leaps of talent and insight that would carry them through mage testing. Most never made those leaps and never returned, remaining minor practitioners of the art under strict Camarilla supervision.

"Glad to hear I was useful," I said, unable to recall Jacard or his talents. "This new direction my life has taken . . . I'm not sure it suits as well. Which leads to business: I must inform Master Dante about the errands I've run for him—my last, as it seems."

"We can try."

Jacard popped up from his stool, tapped on the door, and pressed the latch. He did not flinch, nor did he examine his fingers as I did every time I touched one of Dante's wards. Nor did he seem to sense the flood of magical energy that rushed through the open doorway like a herd of newborn lambs. The whorls and eddies of power made me feel sixteen again, full of vigor and unsullied hopes.

"Master," said Jacard, as he stepped through the doorway, "Sonjeur de Duplais wishes to speak with you."

When I stepped out from behind the adept, shock stole my tongue. Illness or exhaustion had rewritten Dante's body in the five days since we'd visited Calvino de Santo and his spectre. He stood in the center of his circumoccule, leaning heavily on his staff. His eyes, circled in gray, had sunk deeper under his already-heavy brows. His gaunt cheeks were faded, as if these weeks of palace life had not just paled the sun-darkening

of his skin, but sucked out its natural coloring, as well. His thick, wide shoulders bent as if holding up the vault of the sky. Great Heaven, what had he been up to?

"I'll see no visitors today. No flea-wit assistants. And no failed cowards *ever*. Weakness offends me."

Cursing Jacard's presence, I stammered, "Master, I've only a brief—"

"I said *not ever!*" Blue and purple lightning belched from his staff. Gleaming spicules scored exposed flesh and pierced garments, flesh, and bone, stinging like frozen needles. Throat and lungs were seared with frost and my mind with a ferocious repudiation. Only a determined observer would have noticed how Dante's hand trembled as he extended the staff.

Jacard hurriedly dragged me back over the threshold. The door flew shut behind us.

The adept rubbed his arms, as if to make sure his skin remained whole. "Why did he leave the god-blasted door unlocked if he didn't want company?" he mumbled, kicking his stool against the wall so hard it bounced into the middle of the corridor, causing a passing maidservant to squeal and scuttle past.

I knew why. Dante had wanted to warn me off. *Don't come here ever.* Something had changed. My glance flicked to Jacard, reappraising. Did the danger lie in the new assistant himself or some other threat?

"Who can explain one like him?" I said. "When he allows you inside again, inform him that the materials he requested are on their way from Seravain. Father Creator, I'm pleased to leave him to one younger than I. May you learn enough to make your difficulties worthwhile."

"I'll give it a little time," he said. Heaving a sigh, he retrieved the stool, and settled himself on it, feet propped on the desk. As I rounded the corner into the window gallery, he pulled a book from the folds of his gown and began to read. He seemed ordinary enough.

Frustrated and concerned, I set out for Ilario's apartments. My imagining faltered at any *magic* which could cause so great a change. And what could induce Dante to refuse this one last meeting for which I had a reasonable excuse? I needed to tell him all I'd learned.

As I hurried up the broad curved stair to the royal level that housed the

elite of the queen's household, a cluster of ladies in cream-colored silks started down it. They twittered and buzzed softly like moths, the luminous Eugenie de Sylvae at their center. I moved to the side and bowed deeply as they passed.

As I straightened, the queen glanced over her shoulder and smiled ever so slightly. A tweaked corner of her mouth, crinkles at the corners of dark, sad eyes . . . I could not have said exactly how she framed an expression that left me awash in the knees. How could such ethereal beauty be tainted with the vileness of this conspiracy?

But then, I thought, as I moved on down the passage, Ophelie de Marangel might have grown into such a graceful woman. Who was left to weep for Ophelie but Lianelle ney Cazar and I? And if I didn't see to it, Lianelle's fate might mirror her friend's. I rapped on Ilario's elaborately carved door harder than I might have otherwise.

Oddly, the door opened but a crack.

"Lord?" I said, recognizing the pale blue eye that peered out at me.

"Heaven's mercy!" breathed Ilario as he opened the door just enough I could squeeze into his private sitting room. "I am not at all suited to hidings and sneakings."

As Ilario threw the latch, I watched in astonishment as another visitor stepped through a narrow gap in the red brocade wall, then shut a hinged panel, quickly rendering the wall whole again. Dante leaned his back against the hidden door and slid slowly to the floor.

"I JUST NEED SLEEP," SAID the mage, once Ilario and I had hauled him up and over to a couch. "Stop fussing."

"You look like death," I said, "or near enough. And you're not so fine as all that, if your legs'll not hold you up. When did you last eat?"

"Can't remember." He brushed his shaggy hair from his face and scrubbed his sunken eyes. "What did you want to see me about? I need to get back. Gaetana might come for me."

Ilario held a glass of wine under Dante's nose. "Start with this. I'll send for food."

Dante hesitated.

"Shall I sip from it first?" snapped Ilario. He slammed the glass onto the table he'd shoved next to Dante's knees, slopping the dark liquid over the rosy marble.

"I just . . ." The mage reached for the glass. His hand trembled so violently, he could scarce get it to his mouth without spilling it over himself. "Gods."

Making any plans or decisions in his state would be unlikely to serve us. "If you would, Chevalier, food is an excellent idea," I said. "I've not eaten since I got back last night. And you must partake, Master. I'd not like to waste my time on a corpse."

Ilario marched off to the next room to ring for a servant, slamming the door behind him.

"What is this about?" I said.

"Naught to concern you."

"Not so. We cannot afford you to be incapable. If you're ill, we'll fetch a healer. If it's something else, I want to know. We're nearing the crux of this mystery. I need you fit."

"I am not ill."

He would not meet my eye. Rather, his gaze traveled Ilario's apartment, as if to make sure no one lurked behind drape or statue. Certain marvels, like the Syan silk hanging of human-sized dancers, the elephantine urns trimmed in gold and bursting with flowers, and the round table-top of pink marble supported by intricately worked castings of fanciful beasts, caused his gaze to linger. Each time, he wrenched his attention away and fixed it on his staff for a moment before returning to his inspection. His color deepened when he noticed me watching.

Odd how that simple reaction forced me to look at him with new eyes. Curious, yet embarrassed to be caught gawking, he'd likely never been inside a wealthy man's private apartment. No matter his formidable talents, or his unique and powerful insights into magic, he was only a man, still young in countless ways. I needed to remember that.

"If not ill, then what?"

"There is a thing I can do . . . that I am learning to do . . . to read

another mage's spellwork from a distance and draw it into myself. So I can see the exact pattern of the enchantment—its keirna—even as it's being shaped." He gripped his staff and shifted uncomfortably on the thick blue cushions, as if he were eighty years old with grinding joints. "All sorcery requires certain expenditures. This requires more. That's all. I can manage it."

"To see into a living enchantment . . ." So casually he spoke of it. To make his mind an opticum that could see the invisible cells, not of stems and leaves and crystals, but of spells. He would be able to understand a spell's composition and intent far more completely than by analyzing its residue. He might be able to devise magic to counter it. Not even in the vault texts had I heard a glimmer of such a possibility. "Gates of Heaven, man, have you accomplished this?"

Counterspells, as I knew them, required endless trial and error and an assumption that a particular enchantment would be repeated to an exactitude. If we could know what the other mages were doing, we'd not have to insinuate Dante into their trust, and hope to make them spill their secrets in words.

He grimaced and ground the heel of his staff into Ilario's fine carpet. "I'm no good at it yet. But the last few attempts . . ." He glanced up, and I caught the feral gleam I'd espied in him so often. "Orviene has all the magical skills of a tool grinder, but he's careful. His poison wards are clean and meticulous. His sleep spells follow common practice and work as well as any. But Gaetana brings far more talent and a sharper will. Her work is complex; things like honing the fighting skills of the queen's bodyguards; sharpening their awareness. I've yet to pattern one of her works completely."

But he would. I could read it in him. Though it might kill him, he would.

Fed by his fever, ideas bloomed in my head like night lilies. "Perhaps we've been mistaken, assuming Orviene and Gaetana work together. Just an hour since . . ." I told him of the missing Fedrigo and Orviene's hesitation to report his suspicions of Gaetana. "He seemed sincere. Perhaps Gaetana's worked the transference alone or partnered with someone else."

"Mayhap." He considered for a long moment. "Orviene craves to be more than he is. But his magic doesn't *reach*. I'm no good to judge more than that. But the woman . . ."

Dante shifted again, and downed the remainder of his wine, wiping his mouth on his sleeve. Then he stared at the heel of his staff without speaking. I refilled his glass and summoned patience.

"I completed Gaetana's little translation task," he said, after a while. "A simple magical cipher. It was no treatise on the divine elements, but a few pages of a mage's scribblings. He was trying to prove that animals have souls by teaching them to understand human words, exploring techniques to disrupt their natural behaviors with regard to hunting, mating, pain, and the like. Some very unpleasant techniques." His lip curled. "I think Gaetana wanted to see if I balked at such practice. When I didn't, she said she had another text for me to unlock and translate, a manuscript buried deep in layers of wards and ciphers. Even less savory, but carrying knowledge of the uses of magic that have been lost for generations. She prates that a practitioner of 'exceptional talents and proper ethics' can convert any knowledge to good purpose. I've yet to see that text."

The fever of the hunt rose in *me* then. "Was this why you warned me off today?"

"I'm watched closer every hour," he said. "Gaetana walks in at odd times, often without leave. Adepts and acolytes trot over with messages or requests for information. Orviene pesters me to collaborate on his puling little projects. Now I've this fool adept lurking about, thinking he's the god's own son, and he was once their lackey. I'm attempting to discourage visitors. We need to—"

Dante broke off when Ilario returned with a tray of cold roast lamb, sugared oranges, and hot cider. While the mage dug in, and Ilario propped himself at the doorway in a sulk, I inspected the brocade wall. No enchantment, seam, or mechanism marked the secret entry.

"Oh, here, Portier," snapped Ilario, after I had fumbled about for a while. He marched across the carpet, tapped a brass gargoyle tucked into the corner beside his marble hearth, and slid the ugly little visage to the

side. The panel in the wall swung open, revealing a gap that might have been a coal chute at middle-night.

"How long have the two of you shared this little connection?" I said, recalling Ilario's prattlings of hidden passages, trapdoors, and spelled closets that he and Eugenie had explored as children.

"When I heard about Dante's new assistant, it seemed reasonable that the two of you would be less free to talk together from now on in *his* rooms . . . which I know you do, though you never tell me half of what you discuss. So I found occasion to inform the mage about the route between here and there." Ilario hooked a thumb in his belt and returned to his aloof stance by the door. "Never imagined he'd actually use it. Has not my fool's wit exposed our every secret?"

"It will be most useful, lord chevalier," I said, fully sincere.

A glare seemed enough to move Dante to speech, or perhaps the rapidly vanishing food and wine had soothed his brittle edge as well as his exhaustion. He cleared his throat with a growl. "You have shown . . . resources, Chevalier. And the food is welcome."

"Have you a response, my lord?" Truly I felt like one of the women who minded the youngest students at Seravain, settling their fights when they dropped mice into one another's boots or dumped cold tea on one another's sheets.

Ilario fondled his lace and fluffed his ruffles while gazing at the ceiling. "Shall you provide an exhibit for my exposition, mage?"

Dante swallowed the last bite of meat with a grateful sigh. "Aye. It's another thing I've been working at. I aim to shock the twittering birds around this palace, including some murk-headed beginners not so far from here. Did you bring my other books and materials, student?"

I took what peace I could and resisted falling prey to his taunt. "Most. And I learned a bit. . . ."

As Dante devoured the last of the bread and oranges, I launched my tale of Lianelle, Ophelie, Michel de Vernase, and bodies in crates.

"The Cazars are an old-fashioned lot," said Ilario, who now sat on an exotic footstool, tapping his fingers thoughtfully on his chin. "They build on clifftops and keep close behind their walls, playing knife games and

dancing until dawn. But something tweaks me about the name. One of Philippe's envoys might be a Cazar or related to one. I'll inquire about it . . . yes, *discreetly*, sir mage! But Damoselle Maura a villain? That seems unlikely. She is so . . . ordinary."

Ordinary. Unlikely. The very qualities I brought to Philippe's clandestine service.

No. I could not be so wrong about Maura.

Dante's demeanor had hardened as I spoke of Seravain. "This Kajetan," he said, "your *friend* who asks you to spy on me . . . Should I be expecting visits from Camarilla inquisitors?"

"Certainly not. The transference worries him, and the consequences should relations between the Camarilla and the king break down further. He's the only surviving mage in his bloodline. I wish we dared ask his help."

"Keep your friends *out* of my business," Dante snapped, wiping sticky fingers on his sleeve. "You'd do well to consider what kind of mentor locks his student in a tomb when he fails. If he can't teach, he should find someone who can."

"You know nothing about him," I riposted, anger flared all out of proportion to his jab. "Or me."

The green eyes burned. "I know what it is to believe life's dropped you in a shaft you can't crawl out of. And I know what the hand that reaches down to you looks like. I'd wager my eyes 'tis not the hand of this mentor of yours."

Dante, gifted with talent beyond imagining, could never understand. Kajetan's library had saved my sanity. "Your interpretation of my life is irrelevant to our task, mage," I said, "and I'll thank you not to speculate on my personal situation. Kajetan will not have occasion to query you unless you do something to warrant it. On the other hand, I think this mystery of Eltevire must be followed without delay. The Marangels, the dead seamstress, the cell in the crypt . . . The murderers are cleaning up after themselves. They know someone's after them."

"I agree," said Dante, tapping his staff on the carpet. His head was cocked my way in a most annoying manner, as if his mouth were engaged

with the present conversation while his mind yet dealt with the last. "We oughtn't be seen leaving Merona together. I'll meet the two of you at the shrine at Canfreg Spring, what . . . seven days hence?"

"Both?" Ilario straightened his back. "Yes, I could possibly make the time to accompany you. You may have need of a knight. I'll spread it about that I've gone back to the country for a cleanse, as I do every summer, but I'll tell John Deune I've a liaison with a lady. He's quite discreet for a valet, but none too clever, so someone will wheedle the news from him. I'm attentive to so many ladies, some will think it's one and that one will think it's another, until everyone is in a merry muddle and won't know where I've gone."

Dante wiped his mouth and rolled his eyes.

On another day I would have laughed, but on that morning, I felt only urgency. "Canfreg Spring," I said. "Midday of the seventh from this. Then on to Eltevire."

CHAPTER SIXTEEN

"He'll come," I murmured, dribbling wine onto the stained rock and passing the pewter cup to Ilario. "He's a man of his word. We'll finish our prayers, leave him some kind of token, then ride out. He'll catch up. We cannot remain here."

I bowed to the tarnished ikon and moved toward the round door of the little stone shrine, one of a hundred such shrines that lined a pilgrim way stretching from the western sea to the city of Abidaijar in Aroth—the home of the Cult of the Reborn. We had arrived at this barren holy place well before midday of the seventh day out of Merona, and had lingered through a blistering afternoon and a devilishly cold night awaiting Dante. Now the sunlight had again begun its crawl up the jumbled crags to the east.

Ilario made a quick oblation and hurried after me, the low ceiling forcing him to hunch as if his neck were broken. The soot from centuries of smoldering herbs had already soiled his soft gray hat and its soft gray cryte's feather. "But what if his horse has pitched him in a ditch or he's gotten himself sick again with his sorcery?"

"We can't help him by dawdling," I said, pausing at the doorway. I felt exposed here. Every birdcall raised the hair on my neck. The dry breeze

whispered of treachery. The chevalier and I were too conspicuous even for the small traffic that traveled this red-rock wasteland.

I should never have brought Ilario. At my insistence he had traded his satin and lace for canvas breeches, plain shirts, and buff jerkin, and his horse for a pilgrim's donkey. But Father Creator had surely designed the fop to fit in Castelle Escalon's halls like the gilded caryatids and fluted columns. In places like this wayside shrine, where one met few but goatherds, pilgrims, and scoundrels or adventurers bound overland for the exotic lands of Aroth and Syan, Ilario stood out like a magpie among sparrows.

A nosy tinker had spent the night near our encampment. A trio of surly pilgrims—a balding, fleshy fellow of thrice Ilario's girth, his gaptoothed brother, and a wan, flat-eyed woman—had ridden in at dawn to fill their waterskins at the muddy Canfreg Spring. For pilgrims they were exceedingly well armed. Dirks at belt and boot. The big man carried a war ax and a looped chain. They had stared at us for an hour before moving on east.

A temple reader had arrived at midmorning in a heavily laden donkey cart. The reader, a thickset provincial with a profusion of black, wiry hair, and his red-haired manservant, a hungry-looking, agitated sort of man with a wolflike jutting nose and chin, set up a small booth and altar across the road from the shrine. Temple servitors disdained the Cult of the Reborn, yet the bluff, friendly reader invited Ilario and me to join him for devotions. He had exposed his left hand. A man of the blood, then. Though my own gesture was quick, his keen-eyed manservant took full note of my own family mark. The two settled in for the day.

We needed to move on.

As we stepped into the heat-blasted afternoon, Ilario returned the offering cup to a niche above the doorway. I clutched our wine flask.

"Your lengthy devotions send a fair odor to Sante Marko," said the leather-skulled mendicant brother squatting just outside the shrine. "The sweet smokes will lure our beloved saint back through the Veil to stand stalwart in our earthly battles."

"We await the day," said Ilario, crossing his arms over his heart in

pious fashion. Ilario's familiarity with Cult customs made me suspect him a believer.

Relentless sun and wind and the incessant inhalation of "sweet smokes" had withered the mendicant brother to a husk and left his mind adrift somewhere between the barren landscape and Heaven. His ragged garments—the cast-off donations of myriad travelers—flapped in the dry breeze. Dangling from his neck was the same green pilgrim badge Ilario and I wore, marked with the red phoenix insignia of the Cult.

As if of their own accord, the mendicant's bony fingers tapped the side of his rusted cup, reminding us of our obligation to make a more solid offering to keep his herb basket full. Ilario dropped a silver kivra in the cup and one of our bread rolls in the old man's lap, then strolled across the dusty ground toward our tethered donkeys.

I tossed a few coins after Ilario's and followed, studying the rock-lined path, the hivelike shrine, and the rubble walls of the sacred enclosure for some way to leave a sign, so Dante would know we'd come and gone. Gruchin's silver coin, tucked into my boot since Tigano, would be too tempting to any passerby. We'd need my compass to locate Eltevire. I had no scarf or gloves. . . .

"Sweet Heaven, it's a ruin," Ilario grumbled, brushing at his hat. His efforts had succeeded only in spreading the thick soot from his hat to his favorite leather riding gloves.

Inspired, I snatched the modestly feathered hat from Ilario's grasp and returned to the mendicant brother. "My master especially reveres Sante Marko," I said, dropping my voice. "He holds a belief that he once met Sante Marko Reborn, the elderly swordmaster who taught him all his knightly skills. But in the shrine yestereve, he experienced a revelation that he should bare himself to the elements to mellow his pride in that encounter. It's why we've stayed to proffer additional devotions. As his prayers provided no relief from the saint's geas, he offers you this fine hat."

The mendicant brother spread his arms as if to embrace the sky, then reverently brought his fingertips to heart, forehead, and lips. "Sante Marko ever fills our needs," he said, his voice as arid as the wind across the stony

landscape. "Warn your master to heed the letter of the saint's instruction. Where the Veil is thin, the Saints Awaiting view us clearly."

"Where the Veil is thin, brother? What does that mean?"

"'Twas in these lands first blood was shed in anger between human and human."

"The Lay of Goram and Vichkar?" I said. The tale of two friends who battled to the death over a bronze knife had been told since long before the rise of the Sabrian kingdom, before cities, before vineyards, before writing. "You believe it occurred near here."

"Aye. Their battle is our blessing and curse, as is all of creation save Heaven. The saints draw back the Veil to witness such terrible deeds."

Certain places on the earth provided a potent venue for spellwork: deep caves where ancients had painted beast images on the walls, an ancient vineyard in Louvel, a desolate plain in the heart of verdant Challyat. Devout Sabrians claimed such extraordinary magical places to be the actual venues for the creation stories—the cave where humankind first mastered fire, the plain where we first shaped a wheel, or the field where the Pantokrator planted the first grapevine—inevitably linking magic and holiness. They believed the tales collected in the *Book of Creation* to be history as true as the founding of our kingdom, their lessons a message from the divine.

The Camarilla deprecated such factual interpretation, insisting that each "location of magical significance" exemplified but a fortuitous confluence of the five divine elements. Such a site would inevitably attract those who practiced sorcery, imbuing the places with history alongside the layered residue of their magics. This position made more sense to me.

A few mages who lived before the Blood Wars had proposed a truth somewhere in between—that stories of such longevity must hold some secrets of gods or nature that we ought to be able to decipher. However, even they had never hinted that the tales might witness to a *physical* proximity of the human and divine worlds.

"What have you seen, brother?" I said, crouching beside him, my hands flexing as if to wrest his knowledge from inside his bald head.

"What witness do you bear of Goram and Vichkar's blood in this land? Or the thinning of the Veil?" It was easy to believe this dry, red wasteland had witnessed humankind's first murder.

The mendicant brother clasped his hands before his breast. "I have witnessed marvels and terrors: the Stone That Does Not Fall, the Stream That Runs Uphill, the Shadow That Burns. The Pantokrator's Aurora shines through the Veil from time to time, and I've seen the Souleater's servants fly from the god in terror, drenched in blood, passing so close as to freeze my soul."

These marvels he spoke of came from no lore I knew. But what if the conspirators had heeded such rumor and had chosen to pursue their magics here, thinking to find the area a potent field for spellwork? Perhaps, the Mondragoni, preoccupied with necromancy and demonology, had claimed this region for their demesne based on such stories.

I pressed the brother to tell me how and where these strange things manifested themselves, but he rambled on of holy mystery and Sante Marko's blessings. My questions made no more sense to him than asking how did the earth manifest its solidity or the Arch of Heaven—the Tenth Gate—position itself in the night sky. Some things just were. The perpetual smokes of Sante Marko's shrine took him wandering the land. Whether in his mind or in his body, today or twenty years past, it was all one to him.

Jittery and frustrated, I bowed and bade him farewell. "Until Sante Marko comes."

"We await the day." His lips widened over broken teeth, and he plopped Ilario's smudged hat atop his sun-scalded head. Dante could not miss it.

"No matter my poor lost hat, the mage will never find us." Ilario planted his backside on a boulder and blotted his forehead, as I examined another thread of hard-packed dirt and gravel in search of tracks, hair, or droppings. "And we'll never find the way back to our beasts. Holy saints, Portier, we'll languish on this wretched rock forever—starving, filthy,

mad like that cult brother. Were there ever any two more useless wilderness travelers?"

A chukar, flushed from the scattered rocks, clucked and squawked, mocking us.

We had ridden eastward from the shrine on the pilgrim road until well out of sight of the mendicant brother and curious travelers. Tethering our donkeys where clumps of blue-green wheatgrass sprouted thickly in the shade of an overhang, we had scrabbled up the tilted slabs and scree as best we could to reach the higher ground. Once above the scarp, we circled back westward across a stony tableland, hunting the elusive goat track that should lead us up the jagged ridge where the Survey said Eltevire must lie, straight north of Canfreg Spring.

"My compass keeps our heading true, lord. Besides, a simple snare could take yon partridge; I've read how to make them. And your sword could skewer it. We'd not starve."

Ilario scowled and stripped off his jerkin, stuffing it into his already crammed rucksack. " 'Tis ungentle to patronize me, Portier. I already feel like a sheep being driven to the slaughterhouse."

My search futile, I waved him onward. "Consider yourself fortunate," I said, as we struggled up the mountain of stone shards that pulsed with afternoon heat. "The cult brother would have you shed *all* your garments on this journey as an offering of humility."

"*All?* What saint could see merit in fried bones? I've scarce meat enough to cover them all as it is, and surely even . . . *everything* would shrivel away. Sweet patroness of love, defend me!"

My deeper coloring prevented much scalding from the incessant barrage of sun and wind. Fair-skinned Ilario's forehead, ears, and long nose were going to pain him fiercely.

Despite a monologue of complaints and fervid intercessions over the eight days since we'd left Merona, Ilario had shown himself more resilient than I could have imagined. Better than me in the rough. Able to sleep on rock, and as nimble as a goat on these treacherous slopes. More than once his hand had hauled me up steps where my cheaply made boots found no purchase. I was glad he'd come.

Two hours after leaving the donkeys, a clump of coarse hair, snagged on a clump of thistle, hinted we'd found the way. A few more precarious steps, and we climbed onto a well-beaten path that hairpinned up the rubble slope, invisible to all but those who stood upon it. Surely, this was the route to Eltevire. Power . . . magic . . . I could see no other reason to settle in such desolation.

I waved my hand at Ilario and he pulled a small, elegantly engraved spyglass from his belt pouch. As it had all day, the little glass—a "gift from a lady"—revealed no telltale puff of dust or movement behind us.

An hour later, we thought we'd gone wrong again. No sign of goat, house, or ruin was to be found in the forest of sandstone rock spires atop the ridge. The path ended abruptly at two massive boulder stacks standing outlined against the indigo sky like one of Ixtador's Gates. Between them naught was visible but a lip of downsloping ground and the expansive sky. But our next step forward stole our breath.

Beyond the pillars and a few crumbling downward steps, the land took a precipitous plunge into a chasm so deep, its bottom was already lost in night. Only a narrow span of rock, perhaps one and one-half metres wide and fifty long, bridged the chasm. At its far end lay a sun-drenched plateau of crumbled stone and scrubby grass.

"Saints Awaiting!" Ilario's outburst was no less explosive for its being whispered.

I peered eagerly into the glare. The plateau's elevation was enough lower than our own that we could pinpoint the features listed in the Survey. Eight stone houses, built in the same beehive style as Sante Marko's shrine, clustered about a stone ring that must mark the dry well. A splotch of richer green near the center of the plateau evidenced the watering pond. Ilario's little spyglass revealed the ruined temple and watchtower as little more than a square of broken steps and fractured paving, almost lost in the golden haze.

The eighteen-year-old Survey had listed a population of seven-and-thirty people and one hundred eleven goats. We saw no sign of either. Save for its dramatic setting, nothing appeared at all extraordinary about the place.

Fighting off disappointment, I tried to be sensible. If this village was Eltevire, and Eltevire was the heart of our mystery—*the place where everything began*—we needed to be wary before blundering in.

Ilario grumbled when I insisted we sit for a quarter of an hour before proceeding. "Are you so tired, Portier?" he said, damping his voice when I scowled at him. "Honestly, you must get out more. And if you wish to see yonder ruin any closer, we'd best go now. The Souleater himself could not persuade me to cross that ridiculous sliver of rock in the dark."

Indeed, though deep gold light yet mantled Eltevire, our position already lay in shadow. But I wouldn't budge. "We need to listen," I whispered. "Our own footsteps and hard breathing mask sounds. If someone's following, I want to hear it."

Afternoon waned quietly. Dry gusts ruffled our hair and clothing. A scuttling vole rattled pebbles beyond the gate, rousing a cloud of swallows from the cliffs below us. No sounds of life emanated from the village across the bridge or behind us. I desperately wished Dante at my side.

Soon, I could put it off no longer. Dante might never come. "Have you your crocodile charm, lord chevalier?"

Ilario near dropped his rucksack into the chasm. "You don't think . . ."

I summoned patience. "No, lord. No crocodiles here. But we may need a light later on."

Reluctantly, he pulled the charm from his jerkin. "The key to the light spell is *crassica*."

A most unlikely grin forced itself through the foreboding that had weighed on me all day. Ilario's spellkey meant *large teeth*. "It is good you are here, Chevalier," I said. "Tuck yourself behind one of these rocks where you can still watch. Stay hidden until I signal."

"I ought to go with you," he said, face screwed into a grimace and hand tapping his sword hilt. "You've no weapons. But I immensely dislike bridges; we should wait for the mage."

"From the look of the place, I doubt I'll need defending. But we don't know for sure. If you see the least hint of something awry, get away. Don't stop. Don't speak to anyone. Don't let anyone delay you. If you can't find

Dante, go straight to the king." After a moment's hesitation, I passed him my journal. "Give him this. The cipher is not magic."

Ilario glanced at the worn little book and back at me, swallowed hard, then tucked it inside his shirt. "You'll have a care, Portier, yes?"

"Absolutely." More excited than fearful, I hopped and skidded down the unstable gravel and dirt steps. As I stepped onto the stone span, a humming cloud of gnats and sand fleas descended on me. Brushing at my skin, I took a second step. . . .

The world reeled. The chasm yawned. The cliff walls writhed, expanded, contracted, braiding the sunlight and shadow. My skin flushed hot, then cold, then hot again, and my belly heaved. Enchantments!

I dropped into a crouch, planting elbows on my knees and spinning head on my fists before I could topple into the chasm. In the moment I closed my eyes, the sensations vanished.

A visual ward, then—simple and indeed deadly, considering the narrow span of the bridge.

"Great Heaven, Portier, are you well?"

I winced as my name bounced repeatedly between the cliffs and Eltevire's plateau. Why did he have to shout?

Raising my hand to reassure him, I opened my eyes and fixed them on the mottled stone surface of the bridge. Cautiously, I stood. The world and my stomach remained calm. I took one step forward. The world sloshed only slightly, like the liquid in a carefully moved cup. I took another step.

Much as I hated to waste progress already made, I reversed course. Ilario's shout had likely alerted any lurkers. Nonetheless, my tongue refused to call out from such a distance.

"The bridge is warded, lord," I said when I stepped back onto the land. "When I signal you to come over, keep your eyes fixed on the span itself. Look neither right nor left nor up nor down, and pay no mind to anything beyond it. If you feel dizzy or your skin begins to itch, do as I did: Get low and close your eyes. Let the sensations ease; then try again. Do you understand?"

Ilario edged backward. "Perhaps you'll not need me. I'm no use around

enchantments. I've no idea why the mage wanted me to come. He'd as soon push me over this edge."

"He'd never do that, lord. You are just very different from anyone he's known. He does not trust easily." Though truthfully, Dante's insistence on Ilario's company on this venture mystified me, as well. "When I'm sure all is clear, I'll call out or shine the light from your charm."

Blood thumping, I turned back to the bridge. No ordinary ruin would be so viciously warded. I crossed the rock span without further difficulty and strolled down the path into Eltevire and late-afternoon sunlight. The gusty breeze shifted dust about my boots, whipping it into small whirl-winds.

Two of the stone houses in the circle had collapsed. Tattered scraps of leather flapped in several doorways. The rest gaped open or were blocked with rubble, tangled peashrub, or gangly stems of asphodel, thick with white flowers. A peek inside evidenced soot, dust, and a few oddments: shards of pottery; a great deal of goat hair; three broken bone needles; a splintered piece of wood with closely spaced holes, which might have been a piece of a loom.

Bones lay in heaps, inside and outside—the fine bones of chukars and other fowl, of voles, rock pigs, and other scuttering creatures, the larger bones of goats and foxes. A stained stone tub, numerous worn-out tools, and bone pegs bore witness to a village tannery. Had not the Survey con-tradicted me, I'd have said no one had inhabited Eltevire for centuries, and no magic ever had been worked here. Why had Michel risked Oph-elie's life to learn its name?

Crossing the field toward the temple ruin, I strained for some hint of magic. The rocks and grass and blowing dust almost glittered in the ocher light, as if ground glass infused the air. The breeze smelled of dry grass touched with pungent herbs I could neither locate nor identify. But I sensed no spellwork. None.

The temple ruin, situated at the far end of the plateau, revealed no more than the village itself. Sun and scouring wind had faded the temple floor mosaics, obliterating any meaningful design or inscription. What few dressed stones had not been carted off to build the beehive houses

displayed no carving or painted surface, nothing to link the place to the story of Goram and Vichkar or to the Veil, to conspiracy or torment or to magic itself, come to that.

I squatted in the center of the temple floor. Broken bits of once-colored tile, sand, pebbles, and grit sifted through my fingers, scattering on the paving whence I'd gathered them. I was flummoxed.

Spluttering in frustration, I strode down the temple steps and across the rock-strewn field of tufted hare's tail and gray-green stipweed to the pond. The sun, bloated and wavering in the dust haze, settled toward the jagged horizon.

The watering pond was no gritty mudhole like the shrine spring. The clear, bottomless pool lay in a snail-like shell of rock, a catch basin gouged from a knob of the plateau bedrock by centuries of wind and rain. Examination revealed naught unusual.

Swearing, I threw in the temple debris yet clenched in my fist. The obstinate bits and pieces floated atop the dark water, circling slowly, as if a giant's spoon stirred the pool.

One side of the hollowed basin formed an overhang. Trampling the green onion grass that grew on the bank, I circled the pond and climbed atop the protruding rock, sighting back toward the bridge. Ilario might as well come and see the *nothing* we'd traveled so far to find.

A haze drifted across the plateau like mist or smoke in a direction wholly opposite the direction of the wind. I squinted, but Ilario had hid himself well. Still stupidly reluctant to yell, I spoke the key to trigger his charm. *"Crassica."*

Light flamed from my hand like a blue sunrise.

Sainted ancestors! I released my grip on the shells, and the light vanished. But it took moments for my vision to clear, and longer yet for the spell's residue to settle over my spirit like silken sheets. I'd felt no such vigorous energy when Ilario triggered the charm in the crypt.

Without waiting for Ilario's response, I trotted back to the temple ruin. If the nature of Eltevire—its confluence of divine elements or inherited holiness—could so enhance worked spells, what might it do for spellmaking? Selfish. Foolish. My sudden hunger had naught to do with assassina-

tion plots or cruel hauntings, but solely with magic. *My* magic. *Please, gods . . .*

Dropping to my knees on the faded mosaic, I laid out my compass and whispered the key to a spell I had created when I first bought the little instrument. *Locuti.* Locate.

The bulging sun touched the horizon. My eyes near stretched from their sockets as I tried to detect the wisp of white smoke that should indicate the compass's location—and my spell's successful execution. But all I sensed was a shiver that passed through me to settle on the paving like spilled wine ready to stick to my shoes—the residue of failure.

Perhaps a weak spell bound so long ago would never work, even in a place of magical potency. But something new . . .

Manic, I stripped leaves from a stalk of asphodel that poked through the broken paving and laid them beside my compass. I added my handkerchief, and a pebble fetched from the crumbled temple steps, encircling my chosen particles with a thread ripped from my snagged hose. The brass of the compass supplied the elements of base metal and spark. The pebble brought the steadiness of its composite elements—base metal and wood. The leaves added the element of water into the balance, needed for transparency and sinuous movement. The kerchief supplied wood and air, essential for combustion. My mind raced, estimating, adding, and subtracting. Perhaps a smaller stone, lest the working grow too large.

I near cackled at the ridiculous image of uncontrollable fire coming from any work of mine.

The particles appeared correct, their arrangement as prescribed. My will stood ready. Yet instinct would not allow me to begin. I recalculated. Without tinder or kindling, the spell would require a great deal of spark. Brass did not provide enough. I needed silver.

I ripped open my belt purse, cursing as I sorted only twelve silver kentae. But Gruchin's silver double strike was larger and heavier, bearing my royal cousin's raised likeness on both faces. I extracted the coin from my boot and laid it atop the stack inside the loop of string. Another quick calculation. Ten thousand times had I worked this spell, always failing,

and ten thousand times had I imagined it, always succeeding. Trained instinct called the balance perfect. Ready.

Mustering every scrap of will inside me, every remnant of longing, belief, and desire, I called on the magic of my blood and spoke the proper words to complete the formula for fire, the most fundamental of spells.

Faint as a snake's heartbeat in winter, cold as a dead man's nose, a rill of power threaded my veins. Gold sparks burst from the center of the looped thread like grains of sunlight scattered in the encroaching dark, promising warmth and safety. My heart swelled to bursting . . .

. . . and shriveled again, as one-by-one the sparks winked out, my veins warmed, and the heartbeat of my magic stilled. As ever.

The sky dulled to ocher, streaked with purple. The land lay silent and empty.

I could not swear. Could not weep. Could not allow myself to feel this yet again.

And so I did as I had always done. Forced my lungs to pump. Forced myself to move. I folded the handkerchief and tucked it away with my compass. I brushed the leaves, the stone, and the thread aside, lest someone notice their particular arrangement. Certainly the balance of elements had been inexpert. Rushed. So many untried particles. Just because Adept Fedrigo's crocodile charm had worked so explosively, it didn't follow that this place would enhance *new* spellwork. Excuses. Explanations. Anything but admitting the unshakable truth.

"Aaaagh!" Irrational, uncontrollable, a lifetime's disappointment exploded from my every pore. I snatched up the piled silver and flung the coins across the temple floor. The kentae scattered, bouncing and rolling. The double strike coin flew farther, spinning in the air, catching the last stray beam of the vanishing sun. Then, like a hummingbird feeding, the coin paused in its flight and hung suspended in the air . . .

And hung.

Moments passed. I blinked. Squinted. Surely this was some trick of evening light. Tired limbs propelled me to my feet. The breeze of dying day wafted over the plateau. Mesmerized, I moved to stand beneath the coin, scarce an arm's reach above my head. It remained stalwart in its defi-

ance of de Vouger's acclaimed treatise, *Principles of Falling Objects*. It gleamed as if it were the first star awaiting a blackening sky.

I plucked it from its hovering, and it sat heavy in my hand; ice cold, not warm as it should have been from its recent housing in my boot. Dante had declared the thing magically inert, and even yet, I detected not the slightest trace of enchantment about it. I launched it again. It bounced across the paving as any coin would do.

Accuracy. Precision. Repeatability. Without them, you've naught but accidents and happenstance. Dante's teaching echoed as if he stood at my shoulder. I threw the coin again.

It hung in the air, spinning slowly like a gear wheel in a mill. I reined in soul, body, and mind, not daring to feel, not daring to admit, even by wondering, that an object could so violate the simplest, clearest laws of nature without aid of enchantment.

Again, I threw the coin, Gruchin's luck charm, the sole object found in the assassin's pocket. And again . . . Never did it behave the same way twice running.

I tucked the double strike into my boot, gathered the scattered kentae, and repeated the tests. The silver coins behaved properly. I tried copper kivrae, a gold kesole, the crocodile charm, a button, a buckle cut from my boot. No oddity. What was different about the two-faced coin?

I snatched up a shard of mosaic half the size of my palm and tossed it across the temple floor. It rolled lazily, end over end, drifted to the floor, bounced higher than my head in an entirely unlikely direction, and landed back at my feet. A pebble flew ten centimetres, then plummeted to the ground as if it had slammed into a wall, though I used the same motion, the same strength for its launch. A handful of dirt tossed into the air drifted slowly onto my shirt, as if the grains were dandelion cotton. Merciful angels, this was madness.

Recalling the debris I'd thrown into the pond, I gathered a handful of variously sized stones and ran across the field, trying to outrace the settling dark. I threw one of my coppers into the water. It sank as I would expect. Another, and it did the same. Then I tossed the stones into the pond. Some sank. Some floated. I knelt on the bank, the scent of onion

grass sitting like thickened paste on my tongue, and retrieved three of the floating stones as they circled past. They weighed solidly, one near the size of an egg. I tossed them in again. One sank. One bounced off the surface of the water and onto the shore beside me. The egg-shaped one settled to the surface as gracefully as a black swan.

Footsteps crunched on the weedy field behind me. "Lord chevalier, hurry! Come look at this!" I called over my shoulder. "By the Creator, you'll never believe it!"

But this time, *I* fell. A bludgeon slammed into my back, just between the shoulder blades. My face met the ground with all expected force.

CHAPTER SEVENTEEN

31 QAT
30 DAYS UNTIL THE ANNIVERSARY

"Now who exactly might you be?" said the owner of the boot grinding my nose and cheek into the crushed onion grass and the rocky soil beneath. "And where bides your pretty, sneaking *lord* who carries such a fine sword?"

"Ow! Stop!" I said, though the words came out somewhat garbled. "I'm Damiano de Sacre Vaerre. Pilgrim. Ho—pthew—holy place." I spat out the words along with dirt and grit, and grabbed on to the ankle attached to the offending boot, determined to remove it from my cheekbone. And perhaps break it.

Pain exploded in my side. Yet another boot. My breath seized, and my arms flopped to the ground, limp as a dead bird's wings.

A huge, warm weight settled on my back, pressing the remaining air from my lungs, and then a hand snarled my hair and wrenched my head backward. Wiry hair pressed against my cheek, accompanied by warm, beery breath. "What common pilgrim ventures a warded bridge?"

"Or travels with a lord knight dressed common? They've secrets, Quernay. Secrets. He's blood born sure." This voice, more excited than the first, came from in front of me, though my watering eyes revealed only a black blur. Two men. At least two. Friendly as jackals.

"The holy brother told us—aagh!" My scalp threatened to rip. "Please, let me spea—"

The one on my back—Quernay—jerked and twisted my neck into an impossible angle and spat on my cheek. "Answer our questions. Where be the noble swordsman?"

"Out east, waiting for me at Fe-hikal. He dresses poor to discourage thieves. Please, he'll travel on without me."

"Are you so worthless? Why are you here?"

"Awaiting the Reborn."

This time the boot landed on my chin. Blood spurted from my lips and chin. Pain lanced through my jaw, trebling the strained agony of my neck.

"Try again," said Quernay's overeager friend with the boots, mashing his gritty sole into my face.

"Back off, Merle," growled the one at my ear. My stomach churned at the stink of him and the onion grass and the strained posture. "You've been working spells, oddments. To what purpose?"

My prepared story thinned like wafting smoke. I needed something better, perhaps closer to the truth lest I be tested worse; dizziness already clouded my thinking. "I am a failed acolyte," I said. "The mendicant's tales . . . thought I might succeed up here."

"And your pretty lord?"

"Despises me. Calls me lackwit. Dunce. Wanted to show him. Please, take what you will and let me go. Master said he'd leave me behind did I not join him by sunrise."

"Mmm," wheezed Quernay. "Methinks you've seen a bit too much to let you go." The heavy man slammed my face to the ground as he climbed off my back, then snagged my clothing when I attempted to scramble away.

Without wasted word or breath, the two immobilized my legs with cords wrapped from ankles to knees. They bound my wrists behind my back and wound the rope all the way to my elbows, pinching my arms together so tightly they near left their sockets. I could not inhale a full breath.

Blessed angels, keep Ilario hidden. These two were no common bandits. They'd not touched my purse or scattered silver, and, certainly, they themselves had crossed a warded bridge. At least one of them must have some trained sensitivity to magic.

"Get him through the trap," said Quernay. "I'll take a look around."

As the bigger man strode away, his excitable partner looped a rope around my chest and under my cramping shoulders and dragged me across the field. Sharp-edged grass slashed my face. Rocks ripped my clothes and gouged my chest and thighs. I fought to keep my head up, so as not to have it bashed against the rocks. Oblivion would have suited better.

Once he had bumped me up the steps, my captor dropped me on the faded mosaic like a goat brought for sacrifice. The world drifted lazily, like the water in the pool.

"*Aberta*," he spat.

A great whipcrack of magic split the air, trembling the ground beneath my cheek. I tried to press myself into the stone.

Grunts of effort, mumbles, thumps, and creaks located the brutish Merle to my left. "Why the frigging saint did you have to show up here at sunset?" he grumbled. "Oughta slit your throat just for the trouble. Quernay's, too. *Get 'im through the trap. I'll take a look around.* Dung-eating goatherd thinks I'm his slavey. Thinks he's aristo 'cause he can conjure a spell or two."

Accepting that a mountain was not about to fall on me, I drew my bound legs toward my belly and rocked onto my side to get a look. My captor's black shape was outlined against the violet afterglow. The temple reader's red-haired manservant from the shrine—Merle—was wrestling with . . . I blinked dirt away. Everything looked wrong.

No matter my blinking and squinting, the view did not change. The slight, wolfish Merle was raising a rectangular slab that must surely weigh ten times his body's total. Grunting, he gave a prodigious shove, and the slab . . . drifted . . . to the pavement. Yet it landed with a teeth-rattling thud. Then he reached *through the floor* and withdrew a paned lantern. My stomach heaved.

I blinked again, and my perceptions shifted. A layer of illusion masked

a rectangular gap in the temple floor. But was the slab that had closed it granite or silk? Experience and estimation no longer sufficed.

Merle set the lantern on solid ground, then stepped back a few paces. *"Illuminatio."*

Ah, not fair at all that a brutish thug should key a fire spell so soon after my abortive attempt to create one. But indeed, flame blossomed atop the thick white candle inside the lantern. Yet its light entirely contradicted Watt the lens maker's tidy diagrams and explanations. My eyes did *see* the light, but not a beam illumined anything beyond the glass. The night, deeper black than before, snugged up around the lantern panes and trapped the fiery glow inside the glass walls.

"Illuminatio."

This time, flame engulfed the lantern, a wind-whipped bonfire of gold and yellow that could likely be viewed as far west as Tallemant. Merle stood well away from it, his outstretched hand held flat against the flame as if to shield himself. The light beams curled about his outlined fingers.

"Illuminatio, you demon-cursed bit of wax."

The third invocation of the key quenched the bonfire instantly. But a new flame sprouted like an eager weed from the blackened wick and burned brightly within the lantern's confines. The beams spread softly across the paving, clean and straight as they ought.

The wolfish man bellowed laughter. "Guess you're fuddled, eh?" He swung the lantern at my bruised face. I jerked my head back, the glare near blinding me. "We'll fuddle you all."

Truly my senses were entirely fuddled. The first two attempts to key the spell had not satisfied him, yet, had my eyes been closed, I would have been unable to distinguish their residue from the third, successful attempt. Impossible, I would have said a day before, yet perhaps no more extraordinary than coins that flew, stones that floated or sank as if by whim, or light beams that cast no reflection save in a human eye.

My captor gave me little time to sort it out. He lowered the bright lantern back through the hidden gap in the floor, then took up my leash and hauled me toward the same location. Gods . . .

Though the sharp edge between *floor* and *no floor* was not wholly un-

expected, the gut-plummeting drop near sliced my arms off when the rope reached its abrupt limit. Gasping for air, I spewed curses as I had never in my life produced. I hadn't realized I knew so many.

After three or four jerky lowerings, my toes touched ground, slackening the rope. I toppled like the stone slab onto the very hard, very cold floor.

Lamplight spun. The world blurred and bent. Harsh whoops dragged air into my burning chest. "Souleater's servant!" I spoke in true conviction of Merle's identity.

The heavy leash rope smacked the back of my head.

Boots ground on steps. Merle's warm body stank as he bent over me. Quivering fingers pried at my pockets, unbuttoned my shirt collar, pawed my neck, tugged at my sleeves . . . searching. He crowed when he snapped the courret from its slender chain about my neck and stuffed it in his pocket. Everything else—purse, knife sheath, spall pouch, compass, crocodile charm, Gruchin's coin, and the boots from my feet—he lobbed into the corner. I didn't regret the wardstone's loss. It hadn't warned me about him.

"The Aspirant will be quite interested in your mark." Somewhere beyond the red-hot skewers inside my shoulders, he shook my needling-numb left hand. "You'll keep no secrets from *him*."

Damnable incautious fool! I swore at myself, not at Merle. All our efforts would be wasted if the conspirators learned my identity or, angels defend us, Ilario's or Dante's. Who were these people? An aspirant was a magical apprentice, not even a student of my own rank.

"I've no secrets," I mumbled into the floor. "Blood's sour. Can't conjure a dewdrop."

"We'll see to that." Somewhere behind my back a blade left a stinging track across my palm.

"Sante Marko, defend!" I bucked and twisted.

"Merle! Get off him!" The voice came from above my head. Heavy boots pounded the steps, skipping the last few to drop hard on the floor close by. "We want a body left to question."

"Look at his mark, Quernay. See what's fallen into our lap."

The bigger man's noisy breathing soon placed him close. Cool, hard hands forced my clenched fist open. Belying any implication that his object was mercy, he twisted my hand to expose its back, then gripped my bloody chin, and used it to wrench my face up into the lantern light. My tight-bound arms prevented my body following all the way.

"So, who is he?" Quernay's broad face swam in the glare—wiry black hair, wide brow, chin like an anvil. He was none but the temple reader from the shrine, not so friendly anymore. Above him a rectangle of night marked the entry through the temple floor. No illusion masked the opening from below.

"Don't know the mark exactly, but I'm sure I've seen it. It's a good mark, I know. He's blood, for certain, and we need—" A vicious thwack of flesh on bony flesh silenced Merle's views.

"The Aspirant will decide what we need," growled Quernay. "While I fetch the supplies, you get this one into the hole and yourself off to the bridge. Wouldn't want that swordsman to lack a proper welcome should he come looking for his sorcerer."

"Told you, I'm no confounded sorcerer," I croaked. "And my master won't come for me. He's off to Abidaijar to vow himself to the Saints Awaiting. He'll ne'er be back to Sabria. *I'll* ne'er be back do you let me go. Please, I'd no intent to trespass or blaspheme. I didn't know. . . ."

Quernay shoved me into an awkward heap. A better view did naught to soothe a rising panic. A few metres away, between me and a white-washed wall lined with cluttered benches and shelves, a wooden armchair had been bolted to the floor. Leather straps were affixed to its flat arms and the thick, narrow plank that served as its back. Black splatters stained chair, straps, and floor, as well as a fire-glazed urn that stood next the thing. Old blood. Everywhere. Blessed saints . . .

The excitable Merle did not argue. He just watched and quivered as Quernay clambered up the stair and through the entry. Then, exposing his pointed teeth in a grin that made my skin creep, he lashed an arm-length truncheon to his wrist with a leather thong. "Need some practice," he said, raising the club. "Need to make you tender for the blades."

I thrashed and yelled, trying to dodge his precisely placed blows. I butted my head and shoulders against his ankles and slammed my bound legs into his, hoping to trip up his dancing steps. My antics only made him laugh the louder.

Logic screamed that Merle's virulence made no sense. Such reasoned brutality arose from fanatical dispositions, as with the Kadr witchlords who viewed those without their particular power for magic as prey. Or it stemmed from personal bias, passion-wrought grudges over property or family, or overstretched fathers whose profound disappointments prompted them to slay their failed sons. Merle didn't even know me.

Trussed as I was, defensive postures were futile. All too soon, I lay limp as a dead fish, logic as impossible as resistance. At one distinctive instant, my temple slammed against the bolted legs of the chair, and the world went dark. . . .

"I am no one," I whispered as he slapped me awake again. Spittle and blood had pooled under my cheek. "Nothing. My blood is weak. Please—"

Merle didn't seem to hear. Or perhaps he didn't care. Sweating, roaring in high spirits, he took his brutal pleasure. To my sorrow he did not kill me.

Eventually he dragged me into a small, dark room, redolent with pungent scent, and shoved me to my knees. By the time he had fixed my wrist bindings to an overhead loop, drawing my cinched arms so high and tight behind my back as to bend my head near the floor, I could not have told him my true name, much less where I was or why I'd come.

ABSOLUTE DARKNESS. A PUNGENT SCENT that roiled my stomach. A shearing, lacerating agony in my skull. The viciously cramped rack of my upper body that left every breath a struggle. A paralyzing terror of what was to come.

As the lightless hours flowed one into the other, indistinguishable, a bitter litany beat in time with my stuttering heart. *Inexcusable to let them take you. Blind. Inattentive. Caught up in selfish dreams. Unworthy.* Eventually,

inevitably, a warm flood soaked my breeches, firing my skin with shame and my soul with humiliation.

Unable to sit or recline, I tried once to ease the strain of my position by standing, but my wobbling knees refused to hold me. The resulting collapse dropped my entire weight on my overstrained shoulders, near wrenching my arms from their sockets. My cry reflected sharply from the enclosing walls, a knife blade prying at my cracked skull. Sobbing, desperate, I scrabbled aching knees back under me, and there I remained, vowing to every divine being never to move again.

Blackness swelled and flowed, puddled and pooled. Overwhelming. Enveloping. Cocooned in silence, my mind had difficulty holding to any sensible course. Incapable of sleep, I dreamed of faces: my dead father, whom I did not mourn; Kajetan, living, whom I did; Philippe, who had graced me with his confidence; kind, graceful, intelligent Maura, whom I had determined to trust. Ideas, imaginings, and a few small threads of logic floated past me in the dark, like coins and stones on Eltevire's strange pond. And from time to time, a clearly formed conclusion would waggle its tail, troutlike, and attract my notice.

Materials native to this place refused obedience to the prescriptions of natural science; materials brought from elsewhere behaved themselves, the sole exception being Gruchin's coin. Perhaps Gruchin, the not-assassin, the mule, had been bled here. Perhaps his lucky coin had been in his pocket or his boot when he was subjected to the torments of Eltevire. What kind of spellwork could ensorcel silver—the perfect amalgam of the five elements—beyond the bounds of nature, yet leave no residue? *The place where it all began.*

These people were going to bleed me until my soul and body shriveled like a grape left too long in the sun. Another strained inhalation. Another deluge of cold sweats. I shivered uncontrollably.

A small victory when I identified the aroma exuded by the walls. Camphor bespoke the rare whitebud laurel. Whitebud laurel, and walls so close I could feel the reflections of my own breath, bespoke a sorcerer's hole. Lined with cypress, inlaid with camphor laurel, the exterior locked and banded with iron, such windowless closets were the single enclosure

ever discovered that could completely frustrate the use of magic. If my posture had allowed me a full breath, I might have laughed at the irony of such a space wasted on me.

Another fish twitched its tail: Perhaps Merle and Quernay were actually Goram and Vichkar, the blood-thirsty companions of holy legend who had blighted history by perpetrating its first joint and mutual murder. Perhaps demonic spirits could be reborn to do mischief, just as the saints sacrificed their heavenly sojourn to come back and aid sorry humankind.

I dismissed this fishy theory quickly. I could not imagine these two as bosom friends who loved their mothers, as legend bespoke.

Father Creator, how had I come to this? What fool's illusions of purpose had led me so beyond my safe library? Not mother's love. My mother doused herself with lavender scent and tormented her serving girl. Since my father's death, she would dissolve into hysterics whenever she saw me.

A scraping noise heralded a thin, vertical band of gray light that split the wall in front of me. Despite its painful brilliance, I inhaled the light, longing to be a lumenfish, able to drink in the sun's rays, only to release them again in the long dark of sea nights. "D-did you love your m-mother, Quernay?" I croaked through chattering teeth, feeling madly brave. "Are you a f-fish?"

When he failed to answer, I ventured a glance upward, and near pissed myself again. The black-gowned form was not Quernay. Taller, surely, but less bulky overall, the newcomer wore a leather mask formed to a male's likeness. Severe in its perfectly proportioned beauty, serene in its superiority, the walnut-hued face might have been that of the Pantokrator himself or one of his warrior angels . . . or perhaps the Pantokrator's chief adversary. The *Book of Creation* named the Souleater the most beautiful of the fallen. Ophelie's leech had worn a mask.

"Demon get! Merle's left him pulp!" So Quernay was here, too. "Best send the lackwit back to the city, lord, else he'll have us all dead in our beds."

Back to the city . . . Visions of imprisonment in a crate near stilled my heart until I sorted out that he spoke of mad, wolfish Merle, not me.

The silent visitor squeezed through the slotlike doorway, built purposefully narrow to slow an imprisoned sorcerer's escape.

"I've a guess this one will be too stubborn to die on us." The throaty whisper crawled into my soul, quiet like a spider. Gloved fingers lifted my chin. With the light behind, the mask's eye slits revealed naught but tarry voids. The thought came to me that a demon returned to the world might wear such a mask to hide his corruption. "How did you find me?"

Chilled and sick, I could summon no mettle to control my shaking. I clung to my tale. "I am nothing," I mumbled through swollen lips. "No one. Failed. A pilgrim."

"Let me be more specific," said the Aspirant, low and harsh. "I believe I am addressing a very particular *no one*. Did your royal kinsman send you here, librarian?"

I had thought I could get no colder or sicker. "R-royal? N-not even my m-master—"

He allowed my head to drop, launching new bolts of lightning through my neck and shoulders and catapulting my head into such throbbing agony as could obliterate reason.

"Hear me, failure." He ground the whispers into my ear, into my skull, into my soul. "I am Philippe de Savin-Journia's worst nightmare, and I *will* know his purposes. And lest you maintain some hope that you'll not be required to answer, know that we have eliminated your lordly companion—not much of a swordsman after all."

Eliminated? Dead? Ilario?

"Alas, our eager Merle dispatched him before he could tell us all we wished to know."

He might have been telling me the Souleater had launched his legions against a dragonfly, a mosquito, or a luminous moth flitting about a lamp. For one eternal instant I teetered on the precipice, refusing to believe it.

A sodden lump dropped to the floor beneath my drooping head—a fine leather glove, stained with soot and blood. Unmistakably Ilario's glove. Unmistakable, too, that a severed hand remained inside it. My spirit plummeted into the vastness of horror.

"You are quite alone, Portier de Savin-Duplais. You are nothing. Failed. And we have all the time in the world to learn your secrets."

CHAPTER EIGHTEEN

31 QAT

30 DAYS UNTIL THE ANNIVERSARY

The Aspirant and his henchman left me alone, suspended in the silent dark, to contemplate their promises. The walls of a sorcerer's hole were purposely built thick, lest magical keywords penetrate and quicken a prisoner's balked spellwork. And the hole was purposely left dark. Spark was the single element required for every spell; thus a prisoned sorcerer was stripped of anything that carried spark and was allowed no glimmer of light.

Yet even the painful void in which I existed could not compare to that within—guilt and anger and a sadness that left my spirit aching beyond any physical hurt. Ilario: illogical, foolish, preening, silly, but clever in his way, and generous and honorable, and so earnestly devoted. A man of scarlet finery, ruffled lace, and silly charms and elixirs, of incessant babbling, now forever stilled, leaving a sorry, sober vacancy in the converse of the world. Even the dread of bleeding could not divert my grieving.

Hours passed. My extremities lost all sensation. Back, neck, shoulders, and head felt riven by hot irons. Pain and grief festered, and as the press bears down on the vineyard's harvest, so did the waste and wrongness of Ilario's death render a familiar liquor—disappointment, failure, guilt, and self-loathing—as if my father had taken his knife to me again. Back then,

despair had flavored death with sweetness, and at three-and-twenty, with half my blood left puddled on my parents' floor beside my father's corpse and my dreams of magic, its intoxication had near made an end of me. Now, as then, its seductive aroma promised release.

But this time, the stakes were higher than my incapable self. *Focus, Portier, or you're going to betray them all—Ophelie, Lianelle, Calvino de Santo, Gruchin, Michel de Vernase, Philippe and his vision for Sabria's glory, Ilario and his determination to seek truth. You have no leave to despair. The first lesson of your schooling: Put aside distraction. Make a plan. . . .*

Escape. I had to persuade them to unbind me. That was the extent of my strategizing. Quernay arrived. Agony obliterated thought as he un-hitched my arms and dragged me out.

They had lit torches in the great chamber. Firelight danced on the stone floor. I could not lift my forehead from the gritty stone. It felt as if nails had pierced my temples. I could not stop shivering. "P-please. M-my hands are numb. D-damaged, they'll be useless. My livelihood . . ."

"Who told you how to find me?" Leather muted and distorted the soft words spoken so high above me.

"No one. I came here to test my—"

A boot, not Merle's, nudged my bruised groin. Lightning speared my gut. The floor squirmed underneath my face, as I drew up my knees. Sum-moning my last modicum of pride, I did not vomit on the Aspirant's boot.

"Who told you?" His toe tapped not five centimetres from my nose. "You are not clever enough to discover us on your own."

Gritting my teeth and forcing my wits into order, I glared at that dam-nable boot and dared it to reveal its wearer. Indeed, it was no country-man's cocker like Merle's, nor was it a peasant's nailed brogue, nor an elaborately stitched, wide-toed boot of current fashion as Ilario had worn. This was a horseman's knee-high boot of good leather, rubbed thin on the inside of the leg, the plain, double stitching well waxed to keep out sand and water. Worn leather spur stops protruded from the heel. A well-loved boot. A knight's boot.

Think. Who is this man? Lord, Quernay had called him. A knight, it seemed. A sorcerer, I presumed, though his assumed title said not.

Aspirant—what did that signify? One like Dante, not of the blood? Someone who knew me or knew *of* me. I could think of no one to fit the shape. Not yet. But on my hope of life, I would.

"Be assured, librarian, you've done no mischief that I cannot undo."

But I *had* done mischief . . . if I could keep Dante unknown. More, if I could get free. The thought of my partners, one living, one lost, infused a remnant of strength. Let this devil think me cowed.

"Please loose my hands," I mumbled, wincing as speech ground the cracks in my skull one edge against the other. "I'll tell you whatever you want."

"Indeed, you will." The knight's boot nudged my swollen lips and forced its gritty leather way inside, crushing my cheek, shoving my tongue aside, inevitably stretching and filling my bruised mouth until I gagged repeatedly. "The answers will . . . *leak* . . . out of you . . . *drip* . . . *flow*. What a pitiful thing you are. I will make you more useful than you could ever be to the King of Sabria."

Abruptly he removed his foot. I spat, coughed, and swallowed repeatedly to clear the foul taste, my skin ablaze. Shame fueled my risen determination into fury. I would babble like poor dead Ilario and twist my tale into such knots, the leather-faced villain would never find the end of them.

"Get him in the chair," snarled the Aspirant. "His Savin blood is not so sour as he claims. The blood of failures has fed our best work."

The blood of failures . . . Ophelie? Gruchin? As if I needed more fodder for my hatred.

Quernay unwrapped my arms and legs, and sensation returned to my cramped muscles in a fiery flood. Before I could claim any use from them, he hauled my carcass to the chair and strapped down my awakening limbs with the wide strips of supple leather. An extra strap bound my neck to the tall, narrow slat of the chair back.

Above the stair, the doorway to the night remained open. I could not go anywhere trussed like a goose and locked in a sorcerer's hole, but in the chair . . . if I could stay sensible . . . recover some use of my extremities . . . break the damnable straps . . .

A bronze tray sat atop a wheeled trolley next to my chair. Quernay laid out thin tubes of silver on it, alongside a porcelain bowl, pots of herbs, flasks of oils and liquids, and glass cups and tubes, some fitted with brass or ivory handles. The Aspirant opened a flat wood case containing neatly arranged lancets of every size, but he picked out a small brass block and flicked a lever on its top. Ten or more small blades popped out of its polished base.

Saints defend . . . Horror shivered my skin. I had seen sketches of scarificators in histories of the Blood Wars. I clamped my jaw tight.

"Clean him up and we'll draw a sample."

As the masked man watched, Quernay snatched a dagger from his waist and sliced through my ripped and filthy shirt. Grinning, he traced his blade lightly across the bloodied bruises his red-haired friend had left me. "Pity for you we can't use what's already let," he said. "But the Aspirant likes it clean. Fresh."

I shrank into the unyielding chair, needing no player's skill to convey my fear. "This is forbidden, p-perverse."

"You'll learn. We've many a lesson to teach."

With a rag doused in pungent oil from one of his flasks, Quernay wiped dried blood and dirt from my chest. Then he plunged the fiery wick of a lit candle into a bulbous glass cup from the tray. So quick I could scarce follow, he removed the flame and laid the mouth of the cup on my chest. The smooth rim, not so hot as I feared, clung to the skin, and I watched in dread fascination as the circle of flesh purpled and swelled into the cooling cup.

Quernay's finger under the edge of the glass loosened the cup, and he tossed it aside. Before I could speak or think, the Aspirant laid his chilly block of brass over the dark circle of swollen flesh and flicked its triggering lever.

The searing shock set me hard against the leather straps.

"And for good measure," the masked man whispered, "because you have set my plans askew . . ." A precise click and he set the metal block askew in the same spot, cool against the fiery wounding. The lever snapped again. Ten blades bit again. My skull threatened to explode.

"Father Creator," I mumbled, weakness radiating from the spot in scalding waves.

Quernay pressed a tubular glass fitted with a brass plunger over the wound, ensuring the oil on my skin sealed its heated mouth. He twisted the plunger's ivory handle and tugged it slowly outward. Blood surged into the glass. I thought my gut might be drawn out with it.

"It's time I looked in on our other friend," said the Aspirant, tossing his nasty implement onto the tray. "The adept's ready. Bring Portier's offering when you've milked enough for a trial." The masked man moved behind me into the passage that led to the sorcerer's hole.

"Aye, lord." Quernay removed the glass tube, deposited my blood into a porcelain jar, and picked up his glass cup and candle to begin again.

The Aspirant's footsteps halted. Locks snapped, and a heavy door scraped open. Then rose a keening as spoke of eternities of misery, of despair so cold and dark I felt the firelight dim, of suffering so profound my soul quailed. Not *friend*. Victim.

"Legions of Heaven bring you mercy." I had scarce breath enough to speak it, scarce mind enough to think who, in the name of holiness, the poor soul might be. Michel de Vernase? The Aspirant had mentioned an adept—so the missing Fedrigo, perhaps, who might have seen too much of Gaetana's work? *Please gods, let it not be Dante.*

Quernay pressed his cup to my chest. I wrestled the cursed straps, until the lout struck me so forcefully, the sand-hued light blurred and spun, smearing his dark face and my blood-striped skin with gleaming glass and fire. Though my head screamed agony, I clung to sense.

Quernay picked up the gleaming scarificator and cocked its blades. *Snick.* And it bit again. . . .

Such shallow cuts give up blood more slowly than a lanced vein. The day could stretch interminably, and I needed to act while I yet retained some wit. Only one thing was sure to halt a leech using a mule. He wouldn't want that mule to die until he was ready.

As Quernay suctioned blood from the fourth or fifth cupping circle, I took a lesson from Dante's discipline. With every scrap of will I could muster, I sent my mind voyaging into a cave darker than the sorcerer's

hole, conjuring the sound of ocean, the rhythmic crashing of implacable wave on resistant rock. I immersed myself in stillness. Retreated, until my head sagged against the neck strap.

Quernay lifted my head by my hair. Shook my chin. Threw water in my face. But failure had prompted me to work diligently at denying feeling. Sensation remained remote, and I remained limp.

"Weak-livered dolt," he grumbled. "Can't have your heart seizing up. Not yet." He pried the suction loose with a thick finger. After depositing the blood-filled instrument on the bench, he unbuckled the neck strap, allowing my head to droop without risk of strangulation. His heavy footsteps faded down the passage.

Raising a fervent prayer to whatever bright angels might frequent this demonish place, I shook off my trance, bent to the right hand wrist strap, and worried the buckle with my teeth.

As in every circumstance since giving up my studies, a spell formula popped to mind. The spell for breaking was not complex. It required base metal, unadulterated by water or air, and proportioned according to the material to be broken—less for paper or thread, more for wood or rope or leather, monumental amounts for thick stone or metal. The metal must be balanced with spark, proportioned as to the metal particle's hardness, as if— gods, I'd begun thinking like Dante—as if to make the spell's edge keen.

Idiot. I needed to bend my mind to escape, not dream of magic. I worked the leather tongue free and yanked the buckle loose, only to realize that freeing one wrist benefited me nothing. A second strap at the elbow held my arm in place. My freed right hand could not reach my other arm to loose either wrist or elbow. Nor could it reach the buckle on my side that held the strap across my waist or the straps across my thighs.

As I swallowed screaming frustration and rejected the impossibilities of gnawing leather straps in twain or bursting them with main strength, magical calculations continued running in my head. The chair's thick bolts were surely dense enough to supply the needed proportion and quality of base metal. But spark . . . My scattered coppers would compromise the metal without supplying enough spark. The torches—their flame pure spark—were stuck in mounted sconces too far away.

In frantic foolishness, my eyes roved the long chamber's furnishings. In one corner stood a water butt, tin cups stacked atop it. The long, low bench was piled with metal basins, towels, flasks, and a thick, leather-bound ledger, propped on a stack of other books. Beside the stack sat Merle's lantern.

Had not my face felt as battered as a tin pot fallen off a mountainside, I would have grinned. A man incapable of creating magic could still invoke a key. Anyone with half a mind kept spellkeys secret. Clearly, damnable, murderous Merle had less than half a mind.

Without touch to access the spell, I had to focus carefully. Quenching fear and frustration, I considered the lantern and mumbled, *"Illuminatio."* Nothing happened. I breathed deep and tried again.

"Illuminatio." The candle winked out. Curls of smoke filled the lantern.

"Illuminatio." The wick sparked into a small steady flame. *"Illuminatio . . ."*

On the seventh invocation of the spellkey, the lantern exploded into a storm of fire, shooting flames and smoke plumes all the way through the rectangular opening above the stair.

Imprisoned in the bleeding-chair, I laughed as the oiled leather binding of the ledger book burst into flame, quickly charring its pages. And I felt no librarian's qualm as the rapacious fire caught the other books and burst the glass flasks of oils and herbs. Nor did I quake when the spilled oils fueled a burning of the bench itself or when a gout of flame caught the tangles of rope so lately used to bind my limbs.

If the spark traversed the ropes all the way to my chair, I would infuse my will into the flame and the other particles bound within the compass of the chair, attempting once again to create magic. But even did I fail, as was certain, my captors must surely note the conflagration and set me loose. Once free of ropes and straps, once dragged up the steps and into open air, then we'd see.

Foolishly, I hadn't counted on smoke filling the chamber so quickly. Gray and yellow plumes billowed and curled. My eyes flooded. Coughing threatened to splinter my broken head. It took all the mind I could muster

to hold the spellwork ready, awaiting the arrival of the flame. My hands clawed the wooden arms in the very grooves and gouges left by those who'd been bled in this cursed chamber. As I gasped for air, a door deep in the passageway behind me crashed open.

"I'll take care of this one," shouted the Aspirant. "You get Portier out!"

Footsteps pounded toward me, Quernay cursing with a production and artistry that made my own pale. He set to my bindings. "Is this fire *your* doing, sniveler?"

He'd loosed only one ankle when a boulder plummeted straight through the thickening murk, near landing on my head. The moment's terror screamed that Heaven was caving the roof to make an end of us all.

But naught else fell. And Quernay shot to his feet, lurched backward, and drew his sword. Soon weapons clanged and hammered amid the growing din of fire and Quernay's roaring curses. I could see naught but two bodies clad in writhing smoke.

I bared my teeth and crowed. This was Dante, surely. Now we would put an end to these devils.

The sound of the unseen combat measured its progress. The scrape and clash of weapons . . . fast, vicious. Harsh breathing, grunts of effort, edged now and again with the keen timbre of pain.

"*Obscuré!*" Quernay bellowed. The firelight dimmed and smoke darkened.

Dante did not counter with magic. Odd. Surely his potent sorcery overmatched his combat skills. I'd spied no sword ever in the mage's rooms, and he had only one useful hand. Families in Coverge, slaveys in the quarries or mines, could not afford swordmasters.

A body crashed into the bench. Glass shattered. The dulled flames spiked, and smoke billowed thicker, reeking of scorched herbs. The figure lunged back into the fray. Flailing bodies bumped my back, my arms, my scorching knees. The raw wounding on my chest screamed as if with its own voice.

A sweating back pressed to my shoulder. "How many are they?" The voice was none I knew. Certainly not Dante's.

"Two here," I croaked between gasps. "One outside. Another prisoner, deeper in."

He darted away, shouting a question back at me. But I could not comprehend it, for rising flames licked the legs of my chair and singed my bare feet, surrounding me. The air became unbearably hot, and my breath came hard . . . hot, too . . . and I could not fill my lungs for the racking cough and the agony of my head, and the fire thundering ever louder and ever closer . . . and I needed to *break* these cursed straps and be *out* of this cursed chair . . . and I wanted to jump overboard, but the *agente confide* within reported I was not on the *Swan* this time and there would be no such easy escape and certainly no magic. . . .

Blind, coughing, sure my skull must crack, I did not feel him slash the leather straps. But someone hefted me across a set of bony shoulders, and hauled me up the steps toward the blessed air. Whether my rescuer was villain or savior, I near wept with gratitude I could not speak. Then my head whacked the edge of the trap. The smoky world wavered between charcoal and black, between stillness and movement, riven by lightning bolts that rendered me wholly speechless and lost in a midnight of misery.

CHAPTER NINETEEN

32 QAT
29 DAYS UNTIL THE ANNIVERSARY

The wet cloth tied across my eyes might have been dampened in Journia's snowmelt. Water droplets dribbled down my nose like pearls of ice. As far as I could remember, I had been shivering, puking, and head-splintered forever. If I only knew why . . .

Cobweb memories floated in the dark. *Held captive. Beaten. Bled.* There'd been a fire. Flame yet raged in proximity to my lungs, within and without. Now I sat on stony ground in the open air, back propped against a rock wall, and my head felt as if the Pantokrator's own mace was bashing it. But I had no idea where I was or who had brought me here. I needed to be careful. I needed to *know*. I needed to *see*.

"Who's there?" Even such a raw whisper started me coughing, but at least my hands were free to clamp the bones of my skull together. While there, my fingers tested the knot of my blindfold. I tugged one tail and felt it loosen.

Firm footsteps crossed a bit of rough ground, halted, and a body knelt down beside me. "None you know. Stay still until we discover who's about."

A hand cupped the back of my head.

I jerked away, which launched fiery spears from skull through spine,

setting me gasping through fire-seared lungs and barking like a maddened hound. . . .

Arms wrapped my shoulders and buried my face in a man's chest, holding me tight and still until the paroxysm quieted. My head did not quite shatter.

"Let us try this again," he said, soft and urgent. "I am not going to hurt you. I'm going to give you a tisane to soothe your throat and clear your lungs. Might make you a bit drowsy, too."

Gently he held my head and poured a litre or more of lukewarm liquid down my gullet. It tasted of anise and the scrapings from a stable floor. I choked and burbled a feeble protest, while pressing the heel of my hand to my throbbing forehead.

Lacking a voice or nerve enough to move again, I could not rebel when he snugged the wet blindfold tighter. "Your eyes are smoke-scalded, and you've clearly broken your head, so you'd best leave this in place for a time. If you *please*." The recommendation sounded very like a command. "You really ought to be dead."

My companion rose, then moved away. His walk bespoke a trained swordsman, sure of himself, light on his feet, but rooted firmly to the ground, one might say. He paused, took a few steps, paused, took a few more, circling from my right to my left before returning to settle beside me. I smelled smoke and death blood on him, at least until he raised another stinking cup under my nose.

I waved it off. But liquid slopped and spattered on the ground beside me. The next thing I knew, he was gently blotting the raw wounding on my chest with a scalding cloth that stank of his tisane. My body near seized with the hurt of it and my stomach with the smell.

"Sorry," he said. "I thought it had cooled."

Cloth ripped. He dabbed at the scorched cuts and tied strips around my torso. I worked at keeping still. At listening. At remembering. At staying awake.

"How many in their party? Use your hand to tell me."

Surely, if he asked, he was not one of them: not the wolfish one who'd

kicked me half to death, nor the brute who'd strapped me in the chair, nor the masked one . . .

The incoming tide of memory and urgency charged my aching body with fury. Ophelie's murderer, I was sure of it . . . and Gruchin's . . . and Ilario's. For certain the Aspirant had caused a man to emit a cry of torment that might have come from the Souleater's caverns.

"The man in the mask," I croaked, struggling to sit up. *Philippe de Savin-Journia's worst nightmare.* A knight. A sorcerer. I ought to know him.

"Hush." The hand with the warm cloth rested heavy on my rapidly pumping chest, while the other touched my mouth. "Use fingers. I can account for only two men. A scrawny one at the bridge. The big hairy fellow down below. How many more?"

I raised one finger. "He wore—"

"Yes, yes, the third wore a mask. Are you sure there were no more? That makes no sense if they were guarding secrets."

"Maybe an adept. And a prisoner," I whispered. "Desperate, dying. Go!" I shoved at him and waved him away.

He remained solidly in place. "Sante Marko himself could not send me back into that inferno. Smoke's still pouring out the hole. But I looked about before I hauled you up. None remained in the cells, and none's come out since. Either they're dead, or there's another way out, or . . . you were confused. There's not a sign of anyone hereabouts."

Coughing racked me again, threatening to turn my raw lungs inside out, and he muzzled me again and held me still, which was a mercy on my head. When I next opened my mouth, he poured another litre of anise-and-barnstraw tea down me, now rimed with ice. It tasted even nastier when cold.

"I've no yearning to stay here, but I'd rather drag you across that devilish bridge with this cough better settled." He laid something over me—a blanket or cloak that reeked of smoke. "And I'd like some notion of how many others might be waiting for us over there. Sleep easy. I'll watch."

The man's voice bled weariness. He rose and walked away again, making the same pattern: a few steps . . . a pause . . . a few steps. A patrol, only this time he halted halfway round.

"Damn and blast." The quiet oath sounded more in the line of annoyance—a banged shin or snagged hair—than emergency. Even so, it raised another brush of cold sweat.

The wind blustered, tainted with smoke and dust. The harsh screech of a hunting bird echoed from the nearby cliffs. Still shivering, I snugged the blanket round chin and neck. As my breathing eased, the head pounding settled to a duller rhythm, and my cobwebby thoughts collected themselves. I slipped my hands behind my head and untied the damp knots. Slowly, I tugged the cloth down and peered through slitted eyelids.

The wall supporting my back was the well enclosure in the center of the ruined village. Just inside one of the beehive houses burned a small, smokeless fire. Leaning gracefully against the doorpost, frowning at the little spyglass in his two uninjured hands, stood Ilario.

He must have glimpsed the movement of the cloth, or heard as much as I could make of a gasp or a laugh. I myself could not have said which. Or perhaps he'd been slammed by the sheer force of my astonishment, pleasure, and relief, for he glanced over at me, his lips pursed in rue, then looked back at his lady's gift. "Should have known you weren't so addled as you seemed. You'll not mention this to anyone, I trust."

"That you're not dead?" I croaked, choking back a cough with all my will. "That you saved my life? That you leapt through an illusion into a holocaust, freed me from that chair, and fought—"

"Just the one down there. The twitchy fellow's at the bottom of the chasm. Hoped nobody would notice he'd been stuck before he fell. Till the fire bloomed out of that cursed hole like sunrise, I'd come to think *you* must have fallen, too. Now stop talking. I don't like it here."

The fire. Resting the back of my head on the wall, I grinned at the thought of the "Pantokrator's Aurora" that had saved my life. Ilario's knightly sword dangled from his belt. I'd thought it naught but show.

"They showed me your riding glove with a severed hand in it," I whispered.

"The little ferret snagged my rucksack as he fell," he said, with a choked laugh. "My best gloves!"

The man peering through his exquisite little instrument, twisting and

shaking it, *looked* like Ilario de Sylvae: the earring, the fair hair cut fashionably ragged since that other fire, the long nose, unblemished skin, and lithe physique. And yet he was someone else entirely. "Untruth seated so deep, it is scarce detectable," so Dante had said, as if such untruth must ever be dangerous and wicked. Which it could be, I supposed.

Sobered, I waggled my hand to catch his attention. "Tell me who you are, lord chevalier."

His complexion took on the tint of firelight. "One who learned very young that elders pay no mind to idiot children. They don't lock them away. They don't murder them in their beds and call it *childhood flux*. They allow them to stay close to those they care about."

Close to Eugenie. "Does even your sister know you?"

He scrubbed tiredly at his forehead. "She sees as she wills. Beyond that, she does not care."

I interpreted this as *no*. "But Philippe . . ."

He stuffed the spyglass inside his jerkin and moved away from the fire and the house, until he was but a darker silhouette against the starry night. "Truly, Portier, I beg you put this out of your mind. You must have the constitution of an ox. The tisane should have put you to sleep three times over. If I'd thought you'd see . . ."

He would have donned his fool's mask. No, far more than a mask. He would have reverted to that other person, a man as vividly real as anyone I'd ever met. Philippe surely knew. It explained why my cousin had such faith in Ilario. Their friendship expressed itself in private games of stratagems, played out over many years.

"You need to sleep," he said again. "We've maybe two hours until first light. Once we're well away from here and Fedrigo's tisane has done its work, you can tell me what you've learned between getting bashed and burnt—or not, as you choose. But I'd prefer not to fight any more of these lunatics. They don't tire." He drifted to the next house. And the next.

Sleep was impossible. My head throbbed. My chest stung. Every portion of my cursed body hurt, and I had to flex my fingers repeatedly to keep them from going numb. The wind moaned about the beehive houses,

swirling dust and grit into my face. My mind leapt from one puzzle to the next without resolution.

Eventually Ilario interrupted my grumbling with more tea. "Eugenie was only eight when Soren chose her to wed," he said as I drank. "Three months she cried. He didn't touch her—not even Soren was so vile as that—but she'd never been from home. She just missed us all, her papa and mama, and her dolls and dogs. And me. We'd always got on. She is so loving—"

He straightened, dropped three weights in my lap, and strolled off to take up his watch. The weights were my journal, my scratched and dented compass, and Gruchin's double strike coin.

"Antonia suggested Papa send one of the dogs to soothe her. On the very day he received her letter, he called me into his study and told me he'd decided to send me instead. Amid all the lessons and warnings one would expect before sending a boy into fostering, he told me how he'd tried to discourage the marriage until Eugenie was older, and how he had petitioned the Temple to have it nullified on the grounds of Eugenie's misery. But King Soren insisted on an alliance with the House of Sylvae, and that was that. Papa charged me to stay close to Geni no matter what. To protect her as he could no longer do.

"And so I went, happy in Papa's trust, happy for the adventure, and happy to be with Eugenie. The moment I arrived at Castelle Escalon, she stopped crying. Ten days after, a fire destroyed our home. Papa, and Geni's mother whom I adored as my own, and all their servants died in the fire, along with our dogs and cats and birds."

"Angel's comfort, did you ever learn who was responsible?"

"I was eleven, Portier," he said, dry as the Arabascan landscape. "Soren's court comprised a thousand people and thrice that many plots and schemes. Even yet I can't swear whether it was murder or no. Antonia was kind and tried to mother Eugenie, though she has no more instinct for mothering than a berry bush. But I remembered how somber Papa had been, and how his hands had trembled as he spoke to me that last morning. And I thought how if he hadn't sent me, I'd be dead, too, and how the people at the palace had wanted a stupid pet. So I became what was

wanted. I've stayed close to Eugenie, and for better or worse, I've stayed alive."

"And somehow Philippe learned the truth."

"That is a private matter. We—hsst!"

Ilario whisked his sword from its scabbard. Without taking his eyes from the direction of the bridge, he extended his left hand and hauled up my creaking bones. He snatched a poniard from his left boot and pressed it into my hand, motioning me into the house where the little fire burned. He himself dissolved into the night.

I scooped dirt over the fire. Telltales of smoke would be less noticeable than live flame on a night when the air was smoke-laced, anyway. Then I wrapped myself in Ilario's dark cloak and huddled, dizzy, by the low doorway.

Quiet, hurrying footsteps crunched the stony ground. A shapeless figure entered the village circle. "Sheathe your weapon, fool of a lord. The both of you come with me if you favor living an hour more." Faint scarlet light flowed up Dante's white staff like warmed honey, twining his maimed hand and illuminating naught else of him but a billowing black cowl.

"Where in Heaven's demesne have you been, mage?" My voice was much too loud, unfortunate for several reasons. The subsequent lung spasm near shattered my head, and it would not stop.

Before my watering eyes could quite make him out, the mage was beside me, wrapping a string round my throat and his luminous stick. As I coughed and clutched my head, he dragged a finger along the string and snapped, *"Kiné sentia."*

A leaden blanket enfolded my chest, silencing me in midspasm. I could breathe, albeit I had to think about it.

Dante's hand caught my elbow just as my knees buckled. "Over here, lordling," he snapped quietly. "Put your hand to Portier."

"Saints Awaiting, mage, you've no idea the dreadful frights we've encountered!" Ilario—the more familiar Ilario—stumbled out of the inky shadows, fumbling sword and dagger as he tried to sheathe them. "That wretched bridge was near the death of me. If Portier hadn't got himself free of that chair and found me, I'd be a quivering—"

"Keep him on his feet, peacock. We *must* move."

Ilario stowed his weapons, including the knife he'd loaned me. As I struggled to draw breath, he thrust a long arm under my shoulders. "How the devil are we to get him across the bridge? It's nowhere wide enough for two. And there may be more villains than the ones Portier bashed with the lantern."

Ilario could not have imagined how unlikely I was to remember these fabrications. Dante's spell pressed me inevitably earthward.

"By all you name holy, keep silent, fool," said Dante. "And hurry. This rock is riddled with unstable enchantments. We do *not* want to be here."

The mage led us out of the village, the gleam of his staff reduced to a puddle of scarlet on the path. His urgency seemed reflected in the night air. The stars had vanished. Wind gusts threatened to knock us from our feet. A wing-spread owl swooped over our heads, shrieking.

Instead of venturing onto the worrisome bridge, we clambered down a rock shelf . . . and then another . . . and another . . . each shallower and narrower than the one before, until we were descending a crude, even-more-worrisome stair, hacked from the plateau's rocky flank. Each step took shape in the scarlet pool of light that slopped underneath Dante's billowing hem to settle about our feet.

I dared not take my eyes from the light. Some shallower steps could support only our heels. Some were but broken stubs, so that Ilario had to go before and help me down to the next. Some crumbled ominously beneath us. Jagged edges and sharp gravel tormented my feet, yet I was almost grateful for the lack of boots. Bare feet gave me better purchase.

The chevalier alone kept me upright. Knees like porridge, I could scarce move air in and out.

It was a madman's descent into the abyss. Only the grazed evidence of my fumbling knuckles proved a solid wall existed on our left. On our right, the air churned like boiling tar.

Ilario jerked and waved his hand, as a shadowy shape, far too big for leaves or birds, flew in front of us. Revulsion fluttered my spirit. An icy whirlwind whipped another dark shape past and sent it howling into a gaping darkness vaster than the chasm below. My senses—who could

imagine they reported faithfully?—insisted they scented dry cedar on the wind and tasted mouldering leaves of trees that had never grown on desert rock. Whisperings that were not quite words raised the hair on neck and arms, speaking hatred . . . anger . . . a gleeful fury. . . . I blessed Ilario for taking our exposed flank, and I thanked all gods that he was not the ninny he professed.

A great rumbling shivered the stair. Rocks and pebbles skittered around our feet. "Hurry!" shouted Dante above the din. "The dawn comes! Dawn is the danger."

Though I could not understand his concern—I yearned for dawn and light—I clung to Ilario and stumbled downward. The cliff wall bulged and split. A hail of rocks bounced across the path. But no longer was it only my lungs needed forcing. My heart's lumbering pace hobbled my feet.

When we reached a step so broad that Dante's light did not drip off its edge, extra arms grabbed me, and the two men together dragged me through a tangle of trees—fragrant myrtle and prickling juniper, cracking limbs sticky with resin. Leafy wands slapped face and torso, as my bare feet squelched in mud and slipped on moss-slicked stones shuddering with the world's upheaval.

"Here," said Dante, even *his* substantial voice gone breathless. "Stow him here. We're at the boundary. That will have to do."

My back grazed earth and stone. I slid downward, near dissolution from the crushing weight of the world's end. Everywhere in or on me hurt. I could not so much as twitch a finger.

In air lightened to charcoal, my bleared vision picked out the soaring bastions of Eltevire two hundred metres in front of me. "Boundary?" I wheezed, laboring to push air out as well as to draw it in. "What—?"

"Aagh!" Face twisted, Dante clapped his hands to his head. . . .

Eltevire's heights erupted in orange, red, yellow, and green flame, a thundering, unnatural dawn that cast cliffs and weedy thicket into high relief, sounding a din of Dimios's battle against Heaven. The earth before, beneath, and behind me heaved and bucked. Sharp reports of cracking rock heralded cascades of earth and stone. My stomach lurched. The lurid

light illumined the impossible steps we had descended in the night, just in time for an avalanche to sweep them away.

Ilario dived to the earth, arms flung over his head. But Dante stood between the both of us and the disintegrating cliff, his dark hair flying in a wild wind, staff upraised. Rocks and earth rained from the sky, causing silvery glints in the air before falling short or bouncing harmlessly away, as if the mage held out a silver shield visible only when it served.

The quake stemmed from naught of nature's work in sky or earth. Deafening, ruinous, its violence pummeled, crumbled, shattered soul and spirit, earth and flesh and bone. Such frigid fury, such visceral hatred lashed about the peripheries of Dante's trembling shield arm that I believed Merle's truncheon pounded me again.

After a small eternity, the rumbling quieted. One last heave, and the earth shuddered and stilled, and the residue of sorcery began to settle, an invisible dusting that stank of scorched bones.

Dante yet held, his every muscle quivering, staff gripped in a bleeding hand. "Let it go, mage," I whispered, dragging air into my starving lungs. My head felt like rubble. "You've done enough, both of you. I thank—"

My weary body could not force another breath. As the rising sun blazed through the dusty length of the abyss, my senses slid back into night.

CHAPTER TWENTY

"   . . . d on't know how he survived it. Besides all this lot, and the hatchwork of his chest where they bled him, I think his skull is broken. He has this lump on his head the size of an ostrich egg, and I tried to put wet compresses on it as my old nurse taught me, but there was blood everywhere, and I scarce knew where to start. Makes me queasy."

"It was my quieting spell near killed him. Gods, why didn't the damnable prig tell me he couldn't breathe?"

Propped up by a boulder amid clumps of sage and nettle, I could not see the two behind me. But my ears were working well enough to hear this not-quite-whispered exchange. It sparked an extraordinary good humor. To hear Dante confess a mistake always raised a grin. Or perhaps it was merely that I was alive and in the company of exceptional friends.

We had descended into the abyssal ravine that separated Eltevire—or the broken heights where Eltevire once existed—from the highlands we'd traveled to get here. Plumes of smoke and dust drifted across the silvered sky, while fog and shadow hung thick in the bottomland. The stone bridge was gone. Not far beyond my toes, the rubble of the mountaintop had buried a forest of locust and juniper.

I carefully inflated my chest to its fullest capacity, ignoring the scabs that stretched and broke and stung under the scratchy remnants of someone's scratchy cloak, and then sighed all that delicious air out again in thorough appreciation. My catalog of miseries had subsided. The exceptionally cold desert dawn had me shivering. A spring bubbling noisily through a tangle of marshwort roused thirst to a fever. And I had learned not to move in an untimely fashion. My head . . . gods . . . every twitch set off its hammering. But my heart paced an easy rhythm, and the cough had eased.

"You warned me you'd no healing skills, mage," I croaked, teeth chattering. "I b-believe now."

"You're awake!" Ilario scrambled into view on hands and knees, bellowing his delight. "What a fright you gave us! The mage had to strip his spell away and blow into your lungs to start them up again. I feared you were dead and whatever would we tell the k—?"

"Hush, lord!" I said, flinching. Relief at living had not made me forget our circumstances.

Dante loomed over the both of us, his haggard mien little improved from my last view of him at Castelle Escalon. "None's within hearing. And I doubt any's coming back here."

More evidence destroyed before we knew what it meant. But at least we had seen it.

Ilario, apparently none the worse for a night spent with the Earthshaker, leapt to his feet and spread his arms like spindly wings. "Truly, I thought the Last Day had come and the earth would disgorge the Souleater. And you did *something* to save us, mage, for which I must profoundly thank you, but I'm not sure I can bear thinking of it again, as I've never been so frighted. I've thought since then that perhaps you caused the whole thing."

"No, you blighted idiot, I did not cause it." Dante's ferocious gaze raked me stem to stern. "Portier, you must move as soon as you can. They've gone, but I cannot. We need to be away from here." His agitation was profound, as was the tremor in his hands and the shadowed exhaustion that leached the life and color from his skin.

I had no wish to linger in a place where cliffs could be launched at my

head. And if Dante was nervous, I most assuredly wished to be gone. "Now I can breathe, I feel like a new man," I said, holding out my hands for assistance. "Or at least the better parts of the old one."

My skull did not actually explode when they hauled me up. But its grinding bones seemed connected straight to my gut, which promptly revolted in humiliating fashion.

"More?" Ilario pointed at the blessed waterskin I had just drained.

"I could do with three more and a bath in yon spring," I said, dumping the gritty dregs over my head. I smeared the droplets around my face and enjoyed the illusion of cleanliness.

"Do either of you understand what *haste* means?" Dante thrust a straight, slender branch into my hand. It was smoothed at the grip and cut to a reasonable length for a walking stick. "They *must not* see us."

"You said they were gone!" I resisted the temptation to swing around to look back at Eltevire's crumbled remains. Thoughts of the man in the leather mask roused a deep-rooted panic that the deep, cool shadows of the chasm did naught to soothe. "Whatever comes, he mustn't find you with me."

Dante's quivering hand pushed back his hair, resting on his temple as if he suffered the same wretched head as I did. "You *heard* them? Were you able—did you recognize a voice?"

"He wore a mask and a knight's boots. Called himself the Aspirant. But he knew Philippe had sent me."

Dante shook his head dismissively. "Fool of a student. There are no *men* here. Now, move."

Before I gathered his meaning, the mage was ten metres downstream. Tentatively, reluctantly, I reached out with the senses I used to detect enchantments. The much-too-cold ravine seemed to buckle and twist. The malevolent presence I had sensed on our descent the previous night was entwined with the mist, its hissing anger blended with the rill's gurgling. Beyond the deep, cold crevices in rock and rubble yawned the deeper void I'd thought morning had dismissed. "Chevalier, please . . ."

Ilario lent me his strong shoulder again. His brow creased in question, but I devoted strength and concentration to movement. Silent,

desperate, Dante swept us down the gorge like a springtime flood. I could not go as fast as he wished. The mage would race ahead, then double back to help Ilario hand me over fallen trees or boulders. Shamefully weak and wobbly at the knees, I had to fight off repeated bouts of nausea. My flesh felt riddled with maggots. The tumbled boulders seemed to crawl alongside us.

Once Ilario and I came upon Dante, shaking violently, forehead pressed to a rock, his arms flung around his head as if to block out the sights and sounds of battle. "Mage," I whispered, not touching him, "can we help you?"

"Keep moving," he rasped. A pocket of frigid air brushed my skin. Naught was visible, but when I blinked, a blur of color streaked through the haze like a darting fish. We moved. Eventually, Dante passed by us, leaning heavily on his staff.

By midday, Dante awaited Ilario and me in the glaring slot of sunlight that signaled the eastern end of the gorge. The shadows had paled, the fog dispersed. My senses no longer detected anything unnatural.

"Portier," said Ilario quietly, while we were yet a goodly distance from the mage. A tortoise could have outrun me just then. "Our story. We need to agree."

"You heard me call and blundered into the hole. Despite my injuries and bindings, I freed myself of the chair and felled Quernay with the lantern. Is that right?"

He nodded. "I merely helped you up the steps and out. Simple enough."

"I dislike lying to Dante," I said. "My mind's a sieve where he is concerned. Besides, he's our partner. I believe him honorable." He had saved our lives the previous night, and just now shielded us from . . . something.

For the five-hundredth time, I stumbled and Ilario's strong hand kept me upright. "This is my *life*, Portier. I beg you honor my choice."

"If the mage somehow got into that cellar and saw the chair, he'll catch us out. He'll know I could never have loosed the straps."

"But certainly you managed it. By the time I had done for the hairy

brute, checked the cells, and retrieved my crocodile charm, you had broken free of the straps. You were just out of your head."

"All right, all right. I'll play." Naught could ever repay his help. But who'd have thought he could slip so effortlessly back into his idiot self after the journey we'd just experienced? "I owe you my life, lord. You needn't fear my loose tongue."

Eyes fixed on the rocky path, he inclined his head. "Now will you tell me what in the name of Heaven just happened? I've a notion I just crawled out of a dung heap."

"Honestly, I've no idea." Only that something had near unraveled Dante. Whether he'd been protecting us or probing mystery, my mind balked at imagining what it might be. My bones yet quaked, and I flinched with every blink.

A careful survey of the bleak country spread out beyond the gorge revealed not the slightest movement, no stirred dust, no whinny, no glint of metal, no untoward scent of man or beast. Half a kilometre into the open country, Dante relented and let me be still for a while in the shelter of a turpentine tree. As Ilario and I shared a waterskin, the mage propped his back on the tree and stared into the wasteland. I wondered if he was afraid to blink, as well.

"These bandages should be tended," said Ilario, dabbing a dainty finger at the blood- and dirt-encrusted rags bound to my chest. "My physician insists we cleanse wounds every day. A disgusting task . . ." Which he took up right away.

I resisted searching Ilario's pruned expression for evidence of the swordsman or probing his babble for hints of the man I had met at Eltevire. I would honor my promise. Besides, I doubted any flaw was to be found.

As Ilario worked, Dante shook off his reverie and joined us. The mage was no longer shaking. He inspected the lacerated purple circles on my chest for several uncomfortable moments, then nudged my ruined shirt aside to expose several older scars—my father's legacy. He reached out as if to touch them, then hesitated and glanced up.

"If you must." I didn't understand his interest.

His finger, firm, sure, and cold—thrumming with magical energies—traced the long scar that creased my left side and the short one just above my navel. The careful scrutiny recalled his inspection of Gruchin's spyglass, and I wondered if he was building the ragged marks into one of his runelike patterns in his head. I shifted uneasily.

"Killing strikes, these," he said, withdrawing his hand.

"Near enough." So Kajetan had told me when I regained consciousness, weak, nauseated, and bathed in blood and cold sweat. "It was a long time ago."

"Maybe nearer than you think. What happened to the one who did it?"

"He travels Ixtador, I suppose."

"Your father. Gods, he bears a fearsome grudge."

Cold iron lodged in my belly. He did not speak in the past. "How would you know that, mage?"

My demand bounced off his impenetrable stubbornness. "That bandage is filthy." He stood and tossed a clean kerchief of cheap linen into Ilario's lap. "Tell us about this Aspirant, student."

After Ilario folded the kerchief and tied it up for me, he forced me to accept the meager supply of cheese and ale from Dante's pack. Once begun eating, I couldn't stop, despite the profoundly unsettling morning and my annoyance with Dante. Likely a good sign that I was ravenous. Mules lost their appetite as their blood was repeatedly drained. As I ate, I told them the story of Merle and Quernay and their master.

Dante sat cross-legged, as intent in his listening as in everything else. "So this Aspirant worked no enchantments as his assistant drew the blood. Did he inject it directly into himself or distill it?"

"I didn't see. He took it back to where the other prisoner was kept. I was glad enough they didn't try to fill their entire urn in that one hour. They took half a litre, more or less. That's not enough to do much with, do you think?" I paused between bites. I hadn't yet considered the part of me I'd left behind, now taken who knew where.

Dante's long speculation gave me no reassurance. "If you start with odd dreams or unusual behaviors, you might want to tell me. To trigger

what we saw this morn, destroying half a mountain in the hour Eltevire
was compromised . . . The spellwork makes the doings on the *Swan* look
like acolyte's play. It means someone has a talent beyond—"

"Beyond the level of a minimally talented hod-carrier?" I could not
resist the jab.

His head jerked in assent. "Aye. Even allowing for transference to enhance inborn skills. Even allowing that the worst of this day and night was
worked two hundred years past. We've a foe I didn't think existed."

This trace of humility on Dante's part frightened me more than anything we'd encountered.

"What was so mysterious about a cursed ruin?" asked Ilario, giving me
a hand up. "They had a bleeding cell in the royal crypt and didn't see it
necessary to explode the temple to hide it. What *began* here?"

"The whole place was enchanted," I said. "Objects in motion, light,
fire, water . . . nothing behaved properly or consistently. At least nothing
that originated in Eltevire. . . ."

As we plodded along a faint cart path that skirted the end of the ridge,
I told them of my experiments—not of my attempts at magic, which
proved naught but that "place" could not make an incapable sorcerer capable, but of the coins, Gruchin's silver, and the pool, the crocodile charm,
and the lantern. ". . . think of your tisane that was lukewarm one moment,
boiling the next, and felt like glacial ice but a moment later. Nothing
behaved."

We retrieved Dante's donkey, left tethered beside a shady spring where
we could fill our waterskins. "I arrived early at Canfreg Spring," said the
mage, as we set out again, faster now with me astride. "When I heard the
old man's tales—" He shrugged, and I understood. His hunger for knowledge had driven him to Eltevire ahead of us. "I intended to rejoin you, but
three men rode in behind me and I dared not counter the bridge ward or
its trip signal."

He slowed his steps and waved his staff at me. "You should have more
care, student. You sense enchantments and residues. To disentangle a trip
signal from a common ward is only one step more. It could have saved you
this thrashing."

"Then *teach* me, if magic is so damnably easy," I mumbled. The donkey's jarring gait had my head pounding too awfully to yell at him. Despite his air of hard-won wisdom, the mage's brittle arrogance surely named him far younger than only six years my junior. Naturally, he didn't answer.

"So you were in the village while Portier was tortured?" Ilario burst out. "Ill done, mage! Unkind!"

"I never crossed the bridge, never went up to the village until I came for you. I let them pass and came around here. The mendicant had told me of the chasm stair."

"But if you kept away, how did you know they were going to explode the mountain?" spluttered Ilario. "Magework cannot predict the future, no matter what's said, else I'd have never come on this nasty trek! And why didn't the wards along *this* path bring them down on you?"

"I learned what I needed in the chasm. The destruction was writ in Eltevire's bedrock. A very long time ago, I think. Last night the rock's pattern shifted, and I could see a danger building. And just then, three men descended the stair in a hurry—though one was slow and weak—your prisoner, I'd say. Magic takes on extra potency at sunrise and sunset, so I expected the blow at dawn. Fortunately for you, peacock, I guessed right."

Three men had arrived at Eltevire: Quernay, Merle, and the Aspirant. And three men departed: the Aspirant, the prisoner, and who? The prisoner's guard, perhaps. Or perhaps "the adept" was not a prisoner, but another guard. I blotted the sweat from my bruised temples and squinted into midday.

"Over a day and a night I explored these physical anomalies," Dante continued, "though not so systematically as with your coins and pebbles. But it's the *mechanism* of Eltevire's madness that bears most significance." He halted the donkey for a moment and made sure I was listening. "To leave the gorge we had to travel along a boundary—a separation of two natural entities as distinctive as sea and land, or stem and leaf, or wing and air. Even as we walked that boundary, it was disintegrating, soon to be gone entirely. Until this morning, it completely encircled Eltevire's plateau."

"Separating *what*?" I said. "The two sides appear the same—land, veg-

etation, rock, wind. You're saying these villains enchanted *everything* within this boundary, creating some new kind of natural separation."

"No, Portier. Much more than that. Eltevire was not enchanted. Yes, the boundary was created with sorcery, but within the boundaries of that rock, nature itself was altered, *including* magic, for magic is *of* nature." Dante might have been a once-blind man explaining the wonder of his first sunrise. "A stone behaves like a stone, or a sparrow like a sparrow, because the pattern of natural law is written into the pattern of its being— its keirna. If you toss your coins into the air in Castelle Escalon, they behave according to their keirna. When a Merona sparrow takes wing, its flight reflects the physical laws we know. I believe that when the natural laws of bounded Eltevire were altered, the pattern of natural law written into the keirna of every object within that boundary was revised, as well. Did you find any spelled object in Eltevire?"

"None," I said, my mind racing to keep up with him.

"Aye, because your methods of detection are based upon the nature that you know, on the *magic* that you know. What if Gruchin's coin were brought to Eltevire and enspelled with a locator charm so he couldn't escape them? Its keirna, once solely of the world we know, would have been altered. But you or I would never detect the spell, because we don't know how to detect *Eltevire's* magic."

"And what of the crocodile charm?" I said. "It was enspelled in Merona, not Eltevire, yet its behavior changed when I invoked it in there."

A ruddy heat suffused Dante as from a lathered horse nearing its home ground. "The light charm worked exactly as its keirna was laid down. When the keyword is spoken, the spell is triggered and the charm emits blue light. But in Eltevire, the properties of *light* are not immutable as our natural philosophers demonstrate. Use the charm fifty times in Merona, and it will always trigger blue light of a certain quality, but do the same in Eltevire and the manifestation could vary every time."

Ilario pulled his spyglass from his shirt and stared at it as if it were a demon's trinket. "I don't understand half of what you say. But I'm thinking perhaps my lady's glass is not broken after all. In Eltevire, sometimes it would show me my own feet, sometimes the stars, sometimes nothing."

Dante extended a hand, and Ilario passed him the glass. The mage's long fingers caressed the engraved case. He sighted through it up the slope we had to climb to retrieve our mounts, then passed it back to Ilario.

"It's not spelled. And it functions as it should. Light passes through its lenses and is bent, allowing our eyes to see what is directly in front of us, only drawn close. But in Eltevire, light beams do not always follow the rules. Our glass lenses would never work reliably there. Nor our eyes, I'd guess. Nor our magic."

"Father Creator," I said, as my own mind grasped his conclusions: a land where nature itself was altered, where neither physics nor magic could be predicted. *Guess you're fuddled*, Merle had said. *We'll fuddle you all.* "Such a place would be chaos."

"Aye," said Dante. "Chaos. Especially when you add in that there was more inside that boundary than the land you walked. Voices that had no right to be there. Sights you couldn't quite see. More than you know. Naught that I can explain . . . yet. But it's no mystery why they're wanting a handy necromancer."

Father Creator, send your angels. I could not speak. I could not think in aught but prayer, though instinct had whispered it all morning, and Dante had told me, *Your father . . . bears a fearsome grudge.*

The day was heating rapidly. Dante threw his dark cloak back over his wide shoulders, clicked his tongue at the donkey, and planted his white staff on an upward path. "I'll tell you one more thing, my partner *agentes*. The keirna of that boundary was far older than our conspiracy. Think about it: The cult brother's stories of this region have existed for centuries; the Mondragoni settled here well before the Blood Wars. Neither your Aspirant, whoever he is, nor Gaetana nor Orviene *worked* the enchantments that created Eltevire's aberrant nature. They don't know how."

He glanced over his shoulder at me, his green eyes flashing. The beginnings of a smile transformed his gaunt face into something younger and less haunted. "So now I know what they want me for."

WE DIDN'T TALK MUCH THROUGH that long afternoon. Even Ilario's determined idiocy found little outlet. The path was too steep, the day too hot. We moved carefully, scanning the landscape in every direction, but we saw no sign of human or beast . . . or anything else. The lump on my head belonged in a smithy.

Dante had implied that some connection with Ixtador lay beyond Eltevire's boundary. I tried to comprehend what that meant, but exhaustion had its way, and for the first time in nine years, I slipped into my vivid dreaming. I was wielding lightning to hold a mountain pass against a barbarian horde, while a fleeing populace reached safety. Fire threaded my arms and the heated charge of sorcery stank like seared stone. When my magic failed and the enemy bludgeons began to crack my bones, I blinked awake to the wastes of Arabasca and honest bruises and mysteries too deep for comprehension. Then the cursed donkey missed its footing, and in my distraction, I failed to brace. The pain in my head caused me to waste everything I'd eaten.

Vowing not to sleep again, I spent the next miserable hours contemplating everything we had learned from the day Philippe led me into Lady Susanna's dungeon until Dante's fierce conclusion. Perhaps the feigned assassination of Sabria's king had not been a mere distraction, but a first skirmish in a new war, a feint designed to test their plan. The conspirators were gathering power through transference, and if Dante was correct, exploring ways to upend the rule of reason. Chaos. Discord. Fear. So who would benefit from chaos?

Some two hours later, we stopped to drink and rest on the stepped tableland above Sante Marko's shrine. Only then did I speak to a disturbing possibility that had presented itself.

"Chevalier," I said, "what does Michel de Vernase look like?"

Ilario frowned and blotted his sun-scalded forehead with a filthy kerchief. "He's a big man. Near tall as I, but built for a fight. Muscled like a bull, head as well as body. Darker complected than Philippe, gold-brown hair starting to gray. Rough as a battlefield, but ladies fall all over him, which I've never understood."

"Knightly," I said. "Horseman, swordsman, all that. No grandiose reports hiding poor truth?"

Ilario rolled his eyes. "No false reports. Whatever a man can do, Michel de Vernase can do better. Rides like the Arothi. Fights like the warrior angel. Drinks like a sailor. Carries himself like a Linguan stallion."

I persisted, seeking to escape my logic. "But common, you said. Who are his people? Vernase village is the seat of the Ruggiere demesne. Was he born there? Educated?"

Dante looked up from relacing his dusty boots, his face sharp with curiosity.

Ilario draped the filthy kerchief over his forehead. "No family. I've heard he was a basket child, found and raised by an unlanded knight at a military outpost in . . . Grenville, I think it was. No doubt he's clever, and supposedly he's remedied the lack of education since Philippe raised him up. His wife gentled him enough to come to court. Mayhap she set him to his books, as well. Madeleine's worth a hundred of him. Old family . . ." He paused, his hands still for a moment. Then he peered over his kerchief. "What does all this matter?" Eyes widening, he caught his breath. "Was he the Aspirant's prisoner?"

"I thought so," I said, "but now . . . Listen to me. Michel de Vernase was raised up to First Counselor, the highest post in Sabria, short of her sovereign. He was granted a demesne that had ever been reserved for the nobility. How many resentments has he faced on those accounts, as well as for his bullish manner? Yours, Chevalier, and others, I'm sure. He owns Philippe's implicit trust, yet knows he will forever be seen as a product of Philippe's favor. A second part: When the infant prince died, Philippe named a new heir, a secret no one in this kingdom shares—save perhaps Michel, the friend of his youth, closer than a brother, closer even than the estranged wife Philippe loves so dearly. As you put it, lord, Philippe and Michel have always covered each other's sins and drunk each other's wine. One month after the new heir's name was scribed in stone, Philippe's horse went mad and threw him."

Ilario scowled and shook his head, but I hushed him with a gesture. Perhaps he sensed where I was headed.

"Michel publicly scorns magic, as does his friend and liege. The spyglass implicated sorcerers, as did Gruchin's body, mutilated by transfer-

ence. Yet Michel had Philippe's horse and saddle burned, and he neglected to have a mage examine the arrow. He bullied the Camarilla and the mages at Seravain. Ham-handed we called him, yet Philippe considers him a skilled, successful diplomat. And Michel instantly accused, not a sorcerer, but Calvino de Santo."

As I reconstructed my chain of reasoning, a certain fury took fire within me, from embers left smoldering since witnessing Calvino de San-to's testimony. Michel de Vernase had brutalized the guard captain, making him a public scapegoat when Queen Eugenie, the one witness who could aid him, had stubbornly refused to testify. Yet Michel had never extracted Gruchin's name from de Santo—which could have led the investigation back to Gaetana. And Michel had used two young girls, persuading—coercing?—one to return to terrible danger to discover the name of Eltevire. At the least his actions had killed Ophelie and left her young friend at equal risk. But there were other ways to interpret his course.

"What if Michel de Vernase had his own motive for prying the name of Eltevire from the mage who bled Ophelie? All along we've seen clues thrown in for confusion's sake, the trail of evidence obscured almost as quickly as it was laid. What if he wanted to make Eltevire his own?"

"But his name was scribed on the crypt wall," Ilario insisted. "Ophelie spoke it as she died. *Michel . . . captive . . .*"

The more I voiced my theory, the more I was convinced—possessed—of it. "Perhaps she didn't mean that Michel *was* captive, but that Michel had *taken* her captive. The *good man* she hoped to save from the fire could have been someone else altogether. Someone whose name she didn't know, but who possessed magic enough to break her manacles. Perhaps your charm maker, Adept Fedrigo. I don't know that anyone has seen him since Ophelie's escape. Perhaps Fedrigo scratched the Ruggiere symbol on the crypt wall because Michel was there, not as a prisoner, but as captor."

"Well reasoned, student," said Dante softly, his chin propped on his staff. "Very well reasoned."

"Michel de Vernase is this Aspirant? The leader of this conspiracy?"

Ilario's shocked face had paled under his sunburn. "True, I never liked him, but many do. And Philippe . . . He'll never accept it. How could you possibly come to this?"

"Boots," I said. "The Aspirant's boots belonged to a knight, not a mage. They belonged to someone who guessed my identity easily and assumed Philippe had sent me. My cousin said he has been gathering reports of me for years. Who else but Michel would have been assigned such a delicate family task for his king? Who else might guess what *agente confide* Philippe might tap should his good friend vanish? Perhaps, before he went away, Michel himself suggested my name." Perhaps he suggested Portier de Duplais should head an investigation which a dull, failed student of magic could not possibly unravel.

"It would explain why he didn't worry about leaving that Cazar girl at Seravain," Ilario mumbled, wilted by distress. "She's likely in no danger at all. You see, I finally remember about the name. Michel's wife is Madeleine de *Cazar* y Vernase-Ruggiere."

And so did another link snap into place. Lianelle ney Cazar was Michel de Vernase's daughter. As I had done, she had dropped a father's name that would see her scorned or snubbed among a society of mages. I did not believe the child herself involved in transference and murder. When I had accused Michel of callous disregard of Ophelie's safety, Lianelle's distress had been unfeigned. But the father . . .

I could not deny my lust at the prospect of justice for crimes of such magnitude. And amid my sympathy for those like Lianelle, cruelly used by a father's ambition, lay hope for Maura. If the queen herself was innocent, then surely Maura's involvement was but another diversion.

Reasons, motives, the sorcerers who most assuredly had abetted the traitor, the methods to be used to create a kingdom of chaos—the precise construction of this plot could align in a thousand different ways. More than ever we needed Dante to pursue the magic. But the most difficult part would be to convince the king of the danger—that Philippe de Savin-Journia's worst nightmare was not his wife, but his beloved friend.

CHAPTER TWENTY-ONE

"**H**is Majesty will see you now." The satin-garbed undersecretary's lips squeezed to a fleshy knot as he called me from the waiting chamber. Whether his disapproval addressed my cheap, ill-fitting garb, the massed green and purple of my healing bruises, or the king's overgenerosity in granting a coveted private audience to an embarrassment of a fifteenth cousin, I did not care. Too much else weighed on my mind on the first morning of my return to Castelle Escalon.

The undersecretary led me down a soft-lit passageway, his velvet slippers whispering on the cool travertine. Others glided by—a footman bearing a tray of sliced fruit, a perfumed woman herding a swaggering youth of an age to be squired, a lesser temple reader juggling a box. As my escort gestured toward an unpresuming door at the end of the hall, I bowed and exposed my hand to the portly, bearded man who had just come out of it. Baldwin de Germile, a man whose expansive girth and genial manner often saw his intellect underestimated, had yielded his position as First Counselor to Michel de Vernase gracefully, only to reclaim it after the Conte Ruggiere's disappearance. He flicked forefinger to temple in a cheery greeting, though he clearly did not recognize me.

Angels defend, what would such honorable men as Baldwin make of

my tale? Every night of the return journey from Eltevire, I had labored over my journal, recording every detail of our experience in Arabasca, every connection I had drawn to events already described, every assumption, every unanswered question. On the previous night, newly arrived, I had foraged the palace library for historical details that might give background to the story. More and more I believed that Michel de Vernase had conspired with an unknown sorcerer not to murder, but to destroy his king.

Michel's personal history with my cousin must surely outweigh any single bit of evidence I brought in, no matter how damning. Philippe, no blind simpleton, had named Michel his infant son's goodfather. Even those Sabrians who maintained a casual distance from temples and tessilae would entrust guardianship of their children's education, estate, and marriage, and the welfare of those children's soul beyond death, *only* to a person of proven honor. Someone closer than blood kin. Which meant the chain of my story must be unbreakable, each link, in its turn, able to withstand hostile scrutiny.

The door swung open. "Your Majesty, Portier de Savin-Duplais."

The undersecretary stepped aside for me to pass into a map-lined study. Then he retired, closing the door soundlessly behind me.

I sank to one knee, my eyes on the jewel-hued Syan rug. Though I had caught but a glimpse of the man standing across the room, I sensed a fierce appraisal. The bruise on my temple was fairly horrible and the cuts on my lip scabbed over. My hair, never luxuriant, had been clotted with blood and singed into ragged ugliness by the Eltevire fires. Heurot's fussing attention and skillful knife could do naught but whack it off—a convict's shearing.

"Cousin Portier, I believed our understanding precluded any direct encounter." Though this greeting held none of the familial warmth of our first meeting, I did not permit my resolve to waver. My cousin likely feared what I might tell him. Rightly so.

Given no leave to stand, I remained on my knee, eyes down. "Circumstances have changed, sire. I am known to your enemies, though my fellow *agentes* remain hidden in place, ready to pursue these matters until

they are resolved. Both have brought exceptional courage and skill to your service."

"And you have news for me?"

A scarlet thread in the carpet might have been an image of the story I must tell, twisting upon itself, hiding behind the lapis-hued warp threads, only to emerge somewhere altogether unexpected. "We have uncovered much that is dire and terrible, and I would give my arm not to speak the painful words I must. Will you hear me out, Majesty, all the way to the conclusion?"

I felt, more than heard, him move toward me, thus did not startle when he touched my bruised temple. "It appears you have suffered your own hurts to bring me answers. How can I refuse mere words?" His ringed hand brushed my shoulder, but did not pause for me to kiss it.

I rose and took the straight-backed seat he indicated, while he settled in a deep armchair, cushioned with maroon velvet.

"To the conclusion," he said, propping elbows on the chair arms and his chin on tented fingers. "I shall not interrupt."

I inclined my head. "I know you have received some intermediate reports of our investigation, courtesy of Chevalier Ilario, but I would ask you to forget all you've heard, imagined, or assumed about these plots. The story truly begins long before the Blood Wars, when the Mondragoni clan laid claim to an ugly little corner of Arabasca and made it their hereditary demesne. . . ."

An hour I spoke without pause, first outlining the disturbing nature of the magic the Mondragoni had worked at Eltevire. My hour in the palace library had confirmed that no other family had ever held that corner of Arabasca. Then I laid out the threads of our investigation—brave Ophelie and old Audric; Gruchin and his spyglass and an arrow that was never meant to kill; de Santo and his haunting; the fire on the *Swan*.

When I spoke of Lianelle and Ophelie, and Michel de Vernase's visits to Seravain, Philippe closed his eyes as if he could not bear to hear more. But his stony expression did not change, and I continued without pause to tell of Ophelie's family dead, and Gruchin's family dead, and suicidal seamstresses and missing adepts. I explained how Gaetana's approaches to

Dante, the nature of the spyglass, the missing Mondragoni texts, and the mysteries of Eltevire hinted at sorcery so disturbing, he dared not fail to pursue and understand it.

"We cannot ignore the congruence of your enemy's work and the Veil—the natural boundary between life and death—and this unnatural boundary created at Eltevire, where natural law, as we know it, borders on a chaotic otherness. But the most significant question to be answered is the identity of your enemy—the leader of this conspiracy. Who dares use your safety, your wife's grief, and relentless murder to hide this exploration of death and chaos? And why?"

Dante himself could not impose such pressure of will upon me as did my cousin, sitting expressionless in his chair.

I inhaled deeply. "From the beginning, I believed one or both mages of the queen's household stood at the center of these events. That may yet be true. I see now that in my deepest self, I also assumed your wife responsible. But an investigator must not blind himself to possibility. Dante and I have come to believe that the queen's yearning to comfort her dead children has provided a smoke screen for those who pursue an interest in profound and unnatural mysteries. Yet it was only at Eltevire that a glimpse of a man's boots forced me to shift my eyes. This masked man who called himself *Aspirant* never worked magic in my presence. . . ."

As I recounted my tale of beatings, bleeding, and boots, Philippe grew rigid in his chair. And when I reported the Aspirant's claim that he was Philippe de Savin-Journia's worst nightmare, the king shot from his seat and strode to the window.

I paused, heart hammering. I had not yet spoken Michel's name.

His back to me, my silent cousin motioned me to continue.

"It is only in assembling all these bits and pieces, and imbuing them with . . . aspirations . . . that we see a larger story. Let us return to the day that Gruchin, near madness from two years' bleeding and compelled by unknown torments to loft an arrow at his king, stole his crude spyglass from his old partner's shop. Hoping to direct attention to the nefarious activities of his masters, and thus avenge his family's murder, he brought his spyglass and his coin to the field and made sure his own corpus would

be left alongside them as evidence. You assigned your friend and counselor the Conte Ruggiere to investigate the matter. . . ."

Never did Philippe interrupt my account. I did not offer my interpretations of Michel's state of mind, as I had to Dante and Ilario, nor did I dare ask whose name my cousin had scribed on the Heir's Tablet in the royal crypt or what Michel de Vernase had thought of his choice. I did not soften my telling with apologies or implied excuses designed to flatter the king or his friend. Philippe would accept what I said or not. He knew the conte better than anyone.

"Majesty, you told me at the beginning of this journey that Michel de Vernase is either dead or hostage to those who wish you harm. Yet, in most of a year, you have received no request for ransom or favor. I say, either he is dead, or he is one of them."

I did not beg pardon or forbearance. I merely stopped speaking and waited. Any number of reactions seemed likely: denial, argument, imprisonment, interrogation, accusation.

For interminable moments, Philippe remained motionless. Then he whirled about, snagged my arm, yanked open the door, and propelled me through the halls of his palace.

My eyes refused to meet those of the myriad curious courtiers and servants who stepped aside, bowing, to let us pass. My skin burned. I was unsurprised when Philippe burst through a door on the second level of the northwest tower—the headquarters of the Guard Royale—but my spirit quailed, nonetheless. House arrest? Or Spindle Prison, the desolate finger of stone thrust up from the river Ley? My heated skin broke into a cold sweat.

A mustachioed captain, built like a bridge piling despite modest height, leapt up from behind a scarred table and dropped to his knee, alongside several officers and orderlies. "Majesty!"

Philippe twitched his hand to get them up, and his head to clear the room of all but the sturdy captain. "Captain de Segur, since fifteen Cinq of last year, the Conte Ruggiere has been away from Merona on a diplomatic mission. I have just received information that on thirty-four Siece last, he was taken captive. By midday today, you will dispatch the fifth

gardia to find him, beginning the search at Collegia Seravain and working outward in every direction, questioning every man, woman, and child in the demesne if needs must. You will dispatch the seventh gardia to Challyat. I will draw up orders for the Challyat's chief magistrate to investigate the recent fire that killed the Marqués de Marangel and his family. It was no accident. As Magistrate Polleu looks into the murders, the gardia will conduct a search for Conte Ruggiere from Marangel outward. You will dispatch the eighth gardia to search— Tell him where, Portier."

My gaping mouth had already closed, but I could scarce control a stammer. "Ah—Arabasca. Begin at Mattefriesse and work both east and west along the pilgrim road. Suspect any man of more than middling size, especially one who carries a finely sculpted leather mask."

Philippe believed me, at least so far as to act upon my word. I should be pleased. Yet I could not shake the sense that I saw but the outliers of this royal storm and might still end up drowned.

"The ninth gardia will proceed immediately to Vernase," snapped the king. "They shall maintain a cordon two hundred fifty metres distant from the estate of Montclaire. The contessa and her children will be treated with respect, but no one else is to be allowed in or out without identity vouched by three local citizens or an order sealed by this ring." The royal signet of Sabria glinted from his clenched fist.

"Understand, Captain, and make this clear to every officer and man: Michel de Vernase has been the captive of sorcerers and tortured to break his mind. He *must* be apprehended, controlled, and kept in isolation until he stands in my presence. But no matter *what* he says or does not say, he is my First Counselor, a peer of the realm, and my friend. He will be offered every consideration and treated with the full honors of his rank. Have you any question?"

The captain did not waver from his stance. "No, Majesty. All shall be done as you say."

Did Philippe believe what he said? Did he truly believe Michel a pawn? I could not guess.

"Nothing shall serve as excuse for failure."

De Segur bowed. Philippe's grip on my arm tightened, and we were

out of the tower and forging yet another path through Castelle Escalon before the captain could have straightened up again. I could only brace for the unexpected.

Our destination became apparent as we barged through gawking crowds in the curved window gallery and on the broad stair leading to the queen's household wing. My cousin bypassed Ilario's apartments and charged through a small atrium, adorned with alabaster statues of dancers and horses. Even the pair of opalescent doors centering the curved wall did not slow us. Philippe slammed through them as if they were a leather swag over a peasant's shanty.

Jeweled ladies in cream-colored silk covered their mouths or halted their embroidery in midstitch. Lady Antonia, plucked eyebrows exacerbating her shocked expression, stared up from a tête-à-tête conversation with Maura. Maura's face clouded with concern as she took in my bruised face and the shoulder of my doublet wadded in the king's fist.

Though I longed to reassure her, I dared not. My feet stood too near a chasm . . . as did hers. I looked away.

Near an open window, eight or ten ladies clustered on a plush couch and the floor cushions in front of it. Eugenie de Sylvae sat in the center of them, holding an open book, a soft flush draining rapidly from her cheeks.

Stiff and controlled, the king inclined his back to his wife. "A private word with you, madam." No one would mistake this politeness for a request.

In a wave of shining hair and billowing skirts, the queen's friends and attendants dropped into deep curtsies. Eugenie herself rose from her cushion. Tall—but a handsbreadth less than Ilario—and regal, she waited just long enough, and then sank, perfectly composed, into her own obeisance.

The queen did not wait for the king's permission to rise. Her ladies followed her up in practiced unison. Most of them scurried immediately for adjacent chambers. A few, older women for the most part, awaited the queen's gesture of dismissal. Even then, Lady Antonia went to Eugenie and kissed her on the cheek before sweeping from the room.

The last door snicked shut. Eugenie's dark eyes fixed on her husband. Her chin, at once firm and fragile, lifted.

Philippe released my arm. "All these months I have yielded to your determination to rule your household as you desire and demonstrate your confidence in your servants. No matter that my every counselor has entreated me to set you aside, I have trusted that you hold this kingdom's welfare paramount and would allow no grievance with me to change that. And whether or not you deem me fit as sovereign or husband, I could not—and cannot—believe you wish me dead. No longer can I afford forbearance."

Though the queen maintained her silence, the stretched emotions in that room made my forced posture in Eltevire's sorcerer's hole seem comfortable.

"Sit." Philippe waved at her couch.

The lady's entire demeanor stiffened like setting plaster, as if the matter of her sitting was a skirmish in their private war. The king waited, immovable as the palace wall.

Eventually, with a small shrug, the queen settled, graceful and dignified, to the edge of the cushioned seat. Yet she did not yield as might some bullied child, but as a mature woman who made her own choices.

Philippe acknowledged her acquiescence with a stiff nod. Then he shook a finger at me. "This man, Savin-Duplais, is a distant kinsman, a fawning favor-seeker who aspires above his place. In some fevered campaign to *protect* me, he chose to take up the question of last year's attempted assassination where Michel left off. . . ."

So did I come to understand my punishment for bringing the king such news. I had hardly expected thanks, and logic must approve my cousin's play. Yet, for my humiliating ruse to become the definition of my character was an ugly sentence.

As Philippe gave an abbreviated, remarkable, and almost entirely truthful rendition of my morning's recital, the queen's defensive posture yielded to intense listening and growing horror. While omitting all mention of Dante, Ilario, hauntings, the Veil, or his own cooperation, he revealed how my efforts had uncovered a conspiracy to revive transference

and possibly destabilize the Concord de Praesta, the peace between the Camarilla and the crown.

I listened carefully, beginning to think he intended me to play some further role. Why else allow me to witness this painful encounter?

"Michel?" Eugenie's first word burst forth with full shock. "Working with sorcerers to destroy you? Philippe, how can you bear it? It's even worse"—the momentary gap in her self-possession closed quickly—"worse than believing your wife a dupe. Or a traitor. Or a traitorous dupe incapable of keeping her children alive. Or do you believe I have been seduced into *this* conspiracy, as well? Perhaps wife and friend are not such bitter enemies as everyone believes!"

Philippe acknowledged neither her moment's sympathy nor its bitter afterword. "Portier fears that one Adept Fedrigo may be another victim of these conspirators. If we could trace the young man's movements, we might save him before he suffers the Marangel girl's fate. Thus, we must and will question your mage, Orviene. And you, lady, must tell me anything you know that might bear on this tale. Firstly, why, in the name of the Pantokrator, did you suggest to Calvino de Santo that I might wish to wrestle on that day?"

She shot to her feet, confronting him squarely. Fire had returned to her cheeks. "Is it so inconceivable that I should care for your pleasure, husband?"

"On *that* day? When a poisoned arrow lay in wait for me? When my *pleasure* ensured unarmored flesh would await its strike?" The few paces of soft carpet that separated them yawned as an indescribable gulf. "I do not believe in such coincidence. How can I?"

For a moment I believed she might yield her secrets, so deep did her gaze search the man. And truly I wanted to remind them both that the arrow was never meant to strike him.

Eugenie folded her arms across her breast. "You have my permission to question Orviene about his missing adept. Nothing more, though, as always, my liege may do as he wills. As to the wrestling: Earlier that day I engaged in conversation with several friends. Our discussion ran to the manly arts, and it reminded me of things you told me in days when we

did not know each other so well. Do not ask me names. My judgment names my friends trustworthy, and I will not have persons like your sly kinsman subject them to demeaning interrogation. I cannot possibly enlighten you further. Now, if that's all . . ." She extended a hand toward the door.

"I will ask you to consider *this*, lady," said the king, unchastened. "Was it you or your 'trustworthy friends' who raised the subject of *manly arts* that day? And if it was you, then why did it strike you on that particular day, when our personal pleasures had not been a matter between us for so very long? I will not believe Michel my enemy until I hear it from his own mouth. But if such a friend as he can turn traitor and murderer, then no person in this world is above suspicion." *No wife, either*, he did not say.

He snapped a hand toward the door. I bowed to the queen and followed him out. He could not have seen her hands clenched fiercely to her breast or her grief-filled eyes locked to his back.

The king did not manhandle me as we hiked through the corridors. Neither did he dismiss me. Like a bruised duckling, I trailed after him to the study where we had begun. He sat down at a small writing desk and pulled out several sheets of paper, pen, and ink.

"Sit," he said. Without looking at me, he waved at a side table. "Drink if you wish."

I sat, gazing lornly at the decanter and cups, but could not imagine swallowing anything.

My cousin's pen moved in bold strokes. When three papers were written, signed, and sealed with his ring, he rang for the pinch-mouthed undersecretary and dispatched one missive to the Grand Magistrate of Challyat, and one to the commander of the garrison nearest Vernase. The king dropped the third letter into my lap. It bore my name.

I clutched the sealed parchment as he moved to the sideboard, poured wine for each of us, then settled in his armchair. "I apologize for forcing you into that most awkward interview," he said, quite unapologetically. "You needed to be there."

"What would you have me do now, sire?"

"Go to Montclaire and continue your investigation publically. That letter is your commission. You can be sure Madeleine will demand to see it."

I swallowed my astonishment. "The Conte Ruggiere's home? His family . . ." Philippe's own goodchildren.

"It will be impossible to silence the news that I am searching for Michel or to hide the particular nature of my orders to the Guard Royale. Suspicions will swarm this palace as insects swarm the maquis in high summer." He drained his cup and set it aside. Distaste hardened his fair visage. "When he is found—alive, I pray—and proved innocent—which I believe absolutely—then the worst thing I could have done for him is feed ill rumor with the perception of indulgence. As with my wife, I cannot and will not express anything less than full faith in Michel de Vernase. Your theory demands investigation, cousin, and the court and the kingdom must see it pursued diligently, but *against* my personal inclinations. This lays the awkward burden squarely on you. You must continue serving as the efficient *agente* you are, while playing the diligent fool we have made you."

"I understand, sire."

I had resigned myself to the role of Portier the Sycophant, the overeager kinsman who aspired above his place, when I first took it on. Though my notions of destiny had never involved public humiliations, I should have been relieved that playacting was the worst penalty I reaped. Yet Philippe's scarcely concealed contempt pained me, even as I came to understand it. The king viewed sorcery as lies, trickery, and subterfuge, and the belief had fueled his disdain for the mystic art. Now lies and subterfuge—the province of spies—had entangled his heart and limbs, as well. And we were not done yet. Not by half.

"Before you go, you will question this Mage Orviene." Philippe's lips thinned and hardened. "I give you leave to extend that questioning beyond my lady's bounds, even to the woman mage if you judge it needful. Some sorcerer or other is a part of these works you describe. Michel has no connection to a blood family. Over twenty years, I've seen no hint of magical talent."

"I'll certainly question Orviene," I said, mulling the tangles ahead. "But I don't think . . . It's not yet time to wring out the mages. Dante is yet in play to observe them. Perhaps—" How far would his tolerance extend? "You have already acknowledged to Her Majesty that sorcery is involved in this case. Perhaps you could confess you need her help. You could suggest that the overreaching Portier, a failed sorcerer, is clearly incompetent to judge the signs of nefarious sorcery. As you employ no sorcerers of your own, she might provide one to . . . supervise me on the journey to Vernase."

Philippe's knuckles glared white against the dark wood of his chair as he considered this. His gaze fixed on the cold hearth across the room.

"My wife is ever eager to impress her belief in magic on me," he said after a few moments. "But she might choose any of the three. Which would you want—this Dante or one you suspect?"

"If she chooses Orviene or Gaetana, I'll have a chance to observe that one closer," I said. "A fool is easily discounted, as we well know."

His darting glance at me, as quickly returned to the hearth, removed all doubt that he was privy to Ilario's long deception.

"But I could use Dante better," I said. "Sire, would your lady not respond to your suggestion that selecting the mage who was *not* in her employ on the day of the attempted assassination might lead you to a more objective view of her servants? Might she not think such a partnership could lead even you to appreciate magical talents?"

He pressed his fingers to his forehead that could not possibly be throbbing more wretchedly than my own. The shredded remnants of dignity that I'd preserved so carefully these past years lay scattered from his court to the rubble of Eltevire. Perhaps it was that which impelled me to bait a powerful man as he wrestled the maddening truth that he could not trust either of the people he loved most; or perhaps it was only my tired, foolish attempt to raise his better humor.

"Indeed, cousin," I said, "one might argue that your views shifted on the day you summoned a 'kinsman sorcerer' from Seravain. Surely, admitting faulty judgment in a marital dispute could not be received amiss."

In a move so swift as to blur my vision, the king sprang from his seat,

hefted his chair, and smashed it onto the writing desk, splintering the delicate furnishings in a storm of falling cushions, breaking glass, and splattering ink.

"Get out," he yelled, reaching for the broken chair, as if to ready it for a new target. "Do your vile business and crawl back into your hole."

CHAPTER TWENTY-TWO

4 CINQ
21 DAYS UNTIL THE ANNIVERSARY

"Will that be all, lord sir?"

Heurot shut the clothes chest after storing my clean linen. It was the first he'd spoken that evening, which was entirely unlike the chatty young manservant. Before I'd gone to Eltevire, he'd habitually come to attend me in the evenings only after his other gentlemen were satisfied, lingering in my chamber to speak of such matters as his brothers and sisters in service, his latest reading from the chapbooks he picked up in the markets, and the progress of the giant pendulum the king was having constructed in the palace Rotunda. Perhaps he'd sensed my dismal mood.

"Not quite." I handed him a sealed note and sixty kivrae. "Deliver this message to Secretary de Sain in the steward's office right away. And I'd be most grateful if you'd have my new boots picked up from Tick the Cobbler before morning. I'll be leaving Merona tomorrow early, and these bought on my last journey would better fit a twelve-year-old maiden with square feet."

"Certainly, sir lord." The youth accepted my missive for Henri, finalizing arrangements for the journey to Vernase, and slipped the coins into his tunic's voluminous pocket. Then he bowed, as he'd never found nec-

essary before, and backed awkwardly toward the door. But he bumped into the clothes chest, then stumbled over the horrid boots Ilario had bought me in Mattefriese to replace those lost at Eltevire. "I can fetch your new boots right now. Tick works late. Divine grace shine upon you, sir, sonjeur."

"Divine grace, Heurot. Are you quite all right?" His behavior was altogether odd.

"Aye, lord sir. Definitely. Thank you for asking, lord . . . Sonjeur de Duplais." After another jerky bow, he backed out of the door into the passage.

Amused and puzzled, I returned attention to my journal. Dipped my pen.

The door slammed shut, but tight breathing raised my eyes again.

"Will ye be back this time, sir, lord sir, sonjeur?" Heurot pressed his back to the closed door.

"Barring misfortune. Why? Are you sure you're all right, lad? Speak up. And *sir* or *sonjeur* is quite enough."

He stared down at the ugly Arabascan boots. "It's just, I've heard . . . this disgrace . . . that the king's so angry with ye, and dullard me didn't even know ye were his kin, and I've been so free, joking and not acting properly respectful all these days. But I wanted to say, if I wasn't to see ye again, that ye've been kind to me and ye don't seem a lackwit or craven or mercenary at all. Only I didn't know whether it was proper to speak of such."

I suppressed a smile and a sigh of regret. Rumor progressed rapidly, as the king had foretold. More so after his destructive outburst of the morning. Yet rumor served.

"Ah, Heurot, my blood is so remotely related to His Majesty that his wolfhounds are more familiar to him, and more valued. Indeed, my efforts to remedy our distance have put him in a foul temper, and he's sent me off on a wild errand, subordinate to the worst possible taskmaster." I grimaced and shuddered.

Few would understand my early-evening pleasure at hearing that Dante would accompany me to Vernase. Where had I learned how to

move a king to bend his neck to his wife's whims? Sometimes I felt far older than two-and-thirty years.

"Yet I am at little personal risk, and ever hopeful to serve the crown honorably to forward my father's Veil journey. Though it were well"—I beckoned the lad close and whispered—"if perhaps you did not proclaim my better qualities aloud. I'd not have you tainted should I fail to satisfy the royal pleasure."

The lad tossed his yellow hair out of his widened eyes. "Aye, I see what ye mean. I'll pray the holy saints to serve your honor and your . . . satisfyin'."

"I could ask no more."

Smiling, I returned to recording the results of my interview with Mage Orviene. I'd questioned him shortly after leaving the king's study. The mage had offered me little new. Evidently, Adept Fedrigo was perpetually short of money, a matter Orviene did not wish to overemphasize, but feared might have sent the young man to the docks to gamble on the day of his purported murder. And no, the mage could not recall who had told him the story of the ill-fated tavern brawl. One of the palace servants, he thought. He would inquire and let me know. The city magistrate's written report had portrayed the brawl as no different from any other in the history of Riverside taverns.

As before, Orviene impressed me as sincerely grieved about his assistant's fate. He had not himself seen Fedrigo since shortly after I had first arrived at Castelle Escalon. When I mentioned our earlier encounter, and the suspicions he had voiced with regard to the *Swan* fire, he reiterated that he had no evidence of improprieties. But his eyes pointedly told me that his beliefs had not wavered. And that was that.

I hoped writing the details of the interview would grant me some marvelous insight, but not long after the palace bells rang eighth hour of evening watch, a footman delivered me a note, sealed without any device. Unsigned, its blockish characters set down ungracefully one by one, it comprised but one line: *Friend, I await you in the heart of Escalon. Please.*

"Hold!" I caught the messenger before he could disappear down the passage. "Who sent this?"

"Don't know, sir. A lamp boy caught me as I was coming from supper. Said he was given it to be delivered to Sonjeur de Duplais. The donkey hadn't asked on whose authority."

I sent the fellow on his way and scoured the message as if the sparse words hid something I could not see. For a blood-marked man to venture out in answer to so enigmatic a request in these dangerous times was idiocy. Yet the sender could be Ilario, returned early from the country, or Dante, whom I had not seen since we parted ways on the road from Eltevire. Our meetings must be conducted with redoubled caution now I was so exposed. I had to go.

Hoping to arrive while the dusky light yet held, I sped through the north wing and down the back stair to the underground labyrinth that delivered servants speedily to the principal areas of the palace. The branch under the south wing and a damp slanting tunnel delivered me to the south gardens. *The heart of Escalon* was not found within the palace proper.

Before the current residence was built, and long before the current fashion of elaborate, precisely laid-out gardens and follies, some Sabrian queen had grown the *escalon* or garden maze for which the palace was named. Instead of common boxwood or privet, she had chosen colorful plantings of the wildlands—gorse and flowering broom, brilliant yellow nestled amid the budding scarlet of hibiscus, and thick growths of purple-flowered bougainvillea—to disguise those who trod the maze paths. In the center of it all she had built a fair summerhouse of rustic floors and latticed arches, rotted and replaced a dozen times through the decades.

Scents of damp earth, sweet gorse, and freshly trimmed grass hung thick as I hurried through the narrow paths, increasingly anxious. Neither Ilario or Dante would have written *please*.

Holding quiet at the edge of the clearing, I peered through the advancing gloom. A solitary figure, mostly obscured by the latticed walls and deeper twilight inside the elliptical summerhouse, moved slowly back and forth between the peaked ends, pausing at each terminus as if to stare outward through its open arch. When I estimated the person's stature as considerably less than my own, I perused the note again and my heart leapt. *Friend*. Maura.

She halted her pacing the moment I raced up the steps. "Portier! Thank all angels you've come." Anxiety and relief twined together like the flowering vines.

I longed to answer as my own self and not the creature of conspiracy's invention. But the risks were far too high. Maura stood too near the quaking center of this earth tremor.

"Divine grace, damoselle," I said, bowing and exposing my hand, keeping my distance, even as heart and conscience clamored to soothe her trouble. "So secret a summons, lady?"

"I just couldn't— But I needed to find out: All these rumors about Michel de Vernase, about you. These dreadful events: the fire on the *Swan*; Filamena, the sewing woman, found dead in her bed; Adept Fedrigo gone missing. This morning, Henri de Sain tells me you've been asking about shipping crates and—and corpses. This afternoon I see your awful bruises, and I hear you've driven the king to violence. And this evening I'm tasked to arrange transport for you and that vile mage to Vernase. Friend Portier, what is happening?" She sank onto a circular bench, as if spilling her worries had emptied her of strength. "You're the only person I trust."

Her quiet sob near broke my resolution. But caution shaped more lies and kept me away.

"I cannot imagine any reason for you to be afraid." Hands clasped behind my back, I sauntered along the peripheries, underneath the gargoyles carved in the latticed arches. "Though you were wise to meet me in secret. My fool's quest is like to get me hanged. I've uncovered some distinct coincidences that shine unfortunate light on the king's friend, Conte Ruggiere, forcing His Majesty to decisions he detests. Not a path to royal favor. Forgive me for not revealing my—"

"Michel de Vernase would never betray his king." My words had infused iron in her spine. "He is honorable, compassionate, devoted entirely to His Majesty's service and to his family. This evidence cannot be credible. Tell me of it, Portier. Perhaps the answer's somewhat of common knowledge that I could easily provide."

This poorly disguised probing wormed its way beneath my skin like a

glass splinter. I riposted. Lies came easy now. "A taverner at Seravain told me she posted a letter for the conte to a woman here at court. After so long, she couldn't remember the name, but the conte had teased her that this woman 'aided him in secret work.'"

Were I not listening with senses raised, I might have missed Maura's sharp breath. The splinter speared deeper, chilling my heart.

I lowered my voice and tightened the snare. "As I came to consider that Michel might not be so much a friend to His Majesty as everyone assumed, this report turned my thoughts to Mage Gaetana, as it is well-known that sorcerers instigated last year's assault on the king. Do you think it possible *she* is Michel's female accomplice?"

"None of this is possible," Maura said, in growing desperation. "How can circumstances appear so awful—so wicked—when no shred of ill intent lies back of them?"

I did not sense that she was answering my question. *Press harder, Portier.*

"What circumstances, lady? What do you know of the conte's activities?" And then I played my vilest trump. "Should I fail to demonstrate some confirmation of my accusations soon . . . Damoselle, I do fear for my life. I had not reckoned on such staunch friendship between the king and a low-birthed warrior like Michel de Vernase."

Maura's cloak rustled. She moved as if to rise . . . but rocked back again . . . and forward . . . again and again. Her fear burgeoned to fill the summerhouse, and her mouth moved soundlessly, as if words battled to escape her control. Gods, what did she know? I held silent, afraid to remind her of my presence, lest she hold back.

"Gaetana asked me to send that crate to Mattefreise," she said, the hoarse phrases scarce more than a whisper. "It never occurred to me to refuse. Members of the household send things all the time. But who ever will believe that? Because last year, in the month of Siece, I *did* receive a letter from Conte Ruggiere. He asked me to have some girls' clothing made to specification and sent to Tigano in a large crate along with supplies for a tenday journey. Not two months past, I received two similar crates to be delivered to the temple. I did not question who the sender was or what the contents

might be. I've always done favors for the conte. I believed—I still believe the conte is in hiding for good reason. I did not mention these incidents to anyone, as I had pledged him secrecy. I owe him— Sante Ianne! *I* ordered the banners made for the launch of the *Destinne* and arranged for their delivery to the *Swan*. It was my duty to relieve my mistress's burden. But who will believe that?" Her rocking stilled and she pressed her fist to her heart. "Merciful saints, Portier, I suggested the wrestl—"

"Silence!" I blurted. Dismay tore through my layered deceptions like the Aspirant's scarifying blades through flesh. "Say not one more word to me."

No sooner had I spoken than my arms gathered her to my breast. Somehow feet, hands, and heart had taken me where reason forbade me go. Her hair smelled of dusk roses. Her throat fluttered under my stroking fingers like a captive bird's heart.

"Easy, easy, sweet lady." The ragged edge of caution slipped from my grasp. "I will see you through this. But I am surely a sworn witness in this matter. Say naught to me that I cannot report." Her next word would have linked her with treason . . . regicide. I could *not* hear it.

"I did not conspire to evil, Portier. I swear it. Those poor people on the *Swan* . . . murder . . . I could never . . ."

"I believe you."

And I did—utterly and completely—which was wholly unexplainable save by some conviction passed between her body and mine. Was I so experienced with subterfuge that I could recognize truth and lies, so experienced with women that I could untangle wishing belief from desire and sympathy?

"Go back to your apartments and back to your work. Be yourself. Speak nothing of this night. Nothing of me, save ordinary converse about these rumors. And by your hope of Heaven, lady, go nowhere alone until these matters are settled. Even during the day, keep constantly in company." Murder had dogged my footsteps. "If you receive letters, messages, packages . . . anything from Michel, anything related to him, anything from Gaetana . . . get them to me. You are exceptional—clever, efficient, trusted. Of all people, you can do these things without suspicion."

"I'll *not* compromise Michel de Vernase," she said, pulling away.

"Do not speak of him again," I said. "Neither defend nor condemn him." My hands slipped down her arms until they grasped her cold fingers. I gathered them and brought them to my lips. "It is not our place to choose what we will or will not see. We must have faith that unfolding truth will expose your actions in their proper proportion and his as worthy of your beliefs. Trust me"—I kissed her fingers, which tasted faintly of honey and springtime—"and don't be afraid."

"You make me believe that's possible," she said softly. "I've never— Who are you, who can bring me such comfort?"

"As you said, damoselle, I am your friend." Her lips tasted sweeter than her fingers.

IDIOT! WHAT KIND OF AGENTE confide *kisses his witness? Or, angels defend us, his quarry?* As I waited for lovely Maura and her rose-scented hair to leave the maze well behind, I longed for a time when I did not have to consider such things as duplicity after a kiss of such blessedly enveloping heat as could melt a man's boots. The records at Seravain named Maura ney Billard a talented, accomplished sorceress of adept's level. *She* could be Michel de Vernase's magical accomplice, the woman who had tormented Ophelie, playing on my inexperience and pity to learn what I knew.

My soul refused to accept it. Or was it only my body telling my soul what to believe? Why had I not asked what she *owed* Michel?

These circular musings halted upon my return to my apartments. Another message waited.

Sonjeur Duplais:

Regarding my promised inquiries: My valet reminded me that it was Mage Gaetana who brought me the story of poor Drigo's fatal night at the docks. In the spirit of completest candor, as urged by my lady queen, I must add that Mage

Gaetana strongly disapproved of Fedrigo and had repeatedly urged me to dismiss him, complaining that he had invaded her private laboratorium a number of times unasked. I apologize for not mentioning this before. Scruple struggles at passing on such trivia. But conscience cannot permit silence. Fedrigo would have been collared by autumn, and his loss to our community and his family cannot be measured by petty scruple.

Regretfully,
Orviene de Cie, Mage of the
Camarilla Magica

Gaetana. Gruchin had been her creature, her adept, nurtured, discarded, and bled dry. Gaetana had frequent access to the missing Mondragoni manuscripts, as well as to the royal crypt and Maura's services. News of Ophelie's exposure had infuriated her. She had invited Dante onto the *Swan* and approached him with unsavory "translation projects." She had wielded sophisticated magic to douse the *Swan* fire. Most telling, Ophelie had named a *woman* as her tormentor. Gaetana had ordered the "mushroom crate" shipped to Mattefriese.

All of these things could be innocent circumstance, as could Adept Fedrigo's disappearance in the face of her displeasure. Orviene's "suspicions" could be opportunistic lies or spiteful gossip. Yet in their accumulation, the reports cast an aura of conspiracy over the formidable sorceress. We just needed direct evidence that she had engaged in transference.

My battered body and mind begged for sleep. I pressed the heels of my hands to my eyes as if I might squeeze out some plan to make the sorceress speak. Perhaps it was time to compose my own letter.

Over the next hour, I wrote a brief explanation of my search for evidence to prove Michel de Vernase responsible for the attempt on the king's life. To this, I appended an account of a horrifying incident, wherein I had been waylaid in the alleyways of Castelle Escalon, dragged to a subterra-

nean laboratorium, and leeched by a tall, masked woman wearing a silver collar, who threatened to drain every drop of my "royal blood." Lies flowed as fluently from my pen as from my mouth. I described my scarified wounds, and her implements and techniques, and finished with the tale of my harrowing escape by way of an exploding lantern and a passing guardsman.

Shortly before middle-night, I roused a palace messenger and posted copies of this great fiction to Kajetan, my mentor, who had solicited news of transference, and to Angloria, a methodical, painstakingly honest, former instructor of mine, newly raised to the Camarilla prefecture. As guardians of the Concord de Praesta, they could not fail to investigate. Gaetana, the only female mage at Castelle Escalon, would find Angloria's inquisitors at her door by midday. The story was near enough the truth that they would ask her the right questions. Unlike me, they had means to judge the truth of her answers.

My instincts claimed I had done right. At some point I had to take action, lest we swirl in evidence until we were all dead by fire and chaos. I would apologize for the deception later.

"PORTIER! COME, WAKE UP." A hand rattled my bruised shoulder bones.

"Heaven's gates, what is it?"

A candle burned on my bedside table. Ilario's anxious face loomed near. "Come along, Portier, he wants to see you."

"The damnable mage?" I scraped the grit from my eyes and blotted my chin with my sleeve.

Ilario shook his head and tossed my crumpled shirt at me. "Philippe."

That woke me. Mayhap my cousin had reconsidered having a poor relation dictate the course of his marriage, friendships, and sovereignty.

The air from the open window spoke of lapsing night as I laced my traveling breeches and buttoned my shirt. By the time this errand was done, Dante would be waiting for me in the stableyard, ready to set out for Vernase. Unless I wasn't available.

"I didn't know you were come back to Merona, lord," I said as I pulled on my new boots and made to follow Ilario.

"Eugenie sent to me," he said, peeking out of the outer door before pulling it open. "Seems she had a wretched day and needed diversion."

I could well imagine Eugenie's need for comfort.

We tiptoed down the householders' hall, rounded into the northwest tower, and slipped into an abandoned stool closet. Alert now, I noticed Ilario shift the brick in the upper corner. Thus I was not surprised when a narrow panel swung out of the scuffed wooden wall. Once the door clicked shut behind us, Ilario unshuttered a lamp. A quarter of an hour, six turnings, two halts to scurry across public passages and through more hidden panels, and we ended in a capacious wardrobe closet.

"Portier," whispered Ilario, the lamp exposing lines of worry on his boyish face, "I don't like all this, people knowing you're on the hunt. You're awfully . . . exposed. And Philippe—" He puffed his cheeks and blew an unhappy note, shaking his head until his fair hair fell over his eyes. "I've not seen him so angry. So uncertain."

"I appreciate your concern, lord." Truly it warmed me more than I could say, even if he could only express it in the King of Sabria's closet. "But I can't exactly have a bodyguard trailing me around, can I? Not if we're going to find the answers we need. As for my cousin . . . none of us is immune to royal displeasure. At least I've blood kinship on my side."

He grunted a quiet laugh. "That's served *me* well. I'll be waiting here to take you back." He rapped on the wall and shoved open a panel, allowing me to enter the very study I'd been tossed out of half a day earlier.

The damaged desk and chair had been cleared away and the ruined carpet removed to expose patterns of dark and light wood. A small, bright blaze illuminated the tiled hearth. Philippe, gowned in fur-lined silk, hunched in a chair beside it, as if he were eight-and-seventy years and not eight-and-thirty.

I dropped to one knee beside his chair. Before I could rise, he thrust a paper into my hand. Sitting back upon my heels, I read it by the light of the flames.

—

Sire:

I must assume that your battered cousin has limped back to Merona and whispered dreadful tales in your ear. If his story is at all coherent, then you, my friend, my liege, have surely guessed his tormentor's identity and are engulfed in rightful fury.

You must believe me. Things are not at all what they seem. Something extraordinary happened when your servant went searching for your enemies. He found them. And then he discovered things about himself, about magic and power, about the truth of the world. We have been wrong, Philippe. Terribly, blindly wrong.

There is too much to write, and our enemies are ever close. I am forced into hiding. As poor Portier experienced, the dangers are very real. Convey my apologies that I could not protect him better. Good fortune that he had a doughty companion to salvage him!

I do not expect you to meet with me yourself nor dare I trust just any messenger. Your court is riddled with treachers. In honor of our long friendship, the debts we have owned and paid, I beg you send the bearer of this letter—a noble heart well-known to both of us, utterly trustworthy and capable of defending himself—to meet with me, one to one. He will be met at Vigne Caelo at next moonrise and brought to my hiding place. I will send him back on my goodson's deathday with clear evidence of my discoveries.

Ever your servant, M.

—

"YOU'LL NOT SEND ANYONE, SIRE?" I said, appalled. "Certainly not alone? This is but a lure." The high, open ground of Vigne Caelo, Heaven's Vineyard, was completely surrounded by rugged hills, notched with verdant vales—a thousand escape routes and a thousand hiding places.

My cousin's face might have been chiseled in coldest marble. "Is the letter magicked? Do I see what is not there?"

"There's nothing. No enchantment. No residue."

"The hand is Michel's. How can I refuse?" Yet clearly Philippe was torn. He was asking, quite explicitly, for a reason not to acquiesce, a shocking reverse from the morning's stalwart faith.

The wrongness of the words on that page seemed clear to me. Not only had the Aspirant not *protected* me, but he had helped extract my blood, which he yet held. His harsh voice still sounded clearly in my ears: arrogant, lustful, resentful. He had relished my groveling, exploited my history of despair against me, stuck his filthy boot in my mouth. Even discounting personal humiliation, I could summon no belief that he had only *feigned* cruelty.

"The screams I heard in Eltevire allow me no grace for the Aspirant, sire, be he Michel de Vernase or any other. Even now, he makes you doubt yourself. Heed your instincts, lord."

"We cannot fail to collect this evidence he offers. If he is villain and sends us lies, even that would provide grist for your mill of logic, would it not?"

He'd thrown my own words back in my face. "True, but—"

"Will you swear to me upon your life that the danger we face is of greater moment than my own safety? Greater than the normal consequence of a sovereign falling before his time?"

An odd swearing, but easy. Philippe himself had stated this condition when he recruited me. What passing doubts I might have harbored in those early days were long dismissed.

"Your enemies"—I purposely did not mention the Aspirant—"pursued forbidden magic in a place where nature itself is maimed. I swear upon my ancestors that your death is not their sole object and may never have been their object at all. Think what would have been the outcome of the Blood

Wars, if those who battled the savagery had been unable to loft an arrow that would reliably hit its mark, or if those who wielded magic in the cause of right could not predict the outcome of their spellwork?"

Even I, who yearned for magic, could not imagine nature wholly unbound by law and logic. What would sway the balance of sovereignty in such a world? *Fear*, I thought. The power to outwit nature, to compose illogic and harness chaos. Sorcery.

After one moment resting his head on coupled fists, Philippe pulled a sealed dispatch from his lap and waved it and me to the outer door. "Give this to the one who waits outside."

I bowed, forced to swallow the questions and arguments his face forbade me speak.

The moment I opened the door to the anteroom, a rangy young officer in the colors of the Guard Royale jumped up from a waiting bench. "Sonjeur de Duplais! Divine grace." He bowed crisply. "Edmond de Roble-Margeroux. Do you remember me, sonjeur?" A ready grin illumined the young man's dark eyes and well-hewn features that surely sapped the knees of every young lady he encountered.

"Certainly, Greville Margeroux," I said. His thick black hair and cinnamon-hued complexion must instantly recall the luminous Lady Susanna to any who had ever met her—along with old Conte Olivier, and this, their striking son. The king's dear and trusted friends. No wonder, then, at Philippe's reluctance to send him into danger.

"How does my testy pupil?" said Edmond, leaning down from his height in cheery confidence. "Truly that was the most terrifying sevenday of my life. Never have I been threatened with dismemberment, transmutation, disordering, accelerated aging, scabs, leprosy, and worms all in one hour, and all over the matter of learning to use a fork. Is he here? Has he transmuted anyone into vermin as yet?"

"You did well, lord. The mage has made a place for himself in the queen's household, though he dines alone. Everyone in the palace, including me, is terrified of him." I glanced at the three doors that led to adjacent rooms and passages. No one lurked, so late at night. "You've never mentioned your venture into mage-schooling?"

"On my mother's back," he said, his smile vanishing as he uttered a soldier's most solemn swearing. For this young man, that particular bond would be formidable.

"I've brought your orders," I said, handing over the sealed document. The return of his good cheer did not dismiss my wish that I could withhold the page.

His eyes sparked with excitement, flicking over my shoulder into the near-dark study. "Am I to go, then?" he whispered. "The letter was delivered to my barracks sealed. But the note delivered with it warned me to ask extended leave, as I'd likely be sent on a critical mission for the king."

"I've not read these orders," I said, dread and warning near deafening me. "But if so . . . Young lord, be on your guard every moment. *Every* moment."

He sobered properly. "Naturally, sonjeur. This is my first mission for my liege, who has ever shown my family kindness and favor. I shall not fail him."

"There are things worse than failure, Lord Edmond." Hearing myself blurt this platitude, I felt a righteous ass, and though the young man bowed politely, his demeanor spoke disbelief and a youthful assurance of immortality.

I grimaced and shook my head. "His Majesty has set you free to go. Yet, hold . . ."

"Sonjeur?"

"Do you carry the note that brought you here tonight?"

"Indeed. I thought it might be wanted." He pulled a folded page from his pocket.

The brief message reflected exactly what he'd said. Though the hand appeared the same that scribed Philippe's letter, Edmond's note was not signed and the broken seal was plain. "What made you believe an anonymous message to be of such import that you sought leave from your post and rode through the night to deliver it to the King of Sabria?"

"Certain references in the message revealed the sender's identity. I've known him all my life and knew the king would welcome word from him."

"Ah. The conte is a friend of yours, then."

He flushed. "Taskmaster more than friend. He sponsored my appointment to the Guard and trained me to be worthy of it. I was inclined to . . . withhold . . . in confrontation, not a useful quality in soldier or lord. Lord Michel taught me otherwise—a lesson neither easy nor pleasant."

"Indeed. But your families were friendly?"

"Not at all." He blurted this quite vehemently, then attempted to remedy it. "My parents, as you saw, do not go much in company. But I visited Montclaire once. The conte's family is most generous and welcoming, all of them so different from one another and so . . . astonishing. On one evening, the younger girl gathered every cat from the neighborhood into the house using sorcery, while Ambrose, spouting verse, dueled with a manservant in the drawing room. The contessa cajoled servants, family, and guests alike to dance a pateen, while Anne—Damoselle Anne— argued the movement of the planets with her father in three languages at once. I've always wanted to go back. This year past must have been awful for them—not knowing."

"Aye. Awful." But not the worst it could be. By far, not the worst. "Divine grace, Edmond, and godspeed."

He inclined his back briskly and left. Fraught with misgivings, I returned to the study. Philippe's gaze did not shift from the fire. Dismissed already, I bowed, slipped through the hidden panel, and threaded the dark passage in search of Ilario. Michel's two missives sat safely tucked inside my doublet.

CHAPTER TWENTY-THREE

5 CINQ
20 DAYS UNTIL THE ANNIVERSARY

"Get tha gone, sonjeur! I've four mounts come in early need to be tended, all the mornin' usual to be done for our own, and you demanding this 'n that on the skimmy. The upset's took Wek from his duties, when I've my two best lads puking from overmuch ale. The beasts *know*. . . ."

"What about *my* upset?" I grumbled, once old Guillam had limped away. If the grizzled dotard planted his feet in front of me once more, sucking his toothless gums, whacking a cane on his breeches, and blaming me for his unruly stable, my teeth would be ground to nubs.

Our delayed departure from Castelle Escalon could not be unnerving the king's horses any more than it was unsettling me. Just when my cracked head seemed to be healing itself, the cursed Dante had set it hammering again by failing to meet me as arranged. I did *not* want to be here when the Camarilla came for Gaetana. By the time we returned from Vernase, they would know something—the truth of her activities, I hoped—and I could apologize for my fabrications.

For an hour, I'd resisted the urge to go rip the mage from whatever was keeping him. The arrogant devil was probably working on some new line of inquiry that he could not be bothered to tell me. And yet . . .

I peered yet again through the stableyard arch. Rosy dawn light bathed the palace's eastern portico, the logical route for a man leaving the queen's household wing for the stables. The doors remained firmly shut.

What if Dante lay in a heap on his floor, collapsed again?

Unable to dismiss this image, once it settled, I set out to roust the mage. Midway across the carriageway, a flash of color from behind the fluted columns caught my eye. Crimson and olive green—Camarilla colors. Anxiety swelled to panic, the certainty of danger a drover's whip, as real as the boots on my feet, as vivid as the out-of-time hero dreams of my youth.

God's teeth, how could inquisitors be here so quickly? Never had I known Prefect Angloria to make a decision in less than a tenday—especially one of such import. And Dante . . . One hint of suspicion, a single unpleasant encounter, and he would himself become the focus of an inquisition. They'd never forgo an opportunity to examine the legendary *Exsanguin*. Not only did I fear for our investigation, which already felt balanced on a hair, but for Dante himself. He would not bend well to Camarilla questioning. I had to get him away.

Though heart and mind galloped, I maintained my steady pace toward the portico. Nothing attracts a watcher's attention so much as reversing course or speed at first glimpse. I mounted the steps, inclining my head to the balding man and the square-jawed woman who flanked the doors, as if I were any common courtier out to enjoy the fair morning.

Neither responded. Bless the saints, neither looked familiar. I hoped my newly shorn hair, my mottled bruising, and the fringe of beard let grow where it was too painful to scrape would keep me unrecognized. Prefect Angloria, once my formulary instructor, would be somewhere inside.

Fierce urgency propelled me through the east wing passages. But as I arrived in the queen's household, I slowed my steps and smoothed my clothes. Courtiers huddled in conversation or ambled along the window gallery, enjoying the air and the view and gleaning gossip to fuel the day's conversations. More had come than usual today, titillated by mages' mysteries.

A craggy-faced, red-haired woman stood at the intersection of the gallery and the passage to the mages' apartments. Entirely unaffected by the attention she garnered, the scarlet-mantled Prefect Angloria waited like a rock in the confluence of streams. Her gaze roved the gallery and its denizens, the mages' passage, the royal staircase, and the bright scenery beyond the windows with equal disinterest.

Philippe's First Counselor, Lord Baldwin, no longer cheery, hovered at her elbow. From time to time he flicked a commanding dismissal at some lordling drawn too near or servant grown too bold with gawking. The gold-tied scroll in his hand would be the Camarilla warrant.

As specified by the Concord de Praesta, the warrant secured the Camarilla's right of entry, their privilege to enter any home to fetch Witnesses—suspected magical transgressors or potential informants. No civil authority was permitted to intervene.

I hung back, choked by frustration. No one seemed willing to pass by the prefect to access the stair to the queen's residence. I dared not be the first, thwarting my intent to use Ilario and his secret passages to smuggle Dante away.

"Portier!" My heart stuttered when Jacard, Dante's sharp-featured adept, snatched at my sleeve. His skin was flushed and damp. His blood pulsed at a gallop, noticeable even through my sleeve as he drew me into a window niche. "Have you heard the news?"

"I see Camarilla."

"Inquisitors have come for Gaetana," he said, scarce able to contain himself. "Broached her door an hour since, and her yet in her nightdress! Is this something to do with the mess you've dug up? What a paladin you are, out investigating on your own! Everyone's aflutter with the story. I've heard rumor of unholy practice, bleeding. Corpses, even."

"It's no secret that sorcery caused the fire on the *Swan*," I said, keeping my voice low and my back to the strolling courtiers. "I've only pointed out that others must be involved as well. Are the inquisitors questioning anyone else?" I rubbed the mark on my hand. "They wouldn't be rounding up just anyone of the blood, would they?"

Jacard's color deepened. "To say truth, I tiptoed away as soon as they

arrived. I didn't want them deciding they'd drag me along if Dante chose not to be at home."

"I feel quite the same."

Danger drummed in my veins. Camarilla inquisitors could use whatever techniques they deemed necessary to get answers. Rumor spoke of spelled artifacts created before the Blood Wars—effective things, uncomfortable things. The arrogant, impatient Dante's heretical teachings could get him branded and hung up in a cage.

"Jacard, I'm desperate to get to Dante's chambers. The king has charged me to follow the damnable mage on some ghost chase this morning. If we get delayed by inquisitors, it's *my* backside will be aflame. I'd be forever grateful if you could distract the prefect and Lord Baldwin long enough for me to creep past them."

"Fiddle a prefect? Are you mad?"

Ilario would have done it, but he wasn't there, and I knew no one else to ask. "I was mad to begin this holy venture, yes. Now I'm reaping havoc. So, never again. But for now, I'd give you—" Only one thing I knew might buy Jacard's aid. "Help me and I'll tell you the composition of Dante's circumoccule."

In an instant Jacard's nervous excitement was supplanted by calculation. "You saw it made?"

"He had me sear the trough in the floor and build the ring with no fewer than fifteen distinct particles. I can tell you at least twelve of them, and how they were laid."

"He works marvels there." Jacard's hunger echoed my own. "All right, all right. Give me a moment. Don't want the prefect imagining I'm trouble. Be ready to move."

Garbed in sober shirt and breeches rather than an academic gown, the sharp-chinned adept easily merged into a passing group of gentlemen and vanished down the gallery. Meanwhile, I slipped closer to the passage, gliding from one window niche to the next whenever a passing body shielded me from the prefect's view.

I'd almost given up on Jacard, when a sharp popping noise heralded a spray of tinkling glass scattering on the tile floor. The crystal lamp

mounted above the intersecting passages had shattered. Moments later another lamp, a short span from the first, did the same. Passersby ducked and shouted, and everyone, including the prefect and the First Counselor, spun to watch the lamps, bursting one and then another, each farther down the gallery in the direction Jacard had gone. I stepped out of my niche and slid round the corner not two metres from Prefect Angloria's back.

Chest heaving entirely out of proportion to effort, I flattened myself into a niche alongside a tall, cedar cupboard. No one cried out the trespass. No boots pounded after me. A man's conversational tone emanated from deeper in the passage.

". . . entirely understand, Mage Inquisitor. I've no fear of questioning, though I would certainly have appreciated some forewarning. I could have come to the Bastionne on my own." Orviene's clear tenor carried down the way. "Allow me to don more seemly garb, while you examine my laboratorium. Do have a care with that box, Adept. . . ." The voice receded.

So they were taking Orviene as well. No time to dawdle. My only hope was to act as if I belonged here. The cupboard held a collection of refuse—a dented brass pitcher, a soiled towel, a cracked night jar, broken fans, and a torn pillow leaking feathers. I grabbed enough items to make a pile sufficiently tall to obscure my face.

Courage flagged as I stepped into the passage. The two mages outside Gaetana's door wore close-fitting, dull green caps that covered their hair and ears. Sewn with long jowl strips that buttoned over the wearer's mouth, an inquisitor's cap left only eyes, nose, and cheeks exposed above the mage's collar. The caps served as a reminder that inquisitors would neither hear pleas or testimony, nor speak comfort, reasons, or bargains, until their selected Witnesses were secure inside the Bastionne Camarilla, the fortress of the prefects.

Between the two inquisitors and two Camarilla adepts stood one such Witness, shrouded in a dark blue mantle and a thick, all-encompassing hood. Both mantle and hood had been sewn with iron rings to damp the effects of spellwork. Tradition mandated that none should know the Wit-

nesses put to question by the Camarilla, lest rumor forever taint their works. Yet this particular Witness, taller than any other magical practitioner in the palace, could only be Gaetana.

I had always accepted strict, unbending inquisitors as necessary to ameliorate the risks of dangerous or reckless magic, dismissing rumors of cruelly forced testimony as the protestations of the guilty. But, somehow, witnessing this grotesque solemnity in the flesh upended my certainties. And I had brought it down on these people with lies. Holy saints, what had I been thinking?

Juggling my awkward armful of oddities, I strode down the passage past the somber group, as if well accustomed to macabre invaders. Without hesitation, I pushed through the charged enchantments of the door ward and into Dante's apartments.

The mage's great chamber was even more cluttered than usual. The man himself was nowhere to be seen, yet the air quivered with magical energies. Something was very odd. I spun slowly in place. Worktables, heaped with materials. Locking cupboards, doors hanging open. The amber circumoccule fixed in the scuffed mahogany floor. The couch, bathed in rosy light from the great east windows, unhindered by draperies. Ceiling, walls, plain and unbroken.

I blinked. Where was his bedchamber?

Memory insisted the doorway to the adjacent room ought to be midway along the west wall. I ran my hands over the smooth plaster. No mistaking when I found the doorway; the jolt of enchantment near set me on my backside. But only as long as my fingers touched the door frame did the spell allow me to see into the lesser chamber.

Dante sat at his desk, as I had seen him on my first visit so long ago— head bowed, eyes closed, white staff in the rigid grip of his maimed hand. His left hand rested on a small book, forefinger traversing a line of handscribed text on a yellowed page. Naught so extraordinary, save that purple sparks sprayed from the blackened tip of his finger, and plumes of frosty air billowed from his staff. The man himself trembled with such violence, his bones must have been near shattering.

I could spare no time for wonder. "Dante, we must get you away."

He demonstrated no sign that he'd heard me.

One step past the threshold immersed me in a maelstrom of discordant energies—as if the sun and moon tried to shine at once in that chamber or the tide ebbed and flowed in confluence. I squatted at his side. His eyes remained fixed on the page. "Can you hear me? Stop this and listen."

His brow creased, and his finger slowed, but more in the way of pushing on through a disturbance than deciphering my speech.

"Dante!" Gingerly I laid my hand on his shoulder.

He reared backward, near rising bodily into the air. His staff clattered to the floor.

"The Camarilla's come for—"

The mage burst roaring from his chair, shoved me across the room, and slammed me to the wall, his formidable shoulders proving themselves no mere decorative accident of nature. Heat poured from his twisted face, darkened to the color of dried blood.

It took both my hands and all my strength to pry his forearm from my neck. "Let. Me. Go."

In an instant, he released me and stumbled backward. A moment's frantic search and he snatched up his staff and pressed his forehead to the wood, clinging to it as a seaman to his lifeline. "Did you ever consider that what I'm doing outside your presence might have *some* importance?" he said, tight jawed and breathless.

"Father Creator, how could I not know that?" I said, forcing equanimity. "But the Camarilla's come for Gaetana. They're taking Orviene as a Witness. You'll be next . . . and perhaps me. You remember we were traveling to Vernase this morning?"

"Yes." He bit off the word, the storm of violence scarce under his control.

"Our journey's even more important now. The king's had a letter from Michel de Vernase, all but admitting he's the Aspirant. The conte claims innocence and promises to send evidence of his 'discoveries' by Prince Desmond's deathday. We cannot let the Camarilla delay us."

As I forced myself to patience, his breathing slowed and his back straightened. Eventually he looked up, and only the familiar hauteur was

written on him. "Never touch me when I'm in trance, fool of a student," he said. "I could have killed you. Without intent."

"So I've learned," I said, appreciating the concession, while yet rubbing my overbruised throat. Someday I would know the roots of this violence that lay so close to his skin. Only a fool wielded a blade without understanding the irregularities in its tempering. "Now can we leave here before you're hauled off to the Bastionne? They'll be scratching at your door any moment."

"Certainly, I know the officious little pricks are closing in. What took you so blasted long to get here?" It was as if the blazing orange sun had retreated below the eastern horizon, only to bounce back up again arrayed in soft green or lilac. And as it shone so peaceably, the overpowering dread that had driven me since waking dissipated. I was left speechless and limp as old linen.

He tapped the end of his staff on his desk. "I couldn't afford to stop working. This could be my last chance to glean aught from this cursed book. *Gaetana's* book."

My breath halted, interrupting my rising fury at his manipulation. Gaetana's book: *a manuscript buried deep in layers of wards and ciphers. Perhaps even less savory, but carrying knowledge of the uses of magic that have been lost for generations.* A manuscript that people of ethics might have difficulty with.

"Aye, the one I spoke of after Eltevire. If they've taken her, they'll learn of it, too, yes? And when they take me as Witness, I must offer to yield it without coercion. But if I leave it here among my other reading material and fail to reset my flimsy and easily detectable chamber wards, it might not be here when they come back to search for it. Hardly my fault."

"You want me to hide it." We certainly could not allow them to confiscate the book before we knew what it was. "Better we both take it and go."

Dante twisted and stretched his shoulders as if he'd been hunched over the book for a very long time. "Better I get this encounter over with. It has to come sometime, and I'd rather inquisitors not dog our steps as we

go forward. Besides"—he twisted his mouth in his wry semblance of a smile—"we can always hope I'll learn something of interest in the Bastionne Camarilla. The prefects have either deliberately overlooked these episodes of transference or kept their own investigation very close."

"They'll dig deep," I said. "They've old magic that even you—"

"Be sure, I shall yield the butchers only what I wish them to have." The mage's brittle edge reasserted itself, like keen lancets snapped out of a shiny brass block.

"The Camarilla is pledged to preserve the art from those who would pervert it," I said, hating this defensiveness his prejudices roused. "They *must* be strict, and they must keep their counsels, just as we do, to make their work effective. But Edmond de Roble is on his way to meet with Michel de Vernase. Every instinct and every reasoning bone in me is convinced that some piece of this conspiracy will come to a head twenty days from now—whether or not Gaetana is guilty. Someday the prefects need to hear what you can teach, but not today. I need you free. Alive."

The mage looked at me askance, as might a healer observing a hopeless patient. "I promise to watch my mouth, student."

Shifting uncomfortably inside my skin, I pointed at the book. Surely it pointed the way to Gaetana's deeper purposes. To her guilt. "So what is it? What have you learned?"

He scooped it up and waggled his dark brows, his best humor peeking out like sunglints through breaking storm clouds. "A beginning. I've scarce unlocked ten pages and the language is as murky as a pond choked with algae. But the title is *Diel Revienne—The Book of Return*—and we're not speaking of returning from a day's outing to Vernase. It's one of three. I'll tell you more once we're traveling. When the time is right, I'll astonish you!"

A thunderous knock set off a searing whine almost beyond hearing.

Dante shoved me against a stretch of blank wall opposite the door between the chambers. "Stay exactly here. I've set a barrier to hide you—far better than the wall closure. And heed this, student: These barriers inside you are ridiculously strong. *Anger* stiffens them."

I had no idea what he meant. Fingers of enchantment snugged me

against the bedchamber wall like a well-fitted jacket, though naught hindered my view into the adjoining room. Dante stuffed the book inside my shirt. "Best keep still," he said with a sidewise grin, then grabbed his staff and stepped into his great chamber. Bellowing, *"Eximas!"* he stretched the staff toward the outer door.

The whine of the wards ceased. The door flew open. An adept, thick folds of dark fabric draped over his arm, crossed the threshold and intoned, "Master Dante of unknown family and demesne, the Camarilla Magica summons thee to Witness."

Though the man's elongated face wore the habitually haughty expression of Camarilla adepts, his eyes circled quickly, as if to determine whether the ceiling might fall or furniture start flying. He passed Dante a rolled paper, which would be the personal warrant, indicating whether the mage was to be taken as a violator or informant.

Dante tossed the scroll unread onto one of his worktables. He did not respond to the adept's greeting, nor did he bow to the inquisitor who followed the adept inside and began a cursory examination of the great chamber.

The inquisitor—whether man or woman was impossible to judge—brushed fingertips on the circumoccule, then moved on quickly to the cluttered worktables. The fleshy hands touched only one or two items, lifted a few lids, opened a book or two. Ripples of enchantment flowed through the room, splashing on me even where I sat. Dante, wreathed in disdain, remained near the door.

I swore under my breath when the inquisitor drew a flat leather case the length of my arm from a cabinet. Dante had assured me the spyglass and arrow were safely hidden. But the opened case revealed only three wicked-looking knives. I breathed again. Dante's mouth twitched, and I would have sworn by all I held holy that he winked. Father Creator, he was enjoying this!

From then on, I observed Dante's reactions, not solely the inquisitor's. Even when the eyes peering out of the green cap heated at discovering the masked door, Dante remained cool. The hooded mage entered the bedchamber, but, astonishingly, took no note of me. A quick perusal of bed,

desk, cupboard, and chest, and it was done. As I exhaled slowly, the inquisitor returned to the great chamber and waved a finger.

The adept held out his hand for Dante's staff. Dante thumped his staff on the floor, and flame burped from its head. "My ancille goes where I do, Mage Inquisitor. If I'm forbid to carry it into the Bastionne, then you must do so yourself. 'Tis less stable than I would like. My finer skills remain imperfect." No one would mistake his statement for either apology or humility.

"The inquisitor will carry it, Master," said the adept. The inquisitor, naturally, did not speak.

Dante propped the staff against the wall and did not protest as the adept draped him in the shapeless gown of deepest blue, weighted with iron rings. Nor did he lash out as the adept dropped the heavy hood over his head. He wanted to, though. As clearly as blood pulsed in my veins, I experienced a smothered rage—a desire to break the cocky underling who led him, blind and suffocating, into the passage—and something else. . . .

I shook off the fancy. Dante would not fear the Camarilla.

The inquisitor spent a goodly time examining the markings on Dante's staff, before laying a tentative finger on it. First one, then another; then he lifted it gingerly and departed. The door slammed behind him.

Not overeager to venture out of my hiding place, I pulled out the little book. Its binding of faded, brittle leather was crudely stitched, its lettering unreadable, the fore-edge of the pages ragged and stained. An oily residue of spent enchantment made me grip it fiercely. Yet it remained enspelled. I opened to the first thin page. Though scribed in familiar characters— Sabrian script of approximately two centuries earlier—the words formed no familiar language. Indeed, all characters but the few fixed at a time by my eyes' focus shifted their order at random.

Magical encryption, then. But I needed no magic to unravel the book's origin. Inked on the opening page was a pair of dueling scorpions, the blazon of the Mondragoni.

Of a sudden, Dante's good humor and promises of revelation lost flavor, as will tender shoots and leaves left too long in summer sun. Always

in my life, I had desired to know everything of magic. Yet for days after we first stored the Mondragoni texts in Seravain's vault, squeamish sensibility had prevented me pulling them out. Eventually I had yielded to temptation. Finding the pages locked away by the Gautieri wards, I'd convinced myself I was relieved. Now I saw the truth. I wanted to learn everything, even from the decadent masters of Eltevire.

Stuffing the little volume back into my doublet, I crossed to the window, careful not to be seen. On the carriageway, Guillam, the stableman, had brought up four horses. The Camarilla adepts aided the three shrouded Witnesses to mount. Prefect Angloria rode the fourth beast, and the inquisitors and adepts formed up marching ranks behind her. A wave from Angloria, and the bizarre procession moved around the corner of the palace, out of view.

The Camarilla warrant named Dante as informant, not accused. A relief, that. Unless they provoked him to some revelation of his ideas or his true power, he should be held only a short time.

I had not asked Dante what I should do to avoid being killed were I to find him "in trance" again, nor why an interruption should cause such rage. Nor had I inquired how, in Heaven's truth, he had summoned me to his side. . . . *barriers inside you . . . anger stiffens them.* Certainly I had been angry that morning, with Dante, with Philippe, with Michel de Vernase, with the world that used such people as Maura and Edmond de Roble-Margeroux as pawns in terrible, dangerous games. It had taken the mage more than an hour to fetch me to protect this little book.

But how had he done it? I stared at my hand, pocked with the burn scars he had soothed and dressed after the fire on the *Swan*, as if it had taken on a wholly unfamiliar shape. Never in all my studies had I come upon a formula to embed enchantment into a man's very blood and flesh. Into his mind.

CHAPTER TWENTY-FOUR

6 CINQ
19 DAYS UNTIL THE ANNIVERSARY

"You said twelve of fifteen elements." Jacard frowned at my sketch of Dante's circumoccule. We sat beside the tall casements at the end of the mages' passage on the morning after the Camarilla had taken the three away. "It's none of my doing that Dante was hauled off before you could get him out. I risked my career."

"Sorry. Ten are all I can remember. Truly I appreciate your help, Adept, and as soon as I've a chance to consult my journal pages, I'll let you know the rest." Not that better instructions would do him any good without Dante's power to seal and charge the thing. So deeply shaken were my magical certainties, I could no longer assert that any particle embedded in the ring affected the mage's enchantments in any fashion whatsoever.

My skin buzzed with lack of sleep. I had not dared return to my apartments or be seen in public lest someone decide to enshroud me in dark wool and iron and haul me off to the Bastionne. I'd spent the entire previous day in a rose arbor, watching the carriageway for Dante's return. The night I'd spent huddled in the summerhouse, hoping to see a light in his window and trying to decide if the thoughts and fears and urgencies in my head were my own or a product of his enchantment. No enlightenment had been forthcoming. At dawn, rabid for news, I had given up and set out

for the east wing. On my way to Dante's apartments, I had run straight into Jacard.

He folded the page and slipped it into his sleeve. "Acolyte Nadine's uncle is a house mage at the Bastionne. He hasn't been home since yesterday, but he sent her father a message that Gaetana's assistants are not to be summoned. And if hers aren't, the rest of us aren't likely. You're something of a special case I suppose, with this 'holy mission' to root out treachery, but I've not heard your name mentioned. They'd surely have come for you already if they thought you had something useful to say."

"That seems good news," I said. "Perhaps none of this is as serious as it seems." But it was, of course. Too many hours had passed. Camarilla inquisitors did not indulge in drawing room chatter with their held Witnesses.

"Head up," whispered Jacard. "Someone's coming."

"Let me pass. Let me pass." A disheveled Mage Orviene swept down the passage toward his grandly carved door, drawing acolytes and adepts behind him as a comet leads its tail of stars. "I must sit in my own chair. But follow me in, all of you. You must hear what I've to report. And by your hope of Heaven, recall that your lips are sealed by the oaths you have sworn to the Camarilla."

"I'll find you later." Jacard jumped up and joined his fellows, eight or nine of them crowding through the doorway after Orviene.

I slipped onto the back of the group as if I belonged, remaining nearest the door.

Orviene's expansive great chamber vied with Ilario's in overblown elegance, if not so obviously in cost. The mage sagged into a cushioned chair, carved in the shape of a rampant lion, motioning for one of his acolytes to light a man-high lamp of fluted brass. Though the hour was early on a bright day, thick draperies covered the chamber's sole window.

The lamplight only clarified the mage's out-of-character turnout. His chin-length hair, customarily pomaded and combed, straggled on a soiled collar. His skirted doublet hung unbuttoned; his meticulously tailored sleeves flapped about his wrists. But his round face carried worse news, his complexion gray, his eyes dull and uncertain.

"Mage Gaetana was beheaded by the Camarilla Magica at the first hour of morning watch . . ."

The news slammed my chest like a battering ram. Warning, denial, horror, guilt exploded in my head and heart. Only with difficulty could I follow the rest of his words.

". . . unholy practice . . . transference . . . a former adept in her charge . . . and an innocent girl . . . murder . . . confession after intensive questioning . . ."

I had killed her, as clearly as day followed night. As coldly heedless as a child who burns an insect to see how it reacts, I had set the Camarilla on her. *Intensive questioning.* Holy angels, Father Creator . . . I'd never have written the letter had I truly doubted the woman's involvement in terrible crimes. I'd wanted her out of play, prevented from tormenting anyone else. Yet I had expected a prolonged investigation, time to be certain. And what of Dante? Saints defend him.

". . . shock . . . dismay . . . private quest for arcane knowledge . . . thankfully, no evidence of collaboration . . ."

No sense. No sense. No sense. Even amid this nauseating self-reproach, the *agente confide* in my head bullied me with reason. Why had they not come for the lunatic who had written the accusing letter? Great gods, I had signed my name. And these young colleagues were inexperienced, yes, most of them new to court, overawed at their privilege to study with the queen's own. Those I recognized were not Seravain's elite, to be sure, but capable. Yet they had not been asked for their own observations. That must mean the Camarilla possessed other evidence implicating Gaetana.

". . . who worked for her are dismissed without prejudice. I shall personally write recommendations. For my own self and my staff, we must wait to see how Her Majesty reacts to the news as the prefects present it to her. Information may be curtailed or held entirely in confidence. Such scandal so near her royal person! Truth be told, I am tempted to resign."

Her Majesty. When the world learned the queen's mage had been executed for illicit magic, Philippe would be forced to act—to declare his support or arrest her. And if he declared his wife innocent of murder and corruption, he must have the truth to offer his people instead.

The Concord de Praesta had been wrought to prevent civil and magical life from swallowing each other. It ensured that magical practitioners were subject to a law that took into account the particular demands, requirements, and possibilities of their deeds, and it ensured that those lacking magical talents would never be judged by those with talents so alien to their own. Only the Camarilla could judge matters of magical practice. Only the crown could judge civil matters. On the day I had been admitted to the study of magic's secrets, I had sworn the oath to uphold the Camarilla's prerogatives as set by the Concord, believing fully in their value. No argument had yet convinced me otherwise. I had to pursue my own part of this investigation, trusting Philippe to give me time to bring him the truth.

Shaken to the marrow, bursting with questions to which I had no answers, I slid round the door frame into the passage before anyone noticed me. With such alarm and upheaval, none present were looking beyond their own futures. I sped lightly to Dante's door and slipped inside, only to receive another jolt. One might imagine a herd of elephants had arrived before me.

The contents of the worktables had been scattered from one end of the room to the other. Every box had been opened. Every bottle emptied. Every book unstacked. Every paper . . . I spun in place. Not a paper was to be seen. Dante had predicted the Camarilla would come looking for the book. Better they than Michel de Vernase.

It was tempting to run to Ilario. More than four-and-twenty hours Dante had been held. Yet even were we willing to risk our partnership, Ilario, a man outside the magical community, could not intervene with Camarilla business, even to ask for news, nor could his half sister or the king. And I was oath-sworn not to speak of Camarilla business to an outsider.

And so I sat for a while in the midst of the destruction, worried, guilty, and wholly unsure what to do next. I did not so much doubt Gaetana's guilt, as wonder at the circumstances of her "confession." Haste implied a wish to avoid probing too deep, a wish to hide unpleasant truth, a wish to contain and conceal. What if someone in the Camarilla itself wanted

Gaetana's testimony cut short? How likely was it that Gaetana and Michel de Vernase worked alone? And why, why, why did they keep Dante so long?

Near midday, unable to sit still any longer, I began to tidy up the mess, blotting oils and inks, stacking books, and gathering the scattered leaves and scraps, the beads of coral, jade, and lapis, and slips of varied metals onto a sheet. As the afternoon waned, I collected the emptied bottles and jars, settled on the floor beside the heaped sheet, and began to sort the materials into their proper containers. The sun slid westward. . . .

"So when do we ride?"

I jerked upright to the chinking clatter of glass and stone. The world had gone black, save for the soft glow of a white staff.

"Dante! God's teeth!" I jumped to my feet, the sorting debris showering to the floor. "Are you all right? Is it true about Gaetana? What, in the god's creation, did they do to you? What did they ask? So many hours . . ."

I could not slow the spill of questions, even as he moved away, raising his staff high enough to cast its soft light on the jumbled cupboards and filthy floor.

"A blighted mess here. I presume you did not cause it."

"Certainly not." How could he speak of such trivialities? "Dante, tell me about Gaetana."

"The Camarilla killed her for bleeding the girl. She confessed to it."

A statement of fact, entirely dispassionate. I expected rage—or gloating, perhaps—anything but glassy calm.

"And what of you, Master? What did they ask? Did they use . . . extraordinary methods?"

"I am neither dead nor accused." He nudged the broken night jar with his toe, then strolled across the room and touched his staff to the wall. A spike of red light split the dark, and the bedchamber doorway stood revealed. He picked up an emptied rucksack from a worktable and carried it into the bedchamber.

"Shall we get a start on the morning?" he called through the opened doorway. "I've no wish to field idiot questions from slobbering ladies-in-waiting or devious assistants. The moon's just past full, and I've been told the road to Vernase is a good one."

The suggestion surprised me. Dante hated riding, and night travel could be slow and unsettling. But, then, perhaps he was as anxious to be away as I was. Perhaps he dared not speak of the Bastionne inside the palace, where listening ears were everywhere.

"Certainly. Yes, of course, we should go. I'll roust the stableman and meet you in the yard."

"I've a few things to gather; then I'll be down." As I touched the door latch, he called after me. "You do still have my book, yes?"

His will nudged my hands and tongue, subtler than his earlier attempts to influence me, but unmistakable now I knew to watch. Yet even so small a move unleashed a fury in me. I no longer even questioned that he was capable of magic my studies deemed impossible, but that did not mean I would ignore this crude manipulation.

"So tell me, Master, do you still not trust me, or is it you believe me a pure dullard? Would it make a difference if I repeat that these spell tricks are unnecessary? Or that I prefer us to deal with each other as honest men? Or if I told you that an armed assassin would not have kept me from your side once I saw Camarilla in the palace?"

He appeared in the doorway, the rucksack on his shoulder. To my astonishment, he had donned a mage's formal blue gown instead of his favored russet tunic and scuffed trousers. Though his silver collar gleamed in the light of his staff, his face remained shadowed. I could imagine its ascetic arrogance well enough.

"I don't know what to make of you, student. On the one hand, I never met a man who understood himself so little as you. Your own excessively rigid mind plays more tricks on you than I ever could. But on the other hand . . . So tell me, honest man, where is my book?"

"I've put it away, as I presumed you wished." Underneath a bench in the summerhouse, to be precise, as my "excessively rigid mind" had not completely failed me.

"Exactly so. But if I'm to discover anything of interest in it, I'll need it back, won't I?"

I bit back a useless retort. We were not children, and the past two days had surely overstretched him as well as me. I'd known from the first he was subject to this choler. "I'll fetch it with us, certainly. And as we ride, you'll tell me what you've learned from it."

He stooped to rummage through the heaped contents fallen from a gaping cupboard. "Little enough. A few tricks. Some tedious history. The Mondragoni had no use for this other family, the Gautieri, I'll say. Evidently the other way round, as well, as the encryption is hideously complex, doubly so for what puling spellwork is written in it. I doubt I'll ever be able to finish reading the thing, much less grasp its full meaning." He picked a few items from the heap, carried them into his bedchamber, and stuffed them into his leather satchel.

I gaped for a moment, not sure what I was hearing. Dante, suggesting a magical task he could not perform? A conclusion that wholly contradicted his statement of a day earlier that he would "astonish" me with what he learned from the Mondragoni text. "What foolery is this? You said—"

Caution aborted my retort. Did he speak this way for my benefit or for some other listener—perhaps someone who also knew of Gaetana's book? His deliberate preoccupation offered no prospect of immediate enlightenment. I would challenge him again, once we were on the road.

So I left him at his packing. It would not pain me to rouse the stableman, Guillam, from a sound sleep. Perhaps with a cannon.

OTHERS WERE AWAKE IN THE middle-night hours of Castelle Escalon. As I awaited the mage in an unlit corner of the carriageway, an increasing number of footmen and guards raced in and out of the east wing doors. Extra torches were brought out to light the portico steps. Before very long, old Guillam himself led out two palfreys, one white, one sleek bay, both saddled for ladies.

"We'd best be off before we get caught in this lot. The house is in an

uproar." Engrossed in the activity, I near shed my skin when Dante spoke from behind me. He snatched his mount's reins from my hand.

A troop of guardsmen marched round the corner from the direction of the barracks, just as a knot of people emerged from the east wing: guards, ladies, court officials. Lady Antonia, unmistakable in a yellow cloak, hair piled in billowing curls, descended the steps and was assisted into her saddle. Her voice carried, but not her words. Two more followed her—a tall, slender figure, draped head to toe in black and leaning on Ilario's arm. It could be no one but Eugenie de Sylvae.

"He's sending her away," I whispered. It was the only conclusion that made sense. But was my cousin dispatching his wife to her family's home in Aubine or his own mountain fortress Journia, or had Gaetana's treachery pushed him past patience?

The answer came swiftly. The queen and Ilario were bustled down the steps and wrenched apart, amid a flurry of sharply announced commands. The lady, surrounded by a bristling forest of spears, was aided to mount. No coach. No baggage. No attendants but her foster mother. A snapped order moved the party forward, and the milling courtiers dissipated like smoke in wind, leaving the pale-haired Ilario alone in the carriageway.

One other watched alone from the east portico as the queen's party vanished into the dark. Ilario marched up the steps and past my royal cousin without so much as a word. When the king slowly followed the chevalier inside, footmen stepped out and doused the extra torches. A sense of utter failure settled over me like a leaden mantle.

The yard quiet again, Dante and I rode out into a restless city. Lamps blazed. Doors stood open. Knots of citizens had gathered in the streets. Many an eye glared at Dante as we rode by. "Ought to burn 'em all," yelled a burly taverner, just after we'd passed his doorway.

A crowd of boys and rowdies surged across the road, heading down toward the river. When I asked where they were headed, a boy yelled back, "Sorcerer's whore is headed to the Spindle."

I was relieved when we left Merona behind without further incident. For beyond all this, we had still to determine if Michel de Vernase, king's friend and confidant, who called himself the Aspirant, was trying to drive

Sabria into chaos with Mondragoni sorcery or save her from those who were. If any clues were to be found in Michel de Vernase's house, we needed to get there before his family or co-conspirators thought to remove them.

Surely Philippe would wait for my report from Vernase before he judged Eugenie—surely.

THE GIBBOUS MOON HUNG HUGE and yellow in the cloudless void, bathing the quiet vineyards south of Merona in ocher and gold. As the road led us into the soft hills, the shadows of clustered hornbeams and downy oaks mottled the roadway, requiring a rider to keep alert for pits and obstacles as well as the ever-present possibility of thieves. Fortunately the horses could see better than either of us.

Dante continued to put off my questions, claiming the concentration required to stay on his horse quite consumed him. When I persisted, he insisted I shut my mouth unless I had something useful to tell him. We had scarce exited Merona's gates when he had demanded the Mondragoni book. Perhaps if I'd been clever enough to hold it back, I could have pried a few answers from him in exchange.

Well along in the night, the road dipped into a thickly wooded vale creased by a shallow river. "The moon's too low to do us good," I said, weary to the bone. "We should halt until sunrise and rest the horses here by the water."

"Can't say an hour's sleep would go amiss," said the mage, yawning. "Inquisitors don't heed day or night. They pursue what clues they're given." A white glow swelled from his staff, and he urged his mount ahead of mine.

Using his muted, steady light, we found a clearing by the water, a few hundred metres down a side path. Old dung, wheel tracks, and scattered ash evidenced that other travelers had used the clearing. We tended the horses and set them to graze, matters for which the inexperienced mage needed constant direction.

As I wiped sweat and dirt from our saddles, Dante touched his staff to

a blackened ash ring and murmured, *"Incendio, confinium a circumna."* Sparks snapped and flew from the heel of the white stick—and inside my skin. The mage tossed in twigs and bits of dry moss he'd gathered from the trampled ground, and in moments flames had sprouted. The bright enchantment devoured me, a surge of cold fire from feet to head that shivered my bones. The questions I'd prepared for him along the way, the arguments, the appeals to his agreement and our effective partnership, all fled before my longing.

"Creator's Hand, what makes the difference?" I said. No urgency gripped me more than this most fundamental one. "Your enchantments live and breathe. Beside them, every other I've known seems but an image of an image."

Instead of answering, Dante walked. A quarter of an hour . . . half an hour . . . he strode the perimeter of the clearing: thick trees, tangled underbrush, the river, broad and swift-flowing, aglint with the beams of the sinking moon. I could not see his face. He had cleanly and purposefully chosen reticence about the past night's encounter, but *this* silence seemed a struggle.

When he returned to the fire, he crouched and planted his staff between his knees, gripping it so tightly that his knuckles gleamed pale. Poised on edge, I sensed revelation but a decision away.

"Magic must rise unhindered from one's own depths," he said at last. "Only then can it encompass and magnify the entwined keirna of its objects. As I told you, your mind is riddled with barriers solid as mortared walls. And you maintain this stubborn belief in elements, particles, and formulas, as do all those taught at Seravain. Here . . ."

Near spitting with impatience, now he'd sloughed off indecision, he jumped to his feet and beckoned me after him. He halted at the path that had brought us into the clearing. "Learn this path," he said, brightening the glow of his staff, scooping a handful of the black dirt and cramming it into my hand. "Squeeze this. Smell it. Examine its color and composition. Dark and rich here by the river. Mixed with old dung, bark, the rot of fallen leaves and decaying trunks, and all that's washed in from the river in flood."

He scuffed his boots in the rutted track. "See how worn the path is, this wide trough. Consider its uses—tired travelers, maybe fearful ones, scavengers, wheels, horses, mules. This camp is decently protected by the water and the tangled trees, but we ought to build a ward that will warn us if any approach by the path. Where do you begin?"

"Wards require impermeability—base metal. . . ." Rote memory spat out the answer.

"Use your mind, Portier! Think not of divine elements, but of what's here before you." Dante crouched down and tapped a pale knot protruding from the dark soil of the path. "The path is laced with roots. Hornbeam clearly, from the color, and the branches hanging over your head. So, examine the tree roots with your fingers. Then look up, recalling everything you know of hornbeam—modest in height, its wood pale as birch but hard as iron, seeds winged like insects. Feel these leaves, crimped like women's hair."

He swept his arm back the way we'd come. "Someone's coppiced most of the hornbeam in this wood, as the shoots make good poles. But the wood has been ill tended, left to grow for a long time—perhaps the Blood Wars wiped out those who minded it. My staff is hornbeam. The wood is strong, almost impossible to work. It binds magic well. Now wait. . . ."

He crashed off into the tangled underbrush. I studied the path and the dirt in my hand, not at all sure what I was doing. Questions and mysteries and sleeplessness nagged at me, yet magic lay at the heart of our mystery. I had to understand it. And Dante was the only mentor I wanted.

The mage emerged from the thicket and thrust a slender limb into my hand. "Here. Use this to scribe your enclosure about the snarl of roots and the dirt from your hand. Encircle them in your mind, as well."

"Ow!" The hornbeam shoot was approximately the length of my arm, the diameter of a finger, and smooth, straight, and pale, save for one blackened end—still hot, where he'd burned through to cut it.

As commanded, I dumped my handful of dirt atop the exposed roots and used the shoot to draw an elliptical pattern around the pile. Before closing the oval, I hesitated. "Perhaps it's not wide enough. If I need to block the entire path, or if there are more parti—more objects to contain."

"The size of the enclosure does not matter," said Dante. "Stretch it as you work if need be."

I took his word that this would eventually make sense.

"Now fashion a simple crossing ward: You're to be wakened when a warm body passes the barrier. Build the spell pattern in your mind. Your hand can serve as the warmth needed. Surely you know your own hand better than anything in the world, just as you know best what warning can wake you from sleep. So, lay your hand atop the roots and dirt within your enclosure. When the pattern is prepared, seek the power that exists in it already, joining it with what lives in you."

Spell pattern—not so easy as it sounded. As I had learned magic, particles enclosed by a physical boundary—rope or string or circumoccule—provided both the physical and mental structure for spellwork. Formulas prescribed the placement, as well as the balance, of particles—the metal used for spark must sit beside the fabric used for wood and air in the fire spell, for example. I had been taught to hold that exact physical arrangement in my mind as I infused it with will and magic. I'd never been required to create a pattern in my head, a structure of understanding, of random ideas like *crossing* or of properties like *warmth*, provided by physical objects that could be stretched, arranged, molded solely by force of will and inner vision.

But I recalled the runelike structures Dante had shown me, and I worked at creating something similar. Carefully, precisely, as if nurturing the last flame that might keep me living in a tempest, I considered *warmth, crossing, strength, barriers, waking* . . . and I imagined each of them as an abstraction of shape and color. My creation looked something like a gate. And then I reached for what magic might live in hornbeam and soil and the night and the warmth of my own hand, as well as that born in my blood. . . .

As a blizzard wind, enchantment rushed upon me, billowing, thrumming, slamming, sweeping through my heart and soul and mind in a sere glory . . . and vanished two heartbeats after.

Gutted, bereft, I crouched in the dirt in the dark of a woodland after moonset. My skin could not sense the night damp, much less any enchant-

ment. The river's burbling slop sounded a thousand miles distant. Dante had gone off again, taking his staff and its quiet glow.

Gods, fool. What were you thinking? That nature would relent because you've had a difficult few days? That Dante would lend you the keys to Heaven's gates? He's off laughing at you.

I tromped back to the fire, rolled up in my cloak, and closed my eyes in search of sleep. Dante did not return. Sleep was a long time coming. . . .

WHEN THE TRUMPET FANFARE SOUNDED inside my skull, I leapt out of the tangle of sleep as if bit by a viper. Dante leaned on his glowing staff, standing in the path just on the near side of the lumpy hornbeam roots. "Decently done, student. Naught to raise you into the Camarilla, but decently done."

CHAPTER TWENTY-FIVE

7 Cinq
18 days until the Anniversary

Magic! Half-giddy, disbelieving, I made Dante step back and cross the ward thrice over. I insisted he leave his staff behind and do it three times more. When I shamelessly implored him yet again to swear he had not himself sounded the warning trump in my head, he glowered and waved his stick to move me out of his path. "Enough. I would like an hour of sleep before the sun rises. We've three days on the road ahead."

As I squatted in the path and gazed fondly on the gnarled hornbeam roots, he wrapped himself entirely in his cloak. Sitting with his back to the tree nearest the fire, he appeared naught but a shapeless appendage of night. When I gave in and returned to my own resting place, his muffled breathing had already taken on the shallow regularity of sleep.

Though sorely tempted, I did not attempt to create another spell. Depleted as I was, I would surely fail. It seemed more important to relive every moment of the ward's creation, etching each word of Dante's instruction upon my bones. My soul ached at the implications of his teaching. Every spell of a kind could be different—every ward, every bending of light, every cleansing spell, every weather charm—differing not only in quality, but in its very creation. Blind . . . holy Creator, it was as if sor-

cerers had lived with senses chained these many years, and no twisting of logic or drawing down of history could explain to me why that was so.

Eventually even the satiety of a lifetime's yearning must yield to exhaustion, and I fell into vivid dreaming—of a bloody battlefield where my arm strained to breaking as my luminous staff held off a ravening multitude, of rescuing a besieged caravan in high mountains, of conjuring a floodwall for a city threatened with annihilation, of being chained to a bleak and barren rock through season upon agonized season as penance for some brave deed long past remembrance. Every dream story I had glimpsed throughout my youth came full-blown upon me in that waning night. Surely I smiled in my sleep. If my hand could conjure enchantment, then even the wildest fantasies of heroic service might take on true life.

I WOKE TO THE SOUND of rain . . . or the river . . . or . . . I propped myself on my elbows. Bleared eyes noted Dante standing in the path, relieving himself on my treasured hornbeam roots. No trumpet sounded in my head. No magical residue settled on my spirit.

"The sun's been up an hour," he said, when he was done. "Could I saddle a beast one-handed, I'd have headed for Vernase without you." Cold as a marble tomb, he stepped over me and kicked dirt over his fire that had burned through the night without feeding.

Lurching to my feet, I chose to douse my head in the river before thinking too deeply. It served. Not only did the cool water cleanse me of road dust, sleep grit, and Dante's sour greeting, but of naive hopes and childish dreams.

Gaetana was dead. Dante had spent six-and-thirty hours in the Bastionne Camarilla and had chosen to tell me exactly nothing more than that, diverting my attention with the one thing he knew would erase all other concerns. He had played me like a dulcian.

As I saddled the horses, the mage sat on a log, eating a dried fig. The Mondragoni book lay beside him. "Did *you* work the ward?" I rasped, swollen anger and humiliation lodged in throat and chest. "Or did it ever exist at all?"

He accepted the reins and climbed into the saddle, as out of comfort with the horse as a fish in a barnyard. Yet his arrogance remained unyielding. "Did you not sense the spell binding, then? Pity. Even if a slattern despises her bastard, she cannot fail to recognize it as her own."

His vehement ugliness stunned me speechless.

Naturally, I examined the roots. Though I brought every inner sense to bear, no bound enchantment existed on the path or anywhere in the camp. Slight residue of spent magic hung about the defiled hornbeam roots, like morning fog in a hollow, but even if I'd had the skill to disentangle it, it was masked quite effectively by the physical residue Dante had left there.

And naturally, I spent a painstaking half hour attempting to reproduce the pattern I'd created in the night. Nature did not so much as sputter in contempt.

When I caught up to Dante, I passed right on by without a word. I could not bear to look at him. Serving a pitiful vengeance, I raised the pace too high for his inexperienced horsemanship. Stiff as starched sheets, he bounced and jostled, jerking on the reins so that he repeatedly had to coax his confused mount to keep moving at all. By nightfall the mage would think he'd been beaten with Merle's truncheon. Perhaps by then I could put grief and humiliation aside and put him to the question yet again.

The road took us through the grand estates of southern Louvel. Budding vineyards teemed with laborers hauling away weeds and winter's trimmings, or dredging ground limestone and dung into the soil. Farther south, a few tenant farms and freeholds appeared, squeezed between the endless ranks of vines. Here and there a laborer shouted as we passed. I could not hear what they called, and Dante did not say, but the rude gestures were easily interpreted, as well as their pointed reference to Dante's collar. Dante paid them no mind.

The Camarilla's diligence in eliminating false practitioners had left bitter resentments in the countryside. Villagers deprived of their wise women and potion makers could not afford trained mages or adepts. Yet the penalties for purveying false spellwork could be anything from lashes

to branding to ruinous fines. The penalties for practicing magework without a collar or adept's work without Camarilla supervision were far more severe.

As the morning waned, rage leaked away, swallowed by profound misgiving. The inquisitors would have questioned what Dante knew of Gaetana, of transference, perhaps of necromancy or other kinds of unholy magic. They might have pushed to know of his training or his methods. If he had spoken his beliefs about magic, they would never have let him go. If he had exposed his role in our investigation, the prefects would have complained so vociferously that the king was violating their authority as laid down in the Concord, everyone in Merona would have heard the uproar. Neither had transpired.

Ever had the mage been blunt and inconsiderate, but never had he been cruel in our private dealings. And never once in our partnership had he told me an untruth, until he allowed me to believe I had worked magic. Something in his hours at the Bastionne had aimed his deepest rage straight at me.

Two more days—one, if we pushed hard—would take us into Aubine. The Ruggiere demesne lay just inside its boundaries. Dante and I needed a plan to approach our investigation, which meant I had to clear the fouled air between us.

As we neared the market town of Sciarra, the traffic picked up. Forced to a walking pace, we had to thread a path between bawling pack mules laden with early vegetables, dung carts bound for the vineyards, and a youthful swineherd and his unruly charges. A roadside fruit seller spat in our wake. "Cheat! Conniver! Camarilla whore!"

Sciarra's town gates had rusted open and were overgrown with chickweed and trailers of black bryony. I nudged my mount alongside Dante as we rode through. "We are partner *agentes confide*, Master," I said, sucking in my tattered pride. "What have I done to earn your despite?"

Stone-faced, he stared straight ahead, ignoring the stares of townsmen unused to seeing a collared mage guiding his horse through a sea of pigs. His gloved hand tightened on the reins and his nostrils flared. "I warned you to keep your Camarilla friends out of my business. So you promised.

I warned you I detested liars. But it seems I've you to thank for my visit to the Bastionne. And you persist in the lie by pestering me for information. Surely you know your mentor is a skilled and ruthless interrogator. Has he not given you the full report?"

The Camarilla letter. I'd never had a chance to tell him of it. He thought I'd set the inquisitors on him apurpose. And Kajetan . . .

"Father Creator, Dante, I never intended you to be taken. We should have been well away by the time they came for Gaetana. And I'd no idea Kajetan was in Merona. I swear—"

"No more swearing. Better we make an end to this demeaning confederacy. Sooner will please me best."

It was as if a gate had been slammed in my face. This was no afternoon's offense, as when I had challenged his actions on the *Swan*, no playacting, no testy independence that would eventually yield to shared purpose, as our every dispute had done. Though my accusations had not named him, my thoughtless, careless, desperate play had risked his freedom to practice sorcery—the one thing he held more valuable than life. Naturally, he would see it as betrayal. And forgiveness was not a word in Dante's vocabulary.

Eyes darting hither and yon, the mage shifted in his saddle and loosed the strap on his staff. The town's tall houses throttled the road, crowding travelers, carts, and beasts. The pigs had toppled an onion cart, and the onion seller screamed at the swineherd to keep his charges from eating what was spilled.

I felt as incapable as the hapless swineherd. Certainly no words would repair this breach. Yet, at the least, I had to know how it would affect our work. "Was Gaetana guilty?" I blurted.

"I told you, they executed—"

"But was she guilty? Did she bleed Gruchin? Do *you* believe it?"

"Yes." The answer struck square as hammer to nail.

"And Ophelie?"

"Yes."

Every instinct at my command testified that his conviction was not feigned. This eased my conscience somewhat, but not my regret. "You

agreed to the terms of our partnership," I said. "But, altogether without intention, I've betrayed your trust. I understand that will be difficult to mend, though I will do my best. Master, do we finish this or not?"

"Eltevire is destroyed," he said, cold as spring frost. "Gaetana did not know how to formulate such magic, nor did she know anyone who could. None of them know. Camarilla hounds can dig out her confederates. But I will witness to any who listen that her interests did not extend beyond the magic. Once we identify this Aspirant, the instigator of this plot, the matters of *our* investigation will be closed, and we can each return to our own business. The sooner I'm out of that nest of aristos—"

A thump caused Dante to jerk and grunt. A second caused him to throw up a hand protectively. A third projectile bounced off his back and struck my knee. Stones.

"False! Liar! Cheat! Souleater's tool!" Shouts and more missiles flew from a yawning upper window, peopled by shadowed faces. I covered my head, but the sudden barrage caused a squealing riot among the meandering swine that now filled the road side to side hunting onions. My mare jinked and whinnied, and it required all my skill to keep her from panic.

Thank the Creator, a few excited pigs did not rattle Dante's stolid carthorse. A thudding impact on the mage's shoulder had him growling and yanking his staff from its straps.

"Master, no!" I snapped. "No magic! Just get out of here." A hostile magistrate could cause us days of trouble. We could afford no more delays.

Dante did not call up lightning, but only whacked a sow or two on the nose with the staff, then squeezed out of the press into a side lane. Swept past the same turning, I guided my nervous mare through the melee. By the time I left the squealing mass of pork behind, the mage had emerged half a kilometre down the road. Before I could catch up to him, he had vanished through a rickety gate that sported a peeling signboard labeled THE ARBOR.

Swearing at pigs and troublemakers and recalcitrant mages, I followed him into a close, stinking innyard. My jaw dropped.

Dante had already dismounted. He stood between a ramshackle hos-

telry and its dung-fouled stable, yelling at Adept Jacard. ". . . incompetent lout. I told you to bring the kit I'd left on the bench. Before we arrive at Vernase, I'll expect to have at least the bergamot, juniper, cedar, vetiver, and hyssop oils in hand. The artemesia, as well."

Jacard, filmed with sweat and road dust, frowned as if Dante had handed him a snake. "But, Master, you stressed promptness above all. Surely we can acquire these on our way to Vernase."

"Vetiver is near unobtainable outside a seaport. You can sell your body to a whoremaster or your soul to the devil to get it for all I care, but *get* it."

I dropped to the filthy ground beside them. "What, in the Souleater's demesne, is Jacard doing here?" Invited, apparently. Intended to accompany us, though to take the ambitious, curious adept along as we searched Michel de Vernase's home was idiocy.

"I'll not be questioned by a mewling secretary," snapped Dante, "no matter who his relatives are. Nor will I hear excuses from a lead-wit who cannot seem to follow the simplest instruction."

Surely a mage in full regalia had never graced this yard. He had lowered his voice at the least, frustrating the curiosity of two gawking drovers, a blowsy tap girl peering through a skewed doorway, and the pair of piggy eyes squinting over her shoulder from the dark interior of the inn.

Dante spun to glare at the drovers, who quickly busied themselves with loading a pair of mangy hounds into a cage on their wagon. The piggy eyes blinked, and a fat, pale hand drew the tap girl deeper into the inn.

"Hold, girl!" Dante's shout near startled her out of her overfull bodice. "I'll have a stoup. Out here."

"A w-what?" She gawped at the wooden steps at her feet, then back at Dante. "I can't give—"

"A *cup* of your best ale or cider," I called to her, as Dante's color deepened. "An ordinary tasset. I'll have one, as well." No tap girl south of Merona would recognize the peculiar terminology of Coverge's mining settlements.

"Nasty inside there," Dante mumbled as he secured his staff in its

leather straps. His eyes did not leave the doorway. "More's gone in than out that door."

Jacard shrugged and rolled his eyes at me. I grimaced in return, less concerned with disreputable hostelries than with this convoluted mess. The mage knew how fiercely I would object to Jacard's company. Though pleasant enough, Jacard was yet a stranger who had once worked for Gaetana. The adept's presence must quench all honest talk between us. Dante would undoubtedly laugh at the idea of *honest* talk. Gods, how could I have been so stupid?

The tap girl brought out two dripping tassets, the cleanliness of both girl and cups justifying the mage's reluctance to enter the inn. Running his thumb along the cup's rim, Dante mumbled an incantation. The dirty vessel began to glow. The drovers' hounds howled. The gaping girl bobbed a knee and scrambled backward.

"*Mine's* safe to drink now," Dante said when the dogs quieted. He downed it in one long pull and wiped his mouth on the sleeve of his blue gown. "Shall we go?"

More's gone in than gone out . . . My attention snapped to the piggy eyes still watching us, relishing decently dressed travelers, silver collars, and imaginings of a mage's reputed wealth. Cursing under my breath, I emptied my tasset into the muck and tossed the cup to the girl.

JACARD WAS NOT A TERRIBLE companion when it came to tending horses, fetching supplies, or the other tedious necessities of travel, and he maintained an admirable good humor in the face of Dante's unmitigated contempt. But his presence had me entirely on edge for two very long days.

He chattered like Ilario, boasting a great deal of his studies with this or that master at Seravain. He had naught but scorn for Orviene. "His spells are flimsier than paper, Portier, and wholly unreliable. How he earned his collar is a mystery for the ages!"

"Gaetana was better?" I said.

As ever when her name was mentioned, Jacard shuddered. "Praise the saints, she hated adepts and gave us naught but bits and pieces to work on:

deriving a formula for warming feet or making a ball roll uphill—which is impossible, I can tell you—or producing a potion to liquefy a particular bit of charmed paper she owned. Such trivialities chafed a bit after training with Elgin and Corrusco! Worse, she'd never tell us the use of our tasks, nor demonstrate any but the most mundane magic. Then she would scream that we never met her requirements, though she'd not show us why, either. She pawned me off on Conte Bianci two months after I arrived in Merona, and I was glad of it." He dropped his voice. "Dante's even less agreeable or talkative, but his magic . . . Sante Moritzio! . . . at least there's meat to it. I'm sure to learn something if I stay close. Mage Elgin says I've exceptional skills at disentanglation. . . ."

Though interested to hear of Gaetana's work that explained disintegrated manuscripts and revealed her interest in upended physics, I wished Jacard gone. His unending curiosity led inevitably to my own history, to my peculiar quest to serve the king, and to my relations with my royal cousin, with Dante, and even Maura. It required my best wits to keep ahead of him and guide the subject elsewhere. By afternoon of the second day, I was babbling the tales of my youthful dreaming, anything to avoid more tales of his education or the risky topics of transference and forbidden books. I went on longer than I intended about the dreams, as Jacard was so clearly bored by it. Perhaps boredom would still his tongue.

Dante rode behind us, unspeaking. At every stop, he pulled out Gaetana's book and wandered off by himself. To interrupt him was to call down Heaven's wrath. And he knew very well that I would not wish Jacard to take note of a Mondragoni text.

When we passed through the market town of Florien, and the mage dispatched Jacard to find the supplies he required, Dante insisted I go, as well. I could not defy him without breaking role. Clearly the mage did not wish to be alone with me. Our arrival at Vernase, the village nearest Michel's home at Montclaire, came as a divine mercy.

AFTER THE ONE NIGHT SPENT with Dante on hard ground, and a second sharing a dampish pallet with Jacard at a hostelry little better than the

Arbor, the little crossroads tavern in Vernase seemed a paradise. The Cask was clean, genteel, and in possession of an efficient stove and a most excellent bathing tub. Jacard and I shared one of the tavern's two rooms, kept for wine merchants, royal messengers, and other respectable sorts who came to do business with the Conte Ruggiere or his lady. Dante contrived to arrive later and took the other room.

That evening I sat alone in the taproom. The mage took supper in his room, and Jacard spent the evening in the outhouse, complaining of a turbulent belly. As a hearty portion of Mistress Constanza's well-roasted lamb soothed what aches the bath had left, I engaged the taverner in talk of the countryside and my purported mission to offer my services to the conte as a private secretary. "My former employer recommended the Conte Ruggiere as a noble lord who treats his employees fairly."

"Oh, aye, he does that," said the hearty Constanza, a woman of robust appetites, good cheer, and oft misappropriated verbiage. "Them as work for the lord are loyal to the bonesprits. A nobler collaboration'll not be found than the family at Montclaire—lord, lady, and their youngers that's mostly grown now—always generous and lively about the house and countryside, but close and companionable with one another, you know, as you'd want your own family to be. At least that's what we here in Vernase have circumspected these years since the king, divine grace to his name, give him the manor, though Lord Michel weren't even a noble born."

"Good folk, then. I'm glad to hear it," I said, tweaking a finger to bring the woman's broad face closer. "Some few in Merona name the lord more bull than lamb, if you know what I mean."

She gave my rumor due consideration, drawing her mouth and her opinions up tight. "The conte's firm, no doubt, and determined, but any man can drink a dozen tassets in a night while he holds his quarterlies, yet keep a fair good humor with the common dunderheads that happen by to puke their grievlings in his lap, has a good heart beneath, to my mind. But then again, I've got to pass the direful news that the king's own soldiery has set up a line, tight as a tinker's purse, about the manse. The soldiers say the conte is suspicioned of treason, which is wholesomely outlandish to anyone knows a gnat's brow about him."

"Treason!" Appropriately shocked, I begged the good Constanza to forget all I'd said, and asked her about other families and businesses round the area that might have need of a secretary.

She knew no locals with such needs. "But you might try the mage what's rented my other room. He's a dour sort. Slammed Remy into a straw bale for naught but trying to unload his horse. The lad near broke his wing bone from it. Course, I've a vile temper for sorcerers as I was conflicted with a rheumy eye for a year by a rogue mage. But what high and mighty parsonage like a mage wouldn't need a man of business, eh?"

This news struck me with a chilly bite. It was one thing to erupt when startled out of spellworking in dangerous circumstances, as the mage had done in his chambers. But to let fly at a stable lad seemed out of character as well as foolish. Dante played the simmering volcano for our public purposes, but why put on a show for no witness but a boy and a horse? Unless it was no show.

THE CINCH STRAP OF THE Guard Royale encircled Montclaire at a discreet but firm distance. Each soldier stood within hailing distance of the next, so none could pass between without proper identification. My official orders from the king gave Dante and me passage, and, at Dante's glaring insistence, Jacard as well.

I had dispatched a young officer up to the manse that morning to inform Lady Madeleine that a master mage of Queen Eugenie's household and a special envoy of King Philippe would be pleased to wait upon her and her children. We had not waited for an answer, but followed the messenger up the long swell in the green landscape to a hilltop prospect rivaling any in Louvel or Aubine.

Montclaire. The crystalline morning etched the horizons with the snowcapped peaks of Journia far to the northeast and the sultry green crags of Nivanne to the southwest. And beyond the dry, wildflower-mottled ridges to the south shimmered the sea, scarce but a silvered imagining. In between, the sun-splashed fields and vineyards of Aubine spread

over gentle hills, encircled with vines and notched with red-roofed villages. Everywhere bloomed the flowers of early summer—anemones, crown daisies, marigolds, and scarlet pimpernel—amid healthy groves of olive, almond, and lemon trees. If Louvel was Sabria's pumping heart, Tallemant her industrious arm, and thin-aired, pristine Journia her ethereal soul, then Aubine was surely her fertile womb. Philippe had granted Michel de Vernase a prize, indeed.

A broad lane took us through the outer wall into the sunny precincts of the manor. Cascades of purple and pink bougainvillea draped the rambling stone-walled house and gardens. On a flagged terrace, beneath the spreading branches of a walnut tree, the young soldier held a polite distance as a small woman read my note and Philippe's order.

In the yard, a balding man supervised a boy walking our messenger's horse. As we three rode in, the man, his plain black breeches and hose, collarless white shirt, and dark jerkin naming him a servant, drew his spiky gray brows into a knot and stepped forward, as if to bar us from closer approach.

"We're the visitors announced by yon messenger," I said. "All is in order."

"I doubt that, sonjeur," he said, politely holding my horse as I dismounted. "Will you be long?"

"Most of the day, I should think," I said, glancing at Dante, who was no help at all. His brooding gaze roamed the windows that overlooked the terrace and the yard, and his fingers were already loosing the straps that held his staff and the bag of oils and herbs Jacard had filled in the Florien market.

"I'll see the beasts tended," said the stableman, assisting Dante and Jacard to dismount. "You can wait—"

"We'll wait right here," I said, clasping my hands at my back as if I'd all the time in the world.

As he led the horses away, the man raised a decisive finger and another boy came running from the tile-roofed stable to take charge of the three animals. Once his instructions were conveyed, the man lounged against a flower-decked wall, observing us.

"Why don't we just set to?" whispered Jacard, standing at my shoulder. "It's not as if the contessa can refuse us. And she's naught but a slip of a thing." Indeed the messenger towered over the slender woman whose long dark hair fell over one shoulder.

"Manners," I said. It seemed reasonable that diplomacy would gain us more answers than a frontal assault, though truly I had no basis for such a notion. "Lady Madeleine comes from an old and influential family. Her husband is the king's dearest friend—as yet—and her children the king's goodchildren. Even if my suspicions are proved true, we've no reason to believe the conte's family involved in any misdeed." Happily, Sabrian law did not hold blood kin forfeit for a relative's treachery. Society and custom were other matters entirely.

The lady folded the papers and spoke to the soldier, who bowed, pivoted crisply, and joined us. "The contessa agrees to speak with one person. Her children, the young lord Ambrose and Damoselle Anne, are not to be approached outside her hearing."

"But she has no say in the matter," said Jacard, altogether too excited about this interview to my mind.

I ignored the adept. "Thank you, Greville. Please to remain at the lower gate lest we need messages taken."

The young officer snapped a bow and departed. I turned to Dante, measuring my words. "We seek evidence of illicit sorcery, specifically transference, evidence of dealings with assassins or other suspicious persons, links with the fire on the *Swan*, and whatever insights the family can provide as to Michel de Vernase's ambitions and state of mind. Shall I speak to the contessa or shall you?"

It was risky—giving the mage an opportunity to shut me out of the most significant interview of this investigation thus far, but if he was bound to thwart me, best to know straightaway.

Dante had tossed his black bag to Jacard. His hands had vanished into his flowing sleeves, and he had raised the hood of his gown, so that the merest arc of his chin was the only flesh showing above his silver collar.

"I must meet the woman briefly, no matter her wishes," he said. "But then I will examine house and grounds. The adept will follow me, keep-

ing at least ten paces behind and following my instructions exactly. You may have the pleasure of questioning the treacher's kin."

I breathed a little easier. That Dante planned to keep Jacard at arm's length was reassuring. Had he only brought the adept along to distance himself from me?

"As you wish," I said. "I'll join you when I can."

I straightened my doublet and set out for the terrace, where the Contessa Ruggiere waited beneath the walnut tree.

CHAPTER TWENTY-SIX

9 CINQ
16 DAYS UNTIL THE ANNIVERSARY

"Divine grace shine upon thee and thy ancestors, my lady," I said, bowing deeply and exposing my hand. "I am Portier de Duplais. My sincerest apologies for this intrusion."

"You may choke on your apologies, sonjeur." The contessa exposed her left hand in passing as she returned the king's warrant to me. Voice and glare mimed flint and steel as Dante joined us under the walnut tree, Jacard ten steps away. "Only a cretin would believe you and your brethren have come merely to *locate Conte Ruggiere*. Not after a year. Not with an entire gardia camped round our home, choosing who will or will not enter our gates."

I had not expected the contessa to be welcoming, but neither did I expect her to so clearly reflect the ferocity of her bandit ancestry. Cazar nobles held to clannish customs, so I had read, and kept their women . . . tame.

"As my message stated, we have come at the king's behest to gather information. Master Dante, a mage of Queen Eugenie's household, and his assistant, Adept Jacard"—I extended a hand toward each—"must necessarily examine your house and grounds. They will not interview your children, but will leave that to me . . . in your presence, as you

have requested. If you would like to inform your children of these arrangements . . ."

"Our servants will see to that."

"Lady—"

"Let me make this clear to you, sir. My husband has ever been Philippe de Savin-Journia's friend, devoted subject, and loyal servant. I will not help you or your king brand him a traitor, even if it might soothe Philippe's guilt at imprisoning poor, confused Eugenie. And if you make the least attempt to taint my children with this folly, or use this mage to seduce any of us into some confessional, your blood will feed our grapes for next year's harvest."

It had not escaped my notice that the sylphlike contessa wore a slim leather belt around her layered draperies of crinkled white gauze, nor that a sheathed zahkri hung from that belt. The angled Fassid knife was as suitable for gutting an enemy as for gouging a furrow in stony ground or harvesting a cluster of grapes. Nor had I failed to note that the contrast of the white garments with the lady's dusky skin, dark eyes, and dark hair—not black but deepest brown, burnished with copper—was as breathtaking as the view from her hilltop home. Wars had been fought over less treasure than Madeleine de Cazar y Vernase-Ruggiere.

Dante stepped forward, formidable in his shrouded mystery. He extended his hand—his healthy left—palm up, asking for a trust bond, an obsolete custom foreswearing use of magical coercion. "I swear to truth, lady. Will you?"

She did not quail at his forbidding appearance or at the unusual request, delivered as it was without shred of warmth or emotion, but readily laid her slender hand atop his wide, rough one. "That you would ask tells me that lies fester in your heart," she said. "No finding of yours will alter my beliefs."

Startled at Dante's gesture, it took me a moment to register the surge of enchantment at the moment of their touch. By their very nature, trust bonds rarely involved magic, and never of a quality that left an *observer's* fingers tingling. Yet I had felt this before, whenever Dante took the measure of something new—be it human, stone, or magical spyglass.

The contessa did not seem to notice. Her expression was all contempt as Dante departed the terrace in a swirl of robes, Jacard trailing behind. The lady's fearless candor gave me heart in a way. I felt no need to soften what I'd come to say. She needed to comprehend the danger she faced.

"Madame, please believe that concern for the safety of one of your own children has brought me here. Your daughter Lianelle lives in mortal danger."

"Lianelle? At school? What danger?" Her guards fell away instantly, to reveal a mother's dismay.

"Reliable evidence has convinced me that the Conte Ruggiere has allied himself with a conspiracy of sorcerers who threaten to renew the Blood Wars. However impossible this alliance seems, you have already witnessed a measure of its gravity. Its merest suggestion has persuaded King Philippe, who staunchly refuses to believe his friend a betrayer, to send these soldiers to detain and question him. I believe your husband delved into this conspiracy in pursuit of knowledge and became enamored of immense and unholy magic."

I ordered my phrases particularly, and observed her expression as I spoke. Curiously, it was not the mention of conspiracy, war, danger, betrayal, or even the king that transformed her yet again. It was instead the words *unholy magic* that caused her eyes to darken and her lips to compress hard enough to stifle an oath.

I held that recognition close, to use when the time seemed right. "Your dilemma, lady, is as difficult as the king's."

"What dilemma? What choice am I given?" Her zahkri could be no better honed than her scorn.

"Last year, near the time of the assassination attempt on the king, your younger daughter learned a terrible secret. These conspirators, who have left a trail of torture and murder across this kingdom, have every cause to silence her. One student from Seravain already lies dead, as does her family. If Michel de Vernase is innocent, then your daughter lives only at a villain's whim. In order to protect her, we must discover what your husband learned of this plot before he vanished. On the other hand, if the conte works in concert with these people, then only his care for Lianelle

keeps her safe—and you, of all people, must judge if that is enough. I have not come here seeking confirmation of your husband's guilt, but evidence that can lead us to the truth. I ask you, in all sincerity, to assist me."

Her lips parted, but, for a moment, no sound emerged.

I gestured to a wrought-iron bench. "Shall we sit?"

She shook her head. "We walk. I cannot take tea and chat about high treason and my child's danger as if they were Pollamai's new musicale. Explain to me what sorcerer could have lured my husband, who has deemed every collared mage either fool or fraud, to endanger his child and conspire against a friend he pledged to die for." She struck out across the terrace, and I hurried after. Only when we left the paving for a well-worn footpath did I notice she wore no shoes.

The contessa's every word rang like steel on bronze. Where was the weakness, the bruise I could pressure to break through her armor, the keystone to remove that the structure of her belief would fall open to me? Families were not impregnable fortresses, but human constructs riddled with grievance and secrets. Perhaps I'd caught a hint of one already— sorcery.

"I have no idea who did the luring," I said. "Perhaps this unholy alliance grew out of some advance on the conte's own part. Best we—"

"You think Michel approached a sorcerer to do what . . . work a spell to give him more than this?" She waved at the glorious prospect. "To give him fairer, cleverer children than these he dotes on, or a younger wife to dance with? Or do you suppose it was the hunger for greatness, the driver of all men, that urged him to make his life forfeit and his family outcast?"

This last sounded like old argument, not prompted by my presence. Perhaps Michel's ambition was the bruise on this family's body.

The path descended into a red-painted pergola, twined with blooming roses. "I would rather learn than speculate, Contessa, and I needs must learn one step at a time. Let me begin simply. When was the last time you saw your husband?"

She strolled a few steps, riffling the last year's leaves with her toes, her arms folded tightly. "On the thirty-second day of Siece last, Michel re-

ceived a letter from Lianelle, a letter he claimed private, though what business could be so private a child's mother could not see? Within the hour he rode out without naming his destination or estimating his return. I've not seen him since."

A bitter, angry parting, I judged, leaving resentments so deep that faith, fear, and anguish had not vanquished them after almost a year. The letter would have been Lianelle's report that Ophelie had obtained the name Michel sought—*the place where it all began*. Eltevire.

"What does your daughter say of this letter and the circumstances that led to it?"

"She's told me nothing, sonjeur. She does not write. She refuses to come home, as she knows I would not permit her to go back to that place. My daughter is . . . uncompromising." The contessa's odd display of conjoined exasperation and pride struck me as a marvel. My own parents had reacted quite differently to bald defiance.

"So, tell me your theory, lady. Surely in all these months you have put together some chain of events to explain your husband's disappearance."

She peered at me through leafy shadows, curious, as if of all questions in the world, she had not expected that one. "I've given it thought," she said. "But I've no supporting evidence a royal investigator would approve."

"My mind is ever open to change."

She dipped her head. "I know Michel was investigating the attempt on Philippe's life. I saw little of him in those two months. That was nothing extraordinary. We chose to raise our children in the countryside rather than in Merona. Thus his duties often kept him away. But for all these years, he has written faithfully—to me and to one of the children in turn almost every day. Rarely did he write of business. He was a diplomat, negotiating border agreements, modifications to treaties, property encroachments, agreements on trade, ports, and marriages, all manner of things, much of it private. This case was no different. But the world is filled with interesting topics, especially for a mind like his." And hers, I thought, and those of three talented children.

We emerged from the pergola into a grassy bowl dotted with willows.

Old stone walls followed the contours of the hillside, harboring rock roses, yellow flax, and stonecrop. A small lake, afloat with ducks and swans, graced the heart of the meadow. Lady Madeleine paused and inhaled deeply, like a prisoner newly released, then continued on the path of brown earth and wood chips that wound down to the lake. I followed. Silent. Listening.

"From the day he took on this task for Philippe, Michel's letters changed in character," said the lady after we'd hiked twenty or thirty metres. "You would say he became secretive. I would say he was consumed, preoccupied. His mind had engaged with something extraordinary—something that intrigued as well as absorbed. My husband does nothing by halves. Since the evening he rode out—"

"Mama! Don't speak to him!" A young man burst from the end of the pergola and cut straight down the hillside, a blur of gangling limbs, red-brown hair, and a voice not yet certain of its timbre. He slid to a breathless halt three metres from us, rapier in one hand, poniard in the other. "Greville de Grouenn says he's but a sniveling poor relation of the king who spreads lies about Papa to gain royal favor. He's brought a *mage* to spy on us."

The youth, a reflection of his mother's beauty on a frame that promised a warrior's stature, quivered in all the righteous fury of fifteen summers.

"Put away your weapons, Ambrose, and behave as a civilized man. Sonjeur de Duplais is here at your goodfather's behest, inquiring into your father's fate. We shall judge his motives for ourselves, not heed soldiers' gossip." The lady glanced back to me, her brows raised, and the sunlight probing her eyes to reveal a hint of lavender in their depths. "Are you indeed Philippe's kinsman? You don't resemble him."

"Fifteenth cousin. Scrawny, yes, and poor, as librarians are wont to be, but I snivel only rarely. My beliefs have granted me no favor with my liege." I swiveled crisply and bowed to the flustered youth as his rapier wavered between sheath and ready. "Divine grace, young sir."

"You're the librarian from Seravain," said the lady, some understanding awaked in her mind. Perhaps I'd been correct in my guess that her

husband had acted as Philippe's eyes on me these several years. "So you *do* know Lianelle."

"Indeed, my lady. Three years I lived subject to your daughter's intellectual whims and frank assessments."

Amusement glanced across the contessa's sorrows like a beam of sunlight on storm water.

Young Ambrose scowled, fiercer than ever. "Mama, how can you tolerate him? He's persuaded the king that Papa's a *traitor.* All these months we've waited for someone to give a rat's ear that Papa's gone missing, and all we've got for it is house arrest and this liar, worming scraps from you to twist into a hangman's noose. He likely wants Montclaire for himself. I'll see him—"

"Ambrose!" snapped the contessa. "Your insults demean *me,* not Sonjeur de Duplais. Heed my word: Take yourself away from here. Now!"

The lad glared at his mother in disbelief. But he slammed his weapons into enfolding leather and raced up the path. Only then did I notice a young woman standing at the mouth of the pergola, watching this display. At such a distance I could judge naught but an unremarkable stature and a fairer complexion than the contessa or her son. Yet the rare shade of indigo that colored her skirt hinted she was no servant.

"Though I may reprimand my son, I will not apologize for him," said Lady Madeleine, following the direction of my gaze. "He but expresses the frustration we've felt these months. Ambrose was squired to an honorable knight, but gave up his place to companion Anne and me. Yet every morn I must apply a mighty tether of duty and guilt to prevent his setting out to search for his father on his own. For my elder daughter, the ordeal has perhaps been worse. Waiting is the slimmest of stilettos, Sonjeur de Duplais, tormenting with wounds that cannot be seen, save in the blood that flows after."

"Indeed so, my lady." So the watcher at the top of the hill was Damoselle Anne, at seventeen the eldest of Michel de Vernase's children, a young woman who could argue the movement of the planets with her father in three languages at once, according to the admiring Edmond de Roble. "I am not alone in sympathy for these months you have endured. All the more reason to seek the truth, be it good or ill."

When young Ambrose passed by her, the girl remonstrated with him. The brother forcefully removed her hand from his back. No family could be so congenial as Edmond and the taverner described.

"You were speaking of the morning the conte left . . ." In search of something extraordinary. Her words had come right off the paper tucked in my shirt: *Something extraordinary happened when your servant went searching for your enemies. He found them. And then he discovered things . . .* What had Michel discovered about himself, and magic, and the truth of the world? About *unholy* magic?

The contessa's vision melted from her children into a deep and somber reach. "I've received no letter since that day. Not a word. Not a scrap. I have walked this land, touched its living bones, felt the sunlight that clothes it, listened to the music of wind, star, and beast song. But the universe no longer speaks love's name to me. I believe Michel found the answer to his great mystery and it killed him."

She left the path and strode through the mead to the marshy borders of the lake, where her zahkri made short, vicious work of cutting an armful of reeds. As I yet stepped gingerly from one tussock to the next, she was already climbing the terraced slopes again, the muddy hem of her gauze skirts slapping wetly against her bare ankles.

Such certainty. Did it derive from her blood-born magic or from some aspect of her marriage, convincing her of that which caused her mortal grief? I was tempted to believe her. Yet logic and evidence declared Michel de Vernase and the Aspirant to be one and the same. And I did not wish him dead, but rather in my clutches, that I might call him to account for the horrors he had caused.

One thing was clear: Madeleine's conviction explained both her willingness to entertain my questions and her lack of interest in pursuing Lianelle's secrets. Her children's future drove her. Forcing Lianelle to speak would not bring Michel de Vernase back to life, and antagonizing Philippe could make her children's lives infinitely worse. Should treason be proved, Montclaire would surely be granted elsewhere, as Ambrose had guessed. And Philippe, as king, judge, and goodfather, would determine their very freedom, as well as marriage, occupation, and sustenance. Only Lianelle,

if she remained subject to the Camarilla, might retain some choice in her fate, assuming she survived the Aspirant's plots. This recalled a jarring note in the lady's explanations.

I scrambled up a rock-walled terrace. "Why would you keep Lianelle from Seravain, lady? She is intelligent and gifted. As the daughter of a blood family, I would expect you to encourage her to develop her talents."

"After the Blood Wars, my family renounced magic," she said, snapping off leaves of thyme and rosemary as if they were an enemy's limbs. "Sorcery and overreaching had driven many of our kinsmen to depravity, and my grandsires and grandmeres declared it would never happen again. They deliberately sapped the power in our blood and vowed our future generations to uphold their binding. Cazars do not train. We do not explore our talents. We do not use spellwork produced by others. Our abilities have dwindled near to extinction—except, as it happens, for Lianelle."

I blinked in astonishment. "Then how in the name of Heaven did Lianelle end up at a collegia magica? A father who disdains magic. A mother who denies it, and whose family forbids even the *use* of it."

She grimaced. "My daughter refuses to be bound by anyone's vows. And you must understand, my husband did not so much despise the possibilities of magic as its current practice and its importance in a world 'awakening to its own true nature,' as he said it. But when Lianelle woke us one morning with light streaming from her fingertips and fifty of Aubine's most beautiful moths captured in the beams, even Michel could not deny her. Nor could I. Her raw talent surpasses any in my family's remembrance. Michel encouraged her desire to go to Seravain and explore it. But if your warnings are true, if the least harm comes to my child at that place"—she raised her arms skyward, and the breeze swirled her skirts as if her weakened blood called out with one last gasp—"by the blades of my ancestors, I will call down such a curse on his name that a thousand millennia will not see his shade at peace."

Her cry of anguish echoed from lake and rock and hillside, and she threw down the green mass of herbs that her fist had crushed into a shape-

less, scented glob. Clutching her bundle of reeds to her middle, she stormed straight up the hill.

The girl flew down to meet the distraught contessa. "I heard you cry out. What did he say?"

Lady Madeleine, her lips pressed tight, tried to wave off her concern, but the lady's hand was trembling and her complexion flushed.

"Mama, did he hurt you?"

The contessa shook her head.

"At least come inside where it's cooler." The young woman's voice was quiet without being whispery, and her demeanor seemed plain and unelaborated, much like the rest of her. Her eyes darted only briefly my way, as she took the bundle of reeds under one arm and wrapped the other round her mother's shaking shoulders. "Come along if you must."

I almost missed the quiet invitation, and only after a moment did I realize it was addressed to me. "Damoselle," I said. My quick bow was roundly ignored as the two ascended the path.

Though small and slender, like her mother, Anne de Vernase lacked her mother's and brother's earthy beauty, as well as their resonant energies. Curling wisps of straw-colored hair escaped a single tight braid. Pale skin freckled from the sun, eyes too large, and mouth too wide for a narrow face, she appeared unripe for seventeen, like a plum fallen too early from the tree. Walking any street or corridor in Sabria, she would never draw a second glance.

When we reached the terrace, the contessa shook off her daughter's supportive arm. Anne tossed the reeds onto the bench. Interested in watching as much as hearing, I held back as the two spoke quietly, the girl in an earnest, persuasive posture, yet, in the end, disappointed. The contessa laid her hand on her daughter's shoulder, then walked into the house.

Anne called to me across the terrace. "Come inside and finish your interrogation, sonjeur. But please, make it brief. My mother is feeling unwell, but refuses to retire until you and your companions have left Montclaire."

I bowed again and followed her through a breezy arcade into an oc-

tagonal entry hall. Pale yellow walls rose three stories from the blue slate floor, framing open arches that led deeper into the expansive house. The curved arms of a great staircase embraced a gilt-edged mirror taller than two men. The mirror splashed color and sunlight on the unlikeliest of artworks below—a brass telescope with a barrel twice the length of my arm, and an exquisite planetary of silver-inlaid brass. In an odd, lively contrast, earthenware pots and copper urns of fresh flowers had been tucked into every nook and corner. Dante and Jacard were nowhere in sight.

The daughter hurried off toward the back of the house, while the contessa led me into a reception room. The afternoon breeze shifted filmy draperies. Sitting in a high-backed chair where the air from the courtyard could cool her, the contessa leaned her forehead wearily on her clenched fist. I'd never have judged Lady Madeleine fragile. Yet the sultry heat or perhaps the hour's expense of emotion had left her looking drawn and ill. "What else would you have from us, sonjeur?"

Damoselle Anne returned and took a place behind her mother's chair, laying a hand protectively on the lady's shoulder. Though the girl's fair skin was marked properly with the Cazar sign, she had violated the law by failing to expose it to me. Her right hand gripped the chair back, her knuckles entirely bloodless.

Lady Madeleine was a striking person in all ways, but, somehow, the girl intrigued me more. "My lady, may I address your daughter?"

The lady's long fingers caressed the paler ones that rested on her shoulder. "I suppose you must."

"Damoselle, as I've told your mother, I am here seeking information about your father's activities. I will not lie to you. We've well-grounded suspicions that he may be involved in terrible crimes. But I am interested only in truth, in facts—those that may explain away evidence that we have, as well as those that may support it."

"I don't know anything that could help you." This scarcely audible response reminded me of Lianelle, who, of course, had known a great deal.

"We all know more than we think, damoselle. Tell me, what interests did you and your father share?"

Her brows knitted, as if trying to fathom to what wicked purpose I could put such information. "Natural science," she said at last, pushing several escaped curls behind her ear. "Languages. Foreign lands. Stories. Books." She offered each topic slowly, as a small bite from a much larger feast—a private feast.

"Mathematics?" I asked, and she dipped her head.

"Medicine?" A negative shake.

"Sorcery?"

"No!" Genuine distaste here.

"Yet your sister studies sorcery. She summons animals. . . ."

"Drafi, our stable lad, can make horses follow him about like puppies. That doesn't make it magic."

"And your father's belief?"

Not so quick to answer this time. Again I felt her running through the implications of anything she might say. "Papa believes we should explore what branches of learning fascinate us."

"But does he believe magic to be trickery, ready to be unmasked by scientific advancement, or a true branch of learning, in the same vein as physics or alchemistry?"

"Papa believes—" A quick, tight breath hinted at deeper feeling. "How can I say what he believes? He's gone away." Not *He's dead.*

"Damoselle, do you understand the concept of blood transference—an immoral, illicit, and dangerous practice used to enhance a mage's power?"

"Yes. I've read histories of the Blood Wars."

"Have you ever discussed this practice with your father?"

"Never. Why would we?" Brittle. Short. Out of breath. But not at all weak. Eliciting a reaction from the girl felt akin to pecking stone with a needle.

Hoping to nudge her off balance, I kept up the pace. "You studied with your father for many years, played verbal and logic games, practiced languages, wrote stories and mathematical proofs, I would guess, exchanged correspondence frequently when he was away."

"Yes. All those things," she said without a hint of boasting. But then,

I didn't think revealing her thoughts or feelings was Anne's vice. An extraordinary mind must be hidden inside those solid walls.

"Damoselle Anne, have you received a letter from your father since the day he last departed Montclaire?"

Her complexion lost what color it held. "No." So definite, yet so fast—too fast.

"And you've received no letter that could possibly be from him. For if you received a letter lacking a signature or seal . . ."

"He has not written to me. I would recognize his hand anywhere."

"Certainly you would." I pounced without hesitation. Holding my breath, I pulled out the unsigned note addressed to Edmond de Roble-Margeroux and passed it to the young lady. "Tell me, damoselle, is this your father's hand?"

Her eyes scanned the note rapidly. The text contained naught to indict or condemn. Naught that should induce her to lie.

Here at last is the occasion you have pressed for, a chance to return my several favors. Please deliver the accompanying missive to our king in all immediate haste, for his eye and hand only. I'd recommend you seek extended leave from your captain for this journey, as an extended commission will likely follow. As ever, lad, commit. Do not withhold.

"WHEN WAS THIS WRITTEN?" she said, voice dropped to a whisper, which question told me the answer I needed to know.

"I've no way to ascertain that. Perhaps a year ago. Perhaps a month." Let her reveal what she knew.

"Papa scribed it. To Edm— I suppose you know to whom it was written." She hated slipping.

"Your father was young Edmond de Roble's sponsor in the Guard." One step, then another. For the first time, I felt as if matters were coming to a head.

Anne offered the paper to the contessa, who waved it away, covering her eyes with her hands.

"What does it mean?" The girl's soft question did not sound as if she expected an answer.

"We're not sure," I said. But I did know, of course. It meant Michel de Vernase was alive.

Another question had arisen before this diversion, something about letters, but before I could recapture it, a ruddy-cheeked, comfortable sort of woman in a floury apron joined us. She set down a tray holding decanter and cups, and poured wine for the contessa. Lady Madeleine accepted it gratefully, inhaling the rich fragrance before she drank.

The serving woman straightened up, taking my measure with a disdain worthy of an empress. "I suppose you're 'the priggish aristo investigator,'" she said. "Your mage insists you come to His Grace's library right away."

I suppressed a childish retort. Annoyed, not so much with Dante's insulting address or peremptory instruction, but with losing progress to this interruption, I had come near wasting an opportunity. A trusted servant could know a great deal and might not be so carefully schooled as wife or children. "Lady Madeleine, may I speak to your housekeeper?"

The contessa looked up. "Is that necessary?" Evidently my posture spoke answer enough. "Melusina, please tell Sonjeur de Duplais whatever he wishes to know."

"Mistress Melusina, I've only one question. A small thing. How are mages perceived in the village of Vernase? We faced an unfortunate incident on our travels here, and I'm concerned for my companion's safety. He is quite ill mannered, as you've seen."

Melusina flushed and wiped her hands on her apron. "Well, I don't know. We've not had a mage visiting in Vernase in ever so long. My lady, can you recall when the last might have been? Long before the little one went off to school, I think."

The contessa shifted her gaze to me. Despite a weary sadness that seemed to sap her strength more every moment, she understood very well what I was asking. "We've not entertained a mage at Montclaire since

Lianelle was three and that woman came from Seravain to validate her handmark."

A woman . . . "Was it Mage Eliana, perhaps, bright red cheeks, one foreshortened leg?"

"No, she was extremely tall," said Melusina, "almost as tall as His Grace and sturdy as a smith. Our little one was but a mite in her hand. She brought that young adept with her—the pretty girl that was so spindly— and as far as I can recall, everyone in house or village treated them both most respectful."

Gaetana and Michel de Vernase. Father Creator! Ten years past and tenuous, but I'd found a connection.

"I really must go." The contessa made as if to get up, but sagged back into her chair.

"Mama, what's wrong?" Anne dropped to her knees beside her mother's chair, chafing her flaccid hands and patting her scarlet cheeks. "Look at me."

The lady did not respond, and Melusina's speedy provision of damp towels and smelling salts and extra cushions changed nothing.

"Has she been unwell?" I said, feeling entirely out of my experience. "Fevered?"

"Please leave us, sonjeur," said Anne, tight-lipped. "You've clearly pushed my mother beyond all bounds of mercy."

"Do whatever is necessary for your mother's health and comfort, damoselle," I said, bridling at the accusation. "But sometime before this day is out, we must take up this conversation again, whether the contessa is fit to supervise it or not." It shamed me a bit to imagine the lady's illness feigned, yet I could not discount the possibility. Beautiful women of good family were not exempt from conspiracy.

Though the desire to pursue my questions had trumped Dante's summons, the contessa's plight induced me to reverse course. "Melusina, please guide me to the conte's library," I said.

"I should stay—"

"Unfortunately, we are not always free to choose our roles in these matters, mistress. Please show me the way. Then you and your staff may

attend the ladies. Later, when I resume my conversation with Damoselle Anne, perhaps you could sit as her mother's surrogate."

The grumbling Melusina led me up the stair and along a winding gallery into a library worthy of any collegia. Two walls of book-laden shelves so high as to need stepladders were only the beginning. More shelves held models of temples, bridges, towers. Another wall of shelves held stacked boxes of papers, labeled POETRY, ANNE'S STORIES, MAMA'S WILDFLOWER SKETCHES, and the like. More papers, books, and maps lay heaped on two long tables, or spread on one of three desks that crowded the room. Even the ceiling was in use, with a great star chart fixed to it at one end, and the largest map of the world I'd ever seen fixed to the other.

How could I not compare such a place to the library at Manor Duplais? We owned ten books of Sabrian genealogy bound in red leather, a general history of the kingdom, and a chart detailing the Savin family line back twenty generations—far enough to expose our flimsy connection to the reigning monarch. My blood yet stained that chart, as my father had pressed me against it after he pulled his knife, as if to make sure I would recognize my shame before he gutted me.

As always, my hand massaged my belly. A good thing my father had not studied anatomical charts like those propped on Michel's easel stuck off in a corner.

"Here he is, Master," said Jacard, popping up from behind one of the desks.

Dante had already risen. Though his eyes remained shadowed by his hood, I felt their heat, as always.

"What is it?" I shook off my maudlin history and glanced over my shoulder to make sure Melusina had gone. "I could ill afford interruption."

"Over here," said Dante. "Can you use your senses, student, or must I hold your hand as usual?"

A dozen or more wooden storage boxes seemed to have vomited their contents across the floor. Mostly letters, it appeared. Drawings, scribbles, a litter of broken jewelry, buckles, and pen knives. Opening myself to the touch of magic, I stepped through the jumbled heaps. I assumed I searched

for bound enchantment. In the ordinary way, I could detect magical residue only for an hour or two after its expenditure—Dante's for much longer.

In the end, this was easy. When I touched a cube-shaped tin box that sat amid the conte's relics, a sensation of steel nails scraping glass set my teeth aching. I crouched and flipped its lid open.

My breath near left me entirely. A jumble of cloudy glass and tarnished brass and steel filled the box. I pulled out the thin tubes first, and then three small rusted knives and the smooth-rimmed glass cups, nested one within the other. Last came the stained brass blocks, one small, one large, with levers cocked, ready to pop out the lancet blades.

"Blessed angels," I breathed. "We have him."

CHAPTER TWENTY-SEVEN

No one in the manse, meaning Damoselle Anne, Melusina, Bernard—the balding steward from the stableyard—the house-maids, the gardener or his daughter, the cook or cook's help, or even Drafi, the Arothi stable hand, admitted to having seen the tin box before. None but Anne had ever heard a whisper of transference, save in the same unsavory context as necromancy or death curses or spirit slaves. None knew what a scarificator might be used for.

When I showed her how the little blades snapped out to nick the skin, Damoselle Anne looked as if she might collapse. I told her that even a man with no talent himself could collect blood to infuse a mage. The needed spells could be affixed to blades and vessels—as they were with these arti-facts. But the girl squared her chin and said again, "I've never seen such a horrid thing. I can't say why my father would have one, save that he had an interest in learning." She ventured no guess as to whose blood yet crusted the instruments.

Young Ambrose could not be found anywhere in the house, stables, or gardens. Dante did not object when I dispatched Jacard to query the young officer we'd left at the gate. The mage had observed the afternoon's inter-rogations in silence.

The contessa, rebounded from her faint, wandered into the kitchen as I finished questioning the cook. "Forgive me, sonjeur," she said, puzzling over my simple question. "Transference? Ask Michel. I've told him I've no head for business. Ani"—she waved at her daughter—"dearest, we have guests. Where is Melusina? Why have we not set out refreshments? You must pay more attention to hospitality, Ani. You're almost eighteen."

The lady began to hum a Fassid love song, closing her eyes and smiling as if lost in dreaming. But her voice soon faltered, tears coursing down her feverish cheeks.

"Mama!" Anne grabbed the contessa as the lady swayed and stumbled. "Melusina, help me!"

Daughter and servant coaxed the lady to her feet. The three of them vanished up the nearby servant's stair.

"I doubt her condition feigned," said Dante from the doorway. "Secrets always break those who believe themselves unbreakable."

That could certainly be true. But Lady Madeleine had impressed me as an open heart, not welcoming to secrets. Perhaps that's why Michel did not confide in his wife. The daughter, though . . . Anne's secrets preyed on her.

Jacard tramped into the kitchen, winded from his run up the hill. "The boy's not ridden out."

"Ah! Then it's time to examine my perimeter," said Dante, planting his staff firmly on the slate floor. "Come, Adept!" He vanished through the kitchen door Jacard had just entered.

"Perimeter?" I said.

"The man moves like a greyhound," said Jacard, sagged against a kitchen cupboard, still puffing. "First thing this morning, he raced around the lawns and gardens, dragging that blasted stick in the dirt to create this 'perimeter.' I'll swear he never bound a spell, spoke a key, touched a particle . . . anything, but the dirt turned black behind him. Next he drew a binding circle on the terrace and did some actual spellcasting with silver nuggets and hair and bits of those blasted roots and powders he had me chasing down, but the particles fit no formula I've ever read. I'll swear he's got me twisted end around trying to figure it all out. At least he's let me

do his dog work for once: rifling the kitchen pots, examining the ladies' closets, and dragging out every book and box in that damnable library. Naturally, he himself discovered the only useful bit." He sighed heavily. "I'd best go. He doesn't yell quite so much if I keep running, and I've hopes to graduate from dog work before I die. Someday, you must tell me how to figure out what he's doing."

Would that I knew!

As a bellow from outside set Jacard running, a blur of indigo in the passage drew my eye. I set off after it. "Damoselle!" I caught up to the girl in a small yard, walled by red brick service buildings. "Do not think to run away."

She halted immediately. "I am not running away. I just . . ." She tugged her wayward curls behind her ear again. "Why don't you leave? You have what you want. You've pushed my mother to exhaustion. I've never seen her so . . . overthrown."

"Where is your brother, lady?"

"I don't know." Every strained line of her body said otherwise.

"He is not accused. But matters will look very ill if he runs away. Does he know where your father is?"

"How could he know?" she cried, impatience bursting through her reserve. "How could any of us know? Papa has not written in a year. He's sent no message. I've not heard his voice since the hour—" She near swallowed her tongue.

"Since what hour, damoselle?" I said softly. And when she did not answer, I pushed ever so slightly, recalling my lost question at last. "Did your father speak to you in the hour he left Montclaire?"

"Yes." I could scarce hear her answer. "Just ordinary cautions. He asked me to comfort my mother. That's all." I didn't believe her.

"Lianelle would not wish to worry your mother, but I'd guess she confides in her elder sister. She wrote you about Ophelie, didn't she? About the bleeding?"

"Yes. Those vile instruments . . ."

She pressed her lips together for a moment, her hands plucking at her skirt. She was so controlled for a young woman, so inward, so blank a

page when one considered the knowledge and intelligence contained within. The daughter of a worldly man, she could not be so naive as she seemed. If ever a child could be lured into conspiracy, would it not be one like this?

"Lianelle pretends Papa is hiding from those who hurt her friend," she went on. "But *you* think— Sonjeur, my father could not do that to anyone. Ever."

"He spoke with you about transference at some time. Mentioned it."

The sun dropped below the red tile roof, shadowing the girl's pale face. "He spoke of it when we studied Sabrian history. He refuses to hide the world's horrors from us."

Her words fell cold and dry, as if she had focused her good intellect on being a better liar. I cursed the obscuring shadow. "But he *did* hide horrors. Why would he have the leeching implements here? Why would he not show them to you, if they were merely for education?"

"I don't know." She folded her arms and turned halfway round away from me. Fear had tied the girl in knots. Not fear of me, I deemed; Anne de Vernase feared the truth.

"Damoselle, King Philippe cannot ignore the evidence we've gathered, and for right or wrong, innocent or guilty, he will judge your father's fate. And yours. You *must* speak those things you know—for your own future, for the future of your family. I am skilled only in guessing, but you, an intelligent young scholar, must know there are spells to detect lies. Believe me, you are not good enough to evade them. Tell me what your father said about his journey on the morning he left Montclaire."

As from a septic wound touched by a blade, the words burst forth. "He said that some men present a face of such reason and nobility to the world that the world cannot conceive the cruelty and corruption behind it. He said it was his duty to take down such a person, no matter—no matter how highly placed or how close to our family. No matter consequences. And he said someone at Seravain had given him the means to do so."

Father Creator . . . the last link in the chain. "Who, damoselle? Who was your father planning to take down?"

"He said it was better for us not to know such terrible secrets," she said,

all fever drained away, along with hope and self-deception. "Because we would have to live on if his plan went awry."

Better, indeed! His children had to face Philippe's wrath.

"And it all went awry, didn't it?" she said. "My mother believes he's dead. My sister now believes it, too. Our servants, his soldiers . . . even his friend in Merona has stopped writing. So he must be dead."

"What friend?"

She waved her hand in dismissal. "Some woman at court."

Woman? The world paused. "*Who*, damoselle?"

Anne's chin lifted sharply, her guard up again. "I don't recall her name."

I kept my voice even, trying to repair my slip. "So all these months, you've held faith that your father will come home, innocent of any wrongdoing."

"Yes."

"Then, naturally, you've kept all the incoming letters addressed to him."

"Yes, but—"

"I'll see them. Now, if you please."

"But you've no right to see his letters!"

"Ah, damoselle, I do. Your king has given it."

No matter the girl's soft-spoken ways; had she a dagger, it would have flown at that moment. As we returned to her father's upended library, her eyes glinted with angry tears.

Michel de Vernase's unread letters lay in the bottom drawer of the smallest desk in the room. Ten months of letters—letters from diplomats in Aroth, in Syan, one bearing the seal of the Military Governor of Kadr. The conte's correspondence was wide and varied: personal notes about family and friends, minor business of meetings and visits, essays from scholars on a wide variety of topics, none of which interested me at the moment, but might on another day.

When I encountered the letters of importance, I knew. Four of them in a now-familiar hand. Three softened by a year's aging, one crisp as new lettuce. My fingers trembled. My soul rebelled. The day's triumphs fell to

ash. But the *agente confide* inside me nodded. *She told you herself. Gave you the clue.* "He is an honorable man. Compassionate. Your evidence cannot be credible. I owe him—"

"You may return to your mother now, damoselle." I charged down the stair. What did Maura owe Michel de Vernase?

One more question for the housekeeper. Melusina busied herself about the terrace, setting a table for three. "A small inquiry before I go, mistress, a matter of curiosity. Damoselle Maura ney Billard, a good friend of the conte, visited Montclaire in the years before he vanished. She is of small stature, like the contessa and her daughter, but somewhat more . . . womanly . . . with smooth, earth-hued skin. Do you remember her?" This was merely a guess, but I scarce noted anymore whether what fell from my lips was truth or lie.

"Oh, aye, certain I do," said the serving woman, each word a coin upon my eyelids. "Such a sweet, refined sort of person. Never comfortable in the country, but 'twas only twice or three times she came, all in that last year. She told me once that the conte had saved her life when she was a girl no older than Ani."

A year ago Anne would have been fifteen or sixteen. The next question popped into my head as if the sky had cracked and revelations come tumbling down like hailstones.

"Melusina, do you think . . . Is it possible Maura ney Billard was the girl who accompanied the woman mage ten years ago?"

The serving woman's thick hands fell still in the midst of spoons and saltcellars. "I'd never thought of it, but, indeed, such shining hair and skin she had, the color of dark honey. Certain and that would explain why she was familiar with the house and family, though she hadn't been back here since she was so very ill that same year. . . ."

And though my mouth tasted of ashes, it was not so very difficult to draw out Melusina's story of how the conte had brought the "pretty, spindly adept" to Montclaire for one night, when she was too ill to remain at Collegia Seravain, some year or so after her initial visit. Michel had whisked her away to relatives the next day, before Melusina could fatten her up with Montclaire's bounty or provide her gammy's remedies for the

girl's dulled hair or dry skin or weakness so profound the child could scarce lift her arm.

"Thank you, Melusina." I could scarce speak for heartsickness. "I believe we are done here. I hope your mistress recovers swiftly. Terrible events, such matters as the king has set me to uncover, touch us all with pain and sorrow."

All of us. Father Creator, forgive us all.

The woman raised her spread hands in helpless resignation. "I'll not say I'm sorry to see you go, but the pain and trouble was here long before you. 'Tis the world's way, not yours. I regret my rudeness this morning."

Numb and weary, I walked away clutching Maura's letters, clinging to a scrap of hope that they might exonerate, not condemn. I stopped under the walnut tree and opened them one by one. They had been encoded with an elementary cipher, not magic, easy to read, even without transcription.

———

Dear friend: The lady remains resolved to maintain her prerogatives, giving you room to work. Suspicions rise, certainly, but the king will not overrule her. As you predicted. The clues are there to be had should someone clever pick them up. As ever, your debtor.

———

Dear friend: The money and clothes will be waiting. Gaetana has the lady entirely befuddled, believing she will see the resolution of her desires. The lady is wholly lost in sadness and has no idea of her danger. I hear awful rumors about poor de Santo, but I understand the necessity. Until I know where else to direct my reports, I'll continue to send them to your home.

———

Dear friend: Have not heard confirmation of your arrival with the child. QE is restless, and love tempts her to yield, but G soothes her with promises of ghosts. The

calls of the dead continue to drown out the pleas of the living. She is not stupid. She knows well she is being set up as scapegoat but is herself too honest to suspect duplicity from those closest to her. I must confess to some guilt at my own small acts. But my faith in you does not and will not waver.

AND THE MORE RECENT ONE:

Dear friend: My last letter was returned, thus I can only send this to your home. I pray you remain well. The crates arrived at the temple. Food supplies more difficult but arranged. What a surprise it will be when you emerge from hiding. The banners are readied, and the queen persuaded to remain behind. I've wind of a new investigation. I'll tell more as I learn of it.

"LADY," I WHISPERED, "WHAT WERE you thinking to commit such words to paper? Spying on your queen for him? Aiding his plots? Even if he rescued you from bleeding, could you not see he was playing you?"

I found Bernard in the stableyard, told him we would be leaving within the hour, and asked if he had seen the mage.

"He's up to some of his devilry behind the well house," rumbled the steward. "When Saint Ianne returns, he'll banish these demon mages for good. Mayhap he'll banish you, too, for bringing such a one to this blessed house."

I offered no apology to Bernard's righteous fury, but walked the direction his trembling finger pointed, past a well house and into a juniper thicket. If the greatest of the Reborn ever returned to Sabria, I would gladly hand over all matters of justice to him.

The prickly juniper trees stretched across a dry slope before the land dropped away steeply toward the backside of the village. Jacard straddled a narrow footpath, maintaining the required ten paces from Dante. For the first time, the adept's face held a trace of fear alongside awe. I halted at his side, no longer surprised to view wonders.

The heel of Dante's ancille rested in a blackened groove in the dry earth. From its white shaft extended a flat film of silver light taller than a man and stretched two metres to either side. The mage shifted the staff along the charred groove, and the film of light shifted with it. When a shift positioned the translucent film across the footpath, a haloed purple shadow hinted at the shape of a person.

"Ah, the lackwit secretary. You've joined us just in time to discover that someone has crossed my little barrier here," said Dante without even a glance over his shoulder. "Were you capable of the simplest disentanglement, Portier—which skill seems to be lacking in all those who study at Seravain—you might discover which of Montclaire's denizens passed here and when."

No magical disentangling was required. "Damnable, stupid boy," I said, cursing idiot children, incautious, duplicitous women, and my own blindness. "He crossed approximately four hours ago, just before the contessa returned to the house."

Bad enough we'd found implements of transference in the house, but the fool lad had heeded his mother's direction and left her. No judge in the world would believe she had not sent him running to his father. And his elder sister, who had remonstrated with him at the top of the hill, knew very well what he planned. The fainting spells. Just enough answers. Stupid of me not to see it coming.

"I can't be sure," said Dante. "I didn't have an opportunity to take an . . . impression of the boy."

"Can you find him?"

"Unfortunately my lack of contact with the lad means I can't trace him, especially with his four-hour head start on home ground."

"Then our work here is done," I said. "I'll leave word with the guard commander to mount a search for the boy and tighten his watch on the rest of them. We must bring our findings to the king with all haste. Michel de Vernase expressed his intent to take down a 'highly placed' man he deemed corrupt, a man close to his family, a man who presents a face of reason and nobility to the world. His daughter, Anne, can testify to it."

"Remarkable." Gowned and hooded, Dante remained unreadable, the chill timbre of his voice unchanged. "And the magic?"

"He met Gaetana ten years ago, and was fully aware of her interest in transference. Along with the implements you found and my experience at Eltevire, I say we've enough."

"As you will, then. I've no sorrow at putting this idiocy to rest."

Dante hissed, and the silver film vanished. The spent magic showered me as Heaven's light.

CHAPTER TWENTY-EIGHT

11 CINQ
14 DAYS UNTIL THE ANNIVERSARY

I leaned back in the chair, forcing the raw knot that was my gut to relax. "I had to show you first," I said. "There is no hiding them."

Maura laid the letters on her writing table and folded her hands. Her ringed fingers did not quiver. No tears rolled down the silken cheeks that my own fingers ached to touch. No frantic explanations burst forth, no fractured emotions, no demeaning denials or demands for loyalty. Each instance of her serenity served as an incitement to cherish and admire her. And no matter the preachment of reason, my heart yet did so.

She drew her folded hands to her chin. "When the king sent my poor lady to the Spindle, I knew everything had gone wrong. I hoped, naturally. I've lived a year on faith alone—perhaps misplaced, as you assume—though I will not believe that until Michel himself tells me. But I am prepared to answer everything raised by these letters."

Three-quarters of an hour had elapsed since my arrival at Castelle Escalon—much of that waiting until a break in the flow of Maura's supplicants allowed me into her presence to lay out the questions she must prepare to face. Surely by now the king would know I was returned. Our remaining time could be measured in minutes, not hours.

"You should not have risked coming here. Saint's mercy, Portier, you look so tired, so . . . harrowed. Bless you for your care."

"What blessing do I deserve? All the way from Vernase, I tried to imagine some way to spirit you to safety, some way to discover the entirety of truth. I've no confidence the king will even listen to your explanations. But I swear to you, I will do everything—"

"No oaths, Portier. Once you hear what little I have to offer in the way of explanation, at best you'll think me the world's most pitiful gull. But you must understand: In one moment, I was facing Gaetana's lancet four times in a day, certain I would die soulless before I turned sixteen. In the next moment, this great, strong, handsome man told me not to be afraid anymore, and he carried me off to his home and then to a friend's haven by the sea, where I learned to eat and drink and smile again. Were he to walk in here at this moment and say, *Little girl, kiss your headsman for me*, I would do it gladly. Ten years ago, Michel de Vernase bought my soul and gave it back to me. He just—he never told me what he paid for it."

Easy to understand the price: Michel had kept silent about an incident of transference—a mortal crime in Sabria. My fear was what the world might now pay for his silence. Saints sustain me, I held no blame to Maura. Despair was a disease that blighted reason. Yet I remained an *agente confide*, and thus had to ask, "When did you last receive orders from the conte?"

"Not since the fire on the *Swan*. This fourth letter answered his last. When I received no response, I—" She had begun to doubt, no matter what she said now. I had visited her office in those days, when we both heard the cries of the dead so distinctly in the night. "I waited, hoping for understanding, but none came. So I sent no more reports."

She rose, came round the table, and kissed me on the forehead, suffusing me in her sweetness. Clasping my cold hand in her warm one, she drew me up and into a corner of her chamber. A key on her belt ring opened a narrow door to a servant's passage. "None must see the kindest man in all the world leaving Damoselle Maura's den. Go, dear Portier, and do your duty by our king."

Leaving was not so simple. I kissed her quiet hands and stroked her shining hair, cherishing the weight of her head on my shoulder. "This is not over until I say. Remember that, dearest lady, whatever comes."

I MEANDERED THROUGH THE DARKENING maze, reviewing the long afternoon spent with Philippe, trying to capture what details I might have left out of my report, or where I could have said this or that to be more persuasive, or how, in the Creator's wide universe, I was to move forward. Night was creeping into the world again, and body and mind craved sleep. But it seemed like such a waste of precious hours.

Maura's flimsy explanations had indeed failed to satisfy an angry king. Her implicit trust in Michel's unexplained plan to expose the assassins, including, at the least Mage Gaetana, appeared ingenuous. Her unquestioning compliance with orders she swore were scripted in Michel's hand, and dispatched in letters sealed with his signet—and conveniently burnt once she'd read them—displayed an unbelievable naivete. Philippe had declared her life forfeit.

Oh, he had listened to my arguments, agreed that we had evidence yet to hear, and expressed sympathy with her experience of despair and my own, offered to explain Maura's unshakable devotion. He did not deny that Maura's faith in Michel de Vernase mirrored his own. But he refused to reconsider his judgment, save in the timing of its inevitable conclusion. "She has betrayed her queen, and by her own admission, her actions aided those who tortured a child in the royal crypt and set murderous fire to the *Swan*. Her faith cannot matter. If Michel issued the orders she so blindly obeyed, he will die with her."

The mustachioed Captain de Segur had marched Maura through the crowds of shocked courtiers, her capable hands bound at her back. From the window gallery, I had watched the shallop bear her across the golden thread of the Ley and through the iron water gates to join her queen in the Spindle. The desolate image was scored into my heart.

No wild-eyed feat of arms or magic was going to free her. My only weapon was reason. And so I paced the garden maze, yanking my hair and

clawing my arms to drive exhaustion away. *Think, Portier. The Spindle gates are warded by old magic not even its keepers can counter. . . .*

As I rounded a thick wall of gorse and flowering broom, a raven fluttered the branches. Moments later, when hands gripped my shoulders and shoved me into the vine-covered bricks, I recognized the intruder as no bird, but a very tall, very strong, and very angry Ilario, draped in a black cloak.

"You sliming weasel! You scheming toad! How in the name of mercy could you persuade him to leave Geni in that place when she is *innocent*?" He wrenched me up from where I'd fallen and shoved me backward again, this time into a tangle of thorns. "I should wring your scrawny neck, but that would be too kind. By all the Saints Awaiting, I'll see your bowels cut out and burnt do you not go right back and tell Philippe you have no *plan* that requires my sister to stay there another moment. Prisoning will *kill* her."

Without regard to ripped skin or ruined garments, accompanied by a continuum of invective I had not imagined he knew, the chevalier hauled me up from wherever he'd last sent me and shoved me down again, tumbling me head over heels, tangling me in creeping vines, tree limbs, and thorny branches, rendering me incapable of protecting myself, much less providing any sensible answer.

"The *king's* idea," I babbled, "his counselors . . . subjects rabid for justice . . ." *Lord, I understand your anger . . . . It was the only way.*

He batted my hands away whenever I fought to prevent the next uncomfortable segment of my journey through the maze. "To think I had begun to believe you a Saint Reborn. Do you know the Two Invariant Signs?" Another shove. "Refusal to die without meaningful purpose. Inerrant perception of righteousness." And another. "Twice you survived what would have killed any other—on the *Swan*, at Eltevire—and I've never known a man whose honor and compassion grew so much from his bones. But, of course, I *am* a fool."

When my head, still tender from my battering in Eltevire, encountered a much too solid tree trunk, livid lights and unreadable runes swirled behind my eyes. My knees lost all cohesion, and a whimsy stung

my thoughts like an angry wasp. Dante . . . everyone would blame Dante for this. When my lifeless body was found, not the finest *agente confide* in Sabria would imagine Ilario de Sylvae had slain me. Me, a Saint Reborn. A most unlikely sensation burbled through my gut, climbing upward until it burst forth, sounding less like wild hilarity than a croaking screech.

The powerful hands gripped yet again and dragged me upright, but only shook me rather than sending me flying. "Blazes, Portier. Are you dead?"

My hands clutched my splitting head. Hilarity faded. "The queen's only held till Edmond's return," I rasped, once he'd let me slump to an earth that wobbled unnervingly.

My stomach heaved bile, and a fit of coughing threatened to finish what Ilario's hand had begun. But he forced a dribble from his silver flask down my throat. Valerian could set a legion puking.

"Try again," he snapped, out of sympathy once the fit was eased. "Why is my sister yet confined when I hear you've brought letters that exonerate her? Her husband refused to address his decisions, and as the royal ass was about to tear down his own palace with his teeth, I chose to go to the source of the confusion. What have you told him, you pigeon-livered stick?"

"Let me tell you what I learned at Vernase," I said, between hawking attempts to clear the nasty taste from my mouth. "Ten years ago, Michel de Vernase made a bargain with Gaetana to stop leeching a young girl. We don't know the terms, or whether that was when he first became intrigued by the power of transference. . . ."

By the time I arrived at Maura's letters, Ilario had settled on the ground beside me. Every time I paused in my recitation, he revisited his litany of swearing.

"Even the leeching tools did not seal his belief about Michel," I said, Philippe's stubbornness maddening me yet again. "He demands more evidence. Yet his heart also demands he free your sister, lord. You know it does. The root of his rage is this dissonance between duty to Sabria and his love and fear for his wife. He believes he must produce the true crimi-

nal before he sets her free. If he cannot relieve the suspicions of his counselors and reassure his subjects that this woman is worthy of his love and theirs, whether or not she can bear him an heir, then his reign is cracked—perhaps the very breach these purveyors of chaos desire. Jousting for position will replace scholarly concords. Demesne wars and assassinations will replace exploration for new trade routes. News of Gactana's execution has already spread like plague. Without confirmation that she was truly rogue, fear and defensive maneuvering will grow between blood and nonblood families. And in whatever case, he must demonstrate his commitment to justice without prejudice of rank. So he leaves his wife imprisoned. He orders Michel's arrest. And he waits fourteen days for Edmond de Roble to bring him Michel's evidence, praying it will solve the mystery, exonerating both of those he loves."

"And if it does not?"

Such was the likely outcome. "He'll not leave her there an hour more than necessary. Think, lord—if he proclaims Queen Eugenie's innocence today, he must reveal the letters, one of the few cards in his hand that Michel cannot suspect he has."

Ilario scraped his fingers through his hair. "She'll die in the Spindle, Portier. They allow only one family member to visit her, and Antonia has precedence, naturally. Antonia is good-hearted, but she talks of nothing but the way the world should be ordered, and she's never understood Geni. As a child, my sister brought nothing but delight to everyone around her. Now she believes she is Death's handmaiden. If she hears that Maura has betrayed her . . . another friend dead . . ."

"Maura lives until the matter of Michel is decided," I said. "Philippe recognizes that he needs her testimony, no matter whether Michel or someone else is guilty."

"Sweet angels, Maura a traitor." Ilario's shudder rattled the dark. "She's always treated me equably, never whispered behind my back, never gained advantage at my expense, and I can tell you that is rare enough in this court. But to deliver those vile banners to the *Swan*. . . ."

"She had them made months ago and stored them in the temple, as one of Michel's letters ordered her to do. The phosphorus was certainly added

in that time, no doubt along with some clue that would link them to Ophelie, and ultimately, through Maura, to your sister. On the morning of the launch, Maura merely had them collected and delivered to the barge."

"What a demon-blasted confusion." Ilario sighed. "I'd likely serve as dupe for anyone who rescued *me* from soul death."

"As would I," I said, glancing at him sidewise. "Though I might ask my own brave rescuer yet two more favors."

A stillness enfolded Ilario like his black cloak. Had he even realized how thin his mask had become in the last hour? "And what would those be?"

"You must convince Philippe to proceed with your Grand Exposition—and to expose himself to the crowd by his attendance. Prince Desmond's deathday has been somehow significant to the conspirators. Perhaps merely to lay suspicion at the queen's feet. But Michel has purposefully set Edmond's return for that day. If we can lure the villain into some move while the queen is yet imprisoned, we've put a public face on her claim of innocence, while at the same time granting ourselves an opportunity to catch the real criminals as they act. If the villains don't play, we've lost nothing."

"And the second favor?"

"Once we've set the exposition arrangements in motion, Lady Antonia needs must fall ill or be otherwise incapable of visiting the queen, so that you can get me inside the Spindle."

Ilario puffed and spluttered. "Saints Awaiting, Portier, I didn't hurt you all that awfully! If Philippe doesn't chew my bones to rags, my foster mother surely will."

ILARIO, AS IN EVERY TASK I had set him and so many I hadn't, proved faithful. On the morning after Maura's arrest, Philippe issued a proclamation that Ilario de Sylvae's Grand Exposition of Natural Sciences and Magical Phenomena Honoring Prince Desmond's Deathday had his blessing to go forward.

... for indeed the despicable, cowardly assault on the Swan blighted our offering of the Destinne's brave launch to speed our beloved son's Veil journey. We invite the Camarilla Magica to join in this festival, for wholesome displays of the fantastical arts shown alongside the glories of natural philosophy, must surely dispel the stench left by the rogue mage complicit in that attack, the canker now excised from Sabria's healthy body.

THIRTEEN DAYS REMAINED UNTIL EDMOND would return with Michel's answer. Thirteen days until Michel de Vernase would prove friend or foe. Thirteen days to plan how I was to get Maura out of the Spindle and away from Merona.

On the first of the thirteen, Ilario and I spent the entire day with the palace steward, detailing our requirements for the Great Hall and the Rotunda, where we would place the exhibits, and the Portrait Gallery, where we would put refreshment tables. Maura's imprint lay on every message, every name, every idea we had sketched in my journal on that one delightful morning before I'd gone to Seravain and learned I dared not trust her.

On the second day, I sent confirmation messages to the Collegiae Physica, Biologica, and Alchemistra, to the Academie Musica, and to the various artists and makers of lenses and instruments Maura or I had contacted previously. Lord Ilario's personal invitation to the Camarilla was delivered to Prefect Angloria, along with a gilt-edged copy of Philippe's proclamation.

On the third, I fielded at least one hundred fifty queries from interested participants at my newly installed desk in a minor bulge of the Rotunda. A more difficult task was to counter the various rumors each messenger reported: that the event was designed to mock and humiliate magical practitioners, or that it was naught but a venue for devious mages to upend the king's righteous cleansing of Camarilla interference, or the one spreading like plague from some cult prophet that the Exposition would mark the return of a Saint Reborn.

Late on that third afternoon, a dispatch arrived from the Guard Royale captain at Vernase.

Thanks to the close watch on Damoselle Anne de Vernase you mandated before your departure, Ambrose de Vernase has been found. While in the village on household business, the young lady attempted to supply her brother with money, clothing, and maps of northern Sabria. The youth and the damoselle have been returned to Montclaire and the watch on the family doubled.

I FORWARDED THE NOTE TO Philippe straightaway. Unfortunately *northern Sabria* was much too large an area to hint as to Michel's whereabouts. Philippe immediately summoned Lady Madeleine and her children to Merona.

Who could not grieve for the young people caught up in this wretched business: Lianelle and Ophelie, Anne and Ambrose, the missing Adept Fedrigo? And Edmond de Roble's fate yet filled me with unreasoning dread. No matter that Gaetana was dead, we would not be done with the evils the Aspirant had wrought until he was in our hands.

On the fourth day—nine remaining until the Exposition—Ilario worked with two painters, a printmaker, and three sewing women to create banners and posters to be hung or distributed throughout the merchant fairs, guild-halls, temples, and academic halls, inviting the distinguished citizens of the royal city to visit the scientific and magical displays. I dispatched personal invitations to the most important scholars and nobles in Merona to attend the climactic events of the festival, and confirmed that the Lestarte brothers were ready to provide a grand fireworks display from a chain of barges to entertain those people we were unable to accommodate at the Exposition itself. In late afternoon, I set out for the east wing to visit the queen's remaining mages.

"WHAT SORT OF EXHIBITION? I am no acrobat or trained dog to perform tricks for ladies, Acolyte Duplais." Mage Orviene's broad face had wrin-kled the moment I broached the subject of the Exposition. And once I had

described the aligned displays of science and magic, and introduced the idea of his participation, his wrinkles had deepened to ravines. "Dante, were you aware they wanted us to *perform* at this festival?"

Dante's back expressed naught of his thoughts on the matter of Ilario's Exposition. Since Mage Orviene and I had arrived for this consultation, his only comments had been addressed to Jacard, who was scraping some foul mess from the floor inside the circumoccule. The mound of yellow and green muck smelled as if it could be a dead dog dissolving in quicklime. As the adept applied a blade, a pail, and himself to the unpleasant task, Dante observed the sun-drenched landscape outside his windows as if we weren't present.

"I've asked Prefect Angloria to sponsor ten fixed displays to parallel the ten fixed displays of the mundane sciences," I said, smoothing the journal in my lap, as if the prefect herself were tucked away inside it. I needed all the authority I could muster. "Those displays will be open to all guests throughout the morning and early afternoon. But Lucan de Calabria and Aya de Gerson, the Royal Astronomers, will be presenting an optical demonstration for the late-afternoon program in front of Merona's most influential gathering since His Majesty's coronation. It is only fitting that we provide magical demonstrations of equal stature, something memorable, that our art might return to the position of prominence it has lacked for so many years. Who better than Castelle Escalon's resident mages to provide them?"

Orviene's small, neat hands kneaded each other in his lap. "But Dante and I have no idea if we hold a position in the royal household any longer, thanks to the cursed Gaetana—may demons plague her Veil journey! Naturally I had noted irregularities, certain dark tendencies in her work, but I don't believe I shall ever recover from the shock of learning her true depravity. And now Maura ney Billard is arrested, as well. So dreadful, that lovely young woman involved with perversion and murder. Naturally, I've never attached the least suspicion to Her Majesty. Truly, Portier, how could we possibly participate in entertainments, even scholarly ones, with our dear mistress so cruelly detained?"

"No one recognizes that grievous situation more than Lord Ilario, sir

mage," I said. "He is confident our good lady will be free in days, if not hours, and feels that elevating her mages to parity with the king's academicians will demonstrate her wisdom and insight before a noble audience. And what wish could she herself hold higher than that her dead son be honored with her own mages' finest works?"

Orviene blew a resigned sigh and sat back on the couch. "Well, that makes sense, doesn't it? We ought to honor the poor boy. Yes, certainly. I'm sure we can devise something worthy, don't you think, Dante?"

"I work alone," snapped Dante.

Orviene's complexion reddened, and his mouth twitched unhappily. Dante, as a master mage, outranked Orviene. Dante's choice would prevail.

"Demon spawn!" Jacard's knife must have caught on something and flipped out of his slimed hand. I glanced up just in time to see the flying blade plop into the gooey middle of the mess. Face curdled like sour milk, the adept stretched out to retrieve it. But his knee slipped, causing his foot to bump the pail, which dumped its contents back onto the floor. A new wave of the vile stench rushed across the room.

Orviene gagged. I clapped my hand across my nose and mouth. Dante erupted.

Across the room before an eye could see him, the mage kicked Jacard sprawling into the muck. "Bumbling toadeater! Get out of my sight!"

The mage's heavy boot gave the adept no time to get to his feet. Jacard, retching, scrambled straight through the mess, clawed at the door, and stumbled into the passage. Face purpled with fury, Dante spun and extended his staff, already belching fire. As Orviene and I gaped, flame consumed the stinking mess, until only charred streaks on the floor and a choking cloud of green smoke remained.

Dante strode to the windows and shoved the casements open so violently, I thought the iron frames might bend. Hands, shoulders, every part of him trembling, he heaved deep breaths of the evening air. Gods, what was wrong with him?

Orviene leapt to his feet and backed toward the door, keeping his chin up and face cold in disapproval. But his eyes were tinged with fear. Likely

my own were as well. As when I'd interrupted his work with Gaetana's book, as when he'd struck the stable lad in Vernase, Dante's eruptive violence was no mere choleric temper, no playacting, no considered display to keep Orviene off balance and Jacard at a distance. It could not stem solely from his anger with me or in any other way from his time in the Bastionne, as the incident with the book had preceded his stay with the Camarilla inquisitors. No, this was something else again. *All sorcery requires certain expenditures*, he'd said once. Was this the price of his brilliance? I hated to consider such a destructive cost, not when I needed him so sorely.

Orviene waved a limp hand in my direction. "Acolyte Duplais, I shall pursue my own demonstration for the Exposition. Visit my chambers tomorrow, and I'll discuss requirements."

Dante did not turn from the window as the door swung shut behind Orviene. His eyes seemed fixed on the deepening sky, indigo and purple smeared with gold. I urgently needed a private word with him, but could not decide where to begin. And so I waited, wishing I could glimpse his face.

"Why are you still here?" Arms clamped tightly across his chest, staff tucked in the crook of one elbow, he spat the question through a clenched jaw.

I edged closer to him, skirting the swathes of charred mahogany. "I need to know if you'll do this. Before we traveled to Eltevire, you told Ilario you'd some exhibit in mind, something that would 'shock the twittering birds in this palace.'"

"You're to attend this display?"

"Yes, certainly." The question surprised me. I couldn't imagine he'd care. "I can see to your requirements—materials, lamps, draperies, parti—objects to be used. Whatever you wish to be provided."

"I'll bring what I need. Be sure to stand where I can see you. Now, if that's all . . ."

Angels preserve. Unfortunately, I'd only begun, and no stomach-addling demands to stand in his sight when he worked magic could interfere with all the things I needed to say.

"Dante," I said, fingering my journal pages, "I know you wish to be quit of our partnership, but we cannot call our work done quite yet. . . ." His simmering hostility urging me to brevity, I sketched out my growing conviction that the Aspirant would strike one more time on the anniversary of Desmond's death.

"I will place guest registers at every entry and require each man and woman who attends to sign the lists, so that their names can be invoked in prayers for the dead prince. If you were to create one of your perimeters about the hall, Rotunda, and Portrait Gallery, crossing every exit, you could then use the signatures to match these imprints of those who come and go, could you not? We would know who leaves when. Who might be there under a false name. Other things that their . . . keirna . . . could tell us."

"A name scribbled on a page hardly provides enough to pattern a person's keirna clearly."

"I understand that." As ever with Dante, I assumed that the spellwork he had demonstrated at Montclaire was only a part of what was possible. "But it would allow us to control the scene. Gaetana could have created any number of weapons for Michel before she died, but she'll not be here to wield them. Michel de Vernase knows we'll be watching for a mule. Perhaps he'll decide to try something himself."

Dante's head angled slightly in my direction, so perhaps I'd drawn his interest.

Without looking up, I pursued one additional avenue. "On the night we went into the deadhouse to see Ophelie, you enspelled a brass ring to foil the lock on the main door. I found the ring in a pocket the other day and wondered what capabilities it has. I'll have guards posted about the Rotunda, and Philippe will have his bodyguards. But if we were to corner an assassin, it could be helpful if I could lock or unlock doors at will."

"The spell breaks locks. It cannot make a lock function properly. Simple logic will tell you the difference in the two problems."

Indeed, it was much easier to kill a man than to put an injured man to rights. But I had learned what I needed. I steeled myself. "So, Master, will you honor your oath and build the perimeter?"

So fast I could not see it, he grabbed my doublet and drew me toward him, until our noses were but a finger's breadth apart. His green eyes smoldered, reflecting the glints of the dying sunlight. "Do not test me, student."

I refused to flinch. Somewhere behind those eyes was the man who had tended my burnt hand and who had stretched his magic to its limits to prevent the ruins of Eltevire from falling on my head.

"The Royal Astronomers and the other exhibitors will arrive at dawn on the morning of the Exposition. I'll be in the Rotunda two hours before. Will that give you sufficient time?"

He shoved me away. "Close enough. Perhaps you'll learn something."

I caught myself on the arm of his couch. Tugging my garments around straight, I clasped my hands behind my back, as if I weren't shaking.

"From the day we began this, I've learned from you, Dante," I said to his back. "You have cracked the foundation of my life, and I should hate you for it. But you've rebuilt that foundation with a perspective so much larger and more wondrous—a view of nature and magic that I've not yet begun to explore. I do sincerely regret our estrangement. My letter to the Camarilla was foolish and dangerous and lazy, and I failed to consider the risks—the considerable risks—to you. I regret that more than you can imagine, and I hope . . . Whatever is going on with you, I hope you will recognize and beware its toll." I didn't think an appeal to friendship would move him. Likely I had only imagined we had progressed so far as that.

He did not move. So I retreated. But as I laid my hand on the door latch, his voice rose from a frigid darkness. "I'll serve our agreement on the day of the festival, because it serves my purposes to do so. But at middle-night after it, our confederacy will be ended for once and all. Now get out, and do not bring your mewling face here again."

All these days, even while pronouncing Dante's enmity irreversible and totting up reasons for it, I'd held some buried hope that I was wrong. Kajetan had always called me tenderhearted. Soft. But the chill of that dark room settled deep this time. Filled with regret and apprehension, I left him to his brooding.

AT SUPPER TWO DAYS BEFORE the Exposition, Lady Antonia de Foucal fell ill with an attack of spleen and was taken to her room. As she was unable to make her evening visit to her foster daughter, the Warder of the Spindle Prison accepted her written request that the prisoner's next nearest kin, Chevalier Ilario de Sylvae, visit in her stead. The chevalier was most distressed at the doleful venue, shrouding himself completely in black and clutching his famous crocodile charm, though crocodiles had never been sighted in the river Ley.

IT TOOK NO MORE THAN one passage of the three iron water gates bound with hoary spells, one long walk up the steep, twisting central stair, one finger touch of sweating walls, one inhalation of the unnatural gloom, to believe Ilario's contention that his fragile sister must surely die if kept in Spindle Prison too long. I certainly would.

"Prisoner, stand forward," shouted the warder, when we halted our climb before a thick oak door with a barred window.

The bronze key cranked in the lock, spitting a magical residue that tasted like metal shavings. The door swung open soundlessly. A pale figure sat up on a narrow bed, drawing the thick blanket around herself. She pushed bare feet into slippers and made to stand up.

"Dearest Geni," I said, rushing past the warder to bury the lady's face in my embrace before she could stand up and the keen-eyed officer notice the disparity in our heights or the puzzled expression on her face. "Beloved sister."

"Here now," said the officer, "every prisoner, no matter rank, is to stand before the warder."

"Honor binds a Sabrian chevalier to kneel before his queen," I said, releasing the stiff Eugenie, "especially when he pledged himself her own true knight on Grennoch Rock so long ago." I remained kneeling by the bed, head bowed, praying sleep, surprise, and despondency would not prevent Eugenie noting the words Ilario had given me.

"Warder," she said softly, "forgive my brother. He is impulsive and"—
she ruffled my hair, pressing downward so firmly as to keep me kneeling—
"known to be a bit foolish from time to time. I humbly request permission
to sit privately with my visitor."

"Granted," said the warder, gruffly, hanging his lamp outside the door.
"The usual time, though. No extension for prattling fools."

"Divine grace, Warder," she said. "And my thanks for the gift of light."

She remained standing until the door swung shut, and the lock clanked.
Her hand remained firmly on my head. "Please tell me you've brought
good news, brother. It is so good to see you. Refreshing. Though I dearly
love Antonia, she says so little of interest. . . ."

Her words died away as nailed boots rang, descending, on the stair.
Then she tweaked my hood aside and turned my chin so the weak lamplight shining through the barred square in the door illuminated my face.

"Duplais!" She snatched her hand away and stepped back. "Who sent
you? Why are you here?"

"Forgive my impertinence, Majesty," I said, remaining in my genu-
flection. "Your noble brother contrived to get me here, sending his dearest love and encouragement. At the last, I near had to truss him to a tree
to prevent his upending our arrangement and coming himself."

"Our mother consented to this?"

"No, my lady. She is indisposed and knows naught of it. Nor will she
ever know, unless you choose to tell her. The chevalier is prepared to reap
the consequence of her anger."

"What could persuade him to such a tempest as that?" Her hand flew
to her mouth, and she sank to the bed. "Mother of angels, has the verdict
come? Am I—?"

"No, no, Your Grace! I bring no resolution to your situation. Of that I
can say only that many keep faith on your behalf."

I would not give her vapid assurances. I had done so for Maura, convinced that truth must win out. But I had learned that lesson.

"What news I bring tonight will be hard for you to hear," I said, rising, "but Lord Ilario insists that your devotion to your friends and your
passion for justice will compel you to act. And I have no one else. . . ."

As succinctly as I could, I told her Maura's story, both what solid evidence had reported, and Maura's own testimony. I spoke without sentiment. Without interpretation. The burden of judgment had to rest with Eugenie, for the risks she took would be considerable, in circumstances when her own position would yet be vulnerable.

Ilario's estimates of Eugenie's reaction were entirely borne out. "The only other prisoner in the Spindle is two turns up from me," she said, pausing in her tenth traversal of her cell. "Never in all the woes of this world could I have guessed it to be Maura . . . clever, kind Maura. And never this side of Heaven will I believe she has purposefully betrayed a soul to murder. I understand the law, and the need for the king to serve it, else I would be banging my head on these cell walls. But the souls one touches in this life are more important than law. Let Philippe condemn those foul, wretched vipers who so torment young girls. No one will die for *my* sake. Not if I can prevent it."

Nailed boots again rang on the stair. Ascending.

She dropped to the edge of the bed beside me. "Quickly, tell me your plan."

Into her pale, slender hand, I dropped the brass ring Dante had enspelled to break locks. "This is chancy, at best. . . ."

CHAPTER TWENTY-NINE

25 CINQ
THE ANNIVERSARY

"Sonjeur Portier, we need more paper for the Portrait Gallery guest registries," said the breathless young squire as he hurried along beside me, his request almost drowned out by new cheers from the Rotunda. "Could we not just skip a few names?"

"Extra pages are stacked on the table by the service entry," I said, dipping my head to Lord Baldwin's wife and five stair-stepped children, as I sped the length of the Great Hall for the hundredth time since well before dawn. "Skip no one. Shall a small inconvenience cheat our dead prince of his honors?"

"No, certainly not, sonjeur." The squire's voice faded as I left him behind like a faltering horse in a race.

One hour remained until the closing program—the two Royal Astronomers, Mage Orviene, and Dante. Some two hours later the honored guests would flood into the Portrait Gallery for wine and supper and discussion of the varied events of the Grand Exposition, while fireworks lit up the river to end it all. But Edmond de Roble had not yet arrived, nor had any other message or *evidence* from Michel de Vernase. Bless the saints, I had been busy enough to prevent excessive thinking. If Philippe did not find reason to release his wife tonight, then my plan to free Maura was

made infinitely riskier. If Philippe did not find reason to release his wife before exacting the penalty for Michel de Vernase's crimes, then Maura was dead.

The day had gone smoothly since I had followed Dante on his circuit of the Exposition venue before dawn, inhaling the vibrant energies of his magic as he embedded a wide gray stripe in the floor at every entrance. Now that thousands of visitors had crossed his boundary, I could only imagine what the shimmering film of enchantment would look like if the mage were to plant his staff in one of the main doorways—uncountable haloed forms jammed one upon the other. Dante expressed no doubt that he could distinguish one from another, though he advised me to require full family names and birthplaces on the registers that he might have more information to distinguish them.

"Heurot!" I called, relieved to see my ever-reliable valet who had been called into service as a footman. "Go round to every entry and remind the door warders that once the tower bell tolls third hour, none but those with court credentials or signed invitations may be admitted to the Rotunda. The morning guests will be escorted out through the Great Hall."

"Aye, lord sonjeur." He'd not gone two steps before he paused and grinned over his shoulder. "Is this day not the world's marvel, sonjeur? Every hour I've thought I'm outside time called to Heaven. The magics are wonders, but these things folk say are not magics have more the look of it than what the mages do! Scholar Rulf conjures sparks with his ball of sulfur and his hand, and that other fellow claims his pump sucks the air right out of his jars! My mind will scarce believe he can silence a bell's ring, the clearest of the god's music. And what I wouldn't give to be allowed to look into the opticum. I heard one gentleman say there were monsters in the water no bigger than a hair from his head!"

"Indeed." I could not but smile at his delight. Though the intentions of the day had little to do with simple exposition, it pleased me to think minds might be opened to nature's marvels, including sorcery, through my efforts. "Now go on about my mission, lad. If I can manage it later, I'll get you a glance at the monsters."

We raced off in opposite directions. The mass of people circling

Philippe's new pendulum in the Rotunda had grown to thirty deep. The heavy golden bob—filled with lead, so I'd been told—had been first released at exactly noonday, the king himself wielding the taper that burned through its thread leash. Suspended from the peak of the Rotunda's dome by fine steel wire, the orb swung in blinding glory, the plane of its swing constantly shifting ever so slightly about its great circle. Philippe's pendulum engineer had set up paper standards about the circle and inserted a slim stylus protruding downward from the center of the golden ball. No other display elicited such noisy delight as did the pendulum whenever the stylus toppled one of the standards.

"Sonjeur de Duplais, what is this horrid marring of the floor? I was told that you were responsible."

Lady Antonia's imperious finger indicated Dante's gray stripe across one entry to the Rotunda. The dowager queen, a living ikon in a cloth-of-gold mantle, clearly disapproved. Her twenty ladies and gentlemen frowned in unison, as if sullied marble ranked among society's worst depredations.

"Divine grace, my lady," I said, bowing. "This is but a fixture in aid of the evening's program, and no permanent defacement." Which latter declaration could well be a lie for all I knew.

"Indeed?" She fluttered a fan, a requirement as the heat and odor of crowded bodies grew ever more oppressive. "Can you give us a hint of what Eugenie's dread mage has in store for us? Dear Orviene has assured me that his exhibition will be soothing, as I was woefully ill these past two days with such spleen as I thought must leave me blind. Such a banging head, such vicious flashes of fever and chills, and a thirst so fierce that I feared I had contracted sweating sickness. So I must insist that no exhibition be too dreadful or too excessive with noise or lights, else it will surely drive me to Ixtador."

Relieved that Ilario's hand had not been recognized in the lady's attack of "spleen," I expressed all sympathy. "Angel's grace, my lady, you appear well recovered for having suffered so terribly. I wish I could reassure you as to the evening's prospects. But in truth, Master Dante does not confide in anyone, certainly not those he holds in contempt."

She touched her fan to her lips, not at all masking a smile. Gossip of ongoing conflict seemed medicament to many courtiers. "'Tis rumored you do not get on with the fiend."

"Not by half," I said with a helpless shrug, imagining the pleasure of chaining her to the pendulum. "But I would suffer far more than scorn to serve Her Majesty."

"Prettily said, sonjeur. Ilario reports you've been most helpful with this grand folly."

"His lordship is more than kind."

"Well, we must not delve too deeply into an imbecile's qualities." She tapped a red silk slipper on the marked floor. "Do remove this blight when the night is done. Vinegar and coarse wool should serve."

Lady Antonia swept into the Rotunda past the pendulum, trailing behind her the potent scent of jasmine, a growing band of admirers, and a barbed commentary on "Philippe's forever inconsiderate expenditure on mechanical fripperies." Her voice grated on the spirit very like the sour plucks of the virginal on display just behind me.

"Adept Voucon, should I have additional materials fetched for you?" I said, peering over the magnificently carved instrument case.

The stooped, gray-robed sorcerer, acclaimed for playing the virginal without touching either keyboard or strings, was hunched over a loop of cotton string on the floor, frantically adjusting particles of silver, linen, dust, and bone. "Rid this venue of its disharmonies," he said angrily. "I understood we were to work in a purified space."

"Prefect Angloria herself approved this venue, Adept," I snapped. "There are no disharmonies here." Nor anywhere else, so my studies had told me. Many practitioners blamed certain alignments of stars, moon, season, and location for local conditions—disharmonies—that disrupted spellwork. No evidence had ever been produced to support the idea.

I moved on, unreasonably irritated. Excuses, always. No wonder people were skeptical of the art.

A hunger for news sent me in search of Ilario. Indeed, no one could miss him. Resplendent in emerald satin, metres of white lace, and a vermillion short cloak, he was perched on a stool near the opticum at present,

offering incoherent explanations of mathematical complexities and magical wonders at a volume that could wake the kings in the royal crypt. As I watched, he theorized that the pendulum's precession about its great circle resulted from a monstrous lodestone being turned by chained demons in the netherworld, and that Adept Voucon's difficulties with the virginal were surely caused by the nearby vacuum pump. The pump must have removed the very bits of air Voucon was attempting to enchant to shiver the virginal's strings, he said. The appalled academicians would be months in their attempts to recover from his assault on scientific principles.

Before I could take Ilario aside, a siren squeal from the Great Hall raked a claw along my spine. I rushed back to the mobbed venue. But the cry signaled only another lady exhilarated by the sparks of the *virtu electrik,* produced by Scholar Rulf's spinning ball of sulfur, and transmitted through his hand to hers.

The tower bells struck third hour of the afternoon watch, signaling the end of the general exhibition. Ranks of footmen politely urged the guests toward the Great Hall, shooing them away from the pendulum and scouring them out from behind the encircling colonnades.

The Rotunda, a remnant of a pre-Sabrian temple, was a gloomy space, encircled with alternating colonnades and bays. The central dome, some fifty metres above the floor, sat on a ring of arched windows that splashed daylight on its mosaic adornment. Below that circle of light, the thick walls were pierced with only a few small windows, shaped like four-petaled flowers. As these were mostly tucked behind the east and west colonnades or in the two largest half-domed bays on the north and south, the space required lamplight even in the day. It would serve perfectly for the day's culminating events.

On the dais installed in the southern bay, Lucan de Calabria, a puffy, tart-tongued little astronomer, screeched at four laborers shifting a painted screen onto its mark twenty metres from one of the four-lobed windows. In between the window and the screen, two assistants arranged a table on which Lucan's partner, the lean, elegant Aya de Gerson, had set up an apparatus of prisms and lenses.

"Have you everything you need, gentlemen?" I said, one eye on the servants setting out rows of chairs, the other on the west doors where Philippe would arrive. Attendants plumped the cushions in an ornate chair set in the cordoned-off bay reserved for the royal party.

Despite de Calabria's streaming oaths and insults, he asserted the optical display was in good order. Behind the dais, Mage Orviene knelt on the floor, pawing through a leather box. "Dear me," he said in answer to my query, "I'm not sure I have the exact weight of silver for my new work."

"Perhaps Master Dante could provide it," I said, though I'd not seen Dante since dawn and was not about to risk his wrath for Orviene's benefit.

"No, no, no need for that. Once the astronomers have had their fun, I'll just lay out two enclosures. If the one doesn't suffice, I can use the reserve." He clapped me on the shoulder. "Perhaps we'll have rain here in the Rotunda instead of starshine!"

As caelomancy was his specialty, Orviene had lamented that we'd confined the Exposition indoors. But he'd promised to come up with something enjoyable, as long as he could offer his exhibition before Dante's. "The fellow does some clever work. Especially if he's in one of his testy moods. All fire and lightning, even if there's no substance behind it. Anything that follows will seem dull, no matter if it's restringing the Archer's bow in the vault of Heaven!"

I was astonished that Orviene considered Dante's work to lack substance. How could any trained practitioner fail to recognize such soul-stirring power? Perhaps the agreeable Orviene, who had never reached master's rank, merely suffered a tot of jealousy. I certainly did.

As merchants, officers, minor officials, and guildsmen flowed out of the room in a noisy, sweaty stream, the glittering nobility and highest-ranking academics flowed in. The favored few occupied the rows of velvet chairs between the dais and the pendulum, while the rest stood round the sides of the cordoned-off pendulum circle and behind it. I stood back to the wall, a quarter way around from the dais, on line with the last row of chairs.

I should have been pleased. What commentary I'd heard on the day's exhibition had been favorable. To direct such a complexity of people and movement, and to forward a joint venture of the Camarilla and the mundane branches of learning was no small accomplishment for a reclusive librarian. Philippe's guards were on alert for every kind of physical attack we could anticipate, and despite his erratic behaviors, I believed Dante would hold to his word and guard against threatening spellwork. Please the god, Maura could be free by morning.

Yet my conviction that this was the day of reckoning only grew. Ophelie and Gruchin and the rest of the Aspirant's victims cried out in my soul, hauntings as vivid as Calvino de Santo's spectre. Where was Edmond de Roble? Where was Michel de Vernase, and what *evidence of his discoveries* might Edmond bring?

As if in answer to my worries, Dante strolled into the Rotunda from the Hall. Staff resting in the crook of his arm, expression composed, he did not deign to notice the guests vacating the space around him as he positioned himself along the wall opposite me.

The west doors swung open and five royal heralds marched forward. The assembly fell quiet. The piercing brilliance of trumpets brought everyone to their feet. Philippe strode into the Rotunda, his First Counselor, Lord Baldwin, just behind, and third . . . Ilario.

Despite all, I smiled. *Well done, cousin.* Few observers would attach any accolade to Ilario for the festival's success. His day's inanities could only reinforce the general opinion of him. But for Philippe to acknowledge him in such fashion honored the Sylvae family, especially Eugenie, whose fondness for her fool of a half brother was well-known. Ilario would be well satisfied.

The king strolled down the center aisle, the guests bowing or dipping a knee as he passed. He touched one or another on the shoulder or offered a word of greeting. He stopped for a moment to speak with his pendulum engineer, who had just started the shimmering bob swinging again. After so many hours, its arc had decayed.

The Camarilla prefects sat near the front. Kajetan, taller than his fellows, caught sight of me and raised a hand in greeting. Though I had

spotted his silver hair in the Hall that the morning, I had determinedly avoided him. We had not spoken since my letter accusing Gaetana, which meant he would have questions I was not prepared to answer. Protocol would prevent him sharing anything he'd learned from the inquisitors—whether about Gaetana or Dante. I smiled and shrugged, waving helplessly at the mob separating us.

Philippe's return to the dais took him past the seven prefects. They inclined their heads in guarded respect, and he spoke a cordial word to each. The king took his seat without addressing the assembly. That did not surprise me. He was likely stretched tight as his pendulum wire.

And so we began. The lamps in the Rotunda dimmed, leaving the gray air lit by a single window to the right of the dais. Without fanfare, de Gerson, the eloquent, aristocratic royal astronomer, began his presentation on the nature of light. He'd gotten through no more than a few sentences, when his partner, Lucan, objected vociferously, beginning a mock debate. Lucan assumed the role of Massilion, the classical philosopher who had asserted that white light was the purest of the Pantokrator's creations and poured down like liquid from the sun, as it clearly leaked around corners and fell into holes shielded from the sun's face.

De Gerson pronounced that light moved through the aether in straight lines and that colors hid inside it. To Lucan's raucous disdain, he covered the four-lobed window behind their display, and a hole pierced in the screen focused a thin beam of afternoon sunlight through his faceted crystal. The crowd, caught up in their spirited performance, laughed and clapped as the white beam split into a rainbow.

As the two men bantered, my gaze swept the Rotunda. Archers roamed the gallery that circled above us. Guards flanked every door, and three swordsmen stood discreetly behind Philippe's chair.

Lucan, with sly braggadocio, moved a second optical apparatus into place on the long table, while loudly proclaiming that a rainbow was itself one color of light, created by the prism. De Gerson, clever and patient, refuted Lucan's assertion by sliding a slotted board across the spreading rainbow and opening one slot. As a solitary red beam struck the Rotunda wall, people clapped appreciatively. And when he moved the second prism

into place and his beam remained red, rather than splitting into another rainbow, onlookers popped from their seats to join the cheers.

Across the Rotunda, Dante stiffened and slid his staff into one hand. The mage's eyes did not rove. His attention, his stillness, his posture, focused entirely inward as they had on the *Swan*. What did he perceive? The optics exhibition involved no magic. I sensed nothing.

The audience murmured and applauded as Lucan, now convinced, closed one slot and opened the next, replacing the red beam with an orange one . . .

Deciding to join the mage, I slipped rearward past a shallow bay and a section of colonnade.

. . . then yellow . . .

I set out across the Rotunda's center, squeezing between the last row of chairs and the roped stanchions that enclosed the pendulum circle.

. . . then green . . .

I had reached some halfway across the row, when Dante's chin came up sharply and his dark gaze met mine. He pushed through the standing courtiers, who paid him no mind. They were laughing as Lucan's slots opened and closed and the beam shifted to blue and then to violet. The pendulum swung, stirring the air. Fouled air. Where? Where?

A man at my elbow snorted, as if he'd fallen asleep, and a woman laughed brashly. Beneath the clapping and laughter, a girl's voice nearby admonished someone named Cato to sit properly.

I rotated slowly, craning my neck, desperate to *see*.

Darkness swallowed Aya de Gerson's violet beam. Lucan must have shuttered the slot in the window screen at the same time, as the entire Rotunda went black as a tar pit. The fouled air shifted as the pendulum swung again, but my eyes refused to accommodate the darkness, no matter how much I blinked or gouged them. It was as if the world had been devoured by the Norgands' Whale of the Beginnings, and I would have thought the guests had vanished with it, save I could yet hear them laughing, clapping, murmuring. In no wise should the room be so dark. Outdoors the sun was yet westering, and we'd left lamps by the doors.

A clatter and a curse, and I could see again. De Gerson was scratching

his head, while Lucan straightened the prism apparatus, tumbled over on the table—both men far from their window screen. And Dante . . .

I spun. Dante had vaulted the silk ropes and was darting past the plane of the pendulum toward the center of the great circle and an object that hadn't been there before the moment's darkness.

In the span of an eye blink, I raced to join him. Purple cloth . . . wrapped . . . two metres in length, it lay near the center of the pendulum circle, parallel to the current plane of the swinging bob. In the soft light of his staff, a kneeling Dante was pulling the purple wrappings away.

"Halt the pendulum," I snapped to the horrified engineer who was waving his hands for us to get out of the circle. "Keep everyone away. And fetch Captain de Segur!"

The astronomers' debate halted. The seated guests turned to see what had drawn the astronomers' attention. The chatter quieted, only to surge again in a wholly different note. Restive. Uncertain. *What is it? Where? Who's that? The mage* . . .

"Let me pass!" Philippe pushed through the stirring assembly, Ilario and First Counselor Baldwin right behind him, Captain de Segur alongside bearing a lamp. As they stepped over the silken ropes, Dante pulled away the last of the wrappings, and Michel de Vernase's message to his king lay exposed.

Edmond. Edmond. Edmond. Forlorn hope demanded to name this ravaged flesh something other—a fiend taken from the gallows, perhaps, or a young man consumed by wasting sickness and now relieved of mortal suffering. Heart and mind knew better.

They had wrapped him naked. The fine strong body predicted by Edmond's handsome face and stalwart grace had been no lie. But what lay before us in Captain de Segur's lamplight was but a bloodless husk. Every squared centimetre—face, torso, limbs, fingers, eyelids, genitalia—had been precisely incised, no single wound mortal nor scarce even painful of itself. But surely the young man must have believed himself aflame . . . for all the days of his dying.

I sank to my knees and opened his curled fingers. Twined about one lacerated hand was a purple ribbon looped through a signet ring. The

ring's device of an *R* circled by a twisted vine was unmistakable. Ruggiere. Michel. A sealed paper, bearing Philippe's name, had been pinned
to the back of Edmond's left hand. I passed the paper and the ring to
Ilario, who stood between me and my cousin.

The Rotunda, the muted, restive crowd, the displays and celebrations,
receded. My eyes fixed on Edmond's ravaged face, willing him to give
testimony to a single critical question. Bleeding was a senseless form of
murder, requiring a meticulous touch. Other torments were just as exquisitely cruel in pain and horror, while easier to manage. So why bleed
Edmond, whose hand bore no blood family's mark?

Terrible as was the sight and the knowledge of a young man's mortal
torment, more terrible yet were the conclusions of simple logic, as relentless in their progression as Philippe's pendulum. A first, terrifying
theory proposed that the Aspirant had devised some way to leech magic
from unmagical blood. However, the practices of transference had been
thoroughly explored during the Blood Wars, in days when sorcerers
knew far more of spellwork. And Dante had sworn Gaetana—and the
current practices of the Camarilla—incapable of such greater magic.
Logic left but one alternative. Edmond's blood was not as we
assumed. . . .

My gaze shot to Philippe, whose face might be the Pantokrator's first
rough shaping of granite at the beginnings of the world, but whose fist,
marked with the Savin seal as mine was and half hidden beneath his purple mantle, pressed to his breast as if to prevent his heart's disintegration.
And into my mind floated the image of the glorious Lady Susanna, retired
to obscurity in the country with Philippe's old commander forty years her
senior. And alongside the image echoed the story of two men who had
drunk each other's wine and covered each other's sins.

I averted my eyes quickly that no one might follow their course and
glean my understanding. No wonder then at Philippe's ambivalence at
Michel's letter. His faith had compelled him to send Edmond as Michel
required, while his every instinct warned him it was a deadly . . . and very
personal . . . trap. The agony in my cousin's posture was not the sorrow of
a king for his young soldier.

"Cover him," said Ilario, softly. "Angel's comfort, there's naught to be gained by this unseemly exposure."

But what saint or angel could ever comfort the noble warrior king of golden Sabria? None. Not when his oldest friend had murdered his only son.

CHAPTER THIRTY

25 CINQ
THE ANNIVERSARY

Philippe de Savin-Journia's worst nightmare, so the Aspirant had named himself at Eltevire. So he had proved. So he would prove again unless we made the correct moves in answer to this mortal taunt.

Philippe accepted the ring and the note with scarce a glance. "We continue with the exhibition."

"My lord, surely not!" said First Counselor Baldwin, who had arrived just as I laid the purple wrap across Edmond's face. "No matter who this is, we must—"

"We must do *nothing*," snarled the king, low enough to keep the exchange at Edmond's side. "I know who is responsible, and his vile act will not sully the honors being offered Prince Desmond. Not again. That is what he wants. Portier, see to this." Philippe stepped out of the lamplight, but did not leave.

"Aye, Your Grace," I said, swallowing hard at the responsibility my cousin had just laid in my lap. *Think, Portier.* First the crowd, their voices already risen in fearful speculation. Philippe wished to keep knowledge of this assault on his person—it could be termed naught else—contained.

"Lord Baldwin, if you would, announce that a young gentleman guest has suffered a spasm of the falling sickness and must be helped out of the

venue. Say the ailing guest requests that the event proceed in due honor to the late prince. His Majesty has offered his own physician."

A troubled Baldwin flicked his shrewd gaze from Philippe to me and back again. "Sire?"

"As he says."

Philippe's brittle response gave Baldwin direction enough. As if he were a much younger and slimmer man, the First Counselor sprang over the silk ropes and strode toward the dais, bellowing cheerfully. "Everyone, return to your seats and ease your concerns. All is well, though we've had a lamentable incident. . . ."

"Captain de Segur." At my sharp enunciation, the mustachioed guard captain raised his eyes from Edmond's corpus, where they had been fixed. "On bond of life and honor, you will not speak of what you have seen here until His Majesty himself releases you with his word and hand. You will support Lord Baldwin's report in every aspect. Do you understand that I speak with His Majesty's voice?"

I exposed my marked hand on my shoulder, hoping the mark might intimidate him with the possibility that I might muster some magical reinforcement for my authority.

"Yes, certainly." The captain squinted, as if not quite sure what I was. Neither was I, just then.

"Summon two of your most trusted men to carry this young man to"— I glanced around—"perhaps to Lord Ilario's apartments? Chevalier?"

"Certainly. Such a terrible . . . Sante Ianne, so vile . . . wicked . . ."

"And, Captain, double the protection for His Majesty's person, and double the watch on the outer gates and on the exits from the Great Hall, the Rotunda, and the Portrait Gallery. Search the alleyways, the courtyards, anywhere someone could hide. The one who's delivered this victim must not slip out with the departing guests."

De Segur slammed his fist to his chest and hurried away.

I had little hope that his search would be useful. Michel himself would not have risked carrying a corpse into the palace. If we could discover *how* the body had been brought here, we might have better fortune finding *who* had done it. Sorcery. I'd wager my eyes on it.

Dante examined Edmond's lacerated skin, his feet, his back, his eyes, touching and not touching, in the meticulous way he examined everything. Philippe watched from the shadows.

"Someone's carried him across Dante's perimeter, sire," I said. "With the god's grace, Dante will divine who it was."

"There can be no grace here," murmured the king, barren as the wastes of Eltevire. "What in the cursed realm of Heaven will I tell his mother?"

Edmond's mother. A young warrior's beloved mistress sacrificed to political necessity, married off to an elderly friend to shield mother and child from disgrace, and to save Philippe, the scion of a blood family, the unexpected king, from Camarilla penalties for promiscuity. The story would explain a great many things.

"He's been dead more than a day," said Dante, kneeling up. "There's no rigor. What blood he had left is well settled in his legs—he was standing or, more likely, hanging." Raw wounding encircled Edmond's wrists. "No bound enchantments cling to the corpus. Given more time, I might be able to determine where he was kept."

"Can you learn how he was brought here?" I asked.

"I doubt that." Dante shrugged, rising.

Restive murmurs among the guests had yielded to excited babbling and pointing fingers. I excused myself and hurried to the back of the pendulum circle where people pressed against the silken ropes, craning to catch a glimpse of the fallen man. Surely someone had noticed the bundle carried in.

"Scholar," I said to a young academician. "A word with you . . ." Two sharp-eyed ladies and a gentleman with a shock of red hair pressed close behind the young man. "Did you—or any of the rest of you—happen to notice our ailing gentleman stumble into the circle? We're seeking the rest of his party. But his tongue is a bit thick, as happens with the falling sickness, so we could not understand the names. He's wearing a purple mantle. . . ."

Though everyone behind the stanchions wished to speak, none had anything useful to report. They had been watching the light beams or the pendulum or had looked away just then. Several mentioned the lights

going dark, but no one had observed anything odd or anyone looking ill.

When I returned, frustrated, to the pendulum, two guardsmen with a litter had joined Ilario and Philippe. Dante had vanished. "Where's the mage?"

"Says he's gone to 'check the perimeter.'" Ilario knelt at Edmond's side, tucking the purple wrappings about the young man's long limbs.

"Bear the poor gentleman carefully, lest he suffer another spasm," I whispered to the guards. "Keep gawkers away. As you can see, his sickness shames him. Chevalier, will you show them where to lay him?"

The soldiers lifted Edmond's enshrouded form gently and followed Ilario through the parting crowd. Once they had gone, Philippe crooked a finger at the lamp. I held it close as he broke the seal on the letter.

After only a moment he refolded the paper and passed it to me. "You need not fear you've erred in your conclusion, cousin."

What have I learned?

First: To explore the new, one must not fail to look behind and inward.

Second: Setbacks on the field of battle winnow the weak.

Third: All secrets are writ in blood.

Never more in your shadow.

Curiosity begged me to probe Philippe's understanding of this message. But the man had receded to an untouchable distance, as if Discord's Worm, lurking beyond the horizon, had sucked down the roiling ocean. Only the king remained. He pulled a slender scroll from his brocade waistcoat. "Dispatch this to the warder at the Spindle. At middle-night I will come down to the docks to welcome my wife home."

An unseemly rush of relief and excitement engulfed me. Father Creator, by morning, Maura could be free. I needed to notify an accomplice that our

game was on. I needed to get to the harbor before the cordon of guards tightened around it to protect Philippe. Yet the Aspirant's accomplice, and all the answers he could provide, might be lurking in the Rotunda.

As I wrestled with the conflicting demands of duty and desire, Philippe strode back down the aisle to the dais, his authority like a gale wind sweeping away his guests' doubts and fears. "We have done for our ailing gentleman what can be done," he announced. "So let us declare this an interlude to savor the wine and delicacies in the Portrait Gallery, then return and proceed with this extraordinary event. I would see what these mages have to offer that can match our astronomers' exceptional presentation." The king bowed to his two astronomers as would his own most gallant chevalier.

The assembly applauded and cheered. Conversation burgeoned as children were released from their seats, and ladies called to friends, and gentlemen expounded on the afternoon's events to any who would listen. Philippe and Baldwin led the way through the wide doors. The glittering guests pooled behind them and flowed like a mighty river into the gallery.

I had never imagined a king's life to be so like a player's, or a spy's, forced to live masked and walk through scenes no matter the state of his health or his heart. As with so many of the grand destinies explored on my boyhood nights, truth was altogether different from the dreaming. I could not run off to play rescuer. Not yet. I had a murderer to catch.

Once I had dispatched a messenger with Philippe's orders to the Spindle, another to the Lestarte brothers that they should delay the fireworks display until middle-night, and left a brass token in a palace alleyway to alert my evening's accomplice, I hurried into the Great Hall. The exhibits had been dismantled. A few, like the virginal, sat atop wheeled carts, waiting to be hauled out.

A sheen of silver flickered beyond the colonnade at the far end of the hall. Even at so great a distance, Dante's magic shimmered in my veins, as unlike the sorry residues of the day's magical displays as this palace was to a bondsman's hovel. I stayed away from him, though, not wanting to associate our activities.

Each of the twelve entrances to the Great Hall remained manned and

guarded. I interviewed the registrars and scanned their lists, paying particular attention to persons who had arrived in the last hour. Most names were familiar, though oddly . . .

"No one at all passed the door between the quarter hour and the half hour?" I asked the registrar at the southwest door. The gap only struck me because the registry for the southeast door had shown the same quarter hour with no entries.

The young woman peered at her page full of time notations and signatures. "None. We don't have the servants sign each time they come through. We just tally them on their own list as you told us. But . . . I suppose not."

I returned to the registries I'd already examined. Every entry register exhibited the same quarter-hour gap. The tower bells had struck sixth hour as Edmond was carried away, which meant the Rotunda would have gone dark no less than a half-hour previous—approximately the same time interval, which meant . . . what? That everyone in Castelle Escalon had gone blind for a quarter hour?

Magic, surely, yielding just time enough for someone to carry a body in and leave again. Perhaps Dante's perimeter could tell us whose magic had left us blind.

Unfortunately, Dante had left the Exposition. Indeed, no one had seen the mage since he'd been "working his devilry" in the Portrait Gallery. Damn the man! Where had he gone?

I raced up the stair and around the long route to the east wing, calculating the time I had to get questions answered. The supper interlude would consume at least another hour and a half. Once the king returned to the Rotunda, Orviene would begin his demonstration. And then Dante would be needed on the dais. And he wanted me in the Rotunda. Saints knew why.

Jacard's chair outside Dante's apartments sat empty. I barged in without knocking. The mage was not at home. I was not tempted to linger. The air in his great chamber squirmed and wriggled as if I were immersed in one of the royal fishponds. He had wanted more time with Edmond's corpus, so I took off for Ilario's apartments.

Michel had surely intended Edmond's murder to demonstrate his own superior strength and cleverness, as well as a serious vulnerability in Philippe's household. Vulnerability to sorcery, to intrusion, instilling fear, uncertainty, and suspicion in the court, and in Philippe himself. The Conte Ruggiere had proclaimed himself an enemy so bold as to murder the son of Philippe's friends and perhaps . . .

My suspicion of Edmond's parentage would explain Philippe's confidence in his choice of heir. How much better than some random courtier would be a son of his own body, a well-educated, well-trained young noble of intelligence and modesty. Though a bastard could not inherit directly, anyone's name could be scribed on the Heir's Tablet in the royal crypt. Perhaps that was when Michel's rebellion had begun. *Never again in your shadow.* Perhaps the common soldier raised so far above his station, for twenty years the king's closest friend, had expected his own name to be etched in stone.

Captain de Segur's two men stood watch outside Ilario's door. "Sorry, sonjeur," one said, barring me from approaching. "Chevalier de Sylvae commanded nonc is to enter."

"I am the chevalier's secretary, Savin-Duplais," I said. "Inquire."

Moments later, Ilario was dragging me toward his small sitting room. "Blessed saints, Portier, the lad was so hurt, so . . . damaged."

Edmond was laid out on the divan. Dante was bent over him, scraping at the lacerations.

"There you are!" I said, relieved. "What have you learned?"

The mage corked a glass vial and tossed it into a cloth bag that rattled as if it held more such vials. "I'm trying to understand what was done here. The spells used on him are the same used when they took your blood—which means only that they used the same implements. It is likely his injuries were inflicted by the same who inflicted the first of your leeching marks—this Aspirant. Not surprising. Clearly they planned from the first to kill him. One-and-twenty days since he left here, and he was dying for most of that time. But whyever would they leech a man with no blood family connection?"

"Cruelty, taunting, smirking. Michel's telling us he still has tricks."

The words burst out of me without thought. For reasons I had no time to explore, I could not tell Dante what I suspected about Edmond's parentage. "Or perhaps this was sheer vengeance. We found Eltevire. Forced him to destroy it and retreat before he knew how to use it. Transference is only a means to some greater magical end, and Eltevire, in whatever perverse way, represents that end. Michel's letter, setting up this murder, came to Philippe the very night we returned to Merona. And then Philippe set the dogs on Michel and his family. The conte must have been furious, doubly so when he lost Gaetana. I doubt we'll know more than that until we question Michel himself."

Dante lifted his dark brows, then turned back to examine Edmond's fingers. The damnable mage likely knew I was withholding. But the matter was too private—for my cousin, for Lady Susanna, for the queen—and it was only a guess. Ilario stood in the doorway, fondling his crocodile charm, eyes averted.

"So, what did you learn from the perimeter?" I said.

Dante untangled the purple mantle from Edmond's long limbs. "Michel's son is here."

"Ambrose!" The startling news pushed aside speculation. This was bold. Brazen. My doubts about Michel's stellar family were rapidly diminishing.

"The boy entered the Exposition early in the day. He lied about his name, but a pattern on the perimeter shield matched the one at Montclaire. I found no evidence of his leaving."

"What of the contessa or the daughters? Have they even arrived in Merona?"

"None of them crossed the boundary, as far as I could tell. Alas, the boy did not accompany our dead man. Mayhap he was a scout, though. An hour or so after he arrived, a gentleman brought in a 'sickly cousin determined to see the displays.' Evidently the cousin had fainted, and two of the guards helped carry the man in. They deposited him on a bench under the colonnade so he could recover. The impression on the perimeter showed only three men crossing the perimeter together at that time, not four, but then, my enchantment reveals only living persons, not dead

ones. Sadly, neither the guards nor your registrar glimpsed the sick man's face. They didn't worry, as the person who brought him was familiar—a householder, too. The fellow made a tick mark by some earlier signature on the servant's list; thus he scribed only the sick man's name on the registry—*Largesse de l'Aspirant*."

"*Gift of the Aspirant*," I said, mouth awash in bitterness. "And, naturally, no one could remember the householder's name or could say which signature on the servant's list he annotated."

"Not a one of them." Dante buckled his bag.

"And so this mysterious householder waited and placed Edmond in the pendulum circle when the Rotunda went black to hide him," I said. "That was done with magic, wasn't it? You sensed it. I was watching you. I'd wager the householder left the palace right then. Every guest register shows a quarter hour gap just at that time."

"Just before the light vanished, I detected a burst of infantile spell-work, scarce stronger than a beginning student's. And you guess rightly. I found a second impression of the mysterious householder, a few hours later than the first—very likely the time of the darkness. He departed."

"Did he work the darkening spell?"

"Perhaps. I'd too little to go on." Dante hefted his bag, retrieved his staff, and slid the hearthside gargoyle that opened the hidden panel in Ilario's wall. "Now, we've twittering birds yet to shock, student. Are you coming?"

"I'd best leave the way I came," I said. "But I'll be there." Considering Dante's erratic behavior, his insistence on my presence could not but leave me uneasy, but I reminded myself that he had saved my eyesight, the use of my hand, and my life twice over. He had earned my trust. Sadly, I was finding it harder and harder to give.

As the panel closed behind Dante, Ilario laid a silk sheet over Edmond. "I'll summon the Verger," he said. "My physician will swear to whatever I tell him. He'll assume he was drunk when he examined the 'ailing guest.'"

"How will my cousin bear this?" I said, softly.

Ilario glanced up sharply, as if to see if I understood fully what I asked.

He nodded slightly and expelled a long breath. "Rock-headed as he can be, abrupt, unforgiving, shortsighted, tyrannical when it comes to matters in which he has no interest, Philippe de Savin-Journia was born to carry his office. He'll do what's necessary to see Sabria safe. Not even this will break him."

"Will you meet with him tonight?"

"Yes. He must set Geni free now. If I have to challenge him to a duel, I'll see he does it."

I smiled at his ferocity, seeing both the Ilarios I knew at once, as if the man stood before his own reflection in a distorted mirror. "No challenges, Chevalier. He's already sent orders to the Spindle. He'll meet her at the harbor at middle-night."

"Saints and angels." Ilario's head sagged against the wall. But after no more than a moment, it popped up again. "What of your mysterious plan to aid Maura? Will this help? Set it back? If you'd just tell me what I stuck my neck into . . ."

"Your sister will send word that she requires her full honors for her return—proper clothes, her ladies. She is vindicated and does not wish to skulk back to the palace like a freed convict. You should support her in her request." I hoped to tell him without *telling* him.

"Certainly, I will support her. Though . . ." No one could twist his face into a mournful knot as could Ilario. "Portier, this is not a night to press Philippe."

"He *must* accede to her requests, lord. Please. Your sister desires it."

After much groaning reluctance, and varied attempts to coerce, threaten, and plead his way into my secrets, Ilario agreed, as he had for the past ten days, to remain ignorant.

"Your sister promised to be sensible, lord. I reminded her there were other ways to help Maura if circumstances did not settle right tonight." In actuality, however, she had recognized, as I did, that her own freedom would likely signal Michel's guilt—and reduce Maura's life to days, if not hours.

Ilario knew these things, too. "If Geni comes to harm from this, I'll come after you, Portier. At which circumstance you'd best remind me that

she would have locked us both in a hermitage for not telling her about poor Maura." He was not jesting.

He walked me to the door. "Do you believe Dante about the magic? A spell that could make twenty door wardens fail in their duties and erase every speck of light in the Rotunda seems more than student's work. The mage seems . . . off . . . since you came back from Vernase. He doesn't so much as insult me anymore."

"I'd think you would appreciate that." A glib answer, but I had no other, save that Dante meant what he said about being finished with us. "I make no guesses about Dante just now," I said. "But I'd not . . . He is cooperating with me today, as he did at Montclaire, but he vows our partnership ends tonight. Something's twisted him—the sorcery he's working, anger about his interrogation at the Bastionne—so I'm inclined to believe he means it. I find myself wary of him, and you should be, as well. But then you've been wary of him for a long while."

He waved off my concession. "I've lived at court many years. I don't trust anyone save you, *student*."

I could not but laugh at his perfect mimicry of Dante's inflection. But he sobered quickly, his palm weighing the green silk spall pouch at his waist. "This is getting much too heavy, Portier. Keep yourself safe."

I laid a hand on his shoulder, wishing I could assure him that all would be well. I had come away from the Spindle with the impression that Eugenie de Sylvae resembled her half brother in many ways of importance, certainly in courage, loyalty, and determination. But belief would be impossible until the queen walked on shore into her husband's arms with no alarm raised.

As I started down the corridor and the east wing stair on my way back to the Rotunda, I considered the "darkening" magic. With Gaetana dead, who would Michel charge with delivering his dreadful message to Castelle Escalon? We had assumed all along that other magical practitioners were involved, like Quernay at Eltevire. Assuming such a spell would take training . . . I paused for a moment and closed my eyes to recall the young men and women lined up with Orviene behind the dais, matching faces and names with the household roster of adepts and acolytes I'd jotted in

my journal not long after I'd arrived here. Only one face was missing, as it had been for more than a month. . . .

"DANTE!" I CALLED, BREATHLESS AFTER pelting down corridors and stairs to catch him on his way across the Great Hall.

Staff in hand, he paused, his glare a heated poker between my eyes.

I kept my voice low. "You use the impression on your perimeter and the signature on the Registry to develop a pattern, yes—this *keirna* that identifies a person?"

"Yes."

"And magical artifacts can tell us a great deal about the practitioner who enchanted them. Like a signature of another kind. You could use it to explore keirna, as well?"

"Yes."

"Try this." He recognized at once what I deposited in his hand, altering his course abruptly for one of the entrances to the Great Hall. I retreated to an adjacent entry and pretended to review the entire day's guest list, while watching Dante.

Holding what I had just borrowed from Ilario in one hand, he planted his staff on the gray stripe that crossed the threshold. As the guards, the registrar, and scattered guests watched in awe, the silver sheen spread from his staff like a stiff curtain to either side, smudged and layered with shapes of every shade of purple, gray, and blue, as if a crowd stood just beyond it.

Moments stretched. Tame applause echoed from the Rotunda. The gawkers and stragglers remained quiet as if the mystery would ultimately be revealed to them, only to sag in disappointment when Dante lifted his staff and walked away without anything exploding, melting, or catching fire.

Eyes and mind yet dazzled with magical residue, I awaited him behind a cart loaded with tables and crates marked VACUUM JARS and PUMP. The mage dropped Ilario's crocodile charm into my hand. "Cleverly reasoned, student," he said. "It appears Adept Fedrigo has not drowned after all."

CHAPTER THIRTY-ONE

"Sonjeur de Duplais!" The swordsman in red and gold livery hailed me from across the Great Hall. "We found the young man."

"Adept Fedrigo?" I bit eagerly at the possibility. "Already?" Having just spent half an hour passing along his description, I was astonished.

"No, sonjeur," said the guardsman, reversing course as I fell into brisk step beside him. "The Conte Ruggiere's lad. Scholar found him hiding in his cart. Rousted him, and the boy bolted. Door guard chased him into the west wing, where we caught him squeezing into a closet."

The west wing. The king's residence. The guard's livery should have told me. "A closet?"

"Captain said we should inform you before questioning the boy."

"Exactly right."

After traversing innumerable ever-wider stairs and more elegantly appointed galleries, the guardsman turned from the broad, well-lit corridor, which I recognized as leading to Philippe's study, into a clean, spare servant's passage. Two soldiers flanked an open door. Standing inside the cramped mop closet, his gangling limbs in a knot, his tanned cheeks exhibiting a distinctly scarlet cast, was a fuming Ambrose de Vernase.

"Am I under arrest, librarian?" Much to his disgust, his voice chose to display its erratic timbre, sorely diluting his attempt at scorn.

A gray-bearded soldier passed me a sleek dagger with an ivory inlaid handle. "He carried this."

"What would you suggest we do with a man found sneaking into the king's residence with a weapon, Lord Ambrose?" I said evenly, slapping the weapon on my palm. Inside, I was cursing politics and hotheaded children and greedy, ambitious men who made children their pawns.

"I wasn't sneaking anywhere. I was going back to *my* residence, my father's apartments, where we're being held prisoner by our betrayer kin—"

I clapped my hand across the boy's mouth. "Are you an entire imbecile? Think where you are and speak in a civilized manner."

The ruddy color drained from his complexion. My suspicions that Michel de Vernase's children knew facts of importance ran high, and I *would* have their secrets from them. But I'd no time for coddling a fool just now, and I'd not see a rightfully troubled youth imprisoned for thoughtless words.

As he stewed, I turned to the guards. "Was no watch placed on Conte Ruggiere's family when they arrived here?"

"Two men outside the door, night and day, sonjeur," said my escort. "We've no idea how he got past them."

"But here he is, not a spit from His Majesty's own rooms," snarled the bearded guard. Clearly *he* believed the worst. "The conte's apartments, where his mam and sisters lie, are two corridors over."

Ambrose lifted his chin and glared at us all. He could not possibly comprehend the danger his father had put him in.

"You've stayed here with your father in the past," I said. "You know your way about. Why would you mistake a closet—?"

Of course. I would wager my year's pay that one would find a hidden panel in the back of this closet. Philippe would have given Michel apartments that communicated with the royal suite by way of the palace's hidden ways. Michel might have shown his son the intriguing passages, but more likely the boy had spied his father using them. It was certainly not my place to reveal them to the guards.

"Well, no matter. It's easy to get confused in so large a place," I said. "So you were visiting the Exposition. Have you an interest in scientific advancement? Or is it the magic draws you?"

He didn't even pretend. "I wanted to see *him*. The king. My own *goodfather*. I wanted to ask him how he could believe a man who saved his life ten times and spent most of every year away from home in his service could ever betray him. I wanted him to tell me with his own mouth."

"And did you see anyone you recognized this evening?"

"I wasn't looking for any but him," he spat. Not the least twitch of guilty withholding marred his youthful fury. If raw passion exposed truth, then Ambrose de Vernase knew nothing of the night's events.

"I don't think there's more to do here," I said. "Lord Ambrose must be returned to his mother, whose welfare he should consider ahead of childish whims. Being His Majesty's goodson, wise in the ways of politics and royalty, he surely knows that until he reaches his majority, his mother is held equally responsible for any libelous word or treasonous act on his part."

Ambrose's rose-gold complexion faded to puking yellow. One would think I had slammed a boot into his groin.

"As for escape, such a noble young man's word should suffice. Is that true, Lord Ambrose?"

Eyes narrowed, he gave something of a positive acknowledgment with head and shoulders.

"Good." I held out the boy's dagger. "Then, of course, you will place your hand on your weapon and swear by your mother's safety and your own honor that you will not leave your father's apartments by *any route*— door, window, or *other*—until such time as your king gives you leave. Do you so swear?"

"I do—" Ambrose had already spoken by the time he comprehended the "any route" part. When his eyes shot up to meet mine, I made sure he could read my understanding of his evasion. His mouth clenched in resentment. "I do. But I'll make him answer. Be sure of it."

Sacre angeli! I gripped his shoulders and shook him. "Treason is not a contest, Ambrose. Nor are you a child, whose thoughtless transgressions

can be indulged and forgiven. Cool your emotions and heed reason. Your path is grown exceeding narrow this night."

His demeanor did not change, which did not mean he failed to comprehend. I hoped.

"Take him back to his mother. Tell her to put a leash on him."

"Whatever my father's done, he has good reason," said the boy, his dark eyes filling with angry tears. "But you and your mage and . . . and the lord who put you up to it . . . have done worse. You think you can hurt people and no one will guess. I'll see you pay for what you've done."

Though he wrestled and squirmed, the guards marched him away held securely between them.

The young palace aide who'd fetched me shut the closet door. "I may be speaking out of turn, sonjeur. Forgive me, if so, but you seem to have the lad's interest at heart. I don't know that the contessa will talk sense to him. The strain of the conte's disappearance . . . his situation . . . she is not the same woman as visited here in the past."

"How could she be?" I murmured as he left me. Confirming that, indeed, a hidden passage could be accessed from the dark corner of the closet did nothing to soothe my unease.

Stars shone inside the Rotunda's dome. Or rather, silver lights dotted the blackness that filled the great vault, some randomly scattered, some clustered into familiar patterns—the Arch of Heaven, the Bowman, the Three Oxen, the Winter Cup. Some of the "stars" above our craning heads whirled and spun. Orviene adjusted a wooden cylinder and a disk of silver in his spell enclosure, made an entirely unnecessary circling wave of his arm, and a fiery chariot drawn by six giant eagles flew across a silver crescent moon. The compact and powerful charioteer was surely meant to be Sante Ianne the Reborn, though the saint of wisdom was commonly portrayed as returning on the back of one eagle rather than driving six. Perhaps Orviene was a cultist like Ilario, or perhaps the chariot was merely a dramatic image, chosen because the mage couldn't think of anything more interesting.

Was pure illusion the best Orviene could offer? Thanks to Ambrose's

misbehavior, I'd arrived at the Rotunda only at the end of Orviene's display, but I was already sorely disappointed.

The chariot circled the vault. The air smelled faintly of rain. My hair and limp shirt collar shifted slightly in a wispy breeze, a poor reality out of proportion to the chariot's size and speed. The children enjoyed Orviene's work best, squealing in delight as he produced pink and yellow lightning and a rain shower that spattered on doublets and bodices, but felt more like swarming gnats than water droplets. The adult onlookers applauded politely as a grand gesture produced a red-orange sunrise entirely lacking in heat.

As the smiling mage bowed to the audience and made the required obeisance to a stone-faced Philippe, footmen turned up the lamps. The true daylight outside the thick walls had faded. But despite the passing hour and whatever drowsiness might have been encouraged by wine and supper and a less than stirring demonstration, not one soul left the chamber. Guests whispered to their neighbors, and fingers pointed to a shadowed space beside the dais where Dante stood, eyes closed, forehead touching his staff, as if in prayer.

Knowing Dante was more likely to be engaged in spellwork than prayer, I felt my own excitement rise, though reason insisted I should be gnawing bricks by now. Maura was waiting.

I planted my back on one of the columns that supported the vault. Let Dante open his eyes, if he wanted to know where I was.

Orviene left the dais to a scattering of applause. Seemingly oblivious to several scornful comments about "tricks to amuse children," he began chatting amiably with guests seated on the front rows, as he packed his materials into a bag.

"Get you gone, mage!" Dante's voice cracked the restive quiet, as he emerged from the shadows, his staff jabbing at Orviene's paraphernalia. "These folk have serious magic yet to see this night! Take your trinkets with you."

When some of the guests tittered, Orviene—complexion purpled—snatched up his bag and hurried off, abandoning his enclosure strings and metal chips.

The shocked murmurs quieted quickly, as Dante stepped onto the dais. His blue silk robes rippled, and his collar gleamed, the fine gold inlay reminding all that this was a master's collar, not the plain silver of a lesser mage like Orviene. His white staff began to gleam of its own light, brighter by the moment, while the lamplight dulled—flames not snuffed or reduced, but muted in quality as if the air grew thicker.

My skin shivered, itched, half numb, half heated, as do pursed lips when one blows a single low note for much too long.

"We've been asked to show wonders," Dante said, leaning on his staff, his ruined hand hidden inside his flowing sleeve, as always, "and I, a crude man, unaccustomed to what noble lords and ladies and celebrated scholars deem wonderful, have watched and learned this night. The astronomers created slotted shades and built apparatus to demonstrate what they cannot explain. But any alley brat lucky enough to find a shard of broken glass on a sunny day might do as well."

The onlookers gasped as a rainbow of light shot from the top of his staff, red, orange, yellow, green, blue, violet. And they clapped as the colored rays bent and joined together into a single white beam, like a single stem emerging from a spread of colorful roots.

I did not applaud. My gut constricted, because I heard his heated scorn glaring like a summer sunrise, and even halfway across the room I tasted the bitterness feeding his magic. Could no one else sense it? Why were those nearest him not squirming backward? Had my body not been pressed against a solid surface already, I would have done so.

"But I celebrate these academicians of the natural world as you do. They attempt to learn. They map the heavens and theorize about its structure and movements. They quantify and record and seek answers, and create"—his white beam bent and moved, traversing the upturned faces, pale and dark, young and old, smiling, amazed, puzzled, until it reached my own, near blinding me with the glare—"magnifying spectacles, so that lowly secretaries with weary eyes may read the words they scribe for trivial men. Useful things."

Laughter rippled through the silk- and satin-clad rows and lapped at my shoulders from those behind me. Heat rushed to my cheeks, and my

hand came up to shield my eyes, which were not wearing the spectacles at the moment. Was this why he'd wanted me here?

Even as humiliation burned, I could not but contrast the searing heat of the beam with Orviene's simulacrum of sunlight. Every person Dante's light touched must realize the same. After what seemed an age, the beam moved on, and so did the mage's introduction.

"But even a king's astronomers cannot lift you into the heavens, any more than they can take you inside their beams of light. Not yet. And so next, we saw the practitioner deemed collar-worthy by the Camarilla Magica attempt such a journey. But he teased you with air painting, no more real than the inhabitants of this ancient dome."

The white beam and its bright-colored roots vanished. Now the staff, raised high, gave off a broad, spreading glow that illuminated the vault, immersing all of us below in a sea of shadows.

Long before the days of Sabria, a people called the Cinnear had built the Rotunda, choosing the ribbed dome, resting on its ring of glass windows, as a repository of their god stories. Centuries later, a Sabrian king had hired artists to cover the painted scenes of beast gods and legends we did not know. In the arced recesses between the vault's ribs, the artists had laid richly colored mosaics of our own god and the stories of our hero saints.

Though much of the gold background had since flaked away, exposing the faded paintings underneath, and the pendulum suspension cog protruded from the dome's peak like an unsightly wart, the luminous figures of the Pantokrator and his servants still had power to awe. In the daytime, the thin bracelet of glass about the dome's base bathed them in sunlight, revealing the richness of lapis and jade, coral and amber. But touched by Dante's shuddering luminescence, the angels' wings seemed to ripple as in a mighty wind, and the eyes of the saints, dark-outlined as prescribed by the Temple, widened as if they had just taken notice of earthly life. Their backs bent, their raised hands reached down toward us all. . . .

The air boiled, thick as a posset. My wind-whipped hair and collar stung my cheeks. Terror wriggled its way into my craw, though it had no name and no shape that made sense.

I shook my head and blinked, and the saints and angels retreated to the ceiling. Shivering, I forced my eyes from the vault.

"Heaven's gates, so beautiful," murmured a woman just beside me, her sighs merging with a chorus of awe from the rest of the chamber. What did she see? Did no one feel the danger? Gowns, scarves, lace, and hair riffled, disarranged by the wind of angels' wings.

Dante lowered his staff, and every eye shifted his way. "Perhaps you would rather travel to places of your own choosing," he said, and he twirled his staff in his hand, now pointing it at the wooden dais. Spinning in place, he quickly scribed a circle with a rill of blue flame.

As one, the onlookers inhaled, but did not cry out or panic, for the fire did not spread or grow. Inside the circle, Dante crouched down—I could not see what he did—then rose up and settled into his meditative posture, eyes closed, head pressed to the carved hornbeam staff. "Consider regrets," he said, "those unfortunate things you would change. We could travel into that demesne. . . ."

All around me, people closed their eyes. Like sheep. Like herdbeasts allowing themselves to be led into worse danger. Oh, I knew regrets, but I would not play. I held my eyes open.

But darkness bloomed from his circle of fire, blinding my common eyes. And with night came memory and a fiery wounding. . . .

The knife rips down my left arm, and five different places on my chest and back and side, as if my father is trying to carve the cursed mark—the interlaced S and V—into every part of my wretched flesh. Into my heart.

Get up, get up! On your feet, Portier, or die this moment. Sweet angels defend! Grab the madman's wrist. Ignore the pummeling; that hand holds no blade. Hold on. . . .

The gut wound, explosive agony moments before, cools. A blessing, save that my legs are losing all feeling at the same time. Blood pulses weakly from my belly and arm. Numb feet stumble sideways, dragging the scrawny madman along with me, his face contorted, bloody.

"Master! Help me! Dufreyne . . . Garol . . . Mother . . . some-one!" My calls bring no succor, and he does not stop his flailing. The earth wavers . . . light shimmers . . . fades into gray . . . Let go and he'll strike again . . . and you'll die. Retain your hold and you'll collapse . . . and die. Choose.

Let go, then. Strike at his throat. You've one chance. . . .

Released, the madman staggers backward. My weakened hand scarce grazes his throat.

The floor rushes upward. Breath will not come. A cold black glove envelopes limbs, belly, back, squeezing the heart . . . inexorably . . . stilling its struggle . . . then brushes lips and tongue with numbing frost . . . and, with two black-clad fingers, closes my eyelids.

No! Please, give back the light! I am not finished. Father Creator, this is wrong! I am destined . . . meant . . .

Smell is the last of the senses to fade, so it's said, and the first to return. Thus the aroma of cedar and juniper, old leaves and dry grass, dampened by mist, should be a reassuring replacement for the odor of evacuated bowels and blood-soaked wool. But I know where I am, and I will not look upon it. And so I shutter thought and belief and the eyes I cannot feel.

Sweet angels carry this plea to the One Who Judges. Was I not born for more than failure? For more than petty striving? I cannot . . . will not . . . accept this.

A soughing wind rattles twigs and grasses—my only answer. Despair replaces breath. Cold stone replaces heart. And two lumps of unfeeling wood shove me upright and set themselves one before the other. I am terrified to look, lest seeing make it real, lest I spy the First Gate barred and know I will wander in this cold, lifeless place for the duration of the world.

Please, I don't belong here! I am Other! Destined! Hear me. . . .

A hammer falls upon anvil, and I am falling . . . falling . . . seared, crushed, starved, burnt. Bursting agony in my lungs sparks streaks of acid on skin, through flesh. My nostrils clog with choking lavender.

"Onfroi went mad and killed my boy. My child." Her sobbing whispers blare through skull bones like trumpet blasts. "I had to stop him."

"Give me the fire iron, Dame Duplais. No one will blame your son for defending himself. If he lives, he'll not remember elsewise."

THE HOLOCAUST RETREATED AS SWIFTLY as it had come. My backside was planted on the Rotunda floor as boots and slippers, skirts and ruffles, breeches, leggings, and old-fashioned puffed pantaloons brushed past me. Murmurs filled my ears—sobs, fear, muted curses. Occasional outbursts of anger or wonder: "The man's a devil . . . My grandfather . . . cruel . . . So cold . . . So real. What pleasure is this? . . . I smelled his stink . . . her scent . . . our garden . . . real . . . So perfect, I could almost touch it . . . Marvelous . . . Demonic . . . Real . . . What kind of Souleater's servant is he? I *saw*."

"Are you well, sonjeur?" An elderly man wearing the sky blue gown of a mathematician held out a hand to me. "I'm not sure what this cruel mage just showed us, but you're not the only person it's struck low."

Wrung out as old rags, I let him draw me up and prop me against the pillar. But I could only shake my head in answer to his queries, and he soon moved on, as the Rotunda emptied of its unsettled population.

Words could not describe what had just happened. Nor could I shudder or weep or rejoice or rage, though reason swore I had justification for all those things. I could not feel anything save the same conviction that had accompanied every enchantment Dante had worked: What I had seen was truth. Three truths, to be precise, and when was Portier de Savin-Duplais anything but precise?

I had not killed my father.

My hysterical mother, she of the too-strong lavender scent and ever-fractured emotions, had slammed a fire iron into his neck, attempting to save my life.

And on that same night, I had died.

CHAPTER THIRTY-TWO

25 CINQ
THE ANNIVERSARY

My head felt hollow as a burnt-out log. Come another magical wind, it could surely blow through one ear and emerge from the other.

I had died. I had felt the Veil's chill finality on my cheek, smelled the sere and lifeless grasses of Ixtador. And then I had come back. Not as an infant, like a Saint Reborn, and probably not because I had pleaded with a distant god that I had died too early. Surely Ophelie had pleaded the same. And yet, I had screamed: "I am Other . . . destined . . . meant. . . ."

The arid wash of sanity smothered my creeping shivers. *Idiot. Saints wield true magic.* The pleas had been but a recurrence of childish dreams, my hope to serve some purpose in this world.

Kajetan had summoned a physician, so he'd told me after. The man must have been blessedly skilled to induce my heart to beat again before my last tether to life was severed. For all these years I'd thanked Kajetan for saving my life, but only now did I understand how near a thing it had been. He'd saved my mother's life as well, for to slay a noble husband was, as yet, a crime indefensible, according to Sabrian law. How could I not have remembered any of this?

Could simple knowledge of the truth leave the quality of the world so

different? The air of the Rotunda sparked and shivered, as with Scholar Rulf's *virtu electrik*. Footmen's boots struck the marble with a brittle snap. Light, color, and space existed in their own right, no longer subordinate to the physical objects that produced, displayed, or shaped them. I inhaled the emerald of the floor medallions and the petal-shaped voids of the windows. The cool curvature of the column at my back inverted, enfolding me as a mantle. Every perception seemed richer, sharper, more intricate in detail, as if my body, knowing it had once been dead, devoured every sensation of life three times over.

None of this was inherently terrifying. I should relish the taste of the human world. I should rejoice at the weight of murder lifted from my soul. I should grieve for my mother's fractured mind, and marvel at an act of maternal feeling from a person I had deemed incapable of such. So why did chill fingers crawl down my back, and my stomach insist it housed naught but writhing snakes? Why did my hands tremble?

Across the Rotunda a clog of courtiers on their way to the refreshment tables blocked the doorway to the Portrait Gallery. The volume of their conversation was rising by the moment, its tenor angry, tense, and fearful. Men glanced over their shoulders uneasily and spoke too loud; couples clung to each other. Some children clutched parents' necks. But a few little ones dragged along behind, facing backward, glowing as if anticipating more . . . More what?

The tower bells rang tenth hour of the evening watch, giving me fair warning. Two hours remained until the queen would be brought from the Spindle, when I had to be in Riverside to steer the future course of my life.

I walked briskly toward the Portrait Gallery. Something brushed my cheek—a moth?—and I near leapt out of my skin. No one stood within ten metres of me. The chairs were empty, shoved out of their orderly ranks. Soon I would be left alone with the servants come to sweep and the curious footmen come to haul out the chairs.

"Portier!" The steward's third secretary hailed me as he emerged from the crowded Portrait Gallery doorway.

"Divine grace, Henri. Do you need help with those?" De Sain's long

fingers clenched three wine cups. The soft slurp of wine against metal carried across the distance between us.

"No, I'm off to relieve Gufee at the west door registry," he said as I joined him.

Our steps echoed in the increasingly empty Rotunda. "You and Gufee can pass along word that the tallies can stop as soon as the king retires to Riverside. I'll be off writing my report." A flimsy cover for my absence, but enough, I hoped.

"Can't say I'm happy to loll about this place another hour," he said. "Now I understand your fear of that mage. I'll have nightmares till I'm gray-headed." His voice had quieted noticeably at *that mage*.

"What did you actually see, Henri? I couldn't get a good look from the back, and I've heard so many different things."

"Ask someone other." He raised his wine cups. "You'll be sure I've drunk fifty of these already."

"Tell me," I said. "For a while, I was thinking the angels were going to fly right out of the vault. Or that Sante Marko and Santa Claire thought to raise me up to the dome and throw me down again. Can't seem to shed it." Which must explain the tremors in my hands.

Though Henri ducked his head as we strolled through the pooled lamplight and past the silently swinging pendulum, his gaze flicked repeatedly about the gloomy Rotunda, as if he did not wish to see anything, but couldn't resist the looking. "When the mage drew the darkness from his ring of fire, I saw my da, who's been dead since the war in Kadr. Only—"

"Only what?"

"Only he didn't look as he did when I saw him last . . . or ever." The secretary dropped his voice even more. "He was wearing a ragged coat covered with sand. In fact he was climbing a great dune, the sand flowing over him and under him like water. And his face was hollow as if he'd starved and scared as he'd never been in life. Portier, I could near touch him, he seemed so real."

"Surely it was only your imaginings taken shape. Knowing he died in a desert war. Recalling the last time you spoke . . ."

"Angels preserve, he didn't speak! My heart would seize if a voice had come from such a haunting. But I could smell . . . When he was off at the war, Da would chew areca nuts till his tongue was red. To keep him square, you know, relaxed, and ready."

"So you imagined you smelled areca?" My mother was forever in debt to a local spice merchant who imported the odd fruits from the south.

"Take a whiff of my sleeve, Portier. I've not been near an areca nut in seven years." He poked his elbow out.

Feeling a bit foolish, I bent close to the dark blue satin and sniffed. Permeating Henri de Sain's sleeve was a rich aroma something kin to spiced olives. Unmistakably areca.

"It doesn't seem likely," I said, trapping my tremulous hands under my elbows. "Yet powerful sorcery did take place here. It lingers."

"Lots saw phantoms tonight, I hear," said Henri. "Lots felt things . . . movements . . . they couldn't see. Lots won't speak of what they experienced. Myself, I've got to get out of these clothes. The stink makes me think he's going to step out from around the next corner."

The bell rang the quarter hour. My steps slowed. "We'll talk again, Henri. Angels' peace this night."

"Aye, and to you, Portier. And all of us." He sped toward the west doors, juggling wine cups.

I needed to go, to make ready for Maura's escape. Yet magic held me in the Rotunda, drawing me to the center of the night's mystery.

Dante's fire had seared a grooved ring some four metres across into the wide, fitted planks of the dais. I almost laughed. The mage had made himself another circumoccule. And he had spilled—splashed— something inside the circle to stain the pale wood dark. So what had he done?

I stepped across the sooty boundary to examine the stain. But before I could take a second step, my chest tried to fly apart. Unseen fingers probed, tweaked, and pinched as if plucking out my body's every hair one by one. Knees, elbows, and hip joints cracked and splintered, scraped like glass on steel, ground bone on bone.

I backed out hurriedly, and the sensations ceased. Was Dante's spell-

work still active inside the circumoccule? This could not be residue; never had I experienced such a complex, physically painful reaction to spent magic. It would not have surprised me to find my bones reattached in some altogether new alignment.

A sweeping lad with a flat face and angled eyes ambled across the dais, pushing his scant litter of sand, soot, crumbled leaves, bits of straw, and broken glass. He touched his forehead politely as he passed me. His path took him straight through Dante's circle and all the way to the edge of the dais until his sweepings cascaded from the edge onto the floor below. Then he reversed course and slogged by again, his broom gathering a new pile of debris, mostly dust.

That he crossed the circle a second time without so much as a start answered the very question I would ask him. He felt nothing. What I had experienced must be residue detected by my trained senses, and not some unfolding enchantment that anyone might experience.

Staring at the circle, I considered whether the effects would be so severe if I breached it with only one hand. As I debated, the sweeping boy passed by again, pushing another pile of debris. Amid the sweepings was an object very like one of the astronomers' prisms. Once the youth had shoved the mess off the end of the dais and started another round, I stepped down and poked a finger into the piled sweepings. What I had thought a valuable prism was but a chunk of broken glass.

However, as I turned away, I noticed a corked vial amid the detritus, which would not have been so remarkable, save that it was clearly labeled EXPOSITION in Dante's distinctive, left-handed script.

Three short strikes of the tower bell reported another half hour lapsed. Time to move. The earthenware vial, painted dark blue or purple, felt empty. Stuffing it into my doublet, I turned to go.

I'd gone only a few steps when a muffled argument back under the colonnade behind the dais rose to a yell. ". . . find it or I'll conjure a hound that rips flesh from idiot slaveys and set him on you!"

Dante burst out of the dark colonnade, robes flying, hesitating only briefly when he caught sight of me. "Have you naught better to do than idle in this empty cavern, secretary?"

"Alas, I'm assigned to all aspects of the Exposition," I said, tagging after him. "The displays, the program, and the cleaning. Though I've hardly a head for business just now, thanks to you."

His determined course took him onto the dais. I followed, stopping at the circumoccule. He kept going until he reached the back of the platform. "I chose not to clean up my mess immediately after my demonstration," he said, reaching behind the dais and pulling out his bag, which contained the vials with the scrapings from Edmond's wounds. "I greatly dislike questions from the ignorant."

"But, as always, I am willing to risk your annoyance in the cause of learning." I stared up into the dome, where the mosaics were scarcely visible in the gloom. "What, in the name of Heaven, did you do here tonight, Dante?"

"The birds are atwitter, are they not? I've always considered lenses more fascinating than prisms, especially for those of limited vision."

"Indeed. What I saw . . ."

"We are finished at middle-night. Did you forget?" He stepped up to the dais, dropped a plug of lead into the charred groove, and set the heel of his staff atop it. A sputter of white fire, and the plug softened just enough to settle solidly into the trough like a well-constructed dam. "There. I'd recommend these planks be burned. You'll see to it?"

"Certainly," I said, stepping into the circumoccule. Naught but heat bothered me this time, a billowing stink of hot lead from the plug, and a waning prickle of fire from the rest of the broken circle. *This* was residue. I could not say what the other had been. "But I need to know—"

"I'll offer you one more thing, student. If you should catch this charm-peddler Fedrigo, ask who taught him blanking spells." From the bag Dante pulled a length of white string, threaded with black silk, and crushed it in my hand. "Now get out of my way. We are quit."

As he strode down the length of the dais, his gaze scanning the platform, I inspected the string. It yielded naught but a magical residue the texture of stonedust. Entirely confused, I crammed it into my pocket.

When Dante stepped off the dais, he paused and poked his staff at the sweepings pile. Then he kicked the large chunk of glass so hard it shat-

tered against a column, spraying shards all over the newly swept floor. He walked away, quickly swallowed by the gloom under the colonnade.

His anger over something missing . . . something dropped, perhaps . . . I pulled out the vial, uncorked it, and sniffed. Cedar, henbane perhaps, and— I upended the vial over my hand, shook it, slammed it into my palm until a single droplet rolled out. Blood.

I stared at the telling bead and again at the dark stain in the center of Dante's ring. So he had worked a *vitet*, a vital spell, an enchantment that incorporated blood as a particle—or in Dante's case, one that incorporated the blood's keirna in the pattern he wove. Vitets were not illicit, as long as the blood was freely given to the practitioner, but they were as complex and unstable as human souls. Theory suggested this particularly affected the one whose blood was used.

A void yawned in my belly. My fingers rubbed my chest, where cross-hatched scars reminded me of pain, blood, and smoke. The Aspirant still had the half litre of blood he had taken from me. *This* blood could not be mine . . . surely . . . else Dante . . .

The tower bell pealed the quarter before eleventh hour, shaking me out of my paralysis. Father Creator! I sped through the Great Hall and snatched up the bundle of clothes I had stashed at my desk early that morning. Shedding my *agente confide*'s responsibilities and my disturbing memories for a task that supported no delay, I charged out into the night.

CHAPTER THIRTY-THREE

25 CINQ
THE ANNIVERSARY

A s I traversed the open arcades, courtyards, and broad stairs of the palace and the upper city, the Rotunda's oppressive anxiety faded. No longer did I have the sense that at any moment I would bump into something I couldn't see. Yet my perceptions remained in their altered state—as if all my senses had been given spectacles to remove the world's blurred edges.

Lamplight glinted through the seams of doors and shutters and winked like fireflies. Laughter and music from taverns shimmered on the air like bronze bells. The darkest, quietest alleyways were redolent with scent—yesterday's fish, smoked pork fat, wood shavings, forged iron, an overflowing midden, tansy growing in the seams of old walls—not a hodgepodge "stench of the city," but each scent distinct in itself, pleasant or not as its nature and my appreciation prescribed. My perceptions gave me an extraordinary confidence. By the Souleater's Worm, the villains would not count Maura among their victims.

No one must see me in the next hour, at least not to remember, so I kept to Riverside's back streets, well away from the Market Way that led from the heart of the upper city to the harbor. A golden haze swelled over

the rooftops—torches blooming along the wide boulevard to light the way for the king. Rumors would be flying.

A dull thud rattled the shutters along the lane and set the dogs howling. White fire blossomed over the river, a cascade of light as if the stars were melting. *Not yet!* I needed to be at the harbor, as near the main pier as I could get before the turn of middle-night.

No further bursts occurred. The Lestarte brothers must only have been testing their launchers. I slipped into a darkened warehouse that smelled of new cut oak, char, and pitch. Inside, dangling his feet from a cooper's wagon bed, waited Calvino de Santo.

The disgraced guard captain had been more than willing to aid in this night's work. I had warned him his actions would be viewed as conspiracy to treason, but he relished the chance to save another pawn from a fate so like his own.

"So it is tonight," he said, returning the brass token I'd left him in a palace alleyway.

"He sent the release order." I kept a wary eye out the doorway. "No one challenged your leaving?"

"My night's taskmaster believes something I ate gave me heaves. I offered him good proof. The gate guards are so accustomed to my skulking about all night, they never noticed me walk out. I'll walk back in when we're done. I've a thought where to take the lady. I know summat—"

"No! You mustn't tell me." My skin popped out in gooseflesh. "If I'm arrested, I must not be able to reveal her destination. I'd take her myself and damn all, save I must be here to bring de Vernase to trial."

"Skin your worry, sonjeur. Under an hour and I'll pass her to someone reliable. None'll be able to get her destination from me, neither."

We confirmed positions and timing, and I left him. Riverside residents flooded the streets, pointing to the sky over the river. Some brought torches or lanterns to light their way home. Some paraded with pipes and tabors, as if this were the grape harvest festival or a frost fair on midwinter's night.

I pulled a black cloak from my bag and donned one of Ilario's out-of-fashion hats, expensive enough to name me respectable, old enough to

bear no connection to Ilario, and wide enough to shield my face from easy view. As I neared the river, I angled through the steep lanes toward the remote slip where Massimo Haile's barge had been moored on the day of the *Swan* fire. No one had used it since that ill-omened day.

The tower bells told the second quarter of eleventh hour, as I scrambled down the muddy bank, tucked in between the old planks and water's edge, and drew the voluminous cloak over my entire self. When the Guard Royale set their protective perimeter around the harbor, I would already be inside it.

The half hour stretched long and anxious in the pitch dark, my every sense twisted to extremity. Cold mud crept into boots and breeches. My mind worried at the earthenware vial and its telltale drop of blood, pawing through evidence—conversations, dates, and times. I longed for light to consult my journal. My conclusion did not change: Dante could not be the Aspirant. Even the thought, dismissed, appalled and terrified me. No matter passing doubts, no matter his erratic behavior, I refused to believe Dante was bent.

When the tower bells rang middle-night, I poked my head from my shroud and gratefully shed every consideration but the present venture. White, gold, vermillion, and emerald fire seared the night sky all up and down the river. No kingdom in the world could produce the intense colors of Sabrian fireworks. Magic, some called it, though I knew our alchemists had found the secret in their minerals. I crept out from my hiding place and straightened my borrowed hat. Another burst of mixed yellow and green provided a springlike bower of light for the shallop emerging from the Spindle's water gate.

Boots squelching, I scuttered along the steep bank toward the central harbor. When the bank began to flatten and voices murmured nearby, I assumed a drunkard's meandering gait.

With a fierce satisfaction, I noted some two hundred courtiers gathered at the pier. Outside the ring of the Guard Royale, a thousand or more citizens of Merona trilled their pipes, thumped their tabors, and set up howls and cheers at each burst of colored fire.

Wandering up the bank, I waved at no one in particular and fumbled

with my breeches, as if I'd relieved myself at the riverside. Unnecessary playacting. The guards faced outward toward the common mob, and the eyes of the courtiers were fixed on the approaching shallop or on the wharfside street above the mudflats where blazing torchlight illumined the waiting King of Sabria.

The heavy night breeze flapped pennons and shifted cloaks. I forced myself to breathe as the rowers shipped oars and glided the last metres into the pier, tossing lines to those on shore.

Liveried dockhands assisted the flock of ladies, fifteen or twenty of them indistinguishable in dark, hooded cloaks, onto the wide pier. The queen, regal in her pale cloak and gown, glittering with diamonds and rubies, stepped out of the shallop last. Every eye was drawn to her.

A lanky man in emerald satin burst free of the waiting nobles and into the chattering cluster of gentlewomen as they walked up the pier. He embraced each of the brave attendants in turn, swinging her round in exuberance, as his great cloak filled like green wings. Ilario.

Rebecs, shawms, and pipes spun a wild and merry gigue, and the crowd erupted in disbelieving laughter as Ilario danced with the ladies along the pier and muddy bank. When the chevalier bellowed at other men to join in the celebration, a goodly number did so.

Reluctant to involve him in our risk, I had not asked Ilario to create such a distraction, but I blessed it. With all eyes at the center, no one noticed when another fellow—I—in black cloak and gray hat, embraced one of the queen's dark-cloaked ladies and danced her away from the new arrivals and into the crowd of dignitaries.

I'd never felt such an embrace—the softness I had imagined the first time I'd seen her, the desperate thanks, the radiant affection that her great eyes spoke with my name. "Dear, kind Portier."

I swept my voluminous cloak about her. "Switch cloaks with the one in my bag." I whispered. "Quickly, as we dance."

In the press of the crowd, it was unlikely that anyone noted that the gray hat was swept from my head and trampled underfoot, or that when I released the lady from my enveloping embrace, she wore a hooded summer cloak of bright blue. On this night, the brighter color was the better

disguise—Eugenie's own suggestion. By the time Ilario released the laughing gentlewomen, and they strung out along the boardwalk laid across the mudflats from pier to wharfside, no one pointed out that there were fewer ladies by one than had been rowed out of the Spindle.

Maura and I ambled up the boardwalk with the rest of the queen's guests. Two sobering, solid lines of the Guard Royale flanked our path, holding back the raucous mob. Maura shook so violently that I feared someone would notice. But I gripped her tight and babbled noisily of kings and queens and the ridiculous Chevalier de Sylvae, and bent down to kiss her once—which was entirely foolish, but seemed to calm her at the least. Her lips were cold as Journian frost.

At last Eugenie, too, stepped onto Sabria's shore. Ilario bent his knee before her. She raised him into a long embrace, but sent him on and walked up the long path from the pier alone. At last, beneath the blazing torches, she knelt gracefully before her king. To the cheers and wonder of the citizens who'd come to the riverside thinking to see only fireworks, Philippe raised her up and bowed before her in turn, greeting her not as a prisoner indulged, but as Sabria's rightful queen.

Only as the royal couple strolled hand in hand down the wharfside toward Market Way did some sharp-eyed observer point out the orange flares spit up from Spindle Prison. Almost lost in the fireworks, the warning of a prisoner's escape caused only murmurs at first. *But the queen's released . . . king's come to fetch her . . . other prisoners? . . . There, look, another flare!*

More serious shouts soon followed. As Maura and I mingled with the protected elite on the wharfside way, guardsmen spread quickly down the shoreline all the way to Massimo Haile's slip.

I blessed my guiding angels that I had not followed my first instinct to get Maura out of the crowd quickly and go back the way I'd come. Unfortunately, the second line of guardsmen constricted about our party of courtiers. Of a sudden, my plan to slip quietly into tiny, dark Fish Lane where Calvino de Santo waited seemed incredibly naive.

The royal couple, oblivious to the rising disturbance, mounted their waiting horses, as did Lady Antonia and Ilario, who waved his feathered hat and blew kisses at every person wearing skirts and some who didn't.

Philippe's bodyguards encircled the four and escorted them on a slow progress up the boulevard. The rest of us, including the queen's ladies, were held back by the orders of Captain de Segur, the very captain I'd sworn to obedience beside Edmond's body. Cursing fortune and my discarded hat, I ducked my head.

The captain dispatched searchers into the dockside lanes, then climbed atop a cart to address the restive party. "Honorable ladies and noble gentlemen, one moment please," he bellowed. "We've signs that a prisoner has taken advantage of this happy occasion to escape the Spindle. For your protection, we ask you to remain here. We'll escort you to your conveyances a few at a time. . . ."

"Portier, move away from me," Maura whispered.

I gripped her hand the harder and scoured our surroundings for a way out. My anxiety was not at all soothed by the sight of another boat lamp halfway across the strait between the Spindle and the shore. Once the boat landed, Captain de Segur would know exactly for whom he was looking.

A soldier burst from one of the steep side lanes and ran to the captain for a hurried conference. My heart lurched as the captain's sharp eyes roved our party of anxious nobility and lit on me. "Sonjeur de Duplais! Please join me here."

"Fish Lane," I said softly, ducking my head in the captain's direction. "Ten houses in. As soon as you're free to go." I squeezed her hand and dropped the bag containing her black cloak.

Spirit aching at abandoning Maura, I pushed through the grumbling party. "What is it, Captain? I've duties."

He jumped down from his perch. "Fortunate you're here. We've found the fugitive."

It required every bit of discipline I possessed to refrain from looking over my shoulder. "Indeed?"

"The sorcerer was hiding on a balcony overlooking Market Way, exactly where the king was to pass. We need you to identify him."

"A sorcerer . . . Fedrigo!" I spluttered, relieved and astounded. "But I thought—"

My racing mind shifted tactics. Captain de Segur surely realized that Adept Fedrigo was unlikely to be the prisoner escaped from the Spindle, but he couldn't be certain until the boat landed. And without doubt the noblemen and ladies surrounding us were entirely unused to standing in the damp wind surrounded by soldiers. They were ready to mutiny.

"Well, heavenly legions, that's excellent, a fine job!" I shouted, slapping the captain on the shoulder. "Certainly, I'll come with you. Now the fugitive is found, we can allow His Majesty's friends to be on their way unhindered. Bravo! His Majesty will be delighted."

No more than that was required to stir the prickly aristocrats. They began to clamor as one and push through the ring of guards. Only a few hours had passed since I was issuing orders under the king's authority. De Segur had little choice but to follow my lead. The captain ordered his men to release the guests to proceed home as they would.

As the party dissolved, I gripped Captain de Segur's hand firmly. "Sir, you are a credit to the Guard Royale. As you witnessed but a few hours ago, this murderous Fedrigo's infamy ranks second only to that of de Vernase himself in the king's mind." That was most certainly true.

"Then we'd best make sure this man's the one we're supposed to be hunting, hadn't we, sonjeur?" said the captain, his syllables crisp.

"Certainly," I said, then held my breath for a moment as a bright blue cloak vanished up Fish Lane. *Godspeed, sweet lady.* An iron yoke slipped from my spirit, leaving me with an odd certainty: Maura would be all right.

My awareness of enchantment grew stronger the farther into the alley the young soldier led me. With every step, it galled my spirit worse, grinding, gnawing, making me want to retreat.

Never had my sense suggested a rightness or wrongness about spells it detected. It merely signaled that one existed and registered its relative strength. Dante's door wards bit, but that was the *effect* of the spell, and had naught to do with my perception of its existence. In the same way, magical residues presented as more pleasurable or less, but I had never corre-

lated a pleasurable sensation with a worthwhile end or vice versa. But this enchantment clamored evil. Whoever had created it, Fedrigo or other, was someone to be wary of.

The fugitive had been trapped at the blind end of the alley—the back of a ramshackle warehouse, flanked by a tall fence and a deserted house. Face down in the weedy corner, the large man bucked and thrashed, while two soldiers sat on his back, one of them attempting to bind the prisoner's ankles. A young officer held a lantern.

"Captain de Segur sent me to identify the fugitive," I said.

"He ought to have sent more hands to hold the toadeater," said one of the soldiers, a burly man whose knees clamped the prisoner's waist and whose fist snarled the prisoner's hair. His own head looked to have been scraped on the splintered fence. "Or mayhap an iron to crush his skull."

"Hold the light down here," I said, and I crouched where I could see the captive's face.

The prisoner growled at me fiercely, but I could see enough. His dark beard was trimmed closer than last time I'd seen him, and other men could have a neck the same width as their heads, but I would never mistake the nose that looked as if it had been broken ten times.

"I do believe you've earned your king's favor, gentlemen. Please sit him up. And you"—I nodded to the young soldier who'd fetched me—"notify Captain de Segur that this is indeed the man we sought. Remind him that His Majesty wished to be notified the moment we found him." The guide sped away.

"Sitting him up" was a violent business. In the end, the two guardsmen had to bind Fedrigo's thick hands and truss knees, arms, and ankles before they could prop him against the warehouse wall.

"What vileness were you about tonight, Adept?" I said. "Bleeding more children? Or delivering another murdered soldier to your king?" In answer, he hawked bloody spittle in my face.

"We've not got a word out of him," said the young officer, cradling his own left wrist to his chest.

I wrenched open the adept's sleeves and shirt, but found no evidence of transference. "So, unlike Gruchin or Ophelie de Marangel, you are

a willing conspirator," I said. "Gaetana's creature. The Aspirant's creature."

He grinned, fresh blood staining his teeth and leaking out the corners of his battered mouth.

"Where is Michel de Vernase? And what's this spellwork hanging about you like a dead man's stink?"

He widened his eyes like an innocent child accused. He was not afraid, though. True, Fedrigo did not know of Dante's perimeter. And we could not use it at trial to link Fedrigo with Edmond's body without revealing Dante's role in the investigation. But we could surely roust the door guards who helped him carry in his "sickly kinsman" wrapped in purple. Why was he not worried?

I snapped my attention to the officer nursing his damaged wrist. "Your messenger implied the prisoner posed a danger to the king. In what way?"

The young greville flushed. "He was lurking on a balcony overlooking Market Way—the place where it gets narrow going round Sweeper's Rock. Looked as if he were going to drop a rock right down on the king's head. Turned out it was only this book."

The officer held the lantern high. A splintered board protruded from the fence as if Fedrigo had been trying to rip an escape route through it. An open book lay over the tip of the board, as if a reader had marked his place. The large, tattered volume—seven or eight centimetres thick, its wide pages limp with the damp—drooped from the narrow slat.

"This was the *weapon* he held on the balcony?"

"Aye. Ready to drop it over the side, till Orin kicked open the door and took him down. He never got a chance. Though it's not exactly a man's weapon, is it, pig snout?" The biggest soldier slammed a boot into Fedrigo's side.

Despite the blow that pumped more blood from his mouth and left him slumped awkwardly, Fedrigo grinned again, sly and wicked. Eager.

I sat on my haunches, at eye level with the book. Perhaps my perception of magic had been stripped and clarified back in the Rotunda, just like my other senses, for, as sure as my name, I knew this book held more death in it than any weapon I'd ever come near.

Thwarted at his game of magical chaos when we destroyed Eltevire and Gaetana, Michel de Vernase had retaliated by eliminating Philippe's heir. But the king had surely not found time to scribe a new name on the tablet in the crypt. His death would ravage Sabria. This time Michel meant to kill.

"Has anyone touched it?" I said. "How did it get in this position?"

The three soldiers looked at one another. "None of us had aught to do with it."

Fedrigo's eyes flicked from me to the book and back again.

"In the fight on the balcony . . . did the book get dropped or juggled?"

Orin, the young greville with the broken wrist, had been puzzling at my questions, but this one triggered something. "It didn't. I thought it was odd. When I came after him, I thought he'd drop it and run, but he curled up around the thing, then kicked me so hard I near took a dive off the balcony myself. By the time the others showed up, the villain had ducked out."

And led them here. Cornered, he had tried to rip through the fence . . . then placed the book.

Carefully I lifted the worn leather cover, so thin a wind would wrinkle it like paper. Recalling the banners on the *Swan*, I shielded my eyes with my free arm, but no spits of fire leapt out. The title page read *Covenants of Civil Properties in the Demesne of Challyat*, which meant nothing to me. Naught seemed hidden between its pages. I lowered the cover gently. The board creaked.

The impact of the book itself wouldn't kill, even with a square hit on someone's head. But memories of the *Swan* would not leave me, nor would Ophelie's family or Gruchin's. "Have you a fondness for fire, Adept?"

Fedrigo shrugged, but the roused hunger on his bruised face answered all. A spark on the Market Way at its narrowest point—the oldest houses in Merona—would rage through Riverside like summer lightning in the maquis, and up the hill into the city proper.

Now his eyes were on the book, Fedrigo could not look away. A man who loved fire. A man unafraid, perhaps because he *intended* to die. Which

meant we all would die . . . and Philippe, too. I had just sent him notice that one of his son's murderers sat in this alley. *Saints defend us.*

So, Portier, you can try to move the book to a safer place—like the river—or you can sit here and wait for this little trap to fall and explode or whatever it's designed to do.

"One of you bring water," I said, in focused urgency. "Enough to douse the book and more. Hurry!"

Fedrigo's smug expression told me that would not be enough.

"Greville Orin, get you to the palace and find one of the mages— Dante, if you can find him, or Orviene—and get him to come here. Tell them that Duplais says there's a challenge here that devil's fire will not explain. And hurry. Whatever you do, make sure the king keeps away. He *must not* return to Riverside. Do you understand?"

"Understood. I'll spread the word of more fireworks to come at the river, as well." He set the lantern well away from Fedrigo's feet. "Hagerd, be alert. The prisoner is your charge."

"Good man." Better than me to think of a way to empty Riverside without causing a riot.

I crouched near the book like a useless schoolboy, Fedrigo's sly grin driving me to distraction. Had he some alternative trigger to ignite the book? Surely he'd not have perched it so precariously, if so. I dared not move it, but the torn plank could give way at any moment. The imagining had sweat beading my brow and the burn scars on my hands twinging.

"Did *you* work this nasty spell?" I mumbled, knowing full well Fedrigo would not answer.

But the answer came anyway. The magic that hung about the book was huge, not simple. Even I could sense so much. But Dante had called Fedrigo's magic that darkened the Rotunda *infantile.* Darkening spell . . . *blanking spell . . .*

I pulled out the wadded loop of silk-threaded string Dante had given me and dangled it in the air. "Perhaps the one who taught you to work blanking spells is the same who ensorcelled this vile book. We're going to discover who it is whether you speak or not. Whether you die or not."

Fedrigo's smirk faded. His thick neck reddened and spittle dribbled from his mouth. Perhaps his voice had been muted like Gruchin's.

"Not a twitch," growled Hagerd, pressing his sword tip to Fedrigo's belly.

Gaetana hadn't bound this spell; Michel's vengeance had flared to murder only after Eltevire was destroyed and Gaetana dead. Nor had Fedrigo; if Fedrigo was capable of sophisticated spellwork, why would he have used something *infantile* as he deposited Edmond's body? Certainly an experienced spellworker could bind his spells poorly if he wanted. If he had reason. If he wished to make investigators think him incapable. . . .

I twined the looped string about my fingers. And I recalled an impatient Dante poking his staff into an enclosure loop before it could be picked up—one of two loops laid side by side behind the dais in the Rotunda.

"Souleater's bones," I whispered. "*Orviene* taught you spellwork." The incapable Orviene, who had somehow earned a mage's collar. So kind he was . . . so concerned for his poor missing adept. Orviene had asked me if Ilario might know why Fedrigo had gone to the docks on the day the adept was supposedly knifed, yet, when questioned, he had reported Fedrigo perpetually short of money and in the habit of gambling. Indeed, Orviene had pointed me repeatedly at Gaetana, and I, like a dotard, had followed his accusing finger. Of all men, I should have known to look harder at a fool.

Narrowing his eyes and curling his lip, the adept squirmed, and the swordsman shifted his blade to Fedrigo's throat. The magic grated at my spirit, growing like a canker, like raw poison. Gods, where was the man with water? What if Dante refused to come?

I glared at the damnable book and imagined how Dante would proceed. He would see an overused book, smudged and worn. My enlivened senses could smell the dusty shelves where it had lain, the smoky lamps that had illuminated it, could hear the voices reading it, discussing, arguing over it. *Covenants* meant lawyers and magistrates and registrars and property disputes. Angry people had used this book. Maybe that's why it was so tattered. None were so angry as Fedrigo, a man who

burned innocents for pleasure, who would burn himself to keep his master's secrets.

Yet those who had made the book's pages—those who shredded the old linen, soaked and washed and pulped it, spread it in its frame, pressed and dried it—had no clue as to what might be written upon them. Paper could hold poems or stories, accounts or covenants—endless possibilities. And those who brewed the ink, and the binders and printers, for this was a printed book . . . all their labor and invention had gone into a volume destined to hold a cruel and evil spell to murder a king and fire his city. I inhaled deeply of the Riverside stench, of the fishy harbor and the dry wood of the warehouses—every sensation crisp and hard-edged and alive.

Fedrigo, scarlet-faced, growled and rocked his massive body, as I pulled off the link belt I wore over my tunic, clipped the ends together, and laid it gently around the book. He roared, even as Hagerd's rapier bit his fleshy neck.

I grabbed a fistful of dirt and laid it atop the book, evenly so as not to upset its balance, and sat down near the warehouse wall. Closing my eyes, I built the rune in my imagining, encircling the book as it lay on the plank, incorporating everything I'd considered. Dark curling lines for the inked words, ragged white strips for the paper, rectangle for the presses . . . and before I knew it, I was painting the rune with red blotches for anger, and orange, blue, and white arrows for flame, black claws for evil intent. . . .

Fedrigo began to slam his bound feet to the ground. The soldier kicked him, and I wanted to scream at them to stop, for I felt the heat rising. Not in my flesh, but in my bones. In the part of me that understood these things, a part of me I had not visited since I was a child and felt the stirrings of power that made me dream of magic.

I considered *coolness*, *damp*, and *stillness*, and the heaviness of dirt that could smother a fire.

Fedrigo yelled, wordless, guttural, gurgling yells. The swordsman grunted and crashed to the ground, his legs kicked out from under him. But I did not see the plank give way and the book fall, because my eyes

were focused inward, where walls and barriers toppled like paper standards struck by the pendulum.

"Sonjeur, the book!" This time the blaze seared my cheeks, and the crackling quickly rose to a thunder like fifty horses galloping together.

Fedrigo's agitation erupted in crows of triumph.

But I sought the power that lived in the pattern I had made, and I joined it with what lived in me, born in my blood. And as if the spout of flame had been sucked into my veins, enchantment roared through me, unruly and awkward, but building, rushing, towering, shivering my foundation, swelling heart and lungs and filling me with torrents of magic. I spread my arms and bellowed in the triumph of a lifetime's longing.

I did not need to open my eyes to know the book was ash or that Fedrigo glared at me with such hatred as would eat a man's heart, for I had built his hate into the keirna of his book, and I had quenched it with the glory of my art.

CHAPTER THIRTY-FOUR

30 CINQ

5 DAYS AFTER THE ANNIVERSARY

The trial of Michel de Vernase-Ruggiere, Maura de Billard-Vien, Orviene de Cie, and Fedrigo de Leuve for murder and high treason began and ended on 30 Cinq in the 877th year of the Sabrian Kingdom in the city of Merona. Philippe de Savin, King of Sabria, Duc de Journia, Protector of the Fassid, Overlord of Kadr, sat in judgment, in company with a Judicial Scribe and seven Magisterial Advisors, drawn by lottery, as prescribed by Sabrian Law.

Of the four accused, only Orviene de Cie and Fedrigo de Leuve were in attendance. The Conte Ruggiere and Damoselle ney Billard remained at large. A mage of the Camarilla Magica sat as family advocate for de Cie and de Leuve. The Chevalier de Vien refused to send a representative to his daughter's trial, stating that the family maintained no further interest in Damoselle Maura's person or fate. Representing the Conte Ruggiere's family was Damoselle Anne de Vernase. . . .

I LEAFED THROUGH THE NEAT pages, meticulously penned by the judicial scribe and delivered to me for review, scratching out a word here or there, replacing a sentence, correcting not the testimony itself, but its articulation. My cousin had insisted I complete the task immediately following the trial's adjournment to ensure that no questions remained unanswered before he announced his verdict publicly.

Countless activities came to mind as preferable for a soft summer evening after such a long and arduous day. I would have liked to close my eyes

and recapture the sweetness of Maura's embrace. I would have liked to write a letter to my mother and tell her I'd be home to visit soon, and express my hope that perhaps she would be feeling well enough to walk in Manor Duplais' lavender beds with me, as I knew she enjoyed that above all activities.

Magic, too, beckoned at this sunset hour, when the world itself donned a mantle of mystery and all things seemed possible. All these days, even when concentrating on this trial, my spirit had existed in a state of exaltation. So much to learn, to explore. Everything I'd read and studied lay before me like mysterious lands and oceans lay before the *Destinne*'s prow. Twice in the days since, I had ridden into the countryside and spent an afternoon creating simple spells, just to confirm this renewal was no cruel imagining. Each success but fed the yearnings that had ever lingered in my innermost heart, a deep and hungry burn like that of raw spirits or swallowed lightning.

But I would work no magic at Castelle Escalon as long as Dante remained there. He would sense it, and I was not ready to tell him. Somehow his terrible spellwork at the Exposition had shattered the walls and barriers he'd claimed stifled my magic, in the same way it had broken through my memory of my own death. I wanted to believe he had given me this unparalleled gift knowingly, as a friend. But until I understood what was happening with him, I would tell him nothing. It grieved me, but I dared not trust him.

So much for the Invariable Signs of sainthood. For those first few moments after magic had scalded my veins, Ilario's beliefs had come upon me in a rush of wonder. I had eluded Death three times, once so close as to smell the grass of Ixtador Beyond the Veil. What if I *was* Other? What if the recurrent dreams of my youth—the battlefields, the flood, the rescue that had gotten me chained to a rock—were the true memory of recurring lives?

I had quickly recovered my sanity. If I were a Saint Reborn, my inerrant perception of righteousness was, if not broken, then entirely confused.

And so I corrected a paragraph, then approved a swan's graceful glide

to its landing in the swan garden pond. Another paragraph and I watched the sky change color. After so many sultry days, the breeze ruffling the pond smelled of rain to come. I breathed deep, hoping that the most refreshing of all scents would cleanse my blood as Dante's sorcery had cleansed my head, for it seemed as if the facts and implications of this investigation had taken up residence in my veins and arteries, so that if I were to cut my arm I would bleed evidence. Appropriate, I supposed.

I turned another page. Two-thirds of the testimony was my own. The remainder I had elicited from witnesses, for my cousin had designated me Principal Accuser.

Calvino de Santo had testified to Michel de Vernase's actions in the aftermath of the previous year's assassination attempt. In return, Philippe commuted his former captain's sentence. De Santo could now find work and rebuild his life—outside of Sabria, I hoped, lest someday his king discover his role in Maura's escape. I wondered if Gruchin's spectre would yet haunt him outside the palace walls.

Audric de Neville had testified haltingly of Ophelie de Marangel's death. Philippe had granted royal clemency for the killing stroke Ophelie had begged from the old chevalier.

Chief Magistrate Polleu of Challyat testified that the fire that killed the Marqués de Marangel and his family had been traced to a carpenter's apprentice, whose money box at home contained receipts for *the building of crates to specification*, signed by Maura ney Billard. The apprentice's wife identified Fedrigo as a customer she had spied delivering "white paste in a jar of water" just before Ophelie's home burned. The carpenter's helper himself could not testify, as he had died in a fall less than a week after the Marangel fire. That small fact I recorded in my journal, another death to the Aspirant's account.

Henri de Sain witnessed to the shipments of crates by Maura ney Billard, bringing a solidity to the case that masked some of its more speculative elements.

A palace guard and a registrar identified Fedrigo as the householder who brought an "ill kinsman" into the Exposition, revealed later to be one Edmond de Roble-Margeroux, dead son of the king's great friend,

Lord Olivier. Captain de Segur's soldiers witnessed to Fedrigo's attempt to murder Philippe by dropping a fire-spelled book on his head.

Orviene had tried repeatedly to defend himself, babbling like a terrified child of his blindness to Gaetana's and Fedrigo's plotting. He claimed never to have seen the spelled book, and that the enclosure string turned over to the Camarilla had never bound a fire spell and was never his at all.

The Camarilla advocate sat silent through all this. His participation would have made no difference. Orviene and Fedrigo would be bound over to the Camarilla as soon as I verified the transcript. They would be dead by middle-night. The imagining did not grieve me.

Lianelle ney Cazar de Vernase initially refused to testify, until the Principal Accuser took her aside and pointed out that she could sit either in the witness chair or in her father's empty prisoner's box, accused of complicity to treason. The prospect of beheading at dawn the next morning tarnished the luster of defiance.

To give full credit to the girl's courage, however, she agreed only to give yea or nay answers. Though it made my questioning more difficult, I was happy at the solution. I was able to squeeze the story of Ophelie and transference out of her, while avoiding the matter of Eltevire or its disturbing nature. I avoided any testimony that might reveal Ilario's or Dante's roles as king's *agentes*. For Ilario's sake, if no other, our confederacy would remain as secret as I could manage.

Certainly, the most damning of all witnesses was Anne de Vernase, who identified Maura's letters, verified her father's signature on the letters that had sent Edmond de Roble to his death, and reported Michel de Vernase's last words to her: that it was his duty to "take down" persons he deemed corrupt, "no matter how highly placed . . . no matter the consequences." Nothing more was required of her.

Throughout the day the girl had listened to every word unflinching, never once meeting the eyes of her royal goodfather or anyone else in the chamber. When I had done with her questioning, it required three prompts for her to remove herself from the chair. She could not seem to take her eyes from the bloody lancets and scarificator we had found in her father's library.

It surprised me that Lady Madeleine would have sent her daughter alone into such an ordeal. Bad enough the girl had been forced to witness to her father's infamy. At the end when Philippe gave Anne an opportunity to speak in Michel's defense, the girl had shaken her head and remained silent.

Philippe's own demeanor, grim and settled more than angry, had not wavered throughout. He did not present Michel's last letter in evidence, but told his advisors that it laid out frustrated ambition as motive for Michel's crimes. I did not believe that was all, but it was enough for the Magisterial Advisors that Philippe was convinced of Michel's guilt. The burden of judgment was the king's alone.

And so we arrived at the verdict.

> *Michel de Vernase to be declared Outlaw, Abductor, Murderer, and Traitor, stripped of Title and Demesne, neither to be housed nor succored in any wise under penalty of Treason. Upon his arrest to be taken to Spindle Prison, there to be stripped, flogged, and executed by beheading, his body burned and ashes scattered in an unknown location, according to the law of Sabria.*
>
> *Maura de Billard-Vien to be declared Outlaw and Conspirator in Treason and Murder, neither to be housed nor succored in any wise under penalty of Conspiracy. Upon her arrest to be taken to Spindle Prison, there to be executed by beheading, according to the law of Sabria.*
>
> *Fedrigo de Leuve and Orviene de Cie to be declared Murderers and Traitors, to be remanded to the Camarilla Magica for the crime of Blood Transference. If the penalty adjudged by the Camarilla is in any wise lesser than the following, then to be returned to Crown custody, taken to Spindle Prison, there to be stripped, flogged, and executed by hanging, their bodies burned and ashes scattered in an unknown location, according to the law of Sabria.*

AND IT WAS DONE.

Without hesitation, I signed the document in the space reserved for the

Principal Accuser, capped my ink, and wiped my pen, and again wondered if I had done right.

My life held too little of faith to understand how Maura could have done what Michel told her without questioning, yet my conviction of her innocence remained unshakable. I had risked my life and carved out a piece of my honor to save her. Never again could I call myself an honest man, else I must give myself up as guilty of conspiracy as outlined in the verdict. And I would do it all again.

It was not love that made me believe. Though it might have grown to that, we scarce knew each other. We had spent perhaps six full hours in each other's company—both of us bound in secrets. Since that last cold kiss, my dreams of her were already altered. Her soft, self-contained beauty had become that of an indelible artwork, not a living, breathing woman. I wished her safe and happy, but the ache of not knowing where she was—and maybe never knowing—had quickly become manageable. Someday I might discover that I had been duped. Until then, I would rejoice in her freedom and believe.

Having tied up the documents and gathered my materials, I returned to the palace, waiting in an anteroom as the transcript was signed by Philippe and the Magisterial Advisors, sealed by Philippe's ring, and installed in the judicial archives. An attendant was dispatched to summon the family representatives to hear the verdict read. By morning, heralds would be spreading news of it throughout the kingdom.

Shortly after the arrival of the Camarilla advocate, two masked inquisitors, and four adepts, Anne de Vernase arrived. I rose when she entered the waiting room, bowed, and exposed my hand. She returned neither the greeting nor the gesture, but rather faced the judiciary chamber door with hands knotted in front of her. Great gods, what cruel mother sends a seventeen-year-old child alone to hear her father condemned?

The girl's flighty curls were already escaping the tight braid she'd worn for the trial. She appeared altogether small and pinched, as well she might. No matter what secrets she yet held, I felt sorry for her.

"Damoselle," I said quietly, when the attendant stepped out, "though

I understand your distraction, I would advise you to maintain protocol while you are here."

Her brow wrinkled, and she flicked a glance at me as if my meaning might be written on my face. I waved the marked back of my hand at her. "It is the law. I don't mind one way or another, but others might. Especially today."

With a shaking breath, she set her lips tight, returned her gaze to the door, and exposed her hand on her shoulder. She was trembling.

"Perhaps we should send for your mother." Out of all the verbiage I had directed at her that day, it surprised me that this suggestion broke her composure, evoking a spearing glance of hatred and contempt.

The door to the judicial chamber burst open, and the masked inquisitors came out, followed by the two sorcerers, shackled and shrouded in dark wool sewn with iron rings. An attendant held open the outer door.

"Damoselle de Vernase," said one of the Magisterial Advisors, poking his head from the inner chamber, "enter."

But the girl stood paralyzed, her face devoid of color, her eyes like copper medallions fixed in horror on the bullish Fedrigo—unrecognizable in his shapeless hood and gown. Holy angels, her father was reportedly a big man, like the adept.

"Creator forgive you, *Fedrigo*," I said, stepping close to the hooded giant. "No other can."

He growled and rattled his chains. The adepts shoved him forward.

The second, smaller prisoner stepped out of line, stumbling in his shackles. "Good, kind Duplais," Orviene babbled, "tell them I'm no good at magic! My father bribed the examiner at Seravain. I swear to every god and saint, I know nothing of spelled books . . . nothing of leeching . . . I didn't see their evils, their depravity. Please, do you know what's done to you in the Bastionne? Help me. Tell them. . . ."

The masked inquisitors wrenched him into line and shoved him through the door. I felt ill.

"Damoselle, present yourself." The summoning advisor waved at the attendant holding the door. "Mardullo, have the boy brought right away. This'll not take long."

Anne swallowed hard and followed the impatient advisor into the judiciary chamber.

For a quarter hour, I sat with throbbing head in my hands, trying to remember why I had ever taken on this investigation. Just as an advisor opened the door of the judiciary chamber, two members of the Guard Royale escorted young Ambrose into the waiting room . "Good," said the advisor. "Bring him in. And you are required, as well, Sonjeur de Duplais."

In the front of the square, somber room, Philippe, his seven advisors, and his judicial scribe sat at the same long, polished table they had occupied the entire day, the empty witness's chair facing them on the right, the four empty prisoners' chairs facing them on their left. The few rows of chairs reserved for observers remained empty, save for one on the first row where Anne de Vernase sat alone.

The guards installed Ambrose beside her. The youth, casting hostile glances about the room, gripped the arm of his sister's chair and bent his head her way. "So he did it, did he? Judged him guilty? Isn't it a relief we've a kindly guardian to care for us?" At least the lad did not bellow as he had on the night of the Exposition. Standing just behind them, I was likely the only person in the room who heard.

"Quiet your tongue," said the girl, intensely still, eyes fixed on her folded hands. "You must *think*, now. For your family. For your life."

Lord Baldwin motioned me to the witness chair. He served as examiner this time. "Sonjeur de Duplais, please recount your knowledge of the traitor Michel de Vernase's son."

As the boy sneered and rolled his eyes, I gave an accurate rendition of what I had seen at Montclaire and at Castelle Escalon. I did not report his insolence word for word, but no one in the room could fail to imagine what *insult* and *exuberant expressions of anger and resentment* meant. This judgment was quick:

"Ambrose de Vernase to be declared a Danger to the Crown and a Risk of collusion with a known Traitor, to be held in Spindle Prison until the Traitor Michel de Vernase is apprehended or until the King of Sabria determines he is no longer a Danger and a Risk, according to the Law of Sabria."

The judicial scribe passed me the document to review and sign. I wished I could argue that the judgment was harsh or unfair. But no sovereign with a mind would leave Ambrose free to carry tales to his father, to join him, or to be used as a pawn in Michel's cause by anyone else. House arrest would have been more generous, but at fifteen, Ambrose was clever and well trained. He had already eluded soft guardianship. And once word got out as to his father's crimes, Ambrose might not be safe outside the Spindle.

"I won't!" said the boy, reaching for his sister. All traces of youthful defiance fled. "Ani, tell them. I don't know anything!"

Michel de Vernase's children, faces pale and rigid with shock, were forced apart, one to be returned to her mother, the other remanded into custody of soldiers who bound his hands and would row him through three iron water gates into a dank and lonely prison. If the conte himself had been in that room, I would have snatched a guard's dagger and shoved it through the blackguard's heart. No matter their secrets and conspiracy, Michel had made these two and put them here. *He* was responsible.

I assumed this was the end of the day's ordeal. But as Philippe thanked and dismissed his advisors and scribe, he commanded me to stay behind.

The cold sweat that popped out under my layered garments had naught to do with the stuffy judicial chamber. Surely my cousin would have kept his advisors behind if he planned to enter another charge to the day's tally. I stood beside the witness box I had so recently left.

Philippe rose, removed his purple robe, and dropped his heavy pectoral chain and diadem onto the table amid the papers, ink bottles, bloody implements, and damning letters. He mopped his damp forehead, stretched his back and shoulders, then moved to the end of the long table where a decanter held enough wine to fill one cup. He lifted the vessel in query. "You've expended more words today than the rest of us together."

"Thank you, sire, but no. I've not the vigor to lift a cup just now."

He refilled his own and sat in one of the advisors' chairs, beckoning me to take a seat across the table from him. Instead of drinking, he set the cup on the table, fingering its stem and the embossed tree on its bowl. "My wife seems well recovered from her ordeal."

"I am gratified to hear that, lord." That he began with this did naught for my simmering nerves.

"She set Maura free, you know. Pretended a fainting fit. While the warder escorted one of her ladies to fetch smelling salts from the boat, she used a spelled ring to unlock Maura's cell. And what guards could keep count of a bevy of queen's ladies dressed in identical black, hooded cloaks on a night when fireworks lit the sky? It is much easier to manipulate your warder when you are the reinstated queen with full honors, rather than a prisoner awaiting release."

Exactly so. I smiled inside, even as my neck shrank with the imagined slide of cold steel.

"I understand why she did it. I forced her to find a place to take her stand. Putting her in the Spindle . . . one of her nature, so fragile in heart. No necessity—none—has pained me so. Payment must be made for such an insult, and this is mine. Indeed, when it comes to it, I am grateful to pay. But *damned* be this rift that must now persist"—his fist slammed the table so hard, the advisors' empty cups rattled and his own near toppled—"*damned* be these corrupted mages and the villain who used them, and *damned* be this office that must shape our privacy. The whispers about her will never be silenced."

Astonished at such a personal confessional, I trod carefully. "Your lady queen may be fragile of heart, lord, but she is a woman of extraordinary strength and conviction. I did not understand that before observing her close to. Perhaps, with your generous reception and public engagement, others will see those qualities, as well."

My cousin's finger dabbed at droplets of wine jarred out of the cup by his outburst. Then he dropped Dante's spelled ring on the table beside his cup. As it spun and settled, he raised his eyes, every bit a king's finest instrument, to meet mine. My body demanded to crawl under the table.

"It is well you told me from the beginning that you were a *failed* sorcerer, Portier, else I'd have to think you conspired with my wife to free the young lady. I apologize for that."

I wondered if vomiting would be excessively dramatic at this point. Philippe made no sign that he noticed how near it I was.

"You've done me great service, cousin, no matter that I detest the truth you've uncovered. It was a difficult task I set you. But your conduct has been exemplary, and you've shown extraordinary intelligence and insight, as Michel himself told me a lifetime ago that you could. I wish you to take a permanent position in my household and continue to sort out such complicated matters. Only a fool would believe the Aspirant has abandoned his ambitions just because we know his name and have lopped off his magical arms."

He sipped his wine.

"You may name the office as you like—aide, special counselor, royal investigator. *Agente confide* is no longer applicable, as my greatest enemy knows you work for me. But I will make clear to all that my earlier public assessments of your character, intellect, and motives were but a screen. Or"—he toyed with Dante's ring, then shoved it in my direction—"less comfortable, but perhaps more useful, we could leave such unjust assessments as they are and install you in some minor post, allowing you to remain . . . underestimated."

I was entirely wrung out, and if he intended that as punishment, it was a clever one. "Sire, you are most generous, and I am so very honored, but . . ."

For my life, I could not have explained why I did not grasp a royal appointment with both hands and crow to the powers of Heaven that now I would have leisure, means, and opportunity to find my way in the world. The art I had just reclaimed could not be practiced in the mouldering halls of Seravain, and I had no desire to live in a forest hovel as Dante had.

"In no wise can I make such a decision tonight."

"I understand," he said. "I've had few days so difficult as this. Take a little time." He tapped a fingernail idly on the table. "Have you heard that my wife plans to retain this other mage—your Dante?"

"No, lord." This news stung like a slap from an icy hand. Dante and I were finished here. The household acolytes and adepts had been advised by the Camarilla to return to Seravain.

"I don't like him."

"He did you good service, lord. Without him we'd never have unrav-

eled the deception of the arrow, Gaetana's interests, or the meaning of the spyglass or Eltevire."

"But tell me, cousin, what he did five nights ago—tell me it was cleaner, healthier than the spyglass magic."

And, of course, I could not. Philippe would not reveal what he'd seen. Perhaps he wasn't ready, as I was not.

He rose and extended his hand. "We did right today, Portier. No decision in this life is perfect. Would I could see ways to make such complexities more just, more nuanced. But that will take someone more subtle than either of us."

I kissed his ring. "Aye, my lord. We'll leave that for the future. And we'd best catch the villain first."

Likely he noticed I spoke only of Michel. And that I was not such a fool as to take Dante's ring.

UNABLE TO CONSIDER SLEEP, I decided to roust Ilario and tell him of the trial. "My lord's off meddling," said his surly valet, John Deune, who answered the chevalier's door. "Summat to do with the traitor's wife, no matter such is no proper concern of a gentleman."

The ever-awkward Deune took as much ridicule as his master, and with far less grace. I wondered that Ilario kept him on. I surmised no danger that the testy, dull-witted valet would decipher his master's secrets or develop ties with more clever courtiers who might.

I trundled off in search of the Lady Madeleine, curious as to Ilario's "meddling." A footman told me the Chevalier de Sylvae had headed off swearing and cursing, "as was wholly unlike himself," after visiting the Conte Ruggiere's private courtyard. "'Twas surely the strange goings out there," he said, embarrassed. He could describe what he meant only as *unlikely* compared to his experience of noble ladies.

Following the young man's direction, I threaded a snarl of west wing passages into the dark corner of a walled garden. The scent of jasmine hung heavy on the summer night, and clicking beetles and trilling

nightbirds were accompanied by the rhythmic scrape of steel on dirt and stone. Someone was digging . . . and humming. I drew aside a cascading vine.

A woman dressed in soiled white gauze sat inside a ring of fifty lit candles, plunging a spade into the dirt. Mounds of freshly turned earth pocked what had once been a square of grass and curving rose beds. The rosebushes themselves were broken and straggling, petals littering the ravaged yard. Cascades of flowering vines lay in great heaps, ripped from the enclosing walls.

"Mama, please come inside." Lianelle de Vernase crouched outside the ring of candles. "Ani's back. We need to tell you about Ambrose."

"But I cannot, my darling!" The woman leapt up and whirled around, her gown knocking several candles to the grass so that Lianelle had to stomp on the little flames before they set the lady or the garden alight. "So much yet to be done. I must bury every blossom before I go in, else how will they grow? Neither father nor son will come home till all the flowers are buried and risen anew."

Madeleine de Cazar's cheeks, arms, and flushed cheeks were smeared with dirt, and spittle ran down her chin. Her hair, unbound and tangled, flew wild in the night breeze. Her eyes flared excessively bright in the candlelight . . . and bore not the least scrap of reason.

No wonder Anne and Ambrose de Vernase harbored such spearing hatred. And no wonder at Ilario's distress . . . ever the chevalier at a woman's trouble. I refused to believe my questions had done this to Lady Madeleine, nor that Ilario would imagine it so.

Father Creator! Fear a viper's fang in my craw, I bolted for the east wing.

Dante's door stood open. Beyond it lay a horror to chill the soul. The mage's staff belched a scarlet whirlwind that had trapped Ilario at its heart. The young lord hung in the red mist above the circumoccule, a blur of pale skin, flailing limbs, and ragged lace and satin, spinning like a child's top.

"Was it the priggish librarian who allowed you to imagine you have a mind, peacock? Perhaps I must send you through the glass and leave you

a splotch on the paving to convince the earnest little insect that I mean what I say."

As I held speechless in the doorway, the red blur raced toward the windows, the garish reflection doubling the dread spectacle. But before a disastrous collision, the scarlet light vanished in an explosive brilliance, and Ilario plummeted to a heap at Dante's feet.

"Th'art a devil, mage. A dastard." Speech slurred, the chevalier pulled himself to his knees. "Don't need a fine education t'see it. You must heal the— Oof."

The heel of Dante's staff slammed Ilario's belly hard enough to shove him backward. "*Must*, cloudwit?"

"Stop this," I said.

"Must heal . . . contessa . . ." Another blow and Ilario gasped and doubled over. His hand twitched toward his sword, but he merely clenched his fist and shook it feebly . . . impotently . . . at the mage. Merciful god, he was not going to break his mask.

"*Must*, fool?" Another vicious blow.

Ilario groaned. "You. Ensorceled. Lady."

The mage raised the staff again.

"Dante!"

The mage's head jerked up, and his cold green eyes met mine. With a snarl, he slammed the staff down on Ilario's shoulder. Ilario bellowed in agony.

I charged. "Stop this, you misbegotten Souleater! Are you mad?"

Ilario bellowed, as the carved hornbeam landed yet again, this time on his upper arm. The bones cracked and ground. A quick blow to his side silenced his cry, just as I skidded to my knees and threw myself over him.

"Get this whining, lying dancepole out of my apartments." Dante raised his staff again, but it did not fall.

Shielding the chevalier's head, I slid my arm under his shoulder on the side opposite his injuries. "What's happened to you, mage?" I said. "Since when is Ilario the enemy?"

"He burst in here, threatening murder and issuing orders. I'll not have it, no matter who he is."

"Did Madeleine de Cazar threaten you?"

"Creeping aristos who dabble with secrets and sorcery break themselves." Much as he had opined at Montclair.

But the lady's sudden collapse violated every expectation . . . and Dante had made a point of touching her. And of all men, I knew that he could influence the minds of others. God's hand, he *had* done it.

I helped Ilario to his feet. Expecting the cursed hornbeam to land on my own back, I guided him into the passage. Though no hand touched it, the door slammed behind us.

Ilario cradled his left arm and gritted his teeth as I half carried him away. The moment we arrived at his apartments, I dispatched a gaping John Deune to fetch the chevalier's physician. "What were you thinking?" I said as soon as I had him on his couch, pillows supporting his arm. His complexion was the color of alabaster.

"Devil drove the woman mad," he spat through clenched teeth. "Jacard saw him work the magic. Couldn't leave it go without a word."

"But you knew you wouldn't draw a sword on him, either."

"Never thought he'd—" He tried to shrug, a disastrous move.

When he had finished puking up his last meal and lay wasted and trembling on his couch, he summoned a wobbling grin. "Could've. Could've taken him. Easy. Some of us have to live on could'ves."

The physician came and went, leaving Ilario trussed in plaster and linen. I shooed away John Deune with a promise to see the chevalier imbibed the prescribed poppy extract.

Despite a posture rigid with pain, Ilario made it clear he would do no such thing. "Can't," he said. "Might blab something I oughtn't."

The consequences of his chosen life seemed worse by the moment. "Can I fetch anything to help you sleep?"

"Stay till I'm snoring," he mumbled. "Might be tempted to throw myself off the balcony if I heave again."

For the next hour, I recounted the events of the trial and its aftermath. "I'd a mind to drop in on Dante after speaking to you," I said when I'd gotten through most of it. "Thought to inquire if it was my blood he used that night."

"Dante's gone rogue, Portier. He's more dangerous than the Aspirant or Gaetana or Orviene or any of them. Geni says not to bother my head, that she has 'an understanding' with him. But Madeleine's been in that courtyard seven days. Refuses to go inside. Refuses to change her garments. Sleeps where she drops. They try to coax her out of the sun, but it's all they can do to get her to eat or drink. Curdled my blood. And my good sense, obviously."

"I've been unconscionably blind," I said. "He has such a unique and marvelous vision of the natural world. I've never met a man whose passion burned so singular . . . and so bright. After Eltevire, I was certain we'd come to the beginnings of true friendship. But he was so angry when he found out I'd written that letter to the Camarilla. . . ."

"You're more a mush-headed idiot than my sister. Risking your lives for Maura against all evidence. Neither of you willing to condemn this villain mage. At least Geni doesn't claim to *like* him." He shifted uncomfortably, and I stuffed a silk cushion under his rapidly bruising left side. "You did not cause this, Portier. The Camarilla might have scared Dante a bit. Any sane man would get over it. And she's no friend of mine, but Michel de Vernase's wife is no weak-minded ninny. No *strain* or *questioning* broke her."

"I know it," I said. The admission wrenched my spirit. To imagine I'd allowed such talent as Dante's to plunge into an abyss of wickedness pained me more deeply than I could speak. But the escalating violence, breaking a woman's mind, coldly and deliberately brutalizing a man who posed no threat to him . . . Such acts demonstrated a ruthless intent far beyond playacting—beyond healthy anger. Beyond humanity. Not even I could excuse him any longer.

"Indeed, I've been the world's greatest fool," I said, wishing I dared down his neglected poppy extract and sleep for a year. "So tell me reasons. Why harm the contessa if he thinks to join Michel's depleted band? Naught in her answers hinted at complicity in anything criminal."

Ilario raised his brows in disbelief. "You really must learn more of the wicked world, Portier. What does one do to announce one's arrival in a new milieu? You demonstrate your power to the elite in a small, but very

important way. Force them to take note of you. If the one whose attention you crave is a villain, then you demonstrate your power in villainous ways. If the elite decide you are a valuable addition to their circle, they invite you inside."

This is exactly what I had set Dante to do, only we had purged the palace of its villains. But perhaps that was not the circle he aspired to. "That cannot explain this particular villainy," I said, feeling the sealed testimony of the day begin to rip open. "This will not endear him to Michel. If *Michel* wanted her silenced, he could have done it any day this past year."

Ilario drained his cup of wine and passed it to me to refill. "Ah, you see, Dante's act will only gain attention if Michel is a part of the circle he wishes to join. Its nature just tells us that Michel is not the *sole* part of it."

My conclusion followed immediately. "And not the most powerful part."

"He's made a bid to join them, Portier."

I returned to my apartments profoundly troubled. I could not disagree with either Ilario's premises or his conclusions, so clear and obvious when I looked back at the days since Eltevire. Why had I held such fierce certainty in Dante's character? I must be the world's purest idiot. Recalling the mage's pitiless face as he splintered Ilario's bones shook my very soul. What could drive a man to such a reversal of character?

Loyalty and causes, no matter how noble, meant nothing to Dante. His mutilated hand testified of pain as wretchedly familiar. For a man of his talents and will, I doubted any physical danger could coerce. And certainly no personal ties could be used to force him to some behavior unwillingly. Family was anathema, and he recognized no friends. Which left desire.

What Dante loved and desired was magic. He had been willing to sacrifice his physical well-being to delve deeper into sorcery. Had something he'd seen or heard in the Bastionne convinced him he would learn more on this divergent course? Certainly scruple would not restrain him in its learning or its use. What Sabria had seen on the night of the Exposition had likely been but the first hints of his delving.

Father Creator. I had brought him here. I was responsible for whatever he wrought.

But so was one decision made, at least. I sat down and penned an answer to my cousin.

My gracious lord:

You have honored me as kinsman and servant, in no wise more than by today's most generous offer. Your trust humbles and gratifies me. Forgive me, sire, but I cannot accept the position. My search for honorable service necessitates a different path. In concern for my fellow ugentes confide, I would ask that no tale of this investigation—and no defense of me— be released beyond what is already public. My deeds and prayers ever seek your welfare and that of our beloved Sabria.

Your kinsman,
Portier de Savin-Duplais

⸺

ON THE TENTH DAY AFTER his queen's release from Spindle Prison, Philippe de Savin-Journia returned to his Presence Chamber to conduct his public business and welcome a troupe of traveling players who would present a masque in celebration of his birthday. To the surprise of his courtiers and the pleasure of the king—and all gossips—Queen Eugenie graced the audience with her presence. Her pale rose gown trailed behind her like shredded clouds as she made her obeisance.

I had never seen such a genuine smile on my cousin's face as when he raised her up. Open, illuminating, transforming, that smile explained a great deal about Philippe's soldiers' and subjects' affection for him.

The king led Eugenie to her chair across the dais and one step lower

than his own. She whispered in his ear. He kissed her hand. The chamber rang with cheers and joyous applause.

I stood in the mass of courtiers along one side of the Presence Chamber observing this happy evidence of reconciliation. Gossips would note that Queen Eugenie's household had taken on a new shape this day. Certainly Lady Antonia was there, as always, her browless eyes scrutinizing the assembly. Ilario stood close, as well, in a rakish, feathered hat and his most outlandish doublet of yellow brocade, skirted to his knees and rife with silver beadwork that rivaled Eugenie's gown in elaboration. Bands of beaded silk strapped his shoulder and arm, broken in a riding accident, so rumor had it. The colorful crowd of acolytes and adepts was reduced to a pale, subdued Jacard and the queen's new First Counselor, the gaunt, dark-browed mage at her right hand. Gaetana's and Orviene's place was now Dante's alone.

Retaining him made sense. Naught had happened to change Eugenie's desire to feel her mother's hand and ensure the happiness of her dead children. The dread I had carried since the Exposition, reinforced at the sight of Madeleine de Cazar's madness, settled deeper in my belly.

"It is our delight that our queen joins us today in the business of the realm," said the king, now returned to his chair in front of the great planetary. "Before we welcome these visiting players, she wishes to announce an appointment. My lady . . ."

"It is my pleasure to name the new administrator for my household," said a beaming Eugenie, ignoring the chill that spread like hoarfrost from her First Counselor's grim countenance. Strong and determined, her voice carried all the way to the back of the Presence Chamber. "Someone to bring order to my frivolous life and see to the comfort of my dear ladies and valued counselors. A gentleman of quiet demeanor and superior skills—and excellent family connections."

Suppressing a sigh as I noted the hard twitch of Philippe's brow, and a shudder as Dante's gaze speared me with green fire, I made my way forward to kneel at my gracious lady's feet.

EPILOGUE

Midsummer

The Midsummer Fete was quiet this year. All celebrations pale after the Grand Exposition, a mere six months ago, and the public notice of Michel de Vernase's trial and conviction. The traitor is not yet found; nor, thank all benevolent angels, is Maura.

My work in the queen's household is satisfying, and I am fading into bureaucratic anonymity—as I intend. But I am free of business for the evening and so wander into the Great Hall and Rotunda for my nightly visit, a habit I took up on the night I finally admitted Dante had turned. It is here I've found confirming evidence of my fears.

Until Ilario's Grand Exposition, and excepting the occasional coronation or royal wedding, the Rotunda and Great Hall had stood quiet and empty for more than three centuries. No longer.

Sitting on a bench placed for viewing the great pendulum, I watch wisps of light dance over my head. The glimmers are not sunbeams, for the sun failed more than an hour since. Nor are they some reflection of the passage lamps kept lit for the pendulum engineer and guards making rounds. Those lamps are few and hooded so that their weak, steady light falls on the floor.

No, these floating threads of blue, purple, and green can be seen ev-

erywhere in the Great Hall and Rotunda, though chiefly in the dome, occasionally illuminating a saintly hand or angel wing or dark-rimmed eye. Staring will not capture them, as they manifest themselves just as the eye gives in and blinks.

The whispers are just as elusive. I'm not sure anyone else has heard them, though every palace conversation since Prince Desmond's deathday speaks of palace hauntings. No one comes here alone anymore except for me, and even a companion's breathing would drown them out. But after so many nights, I know they are getting louder. I dread the day I'll be able to distinguish words.

What disturbs me more is the smell: cedar and juniper, dry grass and old leaves, touched with moisture and laced with a faint tinge of rot. I cannot find a source for it save in my memories of Eltevire and dying.

Dante has caused this.

One evening as I sat here, sensing these changes, watching the lights dance in the vault and spread into the Great Hall, I recalled something he had said just after the Exposition: "I've always considered lenses more fascinating than prisms."

And so I considered lenses. Which led me to think of spyglasses. And of spectres and of perimeters that might identify those who crossed. But magical perimeters could also serve as an enclosure for spellwork—a great circumoccule—a boundary. And if magic rose from every aspect of nature and not solely from the blood of a practitioner, then how much power could be derived from the keirna of seven hundred onlookers opening themselves to magic in a temple that had witnessed a thousand years of the human and divine?

Thus I began to think of the Rotunda as a great lens, and all of us who'd sat here on that night as peering through to see . . . what? Splinters fractured from the world we knew, as the rainbow colors of the Royal Astronomers were fractured from white light? Or had we been given a view into another place altogether?

These ruminations but affirm my decision to remain at Castelle Escalon and discover the truth. To keep watch on the one who made this happen. In the queen's service I can stand close by her mage. And if Dante

and his allies are lulled into believing my uncomfortable service to the king finished, all the better. No matter that my inerrant perception of righteousness is flawed, I see now what I am. I believe I am destined . . . meant . . . to stand against those who seek chaos. Against him.

Reaching into my boot, I pull out a heavy disk of silver and flip it high overhead. The coin catches the light of the lamp as it spins, twirling, glinting, displaying its two faces. For the span of a few heartbeats it hangs in the air, then drifts slowly to the floor.

Saints watch and guard us all.

ABOUT THE AUTHOR

Carol Berg is a former software engineer with degrees in mathematics from Rice University and computer science from the University of Colorado. Since her 2000 debut, her epic fantasy novels have won multiple Colorado Book Awards, the Geffen Award, the Prism Award, and the Mythopoeic Fantasy Award for Adult Literature. Carol lives in the foothills of the Colorado Rockies with her Exceptional Spouse, and on the Web at www.carolberg.com.

Thanks to all those who helped me bring this story to life. It's impossible to say enough about Linda, my brilliant muse, consultant, and friend—the spirit of Lianelle. And then, of course, Susan, Laurey, Glenn, Brian, Catherine, and Curt, who prod me to be better, and Brenda, who prods me to be. Thanks to Markus, the Fighter Guy, for his valuable consultations. But most especially this is for Pete, the Exceptional Spouse, whose patience and care keep life beautiful and together. I love you all.

ROC
Published by New American Library, a division of
Penguin Group (USA) Inc., 375 Hudson Street,
New York, New York 10014, USA
Penguin Group (Canada), 90 Eglinton Avenue East, Suite 700, Toronto,
Ontario M4P 2Y3, Canada (a division of Pearson Penguin Canada Inc.)
Penguin Books Ltd., 80 Strand, London WC2R 0RL, England
Penguin Ireland, 25 St. Stephen's Green, Dublin 2,
Ireland (a division of Penguin Books Ltd.)
Penguin Group (Australia), 250 Camberwell Road, Camberwell, Victoria 3124,
Australia (a division of Pearson Australia Group Pty. Ltd.)
Penguin Books India Pvt. Ltd., 11 Community Centre, Panchsheel Park,
New Delhi - 110 017, India
Penguin Group (NZ), 67 Apollo Drive, Rosedale, North Shore 0632,
New Zealand (a division of Pearson New Zealand Ltd.)
Penguin Books (South Africa) (Pty.) Ltd., 24 Sturdee Avenue,
Rosebank, Johannesburg 2196, South Africa

Penguin Books Ltd., Registered Offices:
80 Strand, London WC2R 0RL, England

First published by Roc, an imprint of New American Library,
a division of Penguin Group (USA) Inc.

First Printing, January 2010
10 9 8 7 6 5 4 3 2 1

Copyright © Carol Berg, 2010
All rights reserved

 REGISTERED TRADEMARK—MARCA REGISTRADA

Library of Congress Cataloging-in-Publication Data:

Berg, Carol.
The spirit lens: a novel of The Collegia Magica/Carol Berg.
p. cm.
ISBN 978-0-451-46311-1
I. Title.
PS3602.E7523S75 2010
813'.6—dc22   2009030454

Set in Bembo
Designed by Ginger Legato

Printed in the United States of America

THE
SPIRIT LENS

A NOVEL OF THE
COLLEGIA MAGICA

CAROL BERG

A ROC BOOK

"Valen is unquestionably memorable—in what is definitely a dark fantasy as much concerned with Valen's internal struggle as with his conflicts with others." —*Booklist*

"Chilling fantasy." —*Publishers Weekly*

"Fast-paced. . . . Berg creates a troubled world full of politics, anarchy, and dark magic . . . fascinating." —SFRevu

"Carol Berg has done a masterful job of creating characters, places, religions, and political trials that grab and hold your attention. . . . Don't miss one of 2007's best fantasy books!" —Romance Reviews Today

"[Berg] excels at creating worlds. . . . I'm eagerly awaiting the duology's concluding volume, *Breath and Bone*. . . . An engrossing and lively tale, with enough action to keep you hungry for more." —*The Davis Enterprise*

The Bridge of D'Arnath Novels

"A very promising start to a new series." —*The Denver Post*

"Berg has mastered the balance between mystery and storytelling [and] pacing; she weaves past and present together, setting a solid foundation. . . . It's obvious [she] has put incredible thought into who and what make her characters tick." —*The Davis Enterprise*

"Berg exhibits her skill with language, world building, and the intelligent development of the magic that affects and is affected by the characters . . . a promising new multivolume work that should provide much intelligent entertainment." —*Booklist*

"Imagination harnessed to talent produces a fantasy masterpiece, a work so original and believable that it will be very hard to wait for the next book in this series to be published." —*Midwest Book Review*

"[Seri] is an excellent main heroine; her voice, from the first person, is real and practical. . . . I'm truly looking forward to seeing what happens next." —SF Site

"Gut-wrenching, serious fantasy fiction." —Science Fiction Romance

"Excellent dark fantasy with a liberal dash of court intrigue. . . . Read this if you're tired of fantasy so sweet it makes your teeth squeak. Highly recommended." —Broad Universe

— Si vous le prenez, vous serez la première depuis un moment.

La voix de l'homme me fait sursauter. Je me retourne et vois une silhouette fluette dans l'embrasure de la porte.

— C'est pas si mal, là-bas ! proteste Bethan. Allez, viens boire ton thé et ensuite tu iras lui faire visiter.

Iestyn a le visage si mat et si ridé que ses yeux sont à peine visibles. Ses vêtements sont cachés sous un bleu de travail poussiéreux avec des taches de graisse sur chaque cuisse. Tout en me dévisageant, il boit bruyamment son thé à travers sa moustache blanche jaunie par la nicotine.

— Pour la plupart des gens, Blaen Cedi est trop loin de la route, explique-t-il avec un fort accent que je m'efforce de déchiffrer. Ils n'ont pas envie de porter leurs bagages aussi loin, vous comprenez ?

— Est-ce que je peux le voir ?

Je me lève, souhaitant que ce cottage abandonné dont personne ne veut soit la réponse.

Iestyn continue de boire son thé, faisant tourner chaque gorgée dans sa bouche avant de l'avaler. Il finit par laisser échapper un soupir de satisfaction et sort de la pièce. Je regarde Bethan.

— Qu'est-ce que je vous disais ? Il n'est pas bavard. (Elle rit.) Allez-y, il n'attendra pas.

— Merci pour le thé.

— Tout le plaisir est pour moi. Passez me voir une fois que vous serez installée.

J'en fais la promesse, tout en sachant que je ne la tiendrai pas, et me dépêche de sortir. Dehors, je retrouve Iestyn assis sur un quad couvert de boue.

Je recule d'un pas. Il ne s'attend quand même pas à ce que je monte derrière lui ? Un homme que je connais depuis moins de cinq minutes ?

— C'est le seul moyen de se déplacer par ici, crie-t-il par-dessus le bruit du moteur.

J'ai la tête qui tourne. J'essaie de peser le pour et le contre entre mon besoin de voir la maison et la peur primitive qui me cloue sur place.

— Bon, il va falloir monter si vous voulez venir.

Je m'avance et m'assois avec précaution derrière lui. Il n'y a pas de poignées et je ne peux pas me résoudre à tenir Iestyn par la taille, je me cramponne donc à mon siège tandis qu'il met les gaz et que le quad part comme une flèche sur le sentier littoral. Nous longeons la baie. La marée est maintenant au plus haut et s'écrase contre les falaises. Mais au moment où nous arrivons à hauteur du sentier qui descend à la plage, Iestyn s'éloigne de la mer. Il crie quelque chose par-dessus son épaule et me fait signe de regarder à l'intérieur des terres. Le quad fait des bonds sur le terrain accidenté et je cherche ce qui, je l'espère, sera ma nouvelle maison.

Bethan l'a décrite comme un cottage, mais Blaen Cedi n'est guère plus qu'une cabane de berger. Autrefois blanc, l'enduit a depuis longtemps abandonné sa lutte contre les éléments, laissant la maison virer au gris sale. La grande porte en bois a l'air dis-proportionnée par rapport aux minuscules fenêtres qui pointent le bout de leur nez sous l'avant-toit, et une lucarne me dit qu'il doit y avoir un étage, bien que l'espace soit réduit. Je comprends pourquoi Iestyn a du mal à le louer pour les vacances. L'agent immobilier le plus inventif qui soit aurait des difficultés à minimiser l'humidité qui remonte dans les murs extérieurs ou les ardoises déplacées sur le toit.

Pendant que Iestyn ouvre la porte, je tourne le dos au cottage et regarde en direction du littoral. Je pensais que je verrais le camping d'ici, mais le sentier a plongé depuis la côte, nous laissant dans une cuvette peu profonde qui nous cache l'horizon. Je ne vois pas non plus la baie, mais j'entends la mer se fracasser à intervalles réguliers contre les rochers. Des mouettes tournoient dans le ciel, gémissant comme des chatons dans la lumière qui faiblit ; je frissonne malgré moi, éprouvant soudain le besoin de pénétrer à l'intérieur.

Le rez-de-chaussée fait à peine quatre mètres de long ; une table en bois rustique sépare la pièce à vivre d'une kitchenette tapie sous une grosse poutre en chêne.

L'étage est partagé entre la chambre et une toute petite salle de bains avec une demi-baignoire. Le miroir a subi les ravages du temps : le verre marbré et craquelé déforme mon visage. J'ai le teint pâle des rousses, mais le faible éclairage rend ma peau encore plus diaphane, d'un blanc éclatant par rapport à mes cheveux roux foncé qui tombent plus bas que mes épaules. Je retourne au rez-de-chaussée et trouve Iestyn en train d'empiler du bois près de la cheminée. Il finit son tas et traverse la pièce jusqu'à la cuisinière.

— Elle est un peu capricieuse, observe-t-il.

Il ouvre le tiroir-réchaud avec fracas, me faisant sursauter.

— Est-ce que je peux avoir la maison ? dis-je. S'il vous plaît ?

Il y a une note de désespoir dans ma voix et je me demande ce qu'il pense de moi.

Iestyn me regarde avec méfiance.

— Vous avez de quoi payer, pas vrai ?

— Oui, dis-je fermement, même si j'ignore combien de temps vont durer mes économies et ce que je vais faire quand elles seront épuisées.

Il n'est pas convaincu.

— Vous avez un travail ?

Je repense à mon atelier recouvert d'argile. Je ne souffre plus autant de la main, mais j'ai si peu de sensations dans les doigts que je crains de ne plus pouvoir m'y remettre. Si je ne suis plus sculptrice, que suis-je ?

— Je suis artiste, dis-je finalement.

Iestyn grogne comme si ça expliquait tout.

Nous nous mettons d'accord sur un loyer qui, quoique ridiculement bas, arrivera vite à bout de l'argent que j'ai mis de côté. Mais le petit cottage en pierre est à moi pour les prochains mois et je pousse un soupir de soulagement.

Iestyn griffonne un numéro de portable au dos d'un reçu qu'il sort de sa poche.

— Donnez le loyer du mois en cours à Bethan, si vous voulez.

Il me fait un signe de tête et se dirige à grandes enjambées vers le quad, qui démarre dans un vrombissement.

Je le regarde partir, puis je ferme la porte et tire le verrou récalcitrant. Malgré le soleil d'hiver, je me précipite à l'étage pour tirer les rideaux de la chambre et fermer la fenêtre entrouverte de la salle de bains. Au rez-de-chaussée, les rideaux collent aux tringles en métal comme s'ils n'avaient jamais été utilisés, et je donne un coup sec, libérant un nuage de poussière d'entre leurs plis. Le vent fait trembler les fenêtres, le froid glacial s'infiltre par les interstices des châssis mal joints.

Je m'assois sur le canapé et écoute ma respiration. Je n'entends pas la mer, mais le cri plaintif d'une mouette solitaire ressemble à un bébé qui pleure, et je me bouche les oreilles.

La fatigue me gagne : je me mets en boule, passant mes bras autour de mes genoux, le visage collé contre la toile rêche de mon jean. J'ai beau la sentir venir, je suis submergée par une vague d'émotion, jaillissant avec une telle force de mes entrailles que je peux à peine respirer. La douleur que j'éprouve est si physique qu'il semble impossible que je sois encore en vie ; impossible que mon cœur continue de battre alors qu'il est en lambeaux. J'aimerais graver une image de lui dans mon esprit, mais tout ce que je vois quand je ferme les yeux, c'est son corps sans vie dans mes bras. Je l'ai laissé tomber et je ne me le pardonnerai jamais.

5

— On peut parler du délit de fuite, patron ?

Stumpy passa la tête par la porte du bureau de Ray, suivi de près par Kate.

Ray leva les yeux. Au cours des trois derniers mois, les moyens consacrés à l'enquête avaient progressivement été réduits afin de traiter des affaires plus urgentes. Ray faisait encore le point une ou deux fois par semaine avec Stumpy et son équipe, mais ils ne recevaient plus d'appels et il n'y avait rien eu de nouveau depuis des lustres.

— Bien sûr.

Ils entrèrent et s'assirent.

— On n'arrive pas à mettre la main sur la mère de Jacob, annonça Stumpy en allant droit au but.

— Qu'est-ce que tu veux dire ?

— Simplement ça. Son téléphone ne marche plus et la maison est vide. Elle a disparu.

Ray regarda Stumpy, puis Kate, qui semblait mal à l'aise.

— S'il vous plaît, dites-moi que c'est une blague.

— Si c'en est une, on ne connaît pas la chute, fit Kate.

— C'est notre seul témoin ! explosa Ray. En plus d'être la mère de la victime ! Comment vous avez fait pour la perdre ?

Kate rougit et il s'efforça de se calmer.

— Qu'est-ce qui s'est passé exactement ?

Kate regarda Stumpy, qui lui fit signe de parler.

— Après la conférence de presse, on n'avait plus vraiment besoin d'elle, expliqua Kate. On avait sa déposition et elle avait été débriefée, on l'a donc confiée à l'agent de liaison avec les familles.

— Qui était l'agent ? demanda Ray.

— Diana Heath, de la circulation, répondit Kate après une pause.

Ray nota le nom dans son carnet bleu et attendit que Kate continue.

— Diana est passée voir la mère de Jacob l'autre jour et elle a trouvé la maison vide. Elle avait filé.

— Que disent les voisins ?

— Pas grand-chose. Elle ne les connaissait pas assez bien pour laisser une adresse et personne ne l'a vue partir. C'est comme si elle s'était volatilisée.

Kate jeta un coup d'œil à Stumpy et Ray plissa les yeux.

— Qu'est-ce que vous me cachez ?

Il y eut un silence avant que Stumpy ne prenne la parole.

— Apparemment, des commentaires violents ont été postés sur un forum local. Un fauteur de troubles qui insinuait que c'était une mère indigne, ce genre de choses.

— Des propos diffamatoires ?

— Possible. Tout a été supprimé, mais j'ai demandé aux techniciens du labo d'essayer de récupérer les fichiers du cache. Et c'est pas tout, patron. Il semblerait que les agents qui l'ont interrogée juste après l'accident y soient allés un peu fort, qu'ils aient un peu manqué de délicatesse. Visiblement, la mère de Jacob pensait qu'on la tenait pour responsable et qu'on avait donc décidé de ne pas tout faire pour retrouver le conducteur.

— Bon sang ! pesta Ray. (Il se demanda si c'était trop beau d'espérer que rien de tout cela ne soit arrivé aux oreilles du préfet.) Est-ce qu'elle s'est plainte du comportement de la police à l'époque ?

— L'agent de liaison est la première personne à nous en parler, déclara Stumpy.

— Allez voir l'école, dit Ray. Il y a bien quelqu'un qui est resté en contact avec elle. Et interrogez les médecins. Il ne doit pas y avoir plus de deux ou trois cabinets de généralistes dans son quartier ; avec un enfant, elle était sûrement suivie par l'un d'entre eux. Si on trouve lequel, il aura peut-être envoyé son dossier à son nouveau médecin traitant.

— OK, patron.

— Et par pitié, faites en sorte que le *Post* ne sache pas qu'on l'a perdue. (Il esquissa un sourire ironique.) Suzy French va s'en donner à cœur joie.

Personne ne rit.

— Mis à part la disparition d'un témoin clé, poursuivit Ray, est-ce qu'il y a autre chose que je devrais savoir ?

— Les enquêtes transfrontalières n'ont rien donné, dit Kate. Deux ou trois voitures volées sont venues dans notre secteur, mais on les a retrouvées. J'ai écarté tous les véhicules qui se sont fait flasher ce soir-là et j'ai fait le tour des garages et des carrosseries de Bristol. Personne ne se souvient de quoi que ce soit de suspect. Du moins, c'est ce qu'ils disent.

— Comment Brian et Pat s'en sortent-ils avec les caméras ?

— Avec un gros mal de tête, répondit Stumpy. Ils ont visionné les enregistrements de la police et de la ville, et ils sont maintenant sur ceux des stations-service. Ils ont repéré sur trois caméras différentes la même voiture qui venait d'Enfield Avenue quelques minutes après le délit de fuite. Elle a fait deux ou trois tentatives de dépassement risquées avant de disparaître des écrans, et on n'a pas réussi à remettre la main dessus. Ils essaient de déterminer la marque, mais rien ne permet de dire qu'elle est impliquée.

— Parfait, merci de m'avoir tenu au courant. (Ray regarda sa montre pour dissimuler sa déception devant l'absence de progrès.) Pourquoi n'iriez-vous pas au pub ? Je dois appeler le commissaire, mais je vous rejoins dans une demi-heure.

— Ça marche, dit Stumpy qui ne se faisait jamais prier pour aller boire une bière. Kate ?

— Pourquoi pas ? Du moment qu'on m'invite.

Ray arriva au Nag's Head presque une heure plus tard et les autres en étaient déjà à leur deuxième tournée. Il leur envia leur capacité à passer à autre chose : sa conversation avec le commissaire lui avait laissé un goût amer. L'officier supérieur ne s'était pas montré désagréable, mais le message était clair : l'enquête touchait à sa fin. Le pub était calme et il faisait bon à l'intérieur. Ray espérait qu'il pourrait oublier le travail pendant une heure et parler de football, du temps ou de n'importe quoi qui n'était pas lié à un enfant de cinq ans et à une voiture disparue.

— Comme par hasard, tu arrives juste après que j'ai commandé, râla Stumpy.

— Ne me dis pas que tu as sorti ton portefeuille ? renchérit Ray. (Il fit un clin d'œil à Kate.) C'est un miracle !

Il alla chercher une bière et revint avec trois paquets de chips qu'il jeta sur la table.

— Comment ça s'est passé avec le commissaire ? demanda Kate.

Il ne pouvait pas ignorer sa question et il ne pouvait certainement pas mentir. Il but une gorgée de sa pinte pour gagner du temps. Kate l'observa, impatiente de savoir si on leur avait accordé plus de moyens. Il avait horreur de la décevoir, mais il faudrait bien qu'elle le sache à un moment ou à un autre.

— Assez mal, à vrai dire. Brian et Pat retournent dans leurs brigades.

— Quoi ? Pourquoi ?

Kate reposa son verre si fort que le vin fut à deux doigts de déborder.

— On a eu de la chance de les avoir aussi longtemps, dit Ray. Et ils ont fait du bon boulot avec les caméras. Mais leurs brigades ne peuvent pas continuer à les remplacer, et la dure réalité, c'est que rien ne justifie de nouvelles dépenses pour cette enquête. Je suis désolé.

Il présenta ses excuses comme s'il était personnellement responsable de cette décision, mais cela n'empêcha pas la réaction de Kate.

— On ne peut pas abandonner comme ça !

Elle s'empara d'un sous-bock et entreprit de le réduire en miettes.

Ray soupira. C'était si difficile, ce juste milieu entre le coût d'une enquête et le coût d'une vie – une vie d'enfant. Comment pouvait-on mettre un prix là-dessus ?

— On n'abandonne pas, répliqua-t-il. Tu es toujours sur les antibrouillards, non ?

Kate acquiesça.

— Soixante-treize feux ont été remplacés la semaine qui a suivi le délit de fuite. Jusqu'ici, les réparations prises en charge par les assurances sont toutes justifiées, et j'essaie de retrouver la trace des propriétaires qui ont payé de leur poche.

— Tu vois ? Qui sait ce que tu vas finir par découvrir ? On lève juste un peu le pied, c'est tout.

Il regarda Stumpy à la recherche de soutien moral, mais n'en trouva pas.

— La direction veut des résultats rapides, Kate, c'est tout ce qui les intéresse, dit Stumpy. Si une affaire n'est pas résolue en quelques semaines – quelques jours, dans l'idéal –, elle n'est plus prioritaire et elle est remplacée par une autre.

— Je sais très bien comment ça marche, affirma Kate. Mais c'est pas pour ça que c'est normal, non ? (Elle poussa les miettes du sous-bock pour en faire un tas au centre de la table. Ray remarqua que ses ongles sans vernis étaient rongés jusqu'au sang.) J'ai le sentiment qu'on y est presque, vous comprenez ?

— Oui, dit Ray. Et tu as peut-être raison. Mais en attendant, tu vas devoir travailler sur d'autres affaires en même temps. La fête est finie.

— Je pensais me renseigner du côté de l'hôpital, indiqua Kate. Le conducteur a peut-être été blessé dans l'accident : coup du lapin ou quelque chose dans le genre. On a envoyé une patrouille aux urgences du Royal Infirmary le soir même, mais on devrait creuser un peu, au cas où il ne serait pas venu se faire soigner tout de suite.

— Bonne idée, dit Ray. (Cette suggestion lui rappela quelque chose, mais il ne savait plus quoi.) N'oublie pas de vérifier aussi à Southmead et à Frenchay. (Son téléphone, posé à l'envers sur la table, vibra et il le prit pour lire le SMS.) Merde !

Les autres levèrent les yeux vers lui, Kate l'air surprise et Stumpy avec un large sourire.

— Qu'est-ce que tu as oublié ? demanda-t-il.

Ray grimaça mais ne répondit pas. Il vida sa pinte et sortit de sa poche un billet de dix livres qu'il tendit à Stumpy.

— Buvez autre chose. Il faut que je rentre.

Mags remplissait le lave-vaisselle lorsqu'il arriva, disposant les assiettes dans le panier avec une telle violence qu'il tressaillit. Elle avait les cheveux ramenés en une vague tresse, et portait un pantalon de survêtement et un vieux tee-shirt à lui. Il se demanda quand exactement elle avait cessé de faire attention à la manière dont elle s'habillait, puis regretta aussitôt cette pensée. Il ne pouvait pas dire grand-chose de ce côté-là.

— Je suis vraiment désolé, fit-il. J'ai complètement oublié.

Mags ouvrit une bouteille de vin rouge. Elle n'avait sorti qu'un verre, remarqua Ray, mais il jugea qu'il serait plutôt malvenu de le mentionner.

— C'est très rare que je te demande d'être quelque part à une heure précise, commença-t-elle. Je sais que parfois le travail passe avant tout. Je le comprends. Vraiment. Mais ce rendez-vous était prévu depuis deux semaines. Deux semaines ! Et tu avais promis, Ray.

Sa voix trembla et Ray passa un bras hésitant autour de ses épaules.

— Je suis désolé, Mags. Ça s'est mal passé ?

— Ça va. (Elle se débarrassa du bras de Ray pour s'asseoir à la table de la cuisine, puis but une lampée de vin.) Enfin, ils n'ont rien dit d'alarmant, mais Tom n'a pas l'air de s'être aussi bien adapté à l'école que les autres enfants et ils sont un peu inquiets à son sujet.

— Et qu'est-ce que font les profs ? (Ray alla chercher un verre dans le placard, le remplit et rejoignit Mags.) Ils ont bien dû lui parler ?

— Tom dit que tout va bien, apparemment. (Mags haussa les épaules.) Mme Hickson a fait tout ce qu'elle a pu pour le motiver et le pousser à être plus impliqué en classe, mais il refuse de participer. Elle dit qu'elle s'est demandé si Tom n'était pas tout simplement quelqu'un d'introverti.

Ray s'étrangla.

— Introverti ? Tom ?

— Eh bien, justement. (Mags regarda Ray.) J'aurais vraiment eu besoin de toi là-bas, tu sais.

— Ça m'est complètement sorti de la tête. Je suis vraiment désolé, Mags. Ça a encore été une journée chargée et je me suis arrêté pour boire une bière après le boulot.

— Avec Stumpy ?

Ray acquiesça. Mags avait un faible pour Stumpy, qui était le parrain de Tom, et elle fermait les yeux sur les bières qu'ils buvaient ensemble après le travail, car elle savait que son mari avait besoin de ces moments « entre hommes ». Il ne parla pas de Kate, il ne savait pas très bien pourquoi.

Mags soupira.

— Qu'est-ce qu'on va faire ?

— Ça va aller. Écoute, c'est une nouvelle école et ce n'est jamais facile pour un enfant d'entrer au collège. Il évoluait en terrain connu jusqu'ici et il se retrouve tout à coup propulsé dans la cour des grands. Je lui parlerai.

— Ne lui fais pas la leçon…

— Je ne vais pas lui faire la leçon !

— … ça ne ferait qu'empirer les choses.

Ray tint sa langue. Lui et Mags formaient une bonne équipe, mais ils avaient des approches très différentes en matière d'éducation. Mags était plus tendre avec les enfants ; elle avait tendance à les couver au lieu de les laisser se débrouiller seuls.

— Je ne lui ferai pas la leçon, promit-il.

— L'école a proposé qu'on voie comment les choses évoluent ces deux prochains mois et qu'on en reparle avec eux après les vacances.

Elle lui lança un regard qui en disait long.

— Fixe une date, dit Ray. Je serai là.

6

Les phares se reflètent sur l'asphalte mouillé, les éblouissant à intervalles réguliers. Les gens filent à toute allure sur les trottoirs glissants, les voitures qui passent éclaboussent leurs chaussures. Des feuilles détrempées s'amoncellent en tas contre les barrières, leurs couleurs vives ternissant peu à peu.

Une rue déserte.

Jacob qui court.

Un grincement de freins humides, le bruit sourd lorsqu'il percute le pare-brise et tourne sur lui-même avant de retomber sur la route. Un pare-brise flou. Une flaque de sang qui se forme sous la tête de Jacob. Un seul nuage d'haleine blanche.

Le cri déchire mon sommeil, me réveillant en sursaut. Il ne fait pas encore jour, mais la lumière de la chambre est allumée : je ne supporte pas l'obscurité. Mon cœur bat la chamade et j'essaie de reprendre mon souffle.

Inspirer, expirer.

Inspirer, expirer.

Le silence est plus oppressant qu'apaisant et j'enfonce mes ongles dans la paume de mes mains en attendant que la panique disparaisse. Mes rêves deviennent plus intenses, plus pénétrants. Je le *vois*. J'entends l'ignoble craquement de sa tête sur l'asphalte...

Les cauchemars n'ont pas commencé tout de suite, mais maintenant qu'ils sont là, ils ne s'arrêtent plus. Chaque soir, en me mettant au lit, je lutte contre le sommeil et imagine des scénarios différents, comme dans ces livres pour enfants où le lecteur choisit sa fin. Je ferme les yeux en serrant fort les paupières et répète ma fin à moi : celle où nous partons cinq minutes plus tôt, ou cinq minutes plus tard. Celle où Jacob est toujours en vie et dort en ce moment même dans son lit, ses cils noirs posés sur ses joues rondes. Mais rien n'y fait. Chaque soir, je me promets de me réveiller plus tôt, comme si en perturbant le cauchemar je pouvais d'une certaine façon changer la réalité. Mais on dirait que c'est devenu systématique. Depuis des semaines maintenant, je me réveille plusieurs fois par nuit au son d'un petit corps qui heurte le pare-chocs et de mon propre cri inutile tandis qu'il roule et retombe sur la route mouillée.

Je me suis transformée en ermite, cloîtrée à l'intérieur des murs en pierre du cottage, ne m'aventurant pas plus loin que le magasin du village pour acheter du lait et me nourrissant presque exclusive-ment de toasts et de café. Trois fois j'ai décidé d'aller voir Bethan au camping ; trois fois j'ai changé d'avis. J'aimerais me forcer à y aller. Cela fait très longtemps que je n'ai pas eu d'amis et jusque-là je n'en avais pas eu besoin.

Je ferme le poing de ma main gauche, puis déplie mes doigts, engourdis après une nuit de sommeil. Je n'ai presque plus mal à présent, mais ma paume et deux doigts sont restés insensibles. Je presse ma main pour chasser les fourmillements. J'aurais dû aller à l'hôpital, bien sûr, mais cela paraissait si insignifiant par rapport à ce qui était arrivé à Jacob. La douleur semblait si justement méritée ! Alors j'ai préféré bander moi-même la blessure, serrant les dents chaque jour en changeant le pansement. Elle a progressi-vement guéri, et la ligne de vie de ma main a disparu pour toujours sous une couche de cicatrices.

Je sors mes jambes de sous la pile de couvertures qui recouvre mon lit. Il n'y a pas de chauffage à l'étage et les murs luisent de condensation. J'enfile vite un pantalon de survêtement et un sweat-shirt vert foncé, laissant mes cheveux coincés dans le col, et je descends l'escalier. Le carrelage froid me coupe le souffle et je glisse mes pieds dans mes baskets avant de tirer le verrou pour ouvrir la porte d'entrée. J'ai toujours été matinale, debout au lever du jour pour travailler dans mon atelier. Je me sens perdue sans mon travail, comme si je cherchais désespérément une nouvelle identité.

Je suppose qu'il y aura des touristes en été. Pas à cette heure-ci et peut-être pas vers le cottage, mais sur la plage, sûrement. Pour le moment elle est à moi, et la solitude est réconfortante. Un pâle soleil d'hiver se fraie un chemin jusqu'en haut des falaises et fait miroiter les flaques gelées qui parsèment le sentier littoral contournant la baie. Je commence à courir, et mon haleine laisse des nuages de buée dans mon sillage. Je n'ai jamais fait de footing à Bristol, alors ici je m'oblige à courir pendant des kilomètres.

J'adopte un rythme en cadence avec les battements de mon cœur et me dirige vers la mer. Mes chaussures butent contre des cailloux mais mon pied devient plus sûr à force de courir tous les jours. Je connais désormais si bien le sentier qui va à la plage que je pourrais le descendre les yeux fermés, et je saute les derniers mètres pour atterrir sur le sable humide. Serrant la falaise, je longe lentement la baie jusqu'à ce que la paroi rocheuse me pousse vers la mer.

La marée est au plus bas, ayant laissé derrière elle une traînée de bois flotté et de déchets pareille au rond de crasse dans une baignoire. Tournant le dos à la falaise, j'augmente l'allure et sprinte à la lisière de l'eau, mes pieds s'enfonçant dans le sable mouillé. La tête baissée pour me protéger du vent cinglant, je lutte contre les vagues et cours à toute vitesse le long du rivage jusqu'à ce que mes poumons me brûlent et que j'entende mon sang siffler dans mes oreilles. Tandis que j'approche du bout de la plage, la falaise opposée se dresse devant moi, mais au lieu de ralentir l'allure, j'accélère. Le vent rabat mes cheveux sur mon visage et je secoue la tête pour me dégager. J'accélère encore et, une fraction de seconde avant de m'écraser contre la falaise, je tends les bras devant moi et plaque les mains sur la roche froide. Vivante. Réveillée. À l'abri des cauchemars.

L'adrénaline baisse et je me mets à trembler. Je reviens sur mes pas pour constater que le sable mouillé a englouti mes empreintes, ne laissant aucune trace de ma course entre les falaises. Un morceau de bois flotté gît près de mes pieds, je le ramasse pour dessiner un vague cercle autour de moi, mais le sable se referme avant que j'aie soulevé le bâton du sol. Contrariée, je vais un peu plus haut, là où le sable sèche, et je trace un autre cercle. C'est mieux. J'éprouve soudain une envie irrépressible d'écrire mon nom sur le sable, comme un enfant en vacances, et ma puérilité me fait sourire. Le bois est encombrant et glissant, mais je termine les lettres et recule pour admirer mon œuvre. C'est étrange de voir mon nom écrit de façon si nette et affirmée. Je suis restée invisible pendant si longtemps. Et que suis-je à présent ? Une sculptrice qui ne sculpte plus. Une mère sans enfant. Les lettres sont bien visibles. Elles s'affichent : assez grandes pour être vues du haut des falaises. Je frissonne de peur et d'excitation. Je prends un risque, mais ça fait du bien.

En haut de la falaise, une barrière inefficace rappelle aux promeneurs de ne pas s'approcher trop près du bord à cause des éboulements. J'ignore le panneau et j'enjambe le fil de fer pour me tenir à quelques centimètres du vide. L'étendue de sable passe peu à peu du gris à l'or tandis que le soleil prend de la hauteur, et mon nom s'étale au milieu de la plage, me mettant au défi de m'en emparer avant qu'il disparaisse.

Je décide de le prendre en photo avant que la marée monte et l'engloutisse, afin d'immortaliser le moment où je me suis sentie courageuse. Je retourne en courant au cottage chercher mon appareil. Mes pas sont plus légers à présent et je comprends que c'est parce que je cours vers quelque chose. Je ne fuis rien.

Te laisser partir

Cette première photo n'a rien de spécial. La composition n'est pas bonne, les lettres sont trop loin du rivage. Je redescends sur la plage et recouvre l'étendue de sable lisse de noms tirés de mon passé, avant de les laisser se faire absorber par le sable mouillé. J'en écris d'autres un peu plus haut ; des personnages tirés de livres que j'ai lus petite, ou des noms que j'aime simplement pour la forme des lettres qu'ils contiennent. Puis je sors mon appareil photo et m'accroupis sur le sable pour jouer avec les angles, prenant d'abord mes mots avec des vagues à l'arrière-plan, puis avec la roche et ensuite avec un joli coin de ciel bleu. Enfin, je grimpe le sentier escarpé jusqu'en haut de la falaise pour prendre mes derniers clichés, en équilibre instable au bord du vide, ignorant la peur qui me tenaille. La plage est recouverte d'inscriptions de toutes tailles, semblables aux gribouillis sans queue ni tête d'un fou, mais je vois déjà la marée montante lécher les lettres, emportant le sable avec elle tandis qu'elle avance sur la plage. Ce soir, quand la mer se sera une nouvelle fois retirée, la plage sera propre et je pourrai recommencer.

J'ignore l'heure qu'il est, mais le soleil est haut et je dois avoir une centaine de photos dans mon appareil. Mes vêtements sont maculés de sable mouillé et, en passant la main dans mes cheveux, je m'aperçois que ceux-ci sont raidis par le sel. Je n'ai pas de gants et mes doigts sont gelés. Je vais rentrer et prendre un bain chaud, puis transférer les photos sur mon ordinateur pour voir le résultat. J'éprouve un sursaut d'énergie ; c'est la première fois depuis l'accident que ma journée a un but.

Je me dirige vers le cottage, mais quand j'arrive à la fourche du sentier, j'hésite. Je repense à Bethan, à la boutique du camping, et à la façon dont elle m'a rappelé ma sœur. J'ai soudain le mal du pays ; avant de changer d'avis, je prends la direction du camping. Qu'est-ce qui pourrait m'amener à la boutique ? Je n'ai pas d'argent sur moi, je ne peux donc pas prétendre venir chercher du lait ou du pain. Je pourrais poser une question, je suppose, mais j'ai du mal à imaginer quelque chose de plausible. Quoi que j'invente, Bethan saura que c'est un prétexte. Elle me trouvera pathétique.

Ma détermination faiblit avant d'avoir fait cent mètres et je m'arrête en atteignant le parking. Je regarde la boutique de l'autre côté et j'aperçois une silhouette à la fenêtre. Je ne peux pas voir si c'est Bethan mais je ne vais pas attendre pour le savoir. Je fais demi-tour et retourne en courant au cottage.

J'arrive à Blaen Cedi et sors la clé de ma poche ; lorsque je pose la main sur la porte, elle bouge un peu et je me rends compte qu'elle n'est pas fermée. La porte est vieille et le mécanisme peu fiable : Iestyn m'a montré comment la tirer et tourner la clé selon un certain angle pour que les pièces s'emboîtent, et j'ai parfois essayé pendant plus de dix minutes. Il m'a laissé son numéro, mais il ne sait pas que je me suis débarrassée de mon portable. Il y a une ligne téléphonique au cottage, pas de téléphone ; je vais donc devoir aller trouver une cabine à Penfach pour lui demander de venir arranger ça.

Je ne suis à l'intérieur que depuis quelques minutes quand on frappe à la porte.

— Jenna ? C'est Bethan.

Je songe à rester où je suis, mais la curiosité l'emporte et l'excitation me gagne en ouvrant la porte. J'ai beau avoir voulu m'enfuir, je me sens seule à Penfach.

— Je vous ai apporté une tourte.

Bethan me montre un plat recouvert d'un torchon et entre sans attendre que je l'y invite. Elle pose la tourte à côté de la cuisinière.

— Merci. (Je cherche un sujet de conversation, mais Bethan se contente de sourire. Elle enlève son lourd manteau de laine et ce geste me galvanise.) Vous voulez du thé ?

— Seulement si vous en faites. Je suis venue voir comment vous alliez. Je me demandais si vous passeriez à la boutique ; je sais ce que c'est quand on s'installe quelque part.

Elle balaie le cottage du regard et cesse de parler en posant les yeux sur le salon dépouillé, qui n'a pas changé depuis que Iestyn m'a amenée ici pour la première fois.

— Je n'ai pas grand-chose, dis-je, embarrassée.

— Comme nous tous, par ici, observe Bethan avec enthousiasme. Du moment que vous êtes au chaud et que vous vous sentez chez vous, c'est le principal.

Je prépare le thé pendant qu'elle parle, heureuse d'avoir quelque chose à faire de mes mains, puis nous nous asseyons avec nos tasses autour de la table en pin.

— Comment vous trouvez Blaen Cedi ? demande-t-elle.

— C'est parfait. Exactement ce dont j'avais besoin.

— Petit et froid, vous voulez dire ? lâche Bethan avec un rire qui lui fait renverser du thé sur son pantalon.

Elle frotte la toile en vain et le liquide s'infiltre jusqu'à former une tache sombre sur sa cuisse.

— Je n'ai pas besoin de beaucoup de place et le feu me tient assez chaud. (Je souris.) Vraiment, j'aime cet endroit.

— Alors, quelle est votre histoire, Jenna ? Comment est-ce que vous avez atterri à Penfach ?

— Le coin est magnifique, dis-je simplement en baissant les yeux vers la tasse que j'entoure de mes mains pour ne pas croiser le regard perçant de Bethan.

Elle n'insiste pas.

— C'est bien vrai. Il y a pire, même si c'est un peu triste à cette époque de l'année.

— Quand est-ce que vous commencez à louer les mobile homes ?

— On ouvre à Pâques, répond Bethan. Et ensuite, c'est parti pour tout l'été jusqu'aux vacances d'octobre. Vous n'allez pas reconnaître le coin. Prévenez-moi si vous avez de la famille qui vient vous rendre visite et que vous avez besoin d'un mobile home. Vous n'aurez jamais assez de place ici.

— C'est très gentil, mais je n'attends personne.

— Vous n'avez pas de famille ?

Bethan me dévisage et je ne peux pas baisser les yeux.

— J'ai une sœur, mais on ne se parle plus.

— Qu'est-ce qui s'est passé ?

— Oh, les tensions habituelles entre sœurs, dis-je d'un air dégagé.

Je revois encore le visage furieux d'Eve alors qu'elle m'implorait de l'écouter. J'étais trop fière, je le sais maintenant, trop aveuglée par l'amour. Si je l'avais écoutée, peut-être les choses auraient-elles été différentes.

— Merci pour la tourte. C'est très gentil.

— Ne dites pas de bêtises, réplique Bethan, nullement perturbée par le changement de sujet. (Elle met son manteau et enroule plusieurs fois son écharpe autour de son cou.) À quoi servent les voisins ? Bon, vous passerez bientôt prendre le thé alors.

Ce n'est pas une question, mais j'acquiesce. Elle me fixe de ses yeux marron foncé et j'ai soudain l'impression d'être à nouveau une enfant.

— Je passerai, dis-je. Promis.

Et je le pense.

Après le départ de Bethan, je retire la carte mémoire de mon appareil et transfère les photos sur mon ordinateur. Si la plupart sont bonnes à mettre à la poubelle, quelques-unes rendent parfaitement les mots sur le sable, sur fond de mer déchaînée. Je pose la bouilloire sur la cuisinière pour refaire du thé, mais je perds la notion du temps et ce n'est qu'une demi-heure plus tard que je réalise que l'eau n'a toujours pas chauffé. Je tends la main et m'aperçois que la cuisinière est complètement froide. Elle s'est encore éteinte. J'étais si absorbée par les photos que je n'ai pas remarqué que la température avait chuté : je commence à claquer des dents sans parvenir à m'arrêter. Je regarde la tourte au poulet de Bethan et je sens mon estomac gronder de faim. La dernière fois que ça m'est arrivé, il m'a fallu deux jours pour la rallumer, je désespère à l'idée que ça puisse encore être la même comédie.

Je me secoue. Quand suis-je devenue aussi pathétique ? Quand ai-je perdu la faculté de prendre des décisions ? de résoudre des problèmes ? Je vaux mieux que ça.

— OK, dis-je tout haut, ma voix résonnant de façon étrange dans la cuisine vide. Voyons voir ça.

Le soleil se lève sur Penfach avant que je sois de nouveau au chaud. J'ai les cheveux maculés de graisse et les genoux ankylosés à force d'être restée accroupie sur le sol de la cuisine. Mais j'ai la sensation du devoir accompli — ce qui ne m'était pas arrivé depuis longtemps — tandis que j'enfourne la tourte de Bethan dans la cuisinière pour la faire réchauffer. Il est plus l'heure du petit déjeuner que du dîner, et mon estomac s'est calmé. Peu importe : je mets la table, et je savoure chaque bouchée.

7

— Allez ! hurla Ray dans l'escalier en regardant sa montre pour la cinquième fois en autant de minutes. On va être en retard !

Comme si le lundi matin n'était pas assez stressant, Mags avait passé la nuit chez sa sœur et ne serait pas de retour avant midi ; Ray devait donc se débrouiller tout seul depuis vingt-quatre heures. De façon plutôt imprudente – il s'en rendait compte à présent –, il avait donné aux enfants la permission de regarder un film avant d'aller se coucher et il avait dû les arracher du lit à sept heures et demie ; même Lucy, elle qui d'habitude débordait d'énergie. Il était maintenant huit heures trente-cinq et il fallait qu'ils se bougent. Ray était attendu dans le bureau du préfet de police à neuf heures et demie : à ce rythme, il serait toujours à cette heure-là en train de crier en bas de l'escalier.

— Remuez vous !

Ray sortit d'un pas résolu en direction de la voiture et mit le moteur en marche, laissant la porte d'entrée grande ouverte. Lucy la franchit en courant, ses cheveux décoiffés flottant autour de son visage, et se glissa sur le siège avant à côté de son père. Sa jupe d'école bleu marine était froissée et l'un de ses mi-bas était déjà au niveau de sa cheville. Une bonne minute plus tard, Tom sortit d'un pas nonchalant en direction de la voiture, les pans de sa chemise claquant dans la brise. Il tenait sa cravate à la main mais n'avait manifestement pas l'intention de la mettre. Il avait beaucoup grandi ces derniers temps et se tenait bizarrement, la tête constamment baissée et les épaules voûtées.

Ray baissa sa vitre.

— La porte, Tom !

— Hein ?

Tom regarda Ray.

— La porte d'entrée ?

Ray serra les poings. Il ignorait comment Mags faisait pour supporter ça tous les jours sans s'énerver. La liste des choses qu'il avait à faire occupait toutes ses pensées et il se serait bien passé de les emmener à l'école, surtout aujourd'hui.

— Ah ! (Tom se traîna jusqu'à la maison et claqua la porte. Puis il revint et s'installa sur la banquette arrière.) Comment ça se fait que Lucy est à l'avant ?

— C'est mon tour.

— Non.

— Si.

— Ça suffit ! hurla Ray.

Personne ne dit plus un mot et, le temps d'arriver à l'école primaire de Lucy, Ray s'était calmé. Il gara sa Mondeo sur des zigzags jaunes et accompagna Lucy d'un pas énergique jusqu'en classe. Il l'embrassa sur le front et revint en courant, juste à temps pour trouver une femme en train de noter son numéro d'immatriculation.

— Oh, c'est vous ! fit-elle quand il s'arrêta en dérapant près de la voiture. (Elle agita le doigt.) Je pensais que la loi n'avait pas de secret pour vous, capitaine.

— Désolé, s'excusa Ray. Une affaire urgente. Vous comprenez.

Il la laissa en train de tapoter son crayon sur son bloc-notes. Maudite association de parents d'élèves, une vraie mafia, pensa-t-il. Ils avaient trop de temps libre, là était le problème.

— Alors, commença Ray en jetant un coup d'œil furtif vers le siège passager. (Tom s'était glissé à l'avant dès que Lucy était sortie, mais il regardait obstinément par la fenêtre.) Comment ça va l'école ?

— Bien.

Le professeur de Tom avait dit que les choses n'avaient pas empiré, mais qu'elles ne s'étaient certainement pas arrangées. Ray était allé au collège avec Mags et ils avaient eu droit à la description d'un garçon qui n'avait pas d'amis, ne faisait que le strict minimum en classe et ne se mettait jamais en avant.

— Mme Hickson dit qu'il y a un club de foot le mercredi après les cours. Ça te dirait pas ?

— Pas vraiment.

— J'étais pas mauvais à ton âge. Peut-être que c'est dans les gènes, hein ?

Même sans le regarder, Ray savait que Tom levait les yeux au ciel, et il grimaça en se rendant compte qu'il parlait comme son propre père.

Tom enfonça ses écouteurs dans ses oreilles.

Ray soupira. La puberté avait transformé son fils en un adolescent grognon et renfermé, et il redoutait le jour où la même chose arriverait à sa fille. Il n'était pas censé avoir de préférence, mais il éprouvait un faible pour Lucy, qui à neuf ans lui demandait encore des câlins et insistait pour qu'on lui raconte une histoire avant de s'endormir. Même avant la crise d'adolescence de Tom, lui et Ray avaient déjà des prises de bec. Ils se ressemblaient trop, disait Mags, même si Ray ne voyait pas vraiment en quoi.

— Tu peux me laisser ici, lâcha Tom en défaisant sa ceinture alors que la voiture était encore en mouvement.

— Mais on est à deux rues du collège.

— Papa, c'est bon. Je vais marcher.

Il mit la main sur la poignée et l'espace d'un instant Ray crut qu'il allait ouvrir la portière et se jeter dehors.

— Ça va, j'ai compris ! (Ray se rangea sur le côté, ignorant les marquages au sol pour la deuxième fois de la matinée.) Tu sais que tu vas rater l'appel, pas vrai ?

— À plus !

Sur ce, Tom était parti, claquant la porte de la voiture et se faufilant entre les véhicules pour traverser la route. Mais qu'est-ce qui avait bien pu arriver à son fils si gentil et si drôle ? Ce laconisme était-il une sorte de rite de passage pour un adolescent ? autre chose ? Ray secoua la tête. Avoir des enfants pourrait paraître une promenade de santé par rapport à une enquête criminelle complexe, mais il aurait préféré interroger un suspect plutôt que parler avec Tom. Et ça aurait plus ressemblé à une conversation, pensa-t-il avec ironie. Dieu merci, Mags irait chercher les enfants à l'école.

Quand Ray arriva à la préfecture, il avait chassé Tom de son esprit. Nul besoin d'être un génie pour comprendre pourquoi le préfet de police voulait le voir. Le délit de fuite avait eu lieu six mois plus tôt et l'enquête était pratiquement au point mort. Ray s'assit sur une chaise à l'extérieur du bureau lambrissé de chêne du préfet, et sa secrétaire lui adressa un sourire compatissant.

— Elle est en communication, indiqua-t-elle. Elle ne devrait plus en avoir pour longtemps.

Le préfet de police Olivia Rippon était une femme brillante mais terrifiante. Ayant rapidement gravi les échelons, elle dirigeait la police de l'Avon et du Somerset depuis sept ans. Un temps pressentie à la tête de la préfecture de police de Londres, Olivia avait choisi « pour des raisons personnelles » de rester dans sa région d'origine, où elle prenait plaisir à faire perdre leurs moyens aux officiers supérieurs lors des bilans mensuels. Elle faisait partie de ces femmes nées pour porter l'uniforme, ses cheveux châtain foncé tirés en un chignon sévère et de solides jambes dissimulées sous d'épais collants noirs.

Ray frotta la paume de ses mains sur son pantalon pour s'assurer qu'elles étaient parfaitement sèches. La rumeur prétendait que le préfet avait un jour bloqué l'avancement d'un officier prometteur au grade de commandant parce que les mains moites du pauvre homme « n'inspiraient pas confiance ». Ray ignorait si c'était vrai, mais il ne souhaitait prendre aucun risque. Ils arrivaient à s'en sortir avec son salaire de capitaine, mais c'était un peu juste. Mags parlait toujours de devenir enseignante, mais Ray avait fait le calcul : s'il parvenait à obtenir encore une ou deux promotions, ils auraient le petit supplément d'argent dont ils avaient besoin sans qu'elle ait à travailler. Ray songea au chaos de ce matin et se dit que Mags en faisait déjà plus qu'assez. Elle ne devrait pas avoir à travailler juste pour qu'ils puissent s'offrir quelques petits plaisirs.

— Vous pouvez y aller, annonça la secrétaire.

Ray respira à fond et ouvrit la porte.

— Bonjour, madame.

Le silence régna tandis que le préfet prenait de copieuses notes de son écriture illisible caractéristique. Ray s'attarda près de la porte et fit mine d'admirer les nombreuses photos et décorations qui ornaient les murs. La moquette bleu marine était plus épaisse et plus luxueuse que dans le reste du bâtiment, et une énorme table de conférence occupait la moitié de la pièce. À l'autre bout, Olivia Rippon était assise derrière un grand bureau arrondi. Elle finit par cesser d'écrire et leva les yeux.

— Je veux que vous classiez l'affaire du délit de fuite de Fishponds.

Elle n'allait manifestement pas lui proposer de s'asseoir, Ray choisit donc le fauteuil le plus proche d'elle et s'y installa malgré tout. Elle haussa un sourcil, mais ne dit rien.

— Je crois que si on avait un peu plus de temps…

— Vous avez eu assez de temps, coupa Olivia. Cinq mois et demi, exactement. Ça nous met dans l'embarras, Ray. Chaque fois que le *Post* publie les soi-disant derniers développements de l'enquête, ça ne sert qu'à rappeler l'échec de la police. Le conseiller municipal Lewis m'a appelée hier soir : il veut que cette affaire soit enterrée, et moi aussi.

Ray sentit la colère monter en lui.

— Ce n'est pas Lewis qui s'est opposé à la demande des habitants de limiter la vitesse à trente kilomètres heure dans les lotissements ?

Il y eut un silence et Olivia l'observa froidement.

— Classez-la, Ray.

Ils se dévisagèrent sans un mot par-dessus le bureau en noyer poli. Contre toute attente, ce fut Olivia qui céda la première. Elle se carra dans son fauteuil et joignit les mains devant elle.

— Vous êtes un excellent policier, Ray, et votre ténacité est tout à votre honneur. Mais si vous voulez évoluer, vous devez accepter que la politique fasse partie intégrante de notre métier, au même titre que les enquêtes.

— Je le comprends, madame.

Ray lutta pour que sa voix ne reflète pas sa frustration.

— Bien, conclut Olivia tandis qu'elle débouchait son stylo et prenait la note de service suivante dans sa bannette. Alors nous sommes d'accord. L'affaire sera classée aujourd'hui.

Pour une fois, Ray était content qu'il y ait de la circulation en allant au poste. Il n'était pas pressé d'annoncer la nouvelle à Kate et il se demanda pourquoi cette pensée venait avant les autres. Parce qu'elle faisait encore ses armes à la Criminelle, supposa-t-il : elle n'avait pas encore connu la frustration d'avoir à classer une enquête après y avoir consacré tant d'énergie. Stumpy serait plus résigné.

En arrivant, il les appela dans son bureau. Kate fut la première à se présenter, avec à la main une tasse de café qu'elle posa près de son ordinateur, à côté des trois autres à moitié pleines qui se trouvaient encore là.

— Les cafés de la semaine dernière ?

— Ouais. La femme de ménage ne veut plus laver les tasses.

— Ça ne m'étonne pas. Tu peux le faire toi-même, tu sais.

Kate s'assit, juste au moment où Stumpy entra et salua Ray d'un signe de tête.

— Vous vous souvenez de la voiture que Brian et Pat ont repérée sur les caméras pour le délit de fuite ? demanda Kate dès que Stumpy fut installé. Celle qui avait l'air pressée de s'en aller ?

Ray hocha la tête.

— On n'arrive pas à déterminer le modèle sur les images qu'on a et j'aimerais les montrer à Wesley. Au pire, ça nous permettra d'écarter cette piste.

Wesley Barton était un individu maigre et anémique qui avait trouvé le moyen d'intervenir auprès de la police en tant que spécialiste des caméras de surveillance. Depuis le sous-sol sans fenêtres d'une maison étouffante de Redland Road, il utilisait toute une panoplie d'équipements électroniques pour améliorer les images jusqu'à ce qu'elles puissent être utilisées comme preuves. Étant donné que Wesley collaborait avec la police, Ray supposait qu'il n'avait rien à se reprocher, mais il y avait quelque chose de sordide dans tout ça.

— Je suis désolé, Kate, mais je ne peux pas autoriser cette dépense, déclara Ray.

Il rechignait à lui dire que tous ses efforts n'avaient servi à rien. Wesley était cher, mais il faisait du bon travail, et Ray était impressionné par l'approche originale de Kate. Il ne voulait pas l'admettre, même intérieurement, mais il avait l'esprit ailleurs ces derniers temps. Toute cette histoire avec Tom le déconcentrait, et l'espace d'un instant il en voulut à son fils. C'était inexcusable de sa part de laisser sa vie de famille affecter son travail, surtout avec une affaire aussi médiatisée que celle-ci. Mais tout cela n'avait plus beaucoup d'importance, pensa-t-il avec amertume, maintenant que le préfet avait arrêté sa décision.

— Ça ne coûte pas si cher que ça, protesta Kate. Je lui ai parlé, et...

Ray la coupa.

— Je ne peux autoriser aucune dépense, assena-t-il.

Stumpy regarda Ray. Il connaissait suffisamment la maison pour savoir ce qui viendrait ensuite.

— Le préfet m'a demandé de classer cette enquête, annonça Ray sans quitter Kate des yeux.

Il y eut un bref silence.

— J'espère que tu lui as dit d'aller se faire voir ! (Kate rit, mais personne ne l'imita. Elle regarda Ray, puis Stumpy, et son visage s'assombrit.) Tu parles sérieusement ? On va abandonner comme ça ?

— On n'abandonne rien, répondit Ray. On ne peut rien faire de plus. La piste des antibrouillards n'a rien donné…

— Il y a au moins une douzaine d'immatriculations qui manquent encore, indiqua Kate. Tu ne peux pas savoir le nombre de garagistes qui ne gardent aucune trace écrite des réparations qu'ils font. Ça ne veut pas dire que je ne vais pas les retrouver, simplement que j'ai besoin de plus de temps.

— C'est une perte d'énergie, dit gentiment Ray. Il faut parfois savoir s'arrêter.

— On a fait tout ce qu'on a pu, intervint Stumpy. Mais autant chercher une aiguille dans une botte de foin. Pas d'immatriculation, pas de couleur, pas de marque ni de modèle : il nous faut quelque chose, Kate.

Ray apprécia le soutien de Stumpy.

— Et on n'a rien, dit-il. J'ai bien peur qu'il faille donc tirer un trait sur cette affaire pour le moment. Évidemment, si une véritable piste se présente, on la suivra, mais sinon…

Il n'acheva pas sa phrase, conscient que ça commençait à ressembler à un communiqué de presse du préfet.

— Tout ça, c'est politique, pas vrai ? lança Kate. Si le préfet vous dit de sauter par la fenêtre, vous le faites.

Ray mesura alors à quel point elle prenait cette affaire à cœur.

— Allons, Kate, tu es dans la maison depuis assez longtemps pour savoir qu'il y a parfois des choix difficiles à faire. (Il s'arrêta brusquement, ne voulant pas se montrer condescendant.) Écoute, ça fait presque six mois et on n'a rien de concret. Pas de témoins, pas de preuves, rien. On pourrait avoir tous les moyens du monde pour cette affaire et on n'aurait toujours aucune piste sérieuse. Je suis désolé, mais on a d'autres enquêtes, d'autres victimes pour lesquelles il faut se battre.

— Est-ce que tu as essayé au moins ? demanda Kate, les joues rougies par la colère. Ou tu t'es contenté de t'écraser ?

— Kate, avertit Stumpy, calme-toi.

Elle ne fit pas attention à lui et défia Ray du regard.

— Je suppose que tu dois penser à ta promotion. Ce ne serait pas une bonne idée de chercher des noises au préfet, hein ?

— Ça n'a rien à voir avec ça !

Ray essayait de garder son sang-froid, mais il parla plus fort qu'il ne l'aurait voulu. Ils se dévisagèrent. Du coin de l'œil, il voyait que Stumpy l'observait attentivement. Ray aurait dû dire à Kate de sortir. De ne pas oublier qu'en tant qu'inspecteur à la Criminelle elle avait du travail, et que si son chef lui disait qu'une affaire était classée, eh bien elle l'était. Point à la ligne. Il ouvrit la bouche mais fut incapable de parler.

Le problème était qu'elle avait vu juste. Ray ne souhaitait pas plus qu'elle classer l'affaire du délit de fuite, et à une époque il aurait tenu tête au préfet et défendu son point de vue comme elle le faisait à présent. Peut-être avait-il perdu la main, ou Kate avait peut-être raison : il pensait sans doute trop à sa promotion.

— Je sais que c'est dur quand on y a consacré autant de travail, dit-il gentiment.

— Ce n'est pas la question. (Kate désigna la photo de Jacob sur le mur.) C'est ce petit garçon. Ce n'est pas juste pour lui.

Ray repensa à la mère de Jacob assise sur le canapé, le visage marqué par la douleur. Il ne pouvait pas contredire Kate et il n'essaya pas.

— Je suis vraiment désolé. (Il se racla la gorge et tâcha de passer à autre chose.) Quoi de neuf sur les autres dossiers ? demanda-t-il à Stumpy.

— Malcolm est au tribunal toute la semaine pour l'affaire Grayson et il a un dossier à boucler pour les coups et blessures de Queen's Street ; le parquet a décidé d'engager des poursuites. Je m'occupe des vols dans les supermarchés Co-op et Dave est affecté au plan d'action contre les armes blanches. Il est à l'université aujourd'hui pour faire de la « sensibilisation ».

Il prononça ce mot comme s'il s'agissait d'une grossièreté et Ray rit.

— Il faut vivre avec son temps, Stumpy.

— Tu peux toujours leur parler, ça n'empêchera pas ces gamins de se trimballer avec une lame.

— Eh bien, peut-être, mais au moins on aura essayé. (Ray griffonna quelque chose dans son agenda.) Tu me feras un compte rendu avant la réunion de demain matin, OK ? Et j'aimerais avoir ton avis sur une collecte d'armes blanches pendant les vacances scolaires. Essayons d'en récupérer un maximum, ça fera toujours ça de moins dans les rues.

— OK.

Kate fixait le sol, s'arrachant les envies autour des ongles. Stumpy lui donna une tape amicale sur le bras et elle se retourna vers lui.

— Un sandwich au bacon ? proposa-t-il doucement.

— C'est pas ça qui va me remonter le moral, marmonna Kate.

— Non, répliqua Stumpy, mais le mien sera peut-être meilleur si tu ne tires pas la tronche toute la matinée.

Kate rit du bout des lèvres.

— Je te rejoins.

Il y eut un silence et Ray vit qu'elle attendait que Stumpy soit parti. Il ferma la porte et retourna s'asseoir à son bureau, les bras croisés.

— Ça va ?

Kate hocha la tête.

— Je voulais m'excuser, je n'aurais pas dû te parler sur ce ton.

— J'ai connu pire, dit Ray avec un large sourire. (Kate ne broncha pas et il comprit qu'elle n'était pas d'humeur à plaisanter.) Je sais que cette affaire compte beaucoup pour toi, ajouta-t-il.

Kate regarda une nouvelle fois la photo de Jacob.

— J'ai l'impression de l'avoir laissé tomber.

Ray sentit ses défenses céder. C'était vrai, ils avaient laissé tomber Jacob, mais l'avouer à Kate n'arrangerait rien.

— Tu as fait tout ce que tu as pu, dit-il. Tu ne peux pas faire plus.

— Mais ça n'a pas suffi, non ?

Elle se retourna vers Ray et il secoua la tête.

— Non. Ça n'a pas suffi.

Kate sortit de la pièce en refermant la porte derrière elle et Ray frappa un grand coup sur son bureau. Son stylo roula et tomba par terre. Il se laissa aller dans son fauteuil et croisa les mains derrière la tête. Ses cheveux lui parurent clairsemés sous ses doigts et il ferma les yeux, se sentant tout à coup très vieux et très fatigué. Ray pensa aux officiers supérieurs qu'il croisait tous les jours : la plupart plus âgés que lui, mais quelques-uns plus jeunes, gravissant les échelons quatre à quatre. Avait-il la force de se mesurer à eux ? En avait-il tout simplement envie ?

À l'époque où Ray s'était engagé dans la police, tout semblait très simple. Arrêter les criminels et protéger les braves gens. Aider les victimes d'attaques au couteau et d'agressions, de viols et de dégradations, et participer à la construction d'un monde meilleur. Mais le faisait-il vraiment ? Il était enfermé dans son bureau de huit heures du matin à huit heures du soir, ne sortant sur une affaire que lorsque la paperasse pouvait attendre, obligé de se plier aux exigences de la direction même quand cela allait à l'encontre de ses principes.

Ray regarda le dossier de Jacob, qui se résumait à une série de fausses pistes et d'enquêtes infructueuses. Il songea à l'amertume sur le visage de Kate et à sa déception en découvrant qu'il ne s'était pas opposé plus vivement à la décision du préfet, et il n'aima pas l'idée d'avoir baissé dans son estime. Mais les mots du préfet résonnaient encore dans sa tête et il savait qu'il valait mieux ne pas désobéir aux ordres, quoi que pût penser Kate. Il prit le dossier de Jacob et le rangea d'un air décidé dans le dernier tiroir de son bureau.

8

La pluie menace depuis que je suis descendue sur la plage à l'aube et je relève ma capuche pour me protéger des premières gouttes. J'ai déjà pris les clichés que je voulais et la plage est couverte de mots. Je suis devenue experte pour garder le sable lisse et intact autour de mes lettres et je maîtrise mieux mon appareil. J'ai suivi des cours de photographie dans le cadre de mes études d'art, mais la sculpture a toujours été ma grande passion. Je redécouvre avec plaisir mon appareil photo, jouant avec les réglages selon la lumière ; je l'emporte partout, si bien qu'il fait désormais autant partie de moi que les mottes d'argile avec lesquelles je travaillais auparavant. Et bien que ma main soit toujours douloureuse après une journée passée à le tenir, je peux suffisamment la bouger pour prendre des photos. J'ai pris l'habitude de venir ici tous les matins, quand le sable est encore assez humide pour être malléable, et de rentrer l'après-midi au moment où le soleil est au zénith. J'apprends l'heure des marées et, pour la première fois depuis l'accident, je commence à penser à l'avenir, attendant l'été avec impatience pour voir la plage baignée de soleil. Le camping est maintenant ouvert aux touristes et il y a du monde à Penfach. C'est drôle, la vitesse à laquelle je me suis adaptée : je râle contre l'afflux de vacanciers, comme les habitants du coin, ne voulant pas partager ma plage tranquille.

La pluie crible la plage et la marée montante tend à balayer les formes que j'ai dessinées dans le sable mouillé près de l'eau, détruisant les réussites comme les échecs. Chaque jour, je commence par écrire mon nom près du rivage et, à présent, je frissonne en voyant la mer l'engloutir. Mes photos ont beau être enregistrées dans mon appareil, ce côté éphémère me perturbe. Avec l'argile, je pouvais travailler encore et encore, la façonnant jusqu'à la perfection pour révéler sa vraie forme. Ici, je suis obligée de faire vite : je trouve ce processus à la fois exaltant et épuisant.

La pluie tombe dru et se glisse sous mon manteau et dans mes bottes. En me retournant pour quitter la plage, j'aperçois un homme qui se dirige vers moi, un gros chien bondissant à ses côtés. Je retiens mon souffle. Il est encore loin et j'ignore s'il s'approche délibérément ou s'il va juste vers la mer. J'ai un goût métallique dans la bouche et je me lèche les lèvres pour m'hydrater, mais je n'y trouve que du sel. J'ai déjà vu cet homme et son chien : je les ai observés hier matin du haut de la falaise en attendant qu'ils partent et que la plage redevienne déserte. Malgré le vaste espace autour de moi, j'ai l'impression d'être prise au piège et je me mets à longer le bord de l'eau comme si j'avais toujours eu l'intention d'aller par là.

— Bonjour !

Il se détourne un peu de sa route pour marcher parallèlement à moi.

Je ne parviens pas à parler.

— Belle journée pour se promener ! dit-il en levant la tête vers le ciel.

Il doit avoir la cinquantaine : des cheveux gris sous un chapeau huilé, une barbe taillée court qui couvre presque la moitié de son visage.

Je laisse échapper un lent soupir.

— Il faut que je rentre, dis-je vaguement. Je dois…

— Bonne journée !

L'homme m'adresse un petit signe de tête et appelle son chien, puis je fais demi-tour et cours à petites foulées en direction de la falaise. Au milieu de la plage, je me retourne : l'homme est toujours au bord de l'eau et lance un bâton dans la mer. Mon pouls retrouve peu à peu son rythme normal et à présent je me sens ridicule.

Le temps d'arriver tout en haut, je suis trempée jusqu'aux os. Je décide d'aller voir Bethan et je marche vite jusqu'au camping avant de changer d'avis.

Bethan m'accueille avec un large sourire.

— Je vais mettre l'eau à chauffer.

Elle s'affaire en continuant de parler d'un ton enjoué de la météo, des menaces de fermeture des lignes de bus et de la clôture cassée de Iestyn, qui a entraîné la fuite de soixante-dix chèvres pendant la nuit.

— Ça n'a pas plu à Alwen Rees, ça, je peux vous le dire.

Je ris – moins de l'histoire en elle-même que de la façon dont Bethan la raconte, ponctuant ses paroles de grands gestes d'actrice. Je flâne dans la boutique pendant qu'elle finit de préparer le thé. Le sol est en béton et les murs sont blanchis à la chaux, garnis de rayons sur deux côtés de la pièce. Ils étaient vides la première fois que je suis venue ici : ils sont désormais remplis de céréales, de boîtes de conserve, de fruits et de légumes, prêts pour l'arrivée des vacanciers. Une grande vitrine réfrigérante abrite quelques briques de lait et d'autres produits frais. Je prends du fromage.

— C'est le fromage de chèvre de Iestyn, précise Bethan. Vous faites bien d'en prendre tant qu'il y en a, ça part vite quand il y a du monde. Allez, venez vous asseoir près du chauffage et racontez-moi comment ça se passe là-haut. (Un chaton noir et blanc miaule près de ses chevilles et elle le soulève pour le poser sur son épaule.) Vous ne voudriez pas un chat par hasard ? J'en ai trois à donner, notre femelle a eu une portée il y a quelques semaines. Allez savoir qui est le père !

— Non, merci.

Le chaton est incroyablement mignon : une boule de poils dont la queue bat comme un métronome. Ce spectacle fait remonter à la surface un souvenir oublié et j'esquisse un mouvement de recul.

— Vous n'aimez pas les chats ?

— Je ne sais pas m'en occuper, dis-je. Je ne réussis même pas à garder un chlorophytum en vie. Tout finit par mourir avec moi.

Bethan rit, bien que je ne plaisante pas. Elle approche une seconde chaise et pose une tasse de thé sur le comptoir à côté de moi.

— Vous avez pris des photos ?

Bethan désigne l'appareil autour de mon cou.

— Oui. De la baie.

— Je peux les voir ?

J'hésite, mais je fais passer la lanière par-dessus ma tête et allume l'appareil, montrant à Bethan comment faire défiler les images sur l'écran.

— Elles sont magnifiques !

— Merci.

Je me sens rougir. Je n'ai jamais su comment réagir face aux compliments. Quand j'étais petite, mes professeurs faisaient l'éloge de mes œuvres et les exposaient dans le hall d'accueil, mais ce n'est qu'à l'âge de douze ans que j'ai compris que j'avais du talent, encore brut et imparfait. L'école avait organisé une petite manifestation pour les parents et les habitants du quartier, et mes parents étaient venus ensemble, ce qui était rare, même à cette époque. Mon père est resté planté sans dire un mot devant la partie où étaient placés mes tableaux ainsi qu'une statue d'oiseau que j'avais faite avec du métal tordu. J'ai retenu mon souffle pendant un long moment en croisant les doigts dans les plis de ma jupe.

— Incroyable, a-t-il dit. (Il m'a regardé comme s'il me voyait pour la première fois.) Tu es incroyable, Jenna.

J'aurais pu exploser tellement j'étais fière, et j'ai glissé ma main dans la sienne pour l'emmener voir Mme Beeching, qui lui a parlé des Beaux-Arts, des bourses d'études et du tutorat. Je suis restée assise là à fixer mon père, qui pensait que j'étais incroyable.

Je suis heureuse qu'il ne soit plus là. Je ne supporterais pas de lire la déception dans ses yeux.

Bethan regarde encore les clichés que j'ai pris de la baie.

— Vraiment, Jenna, vos photos sont superbes. Vous comptez les vendre ?

Je ris presque, mais elle ne sourit pas et je me rends compte qu'elle est sérieuse.

Je me demande si ce serait possible. Peut-être pas celles-ci – j'apprends encore à maîtriser l'exposition –, mais avec du travail…

— Peut-être, dis-je en m'étonnant moi-même.

Bethan fait défiler les dernières photos et rit quand elle tombe sur son nom écrit sur le sable.

— C'est moi !

Je rougis.

— Je faisais un essai.

— Je l'aime bien. Je peux vous l'acheter ?

Bethan lève l'appareil pour mieux admirer la photo.

— Ne dites pas de bêtises. Je vais la faire imprimer pour vous. C'est la moindre des choses : vous avez été si gentille avec moi.

— Il y a une machine pour les imprimer soi-même à la poste, indique Bethan. J'aimerais bien celle-ci, avec mon nom, et celle-là aussi, où la marée est basse.

Elle a choisi l'une de mes préférées : je l'ai prise le soir tandis que le soleil disparaissait derrière l'horizon. La mer est presque plate, avec des reflets roses et orange, et les falaises tout autour ne sont plus que de vagues silhouettes lisses.

— Je les imprimerai cet après-midi.

— Merci, dit Bethan. (Elle pose l'appareil d'un air décidé et se retourne vers moi. Son regard pénétrant m'est déjà familier.) Maintenant, laissez-moi faire quelque chose pour vous.

— Ce n'est pas la peine, vous avez déjà…

D'un geste, Bethan écarte mes protestations.

— J'ai un peu rangé et je dois me débarrasser de quelques bricoles. (Elle désigne deux sacs noirs soigneusement posés près de la porte.) Rien d'extraordinaire : des coussins et des couvre-lits qui étaient dans les mobile homes avant qu'on les réaménage, et des vêtements qui ne m'iront plus même si j'arrête le chocolat jusqu'à la fin de mes jours. Rien de sophistiqué non plus — les robes de bal ne servent pas à grand-chose à Penfach —, mais des pulls, des jeans et une ou deux robes que je n'aurais jamais dû acheter.

— Bethan, vous ne pouvez pas me donner vos vêtements !

— Et pourquoi pas ?

— Parce que...

Elle me regarde droit dans les yeux et je laisse ma phrase en suspens. Elle est si franche que j'aurais mauvaise grâce à me sentir gênée ; et puis je ne peux pas continuer à porter la même chose tous les jours.

— Écoutez, je finirai par bazarder tout ça de toute façon. Jetez-y un coup d'œil et prenez ce dont vous avez besoin. C'est logique, non ?

Je repars du camping chargée d'habits chauds et d'un sac rempli de ce que Bethan appelle des « accessoires de confort ». En arrivant au cottage, j'étale tout par terre comme s'il s'agissait de cadeaux de Noël. Les jeans sont un peu trop grands, mais ils iront très bien avec une ceinture, et je pleure presque en découvrant la douceur de l'épaisse polaire qu'elle a mise de côté pour moi. Le cottage est glacial et j'ai toujours froid. Les quelques vêtements apportés de Bristol — je réalise que j'ai arrêté de dire « chez moi » — sont usés et rêches à cause du sel et à force de les laver à la main dans la baignoire.

Ce sont les « accessoires de confort » de Bethan qui m'excitent le plus. Je recouvre le canapé en piteux état d'un immense dessus-de-lit en patchwork rouge et vert, et la pièce devient aussitôt plus chaleureuse et accueillante. Sur la cheminée, j'ai disposé des pierres polies par la mer que j'ai trouvées sur la plage : j'y ajoute un vase du sac de Bethan et je décide de le remplir de tiges de saule que je ramasserai cet après-midi. Les fameux coussins vont par terre, près du feu, là où j'ai l'habitude de m'asseoir pour lire ou trier mes photos. Au fond du sac, je trouve deux serviettes de toilette, un tapis de bain et un autre couvre-lit.

Je ne crois pas une seconde que Bethan allait se débarrasser de tout ça, mais je la connais désormais assez bien pour ne pas lui poser la question.

On frappe à la porte et je me fige. Bethan m'a dit que Iestyn passerait aujourd'hui, mais j'attends un instant, juste au cas où.

— Alors, vous êtes là ?

Je tire le verrou pour ouvrir la porte. Iestyn me salue avec sa brusquerie habituelle et je l'accueille avec joie. Ce que j'avais d'abord pris pour de l'indifférence, voire de l'impolitesse, est en réalité la marque d'un homme qui ne se mêle pas aux autres, se souciant plus du bien-être de ses chèvres que des sentiments de ses semblables.

— Je vous ai apporté des bûches, dit-il en montrant le bois de chauffage entassé en vrac dans la remorque accrochée à son quad. Vous en aurez besoin. Je vais les mettre à l'intérieur.

— Vous voulez du thé ?

— Avec deux sucres, crie Iesyn par-dessus son épaule en retournant à grandes enjambées vers la remorque.

Il commence à empiler les bûches dans un seau et je fais chauffer de l'eau.

— Combien je vous dois pour les bûches ? dis-je tandis que nous buvons le thé à la table de la cuisine.

Iestyn secoue la tête.

— Ce sont les restes d'une livraison. Elles ne sont pas assez bonnes pour être vendues.

Avec ce qu'il a entassé près du feu, j'ai du bois pour au moins un mois. Je soupçonne Bethan d'être encore derrière tout ça, mais je ne suis pas en mesure de refuser un cadeau si généreux. Il va falloir que je trouve un moyen de lui rendre la pareille, ainsi qu'à Bethan.

Iestyn hausse les épaules quand je le remercie.

— Je n'aurais pas reconnu l'endroit, constate-t-il en regardant le couvre-lit bariolé ainsi que les coquillages et autres trésors trouvés çà et là. Vous vous en sortez avec la cuisinière ? Elle n'a pas trop fait des siennes ? (Il désigne le vieux modèle en fonte.) C'est une vraie saloperie des fois.

— Je n'ai pas eu de problèmes, merci.

Je réprime un sourire. Je suis devenue une experte – capable de la rallumer en quelques minutes. C'est une petite victoire que je range avec les autres, les accumulant comme si un jour elles pourraient annuler les échecs.

— Bon, il faut que j'y aille, fait Iestyn. J'ai de la famille ce week-end et on dirait qu'on attend une visite de la reine, tellement Glynis est stressée. J'ai beau lui dire qu'ils se moquent que la maison soit propre ou qu'il y ait des fleurs dans la salle à manger, elle veut que tout soit parfait.

Il lève les yeux au ciel, apparemment exaspéré, mais il parle de sa femme d'une voix douce.

— Ce sont vos enfants qui vous rendent visite ?

— Nos deux filles avec leurs maris et les petits, répond-il. On va être un peu à l'étroit, mais tout le monde s'en fiche quand c'est la famille, non ?

Il me dit au revoir et je regarde son quad s'éloigner en cahotant sur le sol accidenté.

Je ferme la porte et reste plantée là à contempler le cottage. Le salon, qui semblait si confortable et accueillant il y a quelques instants, a maintenant l'air vide. J'imagine un enfant – mon enfant – en train de jouer sur le tapis devant la cheminée. Je pense à Eve, ainsi qu'à la nièce et au neveu qui grandissent sans moi. J'ai peut-être perdu mon fils, mais j'ai encore une famille, en dépit de ce qui s'est passé entre nous.

Te laisser partir

Malgré nos quatre ans de différence, je m'entendais bien avec Eve quand nous étions petites. Je l'admirais et elle veillait sur moi, n'en voulant jamais à sa petite sœur de la suivre partout. Nous étions assez différentes ; moi avec ma tignasse auburn indisciplinée et Eve avec ses cheveux châtain clair parfaitement lisses. Nous avions toutes les deux de bonnes notes à l'école, mais Eve était plus studieuse que moi, encore plongée dans ses manuels quand j'avais envoyé valser les miens à travers la chambre depuis longtemps. Je préférais passer des heures dans l'atelier d'art de l'école, ou par terre dans le garage – le seul endroit de la maison où ma mère m'autorisait à sortir mon argile et mes couleurs. Ma délicate sœur méprisait de tels passe-temps et poussait des cris aigus en fuyant mes bras tendus, couverts d'argile humide. Un jour, je l'ai appelée « Lady Eve » et c'est resté, même après que nous eûmes toutes deux fondé une famille. J'ai toujours pensé qu'au fond Eve aimait ce surnom, surtout quand au fil des ans je voyais la façon dont elle accueillait les compliments pour un dîner réussi ou un bel emballage cadeau.

Après le départ de notre père, nous n'étions plus aussi proches. Je n'ai jamais pu pardonner à ma mère de l'avoir mis à la porte et je ne comprenais pas comment Eve y était parvenue. Malgré tout, ma sœur me manque terriblement, maintenant plus que jamais. Perdre quelqu'un de vue pendant cinq ans à cause d'une banale remarque, c'est bien trop long.

Je cherche dans mon ordinateur les photos que Bethan m'a demandées. J'en ajoute trois que j'aimerais afficher sur les murs du cottage dans des cadres que je fabriquerai avec du bois flotté. Elles sont toutes de la baie : toutes prises exactement du même endroit, mais toutes différentes. Les eaux bleu vif de la première, avec le soleil qui miroite sur la baie, laissent place au gris mat de la deuxième, où l'astre est à peine visible dans le ciel. La troisième est ma préférée : je l'ai prise quand le vent était si violent que je devais me concentrer pour ne pas perdre l'équilibre en haut de la falaise, et que même les mouettes avaient abandonné leur ronde incessante dans le ciel. Sur la photo, des nuages noirs plongent vers la mer tandis que celle-ci lance ses vagues à leur rencontre. La baie était vraiment animée ce jour-là. Je sentais les battements de mon cœur pendant que je travaillais.

J'ajoute un dernier cliché sur ma carte mémoire, pris le jour où j'ai commencé à écrire sur le sable, quand j'ai recouvert la plage de noms tirés de mon passé.

Lady Eve.

Je ne peux pas courir le risque de dire à ma sœur où je suis, mais je peux lui faire savoir que je vais bien. Et que je suis désolée.

9

— Je vais chercher à manger au Harry's, tu veux quelque chose ?

Kate apparut dans l'embrasure de la porte du bureau de Ray, vêtue d'un pantalon gris fuselé et d'un pull moulant sur lequel elle avait enfilé une veste légère pour sortir.

Ray se leva et prit sa propre veste sur le dossier de son fauteuil.

— Je viens avec toi. J'ai besoin de prendre l'air.

Il mangeait en général à la cantine ou dans son bureau, mais un déjeuner avec Kate ne se refusait pas. En outre, le soleil brillait enfin et il n'avait pas levé le nez de ses dossiers depuis qu'il était arrivé à huit heures ce matin. Il méritait une pause.

Le Harry's était bondé, comme d'habitude, avec une file d'attente qui serpentait jusque sur le trottoir. L'endroit était très apprécié des policiers, non seulement parce que c'était à deux pas du poste, mais aussi parce que le prix des sandwichs était raisonnable et le service rapide. Il n'y avait rien de plus frustrant pour un flic affamé que de recevoir un appel urgent avant l'arrivée de la commande.

Ils piétinaient dehors.

— Je peux t'apporter le tien au bureau si tu es pressé, proposa-t-elle.

Ray secoua la tête.

— J'ai le temps. Je planche sur les préparatifs de l'opération Break et une pause ne me fera pas de mal. Mangeons sur place.

— Bonne idée. Break, c'est l'affaire du blanchiment d'argent, c'est ça ?

Kate parlait doucement, faisant attention aux gens autour d'eux, et Ray acquiesça.

— Exact. Je peux te montrer le dossier si tu veux, comme ça tu pourras voir comment il est ficelé.

— Ce serait super, merci.

Ils commandèrent à manger et trouvèrent deux tabourets hauts près de la vitrine, gardant un œil sur Harry qui, quelques minutes plus tard, agitait leurs sandwichs en l'air. Deux agents en uniforme passèrent devant la boutique, Ray les salua d'un geste de la main.

— Pris en flag ! On va encore entendre que la Criminelle se tourne les pouces, dit-il à Kate en riant.

— Si seulement ils savaient, répliqua-t-elle en enlevant une tomate de son sandwich pour la manger à part. Je n'ai jamais autant travaillé que sur l'affaire Jacob Jordan. Et tout ça pour rien.

Ray remarqua l'amertume dans sa voix.

— Pas pour rien, tu le sais bien. Un jour, quelqu'un finira par avouer ce qu'il a fait et les gens parleront. Et on le coincera.

— Mais ce n'est pas ce que j'appelle du bon travail de policier.

— Qu'est-ce que tu veux dire ?

Ray ne savait pas s'il devait être amusé ou se sentir insulté par sa franchise.

Kate posa son sandwich.

— Qu'on réagit au lieu d'agir. On ne devrait pas rester assis là à attendre que des informations nous parviennent : on devrait être en train de les chercher.

Il avait l'impression de s'entendre à ses débuts. Ou peut-être Mags, même si, dans ses souvenirs, elle n'était pas aussi sûre d'elle. Kate avait recommencé à manger, ce qu'elle faisait avec autant de détermination que tout le reste. Ray dissimula un sourire. Elle disait exactement ce qui lui passait par la tête, sans aucune censure ni retenue. Elle allait en froisser quelques-uns au poste, mais le franc-parler ne dérangeait par Ray. À vrai dire, il trouvait même ça plutôt rafraîchissant.

— Cette affaire t'a vraiment énervée, hein ? observa Ray.

Elle acquiesça.

— Je ne supporte pas l'idée que le conducteur coure toujours en pensant qu'il s'en est tiré. Et je ne supporte pas l'idée que la mère de Jacob soit partie de Bristol en pensant qu'on ne faisait pas tout pour retrouver le responsable.

Elle ouvrit la bouche pour continuer, puis détourna le regard comme si elle s'était ravisée.

— Quoi ?

Ses joues rougirent légèrement, mais elle leva le menton d'un air de défi.

— Je travaille toujours sur cette affaire.

Au fil des années, Ray avait à plusieurs reprises découvert de la paperasse qui moisissait dans un coin, délaissée par des collègues trop occupés ou trop paresseux pour s'en charger. Mais travailler encore *davantage* ? C'était une première.

— Sur mon temps libre, et je ne fais rien qui puisse t'attirer des problèmes avec le préfet, je t'assure. Je regarde les enregistrements des caméras de surveillance et je réexamine les appels qu'on a reçus après la diffusion de *Crimewatch* pour voir si on n'a pas loupé quelque chose.

Ray imagina Kate assise chez elle, les pièces du dossier éparpillées par terre, et passant des heures à visionner des images granuleuses sur l'écran devant elle.

— Et tu fais tout ça parce que tu crois qu'on peut retrouver le conducteur ?

— Parce que je ne veux pas abandonner.

Ray sourit.

— Tu vas me demander d'arrêter ? dit Kate en se mordant la lèvre.

C'était précisément ce qu'il allait faire. Mais elle était si enthousiaste, si tenace ! Du reste, même si cela n'apportait rien à l'enquête, quel mal y avait-il à cela ? Il aurait pu agir de même à une époque.

— Non, répondit-il. Je ne vais pas te demander d'arrêter. Avant tout parce que je ne suis pas persuadé que ça changerait quelque chose.

Ils rirent en chœur.

— Mais je veux que tu me tiennes au courant et que tu n'y consacres pas trop de temps. Et que ça ne passe pas avant les affaires en cours. D'accord ?

Kate le dévisagea.

— D'accord. Merci, Ray.

Il froissa l'emballage de leurs sandwichs.

— Allez, on ferait mieux d'y retourner. Je vais te montrer le dossier de l'opération Break et après je rentrerai à la maison, sinon je vais encore avoir des ennuis.

Il fit mine de lever les yeux au ciel.

— Je pensais que ça ne dérangeait pas Mags que tu rentres tard ? dit Kate tandis qu'ils se dirigeaient vers le poste.

— Je crois que ça ne va pas très bien entre nous en ce moment, confia-t-il, se sentant aussitôt déloyal.

Il parlait rarement de sa vie privée à ses collègues, sauf à Stumpy, qui connaissait Mags depuis presque aussi longtemps que lui. Cela dit, il ne l'avait pas non plus crié sur les toits : c'était juste Kate.

— Tu crois ? dit-elle en riant. Tu ne devrais pas le savoir ?

Ray esquissa un sourire ironique.

— Je n'ai pas l'impression de savoir grand-chose ces temps-ci. Il n'y a rien de précis, juste… On a des problèmes avec le grand, Tom. Il a du mal à s'adapter à sa nouvelle école et il est devenu grognon et distant.

— Il a quel âge ?

— Douze ans.

— C'est normal à cet âge, remarqua Kate. D'après ma mère, j'étais une vraie petite peste.

— Ah, ça je veux bien le croire ! répliqua Ray. (Kate lui montra le poing et il rit.) Je vois ce que tu veux dire, mais honnêtement, c'est vraiment étrange de la part de Tom et c'est presque arrivé du jour au lendemain.

— Tu crois qu'il se fait harceler à l'école ?

— J'y ai pensé. Mais je ne veux pas l'embêter en lui posant trop de questions. Mags est plus douée que moi pour ce genre de choses, mais elle ne peut rien en tirer. (Il soupira.) Faites des gosses !

— Sûrement pas, lâcha Kate tandis qu'ils arrivaient au poste. (Elle passa son badge pour ouvrir la porte de service.) Pas pour le moment en tout cas. Je compte bien en profiter au maximum avant.

Elle rit et Ray ressentit une pointe de jalousie à l'égard de sa vie simple.

Ils montèrent l'escalier. Quand ils atteignirent le palier du troisième étage, où se trouvait la Criminelle, Ray s'arrêta en posant la main sur la porte.

— À propos de l'affaire Jordan…

— C'est entre toi et moi. Je sais.

Elle sourit et Ray réprima un soupir de soulagement. Si le préfet apprenait qu'il avait quelqu'un sur l'affaire qu'elle avait expressément ordonné de classer, même à titre bénévole, elle ne perdrait pas de temps pour lui faire savoir ce qu'elle en pensait. Et il serait de nouveau en uniforme avant même qu'elle ait raccroché.

De retour dans son bureau, il se pencha sur les préparatifs de l'opération Break. Le préfet lui avait demandé de diriger une enquête sur un blanchiment d'argent présumé. Deux boîtes de nuit du centre-ville servaient de couverture pour des activités illicites et il y avait quantité d'informations à analyser. Étant donné que les deux propriétaires des boîtes de nuit étaient de grandes figures du monde des affaires, Ray savait que le préfet le testait et il avait l'intention de se montrer à la hauteur.

Il passa le reste de l'après-midi à examiner les dossiers de l'équipe numéro trois. Le lieutenant, Kelly Proctor, était en congé maternité et Ray avait demandé à l'inspecteur le plus expérimenté de l'équipe de la remplacer. Sean faisait du bon travail, mais Ray voulait s'assurer que rien ne passait à travers les mailles du filet pendant l'absence de Kelly.

D'ici peu, il pourrait confier plus de responsabilités à Kate, pensa-t-il. Elle était si brillante, elle pourrait apprendre une ou deux choses à certains de ses inspecteurs les plus chevronnés, et elle relèverait le défi avec plaisir. Il repensa à son regard au moment où elle lui avait annoncé qu'elle travaillait toujours sur le délit de fuite : son dévouement était indéniable.

Il se demanda ce qui la faisait avancer. Était-ce simplement qu'elle ne voulait pas s'avouer vaincue ou croyait-elle vraiment qu'elle pourrait résoudre l'affaire ? Avait-il accepté trop vite de classer le dossier ? Il réfléchit un instant, tambourinant des doigts sur son bureau. Il avait fini son service et avait promis à Mags de ne pas rentrer trop tard, mais il pouvait y consacrer une demi-heure et être quand même chez lui à une heure décente. Avant de changer d'avis, il ouvrit le dernier tiroir de son bureau et sortit le dossier de Jacob.

Il ne leva le nez qu'une heure plus tard.

10

— Ah, je me disais bien que c'était vous ! (Bethan me rattrape sur le sentier de Penfach, hors d'haleine, son manteau claquant derrière elle.) Je vais à la poste. Ça tombe bien que je vous voie, j'ai une bonne nouvelle.

— Laquelle ?

J'attends que Bethan reprenne son souffle.

— Le représentant d'une société de cartes de vœux est passé hier, explique-t-elle. Je lui ai montré vos photos et il pense qu'elles feraient d'excellentes cartes postales.

— C'est vrai ?

Bethan rit.

— Oui, c'est vrai. Il aimerait que vous en imprimiez quelques-unes, il les récupérera la prochaine fois qu'il passera.

Je ne peux pas m'empêcher de sourire.

— C'est incroyable, merci.

— Et je les vendrai pour vous à la boutique. En fait, si vous pouvez bricoler un site Internet et mettre quelques photos en ligne, j'enverrai l'adresse à notre liste de diffusion. Il y a forcément des gens qui aimeraient avoir une belle photo de l'endroit où ils sont allés en vacances.

— Je vais le faire.

Je n'ai pas la moindre idée de la manière dont on s'y prend pour créer un site Internet.

— Vous pourriez tracer des messages en plus des noms. « Bonne chance », « Félicitations », ce genre de choses.

— Oui, bonne idée.

J'imagine toute une série de cartes disposées sur un présentoir, reconnaissables au J incliné que j'utiliserais comme logo. Pas de nom, juste une initiale. Elles pourraient avoir été prises par n'importe qui. Il faut que je commence à gagner de l'argent. Je n'ai pas beaucoup de dépenses – je ne mange presque rien –, mais mes économies ne dureront pas indéfiniment et je n'ai aucune autre source de revenus. En plus, le travail me manque. Une voix dans ma tête se moque de moi et je m'efforce de ne pas l'écouter. Pourquoi est-ce que je ne me lancerais pas ? Pourquoi les gens n'achèteraient-ils pas mes photos ? Ils achetaient bien mes sculptures. Je répète :

— Je vais le faire.

— Bon, eh bien c'est réglé, conclut Bethan, ravie. Où est-ce que vous allez aujourd'hui ?

Je m'aperçois que nous sommes déjà arrivées à Penfach.

— Je pensais explorer la côte. Prendre d'autres plages en photo.

— Vous n'en trouverez pas de plus jolie que Penfach. (Bethan regarde sa montre.) Mais il y a un car pour Port Ellis dans dix minutes, c'est un bon point de départ.

Quand le car arrive, je suis contente de monter. Il est vide et je m'assois assez loin du chauffeur pour ne pas avoir à faire la conversation. Le véhicule s'enfonce à l'intérieur des terres sur des routes étroites et je vois la mer disparaître, puis je la cherche de nouveau tandis que nous approchons de notre destination.

La rue calme où s'arrête le car est bordée de murs en pierre qui semblent courir tout le long de Port Ellis. Il n'y a pas de trottoir, je marche donc sur la route vers ce que j'espère être le centre du village. Je vais explorer l'intérieur, puis je me dirigerai vers la côte.

Le sac est à moitié caché dans la haie, le plastique noir fermé par un nœud et lancé dans le fossé peu profond au bord de la route. Je le remarque à peine, le prenant pour des ordures jetées par des vacanciers.

Mais il bouge légèrement.

Te laisser partir

Si légèrement que je me dis que ça doit être mon imagination, que c'est sûrement le vent qui fait bruisser le plastique. Je me penche vers la haie pour attraper le sac et j'ai alors la nette impression qu'il y a quelque chose de vivant à l'intérieur.

Je tombe à genoux et déchire le sac-poubelle. Une odeur fétide de peur et d'excrément me prend à la gorge et je réprime un haut-le-cœur en voyant les deux animaux à l'intérieur. Un chiot est immobile, la peau de son dos lacérée par les griffes du chien affolé qui se tortille à ses côtés en poussant des gémissements à peine audibles. Je laisse échapper un sanglot et prends le chiot vivant pour le glisser sous mon manteau. Je me relève maladroitement et regarde autour de moi, puis j'appelle un homme qui traverse la route une centaine de mètres plus loin.

— À l'aide ! S'il vous plaît, à l'aide !

L'homme se retourne et approche sans se presser, ma panique n'ayant pas l'air de l'émouvoir. Il est âgé et a le dos tellement voûté que son menton repose sur sa poitrine.

— Est-ce qu'il y a un vétérinaire par ici ? dis-je dès qu'il est assez près.

L'homme regarde le chiot calme et silencieux sous mon manteau et jette un coup d'œil dans le sac noir par terre. Il secoue lentement la tête avec un claquement de langue.

— Le fils d'Alun Mathews, répond-il.

Il fait un nouveau signe de tête, sans doute pour m'indiquer où trouver le fils, puis ramasse le sac noir avec son contenu macabre. Je le suis, sentant la chaleur du chiot contre ma poitrine.

Le cabinet se trouve dans un petit bâtiment blanc au bout d'une ruelle ; une enseigne au-dessus de la porte indique « Cabinet vétérinaire de Port Ellis ». Dans la minuscule salle d'attente, une femme est assise sur une chaise en plastique avec un panier pour chat sur les genoux. Une odeur de chien et de désinfectant plane dans la pièce.

La réceptionniste lève les yeux de son ordinateur.

— Bonjour, M. Thomas, que puis-je faire pour vous ?

Mon compagnon la salue d'un hochement de tête et hisse le sac noir sur le comptoir.

— Elle a trouvé deux chiots dans la haie, indique-t-il. Si c'est pas malheureux, nom de Dieu ! (Il se penche vers moi et me tapote doucement le bras.) Ils vont bien s'occuper de vous ici, assure-t-il avant de quitter le cabinet en faisant tinter joyeusement la cloche au-dessus de la porte.

— Merci de nous les avoir amenés.

La réceptionniste porte sur sa tunique bleu vif un badge avec le nom « Megan » écrit en noir.

— La plupart des gens ne l'auraient pas fait, vous savez.

Des clés se balancent sur sa poitrine au bout d'un cordon parsemé de badges d'animaux colorés et de pin's d'associations caritatives, comme ceux des infirmières en pédiatrie. Elle ouvre le sac et blêmit un instant avant de s'éloigner discrètement avec.

Quelques secondes plus tard, une porte s'ouvre sur la salle d'attente et Megan me sourit.

— Vous voulez bien l'amener par ici ? Patrick va vous recevoir tout de suite.

— Merci.

Je suis Megan dans une pièce à la forme bizarre avec des placards coincés dans les angles. À l'opposé se trouvent un plan de travail et un petit lavabo en inox dans lequel un homme se lave les mains avec du savon vert qui mousse sur ses avant-bras.

— Bonjour, je m'appelle Patrick. Je suis le vétérinaire, ajoute-t-il en riant. Mais vous vous en seriez doutée, j'imagine.

Il est grand – plus grand que moi, ce qui est rare – avec des cheveux blond foncé coiffés dans un style indéterminé. Sous sa blouse bleue, il porte un jean et une chemise à carreaux aux manches retroussées, et il arbore un sourire qui découvre des dents blanches parfaitement alignées. Il doit avoir environ trente-cinq ans, peut-être un peu plus.

— Je suis Jenna.

J'ouvre mon manteau pour sortir le chiot noir et blanc qui s'est endormi et laisse échapper de petits reniflements, nullement traumatisé par la mort de son frère.

— Et qui c'est celui-là ? fait le vétérinaire en prenant doucement le chiot. (Celui-ci se réveille en sursaut et se met à trembler. Patrick me le rend.) Vous pouvez le poser sur la table et le tenir pour moi ? Je ne veux pas le perturber davantage. Si c'est un homme qui a mis les chiens dans le sac, celui-ci ne refera peut-être pas confiance aux hommes avant un moment !

Il promène ses mains sur le chiot et je m'accroupis pour lui murmurer des mots réconfortants à l'oreille sans me soucier de ce que Patrick peut penser.

— Qu'est-ce que c'est comme chien ? dis-je.

— Un moite-moite.

— Un moite-moite ?

Je me relève en gardant une main sur le chiot, qui s'est à présent détendu sous l'examen délicat de Patrick.

Celui-ci se fend d'un large sourire.

— Vous savez : moitié ci, moitié ça. Principalement épagneul, je dirais, d'après ses oreilles, mais allez savoir d'où vient le reste. Colley, peut-être, ou même un peu de terrier. On ne se serait pas débarrassé d'eux s'ils avaient été des chiens de race, ça c'est certain.

Il prend le chiot et me le tend pour que je le câline.

— Quelle horreur ! dis-je en humant la chaleur du petit chien. (Il enfouit son museau dans mon cou.) Qui peut bien faire une chose pareille ?

— On informera la police, mais il y a peu de chances qu'ils découvrent quoi que ce soit. Les gens d'ici ne sont pas très bavards.

— Et lui ? Qu'est-ce qu'il va devenir ?

Patrick enfonce les mains dans les poches de sa blouse et s'appuie contre le lavabo.

— Vous pouvez le garder ?

Il a des traits plus clairs au coin des yeux, comme s'il les plissait à cause du soleil. Il doit passer beaucoup de temps dehors.

— Étant donné les conditions dans lesquelles il a été trouvé, il est peu probable que quelqu'un vienne le réclamer, reprend Patrick. Et on manque cruellement de place au chenil. Ce serait bien si vous pouviez l'adopter. Ça m'a tout l'air d'être un bon chien.

— Mon Dieu, je ne peux pas m'occuper d'un chien !

J'ai la sensation que tout cela arrive juste parce que je suis venue à Port Ellis aujourd'hui.

— Pourquoi pas ?

J'hésite. Comment lui expliquer que j'attire les malheurs ? J'aimerais beaucoup prendre soin d'un animal, mais en même temps ça me terrifie. Et si je suis incapable de bien m'en occuper ? Et s'il tombe malade ?

— Je ne sais même pas si mon propriétaire serait d'accord, dis-je finalement.

— Où est-ce que vous vivez ? À Port Ellis ?

Je secoue la tête.

— À Penfach. Dans un cottage près du camping.

Une lueur traverse les yeux de Patrick.

— Vous louez la maison de Iestyn ?

J'acquiesce. Je ne suis plus surprise d'apprendre que tout le monde connaît Iestyn.

— Ne vous en faites pas pour lui, poursuit Patrick. Iestyn Jones est allé à l'école avec mon père, et j'en sais assez sur lui pour que vous puissiez adopter un troupeau d'éléphants si ça vous chante.

Je souris. Difficile de faire autrement.

— Je crois que je n'irai pas jusqu'aux éléphants, dis-je en me sentant aussitôt rougir.

Te laisser partir

— Les épagneuls s'entendent très bien avec les enfants. Vous en avez ?

Le silence semble durer une éternité.

— Non. Je n'ai pas d'enfants.

Le chien se tortille pour se libérer de ma main et commence à me lécher furieusement le menton. Je sens son cœur battre contre le mien.

— D'accord, dis-je. Je l'adopte.

11

Ray sortit doucement du lit, tâchant de ne pas déranger Mags. Il lui avait promis un week-end sans travail, mais s'il se levait maintenant, il aurait une heure pour répondre à ses e-mails et avancer sur le dossier de l'opération Break avant qu'elle émerge. Ils allaient faire deux perquisitions simultanées dans les boîtes de nuit, et si leurs sources se révélaient fiables, ils y trouveraient de grandes quantités de cocaïne ainsi que des documents montrant les mouvements d'argent au sein de ces établissements soi-disant honnêtes.

Il enfila son pantalon et partit à la recherche de café. Tandis que l'eau chauffait, il entendit quelqu'un entrer à pas feutrés dans la cuisine et se retourna.

— Papa ! (Lucy jeta ses bras autour de sa taille.) Je savais pas que tu étais réveillé !

— Ça fait longtemps que tu es debout ? dit-il en se libérant de son étreinte pour se baisser et l'embrasser. Je suis désolé, je ne t'ai pas vue hier soir avant que tu ailles au lit. Comment s'est passée l'école ?

— Bien, je crois. Comment s'est passé le travail ?

— Bien, je crois.

Ils échangèrent un sourire.

— Je peux regarder la télé ?

Lucy retint son souffle et leva la tête vers lui avec des yeux suppliants. Mags avait des règles strictes au sujet de la télévision le matin, mais c'était le week-end et cela permettrait à Ray de travailler un moment.

— Allez, vas-y.

Elle se précipita dans le salon avant que Ray puisse changer d'avis, et il entendit le poste se mettre en marche puis les voix haut perchées des personnages d'un dessin animé. Ray s'assit à la table de la cuisine et alluma son BlackBerry.

À huit heures, il avait répondu à la plupart de ses e-mails et se préparait une deuxième tasse de café quand Lucy entra dans la cuisine en se plaignant d'avoir faim et en demandant où était le petit déjeuner.

— Tom dort encore ? dit Ray.

— Oui. Il est feignant.

— Je ne suis pas feignant ! répliqua une voix indignée du haut de l'escalier.

— Si ! cria Lucy.

Des pas lourds résonnèrent à l'étage et Tom dévala l'escalier, le visage grimaçant sous ses cheveux en bataille. Une vilaine éruption de boutons lui barrait le front.

— Je ne suis PAS feignant ! cria-t-il en poussant sa sœur.

— Aïe ! hurla Lucy, et des larmes lui montèrent aussitôt aux yeux.

Sa lèvre inférieure tremblait.

— C'était pas fort !

— Si !

Ray grogna et se demanda si tous les frères et sœurs se chamaillaient autant que ces deux-là. Juste au moment où il allait les séparer de force, Mags descendit l'escalier.

— Se lever à huit heures, ce n'est pas être feignant, Lucy, dit-elle avec douceur. Tom, ne tape pas ta sœur. (Elle prit le café de Ray.) C'est pour moi ?

— Oui.

Ray remit l'eau à chauffer. Il regarda ses enfants, à présent assis à table et qui parlaient de ce qu'ils allaient faire pendant les grandes vacances, leur dispute oubliée – pour l'instant, en tout cas. Mags parvenait toujours à calmer le jeu d'une façon qui lui échappait.

— Comment tu fais ? demanda-t-il.

— On appelle ça être parent, répliqua Mags. Tu devrais essayer quelquefois.

Ray ne répondit pas. Dernièrement, ils passaient leur temps à s'envoyer des piques et il n'était pas d'humeur à se lancer dans un nouveau débat sur le travail et l'éducation des enfants.

Mags s'activait dans la cuisine pour installer le petit déjeuner sur la table, préparant des toasts tout en servant du jus d'orange entre deux gorgées de café.

— Tu es rentré à quelle heure hier soir ? Je ne t'ai pas entendu.

Elle passa un tablier par-dessus son pyjama et entreprit de casser des œufs. Ray lui avait offert ce tablier pour Noël quelques années plus tôt. Il avait fait ça pour plaisanter – comme ces maris horribles qui achètent à leur femme des casseroles ou des planches à repasser –, mais Mags l'avait tout de suite adopté. Il arborait le portrait d'une ménagère des années cinquante, avec le slogan : « J'adore cuisiner au vin… parfois j'en mets même dans les plats. » Ray se revit rentrer chez lui après le travail et passer ses bras autour de sa femme pendant qu'elle était aux fourneaux, sentant le tablier se froisser sous ses doigts. Il n'avait pas fait ça depuis longtemps.

— Vers une heure, je crois, répondit-il.

Il y avait eu un hold-up dans une station-service de la banlieue de Bristol. La patrouille avait réussi à arrêter les quatre responsables en quelques heures et Ray était resté au bureau plus par solidarité envers son équipe que par réelle nécessité.

Le café était trop chaud mais il but quand même une gorgée et se brûla la langue. Son BlackBerry vibra et il jeta un coup d'œil sur l'écran. Stumpy lui avait envoyé un e-mail pour lui signaler que les quatre délinquants avaient été inculpés et présentés à l'audience du samedi matin, où les magistrats les avaient placés en détention provisoire. Ray envoya un rapide message au commissaire.

— Ray ! fit Mags. Pas de travail ! Tu as promis.

— Désolé, je prenais des nouvelles de l'affaire d'hier soir.

— Seulement deux jours, Ray. Ils vont devoir se débrouiller sans toi.

Elle posa une poêle avec des œufs sur la table et s'assit.

— Attention, c'est chaud ! dit-elle à Lucy. (Elle leva les yeux vers Ray.) Tu veux déjeuner ?

— Non, merci, je grignoterai quelque chose plus tard. Je vais me doucher.

Il s'appuya un instant contre le chambranle de la porte et les regarda manger.

— On doit laisser le portail ouvert pour le laveur de vitres lundi, indiqua Mags. Tu pourras penser à l'ouvrir quand tu sortiras les poubelles demain soir ? Ah, et je suis passée voir les voisins pour les arbres, ils vont bientôt les faire élaguer, mais j'attends de voir.

Ray se demanda si le *Post* parlerait du hold-up de la veille. Après tout, ils ne perdaient pas de temps quand la police échouait à résoudre une affaire.

— Ça a l'air super, dit-il.

Mags posa sa fourchette et le dévisagea.

— Quoi ? fit Ray.

Il monta prendre une douche, sortant son BlackBerry pour envoyer un message à l'attaché de presse de service. Ce serait dommage de ne pas tirer profit d'un travail bien fait.

— Merci pour aujourd'hui, dit Mags.

Ils étaient assis sur le canapé, mais ni l'un ni l'autre ne s'était encore donné la peine d'allumer la télévision.

— Pourquoi ?

— D'avoir mis le travail de côté, pour une fois.

Mags rejeta la tête en arrière et ferma les paupières. Les rides au coin de ses yeux se détendirent et elle parut tout de suite plus jeune : Ray s'avisa qu'elle fronçait beaucoup les sourcils ces temps-ci, et il se demanda s'il en faisait autant.

Mags avait ce que la mère de Ray appelait un sourire « généreux ».

— Ça veut simplement dire que j'ai une grande bouche, avait lâché Mags en riant la première fois qu'elle avait entendu ça.

Ray esquissa un sourire en repensant à ce moment. Elle était peut-être un peu moins joviale ces derniers temps, mais c'était toujours la même Mags, après toutes ces années. Elle se plaignait souvent d'avoir pris du poids depuis la naissance des enfants, mais Ray l'aimait bien comme ça ; le ventre rond et mou, la poitrine pleine et tombante. Elle faisait la sourde oreille à ses compliments, et il avait cessé depuis longtemps de lui en faire.

— C'était super, dit Ray. On devrait faire ça plus souvent.

Ils avaient passé la journée à flâner et à jouer au cricket dans le jardin, profitant au maximum du soleil. Ray avait sorti de la remise le vieux spirobole et les enfants s'étaient amusés avec le reste de l'après-midi, bien que Tom ait décrété que c'était « vraiment trop nul ».

— C'était bien de voir Tom rire, remarqua Mags.

— Ça ne lui arrive pas souvent ces temps-ci, hein ?

— Je m'inquiète pour lui.

— Tu veux qu'on retourne au collège ?

— Je ne suis pas sûre que ça serve à grand-chose, dit Mags. C'est presque la fin de l'année scolaire. J'espère que le fait de changer de professeur arrangera les choses. Et puis il ne fera plus partie des plus jeunes, il aura peut-être plus confiance en lui.

Ray essayait de comprendre son fils, lequel avait traversé le dernier trimestre avec le même manque d'enthousiasme qui avait préoccupé son professeur en début d'année.

— J'aimerais au moins qu'il nous parle, ajouta Mags.

— Il jure que tout va bien, dit Ray. C'est un ado, c'est tout, mais il va devoir se secouer, parce que s'il ne s'investit pas plus l'année du brevet, il est foutu.

— Vous avez eu l'air de mieux vous entendre tous les deux aujourd'hui.

C'était vrai, ils ne s'étaient pas disputés une seule fois. Ray n'avait pas répondu aux remarques insolentes de Tom et celui-ci avait moins levé les yeux au ciel que d'habitude. La journée avait été bonne.

— Et ce n'était pas si dur d'éteindre le BlackBerry, non ? observa Mags. Pas de palpitations ? pas de sueurs froides ? pas de tremblements ?

— Ah, ah ! Non, ce n'était pas si dur.

Il ne l'avait pas éteint, bien sûr, et il avait vibré dans sa poche toute la journée. Il avait fini par aller aux toilettes pour regarder ses e-mails et s'assurer qu'il n'avait rien raté d'urgent. Il avait répondu au préfet au sujet de l'opération Break et avait jeté un rapide coup d'œil à un message de Kate à propos du délit de fuite qu'il avait hâte de lire plus attentivement. Ce que Mags ne comprenait pas, c'était que s'il éteignait son BlackBerry tout un week-end, il aurait tant de travail le lundi suivant qu'il passerait la semaine à rattraper le retard sans pouvoir s'occuper d'autre chose.

Il se leva.

— Bon, je vais quand même aller travailler une petite heure dans le bureau maintenant.

— Quoi ? Ray, tu avais dit pas de travail !

Ray était perdu.

— Mais les enfants sont au lit.

— Oui, mais je suis…

Mags s'arrêta et secoua un peu la tête, comme si elle avait quelque chose dans l'oreille.

— Quoi ?

— Rien. C'est bon. Fais ce que tu as à faire.

— Je redescends dans une heure, promis.

Presque deux heures plus tard, Mags poussa la porte du bureau.

— Je t'ai fait du thé.

— Merci.

Ray s'étira et gémit en sentant son dos craquer.

Mags posa la tasse sur le bureau et, par-dessus l'épaule de Ray, jeta un coup d'œil à l'épaisse liasse de documents qu'il lisait.

— C'est l'affaire de la boîte de nuit ? (Elle parcourut la première feuille.) Jacob Jordan ? Ce n'est pas le garçon qui s'est fait renverser l'année dernière ?

— Si.

Mags eut l'air perplexe.

— Je croyais que l'affaire était classée.

— Elle l'est.

Mags s'assit sur l'accoudoir du fauteuil de salon qu'ils avaient mis dans le bureau parce qu'il jurait avec la moquette du rez-de-chaussée. Il détonnait là aussi, mais c'était le siège le plus confortable que Ray ait jamais essayé et il refusait de s'en séparer.

— Alors pourquoi la Criminelle travaille-t-elle encore dessus ?

Ray soupira.

— Elle ne travaille plus dessus. L'affaire est classée, mais j'ai gardé le dossier. On l'examine avec un regard nouveau pour voir si on n'a rien loupé.

— *On ?*

Ray marqua un temps d'arrêt.

— L'équipe.

Il ne savait pas pourquoi il n'avait pas parlé de Kate plus tôt, mais le faire maintenant serait étrange. Mieux valait la laisser en dehors de tout ça, au cas où le préfet aurait un jour vent de cette histoire. Inutile de ternir sa réputation si tôt dans sa carrière.

— Oh, Ray, tu n'es pas déjà assez occupé avec les dossiers en cours sans avoir à revenir sur les affaires classées ? dit Mags d'une voix douce.

— Celle-ci est encore d'actualité, répondit Ray. Et je ne peux pas m'empêcher de penser qu'on nous l'a retirée trop tôt. Peut-être qu'en revenant dessus on trouvera quelque chose.

Il y eut un silence avant que Mags reprenne la parole.

— Ce n'est pas comme Annabelle, tu sais.

Ray serra sa tasse un peu plus fort.

— Arrête.

— Tu ne peux pas continuer à te torturer comme ça pour chaque affaire que tu ne parviens pas à résoudre. (Mags se pencha et lui pressa le genou.) Tu vas devenir fou.

Ray but une gorgée de thé. Annabelle Snowden avait été la première enquête qu'on lui avait confiée en tant que capitaine. La fillette avait disparu à la sortie de l'école et ses parents étaient dans tous leurs états. Du moins, ils semblaient dans tous leurs états. Deux semaines plus tard, Ray avait inculpé le père pour meurtre après la découverte du corps d'Annabelle dans son appartement, dissimulé dans un compartiment sous le lit ; elle y avait été maintenue en vie pendant plus d'une semaine.

— Je savais qu'il y avait quelque chose de bizarre chez Terry Snowden, finit-il par déclarer en regardant Mags. J'aurais dû tout faire pour l'arrêter dès la disparition.

— Il n'y avait pas de preuves. L'instinct de flic, c'est bien beau, mais tu ne peux pas baser une enquête sur ton intuition. (Mags referma doucement le dossier de Jacob.) C'est une autre affaire. D'autres personnes.

— Encore un enfant, constata Ray.

Mags lui prit les mains.

— Mais il est déjà mort, Ray. Tu peux travailler autant d'heures que tu veux, ça ne le ramènera pas. Passe à autre chose.

Ray ne répondit pas. Il se retourna vers son bureau et rouvrit le dossier, faisant à peine attention à Mags qui quitta la pièce pour aller se coucher. Lorsqu'il se connecta à sa messagerie, il avait un nouvel e-mail de Kate, reçu quelques minutes plus tôt. Il lui envoya un message rapide.

Te laisser partir

— Encore debout ?

La réponse arriva quelques secondes plus tard.

— Je regarde si la mère de Jacob est sur Facebook. Et je suis une enchère sur eBay. Et toi ?
— Je fais le tour des véhicules incendiés dans les régions voisines. J'en ai pour un moment.
— Super, tu vas pouvoir me tenir éveillée !

Ray imagina Kate recroquevillée sur son canapé, son ordinateur d'un côté et un tas de friandises de l'autre.

— Ben & Jerry's ? écrivit-il.
— Comment tu as deviné ?

Ray sourit. Il déplaça la fenêtre de sa messagerie dans un coin de l'écran où il pouvait garder un œil sur ses e-mails et commença à parcourir les fax des rapports d'hôpitaux.

— Tu n'avais pas promis à Mags de prendre ton week-end ?
— C'est ce que je FAIS ! Je travaille juste un peu maintenant que les enfants sont couchés. Il faut bien que quelqu'un te tienne compagnie…
— J'en suis très honorée. Quelle meilleure façon de passer son samedi soir ?

Ray rit.

— Tu trouves quelque chose sur Facebook ? écrivit-il.
— Une ou deux possibilités, mais elles n'ont pas de photos de profil. Attends, le téléphone sonne. Je reviens.

À contrecœur, Ray ferma sa messagerie pour se concentrer sur la pile de dossiers. Jacob était mort depuis des mois et une petite voix dans sa tête lui disait que tout cela était vain. Le fragment d'anti-brouillard de Volvo s'était révélé être celui du véhicule appartenant à une femme au foyer qui avait dérapé sur le verglas et percuté l'un des arbres bordant la route. Toutes ces heures de travail pour rien, et ils continuaient malgré tout. Ray jouait avec le feu en allant à l'encontre des souhaits du préfet et, de plus, il laissait Kate en faire autant. Mais il était déjà allé trop loin. Il ne pouvait plus reculer.

12

L'atmosphère va se réchauffer dans la journée, mais pour le moment l'air est frais et je rentre la tête dans les épaules.

— Il fait froid aujourd'hui, dis-je tout haut.

Je me suis mise à parler toute seule, comme la vieille femme qui se promenait sur le pont suspendu de Clifton, les bras chargés de sacs en plastique remplis de journaux. Je me demande si elle est encore là-bas ; si elle traverse toujours le pont matin et soir. Quand on quitte un endroit, on imagine vite que la vie continue comme avant là-bas, même si rien ne reste jamais pareil bien longtemps. Ma vie à Bristol aurait pu être celle de quelqu'un d'autre.

Je chasse cette pensée puis j'enfile mes bottes et enroule une écharpe autour de mon cou. Comme tous les jours, je bataille avec la serrure qui accroche. Je parviens finalement à fermer la porte et je mets la clé dans ma poche. Beau court sur mes talons. Il me suit comme mon ombre, ne voulant pas me perdre de vue. La première fois que je l'ai ramené au cottage, il a pleuré toute la nuit pour venir dormir sur mon lit. Je m'en suis voulu, mais j'ai enfoui ma tête sous l'oreiller pour ne pas l'entendre, sachant que si je me laissais attendrir je le regretterais. Plusieurs jours se sont écoulés avant qu'il cesse de pleurer et il dort à présent au pied de l'escalier, se réveillant dès qu'il entend craquer le plancher de la chambre.

Je vérifie que j'ai bien la liste des commandes du jour – je les ai toutes en tête, mais je préfère être certaine de ne pas me tromper. Bethan continue de faire la promotion de mes photos auprès des vacanciers et aussi incroyable que cela me paraisse, j'ai du travail. Pas autant qu'avant, avec les expositions et les commandes de sculptures, mais j'ai quand même de quoi faire.

J'ai réapprovisionné deux fois la boutique du camping en cartes postales et je reçois quelques commandes sur le site Internet que j'ai bricolé. Il n'a rien à voir avec le joli site que j'avais avant, mais chaque fois que je le regarde, je suis fière d'avoir réussi à le faire toute seule. Ce n'est pas grand-chose, mais je commence lentement à me dire que je ne suis peut-être pas aussi incapable que je le croyais.

Je n'ai pas mis mon nom sur le site : juste une galerie de photos, un système de commandes rudimentaire et assez peu pratique, et le nom de ma nouvelle activité : « Gravé dans le sable ». Bethan m'a aidée à le trouver alors que nous étions ensemble, autour d'une bouteille de vin, un soir au cottage. Elle parlait de mon projet avec un enthousiasme communicatif et n'arrêtait pas de me demander mon avis, ce qui ne m'était pas arrivé depuis très longtemps.

Le mois d'août est la période la plus chargée au camping ; même si je vois encore Bethan au moins une fois par semaine, je regrette le calme de l'hiver, quand nous pouvions discuter pendant une heure ou plus, les pieds collés au radiateur à bain d'huile dans un coin de la boutique. Les plages sont elles aussi fréquentées et je dois me lever à l'aube afin d'être sûre de trouver un coin de sable lisse pour mes photos.

Une mouette crie et Beau court dans le sable, aboyant après l'oiseau qui le nargue dans le ciel. Je donne des coups de pied dans les débris sur la plage et ramasse un long bâton. La marée se retire, mais le sable est déjà chaud et presque sec. Je vais tracer les messages d'aujourd'hui près de la mer. Je sors un bout de papier de ma poche pour me remémorer la première commande.

— Julia, dis-je. Bon, c'est assez simple.

Beau me regarde d'un air interrogateur. Il pense que je lui parle. Peut-être a-t-il raison, même si je dois faire en sorte de ne pas m'attacher à lui. Je le vois de la même manière que Iestyn doit considérer ses chiens de berger : comme un outil ; là pour remplir une fonction. Beau est mon chien de garde. Je n'ai pas encore eu besoin d'être protégée, mais ça pourrait arriver.

Je me penche et trace un grand J, puis je recule pour vérifier les dimensions avant d'écrire le reste du nom. Satisfaite, je me débarrasse du bâton et saisis mon appareil. Le soleil a maintenant franchi la ligne d'horizon et la lumière rasante pare le sable d'un éclat rose. Je prends une douzaine de photos, m'accroupissant pour regarder dans le viseur jusqu'à ce que l'inscription soit nappée d'écume.

Pour la commande suivante, je cherche un coin de plage propre. Je travaille vite, ramassant des bâtons à pleins bras parmi les tas rejetés par la mer. Quand le dernier bout de bois est en place, j'observe ma création d'un œil critique. Des brins d'algues encore luisantes adoucissent les arêtes des bâtons et des cailloux que j'ai utilisés pour encadrer le message. Le cœur en bois flotté fait deux mètres de diamètre : assez grand pour accueillir les lettres ornées d'arabesques avec lesquelles j'ai écrit : « Pardonne-moi, Alice. » Tandis que je tends le bras pour déplacer un morceau de bois, Beau sort de l'eau à toute allure en aboyant, très excité.

— Doucement !

D'une main, je protège mon appareil photo au cas où il me sauterait dessus. Mais le chien m'ignore, passant devant moi dans un nuage de sable mouillé pour se ruer de l'autre côté de la plage et bondir autour d'un homme qui approche. Je crois d'abord qu'il s'agit du promeneur avec son chien qui m'a parlé une fois, mais il enfonce alors les mains dans les poches de sa veste en toile huilée et je retiens mon souffle, car ce geste me dit quelque chose. Comment est-ce possible ? Je ne connais personne ici, à part Bethan et Iestyn, et pourtant cet homme, qui se trouve à présent à moins de cent mètres, se dirige d'un pas décidé vers moi. J'aperçois son visage. Je le connais, mais je suis incapable de l'identifier. Je me sens vulnérable. Une boule de panique se forme dans ma gorge et j'appelle Beau.

— Jenna, c'est bien ça ?

J'ai envie de m'enfuir, mais je reste clouée sur place. Je fais le tour de tous les gens que je connaissais à Bristol. Je sais que je l'ai déjà vu quelque part.

— Excusez-moi, je ne voulais pas vous faire peur, commence l'homme, et je me rends compte que je tremble. (Il a l'air sincèrement désolé et arbore un large sourire comme pour se racheter.) Je suis Patrick Mathews. Le vétérinaire de Port Ellis.

Je me souviens aussitôt de lui et de la façon dont il avait enfoncé les mains dans les poches de sa blouse bleue.

— Désolée, dis-je enfin en retrouvant ma voix qui semble petite et mal assurée. Je ne vous avais pas reconnu.

Je lève les yeux vers le sentier littoral désert. Des vacanciers vont bientôt arriver pour passer la journée à la plage : équipés de paravents, de crème solaire et de parapluies de façon à faire face à tous les temps. Pour une fois, je suis contente que ce soit la haute saison et qu'il y ait du monde à Penfach : le sourire de Patrick est chaleureux, mais je me suis déjà laissé avoir une fois par ce genre d'expression.

Il se penche pour gratter les oreilles de Beau.

— On dirait que vous avez fait du bon travail avec lui. Comment l'avez-vous appelé ?

— Beau.

C'est plus fort que moi : je fais deux pas en arrière, à peine perceptibles, puis je sens le nœud dans ma gorge se desserrer. J'essaie de détendre mes bras le long de mon corps, mais mes mains remontent tout de suite sur mes hanches.

Patrick s'agenouille et cajole Beau, qui roule sur le dos pour qu'on lui gratte le ventre, comblé par cette tendresse inhabituelle.

— Il n'a pas l'air nerveux du tout.

La décontraction de Beau me rassure. Il paraît que les chiens se trompent rarement sur les gens.

— Non, il va bien, dis-je.

— Ça se voit.

Patrick se relève et balaie le sable sur ses genoux. Je reste sur mes gardes.

— Vous n'avez pas eu de problèmes avec Iestyn, j'imagine ? demande Patrick en souriant.

— Aucun. Il pense sans doute qu'un chien est indispensable dans un foyer.

— Je suis assez d'accord avec lui. J'en aurais bien un, mais je travaille tellement que cela ne serait pas raisonnable. Bon, je côtoie assez d'animaux pendant la journée, je n'ai pas à me plaindre de ce côté-là.

Il a l'air dans son élément au bord de la mer, ses bottes incrustées de sable et sa veste usée par le sel. Il désigne le cœur en bois flotté d'un signe de tête.

— Qui est Alice ? Pourquoi est-ce que vous lui demandez pardon ?

— Oh, ce n'est pas moi. (Il doit me trouver bizarre avec mes dessins sur le sable.) Enfin, le sentiment n'est pas le mien. Je le prends en photo pour quelqu'un d'autre.

Patrick semble déconcerté.

— C'est mon travail, dis-je. Je suis photographe. (Je lève mon appareil comme si, sans l'objet, il pouvait ne pas me croire.) Les gens m'envoient des messages qu'ils veulent voir écrits sur le sable. Je viens ici, je les écris et je leur envoie la photo.

Je m'arrête, mais il a l'air réellement intéressé.

— Quel genre de messages ?

— Surtout des mots d'amour, ou des demandes en mariage, mais j'ai toutes sortes de commandes. Là, il s'agit d'excuses, bien sûr, mais les gens me demandent parfois des citations célèbres ou les paroles de leurs chansons préférées. C'est différent à chaque fois.

Je m'interromps, me sentant rougir.

— Et vous gagnez votre vie comme ça ? Quel boulot fantastique !

J'essaie de déceler du sarcasme dans sa voix, mais je n'en trouve pas, et je me laisse aller à ressentir un peu de fierté. C'*est* un boulot fantastique, et je l'ai créé de toutes pièces.

— Je vends aussi d'autres photos. Surtout de la baie. C'est un coin magnifique, beaucoup de touristes veulent en emporter un petit bout avec eux.

— C'est bien vrai. J'adore cet endroit.

Nous nous taisons quelques instants en regardant les vagues se former puis se briser sur le sable. Je commence à me sentir nerveuse et je cherche autre chose à dire.

— Qu'est-ce qui vous amène sur la plage ? Peu de gens s'aventurent ici à cette heure-ci, sauf pour promener leurs chiens.

— J'avais un oiseau à relâcher, explique Patrick. Une dame m'a amené un fou de Bassan avec une aile cassée et on l'a gardé au cabinet quelques semaines, le temps qu'il se rétablisse. Je l'ai amené en haut de la falaise aujourd'hui pour le remettre en liberté. On essaie de les relâcher à l'endroit où ils ont été trouvés pour optimiser leurs chances de survie. Quand j'ai vu votre message sur la plage, je n'ai pas pu résister à l'envie de descendre pour vous demander à qui il s'adressait. Ce n'est qu'en arrivant en bas que je vous ai reconnue.

— L'oiseau a réussi à s'envoler ?

Patrick acquiesce.

— Oui, ça va aller. Ça arrive assez souvent. Vous n'êtes pas d'ici, non ? Si je me souviens bien, vous avez dit que ça ne faisait pas longtemps que vous viviez à Penfach quand vous avez amené Beau. Où est-ce que vous habitiez avant ?

Te laisser partir

Je n'ai pas le temps de réfléchir à une réponse qu'un téléphone sonne, la petite mélodie tranchant avec l'atmosphère de la plage. Je réprime un soupir de soulagement, bien que mon histoire soit maintenant rodée à force de la répéter à Iestyn, à Bethan et aux quelques promeneurs qui viennent faire la conversation avec moi. Je suis une artiste, mais je me suis blessée à la main dans un accident et je ne peux plus travailler, je me suis donc reconvertie dans la photographie. Ce n'est pas si éloigné de la vérité, après tout. On ne m'a pas demandé si j'avais des enfants, peut-être la réponse se lit-elle sur mon visage.

— Excusez-moi, dit Patrick. (Il fouille dans ses poches et sort un petit pager, enseveli sous une poignée de granulés pour chevaux et de brins de paille qui tombent dans le sable.) Je dois le mettre à fond sinon je ne l'entends pas. (Il jette un coup d'œil sur l'écran.) Il faut que je file, désolé. Je suis volontaire au centre de sauvetage en mer de Port Ellis. Je suis d'astreinte une ou deux fois par mois, et apparemment on a besoin de nous maintenant. (Il remet le pager dans sa poche.) Ça m'a fait plaisir de vous revoir, Jenna. Très plaisir.

Il me fait un signe de la main puis traverse la plage en courant et gravit le sentier sablonneux, disparaissant avant que je puisse lui dire que c'est réciproque.

De retour au cottage, Beau s'effondre dans son panier, épuisé. Je transfère sur mon ordinateur les photos prises le matin en attendant que l'eau chauffe. Elles ne sont pas si mal, compte tenu de l'interruption : les lettres ressortent bien sur le sable et le cadre en bois flotté est parfait. Je laisse la meilleure image à l'écran pour y jeter un coup d'œil plus tard et je monte à l'étage avec mon café. Je vais le regretter, je le sais, mais c'est plus fort que moi.

M'asseyant par terre, je pose ma tasse sur le plancher nu et tends le bras sous le lit pour attraper le coffret auquel je n'ai pas touché depuis mon arrivée à Penfach. Je le tire vers moi et me mets en tailleur pour soulever le couvercle, libérant la poussière en même temps que les souvenirs. Je commence à me sentir mal et je sais que je devrais le refermer sans fouiller davantage. Mais je suis comme une droguée en manque, et rien ne peut m'arrêter.

Je sors le petit album photo qui se trouve au-dessus d'une liasse de documents officiels. Un par un, je caresse ces instantanés d'une époque si éloignée qu'ils semblent appartenir à quelqu'un d'autre. Me voici dans le jardin ; me revoici dans la cuisine, en train de faire à manger. Et me voici enceinte, montrant fièrement mon ventre en souriant à l'appareil. Ma gorge se noue et je sens un picotement familier derrière mes yeux. Je refoule mes larmes d'un battement de paupières. J'étais si heureuse, cet été-là, certaine que ce nouvel être allait tout changer et que nous pourrions recommencer à zéro. Je pensais que ce serait un nouveau départ pour nous. Je caresse la photo en suivant le contour de mon ventre et en imaginant où pouvaient se trouver sa tête, ses membres recroquevillés, ses orteils à peine formés.

Doucement, comme pour ne pas déranger l'enfant à naître, je ferme l'album et le remets dans le coffret. Je devrais redescendre à présent, tant que j'en suis encore capable. Mais c'est comme jouer avec une dent douloureuse ou gratter une croûte. Je fouille jusqu'à ce que mes doigts rencontrent le doux tissu du lapin avec lequel je dormais quand j'étais enceinte, pour l'imprégner de mon odeur et le donner à mon fils à sa naissance. Je le tiens contre mon visage pour le sentir, ayant désespérément besoin d'un souvenir de lui. Je laisse échapper un gémissement étouffé et Beau monte l'escalier sans bruit puis entre dans la chambre.

— Descends, Beau.

Le chien m'ignore.

— Sors !

Te laisser partir

Je lui crie dessus, une folle avec un jouet d'enfant à la main. Je crie sans pouvoir m'arrêter, car ce n'est pas Beau que je vois, mais l'homme qui m'a enlevé mon bébé ; l'homme qui a mis fin à ma vie quand il a tué mon fils.

— Sors ! Sors ! Sors !

Beau se ratatine par terre, le corps crispé et les oreilles aplaties contre le crâne. Mais il n'abandonne pas. Lentement, centimètre par centimètre, il s'approche de moi sans me quitter des yeux.

La colère s'en va aussi vite qu'elle est arrivée.

Beau s'arrête près de moi, toujours ramassé sur le plancher, et pose sa tête sur mes genoux. Il ferme les yeux et je sens son poids et sa chaleur à travers mon jean. Spontanément, mes mains se mettent à le caresser, et mes larmes commencent à couler.

13

Ray avait constitué son équipe pour l'opération Break. Il avait nommé Kate responsable des pièces à conviction, ce qui était beaucoup demander à quelqu'un qui n'était à la Criminelle que depuis dix-huit mois, mais il était certain qu'elle s'en sortirait.

— Bien sûr que je vais y arriver ! dit-elle quand Ray lui fit part de ses inquiétudes. Et je peux toujours venir te voir si j'ai un problème, non ?

— Quand tu veux, répondit Ray. On va boire un verre après le boulot ?

— Essaie de m'en empêcher !

Ils avaient pris l'habitude de se retrouver deux à trois fois par semaine après le travail pour se pencher sur le délit de fuite. Comme ils arrivaient au bout des investigations qui avaient été laissées en suspens, ils passaient de moins en moins de temps à discuter de l'affaire et de plus en plus à parler de leur vie privée. Ray avait été surpris d'apprendre que Kate était elle aussi une fervente supportrice de Bristol City et ils avaient passé plusieurs soirées à se lamenter ensemble de la récente relégation du club. Pour la première fois depuis longtemps, il avait l'impression de ne pas être seulement un mari, un père ou même un policier. Il était Ray.

Il veillait à ne pas travailler sur le délit de fuite au bureau. Il désobéissait directement aux ordres du préfet, mais tant qu'il ne le faisait pas sur ses heures de travail, elle ne pouvait rien dire. Et si leurs recherches aboutissaient à une arrestation, elle changerait vite de discours.

Le besoin de dissimuler leurs investigations au reste de la brigade avait poussé Ray et Kate à se rencontrer dans un pub éloigné des repaires habituels de la police. Le Horse and Jockey était un endroit calme – avec des boxes à hauts dossiers où ils pouvaient étaler les documents sans craindre que quelqu'un les voie – et le patron ne levait jamais les yeux de ses mots croisés. C'était une façon agréable de finir la journée et de se détendre avant de rentrer, et Ray se surprenait à surveiller la pendule en attendant la fin de son service.

Bien sûr, un coup de fil le retarda et Kate avait déjà bu la moitié de son verre quand il arriva au pub. Un accord tacite voulait que le premier sur les lieux commande à boire : sa pinte de Pride l'attendait donc sur la table.

— Qu'est-ce qui t'a retenu ? demanda Kate en la poussant vers lui. Quelque chose d'intéressant ?

Ray but une gorgée de bière.

— Des informations qui pourraient nous être utiles, répondit-il. Un dealer de la cité Creston a un réseau de six ou sept petits revendeurs à sa botte pour faire le sale boulot... ça risque de donner une belle petite affaire.

Un député travailliste qui aimait beaucoup se faire entendre s'était mis à se servir du problème de la drogue pour pointer du doigt la menace que représentaient les « zones de non-droit » pour la société, et Ray savait que le préfet tenait à ce qu'on voie la police faire preuve d'initiative. Si l'opération Break se passait bien, Ray espérait être suffisamment bien vu par la patronne pour qu'elle lui confie aussi cette enquête.

— La brigade de protection des familles a eu des contacts avec Dominica Letts, la petite amie d'un des revendeurs, expliqua-t-il à Kate. Ils essaient de la convaincre de porter plainte contre lui. On ne veut pas effrayer notre gars en faisant intervenir la police pour ça alors qu'on essaie de monter un dossier, mais en même temps notre devoir est de protéger sa petite amie.

— Est-ce qu'elle est en danger ?

Ray marqua un temps d'arrêt avant de répondre.

— Je ne sais pas. La Protection des familles l'a classée à haut risque, mais elle refuse tout net de témoigner contre lui, et pour le moment elle ne coopère pas du tout.

— D'ici combien de temps on pourra agir ?

— Ça pourrait prendre des semaines. C'est trop long. Il va falloir envisager de la placer dans un foyer – à supposer qu'elle soit d'accord – et de mettre de côté les allégations de violences jusqu'à ce qu'on le coince pour la drogue.

— C'est un mauvais calcul, dit pensivement Kate. Qu'est-ce qui est le plus important : le trafic de stupéfiants ou la violence conjugale ?

— Mais ce n'est pas aussi simple que ça, non ? et la violence provoquée par la consommation de drogues ? les vols commis par des toxicos en manque ? Les effets du trafic de drogue ne sont peut-être pas aussi immédiats qu'un coup de poing, mais ils sont tout aussi importants et douloureux.

Ray s'aperçut qu'il parlait plus fort que d'habitude et il s'arrêta brusquement.

Kate posa une main apaisante sur la sienne.

— Hé, je me faisais l'avocate du diable, là. Ce n'est pas une décision facile.

Ray sourit d'un air penaud.

— Désolé, j'avais oublié que je m'emportais vite pour ce genre de choses.

À vrai dire, il n'avait plus réfléchi à tout ça depuis un moment. Il faisait ce métier depuis si longtemps que les raisons pour lesquelles il s'était engagé avaient été englouties par la paperasse et les problèmes de personnel. Une petite piqûre de rappel ne faisait pas de mal.

Son regard croisa un instant celui de Kate et Ray sentit la chaleur de sa peau contre la sienne. Une seconde plus tard, elle retira sa main en riant d'un air gêné.

— Un dernier pour la route ? proposa Ray.

Lorsqu'il revint à la table, l'instant était passé et il se demanda s'il l'avait imaginé. Il posa les verres et éventra un paquet de chips qu'il étala entre eux.

— Je n'ai rien de nouveau sur l'affaire Jacob, annonça-t-il.

— Moi non plus, soupira-t-elle. On va devoir abandonner, hein ?

Il acquiesça.

— On dirait bien. Je suis désolé.

— Merci de m'avoir laissée continuer autant de temps.

— Tu avais raison de ne pas vouloir abandonner et je suis content de t'avoir aidée.

— Même si on n'est pas plus avancés ?

— Oui, parce que c'est différent maintenant. On a fait tout ce qu'on pouvait.

Kate hocha lentement la tête.

— C'est vrai.

Elle dévisagea Ray.

— Quoi ?

— Tu n'es peut-être pas le béni-oui-oui du préfet, après tout.

Elle sourit et Ray rit. Il était content d'être remonté dans son estime.

Ils mangèrent les chips dans un silence complice et Ray jeta un coup d'œil à son téléphone pour voir si Mags ne lui avait pas envoyé de message.

— Comment ça va à la maison ?

— Toujours pareil, dit Ray en remettant son téléphone dans sa poche. Tom est toujours aussi désagréable pendant les repas et je me dispute toujours autant avec Mags sur l'attitude à adopter.

Il eut un petit rire mais Kate ne l'imita pas.

— Quand est-ce que vous revoyez son professeur ?

— On est allés au collège hier, répondit Ray d'un air grave. Apparemment, Tom sèche déjà les cours, à peine un mois et demi après la rentrée. (Il tambourina des doigts sur la table.) Je ne comprends pas ce gosse. Tout allait bien pendant l'été, mais dès qu'il est retourné à l'école, il est redevenu comme avant : renfermé, grincheux, têtu.

— Tu penses toujours qu'il se fait harceler ?

— L'école assure que non, mais ils ne vont pas dire le contraire, pas vrai ?

Ray n'avait pas une grande estime pour la principale de Tom, qui leur avait reproché à Mags et à lui de ne pas présenter un « front uni » aux réunions de parents d'élèves. Mags avait menacé Ray de venir le chercher au bureau pour le traîner de force à la prochaine réunion et il avait eu si peur d'oublier qu'il avait travaillé de chez lui toute la journée pour se rendre au rendez-vous avec elle. Mais ça n'avait rien changé.

— Le professeur de Tom dit qu'il a une mauvaise influence sur le reste de la classe, poursuivit Ray. Il aurait une « attitude subversive ». (Il ricana.) À son âge ! C'est ridicule, nom de Dieu ! S'ils ne savent pas gérer des gamins difficiles, ils n'auraient pas dû devenir profs. Tom n'a pas une attitude subversive, il est juste buté.

— Je me demande de qui il tient ça, dit Kate en réprimant un sourire.

— Attention, inspecteur Evans ! Vous voulez vous retrouver en uniforme ? plaisanta Ray.

Le rire de Kate se transforma en bâillement.

— Désolée, je suis crevée. Je crois que je vais rentrer. Ma voiture est chez le garagiste, il faut que je regarde à quelle heure passe le bus.

— Je peux te ramener.

— Tu es sûr ? C'est pas vraiment sur ta route.

— Ça ne me dérange pas. Allons-y... tu vas me montrer ton quartier huppé.

Te laisser partir

L'appartement de Kate se trouvait dans un immeuble chic du centre de Clifton, où les prix étaient vraiment exagérés, selon Ray.

— Mes parents m'ont aidée pour l'acompte, expliqua Kate. Sinon, je n'aurais jamais pu l'acheter. Et puis c'est petit ; deux chambres, en théorie, à condition de ne pas vouloir mettre de lit dans la seconde.

— Tu aurais sans doute pu avoir beaucoup plus grand ailleurs.

— Sûrement, mais il y a tout à Clifton ! (Kate fit un grand geste.) Dans quel autre quartier est-ce qu'on peut manger un falafel à trois heures du matin ?

Comme la seule chose que Ray avait jamais voulu faire à trois heures du matin, c'était pisser, il ne voyait pas l'intérêt.

Kate détacha sa ceinture et s'arrêta en posant la main sur la poignée.

— Tu veux monter voir l'appartement ?

Son ton était désinvolte, mais l'air se chargea soudain d'électricité, et Ray sut à cet instant qu'il franchissait une ligne avec laquelle il flirtait depuis des mois.

— Avec plaisir, répondit-il.

L'appartement de Kate était situé au dernier étage, desservi par un ascenseur cossu qui arriva en quelques secondes. Quand les portes s'ouvrirent, ils se retrouvèrent sur un petit palier moquetté avec une porte d'entrée couleur crème juste en face. Ray sortit de l'ascenseur après Kate et ils restèrent plantés là en silence tandis que les portes se refermaient. Elle le regardait droit dans les yeux, le menton légèrement relevé, une mèche de cheveux lui tombant sur le front. Ray s'aperçut soudain qu'il n'était pas pressé de partir.

— Nous y voilà, dit Kate sans le quitter des yeux.

Il hocha la tête et tendit la main pour remettre sa mèche égarée derrière son oreille. Puis, sans réfléchir davantage, il l'embrassa.

14

Beau enfouit son museau dans le creux de mon genou et je tends le bras pour lui gratter les oreilles. Je n'ai pas pu m'empêcher de m'attacher à lui : il dort donc sur mon lit comme il le voulait depuis le début. Quand les cauchemars viennent me tourmenter et que je me réveille en criant, il me lèche la main et me réconforte. Peu à peu, sans que je m'en aperçoive, mon chagrin a changé de forme, passant d'une douleur vive et irrégulière, impossible à museler, à une souffrance sourde et constante que je peux reléguer dans un coin de ma tête. Et si je ne la réveille pas, je peux faire semblant que tout va bien. Que je n'ai jamais eu d'autre vie.

— Allez, on y va.

J'éteins la lampe de chevet, qui ne peut pas rivaliser avec le soleil entrant à flots par la fenêtre. Je connais à présent les saisons de la baie et je suis heureuse d'avoir passé presque un an ici. La baie n'est jamais la même d'un jour à l'autre. Les marées, le temps imprévisible, même les déchets rejetés par la mer la transforment constamment. Aujourd'hui, la mer est grossie par une nuit de pluie, le sable gris et détrempé sous d'épais nuages noirs. Il n'y a plus de tentes au camping, seulement les mobile homes de Bethan et une poignée de camping-cars de vacanciers venus profiter des remises de fin de saison. Il ne va pas tarder à fermer et la baie sera de nouveau à moi.

Beau me devance et descend à toute vitesse sur la plage. La marée est haute et il fonce dans la mer, aboyant après les vagues froides. Je ris tout haut. Il ressemble plus à un épagneul qu'à un colley maintenant, avec les pattes un peu trop longues d'un chien pas encore adulte. Il a tant d'énergie que je me demande s'il pourra un jour la dépenser toute.

Je scrute le haut de la falaise, mais il n'y a personne et je ressens une pointe de déception. Je la chasse aussitôt. C'est ridicule d'espérer voir Patrick alors que nous ne nous sommes croisés qu'une seule fois sur la plage, mais je ne peux m'empêcher d'y penser.

Je trouve un coin de plage où écrire. Ça se calmera sûrement en hiver, mais pour le moment les affaires marchent bien. Je me réjouis chaque fois qu'une commande arrive et je m'amuse à essayer de deviner les histoires qui se cachent derrière les messages. La plupart de mes clients ont un lien avec la mer, et beaucoup m'envoient un e-mail après avoir reçu leur commande pour me dire à quel point ils ont aimé la photo – et me raconter qu'ils ont passé leur enfance au bord de l'eau ou qu'ils économisent pour partir en famille sur la côte. Ils me demandent parfois de quelle plage il s'agit, mais je ne réponds jamais.

Je suis sur le point de me mettre au travail quand Beau aboie. Je lève les yeux et j'aperçois un homme qui se dirige vers nous. Je retiens mon souffle, mais il lève la main pour me saluer et je comprends que c'est lui. C'est Patrick. Je ne parviens pas à dissimuler mon sourire, et bien que mon cœur batte la chamade, ce n'est pas sous le coup de la peur.

— J'espérais vous trouver ici, commence-t-il avant même d'arriver jusqu'à moi. Qu'est-ce que vous diriez d'avoir un élève ?

Il ne porte pas de bottes aujourd'hui et son pantalon en velours côtelé est maculé de sable mouillé. Le col de sa veste en toile huilée est relevé d'un côté et je résiste à la tentation de tendre le bras pour le lisser.

— Bonjour, dis-je. Un élève ?

Il fait un grand geste du bras gauche, embrassant presque toute la plage.

— Je pensais vous aider dans votre travail.

Je ne sais pas s'il se moque de moi. Je garde le silence.

Patrick me prend le bâton des mains et attend là, suspendu au-dessus de l'étendue de sable lisse. Je me sens soudain fébrile.

— C'est plus difficile que ça en a l'air, vous savez, dis-je en adoptant un ton sérieux pour masquer mon embarras. Il faut faire en sorte qu'il n'y ait pas d'empreintes de pas sur la photo et travailler vite, sinon la marée monte trop près.

Je n'ai pas le souvenir que quelqu'un ait déjà voulu partager cet aspect de ma vie : l'art a toujours été quelque chose que je devais pratiquer à l'écart, seule, comme s'il n'avait pas sa place dans le monde réel.

— Compris !

Son air concentré est touchant. Après tout, c'est juste un message sur le sable.

Je lis la commande à haute voix.

— Simple et efficace : « Merci, David. »

— Ah, ah ! Merci, pour *quoi* exactement, je me demande, ironise Patrick en se penchant pour écrire le premier mot. Merci d'avoir donné à manger au chat ? Merci de m'avoir sauvé la vie ? Merci d'avoir accepté de te marier avec moi malgré cette petite aventure avec le facteur ?

Je réprime un sourire.

— Merci de m'avoir appris à danser le flamenco, dis-je en faisant mine d'être sérieuse.

— Merci pour ce bel assortiment de cigares cubains.

— Merci d'avoir augmenté le plafond de mon découvert.

— Merci pour… (Patrick tend le bras pour terminer le dernier mot et perd l'équilibre. Il bascule en avant et ne parvient à rester debout qu'en plantant un pied au milieu de l'inscription.) Oh, merde !

Il fait un pas en arrière pour observer le massacre et se tourne vers moi d'un air confus.

J'éclate de rire.

— J'ai pourtant bien dit que c'était plus difficile que ça n'en avait l'air.

Il me rend le bâton.

— Je m'incline devant votre talent d'artiste. Même sans l'empreinte, mon œuvre n'est pas très impressionnante. Les lettres ne sont pas toutes de la même taille.

— Vous n'avez pas démérité.

Je cherche Beau du regard puis l'appelle pour qu'il se détourne d'un crabe avec lequel il veut jouer.

— Et ça ? demande Patrick.

Je jette un coup d'œil au message qu'il vient d'écrire sur le sable, m'attendant à un deuxième « merci ».

Un verre ?

— C'est mieux, mais ça ne fait pas partie des… (Je m'arrête, me sentant stupide.) Ah, je vois !

— Au Cross Oak ? Ce soir ?

Patrick parle d'une voix mal assurée et je m'aperçois que lui aussi est nerveux. Ça me redonne confiance.

J'hésite, mais juste une seconde ; mon cœur bat à tout rompre dans ma poitrine.

— Avec plaisir.

Je regrette mon impétuosité pendant le reste de la journée, et quand arrive le soir, je suis si anxieuse que j'en tremble. Je pense à tout ce qui peut mal se passer et à tout ce que Patrick a déjà pu me dire, cherchant des signes avant-coureurs. Est-il aussi honnête qu'il en a l'air ? Est-ce possible ? J'envisage d'aller à Penfach pour appeler le cabinet vétérinaire et annuler, mais je sais que je n'en aurai pas le cran. Pour tuer le temps, je prends un bain si chaud que ma peau rosit, puis je m'assois sur mon lit en me demandant ce que je vais porter. Ça fait dix ans que je n'ai pas eu de rendez-vous galant et j'ai peur de ne pas respecter les règles. Bethan a continué à se débarrasser des vêtements qui ne lui vont plus. La plupart sont trop grands pour moi, mais j'essaie une jupe violet foncé qui ne me va pas trop mal, je crois, même si je dois nouer un foulard autour de ma taille pour qu'elle tienne. Je fais quelques pas dans la chambre. La sensation inhabituelle de mes jambes qui se touchent est agréable ; ainsi que le balancement du tissu contre mes cuisses. L'espace d'un instant, j'ai l'impression de rajeunir, mais quand je me regarde dans le miroir je m'aperçois que l'ourlet se trouve au-dessus de mon genou, découvrant beaucoup trop mes jambes. Je l'enlève et la jette en boule au fond de l'armoire, puis j'attrape le jean que je viens de quitter. Je trouve un haut propre et me brosse les cheveux. J'ai exactement la même allure qu'il y a une heure. Exactement la même que tous les jours. Je repense à cette jeune fille qui passait des heures à se préparer pour sortir : la musique à fond, le maquillage éparpillé dans la salle de bains, l'air saturé de parfum. J'ignorais de quoi la vie était faite à l'époque.

Je me dirige vers le camping, où je dois retrouver Patrick. À la dernière minute, j'ai décidé d'emmener Beau avec moi et sa présence me redonne un peu de courage, comme ce matin sur la plage. Quand j'arrive, Patrick discute avec Bethan sur le seuil de la boutique. Ils rient de quelque chose et je me demande si c'est de moi.

Bethan me voit, puis Patrick se retourne et sourit tandis que j'approche. Je crois d'abord qu'il va m'embrasser sur la joue, mais il se contente de m'effleurer le bras en me disant bonjour. Je me demande si j'ai l'air aussi terrifiée que je le suis.

— Soyez sages, tous les deux ! lance Bethan avec un grand sourire.

Patrick rit et nous prenons la direction du village. Il a la conversation facile, et bien que je sois certaine qu'il exagère les pitreries de certains de ses patients, je me détends un peu en écoutant ses histoires pendant que nous atteignons le village.

Le patron du Cross Oak est Dave Bishop, un Anglais originaire du Yorkshire arrivé à Penfach seulement quelques années avant moi. Dave et sa femme Emma sont à présent totalement intégrés dans le village et, comme le reste de Penfach, ils connaissent le nom et la profession de tout le monde. Je ne suis jamais entrée dans le pub, mais j'ai salué Dave en passant par là avec Beau pour aller à la poste.

L'espoir de boire un verre tranquille s'évanouit au moment où nous passons la porte.

— Patrick ! Tu paies ta tournée ?

— Il faut que tu viennes voir Rosie, elle ne va toujours pas mieux.

— Comment va ton père ? Le temps gallois ne lui manque pas trop ?

Le tumulte des conversations, combiné à l'espace clos du pub, me rend nerveuse. Je referme la main sur la laisse de Beau et sens le cuir glisser contre ma paume moite. Patrick a un petit mot pour tout le monde mais ne s'arrête pas pour discuter. Il pose une main dans mon dos et me guide doucement à travers la foule jusqu'au bar. Je sens la chaleur de sa paume au creux de mes reins et je suis à la fois soulagée et déçue quand il l'enlève pour croiser les bras sur le comptoir.

— Qu'est-ce que tu bois ?

J'aurais préféré qu'il commande en premier. Je meurs d'envie d'une bière fraîche et je scrute le pub pour voir si les femmes en boivent.

Dave tousse poliment.

— Un gin-tonic, dis-je, troublée.

Je n'ai jamais bu de gin. Cette incapacité à prendre des décisions n'est pas nouvelle, mais je ne me rappelle plus quand ça a commencé.

Patrick commande une Becks et je regarde la condensation se former sur la bouteille.

— Vous devez être la photographe qui habite à Blaen Cedi ? On se demandait où vous vous cachiez.

L'homme qui me parle a à peu près l'âge de Iestyn. Il a des favoris et porte une casquette en tweed.

— Je te présente Jenna, dit Patrick. Elle monte son entreprise, tu comprendras qu'elle n'a pas tellement le temps de venir siffler des bières avec des lascars comme vous.

L'homme rit et je rougis, contente de la façon dont Patrick a justifié mon isolement. Nous choisissons une table dans le coin, et je suis consciente des regards posés sur nous et des ragots qui doivent déjà aller bon train, mais au bout d'un moment les hommes retournent à leurs pintes.

Je veille à ne pas trop parler, heureusement Patrick connaît de nombreuses histoires et anecdotes intéressantes sur la région.

— Il fait bon vivre ici, dis-je.

Il étend ses longues jambes devant lui.

— C'est vrai. Même si je n'étais pas de cet avis à l'adolescence. Les jeunes ne savent pas apprécier la convivialité et la beauté de la campagne. Je tannais mes parents pour qu'on déménage à Swansea. J'étais persuadé que ça changerait ma vie et que j'aurais tout à coup beaucoup de succès : une vie sociale incroyable et une ribambelle de petites amies. (Il sourit.) Mais ils n'ont jamais envisagé de déménager et je suis allé au lycée du coin.

— Tu as toujours voulu devenir vétérinaire ?

— Depuis que je sais marcher. Apparemment, j'alignais toutes mes peluches dans l'entrée et je demandais à ma mère de les apporter une par une dans la cuisine pour les opérer. (Quand il parle, tout son visage s'anime, le coin de ses yeux se plissant une fraction de seconde avant qu'il se mette à sourire.) J'ai obtenu mon bac de justesse et je suis parti étudier la médecine vétérinaire à l'université de Leeds, où j'ai finalement eu la vie sociale dont je rêvais.

— Et la ribambelle de petites amies ?

Patrick sourit.

— Peut-être une ou deux. Mais après avoir tant voulu partir, j'ai eu le mal du pays. À la fin de mes études, j'ai trouvé du travail à côté de Leeds, mais quand j'ai appris qu'on cherchait un vétérinaire pour le cabinet de Port Ellis, j'ai sauté sur l'occasion. Mon père et ma mère commençaient à se faire un peu vieux et l'océan me manquait.

— Tes parents vivaient à Port Ellis ?

Les gens proches de leurs parents m'intriguent. Je ne les envie pas, j'ai simplement du mal à l'imaginer. Si mon père était resté, peut-être cela aurait-il été différent.

— Ma mère est née ici. Mon père a emménagé ici avec sa famille à l'adolescence et ils se sont mariés quand ils avaient tous les deux dix-neuf ans.

— Ton père était lui aussi vétérinaire ?

Je pose trop de questions, mais si je m'arrête, j'ai peur d'avoir à répondre aux siennes. Ça n'a pas l'air de déranger Patrick, dont le visage s'éclaire d'un sourire nostalgique tandis qu'il parle de l'histoire de sa famille.

— Il était ingénieur. Il est à la retraite maintenant, mais il a travaillé toute sa vie pour une compagnie de gaz de Swansea. C'est à cause de lui que je suis devenu sauveteur volontaire. Il l'a été pendant des années. Il filait au milieu du repas le dimanche et ma mère nous faisait prier pour que tout le monde soit ramené sain et sauf. Je voyais mon père comme un véritable super-héros. (Il boit une lampée de bière.) C'était du temps de l'ancien centre de sauvetage en mer de Penfach, avant qu'ils en construisent un nouveau à Port Ellis.

— On fait souvent appel à vous ?

— Ça dépend. On intervient plus en été, quand les campings sont pleins. On a beau mettre des panneaux ou dire aux gens que les falaises sont dangereuses et qu'il ne faut pas se baigner à marée haute, ils s'en fichent. (Il prend soudain un air sérieux.) Promets-moi de faire attention dans la baie, il y a beaucoup de courant.

— Je me baigne rarement. J'ai juste trempé les pieds pour le moment.

— Contente-toi de ça, dit Patrick. (L'intensité de son regard me met mal à l'aise et je change de position sur mon siège. Il baisse les yeux et boit une grande gorgée de bière.) La marée en surprend plus d'un, ajoute-t-il doucement.

J'acquiesce et lui promets de ne pas me baigner.

— Ça peut paraître étrange, mais c'est moins dangereux au large. (Son regard s'éclaire.) En été, il n'y a rien de mieux que de prendre un bateau pour aller piquer une tête en pleine mer. Je t'emmènerai un jour, si tu veux.

C'est juste une proposition, mais je frissonne. L'idée de me retrouver seule avec Patrick – avec qui que ce soit – au milieu de l'océan est absolument terrifiante.

— L'eau n'est pas aussi froide qu'on le pense, précise Patrick, interprétant mal mon malaise.

Il se tait et un silence gêné s'installe.

Je me penche pour caresser Beau, qui dort sous la table, et j'essaie de trouver autre chose à dire.

— Tes parents vivent toujours ici ?

Ai-je toujours été aussi ennuyeuse ? Je repense à l'époque où, à l'université, j'étais un vrai boute-en-train ; mes amis éclataient de rire dès que j'ouvrais la bouche. Maintenant, je dois me forcer pour faire la conversation.

— Ils se sont installés en Espagne il y a quelques années, les veinards. Ma mère a de l'arthrite et je crois que la chaleur soulage ses articulations. C'est son excuse, en tout cas. Et toi ? Tes parents sont toujours en vie ?

— Pas vraiment.

Patrick a l'air intrigué et je réalise que j'aurais simplement dû dire « non ». Je respire à fond.

— Je ne me suis jamais trop entendue avec ma mère, dis-je. Elle a mis mon père à la porte quand j'avais quinze ans et je ne l'ai pas revu depuis. Je ne lui ai jamais pardonné.

— Elle devait avoir ses raisons.

Son intonation indique qu'il s'agit d'une question, mais je reste sur la défensive.

— Mon père était quelqu'un d'exceptionnel. Elle ne le méritait pas.

— Tu ne vois donc plus ta mère non plus ?

— On est restées en contact pendant longtemps, mais on s'est brouillées après... (Je m'arrête.) On s'est brouillées. Il y a quelques années, ma sœur m'a écrit pour me dire qu'elle était morte.

Je vois de la compassion dans les yeux de Patrick, mais je n'y fais pas attention. Je gâche tout, comme toujours. Ma vie est trop chaotique pour lui : il doit regretter de m'avoir invitée à boire un verre. Cette soirée va devenir de plus en plus pénible pour nous deux. Nous avons épuisé les sujets bateaux et je ne sais plus quoi dire. Je redoute les questions que je vois se bousculer dans l'esprit de Patrick : pourquoi je suis venue à Penfach, qu'est-ce qui m'a fait quitter Bristol, pourquoi je suis ici toute seule. Il demandera par politesse, sans se rendre compte qu'il ne veut pas savoir la vérité. Sans se rendre compte que je ne peux pas lui avouer la vérité.

— Je ferais mieux de rentrer, dis-je.

— Déjà ? (Il doit être soulagé, bien qu'il ne le montre pas.) Il est encore tôt. On pourrait boire autre chose, ou manger un bout.

— Non, vraiment, je dois y aller. Merci pour le verre.

Je me lève avant qu'il se sente obligé de proposer qu'on se revoie, mais il recule sa chaise au même moment.

— Je vais te raccompagner.

Un signal d'alarme résonne dans mon esprit. Pourquoi voudrait-il venir avec moi ? Il fait chaud dans le pub, et ses amis sont là ; il a encore une bière à moitié pleine. J'ai l'impression que ma tête va exploser. Je pense au cottage isolé ; personne n'entendrait s'il refusait de partir. Patrick a peut-être l'air gentil et honnête maintenant, mais je sais à quelle vitesse ça peut changer.

— Non. Merci.

Je me fraie un passage à travers le groupe de locaux, sans me soucier de ce qu'ils pensent de moi. Je réussis à ne pas courir avant d'être sortie du pub et d'avoir tourné au coin de la rue, et je file alors à toute vitesse sur la route du camping puis sur le sentier littoral qui va me conduire chez moi. Beau galope à mes pieds, surpris par le brusque changement de rythme. L'air glacial me fait mal aux poumons, mais je ne m'arrête pas avant d'être arrivée au cottage, où je bataille une fois de plus pour tourner la clé dans la serrure. Je finis par entrer, puis je tire violemment le verrou et m'adosse à la porte.

Mon cœur bat à tout rompre et je m'efforce de reprendre mon souffle. Je ne suis même pas certaine que c'est Patrick qui me fait peur ; je ne parviens plus à le dissocier de la panique qui s'empare de moi chaque jour. Je ne fais plus confiance à mon instinct – il s'est trompé tellement de fois. Le plus sage reste donc de garder mes distances.

15

Ray se retourna et enfouit sa tête dans l'oreiller pour échapper à la lumière du jour qui filtrait à travers les stores. L'espace d'un instant, il ne parvint pas à mettre le doigt sur le sentiment qui pesait sur sa conscience, puis il le reconnut. La culpabilité. Qu'est-ce qui lui était passé par la tête ? Il n'avait jamais été tenté de tromper Mags – pas une seule fois en quinze ans de mariage. Il repassa dans sa tête les événements de la veille. Avait-il profité de Kate ? Tout à coup, l'idée qu'elle puisse porter plainte lui traversa l'esprit et il s'en voulut aussitôt. Elle n'était pas comme ça. Pourtant l'inquiétude éclipsa presque la culpabilité.

La respiration régulière à ses côtés lui indiqua qu'il était le premier réveillé et il sortit doucement du lit en jetant un coup d'œil à la silhouette endormie près de lui, la couette tirée sur la tête. Si Mags l'apprenait… mieux valait ne pas y penser.

Tandis qu'il se levait, la couette bougea et Ray se figea. Il espérait lâchement filer en douce sans avoir à faire la conversation. Il devrait bien lui faire face à un moment donné, mais il avait d'abord besoin de quelques heures pour comprendre ce qui s'était passé.

— Quelle heure il est ? marmonna Mags.

— Six heures et quelques, chuchota Ray. Je vais au boulot plus tôt. J'ai de la paperasse en retard.

Elle grogna puis se rendormit, et Ray laissa échapper un soupir de soulagement. Il se doucha aussi vite que possible et une demi-heure plus tard il était dans son bureau, la porte fermée et plongé dans ses dossiers comme s'il pouvait effacer ce qui était arrivé. Par bonheur, Kate était sortie, et à l'heure du déjeuner Ray se risqua à la cantine avec Stumpy. Ils trouvèrent une table libre et Ray apporta deux assiettes de ce qui était censé être des lasagnes mais qui n'y ressemblait pas vraiment. Moira, la cuisinière, s'était appliquée à dessiner un drapeau italien à la craie à côté du plat du jour et leur avait adressé un sourire radieux quand ils avaient passé leur commande. Ray se retrouvait donc avec une énorme portion dont il essayait vaillamment de venir à bout, tâchant de faire abstraction de la nausée qui le tenaillait depuis ce matin. Moira était une femme forte, d'un âge indéterminé, toujours joyeuse en dépit d'un problème de peau qui entraînait une pluie de pellicules argentées chaque fois qu'elle enlevait sa veste en laine.

— Ça va, Ray ? Quelque chose te tracasse ?

Stumpy racla son assiette avec sa fourchette. Doté d'un estomac à toute épreuve, il semblait non seulement supporter la cuisine de Moira, mais même en raffoler.

— Tout va bien, répondit Ray, soulagé que Stumpy n'insiste pas.

En redressant la tête, il vit Kate entrer dans la cantine et regretta de ne pas avoir mangé plus vite. Stumpy se leva en faisant traîner sa chaise par terre.

— On se voit au bureau, patron.

Incapable de trouver une raison valable pour rappeler Stumpy ou abandonner son déjeuner avant que Kate s'assoie, Ray se força à sourire.

— Salut, Kate.

Il sentit son visage s'embraser. Sa bouche était sèche et il avait du mal à avaler sa salive.

— Salut.

Elle s'assit et déballa ses sandwichs, ne remarquant apparemment pas son malaise.

Son visage était impénétrable et la nausée de Ray s'intensifia. Il écarta son assiette, estimant que la colère de Moira était un moindre mal, et regarda autour de lui pour s'assurer que personne n'écoutait.

— À propos d'hier soir… commença-t-il en ayant l'impression d'être un ado mal dans sa peau.

Kate l'interrompit.

— Je suis vraiment désolée. Je ne sais pas ce qui m'a pris… Est-ce que ça va ?

Ray souffla.

— Plus ou moins. Et toi ?

Kate hocha la tête.

— Un peu gênée, à vrai dire.

— Tu n'as pas à te sentir gênée, dit Ray. Je n'aurais jamais dû…

— Ça n'aurait jamais dû arriver, coupa Kate. Mais on s'est juste embrassés. (Elle lui sourit, puis mordit dans son sandwich et poursuivit, la bouche pleine de fromage et de pickles.) C'était agréable, mais ça s'arrête là.

Ray laissa échapper un lent soupir. Tout allait rentrer dans l'ordre. Ce qui s'était passé était terrible, et si Mags l'apprenait un jour elle serait dévastée, mais tout allait bien. Ils étaient grands. Ils pouvaient se promettre de ne pas recommencer et continuer comme si de rien n'était. Pour la première fois depuis douze heures, Ray repensa à l'agréable sensation d'embrasser quelqu'un d'aussi vivant et énergique. Il sentit son visage s'embraser à nouveau et toussa pour chasser ce souvenir.

— Tant que ça ne te pose pas de problème, dit-il.

— Ray, c'est bon. Vraiment. Je ne vais pas porter plainte contre toi, si c'est ce qui t'inquiète.

Ray rougit.

— Bien sûr que non ! Ça ne m'a pas traversé l'esprit. C'est juste que, tu sais, je suis marié et…

— Et je vois quelqu'un, coupa Kate sans ménagement. Et on connaît tous les deux la musique. Alors on oublie, OK ?

— OK.

— Bon, reprit Kate, soudain sérieuse. Je suis venue te voir pour te proposer de lancer un appel à témoins pour l'anniversaire du délit de fuite.

— Ça fait déjà un an ?

— Le mois prochain. On n'aura probablement pas énormément de réponses, mais si quelqu'un a parlé, on pourrait au moins avoir quelques infos. Et on ne sait jamais, une personne a peut-être besoin de soulager sa conscience. Quelqu'un doit bien savoir qui conduisait cette voiture.

Kate avait les yeux brillants et cet air déterminé qu'il connaissait si bien.

— D'accord, dit-il.

Il imagina la réaction du préfet, et il savait que cela n'augurerait rien de bon pour la suite de sa carrière. Mais lancer un appel à témoins pour l'anniversaire de l'accident était une bonne idée. Ils le faisaient de temps en temps pour les affaires non résolues, ne serait-ce que pour montrer aux familles que même si la police n'enquêtait plus activement, elle n'avait pas complètement abandonné. Ça valait le coup d'essayer.

— Super. J'ai de la paperasse à finir pour l'affaire de ce matin, mais on pourrait se retrouver cet après-midi pour préparer l'appel à témoins.

Elle salua joyeusement Moira de la main en sortant de la cantine.

Ray lui envia sa capacité à tirer un trait sur les événements de la veille. Il avait du mal à la regarder sans repenser à ses bras noués autour de son cou. Il dissimula le reste de ses lasagnes sous une serviette en papier et déposa son assiette sur le chariot près de la porte.

— C'était délicieux, Moira, lança-t-il en passant devant le guichet.

— Menu grec demain ! lui cria-t-elle.

Il ne faudrait pas qu'il oublie d'apporter des sandwichs.

Il était au téléphone quand Kate ouvrit la porte de son bureau sans frapper. S'apercevant que Ray était occupé, elle articula silencieusement des excuses et s'apprêtait à sortir à reculons, mais il lui fit signe de s'asseoir. Elle ferma la porte avec précaution et s'installa sur un fauteuil en attendant qu'il ait fini. Il la vit jeter un coup d'œil à la photo de Mags et des enfants sur son bureau et il sentit une nouvelle vague de remords le submerger, luttant pour rester concentré sur sa conversation avec le préfet.

— Est-ce vraiment nécessaire, Ray ? disait Olivia. Il y a peu de chances qu'un témoin se présente, et je crains que cela ne serve qu'à rappeler que nous n'avons arrêté personne pour la mort de cet enfant.

Il s'appelle Jacob, songea Ray, se souvenant des mots prononcés par la mère du garçon presque un an plus tôt. Il se demanda si sa supérieure était vraiment aussi insensible qu'elle en avait l'air.

— Et comme personne ne réclame justice, il est inutile de remuer le couteau dans la plaie. Je pensais que vous aviez assez à faire, surtout avec les commissions d'évaluation qui approchent.

Le sous-entendu était clair.

— Je comptais vous confier l'affaire de la cité Creston, poursuivit le préfet. Mais si vous préférez vous occuper d'un vieux dossier...

L'opération Break avait été un succès, et ce n'était pas la première fois ces dernières semaines que le préfet lui faisait miroiter une affaire encore plus importante. Il vacilla un instant, puis croisa le regard de Kate. Elle l'observait attentivement. Travailler avec Kate lui avait rappelé pourquoi il s'était engagé dans la police des années auparavant. Il avait retrouvé sa passion pour le métier, et dorénavant il allait faire ce qui lui semblait juste, pas ce qui arrangeait la direction.

— Je peux faire les deux, assura-t-il. Je vais lancer l'appel à témoins. Je pense que c'est la bonne décision.

Il y eut un silence avant qu'Olivia reprenne la parole.

— Un article dans le *Post*, Ray, et quelques affiches au bord de la route. Rien de plus. Et tout disparaît au bout d'une semaine.

Elle raccrocha.

Kate attendit qu'il parle, tapotant impatiemment son stylo contre l'accoudoir de son fauteuil.

— C'est bon, dit Ray.

Le visage de Kate se fendit d'un immense sourire.

— Bien joué ! Elle est énervée ?

— Ça lui passera. Elle veut simplement faire savoir qu'elle n'approuve pas, pour pouvoir nous faire la morale quand ça se retournera contre nous et qu'on se sera mis l'opinion publique à dos.

— C'est un peu cynique !

— C'est comme ça que ça marche là-haut.

— Et tu espères être promu ?

Kate avait les yeux pétillants de malice ; Ray rit.

— Je ne peux pas passer ma vie ici.

— Pourquoi pas ?

Ray se dit qu'il ne se porterait pas plus mal s'il pouvait ignorer le jeu des promotions et se concentrer uniquement sur son travail – un travail qu'il aimait.

— Parce qu'il y a les études des enfants à payer, finit-il par répondre. Quoi qu'il en soit, je ne serai pas comme ça, je n'oublierai pas la réalité du terrain.

— Compte sur moi pour te le rappeler quand tu seras préfet et que tu ne me laisseras pas lancer un appel à témoins, dit Kate.

Ray sourit.

— J'ai déjà parlé au *Post* : Suzy French ne voit aucun inconvénient à ce qu'on profite de l'article qu'ils vont consacrer à l'anniversaire de l'accident pour publier l'appel à témoins dans le journal. Ils vont revenir sur les événements, mais j'aimerais que tu contactes Suzy pour lui donner les détails de l'appel avec le numéro de téléphone et une déclaration officielle de la police garantissant la confidentialité des témoignages.

— Aucun problème. Qu'est-ce qu'on fait pour la mère ?

Ray haussa les épaules.

— On lance l'appel sans elle. Contacte la directrice de l'école de Jacob et demande-lui si elle accepte de parler aux journalistes. Ce serait bien d'avoir un éclairage nouveau. Ils ont peut-être quelque chose qu'il a fait à l'école ? Un dessin, par exemple. On va attendre de voir ce que ça donne avant de commencer à chercher la mère, on dirait qu'elle a disparu de la surface de la terre.

Ray en voulait à l'agent de liaison avec les familles de ne pas avoir mieux surveillé la mère de Jacob. Il n'était pas vraiment surpris que celle-ci soit partie. Il le savait d'expérience, la plupart des gens manifestent deux sortes de réactions à la perte d'un être cher : soit ils se jurent de ne jamais déménager, gardant leur maison exactement dans le même état pour en faire une sorte de sanctuaire ; soit ils rompent définitivement avec le passé, incapables de se faire à l'idée de continuer à vivre comme si rien n'avait changé alors que leur vie entière a basculé.

Une fois Kate sortie de son bureau, il contempla la photo de Jacob, toujours punaisée au panneau en liège sur le mur. Les bords s'étaient un peu racornis et Ray la décrocha avec précaution pour la lisser. Puis il la cala contre le portrait encadré de Mags et des enfants, où il pouvait mieux la voir.

L'appel à témoins était leur dernière chance, et il était peu probable qu'il aboutisse, mais ils auraient au moins essayé. Et si ça ne marchait pas, il classerait le dossier et passerait à autre chose.

16

Je suis assise à la table de la cuisine devant mon ordinateur, les genoux ramenés sous le gros pull à torsades que je portais dans mon atelier en hiver. Je me trouve juste à côté de la cuisinière, mais je tremble et je rentre mes mains dans mes manches. Il n'est pas encore midi, mais je me suis servi un grand verre de vin rouge. Je tape ma requête dans le moteur de recherche puis je m'arrête. Ça fait des mois que je ne me suis pas torturée avec ça. Ça ne servira à rien – ça ne sert jamais à rien –, mais comment ne pas penser à lui ? Surtout aujourd'hui ?

Je bois une petite gorgée de vin et j'appuie sur la touche du clavier.

En quelques secondes, l'écran est inondé de reportages sur l'accident, de forums et d'hommages à Jacob. La couleur des liens indique que j'ai déjà visité tous ces sites.

Mais aujourd'hui, exactement un an après que ma vie a basculé, il y a un nouvel article dans l'édition en ligne du *Bristol Post*.

Je laisse échapper un sanglot étouffé, serrant les poings si fort que mes jointures blanchissent. Après avoir dévoré le bref article, je le relis depuis le début. Il n'y a aucun élément nouveau : pas de pistes officielles, pas d'informations sur la voiture, juste quelques lignes rappelant que le conducteur est recherché par la police pour conduite dangereuse ayant entraîné la mort. L'expression m'écœure et je ferme le navigateur, mais même la photo de la baie que j'ai mise en fond d'écran ne me calme pas. Je ne suis pas descendue sur la plage depuis mon rendez-vous avec Patrick. J'ai des commandes à honorer, mais j'ai tellement honte de la façon dont je me suis comportée que je ne supporte pas l'idée de le rencontrer là-bas. En me réveillant le lendemain du rendez-vous, j'ai trouvé ça ridicule d'avoir eu peur et j'ai presque eu le courage de l'appeler pour m'excuser. Mais, au fil des jours, je me suis dégonflée. Ça fait maintenant presque deux semaines et il n'a pas cherché à me contacter. J'ai soudain la nausée. Je vide mon verre de vin dans l'évier et je décide d'aller me promener avec Beau sur le sentier littoral.

Nous marchons pendant des kilomètres, longeant le promontoire qui précède Port Ellis. J'aperçois un bâtiment gris en bas et je réalise que cela doit être le centre de sauvetage en mer. Je m'arrête un moment et songe aux vies sauvées par les volontaires. Je ne peux pas m'empêcher de penser à Patrick tandis que je repars d'un pas énergique sur le sentier qui mène à Port Ellis. Je n'ai pas de destination précise, j'avance machinalement jusqu'à arriver au village, puis je prends la direction du cabinet vétérinaire. Ce n'est qu'au moment où j'ouvre la porte en faisant tinter la petite cloche que je me demande ce que je vais bien pouvoir dire.

— En quoi puis-je vous aider ?

C'est la même réceptionniste – je ne l'aurais pas reconnue sans ses badges colorés.

— Est-ce que je pourrais parler à Patrick ?

Je devrais sans doute donner une raison, mais elle ne me demande rien.

— Je reviens tout de suite.

Mal à l'aise, je patiente debout dans la salle d'attente, où une femme est assise avec un jeune enfant et un animal dans un panier en osier. Je retiens Beau, qui tire de toutes ses forces sur sa laisse.

Quelques minutes plus tard, j'entends des pas et Patrick fait son apparition. Il porte un pantalon en velours côtelé marron avec une chemise à carreaux, et ses cheveux sont tout ébouriffés, comme s'il venait de passer la main dedans.

— Il y a un problème avec Beau ?

Il est poli, mais ne sourit pas, et ma détermination faiblit légèrement.

— Non. Est-ce qu'on pourrait parler une minute en privé ?

Il hésite, et je suis certaine qu'il va refuser. J'ai les joues en feu et je sens le regard de la réceptionniste sur nous.

— Entre.

Je le suis dans la pièce où il a examiné Beau la première fois et il s'appuie contre le lavabo. Il ne dit rien. Il ne va pas me faciliter la tâche.

— Je voulais… je voulais m'excuser.

Je sens un picotement derrière mes yeux et je m'efforce de ne pas pleurer.

Patrick esquisse un sourire ironique.

— On m'a déjà envoyé balader, mais jamais aussi vite.

Son regard s'est adouci et je risque un petit sourire.

— Je suis vraiment désolée.

— Est-ce que j'ai fait quelque chose de mal ? Est-ce que c'est quelque chose que j'ai dit ?

— Non. Pas du tout. Tu as été… (J'essaie de trouver le mot juste, puis j'abandonne.) C'est ma faute, je ne suis pas très douée pour ce genre de chose.

Il y a un silence et Patrick me sourit.

— Tu as peut-être besoin de pratique.

Je ne peux pas m'empêcher de rire.

— Peut-être.

— Écoute, j'ai encore deux patients à voir, et ensuite ma journée est finie. Qu'est-ce que tu dirais de venir dîner à la maison ce soir ? J'ai un ragoût qui cuit dans la mijoteuse en ce moment et il y en a plus qu'assez pour deux. Beau aura même droit à une portion.

Si je refuse, je ne le reverrai pas.

— Avec plaisir.

Patrick regarde sa montre.

— Rejoins-moi ici dans une heure. Ça ira d'ici là ?

— Oui. Je voulais prendre des photos du village de toute façon.

— Super, alors on se voit tout à l'heure.

Son sourire est plus large à présent, creusant des plis au coin de ses yeux. Il m'accompagne jusqu'à la sortie et je croise le regard de la réceptionniste.

— Tout est arrangé ?

Je me demande pourquoi elle croit que je suis venue voir Patrick, puis je me dis que ça m'est égal. J'ai été courageuse : je me suis peut-être enfuie, mais je suis revenue, et ce soir je vais dîner avec un homme qui m'apprécie assez pour ne pas être rebuté par ma nervosité.

La fréquence à laquelle je regarde ma montre ne fait pas passer le temps plus vite, et Beau et moi effectuons plusieurs fois le tour du village avant qu'il soit l'heure de retourner au cabinet. Je ne veux pas entrer et je suis soulagée quand Patrick sort avec un grand sourire en enfilant sa veste en toile huilée. Il gratte les oreilles de Beau, puis nous marchons jusqu'à une petite maison mitoyenne dans la rue d'à côté. Il nous fait passer au salon, où Beau s'affale aussitôt devant la cheminée.

— Un verre de vin ?

— Volontiers.

Je m'assois, mais je suis si nerveuse que je me relève aussitôt. La pièce est petite mais chaleureuse, avec un tapis qui recouvre la majeure partie du sol. Le foyer est flanqué de deux fauteuils et je me demande lequel est le sien – rien n'indique que l'un d'entre eux est plus utilisé que l'autre. La petite télévision détonne dans la pièce et deux énormes bibliothèques occupent les alcôves à côté des fauteuils. J'incline la tête pour lire les dos.

— J'ai beaucoup trop de livres, remarque Patrick en revenant avec deux verres de vin rouge. (J'en prends un, heureuse d'avoir quelque chose à faire de mes mains.) Je devrais en donner quelques-uns, mais je n'arrive pas à m'en séparer.

— J'adore lire. Même si j'ai à peine ouvert un livre depuis que j'ai emménagé ici.

Patrick s'assoit dans l'un des fauteuils. Je l'imite et m'assois dans l'autre en tripotant le pied de mon verre.

— Ça fait combien de temps que tu es photographe ?

— Je ne suis pas vraiment photographe, dis-je en m'étonnant moi-même de ma franchise. Je suis sculptrice. (Je repense à mon atelier dans le jardin : l'argile brisée, les sculptures terminées et prêtes à être livrées réduites à l'état de tessons.) Du moins, j'étais sculptrice.

— Tu ne sculptes plus ?

— Je ne peux plus.

J'hésite, puis je déplie ma main gauche, où de vilaines cicatrices me barrent la paume et le poignet.

— J'ai eu un accident. Je peux encore me servir de ma main, mais je ne sens plus rien au bout des doigts.

Patrick laisse échapper un petit sifflement.

— Ma pauvre ! Qu'est-ce qui t'est arrivé ?

J'ai soudain un flash-back de ce soir-là, il y a un an, et je le refoule au plus profond de moi-même.

— C'est plus impressionnant qu'autre chose. J'aurais dû faire plus attention.

Je suis incapable de regarder Patrick dans les yeux, mais il change habilement de sujet.

— Tu as faim ?

— Je suis affamée.

Une délicieuse odeur s'échappe de la cuisine et mon estomac gronde. Je le suis dans une très grande pièce dont un buffet en pin occupe tout un mur.

— Il était à ma grand-mère, explique-t-il en éteignant la mijoteuse. Mes parents l'ont récupéré quand elle est morte, mais ils ont déménagé à l'étranger il y a quelques années et j'en ai hérité. Il est immense, hein ? Il y a toutes sortes de choses entassées là-dedans. Ne t'avise surtout pas d'ouvrir les portes.

Je regarde Patrick servir le ragoût avec précaution dans deux assiettes puis attraper un torchon pour essuyer une goutte de sauce qu'il étale plus qu'autre chose.

Il apporte les assiettes chaudes sur la table et en pose une devant moi.

— C'est à peu près la seule chose que je sais cuisiner, s'excuse-t-il. J'espère que ce sera bon.

Il en sert un peu dans un récipient en métal et Beau fait son apparition à point nommé dans la cuisine, attendant patiemment que Patrick pose la gamelle par terre.

— Une seconde, bonhomme, dit Patrick.

Il prend une fourchette et remue la viande dans la gamelle pour qu'elle refroidisse.

Je baisse la tête pour dissimuler mon sourire. La façon dont une personne traite les animaux en dit long sur elle, et Patrick commence à me plaire.

— Ça a l'air délicieux, dis-je. Merci.

Je ne me souviens plus de la dernière fois que quelqu'un a pris soin de moi comme ça. C'était toujours moi qui faisais la cuisine, le rangement, le ménage. Tant d'années passées à essayer de fonder une famille heureuse, tout ça pour que tout s'effondre autour de moi.

— C'est la recette de ma mère, indique Patrick. Elle essaie d'enrichir mon répertoire chaque fois qu'elle vient. Elle doit imaginer que je me nourris uniquement de pizzas et de frites quand elle n'est pas là, comme mon père.

Je ris.

— Cet automne, ça fera quarante ans qu'ils sont ensemble, ajoute-t-il. J'ai du mal à imaginer une chose pareille, pas toi ?

Moi aussi.

— Tu as déjà été marié ? dis-je.

Le regard de Patrick s'assombrit.

— Non. J'ai cru que j'allais me marier une fois, mais les choses ont pris une autre tournure.

Il y a un bref silence et je crois voir du soulagement sur son visage quand il comprend que je ne vais pas demander pourquoi.

— Et toi ?

Je respire à fond.

— J'ai été mariée un moment. Mais on ne voulait pas les mêmes choses, en fin de compte.

Je souris de l'euphémisme.

— Tu es très isolée à Blaen Cedi, observe Patrick. Ça ne te dérange pas ?

— J'aime vivre là-bas. C'est un endroit magnifique, et Beau me tient compagnie.

— Tu ne te sens pas seule sans voisins ?

Je songe à mes nuits agitées, quand je me réveille en criant et qu'il n'y a personne pour me réconforter.

— Je vois Bethan presque tous les jours.

— C'est quelqu'un de bien. Je la connais depuis des années.

Je me demande à quel point Patrick et Bethan ont été proches. Il commence à me raconter qu'ils ont un jour emprunté une barque à son père sans sa permission pour aller dans la baie.

— On nous a repérés au bout de quelques minutes. Je voyais mon père debout sur le rivage, les bras croisés, à côté du père de Bethan. On savait qu'on allait avoir de gros ennuis, alors on est restés dans la barque et ils sont restés sur la plage. Ça a duré des heures.

— Qu'est-ce qui s'est passé ?

Patrick rit.

— On a fini par céder, bien sûr. On est rentrés et on a affronté l'orage. Bethan avait quelques années de plus que moi, du coup c'est surtout elle qui a pris, mais j'ai été privé de sortie pendant deux semaines.

Je souris tandis qu'il secoue la tête, comme si la punition avait été un calvaire. Je n'ai aucun mal à l'imaginer adolescent, les cheveux aussi ébouriffés que maintenant et prêt à faire les quatre cents coups.

Mon assiette vide est remplacée par un bol de crumble aux pommes avec de la crème anglaise. L'odeur de cannelle chaude me fait saliver. J'écarte la crème pour manger le gâteau du bout des dents et ne pas paraître impolie.

— Tu n'aimes pas ? me demande-t-il.

— C'est délicieux. C'est juste que j'évite les desserts.

Difficile de se défaire des habitudes d'un régime.

— Tu rates quelque chose. (Patrick termine sa portion en quelques bouchées.) Ce n'est pas moi qui l'ai fait, une des filles du boulot me l'a apporté.

— Désolée.

— Ce n'est rien. Je vais le laisser refroidir un peu et le donner à Beau.

Le chien dresse l'oreille en entendant son nom.

— C'est vraiment un bon chien, dit Patrick. Et il a de la chance.

J'acquiesce, même si je sais à présent que j'ai autant besoin de Beau que lui de moi. C'est moi qui ai de la chance. Patrick a un coude sur la table et le menton appuyé dans la main tandis qu'il caresse Beau. Détendu et satisfait : un homme sans secrets ni tourments.

Il lève les yeux et me surprend à l'observer. Gênée, je détourne le regard et remarque une autre étagère dans un coin de la cuisine.

— Encore des livres ?

— C'est plus fort que moi, répond Patrick avec un grand sourire. Il y a surtout ici des livres de cuisine que ma mère m'a donnés, mais il y a aussi quelques polars. Je peux lire n'importe quoi du moment que l'intrigue tient la route.

Il commence à débarrasser la table et je m'adosse à ma chaise pour l'observer.

Et si je te racontais une histoire, Patrick ?

L'histoire de Jacob et d'un accident. L'histoire de quelqu'un qui n'a pas trouvé de meilleure solution pour survivre que de s'enfuir pour tout recommencer à zéro ; de quelqu'un qui se réveille chaque nuit en criant, incapable d'oublier ce qui s'est passé.

Et si je te racontais cette histoire ?

Je le vois m'écouter, écarquillant les yeux tandis que je lui parle du grincement des freins, du craquement de la tête de Jacob sur le pare-brise. J'aimerais qu'il me prenne la main, mais il ne le fait pas, même dans mon imagination. J'aimerais l'entendre dire qu'il comprend, que je n'y suis pour rien, que ça aurait pu arriver à n'importe qui. Mais il secoue la tête, se lève de table, me repousse. Il est écœuré. Dégoûté.

Je ne pourrai jamais lui raconter.

— Ça va ?

Patrick me regarde bizarrement et, l'espace d'un instant, j'ai l'impression qu'il peut lire dans mes pensées.

— C'était très bon, dis-je. (J'ai deux possibilités : soit je ne revois plus Patrick, soit je lui cache la vérité. Je n'ai aucune envie de lui mentir, mais je ne supporte pas l'idée de le perdre. Je regarde l'horloge au mur.) Je vais devoir y aller.

— Tu ne vas pas refaire ta Cendrillon ?

— Pas cette fois-ci. (Je rougis, mais Patrick sourit.) Le dernier car pour Penfach est à neuf heures.

— Tu n'as pas de voiture ?

— Je n'aime pas conduire.

— Je vais te ramener, je n'ai bu qu'un petit verre de vin. Ça ne me dérange pas.

— Vraiment, je préfère rentrer toute seule.

Je crois déceler un soupçon d'exaspération dans les yeux de Patrick.

— Peut-être qu'on se croisera sur la plage demain matin ? dis-je.

Il se détend et sourit.

— Ce serait super. Ça m'a fait vraiment plaisir de te revoir, je suis content que tu sois revenue.

— Moi aussi.

Il va chercher mes affaires et nous nous tenons tous les deux dans la petite entrée pendant que j'enfile mon manteau. J'ai à peine la place de bouger les coudes et cette proximité me rend gauche. Je bataille avec la fermeture éclair.

— Attends, dit-il. Laisse-moi faire.

Je regarde sa main réunir les deux parties de la fermeture éclair avec précaution puis la remonter. Je suis paralysée par l'angoisse, mais il s'arrête juste avant mon menton et enroule mon écharpe autour de mon cou.

— Voilà. Tu m'appelles quand tu arrives chez toi ? Je vais te donner mon numéro.

Je suis déconcertée par sa prévenance.

— Je voudrais bien, mais je n'ai pas de téléphone.

— Tu n'as pas de portable ?

Son incrédulité me fait presque rire.

— Non. Il y a une ligne au cottage, pour Internet, mais pas de téléphone. Ça va aller, je t'assure.

Patrick pose ses mains sur mes épaules et, avant que j'aie le temps de réagir, il se penche pour m'embrasser tendrement sur la joue. Je sens son souffle sur mon visage et je vacille.

— Merci, dis-je.

Te laisser partir

Bien que ce soit inapproprié et banal, il me sourit comme si j'avais dit quelque chose de profond et je me rends compte à quel point il est facile d'être avec quelqu'un d'aussi peu exigeant.

J'attache la laisse au collier de Beau et nous nous disons au revoir. Je sais que Patrick va nous regarder partir, et quand je tourne au bout de la rue je le vois encore debout devant la porte.

17

Le portable de Ray sonna tandis qu'il était assis pour le petit déjeuner. Lucy essayait d'obtenir son badge de cuisine chez les jeannettes et prenait ça beaucoup trop au sérieux. Le bout de sa langue dépassait au coin de ses lèvres tandis qu'elle s'appliquait à servir des œufs caoutchouteux au bacon brûlé dans les assiettes de ses parents. Tom avait passé la nuit chez un ami et ne serait pas de retour avant midi : Ray avait acquiescé quand Mags avait remarqué que c'était bien que Tom se fasse des amis, mais au fond il appréciait simplement la tranquillité de la maison sans les cris et les claquements de portes.

— Ça a l'air délicieux, ma chérie.

Ray sortit son téléphone de sa poche et jeta un coup d'œil à l'écran.

Il regarda Mags.

— Le boulot.

Il se demanda si c'était au sujet de l'opération Falcon – le nom donné à l'enquête sur le trafic de drogue de la cité Creston. Le préfet lui avait fait miroiter l'affaire une semaine de plus avant de finalement la lui confier avec ordre de se concentrer là-dessus en priorité. Elle n'avait pas mentionné l'appel à témoins. C'était inutile.

Mags jeta un coup d'œil vers Lucy, occupée à disposer la nourriture dans les assiettes.

— Déjeune d'abord. S'il te plaît.

À contrecœur, Ray appuya sur le bouton rouge pour rejeter l'appel et le transférer vers sa messagerie. À peine eut-il le temps de garnir sa fourchette d'œufs au bacon que le téléphone de la maison sonna. Mags décrocha.

— Oh, bonjour, Kate. Est-ce que c'est urgent ? On est en train de déjeuner.

Ray se sentit tout à coup mal à l'aise. Il fit défiler ses e-mails sur son BlackBerry pour avoir quelque chose à faire, levant furtivement les yeux vers Mags, dont les épaules bien droites indiquaient qu'elle n'appréciait pas d'être dérangée. Pourquoi Kate téléphonait-elle chez lui ? Un dimanche en plus ? Il tendit l'oreille pour saisir ce que disait Kate au bout du fil. En vain. La nausée qui l'avait tenaillé ces derniers jours réapparut et il fixa ses œufs au bacon sans enthousiasme.

Mags passa le téléphone à Ray sans un mot.

— Salut, Ray. (Kate était joyeuse, inconsciente de son embarras.) Qu'est-ce que tu fais de beau ?

— Je suis en famille. Qu'est-ce qu'il y a ?

Il sentit le regard de Mags et sut que ce laconisme ne lui ressemblait pas.

— Je suis vraiment désolée de te déranger, fit sèchement Kate. Mais je me suis dit que tu préférerais être au courant tout de suite.

— Qu'est-ce qu'il y a ?

— Une réponse à l'appel pour l'anniversaire du délit de fuite. On a un témoin.

Ray arriva dans son bureau moins d'une demi-heure plus tard.

— Alors, qu'est-ce qu'on a ?

Kate parcourut l'e-mail du central qu'elle avait imprimé.

— Un type affirme qu'une voiture rouge qui roulait n'importe comment lui a fait une queue de poisson à peu près au moment où a eu lieu l'accident, dit Kate. Il comptait le signaler, mais il ne l'a jamais fait.

Ray ressentit une poussée d'adrénaline.

— Pourquoi est-ce qu'il n'a pas contacté la police quand les premiers appels à témoins ont été lancés ?

— Il n'est pas d'ici, expliqua Kate. Il venait rendre visite à sa sœur pour son anniversaire – voilà pourquoi il est certain de la date –, mais il est reparti à Bournemouth le jour même et il n'a pas du tout entendu parler du délit de fuite. Bref, il n'a fait le rapprochement que quand sa sœur a évoqué l'appel à témoins hier soir au téléphone.

— Il est fiable ? demanda Ray.

Les témoins sont une espèce imprévisible. Certains se souviennent des moindres détails, d'autres ne peuvent pas vous dire la couleur de leur chemise sans avoir d'abord vérifié, et ils sont encore capables de se tromper.

— Aucune idée. On ne lui a pas encore parlé.

— Et pourquoi ça, bon sang ?

— Il est neuf heures et demie, se défendit-elle sèchement. On a eu l'information cinq minutes avant que je t'appelle et je me suis dit que tu voudrais lui parler toi-même.

— Excuse-moi.

Kate haussa les épaules.

— Et désolé pour ce matin au téléphone, poursuivit-il. C'était un peu délicat, tu comprends.

— Tout va bien ?

La question était tendancieuse. Ray acquiesça.

— Oui. J'étais mal à l'aise, c'est tout.

Ils se dévisagèrent un instant avant que Ray détourne les yeux.

— Bon, eh bien on n'a qu'à le faire venir, reprit-il. Je veux tous les renseignements qu'il peut nous donner sur cette voiture. La marque, la couleur, le numéro d'immatriculation. Et tout ce qu'il a sur le conducteur. On dirait qu'on a droit à une seconde chance : faisons les choses correctement, cette fois-ci.

— Il sait que dalle, putain ! (Ray faisait les cent pas devant la fenêtre de son bureau sans chercher à dissimuler sa frustration.)

Il ne peut pas nous dire l'âge du conducteur ni s'il était blanc ou noir... Nom de Dieu ! Il ne sait même pas si c'était un homme ou une femme !

Il se frotta vigoureusement la tête comme pour en faire jaillir une idée.

— La visibilité était mauvaise, lui rappela Kate. Et il était concentré sur la route.

Ray n'était pas d'humeur à se montrer indulgent.

— Il n'aurait pas dû prendre le volant si un peu de pluie le gênait tant. (Il s'assit lourdement et but une gorgée de café, puis grimaça en s'apercevant qu'il était froid.) Un de ces quatre, j'arriverai à boire un café en entier, marmonna-t-il.

— Une Ford avec un pare-brise fissuré dont la plaque d'immatriculation commence par un J, récapitula Kate en lisant ses notes. Sûrement une Fiesta ou une Focus. C'est déjà ça.

— Bon, c'est mieux que rien, concéda Ray. Allez, au boulot ! J'aimerais que tu t'occupes en priorité de retrouver la mère de Jacob. Si on coince le responsable, ou plutôt quand on le coincera, je veux qu'elle voie qu'on n'a pas laissé tomber son fils.

— Compris, fit Kate. Le courant est bien passé avec la directrice de l'école quand je l'ai eue au téléphone pour l'appel à témoins. Je vais la rappeler pour creuser un peu de ce côté-là. Quelqu'un doit bien être resté en contact avec la mère.

— Je vais mettre Malcolm sur la voiture. On va chercher sur l'ordinateur central toutes les Fiesta et les Focus immatriculées à Bristol et je te paie à manger pendant qu'on épluche la liste.

Écartant les restes de ce que Moira avait eu l'optimisme de présenter comme de la paella, Ray posa une main sur la pile de dossiers devant lui.

— Neuf cent quarante-deux.

Il siffla.

— Uniquement dans la région, observa Kate. Et si la voiture ne faisait que passer ?

— Voyons si on peut réduire un peu les possibilités. (Il plia la liste et la tendit à Kate.) Compare ces numéros avec ceux enregistrés par le LAPI : disons à partir d'une demi-heure avant le délit de fuite jusqu'à une demi-heure après. On verra combien d'entre elles étaient sur la route au moment de l'accident et on commencera à les éliminer à partir de là.

— On se rapproche, dit Kate, les yeux pétillants. Je le sens.

Ray sourit.

— Ne nous emballons pas. Sur quoi tu bosses en ce moment ?

Elle compta les affaires sur ses doigts.

— Le vol du supermarché Londis, une série d'attaques contre des chauffeurs de taxi asiatiques et une possible agression sexuelle que devrait nous refiler la patrouille. Ah, et j'ai deux jours de formation sur la diversité la semaine prochaine.

Ray ricana.

— Oublie la formation. Et apporte-moi tes dossiers pour que je les confie à quelqu'un d'autre. Je veux que tu travailles à plein temps sur le délit de fuite.

— Officiellement, cette fois-ci ? demanda Kate en haussant un sourcil.

— Absolument, répondit Ray avec un grand sourire. Mais vas-y mollo sur les heures sup'.

18

Quand le car arrive à Port Ellis, Patrick est déjà là. Depuis deux semaines, nous nous voyons tous les matins sur la plage, et quand il a proposé que nous nous retrouvions pour son jour de congé, je n'ai pas hésité longtemps. Je ne peux pas passer ma vie à avoir peur.

— Où est-ce qu'on va ? dis-je en cherchant des indices autour de moi.

Sa maison se trouve dans la direction opposée et nous passons devant le pub du village sans nous arrêter.

— Tu verras.

Nous sortons du village et suivons la route qui descend vers la mer. Tandis que nous marchons, nos mains se touchent et ses doigts se faufilent entre les miens. Je sens une décharge électrique et laisse ma main se relâcher dans la sienne.

La rumeur selon laquelle je fréquente Patrick s'est répandue à une vitesse ahurissante dans Penfach. J'ai rencontré Iestyn par hasard hier au magasin.

— Il paraît que vous voyez le fils d'Alun Mathews, m'a-t-il dit avec un sourire en coin. Patrick est un bon gars, vous auriez pu tomber sur pire.

Je me suis sentie rougir.

— Quand pourrez-vous venir jeter un coup d'œil à la porte ? lui ai-je demandé en changeant de sujet. C'est toujours pareil : la serrure accroche tellement que certaines fois la clé ne tourne même plus.

— Ne vous inquiétez pas pour ça. Il n'y a pas de voleurs par ici.

J'ai respiré à fond avant de répondre, sachant bien qu'il trouvait bizarre que je ferme la porte à clé.

— N'empêche que je me sentirais mieux si elle était réparée.

Iestyn a une fois de plus promis de venir au cottage pour arranger ça, mais quand je suis partie à midi il n'était toujours pas passé et j'ai mis dix bonnes minutes à fermer la porte.

La route continue à se rétrécir et j'aperçois l'océan au bout du chemin. L'eau est grise et déchaînée, l'écume jaillissant des vagues en furie. Les mouettes décrivent des cercles vertigineux, ballottés par les vents qui s'engouffrent dans la baie. Je comprends enfin où Patrick m'emmène.

— Le centre de sauvetage ! Est-ce qu'on peut entrer ?

— C'est l'idée, répond-il. Tu as vu le cabinet vétérinaire, je me suis dit que tu voudrais peut-être voir cet endroit. J'ai l'impression d'y passer presque autant de temps.

Le centre de sauvetage en mer de Port Ellis est un bâtiment trapu et étrange qui pourrait être pris pour une usine sans la tour d'observation perchée sur le toit, ses quatre baies vitrées évoquent une tour de contrôle d'aéroport.

Nous passons devant deux énormes portes coulissantes bleues à l'avant du bâtiment et Patrick tape un code sur un boîtier gris pour ouvrir une petite porte située sur le côté.

— Viens, je vais te faire visiter.

À l'intérieur, le centre de sauvetage sent la sueur et la mer, l'odeur âcre du sel qui s'imprègne dans les vêtements. Le hangar à bateaux est dominé par ce que Patrick appelle « l'engin » – un Zodiac orange vif.

— On est attachés, indique-t-il. Mais par gros temps c'est un vrai défi de ne pas passer par-dessus bord.

Je me promène dans le hangar, déchiffre les affiches sur la porte, les grilles de vérification du matériel soigneusement remplies. Sur le mur se trouve une plaque commémorant la mort de trois volontaires en 1916.

— Le patron P. Grant et les matelots Harry Ellis et Glyn Barry, lis-je tout haut. Quelle horreur !

— Ils répondaient à l'appel d'un bateau à vapeur en perdition au large de la péninsule de Gower, raconte Patrick tandis qu'il me rejoint et passe un bras autour de mes épaules. (Il doit voir ma tête, car il ajoute :) C'était très différent à l'époque, ils n'avaient pas la moitié du matériel qu'on a aujourd'hui.

Il me prend par la main et me conduit dans une petite pièce où un homme en polaire bleue prépare du café. Il a le visage tanné de quelqu'un qui a passé sa vie dehors.

— Ça va, David ? dit Patrick. Je te présente Jenna.

— Il tenait à vous montrer son engin, hein ?

David me fait un clin d'œil et je souris de ce qui semble être une vieille plaisanterie entre eux.

— Je ne m'étais jamais interrogée sur le fonctionnement des centres de sauvetage, dis-je. J'ai toujours considéré qu'ils faisaient partie du paysage.

— Ils n'en ont plus pour très longtemps si on ne les défend pas plus, explique David en versant une grosse cuillerée de sucre dans son café sirupeux avant de le remuer. Nos frais de fonctionnement sont pris en charge par la Royal National Lifeboat Institution, pas par le gouvernement, on est donc toujours à la recherche de financements, en plus d'essayer de trouver des volontaires.

— David est le responsable des opérations, dit Patrick. C'est lui qui gère le centre. Il est là pour nous surveiller.

David rit.

— Il n'a pas tort.

La sonnerie stridente d'un téléphone retentit dans la salle de contrôle vide et David s'excuse. Il revient quelques secondes plus tard et se rue dans le hangar à bateaux en défaisant la fermeture éclair de sa polaire.

— Un canoë s'est retourné au large de la baie de Rhossili ! crie-t-il à Patrick. Un père et son fils sont portés disparus. Helen a appelé Gary et Aled.

Patrick ouvre un casier et en sort une combinaison en caoutchouc jaune, un gilet de sauvetage rouge et un ciré bleu foncé.

— Désolé, Jenna, il faut que j'y aille. (Il enfile sa combinaison par-dessus son jean et son sweat-shirt.) Prends les clés et attends-moi à la maison. Je n'en ai pas pour très longtemps.

Avant que j'aie le temps de répondre, il se précipite dans le hangar, juste au moment où deux hommes pénètrent à toute vitesse par la porte coulissante grande ouverte. Quelques minutes plus tard, les quatre hommes traînent l'embarcation sur la plage pour la mettre à l'eau puis sautent à l'intérieur. L'un d'eux – j'ignore lequel – actionne le lanceur pour démarrer le moteur et le bateau part comme une flèche en bondissant sur les vagues.

Je regarde le point orange rapetisser jusqu'à être englouti par le gris.

— Ils sont rapides, hein ?

Je me retourne et vois une femme appuyée contre la porte de la salle de contrôle. Elle a la cinquantaine passée, des cheveux bruns grisonnants et un chemisier à motifs avec un badge de la Royal National Lifeboat Institution.

— Je suis Helen, dit-elle. Je réponds au téléphone, je fais visiter les lieux aux invités, ce genre de chose. Vous devez être la copine de Patrick.

Je rougis.

— Je m'appelle Jenna. Je suis impressionnée, ils n'ont pas dû mettre plus d'un quart d'heure.

— Douze minutes et trente-cinq secondes, précise Helen. (Elle sourit de ma surprise évidente.) On doit garder une trace de tous les appels et de nos temps de réponse. Tous nos volontaires vivent à quelques minutes d'ici. Gary habite un peu plus haut et Aled tient la boucherie dans la rue principale.

— Qu'est-ce qu'il fait de son magasin quand on l'appelle ?

— Il laisse un mot sur la porte. Les gens du coin sont habitués, ça fait vingt ans qu'il fait ça.

Je me retourne vers la mer désertée par les bateaux à l'exception d'un énorme navire au large. D'épais nuages sombres sont tombés si bas que l'horizon a disparu, le ciel et l'océan ne formant plus qu'une seule masse grise tourbillonnante.

— Ça va aller, souffle Helen. On n'arrête jamais vraiment de s'inquiéter, mais au bout d'un moment on s'habitue.

Je la dévisage, intriguée.

— David est mon mari, explique-t-elle. Quand il a pris sa retraite, il passait plus de temps ici que chez nous, alors j'ai fini par me joindre à lui. La première fois que je l'ai vu partir, je n'ai pas supporté. C'est une chose de lui dire au revoir à la maison, mais de les voir monter dans le bateau... et avec un temps pareil, eh bien... (Elle frissonne.) Mais ils reviennent. Ils reviennent toujours.

Elle pose une main sur mon bras et j'apprécie le soutien de cette femme plus âgée.

— C'est dans ces moments-là qu'on se rend compte à quel point...

Je m'arrête, incapable de l'admettre, même intérieurement.

— À quel point on a besoin d'eux ? dit Helen avec douceur.

J'acquiesce.

— Oui.

— Vous voulez que je vous fasse visiter le reste du centre ?

— Non, merci. Je vais aller attendre Patrick chez lui.

— C'est quelqu'un de bien.

Je me demande si elle a raison. Je me demande comment elle le sait. Je gravis la colline en me retournant de temps à autre dans l'espoir d'apercevoir le zodiac orange. Mais je ne vois rien et j'ai l'estomac noué par l'angoisse. Quelque chose va arriver, je le sais.

C'est étrange de me retrouver chez Patrick en son absence, je résiste à la tentation d'aller jeter un coup d'œil à l'étage. Pour m'occuper, j'allume la radio sur une station locale et j'attaque la vaisselle qui déborde de l'évier.

« *Un homme et son fils sont portés disparus après que leur canoë s'est retourné à un kilomètre et demi au large de la baie de Rhossili.* »

La radio grésille et je tourne le bouton des fréquences afin de trouver un meilleur signal.

« *Des habitants ont donné l'alerte et le canot de sauvetage de Port Ellis est parti à leur recherche. Pour le moment, les sauveteurs n'ont retrouvé personne. On en saura plus tout à l'heure.* »

Le vent cingle les arbres jusqu'à les faire plier. Je ne vois pas la mer depuis la maison ; je ne sais pas si c'est mieux ainsi ou si je devrais céder à l'envie de descendre au centre de sauvetage pour guetter le petit point orange.

Je finis la vaisselle et me sèche les mains avec un torchon en arpentant la cuisine. Le buffet est recouvert de papiers et je trouve ce désordre étrangement rassurant. Je pose la main sur la poignée du placard et j'entends les mots de Patrick résonner dans ma tête.

Ne t'avise surtout pas d'ouvrir les portes.

Qu'est-ce qu'il ne veut pas que je voie là-dedans ? Je regarde par-dessus mon épaule, comme s'il pouvait rentrer d'un instant à l'autre, puis j'ouvre la porte avec décision. Quelque chose tombe aussitôt vers moi et je retiens mon souffle en tendant la main pour rattraper un vase avant qu'il ne se fracasse sur le carrelage. Je le remets à sa place au milieu d'autres objets en verre ; l'air à l'intérieur du buffet est imprégné d'une odeur de lavande défraîchie qui émane d'un tas de linge. Il n'y a rien de sinistre ici : juste des souvenirs.

Je suis sur le point de refermer la porte quand j'aperçois le bord argenté d'un cadre qui dépasse d'une pile de nappes. Je le sors avec précaution. C'est une photo de Patrick, le bras autour d'une femme aux cheveux blonds coupés court et aux dents blanches bien alignées. Ils sourient tous les deux, pas à l'appareil mais l'un à l'autre. Je me demande de qui il s'agit et pourquoi Patrick m'a caché cette photo. Est-ce la femme avec laquelle il pensait se marier ? J'observe le cliché en essayant de trouver une indication sur la date à laquelle il a été pris. Patrick a la même allure qu'aujourd'hui et je me demande si cette femme appartient au passé ou si elle fait encore partie de sa vie. Je ne suis peut-être pas la seule à avoir des secrets. Je remets le cadre entre les nappes et referme la porte du placard, laissant son contenu comme je l'ai trouvé.

Je fais les cent pas dans la cuisine, je commence à fatiguer. Je prépare une tasse de thé et m'assois à la table pour la boire.

La pluie me fouette le visage, me brouillant la vue et faisant défiler des formes imprécises devant mes yeux. Le vent couvre presque le ronronnement du moteur, mais pas le bruit sourd lorsqu'il percute le capot avant de retomber sur l'asphalte.

Soudain, ce qui trouble ma vision n'est pas de la pluie, mais de l'eau de mer. Et le moteur n'est pas une voiture, mais le teuf-teuf d'un canot de sauvetage. Bien que le cri soit le mien, le visage qui lève les yeux vers moi – ces grands yeux sombres avec leurs cils mouillés –, ce visage n'est pas celui de Jacob mais de Patrick.

— Je suis désolée, dis-je sans trop savoir si je parle à haute voix. Je ne voulais pas...

Je sens une main me secouer l'épaule, me tirant du sommeil. Désorientée, je relève la tête de mes bras croisés sur le coin de table encore chaud et sens l'air frais de la cuisine me mordre le visage. Je plisse les yeux à cause de la lumière crue de l'ampoule et lève le bras pour me protéger.

— Non !

— Jenna, réveille-toi. Jenna, c'est un rêve.

Je baisse lentement le bras et ouvre les yeux pour découvrir Patrick agenouillé devant ma chaise. J'ouvre la bouche, mais je ne parviens pas à parler, encore sous le coup du cauchemar et soulagée qu'il soit là.

— Tu rêvais de quoi ?

Je rassemble mes mots.

— Je... je ne sais plus. J'avais peur.

— C'est fini, dit Patrick. (Il écarte mes cheveux humides de mes tempes et prend mon visage entre ses mains.) Je suis là.

Il est pâle, avec les cheveux mouillés et des gouttes de pluie accrochées aux cils. Son regard, d'ordinaire si éclatant, est vide et sombre. Il a l'air abattu, et sans réfléchir je me penche et l'embrasse. Il répond avidement, sans lâcher mon visage, puis me libère pour poser son front contre le mien.

— Les recherches ont été suspendues.

— Suspendues ? Tu veux dire qu'ils n'ont pas été retrouvés ?

Patrick secoue la tête et je vois ses yeux se remplir d'émotion. Il se laisse retomber sur ses talons.

— On y retourne au lever du jour, dit-il d'une voix éteinte. Mais personne n'y croit plus.

Il ferme les yeux et pose sa tête sur mes genoux, pleurant pour ce père et son fils qui ont pris la mer en toute confiance malgré le ciel menaçant.

Je lui caresse les cheveux et laisse couler mes larmes. Je pleure pour un enfant seul dans l'océan, je pleure pour sa mère, je pleure pour les rêves qui hantent mes nuits, pour Jacob, pour mon fils.

19

Les corps sont rejetés par la mer la veille de Noël, plusieurs jours après l'arrêt des recherches. J'avais naïvement imaginé qu'ils réapparaîtraient ensemble, mais je devrais maintenant savoir que la marée est imprévisible. Le fils a été retrouvé en premier, ramené dans la baie de Rhossili par une mer ondoyante qui semblait trop clémente pour avoir infligé les terribles blessures constatées sur le corps du père, découvert un kilomètre et demi plus loin.

Nous sommes sur la plage quand Patrick reçoit le coup de fil et je devine à sa mâchoire serrée que les nouvelles ne sont pas bonnes. Il s'éloigne un peu de moi, comme pour me protéger, et se tourne vers la mer pour écouter David en silence. Une fois qu'il a raccroché, il reste cloué sur place, scrutant l'horizon comme s'il espérait y trouver des réponses. Je m'approche de lui pour poser la main sur son bras ; il sursaute, comme s'il avait complètement oublié ma présence.

— Je suis navrée, dis-je en essayant désespérément de trouver les mots justes.

— Je sortais avec une fille, commence-t-il sans se détourner de la mer. Je l'avais rencontrée à l'université et on vivait ensemble à Leeds.

J'écoute, sans trop savoir où il veut en venir.

— Quand je suis revenu dans la région, elle m'a suivi. Elle ne voulait pas venir, mais on ne voulait pas être séparés, alors elle a laissé tomber son boulot et elle est venue vivre avec moi à Port Ellis. Elle n'aimait pas du tout. C'était trop petit, trop calme, trop ennuyeux pour elle.

Je me sens mal à l'aise, comme si je m'immisçais dans sa vie privée. J'ai envie de lui dire de se taire, qu'il n'a pas besoin de me raconter ça, mais on dirait que c'est plus fort que lui.

— Un jour, au milieu de l'été, on s'est disputés. C'était toujours le même topo : elle voulait retourner à Leeds et je voulais rester ici pour développer le cabinet. Elle était furieuse et elle est partie surfer, mais elle a été happée par un contre-courant et elle n'est jamais revenue.

— Oh, mon Dieu, Patrick ! (J'ai la gorge nouée.) Quelle horreur !

Il se tourne vers moi.

— Sa planche a été rejetée par la mer le lendemain, mais on n'a jamais retrouvé son corps.

— *On* ? dis-je. Tu as participé aux recherches ?

Je n'arrive pas à imaginer à quel point ça a dû être difficile.

Il hausse les épaules.

— On y est tous allés. C'est notre boulot, non ?

— Oui, mais…

Je n'achève pas ma phrase. Bien sûr qu'il a participé aux recherches – comment aurait-il pu en être autrement ?

Je prends Patrick dans mes bras et il se blottit contre moi, enfouissant sa tête dans mon cou. J'avais imaginé que sa vie était parfaite : qu'il n'y avait rien d'autre que ce visage décontracté et drôle qu'il affichait. Mais les fantômes qu'il combat sont aussi réels que les miens. Pour la première fois, je suis avec quelqu'un qui a autant besoin de moi que moi de lui.

Nous marchons lentement jusqu'au cottage, où Patrick me demande de l'attendre pendant qu'il va chercher quelque chose dans sa voiture.

— Quoi donc ? dis-je, intriguée.

— Tu verras.

Son regard a repris son éclat habituel et je suis éblouie par la capacité qu'il a de vivre avec un tel poids. Je me demande si c'est le temps qui lui en a donné la force et j'espère qu'un jour j'y parviendrai moi aussi.

Te laisser partir

Quand il revient, il porte un sapin sur l'épaule. J'éprouve une pointe de nostalgie en repensant à l'excitation qui me gagnait à l'approche de Noël. Quand nous étions petites, Eve et moi avions un rituel strict pour les décorations : d'abord les lumières, ensuite les guirlandes, puis la pose solennelle des boules et enfin le vieil ange en équilibre au sommet du sapin. J'imagine qu'elle perpétue cette tradition avec ses enfants.

Je ne veux pas de sapin chez moi. Les décorations sont pour les enfants, les familles. Mais Patrick insiste.

— Je n'ai pas l'intention de repartir avec, dit-il tandis qu'il le fait passer par la porte en semant des aiguilles par terre. (Il l'installe sur son croisillon en bois et vérifie qu'il est bien droit.) Et puis c'est Noël. Il te faut un sapin.

— Mais je n'ai rien pour le décorer !

— Jette un coup d'œil là-dedans.

J'ouvre le sac à dos bleu marine de Patrick et y trouve une boîte à chaussures cabossée fermée à l'aide d'un gros élastique. En retirant le couvercle, je découvre une douzaine de boules de Noël rouges au verre craquelé.

— Oh, elles sont magnifiques !

J'en soulève une et elle tourne sur elle-même en reflétant mon visage une centaine de fois.

— Elles étaient à ma grand-mère. Je t'ai dit qu'il y avait toutes sortes de choses dans son vieux buffet.

Je rougis en me revoyant fouiller dans les placards de Patrick et tomber sur la photo de la femme qui – je le comprends maintenant – doit être celle qui s'est noyée.

— Elles sont très belles. Merci.

Nous décorons le sapin ensemble. Patrick a apporté une guirlande électrique et je trouve un ruban que je glisse entre les branches. Il n'y a que douze boules, mais la lumière transforme chacune d'entre elles en étoile filante. Je respire l'odeur du sapin avec l'espoir de conserver à jamais le souvenir de ce petit instant de bonheur.

Une fois que nous avons fini, je m'assois et pose la tête sur l'épaule de Patrick en contemplant les éclats de lumière projetés sur le mur. Il dessine des cercles sur mon poignet dénudé, et cela fait des années que je ne me suis pas sentie aussi bien. Je me tourne pour l'embrasser, ma langue cherchant la sienne, et quand j'ouvre les yeux je constate que les siens sont également ouverts.

— Viens, on monte, dis-je.

J'ignore pourquoi j'en ai envie maintenant, à cet instant précis, mais j'éprouve le besoin physique d'être avec lui.

— Tu en es sûre ?

Patrick recule un peu et me regarde droit dans les yeux.

J'acquiesce. Je n'en suis pas sûre, pas vraiment, mais je veux une réponse. J'ai besoin de savoir si ça peut être différent.

Il me passe la main dans les cheveux en m'embrassant dans le cou, sur la joue, sur les lèvres. Puis il se lève et me conduit avec douceur jusqu'à l'escalier, son pouce se promenant toujours sur ma paume comme s'il ne pouvait pas se passer de me caresser, même un court instant. Il me suit tandis que je monte l'escalier étroit, ses mains effleurant ma taille, et je sens mon cœur s'emballer.

Loin du feu et de la chaleur de la cuisinière, la chambre est froide, mais c'est l'appréhension, et non la température, qui me fait frissonner. Patrick s'assoit sur le lit et m'allonge délicatement à ses côtés. Il lève la main pour écarter les cheveux de mon visage, promenant son doigt derrière mon oreille puis le long de mon cou. J'ai une bouffée d'angoisse : je suis si ordinaire, si fade et timorée, et je me demande s'il voudra encore de moi une fois qu'il s'en sera aperçu. Mais j'ai tellement envie de lui, et ce frémissement de désir m'est si inconnu que c'en est encore plus excitant. Je me rapproche de Patrick, si près que nos souffles se confondent. Nous restons allongés ainsi pendant une bonne minute, nos lèvres s'effleurant sans s'embrasser, se touchant sans se donner. Il défait peu à peu mon chemisier, sans me quitter des yeux.

Je ne peux plus attendre. Je déboutonne mon jean et l'enlève, l'envoyant valser d'un coup de pied hâtif, puis je défais maladroitement les boutons de sa chemise. Nous nous embrassons avec fougue et nous débarrassons de nos vêtements jusqu'à ce qu'il soit nu et que je ne porte plus qu'une culotte et un tee-shirt. Il saisit l'ourlet de celui-ci et je secoue la tête.

Il s'arrête. Je m'attends à ce qu'il insiste, mais il soutient un instant mon regard, puis baisse la tête pour embrasser mes seins à travers le coton soyeux. Tandis qu'il descend le long de mon corps, je me cambre et m'abandonne à ses caresses.

Je m'assoupis dans un enchevêtrement de draps et de membres quand je sens, plus que je ne vois, Patrick tendre le bras pour éteindre la lampe de chevet.

— Laisse-la allumée, dis-je. S'il te plaît.

Il ne demande pas pourquoi. Il préfère m'enlacer et déposer un baiser sur mon front.

Quand je me réveille, je m'aperçois aussitôt que quelque chose a changé, mais je suis encore à moitié endormie et ne comprends pas tout de suite de quoi il s'agit. Ce n'est pas la présence de quelqu'un dans mon lit, bien que la sensation soit étrange, mais le fait d'avoir réellement dormi. Un sourire se dessine sur mon visage. Je me suis réveillée naturellement. Aucun cri ne m'a tirée du sommeil, aucun grincement de freins, aucun bruit de crâne percutant un pare-brise. Pour la première fois depuis plus de douze mois, je n'ai pas rêvé de l'accident.

Je songe à me lever pour préparer le café, mais la chaleur du lit me retient sous la couette et je préfère enlacer le corps nu de Patrick. Je promène ma main sur sa hanche, son ventre ferme, sa cuisse musclée. Je sens un frémissement entre mes jambes et je suis à nouveau stupéfaite de la réaction de mon corps qui brûle d'être caressé. Patrick bouge. Il relève un peu la tête et me sourit, les yeux encore fermés.

— Joyeux Noël.

— Tu veux un café ?

J'embrasse son épaule nue.

— Plus tard, répond-il en m'attirant sous la couette.

Nous restons au lit jusqu'à midi, nous délectant l'un de l'autre et savourant des petits pains moelleux avec de la confiture de cassis sucrée et collante. Patrick descend pour se resservir du café et revient avec les cadeaux que nous avons mis sous le sapin hier soir.

— Un manteau ! dis-je en déchirant le papier du paquet mou et mal emballé que Patrick me tendait.

— Ce n'est pas très romantique, dit-il d'un air penaud. Mais tu ne peux pas continuer à porter ce vieil imperméable usé alors que tu passes ton temps sur la plage. Tu vas attraper froid.

Je l'enfile aussitôt. Il est épais, chaud et imperméable, avec de grandes poches et une capuche. Il est mille fois mieux que celui que j'ai trouvé sous le porche du cottage quand j'ai emménagé.

— Vouloir me préserver du froid et de l'humidité est très romantique de ta part, dis-je en embrassant Patrick. Je l'aime beaucoup, merci.

— Il y a quelque chose dans la poche, ajoute-t-il. Pas vraiment un cadeau, juste quelque chose dont tu as besoin, à mon avis.

J'enfonce les mains dans les poches et en sors un téléphone portable.

— C'est un vieux téléphone qui traînait chez moi. Il n'a rien d'exceptionnel, mais il marche. Tu n'auras plus à aller jusqu'au camping pour passer un coup de fil.

Je suis sur le point de lui répondre qu'il est la seule personne que j'appelle quand je réalise que c'est peut-être ce qu'il a voulu dire ! Qu'il n'aime pas le fait que je sois injoignable. Je ne sais pas trop comment le prendre, mais je le remercie et me dis que je ne suis pas obligée de le laisser allumé.

Il me tend un deuxième cadeau, parfaitement emballé avec du papier violet foncé et un ruban.

— Ce n'est pas moi qui ai fait le paquet, confesse-t-il.

Je défais soigneusement le papier et ouvre la petite boîte avec la précaution qui s'impose. À l'intérieur se trouve une broche de nacre en forme de coquillage. Elle reflète la lumière et une douzaine de couleurs dansent à sa surface.

— Oh, Patrick ! (Je suis comblée.) Elle est magnifique.

Je la prends et l'épingle sur mon nouveau manteau. J'ai honte de sortir le dessin au crayon de Port Ellis que j'ai fait pour Patrick, la plage avec le canot de sauvetage qui ne part pas mais rentre à bon port.

— Tu as tellement de talent, Jenna ! s'exclame-t-il en levant le dessin encadré pour l'admirer. Tu perds ton temps ici. Tu devrais exposer, te faire connaître.

— Je ne peux pas, dis-je.

Mais je ne lui explique pas pourquoi. Je lui propose plutôt d'aller faire un tour pour étrenner mon nouveau manteau et nous emmenons Beau sur la plage.

La baie est déserte, la marée est au plus bas, découvrant une vaste étendue de sable pâle. Des nuages chargés de neige s'amoncellent au-dessus des falaises, leur blancheur tranchant avec le bleu profond de la mer. Les mouettes tournoient dans le ciel. Leurs cris plaintifs résonnent dans le vide, et les vagues déferlent en rythme sur la plage.

— C'est presque dommage de laisser des traces de pas.

Je glisse ma main dans celle de Patrick tandis que nous flânons. Pour une fois, je n'ai pas pris mon appareil photo. Nous marchons dans l'eau, laissant l'écume glaciale engloutir le bout de nos bottes.

— Ma mère avait l'habitude de se baigner le jour de Noël, raconte Patrick. Ça mettait mon père hors de lui. Il savait que les marées peuvent être dangereuses, et il la traitait d'irresponsable. Mais dès que tous les cadeaux étaient ouverts, elle attrapait sa serviette et fonçait piquer une tête dans la mer. On trouvait tous ça hilarant, bien sûr, et on l'encourageait de loin.

— C'est fou !

Je songe à la fille qui s'est noyée et me demande comment il peut supporter d'être au bord de la mer après une telle tragédie. Beau se rue sur les vagues, faisant claquer sa mâchoire à chaque déferlement d'eau salée.

— Et toi ? reprend Patrick. Il y avait des traditions un peu folles dans ta famille ?

Je réfléchis un moment et souris en repensant à l'excitation que je ressentais quand les vacances de Noël approchaient.

— Pas vraiment. Mais j'adorais les Noëls en famille. Mes parents commençaient les préparatifs en octobre et la maison était pleine de paquets excitants cachés dans les placards et sous les lits. On a continué après le départ de mon père, mais ce n'était plus pareil.

— Tu as déjà essayé de le contacter ?

Il me presse la main.

— Oui. Quand j'étais à l'université. J'ai fini par le retrouver et j'ai découvert qu'il avait une nouvelle famille. Je lui ai écrit et il m'a répondu qu'il valait mieux laisser le passé là où il était. Ça m'a brisé le cœur.

— Jenna, c'est affreux.

Je hausse les épaules, comme si ça m'était égal.

— Tu es proche de ta sœur ?

Te laisser partir

— On s'entendait bien avant. (Je ramasse un galet et essaie de faire des ricochets à la surface de l'eau, mais les vagues sont trop rapides.) Eve s'est rangée du côté de ma mère quand mon père est parti. Et même si j'en voulais beaucoup à ma mère d'avoir mis mon père à la porte, ça ne nous a pas empêchées de nous serrer les coudes, Eve et moi. Mais je ne l'ai pas revue depuis plusieurs années. Je lui ai envoyé une carte il y a quelques semaines. Je ne sais pas si elle l'a reçue. Je ne suis même pas certaine qu'elle vive toujours au même endroit.

— Vous vous êtes brouillées ?

J'acquiesce.

— Elle n'aimait pas mon mari.

Ça paraît osé de le dire à haute voix et un frisson me parcourt le dos.

— Et *toi*, tu l'aimais ?

C'est une question étrange et je prends le temps d'y réfléchir. J'ai passé tant de temps à haïr Ian, à en avoir peur.

— Au début, dis-je finalement.

Il était si charmant, si différent des étudiants maladroits et potaches.

— Ça fait combien de temps que tu es divorcée ?

Je ne le reprends pas.

— Un moment. (Je ramasse une poignée de galets et commence à les lancer un par un dans la mer. Un pour chaque année passée sans amour. Sans tendresse.) Parfois, je me demande s'il ne va pas revenir.

J'ai un petit rire, mais il sonne faux et Patrick me regarde pensivement.

— Et tu n'as pas eu d'enfants ?

Je me penche et fais mine de chercher des cailloux.

— Il n'en voulait pas.

Ce n'est pas si éloigné de la vérité, après tout. Ian n'a jamais voulu entendre parler de son fils.

Patrick m'enlace les épaules.

— Excuse-moi. Je pose trop de questions.

— Ça ne me dérange pas.

Et je me rends compte que c'est vrai. Je me sens en sécurité avec Patrick. Nous remontons lentement la plage. Le sentier est verglacé et je suis contente de son bras autour de moi. Je lui en ai dit plus que prévu, mais je ne peux pas tout lui raconter. Si je le fais, il partira et je n'aurai personne pour me rattraper dans ma chute.

20

Ray se réveilla optimiste. Il avait pris des congés pour Noël, et même s'il avait fait un ou deux sauts au bureau et rapporté du travail chez lui, il devait admettre que ces vacances lui avaient fait du bien. Il se demanda où Kate en était avec le délit de fuite.

Sur leur liste de neuf cents et quelques Ford Focus et Fiesta rouges immatriculées à Bristol, un peu plus de quarante avaient été repérées par le système de lecture automatisée des plaques d'immatriculation. Les images étaient effacées au bout de quatre-vingt-dix jours, mais armée d'une liste de numéros d'immatriculation Kate faisait le tour des propriétaires pour les interroger au sujet de leurs allées et venues le jour du délit de fuite. Au cours du dernier mois, elle avait bien avancé dans la liste, mais les choses commençaient à se compliquer. Des voitures vendues sans les papiers nécessaires, des propriétaires partis sans laisser d'adresse… c'était déjà un miracle qu'elle en ait éliminé autant, surtout à cette période de l'année. Maintenant que les vacances étaient finies, ça allait certainement se débloquer.

Ray passa la tête par la porte de la chambre de Tom. Seul le sommet de son crâne dépassait de la couette et Ray referma la porte sans bruit. Son optimisme du nouvel an ne s'appliquait pas à son fils, dont le comportement avait empiré au point qu'il avait reçu deux avertissements officiels de la part de la principale. Le prochain entraînerait son exclusion temporaire, ce qui, d'après Ray, était une sanction absurde pour un enfant qui séchait plus de cours qu'il n'en suivait et avait horreur d'être à l'école.

— Lucy dort encore ? demanda Mags quand il la rejoignit dans la cuisine.

— Ils dorment tous les deux.

— Il va falloir qu'ils aillent au lit de bonne heure ce soir, dit Mags. Ils reprennent l'école dans trois jours.

— Est-ce que j'ai des chemises propres ? demanda Ray.

— Tu veux dire que tu n'en as pas lavé ? (Mags disparut dans la buanderie et revint avec une pile de chemises repassées sur le bras.) Heureusement que quelqu'un l'a fait. N'oublie pas qu'on va boire un verre chez les voisins ce soir.

Ray grogna.

— On est obligés ?

— Oui.

Mags lui tendit les chemises.

— Qui invite ses voisins le lendemain du jour de l'an ? pesta Ray. C'est ridicule !

— D'après Emma, tout le monde court tellement pendant les fêtes qu'organiser une soirée juste après est un bon moyen de reprendre du poil de la bête.

— Elle a tort, répliqua Ray. Leurs soirées sont toujours emmerdantes. Les gens passent leur temps à me raconter qu'ils se sont fait arrêter à trente-sept dans une zone limitée à trente et à crier à l'injustice. Ça tourne au dénigrement systématique de la police.

— Ils essaient juste de faire la conversation, Ray, dit patiemment Mags. Ils ne te voient pas souvent...

— Il y a une très bonne raison à ça.

— ... du coup la seule chose dont ils peuvent te parler, c'est de ton travail. Sois indulgent avec eux. Si ça te dérange tant que ça, change de sujet. Parle de la pluie et du beau temps.

— J'ai horreur de ça.

— OK. (Mags posa violemment une casserole sur le plan de travail.) Alors ne viens pas, Ray. Franchement, si c'est pour faire la tête, autant ne pas venir.

Ray n'aimait pas quand elle lui parlait comme à un enfant.

— Je n'ai pas dit que je n'allais pas venir, j'ai juste dit que ça allait être ennuyeux.

Mags se retourna pour lui faire face. Elle avait l'air à présent plus déçue qu'agacée.

— Tout n'est pas passionnant dans la vie, Ray.

— Bonne année, vous deux. (Ray entra dans les locaux de la Criminelle et déposa une boîte de Quality Street sur le bureau de Stumpy.) Je me suis dit que ça pourrait compenser le fait d'avoir travaillé à Noël et au jour de l'an.

La brigade tournait avec une équipe réduite pendant les jours fériés et Stumpy avait tiré le mauvais numéro.

— Il faudra plus qu'une boîte de chocolats pour compenser le fait d'avoir commencé à sept heures du matin le 1er janvier.

Ray sourit.

— De toute façon, tu as passé l'âge de faire la fête jusqu'au petit matin, Stumpy. Mags et moi, on était couchés bien avant minuit le soir du réveillon.

— Je crois que je ne suis pas encore tout à fait remise, fit Kate en bâillant.

— Ton réveillon s'est bien passé ? demanda Ray.

— Oui, enfin le peu dont je me souviens.

Elle rit et Ray ressentit une pointe de jalousie. Les fêtes de Kate ne se résumaient sûrement pas à des conversations insipides à propos de contraventions pour excès de vitesse ou pour avoir jeté des détritus sur la voie publique, contrairement à ce qui l'attendait ce soir.

— Qu'est-ce qu'on a aujourd'hui ? demanda-t-il.

— Une bonne nouvelle, répondit Kate. Une immatriculation.

Ray se fendit d'un large sourire.

— Il était temps. Vous pensez que c'est la bonne ?

— Oui. Elle n'a pas été repérée par le LAPI depuis le délit de fuite, et la vignette est périmée, mais la voiture n'a pas été déclarée hors route, donc, d'après moi, elle a été abandonnée ou brûlée. La carte grise mentionne une adresse sur Beaufort Crescent, à une dizaine de kilomètres de l'endroit où Jacob a été renversé. On y est allés hier avec Stumpy, mais c'est vide. Il s'agit d'une location, du coup Stumpy va essayer de joindre le propriétaire aujourd'hui pour voir s'il a une adresse où faire suivre le courrier.

— Mais on a un nom ? demanda Ray, incapable de dissimuler son excitation.

— On a un nom, répondit Kate rayonnante. Aucune trace dans l'ordinateur central ou dans le registre des électeurs, et je n'ai rien trouvé sur Internet, mais on va y arriver. J'ai obtenu la levée de la protection des données et j'ai envoyé des demandes de renseignements aux entreprises de service public. Maintenant que les fêtes sont passées, on devrait avoir quelques retours.

— On a aussi avancé sur la mère de Jacob, indiqua Stumpy.

— Formidable ! fit Ray. Je devrais prendre des vacances plus souvent. Tu lui as parlé ?

— Il n'y a pas de numéro de téléphone. Kate a fini par dénicher un professeur vacataire à St. Mary's qui la connaissait. Après l'accident, elle avait l'impression que tout le monde la tenait pour responsable. Elle était rongée par la culpabilité et furieuse qu'on ait laissé le conducteur s'en tirer impunément…

— « Laissé le conducteur s'en tirer impunément » ? dit Ray. On est restés assis sans rien faire, c'est ça ?

— Je ne fais que répéter ce qu'on m'a dit, se défendit Stumpy. Bref, elle a coupé les ponts avec tout le monde et elle a quitté Bristol pour prendre un nouveau départ. (Il tapota le dossier, qui semblait s'être épaissi de plusieurs centimètres depuis la dernière fois que Ray l'avait vu.) J'attends un e-mail de la police locale, mais on devrait avoir une adresse d'ici la fin de la journée.

— Bon boulot. C'est très important qu'on ait la mère de notre côté si on va au tribunal. La dernière chose dont on a besoin, c'est qu'un militant antipolice aille se répandre dans les journaux sur le temps qu'on a mis pour inculper quelqu'un.

Le téléphone de Kate sonna.

— Brigade criminelle, inspecteur Evans à l'appareil.

Ray commençait à se diriger vers son bureau quand Kate se mit à gesticuler dans tous les sens pour attirer son attention ainsi que celle de Stumpy.

— Fantastique ! dit-elle. Merci beaucoup.

Elle griffonna furieusement quelque chose sur un bloc-notes A4 et souriait encore en reposant le téléphone un instant plus tard.

— Ça y est, on l'a ! fit-elle en agitant triomphalement le bout de papier.

Stumpy se fendit d'un rare sourire.

— C'était British Telecom, expliqua Kate en se trémoussant sur son fauteuil. Ils ont consulté leurs fichiers de clients sur liste rouge et ils ont une adresse pour nous !

— Où ça ?

Kate détacha la feuille de son bloc-notes et la donna à Stumpy.

— Excellent travail, dit Ray. Allons-y. (Il saisit deux trousseaux de clés de voiture dans l'armoire murale et en lança un à Stumpy, qui le rattrapa habilement.) Stumpy, prends le dossier avec ce qu'on a sur la mère de Jacob. Va voir la police locale et dis-leur qu'on ne pouvait pas attendre leur coup de fil, il nous faut cette adresse maintenant. Ne reviens pas avant d'avoir retrouvé la mère, et quand tu seras avec elle, fais-lui bien comprendre que personne ne va s'en tirer impunément, on fait tout ce qu'on peut pour traduire quelqu'un en justice pour la mort de Jacob. Kate et moi, on se charge de l'arrestation. (Il s'interrompit et lança l'autre jeu de clés à Kate.) En fait, c'est mieux si tu conduis. Il faut que j'annule ma soirée.

— Tu avais prévu un truc sympa ? demanda Kate.

Ray sourit.

— Crois-moi, je préfère être ici.

21

On frappe à la porte et je sursaute. Déjà ? Je ne vois pas le temps passer quand je travaille sur mes photos. Beau dresse l'oreille mais n'aboie pas, et je lui ébouriffe les poils du crâne en me dirigeant vers la porte. Je tirc le verrou.

— Tu dois être la seule personne de la baie qui ferme sa porte à clé, rouspète gentiment Patrick.

Il entre et m'embrasse.

— Ça doit être une habitude de la ville, dis-je d'un air détaché.

Je remets le verrou en place et bataille pour tourner la clé dans la serrure.

— Iestyn n'a toujours pas arrangé ça ?

— Tu sais comment il est. Il n'arrête pas de promettre qu'il va s'en occuper, mais il ne trouve jamais le temps. Il a dit qu'il viendrait ce soir, mais je ne me fais pas trop d'illusions. Je crois tout simplement qu'il trouve absurde de fermer à clé.

— Eh bien, il n'a pas tort. (Patrick s'appuie contre la porte et empoigne la grosse clé pour forcer le mécanisme.) Je crois qu'il n'y a pas eu de cambriolage à Penfach depuis 1954.

Il sourit et j'ignore le sarcasme. Patrick ne sait pas que je vérifie chaque recoin de la maison les soirs où il n'est pas là, ni que je me réveille en sursaut au moindre bruit dehors. Les cauchemars ont peut-être cessé, mais la peur est toujours présente.

— Viens te réchauffer près de la cuisinière, dis-je.

Il fait un froid glacial dehors et Patrick a l'air gelé.

— Ce temps est parti pour durer un moment. (Il suit mon conseil et s'appuie contre l'antique cuisinière.) Tu as assez de bois ? Je peux t'en apporter demain.

— J'ai de quoi tenir des semaines avec ce que Iestyn m'a donné. Il passe récupérer le loyer le premier du mois, et en général il vient avec un tas de bûches dans sa remorque, qu'il refuse de me faire payer.

— C'est un bon gars. Mon père et lui se connaissent depuis un bail. Ils passaient des soirées entières au pub, débarquaient ensuite à la maison et essayaient de faire croire à ma mère qu'ils n'étaient pas bourrés. Ça m'étonnerait qu'il ait beaucoup changé.

Je ris en imaginant la scène.

— Je l'aime bien. (Je prends deux bières dans le frigo et en tends une à Patrick.) Alors, c'est quoi cet ingrédient mystère ?

Il a appelé ce matin pour dire qu'il se chargeait du dîner et je suis curieuse de voir ce qu'il y a dans le sac isotherme qu'il a laissé près de la porte d'entrée.

— Un client me l'a apporté aujourd'hui pour me remercier.

Patrick ouvre le sac et plonge la main à l'intérieur. Puis, tel un magicien sortant un lapin de son chapeau, il brandit un homard noir aux reflets bleutés dont les pinces s'agitent mollement dans ma direction.

— Mon Dieu ! (Je suis à la fois ravie et intimidée par le menu proposé, n'ayant jamais rien cuisiné d'aussi compliqué.) Beaucoup de clients te paient en homards ?

— Plus que tu ne l'imagines, répond Patrick. D'autres paient en faisans ou en lapins. Ils me les donnent parfois en mains propres, mais la plupart du temps je trouve quelque chose devant la porte en arrivant au travail. (Il sourit.) J'ai appris à ne pas demander d'où ça venait. C'est difficile de payer ses impôts en faisans, mais heureusement on a encore assez de clients munis d'un chéquier pour que le cabinet ne coule pas. Je ne peux pas refuser de soigner un animal juste pour une question d'argent.

— Tu es un sensible, toi, dis-je en l'enlaçant pour l'embrasser.

— Chut, fait-il quand nous nous séparons. Tu vas ruiner la réputation de macho que j'essaie de me forger. Et puis je ne suis pas trop sensible pour écorcher un joli petit lapin ou ébouillanter un homard.

Il part dans un rire exagéré, comme le méchant d'un dessin animé.

— Tu es bête, dis-je en me moquant de lui. J'espère que tu sais comment cuisiner ça, parce que moi je n'en ai aucune idée.

J'observe le homard avec méfiance.

— Laissez-moi faire, madame, dit Patrick en posant un torchon sur son bras avant d'exécuter une jolie courbette. Le dîner sera bientôt servi.

Je sors ma plus grande casserole et Patrick remet le homard dans le sac isotherme en attendant que l'eau bouille. Je remplis l'évier pour laver la laitue et nous nous mettons au travail dans un silence complice, Beau se faufilant de temps à autre entre nos jambes pour nous rappeler sa présence. C'est simple et tranquille, et je souris toute seule en jetant un coup d'œil furtif vers Patrick, occupé à préparer la sauce.

— Tout va bien ? demande-t-il en croisant mon regard tandis qu'il pose la cuillère en bois contre la casserole. À quoi tu penses ?

— À rien, dis-je en retournant à ma salade.

— Allez, dis-moi.

— Je pensais à nous.

— Maintenant, tu *dois* m'en dire plus ! s'exclame Patrick en riant.

Il mouille sa main dans l'évier et m'envoie quelques gouttes d'eau.

Je crie. C'est plus fort que moi. Avant que mon esprit puisse me raisonner et me dire qu'il s'agit de Patrick – juste de Patrick qui fait l'idiot –, je me détourne vite de lui en me protégeant la tête. Une réaction viscérale, instinctive, qui accélère mon pouls et fait transpirer mes mains. L'air tourbillonne autour de moi et l'espace d'un instant je suis transportée à une autre époque. À un autre endroit.

Le silence est palpable et je me redresse lentement ; mon cœur bat à tout rompre. Patrick a les bras ballants et l'air horrifié. J'essaie de parler, mais j'ai la bouche sèche et une boule de panique dans la gorge qui refuse de s'en aller. Je regarde Patrick. La confusion se lit sur son visage et je sais que je vais devoir m'expliquer.

— Je suis vraiment désolée, dis-je. Je...

Je porte mes mains à mon visage d'un air consterné.

Patrick fait un pas en avant. Il essaie de me prendre dans ses bras mais je le repousse. J'ai honte de ma réaction et je lutte contre cette soudaine envie de tout lui raconter.

— Jenna, commence-t-il avec douceur. Qu'est-ce qui t'est arrivé ?

On frappe à la porte et nous nous dévisageons.

— J'y vais, dit Patrick.

Je secoue la tête.

— Ça doit être Iestyn. (Je me frotte le visage, heureuse de la diversion.) Je reviens tout de suite.

Quand j'ouvre la porte, je sais exactement ce qui se passe.

Tout ce que je voulais, c'était m'enfuir : faire semblant que la vie vécue avant l'accident était celle de quelqu'un d'autre et me convaincre que je pourrais à nouveau être heureuse. Je me suis souvent demandé quelle serait ma réaction quand on me retrouverait, quel effet ça ferait d'être ramenée à la réalité et si je m'y opposerais.

Mais quand le policier prononce mon nom, je me contente d'acquiescer.

— Oui, c'est moi, dis-je.

Il est plus âgé que moi, avec des cheveux bruns coupés ras et un costume sombre. Il a l'air gentil et je me demande à quoi ressemble sa vie, s'il a des enfants, une femme.

La femme à côté de lui fait un pas en avant. Elle a l'air plus jeune, avec des cheveux châtain foncé qui tombent en boucles autour de son visage.

— Inspecteur Kate Evans, dit-elle en ouvrant un portefeuille en cuir pour montrer sa plaque. Brigade criminelle de Bristol. Je vous arrête pour conduite dangereuse ayant entraîné la mort et délit de fuite. Vous pouvez garder le silence, mais si vous invoquez ultérieurement devant le tribunal un élément que vous avez omis de mentionner auparavant, cela pourra nuire à votre défense...

Je ferme les yeux et laisse échapper un long soupir. Il est temps d'arrêter de faire semblant.

Seconde partie

22

La première fois que je t'ai vue, tu étais assise dans un coin du bar de l'université. Tu ne m'as pas remarqué, pas encore. Je devais pourtant sortir du lot : le seul homme en costume au milieu d'une foule d'étudiants. Tu étais entourée d'amies et riais aux larmes. Je me suis installé avec mon café à la table d'à côté, où j'ai feuilleté le journal en écoutant vos conversations, qui passaient inexplicablement d'un sujet à l'autre, comme la plupart des bavardages féminins. J'ai fini par poser mon journal pour vous observer. J'ai appris que vous étiez toutes des étudiantes en dernière année d'arts plastiques. J'aurais pu le deviner à votre façon de vous approprier le bar : vous passiez votre temps à appeler vos amis à l'autre bout de la salle et à rire sans vous soucier des autres. C'est à ce moment-là que j'ai entendu ton nom : Jenna. J'ai été un peu déçu. Tes magnifiques cheveux et ton teint pâle te donnaient un air préraphaélite et j'avais imaginé quelque chose d'un peu plus classique. Aurelia, peut-être, ou Eleanor. Cependant, tu étais incontestablement la plus séduisante du groupe. Les autres étaient trop m'as-tu-vu, trop vulgaires. Tu devais avoir le même âge qu'elles – quinze ans de moins que moi, au moins –, mais ton visage reflétait déjà une certaine maturité. Tu as regardé autour de toi comme si tu cherchais quelqu'un et je t'ai souri, mais tu ne m'as pas vu et j'ai dû partir quelques minutes plus tard.

J'avais accepté de donner six cours en tant qu'intervenant extérieur dans le cadre d'un programme visant à nouer des liens entre l'université et le monde de l'entreprise. C'était assez simple : les étudiants étaient soit à moitié endormis, soit très intéressés, penchés en avant pour ne rien rater de ce que j'avais à dire sur l'entrepreneuriat. Pas mal pour quelqu'un qui n'a jamais mis les pieds à la fac. Chose étonnante pour un cours sur le commerce, il y avait un certain nombre de filles dans l'auditoire, et les regards qu'elles ont échangé quand je suis entré dans l'amphithéâtre le premier jour ne m'ont pas échappé. J'étais une curiosité, je suppose : plus vieux que les garçons du campus, mais plus jeune que leurs professeurs et maîtres de conférences. Mes costumes étaient faits sur mesure, mes chemises bien ajustées, avec des boutons de manchettes argentés. Je n'avais pas de cheveux blancs – pas encore – et pas de bedaine à dissimuler sous ma veste.

Pendant le cours, je m'arrêtais délibérément au milieu d'une phrase pour fixer une étudiante – différente chaque semaine. Mon regard les faisait rougir et elles me rendaient mon sourire avant de détourner les yeux. Je prenais un malin plaisir à découvrir quel prétexte elles inventaient pour rester à la fin du cours, s'empressant de venir me voir avant que je range mes affaires pour partir. Je m'asseyais alors au bord de la table, appuyé sur une main et penché pour écouter leur question, et je voyais la lueur d'espoir dans leurs yeux disparaître quand elles comprenaient que je n'allais pas les inviter à boire un verre. Elles ne m'intéressaient pas. Pas comme toi.

La semaine suivante, tu étais encore là avec tes amies, et quand je suis passé devant votre table tu m'as regardé et souri ; pas par politesse, mais un large sourire qui a illuminé ton visage. Tu portais un débardeur bleu vif, qui laissait apparaître les bretelles et les bordures en dentelle d'un soutien-gorge noir, et un ample treillis taille basse. Un petit bourrelet lisse et bronzé dépassait entre les deux, et je me suis demandé si tu t'en rendais compte, et si oui pourquoi ça ne te dérangeait pas.

La conversation est passée des devoirs à rendre aux relations amoureuses. Les garçons, je suppose, même si vous parliez d'« hommes ». Tes amies ont baissé la voix et j'ai dû tendre l'oreille, retenant mon souffle en attendant ton tour au milieu de cette litanie d'aventures d'un soir et de flirts sans lendemain. Mais je t'avais bien jugée : tout ce que j'ai entendu de ta part, ce sont des éclats de rire et des piques amicales envers tes camarades. Tu n'étais pas comme elles.

J'ai pensé à toi toute la semaine. À l'heure du déjeuner, j'ai fait un tour sur le campus dans l'espoir de te croiser. J'ai vu l'une de tes amies – la grande aux cheveux teints – et je l'ai suivie un moment, mais elle a disparu dans la bibliothèque et je n'ai pas pu entrer pour voir si elle allait te retrouver.

Le jour de mon quatrième cours, je suis arrivé en avance et j'ai été récompensé de mes efforts en te voyant assise toute seule, à la même table que les deux fois précédentes. Tu lisais une lettre et je me suis rendu compte que tu pleurais. Ton mascara avait coulé sous tes yeux, et tu ne m'aurais sans doute pas cru, mais tu étais encore plus belle comme ça. Je suis venu avec mon café à ta table.

— Ça vous dérange si je me mets là ?

Tu as fourré la lettre dans ton sac.

— Allez-y.

— On s'est déjà vus ici, il me semble, ai-je dit en m'asseyant en face de toi.

— Ah bon ? Je ne m'en souviens pas, désolée.

J'étais contrarié que tu aies oublié aussi vite, mais tu étais bouleversée et tu n'avais peut-être pas les idées claires.

— Je donne des cours ici en ce moment.

J'avais vite découvert que faire partie du corps enseignant attirait les étudiantes. J'ignorais si c'était lié au désir d'avoir quelqu'un pour « glisser un mot en leur faveur » ou si c'était simplement dû au contraste avec leurs camarades masculins à peine sortis de l'adolescence, mais jusqu'ici ça avait toujours fonctionné.

— Vraiment ? (Ton regard s'est éclairé.) Quelle matière ?

— Le commerce.

— Ah.

L'étincelle a disparu et je t'en ai voulu de te désintéresser aussi vite de quelque chose d'aussi important. Après tout, ton art n'allait pas subvenir aux besoins d'une famille ou régénérer une ville.

— Et vous faites quoi quand vous ne donnez pas de cours ? m'as-tu demandé.

Ce que tu pensais n'aurait pas dû avoir d'importance, mais j'ai soudain eu envie de t'impressionner.

— J'ai une société d'informatique. On vend des programmes dans le monde entier.

Je n'ai pas parlé de Doug, qui possédait soixante pour cent et moi seulement quarante, et je n'ai pas précisé que « le monde entier » se limitait pour l'instant à l'Irlande. Notre société était en plein essor et je ne te disais rien que je n'avais pas déjà dit au banquier lors de notre dernière demande de prêt.

J'ai changé de sujet.

— Vous êtes en dernière année, non ?

Tu as acquiescé.

— J'étudie…

J'ai levé la main.

— Ne me dites rien, laissez-moi deviner.

Tu as ri, le jeu te plaisait. J'ai fait semblant de réfléchir un moment en promenant les yeux sur ta robe en Lycra rayée, sur le foulard noué autour de tes cheveux. Tu étais plus ronde à l'époque et tes seins tendaient le tissu sur ta poitrine. Je distinguais le contour de tes mamelons et je me suis demandé s'ils étaient clairs ou foncés.

— Vous faites des études d'arts plastiques, ai-je finalement dit.

— Oui ! (Tu avais l'air stupéfaite.) Comment vous avez deviné ?

— Vous ressemblez à une artiste, ai-je répondu comme si c'était évident.

Tu n'as rien dit, mais deux taches de couleur sont apparues sur le haut de tes pommettes et tu n'as pas pu t'empêcher de sourire.

— Ian Petersen.

Te laisser partir

J'ai tendu le bras pour te serrer la main et je l'ai gardée un peu plus longtemps que nécessaire, sentant la fraîcheur de ta peau sous mes doigts.

— Jenna Gray.

— Jenna, ai-je répété. Ce n'est pas commun. C'est le diminutif de quelque chose ?

— Jennifer. Mais on m'a toujours appelée Jenna.

Tu as ri avec insouciance. Les dernières traces de larmes sur ton visage avaient disparu, et avec elles la vulnérabilité que j'avais trouvée si irrésistible.

— Je n'ai pas pu m'empêcher de remarquer que vous étiez un peu triste. (J'ai montré la lettre dans ton sac ouvert.) Vous avez eu de mauvaises nouvelles ?

Ton visage s'est tout de suite assombri.

— C'est une lettre de mon père.

Je n'ai rien dit. Je me suis contenté d'incliner la tête sur le côté et d'attendre. Les femmes ont rarement besoin d'être encouragées pour parler de leurs problèmes et tu ne faisais pas exception.

— Il est parti quand j'avais quinze ans et je ne l'ai pas revu depuis. Le mois dernier, j'ai fini par le retrouver et je lui ai écrit, mais il ne veut plus entendre parler de moi. Il dit qu'il a une nouvelle famille et qu'on devrait « laisser le passé là où il est ».

Tu as mimé des guillemets et pris un air sarcastique qui ne dissimulait pas ton amertume.

— C'est affreux. J'ai du mal à imaginer qu'on puisse ne pas avoir envie de vous voir.

Tu t'es aussitôt adoucie et tu as rougi.

— Tant pis pour lui, as-tu dit en fixant la table, les larmes te montant à nouveau aux yeux.

Je me suis penché.

— Est-ce que je peux vous offrir un café ?

— Avec plaisir.

Quand je suis revenu, un groupe d'amis t'avait rejointe. J'ai reconnu deux des filles, mais il y en avait une troisième, ainsi qu'un garçon aux cheveux longs et aux oreilles percées. Ils avaient pris toutes les chaises et j'ai dû aller en chercher une à une autre table pour m'asseoir. Je t'ai donné ta tasse et j'ai attendu que tu expliques aux autres qu'on était en pleine conversation, mais tu t'es contentée de me remercier pour le café et de me présenter tes amis, dont j'ai aussitôt oublié les noms.

L'une de tes amies m'a posé une question, mais je ne pouvais te quitter des yeux. Tu étais lancée dans une discussion sérieuse à propos d'un travail de fin d'année avec le garçon aux cheveux longs. Une mèche de cheveux est tombée sur ton visage et tu l'as ramenée impatiemment derrière ton oreille. Tu as dû sentir mon regard parce que tu as tourné la tête. Tu m'as souri d'un air confus et je t'ai pardonné sur-le-champ l'impolitesse de tes amis.

Mon café a refroidi. Je ne voulais pas être le premier à partir et devenir le sujet des conversations, mais mon cours commençait quelques minutes plus tard. Je me suis levé et j'ai attendu que tu le remarques.

— Merci pour le café.

Je voulais te proposer qu'on se revoie, mais comment aurais-je pu avec tous tes amis autour de toi ?

— À la semaine prochaine, peut-être ? ai-je dit, comme si ça n'avait aucune importance.

Mais tu t'étais déjà retournée vers tes amis et je suis parti en entendant ton rire résonner dans la salle.

Ce rire m'a dissuadé de revenir la semaine suivante, et quand on s'est revus quinze jours plus tard, le soulagement sur ton visage m'a prouvé que j'avais bien fait de laisser passer un peu de temps. Je ne t'ai pas demandé si je pouvais m'asseoir à ta table cette fois-ci, j'ai juste apporté deux cafés – noir avec un sucre pour toi.

— Vous vous rappelez comment j'aime mon café !

Te laisser partir

J'ai haussé les épaules, l'air de rien, mais je l'avais noté dans mon agenda à la date du jour où on s'était rencontrés, comme je le fais toujours.

Cette fois-ci, j'ai veillé à te poser davantage de questions sur toi, et tu t'es ouverte comme une feuille sous la pluie. Tu m'as montré tes dessins et j'ai feuilleté des pages de croquis honnêtes mais banals en te disant qu'ils étaient exceptionnels. Quand tes amis sont arrivés, j'étais sur le point de me lever pour aller chercher plus de chaises, mais tu leur as dit que tu étais occupée, que tu les rejoindrais plus tard. À ce moment-là, tous mes doutes te concernant se sont dissipés et je t'ai fixée jusqu'à ce que tu détournes les yeux en souriant, toute rouge.

— On ne se reverra pas la semaine prochaine, ai-je dit. C'est mon dernier cours aujourd'hui.

J'étais touché de lire de la déception sur ton visage.

Tu as ouvert la bouche pour parler, mais tu t'es arrêtée, et j'ai attendu, savourant ce moment d'incertitude. J'aurais pu te le proposer moi-même, mais je préférais te l'entendre dire.

— On pourrait peut-être aller boire un verre un de ces jours ? as-tu demandé.

J'ai pris mon temps pour répondre, comme si ça ne m'était pas venu à l'esprit.

— Et pourquoi pas un dîner ? Un nouveau restaurant français a ouvert en ville. On pourrait peut-être l'essayer ce week-end ?

Ta joie non dissimulée était émouvante. J'ai pensé à Marie, si indifférente à tout, si désabusée et fatiguée de la vie. Jusque-là, je n'avais pas songé que ça pouvait être une question d'âge, mais quand j'ai vu ton enthousiasme enfantin à l'idée d'aller dans un restaurant chic, j'ai su que j'avais bien fait de chercher quelqu'un de plus jeune. Quelqu'un de moins expérimenté. Je ne te prenais pas pour une parfaite ingénue, bien sûr, mais au moins tu n'étais pas encore devenue cynique et méfiante.

Te laisser partir

Je suis venu te chercher à la résidence universitaire, ignorant les regards curieux des étudiants qui passaient devant ta porte, et j'étais content de te voir apparaître dans une élégante robe noire, tes longues jambes moulées dans d'épais collants sombres. Quand je t'ai ouvert la portière de la voiture, tu as sursauté de surprise.

— Je pourrais m'y habituer.

— Tu es ravissante, Jennifer, ai-je dit.

Tu as ri.

— Personne ne m'appelle Jennifer.

— Ça te dérange ?

— Non, je ne crois pas. C'est juste que ça fait bizarre.

Le restaurant ne méritait pas les critiques élogieuses que j'avais lues, mais ça n'a pas eu l'air de te gêner. Tu as commandé des pommes de terre sautées pour accompagner ton poulet et j'ai commenté ton choix.

— C'est rare de tomber sur une femme qui ne fait pas attention à sa ligne.

J'ai souri pour te montrer que je n'y accordais aucune importance.

— Je ne fais pas de régime. La vie est trop courte.

Tu as fini la sauce à la crème de ton poulet, mais tu as laissé tes pommes de terre. Quand le serveur a proposé la carte des desserts, j'ai refusé d'un geste de la main.

— Deux cafés, s'il vous plaît. (J'ai remarqué ta déception mais tu n'avais pas besoin de dessert riche en calories.) Qu'est-ce que tu comptes faire quand tu auras ton diplôme ? t'ai-je demandé.

Tu as soupiré.

— Je ne sais pas. J'aimerais avoir ma propre galerie un jour, mais pour le moment il faut juste que je trouve du boulot.

— En tant qu'artiste ?

— Si seulement c'était aussi simple ! Je fais surtout de la sculpture, et j'essaierai de vendre mes œuvres, mais il faudra que j'accepte de travailler dans un bar ou un supermarché pour payer les factures. Je finirai sûrement par retourner chez ma mère.

— Tu t'entends bien avec elle ?

Tu as froncé le nez à la manière d'un enfant.

— Pas vraiment. Elle est très proche de ma sœur, mais on n'a jamais été sur la même longueur d'onde. C'est sa faute si mon père est parti du jour au lendemain.

Je nous ai resservi du vin.

— Qu'est-ce qu'elle a fait ?

— Elle l'a mis à la porte. Elle m'a dit qu'elle était désolée, mais qu'elle avait une vie à vivre elle aussi et qu'elle ne pouvait plus continuer comme ça. Et elle n'a plus voulu en reparler. Je crois que c'est la chose la plus égoïste que j'aie jamais vue.

Tes yeux étaient emplis de chagrin et j'ai posé ma main sur la tienne.

— Est-ce que tu vas répondre à ton père ?

Tu as violemment secoué la tête.

— Il m'a bien fait comprendre de le laisser tranquille dans sa lettre. Je ne sais pas ce qu'a fait ma mère, mais c'était assez grave pour qu'il ne veuille plus nous revoir.

J'ai glissé mes doigts entre les tiens et j'ai caressé la peau lisse entre ton pouce et ton index.

— On ne choisit pas ses parents, ai-je remarqué. C'est bien dommage.

— Tu es proche des tiens ?

— Ils sont morts.

J'avais si souvent raconté ce mensonge que je m'en étais presque convaincu. C'était peut-être même vrai... comment aurais-je pu le savoir ? Je ne leur avais pas envoyé mon adresse quand j'avais déménagé dans le sud, et ça m'étonnerait que mon départ les ait empêchés de dormir.

— Je suis désolée.

Tu as serré ma main, les yeux brillants de compassion.

J'ai senti un picotement à mon entrejambe et j'ai fixé la table.

— C'était il y a longtemps.

— Ça nous fait quelque chose en commun, as-tu observé. (Tu as affiché un sourire courageux, montrant que tu croyais me comprendre.) On regrette tous les deux notre père.

Tu avais tort, mais je t'ai laissée penser que tu m'avais cerné.

— Oublie-le, Jennifer. Tu ne mérites pas d'être traitée comme ça. Tu es mieux sans lui.

Tu as acquiescé, mais je voyais bien que tu ne me croyais pas. Pas encore, en tout cas.

Tu t'attendais à ce que je vienne chez toi, mais je n'avais aucune envie de passer une heure dans une chambre d'étudiant à boire du café bon marché dans des tasses ébréchées. Je t'aurais bien ramenée chez moi, mais les affaires de Marie étaient encore là et je savais que ça t'aurait gênée. Et puis c'était différent. Je ne voulais pas d'une aventure d'un soir : je te voulais, toi.

Je t'ai raccompagnée jusqu'à ta porte.

— La galanterie a encore de beaux jours devant elle, finalement, as-tu plaisanté.

Je me suis incliné, et quand tu as ri je me suis senti ridiculement content de t'avoir rendue heureuse.

— Je crois que c'est la première fois que je passe la soirée avec un vrai gentleman.

— Eh bien il va falloir t'y habituer, ai-je répliqué en te prenant la main pour la porter à mes lèvres.

Tu as rougi et tu t'es mordu la lèvre. Puis tu as un peu relevé le menton, attendant mon baiser.

— Dors bien, ai-je dit.

J'ai fait demi-tour et ai regagné ma voiture sans me retourner. Tu avais envie de moi – c'était évident –, mais pas encore assez.

23

Ray était dérouté par l'absence de réaction de Jenna Gray. Il n'y avait ni cri d'indignation, ni déni acharné, ni explosion de remords. Il scruta son visage tandis que Kate procédait à l'arrestation, mais il ne distingua qu'une infime lueur de ce qui ressemblait à du soulagement. Il était déboussolé, comme si le sol s'était dérobé sous ses pieds. Après plus d'un an passé à chercher la personne qui avait tué Jacob, il ne s'attendait pas à tomber sur quelqu'un comme Jenna Gray.

Elle était d'une beauté saisissante. Son nez était fin mais long, et sa peau claire couverte de taches de rousseur qui se rejoignaient par endroits. Ses yeux verts étaient un peu retroussés, lui donnant une allure féline, et ses cheveux auburn virevoltaient autour de ses épaules. Elle ne portait pas de maquillage, et même si ses vêtements larges dissimulaient sa silhouette, on devinait à ses poignets étroits et à son cou mince qu'elle était svelte.

Jenna demanda si elle pouvait avoir quelques instants pour rassembler ses affaires.

— J'ai un ami ici, il va falloir que je lui explique la situation. Vous pourriez nous accorder une minute ou deux ?

Elle parlait si doucement que Ray devait se pencher pour l'entendre.

— J'ai bien peur que non, répondit-il. On vous suit à l'intérieur.

Elle se mordit la lèvre et hésita un instant, puis recula pour laisser Ray et Kate entrer dans le cottage. Un homme se trouvait dans la cuisine, un verre de vin à la main, et Ray supposa qu'il s'agissait de son petit ami. Contrairement à Jenna, l'émotion se lisait sur son visage.

L'endroit était si petit qu'il n'y avait rien d'étonnant à ce qu'il ait entendu leur conversation, pensa Ray en balayant du regard la pièce encombrée. Des pierres alignées prenaient la poussière au-dessus de la cheminée, devant laquelle était étendu un tapis rouge foncé parsemé de petites marques de brûlures. Une couverture recouvrait le canapé dans un kaléidoscope de couleurs, sans doute pour tenter d'égayer la pièce, mais l'éclairage était faible et les plafonds bas du cottage obligèrent Ray à baisser la tête pour éviter la poutre entre le coin salon et la cuisine. Quel endroit horrible ! Loin de tout et glacial, malgré le feu dans la cheminée. Il se demanda pourquoi elle avait choisi de s'installer ici. Elle pensait peut-être que c'était la cachette idéale.

— Voici Patrick Mathews, dit Jenna, comme s'il s'agissait d'une réunion entre amis.

Mais elle tourna alors le dos à Kate et Ray, et celui-ci eut tout de suite l'impression d'être de trop.

— Je dois suivre ces policiers. (Elle parlait d'un ton sec et détaché.) Quelque chose d'affreux est arrivé l'année dernière et je dois m'en occuper.

— Qu'est-ce qui se passe ? Où est-ce qu'ils t'emmènent ?

Soit il ne savait rien, soit c'était un sacré menteur, pensa Ray.

— À Bristol, pour l'interroger, indiqua-t-il en s'avançant pour tendre une carte à Patrick.

— Ça ne peut pas attendre demain ? Je peux la déposer à Swansea dans la matinée.

— M. Mathews, commença Ray, à bout de patience. (Ils avaient mis trois heures pour arriver à Penfach et une heure de plus pour trouver le cottage.) En novembre de l'année dernière, un garçon de cinq ans a été renversé et tué par une voiture qui ne s'est pas arrêtée. Je crains que ça ne puisse pas attendre demain.

— Mais qu'est-ce que ça a à voir avec Jenna ?

Il y eut un silence. Patrick regarda d'abord Ray, puis Jenna, et secoua lentement la tête.

— Non. Il doit y avoir erreur. Tu ne conduis même pas.

Elle soutint son regard.

— Il n'y a pas d'erreur.

La froideur de sa voix fit frissonner Ray. Pendant un an, il avait essayé d'imaginer quel genre de personne pouvait être assez insensible pour ne pas venir en aide à un enfant mourant. Maintenant qu'il l'avait en face de lui, il luttait pour rester professionnel. Il savait qu'il ne serait pas le seul : ses collègues aussi trouveraient ça difficile à gérer, tout comme ils avaient du mal à rester polis avec les délinquants sexuels et les pédophiles. Il jeta un coup d'œil à Kate et vit qu'elle ressentait la même chose. Plus vite ils seraient rentrés à Bristol, mieux ce serait.

— Il faut qu'on y aille, dit-il à Jenna. Une fois au poste, vous serez interrogée et vous aurez l'occasion de nous raconter ce qui s'est passé. D'ici là, pas un mot sur l'affaire. Est-ce que c'est compris ?

— Oui.

Jenna prit un petit sac à dos suspendu au dossier d'une chaise. Elle regarda Patrick.

— Est-ce que tu peux rester pour t'occuper de Beau ? J'essaierai de t'appeler quand j'en saurai un peu plus.

Il hocha la tête, mais ne dit rien. Ray se demanda à quoi il pensait ; quel effet ça faisait de découvrir qu'on avait été mené en bateau par quelqu'un qu'on pensait connaître.

Ray passa les menottes aux poignets de Jenna et vérifia qu'elles n'étaient pas trop serrées. Elle n'eut pas l'ombre d'une réaction et il aperçut des cicatrices au creux de sa main avant qu'elle referme le poing.

— La voiture n'est pas tout près, indiqua-t-il. On n'a pas pu aller plus loin que le camping.

— Oui, la route s'arrête à huit cents mètres d'ici, confirma Jenna.

— C'est tout ? s'exclama Ray.

Cela lui avait paru plus long en suivant le sentier avec Kate. Ray avait trouvé une lampe de poche qui traînait dans le coffre de la voiture, mais les piles étaient presque à plat et il avait dû la secouer tous les deux ou trois mètres pour la faire fonctionner.

— Appelle-moi dès que tu peux, dit Patrick tandis qu'ils escortaient Jenna dehors. Et prends un avocat ! cria-t-il ensuite, mais ses mots se perdirent dans la nuit et elle ne lui répondit pas.

Ils formaient un trio insolite, trébuchant sur le sentier qui menait au camping, et Ray était content que Jenna coopère. Elle était peut-être mince, mais elle était aussi grande que lui et semblait bien connaître le sentier. Ray était désorienté et ne savait même pas à quelle distance ils se trouvaient de la falaise. Par moments, le fracas des vagues était si assourdissant qu'il s'attendait presque à recevoir des gouttes sur la joue. Il fut soulagé d'atteindre le camping sans encombre, et il ouvrit la porte arrière de la Corsa banalisée à Jenna, qui monta sans broncher.

Ray et Kate s'éloignèrent de la voiture pour parler.

— Tu crois qu'elle a toute sa tête ? demanda Kate. Elle n'a presque rien dit.

— Qui sait ? Elle est peut-être en état de choc.

— J'imagine qu'elle pensait s'en tirer impunément, après tout ce temps. Comment peut-on être aussi insensible ?

Kate secoua la tête.

— Attendons de voir ce qu'elle a à nous dire avant de l'envoyer à l'échafaud, tu veux bien ? fit Ray.

Après l'euphorie d'avoir enfin identifié le conducteur, l'arrestation avait été décevante.

— Tu sais que les jolies filles peuvent aussi être des meurtrières, pas vrai ? lâcha Kate.

Elle se moquait de lui. Mais il n'eut pas le temps de répliquer qu'elle lui avait déjà pris les clés des mains et se dirigeait à grandes enjambées vers la voiture.

Le retour fut interminable, avec des ralentissements tout le long de la M4. Ray et Kate discutaient à voix basse de sujets anodins : les intrigues de bureau, les nouvelles voitures, les offres d'emploi parues dans le bulletin d'information interne. Ray pensait que Jenna dormait, mais elle parla tandis qu'ils approchaient de Newport.

— Comment m'avez-vous retrouvée ?

— Ce n'était pas si difficile, dit Kate en voyant que Ray ne répondait pas. Vous avez une connexion Internet à votre nom. On a contacté votre propriétaire pour vérifier qu'on avait bien la bonne adresse. Il s'est montré très coopératif.

Ray se retourna pour voir la réaction de Jenna, mais elle regardait la circulation par la fenêtre. Seuls ses poings serrés sur ses genoux indiquaient qu'elle n'était pas détendue.

— Ça a dû être dur de vivre avec ce que vous avez fait, poursuivit Kate.

— Kate ! l'avertit Ray.

— Moins dur que pour la mère de Jacob, bien sûr...

— Ça suffit, Kate ! dit Ray. Attends l'interrogatoire.

Il lui décocha un regard noir et elle le fixa d'un air de défi. La soirée allait être longue.

24

Dans l'obscurité de la voiture de police, je me laisse aller à pleurer. Des larmes chaudes tombent sur mes poings serrés tandis que la femme me parle, ne faisant aucun effort pour dissimuler son mépris. Je n'en mérite pas moins, mais c'est quand même dur à accepter. Je n'ai jamais oublié la mère de Jacob. Je n'ai jamais arrêté de penser à son chagrin, sans commune mesure avec le mien. Ce que j'ai fait m'écœure.

Je respire à fond pour cacher mes sanglots, ne voulant pas attirer l'attention des policiers. Je les imagine en train de frapper à la porte de Iestyn et mes joues s'embrasent de honte. La rumeur selon laquelle je sortais avec Patrick a si vite fait le tour du village : les ragots se sont peut-être déjà emparés du dernier scandale.

Rien ne peut être pire que le regard de Patrick quand je suis revenue dans la cuisine avec la police. J'ai lu la trahison sur son visage aussi clairement que si c'était écrit en toutes lettres. Tout ce qu'il croyait savoir sur moi était un mensonge, et un mensonge destiné à cacher un crime impardonnable. Je ne peux pas lui en vouloir de m'avoir lancé ce regard. Je n'aurais jamais dû m'attacher à quelqu'un – ni laisser quelqu'un s'attacher à moi.

Nous approchons déjà de Bristol. Il faut que je retrouve mes esprits. Ils vont m'emmener dans une salle d'interrogatoire, je suppose, me suggérer de faire appel à un avocat. Ils vont me poser des questions et je vais répondre le plus calmement possible. Je ne vais pas pleurer ni chercher des excuses. Ils vont m'inculper, j'irai au tribunal et ce sera fini. Justice sera enfin faite. Est-ce que c'est comme ça que ça marche ? Je n'en suis pas certaine. Tout ce que je sais de la police, je l'ai glané dans les polars et la presse – je ne comptais pas me retrouver un jour de l'autre côté. J'imagine une pile de journaux avec ma photo en première page, agrandie pour montrer tous les traits de mon visage. Le visage d'une meurtrière.

Une femme a été arrêtée dans le cadre de l'enquête sur la mort de Jacob Jordan.

J'ignore si les journaux publieront mon nom ; même s'ils ne le font pas, ils parleront à coup sûr de l'arrestation. Je pose la main sur ma poitrine et sens les battements de mon cœur. J'ai chaud et je transpire comme si j'avais de la fièvre. Tout est en train de s'effondrer.

La voiture ralentit et s'engage sur le parking d'un ensemble de bâtiments gris et austères, que seul le blason de la police de l'Avon et du Somerset, au-dessus de l'entrée principale, permet de distinguer des immeubles de bureaux alentour. La voiture est garée d'une main experte dans une petite place entre deux véhicules de patrouille et la femme m'ouvre la portière.

— Ça va ? me demande-t-elle.

Sa voix est plus douce à présent, comme si elle regrettait les mots cruels qu'elle m'a jetés tout à l'heure à la figure.

J'acquiesce avec une gratitude pathétique.

Il n'y a pas assez de place pour ouvrir la portière en grand et j'ai du mal à descendre avec les poignets menottés. Je me sens d'autant plus effrayée et désorientée, et je me demande si ce n'est pas le véritable but des menottes. Après tout, si je m'enfuyais maintenant, où est-ce que je pourrais bien aller ? La cour est entourée de hauts murs et un portail électrique bloque la sortie. Quand je suis enfin debout, l'inspecteur Evans me saisit le bras et m'éloigne de la voiture. Elle ne serre pas fort, mais ce geste m'oppresse et je réprime l'envie de me dégager de son étreinte. Elle me conduit jusqu'à une porte métallique où l'homme appuie sur un bouton avant de parler dans un interphone.

— Capitaine Stevens, annonce-t-il. Une femme en garde à vue.

La lourde porte s'ouvre avec un déclic et nous entrons dans une grande pièce aux murs blanc sale. La porte claque en se refermant derrière nous et j'ai l'impression que ce bruit résonne une minute entière dans ma tête. Le bâtiment sent le renfermé, malgré la climatisation bruyante au plafond, et un martèlement régulier provient du dédale de couloirs qui partent de l'espace central. Un jeune homme d'une vingtaine d'années est assis sur un banc métallique gris dans un coin de la pièce, occupé à se ronger les ongles et à recracher les rognures par terre. Il porte un bas de survêtement bleu aux ourlets effilochés, des baskets et un sweat-shirt gris crasseux avec un logo illisible. L'odeur nauséabonde qu'il dégage me prend à la gorge et je me détourne avant qu'il puisse voir le mélange de peur et de pitié qu'il m'inspire.

Pas assez vite.

— Tu t'es bien rincé l'œil, hein, ma chérie ?

Sa voix est nasale et aiguë, comme celle d'un petit garçon. Je me retourne vers lui sans un mot.

— Viens tâter la marchandise, si tu veux !

Il se tient l'entrejambe et part dans un éclat de rire incongru dans cette pièce grise et sinistre.

— Mets-la en veilleuse, Lee, jette le capitaine Stevens.

Le jeune homme s'affale contre le mur en ricanant d'un air satisfait, amusé par son trait d'esprit.

L'inspecteur Evans me reprend le bras, ses ongles s'enfonçant dans ma peau tandis qu'elle me guide jusqu'à un haut comptoir de l'autre côté de la pièce. Un policier en uniforme est calé derrière un ordinateur, sa chemise blanche tendue sur son énorme bedaine. Il adresse un signe de tête à l'inspecteur Evans mais ne m'accorde rien de plus qu'un rapide coup d'œil.

— Je vous écoute.

L'inspecteur Evans m'enlève les menottes et j'ai aussitôt la sensation de pouvoir respirer plus facilement. Je frotte les sillons rouges sur mes poignets et la douleur me procure un plaisir pervers.

— Brigadier, voici Jenna Gray. Le 26 novembre 2012, Jacob Jordan a été renversé par une voiture à Fishponds. Le conducteur ne s'est pas arrêté. La voiture a été identifiée comme étant une Ford Fiesta rouge, immatriculation J634 OUP, propriétaire Jenna Gray. Plus tôt dans la journée, nous nous sommes rendus à Blaen Cedi, un cottage près de Penfach au pays de Galles, où à 19 h 33 j'ai arrêté Gray. Elle est soupçonnée de conduite dangereuse ayant entraîné la mort et de délit de fuite.

Un petit sifflement provient du banc au fond de la pièce, et le capitaine Stevens se retourne pour fusiller Lee du regard.

— Qu'est-ce qu'il fait là, au juste ? demande-t-il en ne s'adressant à personne en particulier.

— Il attend son avocat. Je m'en occupe. (Sans se retourner, le brigadier hurle :) Sally, tu peux ramener Roberts dans la cellule numéro deux ?

Une gardienne trapue sort du bureau derrière le brigadier, un énorme trousseau de clés accroché à la ceinture. Elle a la bouche pleine et essuie sa cravate couverte de miettes. Elle conduit Lee dans les entrailles du bâtiment et, en quittant la pièce, il me lance un regard de dégoût. Ça se passera sûrement comme ça en prison quand on apprendra que j'ai tué un enfant. Une expression de dégoût sur le visage des autres détenus, les gens détournant les yeux sur mon passage. Je me mords soudain la lèvre inférieure en réalisant que ce sera pire, bien pire que ça. La peur me prend au ventre et, pour la première fois, je me demande si je tiendrai le coup. Puis je me dis que j'ai connu pire.

— Ceinture, fait le brigadier en tendant un sac en plastique transparent.

— Pardon ?

Il me parle comme si je connaissais les règles, mais je suis déjà perdue.

— Votre ceinture. Enlevez-la. Vous avez des bijoux ?

Il s'impatiente, et je défais maladroitement la boucle de ma ceinture avant de la faire glisser hors des passants de mon jean pour la mettre dans le sac.

— Non, pas de bijoux.

— Une alliance ?

Je secoue la tête en touchant instinctivement la marque à peine visible sur mon annulaire. L'inspecteur Evans fouille mon sac. Il n'y a rien de personnel à l'intérieur, mais j'ai quand même l'impression d'assister au cambriolage de ma propre maison. Un tampon roule sur le comptoir.

— Vous en aurez besoin ? demande-t-elle.

Elle parle d'un ton neutre, et ni le capitaine Stevens ni le brigadier ne disent quoi que ce soit, mais je rougis furieusement.

— Non.

Elle le met dans le sac en plastique avant d'ouvrir mon portefeuille pour en vider le contenu. Je remarque alors la carte bleu pâle au milieu des reçus et des cartes bancaires. Le silence semble s'installer dans la pièce et j'entends presque mon cœur battre. Quand je jette un coup d'œil à l'inspecteur Evans, je m'aperçois qu'elle a cessé d'écrire et me fixe. Je ne veux pas la regarder, mais je suis incapable de baisser les yeux. *Laissez ça, ce n'est rien.* Elle prend lentement la carte et l'examine. Je m'attends à ce qu'elle me questionne à ce sujet, mais elle l'inscrit sur le formulaire et la glisse dans le sac avec le reste de mes affaires. Je pousse un soupir de soulagement.

J'essaie de me concentrer sur ce que dit le brigadier, mais je suis submergée par une litanie de règles et de droits. Non, je ne veux prévenir personne que je suis ici. Non, je ne veux pas d'avocat...

— Vous en êtes sûre ? coupe le capitaine Stevens. Vous pouvez bénéficier des conseils d'un avocat pendant que vous êtes ici, vous savez.

— Je n'ai pas besoin d'avocat, dis-je doucement. J'ai renversé ce garçon.

Il y a un silence. Les trois policiers échangent un regard.

— Signez ici, fait le brigadier. Et ici, et ici, et ici. (Je prends le stylo et griffonne mon nom à côté de grosses croix noires. Il se tourne vers le capitaine Stevens.) On passe directement à l'interrogatoire ?

La salle est étouffante et sent le tabac froid, malgré l'autocollant « Interdiction de fumer » qui se détache du mur. Le capitaine Stevens m'indique où je dois m'asseoir. J'essaie de rapprocher ma chaise de la table, mais elle est fixée au sol. Sur la table, quelqu'un a gravé une série d'injures au stylo-bille. Le capitaine Stevens actionne l'interrupteur d'un boîtier noir sur le mur et un bip aigu retentit. Il s'éclaircit la gorge.

— Nous sommes le jeudi 2 janvier 2014, il est 22 h 45, et nous nous trouvons dans la salle d'interrogatoire numéro trois du commissariat de Bristol. Je suis le capitaine Ray Stevens, matricule 431, et j'ai avec moi l'inspecteur Kate Evans, matricule 3908. (Il me regarde.) Pouvez-vous donner votre nom complet et votre date de naissance pour l'enregistrement, s'il vous plaît ?

J'avale ma salive et tâche d'articuler.

— Jenna Alice Gray, 28 août 1976.

Je le laisse parler de la gravité des faits qui me sont reprochés et des conséquences du délit de fuite sur la famille, sur la population dans son ensemble. Il ne m'apprend rien, et rien de ce qu'il me dit ne pourrait alourdir mon fardeau.

C'est enfin mon tour.

Je parle doucement, les yeux rivés sur la table entre nous, en espérant qu'il ne va pas m'interrompre. Je ne veux le dire qu'une fois.

— La journée avait été longue. J'avais exposé à l'autre bout de Bristol et j'étais fatiguée. Il pleuvait et la visibilité était mauvaise.

Je garde une voix mesurée et calme. Je veux expliquer ce qui s'est passé sans donner l'impression de chercher à me justifier – comment pourrais-je justifier une chose pareille ? J'ai souvent pensé à ce que je dirais si on en arrivait là, mais maintenant que je suis ici, les mots semblent maladroits et hypocrites.

— Il est sorti de nulle part, dis-je. La route était dégagée, et d'un coup il la traversait en courant. Ce petit garçon avec son bonnet de laine bleu et ses gants rouges. C'était trop tard, trop tard pour faire quoi que ce soit.

J'agrippe le bord de la table des deux mains pour m'ancrer dans le présent tandis que le passé menace de resurgir. J'entends le grincement des freins, je sens l'odeur âcre du caoutchouc brûlé sur l'asphalte mouillé. Quand Jacob a percuté le pare-brise, il s'est retrouvé un court instant à quelques centimètres de moi. J'aurais pu tendre le bras pour toucher son visage à travers le verre. Mais il est reparti en tournant sur lui-même avant de retomber sur la route. C'est seulement là que j'ai vu sa mère, penchée sur le garçon inanimé, cherchant un pouls. N'en trouvant pas, elle s'est mise à crier ; un son primitif venu du plus profond de son être, et j'ai vu à travers le pare-brise flou, horrifiée, une flaque de sang se former sous la tête du garçon, souillant la route mouillée jusqu'à ce que l'asphalte vire au rouge sous le faisceau des phares.

— Pourquoi ne vous êtes-vous pas arrêtée ? Pourquoi n'êtes-vous pas descendue ? Pourquoi n'avez-vous pas appelé les secours ?

Je suis ramenée à la salle d'interrogatoire et je fixe le capitaine Stevens. J'avais presque oublié qu'il était là.

— Je n'ai pas pu.

25

— Bien sûr qu'elle aurait pu s'arrêter ! lança Kate en faisant les cent pas entre son bureau et la fenêtre. Elle est si froide, j'en ai des frissons.

— Tu ne veux pas t'asseoir ? (Ray finit son café et étouffa un bâillement.) Tu m'épuises, et je suis déjà assez crevé comme ça.

Il était plus de minuit quand Ray et Kate avaient à contrecœur mis fin à l'interrogatoire pour permettre à Jenna de dormir un peu.

Kate s'assit.

— À ton avis, pourquoi elle s'est mise à table aussi facilement, après plus d'un an ?

— Je ne sais pas, répondit Ray tandis qu'il se laissait aller dans le fauteuil et mettait les pieds sur le bureau de Stumpy. Il y a quelque chose qui cloche dans tout ça.

— Quoi ?

Ray secoua la tête.

— C'est juste une impression. Je suis sûrement fatigué. (La porte de la Criminelle s'ouvrit et Stumpy fit son apparition.) Tu rentres tard. C'était comment, Londres ?

— Stressant, dit Stumpy. Va savoir pourquoi les gens veulent vivre là-bas.

— Tu as rallié la mère de Jacob à notre cause ?

Stumpy acquiesça.

— Elle n'est pas près d'ouvrir un fan-club, mais elle est avec nous. Après la mort de son fils, elle a été la cible de nombreuses critiques. C'était déjà difficile pour elle d'être acceptée en tant qu'étrangère, et l'accident a jeté de l'huile sur le feu.

— Elle est partie quand ? demanda Kate.

— Juste après l'enterrement. Il y a une grosse communauté polonaise à Londres, et Anya est allée s'installer chez des cousins dans une maison partagée. En lisant entre les lignes, j'ai cru comprendre qu'elle n'avait pas de permis de travail, ce qui n'a pas aidé pour la retrouver.

— Elle t'a parlé facilement ?

Ray s'étira et fit craquer ses doigts. Kate grimaça.

— Oui, répondit Stumpy. En fait, elle avait l'air soulagée de pouvoir parler de Jacob avec quelqu'un. Elle n'a pas annoncé la nouvelle à sa famille au pays. Elle dit qu'elle a trop honte.

— Honte ? Mais pourquoi est-ce qu'elle aurait honte ? s'exclama Ray.

— C'est une longue histoire, dit Stumpy. Anya a débarqué au Royaume-Uni à dix-huit ans. Elle s'est montrée un peu évasive sur la façon dont elle a atterri ici, mais elle a fini par trouver un boulot au noir en tant que femme de ménage dans les bureaux de la zone industrielle de Gleethorne. Elle s'est rapprochée d'un des types qui travaillaient là-bas et elle s'est retrouvée enceinte.

— Et elle n'est plus avec le père ? supposa Kate.

— Exact. Apparemment, les parents d'Anya étaient horrifiés qu'elle ait eu un enfant hors mariage et ils voulaient qu'elle rentre en Pologne pour l'avoir à l'œil, mais elle a refusé. Elle souhaitait leur prouver qu'elle pouvait se débrouiller toute seule.

— Et maintenant elle s'en veut. (Ray secoua la tête.) Pauvre fille. Elle a quel âge ?

— Vingt-six ans. Quand Jacob s'est fait renverser, elle a eu le sentiment d'être punie pour ne pas les avoir écoutés.

— C'est tellement triste. (Kate était sagement assise, les genoux ramenés contre la poitrine.) Mais elle n'y est pour rien, ce n'est pas elle qui conduisait cette foutue bagnole !

— C'est ce que je lui ai dit, mais la culpabilité la ronge. Bref, je lui ai signalé qu'on avait un suspect en garde à vue et qu'on espérait l'inculper, en supposant que vous aviez fait votre boulot bien sûr.

Il jeta un regard en coin à Kate.

— Ne me cherche pas, répliqua-t-elle. Mon sens de l'humour est aux abonnés absents, à cette heure-ci. Il se trouve que Gray a craché le morceau, mais il se faisait tard et on l'a laissée dormir jusqu'à demain matin.

— Je crois que je vais en faire autant, indiqua Stumpy. Si je peux, patron ?

Il défit sa cravate.

— Oui, moi aussi d'ailleurs, fit Ray. Allez, Kate, ça suffit pour aujourd'hui. On réessaiera de lui faire dire où est la voiture demain matin.

Ils descendirent dans la cour. Stumpy fit un signe de la main en franchissant le grand portail métallique au volant de sa voiture, laissant Ray et Kate seuls dans l'obscurité.

— Longue journée, observa Ray.

Malgré la fatigue, il n'avait soudain plus envie de rentrer chez lui.

— Oui.

Ils étaient si proches qu'il pouvait distinguer le parfum de Kate. Il sentit son cœur s'emballer. S'il l'embrassait maintenant, il ne pourrait plus faire marche arrière.

— Bon, bonne nuit, dit Kate sans bouger.

Ray fit un pas en arrière et sortit ses clés de voiture de sa poche.

— Bonne nuit, Kate. Dors bien.

Il souffla en sortant du parking. Il avait été si près de céder à la tentation.

Trop près.

Il était plus de deux heures quand Ray s'effondra dans son lit, et il eut l'impression qu'une poignée de secondes s'étaient écoulées quand son réveil le renvoya au travail. Il avait mal dormi, incapable de cesser de penser à Kate, et il lutta pour la chasser de son esprit pendant le briefing matinal.

À dix heures, ils se croisèrent à la cantine pour le petit déjeuner. Ray se demanda si Kate avait passé la nuit à penser à lui et s'en voulut immédiatement. Ça devenait ridicule, et plus vite il aurait tiré un trait sur tout ça, mieux ce serait.

— Je suis trop vieux pour me coucher si tard, remarqua-t-il tandis qu'ils faisaient la queue pour déguster un « caillot », l'une des spécialités de Moira, ainsi surnommée pour sa capacité à boucher les artères.

Il espérait qu'elle allait le contredire et se sentit aussitôt ridicule.

— Je suis bien contente de ne plus faire les trois-huit, fit-elle. Tu te souviens du coup de pompe de trois heures du mat' ?

— Et comment ! Lutter pour rester éveillé en attendant désespérément une course-poursuite pour avoir une montée d'adrénaline. Je ne pourrais plus faire ça.

Ils emportèrent leurs assiettes garnies de bacon, de saucisse, d'œufs, de boudin noir et de pain frit jusqu'à une table libre, où Kate feuilleta un exemplaire du *Bristol Post* tout en mangeant.

— C'est passionnant, comme d'habitude, ironisa-t-elle. Les élections municipales, les kermesses des écoles, les habitants qui se plaignent des merdes de chien.

Elle replia le journal et le posa sur le côté, où la photo de Jacob en première page semblait les fixer.

— Tu as réussi à tirer autre chose de Gray ce matin ? demanda Ray.

— Elle a répété ce qu'elle avait dit hier. Au moins, elle est cohérente. Mais elle n'a pas voulu répondre quand je lui ai demandé où était la voiture et pourquoi elle ne s'était pas arrêtée.

— Eh bien, heureusement, notre boulot consiste à découvrir ce qui s'est passé, et non *pourquoi* ça s'est passé, lui rappela Ray. On en a assez pour l'inculper. Transmets le dossier au parquet et vois s'ils peuvent prendre une décision dans la journée.

Kate avait l'air pensive.

— Quoi ?

— Quand tu as dit hier que quelque chose clochait...

Elle n'acheva pas sa phrase.

— Oui ? insista Ray.

— J'ai la même impression.

Kate but une gorgée de son thé et le reposa avec précaution sur la table, fixant sa tasse comme si elle espérait y trouver la solution.

— Tu crois qu'elle pourrait tout inventer ?

Cela arrive parfois – surtout avec les affaires très médiatisées comme celle-ci. Quelqu'un vient avouer un crime, et au milieu de l'interrogatoire on s'aperçoit qu'il ne peut pas l'avoir fait. Il omet un fait essentiel – quelque chose qui a été délibérément caché à la presse – et toute son histoire tombe à l'eau.

— Pas tout inventer, non. C'est sa voiture, après tout, et son témoignage concorde avec celui d'Anya Jordan. C'est juste que... (Elle se laissa aller sur sa chaise et regarda Ray.) Tu te souviens, pendant l'interrogatoire, quand elle a décrit l'accident ?

Ray lui fit signe de continuer.

— Elle a donné beaucoup de détails sur Jacob : ses vêtements, son sac...

— Eh bien, elle a une bonne mémoire. Un truc pareil ne s'oublie pas, j'imagine.

Il se faisait l'avocat du diable, anticipant ce qu'allait dire le commissaire – ainsi que le préfet. Au fond, Ray avait toujours la même impression que la veille. Jenna Gray cachait quelque chose.

— D'après la mère de Jacob, la voiture n'a pas ralenti, reprit Kate. Et Gray a dit elle-même que Jacob était sorti « de nulle part ». (Elle mima des guillemets.) Donc si tout est arrivé si vite, comment est-ce qu'elle a pu voir autant de choses ? Et si ça ne s'est pas passé aussi vite et qu'elle a eu tout le temps de l'observer et de faire attention à ce qu'il portait, comment ça se fait qu'elle l'ait quand même renversé ?

Ray garda un instant le silence. Kate avait les yeux brillants, malgré le manque de sommeil, et il reconnut son air déterminé.

— Qu'est-ce que tu proposes ?

— D'attendre avant de l'inculper.

Il hocha lentement la tête. Relâcher un suspect après des aveux complets : le préfet allait sauter au plafond.

— J'aimerais retrouver la voiture.

— Ça ne changera rien, répliqua Ray. Au mieux, on trouvera l'ADN de Jacob sur le capot et les empreintes de Gray sur le volant. Ça ne nous apprendra rien de nouveau. Je préférerais retrouver son téléphone portable. Elle affirme qu'elle s'en est débarrassée quand elle a quitté Bristol parce qu'elle ne voulait pas qu'on la joigne. Et si elle s'en était débarrassée pour dissimuler une preuve ? J'aimerais savoir qui elle a appelé juste avant et juste après l'accident.

— Alors on la libère avec l'obligation de se présenter au poste dans quelques semaines, dit Kate en le regardant d'un air interrogateur.

Il hésita. Inculper Jenna serait la solution de facilité. Des applaudissements lors du briefing matinal, les félicitations du préfet. Mais pouvait-il l'inculper tout en sachant qu'il y avait peut-être autre chose ? Les preuves faisaient pencher la balance d'un côté, son instinct de l'autre.

Ray songea à Annabelle Snowden, toujours en vie dans l'appartement de son père alors que celui-ci suppliait la police de retrouver le ravisseur. Son instinct ne s'était pas trompé à l'époque, et il ne l'avait pas suivi.

S'ils la relâchaient quelques semaines, ils pourraient essayer d'y voir plus clair et faire en sorte qu'aucun détail ne soit négligé avant de la présenter au juge.

Il fit un signe de tête à Kate.

— Laisse-la partir.

26

J'ai attendu presque une semaine avant de te rappeler après notre premier rendez-vous, et j'ai noté l'incertitude dans ta voix quand je t'ai eue au bout du fil. Tu te demandais si tu avais mal interprété les signes, pas vrai ? Si tu avais dit quelque chose qu'il ne fallait pas, ou choisi la mauvaise robe...

— Tu es libre ce soir ? ai-je demandé. On pourrait peut-être sortir tous les deux.

En te parlant, je me suis rendu compte à quel point j'avais hâte de te voir. Attendre une semaine avait été étonnamment difficile.

— J'aurais bien aimé, mais j'ai déjà quelque chose de prévu.

Il y avait du regret dans ta voix, mais je connaissais cette tactique depuis longtemps. Les petits jeux auxquels se livrent les femmes au début d'une relation sont variés mais en général faciles à déchiffrer. Tu avais sans doute disséqué notre rendez-vous avec tes amies, qui avaient dû te prodiguer leurs conseils comme des ménagères n'ayant rien de mieux à faire que de se mêler de la vie des autres.

Ne lui montre pas tout de suite qu'il te plaît.

Fais-toi désirer.

Quand il appellera, dis-lui que tu es déjà prise.

C'est fatigant et puéril.

— Dommage, ai-je répliqué, comme si de rien n'était. J'ai réussi à avoir deux places pour le concert de Pulp ce soir et je me disais que tu voudrais peut-être venir.

Tu as hésité et j'ai cru t'avoir convaincue, mais tu as tenu bon.

— Je ne peux vraiment pas, désolée. J'ai promis à Sarah de sortir entre filles au Ice Bar. Elle vient de se séparer de son copain et je ne peux pas la laisser tomber moi aussi.

C'était convaincant et je me suis demandé si tu avais préparé ce mensonge à l'avance. J'ai laissé le silence s'installer.

— Je suis libre demain soir ? as-tu dit, ton intonation transformant cette affirmation en question.

— Désolé, j'ai déjà quelque chose de prévu demain. Une autre fois, peut-être. Amuse-toi bien.

J'ai raccroché et je suis resté un moment assis à côté du téléphone. Une veine s'est mise à palpiter sur ma tempe et je l'ai frottée nerveusement. Je ne m'attendais pas à ce que tu te livres à ce petit jeu, j'étais déçu que tu t'y sentes obligée.

Je n'ai pas réussi à me calmer de toute la journée. J'ai fait le ménage et ramassé toutes les affaires de Marie qui traînaient un peu partout dans la maison pour en faire une pile dans la chambre. Il y en avait plus que je pensais, mais je ne pouvais pas les lui rendre maintenant. J'ai tout mis dans une valise pour les emporter à la décharge.

À sept heures, j'ai bu une bière, et puis une autre. Je me suis installé dans le canapé devant un jeu télévisé débile, les pieds posés sur la table basse, et j'ai pensé à toi. J'ai failli téléphoner à ta résidence pour te laisser un message et faire semblant d'être surpris de te trouver là. Mais au bout de ma troisième bière, j'ai changé d'avis.

J'ai pris la voiture jusqu'au Ice Bar et j'ai trouvé une place près de l'entrée. Je suis resté un moment assis sur mon siège à observer les gens qui franchissaient la porte. Les filles étaient en minijupe, mais cela n'éveillait en moi que de la curiosité. Je pensais à toi. J'étais troublé par la façon dont tu occupais mes pensées, déjà à cette époque, et par l'importance que revêtait tout à coup le fait de savoir si tu m'avais dit la vérité. J'étais allé là-bas pour te prendre sur le fait : pour entrer dans le bar bondé et constater que tu n'y étais pas, parce que tu étais dans ta chambre, assise sur ton lit avec une bouteille de vin bon marché et un film avec Meg Ryan. Mais j'ai réalisé que ce n'était pas ce que je voulais : je voulais te voir passer devant moi, prête pour ta soirée entre filles avec ta copine déprimée qui venait de se faire larguer. Je voulais avoir tort. Cette sensation était si nouvelle que j'en ai presque ri.

Je suis descendu de la voiture et je suis entré dans le bar. J'ai acheté des Becks et j'ai commencé à me faufiler à travers la foule. Quelqu'un m'a bousculé et a renversé de la bière sur mes chaussures, mais j'étais trop occupé à te chercher pour exiger des excuses.

Et puis je t'ai vue. Tu étais au bout du comptoir, agitant en vain un billet de dix livres sous le nez des serveurs assaillis par une horde de clients. Tu m'as vu et tu as d'abord eu l'air perdue, comme si tu ne voyais pas qui j'étais, puis tu as souri – un sourire plus réservé que la dernière fois.

— Qu'est-ce que tu fais ici ? m'as-tu demandé quand je suis enfin arrivé jusqu'à toi. Je croyais que tu étais au concert de Pulp.

Tu étais sur tes gardes. Les femmes prétendent aimer les surprises, mais en réalité elles préfèrent être prévenues afin de pouvoir se préparer.

— J'ai donné mes places à un gars au boulot, ai-je répondu. Ça ne me disait rien d'y aller seul.

Tu as eu l'air embarrassée d'être la cause de mon changement de programme.

— Mais comment as-tu atterri ici ? Tu es déjà venu ?

— Je suis tombé sur un copain, ai-je dit en levant les deux bouteilles de Becks que j'avais eu la bonne idée d'acheter. Je suis allé au comptoir et maintenant impossible de le retrouver. Il a dû faire une rencontre !

Tu as ri. Je t'ai tendu une bouteille de bière.

— Ce serait dommage de la jeter, non ?

— Il faut que j'y retourne. Je suis juste venue commander, si j'arrive à être servie un jour. Sarah garde une table là-bas.

Tu as jeté un coup d'œil dans un coin de la salle où la grande fille aux cheveux teints était assise à une petite table, en pleine conversation avec un type d'une vingtaine d'années. Au moment où on regardait, il s'est penché en avant et l'a embrassée.

— Elle est avec qui ? ai-je demandé.

Tu as réfléchi avant de secouer lentement la tête.

— Aucune idée.

— Eh bien on dirait qu'elle a du mal à se remettre de sa séparation, ai-je observé.

Tu as ri.

— Bon...

Je t'ai à nouveau tendu la bière. Tu as souri et tu l'as prise, trinquant avec moi avant de boire une grande gorgée, puis tu t'es léché la lèvre inférieure en baissant ta bouteille. C'était délibérément provocant et ça m'a excité. Tu as soutenu mon regard d'un air de défi en avalant une autre lampée de bière.

— Allons chez moi, ai-je soudain dit.

Sarah avait disparu, sans doute avec son nouveau copain. Je me suis demandé si ça ne le dérangeait pas de tomber sur une fille aussi facile.

Tu as hésité un instant, sans me quitter des yeux, puis tu as légèrement haussé les épaules et glissé ta main dans la mienne. Le bar était plein à craquer et je me suis frayé un chemin en serrant ta main pour ne pas te perdre. Ton empressement à me suivre m'excitait tout en me consternant : je n'ai pas pu m'empêcher de me demander combien de fois tu avais fait ça, et avec qui.

Après la chaleur étouffante du Ice Bar, l'air frais de la rue t'a fait frissonner.

— Tu n'as pas pris de manteau ?

Tu as secoué la tête et j'ai enlevé ma veste pour te la mettre sur les épaules tandis qu'on se dirigeait vers la voiture. Tu m'as souri avec gratitude et ça m'a réchauffé.

— Tu es en état de conduire ?

— Ça va, ai-je répondu sèchement.

Te laisser partir

On a roulé un moment en silence. Ta jupe avait remonté quand tu t'étais assise et j'ai posé ma main gauche juste au-dessus de ton genou, mes doigts effleurant l'intérieur de ta cuisse. Tu as bougé la jambe : juste un peu, mais assez pour que ma main se retrouve sur ton genou et non sur ta cuisse.

— Tu es superbe ce soir.

— Tu crois ? Merci.

J'ai retiré ma main pour changer de vitesse. Quand je l'ai reposée sur ta jambe, je l'ai glissée un centimètre plus haut, mes doigts caressant délicatement ta peau. Cette fois-ci, tu n'as pas bougé.

Chez moi, tu as fait le tour du salon en touchant à tout. C'était gênant, et j'ai préparé le café aussi vite que possible. Ce rituel était absurde : aucun de nous n'avait envie de boire quelque chose, même si tu avais dit le contraire. J'ai posé les tasses sur le plateau en verre de la table et tu t'es assise à mes côtés sur le canapé, à moitié tournée vers moi. J'ai remis tes cheveux derrière tes oreilles, laissant un instant mes mains autour de ton visage, avant de me pencher en avant pour t'embrasser. Tu as aussitôt réagi, ta langue explorant ma bouche et tes mains parcourant mon dos et mes épaules. Je t'ai fait lentement basculer en arrière tout en continuant de t'embrasser jusqu'à être allongé sur toi. J'ai senti tes jambes s'enrouler autour des miennes : ça faisait du bien d'être avec quelqu'un d'aussi enthousiaste et réactif. Marie était si froide que j'avais parfois l'impression qu'elle était absente, son corps bougeant machinalement tandis que son esprit était ailleurs.

J'ai promené ma main le long de ta jambe et j'ai senti la peau douce et lisse de l'intérieur de ta cuisse. En remontant, le bout de mes doigts a effleuré de la dentelle et tu as brusquement cessé de m'embrasser en te tortillant sur le canapé pour te dégager de ma main.

— Va moins vite, as-tu murmuré, mais ton sourire indiquait que tu ne le pensais pas.

— Je ne peux pas. Tu es si belle, c'est plus fort que moi.

Tu es devenue toute rose. Je me suis appuyé sur un bras et de l'autre j'ai remonté ta jupe sur tes hanches. Lentement, j'ai glissé un doigt sous l'élastique de ta culotte.

— Je ne...

— Chut, ai-je susurré en t'embrassant. Ne gâche pas tout. Tu es magnifique, Jennifer. Tu m'excites tellement.

Tu m'as embrassé et tu as arrêté de faire semblant. Tu le désirais autant que moi.

Le train met presque deux heures pour relier Bristol à Swansea, et même si j'ai hâte d'apercevoir la mer, je suis contente d'être un peu seule et d'avoir du temps pour réfléchir. Je n'ai pas dormi du tout en garde à vue, les pensées se bousculant dans mon esprit tandis que j'attendais le matin. Je craignais que les cauchemars reviennent si je fermais les yeux. Je suis donc restée éveillée, assise sur le mince matelas en plastique à écouter les cris et autres bruits en provenance du couloir. Ce matin, la gardienne m'a proposé de prendre une douche, m'indiquant une cabine en béton dans un coin de l'aile réservée aux femmes. Les carreaux étaient mouillés et une touffe de cheveux recouvrait le trou d'écoulement comme une araignée prête à bondir. J'ai décliné la proposition et mes vêtements sont encore imprégnés de l'odeur de renfermé du bâtiment.

La femme inspecteur et l'homme plus âgé m'ont interrogée une seconde fois. Mon silence les a contrariés, mais j'ai refusé de donner plus de détails.

— Je l'ai tué, ai-je répété. Ce n'est pas suffisant ?

Ils ont fini par abandonner et m'ont fait patienter sur le banc métallique de l'entrée pendant qu'ils s'entretenaient à voix basse avec le brigadier.

— On vous libère, mais vous devez rester à la disposition de la police, a finalement dit le capitaine Stevens.

Je l'ai regardé d'un air ahuri jusqu'à ce qu'il m'explique ce que cela signifiait. Je ne m'attendais pas à être relâchée, et je me suis sentie coupable d'éprouver du soulagement en entendant que j'avais encore quelques semaines de liberté.

Les deux femmes de l'autre côté du couloir descendent du train à Cardiff dans un tourbillon de sacs de shopping et de manteaux qu'elles oublient presque. Elles laissent derrière elles un exemplaire du *Bristol Post*, et je tends le bras pour le ramasser avec appréhension.

C'est en première page : *Le chauffard arrêté.*

Ma respiration s'accélère tandis que je parcours l'article à la recherche de mon nom, et je laisse échapper un petit soupir de soulagement en constatant qu'ils ne l'ont pas divulgué.

Une femme d'environ trente-cinq ans a été arrêtée dans le cadre de l'enquête sur la mort de Jacob Jordan, un garçon de cinq ans tué en novembre 2012 dans un accident à Fishponds. La femme a été remise en liberté et doit se présenter au commissariat central de Bristol le mois prochain.

J'imagine ce journal dans les foyers aux quatre coins de Bristol, les familles secouant la tête en serrant leurs enfants près d'eux. Je relis l'article pour m'assurer que je n'ai rien raté qui puisse révéler le lieu où j'habite, puis je replie soigneusement le quotidien de façon à masquer la une.

À la gare routière de Swansea, je trouve une poubelle et j'enfouis le journal sous des canettes de coca et des emballages de fast-food. L'encre a déteint sur mes doigts, j'essaie en vain de la faire partir en me frottant les mains.

Le car pour Penfach est en retard et il commence à faire nuit quand j'arrive enfin au village. Le magasin, qui fait également office de bureau de poste, est encore ouvert et je prends un panier pour faire quelques courses. La boutique a deux comptoirs, à l'opposé l'un de l'autre, tous les deux tenus par Nerys Maddock, aidée après l'école par sa fille de seize ans. Il est tout aussi impossible d'acheter des enveloppes au comptoir de l'épicerie que d'acheter une boîte de thon et un sac de pommes au comptoir de la poste, et il faut donc attendre que Nerys ferme la caisse et traverse le magasin en traînant les pieds. Aujourd'hui, c'est sa fille qui est derrière le comptoir de l'épicerie. Je remplis mon panier d'œufs, de lait et de fruits, prends un sac de nourriture pour chien et pose le tout sur le comptoir. Je souris à la fille, qui s'est toujours montrée plutôt sympathique, et elle lève les yeux de son magazine mais reste muette. Elle me regarde brièvement puis retourne à sa lecture.

— Bonjour ? dis-je.

Mon malaise grandissant transforme ce mot en question.

La petite cloche au-dessus de la porte tinte tandis qu'une femme âgée que je reconnais entre dans le magasin. La fille se lève et appelle sa mère dans la pièce d'à côté. Elle dit quelque chose en gallois et Nerys la rejoint quelques secondes plus tard derrière la caisse.

— Bonjour, Nerys, je vais prendre ça, s'il vous plaît, dis-je.

Son visage est aussi impassible que celui de sa fille, et je me demande si elles se sont disputées. Elle m'ignore et s'adresse à la femme derrière moi.

— *Alla i eich helpu chi ?*

Elles entament une conversation. Le gallois m'est toujours aussi incompréhensible, mais les quelques coups d'œil jetés dans ma direction, ainsi que l'expression de dégoût sur le visage de Nerys, ne laissent planer aucun doute sur le sujet de leur échange. Elles parlent de moi.

La femme tend le bras en m'évitant pour payer son journal et Nerys encaisse l'argent. Elle prend mon panier de courses et le pose à ses pieds derrière le comptoir, puis me tourne le dos.

Mes joues s'enflamment. Je remets mon portefeuille dans mon sac et fais demi-tour, si pressée de sortir du magasin que je me cogne contre un présentoir et fais tomber des sauces en sachet. J'entends une exclamation désapprobatrice avant d'ouvrir la porte avec violence. Je traverse rapidement le village en regardant droit devant moi de peur de devoir affronter quelqu'un d'autre, et quand j'arrive au camping, je pleure sans pouvoir m'arrêter. Le store de la boutique est relevé, ce qui signifie que Bethan est là, mais je ne parviens pas à me résoudre à aller la voir. Je continue le sentier jusqu'au cottage et ce n'est qu'à ce moment-là que je réalise que la voiture de Patrick ne se trouvait pas sur le parking du camping. J'ignore pourquoi je m'attendais à ce qu'elle y soit – je ne l'ai pas appelé du commissariat, il ne peut donc pas savoir que je suis rentrée –, mais son absence me laisse perplexe. Je me demande s'il est resté un peu chez moi ou s'il est parti dès que la police m'a emmenée. Il ne veut peut-être plus avoir affaire avec moi. Je me console en me disant que même si c'est le cas, il n'aurait pas abandonné Beau.

J'ai déjà la clé à la main quand je me rends compte que le rouge sur la porte n'est pas une illusion d'optique provoquée par le soleil couchant, mais des traces de peinture étalée à l'aide d'une touffe d'herbes qui gît à mes pieds. Les mots ont été écrits à la hâte, des éclaboussures de peinture recouvrent le seuil en pierre.

DÉGAGE.

Je regarde autour de moi, m'attendant presque à trouver quelqu'un en train de m'observer, mais le crépuscule commence à descendre et je ne vois rien à plus de quelques mètres. Je frissonne et bataille avec la serrure capricieuse, puis je perds patience et, de dépit, je donne un grand coup de pied dans la porte. Un morceau de peinture sèche se détache et je continue de cogner, évacuant ma frustration dans un accès de fureur irrationnelle. Ça n'a aucun effet sur la serrure, bien sûr, et je finis par arrêter, posant le front contre la porte en bois pour me calmer avant d'essayer une nouvelle fois la clé.

Le cottage semble froid et inhospitalier, comme s'il se joignait au village pour me demander de partir. Je n'ai pas besoin d'appeler Beau pour savoir qu'il n'est pas là, et, en allant vérifier que la cuisinière est allumée, je vois un mot sur la table.

« Beau est au chenil. Envoie-moi un message en rentrant. »

P.

Ça me suffit pour comprendre que c'est fini. Les larmes me montent aux yeux et je serre très fort les paupières pour les empêcher de couler sur mes joues. Je me dis que c'est moi qui ai choisi cette voie, et que je dois maintenant l'assumer.

Avec la même concision que Patrick, je lui écris un SMS d'une ligne et il répond qu'il amènera Beau après le travail. Je m'attendais presque à ce qu'il envoie quelqu'un à sa place, et je suis à la fois impatiente et inquiète à l'idée de le voir.

J'ai deux heures devant moi avant qu'il arrive. Il fait nuit dehors, mais je n'ai pas envie de rester ici. Je remets mon manteau et je sors.

C'est étrange de se trouver sur la plage la nuit. Il n'y a personne en haut de la falaise, je me rapproche de la mer pour me tenir à la lisière de l'eau, mes bottes disparaissant quelques secondes après chaque vague. Je fais un pas en avant et l'eau lèche l'ourlet de mon pantalon. Je sens l'humidité remonter lentement le long de mes jambes.

Puis j'avance.

À Penfach, le fond est en pente douce jusqu'à une centaine de mètres du rivage, puis plonge brutalement. Je fixe l'horizon et mets un pied devant l'autre, sentant mes bottes s'enfoncer dans le sable. L'eau m'arrive au-dessus des genoux et éclabousse mes mains, et je repense à ces moments passés à jouer dans la mer avec Eve, quand nous sautions par-dessus les vagues nappées d'écume avec nos seaux remplis d'algues. L'eau est glaciale et j'ai le souffle coupé quand elle atteint mes cuisses, mais je continue d'avancer. Je ne pense plus à rien ; je marche, je marche vers la mer. J'entends un grondement, mais j'ignore s'il s'agit d'une mise en garde ou d'un appel. J'ai plus de mal à progresser à présent : les vagues m'arrivent à la poitrine et je dois lutter contre le poids de l'eau. Et soudain je tombe, mon pied chute dans le vide et je glisse sous la surface. J'essaie de me forcer à ne pas nager, mais ma volonté est ignorée et mes bras s'agitent tout seuls. Je pense tout à coup à Patrick, obligé de partir à la recherche de mon corps jusqu'à ce que la marée le rejette, déchiqueté par les rochers et bouffé par les poissons.

Te laisser partir

Comme si je venais de recevoir une gifle, je secoue violemment la tête et j'avale une grande bouffée d'air. Je ne peux pas faire ça. Je ne peux pas passer ma vie à fuir mes erreurs. Dans ma panique, j'ai perdu la côte de vue et je tourne désespérément sur moi-même jusqu'à ce que les nuages se déplacent et que la lune éclaire à nouveau les falaises. Je me mets à nager. Le courant m'a emportée vers le large depuis que je n'ai plus pied, et j'ai beau tendre les jambes vers le fond à la recherche d'un appui, je ne trouve rien d'autre que de l'eau glaciale. Une vague s'abat sur moi et je bois la tasse, vomissant presque en essayant de respirer à travers ma toux. Mes vêtements mouillés traînent dans l'eau, je ne parviens pas à enlever mes bottes qui m'attirent vers le fond.

J'ai la poitrine compressée et j'ai mal aux bras, mais mes idées sont encore claires ; je prends une profonde inspiration avant de plonger sous l'eau en fendant les vagues. Quand je relève la tête pour respirer, j'ai l'impression d'être un peu plus près de la côte, et je recommence, encore et encore. Je tends la jambe vers le fond et sens quelque chose du bout du pied. Je fais encore quelques brassées, tends à nouveau la jambe, et cette fois mon pied se pose sur la terre ferme. Je nage, cours et rampe pour sortir de la mer, j'ai de l'eau salée dans les poumons, les oreilles et les yeux ; quand j'atteins le sable sec, je me mets à quatre pattes pour reprendre mon souffle avant de me lever. Je tremble sans pouvoir m'arrêter : à cause du froid et de ce que j'ai failli faire.

Arrivée au cottage, j'enlève mes vêtements et les laisse par terre dans la cuisine. J'en enfile d'autres, chauds et secs, puis je redescends pour allumer le feu. J'entends Beau aboyer et j'ouvre la porte en grand avant que Patrick frappe. Je m'accroupis pour dire bonjour à Beau et pour dissimuler mon incertitude quant au comportement à adopter avec Patrick.

— Tu veux entrer ? dis-je en me relevant enfin.
— Il faut que j'y aille.

— Juste une minute. S'il te plaît.

Il hésite puis entre en refermant la porte derrière lui. Il n'a pas l'intention de s'asseoir et nous restons donc debout, Beau à nos pieds. Patrick jette un coup d'œil derrière moi dans la cuisine, où une flaque d'eau s'est formée sous mes vêtements trempés. Il a l'air un peu troublé mais ne dit rien, et c'est à ce moment-là que je comprends qu'il ne ressent plus rien pour moi. Il sc fiche de savoir pourquoi mes vêtements sont mouillés, pourquoi même le manteau qu'il m'a offert est dégoulinant. Tout ce qui l'intéresse, c'est le terrible secret que je lui ai caché.

— Je suis désolée.

Insuffisant, mais sincère.

— Pourquoi ?

Il ne va pas me laisser m'en tirer aussi facilement.

— Pour t'avoir menti. J'aurais dû te dire que j'avais…

Je n'arrive pas à finir ma phrase, mais Patrick prend le relais.

— Tué quelqu'un ?

Je ferme les yeux. Quand je les rouvre, Patrick est sur le point de s'en aller.

— Je ne savais pas comment te le dire. (Les mots se bousculent dans ma bouche.) J'avais peur de ta réaction.

Il secoue la tête, comme s'il ne savait pas quoi penser de moi.

— Dis-moi une chose : est-ce que tu es partie sans t'arrêter ? L'accident, je peux comprendre, mais est-ce que tu es partie sans essayer de venir en aide à ce petit garçon ?

Son regard fouille le mien à la recherche d'une réponse que je ne peux pas lui donner.

— Oui, dis-je. Je suis partie.

Il ouvre la porte avec une telle force que je fais un pas en arrière, puis il disparaît.

28

Tu as passé la nuit à la maison, la première fois. J'ai tiré la couette sur nous et je me suis allongé à tes côtés pour te regarder dormir. Ton visage était calme et serein ; seuls d'infimes mouvements étaient visibles sous la peau translucide de tes paupières. Quand tu dormais, je n'avais pas à faire semblant, à garder mes distances pour que tu ne voies pas que je tombais furieusement amoureux de toi. Je pouvais humer tes cheveux, embrasser tes lèvres, sentir ton souffle doux sur ma peau. Quand tu dormais, tu étais parfaite.

Tu as souri avant même d'ouvrir les yeux. Tu es venue spontanément vers moi et je me suis mis sur le dos pour te laisser me faire l'amour. Pour une fois, j'étais content d'avoir quelqu'un dans mon lit au réveil, et je me suis dit que je ne voulais pas que tu partes. Si ça n'avait pas été ridicule, je t'aurais déclaré ma flamme sur-le-champ. Mais à la place j'ai préparé le petit déjeuner, puis je t'ai ramenée au lit pour te montrer à quel point tu me plaisais.

J'étais heureux que tu proposes qu'on se revoie. Ça voulait dire que je n'aurais pas à passer une autre semaine tout seul à attendre le bon moment pour t'appeler. Je t'ai laissée croire que tu menais la danse et on est allés boire un verre le soir même, puis deux jours plus tard. Et tu n'as pas tardé à venir tous les soirs à la maison.

— Tu devrais laisser quelques affaires ici, ai-je dit un jour.

Tu as semblé surprise et j'ai compris que je dérogeais à la règle : ce n'est pas à l'homme de brusquer une relation. Mais quand je rentrais du travail, la seule trace de ton passage était une tasse posée à l'envers sur l'égouttoir, et ce côté incertain m'angoissait. Tu n'avais aucune raison de revenir ; il n'y avait rien qui te retenait ici.

Ce soir-là, tu as apporté un petit sac avec toi : tu as mis une brosse à dents dans le verre de la salle de bains et des sous-vêtements propres dans le tiroir que je t'avais laissé. Le lendemain matin, je t'ai apporté le thé au lit et je t'ai embrassée avant de partir au travail. J'avais encore ton goût sur mes lèvres en montant dans la voiture. Je t'ai appelée en arrivant au bureau et j'ai su à ta voix pâteuse que tu t'étais rendormie.

— Qu'est-ce qu'il y a ? m'as-tu demandé.

Comment aurais-je pu te dire que j'avais juste envie d'entendre ta voix ?

— Tu pourrais refaire le lit aujourd'hui ? ai-je répondu. Tu ne le fais jamais.

Tu as ri et j'ai regretté de t'avoir appelée. En rentrant à la maison, je me suis précipité à l'étage sans enlever mes chaussures. Mais tout allait bien : ta brosse à dents était encore là.

Je t'ai fait de la place dans l'armoire et tu as peu à peu apporté d'autres vêtements.

— Je ne dors pas là ce soir, m'as-tu dit un jour tandis que je m'asseyais sur le lit pour mettre ma cravate. (Tu étais assise de l'autre côté avec ton thé, les cheveux en bataille et du maquillage de la veille autour des yeux.) Je sors avec des copains de la fac.

Je n'ai rien dit, concentré sur le nœud de ma cravate bleu foncé qui se devait d'être parfait.

— Ça ne te dérange pas, hein ?

Je me suis retourné.

— Tu sais que ça fait exactement trois mois aujourd'hui qu'on s'est rencontrés au bar de l'université ?

— C'est vrai ?

— J'ai réservé une table au Petit Rouge pour ce soir. Le restaurant où je t'ai emmenée la première fois. (Je me suis levé et j'ai enfilé ma veste.) J'aurais dû t'en parler avant, je ne vois pas pourquoi tu te souviendrais de ce jour-là.

— Mais si, je m'en souviens ! (Tu as posé ton thé et écarté la couette, puis tu as traversé le lit pour venir t'agenouiller près de moi. Tu étais nue, et quand tu m'as enlacé j'ai senti la chaleur de tes seins à travers ma chemise.) Je me souviens de tout : tu étais un vrai gentleman et j'avais très envie de te revoir.

— J'ai quelque chose pour toi, ai-je dit soudain. (J'espérais qu'elle était toujours dans le tiroir de ma table de chevet. Je l'ai cherchée à tâtons et je l'ai trouvée au fond, sous une boîte de préservatifs.) Tiens.

— C'est bien ce que je crois ?

Tu as souri et agité la clé en l'air. Je me suis aperçu que j'avais oublié d'enlever le porte-clés de Marie, et le cœur en argent tournoyait dans la lumière.

— Tu es là tous les jours. Autant que tu aies une clé.

— Merci. Ça me touche beaucoup.

— Il faut que j'aille au travail. Amuse-toi bien ce soir.

Je t'ai embrassée.

— Non. Je vais annuler. Tu t'es donné tellement de mal. Ça me ferait plaisir d'aller au restaurant. (Tu as brandi la clé.) Et maintenant que j'ai ça, je serai là quand tu rentreras du travail.

Mon mal de tête a commencé à s'estomper dans la voiture, mais il n'a complètement disparu qu'après avoir appelé Le Petit Rouge pour réserver une table.

Tu as tenu parole, et quand je suis rentré à la maison tu m'attendais dans une robe qui découvrait tes longues jambes bronzées et épousait tes formes de manière provocante.

— Comment tu me trouves ?

Tu as fait un tour sur toi-même et tu m'as souri, une main sur la hanche.

— Ravissante.

Mon manque d'enthousiasme était flagrant et tu as abandonné la pose. Tes épaules sont légèrement tombées et tu as lissé le devant de ta robe.

— C'est trop moulant ?

— Tu es très bien, ai-je répondu. Qu'est-ce que tu as d'autre ici ?

— C'est trop moulant, hein ? J'ai seulement le jean que je portais hier et un haut propre.

— Parfait, ai-je dit en m'avançant pour t'embrasser. Des jambes comme les tiennes sont mieux en pantalon, et ce jean te va comme un gant. Va vite te changer et allons boire un verre avant le dîner.

J'avais peur d'avoir commis une erreur en te donnant une clé, mais tu avais l'air d'aimer les tâches ménagères. Une odeur de gâteau ou de poulet rôti tout juste sorti du four planait en général dans la maison quand je rentrais le soir, et même si ta cuisine n'avait rien d'exceptionnel, tu apprenais vite. Quand tu faisais quelque chose d'immangeable, je n'y touchais pas et tu t'appliquais un peu plus la fois suivante. Un jour, je t'ai trouvée en train de lire un livre de recettes en prenant des notes.

— C'est quoi un roux ? m'as-tu demandé.

— Comment je le saurais ?

La journée avait été difficile et j'étais fatigué.

Tu n'as pas eu l'air de le remarquer.

— Je vais faire des lasagnes maison. J'ai tous les ingrédients, mais on dirait que la recette est écrite dans une autre langue.

J'ai jeté un coup d'œil à la nourriture étalée sur le plan de travail : de beaux poivrons rouges, des tomates, des carottes et du bœuf haché. Les légumes venaient de chez le marchand, même la viande semblait avoir été achetée chez le boucher et non au supermarché. Tu avais dû passer l'après-midi à tout préparer.

Je ne sais pas ce qui m'a poussé à gâcher ton plaisir. C'était peutêtre lié à la fierté qui se lisait sur ton visage, ou à ton air détendu et tranquille. Trop tranquille.

— Je n'ai pas si faim que ça.

Te laisser partir

Ton visage s'est assombri et je me suis tout de suite senti mieux, comme si j'avais arraché un pansement ou gratté une croûte qui me gênait.

— Désolé, ai-je repris. Tu t'es donné beaucoup de mal ?

— Non, ça va, as-tu répondu, mais tu semblais vexée. (Tu as refermé le livre.) Je les ferai une autre fois.

J'espérais que tu n'allais pas faire la tête toute la soirée. Tu es vite passée à autre chose et tu as ouvert une bouteille de ce vin bon marché que tu aimais tant. Je me suis servi un doigt de whisky et me suis assis en face de toi.

— Je n'arrive pas à croire que dans un mois j'ai fini mes études, as-tu dit. C'est passé si vite !

— Est-ce que tu as un peu plus réfléchi à ce que tu allais faire après ?

Tu as froncé le nez.

— Pas vraiment. Je vais prendre des vacances cet été, voyager un peu, peut-être.

C'était la première fois que je t'entendais parler de voyage et je me suis demandé qui t'avait mis cette idée dans la tête, avec qui tu comptais partir.

— On pourrait aller en Italie, ai-je lancé. J'aimerais bien t'emmener à Venise. Je suis sûr que tu adorerais l'architecture, et il y a des musées incroyables.

— Ce serait génial ! Sarah et Izzy vont passer un mois en Inde, j'irai peut-être avec elles une ou deux semaines, ou alors je pourrais voyager en train à travers l'Europe. (Tu as ri.) Ah, je ne sais pas. J'ai envie de tout faire, c'est ça le problème !

— Tu devrais peut-être attendre un peu. (J'ai fait tourner la fin de mon whisky dans mon verre.) Après tout, tout le monde va partir en vacances cet été, et vous allez tous rentrer et vous retrouver sur le marché du travail en même temps. Tu devrais peut-être prendre de l'avance sur les autres pendant qu'ils sont en vadrouille aux quatre coins du monde.

— Peut-être.

Je voyais bien que tu n'étais pas convaincue.

— J'y ai réfléchi, et je crois que tu devrais t'installer ici pour de bon une fois que tu auras terminé tes études.

Tu as haussé un sourcil, comme s'il pouvait y avoir un piège.

— C'est une question de bon sens : tu vis pratiquement déjà ici de toute façon, et tu n'auras jamais les moyens de payer un loyer toute seule avec le genre de boulot que tu comptes faire, du coup tu vas te retrouver dans une colocation minable.

— Je pensais retourner un peu chez ma mère.

— Je suis surpris de t'entendre dire ça, après ce qu'elle a fait à ton père.

— Elle n'est pas si horrible que ça, as-tu répliqué, mais tu étais un peu moins sûre de toi à présent.

— On est bien ensemble, ai-je repris. Pourquoi vouloir changer ça ? Ta mère vit à plus d'une heure d'ici, on ne se verra presque plus. Tu ne veux plus être avec moi ?

— Bien sûr que si !

— Si tu t'installais ici, tu n'aurais pas à t'en faire pour l'argent. Je me chargerais des factures et pendant ce temps tu pourrais tâcher de te constituer un book et essayer de vendre tes sculptures.

— Mais ce ne serait pas juste. Il faudrait bien que je participe, d'une manière ou d'une autre.

— Tu pourrais faire la cuisine de temps en temps, j'imagine, et m'aider un peu à faire le ménage, mais tu ne serais vraiment pas obligée. Me lever à tes côtés tous les matins et te retrouver à la maison le soir me suffirait amplement.

Un sourire s'est dessiné sur ton visage.

— Tu en es sûr ?

— Absolument certain.

Te laisser partir

Tu as emménagé le dernier jour du semestre. Tu as décroché tes posters et mis toutes tes affaires dans une voiture que Sarah t'avait prêtée.

— J'irai chercher le reste chez ma mère le week-end prochain, as-tu indiqué. Attends, il y a une dernière chose dans la voiture. Une surprise pour toi. Pour nous.

Tu es sortie en courant et tu as ouvert la portière passager de la voiture, où un carton était posé au pied du siège. Tu l'as apporté jusqu'à la maison avec tant de précaution que je me suis dit que ça devait être fragile, mais quand tu me l'as donné c'était bien trop léger pour être de la porcelaine ou du verre.

— Ouvre-le.

Tu avais du mal à contenir ton excitation.

J'ai soulevé le rabat du carton et une petite boule de poils a levé les yeux vers moi.

— Un chat, ai-je froidement observé.

Je n'avais jamais compris l'intérêt qu'ont les gens pour les animaux, en particulier les chiens et les chats, qui laissent des poils partout et exigent du temps, de l'affection et de la compagnie.

— C'est un chaton ! as-tu dit. Il n'est pas trop mignon ? (Tu l'as sorti du carton pour le tenir contre ta poitrine.) La chatte d'Eve a eu des petits, et elle a réussi à tous les donner, mais elle a gardé celui-là pour moi. Il s'appelle Gizmo.

— Tu n'aurais pas pu me demander mon avis avant de rapporter un chaton chez moi ? (Je n'ai pas pris la peine de te parler calmement et tu t'es tout de suite mise à pleurer. C'était une tactique si évidente et pitoyable que ça m'a encore plus mis en colère.) Tu n'as pas vu toutes ces pubs où on dit de bien peser le pour et le contre avant d'adopter un animal ? Pas étonnant qu'autant d'animaux soient abandonnés, c'est à cause de gens comme toi, qui agissent sans réfléchir !

— Je pensais que ça te plairait, as-tu répliqué en continuant de pleurer. Je me disais qu'il pourrait me tenir compagnie pendant que tu serais au travail, qu'il pourrait me regarder peindre.

Je me suis calmé. Ce chat pourrait en effet te divertir pendant la journée. Je pouvais peut-être fermer les yeux là-dessus, si ça te rendait heureuse.

— Alors fais en sorte qu'il n'approche pas de mes costumes, ai-je dit.

Je suis monté à l'étage, et quand je suis redescendu tu avais mis un panier et deux bols dans la cuisine, ainsi qu'une litière près de la porte.

— C'est en attendant qu'il soit assez grand pour aller dehors, as-tu précisé.

Tu me regardais d'un air méfiant et j'ai regretté que tu m'aies vu perdre mes nerfs. Je me suis forcé à caresser le chaton et tu as poussé un soupir de soulagement. Tu t'es rapprochée de moi et tu as passé tes bras autour de ma taille.

— Merci.

Tu m'as embrassé de cette façon langoureuse qui précédait toujours le sexe, et quand j'ai légèrement appuyé sur ton épaule tu es tombée à genoux sans un murmure.

Tu es devenue obsédée par le chaton. Sa nourriture, ses jouets, même sa litière dégueulasse t'intéressaient plus que le ménage ou la cuisine. Bien plus que de parler avec moi. Tu passais des soirées entières à jouer avec lui en traînant une souris en peluche par terre au bout d'une ficelle. Tu me disais que tu travaillais sur ton book pendant la journée, mais quand je rentrais le soir je retrouvais tes affaires éparpillées dans le salon, au même endroit que la veille.

Deux semaines après ton emménagement, j'ai trouvé un mot sur la table de la cuisine en rentrant.

« Je suis sortie avec Sarah. Ne m'attends pas ! »

Te laisser partir

On s'était appelés deux ou trois fois dans la journée, comme toujours, mais tu n'avais pas pensé à me le dire. Tu n'avais rien préparé pour le dîner ; tu comptais sans doute manger avec Sarah et tu ne t'étais pas préoccupée de moi. J'ai pris une bière dans le frigo. Le chaton miaulait et essayait de grimper sur mon pantalon en plantant ses griffes dans mon mollet. J'ai secoué la jambe et il est tombé par terre. Je l'ai enfermé dans la cuisine et j'ai allumé la télévision, mais je ne parvenais pas à me concentrer. Je ne cessais de penser à la dernière fois que tu étais sortie avec Sarah : la vitesse à laquelle elle avait disparu avec un type qu'elle venait de rencontrer, et la facilité avec laquelle je t'avais ramenée chez moi.

Ne m'attends pas.

Je ne t'avais pas proposé de vivre avec moi pour passer mes soirées tout seul dans le canapé. J'avais déjà été pris pour un imbécile par une femme – ça n'allait pas se reproduire. Les miaulements ont repris et je suis allé chercher une autre bière dans la cuisine. J'entendais le chaton derrière la porte et je l'ai ouverte d'un coup, envoyant valser l'animal de l'autre côté de la pièce. C'était drôle, et ça m'a momentanément remonté le moral, jusqu'à ce que je retourne au salon et que je voie le bazar que tu avais laissé par terre. Tu avais vaguement essayé de tout entasser dans un coin, mais il y avait une motte d'argile sur une feuille de papier journal – dont l'encre déteignait sans doute sur le parquet – et des pots de confiture remplis d'obscures substances empilés dans une boîte à outils.

Le chaton miaulait. J'ai bu une gorgée de bière. Il y avait un documentaire animalier à la télévision et j'ai vu un renard mettre un lapin en pièces. J'ai monté le volume mais j'entendais encore le chaton miauler. Il me cassait les oreilles et j'ai senti la colère monter en moi, jusqu'à être envahi par une rage chauffée à blanc que je connaissais mais sur laquelle je n'avais aucune emprise. Je me suis levé et je suis allé dans la cuisine.

Te laisser partir

Il était plus de minuit quand tu es rentrée. J'étais assis dans le noir, dans la cuisine, une bouteille de bière vide à la main. Je t'ai entendue refermer la porte d'entrée avec une précaution extrême, enlever tes bottes et entrer sur la pointe des pieds dans la cuisine.

— Tu t'es bien amusée ?

Tu as poussé un cri, et j'aurais trouvé ça drôle si je n'avais pas été furieux contre toi.

— Nom de Dieu, Ian, tu m'as fait une de ces peurs ! Qu'est-ce que tu fais assis là dans le noir ?

Tu as appuyé sur l'interrupteur et le néon s'est allumé en clignotant.

— Je t'attends.

— Je t'ai dit que je rentrerais tard.

Tu articulais moins bien que d'habitude et je me suis demandé combien de verres tu avais bus.

— On est tous allés chez Sarah après le pub et... (Tu t'es arrê-tée en voyant l'expression de mon visage.) Qu'est-ce qui ne va pas ?

— Je t'ai attendue pour que tu ne sois pas toute seule quand tu le découvrirais, ai-je dit.

— Découvrir quoi ? (Tu as soudain dessoûlé.) Qu'est-ce qui s'est passé ?

J'ai montré du doigt la litière, à côté de laquelle le chaton était étendu sur le ventre, immobile. Il avait raidi depuis une heure ou deux et l'une de ses pattes était tournée vers le haut.

— Gizmo ! (Tu as brusquement mis les mains à ta bouche et j'ai cru que tu allais vomir.) Mon Dieu ! Qu'est-ce qui s'est passé ?

Je me suis levé pour te réconforter.

— Je ne sais pas. Quand je suis rentré du travail, il a vomi dans le salon. J'ai essayé de trouver des conseils sur Internet, mais une demi-heure plus tard il était mort. Je suis vraiment désolé, Jennifer, je sais que tu l'aimais beaucoup.

Tu pleurais à présent dans ma chemise tandis que je te serrais contre moi.

— Il allait bien quand je suis partie. (Tu as levé les yeux vers moi à la recherche de réponses.) Je ne comprends pas ce qui s'est passé.

Tu as dû lire l'hésitation sur mon visage, car tu t'es tout de suite éloignée de moi.

— Quoi ? Qu'est-ce que tu me caches ?

— Ce n'est sûrement rien, ai-je répondu. Je ne veux pas te rendre les choses encore plus difficiles.

— Dis-moi !

J'ai soupiré.

— Quand je suis rentré, je l'ai trouvé dans le salon.

— Je l'avais enfermé dans la cuisine, comme d'habitude, as-tu répliqué, mais tu commençais déjà à douter.

J'ai haussé les épaules.

— La porte était ouverte quand je suis rentré. Et Gizmo s'était amusé avec la pile de journaux à côté de ton matériel. Tout ça avait l'air de le fasciner. Je ne sais pas ce qu'il y avait dans ce pot de confiture avec l'étiquette rouge, mais il était ouvert et Gizmo avait le museau dedans.

Tu as pâli.

— C'est le vernis pour mes modelages.

— C'est toxique ?

Tu as acquiescé.

— Il y a du carbonate de baryum dedans. C'est vraiment dangereux et je fais toujours très attention de le ranger en lieu sûr. Mon Dieu, c'est ma faute ! Mon pauvre Gizmo.

— Ma chérie, il ne faut pas t'en vouloir. (Je t'ai attirée vers moi pour te serrer dans mes bras et embrasser tes cheveux. Tu empestais la cigarette.) C'était un accident. Tu essaies de trop en faire. Tu aurais dû rester pour finir ton modelage tant que tout était sorti. Je suis sûr que Sarah aurait compris. (Tu t'es blottie contre moi et tes sanglots ont commencé à se calmer. Je t'ai enlevé ton manteau et j'ai posé ton sac sur la table.) Viens, on monte. Je me lèverai avant toi demain matin et je m'occuperai de Gizmo.

Dans la chambre, tu es restée silencieuse et je t'ai laissée te laver les dents et le visage. J'ai éteint la lumière pour me mettre au lit et tu es venue te pelotonner contre moi, comme un enfant. Ça me plaisait que tu aies tant besoin de moi. J'ai commencé à te caresser le dos en décrivant des cercles et à t'embrasser dans le cou.

— Ça te dérange si on ne le fait pas, ce soir ? as-tu dit.

— Ça va te changer les idées, ai-je répliqué. J'ai envie que tu te sentes mieux.

Tu m'as laissé monter sur toi, mais tu n'as pas réagi quand je t'ai embrassée. Je suis entré en toi et j'ai donné un grand coup pour provoquer une réaction – n'importe laquelle –, mais tu as fermé les yeux sans émettre le moindre son. Tu m'as gâché mon plaisir et je t'ai baisée violemment pour te faire payer ton égoïsme.

29

— Qu'est-ce que c'est que ça ?

Debout derrière Kate, Ray observait la carte qu'elle retournait dans ses mains.

— Quelque chose que Gray avait dans son portefeuille. Quand je l'ai prise, elle est devenue toute blanche, comme si elle ne s'attendait pas à la voir là. J'essaie de comprendre ce que c'est.

La carte de visite était de dimension ordinaire, bleu pâle, avec pour seule information une adresse dans le centre de Bristol. Ray la lui prit des mains et la frotta entre son pouce et son index.

— C'est un papier très bon marché, observa-t-il. Tu as une idée de ce que représente le logo ?

Placé en haut, celui-ci ressemblait à deux huit noirs inachevés, imbriqués l'un dans l'autre.

— Non. Ça ne me dit rien.

— J'imagine que l'adresse ne renvoie à rien dans nos bases de données ?

— Exact, et il n'y a rien non plus dans le registre des électeurs.

— Son ancienne carte de visite ? fit-il en examinant une nouvelle fois le logo.

Kate secoua la tête.

— Ça m'étonnerait, vu la façon dont elle a réagi quand je l'ai prise. Ça lui a rappelé quelque chose. Quelque chose qu'elle veut nous cacher.

— Bon, eh bien, allons-y. (Ray se dirigea à grands pas vers l'armoire murale et prit un jeu de clés de voiture.) Il n'y a qu'un seul moyen de savoir.

— Où est-ce qu'on va ?

Ray brandit la carte bleu pâle en guise de réponse, Kate attrapa son manteau et courut derrière lui.

Ray et Kate mirent un certain temps à trouver le 127 Grantham Street, une habitation quelconque au milieu d'une interminable rangée de maisons mitoyennes en brique rouge, où les nombres impairs étaient inexplicablement loin de leurs homologues pairs. Ils s'arrêtèrent un instant devant la maison, contemplant le jardin broussailleux et les rideaux grisonnants aux fenêtres. Dans le jardin voisin, un chat attentif était affalé sur deux matelas. Il miaula quand ils empruntèrent l'allée menant à la porte d'entrée. À l'opposé des maisons voisines, dotées de portes en PVC bon marché, le 127 avait une porte en bois élégamment peinte et munie d'un judas. Il n'y avait pas de fente pour le courrier, mais une boîte aux lettres métallique fixée au mur à côté de la porte et fermée à l'aide d'un cadenas.

Ray sonna. Kate chercha sa carte de police dans la poche de sa veste, mais Ray posa la main sur son bras.

— Il ne vaut mieux pas, dit-il. Pas avant de savoir qui habite ici.

Ils entendirent des bruits de pas sur un carrelage. Les pas s'arrêtèrent et Ray fixa le petit judas au milieu de la porte. Quel que fût le test, ils le réussirent, car au bout de quelques secondes Ray entendit une clé tourner, puis une seconde. La porte s'ouvrit d'une dizaine de centimètres, bloquée par une chaîne. Compte tenu des mesures de sécurité excessives, Ray s'attendait à voir une personne âgée, mais la femme qui apparut dans l'ouverture de la porte avait à peu près le même âge que lui. Elle portait une robe portefeuille à motifs sous un cardigan bleu marine, avec une écharpe jaune pâle nouée autour du cou.

— Je peux vous aider ?

— Je cherche une amie, répondit Ray. Elle s'appelle Jenna Gray. Elle vivait dans cette rue, mais je ne me souviens pas dans quelle maison. Je suppose que vous ne la connaissez pas ?

— Non, désolée.

Ray jeta un coup d'œil dans la maison par-dessus l'épaule de la femme, qui ferma légèrement la porte en le regardant droit dans les yeux.

— Vous vivez ici depuis longtemps ? demanda Kate, ignorant la réticence de la femme.

— Assez longtemps, répondit-elle sèchement. Bon, si vous voulez bien m'excuser…

— Désolés de vous avoir dérangée, dit Ray en prenant Kate par le bras. Viens, chérie, allons-y. Je vais passer quelques coups de fil pour voir si je peux retrouver son adresse.

Il brandit son téléphone.

— Mais…

— Merci quand même, conclut Ray.

Il donna un petit coup de coude à Kate.

— OK, fit-elle en lui emboîtant enfin le pas. On va passer quelques coups de fil, merci de votre aide.

La femme referma la porte avec énergie et Ray entendit deux clés tourner, l'une après l'autre. Il garda son bras autour de celui de Kate jusqu'à ce qu'ils soient hors de vue de la maison, pleinement conscient de la proximité de ce contact.

— Qu'est-ce que tu en penses ? demanda Kate tandis qu'ils montaient dans la voiture. Est-ce que c'est l'ancienne adresse de Gray ? Ou cette femme en sait-elle plus qu'elle ne veut bien le dire ?

— Oh, elle sait quelque chose, ça c'est certain, répondit Ray. Tu as remarqué ce qu'elle portait ?

Kate réfléchit un instant.

— Une robe et un cardigan sombre.

— Rien d'autre ?

Kate secoua la tête, perplexe.

Ray appuya sur une touche de son téléphone et l'écran s'alluma. Il le donna à Kate.

— Tu l'as prise en photo ?

Ray se fendit d'un large sourire. Il tendit le bras et zooma sur la photo, désignant le nœud de l'écharpe jaune de la femme, où une petite tache ronde était visible.

— C'est un badge, indiqua-t-il.

Il zooma une seconde fois et deux huit noirs nichés l'un dans l'autre apparurent.

— Le symbole de la carte ! s'exclama Kate. Bien joué !

— Il y a un lien entre Jenna et cette maison, ça ne fait aucun doute, dit Ray. Mais lequel ?

30

Je n'ai jamais compris pourquoi tu tenais tant à ce que je rencontre ta famille. Tu détestais ta mère, et même si tu avais Eve au téléphone une fois par semaine, elle n'a jamais fait l'effort de venir à Bristol, alors pourquoi te rendre jusqu'à Oxford chaque fois qu'elle voulait que tu viennes ? Mais tu accourais, comme une gentille petite sœur, me laissant seul toute une nuit – parfois plus – tandis que tu t'extasiais sur son ventre rond et flirtais certainement avec son riche mari. Chaque fois tu me demandais de venir avec toi, et chaque fois je refusais.

— Ils vont commencer à penser que je t'ai inventé, m'as-tu dit. (Tu as souri pour me montrer que tu plaisantais, mais il y avait du désespoir dans ta voix.) J'ai envie de passer Noël avec toi. Ce n'était pas pareil sans toi l'année dernière.

— Tu n'as qu'à rester ici avec moi.

Ce n'était pas une décision difficile à prendre. Pourquoi est-ce que je ne te suffisais pas ?

— Mais j'ai aussi envie de voir ma famille. On n'est pas obligés de passer la nuit là-bas, on peut y aller juste pour midi.

— Et ne rien boire ? Tu parles d'un repas de Noël !

— Je peux conduire. S'il te plaît, Ian, j'aimerais vraiment te présenter.

Tu me suppliais presque. Tu portais moins de maquillage qu'avant, mais ce jour-là tu avais mis du rouge à lèvres et j'ai observé la courbe rouge de tes lèvres tandis que tu m'implorais.

— D'accord. (J'ai haussé les épaules.) Mais l'année prochaine on fait ça juste tous les deux.

— Merci !

Ton visage s'est éclairé d'un sourire radieux et tu t'es jetée dans mes bras.

— Je suppose qu'on va devoir apporter des cadeaux. La bonne blague, comme s'ils en avaient besoin, avec l'argent qu'ils gagnent.

— Ne t'inquiète pas pour ça, as-tu dit, trop heureuse pour remarquer mon commentaire. Eve veut toujours du parfum et Jeff sera content si on lui offre une bouteille de scotch. Tu verras, ça va bien se passer. Tu vas les adorer.

J'en doutais. J'en avais assez entendu au sujet de « Lady Eve » pour me faire ma propre opinion, même si j'étais curieux de voir pourquoi elle t'obsédait tant. Je n'ai jamais regretté de ne pas avoir de frères et sœurs et ça m'agaçait que tu parles si souvent avec Eve. Je venais délibérément dans la cuisine quand tu étais au téléphone avec elle, et si tu te taisais d'un coup je savais que vous parliez de moi.

— Qu'est-ce que tu as fait de beau aujourd'hui ? t'ai-je demandé en changeant de sujet.

— J'ai passé une excellente journée. Je suis allée à un déjeuner-rencontre entre artisans organisé par Three Pillars, une association de professionnels des industries créatives. C'est fou comme on est nombreux à travailler seuls dans un petit bureau. Ou sur la table de la cuisine…

Tu m'as regardé d'un air désolé.

Il était devenu impossible de manger dans la cuisine à cause de la perpétuelle couche de peinture, de poussière d'argile et de croquis éparpillés sur la table. Tes affaires étaient partout, il n'y avait plus un seul endroit où je me sentais chez moi. La maison ne paraissait pas si petite lorsque je l'avais achetée, et même quand Marie était là il y avait assez de place pour nous deux. Marie était plus discrète que toi. Moins exubérante. Plus facile à vivre, en quelque sorte, mis à part les mensonges. Mais j'avais appris à gérer ça et je savais qu'on ne m'y reprendrait plus.

Te laisser partir

Tu parlais encore de ton déjeuner et j'ai essayé de me concentrer sur ce que tu racontais.

— Alors on s'est dit qu'à nous six on pourrait payer le loyer.

— Quel loyer ?

— Le loyer d'un atelier. Je n'ai pas les moyens d'en louer un toute seule, mais je gagne assez d'argent avec les cours que je donne pour en prendre un à plusieurs. Comme ça, je pourrai avoir un vrai four à céramique et mes affaires ne traîneront plus partout dans la maison.

Je ne m'étais pas rendu compte que tes cours te rapportaient autant d'argent. Je t'avais suggéré de donner des cours de poterie car cela me semblait plus judicieux que de passer ton temps à fabriquer des figurines que tu vendais une misère. Je pensais que tu aurais proposé de m'aider à rembourser mon crédit immobilier avant de te lancer dans un partenariat de ce genre. Après tout, tu vivais gratuitement sous mon toit depuis tout ce temps.

— En théorie c'est super, ma chérie, mais qu'est-ce qui se passera quand l'un d'entre vous quittera le navire ? Qui paiera le loyer supplémentaire ?

Je voyais bien que tu n'y avais pas pensé.

— J'ai besoin d'un endroit pour travailler, Ian. C'est bien beau de donner des cours, mais je ne veux pas faire ça toute ma vie. Mes sculptures commencent à se vendre, et si je pouvais les faire plus vite et avoir plus de commandes, je crois que je pourrais monter une affaire rentable.

— Combien de sculpteurs et d'artistes sont dans ce cas ? ai-je observé. Enfin, sois réaliste, ce ne sera peut-être jamais rien d'autre qu'un passe-temps qui te rapporte un peu d'argent de poche.

Tu n'aimais pas entendre la vérité.

— Mais en travaillant à plusieurs on pourra s'entraider. Les mosaïques d'Avril iraient bien avec mes créations, et Grant fait des peintures à l'huile incroyables. Ce serait génial si je pouvais aussi retrouver des amis de la fac, mais ça fait une éternité que je n'ai pas eu de nouvelles d'eux.

— Ce sera un nid à problèmes, ai-je dit.

— Peut-être. Je vais y réfléchir encore un peu.

Je voyais bien que tu avais déjà pris ta décision. J'allais finir par te perdre avec ce nouveau rêve.

— Écoute, ai-je repris, ma voix trahissant mon angoisse. Ça fait un moment que je me dis qu'on devrait déménager.

— Vraiment ?

Tu avais l'air dubitative.

J'ai acquiescé.

— On va chercher une maison avec assez de terrain et je te construirai un atelier dans le jardin.

— Mon propre atelier ?

— Avec un four à céramique. Tu pourras y mettre le bazar que tu voudras.

— Tu ferais ça pour moi ?

Un large sourire s'est dessiné sur ton visage.

— Je ferais n'importe quoi pour toi, Jennifer, tu le sais bien.

C'était vrai. J'aurais fait n'importe quoi pour ne pas te perdre.

Pendant que tu étais sous la douche, le téléphone a sonné.

— Est-ce que Jenna est là ? C'est Sarah.

— Salut, Sarah, ai-je dit. Désolé, elle est sortie avec des amis. Elle ne t'a pas rappelée la dernière fois ? Je lui ai transmis ton message.

Il y a eu un silence.

— Non.

— Ah. Eh bien, je lui dirai que tu as appelé.

Tandis que tu étais encore en haut, j'ai fouillé dans ton sac à main. Il n'y avait rien qui sortît de l'ordinaire ; tes reçus correspondaient aux endroits où tu m'avais dit que tu étais allée. Je me suis détendu. Par habitude, j'ai jeté un œil à la partie réservée aux billets dans ton portefeuille. Elle était vide, mais j'ai senti quelque chose sous mes doigts. En y regardant de plus près, j'ai aperçu une fente dans la doublure, dans laquelle tu avais glissé une petite liasse de billets. Je l'ai mise dans ma poche. Si c'était l'argent des courses, rangé là par précaution, tu me demanderais si je l'avais vu. Sinon, je saurais que tu me cachais quelque chose. Que tu me volais de l'argent.

Tu n'as jamais rien dit.

Quand tu m'as quitté, je n'avais même pas remarqué que tu étais partie. J'attendais que tu rentres à la maison, et ce n'est qu'en allant enfin me coucher que je me suis rendu compte que ta brosse à dents avait disparu. J'ai vérifié les valises, mais rien ne manquait à part un petit sac. Est-ce qu'il t'a promis de t'acheter tout ce dont tu avais besoin ? de t'offrir tout ce que tu voulais ? et qu'est-ce que tu lui as donné en échange ? Tu me dégoûtes. Mais je t'ai laissée partir. Je me suis dit que je serais mieux sans toi et que, du moment que tu n'irais pas voir la police en m'accusant de ce qu'ils appelleraient sans doute de la *maltraitance*, je te laisserais aller où tu veux. J'aurais pu partir à ta recherche, mais je ne l'ai pas fait. Est-ce que tu comprends ? Je ne voulais plus de toi. Et je t'aurais laissée tranquille s'il n'y avait pas eu ce petit article dans le *Bristol Post* d'aujourd'hui. Ils n'ont pas mentionné ton nom, mais tu croyais vraiment que je ne comprendrais pas qu'il s'agissait de toi ?

J'ai imaginé la police t'interrogeant sur ta vie, tes relations. Je les ai vus te pousser à bout, mettre des mots dans ta bouche. Je t'ai vue pleurer et tout leur raconter. Je savais que tu craquerais et qu'ils ne tarderaient pas à venir frapper à ma porte pour me poser des questions sur des choses qui ne les regardent pas. Pour me traiter de tyran, de bourreau, de mari violent. Je ne suis rien de tout ça : tu as toujours eu ce que tu méritais.

Te laisser partir

Devine où je suis allé aujourd'hui. Allez, essaie. Non ? Je suis allé rendre visite à ta sœur à Oxford. Je me suis dit que si quelqu'un savait où tu étais maintenant, ce serait elle. La maison n'a pas beaucoup changé depuis cinq ans. Toujours les mêmes lauriers parfaitement taillés de part et d'autre de la porte d'entrée ; toujours la même sonnette horripilante.

Le sourire d'Eve s'est assez vite évanoui quand elle m'a vu.

— Ian, a-t-elle dit froidement. Quelle surprise !

— Ça fait un bail, ai-je répliqué. (Elle n'avait jamais eu le cran de me dire franchement ce qu'elle pensait de moi.) Tu vas faire entrer le froid, ai-je enchaîné en posant un pied sur le carrelage noir et blanc de l'entrée.

Eve n'avait pas d'autre choix que de s'écarter, et j'ai laissé mon bras effleurer ses seins en passant devant elle pour aller dans le salon. Elle s'est précipitée derrière moi, tâchant de me montrer qu'elle était toujours maîtresse de sa propre maison. C'était pitoyable.

Je me suis assis dans le fauteuil de Jeff, sachant pertinemment qu'elle n'aimerait pas ça, et Eve s'est installée en face de moi. Je la voyais lutter pour ne pas me demander ce que je faisais ici.

— Jeff n'est pas là ? ai-je dit.

Quelque chose dans son regard m'a interpellé. J'ai compris qu'elle avait peur de moi, et cette idée était étrangement excitante. Une fois de plus, je me suis demandé comment Lady Eve était au lit, si elle était aussi coincée que toi.

— Il est en ville avec les enfants.

Elle a remué sur son fauteuil et j'ai laissé le silence s'installer jusqu'à ce qu'elle ne le supporte plus.

— Qu'est-ce que tu fais ici ?

— J'étais dans le coin, ai-je dit en balayant le grand salon du regard. (Elle l'avait repeint depuis la dernière fois qu'on était venus – tu aurais aimé. Ils avaient opté pour ces tons ternes et crayeux que tu voulais dans notre cuisine.) Ça faisait longtemps, Eve.

Elle a légèrement hoché la tête, mais n'a pas répondu.

— Je cherche Jennifer, ai-je poursuivi.

— Comment ça ? Ne me dis pas qu'elle t'a enfin quitté ?

Elle a craché ces mots avec une véhémence que je ne lui connaissais pas.

Je suis resté de marbre.

— On s'est séparés.

— Est-ce qu'elle va bien ? Où est-ce qu'elle vit ?

Elle avait le culot de s'inquiéter pour toi. Après tout ce qu'elle avait dit à ton sujet. Quelle garce hypocrite !

— Tu veux dire qu'elle n'est pas venue se réfugier chez toi ?

— Je ne sais pas où elle est.

— Vraiment ? ai-je fait, ne la croyant pas une seule seconde. Mais vous étiez si proches toutes les deux, tu dois bien avoir une idée.

Une veine s'est mise à palpiter sur ma tempe et je l'ai frottée.

— On ne s'est pas parlé depuis cinq ans, Ian. (Elle s'est levée.) Tu ferais mieux de partir maintenant.

— Tu es en train de me dire que tu n'as pas eu de nouvelles d'elle depuis tout ce temps ?

J'ai étendu les jambes et je me suis laissé aller dans le fauteuil. C'est moi qui déciderais quand partir.

— Exact, a répondu Eve. (Je l'ai vue jeter un rapide coup d'œil vers la cheminée.) J'aimerais que tu t'en ailles, maintenant.

La cheminée consistait en l'un de ces appareils dénués de charme avec un feu alimenté au gaz et de fausses bûches. Sur l'encadrement peint en blanc, une poignée de cartes postales et de cartons d'invitation étaient alignés de part et d'autre d'une pendulette d'officier.

J'ai tout de suite compris ce qu'elle voulait me cacher. Tu aurais dû réfléchir un peu plus, Jennifer, avant d'envoyer quelque chose d'aussi évident. On ne voyait que ça au milieu des cartons d'invitation aux bords dorés : une photo d'une plage prise du haut d'une falaise. Sur le sable, des lettres épelaient *Lady Eve*.

Je me suis levé, laissant Eve me reconduire à la porte. Je me suis baissé pour l'embrasser sur la joue. Elle a eu un mouvement de recul et j'ai résisté à l'envie de la plaquer contre le mur pour m'avoir menti.

Elle a ouvert la porte et j'ai fait semblant de chercher mes clés.

— J'ai dû les poser quelque part, ai-je dit. J'en ai pour une seconde.

Je l'ai laissée dans l'entrée et je suis retourné dans le salon. J'ai pris la carte postale pour regarder au dos, mais il n'y avait pas d'adresse, juste un message mielleux de ton écriture peu soignée que je connaissais si bien. Tu avais l'habitude de me laisser des mots sous mon oreiller et dans mon attaché-case. Pourquoi as-tu arrêté ? Un muscle s'est contracté dans ma gorge. J'ai examiné la photo. Où étais-tu ? J'étais sur le point d'exploser et j'ai déchiré la carte en deux, puis en quatre, puis en huit, me sentant tout de suite mieux. J'ai dissimulé les morceaux derrière la pendulette d'officier juste au moment où Eve est entrée dans la pièce.

— Je les ai trouvées, ai-je lancé en tapotant ma poche.

Elle a regardé autour d'elle, s'attendant sans doute à constater un changement quelconque. Laisse-la chercher, ai-je pensé. Laisse-la trouver.

— Ça m'a fait plaisir de te revoir, Eve, ai-je dit. Je repasserai à l'occasion.

Je me suis dirigé vers la porte d'entrée.

Eve a ouvert la bouche mais aucun mot n'en est sorti, alors j'ai parlé à sa place :

— Vivement la prochaine fois.

Sitôt arrivé à la maison, j'ai regardé sur Internet. Ces hautes falaises encerclant la plage et ce ciel gris avec ses nuages menaçants avaient quelque chose de très britannique. J'ai tapé « plages du Royaume-Uni » et j'ai commencé à faire défiler les images. J'ai cliqué sur « page suivante » un nombre incalculable de fois, mais il n'y avait que des photos de plages de sable pleines d'enfants souriants tirées de guides touristiques. J'ai tapé « plages du Royaume-Uni avec des falaises » et j'ai continué de chercher. Je te trouverai, Jennifer. Où que tu sois, je te trouverai.

Et je viendrai m'occuper de toi.

31

Bethan avance à grands pas vers moi, un bonnet tricoté enfoncé sur la tête. Elle se met à parler alors qu'elle est encore loin. C'est une bonne astuce : je n'entends pas ce qu'elle dit, mais je ne peux pas partir alors qu'elle m'adresse la parole. Je m'arrête et j'attends qu'elle arrive à ma hauteur.

Beau et moi nous promenons désormais dans les champs, à l'écart des falaises et de la mer houleuse. J'ai trop peur de retourner près de la mer, bien que ce ne soit pas l'eau qui m'effraie mais les idées qui pourraient me passer par la tête. Je me sens devenir folle et où que j'aille, je ne peux pas y échapper.

— Je me disais bien que c'était toi, là-haut.

Le camping est à peine visible d'ici : je ne devais être qu'un point sur la colline. Le sourire de Bethan est toujours franc et chaleureux, comme si rien n'avait changé depuis la dernière fois que nous nous sommes parlé, mais elle sait sûrement que je dois rester à la disposition de la police. Tout le village le sait.

— J'allais me promener, indique-t-elle. Tu veux venir avec moi ?

— Tu ne vas jamais te promener.

Bethan esquisse un sourire.

— Eh bien, disons que j'avais très envie de te voir, alors.

Nous marchons ensemble, Beau nous devançant dans son éternelle chasse aux lapins. L'air est vif et le ciel dégagé, et notre haleine forme de la buée devant nous tandis que nous avançons. Il est presque midi, mais le sol est encore dur à cause de la gelée matinale, et le printemps semble loin. Je me suis mise à barrer les jours sur le calendrier, sur lequel le jour où je dois me présenter au commissariat est marqué d'une grosse croix noire. Il me reste dix jours. Je sais grâce au dépliant qu'on m'a donné en garde à vue que mon procès ne se tiendra sans doute pas tout de suite, mais j'ai peu de chances de voir un autre été à Penfach. Je me demande combien je vais en rater.

— Je suppose que tu as appris la nouvelle, dis-je, incapable de supporter le silence plus longtemps.

— Difficile d'y échapper à Penfach. (Bethan respire péniblement et je ralentis un peu le pas.) Même si je ne fais pas très attention aux ragots, continue-t-elle. J'aurais préféré l'apprendre de ta bouche, mais j'ai la nette impression que tu m'évites en ce moment.

Je ne le nie pas.

— Tu veux en parler ?

Je dis instinctivement non, puis je me rends compte que j'en ai besoin. Je respire à fond.

— J'ai tué un petit garçon. Il s'appelait Jacob.

J'entends Bethan souffler légèrement, ou peut-être secouer la tête, mais elle ne dit rien. J'aperçois la mer tandis que nous approchons des falaises.

— Il faisait nuit et il pleuvait. Je l'ai vu trop tard.

Bethan laisse échapper un long soupir.

— C'était un accident.

Ce n'est pas une question, et sa loyauté me touche.

— Oui.

— Ce n'est pas tout, non ?

La machine à ragots de Penfach est impressionnante.

— Non, ce n'est pas tout.

Nous atteignons le haut de la falaise, puis nous tournons à gauche et nous dirigeons vers la baie. J'ai du mal à parler.

— Je ne me suis pas arrêtée. Je suis partie et je l'ai laissé au milieu de la route avec sa mère.

Je ne parviens pas à regarder Bethan, et elle reste silencieuse pendant plusieurs minutes. Quand elle reprend la parole, elle va droit au but.

— Pourquoi ?

C'est la question à laquelle il est le plus difficile de répondre, mais ici, au moins, je peux dire la vérité.

— Parce que j'avais peur.

Je finis par jeter un coup d'œil furtif vers Bethan, mais je suis incapable de déchiffrer son expression. Elle regarde vers le large et je m'arrête pour me tenir à ses côtés.

— Tu ne me détestes pas à cause de ce que j'ai fait ?

Elle m'adresse un sourire triste.

— Jenna, tu as fait quelque chose de terrible et tu vas le payer pendant le restant de tes jours. C'est une punition suffisante, tu ne crois pas ?

— Ils ne veulent plus me servir au magasin.

Je me sens mesquine de parler de ça, mais cette humiliation m'a blessée plus que je ne veux l'admettre.

Bethan hausse les épaules.

— Ce sont de drôles de gens. Ils n'aiment pas les nouveaux venus, et s'ils trouvent un prétexte pour se liguer contre eux, eh bien…

— Je ne sais pas quoi faire.

— Ignore-les. Fais tes courses ailleurs et garde la tête haute. Cette histoire, c'est entre toi et la justice, ça ne regarde personne d'autre.

Je lui adresse un sourire reconnaissant. Le pragmatisme de Bethan est réconfortant.

— J'ai dû emmener un des chats chez le vétérinaire hier, poursuit-elle avec désinvolture, comme si elle changeait de sujet.

— Tu as parlé avec Patrick ?

Bethan arrête de marcher et se tourne vers moi.

— Il ne sait pas quoi te dire.

— Il n'a pas eu trop de mal à trouver les mots la dernière fois que je l'ai vu.

Je me souviens de la froideur de sa voix et de la dureté de son regard quand il est parti.

— C'est un homme, Jenna, ce sont des créatures simples. Parle-lui. Parle-lui comme tu viens de le faire avec moi. Dis-lui que tu avais peur. Il comprendra que tu regrettes ce que tu as fait.

C'est vrai que Patrick et Bethan étaient proches quand ils étaient jeunes, et l'espace d'un instant je me demande si elle a raison : aurais-je encore une chance avec Patrick ? Mais elle n'a pas vu la façon dont il m'a regardée.

— Non, dis-je. C'est fini.

Nous avons atteint la baie. Hormis un couple qui promène son chien au bord de l'eau, celle-ci est déserte. La marée monte, léchant le sable en avançant sur le rivage, et une mouette donne des coups de bec à un crabe au milieu de la plage. Je suis sur le point de dire au revoir à Bethan quand j'aperçois quelque chose sur le sable, près de l'eau. Je plisse les yeux et regarde à nouveau, mais les vagues troublent le sable et je ne parviens pas à lire ce qui est écrit. Une autre vague et ça a disparu, mais je suis certaine d'avoir vu quelque chose, absolument certaine. J'ai soudain froid et je resserre mon manteau. J'entends un bruit sur le sentier derrière nous et je me retourne brusquement, mais il n'y a rien. Mes yeux scrutent le sentier littoral, le haut des falaises, de nouveau la plage en contrebas. Ian est-il là, quelque part, en train de m'observer ?

Bethan me dévisage, alarmée.

— Qu'est-ce qu'il y a ? Qu'est-ce qui ne va pas ?

Je la regarde, mais je ne la vois pas. Je vois l'inscription : l'inscription dont je ne sais plus si je l'ai vue sur la plage ou dans ma tête. Les nuages blancs semblent tourbillonner autour de moi et mon sang gronde dans mes oreilles jusqu'à couvrir le bruit de la mer.

Te laisser partir

— Jennifer, dis-je doucement.

— Jennifer ? demande Bethan. (Elle baisse les yeux vers la plage, où la mer balaie le sable lisse.) Qui est Jennifer ?

J'essaie d'avaler ma salive mais elle reste coincée dans ma gorge.

— C'est moi. Je suis Jennifer.

32

— Désolé, annonça Ray.

Il s'assit sur le bord du bureau de Kate et lui tendit un document qu'elle posa sur la table sans le regarder.

— Le parquet a décidé d'engager des poursuites ?

Il acquiesça.

— Il n'y a aucune preuve pour appuyer la théorie selon laquelle Jenna cache quelque chose, et on ne peut pas retarder les choses plus longtemps. Elle doit se présenter au poste cet après-midi et on va l'inculper. (Il remarqua l'expression de Kate.) Tu as fait du bon boulot. Tu ne t'es pas arrêtée aux apparences, et c'est exactement ce que fait un bon inspecteur. Mais un bon inspecteur sait aussi quand mettre un point final à une enquête.

Il se leva et lui pressa gentiment l'épaule avant de la laisser lire le document. C'était frustrant, mais c'était le risque quand on suivait son instinct. Celui-ci n'était pas infaillible.

À deux heures, l'accueil appela pour signaler que Jenna était arrivée. Ray la conduisit dans les locaux de garde à vue et la fit patienter sur le banc métallique contre le mur pendant qu'il s'occupait de l'acte d'accusation. Ses cheveux étaient ramenés en queue-de-cheval, découvrant ses pommettes hautes et sa peau claire et lisse.

Le brigadier tendit l'acte d'accusation à Ray et celui-ci se dirigea vers le banc.

— En vertu de l'article 1 de la loi sur la circulation routière de 1988, vous êtes accusée de conduite dangereuse ayant entraîné la mort de Jacob Jordan, le 26 novembre 2012. En vertu de l'article 170 (2) de la loi sur la circulation routière de 1988, vous êtes également accusée de délit de fuite. Avez-vous quelque chose à déclarer ?

Ray l'observa attentivement à la recherche du moindre signe de peur ou d'appréhension, mais elle ferma les yeux et secoua la tête.

— Non.

— Vous êtes placée en détention provisoire et vous comparaîtrez demain devant le tribunal de première instance de Bristol.

La gardienne, qui attendait, fit un pas en avant, mais Ray intervint.

— Je m'en occupe.

Il saisit doucement le bras de Jenna et la conduisit dans l'aile réservée aux femmes. Le bruit de leurs semelles en caoutchouc provoqua un concert de demandes tandis qu'ils avançaient dans le couloir.

— Je peux sortir fumer une clope ?

— Mon avocat n'est pas encore là ?

— Je peux avoir une autre couverture ?

Ray les ignora, ne voulant pas empiéter sur les plates-bandes du brigadier en charge des locaux de garde à vue, et les voix se transformèrent peu à peu en grognements de mécontentement. Il s'arrêta devant la cellule numéro sept.

— Enlevez vos chaussures, s'il vous plaît.

Jenna défit ses lacets et retira ses chaussures du bout des pieds. Elle les posa devant la porte, faisant tomber quelques grains de sable sur le sol gris lustré. Elle regarda Ray, qui fit un signe de tête en direction de la cellule vide, puis elle entra et s'assit sur le matelas en plastique bleu.

Ray s'appuya contre le chambranle de la porte.

— Qu'est-ce que vous nous cachez, Jenna ?

Elle tourna brusquement la tête pour lui faire face.

— Comment ça ?

— Pourquoi ne vous êtes-vous pas arrêtée le jour de l'accident ?

Jenna ne répondit pas. Elle écarta ses cheveux de son visage et il aperçut une nouvelle fois cette affreuse cicatrice qui barrait la paume de sa main. Une brûlure, peut-être. Ou un accident du travail.

— Comment vous êtes-vous fait ça ? demanda-t-il en désignant la blessure.

Elle détourna le regard, éludant la question.

— Qu'est-ce qui va m'arriver au tribunal ?

Ray soupira. Il n'obtiendrait rien de plus de Jenna Gray, c'était évident.

— Demain, il ne s'agit que de l'audience préliminaire, indiqua-t-il. On va vous demander ce que vous plaidez et l'affaire sera renvoyée devant la cour d'assises.

— Et après ?

— Vous serez condamnée.

— Je vais aller en prison ? fit Jenna en levant les yeux vers Ray.

— Peut-être.

— Combien de temps ?

— Jusqu'à quatorze ans.

Ray observa le visage de Jenna, où la peur commençait enfin à se lire.

— Quatorze ans, répéta-t-elle.

Elle déglutit.

Ray retint son souffle. L'espace d'un instant, il crut qu'elle allait lui dire pourquoi elle était partie sans s'arrêter ce soir-là. Mais elle se détourna de lui et s'allongea sur le matelas, les paupières serrées.

— J'aimerais essayer de dormir un peu maintenant, s'il vous plaît.

Ray l'observa un moment avant de partir en faisant claquer la porte de la cellule derrière lui.

— Bravo ! (Mags embrassa Ray sur la joue tandis qu'il franchissait la porte.) J'ai vu les infos. Tu as bien fait de ne pas laisser tomber cette affaire.

Il réagit avec retenue, encore troublé par le comportement de Jenna.

— Le préfet est content du résultat ?

Ray suivit Mags dans la cuisine, où elle ouvrit une canette de bière qu'elle lui versa dans un verre.

— Elle est ravie ! Bien entendu, c'est elle qui a eu l'idée de lancer un appel à témoins pour l'anniversaire de l'accident...

Il eut un sourire ironique.

— Ça ne te dérange pas ?

— Pas vraiment, répondit Ray en buvant une petite gorgée de sa pinte qu'il reposa avec un soupir de satisfaction. Peu importe qui récolte les lauriers, tant que l'enquête est bien menée et qu'on obtient un résultat au tribunal. Et puis, c'est Kate qui a fait le plus dur, cette fois-ci.

Peut-être était-ce un effet de son imagination, mais Mags sembla légèrement tiquer au nom de Kate.

— Gray va écoper de combien, à ton avis ?

— Six ou sept ans, peut-être ? Ça dépend du juge, et s'il décide d'en faire un exemple. Ça déchaîne toujours les passions quand un enfant est impliqué.

— Six ans, c'est rien.

Ray savait qu'elle pensait à Tom et à Lucy.

— Sauf quand c'est trop, fit Ray, pensif.

— Qu'est-ce que tu veux dire ?

— Il y a quelque chose d'étrange dans tout ça.

— Comment ça ?

— On a le sentiment qu'elle nous cache quelque chose. Mais c'est fini, on l'a inculpée. J'ai laissé à Kate autant de temps que j'ai pu.

Mags le regarda sévèrement.

— Je croyais que c'était toi qui dirigeais cette enquête. C'est Kate qui a l'impression que Gray ne dit pas tout ? C'est pour ça que tu l'as relâchée ?

Ray leva les yeux, surpris par la dureté du ton de Mags.

— Non, répondit-il lentement. Je l'ai relâchée parce que j'ai estimé qu'il y avait une raison valable de prendre notre temps pour établir les faits et inculper la bonne personne.

— Merci, capitaine Stevens, je sais très bien comment ça marche. Je passe peut-être mes journées à servir de taxi aux enfants et à préparer des paniers-repas, mais j'ai moi aussi été inspecteur, alors ne me parle pas comme à une idiote, s'il te plaît.

— Pardon. Je me rends.

Ray leva les mains en l'air, mais Mags ne rit pas. Elle passa un chiffon sous le robinet d'eau chaude et se mit à nettoyer énergiquement le plan de travail.

— Je suis surprise, c'est tout. Cette femme fuit le lieu d'un accident et abandonne sa voiture pour aller se terrer dans un trou perdu, et quand on la retrouve un an plus tard, elle avoue tout. Pour moi, c'est limpide.

Ray luttait pour dissimuler son agacement. La journée avait été longue, et tout ce qu'il voulait, c'était boire une bière et se détendre.

— C'est un peu plus compliqué, dit-il. Et je fais confiance à Kate, elle a un bon instinct.

Il se sentit rougir, et il se demanda s'il ne défendait pas un peu trop Kate.

— C'est vrai ? fit sèchement Mags. Tant mieux pour elle.

Ray laissa échapper un gros soupir.

— Il s'est passé quelque chose ?

Mags continua de nettoyer.

— Tom ?

Mags se mit à pleurer.

— Bon sang, Mags, pourquoi tu ne l'as pas dit plus tôt ? Qu'est-ce qui s'est passé ?

Il se leva et l'enlaça, puis l'éloigna de l'évier en lui prenant délicatement le chiffon des mains.

— Je crois qu'il vole.

La colère de Ray était telle qu'il fut incapable d'articuler pendant quelques secondes.

— Qu'est-ce qui te fait dire ça ?

C'était le comble. Sécher les cours et piquer des crises à la maison était une chose, mais *voler* ?

— Bon, je n'en suis pas certaine, précisa Mags. Je ne lui ai encore rien dit... (Elle remarqua l'expression de Ray et l'arrêta d'un geste de la main.) Et je ne veux pas le faire maintenant. Pas avant de savoir la vérité.

Ray respira à fond.

— Dis-moi tout.

— Je faisais le ménage dans sa chambre tout à l'heure. (Mags ferma brièvement les yeux, comme si le souvenir lui était insupportable.) Et je suis tombée sur une boîte sous son lit. Il y avait un iPod, des DVD, un tas de bonbons et une paire de baskets toutes neuves.

Ray secoua la tête mais garda le silence.

— Je sais qu'il n'a pas d'argent, poursuivit Mags. Il nous rembourse encore la fenêtre qu'il a cassée. Et je ne vois pas comment il aurait pu avoir tout ça, à moins de l'avoir volé.

— Génial ! ironisa Ray. Il va finir par se faire choper. Ça va faire bien, hein ? Le fils du capitaine arrêté pour vol à l'étalage.

Mags le dévisagea d'un air consterné.

— Et c'est à ça que tu penses ? Ton fils est profondément malheureux depuis un an et demi. Lui qui était si joyeux, stable, intelligent. Il s'est transformé en cancre et en voleur, et la première chose qui te vient à l'esprit, c'est : « Quel effet ça va avoir sur ma carrière ? » (Elle s'arrêta sur sa lancée et leva les mains comme pour le repousser.) Je ne veux pas en parler avec toi maintenant.

Elle fit demi-tour et se dirigea vers la porte, puis se retourna pour faire face à Ray.

Te laisser partir

— Laisse-moi m'occuper de Tom. Tu ne vas faire qu'empirer les choses. Et puis tu as manifestement des soucis bien plus importants.

Ray l'entendit monter l'escalier quatre à quatre puis claquer la porte de la chambre. Il savait que cela ne servait à rien de la suivre – elle n'était visiblement pas d'humeur à discuter. Sa carrière n'avait pas été sa *première* considération, juste *une* considération. Et puisqu'il était le seul à gagner de l'argent dans la famille, c'était un peu fort de la part de Mags de la balayer ainsi d'un revers de la main. Quant à Tom, il la laisserait s'en occuper si c'était ce qu'elle voulait. Et puis, à vrai dire, il n'aurait pas su par où commencer.

33

La maison de Beaufort Crescent était beaucoup plus grande que l'ancienne. Je n'ai pas réussi à obtenir de crédit immobilier pour la totalité de son prix, j'ai donc contracté un prêt en espérant que je réussirais à le rembourser. Les mensualités étaient élevées, mais ça en valait la peine. La maison avait un grand jardin pour ton atelier, et tes yeux brillaient quand on a choisi son emplacement.

— C'est parfait, as-tu dit. J'aurai tout ce qu'il me faut ici.

J'ai pris des congés et j'ai commencé à construire l'atelier la semaine où on a emménagé, et tu te mettais en quatre pour me remercier. Tu m'apportais des tasses de thé fumant au fond du jardin, et le soir tu m'appelais pour déguster une bonne soupe avec du pain fait maison. Je ne voulais pas que ça s'arrête, et j'ai commencé à lever le pied presque sans m'en apercevoir. Au lieu d'être dans le jardin à neuf heures chaque matin, je me mettais au travail à dix heures. Je prenais des pauses plus longues pour manger, et l'après-midi je restais assis dans la carcasse en bois de l'atelier en regardant passer les heures jusqu'à ce que tu m'appelles.

— Il n'y a plus assez de lumière pour travailler, mon chéri, disais-tu. Et regarde, tes mains sont gelées ! Viens à l'intérieur et laisse-moi te réchauffer.

Tu m'embrassais en me disant que tu étais excitée à l'idée d'avoir ton propre espace de travail, qu'on n'avait jamais pris autant soin de toi, que tu m'aimais.

J'ai repris le travail et je t'ai promis d'aménager l'intérieur le week-end. Mais quand je suis rentré à la maison le premier jour, tu avais traîné un vieux bureau dans l'atelier et sorti tes vernis et tes outils. Ton nouveau four à céramique se trouvait dans un coin de la pièce et ton tour de potier au centre. Tu étais assise sur un petit tabouret, concentrée sur l'argile qui tournait entre tes mains, effleurant délicatement le pot pour le façonner. Je t'ai observée par la fenêtre en espérant que tu sentirais ma présence, mais tu n'as pas levé les yeux et j'ai ouvert la porte.

— Ce n'est pas merveilleux ?

Tu ne m'as toujours pas regardé.

— J'adore cet endroit. (Tu as retiré ton pied de la pédale et le tour a ralenti avant de s'arrêter.) Je vais aller me changer et faire chauffer le dîner.

Tu as déposé un petit baiser sur ma joue en veillant à ne pas approcher tes mains de mes vêtements.

Je suis resté un moment dans l'atelier à observer les murs que j'avais prévu de garnir d'étagères – le coin où je comptais mettre le bureau que j'aurais fabriqué rien que pour toi. J'ai fait un pas et brièvement posé le pied sur la pédale de ton tour. Il a tressauté, effectuant à peine une rotation complète, et sans tes mains pour le guider, le pot s'est incliné sur un côté avant de s'écrouler sur lui-même.

À partir de ce jour, j'ai eu l'impression de ne plus te voir. Tu as installé un radiateur pour pouvoir passer plus de temps dans ton atelier et, même le week-end, dès le lever du jour, tu enfilais tes vêtements couverts de taches d'argile pour aller sculpter. Je t'ai construit des étagères, mais je n'ai jamais fabriqué le bureau que j'avais prévu, et ça m'a toujours agacé de te voir travailler sur cette vieille table de récup.

On habitait la maison depuis à peu près un an, je crois, quand j'ai dû aller à Paris pour le travail. Doug avait un contact avec un nouveau client potentiel, et on comptait faire une assez bonne impression pour qu'il nous passe une grosse commande de logiciels. Les affaires tournaient au ralenti et les dividendes étaient de plus en plus petits et de moins en moins fréquents. J'avais pris une carte de crédit pour pouvoir continuer à t'emmener au restaurant et à t'acheter des fleurs, mais les remboursements devenaient difficiles à assumer. Le client de Paris pourrait nous remettre à flot.

— Je peux venir ? as-tu demandé. (C'était la première fois que tu manifestais le moindre intérêt pour mon travail.) J'adore Paris !

J'avais vu la façon dont Doug avait reluqué Marie quand je l'avais emmenée un jour au bureau, et la manière dont elle s'était comportée. Je n'allais pas renouveler cette erreur.

— Je vais travailler non-stop ; ce ne sera pas drôle pour toi. On y retournera tous les deux quand je serai moins débordé. Et puis tu as des vases à finir.

Tu avais sillonné la ville pendant des semaines, faisant le tour des boutiques de cadeaux et des galeries avec des échantillons de ton travail, et tu n'avais trouvé que deux magasins qui te proposaient de prendre chacun une douzaine de pots et de vases en dépôt-vente. Tu étais aussi contente que si tu avais gagné au loto, tu passais plus de temps sur chaque vase que sur tout ce que tu avais fait auparavant.

— Plus tu y consacres de temps, moins c'est rentable, t'ai-je fait remarquer.

Mais on aurait dit que tu ne voulais pas profiter de mon expérience du monde des affaires, et tu continuais à passer des heures à peindre et à vernisser.

Je t'ai appelée en descendant de l'avion à Paris et j'ai soudain eu le mal du pays en entendant ta voix. Doug a emmené le client dîner au restaurant, mais j'ai prétexté une migraine et je suis resté dans ma chambre, où j'ai à peine touché au steak du *room service*. Je regrettais de ne pas t'avoir emmenée avec moi. Le lit impeccablement fait avait l'air immense et ne m'attirait pas le moins du monde. À onze heures, je suis descendu au bar de l'hôtel. J'ai commandé un whisky et je me suis assis au comptoir, puis j'en ai commandé un autre. Je t'ai envoyé un SMS mais tu n'as pas répondu : tu étais sans doute dans ton atelier, loin de ton téléphone.

Te laisser partir

Une femme était assise à une table près du comptoir. Elle portait un tailleur gris à rayures avec des talons hauts noirs, et un attaché-case était ouvert sur la chaise à côté d'elle. Elle épluchait des documents et, quand elle a levé les yeux et croisé mon regard, elle m'a adressé un sourire mélancolique que je lui ai rendu.

— Vous êtes anglais, a-t-elle observé.

— C'est si évident que ça ?

Elle a ri.

— Quand on voyage autant que moi, on finit par avoir l'œil pour ces choses-là. (Elle a rassemblé les documents sur lesquels elle travaillait pour les ranger dans son attaché-case, qu'elle a refermé d'un coup sec.) Ça suffit pour aujourd'hui.

Elle n'avait visiblement pas l'intention de partir.

— Je peux me joindre à vous ?

— Avec grand plaisir.

Je n'avais pas prévu ça, mais c'était exactement ce dont j'avais besoin. Je ne lui ai demandé son nom que le lendemain matin, quand elle est sortie de la salle de bains enveloppée dans une serviette.

— Emma, a-t-elle répondu.

Elle n'a pas voulu savoir le mien et je me suis demandé si elle faisait souvent ça, dans des chambres d'hôtel anonymes de villes tout aussi anonymes.

Quand elle est partie, je t'ai appelée et tu m'as raconté ta journée ; le propriétaire de la boutique de cadeaux était enchanté par tes vases et tu avais hâte de me voir. Tu m'as dit que je te manquais et que tu ne supportais pas qu'on soit éloignés, et ça m'a rassuré.

— Je t'aime, ai-je dit.

Je savais que tu avais besoin de l'entendre : que ça ne te suffisait pas de voir tout ce que je faisais pour toi. Tu as poussé un petit soupir.

— Moi aussi.

Te laisser partir

Doug avait fait du bon travail avec le client au restaurant et, d'après les plaisanteries qu'ils échangeaient lors de notre rendez-vous matinal, ils avaient dû finir la soirée dans une boîte de strip-tease. À midi, l'affaire était conclue, et Doug a téléphoné à la banque pour leur annoncer qu'on était de nouveau solvable.

J'ai demandé au réceptionniste de l'hôtel de m'appeler un taxi.

— Où puis-je trouver les meilleures bijouteries ? ai-je ajouté.

Il m'a adressé un sourire entendu qui m'a agacé.

— Un petit quelque chose pour madame ?

Je l'ai ignoré.

— Le meilleur endroit ?

Son sourire s'est un peu plus figé.

— Faubourg Saint-Honoré, monsieur.

Il est resté courtois tandis que j'attendais le taxi, mais son air présomptueux lui a coûté un pourboire, et il m'a fallu tout le trajet pour retrouver mon calme.

J'ai parcouru toute la rue du Faubourg-Saint-Honoré avant de m'arrêter chez un petit bijoutier banalement appelé « Michel », dont les vitrines regorgeaient de diamants étincelants. Je voulais prendre mon temps pour choisir, mais le personnel en costume discret me tournait autour en me proposant son aide, et je ne parvenais pas à me concentrer. J'ai fini par choisir la plus grosse : une bague en platine sertie d'un diamant carré que tu ne pourrais pas refuser. J'ai tendu ma carte de crédit en me disant que tu en valais la peine.

J'ai pris l'avion du retour le lendemain matin, la petite boîte en cuir me brûlant les doigts. J'avais pensé t'emmener au restaurant, mais quand j'ai ouvert la porte tu t'es jetée sur moi en me serrant si fort que je n'ai pas pu attendre.

— Épouse-moi.

Tu as ri, mais tu as dû lire la sincérité dans mon regard, car tu as cessé de rire et tu as mis ta main devant ta bouche.

— Je t'aime, ai-je ajouté. Je ne peux pas vivre sans toi.

Tu n'as rien dit, et j'ai vacillé. Ça ne faisait pas partie de mon plan. Je m'attendais à ce que tu me sautes au cou, que tu m'embrasses, que tu pleures peut-être, mais par-dessus tout que tu dises oui. J'ai cherché à tâtons la boîte dans la poche de mon manteau et je l'ai mise dans ta main.

— Je suis sérieux, Jennifer. Je veux que tu sois à moi pour toujours. Dis-moi oui, s'il te plaît, dis-moi oui.

Tu as légèrement secoué la tête, mais tu as ouvert la boîte et tu es restée bouche bée.

— Je ne sais pas quoi dire.

— Dis oui.

Tu as hésité assez longtemps pour me faire douter de ta réponse. Puis tu as dit oui.

34

Un bruit métallique me fait sursauter. Après le départ du capitaine Stevens hier soir, j'ai fixé la peinture écaillée du plafond de ma cellule, sentant le froid du socle en béton à travers le matelas, jusqu'à ce que le sommeil me prenne par surprise. Tandis que je me redresse sur le lit, j'ai des courbatures partout et très mal à la tête.

Quelque chose cogne contre la porte, et je comprends que le bruit métallique provenait du passe-plat carré au milieu de celle-ci, à travers lequel une main tend à présent un plateau en plastique.

— Allez, je n'ai pas toute la journée.

Je prends le plateau.

— Je pourrais avoir de l'aspirine ?

La gardienne se tient à côté de l'ouverture et je ne vois pas son visage, juste un uniforme noir et une mèche de cheveux blonds.

— Le médecin n'est pas là. Il va falloir attendre d'être au tribunal.

Elle a à peine fini de parler que le passe-plat se referme avec un bruit sourd qui résonne dans le couloir, et j'entends ses pas lourds s'éloigner.

Je m'assois sur le lit et bois le thé, qui a débordé un peu partout sur le plateau. Il est tiède et sucré, mais je l'absorbe avidement, me rendant compte que je n'ai rien avalé depuis hier midi. Le petit déjeuner consiste en une saucisse et des haricots dans une barquette pour micro-ondes. Le plastique a fondu sur les bords et les haricots sont recouverts d'une sauce orange vif. Je laisse l'offrande sur le plateau avec ma tasse vide et j'utilise les toilettes. Il n'y a pas de siège, juste une cuvette en métal et des feuilles de papier rêche. Je me dépêche de finir avant que la gardienne revienne.

La nourriture que j'ai laissée est froide depuis longtemps quand j'entends à nouveau des pas. Ils s'arrêtent devant ma cellule et sont suivis d'un cliquetis de clés, puis la lourde porte s'ouvre et une fille maussade d'à peine vingt ans apparaît devant moi. Son uniforme noir et ses cheveux blonds et gras m'indiquent qu'il s'agit de la gardienne qui m'a apporté le petit déjeuner, et je désigne le plateau posé sur mon matelas.

— Je n'ai pas réussi à manger ça, désolée.

— Ça ne m'étonne pas, réplique-t-elle avec un petit rire. Je n'y toucherais pas même si je crevais de faim.

Assise sur le banc métallique du couloir, j'enfile mes bottes en compagnie de trois garçons vêtus de pantalons de survêtement et de sweat-shirts à capuche si semblables que j'ai d'abord cru qu'ils portaient une espèce d'uniforme. Ils sont affalés contre le mur, aussi détendus que je suis mal à l'aise. Je me retourne et vois les innombrables affiches au-dessus de nos têtes, mais je n'y comprends rien. Des informations sur les avocats, les interprètes, les infractions « prises en considération ». Suis-je censée savoir ce qui se passe ? Chaque fois qu'une vague d'angoisse me submerge, je me rappelle ce que j'ai fait et je me dis que je n'ai pas le droit d'avoir peur.

Nous attendons une bonne demi-heure, jusqu'à ce qu'une sonnerie retentisse et que le brigadier lève les yeux vers l'écran de contrôle au mur, où apparaît un grand fourgon blanc.

— La limousine est arrivée, les gars, annonce-t-il.

Le garçon à côté de moi fait claquer sa langue et marmonne quelque chose que je ne comprends pas – et que je n'ai d'ailleurs aucune envie de comprendre.

Le brigadier ouvre la porte à deux agents de sécurité, un homme et une femme.

— Vous en avez quatre aujourd'hui, Ash, dit-il à l'homme. Au fait, City a pris une belle raclée hier, hein ?

Il secoue lentement la tête, comme s'il compatissait, mais il arbore un large sourire et l'homme dénommé Ash lui donne une tape amicale sur l'épaule.

— On aura notre revanche, répond-il. (Il jette pour la première fois un coup d'œil vers nous.) Bon, tu as la paperasse pour ceux-là ?

Les deux hommes reprennent leur discussion sur le football et la femme s'approche de moi.

— Ça va, ma belle ?

Un peu ronde, elle a un air maternel en décalage avec son uniforme, et je suis soudain prise d'une ridicule envie de pleurer. Elle me demande de me lever, puis promène le plat de sa main le long de mes bras, de mon dos et de mes jambes. Elle fait le tour de ma taille et vérifie l'élastique de mon soutien-gorge à travers mon chemisier. Je suis consciente des coups de coude échangés entre les garçons sur le banc et je me sens aussi exposée aux regards que si j'étais nue. L'agent menotte mon poignet droit à son poignet gauche et me tire dehors.

Nous sommes conduits au tribunal dans un fourgon cellulaire qui me rappelle les véhicules de transport de chevaux que je voyais dans les foires agricoles où ma mère nous emmenait avec Eve. Les poignets menottés à une chaîne qui court sur toute la largeur du box, je lutte pour ne pas tomber du banc étroit tandis que le fourgon tourne. Le manque de place me rend claustrophobe et je fixe la vitre au verre dépoli qui fait défiler les bâtiments de Bristol dans un kaléidoscope de formes et de couleurs. J'essaie de comprendre où nous allons, mais les nombreux virages me donnent mal au cœur et je ferme les yeux, appuyant le front contre la vitre froide.

Ma cellule ambulante est remplacée par une cellule fixe dans les entrailles du tribunal de première instance. On me donne du thé – chaud, cette fois – et des toasts qui se brisent en mille morceaux dans ma gorge. Mon avocat sera là à dix heures, me dit-on. Comment est-il possible qu'il ne soit pas encore dix heures ? La matinée a déjà duré une éternité.

— Mme Gray ?
L'avocat est jeune et impassible, vêtu d'un costume luxueux aux rayures prétentieuses.
— Je n'ai pas demandé d'avocat.
— Vous devez être représentéc par un avocat, Mme Gray, ou assurer votre propre défense. Souhaitez-vous assurer vous-même votre défense ?
Son sourcil relevé suggère que seul un parfait imbécile envisagerait une telle option.
Je secoue la tête.
— Bien. J'ai cru comprendre que vous avez admis, lors de votre interrogatoire, avoir commis les infractions suivantes : conduite dangereuse ayant entraîné la mort et délit de fuite. Est-ce exact ?
— Oui.
Il feuillette rapidement le dossier qu'il a apporté avec lui, dont le ruban rouge défait traîne négligemment sur la table. Il ne m'a pas encore regardée.
— Voulez-vous plaider coupable ou non coupable ?
— Coupable, dis-je.
Ce mot semble rester comme suspendu dans l'air ; c'est la première fois que je le prononce à haute voix. Je suis coupable.
Il écrit bien plus qu'un seul mot et j'aimerais pouvoir jeter un coup d'œil par-dessus son épaule.
— Je demanderai la remise en liberté sous caution en votre nom, et vous avez de bonnes chances de l'obtenir. Vous n'avez jamais

été condamnée, vous avez respecté les termes de votre précédente remise en liberté, vous vous êtes présentée au commissariat dans les délais... La fuite initiale jouera clairement en notre défaveur... Souffrez-vous de troubles mentaux ?

— Non.

— Dommage. Tant pis. Je ferai de mon mieux. Bon, avez-vous des questions ?

Des dizaines.

— Aucune, dis-je.

— Veuillez vous lever.

Je pensais qu'il y aurait plus de monde, mais, excepté un homme avec un carnet qui a l'air de s'ennuyer dans une partie du tribunal réservée à la presse, il n'y a pas foule. Mon avocat est assis au milieu de la salle et me tourne le dos. Une jeune femme en jupe bleu marine est à ses côtés et surligne quelque chose sur un document. À la même longue table, mais quelques mètres plus loin, se trouve un tandem presque identique : l'accusation.

L'huissier tire sur ma manche et je m'aperçois que je suis la seule encore debout. Le juge, un hommes aux traits tirés et aux cheveux clairsemés, est arrivé et l'audience est ouverte. Mon cœur bat la chamade et mon visage s'embrase de honte. Les quelques personnes présentes dans la tribune du public m'observent avec curiosité, comme si j'étais une pièce de musée. Je me souviens de quelque chose que j'ai lu un jour au sujet des exécutions publiques en France : la guillotine montée sur la grand'place pour que tout le monde puisse voir, les femmes faisant cliqueter leurs aiguilles à tricoter en attendant le spectacle. Un frisson me parcourt quand je m'aperçois que je suis l'attraction du jour.

— Accusée, levez-vous, s'il vous plaît.

Je me remets debout et donne mon nom quand le greffier me le demande.

— Que plaidez-vous ?

— Coupable.

Ma voix semble ténue et je me racle la gorge, mais on ne me demande pas de répéter.

Les avocats débattent de ma remise en liberté sous caution au cours d'un échange verbeux qui me fait tourner la tête.

L'enjeu est trop important ; l'accusée va s'enfuir.

L'accusée a respecté les termes de sa précédente remise en liberté ; il n'y a aucune raison que ce ne soit pas le cas cette fois-ci.

La prison à vie est en jeu.

Une vie est en jeu.

Ils se parlent par l'intermédiaire du juge, comme des enfants passent par un parent pour régler un conflit. Leurs mots sont chargés d'émotion et accompagnés de grands gestes qui se perdent dans le prétoire vide. L'accusation souhaite que je reste en détention provisoire jusqu'à mon procès en cour d'assises, tandis que mon avocat essaie d'obtenir ma libération sous caution pour me permettre d'attendre le procès chez moi. J'ai soudain envie de tirer sur sa manche pour lui dire que ce n'est pas ce que je veux. Mis à part Beau, personne ne m'attend au cottage. Je ne manque à personne. En prison, je serai en sécurité. Mais je reste assise en silence, les mains sur les genoux, incertaine de l'attitude à adopter pour parvenir à mes fins. De toute façon, personne ne me regarde. Je suis invisible. J'essaie de suivre le débat entre les avocats pour savoir qui va gagner cette guerre de mots, mais leurs envolées théâtrales me font rapidement perdre le fil.

Le silence tombe sur le prétoire et le juge me fixe froidement. J'éprouve l'envie absurde de lui dire que je ne suis pas comme les accusés qu'il a l'habitude de voir défiler dans son tribunal. Que j'ai grandi dans une maison comme la sienne et que je suis allée à l'université ; que j'ai organisé des dîners chez moi ; que j'ai eu des amis. Que j'étais autrefois sûre de moi et extravertie. Que je n'avais jamais enfreint la loi jusqu'à l'année dernière et que ce fut une terrible erreur. Mais son regard est indifférent et je sais qu'il se moque de savoir qui je suis ou combien de dîners j'ai organisés. Je ne suis à ses yeux qu'une criminelle comme les autres. J'ai l'impression d'être une nouvelle fois dépouillée de mon identité.

— Votre avocat a défendu avec passion votre droit à la liberté sous caution, Mme Gray, dit le juge. Il m'a assuré que j'avais autant de chances de vous voir vous enfuir que d'aller sur la Lune. (De petits rires se font entendre dans la tribune du public, où deux vieilles femmes sont confortablement installées au deuxième rang avec un thermos. Mes tricoteuses des Temps modernes. Le juge esquisse un sourire.) Il affirme que votre fuite initiale du lieu de ce crime odieux était due à un accès de folie, contraire à votre nature et qui ne se reproduira pas. J'espère, Mme Gray, dans notre intérêt à tous, qu'il a raison.

Il marque une pause et je retiens mon souffle.

— La liberté sous caution est accordée.

Je laisse échapper un soupir qui pourrait être pris pour du soulagement.

Il y a de l'agitation dans la tribune de presse et je vois le jeune homme avec le carnet se faufiler hors de la rangée de sièges, son calepin fourré à la hâte dans la poche de sa veste. Il fait une petite révérence vers la cour avant de sortir, laissant la porte se refermer derrière lui.

— Veuillez vous lever.

Tandis que le juge quitte le tribunal, le bourdonnement des conversations s'amplifie et je vois mon avocat se pencher vers l'accusation. Ils rient de quelque chose, puis il s'approche du banc des accusés pour me parler.

— C'est un bon résultat, dit-il, tout sourire à présent. L'affaire a été renvoyée devant la cour d'assises et sera jugée le 17 mars. On vous donnera des informations sur l'aide juridique et les différentes options qui s'offrent à vous en ce qui concerne votre représentation en justice. Bon retour, Mme Gray.

C'est étrange de sortir libre de la salle d'audience après vingt-quatre heures passées en cellule. Je vais à la cantine pour acheter un café à emporter et je me brûle la langue, trop impatiente de boire quelque chose de plus fort que le thé du commissariat.

Une verrière surplombe l'entrée du tribunal et protège de la bruine de petits groupes de gens qui parlent à toute vitesse entre deux bouffées de cigarette. Tandis que je descends les marches, une femme qui arrive dans le sens opposé me bouscule et du café gicle sur ma main à travers le couvercle en plastique mal fermé.

— Pardon, dis-je machinalement.

Mais quand je m'arrête et lève les yeux, je constate que la femme s'est arrêtée elle aussi et tient un micro à la main. Un flash me fait soudain sursauter et j'aperçois un photographe à quelques mètres de là.

— Que ressentez-vous à l'idée d'aller en prison, Jenna ?

— Quoi ? Je...

Le micro est tendu si près de mon visage qu'il touche presque mes lèvres.

— Allez-vous continuer à plaider coupable ? À votre avis, comment la famille de Jacob vit ces événements ?

— Je, oui, je...

Les gens me poussent de tous les côtés et la journaliste hurle ses questions par-dessus les clameurs de la foule qui scande un slogan que je ne parviens pas à déchiffrer. Il y a tant de bruit que j'ai l'impression d'être dans un stade de foot ou une salle de concert. J'ai du mal à respirer, et quand j'essaie de me retourner je suis repoussée dans la direction opposée. Quelqu'un tire sur mon manteau et je perds l'équilibre, tombant sur une personne qui me remet debout sans ménagement. Je vois une pancarte, faite à la va-vite et brandie au-dessus de la foule de manifestants. Celui qui l'a écrite a commencé avec des lettres trop grandes et les toutes dernières ont été resserrées pour que le message tienne en entier. *Justice pour Jacob !*

C'est ça. C'est le slogan que j'entends.

— Justice pour Jacob ! Justice pour Jacob !

Encore et encore, jusqu'à ce que je sois encerclée par les cris. Je cherche un passage sur le côté, mais il y a des gens là aussi. Le café me tombe des mains et perd son couvercle en heurtant le sol, éclaboussant mes chaussures avant de se répandre sur les marches. Je trébuche encore et, l'espace d'un instant, j'ai l'impression que je vais tomber et être piétinée par la foule en furie.

— Ordure !

Je distingue une bouche déformée par la colère et une paire d'énormes créoles qui se balancent d'avant en arrière. La femme se racle grassement la gorge et me crache le résultat visqueux à la figure. Je tourne la tête juste à temps et je sens la salive chaude atterrir dans mon cou puis dégouliner sous le col de mon manteau. Je suis aussi choquée que si elle m'avait donné un coup de poing et je crie en me protégeant le visage, attendant la prochaine salve.

— Justice pour Jacob ! Justice pour Jacob !

Une main me saisit l'épaule et je me crispe, essayant de me dégager tout en cherchant désespérément une issue.

— Et si on faisait un petit détour ?

C'est le capitaine Stevens. Le visage sombre et résolu, il me tire vers le haut des marches pour me ramener à l'intérieur du tribunal. Il me lâche une fois que nous avons passé la sécurité, mais ne dit rien, et je le suis en silence jusqu'à une cour paisible à l'arrière du bâtiment, où il me montre un portail.

— Ça donne sur la gare routière. Tout va bien ? Vous voulez que j'appelle quelqu'un pour vous ?

— Ça va aller. Merci. Je ne sais pas ce que j'aurais fait sans vous.

Je ferme un instant les yeux.

— Foutus vautours ! s'exclame le capitaine Stevens. Les journalistes prétendent faire leur boulot, mais ils feraient n'importe quoi pour un scoop. Quant aux manifestants... eh bien, disons qu'il y a parmi eux des énergumènes prêts à dégainer leurs pancartes à la moindre occasion ; quelle que soit l'affaire, on les retrouve sur les marches du tribunal. Ne le prenez pas pour vous.

— Je vais essayer.

Je souris d'un air gêné et me retourne pour partir, mais il m'arrête.

— Mme Gray ?

— Oui ?

— Est-ce que vous avez habité au 127 Grantham Street ?

Je sens mon visage se vider de son sang et je me force à sourire.

— Non, capitaine, dis-je avec précaution. Non, je n'ai jamais habité là-bas.

Il hoche la tête et me salue d'un geste de la main. Je jette un coup d'œil par-dessus mon épaule en franchissant le portail et je constate qu'il est encore là à m'observer.

À mon grand soulagement, le train pour Swansea est presque vide, je m'enfonce dans mon siège et ferme les yeux. Je tremble encore à cause de ma rencontre avec les manifestants. Je regarde par la fenêtre et pousse un soupir de soulagement à l'idée de retourner au pays de Galles.

Quatre semaines. Il me reste quatre semaines avant d'aller en prison. C'est inconcevable, et pourtant bien réel. J'appelle Bethan pour lui dire que je rentre ce soir, en fin de compte.

— Tu as obtenu la liberté sous caution ?

— Jusqu'au 17 mars.

— C'est une bonne nouvelle. Non ?

Mon manque d'enthousiasme la laisse perplexe.

— Tu es descendue sur la plage aujourd'hui ? dis-je.

— Je suis allée promener les chiens en haut de la falaise à midi. Pourquoi ?

— Est-ce qu'il y avait quelque chose sur le sable ?

— Rien d'inhabituel, répond-elle en riant. À quoi tu pensais ?

Je pousse un soupir de soulagement. Je commence à me demander si j'ai vraiment vu les lettres sur le sable.

— À rien, dis-je. À tout à l'heure.

Quand j'arrive chez Bethan, elle m'invite à rester pour manger, mais je décline la proposition. Je ne serai pas de bonne compagnie. Elle insiste pour que je ne parte pas les mains vides et j'attends pendant qu'elle verse de la soupe dans une barquette en plastique. Je lui dis enfin au revoir presque une heure plus tard et je rentre au cottage avec Beau.

La porte est tellement gauchie par les intempéries que je ne peux ni tourner la clé ni l'ouvrir. Je donne un grand coup d'épaule dans le bois et elle cède un peu, assez pour libérer la serrure et me permettre de l'ouvrir, mais la clé tourne désormais dans le vide. Beau aboie furieusement et je lui dis de se taire. Je crois que j'ai cassé la porte, mais ça ne me fait plus ni chaud ni froid. Si Iestyn était venu la réparer la première fois que je lui ai signalé le problème, ça n'aurait peut-être pas été sorcier à arranger. Mais j'ai tellement forcé sur la serrure qu'il aura plus de travail maintenant.

Je verse la soupe de Bethan dans une casserole que je pose sur la cuisinière et je mets le pain de côté. Le cottage est froid et je cherche un pull, mais je n'en trouve pas au rez-de-chaussée. Beau est agité, courant d'un bout à l'autre du salon, comme s'il avait passé bien plus de vingt-quatre heures loin d'ici.

Je ne sais pas pourquoi, mais l'escalier a l'air différent aujourd'hui. Il ne fait pas encore complètement nuit, et pourtant il est plongé dans l'obscurité. Quelque chose empêche la clarté de pénétrer par la petite fenêtre de l'étage.

Te laisser partir

Je suis déjà en haut quand je comprends.

— Tu n'as pas tenu ta promesse, Jennifer.

Ian plie la jambe, plaque son pied sur ma poitrine puis me pousse violemment. La rampe en bois m'échappe et je tombe à la renverse, dégringolant les marches pour m'écraser sur le sol en pierre.

35

Tu as enlevé la bague au bout de trois jours, et c'était comme si tu m'avais donné un coup de poing. Tu as dit que tu avais peur de l'abîmer et que tu devais la retirer si souvent pour travailler que tu allais finir par la perdre. Tu l'as donc accrochée à une délicate chaîne en or que tu portais autour du cou et je t'ai emmenée faire les magasins pour trouver une alliance – quelque chose de simple que tu pourrais garder tout le temps.

— Tu pourrais la mettre maintenant, ai-je fait en sortant de chez le bijoutier.

— Mais le mariage n'est pas avant six mois.

Je t'ai serré la main un peu plus fort tandis qu'on traversait la route.

— À la place de ta bague de fiançailles, je veux dire. Pour avoir quelque chose au doigt.

Tu m'as mal compris.

— Ça ne me dérange pas, Ian, vraiment. Je peux attendre qu'on soit mariés.

— Mais comment les gens sauront-ils que tu es fiancée ? (Je ne pouvais pas laisser passer ça. Je t'ai arrêtée et j'ai posé les mains sur tes épaules. Tu as regardé les passants pressés autour de nous et essayé de te dégager de mon étreinte, mais je t'ai tenue fermement.) Comment sauront-ils que tu es avec moi si tu ne portes pas de bague ?

J'ai reconnu ton regard. Le même que celui de Marie – un regard de défi mêlé de méfiance – et ça m'a autant énervé qu'avec elle. Comment osais-tu avoir peur de moi ? J'ai senti mon corps se crisper, et quand je t'ai vue grimacer, je me suis rendu compte que mes doigts s'enfonçaient dans tes épaules. Je t'ai lâchée.

— Est-ce que tu m'aimes ? t'ai-je demandé.

— Tu sais bien que oui.

— Alors pourquoi tu ne veux pas que les gens sachent qu'on va se marier ?

J'ai plongé la main dans le sac en plastique pour en sortir la petite boîte. Je voulais faire disparaître ce regard et spontanément j'ai mis un genou à terre en tendant la boîte ouverte vers toi. Un murmure s'est fait entendre parmi les passants et tu as rougi. Les gens ont ralenti, certains s'arrêtant pour nous regarder, et je me suis senti fier d'être avec toi. Ma belle Jennifer.

— Veux-tu m'épouser ?

Tu as eu l'air émue.

— Oui.

Tu as répondu beaucoup plus vite que la première fois, et mon estomac s'est aussitôt dénoué. Je t'ai passé l'alliance au doigt et je me suis levé pour t'embrasser. Les gens ont poussé des acclamations et quelqu'un m'a donné une tape dans le dos. Je ne pouvais plus m'arrêter de sourire. Voilà ce que j'aurais dû faire la première fois, ai-je pensé : j'aurais dû y mettre plus de cérémonie, plus de formes. Tu méritais plus.

On s'est promenés main dans la main dans les rues animées de Bristol et j'ai caressé ton alliance avec mon pouce.

— Et si on se mariait maintenant ? ai-je lancé. On trouve des témoins dans la rue, on file à la mairie et le tour est joué.

— Mais tout est arrangé pour septembre ! Toute ma famille sera là. On ne peut pas faire ça maintenant.

J'avais usé de toute ma force de persuasion pour te convaincre qu'un grand mariage à l'église serait une erreur : ton père ne serait pas là pour te mener à l'autel, et pourquoi se ruiner en organisant une fête pour des amis que tu ne voyais plus ? On avait prévu une cérémonie civile au Courtyard Hotel, suivie d'un déjeuner pour vingt personnes. J'avais demandé à Doug d'être mon témoin, mais les autres invités seraient les tiens. J'ai essayé d'imaginer mes parents à nos côtés, mais la seule image que j'avais en tête, c'était l'expression de mon père la dernière fois que je l'avais vu. La déception, le dégoût sur son visage. J'ai chassé ce souvenir de mon esprit.

Tu as tenu bon.

— On ne peut pas tout annuler maintenant, Ian. Il y a juste six mois à attendre, ce n'est pas long.

En effet, mais je comptais quand même les jours qui nous séparaient du moment où tu deviendrais Mme Petersen. Je me disais que je me sentirais mieux à ce moment-là, que mes doutes se dissiperaient. Je saurais que tu m'aimais et que tu resterais avec moi.

La veille de notre mariage, tu as insisté pour aller retrouver Eve à l'hôtel, pendant que je passais une étrange soirée d'enterrement de vie de garçon au pub en compagnie de Jeff et de Doug. Ce dernier a vaguement essayé de mettre de l'ambiance, mais personne ne m'a contredit quand j'ai suggéré qu'il valait mieux que je me couche tôt avant le grand jour.

En arrivant à l'hôtel le lendemain, j'ai commandé un double whisky pour me calmer. Jeff m'a tapoté le bras en me disant que j'étais un type formidable, bien qu'on n'ait jamais rien eu en commun. Il n'a pas voulu boire un verre avec moi, et une demi-heure avant la cérémonie il a fait un signe de tête vers la porte, où une femme avec un chapeau bleu marine venait d'arriver.

— Prêt à faire la connaissance de la belle-mère ? a lancé Jeff. Elle n'est pas si horrible que ça, je t'assure.

Les rares fois où j'avais vu Jeff, j'avais trouvé sa jovialité forcée très agaçante, mais ce jour-là j'étais content de l'avoir avec moi. Il me changeait les idées. Je n'avais qu'une envie, c'était de t'appeler pour m'assurer que tu viendrais. J'étais paniqué à l'idée que tu puisses me planter là, m'humilier devant tous ces gens.

J'ai traversé la salle avec Jeff. Ta mère m'a tendu la main et je l'ai serrée, puis je me suis penché pour embrasser sa joue sèche.

— Grace, je suis ravi de vous rencontrer. J'ai tellement entendu parler de vous.

Tu m'avais dit que tu ne ressemblais pas du tout à ta mère, mais elle avait les mêmes pommettes hautes que toi. Tu avais peut-être hérité du teint de ton père, et de ses gènes artistiques, mais tu avais la silhouette élancée et le regard attentif de Grace.

— J'aimerais pouvoir en dire autant, a-t-elle répondu, un sourire amusé au coin des lèvres. Mais c'est à Eve que je dois m'adresser pour avoir des nouvelles de Jenna.

J'ai essayé d'afficher une expression de solidarité, comme si je faisais moi aussi les frais de ce manque de communication. J'ai proposé à Grace de boire quelque chose, et elle a pris une coupe de champagne.

— Santé, a-t-elle dit sans porter de toast.

Tu m'as fait attendre un quart d'heure, comme le veut la tradition, je suppose. Doug a fait semblant d'avoir perdu l'alliance, et ça devait ressembler à n'importe quel autre mariage civil du pays. Mais quand tu as remonté l'allée, aucune mariée n'aurait pu être aussi belle que toi. Ta robe était simple : un décolleté en forme de cœur et une jupe qui épousait tes hanches avec une traîne en satin aux reflets chatoyants. Tu tenais un bouquet de roses blanches à la main et tes cheveux étaient relevés en boucles brillantes autour de ton visage.

Debout à tes côtés, je jetais des coups d'œil furtifs dans ta direction tandis que tu écoutais l'officier de l'état civil célébrer notre mariage. Quand on a prononcé nos vœux, tu m'as regardé dans les yeux et j'ai oublié Jeff, Doug et ta mère. Il aurait pu y avoir un millier de personnes dans la salle avec nous : je ne voyais que toi.

— Je vous déclare unis par les liens du mariage.

Quelques applaudissements hésitants ont retenti et on s'est embrassés avant de redescendre l'allée. L'hôtel avait disposé des boissons et des amuse-gueules dans un coin du bar, et je t'observais tandis que tu faisais le tour des invités, tendant la main pour qu'ils admirent ton alliance.

— Elle est belle aujourd'hui, hein ?

Je n'avais pas remarqué qu'Eve s'était rapprochée de moi.

— Elle est *toujours* belle, ai-je répondu.

Eve a accepté la rectification d'un hochement de tête avant de se tourner vers moi pour me regarder droit dans les yeux.

— Tu ne lui feras pas de mal, hein ?

J'ai ri.

— Ce n'est pas le genre de chose qu'on demande à un homme le jour de son mariage.

— C'est pourtant le plus important, tu ne crois pas ? a dit Eve. (Elle a bu une petite gorgée de champagne et m'a dévisagé.) Tu me rappelles beaucoup notre père.

— Eh bien, c'est sans doute ce qui plaît à Jennifer, ai-je répondu sèchement.

— Sans doute. J'espère simplement que tu ne la laisseras pas tomber toi aussi.

— Je n'ai aucune intention de quitter ta sœur, ai-je répliqué. Et puis, ça ne te regarde pas. C'est une grande fille, pas une enfant traumatisée par un père coureur de jupons.

— Mon père n'était pas un coureur de jupons.

Elle ne le défendait pas, elle énonçait juste un fait, mais j'étais intéressé. J'avais toujours supposé qu'il avait quitté ta mère pour une autre femme.

— Pourquoi est-il parti, alors ?

Elle a ignoré ma question.

— Prends soin de Jenna. Elle le mérite.

Je ne pouvais plus supporter de voir son visage suffisant, ni d'écouter ses sermons ridicules et condescendants. J'ai laissé Eve au bar pour aller glisser mon bras autour de toi. Ma nouvelle femme.

Te laisser partir

Je t'avais promis Venise et j'avais hâte de te faire visiter la ville. À l'aéroport, tu as fièrement tendu ton nouveau passeport et tu as souri quand ils ont lu ton nom à haute voix.

— Ça fait tellement bizarre !

— Tu t'y habitueras vite, ai-je dit. Mme Petersen.

Quand tu as vu que j'avais pris des billets en classe affaires, tu étais aux anges. Tu voulais profiter au maximum de tous les avantages. Le vol n'a duré que deux heures, mais tu as eu le temps d'essayer le masque pour les yeux, de regarder un film et de boire du champagne. J'étais ravi de te voir si heureuse, et que ce soit grâce à moi.

Le transfert jusqu'à l'hôtel a mis plus de temps que prévu et on est arrivés tard. Le champagne m'avait donné mal à la tête, j'étais fatigué et contrarié par la piètre qualité du service. Il ne fallait pas que j'oublie d'exiger le remboursement du transfert en rentrant à Bristol.

— Et si on laissait les valises à la réception et qu'on sortait tout de suite ? as-tu proposé en foulant le hall en marbre.

— On est là pour deux semaines. On va s'installer tranquillement et se faire servir le dîner dans la chambre. Venise sera encore là demain. (J'ai glissé un bras autour de toi et je t'ai pincé les fesses.) Et puis c'est notre nuit de noces.

Tu m'as embrassé, plongeant ta langue dans ma bouche, mais tu t'es ensuite écartée et tu m'as pris la main.

— Il n'est même pas dix heures ! Allez, on fait un petit tour dans le quartier et on boit un verre quelque part. Ensuite on rentre, promis.

Le réceptionniste a souri, sans chercher à dissimuler son amusement devant ce spectacle improvisé.

— Une querelle d'amoureux ?

Il a ri, malgré le regard que je lui ai lancé, et j'ai eu la désagréable surprise de te voir rire avec lui.

— J'essaie de convaincre mon *mari*. (Tu as souri et tu m'as fait un clin d'œil en prononçant ce mot, comme si ça allait changer quelque chose.) On devrait aller se promener dans Venise avant de monter dans la chambre. Ça a l'air tellement beau.

Tu as fermé les paupières un peu trop longtemps quand tu as cligné des yeux et je me suis rendu compte que tu étais un peu soûle.

— C'est très beau, *signora*, mais pas autant que vous.

Le réceptionniste a fait une petite courbette ridicule.

Je t'ai regardée, m'attendant à te voir lever les yeux au ciel, mais tu rougissais et j'ai compris que tu étais flattée. Flattée par ce gigolo, cet homme mielleux aux mains manucurées, avec une fleur à la boutonnière.

— La clé, s'il vous plaît, ai-je dit en passant devant toi pour me pencher sur le comptoir.

Le réceptionniste a eu un moment d'hésitation avant de me remettre un porte-carte contenant deux clés magnétiques.

— *Buona sera, signore.*

Il ne souriait plus.

J'ai refusé qu'on nous aide avec les valises et je t'ai laissée traîner la tienne jusqu'à l'ascenseur, où j'ai appuyé sur le bouton du troisième étage. Je t'ai regardée dans le miroir.

— Il était gentil, hein ? as-tu dit.

J'ai senti un goût de bile au fond de ma gorge. Tout s'était si bien passé à l'aéroport et dans l'avion ; et tu venais de tout gâcher. Tu parlais, mais je ne t'écoutais pas : je pensais à la façon dont tu avais minaudé, à la façon dont tu avais rougi en le laissant flirter avec toi, à la façon dont tu en avais *profité*.

Notre chambre se trouvait au bout d'un couloir moquetté. J'ai introduit la carte magnétique dans le lecteur puis je l'ai retirée, attendant impatiemment le déclic de la serrure. J'ai poussé la porte et fait rouler ma valise à l'intérieur, sans me soucier de savoir si elle se refermait sur toi. Il faisait chaud dans la chambre – trop chaud –, mais les fenêtres ne s'ouvraient pas et j'ai tiré sur mon col pour avoir un peu d'air. Mon sang battait dans mes oreilles mais tu parlais encore ; tu continuais de jacasser comme si tout allait bien, comme si tu ne m'avais pas humilié.

Mon poing s'est machinalement serré, ma peau se tendant sur mes jointures contractées. J'ai senti la pression augmenter dans ma poitrine, comprimant jusqu'à mes poumons. Je t'ai regardée, toujours souriante, toujours bavarde, et je t'ai envoyé mon poing dans la figure.

La pression est tout de suite retombée. Le calme m'a envahi, je me suis senti libéré, comme après le sexe ou une séance de sport. Mon mal de tête s'est atténué et la veine sur ma tempe a arrêté de palpiter. Tu as laissé échapper un sanglot étouffé, mais je ne t'ai pas regardée. J'ai quitté la chambre et ai repris l'ascenseur jusqu'à la réception. Je suis sorti dans la rue sans me retourner vers le comptoir. J'ai trouvé un bar et bu deux bières, ignorant le serveur qui essayait d'engager la conversation avec moi.

Une heure plus tard, je suis retourné à l'hôtel.

— Je pourrais avoir de la glace, s'il vous plaît ?

— *Si, signore.* (Le réceptionniste a disparu avant de revenir avec un seau à glace.) Des verres à vin, *signore* ?

— Non, merci.

J'étais calme à présent. Ma respiration était lente et mesurée. J'ai pris les escaliers, retardant un peu plus mon retour.

Quand j'ai ouvert la porte, tu étais recroquevillée sur le lit. Tu t'es redressée et tu as reculé à l'autre bout du matelas pour t'adosser au mur. Un tas de mouchoirs ensanglantés se trouvaient sur la table de chevet, mais en dépit de tes efforts pour te nettoyer le visage, tu avais du sang séché sur la lèvre supérieure. Un bleu se formait déjà sur l'arête de ton nez et autour de ton œil. Quand tu m'as vu, tu t'es mise à pleurer, et tes larmes prenaient la couleur du sang avant de tomber sur ton chemisier, le maculant de petites taches roses.

J'ai posé le seau sur la table et étalé une serviette que j'ai remplie de glace. Puis je suis venu m'asseoir à tes côtés. Tu frissonnais, mais j'ai délicatement appliqué la poche de glace sur ta peau.

— J'ai trouvé un bar sympa, ai-je dit. Je pense qu'il te plaira. J'ai fait un tour dans le quartier et j'ai repéré un ou deux restaurants pour demain midi, si tu te sens d'attaque.

J'ai retiré la poche de glace et tu m'as dévisagé avec de grands yeux méfiants. Tu tremblais encore.

— Tu as froid ? Tiens, enveloppe-toi là-dedans. (J'ai pris la couverture au pied du lit pour te la mettre sur les épaules.) Tu es fatiguée, la journée a été longue.

Je t'ai embrassée sur le front mais tu pleurais encore. Si seulement tu n'avais pas gâché notre première nuit. Je croyais que tu étais différente et que je n'aurais jamais plus à éprouver ce senti-ment de libération : cette sensation de paix absolue qui suit une dispute. J'étais déçu de constater que, finalement, tu étais comme toutes les autres.

36

J'ai du mal à respirer. Beau se met à gémir. Il me lèche le visage et me donne des coups de museau. J'essaie de réfléchir, de bouger, mais la violence du choc m'a coupé le souffle et je ne parviens pas à me relever. Même si mon corps m'obéissait, il se passe quelque chose en moi, mon monde se rétrécit peu à peu. Je suis soudain ramenée à Bristol, ne sachant pas de quelle humeur sera Ian quand il rentrera. Je lui prépare le dîner, qu'il me jettera sans doute à la figure. Je suis recroquevillée sur le sol de mon atelier, essayant de me protéger des coups de poing qui pleuvent sur moi.

Ian descend l'escalier avec précaution, secouant la tête comme s'il grondait un enfant. Je l'ai toujours déçu ; malgré tous mes efforts, je n'ai jamais su ce qu'il fallait faire ou dire. Il parle doucement, et si on ne s'attardait pas sur le sens des mots, on pourrait croire qu'il s'inquiète pour moi. Mais le son de sa voix suffit à me faire trembler violemment, comme si j'étais allongée dans la glace.

Il se tient au-dessus de moi – jambes écartées – et laisse traîner paresseusement son regard le long de mon corps. Les plis de son pantalon sont impeccables, la boucle de sa ceinture est si brillante que je vois mon reflet terrifié dedans. Il aperçoit quelque chose sur sa veste et arrache un fil qui dépasse, puis le laisse tomber négligemment au sol. Beau gémit toujours et Ian lui décoche un coup de pied dans la tête qui l'envoie un mètre plus loin.

— Ne lui fais pas de mal, s'il te plaît !

Beau pousse de petits cris plaintifs, mais il se relève et s'éclipse dans la cuisine.

— Tu es allée voir la police, Jennifer, dit Ian.

— Je suis désolée.

Ma voix n'est qu'un murmure et je ne suis pas certaine qu'il ait entendu, mais si je répète et qu'il a l'impression que je l'implore, il va s'énerver. C'est étrange la vitesse à laquelle tout me revient : je dois faire exactement ce qu'il me dit en tâchant de ne pas prendre cet air abattu qui le met hors de lui. Au fil des années, j'ai plus souvent échoué que réussi.

J'avale ma salive.

— Je... je suis désolée.

Il a les mains dans les poches. Il a l'air détendu, relax. Mais je le connais. Je sais à quelle vitesse il peut...

— Tu es *désolée* ?

L'instant d'après, il est accroupi sur moi, ses genoux clouant mes bras au sol.

— Tu crois que ça change quelque chose ?

Il se penche, enfonçant ses rotules dans mes biceps. Je me mords la langue trop tard pour retenir le cri de douleur qui provoque chez lui une moue de dégoût. Je sens la bile monter dans ma gorge et je la ravale.

— Tu leur as parlé de moi, hein ?

La commissure de ses lèvres est bordée d'écume et des gouttelettes de salive éclaboussent mon visage. Je repense soudain à la manifestante devant le tribunal il y a quelques heures, mais ça semble loin.

— Non. Non, je n'ai rien dit.

Nous jouons encore une fois à ce jeu, celui où il lance une question et où j'essaie de la reprendre de volée. Je n'étais pas mauvaise. Au début, je croyais voir une lueur de respect dans ses yeux : il s'arrêtait brusquement au milieu de l'échange et allumait la télévision ou sortait. Mais j'ai perdu la main, ou peut-être a-t-il changé les règles, et ai-je commencé à mal juger les questions. Pour l'instant, en tout cas, il a l'air satisfait de ma réponse et change brusquement de sujet.

— Tu vois quelqu'un, pas vrai ?

— Non, je ne vois personne, dis-je rapidement.

Je suis contente de pouvoir dire la vérité, même si je sais qu'il ne va pas me croire.

— Menteuse.

Il me gifle du revers de la main, produisant un claquement sec, comme un fouet, et ce son résonne encore à mes oreilles quand il reprend la parole.

— Quelqu'un t'a aidée à créer un site Internet, quelqu'un t'a trouvé cet endroit. Qui ?

— Personne, dis-je, un goût de sang dans la bouche. Je me suis débrouillée toute seule.

— Tu ne peux rien faire toute seule, Jennifer.

Il se penche jusqu'à ce que son visage touche presque le mien. Je m'efforce de ne pas bouger, sachant à quel point il déteste que j'esquisse le moindre mouvement de recul.

— Tu n'as même pas réussi à te cacher correctement. Tu n'imagines pas comme ça a été facile de te retrouver une fois que j'ai su où tu prenais tes photos. Les habitants de Penfach avaient l'air ravis d'aider un inconnu à la recherche d'une vieille amie.

Je ne m'étais pas demandé comment Ian m'avait retrouvée. J'ai toujours su qu'il y parviendrait.

— Au fait, la carte que tu as envoyée à ta sœur était très jolie.

Cette remarque désinvolte me fait l'effet d'une autre gifle.

— Qu'est-ce que tu as fait à Eve ?

Si quoi que ce soit arrive à Eve et aux enfants à cause de mon imprudence, je ne me le pardonnerai jamais. Je tenais tellement à lui montrer que je pensais encore à elle que je ne me suis pas demandé si je la mettais en danger.

Il rit.

— Qu'est-ce que tu veux que je lui fasse ? Elle ne m'intéresse pas plus que toi. Tu n'es qu'une misérable salope, Jennifer, une incapable. Tu n'es rien sans moi. Rien. Tu es quoi ?

Je ne réponds pas.

— Dis-le. Tu es quoi ?

Du sang coule au fond de ma gorge et je lutte pour parler sans m'étouffer.

— Je ne suis rien.

Il rit, puis déplace son poids pour relâcher la pression, et la douleur s'atténue légèrement dans mes bras. Il fait courir son doigt sur mon visage, le long de ma joue et sur mes lèvres.

Je sais ce qui va se passer, mais ça ne rend pas les choses plus faciles. Il défait lentement mes boutons, ouvrant mon chemisier centimètre par centimètre avant de relever mon débardeur pour découvrir ma poitrine. Ses yeux se promènent froidement sur moi, sans même une lueur de désir, et il tend le bras vers la fermeture éclair de son pantalon. Je ferme les yeux pour me réfugier en moi-même, incapable de bouger, incapable de parler. Je me demande brièvement ce qui arriverait si je criais, ou si je disais non. Si je me débattais ou si je le repoussais, simplement. Mais je ne fais rien, et je n'ai jamais rien fait. Je ne peux donc m'en prendre qu'à moi-même.

J'ignore depuis combien de temps je suis allongée là, mais le cottage est sombre et froid. Je remonte mon jean et roule sur le côté, serrant mes genoux contre moi. Je sens une douleur sourde entre mes jambes, ainsi que de l'humidité que je soupçonne être du sang. Je ne suis pas certaine de m'être évanouie, mais je ne me souviens pas du départ de Ian.

J'appelle Beau. Après une seconde de silence angoissante, il sort prudemment de la cuisine, la queue basse et les oreilles rabattues.

— Je suis vraiment désolée, Beau.

J'essaie de le faire venir vers moi, mais quand je tends la main, il aboie. Juste une fois, pour m'avertir, la tête tournée vers la porte. Je m'efforce de me lever, grimaçant sous l'effet d'une vive douleur, et on frappe à la porte.

Je suis pliée en deux au milieu de la pièce, une main sur le collier de Beau. Il grogne doucement mais n'aboie pas.

— Jenna ? Tu es là ?

Patrick.

J'éprouve une bouffée de soulagement. La porte n'est pas fermée à clé et je réprime un sanglot en l'ouvrant. Je n'allume pas la lumière du salon, et j'espère que l'obscurité est assez épaisse pour cacher mon visage qui doit déjà présenter des marques.

— Tout va bien ? demande Patrick. Il s'est passé quelque chose ?

— Je... j'ai dû m'endormir sur le canapé.

— Bethan m'a dit que tu étais rentrée. (Il hésite et baisse brièvement les yeux au sol avant de me regarder à nouveau.) Je suis venu m'excuser. Je n'aurais jamais dû te parler comme ça, Jenna, j'étais sous le choc.

— Ce n'est rien, dis-je. (Je regarde derrière lui en direction de la falaise plongée dans l'obscurité, me demandant si Ian est là, quelque part, en train de nous observer. Je ne peux pas le laisser me voir avec Patrick. Je ne peux pas le laisser lui faire de mal, pas plus qu'à Eve ni à tous ceux qui comptent pour moi.) C'est tout ?

— Je peux entrer ?

Il fait un pas en avant, mais je secoue la tête.

— Jenna, qu'est-ce qui ne va pas ?

— Je ne veux pas te voir, Patrick.

Je m'entends prononcer ces mots et résiste à l'envie de les retirer.

— Je ne t'en veux pas, dit-il. (Il a l'air fatigué, comme s'il n'avait pas dormi depuis plusieurs jours.) J'ai été exécrable, Jenna, et je ne sais pas quoi faire pour me racheter. Quand j'ai appris ce que tu avais… ce qui s'était passé, j'étais tellement sous le choc que je n'avais plus les idées claires. Il fallait que je prenne mes distances.

Je me mets à pleurer. C'est plus fort que moi. Patrick me prend la main et je n'ai pas envie qu'il la lâche.

— Je veux comprendre, Jenna. Je ne peux pas faire semblant de ne pas accuser le coup – de ne pas trouver ça difficile –, mais je veux savoir ce qui s'est passé. Je veux être là pour toi.

Je reste silencieuse, mais je sais qu'il n'y a qu'une seule chose à faire. Un seul moyen de protéger Patrick.

— Tu me manques, Jenna, murmure-t-il.

— Je ne veux plus te voir. (Je retire brusquement ma main et tâche de mettre de la conviction dans mes paroles.) Je ne veux plus rien avoir à faire avec toi.

Patrick pâlit et recule comme si je lui avais donné un coup de poing.

— Pourquoi est-ce que tu fais ça ?

— Parce que c'est ce que je veux.

Ce mensonge est un supplice.

— C'est parce que je suis parti ?

— Ça n'a rien à voir avec toi. Rien de tout ça ne te concerne. Laisse-moi simplement tranquille.

Patrick me dévisage et je me force à le regarder en face, priant pour qu'il ne voie pas le conflit qui doit se lire dans mes yeux. Il finit par lever les mains, s'avouant vaincu, et fait demi-tour.

Il trébuche sur le sentier et se met soudain à courir.

Je ferme la porte et m'écroule par terre, attirant Beau vers moi pour fondre en larmes dans son pelage. Je n'ai pas pu sauver Jacob, mais je peux sauver Patrick.

Dès que je m'en sens capable, j'appelle Iestyn pour lui demander de venir réparer la serrure.

— Je ne peux plus tourner la clé du tout maintenant, dis-je. Elle est complètement cassée, je n'ai plus aucun moyen de fermer.

— Ne vous inquiétez pas pour ça, réplique Iestyn. Il n'y a pas de voleurs par ici.

— Je veux que ce soit réparé !

Ma fermeté nous surprend tous les deux et il y a un bref silence.

— J'arrive.

Il est là moins d'une heure plus tard et se met vite au travail, mais il refuse le thé que je lui propose. Il sifflote tandis qu'il enlève la serrure et graisse le mécanisme, avant de la remettre et de me montrer que la clé tourne parfaitement à présent.

— Merci, dis-je, sanglotant presque de soulagement.

Iestyn me regarde bizarrement et je resserre mon cardigan. Des ecchymoses marbrées couvrent le haut de mes bras, s'étendant comme des taches d'encre sur un buvard. J'ai mal comme si j'avais couru un marathon, ma joue gauche est enflée et j'ai une dent qui bouge. Je laisse mes cheveux tomber sur mon visage pour cacher le pire.

Je vois Iestyn jeter un coup d'œil à la peinture rouge sur la porte.

— Je nettoierai ça, dis-je, mais il ne répond pas.

Il me salue d'un signe de tête, puis semble se raviser et se retourne vers moi.

— C'est petit, Penfach, observe-t-il. Tout se sait ici.

— C'est ce que j'ai cru comprendre.

S'il s'attend à ce que je me défende, il va être déçu. Je serai jugée par le tribunal, pas par les villageois.

— Je ferais profil bas, si j'étais vous, ajoute Iestyn. En attendant que ça se tasse.

— Merci du conseil, dis-je sèchement.

Te laisser partir

Je ferme la porte et monte à l'étage pour faire couler un bain. J'entre dans l'eau bouillante en serrant les paupières pour ne pas voir les marques qui apparaissent sur ma peau. De petits bleus en forme de doigts d'une délicatesse incongrue parsèment ma poitrine et mes cuisses. J'ai été stupide de croire que je pouvais échapper au passé. Où que j'aille, il me rattrapera toujours.

37

— Tu as besoin d'un coup de main ? demanda Ray, même s'il savait que Mags s'en sortait très bien toute seule, comme toujours.

— Tout est prêt, répondit-elle en enlevant son tablier. Le chili et le riz sont dans le four, les bières dans le frigo et il y a des brownies pour le dessert.

— Ça a l'air parfait, dit Ray.

Il resta planté au milieu de la cuisine, les bras ballants.

— Tu peux débarrasser le lave-vaisselle, si tu cherches quelque chose à faire.

Il commença à sortir les assiettes propres, essayant de trouver un sujet de conversation neutre qui n'entraînerait pas de dispute.

C'était Mags qui avait eu l'idée d'organiser un dîner ce soir. Pour célébrer la fin d'une enquête bien menée, avait-elle dit. Ray se demandait si c'était sa façon de s'excuser pour leurs récentes disputes.

— Merci encore d'avoir proposé ça, fit-il quand le silence devint trop pesant.

Il souleva le panier à couverts du lave-vaisselle, faisant couler de l'eau par terre. Mags lui tendit un chiffon.

— C'est l'une des affaires les plus médiatisées que tu aies eues, observa-t-elle. Il faut fêter ça. (Elle lui prit le chiffon des mains et le mit dans l'évier.) Et puis si l'autre option est que vous alliez fêter ça tous les trois au Nag's Head, le choix est vite fait.

Ray encaissa la critique sans broncher. Voilà donc ce qui se cachait derrière ce dîner.

Ils s'affairaient chacun de son côté dans la cuisine comme si de rien n'était ; comme si Ray n'avait pas passé la nuit sur le canapé ; comme si leur fils ne planquait pas d'objets volés dans sa chambre.

Il risqua un coup d'œil vers Mags sans parvenir à déchiffrer son expression et décida de garder le silence. Ces derniers temps, il avait l'impression de toujours dire ce qu'il ne fallait pas.

Ray savait que comparer Mags et Kate n'était pas juste, mais c'était tellement plus facile au boulot. Kate ne se vexait jamais, il n'était donc pas obligé de réfléchir avant de parler, à l'opposé de ce qu'il faisait désormais avec Mags avant d'aborder un sujet délicat.

Quand il avait proposé à Kate de venir dîner chez lui ce soir, il n'était pas certain qu'elle accepte.

— Je comprendrai si tu refuses, avait-il dit.

Kate avait eu l'air troublée.

— Pourquoi est-ce que je… (Elle s'était mordu la lèvre.) Oh, je vois. (Elle avait essayé de prendre le même air sérieux que Ray, sans grand succès.). Je te l'ai dit, tout est oublié. Ça ne me pose pas de problème, si c'est bon pour toi, bien sûr.

— Ça ira, avait-il répondu.

Il l'espérait, en tout cas. Il se sentit soudain très mal à l'aise à l'idée que Mags et Kate se retrouvent dans la même pièce. La veille, dans le canapé, il avait eu du mal à fermer l'œil, persuadé que Mags était au courant qu'il avait embrassé Kate et qu'elle l'avait invitée dans le seul but de le lui dire. Il avait beau savoir que Mags n'était pas du genre à régler ses comptes en public, cette éventualité lui donnait quand même des sueurs froides.

— Tom est revenu aujourd'hui du collège avec une lettre, dit Mags.

Elle lâcha ça d'un coup, et il eut l'impression qu'elle se retenait de lui annoncer la nouvelle depuis qu'il était rentré du travail.

— Qu'est-ce qu'ils veulent ?

Mags sortit la lettre de la poche de son tablier et la lui tendit.

Te laisser partir

Chers M. et Mme Stevens,

Je vous serais reconnaissante de bien vouloir prendre rendez-vous avec moi auprès de ma secrétaire afin d'évoquer un problème qui se pose au sein de notre établissement.

Je vous prie d'agréer, Madame, Monsieur, l'expression de mes salutations distinguées.

Ann Cumberland
Principale
Collège Morland Downs

— Enfin ! s'exclama Ray. (Il frappa la lettre du revers de la main.) Ils admettent qu'il y a un problème alors ? C'est pas trop tôt, nom de Dieu !

Mags déboucha la bouteille de vin.

— Ça doit bien faire plus d'un an qu'on leur dit que Tom se fait harceler ! poursuivit Ray. Et ils ne voulaient même pas envisager cette possibilité, hein ?

Mags le regarda. L'espace d'un instant, son visage se décomposa et ses défenses cédèrent.

— Comment on a pu passer à côté de ça ? (Elle chercha en vain un mouchoir dans la manche de son cardigan.) J'ai l'impression d'être une mère indigne !

Elle chercha dans l'autre manche, sans plus de résultat.

— Hé, Mags, arrête ça, tu veux. (Ray sortit son mouchoir et essuya délicatement les larmes qui débordaient des cils de sa femme.) Tu n'es passée à côté de rien du tout. Ni toi, ni moi, d'ailleurs. On sait que quelque chose ne va pas depuis qu'il est entré au collège, et on les bassine depuis le premier jour pour qu'ils règlent ça.

— Mais ce n'est pas à eux de régler ça. (Mags se moucha.) C'est nous les parents.

— Peut-être, mais le problème n'est pas ici, non ? Il est à l'école, et maintenant qu'ils l'ont admis, peut-être qu'ils vont enfin faire quelque chose.

— J'espère que ça ne va pas aggraver la situation pour Tom.

— Je pourrais demander aux agents du secteur de faire un saut au collège pour parler du harcèlement scolaire, proposa Ray.

— Non !

La véhémence de Mags le coupa dans son élan.

— Réglons ça avec le collège. Tout ne concerne pas la police. Pour une fois, gardons ça pour nous, d'accord ? J'aimerais vraiment que tu ne parles pas de Tom au boulot.

La sonnette de la porte retentit à point nommé.

— Ça va aller ? demanda Ray.

Mags hocha la tête et s'essuya le visage avec le mouchoir avant de le rendre à Ray.

— Oui.

Ray se regarda dans le miroir de l'entrée. Son teint blême et son air fatigué lui donnèrent soudain envie de renvoyer Kate et Stumpy chez eux pour passer la soirée avec sa femme. Mais Mags avait cuisiné tout l'après-midi, elle n'apprécierait pas d'avoir fait tout ça pour rien. Il soupira et ouvrit la porte.

Kate portait un jean avec des bottes qui lui montaient jusqu'aux genoux et un haut noir à col en V. Sa tenue n'avait rien de très glamour, mais elle avait l'air plus jeune et plus décontractée qu'au travail, et c'était quelque peu perturbant. Ray recula pour la laisser passer.

— C'est vraiment une bonne idée, dit-elle. Merci beaucoup de m'avoir invitée.

— Je t'en prie. (Il la fit entrer dans la cuisine.) Stumpy et toi, vous avez travaillé dur ces derniers mois : je tenais juste à vous montrer que j'apprécie vos efforts. (Il se fendit d'un large sourire.) Et pour être honnête, c'était l'idée de Mags, c'est elle qu'il faut remercier.

Mags accueillit sa remarque avec un petit sourire.

— Bonjour, Kate, je suis contente de faire enfin ta connaissance. Tu n'as pas eu trop de mal à trouver ?

Les deux femmes se faisaient face, et Ray fut frappé par le contraste entre elles. Mags n'avait pas eu le temps de se changer et son sweat-shirt était maculé de petites taches de sauce. Elle était comme d'habitude – chaleureuse, accueillante, gentille – mais à côté de Kate elle avait l'air… il s'efforça de trouver le mot juste. Moins *raffinée*. Il éprouva aussitôt une pointe de culpabilité et se rapprocha de Mags, comme si la proximité était un gage de loyauté.

— Quelle jolie cuisine ! (Kate jeta un œil aux brownies, tout juste sortis du four et nappés de chocolat blanc. Elle tendit une boîte en carton contenant un cheesecake.) J'ai apporté un dessert, mais j'ai peur que ça ait l'air un peu fade maintenant.

— Comme c'est gentil de ta part ! fit Mags en s'avançant pour prendre la boîte. Je trouve toujours les gâteaux meilleurs quand c'est quelqu'un d'autre qui les a faits, pas toi ?

Kate sourit avec gratitude et Ray laissa échapper un lent soupir. La soirée n'allait peut-être pas être aussi pénible qu'il le craignait, mais plus tôt Stumpy serait là, mieux ce serait.

— Bon, qu'est-ce que je te sers ? demanda Mags. Ray est à la bière, mais moi je bois du vin, si tu préfères.

— Je vais t'accompagner.

Ray cria dans l'escalier :

— Tom, Lucy, venez dire bonjour, bande de sauvages !

Des bruits de pas résonnèrent à l'étage et les enfants dévalèrent l'escalier. Ils firent leur apparition dans la cuisine, s'arrêtant dans l'embrasure de la porte, l'air gênés.

— Voici Kate, indiqua Mags. Elle est en formation dans l'équipe de papa pour devenir inspecteur.

Ray écarquilla les yeux à cette annonce, mais Kate ne sembla pas perturbée.

— Encore quelques mois et je serai un véritable inspecteur, répliqua-t-elle avec un grand sourire. Comment ça va, les enfants ?

— Bien, répondirent en chœur Lucy et Tom.

— Tu dois être Lucy, dit Kate.

La petite fille avait les cheveux de sa mère, mais pour le reste, elle tenait de Ray. Tout le monde disait que les deux enfants étaient son portrait craché. La ressemblance ne lui sautait pas aux yeux dans la journée – leurs personnalités étaient trop affirmées –, mais quand ils dormaient, les traits au repos, Ray voyait son visage dans celui de ses enfants. Il se demanda s'il avait déjà eu l'air aussi agressif que son fils, qui fusillait le sol du regard, comme s'il en voulait au carrelage. Il s'était mis du gel dans les cheveux de façon à les coiffer en pics aussi menaçants que son expression.

— Voici Tom, indiqua Lucy.

— Dis bonjour, Tom, fit Mags.

— Bonjour, Tom, répéta-t-il, les yeux rivés au sol.

Mags lui donna un petit coup de torchon, exaspérée.

— Désolée, Kate.

Kate sourit à Tom, et celui-ci jeta un coup d'œil vers Mags pour voir s'il allait devoir rester là.

— Les gosses ! soupira Mags. (Elle retira le film alimentaire qui recouvrait une assiette de sandwichs et la tendit à Tom.) Vous pouvez aller manger ça en haut, si vous ne voulez pas passer la soirée avec les *vieux*.

Elle écarquilla les yeux en prononçant ce mot et Lucy gloussa. Tom leva les yeux au ciel, et ils disparurent dans leurs chambres à vitesse grand V.

— Ils sont sages, observa Mags. Enfin, la plupart du temps.

Elle murmura ces derniers mots, de sorte qu'il était impossible de savoir si elle parlait toute seule ou aux autres.

— Il y a eu d'autres problèmes avec Tom au collège ? demanda Kate.

Ray grogna intérieurement. Il dévisagea Mags, qui évita son regard. Elle serra la mâchoire.

— Rien qu'on ne puisse régler, répondit-elle sèchement.

Ray grimaça et regarda Kate, essayant de s'excuser sans que Mags s'en aperçoive. Il aurait dû la prévenir que Mags était très chatouilleuse à propos de Tom. Il y eut un silence pesant, puis le portable de Ray émit un bip pour signaler l'arrivée d'un message. Il le sortit de sa poche, heureux de la diversion, mais sa joie fut de courte durée.

— Stumpy ne peut pas venir, annonça-t-il. Sa mère a encore fait une chute.

— Elle va bien ? demanda Mags.

— Je crois. Il est en route pour l'hôpital. (Ray envoya un message à Stumpy et remit le téléphone dans sa poche.) Bon, on est juste nous trois, du coup.

Kate regarda Ray, puis Mags, qui se retourna et se mit à remuer le chili.

— Et si on remettait ça à une autre fois ? Quand Stumpy pourra être là ? proposa Kate.

— Ne dis pas de bêtises, répliqua Ray avec une jovialité forcée. En plus, on a une quantité énorme de chili : on ne pourra jamais tout finir si tu ne nous aides pas.

Il observa Mags, souhaitant presque qu'elle abonde dans le sens de Kate et qu'ils annulent le dîner, mais elle continua de remuer.

— Absolument, renchérit-elle vivement. (Elle tendit une paire de gants de cuisine à Ray.) Tu peux apporter la cocotte ? Kate, tu pourrais prendre ces assiettes et les porter dans la salle à manger, s'il te plaît ?

La table n'était pas mise, mais Ray s'assit machinalement au bout et Kate sur sa gauche. Mags posa une casserole de riz, puis retourna chercher un bol de fromage râpé et un pot de crème aigre dans la cuisine. Elle s'assit en face de Kate, et tous les trois furent un moment occupés à se passer les plats et à remplir leurs assiettes.

Quand ils entamèrent le repas, le tintement des couverts sur la porcelaine rendit l'absence de conversation encore plus évidente ; Ray essaya de trouver quelque chose à dire. Mags n'apprécierait pas qu'ils parlent du boulot, mais c'était peut-être le sujet le moins risqué. Avant qu'il ait le temps de se décider, Mags posa sa fourchette sur le bord de son assiette.

— Ça te plaît la Criminelle, Kate ?

— Beaucoup. Par contre, il ne faut pas compter ses heures. Mais le travail est super et c'est ce que j'ai toujours voulu faire.

— J'ai entendu dire que le capitaine était insupportable.

Ray se tourna brusquement vers Mags, mais elle souriait à Kate. Cela n'atténua en rien l'inquiétude qui avait commencé à le gagner.

— Il y a pire, fit Kate en jetant un regard en coin à Ray. Cela dit, je ne sais pas comment on peut être aussi bordélique : son bureau est un véritable désastre. Il y a des tasses de café à moitié pleines qui traînent un peu partout.

— C'est parce que j'ai trop de travail pour en boire un en entier, répliqua Ray.

Être le dindon de la farce était un moindre mal, vu les circonstances.

— Il a toujours raison, bien sûr, renchérit Mags.

Kate fit mine d'y réfléchir.

— Sauf quand il a tort.

Elles rirent toutes les deux, et Ray se détendit un peu.

— Est-ce qu'il passe son temps à fredonner « Les chariots de feu » ici aussi ? demanda Kate.

— Difficile à dire, répondit doucement Mags. Je ne le vois jamais.

L'ambiance retomba et ils mangèrent un moment en silence. Ray toussa et Kate leva les yeux. Il lui adressa un sourire désolé qu'elle ignora, mais en se retournant il s'aperçut que Mags les observait, le front un peu plissé. Elle posa sa fourchette et repoussa son assiette.

— Le boulot ne te manque pas, Mags ? dit Kate.

Tout le monde lui posait cette question, comme si on s'attendait à ce qu'elle rêve encore de la paperasse, des horaires merdiques, des taudis où il fallait s'essuyer les pieds en sortant.

— Si, répondit-elle sans hésiter.

Ray leva les yeux.

— Ah bon ?

Mags continua de parler à Kate comme s'il n'avait rien dit.

— Ce n'est pas vraiment le boulot qui me manque, mais la personne que j'étais à l'époque. Je regrette de ne plus rien avoir à dire, de ne plus rien pouvoir apprendre aux gens.

Ray s'interrompit de manger. Mags était la même qu'avant. La même personne qu'elle serait toujours. Détenir ou non une carte de police ne changeait rien.

Kate hocha la tête comme si elle comprenait, et Ray apprécia ses efforts.

— Tu comptes revenir un jour ?

— Impossible. Qui s'occuperait de ces deux-là ? (Mags leva les yeux vers les chambres.) Sans parler de lui. (Elle se tourna vers Ray, mais elle ne souriait pas, et il tenta de déchiffrer son regard.) Tu sais ce qu'on dit : derrière chaque grand homme...

— C'est vrai, intervint soudain Ray avec plus d'énergie que nécessaire. (Il regarda Mags.) Je ne sais pas ce que je ferais sans toi.

— Le dessert ! fit brusquement Mags en se levant. À moins que tu veuilles encore du chili, Kate ?

— Ça va aller, merci. Tu as besoin d'aide ?

— Ne bouge pas, je n'en ai pas pour longtemps. Je vais débarrasser et faire un tour en haut pour voir si les enfants ne font pas de bêtises.

Elle emporta tout dans la cuisine, puis Ray entendit des pas légers à l'étage, suivis de murmures dans la chambre de Lucy.

— Je suis désolé, dit-il. Je ne sais pas ce qu'elle a.

— C'est à cause de moi ? demanda Kate.

— Non, pas du tout. Elle est un peu bizarre ces temps-ci. Elle se fait du souci pour Tom, je crois. (Il lui adressa un sourire rassurant.) C'est sûrement ma faute, comme d'habitude.

Mags redescendit l'escalier et réapparut quelques instants plus tard avec un plateau de brownies et un pot de crème.

— En fait, je crois que je vais faire l'impasse sur le dessert, Mags, annonça Kate en se levant.

— Tu veux des fruits, plutôt ? J'ai du melon, si tu préfères.

— Non, ce n'est pas ça. Je suis crevée. La semaine a été longue. Le dîner était délicieux, en tout cas, merci.

— Bon, si tu en es sûre. (Mags posa les brownies.) Je ne t'ai pas félicitée pour l'affaire Gray. Ray m'a dit que tout le mérite te revenait. C'est bien pour ton CV, si tôt dans ta carrière.

— À vrai dire, je n'étais pas toute seule, répondit Kate. On forme une bonne équipe.

Ray savait qu'elle parlait de la Criminelle dans son ensemble, mais elle lui jeta un coup d'œil en disant ça et il n'osa pas regarder Mags.

Ils se dirigèrent vers l'entrée, où Mags embrassa Kate sur la joue.

— Reviens nous voir quand tu veux. Ça m'a fait très plaisir de te rencontrer.

Ray espérait être le seul à noter le manque de sincérité dans la voix de sa femme. Il dit au revoir à Kate, hésitant un instant à lui faire la bise. Puis, estimant que ce serait plus étrange encore de ne pas l'embrasser, il fut aussi bref que possible, mais il sentit le regard de Mags posé sur lui et fut soulagé quand Kate s'engagea dans l'allée et que la porte se referma derrière elle.

— Bon, je crois que je ne vais pas pouvoir résister à ces brownies, fit-il avec une gaieté forcée. Tu en veux ?

— Je suis au régime, répliqua Mags. (Elle alla dans la cuisine et déplia la planche à repasser, puis mit de l'eau dans le fer et attendit qu'elle chauffe.) Il y a un tupperware au frigo avec du riz et du chili pour Stumpy. Tu pourras lui apporter demain ? Il aura faim s'il passe la nuit à l'hôpital, et il n'aura pas envie de cuisiner.

Ray apporta son assiette dans la cuisine et mangea debout.

— C'est gentil de ta part.

— Stumpy est quelqu'un de bien.

— C'est vrai. J'ai une bonne équipe.

Mags resta un moment silencieuse. Elle attrapa un pantalon qu'elle se mit à repasser. Quand elle reprit la parole, son ton était désinvolte, mais elle appuyait fermement la pointe du fer sur la toile.

— Elle est jolie.

— Kate ?

— Non, Stumpy. (Mags le dévisagea, exaspérée.) Évidemment, Kate.

— Si tu le dis. Je n'y ai jamais vraiment réfléchi.

Le mensonge était ridicule. Mags le connaissait mieux que personne.

Elle haussa un sourcil, mais Ray fut soulagé de la voir sourire. Il se risqua à la taquiner.

— Tu es jalouse ?

— Pas du tout, répondit-elle. D'ailleurs, si elle est prête à faire le repassage, elle peut emménager ici.

— Désolé de lui avoir parlé de Tom.

Mags appuya sur un bouton et le fer cracha un nuage de vapeur sur le pantalon. Elle continua sans lever les yeux.

— Tu aimes ton travail, Ray, et ça me va. Ça fait partie de toi. Mais c'est comme si les enfants et moi, on n'existait pas. J'ai l'impression d'être invisible.

Ray ouvrit la bouche pour protester, mais Mags secoua la tête.

— Tu parles plus avec Kate qu'avec moi, poursuivit-elle. J'ai bien vu cette complicité entre vous ce soir. Je ne suis pas stupide, je sais ce que c'est quand on travaille toute la journée avec quelqu'un : on lui parle, bien sûr. Mais ça ne t'empêche pas de me parler à moi aussi. (Elle fit jaillir un autre nuage de vapeur et appliqua plus fort le fer sur la planche, le faisant glisser d'avant en arrière.) Personne n'a jamais regretté sur son lit de mort de ne pas avoir passé plus de temps au travail. Mais nos enfants grandissent et tu es en train de passer à côté de ça. Ils seront bientôt partis et tu seras à la retraite. Il n'y aura plus que toi et moi et on n'aura plus rien à se raconter.

Ce n'est pas vrai, pensa Ray, et il s'efforça de trouver les mots pour le lui faire savoir, mais ceux-ci restèrent coincés dans sa gorge et il se contenta de secouer la tête, comme s'il pouvait effacer par ce simple geste ce qu'elle venait de dire. Il crut l'entendre soupirer, mais ce n'était peut-être qu'un autre nuage de vapeur.

38

Tu ne m'as jamais pardonné ce qui s'était passé à Venise. Tu es toujours restée vigilante et tu ne t'es plus jamais abandonnée à moi. Même quand le bleu sur l'arête de ton nez avait disparu et qu'on aurait pu tout oublier, je savais que tu y pensais encore. Je le savais à ta façon de me suivre des yeux quand j'allais chercher une bière, et à cette hésitation dans ta voix avant de répondre à mes questions, même si tu répétais sans cesse que tout allait bien.

On est allés dîner au restaurant pour notre anniversaire de mariage. Je t'avais trouvé un livre sur Rodin relié de cuir chez le bouquiniste de Chapel Road, et je l'avais emballé dans le journal du jour de notre mariage que j'avais conservé.

— Un an, ce sont les noces de papier, t'ai-je rappelé.

Ton regard s'est éclairé.

— C'est parfait ! (Tu as soigneusement replié le journal avant de le glisser à l'intérieur du livre, où j'avais écrit un mot : *Pour Jennifer, que j'aime chaque jour un peu plus*, et tu m'as chaudement embrassé.) Je t'aime, tu le sais, as-tu dit.

Je me posais la question parfois, mais je n'ai jamais douté de mes sentiments pour toi. Je t'aimais tellement que ça me faisait peur ; j'ignorais qu'il était possible d'aimer une personne au point d'être prêt à faire n'importe quoi pour ne pas la perdre. Si j'avais pu t'emmener sur une île déserte, loin de tout, je l'aurais fait.

— On m'a proposé de prendre une nouvelle classe d'adultes, as-tu dit tandis qu'on nous conduisait à notre table.

— C'est bien payé ?

Tu as froncé le nez.

— Pas vraiment, mais ce sont des cours thérapeutiques proposés à tarif réduit pour des personnes souffrant de dépression. Je pense que ça vaut la peine d'accepter.

J'ai ricané.

— Ça va être une vraie partie de plaisir.

— Il existe un lien étroit entre les activités créatives et l'humeur des gens, as-tu précisé. Je serais ravie de les aider, et ce n'est que pour huit semaines. Je devrais pouvoir les caler entre mes autres cours.

— Du moment qu'il te reste du temps pour sculpter.

Tes créations se trouvaient à présent dans cinq boutiques différentes.

Tu as acquiescé.

— Ça ira. Je continuerai à fournir régulièrement les magasins et j'accepterai moins de commandes pendant un petit moment. Cela dit, je ne m'attendais pas à me retrouver avec autant de cours, il faudra que j'en donne un peu moins l'année prochaine.

— Eh bien, tu sais ce qu'on dit, ai-je répliqué en riant. Ceux qui sont capables créent, ceux qui ne sont pas capables enseignent !

Tu n'as rien répondu.

Notre commande est arrivée et le serveur en a fait des tonnes en enlevant la serviette de ton verre pour te servir le vin.

— J'ai pensé que ce serait peut-être une bonne idée d'ouvrir un compte en banque à mon nom pour mes activités, as-tu lancé.

— Pourquoi ça ?

Je me suis demandé qui t'avait suggéré ça et pourquoi tu avais parlé de nos finances avec quelqu'un.

— Ce sera plus simple pour ma déclaration d'impôts, si tout est sur un compte à part.

— Ça te fera juste de la paperasse en plus, ai-je observé.

J'ai coupé mon steak en deux pour vérifier qu'il était bien cuit comme je l'aimais, et j'ai soigneusement enlevé le gras pour le mettre au bord de mon assiette.

— Ça ne me dérange pas.

— Non, c'est plus simple si tout continue d'aller sur mon compte, ai-je tranché. Après tout, c'est moi qui rembourse le crédit immobilier et qui paie les factures.

— Si tu le dis.

Tu as picoré dans ton risotto.

— Tu as besoin de liquide ? t'ai-je demandé. Je peux te donner plus d'argent ce mois-ci, si tu veux.

— Peut-être un peu.

— Pour quoi faire ?

— Un peu de shopping, as-tu répondu. J'ai besoin de vêtements.

— Pourquoi on n'irait pas ensemble ? Tu sais comment tu es quand tu achètes des vêtements : tu vas choisir des tenues qui ne te plairont plus une fois à la maison et tu finiras par en rapporter la moitié. (J'ai ri et je t'ai pressé la main par-dessus la table.) Je vais prendre ma journée et on ira tous les deux. On mangera au restaurant avant d'aller faire les magasins et tu pourras faire chauffer ma carte de crédit, si tu veux. Ça te va ?

Tu as acquiescé, et je me suis concentré sur mon steak. J'ai commandé une autre bouteille de vin rouge et, le temps que je la finisse, il ne restait plus que nous dans le restaurant. J'ai laissé un trop gros pourboire et je suis tombé sur le serveur quand il m'a apporté mon manteau.

— Désolée, as-tu dit. Il a un peu trop bu.

Le serveur a souri poliment, et j'ai attendu qu'on soit dehors pour te saisir le bras et le pincer entre mon pouce et mon index.

— Ne t'excuse plus jamais pour moi.

Tu étais choquée. Je ne sais pas pourquoi : ce n'était pas justement ça que tu redoutais, depuis Venise ?

— Pardon, as-tu dit, et je t'ai lâché le bras pour te prendre la main.

On est arrivés tard à la maison et tu es directement montée à l'étage. J'ai éteint la lumière du rez-de-chaussée pour te rejoindre, mais tu étais déjà au lit. Quand je me suis allongé à tes côtés, tu t'es retournée et tu m'as embrassé en me caressant la poitrine.

— Pardon, je t'aime, as-tu murmuré.

J'ai fermé les yeux et attendu que tu plonges sous la couette. Je savais que c'était inutile : j'avais bu deux bouteilles de vin et j'ai à peine senti un frémissement quand tu m'as pris dans ta bouche. Je t'ai laissée essayer un moment avant de repousser ta tête.

— Tu ne m'excites plus, ai-je dit.

Je me suis retourné vers le mur et j'ai fermé les yeux. Tu t'es levée pour aller dans la salle de bains et je t'ai entendue pleurer tandis que je m'endormais.

Je n'avais pas prévu de te tromper une fois marié, mais tu ne faisais plus aucun effort au lit. Tu m'en veux peut-être d'être allé voir ailleurs ? Mais c'était ça ou la position du missionnaire avec une femme qui gardait les yeux fermés. J'ai commencé à sortir le vendredi soir après le travail et à rentrer au petit matin quand j'en avais assez de celle avec qui j'avais fini au lit. Ça n'avait pas l'air de te déranger et, au bout d'un moment, je ne me donnais même plus la peine de rentrer. Je débarquais à la maison le samedi midi et je te trouvais dans ton atelier. Tu ne me demandais jamais ce que j'avais fait ni avec qui, et c'est devenu une sorte de jeu. Je voulais voir jusqu'où je pouvais aller avant que tu m'accuses d'être infidèle.

C'est arrivé un jour où je regardais un match de football. Manchester United jouait contre Chelsea, et j'étais confortablement installé dans le canapé, les pieds sur la table et une bière fraîche à la main. Tu t'es mise devant la télévision.

Te laisser partir

— Enlève-toi de là, c'est le temps additionnel !

— Qui est Charlotte ? m'as-tu demandé.

— Qu'est-ce que tu veux dire ?

J'ai tendu le cou pour essayer de voir le match.

— J'ai trouvé un reçu avec ce nom et un numéro de téléphone dans la poche de ton manteau. Qui c'est ?

J'ai entendu les supporters exploser de joie à la télévision quand Manchester United a marqué juste avant le coup de sifflet final. J'ai soupiré et pris la télécommande pour éteindre.

— Tu es contente ?

J'ai allumé une cigarette, sachant pertinemment que ça allait te rendre furieuse.

— Tu ne peux pas fumer dehors ?

— Non, je ne peux pas, ai-je répondu en soufflant la fumée dans ta direction. Parce que c'est ma maison, pas la tienne.

— Qui est Charlotte ?

Tu tremblais, mais tu es restée debout devant moi.

J'ai ri.

— Aucune idée. (C'était vrai : je ne me souvenais pas d'elle. Ça aurait pu être un tas de filles différentes.) C'est sûrement une serveuse à qui j'ai tapé dans l'œil. J'ai dû mettre le reçu dans ma poche sans le regarder. (Je parlais avec décontraction, sans la moindre trace de nervosité, et je t'ai vue vaciller.) J'espère que tu ne m'accuses de rien.

Je t'ai défiée du regard, mais tu as détourné les yeux et tu t'es tue. J'ai failli en rire. C'était tellement facile.

Je me suis levé. Tu portais un débardeur sans soutien-gorge et j'avais une vue plongeante sur tes seins, et je pouvais distinguer tes mamelons à travers le tissu.

— Tu es sortie comme ça ? t'ai-je demandé.

— Juste pour faire les courses.

Te laisser partir

— Les nichons à l'air ? Tu veux que les gens te prennent pour une traînée, c'est ça ? (Tu as mis tes mains devant ton décolleté et je les ai enlevées.) Ça ne t'embête pas de les montrer à des inconnus, mais à moi, si ? Il faut choisir, Jennifer : soit tu es une pute, soit tu ne l'es pas.

— Je ne suis pas une pute, as-tu murmuré.

— On ne dirait pas, vu d'ici.

J'ai levé la main et j'ai écrasé ma cigarette entre tes seins. Tu as crié, mais j'avais déjà quitté la pièce.

39

Ray regagnait son bureau à grandes enjambées après le briefing matinal quand il fut arrêté par l'agent de permanence. Rachel était une femme mince d'une cinquantaine d'années aux traits d'oiseau et aux cheveux argentés coupés court.

— C'est vous le capitaine de service aujourd'hui, Ray ?

— Oui, répondit-il, méfiant.

Cette question n'augurait jamais rien de bon.

— J'ai une certaine Eve Mannings à l'accueil qui souhaite signaler une personne en danger : elle s'inquiète pour sa sœur.

— Un agent ne peut pas s'en occuper ?

— Ils sont tous sortis, et elle est très inquiète. Elle attend depuis une heure.

Rachel ne dit rien d'autre ; c'était inutile. Elle se contenta de fixer Ray par-dessus ses lunettes à monture d'acier et d'attendre qu'il prenne la bonne décision. Il avait l'impression de se faire gronder par une tante bienveillante mais intimidante.

Il passa la tête par la porte pour jeter un coup d'œil à l'accueil, où une femme était penchée sur son téléphone.

— C'est elle ?

Eve Mannings était le genre de femme plus à l'aise dans un café qu'au commissariat. Elle avait des cheveux châtain lisses, qui virevoltèrent autour de ses épaules quand elle releva la tête, et portait un manteau jaune vif avec des boutons démesurés et une doublure à fleurs. Elle était toute rouge, mais cela ne reflétait pas forcément son humeur. Le chauffage central du poste semblait n'avoir que deux réglages : glacial ou tropical, et c'était manifestement une journée tropicale, aujourd'hui. Ray maudit en silence le règlement qui voulait qu'un policier se charge de tout signalement d'une personne en danger. Rachel aurait été tout à fait capable de s'occuper de la déclaration.

Il soupira.

— D'accord. Je vais envoyer quelqu'un.

Satisfaite, Rachel retourna à l'accueil.

Ray monta au troisième étage et trouva Kate à son bureau.

— Tu peux faire un saut en bas pour t'occuper d'une main courante ?

— Un agent ne peut pas le faire ?

Ray rit en voyant sa tête.

— J'ai déjà essayé. Vas-y, tu en as pour vingt minutes à tout casser.

Kate soupira.

— Tu me demandes à moi juste parce que tu sais que je ne dis jamais non.

— Fais gaffe, c'est pas tombé dans l'oreille d'un sourd !

Ray sourit avec malice. Kate leva les yeux au ciel mais ne put s'empêcher de rougir.

— Bon, c'est pour quoi ?

Ray lui tendit la feuille que Rachel lui avait donnée.

— Pour signaler une personne en danger. Eve Mannings t'attend à l'accueil.

— OK, mais tu me dois un verre.

— Ça me va ! cria-t-il tandis qu'elle quittait la Criminelle.

Il lui avait présenté ses excuses pour le dîner embarrassant de l'autre jour, mais Kate avait répondu que c'était sans importance et ils n'en avaient plus reparlé.

Il se rendit dans son bureau. Quand il ouvrit son porte-documents, il trouva un post-it de Mags sur son agenda avec la date et l'heure de leur rendez-vous au collège la semaine suivante. Mags avait entouré le message au feutre rouge, au cas où il ne le verrait pas. Ray le colla sur l'écran de son ordinateur avec les autres post-it censés lui rappeler des informations importantes.

Il n'en était qu'à la moitié de sa pile de documents à traiter quand Kate frappa à la porte.

— Ne m'arrête pas, dit Ray. Je suis lancé.

— Tu veux que je te mette au parfum pour la main courante ?

Ray s'arrêta et fit signe à Kate de s'asseoir.

— Qu'est-ce que tu fais ? demanda-t-elle en jetant un œil à la montagne de documents sur son bureau.

— Des papiers. Du classement, surtout, et mes dépenses des six derniers mois. L'administration dit que si je ne m'en occupe pas aujourd'hui, ils n'en autoriseront plus aucune.

— Tu as besoin d'une secrétaire.

— J'ai besoin qu'on me laisse faire mon travail de policier au lieu de ces conneries, s'emporta-t-il. Pardon. Raconte-moi comment ça s'est passé.

Kate regarda ses notes.

— Eve Mannings vit à Oxford, mais sa sœur Jennifer habite ici à Bristol avec son mari, Ian Petersen. Eve et sa sœur se sont brouillées il y a environ cinq ans et elle n'a plus eu de nouvelles d'elle ni de son beau-frère depuis. Il y a quelques semaines, Petersen est passé la voir à l'improviste pour lui demander où était sa sœur.

— Elle l'a quitté ?

— Apparemment. Mme Mannings a reçu une carte de sa sœur il y a plusieurs mois mais elle n'a pas reconnu le cachet de la poste et elle a jeté l'enveloppe. Elle vient de retrouver la carte en petits morceaux derrière une pendule sur sa cheminée, et elle est persuadée que c'est son beau-frère qui l'a déchirée quand il lui a rendu visite.

— Pourquoi il aurait fait ça ?

Kate haussa les épaules.

— Aucune idée. Mme Mannings ne le sait pas non plus, mais ça lui a fichu la trouille, va savoir pourquoi. En tout cas, elle veut signaler la disparition de sa sœur.

— Mais elle n'a pas disparu, fit Ray, exaspéré. Pas si elle a envoyé une carte. Elle n'a juste pas envie qu'on la retrouve. C'est complètement différent.

— C'est ce que je lui ai dit. Bref, tout est là.

Elle lui tendit une pochette en plastique contenant deux pages manuscrites.

— Merci. J'y jetterai un œil. (Ray prit la déclaration et la posa sur l'océan de papiers qui encombrait son bureau.) En supposant que je m'en sorte avec tout ça, tu es toujours partante pour aller boire un verre tout à l'heure ? Je crois que je vais en avoir besoin.

— Plus que jamais !

— Parfait, dit Ray. Tom va quelque part après l'école et je lui ai promis de passer le prendre à sept heures, alors ce sera juste un verre en vitesse.

— Pas de problème. Ça signifie que Tom se fait des amis ?

— Je crois, répondit Ray. Même si ce n'est pas lui qui va me le dire. J'espère qu'on en saura plus quand on ira au collège la semaine prochaine, mais je ne me fais pas trop d'illusions.

— Eh bien, si tu as besoin d'en parler au pub, n'hésite surtout pas, fit Kate. Mais je te préviens, je ne suis pas une experte en adolescents.

Ray rit.

— À vrai dire, ça me fera du bien de parler d'autre chose.

— Alors je serai heureuse de te changer les idées.

Kate sourit, et Ray repensa soudain à ce soir-là, devant chez elle. Kate y repensait-elle aussi parfois ? Il songea à le lui demander, mais elle prenait déjà la direction de son bureau.

Ray sortit son téléphone pour envoyer un message à Mags. Il fixa l'écran, essayant de trouver une formulation qui ne la contrarierait pas sans pour autant être un mensonge pur et simple. Il ne devrait pas avoir à déformer la vérité, pensa-t-il ; après tout, aller boire un verre avec Kate ou avec Stumpy était la même chose. Il ignora la petite voix dans sa tête qui lui expliquait précisément pourquoi c'était différent.

Il soupira et remit le téléphone dans sa poche sans avoir écrit le message. Il était plus facile de ne rien dire du tout. Il jeta un coup d'œil par la porte ouverte et vit le sommet de la tête de Kate tandis qu'elle s'asseyait à son bureau. Elle lui changeait les idées, aucun doute là-dessus, pensa Ray. Mais était-ce vraiment une bonne chose ?

40

J'ai attendu deux semaines avant d'oser me montrer en public, le temps que les bleus sur mes bras passent du violet foncé au vert pâle. Je suis choquée de voir à quel point les contusions ont l'air horribles sur ma peau, alors qu'il y a deux ans elles semblaient faire autant partie de moi que la couleur de mes cheveux.

Je dois sortir pour aller acheter de la nourriture pour chien et je laisse Beau au cottage afin de prendre le car jusqu'à Swansea, où personne ne remarquera une femme déambulant les yeux baissés dans un supermarché, une écharpe nouée autour du cou malgré la température clémente. Je m'engage sur le sentier qui mène au camping, mais je ne parviens pas à me défaire de l'impression que quelqu'un m'observe. Je regarde derrière moi, puis je fais volte-face en me disant que ça doit être de l'autre côté, mais il n'y a personne là non plus. Prise de panique, je tourne sur moi-même, incapable de voir quoi que ce soit à cause des taches noires qui apparaissent devant mes yeux et suivent mon regard partout où il se pose. La peur me noue douloureusement l'estomac et je cours à moitié jusqu'à apercevoir les mobile homes et la boutique de Bethan. Mon cœur commence enfin à ralentir et je m'efforce de retrouver mes esprits. C'est dans ces moments-là que la prison apparaît comme une alternative bienvenue à la vie que je mène.

Le parking de Bethan est réservé aux clients du camping, mais sa proximité avec la plage en fait une option intéressante pour les promeneurs qui désirent emprunter le sentier littoral. Ça ne dérange pas Bethan, sauf en haute saison, quand elle installe de grands panneaux « Parking privé » et sort à toute vitesse de la boutique dès qu'elle voit une famille commencer à décharger son matériel de pique-nique. À cette époque de l'année, quand le camping est fermé, les rares voitures laissées ici appartiennent aux promeneurs de chiens ou aux randonneurs aguerris.

— Vous pouvez l'utiliser, bien sûr, m'a dit Bethan la première fois que je l'ai rencontrée.

— Je n'ai pas de voiture, lui ai-je répondu.

Elle a répliqué que mes invités pouvaient se garer ici et ne m'a jamais fait remarquer que personne n'était venu, à part Patrick, qui laissait son Land Rover sur le parking avant de monter me voir. Je chasse ce souvenir avant qu'il ne s'installe.

Il n'y a pas beaucoup de véhicules aujourd'hui. La vieille Volvo de Bethan, une camionnette que je ne connais pas, et... je plisse les yeux et secoue la tête. Impossible. Ça ne peut pas être ma voiture. Je me mets à transpirer et j'inspire une bouffée d'air en tentant de comprendre ce que je vois. Le pare-chocs avant est abîmé et des fissures dessinent une toile d'araignée de la taille d'un poing au milieu du pare-brise.

C'est ma voiture.

Ça n'a aucun sens ! Quand je suis partie de Bristol, je l'ai laissée derrière moi. Non parce que j'avais peur que la police remonte sa trace – même si ça m'a traversé l'esprit –, mais parce que je ne pouvais plus supporter de la voir. Dans un accès de paranoïa, je me demande si la police l'a retrouvée puis amenée ici pour voir ma réaction, et je balaie le parking du regard comme si des agents armés pouvaient bondir à tout instant sur moi.

Dans ma confusion, je n'arrive pas à savoir si c'est important. Mais ça doit l'être, sinon la police n'aurait pas insisté pour que je leur dise ce que j'avais fait de la voiture. Je dois m'en débarrasser. Je pense aux films que j'ai vus. Est-ce que je pourrais la pousser du haut d'une falaise ? ou la brûler ? Il me faudrait des allumettes et du gaz à briquet, ou peut-être de l'essence – mais comment pourrais-je faire partir le feu sans que Bethan me voie ?

Te laisser partir

Je jette un coup d'œil vers la boutique mais elle n'est pas à la fenêtre, je respire donc à fond et traverse le parking jusqu'à ma voiture. Les clés sont sur le contact et j'ouvre la portière sans hésiter pour m'installer à la place du conducteur. Je suis aussitôt assaillie par des souvenirs de l'accident : j'entends le hurlement de la mère de Jacob, ainsi que mon propre cri horrifié. Je me mets à trembler et tente de me ressaisir. La voiture démarre du premier coup et je sors à toute allure du parking. Si Bethan jette un œil dehors à cet instant, elle ne me verra pas moi, seulement le nuage de poussière qui s'élève derrière le véhicule tandis que je prends la direction de Penfach.

— Ça fait du bien de se retrouver derrière le volant ?

La voix de Ian est mesurée et froide. J'écrase le frein et la voiture vire brusquement à gauche tandis que le volant m'échappe. J'ai déjà la main sur la poignée de la portière quand je réalise que le son provient du lecteur CD.

— Ta petite voiture a dû te manquer, non ? Inutile de me remercier.

Sa voix a un effet immédiat sur moi. Je me fais tout de suite plus petite, m'enfonçant dans le siège comme si je pouvais disparaître à l'intérieur, et j'ai les mains chaudes et moites.

— Tu as oublié nos vœux de mariage, Jennifer ?

Je presse une main sur ma poitrine pour tenter de ralentir les battements frénétiques de mon cœur.

— Tu as promis de m'aimer, de m'honorer et de m'obéir jusqu'à ce que la mort nous sépare.

Il me nargue, reprenant de sa voix froide les vœux que j'ai prononcés il y a tant d'années. Il est fou. Je m'en rends compte à présent, et je suis terrifiée en repensant à toutes ces années passées à ses côtés, sans savoir de quoi il était véritablement capable.

— Tu ne m'honores pas en allant voir la police avec tes histoires, tu ne crois pas, Jennifer ? Tu ne m'obéis pas en leur dévoilant notre intimité. N'oublie pas, tu as toujours eu ce que tu méritais...

Je ne peux plus entendre ça. J'appuie furieusement sur les boutons de l'autoradio et le CD s'éjecte avec une lenteur insoutenable. Je l'arrache de la fente et j'essaie de le casser en deux, mais je ne réussis même pas à le plier et je finis par crier dessus, mon visage hystérique se reflétant sur sa surface brillante. Je sors de la voiture et lance le CD dans la haie.

— Laisse-moi tranquille ! Laisse-moi tranquille !

Je conduis comme une folle, dangereusement, dans les rues bordées de hautes haies de Penfach pour sortir du village et me retrouver dans la campagne. Je tremble violemment et changer de vitesse est au-dessus de mes capacités, je reste donc en deuxième et la voiture hurle son mécontentement. Les mots de Ian résonnent dans ma tête.

Jusqu'à ce que la mort nous sépare.

Je vois une grange délabrée un peu à l'écart de la route, et pas de maisons à proximité. Je tourne dans le chemin cahoteux qui y mène. En approchant, je constate que la grange n'a plus de toit : ses poutres à nu se dressent vers le ciel. À l'intérieur, des pneus et des machines rouillées sont entassés dans un coin. Ça fera l'affaire. Je conduis jusqu'à l'autre bout de la grange et cale la voiture dans un angle. Une bâche vert foncé traîne par terre et je la déplie, me retrouvant couverte d'eau croupie. Je dissimule la voiture dessous. C'est risqué, mais la grange a l'air abandonnée depuis un moment.

J'entame la longue marche jusqu'au cottage, et ça me rappelle le jour de mon arrivée à Penfach, quand ce qui m'attendait était beaucoup plus incertain que ce que je laissais derrière moi. Je sais à présent ce que l'avenir me réserve : il me reste deux semaines à Penfach, puis je retournerai à Bristol pour être jugée, et je serai alors en sécurité.

Il y a un arrêt de car devant moi mais je continue de marcher, réconfortée par la cadence de mes pas. Je me calme peu à peu.

Ian s'amuse avec moi, c'est tout. S'il avait l'intention de me tuer, il l'aurait fait quand il est venu au cottage.

L'après-midi est déjà bien avancé quand j'arrive chez moi, et des nuages sombres s'amoncellent dans le ciel. J'enfile mon imperméable et j'emmène Beau courir sur la plage. Au bord de l'eau, je respire à nouveau, et je sais que c'est ce qui va le plus me manquer.

J'ai la sensation écrasante d'être observée et je tourne le dos à la mer. La peur me prend au ventre quand j'aperçois un homme qui me fait face en haut de la falaise, et mon pouls s'accélère. J'appelle Beau et pose la main sur son collier, mais il aboie et se dégage brusquement de moi pour foncer en direction du sentier, qui monte vers l'endroit où la silhouette se découpe sur le ciel.

— Beau, reviens !

Il ne m'écoute pas et file à toute allure, mais je reste clouée sur place. Ce n'est qu'au moment où il atteint l'autre bout de la plage et gravit agilement le sentier que la silhouette bouge. L'homme se penche pour caresser Beau, et je reconnais aussitôt ces gestes familiers. C'est Patrick.

Je pourrais hésiter à aller à sa rencontre après ce qui s'est passé la dernière fois, mais je suis si soulagée que je marche sans réfléchir dans les traces laissées par Beau pour les rejoindre.

— Comment ça va ? dit-il.

— Bien.

Nous sommes des étrangers cherchant à faire la conversation.

— Je t'ai laissé des messages.

— Je sais.

Je les ai tous ignorés. Au début, je les écoutais, mais ils me rappelaient trop ce que je lui avais fait, et j'ai effacé les suivants. Puis j'ai fini par éteindre mon téléphone.

— Tu me manques, Jenna.

Je trouvais sa colère compréhensible et plus facile à supporter, mais il est à présent calme et suppliant, et je sens ma détermination s'effriter. Je prends la direction du cottage.

— Tu n'as rien à faire ici.

Je suis terrifiée à l'idée que Ian nous voie ensemble, mais je résiste à la tentation de regarder autour de nous pour vérifier que personne ne nous observe.

Je sens une goutte de pluie sur mon visage et je relève ma capuche. Patrick me suit à grandes enjambées.

— Jenna, parle-moi. Arrête de fuir !

Mais c'est ce que j'ai fait toute ma vie, et je ne prends même pas la peine de me justifier.

Un éclair déchire le ciel et la pluie tombe si dru que j'en ai le souffle coupé. Le ciel s'assombrit si vite que nos ombres disparaissent, et Beau se ratatine par terre, les oreilles rabattues. Nous courons jusqu'au cottage et j'ouvre violemment la porte juste au moment où le tonnerre retentit au-dessus de nos têtes. Beau se faufile entre nos jambes et fonce à l'étage. Je l'appelle, mais il ne vient pas.

— Je vais aller voir comment il va. (Patrick monte et je ferme la porte à clé avant de le rejoindre une minute plus tard. Je le retrouve par terre dans ma chambre, Beau tremblant dans ses bras.) Ils sont tous pareils, observe-t-il en esquissant un sourire. Des plus craintifs aux plus féroces, ils ont tous peur du tonnerre et des feux d'artifice.

Je m'agenouille à côté d'eux et caresse la tête de Beau. Il gémit légèrement.

— Qu'est-ce que c'est ? demande Patrick en désignant mon coffret en bois qui dépasse de sous le lit.

— C'est à moi, dis-je sèchement en donnant un grand coup de pied pour le renvoyer à sa place.

Patrick écarquille les yeux mais ne dit rien. Il se met maladroitement debout et emmène Beau en bas.

Te laisser partir

— Ça pourrait être une bonne idée d'allumer la radio pour lui, indique-t-il.

Il parle comme s'il était le vétérinaire et moi la cliente, et je me demande si c'est par habitude ou s'il a décidé que ça commençait à bien faire. Mais une fois qu'il a installé Beau sur le canapé, avec un plaid et Classic FM assez fort pour couvrir les plus petits grondements, il reprend la parole d'une voix plus douce.

— Je m'occuperai de lui.

Je me mords la lèvre.

— Laisse-le ici quand tu partiras, poursuit-il. Tu ne seras pas obligée de me voir, ni de me parler. Laisse-le simplement ici et je viendrai le chercher. Je le garderai pendant que tu seras... (Il marque une pause.) Pendant que tu ne seras pas là.

— Ça pourrait durer des années, dis-je, ma voix se brisant sur ce dernier mot.

— On verra bien, chaque chose en son temps, réplique-t-il.

Il se penche et dépose le plus tendre des baisers sur mon front.

Je lui donne le double de la clé que je garde dans le tiroir de la cuisine et il part sans rien ajouter. Je refoule des larmes qui n'ont pas lieu d'être. C'est mon choix, et je dois l'assumer, peu importe si c'est douloureux. Mon cœur fait un bond dans ma poitrine quand on frappe à la porte à peine cinq minutes plus tard, et j'imagine que Patrick a oublié quelque chose.

J'ouvre la porte.

— Je ne veux plus vous voir ici, dit Iestyn sans préambule.

— Quoi ? (Je m'appuie au mur pour ne pas tomber.) Pourquoi ?

Il ne me regarde pas dans les yeux, préférant cajoler Beau.

— Vous avez jusqu'à demain matin pour faire vos valises.

— Mais, Iestyn, c'est impossible ! Vous savez ce qui se passe. Je suis censée rester à cette adresse jusqu'à mon procès.

— Ce n'est pas mon problème. (Iestyn finit par lever les yeux vers moi et je constate qu'il ne fait pas ça de gaieté de cœur. Il a le visage sévère, mais le regard triste, et il secoue lentement la tête.) Écoutez, Jenna, tout Penfach sait que vous avez été arrêtée pour avoir renversé ce gosse, et ils savent tous que vous êtes là simplement parce que je vous loue ce cottage. Pour eux, j'aurais aussi bien pu être au volant de la voiture. (Il montre le graffiti sur la porte, qui n'a pas voulu partir malgré mes efforts.) Ça, ce n'est que le début. Bientôt, il y aura des crottes de chien dans la boîte aux lettres, des pétards, de l'essence... on lit ça tout le temps dans les journaux.

— Je n'ai nulle part où aller, Iestyn.

J'essaie de l'implorer, mais sa détermination ne faiblit pas.

— Le magasin du village ne veut plus vendre mes produits, continue-t-il. Ils sont écœurés que je donne un toit à une meur-trière. (Je déglutis.) Et ce matin, ils ont refusé de servir Glynis. C'est une chose de s'attaquer à moi, mais s'ils commencent à s'en prendre à ma femme...

— J'ai juste besoin de quelques jours de plus, Iestyn. Mon juge-ment a lieu dans deux semaines, et ensuite je serai partie pour de bon. S'il vous plaît, Iestyn, laissez-moi rester jusque-là.

Iestyn enfonce les mains dans ses poches et fixe un moment l'horizon. J'attends, sachant que je ne peux rien dire d'autre pour le faire changer d'avis.

— Deux semaines, conclut-il. Mais pas un jour de plus. Et si vous avez un minimum de bon sens, vous éviterez le village d'ici là.

41

Tu passais tes journées dans ton atelier, et tu y retournais le soir, sauf quand je te disais de rester. Tu te fichais pas mal que je travaille dur toute la semaine et que je puisse avoir besoin d'un peu de réconfort le soir, qu'on me demande comment s'était passée ma journée. Tu étais comme une petite souris, courant te mettre à l'abri dans ta cabane à la moindre occasion. J'ignore comment, mais tu avais réussi à te faire un nom en tant que sculptrice dans la région ; pas pour tes pots tournés, mais pour tes figurines sculptées à la main. Je ne leur voyais aucun charme, avec leurs visages difformes et leurs membres disproportionnés, mais il y avait apparemment un marché pour ce genre de choses, et tu avais du mal à satisfaire la demande.

— J'ai acheté un DVD pour ce soir, ai-je dit un samedi quand tu es venue dans la cuisine pour faire chauffer de l'eau.

— OK.

Tu ne m'as pas demandé de quel film il s'agissait, et d'ailleurs je n'en savais rien. J'avais décidé de le choisir plus tard.

Tu t'es appuyée contre le plan de travail pendant que l'eau chauffait, les pouces enfoncés dans les poches de ton jean. Tu avais les cheveux détachés, mais coincés derrière les oreilles, et j'ai aperçu l'égratignure sur ta joue. Tu as croisé mon regard et ramené tes cheveux sur ton visage pour la dissimuler.

— Tu veux un café ? m'as-tu demandé.

— Oui, merci. (Tu as versé de l'eau dans deux tasses, mais du café dans une seule.) Tu n'en bois pas ?

— Je ne me sens pas très bien. (Tu as coupé une tranche de citron et tu l'as mise dans ta tasse.) Ça fait quelques jours que je ne suis pas dans mon assiette.

Te laisser partir

— Ma chérie, tu aurais dû me le dire. Viens, assieds-toi.

J'ai tiré une chaise pour toi, mais tu as secoué la tête.

— C'est bon, je suis juste un peu patraque. Ça ira sûrement mieux demain.

Je t'ai enlacée et j'ai pressé ma joue contre la tienne.

— Ma pauvre chérie. Je vais prendre soin de toi.

Tu as passé tes bras autour de moi et je t'ai bercée tendrement, jusqu'à ce que tu te dégages de mon étreinte. Je n'aimais pas quand tu faisais ça. J'avais l'impression d'être rejeté, alors que j'essayais seulement de te réconforter. J'ai senti ma mâchoire se serrer et j'ai aussitôt vu un éclair de vigilance traverser ton regard. J'étais à la fois contrarié et content de le voir – ça me montrait que tu faisais encore attention à ce que je pensais, à ce que je faisais.

J'ai levé le bras vers toi et tu as eu un mouvement de recul, retenant ta respiration en fermant les yeux. Je t'ai effleuré le front et j'ai délicatement enlevé quelque chose que tu avais dans les cheveux.

— Une coccinelle, ai-je dit en ouvrant le poing pour te la montrer. C'est censé porter bonheur, non ?

Tu ne te sentais pas mieux le jour suivant, et j'ai insisté pour que tu restes au lit. Je t'ai apporté des biscuits secs pour calmer ton estomac barbouillé, et je t'ai fait la lecture jusqu'à ce que tu me dises que tu avais mal à la tête. Je voulais appeler le médecin, mais tu m'as promis que tu irais le voir le lundi matin à l'ouverture du cabinet. Je t'ai caressé les cheveux puis j'ai vu tes paupières trembler dans ton sommeil, et je me suis demandé de quoi tu rêvais.

Tu dormais encore quand je suis parti le lundi matin et je t'ai laissé un mot à côté de ton oreiller pour te rappeler d'aller voir le médecin. Je t'ai appelée du travail, mais tu n'as pas répondu, et j'ai eu beau réessayer toutes les demi-heures, le fixe sonnait dans le vide et ton portable était éteint. Je me faisais un sang d'encre, et à midi j'ai décidé de rentrer pour voir si tout allait bien.

Te laisser partir

Ta voiture était devant la maison, et quand j'ai tourné la clé dans la serrure je me suis aperçu que la porte n'était pas fermée. Tu étais assise sur le canapé, la tête entre les mains.

— Ça va ? J'étais mort d'inquiétude !

Tu as levé la tête mais tu n'as rien dit.

— Jennifer ! Je t'ai appelée toute la matinée. Pourquoi tu n'as pas décroché ?

— Je suis sortie, as-tu répondu. Et après...

Tu t'es arrêtée sans raison.

La colère est montée en moi.

— Il ne t'est pas venu à l'idée que je pouvais m'inquiéter ?

Je t'ai attrapée par le col de ton pull et je t'ai relevée. Tu as crié, et ce son m'a brouillé les idées. Je t'ai poussée à travers la pièce pour te plaquer contre le mur, ma main sur ta gorge. J'ai senti ton pouls s'accélérer.

— S'il te plaît, arrête ! as-tu crié.

Lentement, doucement, j'ai enfoncé mes doigts dans ton cou, voyant ma main se refermer comme si elle appartenait à quelqu'un d'autre. Tu as suffoqué.

— Je suis enceinte.

Je t'ai lâchée.

— C'est impossible.

— C'est la vérité.

— Mais tu prends la pilule !

Tu t'es mise à pleurer et tu t'es laissée glisser contre le mur pour t'asseoir par terre, les bras autour des genoux. Je suis resté debout, essayant d'assimiler ce que j'avais entendu. Tu étais enceinte.

— Ça doit être la fois où j'ai vomi, as-tu dit.

Je me suis accroupi pour te prendre dans mes bras. J'ai pensé à mon père, tellement froid et distant, et je me suis juré de ne jamais être comme lui avec mon enfant. J'espérais que ce serait un garçon. Il m'admirerait et voudrait me ressembler. Je n'ai pas pu m'empêcher de sourire.

Tu as lâché tes genoux et tu m'as regardé. Tu tremblais et je t'ai caressé la joue.

— On va avoir un bébé !

Tes yeux étaient encore brillants, mais ton visage s'est lentement détendu.

— Tu n'es pas fâché ?

— Pourquoi je serais fâché ?

J'étais euphorique. Ça allait tout changer. Je t'ai imaginée le ventre rond et plein, dépendante de moi pour manger sainement, ravie que je te masse les pieds ou que je t'apporte le thé. Quand le bébé serait là, tu arrêterais de travailler et je subviendrais à vos besoins à tous les deux. J'ai vu notre avenir défiler dans ma tête.

— C'est un bébé miracle ! me suis-je exclamé. (Je t'ai prise par les épaules et tu t'es crispée.) Je sais que tout n'a pas été parfait entre nous ces derniers temps, mais ce sera différent maintenant. Je vais prendre soin de toi. (Tu m'as regardé droit dans les yeux et j'ai senti une vague de culpabilité me submerger.) Tout va bien se passer maintenant. Je t'aime tellement, Jennifer.

De nouvelles larmes ont jailli de tes paupières.

— Moi aussi.

Je voulais te demander pardon – pardon pour toutes les fois où je t'avais fait du mal –, mais les mots sont restés coincés dans ma gorge.

— N'en parle jamais à personne, ai-je dit à la place.

— Parler de quoi ?

— De nos disputes. Promets-moi que tu n'en parleras jamais à personne.

J'ai senti tes épaules se contracter sous mes doigts, et tes yeux se sont agrandis de peur.

— Jamais, as-tu consenti dans un murmure, à peine plus qu'un souffle. Je n'en parlerai jamais à personne.

J'ai souri.

— Maintenant, arrête de pleurer. Il ne faut pas stresser le bébé. (Je me suis mis debout et je t'ai tendu la main pour t'aider à te relever.) Tu as la nausée ?

Tu as acquiescé.

— Allonge-toi. Je vais te chercher une couverture.

Tu as protesté mais je t'ai accompagnée jusqu'au canapé et je t'ai aidée à t'allonger. Tu portais mon fils, et j'avais bien l'intention de prendre soin de vous deux.

Tu étais inquiète avant la première échographie.

— Et si quelque chose ne va pas ?

— Pourquoi quelque chose n'irait pas ? ai-je rétorqué.

J'ai pris ma journée et je t'ai emmenée à l'hôpital en voiture.

— Il peut déjà fermer le poing. C'est incroyable, non ? t'es-tu exclamée en lisant l'un de tes nombreux livres sur la maternité.

Tu étais devenue obsédée par la grossesse. Tu achetais d'innombrables magazines et tu passais ton temps sur Internet à chercher des conseils sur l'accouchement et l'allaitement. Quoi que je dise, la conversation revenait toujours aux prénoms d'enfants ou au matériel qu'on devrait acheter.

— Incroyable, ai-je répondu, même si je le savais déjà.

La grossesse ne se passait pas comme je l'avais prévu. Tu voulais à tout prix continuer de travailler autant qu'avant, et même si tu acceptais que je t'apporte le thé et que je te masse les pieds, ça n'avait pas l'air de te ravir. Tu faisais plus attention à notre enfant à naître – un enfant qui n'avait même pas encore conscience qu'on parlait de lui – qu'à ton propre mari, qui se trouvait pourtant juste en face de toi. Je t'ai imaginée en train de t'occuper de notre nouveau-né, oubliant jusqu'à mon rôle dans sa création, et je t'ai soudain revue jouer pendant des heures avec ce chaton.

Tu m'as pris la main quand l'échographiste a enduit ton ventre de gel, et tu l'as serrée fort jusqu'à ce qu'on distingue une petite forme sur l'écran, accompagnée d'un battement de cœur étouffé.

— Voilà la tête, a dit l'échographiste. Et vous devriez arriver à voir ses bras... regardez, il vous fait coucou !

Tu as ri.

— Il ? ai-je demandé, plein d'espoir.

L'échographiste a levé les yeux.

— Façon de parler. On ne pourra pas savoir le sexe avant un petit moment encore. Mais tout va bien. (Elle a imprimé un cliché et te l'a donné.) Félicitations.

On avait rendez-vous avec la sage-femme une demi-heure plus tard, et on s'est assis dans la salle d'attente aux côtés d'une demi-douzaine d'autres couples. Il y avait une femme en face de nous avec un ventre monstrueusement gros qui l'obligeait à s'asseoir en écartant les jambes. J'ai détourné le regard, j'étais soulagé quand on nous a appelés.

La sage-femme a pris ton carnet de maternité et l'a parcouru. Elle a vérifié les renseignements et sorti des fiches d'informations sur l'alimentation et l'hygiène de vie pendant la grossesse.

— C'est déjà une experte, ai-je fait. Elle a lu tellement de livres qu'elle doit déjà tout savoir.

La sage-femme m'a dévisagé.

— Et vous, M. Petersen ? Vous êtes un expert ?

— Je n'ai pas besoin, ai-je dit en soutenant son regard. Ce n'est pas moi qui suis enceinte.

Elle n'a pas répondu.

— Je vais prendre votre tension, Jenna. Relevez votre manche et posez le bras sur le bureau, s'il vous plaît.

Tu as hésité et j'ai mis une seconde à comprendre pourquoi. Ma mâchoire s'est serrée mais je me suis adossé à ma chaise, observant les opérations avec une indifférence feinte.

Le bleu sur le haut de ton bras était marbré de vert. Il s'était considérablement estompé au cours des derniers jours, mais il était tenace, comme toujours. J'avais beau savoir que c'était impossible, j'avais parfois l'impression que tu faisais exprès de les garder, pour me rappeler ce qui s'était passé, pour me pousser à me sentir coupable.

La sage-femme n'a rien dit, et je me suis légèrement détendu. Elle a pris ta tension, qui était un peu élevée, et l'a notée. Puis elle s'est tournée vers moi.

— Si vous voulez bien passer dans la salle d'attente, j'aimerais parler un instant avec Jenna en privé.

— Ce n'est pas nécessaire, ai-je dit. On ne se cache rien.

— C'est la procédure standard, a répliqué sèchement la sage-femme.

Je l'ai fixée mais elle n'a pas cédé, et je me suis levé.

— Très bien.

J'ai pris mon temps pour quitter la pièce, et je suis allé attendre près de la machine à café, d'où je pouvais voir la porte du cabinet.

J'ai regardé les autres couples : il n'y avait aucun homme seul – personne d'autre n'était traité de la sorte. Je me suis dirigé d'un pas résolu vers le cabinet de consultation et j'ai ouvert la porte sans frapper. Tu avais quelque chose dans la main et tu l'as glissé entre les pages de ton carnet de maternité. Une petite carte rectangulaire : bleu pâle, avec une sorte de logo.

— Il faut qu'on bouge la voiture, Jennifer, ai-je fait. On n'a le droit qu'à une heure de parking.

— Ah, d'accord. Désolée.

Ce dernier mot était adressé à la sage-femme, qui t'a souri et m'a ignoré. Elle s'est penchée et a posé la main sur ton bras.

— Notre numéro se trouve sur la couverture de votre carnet de grossesse. Si vous avez une question, à propos de quoi que ce soit, n'hésitez surtout pas.

On a roulé en silence. Tu tenais l'échographie sur tes genoux et je te voyais poser de temps en temps une main sur ton ventre, comme si tu essayais de faire le lien entre les deux.

— De quoi voulait te parler la sage-femme ? t'ai-je demandé en arrivant à la maison.

— De mes antécédents médicaux, as-tu répondu, mais c'était trop rapide, trop préparé.

Je savais que tu mentais. Quand tu t'es endormie, j'ai cherché la carte bleu pâle avec le logo rond dans ton carnet, mais elle n'était plus là.

Je t'ai vue changer au fur et à mesure que ton ventre grossissait. Je pensais que tu aurais davantage besoin de moi, mais tu devenais au contraire plus autonome, plus forte. J'étais en train de te perdre à cause de ce bébé, et je ne savais pas comment te récupérer.

Il faisait chaud cet été-là, et tu semblais prendre plaisir à te balader dans la maison avec une jupe baissée sous le ventre et un petit tee-shirt remonté au-dessus. Ton nombril était à l'air et je ne supportais pas de le voir ; je ne comprenais pas pourquoi tu tenais à te trimbaler comme ça, même pour aller ouvrir la porte quand quelqu'un frappait.

Tu as arrêté de travailler, même si l'accouchement n'était pas prévu avant plusieurs semaines, et j'ai donc dit à la femme de ménage de ne plus venir. C'était ridicule de continuer à payer quelqu'un alors que tu restais toute la journée à la maison sans rien faire.

Un jour, je t'ai laissé du repassage, et quand je suis rentré, tu l'avais fini et la maison était impeccable. Tu avais l'air épuisée, et j'étais touché par tes efforts. J'ai décidé de te faire couler un bain, de te bichonner un peu. Je me suis demandé si tu avais envie qu'on commande à manger ou que je cuisine pour toi. J'ai monté les chemises à l'étage et ouvert les robinets avant de t'appeler.

Je pendais les chemises dans l'armoire quand j'ai remarqué quelque chose.

— Qu'est-ce que c'est que ça ?

Tu as aussitôt pâli.

— Une brûlure. Je suis vraiment désolée. Le téléphone a sonné, et j'ai été distraite. Mais c'est en bas, ça ne se verra pas si tu la rentres dans ton pantalon.

Tu étais dans tous tes états, mais ce n'était vraiment pas grave. C'était juste une chemise. Je l'ai posée et j'ai fait un pas en avant pour t'enlacer, mais tu as eu un mouvement de recul et mis un bras autour de ton ventre pour le protéger, détournant le visage en grimaçant. Tu redoutais quelque chose que je n'avais aucune intention de faire, qui n'avait aucune raison d'arriver.

Mais c'est arrivé. Et tu ne peux t'en prendre qu'à toi-même.

42

Le téléphone de Ray sonna tandis qu'il garait sa voiture sur la dernière place libre de la cour. Il appuya sur le bouton « accepter » de son kit mains libres et se retourna pour voir s'il pouvait encore reculer.

Le préfet de police Rippon alla droit au but.

— Je veux que vous lanciez l'opération Falcon aujourd'hui.

La Mondeo de Ray percuta la Volvo bleue garée derrière lui.

— Merde !

— Ce n'est pas vraiment la réponse que j'attendais.

Il y avait dans la voix du préfet une note amusée que Ray n'avait jamais entendue auparavant. Il se demanda ce qui pouvait bien l'avoir mise de si bonne humeur.

— Pardon, madame.

Ray descendit de sa voiture, laissant les clés sur le contact au cas où le propriétaire de la Volvo aurait besoin de sortir. Il jeta un coup d'œil au pare-chocs mais ne vit aucune marque.

— Vous disiez ?

— Le briefing de l'opération Falcon est prévu pour lundi, recommença Olivia avec une patience inhabituelle. Mais je veux que vous l'avanciez. Vous avez peut-être vu aux informations ce matin que plusieurs forces de police ont été critiquées pour leur manque de fermeté envers le trafic de drogue.

Ah ! pensa Ray. Ça expliquait la bonne humeur.

— C'est le moment idéal pour durcir notre position. La presse nationale a déjà été informée de l'opération à venir. Je veux que vous rassembliez vos équipes quelques jours plus tôt.

Le sang de Ray se figea dans ses veines.

— C'est impossible aujourd'hui, dit-il.

Il y eut un blanc.

Ray attendit que le préfet parle, mais le silence s'étira jusqu'à ce qu'il éprouve le besoin de le combler.

— J'ai rendez-vous au collège de mon fils à midi.

Le bruit courait qu'Olivia assistait aux réunions de parents d'élèves à l'école de ses enfants par téléconférence, Ray savait donc que cet argument avait peu de chance de la faire changer d'avis.

— Ray, reprit-elle, toute trace d'humour envolée. Comme vous le savez, je suis extrêmement solidaire des personnes avec des enfants à charge, et j'ai d'ailleurs défendu la mise en place d'horaires aménagés pour les parents. Mais, sauf erreur de ma part, vous avez une *femme*, n'est-ce pas ?

— Absolument.

— Et va-t-elle à ce rendez-vous ?

— Oui.

— Alors, si je puis me permettre, où est le problème ?

Ray s'adossa au mur près de la porte de derrière et leva les yeux vers le ciel à la recherche d'inspiration, mais ne trouva que d'épais nuages noirs.

— Mon fils se fait harceler à l'école, madame. Sérieusement, je crois. C'est la première fois que nous avons la possibilité d'en parler avec le collège depuis qu'ils ont admis qu'il y avait un problème, et ma femme veut que je vienne. (Ray s'en voulut de rejeter la faute sur Mags.) Je veux y être, ajouta-t-il. Je dois y être.

Le ton d'Olivia s'adoucit légèrement.

— Vous m'en voyez désolée, Ray. Les enfants nous causent parfois bien du souci. Si vous estimez devoir aller à ce rendez-vous, allez-y, bien entendu. Mais l'opération sera lancée aujourd'hui, avec la couverture médiatique nationale dont nous avons besoin pour promouvoir notre politique de tolérance zéro. Et si vous ne pouvez pas vous en charger, eh bien je trouverai quelqu'un d'autre. Je vous rappelle dans une heure.

— Tu parles d'un choix ! grommela Ray en remettant le téléphone dans sa poche.

C'était simple : sa carrière d'un côté, sa famille de l'autre. Une fois dans son bureau, il ferma la porte et s'installa dans son fauteuil en joignant le bout des doigts. L'opération d'aujourd'hui était importante et il ne se faisait pas la moindre illusion quant au fait qu'il s'agissait d'un test. Avait-il les qualités requises pour grimper de nouveaux échelons dans la police ? Il n'en était même plus convaincu lui-même – il ne savait même pas s'il le voulait vraiment. Il songea à la nouvelle voiture dont ils auraient besoin dans un an ou deux ; aux vacances à l'étranger que les enfants commenceraient à réclamer d'ici peu de temps ; à la maison plus grande que méritait Mags. Il avait deux enfants intelligents qu'il espérait voir aller à l'université, et où trouverait-il l'argent pour financer cela s'il ne continuait pas à monter en grade ? Rien n'était possible sans sacrifices.

Il respira à fond et décrocha le téléphone pour appeler Mags.

Le lancement de l'opération Falcon fut un triomphe. Des journalistes furent invités dans la salle de conférences de la préfecture pour un point presse d'une demi-heure, au cours duquel le préfet présenta Ray comme « l'un des meilleurs policiers de la région ». Ray ressentit une poussée d'adrénaline en répondant aux questions sur l'ampleur du problème de la drogue à Bristol, les méthodes employées par la police pour faire respecter la loi, et son investissement personnel pour éradiquer le trafic à ciel ouvert et rétablir la sécurité des habitants. Quand le reporter d'ITN lui demanda s'il avait quelque chose à ajouter, Ray s'adressa directement à la caméra.

— Il y a des gens dans cette ville qui vendent de la drogue en toute impunité et qui pensent que la police est incapable de les arrêter. Mais nous avons des moyens et nous sommes déterminés.

Et nous ne relâcherons pas nos efforts tant que les rues ne seront pas débarrassées des dealers.

Il y eut quelques applaudissements et Ray jeta un coup d'œil au préfet, qui hocha presque imperceptiblement la tête. Les perquisitions avaient été menées plus tôt, avec à la clé quatorze arrestations dans six endroits différents. La fouille des maisons allait prendre des heures, et il se demanda comment Kate s'en sortait en tant que responsable des pièces à conviction.

Dès qu'il en eut l'opportunité, il l'appela.

— Tu tombes à pic, fit-elle. Tu es au poste ?

— Je suis dans mon bureau. Pourquoi ?

— Retrouve-moi à la cantine dans dix minutes. J'ai quelque chose à te montrer.

Il s'y trouvait cinq minutes plus tard, attendant impatiemment Kate, qui déboula en trombe avec un grand sourire.

— Tu veux un café ? demanda-t-il.

— Pas le temps, je dois y retourner. Mais vise un peu ça.

Elle sortit un sachet en plastique transparent. À l'intérieur se trouvait une carte bleu pâle.

— Jenna Gray avait la même dans son portefeuille, observa Ray. Où l'as-tu trouvée ?

— Dans l'une des maisons de ce matin. Mais ce n'est pas tout à fait la même. (Elle lissa le plastique pour que Ray puisse lire l'inscription.) Même carte, même logo, mais adresse différente.

— Intéressant. C'était la maison de qui ?

— Dominica Letts. Elle refuse de parler tant que son avocat n'est pas là. (Kate regarda sa montre.) Merde ! Il faut que j'y aille. (Elle tendit le sachet à Ray.) Tu peux la garder, j'en ai une autre.

Elle sourit à nouveau et disparut, laissant Ray examiner la carte. L'adresse n'avait rien de particulier – un quartier résidentiel comme Grantham Street –, mais Ray se dit qu'il devrait quand même pouvoir tirer quelque chose de ce logo. Le bas des huit était ouvert et ils étaient empilés l'un sur l'autre, comme des poupées russes.

Ray secoua la tête. Il devait encore aller voir si tout se passait bien avec les gardes à vue avant de rentrer chez lui, puis vérifier une dernière fois que tout était prêt pour le jugement de Gray demain. Il plia le sachet et le mit dans sa poche.

Il était plus de vingt-deux heures quand Ray monta dans sa voiture et, pour la première fois depuis le matin, il se demanda s'il avait pris la bonne décision en faisant passer son travail avant sa famille. Il y réfléchit pendant tout le trajet ; une fois arrivé devant chez lui, il était convaincu d'avoir fait le bon choix. Le *seul* choix, en réalité. Jusqu'à ce qu'il tourne la clé dans la serrure et entende Mags pleurer.

— Bon sang, Mags, qu'est-ce qui s'est passé ? (Il abandonna son sac dans l'entrée et vint s'agenouiller devant le canapé, lui relevant les cheveux pour voir son visage.) Tom va bien ?

— Non, il ne va pas bien !

Elle repoussa ses mains.

— Qu'est-ce qu'ils ont dit à l'école ?

— Ça dure depuis au moins un an, d'après eux, mais la principale dit qu'elle ne pouvait rien faire sans preuves.

— Et ils en ont maintenant ?

Mags partit dans un grand éclat de rire.

— Ah ça, oui ! Apparemment, ça fait le tour du Net. Défis de vols à l'étalage, *happy slapping*, la totale. Tout a été filmé et posté sur YouTube pour que le monde entier en profite.

Ray sentit son estomac se serrer en pensant à ce que Tom avait dû endurer.

— Il dort ? demanda Ray en faisant un signe de tête en direction des chambres.

— J'imagine. Il doit être épuisé : je viens de passer une heure et demie à lui hurler dessus.

— Lui hurler dessus ? (Ray se leva.) Nom de Dieu, Mags, il en a déjà assez bavé comme ça, tu ne crois pas ?

Il se dirigea vers l'escalier, mais Mags le rattrapa.

— Tu ne comprends vraiment rien, hein ?

Ray la contempla d'un air ahuri.

— Tu es tellement absorbé par ton boulot que tu ne sais même pas ce qui se passe sous ton propre toit ! Tom ne se fait pas harceler, Ray. C'est *lui* qui harcèle les autres.

Ray eut l'impression de recevoir un coup de poing.

— Quelqu'un doit l'obliger à...

— Personne ne l'oblige à faire quoi que ce soit, l'interrompit Mags, plus gentiment. (Elle soupira et se rassit.) Tom semble être le chef d'un petit « gang » influent. Ils seraient six, parmi lesquels Philip Martin et Connor Axtell.

— Évidemment, remarqua Ray d'un ton sinistre en reconnaissant les noms.

— Ce qui est certain, c'est que c'est Tom qui fait la loi. C'était son idée de sécher les cours ; c'était son idée d'attendre les élèves à la sortie du centre d'éducation spécialisée...

Ray eut la nausée.

— Et les affaires sous son lit ? demanda-t-il.

— Volées sur commande, apparemment. Et aucune par Tom lui-même. De toute évidence, il n'aime pas se salir les mains.

Ray n'avait jamais entendu une telle amertume dans la voix de Mags.

— Qu'est-ce qu'on va faire ?

Quand quelque chose n'allait pas au boulot, il y avait un règlement auquel se raccrocher. Des protocoles, des lois, des manuels. Une équipe autour de lui. Ray se sentait totalement démuni.

— On va régler ça, répondit simplement Mags. On va présenter nos excuses aux gens à qui Tom a fait du mal, on va rendre les choses qu'il a volées, et – surtout – on va tâcher de découvrir pourquoi il fait ça.

Ray resta un moment silencieux. Il eut du mal à l'énoncer à haute voix, mais une fois que cette pensée lui eut traversé l'esprit, il ne put la garder pour lui.

— Est-ce que c'est ma faute ? dit-il. Parce que je n'ai pas été là pour lui ?

Mags lui prit la main.

— Arrête, tu vas te rendre fou. C'est autant ma faute que la tienne. Je ne m'en suis pas aperçue non plus.

— J'aurais quand même dû passer plus de temps à la maison.

Mags ne le contredit pas.

— Je suis vraiment désolé, Mags. Ce ne sera pas toujours comme ça, je te le promets. Il faut juste que j'arrive à devenir commissaire, et ensuite…

— Mais tu adores ton boulot de capitaine.

— Oui, mais…

— Alors pourquoi vouloir à tout prix une promotion ?

Ray resta un instant médusé.

— Eh bien, pour nous. Pour qu'on puisse avoir une plus grande maison et que tu ne sois pas obligée de retourner au travail.

— Mais je veux retravailler ! (Mags se tourna vers lui, exaspérée.) Les enfants sont à l'école toute la journée, toi tu es au travail… je veux faire quelque chose pour *moi*. Envisager une nouvelle carrière me permet d'avoir un objectif, et ça ne m'était pas arrivé depuis longtemps. (Elle dévisagea Ray et son regard s'adoucit.) Gros bêta, va !

— Je suis désolé, répéta-t-il.

Mags se pencha pour l'embrasser sur le front.

— Oublie Tom pour ce soir. Il n'ira pas à l'école demain et on lui parlera à ce moment-là. Pour l'instant, parlons plutôt de nous.

En ouvrant les yeux, Ray vit Mags poser doucement une tasse de thé sur la table de chevet.

— Je me suis dit que tu voudrais te lever tôt, fit-elle. C'est le jugement de Gray aujourd'hui, non ?

— Oui, mais Kate peut y aller. (Ray se redressa.) Je vais rester pour parler à Tom avec toi.

— Et rater ton heure de gloire ? Ne t'en fais pas pour ça. Vas-y. Tom et moi, on va s'occuper tous les deux à la maison, comme quand il était petit. J'ai l'impression que ce n'est pas de parler dont il a besoin, mais d'être écouté.

Ray fut impressionné par sa sagesse.

— Tu feras une très bonne prof, Mags. (Il lui prit la main.) Je ne te mérite pas.

Mags sourit.

— Peut-être, mais tu dois faire avec moi, j'en ai bien peur.

Elle lui pressa la main et descendit au rez-de-chaussée, le laissant boire son thé tranquillement. Il se demanda depuis combien de temps il faisait passer son travail avant sa famille, et éprouva de la honte en réalisant qu'il n'avait jamais agi autrement. Il fallait que ça change. Il devait privilégier Mags et les enfants. Comment avait-il pu ignorer à ce point les besoins de Mags et passer à côté du fait qu'elle *voulait* retourner au travail ? À l'évidence, il n'était pas le seul à trouver la vie un peu monotone parfois. Mags avait remédié à ça en envisageant une nouvelle carrière. Et lui, qu'avait-il fait ? Il pensa à Kate et se sentit rougir.

Ray se doucha et s'habilla, puis descendit à la recherche de son veston.

— Il est là ! cria Mags en sortant du salon avec. (Elle désigna le sachet en plastique qui dépassait de la poche.) Qu'est-ce que c'est ?

Ray le prit et le lui tendit.

— Quelque chose qui pourrait être lié à l'affaire Gray. J'essaie de comprendre ce que représente le logo.

Mags leva le sachet et examina la carte.

— C'est quelqu'un qui prend quelqu'un d'autre dans ses bras, non ? dit-elle sans hésiter.

Ray resta bouche bée. Il regarda la carte et vit tout de suite ce que Mags avait décrit. Ce qui lui avait semblé être un huit inachevé et disproportionné était en réalité une tête et des épaules, dont les bras entouraient une silhouette plus petite qui faisait écho aux lignes de la première.

— Bien sûr ! s'exclama-t-il.

Il repensa à la maison de Grantham Street, avec ses multiples serrures et ses rideaux tirés. Il songea à Jenna Gray, à son regard fuyant, et une image commença lentement à se former dans son esprit.

Des bruits de pas résonnèrent dans l'escalier et Tom fit son apparition quelques secondes plus tard, l'air inquiet. Ray le dévisagea. Pendant des mois, il avait considéré à tort son fils comme une victime.

— J'ai tout faux, dit-il à haute voix.

— À propos de quoi ? demanda Mags.

Mais Ray était déjà parti.

43

L'entrée de la cour d'assises de Bristol est cachée dans une rue étroite baptisée à juste titre Small Street.

— Je vais devoir vous déposer là, ma belle, me dit le chauffeur de taxi. (S'il m'a reconnue d'après la photo dans le journal d'aujourd'hui, il ne le montre pas.) Il se passe quelque chose devant le tribunal, je n'amène pas mon taxi là-bas.

Il s'arrête à l'angle de la rue, où une bande de costards-cravates sûrs d'eux sort du All Bar One après un déjeuner arrosé. L'un d'eux me reluque.

— Tu viens boire un verre, ma jolie ?

Je détourne le regard.

— Espèce de salope frigide ! marmonne-t-il, et ses amis éclatent de rire.

Je respire à fond, tâchant de maîtriser ma panique tandis que je scrute la rue à la recherche de Ian. Est-ce qu'il est là ? Est-ce qu'il m'observe en ce moment même ?

Les hauts bâtiments qui bordent Small Street penchent vers la rue, créant une atmosphère sombre et remplie d'échos qui me donne des frissons. Je n'ai pas fait plus de quelques pas quand je comprends de quoi parlait le chauffeur de taxi. Une partie de la rue est bloquée par des barrières de sécurité, derrière lesquelles une trentaine de manifestants sont regroupés. Plusieurs ont une pancarte sur l'épaule, et la barrière juste devant eux est recouverte d'un immense drap où le mot « MEURTRIÈRE ! » est peint en grosses lettres rouges dégoulinantes. Deux policiers en veste fluorescente se trouvent à côté du groupe, nullement perturbés par le slogan que j'entends à l'autre bout de Small Street.

— Justice pour Jacob ! Justice pour Jacob !

Je marche lentement vers le tribunal, regrettant de ne pas avoir pris une écharpe ou des lunettes noires. Du coin de l'œil, je remarque un homme sur le trottoir d'en face. Il est appuyé contre le mur, mais quand il me voit, il se redresse et sort un téléphone de sa poche. J'accélère le pas pour atteindre au plus vite l'entrée de la cour d'assises, mais l'homme marche à la même allure que moi de l'autre côté de la rue. Il passe un coup de fil qui dure quelques secondes. Il porte un sac noir en bandoulière et je m'aperçois soudain que les poches de son gilet beige sont bourrées d'objectifs. Il court devant, ouvre le sac et sort un appareil photo, puis monte un objectif dans un mouvement fluide dû à des années de pratique et me tire le portrait.

Je vais ignorer les manifestants, me dis-je, haletante. Je vais entrer dans le tribunal comme si de rien n'était. Ils ne peuvent rien me faire – la police est là pour les contenir derrière ces barrières –, je vais donc agir comme s'ils n'étaient pas là.

Mais quand je tourne vers l'entrée de la cour d'assises, je vois la journaliste qui m'a abordée à la sortie du tribunal de première instance.

— Un mot pour le *Post*, Jenna ? C'est l'occasion de donner votre version des faits.

Je me retourne, et je reste paralysée en m'apercevant que je fais à présent face aux manifestants. Le slogan laisse place aux cris et aux huées, et il y a tout à coup un mouvement de foule dans ma direction. Une barrière bascule et s'écrase sur les pavés, produisant un son qui résonne comme un coup de feu dans la rue. Les policiers arrivent mollement, les bras écartés, et repoussent les manifestants. Certains crient encore, mais la plupart rient et discutent entre eux comme s'ils étaient juste venus ici passer un peu de bon temps entre amis.

Tandis que le groupe recule et que les policiers remettent les barrières en place autour de la zone réservée aux manifestants, je me retrouve nez à nez avec une femme. Elle est plus jeune que moi — elle ne doit pas avoir trente ans — et, contrairement aux autres manifestants, elle n'a ni banderole ni pancarte, mais quelque chose à la main. Elle porte une robe marron un peu courte avec des collants noirs et des tennis blanches en piteux état qui jurent avec le reste, et son manteau est ouvert, en dépit du froid.

— C'était un bébé tellement sage, dit-elle doucement.

Je vois aussitôt la ressemblance avec Jacob. Ces yeux bleu pâle un peu retroussés, ce visage en forme de cœur se terminant par un petit menton pointu.

Les manifestants se taisent. Tout le monde nous observe.

— Il ne pleurait presque jamais ; même quand il était malade, il se serrait simplement contre moi en me regardant et il attendait que ça passe.

Elle parle très bien anglais, mais avec un accent que je ne reconnais pas – d'Europe de l'Est, peut-être. Sa voix est mesurée, comme si elle récitait un texte appris par cœur, et bien qu'elle ne laisse rien paraître, j'ai l'impression que cette rencontre l'effraie autant que moi. Peut-être même plus.

— Je l'ai eu très jeune. J'étais moi-même encore une enfant. Son père ne voulait pas que je le garde, mais je n'ai pas pu me résoudre à avorter. Je l'aimais déjà trop. (Elle parle calmement, sans émotion.) Jacob était tout ce que j'avais.

Mes yeux se remplissent de larmes, et je m'en veux de réagir comme ça alors que la mère de Jacob a les yeux secs. Je me force à ne pas bouger, à ne pas essuyer mes joues. Je sais qu'elle pense à ce soir-là, comme moi, quand elle a fixé le pare-brise couvert de pluie, les yeux plissés à cause de la lumière aveuglante des phares. Aujourd'hui, il n'y a rien entre nous, et elle me voit aussi bien que je la vois. Je me demande pourquoi elle ne se jette pas sur moi pour me frapper, me mordre ou me griffer. J'ignore si je serais capable d'agir avec autant de retenue à sa place.

— Anya !

Un homme la hèle depuis la foule de manifestants, mais elle l'ignore. Elle me tend une photo, m'obligeant à la prendre.

Ce n'est pas celle que j'ai vue dans les journaux ni sur Internet ; ce large sourire aux dents du bonheur dans son uniforme scolaire, la tête légèrement tournée pour le photographe. Sur celle-ci, Jacob est plus jeune – il doit avoir trois ou quatre ans. Il est blotti au creux du bras de sa mère, tous deux sont allongés sur le dos dans de hautes herbes parsemées d'aigrettes de pissenlit. L'angle de la photo suggère qu'Anya l'a prise elle-même : elle a le bras tendu comme pour attraper quelque chose hors du cadre. Jacob regarde l'appareil. Il plisse les yeux à cause du soleil et rit. Anya rit elle aussi, mais elle est tournée vers Jacob, et le visage de son fils se reflète dans ses yeux.

— Je suis navrée, dis-je.

Ces mots semblent dérisoires, mais je ne trouve rien d'autre à dire, et je ne supporte pas de rester silencieuse face à son chagrin.

— Vous avez des enfants ?

Je pense à mon fils, à son corps atrocement léger enveloppé dans la couverture de l'hôpital, à cette douleur dans mes entrailles qui ne m'a jamais quittée. Il devrait y avoir un mot pour une mère sans enfant, pour une femme privée du bébé qui l'aurait comblée.

— Non.

Je cherche quelque chose à dire, mais rien ne vient. Je tends la photo à Anya, qui secoue la tête.

— Je n'en ai pas besoin, dit-elle. Son visage est là. (Elle pose sa paume à plat sur sa poitrine.) Mais vous. (Elle marque une pause.) Je crois que vous devez vous rappeler. Vous devez vous rappeler que c'était un petit garçon. Qu'il avait une mère. Et qu'elle a le cœur brisé.

Elle fait demi-tour puis passe sous la barrière, disparaissant dans la foule, et j'avale une grande bouffée d'air, comme si l'on m'avait maintenu la tête sous l'eau.

Te laisser partir

Mon avocate est une femme d'une quarantaine d'années. Elle me regarde avec un intérêt professionnel en pénétrant dans la petite salle d'entretien, devant laquelle est posté un garde.

— Ruth Jefferson, se présente-t-elle en tendant une main ferme. C'est une procédure simple aujourd'hui, Mme Gray. Vous plaidez coupable, donc l'audience vise seulement à fixer votre peine. Nous passons juste après le déjeuner, et malheureusement, vous avez hérité du juge King.

Elle s'assoit en face de moi à la table.

— Quel est le problème avec le juge King ?

— Disons simplement qu'il n'est pas réputé pour sa clémence, répond Ruth avec un rire sans humour qui découvre des dents blanches parfaitement alignées.

— À quoi vais-je être condamnée ? dis-je avant de pouvoir m'en empêcher.

Ça n'a pas d'importance. Tout ce qui compte maintenant, c'est que justice soit faite.

— Difficile à dire. Le délit de fuite entraîne un simple retrait du permis de conduire, mais de toute façon la sanction minimale pour conduite dangereuse ayant entraîné la mort est une suspension de deux ans. C'est la durée d'incarcération qui peut varier de façon significative. La conduite dangereuse ayant entraîné la mort est passible de quatorze ans d'emprisonnement ; dans les faits, c'est en général entre deux et six ans. Le juge King penchera pour six ans, et mon travail consiste à le convaincre qu'une peine de deux ans serait plus appropriée. (Elle enlève le bouchon d'un stylo à plume noir.) Avez-vous déjà souffert de troubles mentaux ?

Je secoue la tête et lis la déception sur le visage de l'avocate.

— Parlons de l'accident, alors. J'ai cru comprendre que la visibilité était très mauvaise. Avez-vous vu le garçon avant de le renverser ?

— Non.

— Souffrez-vous de maladies chroniques ? demande Ruth. Ça peut être utile dans ce genre d'affaires. Ou peut-être ne vous sentiez-vous pas bien ce jour-là ?

Je la regarde d'un air ahuri et elle fait la moue.

— Vous ne me rendez pas la tâche facile, Mme Gray. Êtes-vous allergique ? Vous étiez peut-être prise d'une crise d'éternuements au moment de l'accident ?

— Je ne comprends pas.

Ruth soupire puis parle lentement, comme si elle s'adressait à un enfant.

— Le juge King aura jeté un œil à votre dossier, et il aura déjà une condamnation en tête. Mon travail consiste à présenter ce qui s'est passé comme n'étant rien d'autre qu'un malheureux accident. Un accident qui n'aurait pas pu être évité et que vous regrettez profondément. (Elle me lance un regard plein de sous-entendus.) Je ne voudrais pas vous influencer, mais si vous aviez été prise d'une crise d'éternuements, par exemple...

— Mais c'est faux.

Est-ce que c'est comme ça que ça marche ? Un tissu de mensonges destinés à obtenir la peine la plus clémente. Notre système judiciaire est-il à ce point biaisé ? Ça m'écœure.

Ruth Jefferson parcourt ses notes et relève soudain la tête.

— Le garçon s'est-il précipité sous vos roues ? Selon la déclaration de la mère, elle a lâché sa main alors qu'ils approchaient de la route, donc...

— Ce n'est pas sa faute !

L'avocate hausse ses sourcils soigneusement entretenus.

— Mme Gray, reprend-elle d'un ton doux. Nous ne sommes pas ici pour déterminer qui est responsable de ce malheureux accident, mais pour discuter des éventuelles circonstances atténuantes. Essayez de ne pas vous laisser submerger par vos émotions.

— Je suis désolée, dis-je. Mais il n'y a pas de circonstances atténuantes.

— Mon travail consiste à les trouver, réplique Ruth. (Elle pose son dossier et se penche vers moi.) Croyez-moi, Mme Gray, il y a une grande différence entre deux ans et six ans de prison, et s'il y a quoi que ce soit qui puisse justifier le fait que vous avez tué un garçon de cinq ans avant de prendre la fuite, vous devez me le dire maintenant.

Nous nous dévisageons.

— Malheureusement, rien ne peut le justifier.

44

Sans s'arrêter pour enlever son manteau, Ray déboula dans les
locaux de la Criminelle et trouva Kate en train de parcourir les
affaires de la nuit.

— Dans mon bureau, tout de suite !

Elle se leva et le suivit.

— Qu'est-ce qu'il y a ?

Ray ne répondit pas. Il alluma son ordinateur et posa la carte
de visite bleue sur son bureau.

— Rappelle-moi qui avait cette carte.

— Dominica Letts. La petite amie d'une de nos cibles.

— Elle s'est mise à table ?

— Pas un mot.

Ray croisa les bras.

— C'est un foyer pour femmes.

Kate le dévisagea sans comprendre.

— La maison de Grantham Street, expliqua Ray. Et celle-ci.
(Il désigna la carte bleu pâle d'un signe de tête.) Je crois que
ce sont des foyers pour femmes victimes de violences conju-
gales. (Il se cala dans son fauteuil et croisa les mains derrière
la tête.) On sait que Dominica Letts est une victime, c'est ce
qui a failli faire capoter l'opération Falcon. Je suis passé devant
cette adresse en venant au boulot et c'est exactement comme
Grantham Street : des détecteurs de mouvement devant l'entrée,
des rideaux à toutes les fenêtres, pas de fente pour le courrier
dans la porte.

— Tu penses que Jenna Gray est elle aussi une victime ?

Ray hocha lentement la tête.

— Tu n'as pas remarqué qu'elle ne regarde jamais dans les yeux ? Elle a un côté nerveux, tendu, et elle se ferme dès qu'on lui demande des explications.

Avant qu'il puisse développer sa théorie, son téléphone sonna et le numéro de l'accueil s'afficha sur l'écran.

— J'ai quelqu'un pour vous, capitaine, annonça Rachel. Un certain Patrick Mathews.

Ce nom ne lui évoquait rien.

— Je n'attends personne, Rach. Vous pouvez prendre un message et vous débarrasser de lui ?

— J'ai essayé, capitaine, mais il insiste. Il dit qu'il doit vous parler de sa petite amie... Jenna Gray.

Ray écarquilla les yeux. Le petit ami de Jenna. Les recherches que Ray avait effectuées sur son passé n'avaient révélé qu'un avertissement pour ivresse sur la voie publique quand il était étudiant, mais les apparences étaient-elles trompeuses ?

— Amenez-le-moi, fit-il.

Il mit Kate au courant de la situation pendant qu'ils attendaient.

— Est-ce que tu crois que c'est lui le compagnon violent ? demanda-t-elle.

Ray secoua la tête.

— Ça n'a pas l'air d'être le genre.

— Personne n'a jamais l'air...

Kate s'interrompit brusquement au moment où Rachel arrivait avec Patrick Mathews. Il portait une veste en toile huilée usée et un sac à dos sur l'épaule. Ray lui indiqua le fauteuil à côté de Kate, et il s'assit tout au bord, comme s'il comptait repartir d'un instant à l'autre.

— Je suppose que vous avez une information au sujet de Jenna Gray, commença Ray.

— Eh bien, pas vraiment une information, répondit Patrick. Une impression, plutôt.

Ray consulta sa montre. L'affaire de Jenna devait être jugée juste après le déjeuner et il voulait être présent au tribunal pour le verdict.

— Quel genre d'impression, M. Mathews ?

Il regarda Kate, qui eut un haussement d'épaules à peine perceptible. Patrick Mathews n'était pas l'homme dont Jenna avait peur. Mais qui était cet homme ?

— Appelez-moi Patrick, je vous en prie. Écoutez, je sais que vous seriez étonnés si je vous disais le contraire, mais je ne crois pas que Jenna soit coupable.

Cette entrée en matière piqua la curiosité de Ray.

— Il y a quelque chose qu'elle me cache à propos de ce qui s'est passé le soir de l'accident, poursuivit Patrick. Quelque chose qu'elle ne dit à personne. (Il eut un petit rire sans humour.) Je croyais vraiment qu'on pourrait avoir un avenir ensemble, mais je ne vois pas comment ça pourrait être le cas si elle refuse de me parler.

Il leva les mains en signe de désespoir, et Ray songea à Mags. *Tu ne me parles jamais*, avait-elle dit.

— Qu'est-ce qu'elle vous cache, à votre avis ? intervint brusquement Ray.

Tous les couples ont-ils donc des secrets ? se demanda-t-il.

— Jenna garde un coffret sous son lit. (Patrick sembla mal à l'aise.) Il ne me serait jamais venu à l'idée de fouiller dans ses affaires, mais elle ne voulait rien me dire, et quand j'ai touché ce coffret, elle a réagi bizarrement... J'espérais y trouver des réponses.

— Vous y avez donc jeté un œil.

Ray regarda Patrick. Il n'avait pas l'air agressif, mais fouiner dans les affaires de quelqu'un dénotait une tendance à vouloir tout contrôler.

Patrick acquiesça.

— J'ai une clé du cottage : on s'était mis d'accord pour que je passe prendre son chien ce matin, après son départ. (Il soupira.) Je n'aurais peut-être pas dû faire ça. (Il tendit une enveloppe à Ray.) Regardez à l'intérieur.

Ray ouvrit l'enveloppe et aperçut la couverture rouge caractéristique d'un passeport britannique. À l'intérieur, il découvrit une Jenna plus jeune, sérieuse, les cheveux ramenés en une vague queue de cheval. Sur la droite, il lut un nom : Jennifer Petersen.

— Elle est mariée. (Ray jeta un coup d'œil à Kate. Comment avaient-ils pu passer à côté de ça ? L'identité de tout individu mis en garde à vue était minutieusement vérifiée : comment un banal changement de nom avait-il pu leur échapper ? Il regarda Patrick.) Vous le saviez ?

L'audience allait commencer d'ici quelques minutes. Ray tambourina des doigts sur son bureau. *Petersen*. Il avait l'impression d'avoir déjà entendu ce nom quelque part. Mais où ?

— Elle m'a dit qu'elle avait été mariée : je pensais qu'elle était divorcée.

Ray et Kate échangèrent un regard. Ray décrocha le téléphone et composa le numéro du tribunal.

— L'affaire Gray a été appelée ?

Il attendit que le fonctionnaire consulte la liste des affaires du jour.

Petersen, pas Gray. Quelle bourde !

— D'accord, merci. (Il reposa le combiné.) Le juge King a pris du retard, on a une demi-heure.

Kate se pencha.

— La déclaration que je t'ai donnée l'autre jour, quand tu m'as envoyée à l'accueil pour m'occuper d'une main courante. Où est-elle ?

— Quelque part dans ma bannette, répondit Ray.

Kate se mit à fouiller dans les papiers sur le bureau de Ray. Elle prit trois dossiers sur le dessus de sa pile de documents à traiter, et, ne trouvant plus de place sur la table, les lâcha par terre. Elle feuilleta rapidement le reste des documents, se débarrassant de chaque feuille inutile pour s'emparer de la suivante dans la seconde.

— La voilà ! fit-elle triomphalement.

Elle sortit la déclaration de la pochette en plastique et la posa sur le bureau de Ray. Des fragments de photo déchirée s'éparpillèrent sur la table, et Patrick en ramassa un. Il l'examina avec curiosité, puis leva les yeux vers Ray.

— Je peux ?

— Allez-y, répondit Ray, sans trop savoir ce qu'il autorisait.

Patrick rassembla les morceaux et entreprit de reconstituer la photo. Quand la baie de Penfach prit forme sous leurs yeux, Ray laissa échapper un petit sifflement.

— Jenna Gray est donc la sœur pour qui Eve Mannings s'inquiétait tant.

Il passa à l'action.

— M. Mathews, merci de nous avoir apporté le passeport. Je vais devoir vous demander de nous attendre au tribunal. Rachel, à l'accueil, va vous indiquer le chemin. On vous rejoint aussi vite que possible. Kate, retrouve-moi à la protection des familles dans cinq minutes.

Pendant que Kate raccompagnait Patrick en bas, Ray décrocha le téléphone.

— Natalie, c'est Ray Stevens, de la Criminelle. Tu peux regarder ce que tu as sur Ian Petersen ? Un homme blanc, proche de la cinquantaine…

Ray dévala un escalier puis se précipita dans un couloir avant de franchir une porte indiquant « Services de protection ». Kate le rejoignit un instant plus tard et ils sonnèrent ensemble à l'interphone de la brigade de protection des familles. Une femme joyeuse aux cheveux noirs coupés court et aux bijoux voyants ouvrit la porte.

— Tu as trouvé quelque chose, Nat ?

Elle les fit entrer et tourna l'écran de son ordinateur vers eux.

— Ian Francis Petersen, dit-elle. Né le 12 avril 1965. Casier pour conduite en état d'ivresse, coups et blessures et actuellement soumis à une ordonnance restrictive.

— Obtenue par une certaine Jennifer, à tout hasard ? demanda Kate.

Natalie secoua la tête.

— Marie Walker. On l'a aidée à quitter Petersen après six ans de violences systématiques. Elle a porté plainte, mais il s'en est tiré. L'ordonnance restrictive a été émise par le tribunal d'instance et elle est toujours en vigueur.

— Il a été violent avec d'autres compagnes avant Marie ?

— D'après ce qu'on sait, non, mais il y a dix ans il a reçu un avertissement pour voie de fait. Sur sa mère.

Ray sentit la bile monter dans sa gorge.

— On pense que Petersen est marié à la femme impliquée dans l'affaire Jacob Jordan, confia-t-il.

Natalie se leva et se dirigea vers un mur garni de classeurs métalliques gris. Elle ouvrit un tiroir dont elle feuilleta le contenu.

— Je l'ai, dit-elle en sortant un dossier. Voilà tout ce qu'on a sur Jennifer et Ian Petersen, et il y a de quoi faire...

45

Tes expositions étaient d'un ennui mortel. Les lieux étaient différents : des entrepôts reconvertis, des ateliers, des boutiques ; mais les gens étaient toujours les mêmes : des gauchistes râleurs aux écharpes colorées. Les femmes étaient poilues et avaient un avis sur tout, les hommes insipides et soumis. Même le vin manquait de personnalité.

La semaine de ton exposition de novembre, tu t'es montrée particulièrement difficile. Je t'ai aidée à transporter tes œuvres jusqu'à l'entrepôt trois jours avant, et tu as passé le reste de la semaine là-bas, à tout préparer.

— Combien de temps faut-il pour disposer quelques sculptures ? ai-je demandé quand tu es rentrée tard pour la deuxième fois de suite.

— On raconte une histoire, as-tu répondu. Les invités vont se déplacer d'une sculpture à l'autre, et les œuvres doivent leur parler.

J'ai ri.

— Tu devrais t'entendre ! Quel ramassis de conneries ! Contente-toi de bien afficher les prix, c'est tout ce qui compte.

— Tu n'es pas obligé de venir, si tu n'en as pas envie.

— Tu ne veux pas que je vienne ?

Je t'ai dévisagée avec méfiance. Tu avais les yeux un peu trop brillants, le menton un peu trop relevé. Je me suis demandé à quoi était due cette joie de vivre si soudaine.

— Je n'ai juste pas envie que tu t'ennuies. On peut se débrouiller sans toi.

Et je l'ai vue : cette lueur indéchiffrable dans tes yeux.

— On ? ai-je fait en haussant un sourcil.

Tu étais troublée. Tu t'es retournée et tu as fait semblant de te concentrer sur la vaisselle.

— Avec Philip, le commissaire de l'exposition.

Tu t'es mise à laver une poêle que j'avais laissée tremper. Je suis venu derrière toi et je t'ai coincée contre l'évier, ma bouche effleurant ton oreille.

— Oh, c'est le *commissaire*, hein ? C'est comme ça que tu l'appelles quand il *te baise* ?

— Pas du tout, as-tu répondu.

Depuis ta grossesse, tu adoptais un ton particulier pour me parler ; excessivement calme : le genre de ton qu'on emploie pour s'adresser à un enfant en pleurs, ou aux malades mentaux. J'avais horreur de ça. J'ai légèrement reculé et je t'ai sentie souffler, puis je t'ai de nouveau poussée. Tu en as eu le souffle coupé et tu t'es appuyée au bord de l'évier pour reprendre haleine.

— Tu ne baises pas avec Philip ?

J'ai craché ces mots sur ta nuque.

— Je ne baise avec personne.

— Tu ne baises certainement pas avec moi, ai-je observé. Pas en ce moment, en tout cas.

Je t'ai sentie te raidir, et je savais que tu t'attendais à ce que je glisse ma main entre tes jambes ; tu en avais même envie. Ça m'a presque fait de la peine de te décevoir, mais ton derrière maigrichon ne m'excitait plus depuis longtemps.

Le jour de l'exposition, j'étais dans notre chambre quand tu es montée pour te changer. Tu as hésité.

— Ce n'est pas comme si je ne t'avais jamais vue toute nue, ai-je dit.

J'ai sorti une chemise propre que j'ai accrochée à la porte de l'armoire ; tu as étalé des vêtements sur le lit. Je t'ai regardée te débarrasser de ton pantalon de survêtement et plier ton sweat-shirt pour le lendemain. Tu portais un soutien-gorge blanc et une culotte assortie, et je me suis demandé si tu avais fait exprès de choisir cette couleur pour souligner le bleu sur ta hanche. Elle était encore enflée, et tu as grimacé en t'asseyant sur le lit, comme pour me le faire remarquer. Tu as enfilé un pantalon large en lin et un haut ample de la même matière qui dénudait tes épaules anguleuses. J'ai choisi un collier de grosses perles vertes sur l'arbre à bijoux de ta coiffeuse.

— Tu veux que je te le mette ?

Tu as hésité, puis tu t'es assise sur le petit tabouret. J'ai passé les bras par-dessus ta tête pour tenir le collier devant toi, et tu as relevé tes cheveux. J'ai ramené les mains vers ta nuque, serrant le collier contre ta gorge pendant une fraction de seconde, et je t'ai sentie te crisper. J'ai ri, puis j'ai attaché le fermoir.

— Superbe, ai-je fait. (Je me suis baissé pour te regarder dans le miroir.) Essaie de ne pas te ridiculiser aujourd'hui, Jennifer. Tu bois toujours trop à ce genre d'événements et tu fais du rentre-dedans aux invités.

Je me suis levé pour mettre ma chemise, choisissant une cravate rose pâle pour aller avec. J'ai enfilé ma veste avant de me regarder dans le miroir, satisfait du résultat.

— Autant que tu conduises, d'ailleurs, puisque tu ne bois pas, ai-je dit.

Je t'avais proposé plusieurs fois de t'acheter une nouvelle voiture, mais tu tenais absolument à garder ta vieille Fiesta déglinguée. Je montais le moins possible dedans, mais je n'avais plus l'intention de te laisser conduire mon Audi depuis que tu l'avais cabossée en essayant de te garer ; j'ai donc pris place sur le siège passager de ta bagnole pourrie et je t'ai laissée m'emmener à l'exposition.

Quand on est arrivés, il y avait déjà des gens autour du bar, et notre entrée a suscité des murmures d'admiration. Quelqu'un a battu des mains et les autres l'ont imité, mais il n'y avait pas assez de monde pour qu'on puisse appeler ça des applaudissements, et le résultat était plus embarrassant qu'autre chose.

Tu m'as tendu une coupe de champagne et tu en as pris une pour toi. Un homme aux cheveux bruns ondulés s'est approché de nous, et j'ai compris à ta façon de le regarder qu'il s'agissait de Philip.

— Jenna !

Il t'a embrassée sur les deux joues et j'ai vu ta main effleurer si brièvement la sienne que tu as sans doute cru que je ne le remarquerais pas. Si brièvement que ça aurait presque pu être involontaire. Mais je savais que ce n'était pas le cas.

Tu m'as présenté, et Philip m'a serré la main.

— Vous devez être très fier d'elle.

— Ma femme a un immense talent, ai-je répliqué. Bien sûr que je suis fier d'elle.

Philip a hésité avant de reprendre la parole.

— Je suis désolé de vous l'enlever, mais je dois absolument présenter Jenna à certaines personnes. Son travail les a beaucoup intéressées, et...

Il n'a pas achevé sa phrase, préférant frotter son pouce sur ses doigts en me lançant un clin d'œil.

— Loin de moi l'idée de faire obstacle à d'éventuelles ventes, ai-je dit.

Je vous ai regardés faire le tour de la salle ensemble, la main de Philip ne quittant jamais le creux de tes reins, et j'ai alors eu la certitude que vous entreteniez une liaison. Je ne sais pas comment j'ai fait pour garder mon calme pendant l'exposition, mais je ne t'ai pas quittée des yeux. Quand il n'y a plus eu de champagne, j'ai bu du vin, et je suis resté près du bar pour éviter d'avoir à revenir à chaque fois. Je t'ai observée tout le long. Tu arborais un sourire que je n'avais pas vu depuis longtemps, ça m'a rappelé la fille qui riait aux larmes avec ses amies au bar de l'université. Tu ne riais plus, ces temps-ci.

Ma bouteille était vide et j'en ai demandé une autre. Les serveurs ont échangé un regard, mais ils m'ont obéi. Les gens ont commencé à partir. Je t'ai observée tandis que tu leur disais au revoir : tu en embrassais certains, tu serrais la main à d'autres. Aucun n'était traité aussi chaleureusement que ton *commissaire*. Quand il n'est plus resté qu'une poignée d'invités, je suis venu te voir.

— Il est temps de rentrer.

Tu as eu l'air mal à l'aise.

— Je ne peux pas partir maintenant, Ian, il y a encore des gens. Et je dois aider à ranger.

Philip s'est approché.

— Jenna, c'est bon. Ce pauvre Ian t'a à peine vue : il a sûrement envie de fêter ça avec toi. Je vais me débrouiller tout seul et tu viendras récupérer tes œuvres demain. L'expo a eu beaucoup de succès, bravo !

Il t'a seulement embrassée sur une joue cette fois-ci, mais j'étais à deux doigts d'exploser de rage.

Tu as acquiescé. Tu semblais déçue par Philip : tu aurais préféré qu'il te demande de rester ? qu'il m'envoie balader pour te garder avec lui ? Je t'ai pris la main et je l'ai serrée pendant que tu continuais à lui parler. Je savais que tu ne dirais rien, et j'ai serré de plus en plus fort jusqu'à t'écraser les doigts.

Philip s'est enfin tu. Il m'a tendu la main et j'ai dû lâcher la tienne. Je t'ai entendue souffler et je t'ai vue te frotter les doigts.

— Ravi de vous avoir rencontré, Ian, a dit Philip. (Il t'a jeté un rapide coup d'œil avant de me regarder à nouveau.) Prenez soin d'elle, d'accord ?

Je me suis demandé ce que tu lui avais raconté.

— Comme toujours, ai-je répondu d'une voix douce.

Je me suis tourné vers la sortie et je t'ai prise par le coude, enfonçant mon pouce dans ta chair.

— Tu me fais mal, as-tu dit à voix basse. Les gens le voient.

C'était la première fois que je t'entendais me parler sur ce ton.

— Comment oses-tu te payer ma tête ? ai-je soufflé. (On a descendu l'escalier, croisant un couple qui nous a souri poliment.) Tu as passé l'après-midi à flirter avec lui devant tout le monde, à le toucher, à l'embrasser ! (En atteignant le parking, je n'ai plus pris la peine de parler à voix basse, et mes mots ont résonné dans la nuit.) Tu baises avec lui, hein ?

Tu n'as pas répondu, et ce silence m'a mis hors de moi. Je t'ai saisi le bras et je te l'ai tordu dans le dos, le pliant jusqu'à ce que tu cries.

— Tu m'as amené ici pour te moquer de moi, hein ?

— Non !

Des larmes coulaient le long de tes joues, maculant ton haut de petites taches sombres.

Mon poing s'est serré de lui-même, mais juste au moment où mon avant-bras commençait à se contracter, un homme est passé par là.

— Bonsoir, a-t-il dit.

On s'est immobilisés, à cinquante centimètres l'un de l'autre, jusqu'à ce qu'il disparaisse dans l'obscurité.

— Monte dans la voiture.

Tu as ouvert la porte du conducteur et tu t'es installée sur le siège, t'y reprenant à trois fois pour mettre la clé dans le contact et la tourner. Il n'était que quatre heures, mais il faisait déjà nuit. Il avait plu, et tu plissais les yeux chaque fois qu'une voiture arrivait en face, ses phares se réverbérant sur l'asphalte mouillé. Tu pleurais encore, et tu t'es essuyée le nez du revers de la main.

— Regarde dans quel état tu es, ai-je dit. Philip sait que tu es comme ça ? une poule mouillée pleurnicharde ?

Te laisser partir

— Je ne couche pas avec Philip, as-tu répondu.

Tu as marqué une pause entre chaque mot pour insister, et j'ai tapé du poing sur le tableau de bord.

Tu as eu un mouvement de recul.

— Je ne suis pas le genre de Philip, as-tu repris. Il est...

— Ne me prends pas pour un idiot, Jennifer ! J'ai des yeux. J'ai vu ce qu'il y avait entre vous.

Tu as brusquement freiné à un feu rouge, puis tu as redémarré sur les chapeaux de roues quand il est passé au vert. Je me suis tortillé sur mon siège pour t'observer. Je voulais voir ton visage, lire dans tes pensées. Savoir si tu pensais à *lui*. J'ai vu que c'était le cas, même si tu essayais de le cacher.

Dès qu'on arriverait à la maison, je ferais en sorte que ça cesse. Dès qu'on arriverait à la maison, je ferais en sorte que tu ne penses plus à rien.

46

La cour d'assises de Bristol est plus ancienne que le tribunal de première instance, et la solennité transpire de ses couloirs lambrissés. Les huissiers entrent et sortent rapidement du prétoire, leurs toges noires créant des courants d'air qui soulèvent les papiers sur le bureau de la greffière à chacun de leur passage. Le silence est pesant, comme dans une bibliothèque où l'interdiction de faire du bruit donne envie de crier. Je me frotte les yeux et la salle d'audience devient floue. J'aimerais pouvoir garder cette image : les formes brumeuses aux contours imprécis rendent l'atmosphère moins menaçante, moins sérieuse.

Maintenant que je suis là, je suis terrifiée. Mon courage s'est envolé. Bien que j'éprouve une peur bleue de ce que Ian me ferait si je ressortais libre, ce qui m'attend en prison m'effraie soudain tout autant. Je serre les mains et je plonge mes ongles dans la chair de ma main gauche. Dans ma tête des pas résonnent sur une passerelle métallique ; je vois des couchettes étroites dans une cellule grise aux murs si épais que personne ne m'entendra crier. Je ressens tout à coup une vive douleur au dos de la main, et quand je baisse les yeux je m'aperçois que j'ai enfoncé mes ongles si fort que je saigne. Je m'essuie et le sang laisse une traînée rose sur ma peau.

Le box dans lequel je me trouve peut contenir plusieurs personnes ; deux rangées de fauteuils sont fixées au sol, les sièges relevés comme au cinéma. Trois côtés sont vitrés, et je me tortille timidement sur mon siège tandis que le prétoire commence à se remplir. Il y a beaucoup plus de spectateurs aujourd'hui qu'à l'audience préliminaire. La simple curiosité qui se lisait sur le visage des tricoteuses du tribunal de première instance laisse ici place aux regards haineux de ceux qui réclament justice. Un homme, au teint olivâtre et avec une veste en cuir deux fois trop grande pour lui, est penché en avant sur son siège. Il ne me quitte pas des yeux, la bouche déformée par un rictus de colère. Je me mets à pleurer, et il secoue la tête avec une moue de dégoût.

La photo de Jacob se trouve dans ma poche et je glisse ma main autour en tripotant les coins.

Les équipes juridiques se sont agrandies : chaque avocat est assisté de plusieurs personnes, assises derrière lui et penchées en avant pour se murmurer les dernières consignes. Huissiers et avocats sont les seuls à avoir l'air détendus ici. Ils échangent des plaisanteries à voix haute sans se soucier de l'assistance, et je me demande pourquoi il en va ainsi ; pourquoi un système chercherait-il si délibérément à s'aliéner ceux qui en ont besoin ? La porte s'ouvre en grinçant pour laisser entrer une nouvelle vague de spectateurs, mal à l'aise et hésitants. Je retiens mon souffle à la vue d'Anya. Elle se glisse au premier rang à côté de l'homme à la veste en cuir, qui lui prend la main.

Vous devez vous rappeler que c'était un petit garçon. Qu'il avait une mère. Et qu'elle a le cœur brisé.

Les seuls sièges vides de la salle d'audience sont ceux du banc des jurés. Je les imagine occupés par douze hommes et femmes venus écouter les témoignages, m'observer, décider de ma culpabilité. Je leur ai épargné ça ; je leur ai épargné le supplice de se demander s'ils avaient pris la bonne décision ; j'ai épargné à Anya la souffrance de voir la mort de son fils étalée devant le tribunal. Ruth Jefferson m'a expliqué que ça jouerait en ma faveur : les juges sont plus cléments envers ceux qui évitent à la justice les frais d'un procès.

— Veuillez vous lever.

Le juge est âgé. Les histoires d'un millier de familles se lisent sur son visage. Ses yeux perçants embrassent tout le prétoire, mais ne s'attardent pas sur moi. Je ne suis qu'un chapitre de plus dans une carrière pleine de décisions difficiles. Je me demande s'il est déjà fixé à mon sujet – s'il sait déjà combien de temps je vais devoir rester derrière les barreaux.

— Votre Honneur, le ministère public poursuit Jenna Gray… (La greffière lit un document d'une voix claire et neutre.) Mme Gray, vous êtes accusée de conduite dangereuse ayant entraîné la mort et de délit de fuite. (Elle lève les yeux vers moi.) Que plaidez-vous ?

Je m'accroche à la photo dans ma poche.

— Coupable.

Un sanglot étouffé s'échappe de la tribune du public.

Elle a le cœur brisé.

— Vous pouvez vous rasseoir.

L'avocat du ministère public se lève. Il prend une carafe posée sur la table devant lui et se sert lentement. Le bruit de l'eau remplissant son verre résonne dans la salle d'audience silencieuse, et quand tous les regards sont tournés vers lui, il commence.

— Votre Honneur, l'accusée plaide coupable d'avoir provoqué la mort de Jacob Jordan, un enfant de cinq ans. Elle a reconnu que sa conduite ce soir-là ne correspondait absolument pas à ce que l'on est en droit d'attendre d'une personne responsable. De fait, l'enquête de la police a démontré que la voiture de Mme Gray a quitté la route pour monter sur le trottoir juste avant l'accident, et qu'elle roulait à une vitesse comprise entre soixante et un et soixante-huit kilomètres/heure, bien au-delà de la limitation à cinquante kilomètres/heure.

Je crispe mes mains serrées. J'essaie de respirer lentement, calmement, mais la boule dans mon ventre m'en empêche. Les battements de mon cœur résonnent dans ma tête et je ferme les yeux. Je vois la pluie sur le pare-brise, j'entends le cri – mon cri – quand j'aperçois le petit garçon sur le trottoir ; il court, puis tourne la tête pour dire quelque chose à sa mère.

— En outre, Votre Honneur, après avoir renversé Jacob Jordan, le tuant vraisemblablement sur le coup, l'accusée ne s'est pas arrêtée. (L'avocat du ministère public balaie la salle du regard, sa grandiloquence se révélant inutile en l'absence de jury à impressionner.) Elle n'est pas descendue de la voiture. Elle n'a pas appelé les secours. Elle n'a pas manifesté de remords, pas plus qu'elle n'a proposé son aide. Au lieu de cela, l'accusée a pris la fuite, laissant le petit garçon de cinq ans dans les bras de sa mère traumatisée.

Je me souviens qu'elle s'est penchée sur son fils, son manteau le recouvrant presque, le protégeant de la pluie. Les phares de la voiture faisaient ressortir chaque détail, et j'ai mis mes mains sur ma bouche, horrifiée.

— On pourrait imaginer, Votre Honneur, qu'une telle réaction soit due au choc. Que l'accusée soit partie sous l'effet de la panique et que quelques minutes plus tard, peut-être quelques heures – peut-être même un jour plus tard –, elle soit revenue à la raison et soit allée voir la police. Mais au lieu de cela, Votre Honneur, l'accusée a fui la région pour aller se cacher dans un village à cent cinquante kilomètres de là, où personne ne la connaissait. Elle ne s'est pas rendue. Elle plaide peut-être coupable aujourd'hui, mais c'est uniquement parce qu'elle ne peut plus s'enfuir, et le ministère public, avec tout le respect qu'il vous doit, demande que cet élément soit pris en considération au moment de prononcer la peine.

— Merci, maître Lassiter.

Le juge prend des notes sur un bloc de papier, et l'avocat du ministère public incline la tête avant de se rasseoir en relevant sa toge derrière lui. Mes paumes sont moites. La haine du public est presque palpable.

L'avocate de la défense rassemble ses papiers. Même si je plaide coupable, même si je sais que je dois payer pour ce qui est arrivé, j'ai soudain envie de voir Ruth Jefferson se battre pour moi. La nausée monte en moi quand je comprends que c'est ma dernière chance de parler. Dans quelques instants, le juge rendra son verdict, et il sera trop tard.

Ruth Jefferson se met debout, mais avant qu'elle puisse dire quoi que ce soit, la porte du tribunal s'ouvre brusquement. Le juge lève des yeux sévères, manifestement contrarié.

Patrick détonne tellement ici que je ne le reconnais pas tout de suite. Il me regarde, visiblement ému de me voir menottée dans un box aux vitres blindées. Qu'est-ce qu'il fait là ? Je m'aperçois que l'homme qui l'accompagne est le capitaine Stevens, qui adresse un bref signe de tête au juge avant de se diriger vers le centre de la salle d'audience pour se pencher vers l'avocat du ministère public et lui parler à voix basse.

L'avocat écoute avec attention. Il griffonne quelque chose sur un papier, qu'il tend ensuite à Ruth Jefferson à l'autre bout du banc. Le silence est pesant, comme si tout le monde retenait son souffle.

Mon avocate lit le mot et se relève lentement.

— Votre Honneur, puis-je bénéficier d'une courte suspension d'audience ?

Le juge King pousse un soupir.

— Maître Jefferson, dois-je vous rappeler combien d'affaires j'ai cet après-midi ? Vous avez eu six semaines pour vous entretenir avec votre cliente.

— Toutes mes excuses, Votre Honneur, mais j'ai ici des éléments nouveaux qui pourraient avoir une incidence sur la défense de ma cliente.

— Très bien. Vous avez quinze minutes, maître Jefferson. Passé ce délai, j'ai la ferme intention de rendre mon jugement.

Il fait un signe à la greffière.

— Veuillez vous lever, lance celle-ci.

Tandis que le juge King quitte le prétoire, un garde pénètre dans le box pour me ramener au sous-sol.

— Qu'est-ce qui se passe ? dis-je.

— Aucune idée, ma belle, mais c'est toujours la même histoire. Je passe mon temps à monter et à descendre comme un foutu yoyo.

Il m'escorte jusqu'à la pièce étouffante où j'ai parlé avec mon avocate il y a moins d'une heure. Ruth Jefferson arrive presque aussitôt, suivie du capitaine Stevens. Ruth se met à parler avant même que la porte se soit refermée derrière eux.

— J'espère que vous vous rendez compte, Mme Gray, que les tribunaux ne prennent pas à la légère l'entrave au cours de la justice.

Je ne réponds rien, et elle s'assoit. Elle remet une mèche brune rebelle sous sa perruque d'avocate.

Le capitaine Stevens sort un passeport de sa poche et le lâche sur la table. Je n'ai pas besoin de l'ouvrir pour savoir que c'est le mien. Je les regarde, lui et mon avocate exaspérée, puis je tends la main pour toucher le passeport. Je me souviens du jour où j'ai rempli le formulaire pour changer de nom avant le mariage. J'avais essayé une centaine de signatures, demandant à Ian laquelle faisait le plus adulte, laquelle me ressemblait le plus. Quand le passeport est arrivé, c'était la première preuve tangible de mon changement de situation, et j'avais hâte de le montrer à l'aéroport.

Le capitaine Stevens se penche et pose les mains sur la table, son visage au niveau du mien.

— Vous n'êtes plus obligée de le protéger, Jennifer.

J'ai un mouvement de recul.

— S'il vous plaît, ne m'appelez pas comme ça.

— Racontez-moi ce qui s'est passé.

Je ne dis rien.

Le capitaine Stevens parle doucement, et son calme me tranquillise, me rassure.

— On ne le laissera plus vous faire de mal, Jenna.

Alors ils savent. Je laisse échapper un petit soupir et regarde d'abord le capitaine Stevens, puis Ruth Jefferson. Je me sens tout à coup épuisée. Le capitaine ouvre un dossier marron sur lequel je vois écrit « Petersen » – mon nom d'épouse. Le nom de Ian.

— On a reçu beaucoup de signalements, dit-il. Des voisins, des médecins, des passants ont appelé, mais jamais vous, Jenna. Vous ne nous avez jamais contactés. Et quand nous sommes venus, vous avez refusé de nous parler. Vous avez refusé de porter plainte. Pourquoi ne pas nous avoir laissés vous aider ?

— Parce qu'il m'aurait tuée.

Il y a un silence avant que le capitaine Stevens reprenne la parole.

— Quand vous a-t-il frappé pour la première fois ?

— Est-ce que c'est important ? demande Ruth en consultant sa montre.

— Oui, réplique sèchement le capitaine Stevens.

Elle s'adosse à sa chaise en fronçant les sourcils.

— Ça a commencé pendant notre nuit de noces.

Je ferme les yeux en me remémorant la douleur surgie de nulle part et la honte d'avoir raté mon mariage avant même qu'il ait commencé. Je me souviens de la tendresse de Ian quand il est revenu, de la douceur avec laquelle il s'est occupé de mon visage endolori. Je lui ai demandé pardon, et j'ai fait ça pendant sept ans.

— Quand vous êtes-vous rendue au foyer de Grantham Street ?

Je suis surprise qu'il en sache autant.

— Jamais. Ils ont vu mes bleus à l'hôpital et ils m'ont posé des questions sur mon mariage. Je ne leur ai rien dit, mais ils m'ont donné une carte en précisant que je pourrais aller là-bas quand je voudrais, que j'y serais en sécurité. Je ne les ai pas crus – comment est-ce que j'aurais pu être en sécurité si près de Ian ? –, mais j'ai gardé la carte. Le fait de l'avoir me donnait l'impression d'être un peu moins seule.

— Vous n'avez jamais essayé de partir ? demande le capitaine Stevens.

La colère se lit sur son visage, mais elle n'est pas dirigée contre moi.

— Si, des tas de fois, dis-je. Ian allait au travail et je commençais à faire mes valises. Je faisais le tour de la maison pour récupérer les souvenirs que je pouvais raisonnablement emporter avec moi. Je mettais tout dans la voiture… la voiture était toujours à moi, vous voyez.

Le capitaine Stevens secoue la tête sans comprendre.

— La carte grise était encore à mon nom de jeune fille. Ce n'était pas voulu, au départ – juste une de ces choses que j'avais oublié de faire quand on s'est mariés –, mais par la suite, c'est devenu important pour moi. Tout était au nom de Ian – la maison, le compte en banque… j'ai commencé à avoir l'impression de ne plus exister, de lui appartenir moi aussi. Alors je n'ai jamais changé la carte grise. Ce n'était pas grand-chose, je sais, mais… (Je hausse les épaules.) Bref, je chargeais mes affaires dans la voiture, puis je changeais d'avis et je remettais tout exactement au même endroit. À chaque fois.

— Pourquoi ?

— Parce qu'il m'aurait retrouvée.

Le capitaine Stevens feuillette le dossier. Il est incroyablement épais et pourtant il ne doit contenir que les épisodes ayant entraîné un signalement à la police. Les côtes cassées et la commotion cérébrale qui m'ont valu un séjour à l'hôpital. Pour chaque marque visible, il y en avait une douzaine d'autres cachées.

Ruth Jefferson pose une main sur le dossier.

— Je peux ?

Le capitaine Stevens me regarde et j'acquiesce. Il lui tend le dossier et elle commence à le parcourir.

— Mais vous êtes partie après l'accident, observe le capitaine Stevens. Qu'est-ce qui a changé ?

Te laisser partir

Je respire à fond. J'ai envie de répondre que j'ai enfin trouvé le courage de partir, mais c'est faux, bien sûr.

— Ian m'a menacée, dis-je doucement. Il m'a dit que si jamais j'allais voir la police, si jamais je racontais ce qui s'était passé à quiconque, il me tuerait. Et je savais qu'il était sérieux. Ce soir-là, après l'accident, il m'a tellement battue que je ne tenais plus debout. Il m'a ensuite relevée et m'a plaqué le bras dans l'évier. Puis il a versé de l'eau bouillante sur ma main et je me suis évanouie. Après ça, il m'a traînée jusque dans mon atelier et il m'a obligée à le regarder tout casser... tout ce que j'avais fait. (Je ne parviens pas à lever les yeux vers le capitaine Stevens. C'est tout juste si je peux parler.) Et ensuite, il est parti. Je ne sais pas où. J'ai passé la première nuit sur le sol de la cuisine, puis j'ai rampé jusqu'à l'étage pour m'allonger dans le lit. J'ai prié pour mourir, pour qu'il ne puisse plus me faire de mal quand il reviendrait. Mais il n'est pas revenu. Plusieurs jours sont passés et j'ai peu à peu repris des forces. J'ai commencé à imaginer qu'il était parti pour de bon, mais il n'avait presque rien emporté avec lui et je savais qu'il pourrait revenir à tout moment. J'ai compris que si je restais avec lui, un jour il me tuerait. Et c'est là que je suis partie.

— Racontez-moi ce qui s'est passé avec Jacob.

Je mets la main dans ma poche pour toucher la photo.

— On s'est disputés. J'exposais dans un entrepôt. C'était l'exposition la plus importante que j'avais jamais organisée, et j'avais passé plusieurs jours à tout installer avec le commissaire, un homme qui s'appelle Philip. Ça se passait en journée, mais Ian s'est quand même soûlé. Il m'a accusée d'avoir une liaison avec Philip.

— C'était vrai ?

Cette question indiscrète me fait rougir.

— Philip est gay, dis-je. Mais Ian ne voulait pas l'admettre. Je pleurais et je ne voyais pas bien la route. Il avait plu et les phares m'éblouissaient. Il me hurlait dessus en me traitant de salope et de putain. Je suis passée par Fishponds pour éviter les bouchons, mais Ian m'a forcée à arrêter la voiture. Il m'a frappée et il a pris les clés ; il avait tellement bu qu'il tenait à peine debout. Il conduisait comme un fou en hurlant qu'il allait me donner une bonne leçon. On traversait un quartier résidentiel et Ian conduisait de plus en plus vite. J'étais terrifiée. (Je me tords les mains sur les genoux.) Et c'est là que j'ai vu le garçon. J'ai crié, mais Ian n'a pas ralenti. On l'a renversé et j'ai vu sa mère s'effondrer comme si elle avait été renversée elle aussi. J'ai essayé de descendre de la voiture, mais Ian a verrouillé les portes et il a entamé une marche arrière. Il n'a pas voulu me laisser y retourner.

J'avale une grande bouffée d'air et un petit gémissement s'échappe de ma gorge au moment où j'expire.

Le silence s'abat sur la petite pièce.

— Ian a tué Jacob, dis-je. Mais c'est comme si c'était moi.

47

Patrick conduit prudemment. Je me prépare à un millier de questions, mais il attend que Bristol soit loin derrière nous avant de parler. Quand les villes laissent place aux champs verdoyants et que les contours déchiquetés de la côte apparaissent devant nous, il se tourne vers moi.

— Tu aurais pu aller en prison.

— C'est ce que je voulais.

— Pourquoi ?

Il ne me juge pas, il cherche juste à comprendre.

— Parce qu'il fallait que quelqu'un paie pour ce qui s'est passé, lui dis-je. Quelqu'un devait être condamné pour que la mère de Jacob puisse retrouver un peu de tranquillité en sachant que quelqu'un avait payé pour la mort de son fils.

— Mais pas toi, Jenna.

Avant de partir, j'ai demandé au capitaine Stevens ce qu'ils allaient dire à la mère de Jacob, soudain confrontée au procès avorté de la personne qu'elle croyait coupable.

— On va attendre qu'il soit derrière les barreaux avant de lui annoncer quoi que ce soit, m'a-t-il répondu.

Je me rends compte à présent que mon comportement va l'obliger à revivre tout ça.

— Dans le coffret avec ton passeport, dit tout à coup Patrick. J'ai vu... j'ai vu un jouet d'enfant.

Il s'interrompt sans formuler sa question.

— C'était pour mon fils. Ben. J'étais terrifiée quand je suis tombée enceinte. Je pensais que Ian serait furieux, mais il était aux anges. Il affirmait que ça allait tout changer, et même s'il ne l'a jamais dit, j'étais certaine qu'il regrettait la façon dont il m'avait traitée jusque-là. Je croyais que ce bébé serait un tournant pour nous : que Ian se rendrait compte qu'on pouvait être heureux tous les trois.

— Mais ça ne s'est pas passé comme ça, fait Patrick.

— Non. Au début, il était aux petits soins avec moi. Il me traitait comme une princesse et me disait toujours ce qu'il fallait que je mange et ce que je devais éviter. Mais au fur et à mesure que mon ventre a grossi, il est devenu de plus en plus distant. Comme s'il ne supportait pas que je sois enceinte – comme s'il m'en voulait, même. Au septième mois, j'ai fait en repassant une marque de brûlure sur une de ses chemises. C'était stupide de ma part. J'ai été distraite par le téléphone, et je m'en suis aperçue trop tard. Ian est devenu fou. Il m'a donné un grand coup de poing dans le ventre et j'ai commencé à saigner.

Patrick s'arrête au bord de la route et éteint le moteur. Je fixe le terrain en friche devant nous. Une poubelle déborde et des papiers d'emballage dansent dans la brise.

— Ian a appelé une ambulance. Il leur a dit que j'étais tombée. Je pense qu'ils ne l'ont pas cru, mais qu'est-ce qu'ils pouvaient faire ? Les saignements s'étaient arrêtés quand on est arrivés à l'hôpital, mais je savais qu'il était mort avant de passer l'échographie. Je l'ai senti. Ils ont proposé de me faire une césarienne, mais je ne voulais pas qu'on me l'enlève comme ça. Je voulais le mettre au monde. (Patrick me tend la main mais je ne la prends pas, et il la laisse retomber sur son siège.) Ils m'ont donné des médicaments pour déclencher l'accouchement et j'ai attendu à la maternité avec les autres femmes. J'ai vécu les mêmes choses qu'elles : les premières douleurs, le gaz hilarant, les visites des sages-femmes et des médecins. La seule différence était que mon bébé était mort. Quand on m'a enfin emmenée en salle d'accouchement, la femme à côté de moi m'a fait un signe de la main et m'a souhaité bonne chance. Ian est resté avec moi pendant l'accouchement, et même si je lui en voulais, je lui ai tenu la main en poussant, et je l'ai laissé m'embrasser sur le front, car après tout, qui d'autre était là pour moi ? Et je n'arrêtais pas de me dire que si je n'avais pas brûlé sa chemise, Ben serait encore en vie.

Je me mets à trembler et je presse les mains sur mes genoux pour me calmer. Les semaines qui ont suivi la mort de Ben, mon corps a essayé de me faire croire que j'étais une mère. Mes seins étaient douloureux, et je pressais mes mamelons sous la douche pour faire sortir le lait qui s'y accumulait, humant la douce odeur qui remontait jusqu'à mes narines. Un jour, j'ai levé les yeux et j'ai surpris Ian à la porte de la salle de bains en train de m'observer. J'avais encore le ventre arrondi, la peau distendue et flasque. Des veines bleues sillonnaient mes seins gonflés et du lait dégoulinait le long de mon corps. J'ai vu sa moue écœurée avant qu'il fasse demi-tour.

J'ai essayé de lui parler de Ben. Juste une fois – un jour où la douleur de l'avoir perdu était si intense que je pouvais à peine mettre un pied devant l'autre. J'avais besoin de partager mon chagrin avec quelqu'un – n'importe qui – et je n'avais personne d'autre à qui parler à cette époque. Mais il ne m'a pas laissée finir ma phrase.

— Ça n'est jamais arrivé, a-t-il dit. Ce bébé n'a jamais existé.

Ben n'a peut-être pas vu le jour, mais il a vécu. Il a vécu en moi, respiré mon oxygène, partagé ma nourriture. Il faisait partie de moi. Mais je n'ai plus jamais reparlé de lui.

Je ne parviens pas à regarder Patrick. Maintenant que j'ai commencé, je ne peux plus m'arrêter, et les mots se précipitent hors de ma bouche.

— Il y a eu un horrible silence quand il est sorti. Quelqu'un a lu l'heure à haute voix, puis ils me l'ont mis dans les bras, délicatement, comme s'ils ne voulaient pas lui faire mal, et ils nous ont laissés seuls avec lui. Je suis restée une éternité comme ça, à contempler son visage, ses cils, ses lèvres. Je lui ai caressé le creux de la main en imaginant qu'il pouvait attraper mes doigts, mais ils ont fini par revenir pour me l'enlever. J'ai crié en m'accrochant à lui jusqu'à ce qu'ils soient obligés de me donner un calmant. Mais je ne voulais pas dormir, parce que je savais qu'en me réveillant je serais à nouveau seule.

Quand j'ai fini, je regarde Patrick et vois ses yeux remplis de larmes, et quand j'essaie de lui dire que ça va, que tout va bien, je me mets à pleurer moi aussi. Nous nous cramponnons l'un à l'autre dans la voiture au bord de la route, jusqu'à ce que le soleil commence à disparaître, puis nous rentrons à Penfach.

Patrick gare la voiture au camping et m'accompagne sur le sentier du cottage. Le loyer est payé jusqu'à la fin du mois, mais je ralentis en repensant aux mots de Iestyn, au dégoût dans sa voix quand il m'a demandé de partir.

— Je l'ai appelé, indique Patrick en lisant dans mes pensées. Je lui ai tout expliqué.

Patrick parle d'une voix calme et douce, comme si j'étais une patiente qui se remettait d'une longue maladie. Je me sens en sécurité avec lui, ma main blottie dans la sienne.

— Tu pourrais aller chercher Beau ? dis-je tandis que nous arrivons au cottage.

— Si tu veux.

— Je veux juste que tout redevienne normal.

En disant ces mots, je me rends compte que je ne suis pas certaine de savoir ce qu'est la normalité.

Patrick tire les rideaux et me prépare du thé, puis quand il voit que je suis au chaud et confortablement installée, il dépose un petit baiser sur mes lèvres et s'en va. Je regarde autour de moi ces petites choses qui ont fait ma vie ici dans la baie – les photos et les coquillages, le bol de Beau par terre dans la cuisine. Je me sens plus chez moi ici que pendant toutes ces années à Bristol.

Te laisser partir

Je tends spontanément le bras vers l'interrupteur de la lampe à côté de moi. C'est la seule lumière allumée au rez-de-chaussée et elle inonde la pièce d'une chaude lueur abricot. Je l'éteins, et je me retrouve plongée dans l'obscurité. J'attends, mais mon pouls reste régulier ; mes mains sont sèches ; aucun frisson ne parcourt ma nuque. Je souris : je n'ai plus peur.

48

— Et on est sûrs que c'est la bonne adresse ?

Ray posa la question à Stumpy, mais balaya la pièce du regard pour inclure le reste de l'assistance. Moins de deux heures après avoir quitté la cour d'assises, il avait réuni un groupe d'intervention et Stumpy avait contacté le service de renseignements du secteur pour obtenir l'adresse de Ian Petersen.

— Absolument certains, répondit Stumpy. Selon le registre des électeurs, il est domicilié au 72 Albercombe Terrace, et les renseignements ont croisé leurs informations avec celles du service des cartes grises. Petersen a perdu trois points pour excès de vitesse il y a deux mois, et ils ont renvoyé son permis à cette adresse.

— Bon, fit Ray. Espérons qu'il soit chez lui. (Il se tourna pour briefer le groupe d'intervention qui commençait à s'impatienter.) L'arrestation de Petersen est d'une importance capitale, non seulement pour la résolution de l'affaire Jordan, mais aussi pour assurer la sécurité de Jenna. Petersen est un individu violent, c'est ce qui a poussé Jenna à le quitter après plusieurs années de maltraitance.

Les policiers présents dans la pièce hochèrent la tête, l'air farouchement déterminés. Ils savaient tous quel genre d'homme était Ian Petersen.

— Sans surprise, continua Ray, l'ordinateur central fait état d'un avertissement pour voie de fait et de condamnations pour conduite en état d'ivresse et trouble à l'ordre public. Je ne veux prendre aucun risque avec lui, alors on entre, on le menotte et on sort. Compris ?

— Compris, répondirent-ils en chœur.

— Eh bien, allons-y.

Albercombe Terrace était une rue ordinaire avec des trottoirs étroits et trop de voitures stationnées. La seule chose qui distinguait le 72 de ses voisins était les rideaux tirés à toutes les fenêtres.

Ray et Kate se garèrent dans une rue adjacente et attendirent d'avoir la confirmation que deux membres du groupe d'intervention avaient atteint l'arrière de la maison de Petersen. Kate coupa le contact et le silence les enveloppa, uniquement perturbé par le cliquetis du moteur qui refroidissait.

— Ça va ? demanda Ray.

— Ouais, répondit sèchement Kate.

Elle avait cet air résolu qui ne laissait rien transparaître de ses sentiments. Ray sentait son sang bouillir dans ses veines. Dans quelques instants, l'adrénaline l'aiderait à faire le boulot, mais pour le moment elle n'avait nulle part où aller. Il tapota du pied sur la pédale d'embrayage et jeta un nouveau coup d'œil à Kate.

— Tu as ton gilet ?

En guise de réponse, Kate se frappa la poitrine et Ray perçut le bruit sourd du gilet pare-balles sous son sweat-shirt. Un couteau était facilement caché et vite sorti, et Ray avait vu trop de drames évités de justesse pour prendre le moindre risque. Il tâta la matraque et la bombe lacrymogène accrochées à sa ceinture, rassuré par leur présence.

— Reste près de moi, dit-il. Et s'il sort une arme, fous le camp.

Kate haussa les sourcils.

— Parce que je suis une femme ? (Elle ricana.) Je me replierai en même temps que toi.

— Au diable le politiquement correct, Kate ! (Ray frappa le volant du plat de sa main. Il se tut et fixa la rue déserte à travers le pare-brise.) Je ne veux pas qu'il t'arrive quoi que ce soit.

Avant que l'un ou l'autre ait le temps d'ajouter quelque chose, leurs radios grésillèrent.

— Zéro six, patron.

Les équipes étaient en place.

— Bien reçu, fit Ray. S'il sort par la porte de derrière, attrapez-le. On y va.

— Compris, répondit la voix.

Ray se tourna vers Kate.

— Prête ?

— Plus que jamais.

Ils se dirigèrent d'un pas résolu vers l'avant de la maison. Ray frappa à la porte et se hissa sur la pointe des pieds pour regarder par la petite vitre au-dessus du heurtoir.

— Tu vois quelque chose ?

— Non.

Il frappa une nouvelle fois, et le bruit résonna dans la rue déserte. Kate enclencha sa radio :

— Tango Charlie 461 à Central, vous pouvez me passer Bravo Foxtrot 275 ?

— Allez-y.

Elle parla directement avec les deux policiers à l'arrière du bâtiment.

— Du mouvement ?

— Négatif.

— Bien reçu. Restez en place.

— OK.

— Merci, Central. (Kate remit la radio dans sa poche et se tourna vers Ray.) C'est l'heure de la grosse clé rouge.

Deux spécialistes du groupe d'intervention balancèrent un bélier métallique rouge vers la porte. Le bois céda dans un fracas assourdissant et la porte s'ouvrit en claquant contre le mur d'un couloir étroit. Ray et Kate s'écartèrent et les policiers entrèrent, se déployant par groupes de deux pour inspecter chaque pièce.

— RAS !

— RAS !

— RAS !

Ray et Kate les suivirent à l'intérieur sans se perdre de vue en attendant la confirmation de l'arrestation de Petersen. À peine deux minutes plus tard, le lieutenant en charge du groupe d'intervention descendit l'escalier en secouant la tête.

— La maison est vide, patron, annonça-t-il à Ray. La chambre a été nettoyée à fond, et il n'y a plus rien dans l'armoire ni dans la salle de bains. On dirait qu'il a mis les voiles.

— Merde ! (Ray tapa du poing sur la rampe d'escalier.) Kate, appelle Jenna sur son portable. Demande-lui où elle est et dis-lui de ne pas bouger.

Il se dirigea à grandes enjambées vers la voiture, et Kate dut courir pour le rattraper.

— Elle est sur répondeur.

Ray s'installa au volant et démarra.

— Où est-ce qu'on va, maintenant ? fit Kate en bouclant sa ceinture.

— Au pays de Galles, répondit-il d'un air résolu.

Il aboya des instructions à Kate en conduisant :

— Appelle les renseignements pour qu'ils te sortent tout ce qu'ils ont sur Petersen. Contacte la police de la Thames Valley et fais en sorte qu'un agent passe chez Eve Mannings à Oxford ; il l'a déjà menacée une fois, et il y a de fortes chances qu'il y retourne. Appelle nos collègues de la Galles du Sud et lance une alerte au nom de Jenna Gr... (Ray rectifia.) Petersen. Je veux qu'ils envoient quelqu'un au cottage pour s'assurer qu'elle va bien.

Kate nota les consignes au fur et à mesure, puis fit un compte rendu à Ray après chaque coup de fil.

— Personne n'est en service à Penfach ce soir, ils vont envoyer quelqu'un de Swansea, mais il y a un match de foot là-bas et toute la ville est paralysée.

Ray poussa un soupir exaspéré.

— Ils ont compris la situation ?

— Oui, et ils ont dit qu'ils en feraient une priorité, mais ils ne savent pas à quelle heure ils pourront y être.

— Nom de Dieu ! pesta Ray. Il ne manquait plus que ça !

Kate tapota son stylo contre la vitre tandis qu'elle essayait le portable de Patrick.

— Ça sonne dans le vide.

— Il faut à tout prix qu'on ait quelqu'un, dit Ray. Quelqu'un du coin.

— Et les voisins ?

Kate se redressa et se connecta à Internet sur son téléphone.

— Il n'y a pas de voisins... (Ray regarda Kate.) Le camping, bien sûr !

— Je l'ai. (Kate trouva le numéro et le composa.) Allez, allez...

— Mets le haut-parleur.

— Camping de Penfach, bonjour, Bethan à l'appareil.

— Bonjour, ici l'inspecteur Kate Evans de la brigade criminelle de Bristol. Je cherche Jenna Gray. Vous l'avez vue aujourd'hui ?

— Pas aujourd'hui, ma chère. Mais je croyais qu'elle était à Bristol ? (Il y avait une note de prudence dans la voix de Bethan.) Tout va bien ? Qu'est-ce qui s'est passé au tribunal ?

— Elle a été acquittée. Écoutez, je suis désolée de me montrer aussi pressante, mais Jenna est partie d'ici vers trois heures et je voudrais m'assurer qu'elle est bien arrivée. Elle est revenue en voiture avec Patrick Mathews.

— Je ne les ai pas vus, ni l'un ni l'autre, dit Bethan. Mais Jenna est bien là, elle est descendue sur la plage.

— Comment vous le savez ?

— Je viens d'aller promener les chiens, et j'ai vu un de ses messages sur le sable. Mais il était un peu bizarre, ça ne ressemblait pas à ce qu'elle écrit d'habitude.

Ray sentit l'inquiétude monter en lui.

— Que disait le message ?

— Qu'est-ce qu'il y a ? répliqua Bethan. Qu'est-ce que vous me cachez ?

— Qu'est-ce qu'il disait ?

Ray n'avait pas eu l'intention de crier, et l'espace d'un instant, il crut que Bethan avait raccroché. Quand elle reprit enfin la parole, l'hésitation dans sa voix suggérait qu'elle avait compris que quelque chose n'allait pas.

— Il disait juste : « Trahi ».

49

Je ne comptais pas m'endormir, mais on frappe à la porte et je redresse brusquement la tête en frottant mon cou engourdi. Je mets une seconde à savoir où je suis, et on frappe de nouveau, de façon plus insistante. Je me demande depuis combien de temps Patrick attend devant le cottage. Je me mets péniblement debout et grimace tandis qu'une crampe me saisit le mollet.

J'ai un mauvais pressentiment en tournant la clé, mais la porte s'ouvre avec fracas avant que je puisse réagir et je me retrouve plaquée contre le mur. Ian est tout rouge, sa respiration hachée. Je me prépare à recevoir un coup de poing, mais il ne vient pas, et je compte les battements de mon cœur tandis qu'il referme lentement le verrou.

Un, deux, trois.

Rapides et violents, cognant dans ma poitrine.

Sept, huit, neuf, dix.

Le voilà prêt. Il se tourne vers moi avec un sourire que je connais aussi bien que le mien. Un sourire qui n'atteint pas ses yeux, qui laisse présager ce qu'il me réserve. Un sourire qui me dit que même si la fin approche, elle ne sera pas rapide.

Il me prend par la nuque, appuyant le pouce sur mes cervicales. C'est désagréable, mais pas douloureux.

— Tu as donné mon nom à la police, Jennifer.

— Je n'ai pas...

Il m'attrape par les cheveux et me tire vers lui d'un coup sec. Je plisse les yeux en m'attendant à une explosion de douleur. Mais quand je les rouvre, son visage est à quelques centimètres du mien. Il empeste le whisky et la sueur.

— Ne me mens pas, Jennifer.

Je ferme les paupières en me disant que je peux survivre à ça, même si chaque partie de mon corps aimerait le supplier de me tuer sur-le-champ.

De sa main libre, il me saisit la mâchoire et promène son index sur mes lèvres avant de glisser un doigt dans ma bouche. Je résiste à l'envie de vomir quand il appuie sur ma langue.

— Tu m'as trahi, espèce de salope, dit-il d'une voix aussi douce que s'il me faisait un compliment. Tu as fait une promesse, Jennifer. Tu as promis que tu n'irais pas voir la police, et qu'est-ce que j'ai vu aujourd'hui ? Je t'ai vue racheter ta liberté en m'enlevant la mienne. J'ai vu mon nom – mon putain de nom ! – à la une du *Bristol Post*.

— Je vais leur dire. (Je tâche d'articuler malgré son doigt.) Je vais leur dire que ce n'était pas vrai. Je vais leur dire que j'ai menti.

Je bave sur sa main et il a une moue de dégoût.

— Non, réplique-t-il. Tu ne vas rien dire à personne.

Sans lâcher mes cheveux, il me libère la mâchoire et me gifle violemment.

— Monte à l'étage.

Je serre les poings le long de mon corps, sachant que malgré la douleur je ne dois pas me toucher le visage. J'ai un goût de sang dans la bouche et j'avale discrètement ma salive.

— S'il te plaît, dis-je d'une voix ténue qui semble appartenir à quelqu'un d'autre. S'il te plaît, ne...

Je cherche les mots justes, les mots les moins susceptibles de l'énerver. *Ne me viole pas*, ai-je envie de dire. C'est arrivé si souvent que ça devrait m'être égal, et pourtant je ne supporte pas l'idée de l'avoir sur moi une fois de plus ; de l'avoir en moi, m'obligeant à émettre des sons à mille lieues de la haine que j'éprouve pour lui.

— Je ne veux pas faire l'amour, dis-je en maudissant ma voix brisée qui trahit l'importance que j'y accorde.

— Faire l'amour avec toi ? crache-t-il, des gouttelettes de salive éclaboussant mon visage. Ne te flatte pas, Jennifer. (Il me lâche les cheveux et me regarde de haut en bas.) Monte à l'étage.

Mes jambes menacent de se dérober sous moi tandis que je fais les quelques pas qui me séparent de l'escalier, puis je me cramponne à la rampe pour monter, sentant sa présence derrière moi. J'essaie de calculer dans combien de temps Patrick va revenir, mais j'ai perdu toute notion de l'heure.

Ian me pousse dans la salle de bains.

— Déshabille-toi.

J'ai honte de lui obéir aussi facilement.

Il croise les bras et me regarde enlever laborieusement mes vêtements. Je pleure à présent à chaudes larmes, même si je sais que ça va le mettre hors de lui. C'est plus fort que moi.

Ian bouche la baignoire et ouvre le robinet d'eau froide, mais pas celui d'eau chaude. Je suis debout devant lui, nue et grelottante, et il observe mon corps, visiblement écœuré à cette vue. Je me souviens de l'époque où il m'embrassait dans le cou avant de promener ses doigts avec une extrême douceur, presque avec vénération, entre mes seins et sur mon ventre.

— Tu ne peux t'en prendre qu'à toi-même, soupire-t-il. J'aurais pu venir te chercher quand je voulais, mais je t'ai laissée partir. Je ne voulais plus de toi. Tout ce que tu avais à faire, c'était de la boucler, et tu aurais pu continuer ta petite vie minable ici. (Il secoue la tête.) Mais non, hein ? Il a fallu que tu ailles voir la police pour tout leur déballer. (Il ferme le robinet.) Monte dans la baignoire.

Je ne résiste pas. Ça ne sert plus à rien maintenant. J'entre dans la baignoire et m'assois. L'eau glaciale me coupe le souffle et me mord le ventre. J'essaie de me convaincre qu'elle est chaude.

— Maintenant, tu vas te laver.

Il prend une bouteille d'eau de Javel par terre à côté de la cuvette des toilettes et dévisse le bouchon. Je me mords la lèvre. Une fois, il m'a fait boire de la Javel. Un jour où j'étais rentrée tard après un dîner avec mes amis de la fac. Je lui ai dit que je n'avais pas vu le temps passer, mais il a versé l'épais liquide dans un verre à vin et m'a regardée l'amener à mes lèvres. Il m'a arrêtée après la première gorgée et a éclaté de rire en me disant que seule une idiote aurait accepté de boire ça. J'ai vomi toute la nuit, et j'ai gardé le goût chimique dans la bouche pendant plusieurs jours.

Ian verse de la Javel sur mon gant de toilette. Le liquide déborde et goutte dans la baignoire, où les taches bleues s'étendent à la surface de l'eau comme de l'encre sur un buvard. Il me tend le gant de toilette.

— Frotte-toi bien.

Je frotte le gant de toilette sur mes bras, essayant de m'asperger d'eau en même temps pour diluer la Javel.

— Maintenant, le reste du corps, dit-il. Et n'oublie pas le visage. Fais ça bien, Jennifer, ou je le fais à ta place. Peut-être que ça te lavera de tes péchés.

Il m'oblige à nettoyer toutes les parties de mon corps à la Javel, et quand j'ai terminé, ma peau me pique. Je m'enfonce dans l'eau glaciale pour soulager cette sensation de brûlure, incapable d'empêcher mes dents de claquer. Cette douleur, cette humiliation – c'est pire que la mort. Vivement que ce soit fini.

Je ne sens plus mes pieds. Je tends le bras pour les frotter, mais c'est comme si mes doigts appartenaient à quelqu'un d'autre. Je suis frigorifiée. J'essaie de me redresser pour garder au moins la moitié du corps hors de l'eau, mais il me force à rester allongée, les jambes péniblement repliées sur le côté pour tenir dans la petite baignoire. Il rouvre le robinet d'eau froide jusqu'à remplir la cuve à ras bord. Mon cœur ne cogne plus dans mes oreilles, mais bat timidement dans ma poitrine. Je me sens faible et engourdie, et j'entends les mots de Ian comme s'ils provenaient de très loin. Je claque des dents et me mords la langue, mais je perçois à peine la douleur.

Te laisser partir

Ian est resté debout près de la baignoire pendant que je me lavais, mais il est désormais assis sur la lunette des toilettes. Il m'observe froidement. Il va me noyer, je suppose. Ça ne prendra pas longtemps – je suis déjà à moitié morte.

— Ça a été facile de te retrouver, tu sais. (Il s'exprime avec désinvolture, comme si nous étions de vieux amis en train de discuter au pub.) Ce n'est pas difficile de créer un site Internet sans laisser de traces, mais tu es si stupide que tu ne t'es pas aperçue que n'importe qui pouvait trouver ton adresse.

Je ne dis rien, mais il n'a pas l'air d'avoir besoin de réponse.

— Vous autres les femmes, vous croyez pouvoir vous débrouiller toutes seules, poursuit-il. Vous croyez ne pas avoir besoin des hommes. Mais dès qu'on n'est plus là, vous n'êtes plus capables de rien. Vous êtes toutes les mêmes. Et les mensonges ! Nom de Dieu, ce que vous pouvez mentir ! C'est aussi naturel que de respirer, chez vous.

Je suis si fatiguée. Si désespérément fatiguée. Je me sens glisser sous la surface de l'eau, et je me secoue pour rester éveillée. J'enfonce mes ongles dans mes cuisses, mais je les sens à peine.

— Vous croyez pouvoir vous en tirer impunément, mais on finit toujours par vous démasquer. Les mensonges, les coups bas, les trahisons...

Ses mots ne m'atteignent pas.

— J'ai été très clair dès le début, continue Ian. Je ne voulais pas d'enfants. (Je ferme les yeux.) Mais on n'a pas notre mot à dire, hein ? C'est la femme qui décide. C'est elle qui choisit si elle avorte ou pas. Putain, et mon choix à moi dans tout ça ?

Je pense à Ben. Il aurait pu être en vie. Si seulement j'avais pu le protéger quelques semaines de plus...

— Un jour, on m'annonce que je vais avoir un fils, dit Ian. Et je suis censé fêter ça ! Fêter un enfant que je n'ai jamais voulu.

Un enfant qui n'aurait jamais existé si elle ne me l'avait pas fait dans le dos.

J'ouvre les yeux. Les carreaux blancs au-dessus des robinets sont parcourus de fissures que je suis du regard jusqu'à ce que mes yeux se remplissent d'eau et que tout devienne flou. Il dit n'importe quoi. Ou peut-être que c'est moi qui ne comprends pas. J'essaie de parler mais ma langue est engourdie. Je ne lui ai pas fait d'enfant dans le dos. C'était un accident, mais il était heureux. Il affirmait que ça allait tout changer.

Ian est penché, les coudes sur les genoux et les mains près de la bouche, comme s'il priait. Mais ses poings sont serrés et une veine palpite furieusement sur sa tempe.

— Je l'avais prévenue, reprend-il. Je lui avais dit que je ne voulais rien de sérieux. Mais elle a tout gâché. (Il me regarde.) C'était censé être une histoire sans lendemain, un petit coup vite fait avec une fille sans intérêt. Il n'y avait aucune raison que tu l'apprennes un jour. Sauf qu'elle est tombée enceinte, et qu'au lieu de foutre le camp elle a décidé de rester et de faire de ma vie un enfer.

Je m'efforce de comprendre ce qu'il raconte.

— Tu as un fils ? finis-je par parvenir à articuler.

Il me regarde et rit jaune.

— Non, ça n'a jamais été mon fils, rectifie-t-il. C'était le rejeton d'une salope polonaise qui nettoyait les chiottes au boulot. J'étais juste le donneur de sperme. (Il se lève et lisse sa chemise.) Elle est venue me voir quand elle a su qu'elle était enceinte, et je lui ai bien fait comprendre que si elle le gardait, il faudrait faire sans moi. (Il soupire.) Je n'ai plus entendu parler d'elle jusqu'à ce que l'enfant entre à l'école. Et ensuite, elle ne voulait plus me lâcher. (Il grimace en se lançant dans une piètre imitation d'un accent d'Europe de l'Est.) *Il a besoin d'un père, Ian. Je veux que Jacob sache qui est son père.*

Je relève la tête. Dans un effort qui me fait crier de douleur, je m'appuie au fond de la baignoire pour me redresser.

— Jacob ? dis-je. Tu es le père de Jacob ?

Ian me dévisage un instant en silence, puis me saisit brusquement le bras.

— Sors.

Je trébuche sur le rebord de la baignoire et m'effondre par terre, les jambes ankylosées après une heure passée dans l'eau glaciale.

— Couvre-toi.

Il me lance mon peignoir et je l'enfile, m'en voulant d'éprouver de la gratitude. J'ai la tête qui tourne : Jacob était le fils de Ian ? Mais quand Ian a découvert qu'il avait renversé Jacob, il a dû...

Quand je comprends enfin la vérité, j'ai l'impression de recevoir un coup de couteau dans le ventre. La mort de Jacob n'était pas un accident. Ian a tué son propre fils, et maintenant c'est mon tour.

50

— Arrête la voiture, ai-je dit.

Tu n'as pas réagi, et j'ai saisi le volant.

— Ian, non !

Tu as essayé de me le reprendre et on a heurté le trottoir avant de revenir au milieu de la route, évitant de justesse une voiture qui arrivait en sens inverse. Tu n'avais pas d'autre choix que de lâcher l'accélérateur et de freiner. On s'est arrêtés en diagonale sur la chaussée.

— Descends.

Tu n'as pas hésité, mais une fois sortie tu es restée plantée près de la portière, debout sous la bruine. J'ai fait le tour de la voiture pour venir de ton côté.

— Regarde-moi.

Tu n'as pas levé les yeux du sol.

— Regarde-moi, j'ai dit !

Tu as lentement redressé la tête mais tu regardais derrière moi, par-dessus mon épaule. J'ai changé de position pour entrer dans ton champ de vision, et tu as tout de suite regardé de l'autre côté. Je t'ai empoignée par les épaules et secouée de toutes mes forces. Je voulais t'entendre crier, j'arrêterais à ce moment-là, mais tu n'as émis aucun son. Ta mâchoire s'est serrée. Tu voulais jouer, Jennifer, mais je gagnerais. Je te ferais crier.

Je t'ai lâchée, et tu n'as pas réussi à dissimuler ton soulagement. Il se lisait encore sur ton visage quand j'ai fermé le poing pour te l'envoyer dans la figure.

Je t'ai frappée sous le menton et ta tête est partie en arrière, percutant le toit de la voiture. Tes jambes se sont dérobées et tu as glissé par terre. Tu as enfin émis un son, un gémissement, comme un chien battu, et je n'ai pas pu m'empêcher de sourire devant cette petite victoire. Mais ça ne suffisait pas. Je voulais t'entendre me demander pardon, avouer que tu flirtais, avouer que tu baisais avec quelqu'un d'autre.

Je t'ai regardée te débattre sur l'asphalte mouillé. Mais ça ne m'a pas libéré – la boule de rage chauffée à blanc continuait de grossir dans ma poitrine. Je finirais ça à la maison.

— Monte dans la voiture.

Tu t'es péniblement remise debout. Du sang ruisselait de ta bouche et tu l'as en vain étanché avec ton écharpe. Tu as essayé de retourner sur le siège du conducteur mais je t'en ai empêchée.

— De l'autre côté.

J'ai mis le moteur en marche et ai démarré avant que tu aies fini de t'installer. Tu as poussé un cri, affolée, et tu as claqué la portière avant de chercher frénétiquement ta ceinture. J'ai ri, mais ça n'a pas apaisé ma rage. Je me suis demandé si je n'étais pas en train de faire une crise cardiaque : ma poitrine était si comprimée, ma respiration si difficile et si douloureuse. Et tout ça, c'était ta faute.

— Ralentis, tu vas trop vite, as-tu dit en postillonnant du sang sur la boîte à gants.

J'ai accéléré pour te montrer qui commandait. On traversait un quartier résidentiel tranquille avec de jolies maisons, et une rangée de voitures étaient garées de mon côté de la route. J'ai déboîté pour les dépasser, malgré les phares qui arrivaient en sens inverse, et j'ai mis le pied au plancher. Je t'ai vue lever les bras pour te protéger le visage ; la voiture d'en face a klaxonné et fait un appel de phares tandis que je me rabattais juste avant qu'il soit trop tard.

La pression a légèrement diminué dans ma poitrine. J'ai gardé le pied sur l'accélérateur et on a tourné à gauche, dans une longue rue toute droite bordée d'arbres. J'ai soudain reconnu l'endroit, même si je n'étais venu qu'une fois. C'était là que vivait Anya. Là où je l'avais baisée. Le volant m'a échappé des mains et la voiture a heurté le trottoir.

— S'il te plaît, Ian, ralentis !

Il y avait une femme avec un enfant sur le trottoir une centaine de mètres plus loin. L'enfant portait un bonnet à pompon, et la femme… j'ai serré le volant plus fort. Je me faisais des idées. Imaginer que c'était elle, juste parce qu'on était dans sa rue. Ça ne pouvait pas être Anya.

La femme a levé les yeux. Elle avait les cheveux détachés, et malgré le temps, elle ne portait ni bonnet ni capuche. Elle me faisait face et riait, le garçon courant à ses côtés. J'ai soudain cru que ma tête allait exploser. C'était elle.

J'avais mis Anya à la porte après l'avoir baisée. Je n'avais aucune envie de remettre ça, ni de voir sa jolie tête vide traîner au bureau. Quand elle avait réapparu le mois dernier, c'est tout juste si je l'avais reconnue : et maintenant elle ne voulait plus me laisser tranquille. Je l'ai vue se diriger vers le faisceau des phares.

Il veut connaître son père, il veut te rencontrer.

Elle allait tout gâcher. Ce garçon allait tout gâcher. Je t'ai regardée, mais tu avais la tête baissée. Pourquoi est-ce que tu ne me regardais plus ? Tu avais l'habitude de poser ta main sur ma cuisse quand je conduisais, de te tortiller sur ton siège pour pouvoir m'observer. C'est à peine si tu posais les yeux sur moi à présent. J'étais déjà en train de te perdre, et si tu découvrais l'existence de ce garçon je ne te récupérerais jamais.

Ils traversaient la route. J'avais atrocement mal à la tête et tu pleurnichais. On aurait dit une mouche qui bourdonnait à mon oreille.

J'ai écrasé l'accélérateur.

51

— Tu as tué Jacob ? dis-je, presque incapable de prononcer ces mots. Mais pourquoi ?

— Il allait tout gâcher, répond simplement Ian. Si Anya avait gardé ses distances, rien ne leur serait arrivé. Elle ne peut s'en prendre qu'à elle-même.

Je repense à cette femme devant la cour d'assises, avec ses tennis fatiguées.

— Elle avait besoin d'argent ?

Ian rit.

— Si ça n'avait été que ça ! Non, elle voulait que je sois un père. Que je voie le garçon le week-end, qu'il dorme à la maison, que je lui achète des putains de cadeaux d'anniversaire…

Il s'interrompt tandis que je me lève avec précaution en me cramponnant au lavabo au cas où mes jambes endolories ne supporteraient pas mon poids. Mes pieds me piquent en se réchauffant. Je me regarde dans le miroir et je ne me reconnais pas.

— Tu aurais appris son existence, reprend Ian. Et celle d'Anya. Tu m'aurais quitté.

Il est debout derrière moi et pose doucement les mains sur mes épaules. J'aperçois sur son visage cette expression que j'ai vue tant de fois après m'avoir battue. Je croyais y déceler des remords – bien qu'il ne se soit jamais excusé une seule fois –, mais je me rends compte à présent que c'était de la peur. La peur que je le voie comme il est vraiment. La peur que je n'aie plus besoin de lui.

Je me dis que j'aurais aimé Jacob comme mon propre fils ; je l'aurais accueilli, j'aurais joué avec lui, je lui aurais offert des cadeaux rien que pour voir la joie sur son visage. Et j'ai soudain l'impression que Ian ne m'a pas enlevé un, mais deux enfants, et ces deux vies gâchées me redonnent de l'énergie.

Je feins une défaillance et baisse la tête vers le lavabo avant de la rejeter en arrière de toutes mes dernières forces. Un ignoble craquement s'élève quand mon crâne heurte le sien.

Ian me lâche pour porter les mains à son visage, le sang ruisselant entre ses doigts. Je me rue à travers la chambre puis sur le palier, mais il est trop rapide et m'agrippe le poignet avant que je puisse descendre. Ses doigts ensanglantés glissent sur ma peau humide et je me débats pour me libérer. Je lui envoie mon coude dans le ventre et reçois en échange un coup de poing qui me coupe le souffle. Il fait noir comme dans un four et je suis désorientée – de quel côté se trouve l'escalier ? Je tâtonne du pied et mes orteils touchent la tringle métallique de la première marche.

Je plonge sous le bras de Ian, tendant les mains vers le mur. Je plie les coudes comme si je faisais une pompe, puis pousse en arrière de toutes mes forces pour expédier tout mon poids sur lui. Il pousse un cri bref en perdant l'équilibre, puis tombe et s'écrase en bas des marches.

Le silence revient.

J'allume la lumière.

Ian est étendu au pied de l'escalier, immobile. Il est couché à plat ventre sur le sol en ardoise et j'aperçois une entaille à l'arrière de son crâne, d'où s'échappe un filet de sang. Je l'observe, toute tremblante.

Me cramponnant à la rampe, je descends pas à pas l'escalier sans quitter des yeux la silhouette étendue en bas, face contre terre. Je m'arrête sur la dernière marche. La poitrine de Ian bouge imperceptiblement.

Haletante, je tends un pied et le pose avec précaution sur le sol en pierre à côté de lui, m'immobilisant comme un enfant qui joue à un, deux, trois, soleil.

J'enjambe son bras tendu.

Sa main me saisit la cheville et je crie, mais il est trop tard. Je suis déjà par terre et Ian est sur moi, rampant le long de mon corps, les mains et le visage en sang. Il tente de parler, mais aucun mot ne sort de sa bouche déformée par l'effort.

Il s'agrippe à mes épaules pour se hisser au niveau de mon visage et je lui décoche un coup de genou dans les parties. Il hurle et me lâche en se tordant de douleur. Je me lève à toute vitesse et me rue sans hésiter vers la porte, luttant pour tirer le verrou qui me glisse deux fois entre les doigts avant que je parvienne à l'ouvrir et à sortir. La nuit est froide et la lune presque entièrement dissimulée par les nuages. Je fonce à l'aveuglette, mais à peine me suis-je mise à courir que je distingue les lourds pas de Ian derrière moi. Je ne me retourne pas pour savoir à quelle distance il se trouve, mais je l'entends grogner à chaque pas.

Je cours laborieusement, pieds nus, sur le sentier rocailleux, mais les grognements semblent s'atténuer et je crois que je gagne du terrain. J'essaie de retenir mon souffle, de faire le moins de bruit possible.

Ce n'est qu'en entendant le fracas des vagues que je m'avise que j'ai raté l'embranchement pour le camping. Je maudis ma stupidité. Je n'ai plus que deux options : suivre le sentier qui descend à la plage, ou tourner à droite et continuer sur le sentier littoral en m'éloignant de Penfach. J'ai pris ce chemin plusieurs fois avec Beau, mais jamais la nuit – le sentier longe le bord de la falaise et j'ai toujours eu peur que Beau perde l'équilibre. J'hésite un instant, mais je suis terrifiée à l'idée de me retrouver prise au piège sur la plage : j'ai sûrement plus de chances de m'en sortir si je continue de courir. Je tourne à droite et m'engage sur le sentier littoral. La nuit se fait plus claire tandis que le vent se lève et chasse les nuages. Je risque un rapide coup d'œil derrière moi, mais le sentier est désert.

Je ralentis jusqu'à marcher, puis je m'arrête pour tendre l'oreille. Le silence est total, excepté les bruits de la mer, et mon cœur commence à se calmer un peu. Les vagues se brisent en rythme sur la plage et j'entends la sirène lointaine d'un bateau. Je reprends mon souffle et j'essaie de me repérer.

— C'est fini, Jennifer.

Je me retourne brusquement, mais je ne le vois pas. Je scrute l'obscurité et distingue des broussailles, un échalier, et au loin une cabane de berger.

— Où es-tu ?

Je crie, mais le vent emporte mes mots au large. J'inspire à fond, prête à hurler, mais l'instant d'après il est derrière moi, le bras passé autour de ma gorge. Il me tire en arrière en me soulevant, jusqu'à ce que je commence à suffoquer. Je lui donne un coup de coude dans les côtes et il relâche suffisamment son étreinte pour que je puisse respirer. Je ne mourrai pas aujourd'hui. J'ai passé la majeure partie de ma vie d'adulte à me cacher, à m'enfuir, à avoir peur, et maintenant, juste au moment où je me sens enfin en sécurité, il est revenu pour me tuer. Je ne vais pas le laisser faire. J'ai une montée d'adrénaline et je me penche en avant. Ce mouvement le déséquilibre assez pour me permettre de me dégager.

Et je ne m'enfuis pas. Je ne m'enfuis plus.

Il tente de m'attraper, mais d'une poussée, j'écrase le bas de ma paume sous son menton. Le coup le fait reculer et il vacille au bord de la falaise pendant ce qui semble durer plusieurs secondes. Il essaie de s'agripper à mon peignoir, ses doigts effleurant le tissu. Je crie et fais un pas en arrière, mais je perds l'équilibre et l'espace d'un instant j'ai l'impression que je vais l'accompagner dans sa chute. Mais je me retrouve soudain à plat ventre au bord de la falaise tandis qu'il tombe dans le vide, et j'aperçois ses yeux révulsés avant que les vagues l'engloutissent.

52

Le téléphone de Ray sonna tandis qu'ils contournaient Cardiff. Il jeta un coup d'œil à l'écran.

— C'est la Criminelle de Swansea.

Kate l'observa tandis qu'il écoutait les dernières nouvelles de Penfach.

— Dieu merci ! s'exclama-t-il. Pas de problème. Merci de m'avoir tenu au courant.

Il raccrocha et laissa échapper un long et lent soupir.

— Elle n'a rien. Enfin, façon de parler. Mais elle est en vie, en tout cas.

— Et Petersen ? demanda Kate.

— Il n'a pas eu autant de chance. Apparemment, il a poursuivi Jenna sur le sentier côtier. Ils se sont battus et Petersen est tombé de la falaise.

Kate grimaça.

— Pas marrant, comme mort.

— Il n'en méritait pas moins, répliqua Ray. En lisant entre les lignes, je ne crois pas qu'il soit vraiment « tombé », si tu vois ce que je veux dire, mais la Criminelle de Swansea a pris la bonne décision : pour eux, il s'agit d'un accident.

Ils se turent.

— On retourne à Bristol, du coup ? demanda-t-elle.

Ray secoua la tête.

— Pour quoi faire ? Jenna est à l'hôpital de Swansea et on y sera dans moins d'une heure. Maintenant qu'on est là, autant finir le travail, et on mangera un morceau avant de rentrer.

La circulation s'améliora sur la fin du trajet et ils atteignirent l'hôpital de Swansea un peu après sept heures. L'entrée des urgences était bondée de fumeurs avec des bras en écharpe, des chevilles bandées et toutes sortes de blessures invisibles. Ray fit un pas de côté pour éviter un homme plié en deux à cause de crampes d'estomac, et qui réussit malgré tout à tirer une longue taffe sur la cigarette que sa petite amie lui approchait des lèvres.

L'odeur de fumée qui planait dans l'air froid fut remplacée par la chaleur aseptisée des urgences ; à l'accueil, Ray montra sa carte de police à une femme visiblement épuisée. Elle leur indiqua une chambre du bâtiment C, où ils trouvèrent Jenna couchée, adossée à une pile d'oreillers.

Ray éprouva un choc à la vue des ecchymoses violettes qui dépassaient de sa chemise d'hôpital et remontaient le long de son cou. Ses cheveux dénoués tombaient sur ses épaules, raides et ternes ; et son visage était marqué par la fatigue et la douleur. Patrick était assis près d'elle, un journal ouvert à la page des mots croisés abandonné à ses côtés.

— Bonjour, dit doucement Ray. Comment ça va ?

Elle sourit faiblement.

— J'ai connu des jours meilleurs.

— Vous avez traversé beaucoup d'épreuves. (Ray s'approcha du lit.) Je suis désolé qu'on n'ait pas réussi à le coincer à temps.

— Ça n'a plus d'importance maintenant.

— J'ai entendu dire que vous étiez le héros du jour, M. Mathews.

Ray se tourna vers Patrick, qui leva une main en signe de protestation.

— Pas vraiment. Si j'étais arrivé une heure plus tôt, j'aurais peut-être pu me montrer utile, mais j'ai été retenu au cabinet et le temps que je sois là-bas... eh bien...

Il regarda Jenna.

— Je ne crois pas que j'aurais eu la force de rentrer au cottage sans toi, dit-elle. À l'heure qu'il est, je serais sans doute encore allongée là-bas en train de fixer le vide.

Elle frissonna et Ray eut froid dans le dos, malgré l'air étouffant de l'hôpital. À quoi cela avait-il bien pu ressembler, là-haut au bord de la falaise ?

— Ils vous ont dit combien de temps vous alliez rester ici ? demanda-t-il.

Jenna secoua la tête.

— Ils veulent me garder en observation, apparemment, mais j'espère que ça ne durera pas plus de vingt-quatre heures. (Elle regarda Ray et Kate.) Est-ce que je vais avoir des ennuis ? Pour vous avoir menti à propos du conducteur ?

— Il y a bien un risque de poursuites pour entrave à la justice, répondit Ray. Mais ça m'étonnerait qu'on en fasse une priorité...

Il sourit et Jenna poussa un soupir de soulagement.

— On va vous laisser tranquilles, conclut-il. (Il regarda Patrick.) Prenez soin d'elle, d'accord ?

Ils quittèrent l'hôpital et parcoururent en voiture la courte distance qui les séparait du commissariat de Swansea, où leur collègue les attendait. Le capitaine Frank Rushton avait quelques années de plus que Ray, et un physique qui laissait penser qu'il serait plus à l'aise sur un terrain de rugby que derrière un ordinateur. Il les accueillit chaleureusement et les fit passer dans son bureau, leur proposant un café qu'ils refusèrent.

— On doit rentrer, expliqua Ray. Sinon, l'inspecteur Evans ici présent va faire exploser mon quota d'heures sup'.

— Dommage, répliqua Frank. On va tous se faire un resto indien ce soir. Un de nos chefs part à la retraite et c'est son pot de départ, en quelque sorte. Si vous voulez vous joindre à nous, vous êtes les bienvenus.

— C'est gentil, fit Ray. Mais il vaut mieux qu'on rentre. Vous gardez le corps de Petersen ici, ou vous voulez que je contacte le bureau du coroner de Bristol ?

— Si vous avez le numéro, je le veux bien, dit Frank. Je passerai un coup de fil quand on aura retrouvé le corps.

— Vous ne l'avez pas retrouvé ?

— Pas encore. Il est tombé à environ huit cents mètres du cottage de Gray, dans la direction opposée au camping de Penfach. Vous connaissez le coin, non ?

Ray hocha la tête.

— Le type qui a retrouvé Gray, Patrick Mathews, nous a emmenés sur place, reprit Frank. Et c'est bien là-bas que ça s'est passé, ça ne fait aucun doute. Tout concorde avec le témoignage de Gray : il y a des traces de lutte au sol et le bord de la falaise est éraflé.

— Mais il n'y a pas de corps ?

— À vrai dire, ça n'a rien d'exceptionnel. (Frank remarqua les sourcils relevés de Ray et eut un petit rire.) On a l'habitude de ne pas retrouver de corps tout de suite. De temps en temps, on en a un qui saute, ou un gars qui glisse en revenant du pub, et il faut souvent attendre quelques jours, ou plus, avant que le corps soit rejeté par la mer. Quelquefois, il ne réapparaît jamais ; d'autres fois, on récupère juste quelques morceaux.

— Comment ça ? demanda Kate.

— Ça fait une chute de soixante mètres à cet endroit, expliqua Frank. Avec un peu de chance, vous pouvez éviter les rochers en tombant, mais une fois en bas les vagues vont vous projeter encore et encore contre la falaise. (Il haussa les épaules.) Un corps se disloque facilement.

— Bon Dieu ! s'exclama Kate. C'est à vous couper l'envie de vivre au bord de la mer !

Frank se fendit d'un large sourire.

— Bon, vous êtes sûrs que vous n'allez pas vous laisser tenter par un resto indien ? J'avais envisagé de me faire muter dans l'Avon et le Somerset à une époque, j'aimerais bien savoir ce que j'ai loupé.

Te laisser partir

Il se leva.

— On a dit qu'on mangerait un morceau, fit Kate en regardant Ray.

— Allez, insista Frank. On va bien se marrer. Presque toute la Criminelle sera là, et quelques agents. (Il les raccompagna à l'accueil et leur serra la main.) On a rendez-vous dans une demi-heure au Raj, dans High Street. Ce délit de fuite, c'est un excellent résultat pour vous, non ? Vous devriez vous arranger pour passer la nuit ici et fêter ça dignement !

Ils dirent au revoir à Frank, et Ray sentit son estomac gargouiller tandis qu'ils regagnaient la voiture. Un poulet jalfrezi et une bière, c'était exactement ce qu'il lui fallait après cette journée. Il jeta un coup d'œil à Kate et se dit que passer la soirée avec les gars de Swansea était tentant. Ce serait dommage de prendre la route maintenant, et Frank avait raison, il pourrait sans doute prétexter avoir encore quelques détails à régler demain pour passer la nuit ici.

— Allons-y, dit Kate. (Elle s'arrêta et se tourna vers Ray.) Ça va être sympa, et il a raison, on devrait fêter ça.

Ils étaient si proches l'un de l'autre qu'ils se touchaient presque, et Ray s'imagina laisser les collègues de Swansea après le resto, aller boire un dernier verre quelque part avec Kate, puis rentrer à l'hôtel. Il déglutit en pensant à ce qui pourrait arriver ensuite.

— Une autre fois, trancha-t-il.

Il y eut un silence, puis Kate hocha lentement la tête.

— OK.

Elle se dirigea vers la voiture et Ray sortit son portable pour envoyer un message à Mags.

« Je rentre. Ça te dit de manger indien ce soir ? »

53

Les infirmières se sont montrées bienveillantes avec moi. Elles ont soigné mes blessures avec une efficacité discrète, sans jamais se plaindre que je leur demande encore et encore si Ian est bien mort.

— C'est fini, dit le médecin. Maintenant, reposez-vous.

Je ne me sens ni soulagée ni libérée, juste très fatiguée. Patrick ne quitte pas mon chevet. Je me réveille en sursaut plusieurs fois dans la nuit et il est toujours là pour apaiser mes cauchemars. Je finis par accepter le calmant que l'infirmière me propose. Je crois entendre Patrick discuter au téléphone, mais je me rendors avant de pouvoir lui demander à qui il parlait.

Quand je me réveille, le soleil filtre à travers les stores de la fenêtre, striant mon lit de fines bandes de lumière. Un plateau est posé sur la table à côté de moi.

— Le thé doit être froid maintenant, observe Patrick. Je vais aller voir si je peux en avoir un autre.

— Ce n'est pas la peine, dis-je en me redressant péniblement.

Mon cou est douloureux et je le tâte avec précaution. Le téléphone de Patrick émet un bip et il le sort pour lire le message.

— Qui est-ce ?

— Personne, répond-il. (Il change de sujet.) Le médecin dit que ce sera douloureux encore quelques jours, mais il n'y a rien de cassé. Il t'a prescrit de la pommade pour neutraliser les effets de la Javel, et tu devras en mettre tous les jours pour empêcher ta peau de se dessécher.

Je replie mes jambes pour qu'il puisse s'asseoir près de moi sur le lit. Il a le front plissé et je m'en veux de lui causer tant de soucis.

— Je me sens bien, dis-je. Je t'assure. Je veux juste rentrer chez moi.

Je le vois chercher des réponses sur mon visage : il aimerait savoir ce que je ressens pour lui, mais je ne le sais pas encore moi-même. Je sais seulement que je ne peux pas me fier à mon instinct. Je me force à sourire pour lui prouver que je vais bien, puis je ferme les yeux, pour éviter son regard plus que dans l'espoir de dormir.

Je suis réveillée par des bruits de pas devant ma porte et j'espère que c'est le médecin, mais j'entends Patrick parler avec quelqu'un.

— Elle est là. Je vais aller boire un café à la cantine pour vous laisser un peu de temps toutes les deux.

Je ne vois pas qui cela peut être, et quand la porte s'ouvre sur une silhouette élancée dans un manteau jaune vif avec de gros boutons, il me faut encore une seconde pour comprendre ce qui se passe. J'ouvre la bouche mais le nœud dans ma gorge m'empêche de parler.

Eve se précipite et m'étreint de toutes ses forces.

— Tu m'as tellement manqué !

Nous nous cramponnons l'une à l'autre jusqu'à ce que nos sanglots se calment. Puis nous nous asseyons en tailleur en nous tenant les mains, comme quand nous étions petites, installées l'une en face de l'autre sur le lit superposé du bas dans notre chambre.

— Tu t'es coupé les cheveux, dis-je. Ça te va bien.

Eve touche timidement son carré parfaitement lisse.

— Je crois que Jeff préfère plus long, mais j'aime bien comme ça. Il t'embrasse, d'ailleurs. Oh, et les enfants ont fait ça pour toi. (Elle fouille dans son sac et sort un dessin froissé, plié en deux pour faire une carte de prompt rétablissement.) Je leur ai dit que tu étais à l'hôpital, alors ils croient que tu as la varicelle.

Je regarde le dessin de moi au lit, couverte de boutons, et je ris.

— Ils m'ont manqué. Vous m'avez tous manqué.

Te laisser partir

— Tu nous as manqué toi aussi. (Eve respire à fond.) Je n'aurais jamais dû dire ce que j'ai dit. Je n'avais pas le droit.

Je me revois allongée à l'hôpital après la naissance de Ben. Personne n'avait pensé à enlever le petit lit en plexiglas qui me narguait dans le coin de la pièce. Je n'avais pas encore annoncé la nouvelle à Eve, mais quand elle est arrivée, j'ai su à son expression que les infirmières l'avaient interceptée. Malgré ses efforts pour le cacher, un cadeau au papier froissé et déchiré dépassait de son sac. Je me suis demandé ce qu'elle allait en faire – si elle trouverait un autre bébé à qui donner les vêtements qu'elle avait soigneusement choisis pour mon fils.

Elle n'a d'abord rien dit, puis n'a pas pu s'empêcher de parler.

— Est-ce que Ian t'a fait quelque chose ? C'est lui, hein ?

J'ai détourné le regard, vu le petit lit vide et fermé les yeux. Eve n'avait jamais eu confiance en Ian, bien qu'il ait pris soin de ne jamais laisser personne voir son vrai visage. J'avais toujours affirmé que tout allait bien entre nous : d'abord parce que j'étais trop aveuglée par l'amour pour voir les failles de notre relation, ensuite parce que j'avais trop honte de reconnaître que j'étais restée aussi longtemps avec un homme qui me faisait tant de mal.

J'aurais voulu que ma sœur me prenne dans ses bras. Qu'elle me serre fort contre elle pour atténuer cette douleur dans mes entrailles. Mais elle était furieuse, son chagrin exigeant des réponses, une raison, un responsable.

— Ce type n'est pas clair, tu n'auras que des ennuis avec lui, a-t-elle dit. (J'ai serré les paupières.) Tu ne le vois peut-être pas, mais moi si. Tu n'aurais jamais dû rester avec lui quand tu es tombée enceinte. Ton bébé serait peut-être encore en vie maintenant. C'est autant ta faute que la sienne.

J'ai ouvert les yeux, consternée, les mots d'Eve m'atteignant en plein cœur.

— Va-t'en, ai-je dit d'une voix brisée mais déterminée. Ma vie ne te regarde pas, et tu n'as pas le droit de venir me dire ce que je dois faire. Va-t'en ! Je ne veux plus jamais te revoir.

Eve a quitté la maternité, me laissant seule avec mon ventre vide, désemparée. Les mots de ma sœur m'avaient blessée, mais elle m'avait juste dit la vérité. J'étais responsable de la mort de Ben.

Pendant les semaines qui ont suivi, Eve a essayé de me contacter, mais j'ai refusé de lui parler. Et elle a fini par cesser d'appeler.

— Tu avais cerné Ian, lui dis-je à présent. J'aurais dû t'écouter.

— Tu l'aimais, répond-elle simplement. Comme maman aimait papa.

Je me redresse.

— Comment ça ?

Le silence s'installe et je vois Eve réfléchir à ce qu'elle doit me dire. Je secoue la tête, comprenant tout à coup ce que, plus petite, je refusais d'admettre.

— Il la battait, c'est ça ?

Elle se contente de hocher la tête.

Je pense à mon père, beau et intelligent, qui trouvait toujours quelque chose d'amusant à me proposer, qui me faisait encore tournoyer à bout de bras même quand j'étais trop grande pour ça. Je pense à ma mère – toujours calme, distante, froide. Je pense à la façon dont je lui en ai voulu de l'avoir laissé partir.

— Elle a supporté ça pendant des années, explique Eve. Et un jour, je suis rentrée dans la cuisine après l'école et je l'ai vu en train de la battre. Je lui ai crié d'arrêter, il s'est retourné et m'a frappée au visage.

— Mon Dieu, Eve !

Je suis sidérée que nos souvenirs d'enfance soient si différents.

446

— Il ne savait plus où se mettre. Il s'est excusé et m'a dit qu'il ne m'avait pas vue, mais j'ai aperçu son regard avant qu'il me frappe. À cet instant il me haïssait, je suis convaincue qu'il aurait pu me tuer. Et puis maman a eu comme un déclic : elle lui a ordonné de partir et il a obéi sans un mot.

— Il n'était plus là quand je suis rentrée de la danse, dis-je en me souvenant du chagrin que j'avais éprouvé ce jour-là.

— Maman lui a dit qu'elle irait à la police si jamais il s'approchait encore de nous. Ça lui a brisé le cœur de le mettre à la porte, mais elle voulait nous protéger.

— Elle ne m'a jamais rien dit.

Il est vrai que je ne lui en ai jamais vraiment donné l'occasion. Je me demande comment j'ai pu si mal interpréter les choses. J'aimerais que ma mère soit encore là pour pouvoir en parler avec elle.

Une vague d'émotion me submerge et je me mets à sangloter.

— Je sais, ma chérie, je sais.

Eve me caresse les cheveux, comme quand nous étions petites, puis elle me prend dans ses bras et pleure à son tour.

Elle reste deux heures, pendant que Patrick fait des allers-retours entre la cantine et la chambre, voulant nous laisser du temps tout en veillant à ce que je ne me fatigue pas trop.

Eve me donne une pile de magazines que je ne lirai pas et me promet de revenir me voir dès que je serai rentrée chez moi, ce qui, d'après le médecin, sera possible d'ici quelques jours.

Patrick me presse la main.

— Iestyn va envoyer deux gars de la ferme au cottage pour tout nettoyer, indique-t-il. Et ils vont changer la serrure, comme ça tu sauras que tu es la seule à avoir la clé. (Il a dû lire l'angoisse sur mon visage.) Ils vont tout remettre en état. Ce sera comme si rien n'était jamais arrivé.

Non, me dis-je, ça ne pourra jamais être le cas.

Mais je lui presse la main à mon tour. Son visage respire l'honnêteté et la gentillesse, et je me dis que, finalement, la vie pourrait valoir la peine d'être vécue avec cet homme. La vie pourrait être belle.

Épilogue

Les jours sont plus longs et Penfach a retrouvé son rythme habituel, perturbé uniquement par la marée estivale de familles venues profiter de la plage. L'air est imprégné d'effluves de crème solaire et de sel marin, et la cloche du magasin du village semble ne jamais s'arrêter de tinter. Le camping ouvre pour la saison avec une couche de peinture fraîche, les rayons de la boutique remplis à ras bord de produits indispensables aux vacanciers.

Les touristes ne s'intéressent pas aux ragots du coin, et, à mon grand soulagement, les villageois ne se passionnent bientôt plus pour mon histoire. Quand les jours raccourcissent à nouveau, la rumeur s'est presque éteinte, étouffée par l'absence de nouvelles informations et par la vive résistance de Bethan et de Iestyn, qui se chargent de remettre à sa place quiconque affirme savoir ce qui s'est passé. Quand la dernière tente a été démontée, le dernier seau vendu et la dernière glace mangée, tout est oublié. Là où je ne trouvais autrefois que portes closes et mépris, je suis désormais accueillie à bras ouverts.

Comme promis, Iestyn a remis le cottage en état. Il a changé la serrure, posé de nouvelles fenêtres, repeint la porte d'entrée et effacé toute trace de ce qui s'est passé. Et même si je ne pourrai jamais oublier ce soir-là, je veux rester ici, en haut de la falaise, avec pour seul voisinage celui de la mer. Je suis heureuse dans mon cottage et je refuse de laisser Ian détruire aussi cette partie de ma vie.

Je prends la laisse de Beau et il attend impatiemment près de la porte que j'enfile mon manteau pour aller le promener une dernière fois avant de dormir. Je ne peux toujours pas me résoudre à laisser la porte ouverte quand je pars, mais lorsque je suis à l'intérieur je ne m'enferme plus, je ne sursaute pas quand Bethan entre sans frapper.

Te laisser partir

Si Patrick dort ici la plupart du temps, il devine les moments où j'ai besoin d'être seule et retourne alors discrètement à Port Ellis pour me laisser à mes pensées.

Je regarde la marée monter dans la baie, en contrebas. La plage est couverte d'empreintes de promeneurs avec leurs chiens et de mouettes venues se nourrir des vers qui vivent dans le sable. Il est tard, le sentier littoral est désert en haut de la falaise où une toute nouvelle barrière rappelle aux marcheurs de ne pas trop s'approcher du bord. Un frisson de solitude me parcourt. Je regrette que Patrick ne soit pas là ce soir.

Les vagues déferlent sur la plage dans un bouillonnement d'écume blanche. Chacune avance un peu plus loin, découvrant pendant quelques secondes une portion de sable lisse et luisant avant qu'une autre vienne la remplacer. Je suis sur le point de faire demi-tour quand j'aperçois quelque chose de tracé sur le sable. Ça disparaît en un clin d'œil. La mer balaie l'inscription qu'à présent je ne suis plus certaine d'avoir vue, et la plage s'assombrit au moment où le soleil couchant se reflète dans l'eau. Je secoue la tête et reprends le chemin du cottage, mais quelque chose me retient et je retourne au bord de la falaise, me tenant aussi près du vide que possible pour scruter la plage.

Il n'y a rien.

Je resserre mon manteau pour me protéger du froid qui me saisit brusquement. Je me fais des idées. Il n'y a rien, pas de lettres majuscules bien droites. Ce n'est pas vrai. Je ne vois pas mon nom.

Jennifer.

La mer ne vacille pas. La vague suivante se brise sur le sable et les marques disparaissent. Une mouette décrit un dernier cercle dans le ciel tandis que la marée continue de monter, et le soleil glisse sous l'horizon.

Puis vient l'obscurité.

Note de l'auteur

J'ai commencé ma formation de policier en 1999 et j'ai été affectée à Oxford en 2000. En décembre de cette année-là, un garçon de neuf ans a été tué par un chauffard au volant d'une voiture volée dans le quartier de Blackbird Leys. L'enquête a duré quatre longues années, au cours desquelles d'importants effectifs ont été mobilisés. Cette affaire a constitué la toile de fond de mes premières années en tant qu'agent de police et donnait encore lieu à des investigations quand j'ai rejoint la brigade criminelle, trois ans plus tard.

Une grosse récompense a été promise, ainsi que l'immunité, pour le passager de la voiture s'il venait identifier le conducteur. Mais malgré plusieurs arrestations, personne n'a jamais été inculpé.

Les conséquences de ce crime m'ont intriguée. Comment le conducteur de cette Vauxhall Astra pouvait-il continuer à vivre avec ce qu'il avait fait ? Comment le passager pouvait-il garder le silence ? Comment la mère de l'enfant pourrait-elle un jour surmonter la perte tragique de son fils ? J'étais fascinée par les informations récoltées chaque année après l'appel à témoins lancé pour l'anniversaire de l'accident, et par le travail minutieux des policiers qui examinaient chaque renseignement dans l'espoir de trouver la pièce manquante du puzzle.

Des années plus tard, quand mon propre fils est mort – dans des circonstances très différentes –, j'ai constaté par moi-même que les émotions pouvaient altérer le jugement et modifier le comportement. Le chagrin et le remords sont des sentiments puissants, et j'ai commencé à me demander comment ils pourraient affecter le comportement de deux femmes, impliquées de façon très différente dans le même accident. Le résultat est *Te laisser partir*.

Remerciements

Je me suis toujours demandé, en lisant les remerciements, comment autant de personnes pouvaient être impliquées dans l'écriture d'un seul livre. Je comprends à présent. Je tiens à remercier les premiers lecteurs de *Te laisser partir* – Julie Cohen, AJ Pearce et Merilyn Davies, entre autres –, qui m'ont aidée à voir ce qui allait et ce qui n'allait pas, ainsi que Peta Nightingale et Araminta Whitley pour avoir cru en moi. J'ai la chance d'avoir comme agent la formidable Sheila Crowley, mais je ne l'aurais jamais rencontrée sans une conversation fortuite avec Vivienne Wordley, qui a suffisamment aimé mon manuscrit pour le lui transmettre. Merci Vivienne, Sheila, Rebecca et le reste de l'équipe de Curtis Brown pour tout ce que vous faites. Vous n'auriez pas pu me trouver de meilleure maison que Little, Brown. J'ai apprécié la brillante Lucy Malagoni dès l'instant où je l'ai rencontrée et je n'aurais pas pu rêver d'une éditrice plus perspicace et enthousiaste. Merci Lucy, Thalia, Anne, Sarah, Kirsteen et tout le monde chez Little, Brown, y compris la merveilleuse équipe des droits étrangers, qui ont tous beaucoup de travail mais parviennent à me donner l'impression que mon livre est le seul dont ils s'occupent.

Merci à mes anciennes collègues Mary Langford et Kelly Hobson : Mary pour avoir relu une première version et Kelly pour son aide de dernière minute sur quelques points de procédure. Enfin, merci à mes amis et à ma famille qui ont toujours cru en moi, qui m'ont soutenue quand j'ai décidé de quitter mon boulot pour écrire des livres et qui ne m'ont jamais suggéré d'aller trouver un vrai travail. Je n'aurais pas pu – ni voulu – le faire sans le soutien de mon mari Rob et de nos trois enfants, Josh, Evie et Georgie, qui m'ont encouragée, m'ont apporté du thé et se sont débrouillés tout seuls « juste le temps de finir ce chapitre ». Un grand merci à tous.

Photocomposition Nord Compo

Imprimé en France par CPI en janvier 2016

Pour le compte des Éditions Marabout.
Dépôt légal : février 2016
N° impression : 3014854
ISBN : 978-2-501-09633-1
18.7783.7/01